D1756730

ROUTLEDGE HANDBOOK OF PHYSICAL EDUCATION PEDAGOGIES

The first fully comprehensive review of theory, research, and practice in physical education to be published in over a decade, this handbook represents an essential, evidence-based guide for all students, researchers, and practitioners working in PE. Showcasing the latest research and theoretical work, it offers important insights into effective curriculum management, student learning, teaching, and teacher development across a variety of learning environments.

This handbook not only examines the methods, influences, and contexts of physical education in schools, but also discusses the implications for professional practice. It includes both the traditional and the transformative, spanning physical education pedagogies from the local to the international. It also explores key questions and analysis techniques used in PE research, illuminating the links between theory and practice. Its nine parts cover a wide range of topics including:

- curriculum theory, development, policy, and reform
- transformative pedagogies and adapted physical activity
- educating teachers and analyzing teaching
- the role of student and teacher cognition
- achievement motivation.

Offering an unprecedented wealth of material, the *Routledge Handbook of Physical Education Pedagogies* is an essential reference for any undergraduate or postgraduate degree program in physical education or sports coaching, and any teacher training course with a physical education element.

Catherine D. Ennis is a Professor in the Department of Kinesiology at the University of North Carolina at Greensboro, USA. Professor Ennis is past president of the National Academy of Kinesiology and a former president of the Research Consortium of SHAPE America. Professor Ennis has published well over 100 articles and chapters including more than 80 refereed articles in the area of curriculum theory and development. She also has presented over 150 papers or invited addresses at national and international conferences. As a principal investigator, she has received over US$3 million in grants from the U.S. National Institutes of Health to design, implement, and evaluate the Science, PE, and Me! elementary (2003–2008) and

Healthful Living middle school physical education curriculum models (2011–2016). She has served on the editorial boards of *Sport, Education and Society, Physical Education and Sport Pedagogy, European Physical Education Review*, and *Contemporary Educational Psychology*.

Kathleen M. Armour is Head of School in the School of Sport, Exercise and Rehabilitation Sciences at the University of Birmingham, UK.

Ang Chen is a Professor of Kinesiology at the University of North Carolina at Greensboro, USA.

Alex C. Garn is Associate Professor in the School of Kinesiology at Louisiana State University, USA.

Eliane Mauerberg-deCastro is Associate Professor in the Department of Physical Education at São Paulo State University (UNESP), Brazil.

Dawn Penney is Professor of Physical Education and Sport Pedagogy at Monash University, Australia.

Stephen J. Silverman is Professor of Education and Chair of the Department of Biobehavioral Sciences at Teachers College, Columbia University, USA.

Melinda A. Solmon is the Roy Paul Daniels Professor and Director of the School of Kinesiology at Louisiana State University, USA.

Richard Tinning is Emeritus Professor, School of Human Movement and Nutrition Sciences, University of Queensland, Australia.

ROUTLEDGE HANDBOOK OF PHYSICAL EDUCATION PEDAGOGIES

Senior Editor: Catherine D. Ennis

ASSOCIATE EDITORS:

KATHLEEN M. ARMOUR, ANG CHEN, ALEX C. GARN,
ELIANE MAUERBERG-DECASTRO, DAWN PENNEY, STEPHEN J. SILVERMAN,
MELINDA A. SOLMON, AND RICHARD TINNING

Routledge
Taylor & Francis Group

LONDON AND NEW YORK

First published 2017
by Routledge
2 Park Square, Milton Park, Abingdon, Oxon OX14 4RN

and by Routledge
711 Third Avenue, New York, NY 10017

Routledge is an imprint of the Taylor & Francis Group, an informa business

British Library Cataloguing in Publication Data
A catalogue record for this book is available from the British Library

Library of Congress Cataloguing in Publication Data
Names: Ennis, Catherine D.
Title: Routledge handbook of physical education pedagogies /
edited by Catherine D. Ennis.
Description: New York: Routledge, 2016. |
Series: Routledge International Handbooks |
Includes bibliographical references and index.
Identifiers: LCCN 2016004396 | ISBN 9781138820999 (Hardback) |
ISBN 9781315743561 (eBook)
Subjects: LCSH: Physical education and training–Handbooks, manuals, etc. |
Physical education and training–Study and teaching.
Classification: LCC GV341.R689 2016 | DDC 796.07–dc23
LC record available at https://lccn.loc.gov/2016004396

ISBN: 978-1-138-82099-9 (hbk)
ISBN: 978-1-315-74356-1 (ebk)

Typeset in Bembo
by Out of House Publishing

Printed and bound in Great Britain by TJ International Ltd, Padstow, Cornwall

The Routledge Handbook of Physical Education Pedagogy is dedicated to Physical Educators worldwide who work tirelessly every day to provide high quality physical education for their students.

CONTENTS

Contents

Contents

FIGURES

TABLES

CONTRIBUTORS

Nathalie Aelterman, Ghent University, Belgium

Rosa Angulo-Barroso, California State University – Northridge, USA

Kathleen M. Armour, University of Birmingham, UK

Dean Barker, University of Gothenburg, Sweden

Martin Block, University of Virginia, USA

Joy Butler, University of British Columbia, Canada

Lorraine Cale, Loughborough University, UK

Erin Cameron, Memorial University of Newfoundland, Canada

Ashley Casey, Loughborough University, UK

Ang Chen, University of North Carolina at Greensboro, USA

Donetta J. Cothran, Indiana University, USA

Fiona Dowling, Norwegian School of Sport Sciences, Norway

Catherine D. Ennis, University of North Carolina at Greensboro, USA

Eimear Enright, University of Queensland, Australia

Matthew Ferry, George Mason University, USA

Katie Fitzpatrick, University of Auckland, New Zealand

Alex C. Garn, Louisiana State University, USA

Robyne Garrett, University of South Australia, Australia

Karen Lux Gaudreault, University of Wyoming, USA

Kim C. Graber, University of Illinois, USA

Shirley Gray, University of Edinburgh, UK

Leen Haerens, Ghent University, Belgium

Peter A. Hastie, Auburn University, USA

Serap Inal, Yeditepe University, Turkey

Mike Jess, University of Edinburgh, UK

David Kirk, University of Strathclyde, UK

Aija Klavina, Latvian Academy of Sport Education, Latvia

Martin Kudláček, Palacky University Olomouc, Czech Republic

Pamela Hodges Kulinna, Arizona State University, USA

Weidong Li, The Ohio State University, USA

Lauren J. Lieberman, The College at Brockport, USA

Suzanne Lundvall, The Swedish School of Sport and Health Sciences, Sweden

Ninitha Maivorsdotter, Örebro University, Sweden

Kyriaki Makopoulou, University of Birmingham, UK

Eliane Mauerberg-deCastro, São Paulo State University, Brazil

Nate McCaughtry, Wayne State University, USA

Louise McCuaig, University of Queensland, Australia

Bryan A. McCullick, University of Georgia, USA

An De Meester, Ghent University, Belgium

Isabel Mesquita, University of Porto, Portugal

Stephen Mitchell, Kent State University, USA

Moss Norman, University of Manitoba, Canada

Kimberly L. Oliver, New Mexico State University, USA

Alan Ovens, University of Auckland, New Zealand

Melissa Parker, University of Limerick, Ireland

Kevin Patton, California State University – Chico, USA

Dawn Penney, Monash University, Australia

LeAnne Petherick, University of Manitoba, Canada

Kirsten Petrie, University of Waikato, New Zealand

Mikael Quennerstedt, Örebro University, Sweden

Nilo C. Ramos, Oklahoma State University, USA

K. Andrew R. Richards, The University of Alabama, USA

Bo Shen, Wayne State University, USA

Stephen J. Silverman, Teachers College, Columbia University, USA

Cindy Sit, Chinese University of Hong Kong, Hong Kong

Melinda A. Solmon, Louisiana State University, USA

Prithwi Raj Subramaniam, Ithaca College, USA

Haichun Sun, University of South Florida, USA

Isabel Tallir, Ghent University, Belgium

Thomas J. Templin, The University of Michigan, USA

Gary Thomas, University of Birmingham, UK

Malcolm Thorburn, University of Edinburgh, UK

Richard Tinning, University of Queensland, Australia

Teri Todd, California State University – Northridge, USA

C. K. John Wang, Nanyang Technological University, Singapore

Collin A. Webster, University of South Carolina, USA

Shaun D. Wilkinson, Northumbria University – Newcastle, UK

Amelia Mays Woods, University of Illinois, USA

Deborah A. Wuest, Ithaca College, USA

Ping Xiang, Texas A&M University, USA

Sami Yli-Piipari, University of Georgia, USA

ACKNOWLEDGMENTS

The *Routledge Handbook of Physical Education Pedagogies* is the result of a major effort by the eight part editors and 71 authors involved in this very large and complex project. Errors and omissions, of course, are my responsibility. It was a goal of the proposal and author recruiting process to include a diversity of practice, themes, and scholarship along with a blend of senior and emerging scholars' perspectives representative of international physical education pedagogies at this time. To the extent that this text accomplishes this goal I am thankful to the ideas, advice, and suggestions of the prospectus reviewers, Routledge developmental staff, and of course to the efforts of my distinguished colleagues who agreed to take on the major responsibilities associated with part editing. I also am most appreciative to the Routledge editing and production staff and particularly to Simon Whitmore, William Bailey, and Cecily Davey for their patience, responsiveness, and support during the Handbook development process.

Catherine D. Ennis

INTRODUCTION

Catherine D. Ennis, UNIVERSITY OF NORTH CAROLINA AT GREENSBORO, USA

Physical education pedagogy occurs at many levels and reflects diverse interests, philosophies, and perspectives. Pedagogy, itself, is a comprehensive term encompassing a range of educational endeavors from traditional curricular, teaching, and assessment practices to policies and politics that shapes both pedagogical processes and products. Because of professional educators' diverse histories and experiences, pedagogy represents a blend of disciplinary specializations. At the scholarly level, it is informed most intensely by educational philosophy, sociology, and psychology with each contributing an essential perspective that influences our conceptions of the field. Pedagogy can be thought of as a "dynamic interplay between practice, context, and theory" (Connelly, 2008, p. xii). Each stakeholder, administrator, and policy maker uniquely shapes and is shaped by these interactions.

This Handbook focuses on the pedagogical practices, influences, and context of physical education in P-12 schools and teacher education. As such it does not adhere to any single theory or perspective, but instead provides a tapestry of topics, perspectives, emphases, and methodologies. It includes both the traditional and the transformative spanning pedagogical practices from the local to the international. Physical education as a school subject area has endured many twists and turns that have shaped our present perspectives and pedagogies. Certainly, the seminal work by Kirk, O'Sullivan, and Macdonald (2006) and their contributing authors in the Sage *Handbook of Physical Education* has provided both a significant contribution to the physical education scholarly literature and a conceptual and structural framework for this Routledge Handbook. In fact, many editors and authors in this volume sought inspiration from the outstanding authors and topics included there and we collectively "stand on their shoulders" in producing this work.

The Routledge Handbook part editors and authors are in essence the weavers who have embraced opportunities to reflect on the field and to ask what are the central issues and discourses that comprise the pedagogical tapestry in these areas of study. The pedagogical tapestry reflected in this Handbook is less about squeezing perspectives into a preferred pedagogy and more about accurately representing a range of legitimate threads that weave together our scholarship, research, and practice in the early decades of the twenty-first century. In essence, we are asking, "What are the historical events that have shaped our perspectives and how will they continue to influence these key areas of study today and in the future?" For some weavers, the tapestry consists of a brilliant array of colors and figures that depict a vibrant, yet complex set of pedagogical interactions. For others, the physical education pedagogical tapestry is comprised of darker colors representing deep concerns for welfare of the students and teachers who at times are marginalized and alienated from the academic world of schools.

The organizing structure of the *Routledge Handbook of Physical Education Pedagogies* includes both a traditional focus on curriculum and instruction in schools and teacher education and a contemporary and a futuristic look at novel approaches to policy, cognition, and motivation. As such it affords both collaborative and critical perspectives on pedagogical issues and trends shaping physical education. To achieve this unique blend, I made a number of editorial decisions that shaped and structured this Handbook in purposeful ways. I take full responsibility for the opportunities and limitations afforded by these decisions and hope that these discourses stimulate enthusiastic critiques and reconceptualizations of our field. I am indebted to Richard Tinning for suggesting the use of the term "pedagogies" in place of the more standard "pedagogy." I concur with his assessment that the Handbook chapters provide insights into a range of pedagogies that inform our scholarship and practice.

Specifically, in conceptualizing this Handbook, I first identified nine broad areas of pedagogical study in PE and then recruited distinguished international scholars to lead each part. I tasked each scholar to hone their part focus to reflect prominent themes and discourses influencing pedagogical decision-making in the second and third decades of the twenty-first century. Once they had laid out plans for their parts, the editors' second task was to identify and recruit distinguished international scholars to write Handbook chapters within their part. As necessary in a Handbook of this type, author selection was limited to individuals who write in English, understanding that this may have limited the expertise, depth, and breadth of discourses represented.

This process resulted in a blend of senior and emerging scholars who view the field and individual discourses from diverse and, at times, contradictory perspectives. I suggested the number of chapters in each part that could reasonably fit within the publisher's contracted book length and encouraged part editors to submit requests to me for additional chapters or to "return" chapters not needed, to be allocated elsewhere. Thus, the reader will find that the parts include different numbers of chapters; I made no effort to equalize this, working with part editors, instead, to include the topics and discourses that editors and authors felt best represented the area. My goal was to ensure that part editors had ownership of their parts and could work with chapter authors in their own ways to shape part discourses to match their beliefs, expertise, and vision. To that end, part editors were invited to write an introduction to their parts, providing an overview of key discourses and insights into the topics within each chapter.

This process did not and could not possibly include every distinguished scholar in PE as a part editor or chapter author and for that I extend my deeply felt apology. Nor could it reflect every viable topic or theme currently of interest to physical education pedagogy researchers and scholars. When making decisions regarding topics to omit, I considered a number of recently published contemporary handbook-like reviews of literature published in journals accessible to physical education scholars. For example, Richards, Templin, and Graber's (2014) excellent review of the themes and research in education and physical education teacher socialization recently published in *Kinesiology Review* convinced me that any chapter on this topic would be redundant. Likewise, the extensive 2013–2014 multi-issue feature on Teacher Effectiveness published in the *Research Quarterly for Exercise and Sport* contained a very thorough appraisal and critique of the current literature on teaching and teacher effectiveness, allowing me to limit the scope of this topic in the Routledge Handbook. Another new scholarly journal at this writing, the *Journal of Sport and Health Science* published by Elsevier and the Shanghai University of Sport, recently ran two separate features summarizing the exergaming and physical literacy literature, permitting the omission of these topics from this Handbook.

As physical education pedagogy continues to mature as an area of study, the number of influential discourses and topics has grown considerably. Therefore, I limited chapter length while encouraging editors and authors to construct extensive reference lists to assist readers to further explore the topic by accessing the original papers. I provided loose structural guidelines for chapter authors, encouraging them to discuss historical perspectives, pertinent theoretical frameworks, current issues and trends, implications for evidence-based practice, and future directions to provide some level of continuity for the chapters. Authors concluded by summarizing key points and offering reflective questions to stimulate discussion. Although part editors were aware of other editors working on the Handbook, some conferred and consulted while others focused principally on their own parts. This created issue-motivated, polyvocal discourses around highly influential topics that appear several times in different parts. For example, the concerns about obesity discourses appear in chapters by Cameron, Norman, and Petherick (23; Transformative Pedagogies), Makopoulou and Thomas (32; Educating Teachers), and Li (38; Student and Teacher Cognition). Likewise, the importance of inclusion pedagogies is discussed in chapters by Lieberman and Block (17; Adapted Physical Activity) and Makopoulou and Thomas (32; Educating Teachers), while fitness-based programming is critiqued by Thorburn (6; Curriculum Theory and Development) and Cale (27; Analyzing Teaching). Readers will find with these and other chapters that authors often approach topics from quite different perspectives and often disagree.

In an effort to assist novice readers to read and understand research and scholarship in physical education pedagogy, this Handbook begins with a part (I) that Steve Silverman and I edited exploring processes and methodologies scholars use when *Designing and Conducting Research*. Chapters in this part summarize research paradigms and methodologies used frequently to examine a range of pedagogical topics and themes. Authors explain that the breadth of methodologies currently used in educational and physical education research is quite impressive ranging from phenomenological and critical research to advanced statistical modeling. They discuss the value of a focused research question as well as the importance of selecting appropriate methodologies to answer research questions. Authors also embrace interpretive and critical research practices and methodologies that increase depth and clarity of qualitative research. These authors take readers through a step-by-step process for planning and executing qualitative research.

The second Handbook part (II) *Curriculum Theory and Development*, continues in an effort to assist novice readers to become comfortable with curriculum development terminology and basic practices of scope, sequence, standards alignment, mapping, and models. I edited this part placing the initial emphasis on practice-oriented development in PE. The role of pedagogical models is further elaborated in discussions of models-based practice with more in-depth exploration of "families" of games and fitness and physical activity models that hold promise for physical education. The part concludes with two chapters examining curriculum theories of complexity and globalization policy currently impacting physical education.

The policy theme continues in Part III, *Curriculum Policy and Reform*, edited by Dawn Penney. Penney and her colleagues critique the competing forces that attempt to reform physical education within the stabilizing environment of public schools. Simultaneously, a diverse range of private and public organizations and agencies "helpfully" provide externally designed curricula and teachers to "reform" physical education in schools and other public spaces. Authors in this part argue that teachers and teacher educators need to develop new ways to influence policy and reform discourses rapidly entering the physical education arena.

Eliane Mauerberg-deCastro has guided Part IV authors in the *Adapted Physical Activity* part, making a statement about the role and value of programs specifically designed to welcome and assist students with disabilities in inclusive approaches to physical education. Mauerberg-deCastro has recruited an international cohort of scholars with wide-ranging expertise to highlight the many innovations in motor learning and development specifically targeted to assist students with special needs. Chapters in the part continue policy themes by providing a critical analysis of adapted physical education and physical activity discourses and programs around the world, pinpointing areas of innovation and lag in providing needed services to students with disability.

The emphasis on critical discourses with a continuing focus on reform intensifies in Richard Tinning's part (V) examining *Transformative Pedagogies*. This part blends scholarly critique with rich examples of programs and teaching strategies that seek to transform physical education and teacher education, guiding them toward more democratic and socially just pedagogies. Opportunities for personal and social change are articulated through discourses of body culture, gender and sexuality, and body size. Additional chapters examine transformative pedagogies that are life changing for physical education teachers and young migrants, particularly Muslim girls, in a new world in which the majority culture can be oppressive.

Teacher accountability is a topic that holds critical consequences for teachers both in the United States and around the world. Part VI, *Analyzing Teaching*, edited by Ennis and Silverman, includes chapters that review the rapidly emerging literature on performance based and student growth/value added teacher accountability evaluation systems. Critical questions emerge as to whose definitions of teacher effectiveness count within neoliberal perspectives on high stakes testing and teacher accountability. Authors point out the continuing need to develop more appropriate strategies to measure student progress in fitness and physical activity curricula. The widespread use of standardized fitness tests is undermining efforts to design more authentic measures of physical activity within an emphasis on intrinsic motivation for lifetime participation. Authors project that researchers and teachers analyzing teaching and learning in the future will employ a range of innovative technologies, featuring wireless applications that will refocus and reinvigorate authentic measures of teaching and student learning.

Teacher training at the preservice and inservice levels is subject to analysis and critique in Part VII, *Educating Teachers "Effectively" from PETE to CPD*. Part editor, Kathleen Armour, has directed the focus of these chapters analyzing theory and practice in teacher education and continuous professional development. Chapter authors explore the role of learning theories in learning to teach and the role of continuous learning in teachers' quests to meet students' dynamic and diverse needs. Topics such as the role of health in physical education and the need for inclusive pedagogies have unique requirements for teacher training. Experienced teachers are finding professional development workdays focusing on continuous teacher growth to be of value as they strive to include students with diverse needs in their classrooms.

The teaching-learning process continues to take center stage in Part VIII, *The Role of Student and Teacher Cognition in Student Learning*. Part editors Melinda A. Solmon and Alex C. Garn have gathered a cadre of authors who explain the extensive body of research examining the role of physical self-concept, attitudes, teacher efficacy, and beliefs in shaping opportunities for student learning in physical education. Cognition scholars draw on a range of psychological theories, including goal theory and self-determination theory, to explain how students perceive and emotionally respond to class climate in a range of physical education settings.

In the last part (IX), *Achievement Motivation*, part editor Ang Chen focuses on theoretical and practical applications of motivation theories in physical education curriculum design and the selection of instructional strategies and authentic assessments that encourage student learning and participation. Learning in physical education requires students to expend effort directed toward positive educational goals. Chapter authors in this part review a rich body of research based on expectancy-value, intrinsic motivation, individual and situational interest, and goal adaptation to explain ways to focus and enhance student learning in physical education and physical activity settings. This part and the Handbook conclude with a chapter integrating much of the research findings in this area to consider the use of motivation as an explicit learning strategy in physical education.

We have made positive progress in researching the forces, factors, influences, and variables that affect and are affected by the pedagogical process in physical education. Far from the "dismal science" that Locke (1977) observed, scholars today are making legitimate and deliberate progress toward an enhanced understanding of the teaching-learning process. Certainly we still have a long road ahead as we explore new topics and weave new threads in our pedagogical tapestry in PE. We will continue to work to grasp theoretical relationships and design creative applications to enhance our understanding of this complex and fascinating field. On the horizon are new policy and practice discourses, issues, and trends that will require the best we have to offer both to our research and to each new cohort of eager graduate students who seek to contribute and expand our understandings of school and the many opportunities and challenges teachers and students face when becoming physically educated. Many of these challenges will come from forces outside physical education that purposely or inadvertently continue to marginalize physical education as a school subject. Certainly, the ever-present threats to the integrity of our content and instructional time required to learn in the physical domain demand astute negotiations and agile maneuverings to protect students' opportunities to learn in public school settings.

References

Connelly, F. M. (Ed.). (2008). Planning the handbook: Practice, context and theory. *The Sage handbook of curriculum and instruction* (pp. ix–xv). Los Angeles: Sage.

Kirk, D., O'Sullivan, M., & Macdonald, D. (Eds.). (2006). *The handbook of physical education*. London: Sage.

Locke, L. F. (1977). Research on teaching in physical education: A new hope for a dismal science. *Quest*, *28*, 2–16.

Richards, K. A. R., Templin, T. J., & Graber, K. (2014). The socialization of teachers in physical education: Review and recommendations for future works. *Kinesiology Review*, *3*, 113–134.

PART I

Designing and conducting physical education research

Introduction

One of my (Cathy's) graduate students once asked, "Has anyone ever invented a curricular-ometer?" The student went on to explain that there must be a way to put a "sensor" on each aspect of the gymnasium environment – students, teachers, equipment, etc. – to gather "full and complete information" from and about each important aspect of the PE learning environment (Isn't there an app for that?). The curricular-ometer would then assist researchers to integrate these to understand effective teaching and learning practices. As we write this introduction to the research part, we are fairly certain that a curricular-ometer has not yet been developed. Currently, researchers' paper and pencils, cameras, laptops, accelerometers, tablets, and apps (to name a few), as well as their eyes, ears, and intuition will continue to be the primary data collection and analysis tools available. Yet, almost 40 years after William Anderson's and Gary Barrette's (1978) original question, "What's going on in gym?" scholars are still working to answer this question. It is a question which has led us to increasingly more sophisticated insights about the interactions and events in physical education that have motivated several generations of physical education pedagogy researchers from around the world.

Conducting research in physical education can be at once a most exciting, perplexing, and exhilarating experience. The opportunity to pose and answer questions about a subject area that we greatly value is without question an energizing and, at times, frustrating experience for pedagogical scholars and researchers. The research opportunities in physical education are rich and varied. Some researchers are eager to delve deeply into the physical education classroom, broadening our perspectives with in-depth analyses of teachers, and students' many experiences and perceptions. Others are employing statistical modeling techniques to scale research findings, linking variables across classrooms, settings, and geographic areas. They are using complex research designs to reveal insights into relationships among students' cognitions, attitudes, motivation, and impressions of class climate. Currently, researchers are conceptualizing significant research questions using many different research designs. Their graduate students are soon to be the mid-twenty-first century scholars who are as equally comfortable conducting case studies and life histories as designing modeling studies examining complex relationships across rich data sets of pedagogical variables.

The Designing and Conducting Physical Education Research part opens with a chapter introducing readers to a few of the most important paradigms and procedures currently used to conduct physical education research – broadly defined. Templin and Richards begin with a look at research on teaching in physical education and physical education teacher education. They point out the very real challenges of "real world" research and the dizzying array of perspectives, methods, and contexts where researchers seek answers to better understand what is occurring in physical education. After a brief history, these authors begin by describing the development of physical education research questions and the explicit and implicit links from the research question to the selection of study methods. They conclude by addressing the question, "To what extent does research influence practice?"

Certainly, there have been important findings with lasting benefits to teachers and students currently implemented as evidence-based practice. Templin and Richards point out that evidence-based practice research puts children's needs first, encouraging practitioners to adopt an orientation toward life-long learning to stay up-to-date in a rapidly evolving profession. Unfortunately, much of the research supporting best practices has not yet reached some teacher education programs or physical education classrooms. A case in point is the rapidly accumulating findings underpinning pedagogical models which appear to hold promise to revolutionize physical education, although as yet have not been widely accepted by practitioners or implemented in practice.

The second chapter in this opening part places the spotlight directly on interpretive and critical research philosophies and practices. Qualitative research has helped researchers move from their mile-high ivory tower perspective on schools and classrooms to become "up close and personal" with teachers and students in their world. Ethnographers, phenomenologists, and critical scholars have revealed in impressive detail and with riveting analyses the microcosm of the school world. In Chapter 2, Woods and Graber provide a look at qualitative research genres with emphasis on the roles and responsibilities of qualitative researchers. They direct the reader to significant research in each genre and point out essential characteristics of research conducted from each perspective. Woods and Graber conclude by assisting novice researchers to think critically and reflectively about the qualitative research process, assisting with such important elements as planning a study, selecting participants, and collecting and analyzing data. Of utmost importance are the underlying foundations of qualitative research, credibility, dependability, and confirmability essential to the design of research studies of high quality. These key elements make a meaningful difference as we work to understand teacher–learner interactions within varied school and physical education contexts.

Catherine D. Ennis
University of North Carolina at Greensboro, USA

Stephen J. Silverman
Teachers College, Columbia University, USA

Reference

Anderson, W. G., & Barrette, G. T. (1978). What's going on in gym?: Descriptive studies of physical education classes [monograph]. *Motor skills: Theory into practice, 81.*

1

THE RESEARCH ENTERPRISE IN PHYSICAL EDUCATION

Thomas J. Templin, THE UNIVERSITY OF MICHIGAN, USA

& K. Andrew R. Richards, THE UNIVERSITY OF ALABAMA, USA

Compared to some of the most established fields within the social sciences, research on teaching in physical education (PE) and physical education teacher education (PETE) is a relatively young discipline. Since its resurgence as an enterprise once described as a "dismal science" (Locke, 1977), we have witnessed expansive growth of research publication in mainstream PE or sport pedagogy journals. This research has addressed a myriad of topics linked to the study of curriculum, teaching, teachers, and teacher education in PE (Housner, Metzler, Schempp, & Templin, 2009; Kulinna, Scrabis-Fletcher, Kodish, Phillips, & Silverman, 2009; Silverman & Skonie, 1997; Ward & Ko, 2006). Journals such as *Journal of Teaching in Physical Education* (28 volumes), *Research Quarterly for Exercise and Sport* (86 volumes), *Physical Education and Sport Pedagogy* (20 volumes), and the *European Physical Education Review* (21 volumes) represent some of the prominent publication outlets used by PE scholars. As an illustration of the broader reach of PE scholarship, Kulinna and her colleagues (Kulinna et al., 2009) noted 1,819 PE focused research articles within 94 journals worldwide.

Despite this growth, scholarship in the discipline has not come without challenges. It has been argued that the path taken by PE has been uncertain, non-linear, and, at times, tenuous at best (Kirk, Macdonald, & O'Sullivan, 2006). Many PE scholars and PETE programs continue to vie for status and resources in departments of Kinesiology in the midst of ever-changing values and identities (Lawson, 2007; Templin, Blankenship, & Richards, 2014). PE faculty and PETE programs serve two masters. They stand straddled, with one leg in kinesiology and another in educational research. Research in PE is, therefore, likely the only educational discipline informed by scholarship in both the natural and social sciences. While in some instances this diversity has positive implications for the field, the work of PETE faculty is often divorced from that of faculty in other kinesiology sub-disciplines and the practitioners for whom their work has implications (Bailey & Kirk, 2009). Equally, some of the methodologies used by PE scholars to conduct field studies are foreign to experimentalists or laboratory scientists who, in some instances, still marginalize qualitative research designs.

While challenges continue to impact the work of PE scholars, research in the discipline continues to expand through four generations of sport pedagogy scholars. This research has potential to yield important implications for both PE practice and the training of PE teachers. Research tests theories of education and instructional approaches, leading to the development of practices supported by empirical evidence. It similarly helps to uncover the student experience, identifying practices that work best in increasing student physical activity, motivation, and enjoyment (Armour & Macdonald, 2012). While much of the research in PE began rooted in positivism (i.e., an approach to research which begins with the assumption that there is a "real world" out there that can be objectively measured), the field has evolved to include a variety of interpretivist, critical, feminist, and post-modernist perspectives (Macdonald et al., 2009). To some extent, theoretical perspectives guide methodological decisions. Early scholars adopted descriptive methodologies relying on quantitative frameworks for data collection and analysis (Silverman, 1991). As evident in this volume, contemporary scholars now draw on a wider range of methodological approaches, including qualitative, modeling, and mixed-method/multi-method designs (Hemphill, Richards, Templin, & Blankenship, 2012).

Numerous textbooks have been written to address the process of conducting research in education (e.g., Cohen, Manion, & Morrison, 2011) and PE (e.g., Armour & Macdonald, 2012; Sparkes & Smith, 2014; Thomas, Nelson, & Silverman, 2015), as well as those that examine qualitative (Patton, 2015) and quantitative (Tabachnick & Fidell, 2007) research methodologies more generally. Rather than discuss specific research methodologies, this chapter focuses on the broader research enterprise in PE. We begin by discussing motives that influence research and then turn to the importance of crafting research questions to focus a study. Next we consider the need for evidence-based practice and the extent to which research impacts practice before concluding with some recommendations for approaching the research process.

The broad view: reasons and motives for pursuing research directions

The first step in the research process typically involves identifying an area of inquiry in which the scholar has an interest. In commenting on the directions taken by scholars in pursuing research agendas, Armour and Macdonald (2012) noted that one's research "reflects who you are and your interests ... therefore, it is important to reflect on the source of your motivation to undertake research in a particular area and for a particular purpose" (p. 9). Macdonald and McCuaig (2012) also recommend that scholars follow their interests and strengths in pursuing research topics, especially since individual research projects represent long-term commitments that could span months if not years. For many, research motives emerge from first-hand experience teaching in K-12 and PETE settings (see Casey & Fletcher, 2012). The topics scholars pursue, therefore, often arise through their work with children, teachers, and PETE students in the complex, sociopolitical contexts of schools and universities.

Beyond first-hand experience, individual researchers may have a variety of motives for asking research questions. For example, a scholar may be motivated by a desire to learn about the teachers' and children's lived experiences to give voice to underrepresented groups, or to diagnose potential problems in practice and formulate solutions. Siedentop (2009) explained that PETE scholars represent a research profession whose primary purpose is to serve the discipline of PE. Research and scholarship, from this perspective, relate to improving PE practices in schools. Different research traditions and theoretical orientations also lend themselves to certain types of research inspired by different motives. Critical theorists, for example, seek to critique fundamental democratic assumptions prevalent in much of the Western world, viewing research as a "form of social or cultural criticism" (Kincheloe & McLaren, 2005, p. 303). Participatory action researchers view research as being directly relevant to a particular group of people, and they seek to empower those people through the process of constructing and using knowledge (Nieuwenhuys, 2004).

Beyond an individual's motives for pursuing a topic, scholars also acknowledge sociopolitical factors that influence research agendas. The selection of research topics and identification of research questions are influenced by a myriad of factors including epistemological beliefs, interests and methodological orientations, availability of funding, and current trends in the research literature (Armour & Macdonald, 2012). Macdonald and McCuaig (2012) argue that research in PE and sport pedagogy is "overlaid by a research context that is frequently political, of public interest, and potentially attracts a range of opinion" (p. 16). Much of this complexity is attributable to differing expectations and priorities related to the role of PE in the larger school curriculum and in children's lives outside of school.

University and departmental priorities similarly influence research agendas. Funded research is often given priority over the generation of knowledge and understanding for its own sake. As universities have become increasingly entrepreneurial, research has become a commodity and "knowledge is and will be produced in order to be sold" (Lyotard, 1984, pp. 4–5). This is evidenced by faculty reward structures in countries such as the US, UK, New Zealand, and Australia that emphasize grant funding as a key indicator of success (Armour & Macdonald, 2012). Hiring decisions may be based on funding history, the perceived fundability of one's research line, and prospects for tenure and promotion may be connected to the acquisition of grant funding. Scholars who only pursue research that appeases a grant agency may prioritize the interests of others over their own. In these environments, overreliance on one's interests may make research unfundable and have negative implications for the researcher. Researchers thus need to balance their interests for engaging in research with the type of work that is attractive to funding agencies (Armour & Macdonald, 2012).

Narrowing the focus: the development of research questions

Having identified an area of research that one finds to be interesting, the next step is to consider the role of research questions in helping to focus a study. Whether the questions evolve from "logic, practicality, or serendipity" (Locke, Spirduso, & Silverman, 2014, p. 46), the question or set of questions (and hypotheses in quantitative or mixed-method research) should serve as the foundation of one's research project. Nevertheless, it is not uncommon for a neophyte researcher to approach a project without in-depth reflection about the central questions or sub-questions that will guide the project. Consider the following exchange between a graduate student and research advisor:

> **Graduate student**: "Dr. Templin, I have been thinking about my dissertation topic and am really interested in studying how beginning teachers adjust to their first jobs within a school setting."
> **Professor**: "Well that's great. Can you give me a little bit more information to help me understand what you are interested in studying?"
> **Graduate student**: "You know, we have learned about occupational socialization theory, and I would like to study the organizational socialization of beginning teachers. You and your students have been studying this topic for a long time, haven't you?"
> **Professor**: "Ok, that's good, but you will need to focus your study a little more than that. What is the purpose of your study and what are the specific research questions you want to ask? These questions should be grounded in the framework of occupational socialization theory, past literature on beginning teachers, and the precise constructs and variables you want to study. You can't try to do it all, so you need to consider what elements of the first-year experience you are interested in studying. Once you have identified

some questions, think about the type of research methods you will use to answer them. Will your questions call for a quantitative, qualitative, or mixed-methods design?"

The graduate student in the preceding dialogue has identified a broad area of interest, but failed to focus that interest into a manageable set of research questions. The professor's advice is aimed at helping the student narrow the focus as he provides encouragement related to developing questions to guide the inquiry. The professor's advice is mirrored in numerous research methods texts where authors have addressed the necessity of crafting research questions (Armour & Macdonald, 2012; Creswell, 2014; Locke et al., 2014; Maxwell, 2013). Also important in the professor's advice is the need to connect research questions to a theoretical framework related to the purpose of the study. Theories provide researchers with a unified body of literature related to a topic and help to inform assumptions or hypotheses with which the researcher approaches a given study. An appropriate theory can both focus the study and guide the research questions that are asked. Theories also help to identify the contributions of research and situate it within a body of knowledge. Physical education researchers have used a variety of theories to guide their work. Examples include occupational socialization theory (Richards, Templin, & Graber, 2014), experiential learning theory (Kolb & Kolb, 2005), self-determination theory (Deci & Ryan, 1985), the theory of planned behavior (Ajzen, 2012), and different strands of critical and feminist theories (e.g., Acker, 1987).

Research questions should be developed prior to and serve to guide the methods employed by the researcher. Ideally, rather than relying on one's preferences for data collection and analysis techniques, research methods should be guided by the questions one asks (Creswell, 2014). This speaks to the importance of developing an appreciation for and the ability to use both qualitative and quantitative research methods. Generally, questions that are guided by "how" and "why" are qualitative in nature, whereas those that begin with words such as "what" and "how many" are more quantitatively driven (Patton, 2015). Mixed-methods questions lead to both qualitative and quantitative methods independently and in an integrated way. Granted, one cannot expect to be an expert in all research methods, but understanding the type of methods that can be used to address specific research questions can aid in study design. In the following sections we discuss the development of research questions driven by quantitative, qualitative, and mixed-methods approaches. Table 1.1 provides an overview of the stated purposes and research questions from recent studies published in the *JTPE* to which we will refer.

The relationship between research questions and study methods

In quantitative research, research questions are typically crafted in advance and are used to develop hypotheses that guide statistical testing (Creswell, 2014; Maxwell, 2013). Quantitative research questions can be descriptive, predictive, or causal (McBride, 2013). Descriptive questions seek to describe what is occurring in a particular setting. This could involve quantifying a variable, examining the relationship among variables, and examining changes in a variable over time. Predictive questions seek to determine whether one or more variables can be used to predict another. Causal questions seek to determine directional causation in the relationship among variables. The use of causal questions is increasing as more PE faculty apply for large, externally funded grants; however, these questions require experimental manipulation of variables, which has been a rarity in educational research. Further, Locke and colleagues (2014) outline three tests of clarity and inclusiveness typically connected to quantitative research: 1) Is the question free of ambiguity? 2) Is a relationship among variables expressed? and 3) Does the question imply an empirical test? The first row of Table 1.1 provides an overview of a recent quantitative

Table 1.1 Example purpose statements, research questions, and hypotheses from articles in the *Journal of Teaching in Physical Education*

Citation	Design	Purpose	Research questions	Hypotheses
(Webster et al., 2013)	Quantitative	To test a theoretical model of South Carolina's Early Classroom Teachers' (ECTs) adoption of Physical Activity Promotion in the Academic Classroom (PAPAC), and to test the psychometric properties of the measures employed in this study and establish their validity and reliability	1) What are the relationships amongst ECTs' awareness of the Student Health and Fitness Act, perceived school support of PAPAC, perceived attributes of PAPAC, domain-specific innovativeness, and self-reported PAPAC?	1) Direct and positive relationships between policy awareness and perceived school support, perceived school report and intrapersonal factors, and intrapersonal factors and self-reported PAPAC. 2) Indirect and positive relationships between policy awareness and intrapersonal variables, policy awareness and self-reported PAPAC, and perceived school support and self-reported PAPAC.
(Patton et al., 2013)	Qualitative	To examine the pedagogy of facilitation within physical education professional development	1) What were the self-identified pedagogical strategies employed by facilitators in professional development (PD)? 2) From the perspective of the teachers, what strategies contributed to their growth as teachers?	N/A
(Richards et al., 2015)	Mixed method	Provide a comprehensive, in-depth evaluation of college students' experiences participating in a physical activity-based SL program for children with disabilities	1) What is the impact of program involvement on college student participants' perceptions of academic and civic learning? 2) What role do gender, prior program experience, and volunteer status play as moderating variables in participants' civic learning? 3) How do participants view program involvement as relevant to their personal and professional identities?	N/A

study conducted by Webster et al. (2013). Here we illustrate how the stated purpose of the study connects to the research question and study hypotheses.

Whereas the relationship between research questions, hypotheses, and methods is often quite clear in quantitative research, the role of research questions in qualitative inquiry is less straightforward. Some qualitative experts believe that specific questions should be established in advance, while others take the position that they should emerge from a larger, more general question (Patton, 2015). We believe that both approaches should be utilized in a qualitative study. However, locking into a predetermined set of questions can give rise to what Maxwell (2013) referred to as Type III error, which involves "answering the wrong question" (p. 73). Maxwell goes onto explain that "early provisional questions frame the study in important ways, guide decisions about methods, and influence (and are influenced by) the conceptual frame-work, preliminary results, and potential validity concerns"; however, "well focused questions are generally the result of an interactive design process, rather than the starting point for developing a design" (p. 73). As a result, the focus of the inquiry may evolve over time, and the final set of research questions may differ from those that initially drove the inquiry. Regardless of the approach taken, the final set of questions should relate to and elaborate upon the stated purpose of the study. The second row of Table 1.1 provides example research questions from a qualitative study conducted by Patton, Parker, and Pratt (2013). Here we document how the authors' purpose is connected to the research questions.

Beyond purely qualitative and quantitative designs, there has been a trend toward mixed-method and multi-method designs that "combine elements of qualitative and quantitative research approaches … for the broad purposes of breadth and depth of understanding and corroboration" (Johnson, Onwuegbuzie, & Turner, 2007, p. 123). Such approaches capitalize on the strengths of both research traditions, such as the generalizability possible in quantitative inquiry and the detailed description provided through qualitative methods (Tashakkori & Teddlie, 2003). The use of multiple methods, therefore, facilitates triangulation which can increase the reliability and relevance of findings (Patton, 2015). Both "how/why" and "what/how many" questions should be used to guide mixed-method and multi-method designs in order to focus the method on both areas of inquiry. While mixed methods have the potential to yield interesting and meaningful results, the quantitative and qualitative elements of the study should be selected with purpose. Creswell (2014) recommends that qualitative and quantitative methodologies be chosen intentionally to complement one another. The third row of Table 1.1 overviews a mixed-method study conducted by Richards, Eberline, Padaruth, and Templin (in press). Here we illustrate how the purpose of the study relates to its research questions. The first two questions guided quantitative data collection and analysis, while the third focused the qualitative component of the inquiry.

Prevalence of research questions in published studies

Hemphill et al. (2012) conducted a review of all research articles published in *JTPE* from 1998 to 2008. The review focused on the number and type of qualitative research articles published in the journal, as well as the foci of qualitative research and authorship trends. While this study focused on only one of many publication outlets in PE throughout the world, the authors noted an increase in the prevalence of qualitative research compared to that which had been noted in previous reviews (e.g., Byra & Goc Karp, 2000). In considering the importance of research questions as a "signpost" to guide the study design (Creswell, 2014, p. 139), we conducted a small-scale follow-up to Hemphill et al.'s (2012) study and reviewed all of the research published in the *JTPE* in 2013 and 2014 with a twofold purpose. First, we sought to classify the articles by methodology (i.e., qualitative, quantitative, or mixed method) and second we noted whether or not they included identifiable research questions to guide the inquiry. Given the findings of Hemphill et al.'s (2012) review, we anticipated an equal number of qualitative and quantitative studies, with somewhat fewer mixing methods. Further, since several authors cited throughout this chapter stressed the importance of research questions (e.g., Armour & Macdonald, 2012; Creswell, 2014; Locke et al., 2014; Maxwell, 2013), we expected to find clearly articulated research questions and hypotheses (in the case of quantitative research).

To our surprise, in our review of articles published in the 2013 and 2014 issues of *JTPE*, we found that there were nearly twice as many quantitative studies in the two-year period ($n = 31$) as there were qualitative studies ($n = 17$). This led us to wonder whether the research pendulum has swung back toward a quantitative dominance in the *JTPE*, or if this is just a two-year anomaly. As predicted, there were relatively few mixed-methods studies published ($n = 6$). More surprising was the absence of research questions and hypotheses we noted across the studies. Only 5 of the 17 qualitative studies (29.41%), 5 of the 31 (16.13%) quantitative studies, and 2 of the 6 mixed-methods studies (33.33%) clearly articulated research questions. Taken together, only 12 of 54 (22.22%) studies included research questions. Of the quantitative studies, 15 of 31 (48.39%) included hypothesis statements, and only 2 (6.45%) included both research questions and hypotheses. In total, 25 of the 54 studies (46.30%) utilized research questions and/or hypotheses.

The outcomes of our informal review must be interpreted with caution as they reflect a very finite time period and only consider one of the several publication outlets favored by PE researchers. Nonetheless, they do indicate that, within this time period and in this journal, the majority of researchers did not report research questions and hypotheses in their articles. We, however, stand resolute in our belief that the development of research questions is critical in the design and conduct of a study. Equally, these questions should be clearly presented in any proposal and subsequent publication from a study. Research questions keep investigators focused on what they want to explore and aid in the analysis and communication of research. Without considering research questions prior to the inception of a study, it can be difficult for the researcher to focus the methodology on a reasonable topic within a broad area of interest. When questions are crafted, but not included in published manuscript, the reader may not be able to trace the development of the study through the literature, methods, results, and discussion.

Considering impact: to what extent does research influence practice?

The preceding sections of this chapter have dealt with motives for engaging in scholarly inquiry and the crafting of research questions to focus that inquiry. This third and final section will examine the fruits of scholarly inquiry with regard to the impact it has on practice in PE and PETE. Ideally, research allows teachers to engage in evidence-based practice, which involves the interrogation and integration of research knowledge into one's practice (Osmond & Darlington, 2001). Evidence-based practice has been defined as methods of teaching that have been proven effective through rigorous evaluation, ideally in the form of experimental and quasi-experimental studies (Davies, 1999). Large-scale investigations, such as those conducted with the CATCH (Leupker et al., 1996) and SPARK (Sallis et al., 1996) curricula, are required to make definitive statements about the outcomes associated with instructional approaches. Alternatively, evidence can be established over the course of numerous studies that look at the efficacy of a curricular approach, as has been the case with instructional and curricular models such as sport education, teaching games for understanding, and cooperative learning (Metzler, 2011).

Evidence-based practices limit guesswork and place emphasis on systematically generated knowledge over personal interpretations and knowledge gained through experience. In PE, evidence-based practice puts children's needs first, requiring practitioners to adopt an orientation toward life-long learning to stay current in the best pedagogies available at any given time (Gibbs, 2003). Macdonald (2009) adds that teachers should be critical consumers of research who can digest and implement lessons learned from findings to improve their pedagogy. However, this is predicated on the assumption that teachers view research as a meaningful source of knowledge. Macdonald (2009) addresses this supposition by noting that the body of knowledge accumulated through PE research "appears to have had little impact upon teacher's practice … there is a disjunction between PE evidence and PE practice" (p. 199).

For several decades it has been recognized that traditional approaches to teaching PE dominate school settings as teachers draw upon their personal experiences rather than research-based evidence (Bailey & Kirk, 2009). Traditionalism is deeply embedded within the PE profession and is related to the way in which teachers are socialized. As children, potential recruits participate in PE classes that are often taught using traditional methodologies, and these experiences go on to shape their subjective theories of what it means to be a PE teacher (Richards et al., 2014). Subjective theories developed during this time of acculturation are difficult to change and are likely to persevere through preservice training (Green, 2002). Further, colleagues who are resistant to change can make it difficult for teachers who are interested in using research-based practices. This concern has been echoed across decades of research, as Hoffman (1971) noted that, unless evidence-based practices filter down to veteran teachers, "a powerful force for the exclusive perseverance of traditionalism remains unchecked" (p. 57). Richards et al. (2014) made this point more recently by commenting that the sociopolitical climate of schools, which focus on maintenance of the status quo, can make it difficult for new teachers to implement innovative practices.

The inability of research to impact practice goes beyond teachers' reliance on traditional methodologies. Policymakers do not have the time to read the research literature, and there is very little evidence to suggest that research on PE and PETE has had a meaningful impact on public policy (Bailey & Kirk, 2009). Further, the type of research evidence that is most valued by policymakers – that which is derived from randomly controlled, experimental trials (Osmond & Darlington, 2001) – is rare in PE research, making it difficult to build persuasive arguments. While there has been a proliferation of qualitative research within the field (Hemphill et al., 2012), these types of studies are still not widely accepted by policymakers. In the US, the Education Science Act of 2002, which prioritized quantitative methods using experimental designs as the gold standard for educational researchers applying for federal grants (Demerath, 2006), makes this point clear. Armour and Macdonald (2012) note that the inability of PE researchers to obtain the type of funding necessary to form and maintain large researcher teams and tackle big research questions may be one reason why research in the areas has not had a large impact on practice. Further, when this type of work is conducted, it tends to be published outside of PE journals, limiting the likelihood that it will be identified as PE research as well as the possibility of increasing accessibility to or awareness of PE researchers.

Although evidence does not support a strong alignment between research and practice in PE, there are ways that this connection could be strengthened in the future. First, researchers must communicate more with practitioners at venues and in language accessible to them (Bailey & Kirk, 2009). This requires looking beyond publications in empirical journals and presentations at research conferences and considering outlets such as practitioner-focused journals, social media, and in online forums. Unfortunately, this would also require a reconceptualization of faculty reward structures, which tend to prioritize publication in high impact journals.

Ironically, the journals that have the best reputations and are viewed positively by tenure and promotion committees are often the least accessible to teachers.

Professional development programming has been recommended as one option for connecting in-service teachers with evidence-based practices (Armour & Yelling, 2004). While they can be impactful, these opportunities must be designed with the characteristics of adult learners in mind, and focus on factors that promote sustainability and teacher change (see Parker & Patton's Chapter 30 in this volume). Professional development providers should also be aware of teachers' reluctance to implement changes that are forced upon them by administrations (Guskey, 2002). What is needed is a balance. When teachers are held accountable for quality practice, but are provided some flexibility in the determination of what change will be involved, they may be more likely to embrace innovation. Fullan (2007) discussed capacity building with a focus on results as the intersection of top-down and bottom-up change initiatives. These initiatives have some degree of top-down oversight, but also empower grass-roots change.

Finally, PE researchers can design studies that place teachers and students at the center of our scholarly endeavors. Locke (1977) encouraged PE researchers to avoid valuing research for its own sake and instead focus on the potential for research to serve the greater needs of the PE community. More recently, Armour and Macdonald (2012) argued that PE researchers have a professional responsibility for doing research that has implications for the children, teachers, and policymakers they seek to serve through their work. Action research methods, which involve practitioners as collaborators in research aimed at affecting teaching practice (Nieuwenhuys, 2004), have a lot to offer in this arena. Regardless of the particular approach adopted, we should seek to ask the types of research questions that hold meaning for practitioners and have application in their setting.

Conclusions and final thoughts

The purpose of this chapter was to discuss the research enterprise in PE and PETE. We began by describing motivations for conducting research and addressed how these initial ideas for research are narrowed and formalized through the creation of research questions. In the final section, we considered the impact of research on practice and provided some recommendations for strengthening this impact. We offer three general take-away points from the preceding discussion:

1. Scholars can seek to engage in research that is both personally and professionally relevant. That is, research that is personally interesting and which has meaningful implications for the PE community as a whole.
2. Research questions help to guide both the researcher and the reader of published articles through the investigation from conception through conclusions. Research questions are linked to and guide the use of particular methodologies in a study design.
3. Ideally, research should have an identifiable impact on practice. Teacher dispositions toward reading research, the sociopolitical climate in schools, and the larger political climate surrounding education can limit the integration of research in teacher practice. We must find new, innovative ways to communicate research findings to teachers and support them as they implement new pedagogies.

In closing, we must recognize and appreciate the progress we have made over the past 40 years. The research enterprise in PE can no longer be framed as a dismal science, but a thriving field of inquiry. This has resulted from a growing body of scholars; many outlets for publication and presentation of findings, advancement, and diversification in research methodology; an ever-expanding focus on effective teaching, student learning, and PETE; and the sociopolitical climate in which schools are situated and education occurs. The current body of literature related to PE has much to say in terms of teachers' experiences, lives, and careers, and presents evidence-based practices that support student learning. We are, however, less confident in saying that this body of research has been maximally used to inform K-12 practice. Over four decades after Hoffman (1971) called for more innovative approaches to teaching physical education, many teachers continue to embrace traditional methodologies and curricula (Richards et al., 2014). The challenge in the next four decades will be to find a way to have an evidence-based impact on the practice of K-12 PE in schools. Our research has tremendous promise to make a difference in the practice of physical education for generations to come. However, the question remains: will it make a difference?

Reflective questions for discussion

1. What topic areas in physical education are you interested in studying? What is your motivation for pursuing these areas of research?
2. Based on the information presented in this chapter, how will research questions guide your current and future research?
3. What theoretical frameworks support your identified areas of research? How can these theories inform the development of research questions?
4. Do you feel more comfortable with qualitative or quantitative research methods? How does your comfort with particular methods influence the research questions you are able to use in your research?
5. From your perspective, what type of research is most needed in the field of physical education? How will this research help to inform physical education practice in K-12 school settings?

References

Acker, S. (1987). Feminist theory and the study of gender and education. *International Review of Education, 33*, 419–435.

Ajzen, I. (2012). The theory of planned behavior. In P. A. M. Van Lange, A. W. Kruglanski, & E. T. Higgins (Eds.), *Handbook of theories of social psychology: Volume one* (pp. 438–459). Thousand Oaks, CA: Sage.

Armour, K., & Macdonald, D. (Eds.). (2012). *Research methods in physical education and youth sport.* London: Routledge.

Armour, K., & Yelling, M. (2004). Professional development and professional learning: Bridging the gap for experienced physical education teachers. *European Physical Education Review, 10*(1), 71–94.

Bailey, R., & Kirk, D. (Eds.). (2009). *The Routledge physical education reader.* New York: Routledge.

Byra, M., & Goc Karp, G. (2000). Data collection techniques employed in qualitative research in physical education. *Journal of Teaching in Physical Education, 19*, 246–266.

Casey, A., & Fletcher, T. (2012). Trading places: From physical education teachers to teacher educators. *Journal of Teaching in Physical Education, 31*, 362–380.

Cohen, L., Manion, L., & Morrison, K. (2011). *Research methods in education* (7th edn). New York: Routledge.

Creswell, J. W. (2014). *Research design: Qualitative, quantitative, and mixed methods approaches.* Thousand Oaks, CA: Sage.

Davies, P. (1999). What is evidence-based education? *British Journal of Educational Studies, 47*(2), 108–121.

Deci, E. L., & Ryan, R. M. (1985). *Intrinsic motivation and self-determination in human behavior.* New York: Plenum.

Demerath, P. (2006). The science of context: Modes of response for qualitative researchers in education. *International Journal of Qualitative Studies in Education, 19*, 97–113.

Fullan, M. (2007). *The new meaning of educational change* (4th edn). New York: Teachers College Press.

Gibbs, L. (2003). *Evidence-based practice for the helping professions*. Pacific Grove, CA: Brooks/Cole-Thomson.

Green, K. (2002). Physical education teachers in their figurations: A sociological analysis of everyday "philosophies." *Sport, Education and Society, 7*, 65–83.

Guskey, T. (2002). Professional development and teacher change. *Teachers and Teaching: Theory and Practice, 8*, 381–391.

Hemphill, M. A., Richards, K. A. R., Templin, T. J., & Blankenship, B. T. (2012). A content analysis of qualitative research in the *Journal of Teaching in Physical Education* from 1998 to 2008. *Journal of Teaching in Physical Education, 31*, 279–287.

Hoffman, S. J. (1971). Traditional methodology: Prospects for change. *Quest, Monograph, XV*, 51–57.

Housner, L. D., Metzler, M. W., Schempp, P. G., & Templin, T. J. (Eds.). (2009). *Historic traditions and future directions of research on teaching and teacher education in physical education*. Morgantown, WV: Fitness Information Technology.

Johnson, R. B., Onwuegbuzie, A. J., & Turner, L. A. (2007). Toward a definition of mixed methods research. *Journal of Mixed Methods Research, 1*, 112–133.

Kincheloe, J. L., & McLaren, P. (2005). Rethinking critical theory in qualitative research. In N. K. Denzin & Y. S. Lincoln (Eds.), *The Sage handbook of qualitative research* (pp. 303–342). London: Sage.

Kirk, D., Macdonald, D., & O'Sullivan, M. (Eds.). (2006). *The handbook of physical education*. Thousand Oaks, CA: Sage.

Kolb, A., & Kolb, D. (2005). Learning styles and learning spaces: Enhancing experiential learning in higher education. *Academy of Management Learning & Education, 4*, 193–212.

Kulinna, P., Scrabis-Fletcher, K., Kodish, S., Phillips, S., & Silverman, S. (2009). A decade of research in physical education pedagogy. *Journal of Teaching in Physical Education, 28*, 119–140.

Lawson, H. A. (2007). Renewing the core curriculum. *Quest, 59*, 219–243.

Leupker, R. V., Perry, C. L., McKinlay, S. M., Nader, P. R., Parcel, G. S., Stone, E. J., et al. (1996). Outcomes of a field trial to improve children's dietary patterns and physical activity: The child and adolescent trial for cardiovascular health (CATCH). *Journal of the American Medical Association, 275*, 768–776.

Locke, L. F. (1977). Research on teaching in physical education: A new hope for a dismal science. *Quest, 28*, 2–16.

Locke, L. F., Spirduso, W. W., & Silverman, S. J. (2014). *Proposals that work: A guide for planning dissertation and grant proposals* (6th edn). Thousand Oaks, CA: Sage.

Lyotard, J. F. (1984). *The postmodern condition: A report on knowledge*. Minneapolis: The University of Minnesota Press.

Macdonald, D. (2009). Evidence-based practice in physical education: Ample evidence, patchy practice. In L. D. Housner, M. W. Metzler, P. G. Schempp, & T. J. Templin (Eds.), *Historic traditions and future directions of research on teaching and teacher education in physical education* (pp. 199–205). Morgantown, WV: Fitness Information Technology.

Macdonald, D., Kirk, D., Metzler, M. W., Nilges, L. M., Schempp, P. G., & Wright, J. (2009). It's all very well, in theory: Theoretical perspectives and their applications in contemporary pedagogical research. In R. Bailey & D. Kirk (Eds.), *The Routledge physical education reader* (pp. 369–391). New York: Routledge.

Macdonald, D., & McCuaig, L. (2012). Research principles and practices: Paving your research journey. In K. Armour & D. Macdonald (Eds.), *Research methods in physical education and youth sport* (pp. 16–28). New York: Routledge.

Maxwell, J. A. (2013). *Qualitative research designs: An interactive approach*. Thousand Oaks, CA: Sage.

McBride, D. M. (2013). *The process of research in psychology* (2nd edn). London: Sage.

Metzler, M. W. (2011). *Instructional models in physical education* (3rd edn). Scottsdale, AZ: Holcomb Hathaway.

Nieuwenhuys, O. (2004). Participatory action research in the majority world. In S. Fraser, V. Lewis, S. Ding, M. Kellett, & S. Robinson (Eds.), *Doing research with children and young people* (pp. 206–221). London: Sage.

Osmond, J., & Darlington, Y. (2001). *Introducing evidence-based practice*. Brisbane, Australia: University of Queensland.

Patton, K., Parker, M., & Pratt, E. (2013). Meaningful learning in professional development: Teaching without telling. *Journal of Teaching in Physical Education, 32*, 441–459.

Patton, M. Q. (2015). *Qualitative research and evaluation methods* (4th edn). Thousand Oaks, CA: Sage.

Richards, K. A. R., Eberline, A., Padaruth, S., & Templin, T. J. (2015). Experiential learning through a physical activity program for children with disabilities. *Journal of Teaching in Physical Education, 34*, 165–188.

Richards, K. A. R., Templin, T. J., & Graber, K. (2014). The socialization of teachers in physical education: Review and recommendations for future works. *Kinesiology Review, 3*, 113–134.

Sallis, J., McKenzie, T., Alcaraz, J. E., Kolody, B., Faucette, N., & Hovell, M. F. (1996). The effects of a two-year physical education program (SPARK) on physical activity and fitness in elementary school students. *American Journal of Public Health, 87*, 1328–1334.

Siedentop, D. (2009). Research on teaching physical education: Celebrating our past and focusing on our future. In L. D. Housner, M. W. Metzler, P. G. Schempp, & T. J. Templin (Eds.), *Historic traditions and future directions of research on teaching and teacher education in physical education* (pp. 3–14). Morgantown, WV: Fitness Information Technology.

Silverman, S. J. (1991). Research on teaching in physical education. *Research Quarterly for Exercise and Sport, 62*, 352–364.

Silverman, S. J., & Skonie, R. (1997). Research on teaching in physical education: An analysis of published research. *Journal of Teaching in Physical Education, 16*, 300–311.

Sparkes, A. C., & Smith, B. (2014). *Qualitative research methods in sport, exercise and health: From process to product.* New York: Routledge.

Tabachnick, B. G., & Fidell, L. S. (2007). *Using multivariate statistics* (5th edn). Boston, MA: Allyn and Bacon.

Tashakkori, A., & Teddlie, C. (Eds.). (2003). *Handbook of mixed methods in social and behavioral research.* Thousand Oaks, CA: Sage.

Templin, T. J., Blankenship, B. T., & Richards, K. A. R. (2014). End of a golden era: The demise of a PETE program. *pelinks4u, 16*(8). Available at www.pelinks4u.org/articles/templin10_2014.htm.

Thomas, R. J., Nelson, J. K., & Silverman, S. J. (2015). *Research methods in physical activity* (7th edn). Champaign, IL: Human Kinetics.

Ward, P., & Ko, B. (2006). Publication trends in the *Journal of Teaching in Physical Education* from 1981 to 2005. *Journal of Teaching in Physical Education, 25*, 266–280.

Webster, C., Caputi, P., Perrault, M., Doan, R., Doutis, P., & Weaver, R. (2013). Elementary classroom teachers' adoption of physical activity promotion in the context of a statewide policy: An innovation of diffusion and socio-ecologic perspective. *Journal of Teaching in Physical Education, 32*, 419–440.

2

INTERPRETIVE AND CRITICAL RESEARCH

A view through a qualitative lens

Amelia Mays Woods & Kim C. Graber, UNIVERSITY OF ILLINOIS, USA

The term, qualitative research, is derived from its reference to "quality" through detailed narratives and observations. Such research typically involves the examination of phenomena in social settings, in which researchers give voice to participants. Qualitative investigations occur in the natural world, focus on context, and employ multiple methods to gain an understanding of the participants under study (Rossman & Rallis, 2012). Researchers who "support a way of looking at research that honors an inductive style, a focus on individual meaning, and the importance of rendering the complexity of a situation," typically engage in qualitative research (Creswell, 2014, p. 4). The use of words rather than numbers or statistics typically characterizes this form of inquiry, and unlike quantitative researchers who establish external validity in order to generate generalizability, the goal of qualitative researchers is to provide adequate description to enable individual readers to transfer findings from the qualitative study to other settings based on perceived similarities (Lincoln & Guba, 1985).

Qualitative research commonly includes "thick" descriptions, participant quotes, and relevant artifacts. Thick description is not so much about the amount of collected data as it is about the researchers' explanation of the process, description of the setting and participants, and relationship of the data to the conclusions. Qualitative inquiry incorporates data collected through "field notes, interviews, conversations, photographs, recordings, and memos to the self" (Denzin & Lincoln, 2011, p. 3). Such systematic inquiry provides first-hand records of individuals' unique perspectives, thereby enhancing readers' understanding.

Historical perspective

Although anthropologists and sociologists such as Margaret Mead and Willard Waller began conducting qualitative investigations in the 1930s and 1940s, it was not until much later that it became a respectable form of inquiry in physical education (PE). The focus of Mead's work in relation to education in less developed countries and Waller's research on the sociology of education, shed important new insights about how children were educated through the use of descriptive data (Bogdan, 2009). During the last two decades of the twentieth century, at which time there was an evolution of PE research grounded in the naturalistic paradigm, qualitative researchers frequently referenced Mead and Waller as accomplished scholars who made credible contributions to the knowledge base through the qualitative paradigm. They were pioneers who paved a trail for qualitative researchers in the field of PE who sought to understand the human experience through descriptive data. The scholarly merits of their findings were difficult to dispute and qualitative researchers understood that referencing researchers like Mead and Waller would help them to defend the merits of qualitative inquiry to publishers, journal reviewers, and audience members attending conferences.

Interestingly, many studies in PE that are considered the most classic and continue to be heavily referenced were published during the time in which qualitative research was emerging, yet not entirely accepted by all scholars in the field. Thus, their quality had to be outstanding in order to convince skeptics that research questions were relevant, methods were appropriate and rigorous, and the findings made a significant contribution to the field.

Many of the initial published investigations hailed from researchers at the University of Massachusetts. For example, Patricia Griffin, the first scholar to publish qualitative research in *Research Quarterly for Exercise and Sport* (*RQES*) (Griffin, 1985b), the leading PE journal at that time, developed a line of inquiry in which she sought to understand the participation patterns of boys and girls through the use of interviews and observations (1983, 1984, 1985a). Judith Placek, whose multi-case study of teacher planning in PE led her to conclude through interviews, observations, and document analysis, that teachers might be less interested in student learning than keeping them "busy, happy, and good" remains one of the most heavily referenced scholars to publish during this period of time (Placek, 1983, 1984). Finally, Kim Graber's study on studentship (1991) continues to inform teacher educators about behaviors undergraduate students employ to progress through their teacher education program with the greatest ease, most success, and least amount of effort. Her research became the focus of a tutorial in *RQES* dedicated to understanding and critiquing qualitative inquiry (see Locke, 1989).

Tutorials and critiques

All forms of scholarship should be subject to critique and debate to ensure they meet rigorous standards that merit publication and the dissemination of results to the public. The creation of new knowledge should never be taken lightly nor assumed to have merit without being subjected to rigorous peer debate. In large measure, it is due to the early efforts of those who sought to explain the merits of qualitative inquiry and critique its shortcomings, that it is considered to be a viable and important form of inquiry today.

One of the earliest qualitative researchers, Neil Earls, who confronted resistance when proposing a heuristic study for his dissertation, later wrote a monograph for the *Journal of Teaching in Physical Education* (*JTPE*) (Earls, 1986). He understood the need to educate others and pacify the critics if qualitative inquiry was to gain acceptance in the academic community. His goal in writing the monograph was that "future works from a naturalistic perspective can be presented without rehashing many of the points in this monograph and without reference to or justification from the particular perspective of positivism" (p. 8). Subsequently, a tutorial by Locke in *RQES* sought to alleviate critics' concerns by addressing the "question of quality in qualitative research" (Locke, 1989, p. 10). Locke understood that in order to convince others of its merit, they needed to be provided with examples of high-quality research articles, a clear understanding of the philosophical perspectives that ground qualitative inquiry, and information about appropriate methodology. He also had the insight to know that advancing qualitative inquiry would not be accomplished by bashing the perspectives of those who preferred a more positivist form of inquiry: "In the process of addressing ourselves to those issues, no one becomes better informed when questions are deflected by pointing out that the other side has similar problems" (p. 15).

Although no actual blood was shed, debates were often heated and prolonged. For example, after Schempp (1987) criticized the limitations of natural science inquiry (positivist research) and asserted that qualitative inquiry might fill the void, Siedentop responded by stating he was "disappointed that what followed was an exorcism of a caricature rather than a contribution to the ongoing dialogue" (Siedentop, 1987, p. 373). Schempp's (1988) subsequent reply to Siedentop, in which he stated, "There is little to be gained from reducing intellectual discourse to name calling or from cataloguing competing perspectives as misconceptions. Ad hominem attacks are more likely to alienate than illuminate, thus making their contribution to scholarship suspect" (Schempp, 1988, p. 79), demonstrates the passion held by individual researchers toward a particular paradigm.

Critiques by scholars who primarily sought to maintain standards of high quality required qualitative investigators to answer difficult questions and dig deeply into the qualitative literature to learn more about different philosophical perspectives and methods of inquiry. Siedentop's primary concern, for example, was that the qualitative investigator is the instrument through which data are collected and therefore neutrality, which is critical in many research traditions, would be unachievable (Siedentop, 1989). As additional qualitative studies were published and debates provided a forum for considering and reconsidering different perspectives, qualitative inquiry became more welcome in journals as an appropriate mechanism for acquiring important data. For novice researchers interested in pursuing qualitative inquiry and understanding its different form, a recent tutorial by Azzarito (2011) provides an excellent guide.

Today, scholars are more concerned about selecting the method (qualitative or quantitative) that best answers a research question than they are about debating if one paradigm is better than another. The acceptance of both the positivist and naturalistic paradigms in the literature has resulted in many exceptional research studies, some of which incorporate both paradigms within an individual study. For example, of those articles published between the years 1998 and 2008, 47.4% were quantitative, 32.5% were qualitative, and 20.1% were mixed method (Hemphill, Richards, Templin, & Blankenship, 2012).

Descriptive to theoretical

Early qualitative studies were primarily descriptive in nature. Researchers were more concerned about providing thick descriptions and explaining their methodology to convince readers that their studies had rigor than they were about advancing existing theory. Within a few years, however, a few qualitative investigators progressed beyond publishing purely descriptive studies to utilizing a grounded theory approach whereby they sought to develop theory that was grounded in the data of a particular study (Creswell, 2013, p. 83). Developed by Glaser and Strauss in 1967, many researchers, however, found the approach difficult and even the authors eventually disagreed with its meaning and procedures, with Glaser criticizing Strauss' approach as "too prescribed and structured" (Creswell, 2013, p. 84). Thus, qualitative researchers in PE rarely adhered to exact procedures as described by Glaser and Strauss (1967); however, many incorporated elements of the approach by using techniques such as constant comparison (e.g., Fernandez-Balboa, 1991).

As qualitative researchers became more experienced and methods matured, journal reviewers and leading scholars in PE called for qualitative researchers to advance existing theory by grounding investigations in theoretical perspectives developed in fields like education and the social sciences. In response, between the years 1998 and 2008, 38 different theories and frameworks were referenced in qualitative articles that appeared in *JTPE*, which totaled 69.1% of all qualitative articles published during that time (Hemphill et al.,

2012). Today, it is not uncommon to read research articles where investigators ground their investigation in theory while simultaneously employing elements of a grounded theory or inductive approach.

Forms of qualitative inquiry

The extent of the qualitative researcher's involvement in a research setting ranges from non-participant to full participant. The researcher who employs a non-participant approach observes events from the sidelines as they unfold, without involvement in the natural setting. In contrast, the researcher who assumes a participant approach becomes deeply and personally involved in the contexts being studied often becoming one of the participants. In both cases, research questions are typically developed prior to entering the field, and as results begin to emerge, questions and methodology are often revised, facilitating richly textured data.

Those endeavoring to seek awareness through qualitative inquiry assume a variety of philosophical approaches. Denzin and Lincoln (2011) offer nine, Marshall and Rossman (2010) discuss nine, and Saldana (2011) describes thirteen different approaches in which qualitative inquiry can be conducted. Clearly such diversity offers opportunities for researchers to select an approach that best fits their philosophic orientation toward qualitative inquiry. Utilizing a particular or a combination of approaches, such as scaffolding, is essential in establishing the study's credibility. The most frequently used approaches across the literature in PE include case study, ethnography, critical theory, narrative, life history, and phenomenology.

Case study

In using a case study approach the researcher examines a *specific* entity or event for increased understanding. Data are typically gathered through observations, interviews, documents, and audio/video. There are three reasons for opting to conduct case study research: (1) access to enriched disclosure of places others might never go; (2) opportunity to view an event or situation through the lens of the researcher; and (3) reduced defensiveness and resistance among readers (Gomm, Hammersley, & Foster, 2000). Such microscopic views intensify experience and heighten awareness. The researcher's choice to utilize an instrumental, collective, or intrinsic case study approach is governed by purpose. According to Gomm and colleagues (2000), if the study is instrumental, the focus is on a specific issue with one case to illustrate; if collective, multiple cases offer varied perspectives on the same specific issue; and if intrinsic, intent may be simply to evaluate the case itself, whether it is an activity, an individual, or a circumstance.

Scholars in PE who engage in case study research are heavily influenced by the work of Robert Stake (1995), who defined critical aspects of such an approach in his seminal text, *The Art of Case Study Research*. One of the first published case studies in PE pedagogy, authored by Templin (1989), focused on the influence of workplace conditions over time on a secondary school physical educator. More recently, case studies have appeared in journal publications including work by Lux and McCullick (2011), Thorburn (2011), and Woods and Lynn (2014). Each of these cases explores the professional lives of veteran teachers who have persisted in the profession and factors that have invigorated and frustrated them during their careers.

By narrowing examination to a specific circumstance, more thoroughly illuminating context and interaction, a case study provides in-depth observation and understanding. Conclusions drawn in such studies offer insights to applications appropriate in similar contexts.

Ethnography

The complex culture of a group is the core of study in ethnography, a type of research that evolved from the field of anthropology (Wall, 2015). In an ethnographic study researchers immerse themselves long term in the culture and lives of the group of interest, utilizing a variety of data collection methods to explore the rich texture of that culture. They report the behaviors, beliefs, and language of the group. Features of ethnographic research include a focus on one or a small number of cases; data collection obtained through interviews, artifacts, and other sources; and depiction of the ideas and beliefs of the group defined through observable actions. Difficulties inherent in this type of research are acceptance of the individual researcher as a trusted other, the extensive time required, and the storytelling nature of the report.

An example of ethnography in the PE literature is a study conducted by Azzarito (2012) in which she used visual participatory ethnographic research methods to examine "what moving in their worlds" meant to inter-city student-researchers. Her participants used digital cameras to construct visual diaries to express their "thoughts, feelings and ideas [that] 'speak for themselves' about their knowledge of their own bodies, sharing their embodiments" (p. 295).

A more recent form of ethnographic research that has appeared in the PE literature is *autoethnography*, whereby a researcher strives to explain and analyze personal experience. Patton (2002) describes autoethnography as using one's own experiences "to garner insights into the larger culture." He maintains that the distinguishing difference between autoethnography and ethnography is "self-awareness about and reporting of one's own experiences and introspections as a primary data source" (p. 86). Marshall and Rossman (2010) identify this approach as both a method and a product. Invitation for self-disclosure through blogs, reality shows, and YouTube contribute to the increasing utilization of this method. Using a self-study approach, Casey and Fletcher (2012) used teacher socialization as a lens through which they studied their own personal transitions from high school teachers to PE teacher education (PETE) faculty members. They improved their understandings of self and practice by serving as both participants and the instruments through which data were collected.

Critical theory

Critical theory is a research orientation in which investigators study power imbalances and justice, and seek to enable individuals to overcome constraints related to ethnicity, class, gender, and other social contexts (Creswell, 2013). The aim of this approach is not simply to describe the situation from a particular vantage point; instead the goal is to challenge the situation (Cohen & Crabtree, 2006). Critical theorists encourage participants to explore their current experiences through dialogues and reflections so that eventually change can occur. Related to the critical theory approach are the orientations of critical race theory, queer theory, and disability theory (Creswell, 2013).

As an example, when traditional ethnography centers on a political perspective characteristic of a specific group, it may be identified as *critical ethnography*. This type of ethnography is based on *critical theory*. Within PE research, critical ethnography evolved from attempts to drastically alter deeply rooted educational practices. Critical ethnography identifies significant constraints on a specific group in a defined context. Madison (2012) clarifies that through critical ethnography the researcher is bound to address unfair or unjust processes in an effort to improve such conditions.

Katie Fitzpatrick (2011) published a year-long critical ethnography of the lives of a class of 16 students in a multi-ethnic New Zealand high school. She spent more than 150 hours in their PE, health, and sports camp classes to better understand the *place* of PE in their lives. Fitzpatrick reported that, "On the one hand, PE is implicated with narrow body norms while on the other hand it provides a space for relationship building, play and critical resistance." Furthermore, she noted that PE was a key site for learning and was "politically fraught, given its close association with racialized and gendered body discourses" (p. 174).

Life history

In a life history approach, the researcher explores a person's life, usually focusing on the cultural norms that influenced the individual (Hays & Singh, 2012). The researcher works closely with the participant as s/he tells the stories of her/his life. Face-to-face interviews are the most common type of data collection, although Schempp, Sparks, and Templin (1993, p. 450) indicate that any document or artifact that "may in some way describe a person's vision of the world is appropriate for analysis." They published a noteworthy study in the *American Educational Research Journal* in which they utilized life history methodology to reconstruct the micropolitics of teacher induction from the perspectives of three beginning teachers. They found that the teachers' thoughts and actions were swayed and sustained by three streams of consciousness: biography, role demands, and the school culture.

Narrative

Hays and Singh (2012) identify three assumptions that undergird narrative research. First, through stories, individuals connect events over time in a culturally meaningful manner. Second, their identities are shaped by these stories. Third, their narratives change depending upon audience and context. In narrative research, detailed accounts by an individual or group of individuals offer others opportunities to understand groups, communities, and contexts through the lived experiences of the participants.

As an example of narrative research in PETE, Stride (2014) interviewed South Asian Muslim girls regarding their views of school-based physical activities and the way participation influenced their involvement in physical activities away from school. Through analysis of their narratives, Stride discovered that the girls did not fit the passive and fragile stereotype ascribed to them, they enjoyed the social opportunities afforded in PE, and they were also physically active outside of school. Narratives afforded a lens into the girls' perceptions regarding physical activities, dispelling previously conceived notions. By utilizing a narrative approach researchers uncover specificities not necessarily recognizable by other means.

Phenomenology

Testimonies of an experience related to a phenomenon are examined in a phenomenological study. More specifically, a phenomenological approach weaves the researchers' lived experiences with the topic, which Moustakas (1994) calls the epoche, with those of the participants. In so doing both the researcher's and the participants' understandings grow and mature as they build shared meanings. After catastrophes occur, for example, the media often interview all survivors to showcase varied perspectives about the traumatic incident. In a phenomenological study, however, the researcher examines these testimonies to find the common thread that interlaces their stories to build a composite, whereby conclusions about the experience can be drawn. Phenomenology clearly seeks commonalities about a shared experience. Whereas narrative centers on the lived experience of an individual, phenomenology examines meaning derived from a shared experience (Creswell, 2014).

In a phenomenological study of the parental involvement in PE for students with developmental disabilities, An and Hodge (2013) utilized interviews, artifacts (photographs and written documents), and researchers' journals to examine the meaning of parental involvement. The results demonstrated the need for establishing partnerships in PE between parents and physical educators.

Planning a study

A number of considerations must be explored as the qualitative researcher conceptualizes various aspects of a study. Attention to these elements often separates qualitative genres from other research forms.

Selection of participants

After determining the research question, participants should be selected who will best contribute insights toward better understanding the question. Purposeful selection ensures that "particular settings, persons, or activities are selected deliberately to provide information that is particularly relevant" (Maxwell, 2013, p. 97). Determining the number of locations and participants to include is dependent upon the chosen design. Creswell (2014, p. 189) maintains that narrative research typically includes 1 or 2 individuals; phenomenology 3–10, grounded theory 20–30; ethnography one culture-sharing group with numerous artifacts, interviews, and observations; and case studies 4 or 5 cases.

Data collection

In qualitative research the most common methods of data collection include: interviews, observations, and document analysis (Locke, Silverman, & Spirduso, 2010). Each method is detailed below.

Interviewing

Through interviews, a researcher is exposed to the participant's point of view in his or her own words and is granted insights to the meaning of their experiences. The type of interview, its content, and method are based on the research tradition of the investigation with interview approaches ranging from informal to semi-structured to structured. Individual interviews are the most common data collection method in qualitative research. Other methods include interviews of dyads, triads, and focus groups that consist of five to ten participants. Most interviews are audio recorded and conducted in a face-to-face setting, via telephone or video conversations or online via email communication.

Observations

Observation as a means of data collection in qualitative research includes not only formally recording events, actions, conversations, and artifacts at the site, but also informally joining in on-site activities. Such data collection can stand as its own method or complement others (Hays & Singh, 2012). Much of observational data collection occurs in natural or everyday settings, such as in classrooms or on playgrounds, in which the researcher attempts to conduct the observation without disrupting the lived experiences occurring in the venue. There is an observation continuum, however, which spans from the researcher as a complete observer to complete participant (Creswell, 2013).

Document analysis

Alongside interviews and observations, existing documents or writings provide vital sources of qualitative data. The examination of documents is "potentially quite rich in portraying the values and beliefs of participants in a setting" (Marshall & Rossman, 2010, p. 164). Data in the form of documents can be public or private in nature. For example, researchers could analyze a newspaper report of an innovative curriculum in a PE program, which would be a public document. Likewise, the examination of lesson plans represent private documents. Journals, blogs, and email correspondences are also becoming common document data sources.

Quality control

There are as many different forms of qualitative inquiry as there are perspectives about how it should be conducted. At one end of the continuum are those who believe strongly that qualitative inquiry should have rigor and employ standards that promote quality control in a manner similar to quantitative inquiry. They argue that "authors who use positivist terminology facilitate the acceptance of qualitative research in a quantitative world" (Creswell, 2013, p. 146). At the other end are those who argue strongly against equating qualitative inquiry to quantitative inquiry and believe that quality can be established by understanding rather than convincing (Creswell, 2013; Wollcott, 1990). Although authors in PE use a variety of techniques to demonstrate quality, the majority employ procedures that facilitate credibility, dependability, and confirmability. When these exist, readers of qualitative inquiry tend to perceive that trustworthiness also exists. While some of the more commonly applied strategies are highlighted below, it is not an exclusive list, nor should it be interpreted that studies lacking one or more techniques are unworthy of publication. It must be emphasized, however, that peer reviewers in PE are more likely to perceive quality in those studies that employ multiple methods and utilize several quality controls than in those that do not.

Credibility

In qualitative inquiry, it is important to demonstrate that the findings of a study adequately represent participants' perspectives and the context in which the study occurred. Similar to establishing validity in quantitative inquiry (Lincoln & Guba, 1985), qualitative investigators seek to ensure that data are credible. One of the more frequently used ways in which investigators demonstrate credibility is through *triangulation* (Hemphill et al., 2012). Triangulation may involve using different methodological approaches when conducting a study. For example, "this can mean using several kinds of methods or data, including both quantitative and qualitative approaches" (Patton, 2002, p. 247). Triangulation may also involve the use of multiple investigators or multiple theories. It is a technique that enables investigators to make comparisons and test for consistency.

Another technique associated with ensuring the results are credible is *prolonged engagement*. This "is the investment of sufficient time to achieve certain purposes: learning the 'culture,' testing for misinformation introduced by distortions either of the self or the respondents, and building trust" (Lincoln & Guba, 1985, p. 301). By immersing oneself in a setting for an extended period of time, the researcher becomes more familiar with the environment and less likely to mischaracterize what is transpiring. In addition, as participants become increasingly familiar with the investigator, they are more likely to trust the researcher and provide information they may not have shared at an earlier point in time during the study. Whereas it is not unusual for sociologists and anthropologists to immerse themselves in a setting for years, few, if any, researchers in PE have that luxury given job responsibilities at their university. In most cases, researchers who conduct observations can only visit a site for several hours during the day and for no more than a few weeks at a time. Rovegno, however, is one example of a researcher who has achieved prolonged engagement by studying at the same school and with same teacher over a three-year period (Rovegno, 1998; Rovegno & Bandhauer, 1997).

The most commonly employed technique for facilitating credibility in PE research is through *member checking*; employed by 44% of all researchers who published in *JTPE* during a ten-year period of time (Hemphill et al., 2012). This requires investigators to return to participants to check the accuracy of transcripts and confirm emerging themes. In smaller studies, all participants will likely participate in member checks whereas in larger studies, only a representative proportion might engage in the process.

Another popular technique that qualitative researchers in PE use to facilitate credibility is *peer debriefing* (Hemphill et al., 2012). Here a colleague familiar with qualitative inquiry is selected to assist the investigator. The role of this individual is to thoroughly review the data and "keep the inquirer 'honest,' exposing him or her to searching questions by an experienced protagonist doing his or her best to play the devil's advocate" (Lincoln & Guba, 1985, p. 308). Their role, however, is not to demand or discourage but to encourage greater reflection.

Lincoln and Guba (1985) suggest that another valuable technique associated with credibility is through *negative case analysis*. They state that negative case analysis is "a 'process of revising hypotheses with hindsight.' The object of the game is continuously to refine a hypothesis until it *accounts for all known cases without exception*" (p. 309, original emphasis). When using this technique, qualitative investigators examine emerging themes and account for and explain instances where discrepancies may exist. Although time consuming, this approach promotes credibility and allows for new findings, some of which will provide for greater sophistication of results, to emerge. For example, in Graber's (1991) study of studentship, she found that students were more likely to cheat in one observed class than in another. Had she only observed students enrolled in one class, she might have assumed that cheating was a typical behavior commonly employed by undergraduate students. Since her study employed triangulation across settings, however, she had the advantage of observing the same students in two different settings. Although cheating became one of the themes in her results, she had to explain why some students cheated in one class and not the other. A negative case search enabled her to determine that cheating is heavily influenced by contextual factors and not a behavior students employ without consideration of the learning environment.

Dependability

Although dependability is similar to establishing reliability in quantitative inquiry, Lincoln and Guba (1985) emphasize that naturalists understand that the world changes. Therefore, instead of seeking to ensure that results are predictable and consistent, qualitative researchers seek to account for instability. Lincoln and Guba suggest that *overlap of methods*, one form of triangulation, can assist in establishing dependability. Another method they suggest is an *inquiry audit*. This involves inviting an experienced qualitative investigator to carefully examine all aspects of data collection and analysis.

Confirmability

In qualitative inquiry, it is important that findings are "determined by the subjects (respondents) and conditions of inquiry and not by the biases, motivations, or perspectives" of the qualitative researcher (Lincoln & Guba, 1985, p. 290). One technique frequently employed by investigators in PE involves establishing an *audit trail*. Qualitative investigators may seek the assistance of an "auditor" whose role it is to examine both the record keeping *process* and the *product* (data, emerging themes, recommendations) (Lincoln & Guba, 1985). In order to accomplish this, it is important that the investigator maintain impeccable records. By using separate logs, for example, to record observations, describe methodological procedures, and document emerging theories, it will be easier for the investigator to analyze results and for the auditor to confirm that emerging themes and theories are supported in the data.

It is essential that readers perceive study results as trustworthy. By incorporating quality controls during an investigation, the researcher increases the likelihood that peer reviewers and other scholars will believe the results are credible and dependable. Thus, Patton (2002) emphasizes that the investigator must "carefully reflect on, deal with, and report potential sources of bias and error" (p. 51). In order to promote trustworthiness, it is common practice for qualitative investigators to consider personal bias prior to an investigation and disclose bias in written manuscripts. An excellent example of disclosure can be found in a published manuscript that addresses communities of practice in PE (see Parker, Patton, Madden, & Sinclair, 2010).

Data analysis

Unlike quantitative inquiry, in which data analysis does not begin until all data have been collected, qualitative inquiry begins immediately as data are collected and continues until all data have been analyzed and accounted for after data collection ceases (Patton, 2015). This enables research procedures to be revised and new questions to be asked as results begin to unfold. It is an inordinately time consuming and challenging process that can be made easier by having maintained orderly records. Even then, however, sorting through hundreds of documents and making comparisons between and among interview transcripts, observation and method logs, and documents collected in the field, requires an intensive time commitment. Careful analysis is revealed in manuscripts that provide sophisticated insights whereas cursory analysis reveals itself in letters of rejection from a journal editor to an investigator. It has been argued that a good qualitative investigator is able to make the familiar strange and the strange familiar (Delamont & Atkinson, 1995; Erikson, 1986). This occurs when a phenomenon which is considered easily explainable and understood becomes complex and unfamiliar. A good qualitative investigator is able to provoke contemplation and consideration of vantage points that may not have been previously considered by readers. Achieving this goal, however, requires time, continuous consideration of the data, and adequate discussion with others about emerging findings.

There is no singular procedure or technique for analyzing qualitative data. Multiple forms of analysis exist and entire books have been written on the subject. Some researchers prefer to manually analyze data while others use qualitative data analysis software such as NVivo, ATLAS. ti, or QDA Miner to assist with the process. Ultimately, it is the responsibility of the investigator to select those procedures that best meet the philosophic orientation of the study, the purpose of the investigation, and the methods that were used to collect data. In PE, open and axial coding are commonly employed techniques. Open coding is the "process of breaking down, examining, comparing, conceptualizing, and categorizing data" (Strauss & Corbin, 1990, p. 61) whereas axial coding is the process of developing codes in relation to each other. Typically, this latter approach employs both inductive and deductive reasoning and analysis. These techniques were employed in a recent study examining bullying in middle school PE (O'Connor & Graber, 2014).

Inductive analysis occurs when an investigator analyzes data without regard to a particular theory (Patton, 2002). Consistent with grounded theory, it is a deliberative attempt to develop new theory based on the data collected. Patton states, "Inductive analysis begins with specific observations and builds toward general patterns. Categories or dimensions of analysis emerge from open-ended observations as the inquirer comes to understand patterns that exist in the phenomenon being investigated" (2002, pp. 55–56). In contrast, deductive analysis occurs when investigators analyze data in relation to hypotheses generated prior to data collection or in relation to pre-existing theories (Patton, 2002). Both approaches have merit and investigators in PE increasingly employ both during data analysis. For example, Woods and Lynn (2001) initially employed an inductive approach when analyzing how PE teachers matured with experience. Upon locating an existing theoretical framework that accounted for their findings, they conducted a deductive analysis.

Qualitative analysis provides an in-depth perspective from which to view natural experience and context associated with phenomena. Highly trained qualitative researchers work persistently over time to draw an accurate picture of the setting, participants, and events (Patton, 2015). In each instance, these in-depth analyses enhance our understanding and provide important insights into the world. In education and physical education researchers are using multiple data sources and methods to illuminate the teaching-learning process within a rich and highly complex world of schools.

Summary of key findings

- The depth and breadth of published qualitative investigations have enabled our understanding of PE to grow substantially.
- Qualitative researchers today are asking increasingly sophisticated questions and employing mixed methods because of an earlier generation of scholars who blazed a trail.
- Studies can range from an investigation of a single individual using a case study approach to ethnography where the complex culture of a group is examined.
- Investigators rely on a variety of techniques and theories for framing their studies, collecting and analyzing data, and ensuring that findings are trustworthy.
- Studies that have employed qualitative techniques have made a tremendous contribution to the profession.
- The debate about methodology has quieted, and the research question being asked is now the primary factor in determining which methodology is most appropriate.
- Researchers work to design credible and trustworthy studies from the time the study is conceptualized until data analysis is complete.
- Multiple software packages exist to assist researchers in the complex and time consuming tasks associated with data organization and analysis. These programs can reduce the time required while assisting researchers to position data creatively to discern intriguing relationships in highly complex settings.

Reflective questions for discussion

1. To what extent must qualitative investigators continue to defend the significance of their research and its applicability to other settings?
2. If qualitative inquiry is an acceptable and valued form of inquiry, why is it so difficult to successfully compete for external funding for projects?

3. Consider an idea that you have for a research study and identify several different data sources that might provide insight to answer your research questions.
4. What new methods and techniques might emerge for gathering qualitative data?
5. How might emerging technologies influence the manner in which qualitative studies are conducted and interpreted?
6. When designing a qualitative research study, suggest several different strategies you can use to increase the credibility of your research.

References

An, J., & Hodge, S. (2013). Exploring the meaning of parental involvement in physical education for students with developmental disabilities. *Adapted Physical Activity Quarterly, 29,* 147–163.

Azzarito, L. (2011). *E-Guide to qualitative methods in physical activity research.* Reston, VA: American Alliance for Health, Physical Education, Recreation and Dance.

Azzarito, L. (2012). Photography as a pedagogical tool for shedding light on "bodies-at-risk" in physical culture. *Visual Studies, 27,* 295–309.

Bogdan, R. (2009). *Qualitative research.* Retrieved from www.education.com/reference/article/qualitative-research/.

Casey, A., & Fletcher, T. (2012). Trading places: From physical education teachers to teacher educators. *Journal of Teaching in Physical Education, 31,* 362–380.

Cohen, D., & Crabtree, B. (2006). *Qualitative research guidelines project.* Robert Wood Johnson Foundation. Retrieved from www.qualres.org/index.html/.

Creswell, J. W. (2013). *Qualitative inquiry & research design: Choosing among five approaches* (3rd edn). Los Angeles: Sage.

Creswell, J. W. (2014). *Research design: Qualitative, quantitative, and mixed methods approaches* (4th edn). Thousand Oaks: Sage.

Delamont, S., & Atkinson, P. (1995). *Fighting familiarity: Essays on education and ethnography.* Cresskill, NJ: Hampton Press.

Denzin, N. D., & Lincoln, Y. S. (2011). *The Sage handbook of qualitative research* (4th edn). Thousand Oaks, CA: Sage.

Earls, N. (1986). Introduction. *Journal of Teaching in Physical Education, 6,* 7–9.

Erikson, F. (1986). Qualitative methods in research on teaching. In M. C. Wittrock (Ed.), *Handbook of research on teaching* (pp. 119–158). New York: Macmillan.

Fernandez-Balboa, J. M. (1991). Beliefs, interactive thoughts, and actions of physical education student teachers regarding pupil misbehaviors. *Journal of Teaching in Physical Education, 11,* 59–78.

Fitzpatrick, K. (2011). Stop playing up!: Physical education, racialization and resistance. *Ethnography, 12,* 174–197.

Glaser, B., & Strauss, A. (1967). *The discovery of grounded theory.* Chicago: Aldine.

Gomm, R., Hammersley, M., & Foster, P. (2000). *Case study method.* London: Sage.

Graber, K. C. (1991). Studentship in preservice teacher education: A qualitative study of undergraduate students in physical education. *Research Quarterly for Exercise and Sport, 62,* 41–51.

Griffin, P. S. (1983). "Gymnastics is a girl's thing": Student participation and interaction patterns in a middle school gymnastics unit. In T. J. Templin & J. K. Olson (Eds.), *Teaching in physical education* (pp. 71–85). Champaign, IL: Human Kinetics.

Griffin, P. S. (1984). Girls' participation patterns in a middle school team sports unit. *Journal of Teaching in Physical Education, 4,* 30–38.

Griffin, P. S. (1985a). Boys' participation styles in a middle school physical education sports unit. *Journal of Teaching in Physical Education, 4,* 100–110.

Griffin, P. S. (1985b). Teacher perceptions of and reactions to equity problems in a middle school physical education program. *Research Quarterly of Exercise and Sport, 56,* 103–110.

Hays, D. G., & Singh, A. A. (2012). *Qualitative inquiry in clinical and educational settings.* New York: The Guilford Press.

Hemphill, M. A., Richards, K. A. R., Templin, T. J., & Blankenship, B. (2012). A content analysis of qualitative research in the *Journal of Teaching in Physical Education* from 1998–2008. *Journal of Teaching in Physical Education, 31,* 279–287.

Lincoln, Y. S., & Guba, E. G. (1985). *Naturalistic inquiry*. Newbury Park, CA: Sage.

Locke, L. F. (1989). Qualitative research as a form of scientific inquiry in sport and physical education. *Research Quarterly for Exercise and Sport, 60*, 1–20.

Locke, L. F., Silverman, S. J., & Spirduso, W. (2010). *Reading and understanding research* (3rd edn). Thousand Oaks, CA: Sage.

Lux, K. M., & McCullick, B. A. (2011). How one exceptional teacher navigated her working environment as the teacher of a marginal subject. *Journal of Teaching in Physical Education, 30*, 358–374.

Madison, D. S. (2012). *Critical ethnography: Method, ethics, and performance*. Thousand Oaks, CA: Sage.

Marshall, C., & Rossman, G. B. (2010). *Designing qualitative research* (5th ed.). Los Angeles: Sage.

Maxwell, J. A. (2013). *Qualitative research design: An interactive approach*. Thousand Oaks, CA: Sage.

Moustakas, C. (1994). *Phenomenological research methods*. Thousand Oaks, CA: Sage.

O'Connor, J. A., & Graber, K. C. (2014). Sixth-grade physical education: An acculturation of bullying and fear. *Research Quarterly for Exercise and Sport, 85*, 398–408.

Parker, M., Patton, K., Madden, M., & Sinclair, C. (2010). From committee to community: The development and maintenance of a community of practice. *Journal of Teaching in Physical Education, 29*, 337–357.

Patton, M. Q. (2002). *Qualitative research and evaluation methods* (3rd edn). Thousand Oaks, CA: Sage.

Patton, M. Q. (2015). *Qualitative research and evaluation methods* (4th edn). Thousand Oaks, CA: Sage.

Placek, J. (1983). Conceptions of success in teaching: Busy, happy and good? In T. J. Templin & J. K. Olson (Eds.), *Teaching in physical education* (pp. 46–56). Champaign, IL: Human Kinetics.

Placek, J. H. (1984). A multi-case study of teacher planning in physical education. *Journal of Teaching in Physical Education, 4*, 39–49.

Rossman, G. B., & Rallis, S. F. (2012). *Learning in the field: An introduction to qualitative research* (3rd edn). Thousand Oaks, CA: Sage.

Rovegno, I. (1998). The development of in-service teachers' knowledge of a constructivist approach to physical education: Teaching beyond activities. *Research Quarterly for Exercise and Sport, 69*, 147–162.

Rovegno, I., & Bandhauer, D. (1997). Norms of the school culture that facilitated teacher adoption and learning of a constructivist approach to physical education. *Journal of Teaching in Physical Education, 16*, 401–425.

Saldana, J. (2011). *Ethnotheater: Research from page to stage*. Walnut Creek, CA: Left Coast Press.

Schempp, P. G. (1987). Research on teaching in physical education: Beyond the limits of natural science. *Journal of Teaching in Physical Education, 6*, 111–121.

Schempp, P. G. (1988). Exorcist II: A reply to Siedentop. *Journal of Teaching in Physical Education, 7*, 79–81.

Schempp, P. G., Sparks, A., & Templin, T. (1993). The micropolitics of teacher induction. *American Educational Research Journal, 30*, 447–472.

Siedentop, D. (1987). Dialogue or exorcism? A rejoinder to Schempp. *Journal of Teaching in Physical Education, 6*, 373–376.

Siedentop, D. (1989). Do the lockers really smell? *Research Quarterly for Exercise and Sport, 60*, 36–41.

Stake, R. E. (1995). *The art of case study research*. Thousand Oaks, CA: Sage.

Strauss, A., & Corbin, J. (1990). *Basics of qualitative research: Grounded theory procedure and techniques*. Newbury Park, CA: Sage.

Stride, A. (2014). "Let US tell YOU!" South Asian, Muslim girls tell tales about physical education. *Physical Education & Sport Pedagogy, 19*, 398–420.

Templin, T. (1989). Running on ice: A case study of the influence of workplace conditions on a secondary school physical educator. In T. Templin & P. Schempp (Eds.), *Socialization into physical education: Learning to teach* (pp. 165–195). Indianapolis, IN: Benchmark Press.

Thorburn, M. (2011). "Still game": An analysis of the life history and career disappointments of one veteran male teacher of physical education in Scotland. *Educational Review, 63*, 329–343.

Wall, S. (2015). Focused ethnography: A methodological adaption for social research in emerging contexts. *Forum: Qualitative Social Research, 16*(1), 102–116.

Wollcott, H. F. (1990). On seeking – and rejecting – validity in qualitative research. In E. W. Eisner & A. Peshkin (Eds.), *Qualitative inquiry in education: The continuing debate* (pp. 121–152). New York: Teachers College Press.

Woods, A. M., & Lynn, S. K. (2001). Through the years: A longitudinal study of physical education teachers from a research-based preparation program. *Research Quarterly for Exercise and Sport, 72*, 219–231.

Woods, A. M., & Lynn, S. K. (2014). One physical educator's career cycle: Strong start, great run, approaching finish. *Research Quarterly for Exercise and Sport, 85*, 68–80.

PART II

Curriculum theory and development

Introduction

Why does anyone need to learn about curriculum? Everyone knows what a curriculum is; after all we have all been to school, some of us for many years. We have all experienced a curriculum so we might say we know curriculum, if not intimately, certainly experientially. Interestingly, curriculum is one of those topics that the more you know, the more you don't know and the more you need to know to begin to have a comprehensive understanding of schools. As a curriculum specialist, myself, I would assert arguably that curriculum is the center of the educational universe! Because educational programs reflect the values and beliefs of the curriculum developers and the societies in which they live, they are the generators for all other pedagogical process associated with content, teachers, students, teaching, and assessment – to name only a few.

As you get to know curriculum better, you find that there are explicit ties or relationships between and among each of its pedagogical "parts" explicitly and implicitly embedded in a curriculum. Curriculum developers must blend their beliefs and values with an understanding of content to answer key curriculum questions, such as "What knowledge and skills are of most value to my students in this school setting?" and "Why will this unit or lesson be meaningful to my students (that is, *all* of my students, not just the ones 'like me')?" Answers to these questions also require curriculum developers to understand the historical, cultural, political, and economic situations or contexts in which the curriculum will be implemented, who will implement and who will experience it. In many instances, although not all, it is probably easier to experience a curriculum than design one; one that is relevant and meaningful for these students within this very complex educational situation.

In this Handbook, the *Curriculum Theory and Development* part consists of six chapters that reflect both curriculum development – or how content and teaching are planfully integrated to form a coherent unit – and curriculum theory – the theoretical frameworks that bind together the working parts of a curriculum. While curriculum development is often quite concrete and focused on pedagogical information, curriculum theory is often more abstract. Developers work on the nuts and bolts of curriculum content or scope such as the topics to be taught in units and lessons. Developers also are responsible for deciding the order in which the content topics will be presented, described traditionally as sequence. Curriculum theorists define critical elements in the educational process and how they are linked or related to form a coherent plan of study that students will perceive as relevant and meaningful. At times, the theory precedes the development, but usually teachers work iteratively ... back and forth between the theoretical plan and actual student experiences to find just the "right" way to present a topic, invite and encourage student engagement with meaningful tasks, and find authentic and appropriate ways for students to learn and demonstrate their understandings.

In the first chapter (3) in this part, Donetta J. Cothran provides a primer of curriculum development, defining and explaining the curriculum process and how it often works in schools in the United States. She examines the complexity involved in defining traditional curriculum terms and process, the steps involved in curriculum planning, the role of standards in the curriculum process, and the challenges of authentic curricular assessment. Cothran critiques the traditional curriculum design process in the US that has been strongly influenced by the Tyler Rationale. Although incremental and logical, it does not actually reflect the dynamic processes teachers use in contemporary design. She continues to explain a more authentic contemporary, standards-based "backward" design model, Understanding by Design.

Ash Casey's chapter (4) on models-based practice provides an important perspective on theory-based curriculum development. Casey provides an in-depth analysis of ways that "big ideas," described as curriculum themes, can be used as theoretical frameworks to design models. Physical education curriculum models typically have a limited focus on one in-depth physical education content area, such as games, fitness and physical activity, or social justice, to name just a few. Casey problematizes the current implications, issues, and constraints of models-based practice and suggests the need to both understand the longitudinal impact of a model on practice and conduct research to examine multiple model implementation. He concludes by suggesting that future research should clarify the place of curriculum models in our physical education teacher education and school programs.

While Casey's chapter focuses on curriculum models, the next two chapters by Peter Hastie and Isabel Mesquita (5) and Malcolm Thorburn (6) provide descriptions and critiques of two "families" of curriculum models currently influencing physical education worldwide. Hastie and Mesquita's chapter delves deeply into the origins, philosophy, essence, and research associated with Sport Education as well as a number of other games-based approaches, such as Teaching Games for Understanding. Looking critically at "gaps" in games-based research, they suggest future designs and topics ripe for exploration. Thorburn, in turn, focuses on model-based approaches to fitness and physical activity curriculum. He analyzes the policy context in which these models have gained prominence and argues that a strength-based approach to fitness and physical activity emphasizing personal growth would best serve the longer term interests of physical education learners.

The part concludes with two chapters that explore contemporary theories that can help to explain curriculum complexity and constructs impacting implementation. In Chapter 7, Alan Ovens and Joy Butler describe the physical education curriculum implementation process from a complexity theory perspective. They begin with explanations of the terms and processes thought to work within dynamic, complex systems and conclude with three case studies that ground and illustrate complexity thinking in concrete and current practices of physical educators. Mauerberg-deCastro (Chapter 14) later will discuss complexity theory as dynamic systems theory instrumental in adapted physical education practices for students with disabilities.

In the final chapter (8) in this part, I look at the impact of context and the global political process to begin a discussion of curriculum within a globalized world. The world can be a perilous place where neoliberal political policies of privatization, accountability, and resource redistribution can hijack democratic curriculum discourse under the auspices of globalization.

Despite cautions, I argue that as scholars and teachers we have much to learn from each other in a globalized world. I conclude by elaborating the role of external funding to design, scale, and implement themes in globalized curriculum, providing examples using the themes of fair play, culturally sustaining and revitalizing dance curricula, and the central place of knowledge in physical education as a foundation to promote and facilitate positive, nurturing perspectives on youngsters' health and well-being.

As you continue reading through the parts and chapters in this Handbook, you will find that the themes introduced in these introductory chapters will be repeated, elaborated, and contradicted by the distinguished scholars who have contributed to this text. Hopefully, the curriculum seeds planted here will be nurtured as you conceptualize your own understanding of physical education pedagogies.

Catherine D. Ennis
University of North Carolina at Greensboro, USA

3

DESIGNING EFFECTIVE PROGRAMS

Creating curriculum to enhance student learning

Donetta J. Cothran, INDIANA UNIVERSITY, USA

Think back to your favorite PE memories from your K–12 school years. Was it a favorite sport that still makes you smile or was it a piece of equipment like the parachute or scooter that first came to mind? Now reflect on that experience and exactly what made it your favorite. Did you learn something specific that changed how you moved for a lifetime? Is your memory more about a positive emotion that came from being with friends, experiencing a novel task, or expressing yourself in a creative activity? Perhaps your memory is of competence and victory and having your status as a skilled mover publicly acknowledged? Do you believe everyone in the class experienced the unit in the same way you did? Why do you think your teachers even chose that content for your class? What did they hope you learned, if anything, and did they attempt to measure that learning? Did your parents know about that unit and what did they think about your participation in it? These are all questions of curriculum and the goal of this chapter is to discuss key curricular questions like these and offer recommendations for effective practices.

Curriculum definition

The definition of "curriculum" varies across time, theory, and educational settings. The word's Latin root, *currere*, refers to a course to be run and one common definition of curriculum stays true to that meaning with curriculum being described as a series of prescribed courses students must complete to achieve the finish line of graduation. Those Latin roots also show in the plural form of the word as the plural of curriculum is *curricula*. Sometimes curriculum is defined as the "what and why" of what schools teach with instruction being the "how" that material is taught. In curriculum theory, many scholars broaden the definition significantly to capture more of the students' educational experiences. These definitions often vary on two points. First, is a curriculum only *planned* experiences or does the curriculum include everything the student experiences while at school, planned or unplanned? One aspect of these unplanned experiences is the hidden curriculum (Bain, 1975; Kirk, 1992). For example, in PE students often experience very powerful learning about gender and sport. No formal curriculum has ever stated as a learning outcome, "Students will identify specific sports as boy or girl sports and engage more in their gender appropriate sports." Yet many students do believe that volleyball is a girls' team sport and football is for boys, and their participation patterns vary in the two sports accordingly (Azzarito

& Solmon, 2009). These beliefs and behaviors clearly represent student learning, but it was not officially planned for, so should it be considered part of the student experience and therefore part of the curriculum? Second, curricular definitions differ with regard to the impact on the student. Does the student actually have to learn or demonstrate mastery of the content for that content to be considered part of the curriculum or does the fact that the teacher taught it and students participated make it curriculum? A good working definition of curriculum is provided by Lund and Tannehill (2015) who define curriculum as including, "all knowledge, skills, and learning experiences that are provided to students within the school program" (p. 6).

Curricular levels

The concept of a curriculum is an abstract idea and it can be hard to understand and measure without examining it from different perspectives. Glatthorn, Boschee, Whitehead, and Boschee (2015) suggest two ways to think about curriculum levels. One is by viewing it as *prescriptive*, what should happen, or *descriptive*, the curriculum in action as experienced by the participants. Another way to examine curriculum is the level from which the individual is viewing the curriculum. Glatthorn and colleagues (2015) suggest looking at the different levels of a curriculum via these six frames: the *recommended curriculum*, the *written curriculum*, the *supported curriculum*, the *taught curriculum*, the *tested curriculum*, and the *learned curriculum*. See Figure 3.1.

The *recommended curriculum* can be thought of as the "external expert" level of the curriculum. At this level, the curriculum is a formal and political document that provides a framework for programs but rarely does it prescribe specific learning content or activities. For example, most state departments of education provide curricular frameworks for various subject matters, including PE. In Chapter 11, Penney and Mitchell point out a number of factors external to schools, teachers, and students that impact the recommended curriculum.

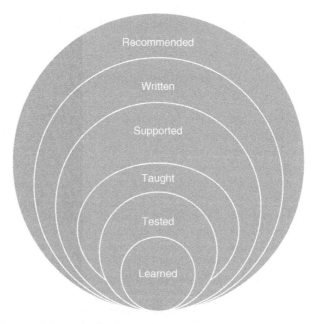

Figure 3.1 Glatthorn et al. (2015) levels of curriculum

The *written curriculum* (Glatthorn et al., 2015) generally focuses on expanding the expert recommendations into a detailed master plan for use by multiple teachers. Often the goal of the written curriculum is to standardize practice within a more defined setting, perhaps a school district. That standardization can sometimes be perceived as an attempt to control the individual teacher's decision making (see Petrie's Chapter 12 for discussion of this perspective). In addition to standardizing, Glatthorn et al. suggest the written curriculum also tries serve as a mediator between the realities of a local environment and the ideals of the recommended curriculum.

Resources as enhancers and constraints on what can and will be part of a planned program are key considerations at the *supported curriculum* level. For example, how much time is given to PE and what class sizes will be allowed and what equipment is available for use? Numerous authors have noted the challenges associated with resources and class size in PE (e.g., Bevans, Fitzpatrick, Sanchez, Riley, & Forest, 2010; Dyson, Coviello, DiCesare, & Dyson, 2009).

The *taught curriculum* may or may not resemble the written and supported curriculum, particularly in a content area like PE which, at least in the United States, does not currently have widespread use of standardizing protocols like textbooks and formal testing that often direct classroom teachers in their practice. It is anticipated that teachers will adapt, not adopt a curriculum based on personal values and individual school and student needs and resources, but how much adaptation can be made and still reflect the recommended or written curriculum varies widely across settings (e.g., Cothran, McCaughtry, Kulinna, & Martin, 2006; Curtner-Smith, Hastie, & Kinchin, 2008).

The *tested curriculum* is revealed by the content and range of assessment tools used. Those include teacher-made tests as well as formal, standardized tests that may be mandated by the school district or state department of education. A common curricular misalignment in PE occurs at this level as many teachers use fitness testing as a primary assessment even though their curricular content is sport skill or participation based. Increasingly student results on the tested curriculum are being used as an indicator of teacher effectiveness (see McCullick, Gaudreault & Ramos, Chapter 25 in this volume; Rink, 2013).

Glatthorn et al. (2015) suggest thinking about the *recommended curriculum* as what "ought" to happen while the *written, supported, taught,* and *tested* levels are what educators intend to happen in a class. The planned and unplanned changes to students' knowledge and skills are the *learned curriculum*. It includes intentional items from the prior levels of curricular planning as well as un-intended learning via the hidden curriculum. Students are not passive recipients at this level as they are actively involved in negotiating the class content (Cothran & Ennis, 1997; see Solmon's Chapter 33 in this volume), and accountability systems (Carlson & Hastie, 1997).

Thus, we can define a curriculum by examining different events or outcomes at each of Glatthorn et al.'s (2015) levels. Thinking about curriculum within levels also assists in assessing outcomes or program quality. By analyzing the curriculum at each level, we can determine if the outcomes listed at the *recommended* and *written* curriculum levels, for example, are the same as those students actually experience (*learned* level) and achieve (*tested* level). Comparing the teacher's purpose and content (*taught* level) with students' experiences (*learned* level) gives us a better idea of curricular implementation and concrete reasons why students may or may not have learned (*tested* level).

Curriculum design and planning

Historically, physical educators have often started their educational planning at a local level with a list of possible activities they might want to teach. Depending on the season as well as time and resources, teachers then decide what will be taught in a school year. Within each of those typically short units (the multi-activity model is discussed more fully in Hastie & Mesquita, Chapter 5) teachers might have educational goals in mind but rarely is the curriculum developed comprehensively beyond perhaps offering a variety of activities (e.g., dance, individual/dual sports, team sports, fitness). In this multi-activity planning model, the content or activity comes first in planning, not student learning. After selecting the activity, the teacher then decides what specifically the student needs to learn about the sport or movement form and plans the unit. Alternately, the planning starts and stops with the unit selection and the program is largely recreational in nature with no specific learning objectives in mind beyond student engagement. Placek (1983) described these programs as having goals of keeping students "busy, happy, and good."

The Tyler Rationale

Until recently, programs that did attempt an educational focus likely used the Tyler Rationale (Tyler, 1949, see also Ovens & Butler, Chapter 7) to guide their planning. Tyler's work was the culmination of over 50 years of American education's focus on a scientific system of efficiency that originated in factory work analysis. The Tyler model dominated educational planning for decades and is still influential today. He suggested these four questions should guide curricular design:

1. What educational purposes should the school seek to attain?
2. What educational experiences are most likely to achieve these purposes?
3. What is the most effective organization of those experiences?
4. How can it be determined if the purposes have been attained?

Part of the scientific analysis of learning was the goal of identifying independent, discrete aspects of learning that could be taught and measured to document teaching effectiveness and student learning. This desire to articulate the specific sub-components of observable learning led to a second extremely influential publication by Bloom (1956). In Bloom's *Taxonomy of Educational Objectives* six levels of student understanding are identified in the cognitive domain. Later work by Bloom and others revised and expanded the original taxonomy of student learning to all three domains.

Standards-based planning

More recently, curricular planning is often guided by a standards-based approach. For teachers who have traditionally started planning with content or by thinking about the activities students will participate in during today's lesson, the standards-based curriculum is a very different way of looking at the curricular planning process. Planning starts not with activities but rather with broad student learning outcomes, and the design moves *backward* from outcomes to the tasks/activities needed to attain them. This concept of backward design will be described more fully in the next section. The Tyler Rationale also shares a focus on student learning outcomes, but the philosophical underpinnings of the two approaches (e.g., behavioral vs. constructivist learning, designing up vs. designing down, linear vs. inter-relational) are arguably quite different.

Both Tyler's (Tyler, 1949) historical focus on educational purposes and the more recent use of educational standards reflect a key question in curriculum design: What is the knowledge of most worth? (Broudy, 1982; Young, 2013). In the past those most valued purposes have often been called goals. In the United States today, broad student learning outcomes are more likely to be called standards. Internationally the terms may differ, but many countries have developed similar guiding principles for PE programs. (See MacPhail [2015] for an overview of different national standards.) Regardless of the nomenclature the basic principle is the same: curriculum planning starts at the end of the learning process by defining what students should know, value, and be able to do. These expectations are made explicit when planning is directed toward these student learning outcomes. In the Society of Health and Physical Educators (SHAPE) America K-12 Standards for PE (Table 3.1, SHAPE America, 2014) note the repeated use of the term *physically literate individual*. The term *physical literacy* is a relatively new one in PE curriculum theory and it is meant as a comprehensive term that captures the multi-faceted nature of student learning in PE (Whitehead & Duncan, 2010). PE is not just about the psychomotor domain, although that contribution does make the content area unique in the school setting, but also is about student learning in the cognitive and affective domains. Incorporating the term *literacy* into the national standards also parallels the terminology used in the broader educational community to reflect student learning outcomes in other content areas.

Additionally, national standards in most countries often include student outcomes at specific points prior to the final year. These are sometimes called benchmarks or levels, and in the SHAPE America standards (SHAPE America, 2014) are referred to as grade level outcomes. Sometimes the benchmarks are provided in groupings of student grades (e.g., K-2, 3–5, 6–8, 9–12) and at other times, yearly guidance is provided. The goal of these sub-standards is to provide checkpoints along the way to guide educators in the planning process. Table 3.2 provides one example from the SHAPE America standards of how the grade level standards are linked building blocks that extend student learning across the years. Notice how the grade level

Table 3.1 SHAPE America national standards for K-12 physical education (reproduced with permission)

1. The physically literate individual demonstrates competency in a variety of motor skills and movement patterns.
2. The physically literate individual applies knowledge of concepts, principles, strategies, and the tactics related to movement and performance.
3. The physically literate individual demonstrates the knowledge and skills to achieve and maintain a health-enhancing level of physical activity and fitness.
4. The physically literate individual exhibits responsible personal and social behavior that respects self and others.
5. The physically literate individual recognizes the value of physical activity for health, enjoyment, challenge, self-expression, and/or social interaction.

Table 3.2 Examples of SHAPE America grade level outcomes (reproduced with permission)

SHAPE America (2014) National K-12 Standards

Standard 1: Demonstrates competency in a variety of motor skills and movement patterns
Kindergarten: Strikes a lightweight object with a paddle or short handled racket
Fifth Grade: Strikes an object consecutively with a partner using a short handled implement over a net or against a wall in either a competitive or cooperative environment
Eighth Grade: Strikes with a mature overhand pattern in a modified game for net/wall games such as badminton, volleyball, or pickleball
9-12 Grade: Refines activity-specific movement skills in one or more lifetime activities

outcomes provide some specific topical guidance but they are not prescriptive with regard to specific content or instructional methods.

Using standards to guide curriculum design

National standards offer a valuable but general direction of intended student learning that represents the totality of student learning across the K–12 educational program. Although standards are not a curriculum, they do supply a foundation and framework from which decisions are made. Often a first step in a school's attempts to offer a standards-based curriculum is to approach the task by adding a link from the newly considered standards to the current curriculum guide and lesson plans. In this approach, the school takes its current curriculum and then looks to see what standards might be addressed by the current structure. For example, if a school offers a weight training unit, the teachers might then declare that unit to be a match for Standard 3 (SHAPE America, 2014) which relates to students' fitness, while the basketball unit is designated as meeting Standard 1's (SHAPE America, 2014) focus on movement skills. This haphazard, after-the-fact standard assigning process is not an appropriate way to build a standards-based curriculum that maximizes student learning. With this approach, the real questions of student learning and curricular decision-making remain unanswered (O'Shea, 2005). Why is weight training an essential life skill for these students to learn in this time and place? What skills are to be learned in basketball and why … and how do those basketball skills relate to other sports in the year's plan, much less how do they relate to the individual student's ability to be a healthy, active mover for a lifetime?

Understanding by Design

To answer those questions and to fulfill the potential of the curriculum to offer meaningful, high impact learning experiences for students, a process of intentional design, starting with the standards, must be undertaken. One comprehensive model for this process is Understanding by Design (UBD; Wiggins & McTighe, 2005). UBD integrates curriculum, assessment, and instruction with an overarching goal of creating a learning environment that produces students who leave school as active problem solvers with understandings and skills relevant to real life. A key tenet of UBD is the concept of backward design. Just as a driver starts a trip with a destination in mind, a UBD approach to curriculum starts at the end with the final destination in mind and the rest of the trip is then planned to ensure arrival at the final destination. There are three steps in the UBD backward design process (Wiggins & McTighe, 2005): 1) identify desired learning results via unpacking the standards, 2) determine acceptable evidence of learning, and 3) plan the instruction, a phase often called delivering forward.

Identify the desired results via unpacking the standards

In UBD, the desired student learning results must be identified first in the planning process. Although the national standards are an important influence on defining outcomes or results, they are just a starting point. The next step in the process is to ask, "What are the enduring understandings and essential questions that underlie the standards?" The essential question is NOT "What do students need to know about basketball?" rather essential questions and enduring understandings examine complex and *interconnected* links. Instead, an essential question might be, "Why and how do people choose to move?" and throughout the PE class specific content, like basketball, is examined from the lens of why might someone want to engage in basketball and how do they do that in their community? In this design step, teachers also examine specifically what skills and understandings do we want our students to know, do, and value? This reflective step is often referred to as "unpacking the standards."

When teachers unpack standards, they identify significant educational values and context that play an influential part in decision making (Lund & Tannehill, 2015). Chapter 36 (Kulinna & Cothran, this volume) discusses in detail teacher beliefs and the role they have in decision making. Although educational values and context influence the development of national standards, in the unpacking stage local stakeholder input starts to differentiate the curriculum. Sometimes that differentiation is influenced by community values and opportunities. One might ask, "What does it mean to be a mover in this time and place in this community?" For example, it may be a common choice to include cross country skiing in a curriculum for students in Maine but skiing is probably not going to be a curriculum choice for schools in southern California. Too many curricular guides ignore the reality of their setting and offer extremely detailed comprehensive plans for multiple sport and movement forms, yet those plans are totally unrealistic. One of the greatest constraints on curriculum development is the instructional time available to teach content to students (Kelly & Melograno, 2004). For example, a secondary student might only have one semester of PE which would be 90 days in most communities. Over the course of a semester that equates to 75 instructional hours (assuming 50 minute classes), not including instructional time lost to locker room time (probably 15 of the 50 minutes) nor the time lost to circumstances outside the teachers' control (typically 10% of the available school year) like school assemblies, field trips, and fire drills. What can be realistically accomplished in the remaining 45 instructional hours each year? Limited time and other factors like class size and available equipment also place constraints on what can be accomplished. Keep in mind the focus of the curriculum is on what students can actually *learn* in the time available, not what the students were exposed to or what the teacher talks about over the course of the year! Thus, when the curriculum is focused on learning outcomes, limited instructional time becomes a major constraint.

Given the limited time available in PE, difficult decisions must be made as to what student learning to prioritize. In addition to community values and resources, a curriculum planner also analyzes student needs and characteristics (Darst, Pangrazi, Brusseau, & Erwin, 2015). What knowledge, experience, attitudes, strengths, and needs do students bring to the program? Probably the biggest change in student needs in the last 15 years is the increasing incidence of overweight and obese students in the K-12 setting. Due to those demographic changes many teachers are actively re-thinking their curriculum to focus more on physical activity than physical skill development and the inclusion of additional wellness and nutrition knowledge in their classes (e.g., Hastie, 2003; Metzler, McKenzie, van der Mars, Barrett-Williams, & Ellis, 2013; for differing views on this topic see Chapter 38 by Weidong Li and Chapter 23 by Cameron, Norman, & Petherick). Other key stakeholders in the curricular decision making process include parents, school administrators, and other teachers. Teachers developing a curriculum attempt to account for all these factors and more when developing their program philosophy and curriculum.

Let us examine an example from a real world curriculum guide. The state of North Carolina (USA) has developed a state level curriculum guide that helps teachers with backward design and curriculum planning. In this guide, the 8th grade essential standard for personal and social responsibility is, The Student will: *Use behavioral strategies that are responsible and enhance respect of self and others and value activity* (North Carolina Department of Public Instruction, n.d.). What does this standard mean that a student will know and be able to do? The guide suggests these as possible answers to that important question:

- willingly join others of diverse culture, ethnicity, and gender during physical activity;
- work cooperatively with peers of differing skill to promote a safe school environment;
- recognize causes and then demonstrates potential solutions to issues as related to a safe school environment and the physical activity setting;
- work cooperatively with a group to achieve group goals in competitive as well as cooperative settings;
- display empathy to the feelings of others during physical activities;
- recognize the diversity and/or different cultures differences in participation in physical activity. (p. 25)

Even these unpacked meanings of the standard can be further analyzed for specific student learning competencies. As one example from the North Carolina document (p. 25), a more specific learning outcome is: "demonstrate conflict resolution skills; importance of positive attitude, sportsmanship, etiquette, fair play, and support to teammates and opponents whether you win or lose during group physical activity."

Determine acceptable evidence of learning

After key ideas and essential learning questions have been developed, the second step in the UBD planning process is to determine acceptable evidence of the learning (Wiggins & McTighe, 2005). How will teachers, students, parents, and any other interested stakeholders know that the essential learning has occurred? In UBD, assessment comes before instructional decisions. Instead of looking at the standards and asking "What would be a fun activity to do related to the standards?", the UBD planner asks "What performance task and/or other assessment tools would demonstrate real understanding by students?" and the answer to that question then guides the instructional decisions. The learning evidence should include a continuum of tools from informal checks on understanding, through traditional observations and tests, to more real world performance tasks and projects to provide multiple perspectives, not a single measure, of student learning (Wiggins & McTighe, 2005). For example, instead of a single fitness assessment of a mile run time, a teacher might collect information about the students' fitness in the form of an outside-of-class physical activity log, in class pedometer or heart rate information, and a test on cardiovascular fitness principles and planning in addition to the mile run time. For an even more authentic assessment task, the student could train for a local 5k race while keeping a training log and running journal. Some curricular documents identify acceptable levels of performance on assessments. When a *content standard* also includes performance criteria it is called a *performance standard*.

Planning instruction, or delivering forward

The third and final step in UBD is to plan the instructional activities (Wiggins & McTighe, 2005). Now that the teacher knows what students need to know, and how they will demonstrate their knowledge, learning activities are designed. This phase is often called the "delivering forward" step where the backward design process starts to move forward to the standards where the planning process began. When designing student experiences, Wiggins and McTighe (2005, pp. 197–222) suggest keeping in mind the acronym W. H. E. R. E. T. O.:

W = Help the students know **W**here the unit is going and **W**hat is expected? Help the teacher know **W**here the students are coming from (prior knowledge, interests)?

H = **H**ook all students and **H**old their interest?

E = **E**quip students, help them **E**xperience the key ideas, and **E**xplore the issues?

R = Provide opportunities to **R**ethink and **R**evise their understandings and work?

E = Allow students to **E**valuate their work and its implications?

T = Be **T**ailored (personalized) to the different needs, interests, and abilities of learners?

O = Be **O**rganized to maximize initial and sustained engagement as well as effective learning? (Reproduced with permission)

All these planning steps are designed to change the educational focus from what will be covered to what will be learned. Although presented linearly in this discussion, the process is actually quite iterative and related as the teacher works to build a coherent, cohesive plan that links essential student learning with assessment and educational experiences (Tannehill, van der Mars, & MacPhail, 2015). The process includes much discussion, reflection, and trial and error to find the right balance and links in the final product ... which is never final. Effective teachers are constantly monitoring their students and learning and making adjustments to maximize student engagement and learning.

Curriculum mapping

A related planning strategy that some teachers and schools use to ensure the right balance and complete links between curriculum, assessment, and instruction are actually in place is the use of curriculum mapping (Jacobs, 1997, 2004; Udelhofen, 2005). Curriculum maps provide an overview of what occurs in a class with regard to what content is covered, how, when, and for how long. Comprehensive maps also include resources used and assessments. You may already have started to think how valuable a document a curriculum map can be. For example, it would be extremely helpful for the middle school PE teachers to know what learning experiences students had in their elementary PE program. With information about what happened previously in the students' learning journey, the teacher is better prepared to design the next learning experience. *Vertical sequencing* is the term used to describe the year-to-year planning process. When the year-to-year planning includes revisiting key concepts that intentionally build on earlier student experiences and competencies, the process is known as *curricular spiraling*. Rather than a content area being a "one and done" topic, spiraling allows for revisiting a topic, systematically deepening students' knowledge and experience over the course of several years. Comparing maps across grade levels is an example of a vertical view or *articulation* of curriculum. Maps also provide a tool for horizontal analysis, a comprehensive look at a single year. For example, the curricular map can show linked concepts of invasion game strategies across units or how fitness is infused throughout the different units to ensure full coverage of the various fitness topics over the course of the year. A horizontal analysis of curricular maps also can provide information to teachers at the same grade level, but in different subject matter areas, about what students are experiencing in other classes. This information can be the start of interdisciplinary planning or supportive activities in multiple areas.

At their most basic level, curriculum maps serve as a curriculum inventory of what was actually taught as teachers record specific lesson content, time spent on the content, and resources used when teaching (Kelly & Melograno, 2004). When used in this way the curriculum map is constructed after the instructional episode and provides a "real time" scope and sequence of how the curriculum was enacted. The *scope* of a curriculum is the intended content; what students will learn and how deeply they will learn it. The *sequence* of a curriculum focuses on the question of timing, specifically when will a topic be taught and how much time will be spent on it (Shimon, 2011). It also includes the order of topics and prerequisites for learning, all of which serves to lay the foundation for knowledge growth. When used in this way the curriculum map can serve as a check on the *fidelity* of the curriculum implementation, or the "accuracy" in which curriculum was enacted. When maps are used as a curriculum *diary*, they can also serve as a tool for curricular revision. By having access to what happened in class with regard to the content and time needed for instruction, teachers can develop more accurate and effective future curricular versions.

More commonly, however, curriculum maps are more complex documents that provide a mechanism for teachers to align curricula with standards and share their curriculum with other teachers in meaningful ways (Jacobs, 2004). Instead of being done after the fact as with the curriculum inventory approach, curriculum maps can also be a valuable planning tool where key aspects of the learning process are documented and linked to one another (Jacobs, 2004). A number of templates are available online for schools and teachers to use when developing maps. Simple maps tend to be more calendar style with designated learning topics, assessments, and standards shared in a column method as in Table 3.3 while more complex maps include essential questions for a unit, standards, student skills/understandings, assessment, activities, and resources like the example items in Table 3.4. A well-structured curricular map should help teachers identify repetition or gaps in a program, prompt conversation and reflection among teachers, and support alignment between standards, curriculum, assessment, and instruction (Udelhofen, 2005). The maps are not static documents and are constantly being evaluated, altered, and shared with other stakeholders. Creating a curriculum map is a time consuming process but the potential for curricular coherence exists not just between standards and teacher practices but between standards, teacher practices, assessment, and student learning.

Table 3.3 Basic curriculum map – organized by month

Month	Content	Skills & knowledge	Assessment
September	Volleyball	–Serving: underhand and overhand –Forearm pass –Set –Floor spike –Rules –4-2 offense	–Teacher observation skill checklist –Rules quiz –Video self-analysis of game play
October	Weight training	–Equipment use and safety-basic muscle anatomy –Training principles Progression Overload –Free weight technique Lunges Squats Bench press Biceps Triceps Overhead press Bent row	Safety quiz Anatomy notebook Training log Peer and teacher observation skill checklist

Table 3.4 Possible items and examples to include in an expanded curriculum map

---

Enduring understanding
>   Movement plays an essential role in lifetime wellness

Essential questions
>   What is wellness and how does movement play a role in it?
>   What wellness resources are available to me and my family?
>   How does my current wellness affect my quality of life?
>   How can I improve an area of wellness in ways I find meaningful and practical?

What will the student know and do?

1. Identify wellness components and explain the role of physical activity in wellness.
2. Use personal wellness assessment tools to develop a baseline status of current wellness practice in physical activity, stress management, and nutrition.
3. Create one SMART goal for each area of the wellness evaluation and a four-week plan for attaining each goal.
4. Maintain a weekly wellness journal that includes analyzing home and community resources to explore physical activity options.

Link to standards: This section would include links to specific curriculum standards and grade level outcomes both within and outside of physical education.

Assessment
>   *Formative:* daily training logs, individual assessment tool results, teacher observation, self-assessment via personal fitness plan rubric
>   *Summative:* 1) Wellness quiz focused on fitness components and training principles; 2) Personal fitness plan and evaluation; and 3) Community resource brochure

Resources: physical education websites, Fitnessgram and Activitygram, wellness portfolio notebook

---

Curriculum assessment

Similar to an effective assessment and evaluation plan for individual students, a curricular evaluation plan includes a range of tools used in various ways at multiple times throughout the school year. Given that the purpose of the curricular planning process is student learning, the starting point in program evaluation should be focused on the collected evidence of student learning. These individual student learning evaluation tools also provide program insights. For example, if individual students were evaluated on a tennis skill rubric during that unit, a holistic analysis of the various student tennis scores can reveal program strengths and weaknesses. Perhaps the students generally scored acceptable or higher on the forehand and backhand but their serving scores were much lower than desired. Those results suggest needed changes to next year's plan with more time designated for the serving skill and/or different teaching methods. Similarly, if the students' end of semester individual fitness plans show a strong understanding of cardiovascular fitness but less mastery of flexibility concepts and life integration, the curriculum can be altered.

The curricular mapping process is both a planning and an evaluation tool (Jacobs, 2004). A thorough curricular map provides ongoing evaluation as the actual class events are constantly being compared to the original plan with adjustments being made and notes recorded about needed changes for the next time the topic is taught. At a more formal level, the United States Centers for Disease Control developed the Physical Education Curriculum Analysis Tool (PECAT) to provide physical educators with a formal assessment tool specific to the

US national standards. The current version of the PECAT form (available at www.cdc.gov/healthyyouth/pecat/) is based on the 2012 national K-12 standards that included six student standards instead of the current version with five standards. The tool, however, is still quite useful to teachers and school districts interested in a comprehensive analysis of their program's strengths and weaknesses.

Given that there are numerous stakeholders involved in the formation of the curriculum, those same groups should also be involved in the evaluation (Jewett, Bain, & Ennis, 1995). The primary stakeholders, the students, are rarely asked what they think about the curriculum yet their engagement is critical to any curriculum's success (Tannehill et al., 2015; Chapter 20 by Oliver & Kirk). Student surveys can easily reveal preferred content, problems in the program, and insights into what students find meaningful in class and outside of school. Focus groups of students can provide immediate and ongoing feedback about program strengths and weaknesses, as well as options. Similar tools could also be used with parents and other community members.

The curriculum of the future

This is an exciting time in PE curriculum design. Although the standards-based movement in the United States has not come without some pitfalls, it has also offered teachers new ways of thinking about, planning for, and achieving long lasting, meaningful student learning. The standards movement and related evaluation metrics are likely to become even more important in PE and teacher evaluation (Rink, 2013). Already several states in the United States have developed state-wide assessment tools that must be used by every school and those test results are shared with parents and other stakeholders. Another trend is that as a field we are actively moving away from a largely ineffective yet dominant model (multi-activity) and are developing new models that show great promise in promoting student learning and engagement (Ennis, 2000; Chapter 4 by Casey). For example, Sport Education (Siedentop, Hastie, & van der Mars, 2011), Teaching Games for Understanding (Griffin & Butler, 2005), and Teaching Social and Personal Responsibility (Hellison, 2011) are all models that have proven effective in a variety of settings. Some of those models are addressed more fully in this handbook (see Chapter 5, by Hastie & Mesquita and Chapter 6 by Thorburn). It seems likely that those models will continue to evolve and new models will be developed to meet the needs of learners in the twenty-first century. Based on current health trends and public health needs, it seems likely and necessary that the field will develop more curricular models to address student wellness specifically. One example of this is a Health Optimizing PE (HOPE) (Sallis et al., 2012) approach to PE that focuses on physical activity as a public health and PE goal.

It also seems likely that current and future models will need to incorporate more technology to enhance planning, instruction, learning, and assessment (Tannehill et al., 2015). How might content, instruction, and evaluation change if every child in class had access to a personal computer or tablet in class? That scenario is already true in some school districts. Do students even need to attend a regularly scheduled PE class during the school day to learn about PE? Already 30 of the 50 US states (National Association for Sport & Physical Education & American Heart Association, 2012) have versions of online PE programs for K-12 students. What should the content of those lessons be? Right now the online courses are designed for individual students but how might online education be an avenue for bringing people together to create a community of likeminded and motivated movers from across a school district, state, or country?

Summary of key findings

- Curricular definitions vary greatly. Lund and Tannehill (2015) provide a representative definition of curriculum by describing it as: "all knowledge, skills, and learning experiences that are provided to students within the school program." (p. 6)
- The hidden curriculum is not part of the school's intended curriculum but is nonetheless student learning. It is often related to unstated expectations about rules and behavior.
- Curricula are developed, implemented, and understood from a variety of perspectives. They often begin with development by experts and then the curriculum is interpreted and adapted by stakeholders including implementation by an individual teacher and meaning making by students.
- Although the Tyler Rationale and the standards-based movement both claim a focus and starting point on student learning outcomes, the underlying assumptions and methods of the two differ.
- The Understanding by Design (UBD; Wiggins & McTighe, 2005) model is a comprehensive tool to help teachers implement content standards in ways that result in significant and meaningful student learning for a lifetime. The three steps are often presented in a linear fashion but the refining and aligning process is continuous and circular.
- The first step in UBD is to identify desired results. If content standards are guiding the process, the standards must be "unpacked" to identify specific meaningful learning components and links.
- The second step in UBD is to identify acceptable evidence of student learning. Multiple assessment tools are recommended.
- The third step in UBD is to plan instructional activities to engage students in mastering the essential knowledge. This step is sometimes referred to as "delivering forward."
- Curricular mapping provides a mechanism for aligning essential questions for a unit, standards, student skills/understandings, assessment, activities, and resources as they apply to a specific unit of time.
- Just as an effective student assessment evaluation plan includes multiple tools and checkpoints in time, a curricular evaluation plan should follow a similar multi-step process and include the perspectives of various stakeholders.

Reflective questions for discussion

1. Think about the curriculum you are currently teaching or enrolled in as a student. Analyze those learning experiences from Glatthorn et al.'s (2015) levels of the curriculum: recommended, written, supported, taught, tested, and learned. Identify consistencies and inconsistencies across the levels and suggest reasons why those might occur.
2. Review the SHAPE America K-12 Standards in Table 3.1. Think of a specific school setting that you are familiar with and rank order those standards based on your knowledge of those specific students and their needs. Now create a list of essential questions based on your top two rankings. Using Tables 3.3 and 3.4 as a guide, create a curricular map for one of your essential questions.
3. Select a specific movement form you would like to teach/currently teach (e.g., volleyball passing, personal walking program). Use the W.H.E.R.E.T.O. (Wiggins & McTighe, 2005) acronym to identify specific strategies you could develop to engage students in more meaningful and deeper learning.

4. The curriculum of the future likely includes more evaluation and technology as well as the development of additional curricular models. Are there any features of today's curriculum that we should be sure to maintain? What do you believe the curriculum of the future will look like?

References

Azzarito, L., & Solmon, M. A. (2009). An investigation of students' embodied discourses in physical education: A gender project. *Journal of Teaching in Physical Education, 28,* 173–191.

Bain, L. L. (1975). The hidden curriculum in physical education. *Quest, 24,* 92–101.

Bevans, K. B., Fitzpatrick, L. A., Sanchez, B. M., Riley, A. W., & Forrest, C. (2010). Physical education resources, class management, and student physical activity levels: A structure-process-outcome approach to evaluating physical education effectiveness. *Journal of School Health, 80,* 573–580.

Bloom, B. S. (1956). Taxonomy of educational objectives: The classification of educational goals. *Handbook 1: Cognitive Domain.* New York: David McKay.

Broudy, H. S. (1982). What knowledge is of most worth? *Educational Leadership, 39,* 574–578.

Carlson, T., & Hastie, P. (1997). The student social system within sport education. *Journal of Teaching in Physical Education, 16,* 176–195.

Cothran, D. J., & Ennis, C. D. (1997). Students' and teachers' perceptions of conflict and power. *Teaching and Teacher Education, 13,* 541–553.

Cothran, D. J, McCaughtry, N., Kulinna, P. H., & Martin, J. (2006). Top down public health curricular change: The experience of physical education teachers in the United States. *Journal of In-Service Education, 32,* 533–547.

Curtner-Smith, M. D., Hastie, P. A., & Kinchin, G. D. (2008). Influence of occupational socialization on beginning teachers' interpretation and delivery of sport education. *Sport, Education, and Society, 13,* 97–117.

Darst, P. W., Pangrazi, R. P., Brusseau, T. A., & Erwin, H. (2015). *Dynamic physical education for secondary students* (8th edn). New York: Pearson.

Dyson, B., Coviello, N., DiCesare, E., & Dyson, L. (2009). Students' perspectives of urban middle school physical education programs. *Middle Grades Research Journal, 4,* 31–52.

Ennis, C. D. (2000). Canaries in the coal mine: Responding to disengaged students using theme-based curricula. *Quest, 52,* 119–130.

Glatthorn, A. A., Boschee, F., Whitehead, B. M., & Boschee, B. F. (2015). *Curriculum leadership strategies for development and implementation* (4th edn). Thousand Oaks, CA: Sage.

Griffin, L. L., & Butler, J. I. (Eds.) (2005). *Teaching games for understanding: Theory, research, and practice.* Champaign, IL: Human Kinetics.

Hastie, P. (2003). *Teaching for lifetime physical activity through quality high school physical education.* San Francisco: Benjamin Cummings.

Hellison, D. (2011). *Teaching personal and social responsibility through physical activity* (3rd edn). Champaign, IL: Human Kinetics.

Jacobs, H. H. (1997). *Mapping the big picture: Integrating curriculum and assessment K-12.* Alexandria, VA: Association for Supervision and Curriculum Development.

Jacobs, H. H. (Ed.) (2004). *Getting results with curriculum mapping.* Alexandria, VA: Association for Supervision and Curriculum Development.

Jewett, A. E., Bain, L. L., & Ennis, C. D. (1995). *The curriculum process in physical education* (2nd edn). Madison, WI: Brown & Benchmark.

Kelly, L. E., & Melograno, V. J. (2004). *Developing the physical education curriculum: An achievement-based approach.* Champaign, IL: Human Kinetics.

Kirk, D. (1992). Physical education, discourse, and ideology: Bringing the hidden curriculum into view. *Quest, 44,* 35–56.

Lund, J., & Tannehill, D. (2015). *Standards-based physical education curriculum development* (3rd edn). Boston: Jones & Bartlett.

MacPhail, A. (2015). International perspectives on the implementation of standards. In J. Lund & D. Tannehhill (Eds.) *Standards based physical education curriculum development* (3rd edn) (pp. 21–36). Boston: Jones & Bartlett.

Metzler, M., McKenzie, T. L., van der Mars, H. Barrett-Williams, S. L., & Ellis, R. (2013). Health optimizing physical education (HOPE): A new curriculum for school programs – part 1: Establishing the need and describing the model. *Journal of Physical Education, Recreation, and Dance, 84*(4), 41–47.

National Association for Sport & Physical Education & American Heart Association. (2012). *2012 Shape of the nation report: Status of physical education in the USA*. Reston, VA: American Alliance for Health, Physical Education, Recreation & Dance.

North Carolina Department of Public Instruction (n.d.). *Middle school physical education unpacked content*. Retrieved from www.ncpublicschools.org/docs/acre/standards/support-tools/unpacking/health/6-8-pe.pdf.

O'Shea, M. R. (2005). *From standards to success*. Alexandria, VA: Association for Supervision and Curriculum Development.

Placek, J. H. (1983). Conceptions of success in teaching: Busy, happy, and good? In T. Templin & J. Olsen (Eds.), *Teaching in physical education* (pp. 46–56). Champaign, IL: Human Kinetics.

Rink, J. E. (2013). Measuring teacher effectiveness in physical education. *Research Quarterly for Exercise and Sport, 84*, 407–418.

Sallis, J. F., McKenzie, T. L., Beets, M. W., Beighle, A., Erwin, H., & Lee, S. (2012). Physical education's role in public health: Steps forward and backward over 20 years and HOPE for the future. *Research Quarterly for Exercise and Sport, 83*, 125–135.

Shimon, J. M. (2011). *Introduction to teaching physical education: Principles and strategies*. Champaign, IL: Human Kinetics.

Siedentop, D., Hastie, P. A., & van der Mars, H. (2011). *Complete guide to Sport Education* (2nd edn). Champaign, IL: Human Kinetics.

Society of Health and Physical Educators [SHAPE America]. (2014). *National standards & grade-level outcomes for K-12 physical education*. Champaign, IL: Human Kinetics.

Tannehill, D., van der Mars, H., & MacPhail, A. (2015). *Building effective physical education programs*. Burlington, MA: Jones and Bartlett.

Tyler, R. W. (1949). *Basic principles of curriculum and instruction*. Chicago, IL: University of Chicago Press.

Udelhofen, S. K. (2005). *Keys to curriculum mapping: Strategies and tools to make it work*. Thousand Oaks, CA: Corwin.

Whitehead, M., & Duncan, W. H. (Eds.) (2010). *Physical literacy: Throughout the lifecourse*. New York: Routledge.

Wiggins, G., & McTighe, J. (2005). *Understanding by design* (expanded 2nd ed., USA). Alexandria, VA: Association for Supervision and Curriculum Development.

Young, M. (2013). Overcoming the crisis in curriculum theory: A knowledge-based approach. *Journal of Curriculum Studies, 45*, 101–118.

4

MODELS-BASED PRACTICE

Ashley Casey, LOUGHBOROUGH UNIVERSITY, UK

> There presently exists a really delightful and vigorous array of approaches to schooling which can be used to transform the world of childhood if only we will employ them. (Joyce & Weil, 1972, p. xiii)

Writing more than 40 years ago Joyce and Weil (1972) argued that at a time of fearsome educational trouble there were "approaches to creating environments for learning" (p. xiii) that could serve different educational purposes and different ways of thinking. The title for their preface "we teach by creating environments for children" seems as apt a way of positioning this chapter as it does for their book. We live at a time when education has become a policy center for national governments and an increasingly fertile ground for global comparisons, where teachers are being de-professionalized and curricula are being written to exclude rather than include their insights and passions (Apple, 1992; Au, 2011; Sloan, 2008; see also Penney, Chapter 9; Parker & Patton, Chapter 30). Like Joyce and Weil, we face some fearsome troubles and we need to create environments that can serve the diverse needs of the learners in our care.

Despite the continued de-professionalization of teachers there have been some "delightful and vigorous" additions made to physical education pedagogy and scholarship in the form of models-based practices and other curriculum innovations. This chapter sets out to explore this particular array of practices and the ways in which they lend to the teaching and learning that occurs in physical education (PE). That is not to say that excellent pedagogical practices do not occur outside of models-based practice. I would not be alone when I respectfully suggest that motivated teachers have always and will continue to design and teach their own models – they just aren't published and scrutinized except perhaps in a few single subject design studies (e.g., Ennis, 2008). That said, this chapter is about models-based practice and it begins with an exploration of the broader history of so-called "models" that serve to support the modern idea of models-based practice.

Before doing that, however, I will explain some of the key terminology that underpins models-based practice (and therefore this chapter). It is my hope that by providing research-informed definitions (see Table 4.1) of some fundamental terms associated with models-based practice the depth and breadth of this field can be better comprehended. Then, and by engaging in a brief discussion of these definitions, it is my hope that, as a reader you

Table 4.1 Key terms used in Chapter 4

Term	Definition
Model	"A plan to carry out effective instruction with different goals, tasks and students. Each model has been designed and developed to help teachers to achieve different outcomes" (Jewett & Bain, 1985, p. 192).
Curriculum model	A general pattern for designing programs that is based around a conceptual framework and which identifies learning goals and program structure (Haerens et al., 2011; Jewett & Bain, 1985).
Instructional model	A unique way for a teacher to make and carry out teaching decisions leading to student learning in physical education. "Each model differs in terms of how they are designed, how they work, how learning occurs and when and where they can be used" (Metzler, 2011, p. 22).
Model-based instruction	The use of one model in a curriculum. It is a process by which the teacher purposefully aligns the desired outcomes with one teaching/instructional style (Metlzer, 2011).
Multi-model curriculum	A teacher selects a main-themed curriculum approach that "will most effectively meet your students' needs and your view of physical education" (Lund & Tannehill, 2015, p. 168). This process is repeated with every unit of work, which results in multiple models being used in the curriculum.
Pedagogical model	A term for the use of a model that is focused on the interdependent and irreducible four-way relationship between learning, teaching, subject matter, and context (Rovegno, 2006). In other words it does not place a focus solely on curriculum or instruction.
Models-based practice	A mechanism or pedagogical approach through which to move away from privileging physical education subject matter (i.e., curriculum) or the teacher (i.e., instructional) and instead aligns outcomes with students, needs and the teaching/instructional style.

can engage more thoroughly and critically in the discussions that take place in the remaining sections of this chapter.

One of the key debates currently occurring in PETE (at least in the face-to-face encounters that occur at conferences) is the notion of a model (be it instructional, curriculum, or pedagogical). Some would argue that we need coherent PE experiences for our young people: experiences that are similarly good and appropriate for all students. Others, critical pedagogues for example, would argue that the term "model" is too prescriptive and that it suggests that there is one "best" way of teaching, which takes little or no account of the teacher, the learner, and/or the context. The notion of model or models that I use in my work could be likened to the idea or notion of chair. Look in any office, home, or shop and you will find thousands of versions of a chair and yet they all serve a purpose. Models, in a similar way, have a purpose. They are often theme-based and are representative of a particular philosophy (for example Sport Education and play or Cooperative Learning and constructivism) but they can also be interpreted and used in different ways. There are some conceptual and pedagogical musts (otherwise the purpose changes) but these are flexible rather than rigid in their conception.

Models, in different forms, have been developed and have evolved over time to meet the needs of teachers and learners across different contexts (Lund & Tannehill, 2015). Significantly, no one model is capable of delivering the entire PE curriculum. Consequently there is a need to select an appropriate model or models and use them for the appropriate purpose and in the appropriate way. Haerens, Kirk, Cardon, and De Bourdeaudhuij (2011) coined the term pedagogical model in an effort to move away from a tight focus on either the subject matter (i.e., curriculum model) of PE or the teacher (i.e., instructional model). Instead pedagogical models is an "institutionally-neutral term that could be used in sports and exercise, artistic and leisure settings beyond the school, such as sports and dance clubs and outdoor adventure center" (Haerens et al., 2011, p. 324).

For the purposes of this chapter, and in an effort to bring the diverse and yet interrelated terminology in the broader field together, I will use only the umbrella terms "pedagogical model(s)" and "model(s)-based practice" going forwards. This is both in an effort to gain clarity in my writing and in an attempt to bring these different ideas together.

Historical overview

There has been a tradition of thinking about teaching in PE in one *way* – be it drills in the late nineteenth century, gymnastics of the late 1950s, the teaching games from the 1960s onwards, or the role of the teacher as the leader of learning (Kirk, 2010). This *way* has manifested itself as a didactic, teacher-led approach that focuses on technique, especially the established techniques of traditional, gendered team games (Flintoff, 2011).

In contrast research has long sought to expand on the limited, one-size-fits-all notions of teaching that seem so obstinate in our field (for example, the multi-activity sport-based approach). Indeed, and for a long time, researchers and curriculum theorists have sought to improve the teaching of PE by developing different ways of thinking about and doing the subject (from the perspective of both teachers and learners [Kirk, 2010]). While this has taken different paths, one enduring theme has focused around the need to diversify the model(s)-based practices that are used when teaching PE and to begin the process of developing curriculum programs around these models. Work in the 1960s on *the spectrum of teaching styles* (Mosston, 1966), the 1970s on *models of teaching* (Joyce & Weil, 1972) and later through *curriculum models* (Jewett & Bain, 1985; Jewett, Bain, & Ennis, 1995; Siedentop & Tannehill, 2000), *instructional models* (Metzler, 2000), and *pedagogical models* (Haerens et al., 2011; Kirk, 2013) have all challenged the idea that there is one single *way* of thinking about the subject. Instead there should be multiple ways of thinking about and doing PE and thinking about the learner, context, teacher, and subject matter. Consequently it is important that we continue to develop and study a wide range of models and how they might (or might not) work in unison. If, as suggested earlier, there is no one *way* of teaching PE, and if different models are positioned to draw on different theories and conceptual frameworks to achieve different aims, then it is vital that we begin to see the bigger picture and are not content to see things from just one angle.

A plethora of models

Thirty years ago Joyce and Weil (1972, p. 24), in their book *Models of Teaching*, gave an outline of what models-based practice should aspire to be:

> Teaching should be conceived as the creation of an environment composed of interdependent parts. Content, skills, instructional roles, social relationships, types of activities, physical facilities, and their use all add up to an environmental system whose parts interact

with each other to constrain the behavior of all participants, teachers as well as students. Different combinations of these elements create different environments eliciting different educational outcomes.

Building on the concept of interdependence a handful of "blue-sky" thinkers (for example Daryl Siedentop and Don Hellison), who have attracted strong global research interest (Kirk, 2006), have created a number of pedagogical models, designed or adapted specifically for PE. Seven of these models (Direct Instruction, personalized system for instruction, Cooperative Learning, Sport Education, peer teaching, Tactical Games, and inquiry teaching) were included in Michael Metzler's (2000) first compendium *Instructional Models in Physical Education*. His intention was to build upon the work detailed in two books *Teaching Physical Education: From Command to Discovery* (Mosston, 1966) and *Models of Teaching* (Joyce & Weil, 1972) and deliver a precise, systematically organized and thorough analysis of the teaching decisions and actions employed in the use of each model. In his subsequent volumes Metzler (2005, 2011) included Teaching Personal and Social Responsibility as a model.

In their recent book, Lund and Tannehill (2015) included the Skill Theme Approach, Adventure Education, Outdoor Education, Teaching Games for Understanding (TgfU), Sport Education, Cultural Studies, and Fitness and Wellness in their list of models (taking the number, including Metzler's, to 13). With the ongoing conceptualization of new models, for example Health-Based Physical Education (Haerens et al., 2011) and Health Optimizing Physical Education (Metzler, McKenzie, van der Mars, Barrett-Williams, & Ellis, 2013; see also Thorburn, Chapter 6), the development of hybrids (such as the Sport for Peace model [Ennis et al., 1999] and Empowering Sport [Hastie & Buchanan, 2000]), and the addition of other scholars' lists (such as Siedentop & Tannehill's [2000] list which includes Developmental Physical Education and Integrated Physical Education) that number will continue to rise. Indeed Kirk (2013, p. 983) recently argued that "a future task for educational theorists in PE is to elaborate the justificatory arguments to support other pedagogical models" so that robust pedagogical solutions can be created for enduring educational concerns.

In a field (i.e., models-based practice) that looks set to increase in number, and therefore, possibly, in its impact, it is important to understand what the key aspects of pedagogical models are and what makes something a model(s)-based practice. In the next section I draw on the work of Jewett and Bain (1985) and, using Cooperative Learning as an example that I am very familiar with (Casey, 2013), undertake to explain the theoretical framework that sits "behind" a pedagogical model.

From theory to model (and back)

Fundamentally a pedagogical model should not be mistaken for national curriculum or national/state standards. Such standards-based curricula use, as their starting point, a set of minimum outcomes that each student should either know or be able to do at fixed time points in his or her schooling. For example, Standard 1 in the most recent *National Standards for K-12 Physical Education* in the USA states, "the physically literate individual demonstrates competency in a variety of motor skills and movement patterns" (Society of Health and Physical Educators [SHAPE America], 2014, see Chapter 3 by Cothran, Tables 3.1 and 3.2). Similarly, the National Curriculum for Physical Education in the UK stipulates that, "by the end of each key stage [there are four key stages in the UK for students aged 5–8, 8–11, 11–14, and 14–16 years old], pupils are expected to know, apply and understand the matters, skills and processes specified in the relevant programme of study" (Department for Education, 2014). Fundamentally, national

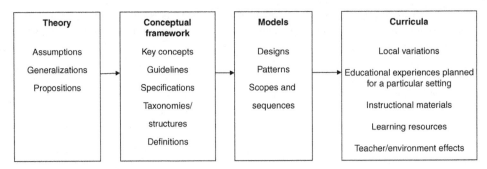

Figure 4.1 From curriculum theory to curriculum practice model (adapted from Jewett & Bain, 1985)

curriculum and/or national and state standards have been developed as the result of public policy and national priorities and are focused on learning outcomes and not pedagogical inputs (see, for example, Penney, Chapter 9).

In contrast, and drawing on the foundational work of Jewett and Bain (1985) (see Figure 4.1 above), pedagogical models are the end result of initially theorizing about learning and then the development of theories (in the form of assumptions, generalizations, and propositions). From such theorizing and the development of specific theories emerges a conceptual framework (i.e., key concepts, guidelines, etc.) around which the models (i.e., Cooperative Learning) themselves are developed and their specific designs are written. Significantly, the initial construction of models should not be considered as a pedagogical model. It is not until they are used and tempered in local curricula contexts and revisited theoretically that they start to become what we would recognize as a pedagogical model.

This process, described in Figure 4.2, which moves from theorizing to use in local curricula, is what separates pedagogical models from national or state expectations. For while such national and state documents focus on outcomes, pedagogical models allow us to think about "what should constitute the world of learning and how to go about making this world" (Macdonald, 1977, cited in Jewett & Bain, 1985, p. 13). In the case of models-based practice, this thinking has occurred in an academic context (at least initially) and has moved from theorizing and towards the form of a conceptual framework. To move from a framework to a model the user needs to a) accept "the basic assumptions underlying that framework and a philosophy consistent with the theoretical base" (Jewett & Bain, 1985, p. 15), and then b) apply these in a curriculum context. Only by moving backwards and forwards between the model, the framework, and the theory in a "process of reconsideration" (something that curriculum/ standards rarely seem to do) does the idea become truly pedagogical as well as being iterative rather than prescriptive.

If we take Cooperative Learning as an example it could be argued that, as a model, its conceptual framework is based around Deutsch's (1949) theory of social interdependence (Johnson & Johnson, 2009). Deutsch (2006) suggests that in cooperative social situations individuals' goals are positively interrelated and correlated with the attainment of that goal by other members of the group, i.e., "you sink or swim together" (Deutsch, 2006, p. 24). Consequently, individuals can be said to have responsibility forces and a membership motive to help each other attain through positively interdependent goals (Deutsch, 1949, 2006). There are many people who might contest those assumptions, but to buy into Cooperative Learning means buying into the basic assumptions of the model and believing that social independence acts as a catalyst for learning.

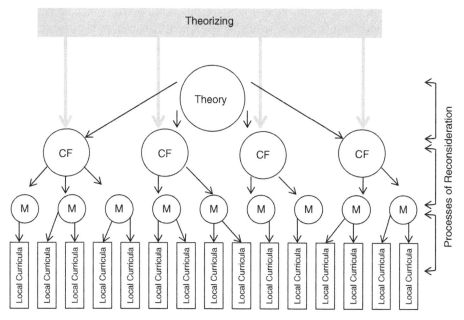

Key: CF = Conceptual Framework, M = Model

Figure 4.2 The process of model development (adapted from Jewett & Bain, 1985)

As Johnson and Johnson (2009) suggest, Cooperative Learning is effective because practice has been derived from a validated and widely researched theory that has allowed effective procedures to be deduced for practitioners to use in classrooms. Once the identifiable theory is framed (i.e., social interdependence theory) then it becomes possible to "translate theoretical generalizations and propositions into proposed curriculum models, each of which offers the curriculum planner a particular pattern for consideration in designing a local curriculum" (Jewett & Bain, 1985, p. 15). In the case of PE and Cooperative Learning this has generally been represented as the "conceptual approach" (Johnson & Johnson, 2009) and has required the use of five critical elements: Positive Interdependence, Individual Accountability, Group Processing, Promotive Face-to-Face Interaction, and Small-Group and Interpersonal Skills (Casey & Goodyear, 2015).

The final process is the development of local curricula. Such curricula (indeed the model itself) allow for numerous variations to occur when implemented in particular settings. Metzler (2011, p. 37) suggested, "a teacher will always have to make some modifications, most often due to context, but those changes should not go against the basic assumptions in the model." Individual aspects of the local context such as the environment, the teacher, the curriculum, the prior experiences of the learners, etc., all have the potential to impact on the model and the way the conceptual framework becomes manifested in the local context but it should not go against the underlying theory (Hastie & Casey, 2014; Kirk, 2013; Zhu, Ennis, & Chen, 2011). To do so would be to change the core of the model.

It is the overall continuum (from theorizing to local curricula and back) that defines and positions pedagogical models as being different to national or state curriculum (Casey, 2014). These are theorized models that have been tempered in multiple contexts; they are not "cookbook" style solutions or approaches to ensuring that individuals have acquired demonstrable and accessible skills and movement patterns. That said, and despite the decades that models have been conceptualized as innovations in PE (Kirk, 2010; Metzler, 2011), they should still not be considered as the finished article. In this way they are seen as evolving and developing entities that continue to move, albeit slowly, through processes of reconceptualization in both research and in local contexts.

Current trends and issues

Pedagogical models are firmly positioned in the prevalent discourses of our field. Love them or hate them they appear to be here to stay. Indeed, given the increasing column inches afforded to pedagogical models in our academic and practitioner journals, and our books (including this one), it seems beyond doubt that this idea currently forms a central theme in the discussion we are having about PE. That said, and despite the plentiful examples (both theoretical and empirical) that enrich our field, there is still a very real sense that far too many children and young people continue to have poor experiences of PE (Ennis, 1996).

It seems that while there is widespread acknowledgment that children need a diverse range of abilities and life experiences if they are to grow and mature into lifelong participants in physical activity, there is little (certainly much less than we would like) evidence that PE has changed (at least not pedagogically) from its days of the drills. Bailey et al. (2009) suggested that PE and youth sport should focus on achieving four diverse outcomes, i.e., cognitive, physical, affective, and social learning and yet physical learning (in the form of technical competence) is frequently seen as the primary outcome of PE (Evans, 2013; Kirk, 2010). Thinking more broadly Siedentop (1996) argued that, as a consequence of PE, children (and the adults they become) should value the physically active life and engage in practices that help them to be physically active. However, such practices, outcomes, and ideals are not readily achievable through a "one-size-fits-all" approach to teaching; and yet that is what we have experienced for decades as a field.

Such is the literature that surrounds models-based practice that we can confidently say they work (Casey, 2014). Indeed, we know more and more about how each of these models works in isolation and in small interventions. In fact, and as I will discuss in the next section, such is the prevalence of short, standalone empirical investigations that many in the field (see Casey, 2014; Casey & Goodyear, 2015; Hastie, de Ojeda, & Luquin, 2011; Harvey & Jarrett, 2014) have called for increasingly complex and longitudinal explorations of the learning that occurs as a result of using pedagogical models over time.

Implications for evidence-based practice

> The first question that needs to be asked when planning a curriculum is not: How can we plan more effectively or teach more effectively? It is: *What curricula are worth planning?* There is no point doing more effectively what is not worth doing in the first place! (Pratt, 1994, p. 2, original emphasis)

Drawing on four recent literature reviews (Casey, 2014; Casey & Goodyear, 2015; Harvey & Jarrett, 2014; Hastie et al., 2011) it is possible to say that pedagogical models are worth doing in the first place. We have a critical mass of research (over 160 studies have been reported on across these different reviews of literature exploring different models) that "shows" that different models can achieve some of the aims of multiple national curricula and/or national/state standards (see Dyson, Griffin, & Hastie, 2004). Therefore, and in answering Pratt's question at the beginning of this section, we have a growing understanding of *what curricula are worth planning*.

Conversely, we still need to know much more about the longer-term impact of pedagogical models; such as how they might work if models-based practice were used to underpin an entire school provision and/or if a model or models was/were used across a whole school year and beyond. We simply do not know what the impact on learning might be when using multiple models, and/or single models over a sustained period, and/or with multiple groups across multiple curriculum contexts.

We need to expand our thinking and develop our understanding of how models might work in unison. Kirk (2013) (along with Lund & Tannehill, 2015) recently concluded "physical education can legitimately aspire to achieve a wide range of educational outcomes for school-age children and youth but to do this it needs to take particular and different forms in contrast to its current and traditional form" (p. 983). To do this Kirk argued for a models-based approach to teaching and learning in PE.

A models-based approach, in contrast to the studies we have to date that represent a single model approach (even when hybrids are used), suggests the need for a number of forms of PE (Kirk, 2013). Consequently, a models-based approach would make use of a range of pedagogical models to achieve the entire aspiration of the curriculum. Much in the same way as Lund and Tannehill (2015), who suggested that to deliver the entire PE curriculum there is a need to first select a main-themed curriculum approach, Kirk (2013) believes that the big picture comes before the selection of an appropriate range of pedagogical models capable of delivering the desired learning.

To date, and to my knowledge, there is only currently one documented example of a models-based approach (Casey, 2010). My doctoral work, undertaken while working as a secondary school PE teacher, explored (across seven school years) my move away from a "one-size-fits-all" traditional approach to teaching and to what we might now recognize as a models-based approach. It explored the role of the teacher, the learner, and the curriculum in models-based practice and various aspects of this work have been published over the last six years. However, this certainly remains an area for future research (both mine and in the field at large) and while I would like to be in a position to talk about this work it would do a disservice to the work I am currently doing with a number of colleagues around this issue.

Issues/constraints associated with implementing models-based practice

Despite the increased prevalence of models in the literature, and my futurist stance around its development, there are still a number of issues that face current research in model-based practice (single model) or models-based practice (multiple models) in the curriculum. In this section I will examine three: fidelity in our reporting of research, teachers' learning to use MBP, and hybridization. It is my intention to tentatively explore these in the rest of this section.

Fidelity

If we are to take forward either a model- or models-based approach then we need evidence of how models have been implemented leading to claims of student outcomes and how researchers have ascertained curriculum fidelity (Zhu et al., 2011) or "model fidelity" (Hastie & Casey, 2014) so that we can better understand how a model or multiple models are able to support learning. Furthermore, evidence shows that while teachers are prepared to try out a model they may not implement it in a manner consistent with the developer's ideas, and when they do, rarely sustain this beyond the honeymoon period of implementation (Goodyear & Casey, 2015; see also Cothran, Chapter 3). But why is "buy in" fairly easy and actionable, fidelity and longer-term practice so difficult to sustain? Launder (2001) suggested that models were so complex that only the teaching equivalent of "test pilots" could use them. In a recent review of literature I asked if models-based practice had the "potential to be the great white hope of ped-agogical change in physical education or, if in fact, it is a white elephant that should be recon-sidered or abandoned" (Casey, 2014, p. 18). I concluded by suggesting that while there was real potential we, as a field, need to do more to make this a reality; which means being open about what we did or did not do in our research.

It is hard enough, however, to establish model fidelity with one tightly focused model and it is likely to prove very difficult in a models-based approach. To this end it is important to con-sider how such a multiple models-based approach will work. Will, perhaps, teachers teach skill/games in the fall through Sport Education, fitness in the spring (through Health-Based PE or Fitness and Wellness) and leadership (through Adventure Education or Cooperative Learning) in the summer? Or, alternatively, will they use all four simultaneously, using aerobic skill-based games in cooperatively-oriented adventure settings year round (although, as I argue later, this creates a hybrid model rather than being models-based practice)? Either way the use of mul-tiple models in a curriculum will need careful consideration if fidelity is to be maintained and hoped-for learning enjoyed.

Teachers' learning to use MBP

A better understanding of the teacher change process is necessary if we are to understand why teachers have not adopted some of these innovations. (Bechtel & O'Sullivan, 2007, p. 222)

In their paper Bechtel and O'Sullivan (2007) identified two themes that acted as enhancers of teacher change – (1) beliefs and visions, and (2) teacher support (with three sub-themes of principal, collegial, and student support). The four teachers in Bechtel and O'Sullivan's (2007) study benefited from these enhancers in their use of innovative pedagogies. Where unsustainable change was noted it was due to a lack of prominence of one, some, or all of these enhancers.

In a similar paper McCaughtry, Sofo, Rovegno, and Curtner-Smith (2004) explored how teachers learned to teach through a new (to them) model. Their paper focused on the learning of Sport Education, but it carried many salient points with regard to pedagogical change in PE. McCaughtry et al. (2004) suggested that (a) teachers retreat from new pedagogical situations when problems arise and, consequently, they need to prepare ways to combat these retreats. They further argued that (b) implementing new practices often requires impromptu adaptations in the midst of lesson and that (c) new pedagogies benefit from a "supportive learning climate" (p. 152) where "new teachers feel free of recrimination for mistakes." Finally, they point out that when (d) teachers experience "relatively short retention of curricular learning, there is a need to revisit new ideas multiple times during pedagogical development." These authors also implied that researchers in PE, in line with their colleagues in other fields of education, have begun to notice a missing link in their investigations: investigations have focused predominately on development of new curricular approaches and on student learning. The area of dereliction has been teacher learning:

An area that has received far less attention, however, has been investigations as to how teachers learn to teach a new curriculum. The logic seems to go: what good is sound cur-riculum that leads to optimal student learning, if teachers routinely struggle in learning to teach it? It would seem that all the benefits of sound curriculum and student learning would unravel if we fail to understand how teachers learn a curriculum and implement it. In other words, it has become clear that assuming teachers seamlessly learn to teach a new curriculum is presumptuous, and that focused research is needed to better understand pitfalls and facilitators to the process. (McCaughtry et al., 2004, p. 136)

Other findings (see Rovegno, 1998) indicate that teachers' oversimplification of the new curriculum, perhaps because of a wish to engage the lower ability pupils in the first instance and an unawareness of connections and progressions in the new curriculum, may be among the key reasons for teachers to fail in the implementation of new models of teaching.

Hybridization

Many authors have suggested that the theoretical and pedagogical considerations of pedagogical models are such that they could be linked to make hybrid pedagogical models. Such an amalgamation may be particularly attractive to teachers struggling with the apparent "teacherless" teaching (i.e., the teacher in the role of observer) emphasis of the Sport Education model (Alexander & Penney, 2005). By placing the "muscle" of TGfU around the "skeletal framework" of Sport Education, Alexander and Penney (2005) and Collier (2005) felt that the complementary features of both could potentially enhance the learning outcomes for students. There is potential for the combination of Sport Education and TGfU – and also, as Dyson et al. (2004) argue, Cooperative Learning – to be thought of as "teammates on a curriculum team" (Collier, 2005, p. 137).

The possibility of a hybrid models approach has only been suggested in the last ten years when Alexander and Penney (2005), Collier (2005), Dyson (2005), Dyson et al. (2004), and Hastie and Curtner-Smith (2006) separately extolled the virtues of a dual model approach to teaching in PE. However, with the exception of Casey and Dyson (2009) and Hastie and Curtner-Smith (2006) there is little empirical research published that looks at the marriage of different models. Where Hastie and Curtner-Smith (2006) reported that students became competent, Casey and Dyson (2009) indicated that teachers themselves needed to become competent in the models before their pupils prosper.

In looking to develop a "teamed" model approach, Mowling, Brock, and Hastie (2006) stated that Sport Education and Cooperative Learning have been shown to aid in the "scaffolding of learning" in that they provide structure in the achievement of physical, social, emotional, and intellectual learning. While they are stand-alone pedagogical models they have also been used as structures within which other pedagogical approaches could work. Barrett (2005) employed Cooperative Learning as a framework for his use of direct instruction "teaching moments" in sixth-grade PE. He used a teacher workshop in which the new skills or strategies were introduced and this, he believed, differed from a traditional classroom as cueing, modelling, and student demonstrations were used. Cooperative learning in this way became a bedfellow of direct instruction rather than the two models being interlinked in a more substantial way. Barrett's wish to utilize the two methods as separate parts of his work is in keeping with the recommendations of Dyson et al. (2004) to keep the models true to their founding principles.

However, there were problems with the linking of models in this way (Hastie & Curtner-Smith, 2006). In their example Hastie and Curtner-Smith (2006, p. 3) attempted to create a hybrid from Sport Education and TGfU but acknowledge that these models "faced" in different directions. Sport Education was positioned as "outward facing" (i.e., looking at sport culture) while TGfU was seen as "inward facing" (i.e., looking at player competency). The reported advantage

'ducation of positioning the teacher as a facilitator of learning was partially negated
›fTGfU and its need to have the teacher closer to the action.

..idering the "ways" in which models-based practice is evolving, it is important to
acknowledge the differing impact of fidelity, teacher learning, and hybridization on the field.
Hastie and Curtner-Smith (2006, p. 24) concluded, "combining the two models also appeared
to change the way" in which the teacher "conceptualized and employed the TGfU approach."
If this is true – and this finding is applied to teachers learning new models, perhaps hybridized
models, and while seeking fidelity – then a number of issues and constraints emerge that need
to be considered when both implementing and advocating for models-based practice.

Future directions

Models-based practice transformed my teaching of PE (Casey, 2010) and understandably I am
a firm advocate of "it" as a potential future for PE. Despite this level of advocacy I am still
unpacking my experiences of developing a models-based practice. Others are doing the same in
their extensive and systematic exploration of different models (see Peter Hastie's body of work
as an exemplar and Hastie & Mesquita, Chapter 5). Models-based practice, however, has not
emerged as a short-term fix for the ills of PE: if it has, then Sport Education and TGfU would
not be described as a 30-year-old innovation. It is though, I believe, a longer-term future for
a subject that is at risk of extinction (Kirk, 2010) but only if we are prepared to continually
engage in further research and future reconsideration of these models. To further the holistic
learning of students in our care we need to consider how both skill and social justice issues,
for example, can be achieved simultaneously. To that end, future directions of research need to
allow us to better understand the place of models-based practice in our PE Teacher Education
and school programs. I end this chapter by reiterating my "Models-Based Practice" paper conclusion, as I believe it holds true.

> Currently, we have failed to change what is done in the name of PE and while MBP
> [Models-based Practice] has the potential to be more the great white hope so many ad-
> vocate rather than a white elephant, we need to do more to make this a reality. (Casey,
> 2014, p. 31)

Reflective questions for discussion

1. What are pedagogical models and how might they be used in PE?
2. Describe three models currently used in PE. Include the model's assumptions (what should students know and be able to do?), content, and role of the teacher in the models you describe.
3. What are the positives and negatives of using models to structure PE curricula?
4. How is a model different from a national curriculum or professional standards?
5. What is the role of a conceptual framework in model development and teaching?
6. Instructional time is a factor in teaching any content for learning. Reflecting on the demands of teaching curricular models (e.g., Teaching Games for Understanding, Sport Education, Self and Social Responsibility, etc.) is PE instructional time adequate to teach the major curricular elements in PE?
7. How should models be blended in "models-based practice"? What are the essential elements that must be taught for the model to retain its character? Which can be left out when

instructional time is limited? Are certain models easier to blend than others? What makes a model "blendable"? Under what curricular and contextual circumstances should models never be blended?

8. What new or innovative PE models are needed in the future? In responding to this question, describe the context and participant needs that might be addressed with this new model.

References

Alexander, K., & Penney, D. (2005). Teaching under the influence: Feeding Games for Understanding into the Sport Education development refinement cycle. *Physical Education and Sport Pedagogy, 10*(3), 287–301.

Apple, M. (1992). *Teachers and texts: A political economy of class and gender relations in education.* New York: Routledge.

Au, W. (2011). Teaching under the new Taylorism: High-stakes testing and the standardization of the 21st century curriculum. *Journal of Curriculum Studies, 43*(1), 25–45.

Bailey, R., Armour, K., Kirk, D., Jess, M., Pickup, I., & Sandford, R. (2009). The educational benefits claimed for physical education and school sport: An academic review. *Research Papers in Education, 24*(1), 1–27.

Barrett, T. (2005). Effects of cooperative learning on the performance of sixth-grade physical education pupils. *Journal of Teaching in Physical Education, 24*, 88–102.

Bechtel, P. A., & O'Sullivan, M. (2007). Enhancers and inhibitors of teacher change among secondary physical educators. *Journal of Teaching in Physical Education, 26*, 221–235.

Casey, A. (2010). *Practitioner research in physical education: Teacher transformation through pedagogical and curricular change.* Unpublished PhD thesis, Leeds Metropolitan University.

Casey, A. (2013). "Seeing the trees not just the wood": Steps and not just journeys in teacher action research. *Educational Action Research, 21*(2), 147–163.

Casey, A. (2014). Models-based practice: Great white hope or white elephant? *Physical Education and Sport Pedagogy, 19*, 18–34.

Casey, A., & Dyson, B. (2009). The implementation of models-based practice in physical education through action research. *European Physical Education Review, 15*(2), 175–199.

Casey, A., & Goodyear, V. A. (2015). Can Cooperative Learning achieve the four learning outcomes of physical education?: A review of literature. *Quest, 67*(1), 56–72.

Collier, C. S. (2005). Integrating tactical games and sport education models. In L. L. Griffin & J. I. Butler (Eds.), *Teaching Games for Understanding: Theory, research, and practice* (pp. 137–148). Leeds: Human Kinetics.

Department for Education. (2014). *National curriculum in England: Physical education programmes of study.* Retrieved from https://www.gov.uk/government/publications/national-curriculum-in-england-physical-education-programmes-of-study.

Deutsch, M. (1949). A theory of cooperation and competition. *Human Relations, 2*, 129–151.

Deutsch, M. (2006). Cooperation and competition. In M. Deutsch, P. T. Coleman, & E. C. Marcus (Eds.), *The handbook of conflict resolution: Theory and practice* (pp. 23–42). San Francisco: Jossey-Bass.

Dyson, B. (2005). Integrating Cooperative Learning and Tactical Games models: Focusing on social interaction and decision making. In L. L. Griffin & J. I. Butler (Eds.), *Teaching Games for Understanding: Theory, research, and practice* (pp. 149–168). Leeds: Human Kinetics.

Dyson, B., Griffin, L. L., & Hastie, P. (2004). Sport Education, Tactical Games, and Cooperative Learning: Theoretical and pedagogical considerations. *Quest, 56*, 226–240.

Ennis, C. D. (1996). Students' experiences in sport-based physical education: [More than] apologies are necessary. *Quest, 48*, 453–456.

Ennis, C. D. (2008). Examining curricular coherence in an exemplary elementary school program. *Research Quarterly for Exercise and Sport, 79*(1), 71–84.

Ennis, C. D., Solmon, M. A., Satina, B., Loftus, S. J., Mensch, J., & McCauley, M. T. (1999). Creating a sense of family in urban schools using the "Sport for Peace" curriculum. *Research Quarterly for Exercise and Sport, 70*(3), 273–285.

Evans, J. (2013). Physical education as porn! *Physical Education and Sport Pedagogy, 18*(1), 75–89.

Flintoff, A. (2011). Gender and learning in physical education and youth sport. In K. Armour (Ed.), *Sport pedagogy: An introduction for teaching and coaching* (pp. 202–225). Harlow, UK: Pearson Education.

Goodyear, V. A., & Casey, A. (2015). Innovation with change: Developing a community of practice to help teachers move beyond the "honeymoon" of pedagogical renovation. *Physical Education and Sport Pedagogy, 20*(2), 186–203.

Haerens, L., Kirk, D., Cardon, G., & De Bourdeaudhuij, I. (2011). Toward the development of a pedagogical model for health-based physical education. *Quest, 63*(3), 321–338.

Harvey, S., & Jarrett, K. (2014). A review of the game centered approaches to teaching and coaching literature since 2006. *Physical Education and Sport Pedagogy, 19*(3), 278–300.

Hastie, P. A., & Buchanan, A. M. (2000). Teaching responsibility through sport education: Prospects of a coalition. *Research Quarterly for Exercise and Sport, 71*(1), 25–35.

Hastie, P. A., & Casey, A. (2014). Fidelity in models-based practice research in sport pedagogy: A guide for future investigations. *Journal of Teaching in Physical Education, 33*, 422–431.

Hastie, P. A., & Curtner-Smith, M. D. (2006). Influences of a hybrid Sport Education unit on one teacher and his students. *Physical Education and Sport Pedagogy, 11*(1), 1–28.

Hastie, P. A., de Ojeda, D. M., & Luquin, A. C. (2011). A review of research on sport education: 2004 to the present. *Physical Education & Sport Pedagogy, 16*(2), 103–132.

Jewett, A. E., & Bain. L. L. (1985). *The curriculum process in physical education.* Dubuque, IA: Wm. C. Brown.

Jewett, A. E., Bain, L. L., & Ennis, C. D. (1995). *The curriculum process in physical education* (2nd edn). Boston: WCB/McGraw-Hill.

Johnson, D. W., & Johnson, R. T. (2009). An educational psychology success story: Social interdependence theory and cooperative learning. *Educational Researcher, 38*(5), 365–379.

Joyce, B., & Weil, M. (1972). *Models of teaching.* London: Prentice-Hall International.

Kirk, D. (2006). Physical education curriculum. In D. Kirk, D. Macdonald & M. O'Sullivan (Eds.), *The handbook of physical education* (pp. 563–564). London: Sage.

Kirk, D. (2010). *Physical education futures.* Abingdon, UK: Routledge.

Kirk, D. (2013). Educational value and models-based practice in physical education. *Educational Theory and Philosophy, 45*(9), 973–986.

Launder, A. G. (2001). *Play practice.* Leeds: Human Kinetics.

Lund, J., & Tannehill, D. (2015). *Standards-based physical education curriculum development* (3rd edn). Sudbury, MA: Jones & Bartlett.

Macdonald, J. B. (1977). Values bases and issues for curriculum. In A. Molner & J. A. Zahorik (Eds.), *Curriculum theory* (pp. 10–21). Washington, DC: Association for Supervision and Curriculum Development.

McCaughtry, N., Sofo, S., Rovegno, I., & Curtner-Smith, M. (2004). Learning to teach Sport Education: Misunderstandings, pedagogical difficulties, and resistance. *European Physical Education Review, 10*(2), 135–155.

Metzler, M. W. (2000). *Instructional models for physical education.* Needham Heights, MA: Allyn & Bacon.

Metzler, M. W. (2005). *Instructional models for physical education* (2nd edn). Scottsdale, AZ: Holcomb Hathaway.

Metzler, M. W. (2011). *Instructional models for physical education* (3rd edn). Scottsdale, AZ: Holcomb-Hathaway.

Metzler, M. W., McKenzie, T. L., van der Mars, H., Barrett-Williams, S. L., & Ellis, R. (2013). Health Optimizing Physical Education (HOPE): A new curriculum for school programs – part 1: Establishing the need and describing the model. *Journal of Physical Education, Recreation & Dance, 84*(4), 41–47.

Mosston, M. (1966). *Teaching physical education: From command to discovery.* Columbus, OH: Charles E. Merrill.

Mowling, C. M., Brock, S. J., & Hastie, P. A. (2006). Fourth grade students' drawing interpretations of a Sport Education soccer unit. *Journal of Teaching in Physical Education, 25*(1), 9–35.

Pratt, D. (1994). *Curriculum planning: A handbook for professionals.* Fort Worth, TX: Harcourt Brace.

Rovegno, I. (1998). The development of in-service teachers' knowledge of a constructivist approach to physical education: Teaching, beyond activities. *Research Quarterly for Exercise and Sport, 69*, 147–162.

Rovegno, I. (2006). Situated perspectives on learning. In D. Kirk, M. O'Sullivan, & D. MacDonald (Eds.), *Handbook of physical education,* London: Sage.

Siedentop, D. (1996). Valuing the physically active life: Contemporary and future directions. *Quest, 48*(3), 266–274.

Siedentop, D., & Tannehill, D. (2000). *Developing teaching skills in physical education.* Mountain View, CA: Mayfield.

Sloan, K. (2008). The expanding educational services sector: Neoliberalism and the corporatization of curriculum at the local level in the US. *Journal of Curriculum Studies, 40*(5), 555–578.

Society of Health and Physical Educators [SHAPE America]. (2014). *National standards & grade-level outcomes for K-12 physical education.* Champaign, IL: Human Kinetics.

Zhu, X., Ennis, C. D., & Chen, A. (2011). Implementation challenges for a constructivist physical education curriculum. *Physical Education & Sport Pedagogy, 16*(1), 83–99.

5

SPORT-BASED PHYSICAL EDUCATION

Peter A. Hastie, AUBURN UNIVERSITY, USA

& Isabel Mesquita, UNIVERSITY OF PORTO, PORTUGAL

If we were to gather a group of experts in sport pedagogy and ask them to word associate with the term "games in physical education," perhaps the most common response would be "double-edged sword." On one side, results from surveys of students across various countries with respect to their overall enjoyment of physical education (PE), show an overwhelming preference for time spent on sport activities (Hill & Hannon, 2008; Smith & St. Pierre, 2009). These data support those from previous studies (e.g., McKenzie, Alcaraz, & Sallis, 1994) that also indicate a much greater preference by students for game play compared with fitness activities.

The intuitive rationale for students' preference for games and sports is that they present the most playful component of PE and also the most significant opportunities for socializing. In fact, this postulate is supported by students' voice where they note that activities that allowed them to "be active, socialize, and work with and against friends and classmates" were those they believed had the biggest impact on enjoyment (see Smith & St. Pierre, 2009, p. 216). Likewise, Rikard and Banville (2006) reported that the most popular curriculum content that fueled enjoyment was team-based activities where students could compete and interact.

The enjoyment of sports within PE is not however universal to all students. Empirical evidence illustrates that some students (mostly those with low skill levels and girls), show high levels of dissatisfaction with games instruction (see Casey, Hill, & Goodyear, 2014; Smith, Green, & Thurston, 2009). Such discontent can be divided into two main themes: the first common to all students, and the second experienced mostly by students who are lower-skilled and often marginalized and alienated.

The first theme could be given the label of "boring and irrelevant content." Here Rikard and Banville (2006) perhaps summarize it best when they report that a focus on repetitive, teacher directed, and molecular approaches to team sports instruction is tied to increasing levels of student dissatisfaction. That is, when students see themselves as being underchallenged by sport activities that do not contribute to their fitness or interest level, they express significant frustration and boredom. Indeed, many students hold perceptions that PE has no impact on their individual skill improvement, and that activities taught had no transfer to their activity choices outside of school (see Dismore & Bailey, 2011; Gard, Hickey-Moodey, & Enright, 2013).

Kirk (2010, p. 41) critiqued this molecular approach that puts the focus on discrete, non-game-like skills as "Physical education as sport techniques." Physical education as sports techniques is perhaps best summarized by a student in Rikard and Banville's (2006, p. 393) study who noted "we don't need to spend most of the class going over them [skills], like in basketball; we already know how to dribble!" While the underlying intent of these units is to provide young people with greater opportunities to find activities to which they are attracted, an unintended consequence seems to be low levels of student commitment, intensity of engagement, and enthusiasm (e.g., Perlman, 2010; Shen, Wingert, Li, Sun, & Rukavina, 2010). Siedentop (1994, p. 7) also criticized "decontextualized physical education" in which teachers teach games and sports in ways that do not resemble authentic sport experiences and infrequently use modified games that promote student decision making and increased understanding of game play. Further, in PE as sport techniques, the teacher controls almost all aspects of the learning process, leading to minimal levels of student autonomy, perceptions of competency, and relatedness (Hastie, 2012).

Another outcome of PE as sport techniques relates to unit length. When units are short, students are unable to achieve any significant mastery of learning outcomes. As early as 1987, Taylor and Chiogioji (1987) noted that the proliferation of and emphasis on teaching many activities in too short a time makes it difficult for students to achieve any PE goal. Indeed, this smorgasbord approach lessens students' opportunities to master any single activity. When students do not see development of their game skills or tactics, they have a concurrent perception that the content lacks meaning.

The second theme of students' discontent concerning games within PE could be given the label of "discriminatory and abusive practices." In the 1990s Ennis and colleagues outlined cases in PE where the aggressive male players were allowed to control both access to and conduct of games, thereby marginalizing and alienating girls and lower-skilled boys (Ennis, 1996, 1999; Ennis et al., 1997). The games taught typically were not developmentally appropriate, involving large numbers of students who were intimidated by the higher-skilled students. They soon became either complete avoiders or at best, "competent bystanders" (see Tousignant & Siedentop, 1983). Pope and O'Sullivan (2003) described these scenarios which privilege success in psychomotor movements and competitiveness in the gym as having "Darwinist" dimensions. Moreover, the non-cooperative and individualized nature of the learning experiences served to sustain the dominant forms of masculinity demonstrated through boys' aggressive game-play behaviors (Griffin, 1985). As a result, teachers' time and attention are essentially divided between constant negotiations for the cooperation of dominant boys and the highly teacher-centered focus on class management. Subsequently, teachers are left with limited opportunities to "protect and support low-skilled pupils, control competitive levels, and nurture social relationships among pupils" (Curtner-Smith & Sofo, 2004, p. 351).

While there still exists a preponderance of PE as sport techniques within many school programs, there is also a concurrent shift in thinking towards game *play* focused PE in what Ennis (2014) calls "second generation" curricular models that build on strong statements of democratic, student-centered practice in PE. In this chapter we focus attention on some prominent models that use student-centered approaches in teaching sport within PE, and examine their philosophical basis, essential elements, and summarize research that has been conducted on each. Next we focus on promoting quality in research on student-centered sport models, addressing issues such as asking "good" research questions, using appropriate research designs, demonstrating implementation fidelity, and selecting meaningful dependent variables. The chapter concludes with a recommendation that future research on games models takes a more interpretative approach, focusing on internal pedagogical practices of sport within PE rather than a "versus" approach that compares one model with another.

Approaches to games teaching and learning

Curriculum developers have designed and tested a number of student-centered sport and games models for physical education. Among those receiving intense scrutiny by scholars and practitioners are Sport Education, and several Games-Centered Approaches, including Teaching Games for Understanding [TGfU] and Tactical Games. In this section we will summarize the essence of each model and present a few notable studies that have investigated each model.

Sport Education

Sport Education is a pedagogical model designed to provide authentic, educationally rich sport experiences for girls and boys in the context of school PE. First conceptualized in the 1980s by Daryl Siedentop, the model was derived from play education. Siedentop argued that cultures of physically active play are fundamentally important to collective social life (Siedentop, 2002). What spurred Siedentop's development of the model in the later part of that decade into a more full-fledged iteration was his view that students were not interested or inspired in many PE programs, even when taught effectively. By consequence, and following his views of what constituted a quality sporting experience, Siedentop (1994) sought to make available to students in schools an "authentic sporting experience." To achieve this, he crafted the model based on what he believed to be the six key features of sport that make it authentically into a workable model. Those features include: (a) that sport is structured in seasons; (b) players are team members who remain with their team for the entire season; (c) seasons are defined by formal competition, interspersed with teacher and student directed practice sessions; (d) a culminating event concludes each season; (e) sport play includes extensive record keeping; and (f) a festive atmosphere pervades the season (and particularly the culminating event). These characteristics are the standard bearers on which units of work within PE can now be identified as Sport Education.

Essential elements

There are four immutable aspects of Sport Education which cannot be compromised if a particular PE is to be called Sport Education. These include (i) the unit of work takes place over an extended period of time, (ii) the idea of a persisting team, (iii) the presence of developmentally appropriate competition consisting of small-sided games, and (iv) that students take upon roles and responsibilities other than that of player (Hastie, 2012). These roles can include coaches, referees, score keeper, statisticians, and members of the sports organizing board. A typical season sees students progressing from initial experiences in refining and practising skills under the guidance of a student coach, through a series of nonconsequented scrimmage games, and ending with a formal team competition in which the spirit of the competition is to compile points for winning matches while showing good sporting behavior. At the end of the formal competition a variety of awards are presented such as final standings, referee, fair play, and participation awards.

Research findings

While the aim of Sport Education is to create "competent, literate, and enthusiastic sports players" (Siedentop, Hastie, & van der Mars, 2011, p. 5), the earliest reviews of research focused on different elements. Organizing their review around what Alexander and Luckman (2001,

p. 254) called the "5 big aims of PE" (namely, motor skill development, knowledge and understanding, fitness, social development, and values and attitudes), Wallhead and O'Sullivan (2005, p. 181) made the following executive summary:

> Evidence suggests that SE, with its emphasis on persistent team membership, promotes personal and social development in the form of student responsibility, cooperation and trust skills. Student leadership within the model has been identified as potentially problematic for effective content development and the promotion of equitable participation. Further research is required to examine the dynamics of peer interaction and subsequent content learning and performance that occurs during student-led tasks of the curriculum.

Kinchin's (2006) review of Sport Education focused more on the perceptions of students and teachers than objective measures of learning. Students described Sport Education as "better than before [multi-activity]." They liked the opportunity to become affiliated with a group of team mates over an extended period of time. Students also endorsed opportunities to have responsibility and take ownership within their teams, and expressed high levels of seriousness with respect to fulfillment of their roles. Teachers particularly appreciated the ability of Sport Education to take them off center-stage and place them in a more supporting role. In addition, teachers were energized by increased student interest in PE, resulting in what Alexander, Taggart, and Thorpe (1996, p. 23) describe as having "a spring in their steps."

Hastie, Martínez de Ojeda, and Calderón's (2011) review of Sport Education used the same five common content standards and aims of PE used in Wallhead and O'Sullivan's (2005) review. In this update, Hastie et al. supported many of the same findings from the 2005 review. However, Hastie and his colleagues' more recent review reported instigation of research in a number of new contexts focusing on new research questions. In particular, research teams had begun to investigate students' motivational responses towards Sport Education, as well as issues related to PETE students' learning how to teach Sport Education. Further, by 2011, research designs had become more sophisticated and researchers were using larger sample sizes.

Hastie's (2012) initial chapter in the text *Sport Education: International Perspectives* was the first to address the central goals of the model. Hastie's executive summary reported that evidence for competency was "burgeoning and developing," support for literacy was "emerging," and that enthusiastic responses by students had been "significantly substantiated." Table 5.1 provides sample references to various studies that provide support for those generalizations.

Table 5.1 Sample outcomes of research on the goals of Sport Education

Competence	*Positive perceptions of skill improvement by students*	Spittle & Byrne (2009)
	Empirical examples of skill competence	Hastie, Sinelnikov, & Guarino (2009)
	Teacher perceptions of tactical development	Clarke & Quill (2003)
	Empirical examples of tactical development	Hastie, Sinelnikov, & Guarino (2009)
	Game knowledge	Hastie & Sinelnikov (2006)
Literacy	*Development of fair play*	Vidoni & Ward (2009)
Enthusiasm	*Greater efforts in both team practices and in game play*	Wallhead & Ntoumanis (2004)
	Valuing of team affiliation and perceptions of inclusion	MacPhail, Kirk, & Kinchin (2004)
	Autonomy supportive social factors	MacPhail, Gorely, Kirk, & Kinchin (2008)

Game-centered approaches

In 1982, the *Bulletin of Physical Education* published a special issue taking a critical look at the teaching of games within PE. The theme of this edition was "it's a different ball game" (Jackson, Jones, & Williamson, 1982, p. 23). In particular, the most significant paper emanating from the journal was that by Bunker and Thorpe (1982) who presented "a model for the teaching of games in secondary schools." The essential premise of this paper (and indeed of the complete special edition) was that the focus on learning technical skills in PE classes with little to no emphasis on strategy was based on a flawed ideology. Instead, Bunker and Thorpe recommended a change in the way games were taught placing emphasis on understanding the logic of play imposed by the rules of the game, and helping students develop an appreciation of the tactical structure of play before being taught highly structured technique.

Since this first paper, a number of iterations of the model known as "Teaching Games for Understanding" (TGfU) have appeared in scholarly papers and practitioner oriented texts. Central to all of these models is the concept that game skill is best developed in circumstances that most closely represent the situations in which the skills will be used (Thorpe & Bunker, 2010). Nonetheless, as Stolz and Pill (2014, p. 37) note, these variants of the original model "may appear to be different, but on closer inspection are defined by subtle rather than distinctive differences." Game-centered approaches examined in this chapter include TGfU, Tactical Games, Game Sense, Play Practice, Invasion Games Competence Model (IGCM), and Tactical Decision Learning Model (TDLM).

Teaching Games for Understanding – TGfU

Essential elements

There are four immutable aspects which cannot be compromised if one is to correctly describe a particular unit within PE as TGfU. These include (i) games are modified to suit the students' skills and experience, (ii) skill learning is tied to developing tactical knowledge, (iii) tactical problems are foregrounded within learning tasks, and (iv) students are given multiple opportunities to problem solve and practice the appropriate tactical response.

To achieve this, Bunker and Thorpe (1982) outlined a model of TGfU that contains six stages in which students follow a cycle beginning with modified game play, through elements of game appreciation, tactical awareness, appropriate decisions, skill practice, and finally returning to the game to determine effectiveness of game play. As Kirk and MacPhail (2002, p. 179) note, "as the players' expertise develops, the game form is changed to continue to challenge the players in terms of game appreciation, tactical awareness, decision-making, and execution of technique."

Research findings

Research on TGfU has tended to focus on two lines of inquiry. The first has been studies of teachers' and students' perceptions of the attractions and drawbacks of using the model. While Harvey and Jarrett (2014) report that both pre-service and in-service teachers experienced some difficulties using the new pedagogies involved with TGfU, the general consensus across studies was that teachers appreciated the change in focus from class management to one focusing more on student learning (Alison & Thorpe, 1997; Butler, 1996; Cruz, 2004). Students believe they learn more about game rules and tactics, and as a result are willing to give greater effort. In particular, there was the consensus that TGfU effectively engaged students regardless of their skill level or gender (e.g., Harvey et al., 2009; Jones, Marshall, & Peters, 2010).

The second line of research on TGfU has followed comparisons of units of this model with those using more direct instruction methods. Both major reviews of research (Harvey & Jarrett, 2014; Oslin & Mitchell, 2006) suggest equivocal outcomes with respect to skill execution, particularly on-the-ball skill execution. However, there does seem to be evidence for improvements in off-the-ball movement (Harvey et al., 2009; Gray & Sproule, 2011; Lee & Ward, 2009).

Tactical Games

Essential elements

In 1997, Griffin, Mitchell, and Oslin proposed a simplified three-stage model of TGfU, which they labeled "A Tactical Games Approach." In this approach, which locates specific skills within games themselves, the essential lesson components of the model include modified game play (that highlights a particular tactical problem), the development of tactical awareness and decision making through questioning, and the subsequent development of skill execution. By consequence, the three immutable elements which cannot be compromised if one is to correctly describe a particular unit within PE as Tactical Games would be that (i) lessons follow a game – skill practice – game pattern, (ii) the game forms typically involve "representation" and "exaggeration", and (iii) teachers frequently use questioning to foster students' critical thinking and problem solving. First introduced by Thorpe, Bunker, and Almond (1986), the game form, representation, is best defined as "a condensed game that contains the same tactical structure of the advanced form of the game (e.g., reduced number of players and modified equipment)." The game form, exaggeration, involves "changing the secondary rules of the game to overstate a specific tactical problem (e.g., long and narrow courts, narrow or wide goals)" (Griffin & Patton, 2005, pp. 3–4).

Research findings

Similar to the TGfU studies, tactical games research typically examines teacher (e.g., Bohler, 2009) or student motivational responses (e.g., Mandigo, Holt, Anderson, & Sheppard, 2008) or to comparisons between these and more skill-based approaches (Harrison et al., 2004). Again, researchers report that teachers believe students can improve game play and understanding, while students report enjoyment in trying to master the tactical dimensions of games. Nonetheless, comparative studies again showed no superior outcomes for the Tactical Games approach.

A new direction in Tactical Games research has been the examination of whether tactical understanding developed during one game would successfully transfer to another game within the same games category. Studies by Mitchell and Oslin (1999; net/wall games) and Martin (2004; invasion games) have both shown the generic tactics of badminton and Frisbee were sustained into units of pickleball and team handball.

Game Sense

Essential elements

Stolz and Pill (2014, p. 40) suggest that the term "Game Sense" was first used by Thorpe and West (1969) "as a description of game intelligence and as a games teaching performance measure." Less prescriptive than TGfU and more open to different interpretations (Light, 2013), the immutable aspects of Game Sense include (i) that instruction is centered on the playing of small-sided, competitive games or game-like activities, and (ii) within these games the teacher (or coach) prioritizes questioning over telling players what they should do. Both of these aspects are aimed at developing tactical game understanding. In Game Sense, there is an attempt to locate all learning *within the game*, with skills learned and developed within play, rather than being identified prior to game participation. As Den Duyn (1997) notes, skill is developed through the coupling of technique to the game context.

Research findings

Like all games-based models, studies investigating Game Sense have shown this model to provide a motivating climate for students, particularly those with previous resistance to sport (Chen & Light, 2006). However, Brooker, Kirk, Braiuka, and Brangrove (2000) did report some instances of resistance from students towards modified games in contrast to playing the "real" version. This resistance was among a number of the challenges that Brooker et al. (2000) suggest face teachers when introducing new pedagogies to students. Among these include significant demands for sport content knowledge as well as the challenges of thinking differently about the nature and purpose of PE, factors supported by Pill (2011) in his study of 64 Australian teachers and also Jarrett (2011) with teacher trainees. Nonetheless, similar to studies using Tactical Games which examined the issue of transfer, Jones and Farrow (1999) found positive transfer in decision-making skills from badminton to volleyball within the Game Sense approach.

Play Practice

Essential elements

First developed by Launder (2001), Play Practice is best described by Holt, Ward, and Wallhead (2006, p. 101) as "a structure for teaching sports ... through the development of closely aligned practice tasks that replicate the demands of the game while maintaining the critical aspect of play." Thus, the three immutable features of Play Practice include (i) a shaping of play to suit the player experiences, (ii) a focus on learning sport skills, and (iii) through play, attention is directed towards areas that need improvement. Stolz and Pill (2014, p. 42) suggest that these are "conceptually similar to the TGfU pedagogy of teaching through the game and directing learning by sampling, exaggerating and representation of game structures." However, unlike TGfU, Launder notes it is not necessary to apply Play Practice as a complete package. Rather, a teacher can make small adjustments to skill practice or a game as they see fit, to maximizing alignment and transfer from practice to game, while ensuring early and continuing success. It is Launder's position (in contrast to TGfU), that it is the technical demands of a sport that determines the instructional emphasis on games sense and technique (see Zhang, Ward, Li, Sutherland, & Goodway, 2012).

Research findings

To date, research on Play Practice has taken place in university PE settings, with studies by Zhang et al. (2012) examining table tennis, and Holt et al. (2006) studying soccer. Zhang's examination of skill performance suggested that Play Practice was effective in increasing students' skill levels. Holt and colleagues investigated the second key goal of Play Practice, skill transfer, and found that instruction via Play Practice promoted transfer for the most able participants. Lower-skilled students, however, while perhaps knowing appropriate skill responses, were unable to perform these during practice, and hence could not transfer them to game situations.

Invasion Games Competence Model

Essential elements

The Invasion Games Competence Model (IGCM) is a conceptual model for teaching invasion games which comprises three main goals: (i) to afford students successful participation in sport-related modified versions of invasion games; (ii) to help them become more self-regulated learners; and (iii) to develop students' ability to transfer problem solving skills to other invasion games (Musch et al., 2002). Similar to Sport Education in creating the "authentic sporting experience," in the IGCM, traditional lessons are replaced by training sessions based on competitive matches. Thus the model emphasizes extensive game practice where equitable participation is guaranteed, assuring an authentic and democratic learning environment.

Within the IGCM, specific invasion games tactical-content and skills are taught through three different categories of game forms; basic and partial game forms and game-like tasks (De Clercq et al., 2005). Basic Game Forms (BGF) are modified versions of the full invasion game; as students' game performance improves, BGF increase in complexity. Partial Game Forms (PGF) and Game-Like Tasks (GLT) are intermediate learning tasks designed specifically to help students respond to game problems that cannot be solved within BGF. PGF emphasizes one of the structural BGF parts (such as scoring/preventing scoring, creating/preventing shooting opportunities, and setting up/preventing the set-up of an attack) (Tallir, Lenoir, Valcke & Musch, 2007). In GLT, students practice specific movement patterns (e.g., dribbling, passing, and shooting) required to solve a specific game problem faced by students within the PGF.

By consequence, there are four immutable aspects which cannot be compromised if one is to correctly describe a particular unit within PE as representing the IGCM. These are (i) that students work within heterogeneous groups, (ii) student learning is developed while learning tactical content and skills specific to invasion games (through basic and partial game forms and game-like tasks), (iii) learning tasks are totally connected with the specific game demands, and (iv) learning outcomes are evaluated as students participate within authentic game performance situations as players and supportive players.

Research findings

To our knowledge, the only study published using the ICGM was that by Tallir et al. (2007). They examined the effectiveness of two approaches (ICGM and traditional) with primary school children with respect to basketball game performance (decision making and motor skill efficiency and efficacy). All three components improved in both groups, but learning profiles were different, with the IGCM group showing a major increase in game performance from pre-test to post-test, while the traditional group caught up at the retention test. In a study combining a Sport Education hybrid model with ICGM during a soccer unit, Mesquita, Farias, and Hastie (2012) demonstrated improvements in students' decision making and skill execution during game play, particularly in girls and lower-skilled students. The authors suggest that the team members' strong commitment and motivation to practice, which accompanies team membership, prolonged engagement with the basic game form.

Tactical-Decision Learning Model
Essential features

Gréhaigne, Wallian, and Godbout (2005) developed the Tactical-Decision Learning Model (T-DLM) to enhance students' tactical knowledge construction and decision-making skill development. In the model students take part in cycles of "play-discuss-play" to progressively gain tactical knowledge while refining decision-making skills. That is, instruction begins with mini game play in which students receive intrinsic feedback about the game performance and extrinsic feedback from the teacher (and sometimes student observers). Following games, teams engage in a "debate of ideas" (Gréhaigne, Richard, & Griffin, 2005, p. 116) to generate an action plan, which they then test in play. The positive and negative aspects of that action plan are then evaluated to form a new game plan, which is then again tested in this recurring cycle. By consequence, the immutable aspects of the T-DLM include (i) play in small-sided games, (ii) the development of action projects though a debate of ideas, and (iii) testing and re-testing game plans.

Research findings

While widely practiced within French PE settings (see Gréhaigne, 2014), there is less evidence of empirical work using the model. Nonetheless, Chang, Wallian, Nachon, and Gréhaigne (2006) examined the efficacy of the "debate of ideas" concept, finding it helped students to understand and appreciate "efficient action rules" (i.e., appropriate ways to respond to strategic challenges) within basketball games.

A later study by Gréhaigne, Caty, and Godbout (2010) following 4 vs. 4 soccer identified eight play configurations that occurred most frequently with novice players. The authors suggested that by studying these play configurations, teachers can help students better predict the evolution of game play situations. While Gréhaigne et al. (2010) acknowledge challenges in developing appropriate pedagogies for this form of game instruction, they do present a didactical model of game play in which students strive to make sense of a new game problem by relating it to their prior knowledge and by collaborating with fellow students to construct shared understandings.

Promoting quality in research on sport-based physical education: moving forward in the research agenda

To date, research on sport within PE has been essentially descriptive, with the key areas being participants' (both teachers and students) responses to second generation sport models, and whether these models are able to achieve their goals. After reviewing the literature across various models, we are fairly confident that these innovative models can provide a more engaging way for students to participate in sports settings, and that in the main, the development of skillful and tactically astute sports players is possible (Harvey & Jarrett, 2014; Hastie et al., 2011).

It is our belief, however, that we need to change the focus of research on sports models. First, with respect to the development of skill and tactical development, there is a need to increase the number and quality of studies using more sophisticated designs that have demonstrated sufficient model fidelity to support their claims. Second, we need studies that concentrate on the internal pedagogical practices that occur within Sport Education and games-based approaches. In those designs, the aim is to achieve a deeper understanding of the dynamics of teachers' and students' interactions, leading to enhanced learning within individual and team sports. These studies would add to those seeking answers to questions such as "Does it work?" with those asking, "Why and how does each model work?" and even more importantly, "How can the model be improved?" This new line of inquiry is particularly important given recent research findings demonstrating differential outcomes according to both students' gender and skill level (Farias, Mesquita, & Hastie, 2015; Mahedero, Calderón, Arias, Hastie, & Guarino, 2015). That is, the attribution of the effects of a single dependent variable to the entire sample of students being studied is too simplistic and can even result in a misleading set of conclusions.

Changing the research design focus

From a quantitative perspective, most studies of Sport Education and games-based approaches to this point have been limited to collecting data from a single site involving only one exposure to the intervention. Further, within single case design studies of Sport Education, for example, over 80% have only studied a single class. In fact, the only quasi-experimental study of Sport Education that examined seasons across schools was that of Hastie, Calderón, Rolim, and Guarino (2013), while only those of Spittle and Byrne (2009) and Wallhead, Garn, and Vidoni (2013) measured students across multiple seasons. In addition, most of the research examining the impact of sport-based models has not included the application of a retention test. In fact, this test is perhaps more crucial for an accurate assessment of all students' improvements than simply a post-test (Haerens & Tallir, 2012). From the analysis of the empirical research focused on this topic, only two studies (Mesquita et al., 2012; Pereira et al., 2015) have adopted this measure. We suggest then, that future studies examining student performance in sport-based PE consider expanding both the scope of the participant pool and the number of measures to include retention (and in the case of tactical learning, transfer) tests.

Future research designs examining student outcomes in sport-based PE might also begin to investigate the impact of multiple variables on student outcomes. Examples of these variables might include those relating to the teacher (e.g., experience with the model, sport content knowledge), students (e.g., sex, gender, and prior sport experience), student motivation (e.g., goal orientation and perceived autonomy), student engagement (measured through either game involvement or physical activity), and student performance (game performance). The development of designs in which regression or path analyses are used to empirically test these relationships would allow for a more sophisticated accounting of the postulates presented in the research to date. Figure 5.1 shows but one possibility.

From a qualitative perspective, researchers also should consider more lengthy case studies and action-research projects. This will facilitate the study of how teachers and students give value and significance to the content. Further, findings from more in-depth research will assist us to improve games-based practice. The rationale here is that these designs provide a richer understanding of the teaching and learning experiences within team sports. In particular, action-research designs allow a close monitoring of the implementation of pedagogical approaches (Casey & Dyson, 2009) and assist teachers to achieve better results associated with pedagogical change (Van Looy & Goegebeur, 2007). In turn, the ability of case studies to investigate a particular phenomenon within real-life contexts can deepen understanding of unique situations. For instance the deep examination of an expert teacher or a school sport department staff teaching team sports is a good example of research which can unearth the key factors that made those cases successful, as well as identifying how the problems faced in each moment were perceived and solved by the actors. Within this participatory research, a wide set of methods exists (including diaries and visual methods such as photo-elicitation and photo voice) that are

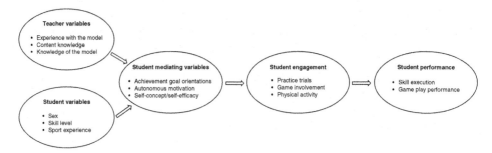

Figure 5.1   Potential variables and interrelationships in future research on sport-based models

considered pertinent ways for participants to engage in research and generated data (Enright & O'Sullivan, 2012).

Action-research and case study designs by nature, require more intensive engagement in the sport setting, and are further strengthened by the collection of data over an extended period of time. Extending time in a sport setting beyond a single season or unit allows for an analysis of the critical elements which have the most significant impact on instruction and learning. This idea clearly supports suggestions for more longitudinal studies echoed in previous reviews of Sport Education and games-based approaches.

Addressing issues of implementation fidelity

When conducting research examining models-based instruction, researchers should demon-strate that the model was implemented within the spirit of its creators. Throughout this chapter we have outlined the immutable aspects of a model that provide its operational definition. Both Harvey and Jarrett (2014) and Hastie and Casey (2014) report, however, that there are severe deficiencies in the games teaching literature with respect to rich descriptions of the unit's cur-ricular elements and detailed validation of model implementation. Further, given that responses to models-based instruction has tended to be very context specific, it is critical that all studies include detailed descriptions of the program context, including the teacher's and students' pre-vious experiences with the model or with models-based practice.

The future of sport-based physical education

Across the globe, sport is too important a cultural entity for it to disappear altogether from the PE curriculum in schools. However, the past two decades have seen a philosophical shift toward a health-related focus to the detriment of sport-based curriculum. We would contend that sport, itself, is not the problem but rather the manner in which it has been taught that has served to marginalize too many students. Further empirical work is needed to describe how teachers can provide positive sport experiences to the majority of students. In addition, this research needs to demonstrate student learning of standards-based objectives.

Summary points

- Within PE, there are stronger preferences by most students for game play compared with fitness activities, due mostly to the fact that game play allows them to be active, socialize, and work with and against friends and classmates.

Table 5.2 Immutable aspects of game-based models

Sport Education	1. The unit of work takes place over an extended period of time
	2. The idea of the persisting team
	3. The presence of developmentally appropriate competition consisting of small-sided games
	4. That students take upon roles and responsibilities other than that of player
TGfU	1. Games are modified to suit the skills and experience of the students
	2. Skill learning is tied into developing tactical knowledge
	3. Tactical problems are foregrounded within learning tasks
	4. Students are given multiple opportunities to problem solve and practice the appropriate tactical response
Tactical Games	1. Lessons follow a game – skill practice – game pattern
	2. The game forms included typically involve "representation" and "exaggeration"
	3. Frequent use of questioning is used to foster students' critical thinking and problem solving
Game Sense	1. Instruction is centered on the playing of small-sided, competitive games or game-like activities
	2. Within these games the teacher (or coach) prioritizes questioning over telling players what they should do
Play Practice	1. There is a shaping of play to suit the experiences of players
	2. The focus is on learning sport skills
	3. Through play, attention is directed towards areas that need improvement
Invasion Game Competence Model	1. Students work within groups or teams consisting of players with different skill levels
	2. Student learning is developed within learning tactical content and skills specific to invasion games (through basic game forms, partial game forms, and game-like tasks)
	3. Learning tasks are totally connected with the specific game demands
	4. Learning outcomes are evaluated within authentic game performance situations as players and supportive players

- Student discontent with game content in PE arises from cases where the content is boring and irrelevant and students see themselves as being underchallenged. In these situations students may experience discriminatory and abusive practices where aggressive male players control both access to and conduct of games, thereby marginalizing and alienating girls and lower-skilled boys
- The last two decades have seen a shift in thinking towards game *play* focused PE in what Ennis (2014) calls "second generation" models that build on strong statements of democratic, student-centered practice.
- Each of the models discussed in this chapter has a number of immutable aspects which cannot be compromised if one is to correctly describe a particular unit within PE as following that model (see Table 5.2).
- The Sport Education model (Siedentop et al., 2011) aims to create competent, literate, and enthusiastic sports players by mimicking many of the components of community sport. This model is the most empirically researched of the second generation models.
- In 1982, Bunker and Thorpe presented a model for teaching games in secondary schools that shifted the focus from learning technical skills to an emphasis on understanding the logic of

play imposed by the rules of the game. Further, it assisted students to develop an appreciation for the tactical structure of play before they experienced highly structured technique teaching. A number of iterations of the model known as "Teaching Games for Understanding" (TGfU) have appeared in scholarly papers and practitioner oriented texts.

- Central to all models is the concept that game skill is best developed in authentic circumstances that most closely represent the situations in which the skills will be used (Thorpe & Bunker, 2010).
- While research on sport within PE has been essentially descriptive, there is enough evidence to suggest that second generation models can provide a more engaging way for students to participate in sports settings, and for them to become more skillful and tactically astute sports players (Harvey & Jarrett, 2014; Hastie et al., 2011).
- Future research on sport in PE should include more sophisticated designs, examining multiple variables. Additionally, researchers need to provide evidence of sufficient model fidelity to support their claims.
- There is a critical need for studies investigating the internal pedagogical practices that occur within Sport Education and games-based approaches. In those designs, the aim is to achieve a deeper understanding of the dynamics of teachers' and students' interactions that lead to enhanced learning within individual and team sports.

Reflective questions for discussion

1. Is there any benefit in continuing to compare the learning outcomes of second generation models with those achieved from more traditional, multi-activity formats?
2. Often research examining sport-based PE has placed a stronger focus on the experiences and achievements of lower-skilled students. What might be appropriate designs for evaluating how sport models can serve both lower- and higher-skilled students?
3. How might research be designed to evaluate the effectiveness of second generation models in promoting out-of-school engagement in sport and physical activity?
4. Second generation models place significant value on the cognitive components of sport engagement which have implications for the accumulation of physical activity within lessons. What argument can you make to justify the potential subjugation of the public health agenda within these models?
5. What are the key questions that need to be addressed by research examining sport-based PE?

References

Alexander, K., & Luckman, J. (2001). Australian teachers' perceptions and uses of the Sport Education curriculum model. *European Physical Education Review, 7*, 243–267.
Alexander, K., Taggart, A., & Thorpe, S. (1996). A spring in their steps? Possibilities for professional renewal through Sport Education in Australian schools. *Sport, Education and Society, 1*, 23–46.
Alison, S., & Thorpe, R. (1997). Comparison of the effectiveness of two approaches to teaching games within PE. A skills approach versus a games for understanding approach. *British Journal of Physical Education, 28*(3), 9–13.
Bohler, H. (2009). Sixth-grade students' tactical understanding and decision making in a TGM volleyball unit. In T. Hopper, J. Butler, & B. Story (Eds.), *TGfU … Simply good pedagogy: Understanding a complex challenge* (pp. 87–99). Ottawa, Canada: PHE Canada.
Brooker, R., Kirk, D., Braiuka, S., & Brangrove, A. (2000). Implementing a game sense approach to teaching junior high school basketball in a naturalistic setting. *European Physical Education Review, 6*, 7–26.
Bunker, D., & Thorpe, R. (1982). A model for the teaching of games in secondary schools. *Bulletin of Physical Education, 18*(1), 5–8.

Butler, J. (1996). Teacher responses to teaching games for understanding. *Journal of Physical Education, Recreation and Dance, 67*(9), 17–20.

Casey, A., & Dyson, B. (2009). The implementation of models-based practice in physical education through action research. *European Physical Education Review, 15,* 175–199.

Casey, A., Hill, J., & Goodyear, V. A. (2014). "PE doesn't stand for physical education, it stands for public embarrassment": Voicing experiences and proffering solutions to girls' disengagement. In S. Flory, A. Tischler, & S. Saunders (Eds.), *Sociocultural issues in physical education: Case studies for teachers* (pp. 37–53). London: Rowman & Littlefield.

Chang, C. W., Wallian, N., Nachon, M., & Gréhaigne, J.-F. (2006). Pratiques langagières et strategies d'action vers une approche semio-constructiviste du basket-ball a Taiwan. / Language productions and action strategies: Towards a semi-constructivist approach to basketball in Taiwan. *STAPS: Revue des Sciences and Techniques des Activités Physiques and Sportives, 27,* 63–77.

Chen, S., & Light, R. (2006). "I thought I'd hate cricket but I love it!": Year 6 students' responses to Game Sense pedagogy. *Change: Transformations in Education, 9*(1), 49–58.

Clarke, G., & Quill, M. (2003). Researching Sport Education in action: A case study. *European Physical Education Review, 9,* 253–266.

Cruz, A. (2004). Teachers' and students' perception of the Teaching Games for Understanding approach in physical education lessons. *Journal of Physical Education and Recreation, 10*(2), 57–66.

Curtner-Smith, M., & Sofo, S. (2004). Preservice teachers' conceptions of teaching within Sport Education and multi-activity units. *Sport, Education and Society, 9,* 347–377.

Den Duyn, N. (1997). *Game sense: Developing thinking players.* Canberra: Australian Sports Commission.

Dismore, H., & Bailey, R. (2011). Fun and enjoyment in physical education: Young people's attitudes. *Research Papers in Education, 26,* 499–516.

Ennis, C. D. (1996). Students' experiences in sport-based physical education: [More than] apologies are necessary. *Quest, 48,* 453–456.

Ennis, C. (1999). Creating a cultural relevant curriculum for disengaged girls. *Sport, Education and Society, 4,* 31–50.

Ennis, C. D. (2014). What goes around comes around … or does it? Disrupting the cycle of traditional, sport-based physical education. *Kinesiology Review, 3,* 63–70.

Ennis, C. D., Cothran, D. J., Davidson, K. S., Loftus, S. J., Owens, L., Swanson, L., & Hopsicker, P. (1997). Implementing curriculum within a context of fear and disengagement. *Journal of Teaching in Physical Education, 17,* 52–71.

Enright, E., & O'Sullivan, M. (2012). Producing different knowledge and producing knowledge differently: Rethinking physical education research and practice through participatory methods. *Sport, Education and Society, 17,* 35–55.

De Clercq, D., Multael, M., Musch, E., Mertens, B., Vonderlynck, V., & Remy, C. (2005). *New didactics in teaching invasion games with applications to basketball and team handball.* Ghent, Belgium: Electronic Sports Education Program.

Farias, C. F., Mesquita, I. M., & Hastie, P. A. (2015). Game performance and understanding within a hybrid Sport Education season. *Journal of Teaching in Physical Education, 34,* 363–383.

Gard, M., Hickey-Moodey, A., & Enright, E. (2013). Youth culture, physical education and the question of relevance: After 20 years, a reply to Tinning and Fitzclarence. *Sport, Education and Society, 18,* 97–114.

Gray, S., & Sproule, J. (2011). Developing pupils' performance in team invasion games. *Physical Education and Sport Pedagogy, 16,* 15–32.

Gréhaigne, J.-F. (2014). *L'intelligence tactique. Des perceptions aux décisions tactiques en sports collectifs.* Besançon, France: Presses de l'Université de Franche-Comté.

Gréhaigne, J.-F., Caty, D., & Godbout, P. (2010). Modelling ball circulation in invasion team sports: A way to promote learning games through understanding. *Physical Education and Sport Pedagogy, 15,* 257–270.

Gréhaigne, J.-F., Richard, J.-F., & Griffin, L. (2005). *Teaching and learning team sports and games.* New York: RoutledgeFalmer.

Gréhaigne, J.-F., Wallian, N., & Godbout, P. (2005). Tactical-decision learning model and students' practices. *Physical Education and Sport Pedagogy, 10,* 255–269.

Griffin, L. L., Mitchell, S. A., & Oslin, J. L. (1997). *Teaching sport concepts and skills: A tactical games approach.* Champaign, IL: Human Kinetics.

Griffin, L. L., & Patton, K. (2005). Two decades of Teaching Games for Understanding: Looking at the past, present, and future. In L. L Griffin & J. I. Butler (Eds.), *Teaching Games for Understanding: Theory, research, and practice* (pp. 1–18). Champaign, IL: Human Kinetics.

Griffin, P. S. (1985). Boys' participation styles in a middle school physical education team sports unit. *Journal of Teaching in Physical Education, 4*, 100–110.

Haerens, L., & Tallir, I. (2012). Experimental research methods in physical education and sports. In K. Armour & D. Macdonald (Eds.), *Research methods in physical education and youth sport* (pp. 149–162). London: Routledge.

Harrison, J. M., Blakemore, C. L., Richards, R. P., Oliver, J., Wilkinson, C., & Fellingham, G. (2004). The effects of two instructional models – tactical and skill teaching – on skill development and game play, knowledge, self-efficacy, and student perceptions in volleyball. *The Physical Educator, 61*, 186–199.

Harvey, S., & Jarrett, K. (2014). A review of the game-centred approaches to teaching and coaching literature since 2006. *Physical Education and Sport Pedagogy, 19*, 278–300.

Harvey, S., Wegis, H. M., Beets, M. W., Bryan, R., Massa-Gonzalez, A.-N., & van der Mars, H. (2009). Changes in student perceptions of their involvement in a multi-week TGfU unit of soccer: A pilot study. In T. Hopper, J. Butler, & B. Story (Eds.), *TGfU … Simple good pedagogy: Understanding a complex challenge* (pp. 101–113). Ottawa, Canada: PHE Canada.

Hastie, P. (2012). The nature and purpose of Sport Education as an educational experience. In P. Hastie (Ed.). *Sport Education: International perspectives* (pp. 3–14). London: Routledge.

Hastie, P. A., Calderón, A., Rolim, R. J., & Guarino, A. J. (2013). The development of skill and knowledge during a Sport Education season of track and field athletics. *Research Quarterly for Exercise and Sport, 84*, 336–344.

Hastie, P. A., & Casey, A. (2014). Fidelity in models-based practice research in sport pedagogy: A guide for future investigations. *Journal of Teaching in Physical Education, 33*, 422–431.

Hastie, P., Martínez de Ojeda, D., & Calderón, A. (2011). A review of research on Sport Education: 2004 to the present. *Physical Education and Sport Pedagogy, 16*, 103–132.

Hastie, P. A., & Sinelnikov, O. A. (2006). Russian students' participation in and perceptions of a season of Sport Education. *European Physical Education Review, 12*, 131–150.

Hastie, P. A., Sinelnikov, O. A., & Guarino, A. J. (2009). The development of skill and tactical competencies during a season of badminton. *European Journal of Sport Science, 9*, 133–140.

Hill, G., & Hannon, J. C. (2008). An analysis of middle school students' physical education physical activity preferences. *The Physical Educator, 65*, 180–194.

Holt, J., Ward, P., & Wallhead, T. (2006). The transfer of learning from play practices to game play in young adult soccer players. *Physical Education and Sport Pedagogy, 11*, 101–118.

Jackson, S., Jones, D., & Williamson, T. (1982). It's a different ball game! A critical look at the games curriculum. *Bulletin of Physical Education, 18*(1), 23–26.

Jarrett, K. (2011). Undergraduate sport students' perceptions of a change to Game Sense pedagogy. *Asian Journal of Exercise and Sport Science, 4*(1), 1–17.

Jones, C., & Farrow, D. (1999). The transfer of strategic knowledge: A test of the games classification curriculum model. *The Bulletin of Physical Education, 25*(2), 103–124.

Jones, R., Marshall, S., & Peters, D. (2010). Can we play a game now? The intrinsic benefits of TGfU. *European Journal of Physical and Health Education, 4*(2), 57–63.

Kinchin, G. D. (2006). Sport Education: A view of the research. In D. Kirk, D. Macdonald, & M. O'Sullivan (Eds.), *The handbook of physical education* (pp. 596–609). London: Sage.

Kirk, D. (2010). *Physical education futures*. London: Routledge.

Kirk, D., & MacPhail, A. (2002). Teaching Games for Understanding and situated learning: Rethinking the Bunker-Thorpe model. *Journal of Teaching in Physical Education, 21*, 177–192.

Launder, A. (2001). *Play Practice: The games approach to teaching and coaching sports*. Champaign, IL: Human Kinetics.

Lee, M.-H., & Ward, P. (2009). Generalization of tactics in tag rugby from practice to games in middle school physical education. *Physical Education and Sport Pedagogy, 14*, 189–207.

Light, R. (2013). *Game Sense: Pedagogy for performance, participation and enjoyment*. London: Routledge.

MacPhail, A., Gorely, T., Kirk, D., & Kinchin, G. (2008). Children's experiences of fun and enjoyment during a season of Sport Education. *Research Quarterly for Exercise and Sport, 79*, 344–355.

MacPhail, A., Kirk, D., & Kinchin, G. (2004). Sport Education: Promoting team affiliation through physical education. *Journal of Teaching in Physical Education, 23*, 106–122.

Mahedero, M., Calderón, A., Arias, J. L., Hastie, P., & Guarino, A. (2015). Effects of student skill level on knowledge, decision making, skill execution and game performance in a mini-volleyball Sport Education season. *Journal of Teaching in Physical Education, 34*, 626–641.

Mandigo, J., Holt, N., Anderson, A., & Sheppard, J. (2008). Children's motivational experiences following autonomy-supportive games lessons. *European Physical Education Review, 14*, 407–425.

Martin, R. (2004). An investigation of tactical transfer in invasion/territorial games. *Research Quarterly for Exercise and Sport, 75* (March Supplement), A73–A74.

McKenzie, T. L., Alcaraz, J. E., & Sallis, J. F. (1994). Assessing children's liking for activity units in an elementary school physical education curriculum. *Journal of Teaching in Physical Education, 13*, 206–215.

Mesquita, I., Farias, C., & Hastie, P. (2012). The impact of a hybrid Sport Education-invasion games competence model soccer unit on students' decision making, skill execution and overall game performance. *European Physical Education Review, 18*, 205–219.

Mitchell, S., & Oslin, J. (1999). An investigation of tactical transfer in net games. *European Journal of Physical Education, 4*, 162–172.

Musch, E., Mertens, B., Timmers, E., Mertens, T., Graça, A., Taborsky, F., Remy, C., De Clercq D., Multael, M., & Vonderlynck, V. (2002). An innovative didactical invasion games model to teach basketball and handball. Paper presented at the 7th Annual Congress of the European College of Sport Science, Athens, Greece.

Oslin, J., & Mitchell, S. (2006). Game-centred approaches to teaching physical education. In D. Kirk, D. Macdonald, & M. O'Sullivan (Eds.), *The handbook of physical education* (pp. 627–651). London: Sage.

Pereira, J., Hastie, P., Araújo, R., Farias, C., Rolim, R., & Mesquita, I. (2015). A comparative study of students' track and field technical performance in Sport Education and in a direct instruction approach. *Journal of Sports Science and Medicine, 14*, 118–127.

Perlman, D. J. (2010). Change in affect and needs satisfaction for amotivated students within the Sport Education model. *Journal of Teaching in Physical Education, 29*, 433–445.

Pill, S. (2011). Teacher engagement with Teaching Games for Understanding – Game Sense in physical education. *Journal of Physical Education and Sport, 11*(2), 115–123.

Pope, C., & O'Sullivan, M. (2003). Darwinism in the gym. *Journal of Teaching in Physical Education, 22*, 311–327.

Rikard, G., & Banville, D. (2006). High school student attitudes about physical education. *Sport, Education and Society, 11*, 385–400.

Shen, B., Wingert, R. K., Li, W., Sun, H., & Rukavina, P. B. (2010). An amotivation model in physical education. *Journal of Teaching in Physical Education, 29*, 72–84.

Siedentop, D. (1994). *Sport Education: Quality PE through positive sport experiences.* Champaign, IL: Human Kinetics.

Siedentop, D. (2002). Sport Education: A retrospective. *Journal of Teaching in Physical Education, 21*, 409–418.

Siedentop, D., Hastie, P., & van der Mars, H. (2011). *Complete guide to Sport Education.* Champaign, IL: Human Kinetics.

Smith, A., Green, K., & Thurston, M. (2009). Activity choice and physical education in England and Wales. *Sport, Education and Society, 14*, 203–222.

Smith, M. A., & St. Pierre, P. (2009). American and English secondary students' perceptions of enjoyment in physical education. *The Physical Educator, 66*, 209–221.

Spittle, M., & Byrne, K. (2009). The influence of Sport Education on student motivation in physical education. *Physical Education and Sport Pedagogy, 14*, 253–266.

Stolz, S., & Pill, S. (2014). Teaching games and sport for understanding: Exploring and reconsidering its relevance in physical education. *European Physical Education Review, 20*, 36–71.

Tallir, I., Lenoir, M., Valcke, M., & Musch, E. (2007). Do alternative instructional approaches result in different game performance learning outcomes? Authentic assessment in varying conditions. *International Journal of Sport Psychology, 38*, 263–282.

Taylor, J. L., & Chiogioji, E. N. (1987). Implications of educational reform on high school PE programs. *Journal of Physical Education, Recreation & Dance, 58*(2), 22–23.

Thorpe, J., & West, C. (1969) A test of Game Sense in badminton. *Perceptual and Motor Skills, 28*, 159–169.

Thorpe, R., & Bunker, D. (2010). Preface. In J. Butler & L. Griffin (Eds.), *More Teaching Games for Understanding: Moving globally* (pp. vii–xv). Champaign, IL: Human Kinetics.

Thorpe, R., Bunker, D., & Almond, L. (1986). *Rethinking games teaching.* Loughborough, UK: University of Technology.

Tousignant, M., & Siedentop, D. (1983). A qualitative analysis of task structures in required secondary physical education classes. *Journal of Teaching in Physical Education, 3*, 47–57.

Van Looy, L., & Goegebeur, W. (2007). Teachers and teacher trainees as classroom researchers: Beyond Utopia? *Educational Action Research, 15*, 107–126.

Vidoni, C., & Ward, P. (2009). Effects of Fair Play instruction on student social skills during a middle school sport education unit. *Physical Education and Sport Pedagogy, 14*, 285–310.

Wallhead, T. L., Garn, A. C., & Vidoni, C. (2013). Sport Education and social goals in physical education: Relationships with enjoyment, relatedness, and leisure-time physical activity. *Physical Education and Sport Pedagogy, 18*, 427–441.

Wallhead, T. L., & Ntoumanis, N. (2004). Effects of a Sport Education intervention on students' motivational responses in physical education. *Journal of Teaching in Physical Education, 23*, 4–18.

Wallhead, T., & O'Sullivan, M. (2005). Sport Education: Physical education for the new millennium? *Physical Education and Sport Pedagogy, 10*, 181–210.

Zhang, P., Ward, P., Li, W., Sutherland, S., & Goodway, J. (2012). Effects of Play Practice on teaching table tennis skills. *Journal of Teaching in Physical Education, 31*, 71–85.

6

FITNESS AND PHYSICAL ACTIVITY CURRICULUM

Malcolm Thorburn, UNIVERSITY OF EDINBURGH, UK

In many countries in the Anglophone world, school-based physical education (PE) programmes have in recent years become an important policy conduit for emphasising the benefits of physically active lifestyles and for establishing wider connections with healthy behaviours and personal well-being (see, for example, Australian Curriculum Assessment and Reporting Authority [ACARA], 2012; New Zealand Curriculum Online, 2007; Scottish Executive, 2006). This policy prioritization has frequently arisen due to concerns (both economic and social) about low participation levels and increases in the number of overweight children (World Health Organization, 2014). However, this position may not last indefinitely, and matters are complicated further by the tendency of policy nowadays to pronounce on aspirations and outcomes with very little elaboration on the in-between implementation details surrounding curriculum planning and pedagogical practices (Priestley & Biesta, 2013). Furthermore, policies, planning and practices in fitness and physical activity have often been poorly thought out; as evident by the overemphasis on performative cultures, energy expenditure metrics, health surveillance and physical fitness testing (Cale, Harris & Chen, 2012). This makes it necessary for those with a responsibility for developing connections between fitness and physical activity and PE to consider how better quality learning and teaching can be achieved, and of how specifically pupils can connect their school-based experiences with their out-of-school interests and active participation goals. In short, how can the qualities of pupils' learning experiences achieve a wider range of outcomes which collectively contribute not only to fitness and physical activity gains but demonstrate as well that PE has a clear educational and societal relevance? Progress on this basis might go some way to overcoming one major concern, namely that as Kirk (2013, p. 974) notes, physical educators to date have "never achieved their most cherished aspiration, that young people would, as a result of their physical education experience, engage in lifelong physical activity".

Achieving these ambitions is likely to be dependent upon recognising from the outset the tensions, complexities, contradictions and messiness that regularly accompany reviews of schooling arrangements, the pedagogical concerns of teachers and wider health and educational priorities (Ball & Junemann, 2012). In addition, government fears of increased childhood obesity levels often fail to acknowledge that pupils can be quite manipulative in their relationships with health and wellbeing, and physical activity knowledge and practices. For example, McDermott (2012) found in a fitness-based programme in Canada that young pupils sought to circumvent the intended instrumental focus on increased physical activity and replace it with an emphasis on the more intrinsic benefits of fun and enjoyment. Furthermore, there has been variable progress in PE's position within curriculum and teacher education arrangements worldwide. McKenzie and Lounsbery (2009) note the lack of time and impact in many United States of America (USA) programmes and Pope (2013) bemoans the rationalisation of teacher education programmes in New Zealand and the impact this is likely to have on pupils' learning experiences. Furthermore, Harris (2013) argues that teacher education programmes insufficiently prepare student teachers with the knowledge, perceptions and experiences necessary to promote healthy active lifestyles.

However, in other countries there have been good gains made since the turn of the twentieth century, e.g. in Scotland plans to markedly increase the number of teachers and the amount of curriculum time for PE for all pupils between 3 and 18 years have largely been met (Scottish Government, 2014). This enhanced policy position reflects an expectation that it is vital to recognise PE's contribution to a greater extent than previously as PE is central to a balanced education and for its capacity to be a key influence in bringing about the cultural change of attitude towards healthy living which is required. This has occurred despite policy ambitions generally advocating an increase in teacher autonomy and school-based decision-making. Thus, PE has recently moved from having a stable but rather peripheral curriculum role to occupying a position as the pivotal component of health and wellbeing. This position is supported by a Scottish Government pledge to double curriculum time (a minimum of two hours per week); the only specified timetable requirement which exists across the entirety of the curriculum (Thorburn, Jess & Atencio, 2011).

Aims of the chapter

Given these multi-various influences, the chapter aims to review various theoretical and practical issues that academics and teachers (as active curriculum decision-makers) might wish to review. If successful, the chapter might play a small part in informing future theory and practice, and also overcome some of the problems of being reliant on taken for granted assumptions and/or narrowly drawn empirical evidence. Accordingly, the chapter aims to offer a forward thinking account of the possibilities for fitness and physical activity; one that gets beyond being burdened by a deficit model of curriculum planning where PE is considered as being something of a corrective for alleviating modern societal excesses. As such, the chapter is designed around considering what fitness and physical activity gains it is possible to realistically achieve as part of a liberal minded PE. The context of fitness and physical activity discussed is one which encourages integrated and holistic learning, and is also one where there is a commitment to pupils' participation being voluntary (or at least voluntary in spirit). Thus, even though 'compulsory' curriculum arrangements are the norm in many countries this should not constrain the ways in which pupils' learning experiences are designed and taught. Consequently, there is an expectation in what follows that through high quality learning and teaching, pupils will be able to take on increased responsibility for their activity futures and build a perspective on participation that considers fitness and physical activity as part of PE to be an essentially valuable endeavour which is worthy of sustained commitment.

Current challenges for physical education

It is well-documented that PE has often been beset by conceptually confused aims and relatively unadventurous policy making (Penney, 2008). This can result in inflexible practices based around yearly repetitions of multi-activity programmes where frequent changes of activity are used to try to secure and retain pupils' interest (Kirk, 2013). Kirk's (2010) futures critique also indicates a series of pedagogical self-inflicted mistakes; most notably an over-reliance on dislocated introductory-level teaching approaches which do little to nurture pupils' growth as teaching is based on limited technique-led approaches rather than on holistic and integrated approaches. Unsurprisingly, therefore, the contribution of PE continues to be open to some doubt and uncertainty with questions continuing over how subject aims and values connect with various health, sport and educational priorities. From a health perspective, Gard (2008) considers that obesity concerns are in danger of distorting educational values and similarly Penney (2008) advises that for PE to align itself too closely with a health-based remit may prove ill-advised. From a sporting perspective, there is also an expectation that major events (e.g. the Olympic Games) will yield a participation dividend among school-age pupils. However, political sentiments and policy connections have often been vague and confused on this matter, and have at times insensitively criticised certain activities and cultural contexts (Thorburn, 2014). Furthermore, fears continue about the relative educational value of PE, e.g. Barrow (2008, pp. 274–275) in a preliminary discussion of education and the body argues that:

> Faced with limited resources, for example, a case might be made for appointing a history teacher rather than a PE teacher. For it is at least arguable that in practice most children will not receive an education without the formal apparatus of schooling, whereas bodily fitness, bodily participation in sport and the like could be relatively easily attained and maintained with or without a school system.

As will be discussed later, the main point raised by Barrow (2008) about lack of educational worthiness is of considerable concern at present given the increasingly mixed market schooling arrangements which now support PE provision (Evans & Davies, 2014, see also Penney & Mitchell, Chapter 11). At this stage however the sum of the concerns raised in this brief overview highlight the need to ensure that being physically educated involves being experienced in practical learning, which is filled with clear personal and educational relevance and where improved levels of fitness and physical activity are one among many of the benefits of active participation (Wellard, 2012).

Conceptual possibilities for fitness and physical activity

Despite the concerns raised there may be less need than anticipated for academics and teachers to be unduly gloomy about PE futures; most notably because in many countries holistic and child-centred curriculum imperatives offer promising conceptual and methodological opportunities for PE. On this basis, different framework (or models-based) ideas are later reviewed: all of which aim to discuss conceptualisations of PE that particularly emphasise fitness and physical activity in the context of a holistic and child-centred focused curriculum, where personalised (and often reflective) experiences are a key contributor to the realisation of educational aims. This latter point matters a great deal when considering the positioning of fitness and physical activity in education. For while most academics and teachers agree that schools should have some form of concern for physical activity this is a long way short of agreeing that fitness and physical activity is of educational value and worthy of a curriculum place relative to other activities and subjects. In fact, it could be argued (as some have, e.g. Barrow, 2008) that fitness and physical activity is just one in a long line of life skills and aspects of socialising that can contribute to schooling but are not worthy of being considered educational; as fitness and physical activity do not sufficiently contribute to the development of understanding. Faced with these concerns there are really three main responses possible: first, accept that practical-based fitness and physical activity lessons are only ever likely to be of peripheral importance in schools (i.e. minimal time; modest status). There has in the past been some recognition (if not advocacy) that this position may not be as bad as anticipated for PE (see, for example, Carr, 1997). However, in light of the current fissure between high levels of public and political support for PE but low levels of support at national, state and local government level (McCullick, 2013) this seems an unwise course to recommend. Second, courses could be designed which specifically highlight the areas of knowledge in fitness and physical activity that pupils need to understand more about. However, as evidence from examinations awards in PE has highlighted, understanding the key concepts of fitness and physical activity has frequently led to PE being studied rather than experienced. As Casey and O'Donovan (2013, p. 17) note "in positioning PE as a legitimate sibling of other academic subjects ... physical educators dismissed the pedagogical approaches that worked well in practical PE lessons and instead embraced a traditional approach to teaching pupils in classrooms". Therefore, the knowledge-led approach, tainted as it is often is by the adverse effects of a high-stakes testing mindset (McCullick, 2013), is problematic as well. Thorburn (2007) found, for example, in senior school examination awards in England and Wales that the emphasis on theoretical propositional knowledge was much greater than that afforded to practical knowledge. This added to the difficulties of teachers blending theory and practice when trying to create rich learning environments. Lastly, lessons, courses or programmes could be designed in fitness and physical activity which combine high levels of practical learning which merge a first-person perspective on experiences with engagement with knowledge-led imperatives which focus on understanding better how the body works and moves. It is developments based on this option which are now considered.

Strengths-based approaches

Recently, there has been a move across a range of public health services to utilise asset (or strengths)-based approaches as a more effective way of helping people to identify the factors which enhance their lives (Scottish Government, 2012). Strengths in this respect are not considered as an aspect of fitness (e.g. muscular endurance) but rather as part of something which is connected and informed by salutogenic health theory (Antonovsky, 1996). Strengths-based approaches are a pivotal part (along with health literacy; educative outcomes; learning in, about and through movement and critical inquiry) of the rationale for health and PE in the draft Australian curriculum proposals (ACARA, 2012). In a PE context, the emphasis with strength-based approaches is on highlighting positive messages about healthy lifestyles rather than dwelling on deficit (or biomedical or pathogenic) influences (McCuaig, Quennerstedt & Macdonald, 2013). As such, policy in the current Australian context aims to move beyond a restrictive focus on health as something which you either have or have not to varying degrees to a futures-focus where fitness and physical activity is a helpful contributor to achieving a range of life goals. Pedagogically, strength-based approaches would be reflected in lessons which emphasise pupil's self-confidence, self-awareness and empathy for others (Quennerstedt, 2011). However, as McCuaig et al. (2013) note, achieving your goals does not involve reaching a fixed end point; rather it is part of something which is much more dynamic: a lifelong learning process or journey.

Going forward on this basis requires considering how health-informed strength-based ideas could articulate with learner-centred holistic priorities such as developing personal growth and improving social interaction. In this respect, revisiting the theorising of John Dewey might help given the prominence of Dewey's writings in discussions on the child and the curriculum (Dewey, 1902), democracy and social justice in education (Dewey, 1916) and experiential learning approaches (Dewey, 1938). Dewey's writings offer valuable insights into how curriculum can help cultivate the habits, skills, values and knowledge which support active lifelong participation. For example, Ennis (2006) notes how in the late 1920s in the USA a new holistic-informed PE curriculum, inspired by the ideas of Dewey, was developed in order to foster democratic citizenship and move the subject on beyond the restrictions of various systems of gymnastics teaching. These programmes remained popular until the 1950s through demonstrating their relevance to motor development and by being grounded in theories of social relationships. However, these types of programmes have become less evident in recent decades with much more attention being focused on developments in sport education, games teaching and programmes designed to improve pupils' sense of personal and social responsibility. As such, there may well be a need for a Dewey-informed reappraisal of how fitness and physical activity learning and teaching could be constructed in ways which enhance personal growth (Thorburn & MacAllister, 2013).

Dewey considered that his focus on the biology of learners made it easier to understand human activity, especially in terms of how deep satisfaction could be gained through effort (Carden, 2006). This led Dewey to argue that curriculum goals need to be informed by their (subjective) relevance to the lives and experiences of pupils as well as by their (objective) subject knowledge merits. Dewey (1938) considered that learning needs to be a rich, fluid and interactive process with teachers being challenged to survey the capacities and needs of their pupils when designing learning environments. Responding to Dewey's call requires an emphasis on practical learning experiences that afford pupils responsibility and some measure of control over the pace and direction of learning. This promotes active deliberation, discernment and decision-making and enables pupils to become acquainted with how their new-found exercise habits and skills can be employed flexibly to the benefit of their active lifelong engagement. Pedagogically, it would be important to recognise however that strength-based thinking and Dewey's focus on cycles of experiences and reflection should not become unduly onerous, repetitive or dull. Therefore, when pupils are working practically and in-the-moment, and when their skills and abilities are thoroughly on-task, there is a need for teachers to avoid interrupting such instances unnecessarily (Thorburn & MacAllister, 2013).

Curriculum and pedagogy

Strength-based approaches and Dewey's theorising agree that there are no final end points to learning. Instead, learning is constantly evolving and dynamic rather than straightforward and linear. However, many current curriculum arrangements make direct (linear-type) connections between experiences and outcomes and second, as McCuaig et al. (2013, p. 119) report, in trials of strength-based approaches in three large secondary schools in Queensland Australia, many teachers found these practices challenging and were considering adaptations "that would reassert a more pathogenic, teacher-directed orientation". Addressing these theory-practice concerns needs teachers to reflect on how they interpret policy advice when planning curriculum and designing pedagogical practices. From a curriculum perspective, there is a need for teachers to appreciate that curricula are not unchallengeable and neutral entities but are to various extents arrangements that teachers can adapt, shape and modify to suit their school circumstances (Thorburn & Horrell, 2014). From a pedagogical perspective, the success of school fitness and physical activity programmes will be enhanced if it is clear to pupils and parents how learning experiences (i.e. from across the domains of learning – physical, social, emotional and cognitive) are interconnected and capable of over-taking formal outcome expectations.

Teachers and academics also need to respond to a number of external concerns at this time. Arguably the greatest of these is recognising how neoliberal influences, i.e. high stakes testing and measurement and outsourcing of teaching to private providers, may come to influence the ways in which teachers negotiate curriculum spaces and organise their teaching (Macdonald, 2011; Penney & Mitchell, Chapter 11). More widely, Evans and Davies (2014) advise that, due to the system-wide changes happening in the governance, organisation and delivery of education, greater attention needs to be paid to the relationship between PE and the political economy of education. This is especially important if commitments to improving social justice and reducing health inequalities through PE are to continue. And, while engaging with economic notions such as cost/benefits analysis might prove uncertain and de-stabilising in the short term, new governance protocols dictate that physical educationalists reset their sights on what can be viably achieved in various education-related contexts. For example, Ennis (2006) posits that due to the drain on resources, facilities and instructional time, PE would be better served by taking place in community centres as opposed to schools. And following Evans and Davies (2014), it is possible to see how continuing decentralisation of education in England could lead to teachers working more widely across school and community boundaries. In addition, McCullick (2013) notes that there is often a problem with parents' perceptions of PE, as many of them consider that there is a strong link between PE and reducing obesity levels, even though it is widely accepted within the academic and teaching community that time spent on moderate to vigorous activity in lessons will not be sufficient to meet national targets (e.g. Cale et al., 2012). Taken together this brief review of current trends and issues highlights some of the challenges involved in pressing for an educational emphasis on personal growth during a period of relative economic austerity; in short, of arguing that a version of fitness and physical activity can be crafted in neoliberal terms as a 'premium product' which is worthy of investment. The remaining sections of the chapter address this pivotal issue.

Implications for evidence-based practice

Noting the McCuaig et al. (2013) evidence of a gap between policy aspirations and teachers' practices should not necessarily be read as a criticism of teachers. For at a policy level policies often lack sufficient philosophical elaboration (Priestley & Biesta, 2013) and in practice, teachers highlight that they often face a plethora of day-to-day concerns (e.g. large class sizes, levels of disruption, poor facilities, limited resources, modest curriculum time, pupils with diverse learning needs), all of which adversely impact on teaching. Nevertheless, a concern of Alfrey and Gard (2014) is that fitness and physical activity time in school could be better utilised, as too much time is directed toward performance and fitness testing relative to highlighting how fitness and physical activity can equip pupils with the experiences, knowledge and skills to make more informed lifestyle decisions. Following Dewey, a main challenge in this regard is on reviewing how habits and skills can transfer from being attributes which can be acquired through training (with little thought or reflection) to something which when sufficiently adapted and extended is of educational value. Thus, what matters is how carefully exercise habits and the mastery of skills are framed in relation to the wider context and goals of PE, so that pupils' personal growth is more obviously at the forefront of learning. To teach effectively in these contexts teachers need to possess high levels of content knowledge expertise (i.e. the ability to understand and demonstrate the basic skills of activities). They also need to possess a wider appreciation of how to extend learning and interact with pupils (pedagogical content knowledge) so that the transformative benefits of sustained engagement in practical activities can be seen by pupils as a helpful and worthwhile endeavour. Meeting these requirements is consistent with Siedentop's (2002) view that effective teaching is underpinned by teachers possessing a high level of content knowledge of activities as the basis for developing their knowledge of teaching and maximising pupils' learning experiences. It chimes as well with McCullick's (2013) exhortation that at its heart PE needs to remain true to its central focus on learning how the body works and moves. It also addresses concerns raised by Harris (2013) who found that student teachers' teaching of health and physical activity largely consisted of discrete blocks (or units) of physiology with minimal attention being paid to how the teaching of physical activities could merge effectively with various health and educational imperatives. In short, the problems of PE being studied rather than experienced were again evident.

Linking fitness and physical activity learning and teaching to wider school and societal goals

As noted earlier curriculum implementation is a complex process which those advocating change rarely focus on sufficiently (Ennis, 2013a). In trying to address this shortfall, the final part of the chapter considers how the ideas associated with strength-based approaches and Dewey's ideas on experiential learning might work in practice. In sympathy with MacIntyre (2007) it is argued that it is from inside practices that pupils and teachers can "encounter thick and distinctive notions about what it is worthwhile to participate in, excellent to achieve and admirable to become" (Higgins, 2011, p. 50). In this light, teachers need to not only be effective and efficient in a technical sense but focus as well on the wider dimensions of education and with pupils flourishing. Once this mix is achieved, the goods internal to practice have transferable gains, as engaging in practice increases the ways in which pupils can make considered judgements about how they wish to lead and construct their lives. Progress in this way is largely consistent with Kretchmar's (2006) view that PE can be a genuine turning point in pupils' lives with challenging and situated learning environments creating opportunities for pupils to reference their activity-based habits against the achievement of clear standards of success. The examples below provide a brief outline of how teachers might take forward strength-based planning ideas in order to provide some insights into the types of gains we might expect to see in practice.

Two national curriculum examples: Scotland and Australia

In Scotland, Thorburn and Horrell (2014) identified how salutogenic approaches offered a broad and largely coherent perspective on health and wellbeing which could support efforts to enhance the centrality of PE as part of new educational ambitions. After reviewing the influences on policy closely the authors considered the methodological possibilities which existed. Key to progress was identifying where teachers are active curriculum decision-makers rather than passive receivers of policy expectations and prescribed outcomes. This highlighted the learning and teaching filter through which teaching interventions could reflect overarching curriculum aims. In turn, this revealed how a heightened emphasis on adopting a more holistic perspective on learning, where there is increased time available for reflection and decision-making, was pivotal to the realisation of policy goals. Teaching in these ways has the capacity to present knowledge in practices which are experienced by pupils as tangible, accessible and relevant to their lives. Through further deliberative practice the potential for links between experiences and associated knowledge (of skills, fitness, training and healthy living) can become increasingly sophisticated and refined, and help learning to become more deeply embedded and sustained. Such a first person perspective on learning can achieve a middle ground between experiential learning, viz. the acquisition of knowledge, and equip pupils with the habits, skills and capacities to make more informed and educationally rounded fitness and physical activity decisions at school and in future years.

In Australia, submissions from across a range of professional sectors have endorsed the holistic strength-based ideas underpinning the draft Australian Health and Physical Education Curriculum (McCuaig et al., 2013). Therefore, the challenge, as with Scotland, is to develop sound pedagogical ideas about how strength-based ideas could be put into effective practice. The focus on promoting healthy behaviours rather than preventing illness is evident in the draft policy documentation. However, as noted earlier, initial attempts at adopting these new approaches were not without their difficulties. So, at this stage, the emphasis is on supporting teachers to emphasise the wide-ranging benefits of fitness and physical activity, e.g. in terms of its social, psychological and cultural benefit, rather than more narrowly focusing on preventive behaviours (McCuaig et al., 2013).

One activity example: exergaming

In exergaming (video games that use technology to track body movements or reactions) how could this relatively new activity become a suitable learning context for the majority of pupils; where participation is voluntary and sustained, and where pupils strive for achieving personal growth and a depth of understanding about how the body functions and moves? This matters as current research shows that as participation in exergaming continues, pupils' interest declines (Ennis, 2013b). So, how can teachers continue with their teaching of exergaming rather than roll out other new activities to try and combat pupils' lack of interest? Ennis (2013b) highlights, in Deweyan-type terms, the holistic and integrated possibilities of merging the physical, affective and cognitive together in ways which are characterised by teaching containing enhanced opportunities for pupils to engage in constructive discussion, problem solve and make decisions. In these settings, skilled teachers would be able to continually challenge pupils across all domains of learning by, for example, altering the demand of tasks and by varying the types and difficulty of questions asked on an individual pupil basis. If successful, the physical benefits of being fitter would coincide with the social development benefits of being able to work constructively together with others on group tasks. It would also be allied to the emotional benefits of showing perseverance when continuing to exercise when fatigued and connect as well with an increased understanding of aspects of fitness and fitness training principles.

Evidence of effectiveness

Critics of the three examples might see the claims made for connecting more closely fitness and physical activity learning and teaching with the realisation of wider school and societal goals as lacking in substantive enough evidence of impact. In this light some indicators of what might count as evidence of effectiveness are provided. This review responds to a key point McCuaig et al. (2013) note, namely that a strengths-based approach can become overly individual and insular. Therefore, positively responding to this concern requires fitness and physical activity teaching to be of whole school relevance as well as being meaningful for pupils at an individual level. The key point in this respect is that the internal goods of fitness and physical activity practice need to merge coherently with the external (institutional) goals of schools. This can happen, it is argued, when there are extended opportunities for pupils to reflect and deliberate on their learning, where experiences are dynamic and interactive and where experiences can be shared more widely across the school (e.g. when reported on in newsletters, school displays). Thus, in brief, as practice experiences become part of pupils' wider social conversations, the school environment can become a context around which the goods of practice can be shared both internally and externally. If this happens in diverse ways which reflect the precise culture and ethos of individual schools, then the wider school community itself will attest to the benefits of continuing to support high quality learning and teaching in PE.

Further issues

However, progressing with examples such as exergaming within a wider strength-based conception of fitness and physical activity does raise some issues which are not easy to resolve or rule over. For example, as Quennerstedt (2011) notes (following salutogenic thinking), it is quite possible that PE could be a negative influence on pupils' health more widely, especially if pupils are required to continue participating in the subject when they do not consider that it benefits their overall health. In this setting, how can teachers recognise the importance of pupils' autonomy as well as nurture the concept of participation being voluntary, even when teaching arrangements dictate that PE is a must-do compulsory subject? Alternately, what would be the consequences if it were possible to make participation in PE optional at certain ages and stages of pupils' development? What might policy stakeholders make of such decision-making, especially in countries where PE is seen as a key contributor to the realising of a series of health and wellbeing outcomes (Thorburn & Horrell, 2014)? Furthermore, what would parents make of such a response; especially as many parents consider that PE is an important contributor to health and academic attainment (McCullick, 2013)? If therefore the status quo is to remain (and pupils' involvement in PE remains obligatory), there is an on-going need as Gao, Lee and Harrison (2008) note to review and better understand the types of learning experiences which motivate pupils towards regular physical activity and which connect with their wider reflections on how they wish to lead their lives in the future.

Conclusion

Ennis (2013a) notes that among all these complexities we need to find ways to bring meaning and learning to many PE programmes worldwide. In Macdonald's (2013, p. 100) terms to "lay a foundation of knowledge, skills and understanding that can be applied across ever-changing priorities and life-phases". In agreement with these sentiments, this chapter has argued that greater conceptual clarity and a degree of methodological change is required if fitness and physical activity as part of PE is to make the most of the rather inexact and variable curriculum opportunities which exist in the Anglophone world.

Future research

Anticipating the future is inherently uncertain and whether the educationally driven ideas in this chapter are helpful in highlighting the main challenges which exist for teaching fitness and physical activity remains to be seen. For it might well be that bolder thinking was required. For example, it could be argued that the quest for active lifelong learning requires clearer and more nuanced links to be drawn between the body and the mind, where the whole person is considered in a holistic and synthesised way based on their feelings and thinking, and their sense of being-in-the-world (Stolz, 2014). By contrast, it could be argued that the chapter has under-acknowledged digitised health and PE developments, where software algorithms underpin pedagogies and where wearable and mobile activity trackers, biosensors and personal analytics apps play an increasing part in how pupils learn about their own bodies and health (Williamson, 2015). These are areas of thinking you may also wish to critique and review in the future.

Summary of key findings

- PE is frequently viewed as an important policy conduit for emphasising the benefits of physically active lifestyles, and for establishing wider connections with healthy behaviours and personal wellbeing.
- Policies, programmes and practices in PE have often overemphasised performative cultures, energy expenditure metrics, health surveillance and physical fitness testing rather than how PE links to active lifelong learning.
- Policy to practice is rarely a straight line issue. It is often messy, complex and prone to contradictions and confusion.
- In terms of fitness and physical activity becoming a 'premium product', pupils need to be able to take increased control over their activity futures and build a perspective on their participation which considers PE as an essentially helpful and valuable endeavour which is worthy of sustained commitment.
- Historically, PE may well have contributed to its own difficulties through its over-reliance on undemanding multi activity programmes.
- The concept of high quality PE developed in this chapter is on where improved levels of fitness and physical activity is one among many of the benefits of active participation.
- Recently, public health services have often sought to utilise asset (or strengths)-based approaches as an effective way of helping people to identify the factors which can enhance their lives.
- John Dewey's writings may be helpful to review in considering how health-informed strength-based ideas could articulate with learner-centred holistic educational priorities.
- Teachers need to be active curriculum decision-makers and recognise that curricula are not unchallengeable and neutral entities but can (to various degrees) be adapted, shaped and modified to suit their school circumstances.
- Academics and teachers need to think through how to constructively respond to the system-wide changes happening in the governance, organisation and delivery of education.
- Effective teaching is underpinned by teachers possessing a high level of content knowledge of activities. This enables teachers to develop their knowledge of teaching and maximise pupils' learning experiences.
- School programmes should create motivational learning environments which strengthen pupils' beliefs about the benefits of voluntarily engaging in high levels of physical activity.

Reflective questions for discussion

1. The central argument in this chapter is that strength-based approaches to fitness and physical activity which emphasise personal growth would best serve the longer term educational interests of PE.
   a. To what extent do you agree or disagree with this argument?
   b. To what extent are these ideas realistic or unrealistic in terms of PE futures in your area?
   c. Are the ideas presented in this chapter bold enough?
2. To what extent are the philosophical ideas of Barrow (2008) on PE teaching reflected in new neoliberal notions of outsourcing PE to private providers?

3. Do you see new forms of school governance arrangements as predominantly a help or a hindrance in promoting high levels of physical activity for personal growth?
4. In the view of some educators, fitness and physical activity is one in a long line of life skills that contribute to schooling but are not worthy of being considered as educational. How would you respond to this claim?
5. Should pupils do equal amounts of fitness and physical activity in schools?
    a. Should participation be compulsory or optional; and if optional at what age?
    b. Should fitness and physical activity be taught on a single sex or co-ed basis in high schools?

References

Alfrey, L., & Gard, M. (2014). A crack where the light gets in: A study of health and physical education teachers' perspectives on fitness testing as a context for learning about health. *Asia-Pacific Journal of Health, Sport and Physical Education, 5*(1), 3–18.

Antonovsky, A. (1996). The salutogenic model as a theory of health promotion. *Health Promotion International, 32*(1), 11–18.

Australian Curriculum Assessment and Reporting Authority [ACARA]. (2012). *Draft Shape of the Australian Curriculum: Health and Physical Education.* Available online at: www.acara.edu.au/curriculum/hpe.html (22 July 2014).

Ball, S., & Junemann, C. (2012). *Networks, new governance and education.* Bristol: Policy Press.

Barrow, R. (2008). Education and the body: Prolegomena. *British Journal of Educational Studies, 56*(3), 272–285.

Cale, L., Harris, J. & Chen, M. H. (2012). Monitoring health, activity and fitness in physical education: Its current and future state of health. *Sport, Education and Society, 19*(4), 376–397.

Carden, S. D. (2006). *Virtue ethics: Dewey and MacIntyre.* London: Continuum.

Carr, D. (1997). Physical education and value diversity: A response to Andrew Reid. *European Physical Education Review, 3*(2), 195–205.

Casey, A., & O'Donovan, T. (2015). Examination physical education: Adhering to pedagogies of the classroom when coming in from the cold. *Physical Education and Sport Pedagogy.* 20(4) 374–365.

Dewey, J. (1902). *The child and the curriculum.* Chicago: The University of Chicago Press.

Dewey, J. (1916). *Democracy in education.* New York: Macmillan.

Dewey, J. (1938). *Experience and education.* New York: Macmillan.

Ennis, C. D. (2006). Curriculum: Forming and reshaping the vision of physical education in a high need, low demand world of schools. *Quest, 58*(1), 41–59.

Ennis, C. D. (2013a). Implementing meaningful, educative curriculum, and assessment in complex school environments. *Sport, Education and Society, 18*(1), 115–120.

Ennis, C. D. (2013b). Implications of exergaming for the physical education curriculum in the 21st century. *Journal of Sport and Health Science, 2*, 152–157.

Evans, J., & Davies, B. (2014). Physical education PLC: Neoliberalism, curriculum and governance. New directions for PESP research. *Sport, Education and Society, 19*(7) 869–884.

Gao, Z., Lee, A. M. & Harrison, L. (2008). Understanding students' motivation in sport and physical education: From the expectancy-value model and self-efficacy theory perspectives. *Quest, 60*(2), 236–254.

Gard, M. (2008). Producing little decision makers and goal setters in the age of the obesity crisis. *Quest, 60*(4) 488–502.

Harris, J. (2014). Physical education teacher education students' knowledge, perceptions and experiences of promoting healthy, active lifestyles in secondary schools, *Physical Education and Sport Pedagogy, 19*(5) 466–480.

Higgins, C. (2011). *The good life of teaching: An ethics of professional practice.* Chichester: Wiley-Blackwell.

Kirk, D. (2010). *Physical education futures.* London: Routledge.

Kirk, D. (2013). Educational value and models-based practice in physical education. *Educational Philosophy and Theory, 45*(9), 973–986.

Kretchmar, R. S. (2006). Life on Easy Street: The persistent need for embodied hopes and down-to-earth games. *Quest, 58*(3), 344–354.

Macdonald, D. (2011). Like a fish in water: Physical education policy and practice in the era of neoliberal globalization. *Quest, 63*(1), 36–45.

Macdonald, D. (2014). The new Australian Health and Physical Education Curriculum: A case of/for gradualism in curriculum reform? *Asia-Pacific Journal of Health, Sport and Physical Education, 4*(2), 95–108.

MacIntyre, A. (2007). *After virtue: A study in moral theory.* London: Duckworth.

McCuaig, L., Quennerstedt, M. & Macdonald, D. (2013). A salutogenic, strengths-based approach as a theory to guide HPE curriculum change. *Asia-Pacific Journal of Health, Sport and Physical Education, 4*(2), 109–125.

McCullick, B. A. (2014). From the cheap seats: One consideration of school-based PE's position in contemporary American schools. *Physical Education and Sport Pedagogy, 19*(5) 533–544.

McDermott, L. (2012). 'Thrash yourself Thursday': The production of the 'healthy' child through a fitness-based PE practice. *Sport, Education and Society, 17*(3), 405–429.

McKenzie, T. L, & Lounsbery, M. A. F. (2009). School physical education: The pill not taken. *American Journal of Lifestyle Medicine, 3*(3), 219–225.

New Zealand Curriculum Online. (2007). *The school curriculum: Design and review.* Available online at: http://nzcurriculum.tki.org.nz/The-New-Zealand-Curriculum/The-school-curriculum-Design-and-review (8 August 2014).

Penney, D. (2008). Playing a political game and playing for position: Policy and curriculum development in health and physical education. *European Physical Education Review, 14*(1), 33–49.

Pope, C. C. (2014). The jagged edge and the changing shape of health and physical education in Aotearoa New Zealand. *Physical Education and Sport Pedagogy, 19*(5) 500–511.

Priestley, M., & Biesta, G. (Eds). (2013). *Reinventing the curriculum: New trends in curriculum policy and practice.* Bloomsbury: London.

Quennerstedt, M. (2011). Warning: Physical education can seriously harm your health. In S. Brown (Ed.), *Issues and controversies in physical education: Policy, power and pedagogy* (pp. 46–56). North Bay City, New Zealand: Pearson.

Scottish Executive. (2006). *Curriculum for excellence: Building the curriculum: The contribution of curriculum areas.* Edinburgh: Scottish Executive.

Scottish Government. (2012). *Health in Scotland: Assets for health. Annual report of the Chief Medical Officer.* Edinburgh: Scottish Government and NHS Scotland.

Scottish Government. (2014). *Statistical bulletin: Summary statistics for attainment, leaver destinations and healthy living.* Available online at: www.scotland.gov.uk/Resource/0045/00453110.pdf (17 June 2014).

Siedentop, D. (2002). Content knowledge for physical education. *Journal of Teaching in Physical Education, 21*(4), 368–378.

Stolz, S. (2015). Embodied learning. *Educational Philosophy and Theory, 47*(5) 474–487.

Thorburn, M. (2007). Achieving conceptual and curriculum coherence in high-stakes school examinations in physical education. *Physical Education and Sport Pedagogy, 12*(2), 163–184.

Thorburn, M. (2014). Values, autonomy and well-being: Implications for learning and teaching in physical education. *Educational Studies, 40*(4) 396–406.

Thorburn, M., & Horrell, A. (2014). Grand designs! Analysing the conceptual tensions associated with new physical education and health and wellbeing curriculum. *Sport, Education and Society, 19*(5), 621–636.

Thorburn, M., Jess, M. & Atencio, M. (2011). Thinking differently about curriculum: Analysing the potential contribution of physical education as part of 'health and wellbeing' during a time of revised curriculum ambitions in Scotland. *Physical Education and Sport Pedagogy, 16*(4), 383–398.

Thorburn, M., & MacAllister, J. (2013). Dewey, interest and well-being: Prospects for improving the educational value of physical education. *Quest, 65*(4) 458–468.

Wellard, I. (2012). Body-reflexive pleasures: Exploring bodily experiences within the context of sport and physical activity. *Sport, Education and Society, 17*(1), 21–33.

Williamson, B. (2015). Algorithmic skin: Health-tracking technologies, personal analytics and the biopedagogies of digitized health and physical education. *Sport, Education and Society, 20*(1), 133–151.

World Health Organization. (2014). *Global strategy on diet, physical activity and health.* Available online at: www.who.int/dietphysicalactivity/en/ (27 June 2014).

7

COMPLEXITY, CURRICULUM, AND THE DESIGN OF LEARNING SYSTEMS

Alan Ovens, UNIVERSITY OF AUCKLAND, NEW ZEALAND

& Joy Butler, UNIVERSITY OF BRITISH COLUMBIA, CANADA

Over the past two decades there has been a rapid growth of interest in complexity and its value to curriculum and the design of learning systems in physical education (PE). We suggest that understanding this 'turn' to complexity is linked to three intertwined ideas. The first is ontological and involves viewing the world as organized through highly connected and interdependent elements so that the focus becomes not about understanding what something is (a focus on being), but how it comes into being (a focus on becoming or emergence). The second is conceptual and involves the value to researchers and practitioners of drawing on a renewed vocabulary that enables generative ways of questioning the assumptions, normalizing logics, and methodologies of educational practice. The third is reflexive and involves researchers and practitioners being aware of the dynamic, partial, layered, and contingent nature of educational practice.

We draw on these ideas to help structure the discussion in this chapter. In the first section we begin with an introduction to complexity and outline some of the concepts that can be applied from complexity to PE settings. In the second, we discuss the implications that complexity has for curriculum design and consider the ways in which prescribed learning systems can evolve into emergent learning networks. Finally, in the last section we present three case studies that help ground and illustrate these ideas as instances of concrete and current practices of physical educators designing and implementing curriculum with a focus on complexity thinking.

An introduction to complexity

There is no easy consensus around what complexity is, what principles it embodies, or quick definitions of its meaning (Davis, Phelps, & Wells, 2004; Ovens, Hopper & Butler, 2013a). Despite the common usage of terms like 'complexity theory' or 'complexity science,' it is neither a unified field nor purely a science. Rather, complexity refers to evolving systems of thought that emerge as disciplinary fields, such as economics, physics, health, and biology, grapple with objects of study that scholars find increasingly difficult to understand through conventional ways of knowing (Byrne, 2005; Cilliers, 1998). Certainly, in PE it is possible to map the interest in complexity back through several genealogical lines (Alhadeff-Jones, 2008; Davis, Sumara, & Luce-Kapler, 2014). For example, in motor learning there has been a strong trajectory through dynamical systems and ecological psychology (Davids et al., 2013; Kelso, 1995,

2009), in pedagogy the trajectory is through complexity thinking and the work of Davis et al. and others (Ovens et al., 2013a; Storey & Butler, 2012), in sport sociology it has been through figurational sociology (Green, 2006), while others draw their lineage through contemporary social theories (Smith & Ovens, 2015; Tinning, 2010).

Viewed in this manner, complexity can be described as a collection of theories, dispositions, and conceptual tools that have evolved in different disciplinary fields to better accommodate the complex issues and realities being studied (Mason, 2008; Morrison, 2008; Walby, 2007). Some researchers have attempted to map this collection into different themes or communities to better represent the divergent positions, purposes, and histories involved (e.g. Alhadeff-Jones, 2008; Byrne, 2005; Morin, 2007; Richardson & Cilliers, 2001). While such descriptions provide a sense of the richness, disorder, and heterogeneity that can be observed in research related to complexity, we will focus this brief introduction on some of the philosophical implications of engaging with complexity.

One of the most fundamental notions in complexity is the way the object of study is modelled as a self-organizing system of interacting entities (Davis & Sumara, 2006; Ovens et al., 2013a). This simple assumption leads to some important ontological implications. First, the focus of attention is shifted to the relationality of all the elements in a particular setting and how they are affected by and affect others with which they are in contact. Theoretically, there is a broad range of metaphors used to describe this patterning of relations, including system, network, entanglement, web, mangle, and assemblage. While not all the same, these different labels allude to the importance of understanding what the elements in a system can do rather than describing what they are (Davis et al., 2004; Richardson & Cilliers, 2001). In complexity, the most common term in usage is 'system'.

Second, when the patterning of interactions in a system leads to uncertain and unpredictable behaviours, the system is said to be complex (as opposed to simple or complicated) (Byrne, 2005; Cilliers, 1998). For example, a computer is complicated, while the internet it connects to is complex. If the system has the added ability to change its structure in response to experience it is said to be a complex adaptive system. A PE lesson is considered to be a complex adaptive system because the lesson as a whole cannot be understood by simply analysing the individual parts, and it has the ability to adapt and change over time in response to the ecosystem in which it is a part (Wallian & Chang, 2012).

Third, the patterning of relations leads to the important insight that the properties that become our objects of study are generated by component interactions that occur at a lower level (Anderson, 1972; Goldstein, 2013; Ovens, Hopper, & Butler, 2013b). Put another way, the 'things' that we see and work with are the results of processes, have uncertain life, and exist only as the emergent product of interactions occurring within the system. This means that teachers and researchers need to shift their focus from trying to understand things as stable, substantive 'beings' to fluid, always contingent 'becomings' that are always in the process of being created and open to change (Davis & Sumara, 2006; Deleuze, 1994). This is not a foreign concept in PE, since the body is readily identified as constantly changing and adapting to its daily environment (think in terms of jogging and getting fit).

Fourth, the belief that entities like curriculum, learning, students, and schools are always the outcome of component interactions opens the possibility to new understandings and descriptions of system behaviour (Doll, 2012; Ricca, 2012). For example, the concept of nestedness draws attention to the way each system is itself composed of smaller subsystems while also contributing to other, larger systems (Davis & Sumara, 2006). Nestedness draws attention to our tendency to only conceptualize phenomena at one scale rather than see them as layered and interconnected.

Related to this, our fifth concept of transphenomenality draws attention to the way the phenomena emerge from the organization occurring at each level (Davis, 2008). For example, it is possible to see learning as occurring at the cellular level in patterns of neuron activity, at the personal level as coordinated patterns of motor behaviour, and at the social collective level as skilful action in game play. In order to better understand learning, one needs to appreciate it as a phenomenon occurring simultaneously and interdependently at each different level of system organization.

Finally, thinking of things as composed through patterns of relations brings attention to the nature of information flow through such patterning. Complex systems are described as open systems because they can exchange information with others in the ecosystem. In terms of education, this implies the component subsystems (students, teachers, schools) are not closed and isolated, but constantly exchanging information and resources and with other systems. There are two points to be made here where education is concerned. First, the concept of perturbance refers to the reaction of a system when it encounters a disturbance in the broader system (or ecosystem). Deleuze (1994) suggests that such encounters force the system to 'think' and invite further inquiry. In this way, perturbance can motivate learning by provoking attention, experimentation, adaption, and structural change (Smith & Ovens, 2015). In a similar manner, the concept of recursivity refers to the way flows of information help the system to interact and develop. Recursivity is an interactive process in that information about the system feeds back into the system to shape and inform future system behaviour (Morin, 2008). It takes place in the tension between system structure and action, moving beyond the notion of feedback and system governance to include the production of knowledge when the system's current knowledge is challenged by the knowledge required to act (Koskinen, 2013).

Complexity thinking

Before moving on, it is important to add that complexity is not just about ontological issues. One of the complexity communities identified by Richardson and Cilliers (2001) was that of complexity thinking. Hardman (2010) suggests complexity thinking has grown to be the dominant form of complexity theorizing in education today. Complexity thinking is, "an attitude which is potentially generative of, and pays attention to, diverse sensibilities without making claims to, or being trapped by, universals or absolutes" (Ovens et al., 2013b, p. 3). Complexity thinkers are concerned with the philosophical implications of assuming that reality is complex rather than predictable. They take a broad, interdisciplinary approach to understanding and researching education (Davis & Sumara, 2008). Thinking in this way encourages us to set aside our desire for certainty and facts in favour of a more open and reflexive stance that acknowledges the multiple, partial, and fluid elements that are complicit in shaping and being shaped by one's focus of interest (Davis & Sumara, 2012).

In relation to this, one of the concepts that we believe is useful is the idea of *currere* (Pinar & Grumet, 1976). The word currere derives from the same root as curriculum, 'to run, or to course'. For Pinar (2012), the concept of currere enables a way to reconceptualize the curriculum away from the impersonal goals of mandated curriculum documents and onto the emergent and collective processes of moving through the melee of present events. In this sense, the curriculum offers a space in which learning emerges, rather than a set of exercises that lead to predetermined outcomes. Rather than being simply described as the course itself (content and predetermined processes), currere is an open field of deterritorialized potential on which a pedagogical life may be run (Deleuze, 1994). In this way, currere takes into account the multiplicity of contexts that support learning, and the way these exist in relationship to each other (see also Cothran, Chapter 3).

Complexity applied to physical education settings

Many of the concepts relating to complexity have a clear application to PE. A comprehensive list of these is presented in the glossary of Ovens et al. (2013a) and we encourage readers new to complexity to investigate additional texts such as Davis and Sumara (2008), Morin (2007), and Davids et al. (2013). For the purposes of this chapter, we have listed those concepts (see Table 7.1) that we feel to be particularly generative in PE.

Introduction to curriculum development and implementation

The turn to exploring curriculum development from a complexity perspective corresponds not only with the development of new language and theoretical frameworks, but also with long-time concerns that the dominant discourse framing curriculum is one oriented around prediction and control (Radford, 2008). Inherent in such a discourse is the belief that learning is an 'input-output' linear process in which teaching methods and learning outcomes can be pre-defined and managed with confidence and certainty. By the mid twentieth century, this belief was exemplified in what came to be known as the Tyler Rationale, in which the processes of curriculum design became simplified to identifying objectives, selecting appropriate learning activities, organizing student activity to maximize effect, and evaluating to see if students attained the

Table 7.1 Complexity concepts relevant to physical education

Concept	Description
Relationality	A sensitivity to the connecting, connectable, connected nature of systems and the webbed patterns such interconnections display that give a sense of 'aliveness' to the system (Doll, 2012).
Emergence	A process that occurs when a network of relations begin to exhibit properties that arise from the interactions of agents and elements that make up the system and cannot be explained from understanding the elements individually.
Nestedness	A belief that complex systems are themselves made up of many subsystems as well as being nested within other systems. Each system can be "simultaneously seen as a whole, a part of a whole, or a network of wholes" (Davis et al., 2014, p. 178).
Transphenomenality	An awareness that educational phenomena emerge across a wide range of phenomena and thus need to be studied at the different nested levels and scales of organization.
Perturbance or disturbance	The act of disturbing or challenging the current state of a system in order to evoke moments in which system change may occur.
Recursivity	A process in which the information produced by the system is used to inform the system and enable it to adjust accordingly.
Currere	A focus on the emergent and collective processes of moving through the melee of present events in order to expand the space of the possible and the as-yet-to-be-imagined (Pinar, 2012).

predefined objective (Tyler, 1949; see Cothran, Chapter 3). The discourse was also evident in the school effectiveness movement that emerged in the 1980s, which developed sophisticated modelling approaches involving a wider range of variables, consideration of contextual factors, and multilevel statistical analyses. Despite this, the underlying assumption remained – that schools were a relatively stable, homogenous, and closed field of operations (Teddlie & Reynolds, 2000).

It is still possible to detect modernist ideas of prediction and control as they continue to frame the wave of curriculum reform discussions at the start of the new millennium (see also Penney, Chapter 9 & Ennis, Chapter 8). While many of these appear grounded in good intentions, such as ideas and plans for 'improving the quality of learning' and 'raising levels of achievement' or 'better preparing students for the 21st century', it is rare that these discussions move beyond attempts to simply revise the outcomes and standards expected, to introduce greater accountability for teachers, to increase evaluation and assessment of students, and to introduce rewards for those who can achieve the outcomes in the most efficient and effective ways (see McCullick, Gaudreault, & Ramos, Chapter 25). Each solution for reform appears hopelessly constrained within an instrumental rationality where curriculum is a design specification for society, teachers are educational technicians enacting the design, and students are commodities whose subjectivity and individuality are mercilessly overlooked and deprived. The turn to complexity provides a means to challenge such notions and instead open a space to rethink curriculum and pedagogy as an organic and living process that is connected to place, community, and local knowledge.

It is worth pausing at this point to reflect on the distinction between a prescribed curriculum and one that is more organic and complex. Table 7.2 lists some of the defining characteristics of these two curriculum systems. Contrasting the systemic nature of curriculum in this way has become a mechanism used by a variety of people to highlight some of the broader shifts occurring in contemporary education (for example, Jess, Attencio, & Thorburn, 2011; Macdonald, 2003; Morrison, 2008; Radford, 2008; Williams, Karousou, & Mackness, 2011). Schools and teachers are constantly evolving and such a comparison highlights the key aspects inherent in these changes. However, there is a risk to thinking of curriculum practice and change in a binary manner (as existing as either one position or the other). Not only does this tend to oversimplify the way curriculum practice is linked to broader social, political, economic, and technological factors and present each pole of the binary as homogenous positions, but also, such binaries are typically organized to favour one side over the other. For many, the list of characteristics under the emergent learning networks would represent favoured positions on key educational and pedagogical issues, leading to the rejection of those characteristics under the prescriptive learning systems column. It should be stressed that not all top-down, prescriptive systems are bad or unworkable (and conversely, not all bottom-up development is good). Rather, the focus should be more on how the learning system engages different stakeholders in webs of relations that co-create value and form value networks (Desai, 2010). There is also a risk that such binaries reify the modernist notion that change represents progress towards better and improved education. In a complex sense, all we can say is that education is in a constant state of emergence and becoming different. The question of whether this is better depends on who is doing the asking.

One way of acknowledging that curriculum is multifaceted and viewer dependent is to view it as a series of simultaneities – phenomena that exist together and are coupled in such a way that they mutually influence each other (Davis & Sumara, 2008). Hussain, Connor, and Mayo (2014) envision curriculum as six partial and incomplete views of curriculum that exist simultaneously (see Table 7.3). By moving between these views and seeing each as a space for problematizing practice, it is possible to position curriculum in an ever-evolving reality that is

Table 7.2 Characteristics of prescriptive and emergent curriculum frameworks

Nature of system	Prescriptive learning systems	Emergent learning networks
System organization	Top down, hierarchical, external and institutional control	Developmental, holonic, collaborative, self-organization
System behaviour	Predictable, complicated, mechanistic	Complex, adaptive, organic
Link to environment	Closed, internally interactive, learning community	Open, highly connected, learning network
Conception of learning	Prescribed, predictable, product driven	Emergent, uncertain, process driven
Learning activity	Passive participation, directed activity, individualized experiences	Active participation, self-organized action, collaborative experiences
Pedagogy	Transmission, de-contextualized experience, summative feedback	Emergent, situated and authentic experiences, formative feedback
Validation and revision	Absolutist, best practice, bureaucratic, informed by large-scale quantitative research. Externally benchmarked	Shared, dynamic practice, networked, informed by transdisciplinary and multi-method forms of research. Reflectively evaluated

Table 7.3 The six simultaneities of curriculum (adapted from Hussain et al., 2014)

Simultaneity	Its focus is on …
Curriculum as structure	Conceptualizing and understanding the systems that exist in the setting, i.e. nested systems of knowers, knowledge, and curriculum/activity.
Curriculum as process	Understanding emergence and the processes of drifts and self-organization that give rise to it.
Curriculum as content	Creating an enabling constraint to enable teachers and children to make decisions about curriculum content.
Curriculum as teaching	Foregrounding the teacher-as-knower and how his/her thinking and actions contribute to curriculum and are influenced by other aspects of curriculum.
Curriculum as learning	Foregrounding the child(ren)-as-knower and how his/her/their interactions with others and participation in activities trigger changes in knowledge and activities.
Curriculum as activity	Generating and enacting the activities at the centre and explaining how these influence and are influenced by teaching and learning.

brought forth in the process of enacting educational practice. It is also possible to acknowledge within this process the deliberate intention to strategically foster learning without knowing or prescribing exactly what will emerge.

Complexity and curriculum design

There is an awkward paradox that exists in relation to designing for complex educational systems. The concept of design, like the related notion of planning, implies an intention to achieve a particular outcome by manipulating form to fit function (Blecic & Cecchini, 2008). However, if the inherent characteristic of a complex system is that they display non-linearity, uncertainty, and unpredictability, then acts of design and planning become somewhat problematic. The complex nature of teaching means that what works in one situation may not work in other situations with other students and may not even work again for the same situation at a later date. In short, teachers (and curriculum planners) should not envisage some generic future state toward which the learners can be moved, since the possible futures open to the learning system are too many and the causes leading to it are too obscure.

One way of resolving this paradox is to begin with the assumption that learning will be emergent whether it is designed for or not (Wenger, 1998). In this way, the design process becomes an intention to foster emergent learning without predetermining or knowing what the specific outcomes will be (Blecic & Cecchini, 2008). Framed in this way, curriculum becomes an ever-evolving reality invented by the ongoing interactions of knowers, knowledge, and activities situated in the different nested layers (or simultaneities) of the education system (Hussain et al., 2014). This process is recursive in the sense that information produced by the system is continually informing the system and enabling it to adjust accordingly. This situation demands that the planning and design should be as emergent as the learning.

This brings us to the concept of *currere*, which frames curriculum and pedagogy as processes that emerge through a learning system that is flexibly organized in ways that allow students to explore what is socially relevant, intellectually engaging, and personally meaningful. Currere requires curriculum planners and teachers to give up the role of 'grand curriculum designers' and instead take on the roles of eco-system architects or engineers who use lesson plans that are open-ended and responsive to student input. It places students in a rich and complexly dynamic environment in which they can be engaged in meaningful learning and able to participate in curriculum conversations that are driven by interaction, relations, and recursions. As the complex web of interactions, relationships, and understanding is woven and develops in the classroom, the curriculum emerges as a conversation.

In Table 7.4, we return to the list of complexity concepts identified in Table 7.1 and consider how these may be applied to the design and implementation of an emergent learning system PE.

Case studies highlighting complexity theory and curriculum implementation in health and physical education

This chapter will highlight three case studies that demonstrate the use of complexity theory as it is applied to the various social, political, and structural complexities affiliated with constructing and implementing health and PE curriculum.

Case study 1: reconfiguring support networks in a secondary school physical education department in order to refocus curriculum planning around emergent student learning

The first case study examines how a PE department in a medium sized urban secondary school in Canada undertook to revise their curriculum and teaching (see McGinley & Kanavos, 2014). As was typical, the department in this study was responsible for scheduling classes and facilities and for teaching and assessing mandatory PE in grades 8–10 (approximately 360 students), and four elective classes in grades 11–12 (80 students). This task was traditionally undertaken by the Head of Department (HoD) in a hierarchical approach, anecdotally described by one

Table 7.4 Complexity concepts applied to physical education

Concept	Possible application to HPE
Relationality	• Students in a class are not just a group of isolated individuals. Rather, they connect with, and relate to, the others in the class so that they also become a networked collective. • The social network of students is not closed or isolated, but extends beyond the boundaries of the lesson. • Patterns of connections within and beyond the classroom influence the depth and richness of learning that emerges within a class of students. Therefore teachers should adapt and take advantage of the relationships of students with others in and outside of the class. • Students need to be coached to develop their own personal learning networks because it is not how smart the individual is, but how smart the network they build that is important. • New technologies have the potential to connect students with other people and knowledge systems.
Emergence	• What students learn from a lesson cannot be predicted or planned with certainty. The teacher can only increase the probability of an outcome through managing the constraints shaping students' engagement with the lesson. • Diversity in groups is important to the creativity, intelligence, and problem solving ability of each group. • Knowledge and skills emerge as solutions to the problems the student encounters in a specific context.
Nestedness	• Learning is always layered, occurring at the cellular, organ, person, classroom, school, school district, and society levels. • Students need help to make the connections between layers meaningful.
Transphenomenality	• Complex events are best understood by observing at least three levels of organization. • Identities are framed by contexts – who one is and where one is are inextricably intertwined.
Perturbance or disturbances	• Allow for and provoke 'teachable moments.' • Game structure (rules and regulations) and game play constraints work in balance to create both spontaneous and planned disturbances (unexpected events). As players adapt due to the disturbances created by one set of structural constraints and integrate those adaptations into their game play, the balance is disturbed and a new game structure is needed to rebalance the system.
Recursivity	• Use feedback generated from students to the teacher to inform pedagogy and curriculum, so that the learning system becomes adaptive and can evolve. • Game structures themselves are also open to feedback in order for the system to evolve. • As players gain new insights into tactical options and their abilities, teachers can use direct, Socratic, or democratic methods to adapt the game structure, thereby extending or expanding the adaptation potential of a game.
Currere	• The curriculum offers a space in which learning emerges, rather than a set of exercises that lead to predetermined outcomes. • Keep learning objectives simple and general to minimize confusion. • Use problems to guide what is needed to be known, i.e. learning from mistakes.

of the teachers as "ticking boxes on a checklist." This included ensuring that the programme addressed the Ministry of Education's prescribed learning outcomes (PLO's) and that teachers could report achievement against established assessment criteria. These criteria focused on students achieving normative standards of fitness, being competent in isolated skill progressions (games, gymnastics, and dance), and having a competent understanding of rules and activity structures. These were all taught within a teacher-centred pedagogy. This implied that learning can be identified ahead of time and assessed by checking that these prescribed outcomes are achieved. In summary, learning was framed as a linear mechanical process.

Initiating and sustaining departmental change is never easy. An important element in this case was the way the HoD could reconfigure the pattern of relations within the department that sustained current practices. He did this by enrolling in a Master's degree (opening a channel for new ideas and information to come into the department) and by inviting a district counsellor from a nearby school to act as a 'critical friend' (creating a means to perturb current practice and enhance feedback). Another key element was the willingness of the HoD to develop a department culture that was more collaborative, democratic, and focused on placing student learning at the heart of all planning and departmental initiatives. Creating a culture of support and trust where each member felt their contributions mattered required a shift in the usual hierarchical traditional approaches to leadership. Enabling this meant the HoD becoming less of a director and more willing to find ways to engage greater participation and sharing of ideas amongst his colleagues and students.

Energy was then focused on developing a 'growth plan' for the department. Once everyone in the department felt this was not another 'flash in the pan' or 'top-down initiative' provided by either the district or school administration, a sense of trust developed. Time during department meetings and other ad hoc meetings was set aside for discussions about teaching, knowing, and learning. The development of the plan involved several phases (similar to action research), including planning, implementation, an action plan, and time to reflect and evaluate before moving onto the next phase. The HoD kept the principal and other essential stakeholders in the loop about developments and reported back to meetings. As the group began working collaboratively around scheduling, resources, teaching methods, implementation strategies, they began to develop a shared language and culture about teaching PE. These became a necessary part of bonding. "*We put a great deal of energy into creating a healthy environment that encouraged dialogue, inquiry, and sharing of ideas.*" The department became vibrant and energized. Its members rediscovered a spirit of idealism more typical of undergraduate students than veteran teachers – including rekindled hope, passion, and interest in their learners.

Through close collaboration, department members re-envisioned and rewrote major goals and policies for their department. By being involved, they became more willing and able to engage in the 'School Growth Plan' (SGP) goals being initiated by the School Administration team. Through a recursive process between school and department discussions, department documents dovetailed well into the child-centred policies of the SGP goals. These in turn fitted well into the wide interpretation of the provincial pupil learning outcomes and assessment guides. Such involvement in broader school policy making was a radical departure for several members of the department.

While very brief, the case helps to highlight some of the elements that enabled this group of teachers to enact an effective change process around their departmental curriculum and teaching. In summary, these were: 1) reconfiguring the professional network to enable new sources of ideas and feedback; 2) deep examination of the educational beliefs and philosophy underpinning current practice; 3) support and time for developing and implementing curricular and pedagogical innovations; 4) supportive, open-minded leadership; 5) development of shared values, beliefs, and resources through collaborative inquiry; and 6) perturbance and recursivity around perceived barriers for change, which provided a means for informing the system. For a more complete report on this case, we suggest reading McGinley and Kanavos (2014).

Case study 2: supporting regional curriculum development with a self-organized professional learning community

The second case study focuses on how a group of teachers in the São Paulo region of Brazil self-organized their own professional community to support curriculum in their region (Sanches Neto, Venâncio, Betti, & Daolio, 2014). Brazil is a huge country divided into 27 states and 5570 municipalities. While it has national curriculum guidelines (Brazil, 1996) each metropolitan region has considerable autonomy for how the school curriculum is implemented in its own area. Complicating this is the fact that a high population density and shortage of schools means education in Brazil occurs in a series of 'shifts'. Each school can operate up to three shifts each day to meet the population demand and this means that students attend school only in the morning, afternoon, or evening. For the PE teachers working in the São Paulo region, who commonly have to work across several school districts, with different curriculum regulations and insufficient equipment and facilities, the job of creating quality PE programmes is particularly complex.

In 2005, a group of PE teachers decided to look at ways to work collaboratively to help support and enhance their teaching. They were inspired by Elliott's (1998) notion of 'teacher-researcher' as a way they could create an inquiry-oriented approach to solving the unique problems they encountered in their daily work. Initially they met in person to share vignettes of their individual experiences (similar to the method proposed by Tsangaridou & O'Sullivan, 2003) and support each other. Later, a website was developed that could help link the group, provide a means to coordinate activities and share resources, and encourage additional members (Sanches Neto et al., 2014). Over time, this group has grown and there are currently more than 265 teachers registered on the group's website.

Questioning the nature of curriculum practice in São Paulo schools and the role PE played in enhancing the lives of young people was always a central concern for the teachers in the group. What became important was acknowledging that PE was an expression of the interdependent and specific factors in play in any school setting and not the application of generic solutions. What emerged from their work was the idea that curriculum should be broadly organized around the four 'thematic content sets' of the dynamics of culture (cultural elements), body (personal and interpersonal aspects), movement, and environment (environmental demands) (see Table 7.5). When implementing this curriculum the aim for teachers is not only to include at least one topic from each set, concurrently, in each lesson, but also to treat them pedagogically in an integrated mode in order to enhance the efficacy of the experience for the students involved (Sanches Neto et al., 2013).

While brief, the snapshot provided in this case study reveals something of the passion and commitment of the teachers involved to participate in the complex work of bringing a meaningful curriculum to life for the students in their particular region of Brazil. In effect, the teachers began to self-organize their own professional learning community that had no institutional or governmental affiliation (Sanches Neto, 2014). By working as a collective, they were able to extend support and encourage discussion about issues that were particular to their situation that did not lend themselves easily to generic solutions. Working collaboratively, the group not only developed resources and teaching methods appropriate for these settings, they also shared a common culture and language about teaching PE. The result is a curriculum that is

Table 7.5 Content sets for physical education (adapted from Sanches Neto, 2003, 2014)

Cultural elements	Movement	Transdiscipline approach	Environmental demands
Play and games	Combination and specialization	Anatomy and biomechanics	Administration and economy
Circus and gymnastics	Stabilization skills	Anthropology and psychology	Aesthetics and philosophy
Dance	Abilities and training	Biochemistry and nutrition	Physics and nature
Wrestling and capoeira	Manipulation skills	Embryology and physiology	History and geography
Sports	Rhythm	Motor behaviour	Sociology and politics
Daily life activities	Locomotion skills	Health and pathology	Virtual

shared, transdisciplinary, meaningful for all participants, contextually relevant and fluid enough to adapt to the changing issues and settings the teachers encounter in their daily work (Sanches Neto, 2014).

Case study 3: creating a complexity framework at the macro level (national curriculum) that enables curriculum frameworks at the micro level (individual schools)

The third case study focuses on curriculum complexity at a national level. Like many countries around the globe, Scotland has grappled with ensuring its national curriculum meets the needs of learning to live and work in the twenty-first century. This has led to an increasing level of discussion at the policy level of the education system for revising curriculum around aspirational claims for young people to become 'successful learners,' 'confident individuals,' 'effective contributors,' and 'responsible citizens' (Scottish Executive, 2004a). It was also seen that to achieve such goals there was a need for teachers to be more flexible in how they interpreted the curriculum and use more active learning approaches to enable "the creative, adaptable professional who can develop the ideas that arise when children are immersed in their learning" (Scottish Executive, 2004a, p. 19). Coupled with this was the view that PE contributed significantly to achieving national health outcomes and, consequently, was "an area of the curriculum which, exceptionally, needs greater priority to support the health and well-being of young people in Scotland" (Scottish Executive, 2004b, p. 1).

One of the groups charged with working with primary schools and their teachers to help implement this vision was the Developmental PE Group (DPEG) at the University of Edinburgh. To effect curriculum change at the national level, the DPEG recognized that there was a complex mix of factors that influence how curriculum is enacted in schools. Key amongst these was the influence of primary teachers' experiences during their own schooling and teacher education to shape their knowledge and beliefs about the purpose of PE, its content, and teaching approaches (Elliot, Atencio, Campbell, & Jess, 2013). Associated with this, the DPEG group also saw the need to challenge the fragmented and compartmentalized nature of the traditional curriculum model in which student activity was often marginalized, rarely developed within a situated and authentic context, and usually failing to provide deep learning experiences.

In embarking on the ambitious project to lead a complexity-informed curriculum development programme, the DPEG encouraged teachers to tap into the potential of students to self-organize their own learning. This meant supporting teachers to use exploratory and open-ended tasks within different environmental settings. The emphasis was on working with teachers to help them create an inclusive learning culture where learning emerged through the posing of problems, the encouragement of dialogue and critique, and the scaffolded discovery of movement patterns. The DPEG emphasized the need for teachers to recognize and support young people's 'edge of chaos' explorations so that students could view 'mistakes' as an important, necessary, and even enjoyable part of the movement learning process. Coupled with this the DPEG encouraged teachers to look beyond the idea that learning to move was about developing sport specific techniques and should rather be focused on the development of broader movement foundations, including adaptability and creativity, which enhance participation in most physical activities across the lifespan (Jess et al., 2011).

This case study not only highlights the transphenomenal nature of curriculum, by demonstrating how concerns around the nature and practice of curriculum emerge at various levels of the education system, it also acknowledges the uncertainty and non-linear nature of curriculum change. That is, it helps demonstrate how the aspirational and flexible outcomes relevant to physical activity, health, and well-being at the macro level of national curriculum policy provide the enabling framework for curriculum at the micro level of individual school practice rather than determining those practices. The results from the work of the DPEG reveal encouraging signs that schools, teachers, and young people have moved to a more complex and constructivist approach to learning movement. Importantly, by informing their work from constructivist, ecological, and dynamic systems theories, they have effectively created a complexity framework that enables them to articulate a vision of teaching PE while still acknowledging the 'messiness' and 'chaos' of doing this in practice (Jess et al., 2011).

Conclusion

The turn to working with complexity has value to those seeking to research curriculum and design of learning systems in PE. As we have outlined in this chapter, complexity can be generative in a number of ways. By viewing the world as organized through highly connected and interdependent elements, attention becomes more focused on affect and process rather than substance and being. This provides researchers and practitioners a vocabulary that enables new ways of questioning the assumptions, normalizing logics, and methodologies of educational practice. As our case studies demonstrate, it also provides researchers and practitioners a means to work with the dynamic, partial, layered, and contingent nature of educational practice in order to find the spaces in which they may make a difference.

Reflective questions for discussion

1. Describe six principles associated with contemporary approaches to complexity theory/thinking.
2. In what ways do schools reflect complex systems?
3. To what extent can we use complexity thinking as a conceptual framework to explain or account for (some of) the multiple processes and individuals influencing school-based curriculum development?
4. Explain how each case study reflects complexity thinking as described in this chapter.

References

Alhadeff-Jones, M. (2008). Three generations of complexity theories: Nuances and ambiguities. In M. Mason (Ed.), *Complexity theory and the philosophy of education* (pp. 62–78). Chichester, UK: Wiley-Blackwell.

Anderson, P. (1972). More is different. *Science, 177*, 393–396.

Blecic, I., & Cecchini, A. B. (2008). Design beyond complexity: Possible futures – prediction or design? (and techniques and tools to make it possible). *Futures, 40*(6), 537–551.

Brazil. (1996). *Lei de diretrizes e bases da educação nacional: Lei n.9394/96 [Law of guidelines and basis for national education].* Brasília-DF: Congresso Nacional. Retrieved from www.planalto.gov.br/ccivil_03/Leis/L9394.htm.

Byrne, D. (2005). Complexity, configurations and cases. *Theory, Culture & Society, 22*(5), 95–111.

Cilliers, P. (1998). *Complexity and postmodernism: Understanding complex systems.* London: Routledge.

Davids, K., Araújo, D., Hristovski, R., Serre, N. B., Button, C., & Passos, P. (Eds.). (2013). *Complex systems in sport (Vol. 7).* London: Routledge.

Davis, B. (2008). Complexity and education: Vital simultaneities. *Educational Philosophy and Theory, 40*(1), 50–65.

Davis, B., Phelps, R., & Wells, K. (2004). Complicity: An introduction and a welcome. *Complicity: An International Journal of Complexity and Education, 1*(1), 1–7.

Davis, B., & Sumara, D. (2006). *Complexity and education: Inquiries into learning, teaching and research.* London: Routledge.

Davis, B., & Sumara, D. (2008). Complexity as a theory of education. *Transnational Curriculum Inquiry, 5*(2), 33–44.

Davis, B., & Sumara, D. (2012). Fitting teacher education in/to/for an increasingly complex world. *An International Journal of Complexity and Education, 9*(1), 30–40.

Davis, B., Sumara, D., & Luce-Kapler, R. (2014). *Engaging minds: Cultures of education and practices of teaching* (3rd edn.). London: Routledge.

Deleuze, G. (1994). *Difference and repetition* (P. Patton, Trans.). London: Athlone.

Desai, D. (2010). Co-creating learning: Insights from complexity theory. *The Learning Organization, 17*(5), 388–403.

Doll, W. (2012). Complexity and the culture of curriculum. *Complicity: An International Journal of Complexity and Education, 9*(1), 10–29.

Elliot, D., Atencio, M., Campbell, T, & Jess, M. (2013). From PE experiences to PE teaching practices? Insights from Scottish primary teachers' experiences of PE, teacher education, school entry and professional development. *Sport, Education and Society, 18*(6), 749–766.

Elliott, J. (1998). Recolocando a pesquisa-ação em seu lugar original e próprio [Replacing action-research in its own original place]. In C. M. G. Geraldi, D. Fiorentini, & E. Pereira (Eds.). *Cartografias do trabalho docente: Professor(a)-pesquisador(a) [Cartographies of teacher work: Teacher-researcher]* (137–152). Campinas-SP: Mercado de Letras.

Goldstein, J. (2013). Reimagining emergence: Part 1. *E:CO, 15*(2), 78–104.

Green, K. (2006). Physical education and figurational sociology: An appreciation of the work of Eric Dunning. *Sport in Society: Cultures, Commerce, Media, Politics, 9*(4), 650–664. Retrieved from www.informaworld.com/10.1080/17430430600769031.

Hardman, M. (2010). *Is complexity theory useful in describing classroom learning?* Paper presented to The European Conference on Educational Research, Helsinki, 26th August 2010.

Hussain, H., Connor, L., & Mayo, E. (2014). Envisioning curriculum as six simultaneities. *Complicity: An International Journal of Complexity and Education, 11*(1), 59–84.

Jess, M., Atencio, M., & Thorburn, M. (2011). Complexity theory: Supporting curriculum and pedagogy developments in Scottish physical education. *Sport, Education and Society, 16*(2), 179–199.

Kelso, J. A. S. (1995). *Dynamic patterns: The self-organization of brain and behavior.* Cambridge, MA: MIT Press.

Kelso, J. A. S. (2009). Coordination dynamics. In R. Myers (Ed.), *Encyclopedia of complexity and system sciences* (pp. 1537–1564). Berlin, Germany: Springer-Verlag.

Koskinen, K. U. (2013). *Knowledge production in organizations: A processual autopoietic view.* Sydney: Springer International.

Macdonald, D. (2003). Curriculum change and the post-modern world: Is the school curriculum-reform movement an anachronism? *Journal of Curriculum Studies, 35*(2), 139–149.

Mason, M. (2008). *Complexity theory and the philosophy of education.* Chichester, UK: Wiley Blackwell.

McGinley, S., & Kanavos, G. (2014). *Enacting change in a secondary physical education department.* Master of Education graduating project, Vancouver, BC: University of British Columbia.

Morin, E. (2007). Restricted complexity, general complexity. In C. Gershenson, D. Aerts, & B. Edmonds (Eds.), *Worldviews, science and us: Philosophy and complexity* (pp. 5–29). London: World Scientific.

Morin, E. (2008). *Advances in systems theory, complexity, and the human sciences.* New York: Hampton Press.

Morrison, K. (2008). Educational philosophy and the challenge of complexity theory. In M. Mason (Ed.), *Complexity theory and the philosophy of education* (pp. 16–45). Chichester, UK: Wiley-Blackwell.

Ovens, A., Hopper, T., & Butler, J. (2013a). Reframing curriculum, pedagogy and research. In A. Ovens, T. Hopper, & J. Butler (Eds.), *Complexity thinking in physical education: Reframing curriculum pedagogy and research* (pp. 1–13). London. Routledge.

Ovens, A., Hopper, T., & Butler, J. (2013b). *Complexity thinking in physical education: Reframing curriculum pedagogy and research.* London: Routledge.

Pinar, W. (2012). *What is curriculum theory?* New York. Routledge.

Pinar, W., & Grumet, M. (1976). *Toward a poor curriculum.* Dubuque, IA: Kendall/Hunt.

Radford, M. (2008). Prediction, control and the challenge to complexity. *Oxford Review of Education, 34*(5), 505–520.

Ricca, B. (2012). Beyond teaching methods: A complexity approach. *Complicity: An International Journal of Complexity and Education, 9*(1), 31–51.

Richardson, K., & Cilliers, P. (2001). What is complexity science? A view from different directions. *Emergence, 3*(1), 5–23.

Sanches Neto, L. (2003). *Educação física escolar: Uma proposta para o componente curricular da 5ª à 8ª série do ensino fundamental [School physical education: A proposal for the curriculum from 6th to 9th grades].* Rio Claro-SP: UNESP. Dissertation (Master's in School Physical Education).

Sanches Neto, L. (2014). *O processo de elaboração de saberes por professores-pesquisadores de educação física em uma comunidade colaborativa [The process of knowledge elaboration by physical education teacher-researchers within a collaborative community].* Rio Claro-SP: UNESP. Thesis (Doctorate in Professional Education in Physical Education Working Field).

Sanches Neto, L., Conceição, W. L., Okimura-Kerr, T., Venâncio, L., Vogel, A. J. Z., França, A. L., Corsino, L. N., Rodrigues, J. C. R., & Freitas, T. P. (2013). Demandas ambientais na educação física escolar: perspectivas de adaptação e de transformação [Environmental demands in school physical education: Perspectives towards adaptation and transformation]. *Movimento, 19*(4), 309–330. Retrieved from www.seer.ufrgs.br/Movimento/article/viewFile/41079/27456.

Sanches Neto, L., Venâncio, L., Betti, M., & Daolio, J. (2014). Propostas curriculares de educação física: Podemos esperar por mudanças? O caso da rede estadual de ensino de São Paulo [Physical education curricular proposals: Can we expect changes? The case of São Paulo state teaching network]. In M. I. P. Soeiro & M. I. Silva (Eds.), *Educação física escolar: Pesquisas e reflexões [School physical education: Research and reflections]* (pp. 24–42). Natal, Brazil: UERN. Retrieved from www.uern.br/controledepaginas/edicoes-uern-ebooks/arquivos/1205educacao_fisica.pdf.

Scottish Executive. (2004a). *A curriculum for excellence: The curriculum review group.* Edinburgh, UK: Scottish Executive.

Scottish Executive. (2004b). *Response from Peter Peacock, Minister for Education and Young People, June 15th, 2004.* Edinburgh, UK: Scottish Executive.

Scottish Executive. (2007). *Reaching higher: Building on the success of Sport 21.* Edinburgh, UK: Scottish Executive.

Smith, W., & Ovens, A. (2015). Learning bodies: Embedded, embedding and always emerging. In P. O'Connor & K. Fitzpatrick (Eds.), *Education and the body* (pp. 115–126). Auckland, New Zealand: Edify.

Storey, B., & Butler, J. (2012). Complexity thinking in PE: Game centered approaches, games as complex adaptive systems, and ecological values. *Physical Education and Sport Pedagogy, 18*(2), 133–149.

Teddlie, C., & Reynolds, D. (Eds.). (2000). *The international handbook of school effectiveness research.* London: Falmer Press.

Tinning, R. (2010). *Pedagogy and human movement: Theory, practice and research.* London. Routledge.

Tsangaridou, N., & O'Sullivan, M. (2003). Physical education teachers' theories of action and theories-in-use. *Journal of Teaching in Physical Education, 22,* 132–152.

Tyler, R. W. (1949). *Basic principles of curriculum and instruction.* Chicago: University of Chicago Press.

Walby, S. (2007) Complexity theory, systems theory, and multiple intersecting social inequalities. *Philosophy of the Social Sciences, 37,* 449–470.

Wallian, N., & Chang, C. (2012). The complex thinking paradigm in physical education teacher education: Perspectives on the 'reflective practitioner' concept in France. In A. Ovens, T. Hopper, & J. Butler (Eds.), *Complexity thinking in physical education: Reframing curriculum pedagogy and research* (pp. 168–180). London: Routledge.

Wenger, E. (1998). *Communities of practice: Learning, meaning and identity.* Cambridge, UK: Cambridge University Press.

Williams, R., Karousou, R., & Mackness, J. (2011). Emergent learning and learning ecologies in Web 2.0. *The International Review of Research in Open and Distance Learning, 12*(3), 39–59. Retrieved from www.irrodl.org/index.php/irrodl/article/view/883.

8

GLOBALIZED CURRICULUM

Scaling sport pedagogy themes for research

Catherine D. Ennis, University of North Carolina at Greensboro, USA

Globalization is a multidimensional construct used to structure international initiatives in economics, politics, technology, population studies, and education, to name just a few. Economist, Theodore Levitt, was the first to describe globalization phenomena, events, and consequences of changes in global economics. Levitt's particular expertise was the complex world of production, consumption, and investment (Stromquist, 2002). Scholars and governments quickly embraced the term using it to describe political and cultural changes rapidly transforming nations and people worldwide (Spring, 2008).

By its very definition, globalization assumes an interdisciplinary perspective, in which societies, cultures, and even civilizations bend and transform under the weight of economic, political, and social pressures (Stromquist & Monkman, 2014). Policies, of course, exist within a context and in the case of globalization context, is not limited to international influences but also influences and is influenced by decisions made at the local, regional, and national levels. Therefore, the term, globalization, embraces both positive and negative forces from the local to the international as each level changes and is changed by informational awareness, economics, and the force of rapidly evolving public opinion (Rizvi & Lingard, 2010).

As societies shift and adjust to world trends, societal institutions, such as education, also feel the weight of globalized policies. Neoliberal influences on government and economics have greatly molded educational perspectives in both developed and developing countries and reflect in no small way the desires of developed countries to influence education from systems to an individual level. Current discussions of globalization must acknowledge and explore this force and its impact globally through World Bank and International Monetary Fund (IMF) policies (Chepator-Thompson, 2014) and locally based on resource allocations to community schools.

In this chapter, I begin with an overview of globalization discourses that are currently shaping economic, political, and social policies. I then apply these discourses to the construct of globalized curriculum in physical education (PE), emphasizing both current and future trends. I conclude by considering several sport pedagogy-related themes that hold global attention and value. In the final section, I discuss current and potential research initiatives that can be scaled and externally funded in the evolving contexts of fair play, cultural revitalizing pedagogy, and health and well-being to provide students with relevant and meaningful opportunities to develop active, healthy physical experiences.

Globalization discourses

Spring (2008) identifies four globalization discourses that influence educational models around the world. These include world culture, world systems, postcolonial, and culturalist discourses. Discourses surrounding *world culture* propose that, "all cultures are slowly integrating into a single global culture" (Spring, 2008, p. 334). From this perspective, often described as neo-institutionalist, nations draw on a single Western conception of mass schooling when planning their school systems. This single global model for schooling assumes that Western perspectives should be set as the standard for all nations and cultures regardless of history, ethnic origins, or localized schooling practices (Lee & Cho, 2014). In PE, one might consider the relatively rapid exportation of models-based practice especially as related to the games-based approaches and the impact of fitness and wellness approaches which in the United States have an overwhelming neoliberal appeal (see Casey, Chapter 4). Likewise, when curricula are embraced by ministries of education and written as national curricula (see Thorburn, Chapter 6), the world cultures globalization thread becomes pervasive and powerful, shaping programming and teacher and student accountability (Evans, 2014; Macdonald, 2014).

Advocates of the *world systems* discourses conceptualize the world into two major, but unequal zones. The core or Northern Zone (Rizvi & Lingard, 2010) consists of the United States, the European Union, and Japan which allocate resources purposefully to inculcate Northern Zone values to dominate and influence national (and educational) policy in the Southern Zone (i.e., Africa, South American, Caribbean, South Pacific Island nations). Northern Zone nations further these aims through their influence on funding available through international organizations such as the World Bank, the Organisation for Economic Co-operation and Development, and the World Trade Organization, or the General Agreement on Trade in Services. For example, the World Bank provides educational loans to developing countries for the express purpose of economic and educational development. In this way, it directly influences educational ideology, planning, and institutional structures in developing countries (Chepator-Thompson, 2014). Neoliberal policies such as privatization of school systems and support of private and religious schools with public and World Bank/IMF funding limit access to liberal education and funnel curricular into vocational orientations. In PE, Chepator-Thompson (2014) points out the seductive pull of these forces as they shape curricula in a blatantly colonial scenario.

Postcolonial perspectives on globalization are a special case of the world systems theories. Postcolonials attempt to impose an economic and political system that benefits wealthy and rich nations (both individuals and large multinational corporations) to the detriment of the world's poor countries and individuals (Stromquist & Monkman, 2014). In current manifestations of postcolonial globalism, wealthy nations attempt to impose market economies, human capital education, and neoliberal school reforms designed to further the agenda of rich nations and multinational corporations. From this perspective, education is an economic investment designed to produce skilled labor to serve corporations (Spring, 2008). Postcolonial analyses include those of slavery and migrations, race, culture, class, and gender manifest in resistance and struggle, identity complexity, and language rights.

Culturalist theories of globalization emphasize the role of "cultural variations and the borrowing and lending of educational ideas within a global context" (Spring, 2008, p. 334). On a positive note, this model of schooling argues for inclusion and educability of all, the right to a quality education, and the importance of perpetuating economic and democratic rights (Artiles, Kozleski, & Waitoller, 2011). To an extent, the culturalist perspective appears compelling until one examines the processes used to implement this aim. The argument is that when affluent nations design curriculum they incorporate best models and practices available. Disseminating these curricular prototypes globally can provide uplifting educational experiences for poor nations unable to fund the development of curricula that meet world standards. Thus, the rationale for a world or globalized curricula from culturalists' perspectives focuses again on a Western school model that *should* be globalized because it represents a universal, absolute conceptualization of best practice.

Neoliberalism

Set and entwined within these discourses are powerful strands that have evolved from and influenced economic and political policies impacting national and multinational educational systems. Among these discourses are Northern Zone products of neoliberalism, global uniformity, and knowledge economies (Spring, 2008). Neoliberalism has become a central plank in the political platforms of conservative governments and politicians. Neoliberalism can be traced to the work of Friedrich Hayek, an Austrian economist and Nobel Prize winner. His work is based on a strong criticism of large government and unwieldy government bureaucracies. He favored free markets and minimal government regulations on markets and business. Within this perspective, sanctioned and regulated institutions such as schools should be privatized and control shifted to the marketplace (Rizvi & Lingard, 2010). Thus, society, students, and their families could choose schools based on their interests and judgments of quality without the need to attend schools based on geographic region or family income (e.g., charter and magnet schools).

To facilitate free choice, neoliberal governments and taxpayers fund mechanisms such as vouchers permitting students to attend any public, private, or religious school. Schools would be free and influenced by marketplace competition to market their curriculum and recruit students based on their offerings. Conservative neoliberalists, however, are unwilling to relinquish control of key educational drivers such as curriculum standards, testing requirements, or teacher credentialing, tenure, and salary scales (e.g., Sloan, 2008). In other words, neoliberalists advocate individual choice and minimal government regulation while simultaneously protecting accountability structures which in fact limit choice and impose government regulations. The goal is to shape policies and, in the case of schools, require administrators and teachers to conform within a highly regulated environment. Thus, neoliberal school reforms are designed to privatize traditional school services and return them to the marketplace in the form of school choice and for-profit schooling (Apple, Kenway, & Singh, 2005; Macdonald, 2011). World system and postcolonial advocates argue for neoliberalist ideologies to ensure that privileged nations and people retain their wealth and power in a globalized economy (Stromquist & Monkman, 2014).

Historically, the relative low status of school-based PE actually has protected it from some of these neoliberalistic forces while making it the victim of others. While physical educators have successfully avoided many of the regulations associated with prescribed curriculum and accountability-based testing experienced by classroom teachers and their students in high profile subjects, they have, in turn, been whipped by the consequential redistribution of already limited school resources to these 'tested subject areas' (Ennis, 2014; McCullick, 2014). Recently, though, this too has changed in the United States as the neoliberal government funding programs such as the 'Race to the Top' initiatives have provided millions of dollars in resources to develop accountability systems for all teachers, including physical educators (United States Department of Education, 2009). Physical educators in some states and school districts are compelled to comply with ASW (Assessments of Student Work) policies, focusing on PE students' performance within specific standards and objectives.

A second aspect of neoliberal agenda, *global uniformity*, is a double-edged sword of educational globalization policies. World culturalists perceive a world curriculum in which supposedly all individuals have equal opportunities to flourish in a competitive marketplace. This perspective resonates in Northern Zone countries that simultaneously welcome, resist, and struggle to assimilate migrants from diverse cultures. Yet, uniformity comes with a substantial price as ethnic minorities must subsume their identities within a Northern Zone world and work view. Homogenization of curriculum and peoples may be a consequence of efforts to find the 'best' curriculum from a globalized perspective (Anderson-Levitt, 2008). This perspective on the converging curriculum suggests that nations increasingly agree on core curricula with 'subject areas' as the unit of commonality (in PE: games/sport; physical activity). However, simply because most countries include a subject, topic, or concept in their core curricula does not mean that it is taught in a uniform manner.

While national economies benefit from the 'brain gain' that occurs as skilled workers arrive, this increase in multicultural populations can result in cultural and religious conflicts and resistance to uniform, assimilationist curriculum practices. Only recently have educators attempted to view globalization through a pluralistic lens. As multicultural advocates argue for sustaining curricula that permit ethnic and cultural minorities to maintain and embrace content and schooling practices from their cultures (see Barker & Lundvall, Chapter 24) there is hope that the resulting globally inclusive educational environment becomes more welcoming and stabilizing for both cultural minorities and majority populations. Culturalists point to these benefits as they advocate for curricular globalization.

Globalized curriculum

A global perspective emphasizes national and regional settings that shape curriculum. Worldwide initiatives and struggles for power that consume peoples, resources, and lives influence what we teach and how we teach it. The dramatic increase in the number and diversity of migrants, the instantaneousness of communications, and the speed of travel suggest that many curricula are already globalized, impacting considerably larger numbers of individuals across large geographic spaces. Anderson-Levitt (2008) argues that another characteristic of curricular globalization is that most countries tend to agree to disagree about a similar set of issues. This is particularly true about those stemming from a neoliberal agenda. The role of market reforms, school choice, educational privatization, and deprofessionalization of teacher roles in teaching and curricular development resonate in developing countries eager to win World Bank/IMF grants.

Anderson-Levitt (2008) notes, however, that more than one type of curriculum and pedagogy can lead to high achievement. Yet, because of a uniform commonality or globalization of curriculum in mathematics and science, for example, it becomes increasingly difficult to differentiate curriculum by country. This can be true in PE with the globalizing influence of sport and health-related fitness. Academic success may also be attributed to a nation's wealth distributed across schools, school districts, and regions making it difficult to determine if high achievement should be attributed to a country's wealth or to a globalized curriculum of best practices. It is also possible to look at a country's Ministry of Education as a culprit in the drive for globalization of successful practices. In PE, globalization of model-based and games-based approaches are central to national curricula attempts to inculcate best practices for teaching while enhancing nationalistic pride and Olympic and World Cup success. Ministries of Education often promote agenda at the expense of teacher reflection and community input. Yet, to the extent that games- and movement-based models replace more traditional, authoritarian, and teacher-centered approaches, they provide hope for better student experiences in PE.

Community schooling

Farrell (2008) reports that a strengthening global focus on models of community school-ing also holds promise to strengthen the connections between communities and their local schools. Although the model varies by location based on unique histories and social struc-tures, a growing body of research is tracking student success in terms of enrollment, retention, grade completion and promotion, and academic success. Farrell (2008) identifies 200 of these community programs that roughly fit within the community-schooling model, arguing that community schools represent the best current model for enhancing learning on a large scale in developing countries with very poor and disadvantaged students. He concludes that the traditional model of schooling can be changed on a large scale even in very poor places with very limited resources.

Globalization of community schools depends on characteristics of effective schooling institutionalized as 'best practices' pedagogy. Child-centered curriculum, active learning, and engagement of parents and the community in the educational process propel community schools and their students to strong learning results. Community schools reflect an in-depth reorganization and revisioning of traditional schools leading to new models of schooling that are far different and far more effective than current neoliberalist schools (Coalition of Community Schools, 2016).

Culturally sustaining pedagogy

Gloria Ladson-Billings (1995) elegantly articulated the importance of community and cultural relevance in her study of successful teachers of African-American students. She proposed "a theoretical model that not only addresses student achievement but also helps students to accept and affirm their cultural identity while developing critical perspectives that challenge inequities that schools (and other institutions) perpetuate" (p. 469). She provided strong evidence to refute the value of traditional behaviorist school and class structures in favor of inclusive approaches to education.

Paris (2012) has reconceptualized this concept to focus on culturally *sustaining* peda-gogy. This stance focuses on the need to "perpetuate, foster and sustain linguistic, literate, and cultural pluralism as part of the democratic project of schooling" (p. 93). In a sym-posium published in *Harvard Educational Review*, Ladson-Billings (2014) reconceptualized cultural relevance to add the dimension of sustenance for ethnic and racial minorities. In this symposium, Paris and Alim (2014) argue that culturally sustaining pedagogy expands on Ladson-Billings' original construct to include (a) a focus on "the plural and evolving nature of youth identity and cultural practices and (b) a commitment to embracing youth culture's counterhegemonic potential while maintaining a clear-eyed critique of the ways in which youth culture can also reproduce systemic inequality" (p. 85). They argue that this per-spective is desperately needed as traditional schools continue to emphasize deficit learning (Artiles et al., 2011; Paris & Alim, 2014). Within the symposium papers, McCarty and Lee (2014) expand the 'sustaining' construct further to advocate for culturally *revitalizing* peda-gogy; curricula that mend and heal indigenous cultures through a dynamic reenactment of responsive schooling focused on heritage, language, and culture.

Traditional schooling practices continue to oversimplify cultural practices, ignoring ways that youth express and communicate their understandings through movements and dance-rap, such as hip-hop and Reggaeton. These diverse, non-traditional forms hold promise as a deeper form of expression that resonates with youth within their popular community (Hill & Petchauer,

2013; Toscano, Ladda, & Bednarz, 2014). Further, Paris and Alim (2014) argue that multicultural and culturally relevant pedagogies are often:

> enacted by teachers and researchers in static ways that focus solely on the important ways racial and ethnic difference was enacted in the past without attending to the dynamic enactments of our equally important present or future. As youth continue to inhabit a world where cultural and linguistic recombinations flow with purpose, we need pedagogies that speak to this new reality – as Pennycook (2007) puts it, pedagogies that "go with the flow." (pp. 91–92)

Knowledge foundations for lifelong learning

Lifelong learning is inherent in discourse surrounding the global knowledge economy. Schools begin the preparation of students to use, attain, and apply skills to embrace rapidly changing technology (Spring, 2008) and to possess the capabilities to convert educational opportunities to their benefit (Scherrer, 2014). Knowledge is certainly one of the primary prerequisites and products of educational opportunity. Students first must be prepared to learn and must possess good health, skillfulness, and motivation to apply knowledge to their benefit (Scherrer, 2014). Although this message resonates within a neoliberal economic agenda of human capital enhancement (Bailey, Hillman, Arent, & Petitpas, 2012), there are other more substantive goals that are achieved through knowledge development.

The European Commission's statement in the Horizon 2020 guidelines (European Union, 2011) defines lifelong learning as "all purposeful learning activity, undertaken on an ongoing basis with the aim of improving knowledge, skills and competence" (European Union, 2000, p. 3). Lifelong learning is considered to be essential for individuals to compete successfully within the dynamic global job market and technology. While the explicit focus on purposes of economic development in some ways represents a neoliberal agenda, it is critically important that students have opportunities to use knowledge as part of a healthy and productive life. When discussing the knowledge economy, advocates argue first for learning basic skills, including mathematics, interpersonal, problem-solving, and the openness and ability to learn new things (Spring, 2008).

The centrality of community schools (Farrell, 2008), sustaining and revitalizing pedagogies (McCarty & Lee, 2014; Paris, 2012) and lifelong learning are essential to the development of positive and productive aspects of a globalized society. Globalized curricula, while resisting the urges to create uniform pedagogical systems, provide opportunities to connect communities of culture and learning while sustaining and revitalizing ethnic and cultural foundations. It is naïve to think, however, that sustaining pedagogies can provide necessary resources without also enhancing the children's capabilities and knowledge to use those resources to create a better life (Scherrer, 2014). Knowledge of disciplinary principles, social concepts, and a deep understanding of relational knowing are critical in curricula of lifelong learning.

Sport pedagogy themes within globalized curriculum

While there are a number of viable sport pedagogy themes that can play a central role in positive, revitalizing globalized curriculum (e.g., Binder, 2001), I will discuss three holding promise for multinational, multisite collaborations such as those crafted within the European Union's Horizon 2020 funding initiative. Although external funders often have a neoliberalistic agenda, there are opportunities for reflective scholars and practitioners to transform these guidelines into

117

cross-cultural, student-centered approaches that can provide relevant, appropriate programs for children and youth. For the remainder of this chapter, I will develop research scenarios for three themes, fair play, ethnically sustaining and revitalizing sport pedagogies, and knowledge-based curricula for healthful living. Each is founded in an extensive literature complete with theoretical frameworks, extensive bodies of research, and compelling human and political issues and concerns. With careful attention to individual goals and input from community-based groups, these initiatives can be shaped and molded to provide a positive and uplifting starting point for curriculum development. While it is important to avoid the seduction of neoliberal tactics, opportunities abound for scholars to design and scale flexible, reflexive programs to focus the curriculum toward positive, democratic aims. Although we have learned a great deal from single-class, site-specific research, we cannot disregard opportunities to identify central variables influential across many PE settings. These variables can be identified and shaped within local social settings to provide individual and unique opportunities specific to students' needs and interests. It is very likely that these common structuring programmatic concepts exist and can lead to positive PE opportunities for students and teachers.

Funding to examine variables in multisite environments is available to PE scholars and researchers with the resulting programs enacted to benefit teachers and students. I describe these dynamic programs as 'curricula of possibility.' By this I mean flexibly constructed curricula with the individual student and teacher at the center of the planning process. Options, suggestions, and alternatives embedded in curricular materials provide opportunities for teachers and students working at the local level to own the curriculum by shaping it to provide relevance and meaning. In this section, I will briefly sketch out specific aims, rationale, and a research design, all in broad strokes, for each of these globalized PE curricular themes.

Fair Play

Beginning in the mid 1990s Gibbons, Ebbeck, and Weiss (1995; Binder & the Commission for Fair Play, 1990) proposed fair play curricula for sport pedagogy founded on the principles of equity and sportsmanship. The Fair Play curriculum was developed from a conceptual framework of moral development education, emphasizing concepts of moral judgment, reason, intention, and prosocial behavior for children and adolescents. Units and lessons are based on a progression of moral dilemmas, dialogue among peers and leaders, and tasks and experiences that create opportunities for moral balance. These task sequences and events lead students and teachers to develop a greater understanding and deeper appreciation for fair play, respect for others, and the value of equal opportunities. While numerous efforts at sportsmanship curricula exist, the program developed by Gibbons, Weiss, and their colleagues (Gibbons & Ebbeck, 1997; Gibbons et al., 1995; Romance, Weiss, & Bockoven, 1986; Vidoni & Ward, 2009) provides a thoughtful, scalable opportunity that can benefit both students and their teachers. When developed as the centerpiece in a proposal for external funding the specific aim might read:

> To design, implement and evaluate an elementary fair play curriculum in sport pedagogy to increase children's knowledge, reflective abilities, and intentions to play fairly in sporting competitions.

Certainly, parents, physical educators and youth sport coaches are supportive of fair play curricula. Enticing neoliberal agencies and review panels' support for PE programs with this focus requires linking Fair Play aims to world issues and events that resonate beyond the PE classroom. For example, football and sport hooliganism is a major cause for concern throughout the European Union, the United States, and many other world sporting venues. Incidents frequently occur surrounding sporting events worldwide, with one recent review identifying incidents in over 50 nations. The seriousness of these practices can be cataloged through incidents ranging from brawling, bullying, vandalism, intimidation, and death. These behaviors, however, are not limited to peripheral off-the-field spectators and events; players themselves are increasing engaging in purposefully violent behaviors in which the intent is to injure the opponent in retaliation or to gain a tactical advantage. Opportunities to address these behaviors as part of a Fair Play curriculum through instruction in moral judgment, reasoning, and respect, positive dialogue with peers, socially and morally acceptable behaviors during sporting contests, sportsmanship training, and identification and application of alternative behaviors hold promise for assisting youngsters to reflect on their personal and team behaviors in sporting environments. Fair Play curricula, while explicitly addressing these concerns, retain flexibility to permit teachers to adapt and adjust the concept of fair play to local and community issues.

Qualitative research designs have provided critically important information at the micro classroom or school level. I have conducted a fair amount of research using these designs and understand their benefits (e.g., Ennis, 2008). Yet, used alone, they are less likely in the United States or the European Union to receive levels of external funding necessary to scale PE programs to a range of school environments necessary to understand a curriculum's potential to be a Curriculum of Possibility. Scaling requires curricula to be examined in multiple settings, taking into account both unique, context-specific factors and those common to multiple settings. This is necessary to identify factors that are unique to a particular school but still likely to exist at some level at many other schools. By broadening the school, classroom, teacher, and student populations, we gain a more complex understanding of how specific pedagogical elements impact students' understandings of fair play concepts within the learning process.

In designing scalable research, in this case, to examine the opportunities and impact afforded by Fair Play curriculum, it is important to provide funders with information to compare the new program with existing curricula. A mixed method design permitting both individual school and student-level analyses as well as a broader understanding of student experiences can provide the right combination to enhance our cross-school understanding while addressing funders' need for accountability. Development and testing (pre/post controlled trial) can focus on the same curricular and instructional variables (e.g., moral judgment, reasoning, and respect, positive dialogue with peers, socially and morally acceptable behaviors during sporting contests, sportsmanship training, and identification and application of alternative behaviors) across sites to identify those with cultural relevance and sustainability. Data collection might include pre/post assessments of moral development in authentic situations; qualitative observations of lessons and practices; interviews and focus groups with children, physical educators, and coaches; scenario analysis and the use of virtual reality experiential cases to assist students and players to become emotionally involved in fair play settings. While small unfunded research teams might examine a few of these variables within local contexts, external funding provides opportunities for in-depth exploration of curricular options and analyses of both the unique-to-the-setting and more comprehensive factors integral to meaningful programming.

Culturally sustaining and revitalizing pedagogies

Migrations of peoples have occurred throughout history in the countries around the world and continue today as families move to create a safe and economically secure life. Yet, with few exceptions, the dominant politics of education and educators continue to sustain a white, male privileged perspective on content and process reflected in national curricula. This is true in sport pedagogy as represented in traditional, multi-activity programming. While skilled boys' interest in football appears to cross many political, cultural, and ethnic boundaries, this sports-oriented perspective may not have the same meaning and value to girls and unskilled boys (see Fitzgerald & Enright, Chapter 21). Likewise, other traditional Eurocentric sports may not resonate with boys or girls from countries outside the United States, the Commonwealth of Nations, or the European Union.

Sport pedagogy curricula with potential to sustain and revitalize ethnic and cultural minority students can strengthen and enhance student identities, self-confidence, and feelings of security. Importantly, they can assist students representing majority populations to enhance and deepen their value for diverse cultural groups and practices. Rovegno and Gregg (2007) constructed and tested an interdisciplinary unit for elementary PE to provide a more authentic picture of Native American cultures (Hawaiian and Native American Indian Tribal). Instead of a traditional dance unit that privileges White dance forms, Rovegno and Gregg's unit emphasized folk dance to emphasize diverse dances of native and ethnic Americans. Toscano and her colleagues (2014) also used a variety of dance forms from popular culture as the basis for dance curriculum. These dance forms assist students to follow the music while developing the rhythm of the dances. Their unit combined aerobic dance and fitness principles with contemporary dance patterns assisting students to develop competence in three dance activities: Zumba, Squaring the Rap, and Hip-Hop Hoedown. Zumba emphasizes aerobic dance steps with Latin American dance movements and music, Squaring the Rap combines basic square dance steps with rap music, while Hip-Hop Hoedown combines square dance with Hip-hop music. A proposal for external funding for this project may have as its specific aim:

> To design and test a culturally sustaining and revitalizing middle grades dance curriculum that features migrant students' heritage and contemporary dance to assist cultural and ethnic minority and majority students to engage in enjoyable physical activity while increasing their understanding and value for diverse cultures.

Migrant students are asked to assimilate into contemporary school sport pedagogy programs with typically little opportunity to share their culture and traditions with majority students. Likewise, majority students rarely have opportunities to learn dances and participate in ethnic and cultural traditions embraced by immigrant students in their classes. Culturally sustaining and revitalizing pedagogy acknowledges the pluralistic and evolving nature of youth identity and cultural practices and embraces youths' cultural and ethnic heritage. By foregrounding ethnicity within an enjoyable dance context, migrants and majority students interact around dance within a physical activity context that foregrounds these cultures.

Investigators from different countries working as research teams can design, scale, and test community-focused dance curricula that feature dances from both majority and minority/migrant cultures within the community. While the specifics of dance selection, and cultural influences will be unique to each community, students learn to reflect on differences in dance forms as they are encouraged to embrace difference. Students learn the dance steps, music, and rhythmic patterns valued by ethnic groups within their geographic region and discuss the meaning and place of dance in these cultures. Factors and variables examined within this curricular research might include cultural awareness, openness to difference, sensitivity and respect, as well as ability to work cooperatively. In addition to class observations and teacher and student interviews across schools and countries, social protocols such as sociograms can be used to identify changes in student friendship groups and willingness to partner with others from different cultural and ethnic backgrounds.

Again, the importance of 'scale' within the research both requires and attracts external funding to the project and provides opportunities to explore options across different cultures and communities. Intentionally building research designs with flexibility and site specificity permitting researchers to examine factors unique to their own communities within a comprehensive research structure retains individual site uniqueness while placing these differences within a larger national or international context.

Knowledge as a foundation for lifelong learning

The economic and social impact of health concerns associated with physical activity are a dominant force in many societies. This obsession is particularly evident in the United States where data from numerous epidemiological and medical studies have focused a national spotlight on health. While fully acknowledging the underlying (neoliberal) factors giving impetus to these initiatives, researchers have found opportunities to examine positive factors associated with health and well-being as a theme of PE curricula. Thorburn (Chapter 6) describes an asset- or strength-based approach to fitness and physical activity curricula that provides a nurturing environment for students to learn about physical activity and nutritional factors that can benefit their health. This can be done effectively without glorified, false claims for exercise or accusations associated with weight or obesity (McCullick, 2014), and with a sincere interest in assisting children and youth to reflect on the value of different healthy practices based on a range of informational sources. Students can construct their understanding while they examine truth claims associated with the effects of exercise on their bodies (Ferkel, Judge, Stodden, & Griffin, 2014).

Sometimes described as health-related science PE initiatives, scholars are proposing physically active curricula focused on concepts and principles with a sound scientific basis (e.g., Finn & McInnis, 2014). These proposals are winning external funding to examine the impact of health-related science-based curricula on students' physical activity interest and enjoyment. In the United States, where traditional PE is at great risk, these health and physical activity-oriented programs are seen as opportunities to increase resources and literally 'save' PE and PETE programs pushed aside in the rush toward high-stakes testing (McCullick, 2014). They are redirecting parents' and administrators' interest back to PE as an opportunity to enhance student health and reinforce science concepts, permitting PE to become a partner in the holistic mission of schools.

When PE is seen as 'essential' to schools, physical educators gain status and students place greater value on the content. Additionally, instructional time and other resources, such as staffing, may increase while learning-specific facilities and equipment become more available, making it possible to provide a positive environment for student learning. PE curricula are increasingly focusing on best practices in the promotion of physical activity and healthy nutrition (see Cale, Chapter 27). Health is central to improving and continuing prosperity in all countries and drives resource allocations for medical, educational, and public health professions.

Although sport pedagogy curricula currently are turning to examine physical activity/ health and well-being-oriented approaches (Thorburn & Horrell, 2014), a few curricula afford a science-enriched knowledge-based perspective on physical activity and nutrition. The *Science, PE, and Me!* and the *Science of Healthful Living* curricula provide a coordinated curriculum for children ages 8–14 (Sun, Chen, Zhu, & Ennis, 2012). The US National Institutes of Health has embraced this concept and provided $3 million to design, evaluate, and disseminate science-enriched approaches to PE. The lessons are designed using a constructivist learning cycle strategy entitled the 5Es (Engagement, Experiment, Explanation, Elaboration, and

Evaluation) to assist students to use a reflective, scientific inquiry process to examine the effects of exercise and nutrition on their bodies. Students (8–11 years old) examine fitness components in three constructivist-oriented physically active units, *Dr. Love's Healthy Heart*, *Mickey's Mighty Muscles*, and *Flex Coolbody's Fitness Club*, while 11–14 year old students examine exercise and motivation principles (e.g., overload, progression, specificity, frequency, intensity, duration, caloric balance, stress management, goal setting) in two physically active units, the *Cardio Fitness Club* and *Healthy Lifestyles*.

This external funding has been used in a range of productive ways. For example, master teachers were hired to develop curricula and to provide professional development to teachers implementing the curriculum. Funding facilitated a large-scale evaluation of the curriculum using a pre-post test randomized controlled design in over 60 elementary and middle schools. Students in the experimental schools in all grades (3–8; ages 8–14) demonstrated statistically significant knowledge gains when compared to students participating in a traditional PE program in the control group schools (Sun et al., 2012). Student knowledge gains were traced to the 5Es learning cycle strategy lesson format and the practice of student reflection on health-related science (fitness) knowledge using student science journaling. Students use the journals in each lesson to record their personal data in the form of heart rate, ratings of perceived exertion, exercise repetitions and sets, and steps. They reflect on the meaning of their findings for their own health and well-being, and transfer knowledge necessary for solving physical activity-related challenges in their lives. A specific aim of research to examine this curriculum might be:

> To design and field test science-enriched PE curricula to increase students' knowledge and interest in health-related science, physical activity, and the role of a healthy diet in their health and well-being.

Research has provided compelling evidence to support the value of healthy behaviors, such as regular physical activity and healthy eating choices. This life- and health-science research provides critical evidence necessary to understand students' healthy choices. Young adolescents are at a critical age when they question and test a range of personal and social behaviors, some of which place them at great risk for illness or injury. Adolescence also is a period when teachers have an opportunity to discuss health-related science concepts and teach the scientific inquiry process, guiding young teens toward the selection of personally relevant, research-supported healthy behaviors.

A proposal for external funding to scale this curriculum investigating its influence on students, teachers, and the community might be based on a pre/post-test controlled, randomized modeling design in which the experimental group participates in the curriculum while the comparison schools participate in traditional PE. Variables include science knowledge, interest in science and science careers, physical activity, reflection and application of concepts to life decisions, and motivation to participate in physical activity outside of school. By providing flexibility in curriculum implementation, content options and alternate health-focused scenarios, parents, teachers, and students can work collaboratively to shape a curriculum addressing issues and events within their community. This 'curriculum of possibility' provides multiple outlets for implementation at the local level while conveying science-based information to counter media, consumer, and crisis discourses.

Each of these three proposals presents opportunities for funding within curricular globalization initiatives. Research teams representing different universities and countries can compete successfully for external funding by proposing broadly based research initiatives that resonate with the contemporary themes and address key social and cultural issues.

Future directions

Anderson-Levitt (2008) argues that when viewed along many dimensions, curricula are global and becoming more uniform as the trends that began in the 1950s of Western-style schooling have spread to Southern Zone developing countries. While many schools will advocate for reforms in the twenty-first century, the nature, complexity, and systemic nature of reform initiatives will be quite diverse across nations and world regions. It will remain true from a global sense that "whatever educators borrow they adapt, wittingly or not, to national culture and local ways of doing school" (Anderson-Levitt, 2008, p. 364). Most loosely coupled educational systems whether 'controlled' by a Ministry of Education or a small township, cannot prevent teacher-initiated curricular modification and differentiation. Thus, in the future, the actual risks of a uniform, globalizing curricular effect are really quite remote. Microanalyses of curricula at the classroom level continue to demonstrate significant diversity even among nations whose students receive the highest scores on the Trends in International Mathematics and Science Study (TIMSS) and the Programme for International Student Assessment (PISA).

When globalization is viewed *outside* the neoliberal perspective, it can encourage more idealistic and somewhat more positive experiences. Stromquist and Monkman (2014) point out that although the economical and technological phenomena will continue to dominate at the national level, communities are still able to focus on specific educational and cultural goals. They can address national and global initiatives while still maintaining and sustaining unique cultural and ethnic perspectives. Education for All (UNESCO, 2000) and the United Nations Millennium Development Goals (United Nations, 2015) emphasize the dynamic nature of globalization and its wide range of opportunities and consequences. In developing countries, globalization can be transformative, providing opportunities to construct and reconstruct local cultures as knowledge is created and recreated at multiple sites. This coupling, decoupling, and loose coupling of systems with local cultures and communities will permit communities to foreground a form of globalization that values heritage and local knowledge while bringing broad-ranging knowledge and insights into the local conversation.

Summary of key findings

- Globalization is a multidimensional construct that has been used to structure international initiatives in economics, politics, technology, population studies, and education.
- Globalization embraces both positive and negative forces from the local to the international, changing and changed by increasing awareness, economics, and the force of rapidly evolving public opinion (Rizvi & Lingard, 2010).
- Spring (2008) reports four educational globalization discourses that influence educational models around the world. These include discourses of a world culture, world systems, post-colonial, and culturalist approaches.
- Neoliberalism is a conservative ideology that seeks to spread policies that appear beneficial, yet when examined often constrain individual freedom and individuality.
- Neoliberalists advocate individual choice and minimal government regulation while simultaneously protecting accountability structures. In schools these tendencies are reflected in school choice, accountability testing, and efforts to superficially homogenize school curricula around 'effective' programming.
- Neoliberalism reflects the 'dark side' of schooling, limiting student and teacher opportunities to implement curricula that are meaningful and relevant to students at the local level.

- Globalization, though of concern for its homogenizing tendencies, can be useful as an initiative to provide opportunities for teachers and students to consider 'curricula of possibility.'
- Curricula of possibility are programs that provide flexibility of content and implementation to permit teachers and students to select topics and methods that match individual and community diversity within a relatively uniform curricular structure.
- Scaling curriculum provides opportunities to better understand the impact of a specific curriculum across diverse school sites, permitting a focus on diverse needs and interests as integral to curricular reach and impact.
- External funding is often essential in scaling research designs to embrace diverse communities and interests. Broad topics and flexible implementation protocols permit scholars to examine opportunities provided by curricula of possibility.
- In this chapter three scenarios for externally funded projects were considered: fair play, culturally sustaining and revitalizing pedagogies, and knowledge as a foundation for lifelong learning. Each provides opportunities to engage teachers and students in a reflective, thoughtful approach to PE.

Reflective questions for discussion

1. In what ways do you see the effects of globalization in your community? To what extent are curricula in PE and teacher education impacted by globalizing concepts?
2. Neoliberal perspectives are influential in many school policy, curricular, and accountability decisions. Describe those most influential in your school or community. Which of these do you see as positively and negatively affecting educational decisions?
3. Globalization suggests that concepts that are effective in one setting might hold benefits for other settings. What factors might negate this premise? How can programs be designed to 'scale' so they reflect both broadly based and uniquely local interests and knowledge?
4. Fair play, culturally sustaining and revitalizing pedagogies, and foundations for lifelong learning were proposed as scalable concepts providing benefits at national and community levels. To what extent do you agree and what concerns do you have for teachers, students, and the educational environments where these curricula are implemented? Are they curricula of possibility or simply another crafty neoliberal plan to impose conservative privatization goals on education?
5. What other themes might be conceptualized and scaled or globalized to become curricula of possibility in PE? Select a theme and identify a specific aim, rationale, and research design to attract external funding to explore your idea in multiple schools.

References

Anderson-Levitt, K. M. (2008). Globalization and curriculum. In F. M. Connelly with M. F. He & J. Phillion (Eds.), *The Sage handbook of curriculum and instruction* (pp. 349–368). Los Angeles: Sage.

Apple, M., Kenway, J., & Singh, M. (Eds.). (2005). *Globalizing education: Policies, pedagogies, & politics.* New York: Peter Lang.

Artiles, A. J., Kozleski, E. B., & Waitoller, F. R. (Eds.). (2011). *Inclusive education: Examining equity on five continents.* Cambridge, MA: Harvard Educational Press.

Bailey, R., Hillman, C., Arent, S., & Petitpas, A. (2012). Physical activity as an investment in personal and social change: The human capital model. *Journal of Physical Activity and Health, 9*(8), 1053–1055.

Binder, D. (2001). 'Olympism' revisited as context for global education: Implications for physical education. *Quest, 53*(1), 14–34.

Binder, D., & the Commission for Fair Play. (1990). *Fairplay for kids: A resource manual.* Ottawa, ON: Commission for Fair Play.

Chepator-Thompson, R. (2014). Public policy, physical education, and sport in English-speaking Africa. *Physical Education and Sport Pedagogy*, *19*(5), 512–521.

Coalition of Community Schools. (2016). *Vision, mission principles and strategies for the coalition for community schools through 2020*. Retrieved from www.communityschools.org/about/overview.aspx.

Ennis, C. D. (2008). Examining curricular coherence in an exemplary elementary school program. *Research Quarterly for Exercise and Sport*, *79*(1), 71–84.

Ennis, C. D. (2014). The role of students and content in teacher effectiveness. *Research Quarterly for Exercise and Sport*, *85*(1), 6–13.

European Union. (2000). *Lifelong learning*. Retrieved from http://ec.europa.eu/education/tools/llp_en.htm.

European Union. (2011). *Horizon 2020*. Retrieved from https://ec.europa.eu/programmes/horizon2020/en/what-horizon-2020.

Evans, J. (2014). Neoliberalism and the future of socio-educative physical education. *Physical Education and Sport Pedagogy*, *19*(5), 545–558.

Farrell, J. P. (2008). Community education in developing countries: The quiet revolution in schooling. In F. M. Connelly with M. F. He & J. Phillion (Eds.), *The Sage handbook of curriculum and instruction* (pp. 369–389). Los Angeles: Sage.

Ferkel, R. C., Judge, L. W., Stodden, D. F., & Griffin, K. (2014). Importance of health-related fitness knowledge to increasing physical activity and physical fitness. *The Physical Educator*, *71*(2), 218–233.

Finn, K. E., & McInnis, K. J. (2014). Teachers' and students' perceptions of the Active Science Curriculum: Incorporating physical activity in two middle school science classrooms. *The Physical Educator*, *71*(2), 234–253.

Gibbons, S. L., & Ebbeck, V. (1997). The effect of different teaching strategies on the moral development of physical education students. *Journal of Teaching in Physical Education*, *17*(1), 85–98.

Gibbons, S. L., Ebbeck, V., & Weiss, M. R. (1995). 'Fair Play for Kids': Effects on the moral development of children in physical education. *Research Quarterly for Exercise and Sport*, *66*(3), 247–255.

Hill, M. L., & Petchauer, E. (Eds.). (2013). *Schooling hip-hop: Expanding hip-hop based education across the curriculum*. New York: Teachers College Press.

Ladson-Billings, G. (1995). Toward a theory of culturally relevant pedagogy. *American Educational Research Journal*, *32*(3), 465–491.

Ladson-Billings, G. (2014). Culturally relevant pedagogy 2.0: a.k.a. the remix. *Harvard Educational Review*, *84*(1), 74–84.

Lee, K-C., & Cho, S-M. (2014). The Korean national curriculum for physical education: A shift from edge to central subject. *Physical Education and Sport Pedagogy*, *19*(5), 522–532.

Macdonald, D. (2011). Like a fish in water: Physical education policy and practice in the era of neoliberal globalization. *Quest*, *63*(1), 36–45.

Macdonald, D. (2014). Is global neo-liberalism shaping the future of physical education? *Physical Education and Sport Pedagogy*, *19*(5), 494–499.

McCarty, T. L., & Lee, T. S. (2014). Critical culturally sustaining/ Revitalizing pedagogy and indigenous education sovereignty. *Harvard Educational Review*, *84*(1), 101–124.

McCullick, B. A. (2014). From the cheap seats: One consideration of school-based PE's position in contemporary American schools. *Physical Education and Sport Pedagogy*, *19*(5), 533–544.

Paris, D. (2012). Culturally sustaining pedagogy: A needed change in stance, terminology, and practice. *Educational Researcher*, *41*(3), 93–97.

Paris, D., & Alim, A. S. (2014). What are we seeking to sustain through culturally sustaining pedagogy? A loving critique forward. *Harvard Educational Review*, *84*(1), 85–100.

Pennycook, A. (2007). *Global Englishes and transcultural flows*. New York: Routledge.

Rizvi, F., & Lingard, B. (2010). *Globalizing education policy*. London: Routledge.

Romance, T. J., Weiss, M. R., & Bockoven, J. (1986). A program to promote moral development through elementary physical education. *Journal of Teaching in Physical Education*, *5*(2), 126–136.

Rovegno, I., & Gregg, M. (2007). Using folk dance and geography to teach interdisciplinary, multicultural subject matter: A school-based study. *Physical Education and Sport Pedagogy*, *12*(3), 205–223.

Scherrer, J. (2014). The role of the intellectual in eliminating the effects of poverty: A response to Tierney. *Educational Researcher*, *43*(4), 201–207.

Sloan, K. (2008). The expanding educational services sector: Neoliberalism and the corporatization of curriculum at the local level in the US. *Journal of Curriculum Studies*, *40*(5), 555–578.

Spring, J. (2008). Research on globalization and education. *Review of Educational Research*, *78*(2), 330–363.

Stromquist, N. P. (2002). *Education in a globalized world: The connectivity of economic power, technology and knowledge.* Lanham, MD: Rowman & Littlefield.

Stromquist, N. P., & Monkman, K. (Eds.). (2014). *Globalization and education: Integration and contestations across cultures.* New York: Rowman & Littlefield Education.

Sun, H., Chen, A., Zhu, X., & Ennis, C. D. (2012). Learning science-based fitness knowledge in constructivist physical education. *Elementary School Journal, 113*(2), 215–229.

Thorburn, M., & Horrell, A. (2014). Grand designs! Analysing the conceptual tensions associated with new physical education and health and well-being curriculum. *Sport, Education and Society, 19*(5), 621-636.

Toscano, L., Ladda, S., & Bednarz, L. (2014). Moving to the beat: From Zumba to hip-hop hoedown. *Strategies, 27*(2), 31–36.

UNESCO. (2000). *Education for all.* Retrieved from www.unesco.org/new/en/education/themes/leading-the-international-agenda/education-for-all/.

United Nations. (2015). *United Nations millennium development goals.* Retrieved from www.un.org/millenniumgoals/ and www.un.org/ga/search/view_doc.asp?symbol=A/69/L.85&Lang=E.

United States Department of Education [USDE]. (2009). *American Recovery and Reinvestment Act of 2009 (ARRA),* Section 14005–6, Title XIV, (Public Law 111–5). Washington, DC. Retrieved from http://www2.ed.gov/programs/racetothetop/legislation.html.

Vidoni, C., & Ward, P. (2009). Effects of Fair Play instruction on student social skills during a middle school Sport Education unit. *Physical Education and Sport Pedagogy, 14*(3), 285–310.

PART III

Curriculum policy and reform

Introduction

Curriculum reform is many things to many people. It can be an opportunity to change or influence what skills, knowledge and understanding are at the fore of children's experiences in physical education, a chance to make a political statement about the status of particular learning, something that can be exploited for financial gain, a source of frustration, something that seems little more than rhetoric, or something with profound implications for teaching and learning. This part of the handbook connects with these and other views of curriculum reform. Most of the chapters in reflect that curriculum reform has been and needs to remain an important focus for research in physical education.

While curriculum reform may well be something that we are familiar with and that, at least to some extent, we appreciate the significance of, much about curriculum reform can appear frustratingly opaque. This set of chapters therefore seek to challenge established familiarity with curriculum reform and extend understanding of its significance for physical education as a field and profession. In various ways the chapters that follow all strive to give more transparency to a process that is accepted as complex and always value laden. It is a part of the handbook that, as a result, openly aims to prompt more questions to be asked of current and prospective future curriculum reform. As a group of authors we make no apologies for raising many questions and not providing simple or definitive answers. The issues that we raise are undeniably complex, always need to be contextualised in relation to unique political, policy, demographic, institutional and professional settings, and remain matters that are open to different standpoints. Each of us has our own personal standpoint on a range of issues associated with curriculum reform in physical education. Collectively, however, the chapters reflect that we adopt a socio-critical stance and as a consequence have pursued research that seeks to 'dig deeper' into curriculum matters in physical education.

How can we, for example, explain stability in significant aspects of school curricula amidst major curriculum reform initiatives? Why is it that policy developments originating beyond education continue to have an apparently defining influence upon physical education curriculum? Are contemporary policy developments aiding or inhibiting efforts to challenge long-standing inequities inherent in physical education curriculum? How can curriculum reform in physical education be effectively progressed and supported in increasingly complex policy contexts?

These are amongst the challenging questions that our chapters address. Insights from education policy sociology provide foundational understanding of complexities that characterise the contemporary policy landscapes and contexts within which curriculum reform is set, and the process of curriculum reform. The first chapter (9) in this part, *Policy and possibilities*, opens by problematising what we understand curriculum reform 'to be' – and, therefore, what it involves and extends to. I present conceptualisations that are intended to go some way towards providing a platform for theoretically and empirically extending curriculum research in physical education, and for fresh thinking about the professional and practical dimensions of curriculum reform. Rather than denying tensions inherent in curriculum reform, the chapter argues for these to be reframed as critical opportunities for 'policy action'. Jess and Gray's chapter (10) and Penney and Mitchell's chapter (11) both vividly illustrate that these opportunities are being pursued in various curriculum settings, by an increasingly diverse range of organisations and agencies. In Chapter 9 I specifically prompt teachers and teacher educators to engage more proactively with curriculum texts that openly offer the scope for various readings and responses. The tensions and gaps in curriculum texts and their positioning in and amidst other policy developments relating to education, but also sport, health and public services as a whole, are identified as critical spaces for action and influence in curriculum reform. They are spaces that several of the chapters in this part very clearly indicate are being exploited by an increasing number of agencies. Hence, Chapter 9 raises the issues of ownership of curriculum reform and professional responsibility for the curriculum futures that will materialise in schools.

Chapter 10, entitled *Curriculum reform and policy cohesion in physical education*, by Mike Jess and Shirley Gray, presents historical and contemporary analyses to illustrate the parallel influences that the 'internal dynamics' of physical education and external factors have on curriculum reform. A chronological account reveals the tensions that can be created amidst shifts in discourses internal to physical education and changes in the discourses shaping the political, economic and policy context. Jess and Gray's discussion prompts us to reflect on the flow of influences shaping curriculum reform in physical education from a long-term, rather than short-term and reactionary viewpoint. Their analysis leads them to suggest that "the profession's capacity to create robust but flexible curriculum structures to cope with, negotiate and influence the dynamic and crowded policy landscape" is likely to be critical in shaping physical education curriculum futures. The developments in Scotland that Jess and colleagues have been centrally involved in also vividly illustrate that work directed towards achieving greater coherency between various policies and sites of influence associated with developing physical education curriculum, is equally important in this endeavour.

In Chapter 11, *Reforming curricula from the outside-in*, Dawn Penney and Steve Mitchell arguably reveal the scope of the challenge involved in thinking about, let alone achieving, such coherency. Their chapter takes a close (and professionally 'hard') look at the extent to which 'external' forces stemming from multiple government arenas, non-government, charitable and commercial sources influence the development and enactment of curriculum reform in physical education. The research that they report paints a picture of many organisations filling a vacuum and openly re-populating the curriculum, policy and professional spaces of physical education. Penney and Mitchell describe contexts of curriculum reform and prospects for reform that clearly demand that physical education teachers, teacher educators and researchers all need to develop new ways of connecting with and influencing the flow of discourses and practices within and across complex policy communities and networks.

In Chapter 12, *Curriculum reform where it counts*, Kirsten Petrie offers us insight into the sorts of shifts in thinking and approaches to curriculum reform that can help in addressing this need. The chapter directs attention particularly to ways in which teachers can be effectively supported as drivers of curriculum reform that is directed towards enhancing equity and opportunity in physical education classrooms. Drawing on her own and international research, Petrie engages us with the creativity inherent in curriculum reform that is underpinned and driven by shared ownership, investment and characterised by ongoing, open negotiation between teachers and teacher educators as collaborators and co-constructors of reform.

All of the chapters to this point variously illustrate the importance of equity in curriculum reform in physical education and identify it as an ongoing agenda for curriculum reform and research. In Chapter 13, Shaun Wilkinson brings the spotlight firmly onto equity issues. *Equity and inequity amidst curriculum reform* critically explores the curriculum and pedagogical realities of 'reform' in physical education and education, over time and internationally. Extending theoretical perspectives introduced in other chapters, Wilkinson pursues ways in which the interplay between policy texts and policy contexts play out to directly and subtly advance or, alternatively, inhibit advances in equity in physical education curriculum. Wilkinson's chapter unequivocally makes a case for equity to be at the fore of thinking about curriculum reform and curriculum futures. My hope is that collectively, the chapters in this section will both inspire and enable physical education professionals internationally to ensure that ongoing inequities in physical education are meaningfully challenged in and by future curriculum reform.

Dawn Penney
Monash University, Australia

9

POLICY AND POSSIBILITIES

Dawn Penney, MONASH UNIVERSITY, AUSTRALIA

This chapter focuses on the complexity of curriculum reform in physical education (PE) and specifically directs attention to the 'possibilities' for curriculum reform that are inherent in contemporary policy developments and policy contexts. Key issues that underpin the chapter are the ownership of, and professional responsibility for, curriculum reform in PE. The stance I take is that professional responsibility for curriculum reform is tied to the challenge of advancing quality and equity in PE (UNESCO, 2015). This is a challenge that I argue is as relevant in any local setting as it is internationally, and that any analysis of curriculum reform should address. This and other chapters that follow present research evidence that illustrates that despite many curriculum reforms that would be regarded as 'landmarks' for state or national education systems, longstanding inequities remain engrained and expressed in the PE curriculum that is enacted and experienced in many schools. Understanding more about curriculum reform 'as policy' and as also fundamentally about teaching and learning in PE, is arguably a critical prerequisite to challenging this status quo.

Theoretically, the chapter is therefore grounded in education policy sociology. It draws on mainstream education research and specialist research in PE to present a series of conceptualisations that challenge how we think about curriculum reform in PE and that help to reveal the many ways in which curriculum reform is advanced, resisted and/or redirected. Advancing, resisting or influencing the direction of curriculum reform are all processes that I emphasise are inherently complex, associated with many sites, and that implicate many people in the pursuit of various interests in and for PE curriculum. The processes directly and indirectly involve people and organisations that we regard as legitimate players in curriculum reform in PE – and others whose influence we perhaps question. From the outset, then, curriculum reform is presented as always political and value laden; a process that both historical and contemporary studies show is characterised by contestation. It is, essentially, the negotiation of possibilities for future policy and practice, and always involves opportunities and constraints that impact what can appear in the text of official curriculum documents; what can happen in the name of PE in schools; and what we imagine as possible and desirable directions to pursue in curriculum development.

This chapter reflects that as a social, political and, ultimately, pedagogic process, curriculum reform includes but goes well beyond the production of new official curriculum texts. As I discuss further below, 'curriculum' and, hence, 'curriculum reform' is conceptualised as a process that spans and connects policy and pedagogy. In the chapter I try to reveal more about the opportunities and constraints pertaining to current and prospective future curriculum reform – conceived as encompassing official policy texts *and* extending to the lived experiences of PE curriculum. In doing so, I emphasise *agency* as a critical issue for all professionals in the field to address. From this perspective, teachers and teacher educators are key actors in increasingly complex policy communities and networks that shape, influence, enable and constrain curriculum reform in PE. I suggest that as PE professionals we need to see ourselves as active players in these communities and networks, and recognise that our actions play a part in enabling or inhibiting *particular* curriculum futures for PE and for children in PE (Kirk, 2010; Penney, 2013a; Penney & Chandler, 2000). I argue that whether we acknowledge it or not, on a daily basis we are implicated in either extending possibilities for curriculum reform or closing possibilities down. Those possibilities relate simultaneously to the future of the field and to what children experience as PE.

Below I provide a brief historical backdrop to the ways in which curriculum reform is explored in this chapter. This leads into a section that adds depth to the theoretical basis of my approach and explains some of the key conceptualisations that are important reference points for analysis of trends and issues emerging from research pertaining to curriculum reform and PE. My discussion of trends and issues deliberately features insights from mainstream education and from specialist PE research. It focuses on research that collectively establishes a socio-critical orientation to analysis of ongoing curriculum reform in PE and prospects for the future. The studies and approaches discussed illustrate inquiry that goes beyond '*what*' is happening in curriculum reform in PE to also engage with questions of '*how*' and '*why*' reform follows the paths it does, and that direct attention to the *curriculum consequences* of particular interests and discourses gaining prominence in education and physical education.

Issues that I identify as particularly significant in considering curriculum reform 'possibilities' amidst policy contexts that are dynamic and increasingly complex, are: the collective impact of seemingly unconnected or incoherent policy developments; the importance of the people and organisations influencing interpretations and enactment of curriculum; the fact that official curriculum texts are always an expression of compromise; and the relationship between curriculum, pedagogy and assessment. I also draw attention to research that highlights that 'context matters' greatly in terms of the possibilities for curriculum reform that will be (and can be) pursued in any individual school context. Theoretical and empirical insights from research are then used to address implications for future approaches to curriculum reform in PE and future directions for research. The chapter concludes with a summary of key findings and a series of questions that are designed as prompts for reflection and discussion of PE curriculum developments and futures.

Insights from history: politics, process and contexts

The limitations of length mean that it is neither feasible nor appropriate to attempt to engage with the full spectrum of research in PE that has, at various points in time, directly addressed or provided insight into matters of curriculum reform in PE. Rather, the chapter centres on education policy and the use of policy as a conceptual tool for analysis of curriculum reform. This reflects that there is now a sustained line of curriculum research in PE, particularly in the UK, other parts of Europe and Australasia, that has used policy developments as a catalyst for research while also seeking to extend the theorising of policy as it relates to curriculum reform. Here I introduce some of the insights about the 'policy-curriculum' relationship that have emerged from research within and beyond PE over approximately the past 25 years. This period has been particularly rich in relation to the development of education policy sociology and is also characterised as a period of unprecedented and ongoing changes in political, economic and education landscapes and agendas (see also Evans & Davies, 2015; Jess & Gray, Chapter 10: Penney & Mitchell, Chapter 11).

Research that has taken curriculum and/or other policy developments as its focus during this period has repeatedly revealed curriculum reform as an openly political process, with challenges, tensions and negotiations involved in reaching a point of 'settlement' (Luke, Woods & Weir, 2013) marked by publication of a new official curriculum text (see for example, Davies, Evans, Penney & Bass, 1997; Dinan, 2000; Ovens, 2010; Penney & Evans, 1999; Thorburn & Horrell, 2011). At the same time, this research has highlighted that such publications are far from the end of tensions and negotiations. Hence, I have previously emphasised the need to understand curriculum as always 'unfinished' (see for example, Penney, 2013a). An increasing number of studies in PE have demonstrated the significant role that various 'intermediary' sites, parallel policy developments (associated for example, with sport policy) and school contexts themselves play in shaping interpretations and enactment of official texts. Curtner-Smith's (1999) study still stands out for revealing the shortcomings of simplistic notions of 'implementation' and the potential for the ongoing negotiation of curriculum reform mandates and recommendations to result in 'no change' in pedagogical practice.

The concept of 'slippage' (Bowe & Ball with Gold, 1992; Penney & Evans, 1999) has been central to analyses seeking to explain such an outcome and also reveal the creation of multiple hybrid texts as an integral feature of curriculum reform processes. Research has also increasingly illustrated, however, the complex composition of the political and policy 'space' impacting curriculum reform in PE (see for example, Houlihan, 2000; Houlihan & Green, 2006; Thorburn & Horrell, 2011). To a great extent, the theoretical section that follows reflects that 'slippage' is now a seemingly inadequate analytic tool for curriculum studies that are located within education systems that have been transformed by neoliberal and market discourses, and that need to engage with the particularly complex policy dynamics that impact curriculum reform in PE. In Chapter 11 Penney and Mitchell discuss a body of research that highlights the need to critically examine who the dominant voices are in contemporary PE policy networks that are anything but linear.

Finally, I highlight three points from a historical perspective. First, the history of curriculum reform in PE repeatedly illustrates that specific contexts matter in the sense that they create conditions of possibility for particular reform agendas to be pursued. Below, I expand on the complex interplay between curriculum reform and curriculum contexts. Second, a historical perspective prompts exploration of how and why particular discourses and practice maintain their dominance in PE curriculum over time, amidst the rhetoric of 'reform'. Third (and a related point), I suggest that an important argument for renewed attention to be given to a historical perspective in curriculum reform studies in PE is that it has the capacity to reveal the *cumulative impact* of multiple policy developments over time. I suggest that we have limited insight into how, subtly and progressively, a catalogue of policy initiatives impact official curriculum developments and the ways in which official reforms are interpreted and enacted. Such inquiry is highly pertinent to pursue in political contexts that research shows are premised on increasingly distributed and opaque governance of education (Ball, 2007; see Penney & Mitchell, Chapter 11).

Theoretical insights

Contemporary education contexts are such that we need "a set of analytic concepts which are potent and malleable" (Ball, 2007, p. 1) to effectively engage with what is happening in relation to curriculum reform in PE, but also, how and why it is happening, and with what effects.

This commentary offers an introduction to some such concepts and certainly is not exhaustive. I discuss concepts and insights about curriculum reform generated from three areas of literature: curriculum theory within sociology of education; network theory as utilised and developed in recent work in education policy sociology; and complexity theory. These are presented as complementary rather than oppositional approaches to theorising contemporary curriculum reform in PE.

Curriculum policy

Preceding discussion has already illustrated that talking about curriculum reform is inherently problematic, as people have different understandings of what 'curriculum' encompasses. Connelly and Connelly (2013) offer a 'three-pronged' conceptualisation of curriculum policy that can counter the tendency for vagueness and, at the same time, extend and give clear foci for curriculum research. They distinguish between (i) "formal curriculum policy", centring on official, mandatory written curriculum texts; (ii) "implicit curriculum policy", referring to policy documents and resource materials arising from government and non-government sources, that influence either curriculum practices or the writing of formal curriculum policy (p. 58); and (iii) "prudential curriculum policy" that directs attention to the "prudence, practical wisdom and practical knowledge" (p. 59) that features in the adaptation of curriculum requirements and recommendations for specific local and institutional contexts. As curriculum researchers in health and PE have identified, this conceptualisation aligns with the Ball, Maguire, Braun, with Hoskins and Perryman's (2012) call for a shift in language from policy 'implementation' to 'enactment' (see Leahy, Burrows, McCuaig, Wright & Penney, 2016; Penney, 2013a). Ball et al.'s (2012) intention was to bring to the fore the "originality and creativity" in teachers' contextualisation and enactment of policy, albeit within limits arising from "the possibilities of discourse", such that teachers are simultaneously "policy subjects and actors" (Ball et al., 2012, p. 3). I advocate for this shift to talk of *enactment* of curriculum policy and for curriculum reform to be conceptualised as encompassing all three of Connelly and Connelly's (2013) dimensions of curriculum policy.

Sites of influence and sources of possibility

Reflecting the above stance, I also point to the utility of Bernstein's (1990, 2000) theoretical work. Again, my commentary is necessarily selective. Connelly and Connelly (2013) allude to the blurred boundaries between formal and implicit curriculum, highlighting that curriculum policy 'users' rarely distinguish between requirements and recommendations. Penney and Mitchell's chapter (11) looks further at how changes in the composition of policy communities and networks mean that we should also be posing questions about who is influential in producing materials that amount to "implicit curriculum policy" (Connelly & Connelly, 2013) and prospectively supersede official texts as the prime point of reference in enactment. In his theorising of pedagogic discourse, Bernstein (1990) identified "recontextualising fields" (specifically, the "official recontextualising field" and "pedagogic recontextualisation field") as playing a critical role in the creation, legitimation and transmission of discourse, through the selective appropriation and transformation of texts. This is a process of "re-positioning them [i.e. texts] in relation to other texts and practices, and modifying and re-focusing them through 'selection, simplification, condensation, and elaboration' (Bernstein, 1990, p. 192) of content" (Penney, Petrie & Fellows, 2015, p. 46). From their research in New Zealand, Penney et al. (2015) identified recontextualisation and, more particularly, the composition of the "official recontextualising field" and the "pedagogic recontextualising field" (Bernstein, 1990), and the relations between them, as critical issues in relation to changes in the influence of various policy actors and agencies in health and PE curriculum (see also Penney & Mitchell, Chapter 11).

If we consider curriculum reform as encompassing formal, implicit and prudential curriculum policy (Connelly & Connelly, 2013), I also suggest that matters of assessment and pedagogy are intertwined with curriculum policy and that they should be integral to our conceptualisation of curriculum reform. Bernstein's (1990) conceptualisation of curriculum, pedagogy and evaluation (incorporating assessment systems) as three inter-related "message systems" of schooling, then offers further insight for analyses of reform. For example, it directs our attention to the ways in which formal assessment requirements that accompany new curriculum frameworks, or assessment texts that take on the status of "implicit curriculum policy" (Connelly & Connelly, 2013) can have a defining influence in interpretations and enactment of new official curriculum texts. As I discuss below, this is particularly evident in examination PE contexts. Bernstein's conceptualisation points particularly to the *alignment* of curriculum, pedagogy and assessment as being fundamental to coherency in curriculum reform efforts (see Penney, Brooker, Hay & Gillespie, 2009). Again research focusing on examination PE has revealed the consequences of misalignment (see below and e.g. Thorburn, 2007). Relationships between curriculum, pedagogy and assessment are also identified as presenting opportunities to challenge the positioning of various discourses in PE curriculum 'reform'. Jess, Antencio and Thorburn's (2011) research grounded in complexity theory (see below) has particularly illustrated pedagogy (and processes to support pedagogical change) as vitally important in advancing curriculum reforms in Scotland that have sought to challenge long-established curriculum practices in PE.

Finally from Bernstein's (1990, 2000) work, curriculum structures and knowledge boundaries are issues that I have directed attention to previously in openly challenging the scope of thinking about curriculum futures in PE (Penney 2013b; Penney & Chandler, 2000). From Bernstein's (1990, 2000) work, challenging knowledge boundaries that are embedded in and sustained by curriculum policy (formal, implicit and prudential, see above) is central to what we might regard as "radical reform" (Kirk, 2010). Following Kirk (2010), I suggest that much 'reform' has acted to legitimate rather than challenge the dominance of established curriculum structures, practices and discourses – and their inherent inequities (see Wilkinson, Chapter 13). Conceptualising curriculum reform in terms of formal, implicit and prudential curriculum policy, and as an ongoing interplay between curriculum, assessment and pedagogy, can prospectively help in efforts to break that trend.

Network theory

In employing network theory, Ball (2007) makes the observation that the new policy networks and communities that now characterise education policy and, I contend, curriculum policy, need to also be understood as "discourse communities" that "bring into play new policy narratives" (p. 123) and give authority to new policy actors and the discourses that they speak (see also Ball & Junemann, 2012). I suggest that as a new mix of discourses "re-populate the field of [education] policy" (Ball, 2007, p. 123), they progressively change the discursive boundaries of thinking about curriculum and curriculum reform. In Chapter 11 Penney and Mitchell draw on research addressing the role and influence of 'external providers' in PE curriculum to further explore this proposition.

Also relevant in the conceptualisation of curriculum reform 'as a network activity' is the recognition that new policy communities do not simply replace existing structures and actors. Rather, they "both circumvent and incorporate, overlay or extend beyond" (Ball, 2007, p. 122) established policy communities associated with the development and delivery of PE curriculum. A network perspective thus necessarily also encompasses a historical perspective and prompts examination of how organisations and individuals that historically have been at the centre of curriculum reform are repositioned in and by changing policy networks.

Complexity theory

PE researchers in Scotland (Jess et al., 2011) and New Zealand (Ovens, 2010) have also illustrated that complexity theory offers another conceptual tool for analyses of current curriculum practice, but also is a framework that offers an alternative view of possible curriculum futures. As Jess et al. (2011) explain, the strength of complexity theory in relation to thinking about curriculum reform is the grounding of the theory in uncertainty and unpredictability, such that there is not an expectation that order and set, singular logic will characterise processes of policy development, interpretation and enactment. Instead, complexity theory offers a platform for an ecological orientation, "viewing curriculum as a complex, emergent and self-organising phenomenon" (Jess et al., 2011, p. 183). Jess et al. (2011) highlight that adopting a complexity perspective generates a distinct view of the sorts of policy and pedagogical relationships that are inherent in curriculum reform conceived as a process spanning education systems and extending to teaching and learning in PE. In many respects, the characteristics (including shared vision and collaboration within networks) that they associate with thinking about curriculum as "a complex connective system" as compared to a "behaviourist hierarchical system" align with Petrie's (Chapter 12) call for a shift in thinking about the positioning and role of teachers in curriculum reform. Jess et al. (2011) illustrate that a complexity perspective re-orientates our thinking about teachers as actors in curriculum and learning networks and systems that are complex and dynamic. It therefore also challenges our thinking about the nature and process of curriculum and pedagogical reform in PE. Based on their experiences in working centrally amidst major curriculum reform initiatives in Scotland, Jess et al. (2011) advocate for approaches to curriculum reform to be informed by complexity theory, but also acknowledge that their experience also shows the challenges that teachers and other curriculum stakeholders can have in engaging with a perspective that can prove "frustrating, vague, too complicated and, ultimately, uncomfortable to grasp and implement" (Jess et al., 2011, p. 194).

Current trends and issues

Each of the chapters in this part provides further commentary on trends and issues relating to curriculum reform that connects in various ways with the perspectives discussed above. Here I focus on points that particularly connect with the notion of 'possibility' in ongoing and prospective future curriculum reform.

The progressive and collective impact of policy developments

Education policy sociology particularly prompts the realisation that amidst neoliberalism, significant impact lies not in any single policy initiative but rather in the collective impact over time of a sustained 'package' or series of initiatives. In PE, research is beginning to reveal this sort of cumulative policy impact on curriculum. Studies featuring in Chapter 11 (Penney & Mitchell) show political and policy developments clearly changing the context within which curriculum policy is developed, interpreted and enacted. The chapters by Jess and Gray (10) and Wilkinson (13) also illustrate multiple policy interests and initiatives 'coming together' 'over' matters of PE curriculum – and powerfully shaping the discourses gaining prominence in official curriculum texts and informing patterns of curriculum provision and support. Below I identify that a key challenge for future research is to further examine the impact that is associated with changed conditions of and for curriculum reform in PE.

Who are the key policy actors in physical education curriculum?

In any national or local setting and indeed, internationally, there are people who stand out as influential figures in PE curriculum – and such influence is by no means new. Yet, I suggest that the people and organisations influencing interpretations and enactment of curriculum is an important 'current issue'. Ball's (2007) and Ball and Junemann's (2012) analyses bring to the fore the significance of the personal as well as structural dimension of policy networks. Their research highlights that individuals and inter-personal relations are increasingly important to pursue in seeking to reveal how and why particular discourses gain credibility and become a 'natural' part of curriculum reform discussions. "People move across and within" networks and some "who occupy multiple positions join things up" (Ball, 2007, p. 19) creating an accepted logic in relation to both curriculum problems and 'obvious' solutions. In PE there is a lack of contemporary empirical insights into who, specifically, is playing a key role in 'making connections' via involvement 'across' arenas of formal, implicit and prudential curriculum policy (see above), and what the 'curriculum consequences' are of changing patterns of policy influence. However, I suggest that the research evidence discussed by Penney and Mitchell (Chapter 11) supports the contention that this is an increasingly important issue to examine in relation to curriculum reform in PE. Further, Petrie's chapter (12) calls for shifts in thinking and practice to ensure that curriculum reform is conceived and approached as a process that accords central status to teachers.

Compromise and curriculum reform

As indicated above, curriculum research has repeatedly illustrated tensions and compromises featuring in curriculum reform initiatives in PE and being expressed openly in official texts (see for example, Ovens, 2010). The development of a new Australian Curriculum and, specifically, Australian Curriculum Health and PE (AC HPE), that has involved the production of a series of texts to reach the point of an endorsed official curriculum text, is a recent example of curriculum reform characterised by tensions and compromise that will continue to 'play out' amidst enactment across states and schools in Australia (see Macdonald, 2013; Penney, 2013a). Limitations of space preclude in-depth discussion of specific features of the AC HPE official texts and associated development process. The point I want to make, however, is that it is an example of formal curriculum policy that in many respects, *because* of the tensions and compromises expressed in the official text, openly gives rise to notably wide-ranging possibilities for readings of and responses to the text – spanning the spectrum from 'status quo' to 'radical reform' (Kirk, 2010). It is a text that I have suggested has openly been designed with the anticipation that this range of readings and responses will materialise (Penney, 2013a). In these circumstances and arguably any contemporary context of curriculum reform, critical issues then are: what readings gain the status of *preferred* readings?, how?, why?, and what curriculum possibilities are therefore legitimated or effectively denied amidst the progressive uptake of 'reform'?

Reform dynamics: curriculum, pedagogy and assessment

At least part of the answer (or one answer) to the questions just posed lies in the relationship between curriculum, pedagogy and assessment. Research relating to curriculum developments in examination PE evidences ways in which requirements relating to assessment influence what teachers will perceive as approaches that are legitimate, desirable, or 'too risky' in enacting new curriculum (see, for example, Brown & Penney, 2016; Thorburn, 2007). Examination PE is also a context where assessment materials produced as 'guidance' clearly take on the status of implicit curriculum policy and, as such, influence decisions about curriculum content and pedagogy (Brown & Penney, 2016). While this research has shown curriculum and pedagogical possibilities being constrained by the dynamic between assessment, curriculum and assessment, I suggest that at the same time it highlights the potential for the reverse effect – that is, for progressive approaches towards assessment and pedagogy to notably extend the possibilities arising in and from curriculum reform. Research on the development of innovative pedagogical and/or instructional models (such as Sport Education) supports this contention. Jess et al.'s (2011) work in Scotland and Petrie and colleagues' work with teachers in New Zealand (see Chapter 12) both provide further evidence that focusing on pedagogy can be a productive route to curriculum transformation.

Context matters

'Context' – global, national and local – is undeniably important in curriculum reform. As indicated above, research within and beyond PE indicates that the consequences of changes in the political, economic and policy contexts for PE curriculum reform are potentially profound (see Penney & Mitchell, Chapter 11). Returning to Ball et al.'s (2012) talk of enactment, these changes are about new discursive limits being placed on engagement in and with curriculum reform. While I certainly do not deny the importance of such changes, I also highlight that the individual particularities of any school context and any PE classroom matter greatly. They are vital to address in seeking to understand the *different* possibilities for reform that are recognised by teachers in any given school, and that can be pursued in practice.

Anyone undertaking or engaging in case study research, or working with a group of teachers from different schools, will readily relate to this emphasis that characteristics of individual school contexts are very significant in shaping curriculum reform – and, furthermore, that teachers are uniquely placed to exploit the curriculum and pedagogic possibilities that their particular school context presents. Indeed, many official texts, including the AC HPE referred to above, are consciously designed to enable these possibilities to come to the fore in teachers' interpretation and enactment. Ball et al. (2012) usefully identify that analyses of contexts need to explore professional culture, as well as matters of history, locale and material aspects of resourcing, and the interplay between 'internal' dimensions of context and the external (state, national, global) policy context. Professional culture and professional responsibility for curriculum reform in PE are issues that I see as critical for all physical educationalists to reflect on, particularly in contexts that are openly being reshaped by neoliberal and market discourses (see, e.g., Evans & Davies, 2015; Macdonald, 2011, 2015; Penney & Mitchell, Chapter 11).

Implications for practice: teachers as policy actors and knowledge brokers

Jess et al.'s (2011) research illustrates that re-conceptualising curriculum reform prospectively impacts all stakeholders in PE curriculum. It is tempting to add 'and every stage of the curriculum reform process'. However, such a comment sends us back to linear and hierarchical thinking that I want to avoid further legitimating. Hence, one of the notable implications of the theoretical and empirical research insights presented in this chapter relates to how we talk about and, therefore, think about, curriculum reform. For me the appeal of network theory is that we can see ourselves as a part of curriculum reform communities and networks and, furthermore, then consider the position/s, roles and influence that we have and that we also aspire to. In then talking of teachers as key policy actors (Penney, 2013a) and encouraging physical educators in Australia to think about personal policy action, I was identifying that in Australia over the coming months and years, it is teachers and teacher educators who will determine whether progressive ideals that are embedded in the AC HPE text, ultimately find expression in the curriculum enacted as the AC HPE in schools. The official text is one that I maintain offers clear possibilities for, but very little assurance that the 'reform' will be a landmark for, advances in quality and equity in PE curriculum.

The research insights presented in this chapter reaffirm that global policy contexts impacting education and PE, national and state policy contexts, and individual school contexts are *all* influential and important for future practice and research to engage with. Yet, research also repeatedly reaffirms that teachers are always critical mediators and negotiators of policy texts and policy contexts (albeit, texts and/or contexts that are seen as constraining). As Macdonald (2015, p. 37) has discussed, talk of 'brokering' can be seen to imply an essentially "technical rather than intellectual or creative" set of tasks. Hence, she has questioned whether

> to talk of teacher-as-knowledge broker is to buy into discourses that position teachers as technicians, functionaries of state-sponsored surveillance systems of teacher and student performance standards, and abandon aspirations such as teachers as intellectual or creative workers. (p. 37)

As Macdonald (2015) also recognises, however, if we re-frame the notion of brokering to foreground a critical perspective and critical judgement calls about whether and how any resources and services feature in PE curriculum, it is clearly an intellectual and important role, not a merely technical one. I see the adoption of such a perspective as vitally important for the curriculum future(s) of PE.

Future directions for research

Evans and Davies (2015) recently observed that contemporary developments in education policy and governance are "not only affecting the forms, structures and modalities of educational provision and organisation" (p. 5), but are also 'outrunning' research agendas in PE. This chapter reflects the view that we need to respond by considering not only the empirical focus of those agendas, but also their theoretical and methodological underpinnings. It has endeavoured to foreground new ways of theorising curriculum reform as a social and political process that has structural and discursive dimensions, and present conceptualisations that convey curriculum reform as being as much a pedagogical issue as a policy issue. Looking beyond the immediate field of PE is undoubtedly important to locate conceptual tools that enable us to explore the relationship between the structures we now associate with PE curriculum reform and the discourses that are dominant in the thinking and practice of reform – or, alternatively, are marginalised amidst it.

Hence, my hope is that the theoretical discussion in this chapter will prompt further theoretical work in the field. I echo Ball and Junemann (2012) in identifying that the challenge "is to theorise continuity and change together" (p. 134) and, in doing so, also embrace the notion that "[p]olicy creates context; but context precedes policy" (Ball et al., 2012, p. 18). Research focusing on curriculum reform in PE arguably needs to become more expansive and sophisticated in scope, depth and methodological approach if it is to 'catch up with' and 'keep pace with' the developments that Evans and Davies (2015) describe. Pursuing the complex (and changing) dynamics between official, implicit and enacted curriculum policy (Connelly & Connelly, 2013) is certainly not an easy task. Ball and Junemann (2012, p. 15) have articulated some of the inherent challenges of network research, highlighting for example, that network relations are typically "opaque" and networks themselves are dynamic, often featuring "fleeting" and "fragile" components. There are no simple methodological answers to the challenges, for example, of how to access, meaningfully engage with, and track the influence and impact that exchanges occurring amidst changing relations have on curriculum matters in PE. Engaging with such issues analytically and methodologically, is, however, a necessary research endeavour if we are to understand more about curriculum reform possibilities and, furthermore, actively extend those possibilities.

Summary of key findings

- Curriculum reform always needs to be understood as a complex political and social process that is characterised by compromise and negotiation.
- Connelly and Connelly's (2013) three dimensions of curriculum policy – formal, implicit, and prudential – provide a framework for exploring the dynamic between official curriculum texts, guidance materials and resources, and the interpretation, adoption and application of these as curriculum in schools.
- Network theory and complexity theory provide conceptual insights that can extend the depth and sophistication of curriculum reform research in PE to align with contemporary curriculum policy contexts.
- The relationships between curriculum, pedagogy and assessment are significant in relation to interpretations and enactment of new official curriculum, and the potential to challenge the dominance of particular discourses in curriculum reform.
- The tensions inherent in official curriculum texts represent avenues for 'alternative' readings and responses to be developed. By design official curriculum texts will typically enable and legitimate a range of readings and responses.
- The cumulative impact of multiple policy developments on curriculum reform texts and contexts is emerging as increasingly significant to engage with.
- Conceptualising teachers and teacher educators as policy actors and critical knowledge brokers positions them as having a key professional responsibility for curriculum futures in PE.

Reflective questions for discussion

Readers are encouraged to relate the issues discussed in this chapter to their specific context and experiences of curriculum reform.

1. Who do you see as the legitimate players in curriculum reform in PE?
2. Whose influence in contemporary curriculum reform do you question or oppose – and why?
3. The notion of "implicit curriculum policy" (Connelly and Connelly) relates to guidance materials and resources that accompany new official curriculum developments. Who do

you recognise as producing influential materials and resources? What particular reading/s of official curriculum texts do they promote?

4. Can you recognise ways in which assessment policies or practices influence approaches to curriculum reform?
5. What aspects of your professional context do you associate with constraining, and enabling, curriculum reform?
6. What position/s do you hold or aspire to in relation to the policy networks and communities associated with curriculum reform in PE?

References

Ball, S. J. (2007). *Education plc. Understanding private sector participation in public sector education.* Abingdon, Oxon: Routledge.

Ball, S. J., & Junemann, C. (2012). *Networks, new governance and education.* Bristol: The Policy Press.

Ball, S. J., Maguire, M., Braun, A., with Hoskins, K., & Perryman, J. (2012). *How schools do policy. Policy enactment in secondary schools.* Abingdon, Oxon: Routledge.

Bernstein, B. (1990). *The structuring of pedagogic discourse. Volume IV: Class, codes and control.* London: Routledge.

Bernstein, B. (2000). *Pedagogy, symbolic control and identity. Theory, research, critique* (Revised edn). Oxford: Rowman & Littlefield.

Bowe, R., & Ball, S. J., with Gold, A. (Eds.). (1992). *Reforming education and changing schools. Case studies in policy sociology.* London: Routledge.

Brown, T., & Penney, D. (2016). Interpretation and enactment of Senior Secondary Physical Education: Pedagogic realities and the expression of Arnoldian dimensions of movement. *Physical Education and Sport Pedagogy.*

Connelly, F. M., & Connelly, G. C. (2013). Curriculum policy guidelines. Context, structure and functions. In A. Luke, A. Woods & K. Weir (Eds.), *Curriculum syllabus design and equity: A primer and model* (pp. 54–73). New York: Routledge.

Curtner-Smith, M. D. (1999). The more things change the more they stay the same: Factors influencing teachers' interpretations and delivery of national curriculum physical education. *Sport, Education and Society, 4*(1), 75–97.

Davies, B., Evans, J., Penney, D. & Bass, D. (1997). Physical education and nationalism in Wales. *The Curriculum Journal, 8*(2), 249–270.

Dinan, M. (2000). Public concerns and private interests in the construction of a health and physical education policy document in Queensland: A preliminary analysis. *Curriculum Perspectives, 20*(1), 1–7.

Evans, J., & Davies, B. (2015). Physical education, privatisation and social justice. *Sport, Education and Society, 20*(1), 1–10.

Houlihan, B. (2000). Sporting excellence, schools and sports development: The politics of crowed policy spaces. *European Physical Education Review, 6*(2), 171–193.

Houlihan, B., & Green, M. (2006). The changing status of school sport and physical education: Explaining policy change. *Sport, Education and Society, 11*(1), 73–92.

Jess, M., Atencio, M. & Thorburn, M. (2011). Complexity theory: Supporting curriculum and pedagogy developments in Scottish physical education. *Sport, Education and Society, 16*(2), 179–199.

Kirk, D. (2010). *Physical education futures.* London: Routledge.

Leahy, D., Burrows, L., McCuaig, L., Wright, J. & Penney, D. (2016). *School health education in changing times. Curriculum, pedagogies and partnerships.* London: Routledge.

Luke, A., Woods, A. & Weir, K. (2013). Curriculum design, equity and the technical form of the curriculum. In A. Luke, A. Woods & K. Weir (Eds.), *Curriculum, syllabus design and equity. A primer and model* (pp. 6–39). New York: Routledge.

Macdonald, D. (2011). Like a fish in water: Physical education policy and practice in the era of neoliberal globalization. *Quest, 63*(1), 36–45.

Macdonald, D. (2013). The new Australian Health and Physical Education Curriculum: A case of/for gradualism in curriculum reform? *Asia Pacific Journal of Health, Sport and Physical Education, 4*(2), 95–108.

Macdonald, D. (2015). Teacher-as-knowledge-broker in a futures-oriented health and physical education. *Sport, Education and Society, 20*(1), 27–41.

Ovens, A. (2010). The New Zealand Curriculum: Emergent insights and complex renderings. *Asia-Pacific Journal of Health, Sport and Physical Education, 1*(1), 27–32.

Penney, D. (2013a). From policy to pedagogy: Prudence and precariousness: Actors and artifacts. *Asia-Pacific Journal of Health, Sport and Physical Education, 4*(2), 189–197.

Penney, D. (2013b). Points of tension and possibility: Boundaries in and of physical education. *Sport, Education and Society, 18*(1), 6–20.

Penney, D., Brooker, R., Hay, P. & Gillespie, L. (2009). Curriculum, pedagogy and assessment: Three message systems of schooling and dimensions of quality physical education. *Sport, Education and Society, 14*(4), 421–442.

Penney, D., & Chandler, T. (2000). Physical education: What future(s)? *Sport, Education and Society, 5*(1), 71–87.

Penney, D., & Evans, J. (1999). *Politics, policy and practice in physical education.* London: FN Spon, an Imprint of Routledge.

Penney, D., Petrie, K. & Fellows, S. (2015). HPE in Aotearoa New Zealand: The re-configuration of policy and pedagogic relations and privatization of curriculum and pedagogy. *Sport, Education and Society, 20*(1), 42–56.

Thorburn, M. (2007). Achieving conceptual and curriculum coherence in high-stakes school examinations in physical education. *Physical Education and Sport Pedagogy, 12*(2), 163–184.

Thorburn, M., & Horrell, A. (2011). Power, control and professional influence: The curious case of physical education in Scotland. *Scottish Educational Review, 43*(2), 71–83.

UNESCO. (2015). *Quality physical education guidelines for policy-makers.* Paris: UNESCO.

10

CURRICULUM REFORM AND POLICY COHESION IN PHYSICAL EDUCATION

Mike Jess & Shirley Gray, UNIVERSITY OF EDINBURGH, UK

As other chapters in this part reaffirm, physical education (PE) reform brings a number of paradoxes to the fore. Amidst and despite 'reforms' PE is invariably still viewed as sport, games or play, and has tended to have "a shadowy, marginal existence in education" (Osliņš & Stolz, 2013, p. 888). Whilst PE has remained a constant feature of most national curricula globally (Puhse & Gerber, 2005), attention has often been drawn to the subject's low status and perceived failings, resulting in calls for curriculum reform (e.g. Penney & Chandler, 2000). This chapter reflects that research has highlighted a lack of clarity and/or agreement about the nature of the PE curriculum, revealed the limited influence that the profession has at government level (Evans & Davies, 2015), and increasingly drawn attention to 'external' stakeholders (mostly from sport and health) setting specific directions for the PE curriculum (see Penney & Mitchell, Chapter 11). Thus, the interaction between the PE profession and national policy makers and the associated synergies and tensions in respective agendas are now of particular interest to the profession (e.g. Evans, 2013). Alongside this, as Petrie's chapter (12) discusses, the limited role that teachers play in the curriculum development process has also repeatedly been evidenced.

In an effort to better understand the issue and process of policy coherence, we take a 'big picture' view, exploring how the complex relationship between the PE profession and policy makers has shaped, and continues to shape, the nature of PE. Historical and contemporary policy relationships are then positioned as fundamental to the analysis and understanding of the directions pursued in curriculum reforms and the practices that are consequently advanced or inhibited. We first direct attention to the significance of a historical perspective and discuss how, during much of the twentieth century, physical educators developed a 'school subject' with limited government input. This evolutionary process is identified as far from smooth so that by the latter part of the century, as governments began to take more interest in curriculum development, the PE profession was not in a strong position to influence policy direction. Building from this, we scrutinise how recent shifts in conceptual thinking and curriculum initiatives stemming from within the profession have interacted with differing government views on the nature of PE. We identify tensions in policy agendas across government arenas as a key issue in understanding both the processes and outcomes of contemporary curriculum reform in PE. While the chapter reflects research that has been focused particularly on the UK context, the lines of analyses and emergent trends discussed are ones that have international currency. In looking to the future we direct attention to the need for the profession to be astute in responding to the evidence from historical developments and contemporary policy contexts. We suggest that PE futures will likely be governed by the profession's ability to create robust but flexible curriculum structures that have the capacity to cope with, negotiate and influence policy landscapes. This stance underpins our recommendations for future curriculum scholarship, research and practice.

The evolving nature of physical education in the twentieth century

PE's evolution has been complex as events within and beyond the profession have interacted to create a non-linear and often messy trajectory. Whilst observations about physical culture go back to Ancient Greece, Kirk's (1992) work located in the UK identifies that it was not until the late nineteenth century with the introduction of mass schooling that PE emerged as a 'school subject'. It is evident, however, that this introduction stemmed more from concerns about the poor physical health and fitness levels of the military rather than claims about how it can contribute to the *education* of young people in schools (Kirk, 1992). Hence, it is important to acknowledge that both the prominence of 'other discourses' in establishing curriculum directions for PE, and curriculum marginality, are historical features of PE.

With governments having limited involvement in curriculum development during much of the twentieth century (Ball, 2008), physical educators had some autonomy to develop the curriculum as best they saw fit (Kirk, 1992). Yet, as an area of study in its relative infancy, PE had a limited 'intellectual tradition' (Gard, 2008) which made it difficult to create a cohesive and robust vision for PE as different groups positioned the subject in line with numerous, and sometimes conflicting, interests (Goodson, 1987). As Jewett and Bain (1985) have noted, PE's engagement with the curriculum process was relatively limited with the result that "the state of the art of physical education curriculum does not permit presentation of several comprehensive, sophisticated, competing theories of physical education" (p. xi). Rather, lack of clarity has been seen as characteristic of PE and a cause of concern for many within the profession. Countering such concern, Kirk (1992) suggested that conflicts should not be seen as "episodes of abnormal chaos punctuating a normal state of calm tranquillity and consensus, but are instead a common and entirely healthy feature of social life" (p. 156). In essence, as an emergent profession, non-linear evolution should be seen as part of the normal development process.

A historical perspective extending through the twentieth century, and considering the second half of the century in particular, illustrates that a lack of linearity characterises curriculum reform in PE. Further, it brings to the fore the ways in which key developments within and external to the profession have had a significant influence on how PE developed. The sections that follow draw upon research that has variously utilised historical, sociological and philosophical perspectives to explore the changing internal and external 'dynamics' that have impacted on the focus and direction of curriculum 'reform'. Key 'internal' developments we direct attention to are:

(i) the shift from physical training to physical education;
(ii) scientisation and the multi-activity curriculum approach; and
(iii) a focus on the secondary school years.

We then direct attention to the following parallel 'external' developments:

(i) the mind-body dualism and status; and
(ii) increased government intervention.

Throughout, however, we point to the important interplay between internal and external developments.

Internal developments

Kirk's (1992, 2001) research has documented that until the end of the Second World War, PE (or physical training as it was often called) was largely a female profession with a curriculum dominated by Swedish or German gymnastics focused on regimented physical drill. As historical studies have illustrated (Fletcher, 1984), the history of the profession and of curriculum reform in PE are firmly identified as gendered and as inherently related to one another. This line of research also highlights the way in which the respective curriculum histories of PE teacher education and of PE as a school subject are intertwined. Later in the chapter we return to this issue in considering contemporary issues and future directions for curriculum reform.

With the introduction of mass secondary schooling after the Second World War, male teachers began to enter the profession in significant numbers and efforts were made to extend the nature of PE curriculum (Kirk, 1992). However, in various parts of the world, this caused considerable tension. While female physical educationists tended to favour a more aesthetic, creative and progressive movement education approach, the males concentrated on a scientifically oriented movement mastery approach focused on games and sports (Whitson & McIntosh, 1990). This more scientific approach, fitting well with the educational worldview of the time, began to dominate the curriculum and was initially viewed with some optimism in terms of its educational potential (Kirk, 2013). The model, later termed the multi-activity approach (Siedentop, 1982), was underpinned by behaviourist learning theories and characterised by teaching concentrated on technical movements and curriculum design in short 6–8 week 'blocks' of lessons focused on specific physical activities, particularly team games (Jess, Atencio & Thorburn, 2011). While this approach gradually extended to include a range of physical activities (e.g. gymnastics, dance, aquatics, etc.), as others have discussed (e.g. Locke, 1992; Penney & Chandler, 2000) the model has continued to set a strong frame for curriculum thinking and notions of 'reform'.

Towards the end of the century, other curriculum models began to feature as part, albeit a small part, of PE. These included Movement Skill Themes, Humanistic PE, Fitness for Life, Health-Related Activity, Teaching Games for Understanding (TGfU) and Sport Education; all of which have variously played a prominent role in subsequent developments internationally. By the end of the century, however, there was some consensus that "the PE curriculum has been structured with a subject matter orientation" and more specifically that "sports, dance and gymnastics units have dominated" (Jewett & Bain, 1985, pp. 32–33). Concurrently, concerns were being raised about the educational worthiness of this approach and of the conceptualisation underlying thinking about the curriculum (Fernandez-Balbao, 1997).

External-internal interplay is particularly evident when we consider the impact that the introduction of compulsory secondary schooling had on the profession, as initial teacher education increasingly focused on the specialist training needed to teach PE across the secondary school years (Kirk, Tinning & Macdonald, 1997). Less attention was given to primary school developments as curriculum projects increasingly concentrated on the secondary years. Some observers suggested that this marginalising of primary PE would result in many children entering secondary school lacking the movement competence, knowledge or motivation to engage in PE (Gallahue, McLenaghan & Luedke, 1975). These concerns were compounded by research reporting few specialist teachers working in primary schools (Physical Education Association, 1987), weaknesses in the quality of teaching (Graber, Locke, Lambdin, & Solmon, 2008), limited initial teacher education (Kerr & Rodgers, 1981) and a general lack of confidence to teach PE

(Faucette, Nugent, Sallis, & McKenzie, 2002). By the end of the century concerns about the state of primary PE were common in the literature across the world (Hardman & Marshall, 2000) – and they continue to frame curriculum reform in PE (see Petrie, Chapter 12; Penney & Marshall, Chapter 11).

So, with PE initially introduced to the school curriculum on health grounds, mass secondary schooling and the introduction of male teachers in the post-Second World War period saw primary PE being marginalised and a move towards a more scientifically oriented multi-activity approach. However, while curriculum 'reforms' were largely framed within this overarching structure, concerns were beginning to be raised about its appropriateness to meet broader educational objectives.

External developments

As indicated above, external events concurrently impacted on the evolution of PE in the UK particularly, but also internationally. Drawing on research within and beyond PE we direct attention to two issues that internationally had a particularly significant impact in the post-war period: the positioning of the subject within the overall curriculum and, towards the end of the century, government intervention.

Within the UK, while the subject's position within the overall curriculum had been a long-standing concern for the profession, this debate was re-ignited to a wider audience in the 1960s when two prominent educational philosophers, Peters (1966) and Hirst (1968), questioned PE's role in the curriculum. Writing from the Platonic-Cartesian liberal-analytical tradition of philosophy that dominated education thinking in the West, they presented a view of the curriculum that distinguished between mind and body and privileged different intellectual modes of enquiry. Peters (1966, p. 159) considered that games, the dominant feature of the multi-activity curriculum, were non-serious and morally unimportant activities because they lacked "a wide ranging cognitive content" as they were based on "mere know-how". In contrast, he suggested that the study of science, for example, offered limitless potential for increasing knowledge and for making discerning judgements. PE's position within this academically inclined curriculum was problematic, and it was with some relief, for some, that PE was later included in the cognitively focused, high-stakes assessment programmes in some countries (Ayers, Sawyer & Dinham, 2004). However, views such as that expressed by Ozoliņš and Stolz (2013), in stating that PE "is concerned with the exercise and development of the body and not the mind, so it is non-cognitive" (p. 849) highlight that while Peters (1983) and Hirst (1993) were later to acknowledge the value of practical activities, the impact of their earlier work has had a lasting effect. PE has repeatedly faced the challenge to justify its academic worth and research internationally continues to highlight this as a prime issue amidst curriculum developments in the senior secondary years (Fitzclarence & Tinning, 1990).

During the 1980s and 1990s, developments in many parts of the world reaffirmed the need for curriculum reform in PE to be acknowledged as inherently tied to wider political and social change (see Chapter 9 by Penney and Chapter 13 by Wilkinson). Policy and curriculum research in education revealed that while governments had taken a 'hands-off' approach to curriculum development (Ball, 2008), globalisation, the knowledge economy and performativity were emerging concepts gaining precedence in policy arenas, with profound implications for educational reform. A growing body of research illustrated reforms positioning education within a market ideology focused on attainment and teacher accountability (Day & Smethem, 2009), and increasingly resulting in educational developments being initiated outside the profession (Webb

& Vulliamy, 1999). Educational research internationally further highlighted that long-held social justice goals were often sidelined as moves were made towards an "overriding emphasis on policy making for economic competitiveness" (Ball, 2008, p. 12).

Over time, research has revealed the subtle and sometimes overt impact of this emerging political context on PE curriculum reform. Developments in England highlighted a shift from a situation where PE was of limited interest to policy makers to one in which governments pushed ideologically driven agendas in the context of national curriculum reforms and policy developments spanning education and sport. Acknowledging poor physical activity levels and limited sporting success, a 'restorationist' discourse was embedded in a PE national curriculum and in sport policy (Penney & Evans, 1999). John Major, then Prime Minister, promised to "put competitive team games at the heart of school life" (cited in Carney & Armstrong, 1996, p. 69) and set in train policy and structural changes to achieve this. The Youth Sport Trust (YST), founded in 1994 with the aim of developing and implementing PE and sport programmes for young people was central to this traditional sport revival. The YST rapidly came to prominence by supporting the government's sport policy, articulating the value of school sport (and PE) in relation to whole school improvements and undertaking large-scale national professional development programmes. Conversely, the PE professional associations were reluctant to follow these narrow sporting priorities and were effectively excluded from the national policy discourse (Houlihan & Green, 2006). In a short period of time, this type of government intervention occurred in many countries and saw PE move from being in "a world of its own" (Thorburn & Horrell, 2011, p. 74) to a position amidst the wider world of policy discourse: a position that the profession has found particularly difficult to impact upon (Hardman & Marshall, 2000).

Hence, we can reflect that after the Second World War PE sought to expand its horizons and align itself with broader, 'more worthy' educational goals. However, the result of this was that the profession became embroiled in internal and external debates about curriculum structures, primary PE and positioning within the overall curriculum. As governments around the world became more prominent in curriculum development processes, Macdonald and Brooker (1997) identified that the challenge for the profession was to construct curricula that were "sufficiently defensible, rigorous, and relevant within contemporary school cultures to ensure that the subject [or learning area] is positioned as legitimate work" (p. 155). As the new century approached, the manner in which this curriculum challenge was tackled would have an important impact on how the profession would achieve recognition of legitimacy within and beyond education.

Physical education in the twenty-first century: changing thinking, emerging connections

At the beginning of the twenty-first century, a series of events occurred to, once again, influence the direction of 'reform' in PE. Reports of an impending global childhood 'obesity epidemic' (James, Leach, Kalamara, & Shayeghi, 2001) and increasing recognition of the lifelong benefits from regular physical activity (Paffenbarger, Hyde, Wing, & Hsieh, 1986) helped raise the profile of PE in many countries (Hardman & Marshall, 2005). While the enhanced interest was to be welcomed, the extent to which it would impact on prospects for PE was soon apparent. The context in which PE developments were now placed was characterised by greater complexity as health, sport and education stakeholders became the prominent actors in curriculum matters. As the PE profession tried to move beyond the multi-activity approach, the policy space in which it was operating was more crowded, contested and diverse (Petrie & lisahunter, 2011).

Again, a combination of internal and external developments impacted prospects for curriculum reform and placed PE in both a challenging and potentially precarious position. Key (and again parallel) influences that we identify with the evolution of PE in the early part of the twenty-first century are summarised as:

- Internal: (i) a conceptual shift; (ii) new curriculum models; and (iii) models-based practice, connective specialism and lifelong learning.
- External: (i) sport, health and education agendas; and (ii) ongoing government intervention.

Internal developments

The turn of the century saw PE increasingly question its association with positivist views of knowledge and practice, and calls were made for change in response to the emergence of new postmodern theoretical perspectives (Fernandez-Balboa, 1997). A growing number of academics supported the view that the knowledge and practices associated with PE were not fixed entities and that there was a need for learning experiences to be more relevant to the complex needs of young people (Tinning & Fitzclarence, 1994). PE began to negotiate notions of uncertainty and contradiction and explore a curriculum process aimed at developing learners who could "deal with the uncertainty of conflicting and changing knowledge" (Wright, 2004, p. 6). The move from its positivist tradition saw PE engage with principles from interpretive, critical, feminist, poststructuralist and complexity perspectives (see Kirk, Macdonald & O'Sullivan, 2006). Aligned to these conceptual shifts, the research and curriculum reform discourse was being informed by constructivist (Azzarito & Ennis, 2003), situated (Kirk & Kinchin, 2004), critical (Sicilia-Camacho & Brown, 2007), ecological (Hastie & Siedentop, 2006), dynamical systems (Chow et al., 2007) and complexity (Jess, Keay & Carse, 2014) perspectives on learning. Accordingly, participative, interactive and situated learning experiences became a feature of more integrated curriculum, pedagogy and assessment developments that, as Penney discusses in Chapter 9, are as much about pedagogy and assessment issues as they are about curriculum.

As these developments emerged, there was broad acknowledgement that the multi-activity approach offers a limited educational experience (Kirk, 2010). Grounded in behaviourism, the approach attempts to reproduce specific knowledge drawn from different sports and has been criticised for being fragmented and de-contextualised (Siedentop, 1994). In addition, by offering samples of different activities (Cothran, 2001), it has been suggested there is limited opportunity for any sustained engagement to enable transfer of learning across ages, curriculum areas and out-of-school contexts (Penney & Jess, 2004). Therefore, although the multi-activity approach may still dominate in many countries, there have been repeated calls to create more relevant curriculum approaches (Ovens, Hopper & Butler, 2013).

As preceding sections have acknowledged, calls for reform are not new. Sport Education (Siedentop, 1994) and TGfU (Bunker & Thorpe, 1982) are the most notable 'alternative' models to counter the dominant curriculum approach. Yet, it is arguably only recently that efforts have been made to overtly integrate these models with new conceptualisations of knowledge and learning (Hastie, 2012). While neither model addresses the entire PE curriculum, both offer an insight into the application of more open-ended, situated and complexity-oriented thinking and opportunities for curriculum reform. Although they have grown in popularity globally and garnered significant research support (e.g. Butler & Griffin, 2010), the ongoing dominance of the multi-activity discourse is highlighted by the fact that these approaches remain at the periphery of many official curriculum reforms.

TGfU proposes that games teaching can be designed to be developmentally appropriate and conditioned to develop tactical awareness. By creating four game categories, i.e. invasion, central net, striking and fielding and target, TGfU sets a context for learners to make decisions about the nature of games, tactics and movement skills. As such, the focus is more on cognitive and affective learning and moves beyond behaviourist instruction focused on movement mastery. Aimed at children in the late primary and secondary school, Sport Education sets out to offer more 'authentic' learning experiences, with key features that include sustained teams, 'blocks' re-framed as seasons, student roles and structured competition (see Hastie & Mesquita, Chapter 5). Other curriculum models linked to the contemporary thinking noted above have been (and continue to be) introduced and developed. Examples include cooperative learning, place-based learning, critical pedagogy, health optimising PE, Taking Personal and Social Responsibility (TPSR) and Cultural Studies. Central to these models is the different physical, cognitive and affective learning intentions aligned with a more holistic vision of PE (Bailey et al., 2009).

From one perspective, these developments signal enhanced engagement in curriculum reform and growing strength in curriculum thinking and research. Yet, as the number of these varied models expands, issues of curriculum cohesion, robustness and flexibility have received renewed attention. Penney (2013) brings these issues into focus by exploring Maton's (2011) distinction between cumulative and segmented learning. Cumulative learning is characterised by integrated progression and transfer across contexts while segmented learning is seen as "educational practices where learned knowledge is strongly bounded from other knowledges and contexts" (p. 128). This distinction is useful because it draws attention to the weakness of the multi-activity approach and signals the need to develop the knowledge and skills that can be applied across different contexts both now and in the future. Building on this idea of cumulative learning, two 'curriculum perspectives' are discussed below that again reflect research developments relevant to our focus on reform: models-based practice (MBP) (e.g. Kirk, 2013) and connective specialism (e.g. Penney, 2008).

While MBP appears to have similarities with the multi-activity approach, it is built on the notion that different forms of PE have the potential to contribute to a range of educational outcomes (Kirk, 2013). Different curriculum models, therefore, are used to create an overarching curriculum that sets out to achieve a range of educational outcomes within local contexts. Teachers can select sequences of models based on learners' needs and on each model's capacity to support cumulative learning over time. Quay and Peters (2008) highlighted the possibilities of this approach by connecting fundamental motor skills, creative games making, TGfU, Sport Education and TPSR in a primary PE programme that set out to support children's skill and fitness, personal and social development and physical activity learning.

In a similar vein, the idea of PE as a connective specialism (Penney & Chandler, 2000) has also received attention. Building on the core knowledge and skills towards which teaching and learning should be directed (Jess et al., 2011), the connected curriculum is seen as the catalyst for experiences that contextualise learning within situated contexts (Rovengo, 2006). Situating learning captures the lived experiences of learners and demonstrates how they can integrate school knowledge with their lives (Kirk & Macdonald, 1998). This connected and situated thinking has also been directed towards lifelong agendas (Green, 2004) in which the curriculum not only engages with lifelong and lifewide learning but also with lifelong physical activity and health (Penney & Jess, 2004). It has been argued that these lifelong agendas will need to be represented consistently as a focal point for curriculum innovation and will have implications for the nature of future learning in PE as it moves beyond the curriculum and the school gates (Penney, Jess, & Thorburn, 2006). However, while there have been some efforts to develop a connected curriculum in primary schools (e.g. Jess, 2012), the ongoing dominance of the multi-activity approach has made developments of this nature more difficult in secondary schools (Penney, 2013).

The early twenty-first century has, therefore, seen a shift in thinking about curriculum by researchers, towards initiatives focused on the knowledge and skills connected to a more participative, cumulative and situated vision of school PE as the foundation for lifelong physical activity. However, history clearly shows that an issue for the profession is its capacity to articulate a coherent vision of this new curriculum and to demonstrate the potential that new practices offer across and beyond the classroom.

External developments

While PE has taken up more contemporary thinking and practice, as Penney and Mitchell (Chapter 11) discuss, external influences have become more varied and more intense. The increased engagement of health, sport and education actors (Petrie & lisahunter, 2011) aligned with government moves towards greater marketisation, performativity and outsourcing (Williams & Macdonald, 2015) have created a complex policy arena in which PE must now compete. Internationally, therefore, while PE's position within the curriculum may appear more secure (Thorburn, Jess & Atencio, 2009), as in earlier times, the upturn in fortune arises mostly from increased support and pressure from health and sport (Petrie & lisahunter, 2011). Uncertainty remains about the specific nature of the curriculum as health agendas, particularly obesity and physical inactivity, have become notably influential in some countries (see e.g. Burrows & Ross, 2003; Petrie & lisahunter, 2011), while sport remains a driver for policies in others (e.g. English Department for Education, 2013). Again, we recognise mixed implications for PE. Increased attention bringing other policy agendas and players 'into' the PE curriculum space has created more funding opportunities, with many new projects stemming from health and/or sport sources (Evans & Davies, 2015). These interests have, however, been identified as filling a void in terms of input by education departments in the development of PE (Evans, 2004). Therefore, the profession is conscious that this new-found prominence arises from an engagement with 'other' political agendas being pursued in schools and, as such, has the potential to promote a profession and curriculum that is "positioned instrumentally as cure-alls for a range of social and private ills" (Burrows & Ross, 2003, p. 15).

Within this context, the economic recession has seen rapid changes in education systems as governments of different political persuasions adopt neoliberal agendas to address the prevailing socio-economic conditions (Rizvi & Lingard, 2010). These developments have seen a re-focusing on the instrumental goals of education (Macdonald, 2011) as performativity agendas emphasising accountability, measurement and inspection become more common. The reality for many PE teachers engaging with curriculum reform is that their deliberations are framed by pressure to produce evidence of raised standards that meet performative outcomes (Montague, 2012) and teaching and learning agendas focused on 'cost effective' curriculum and pedagogies. Connecting this agenda with sport and/or health agendas could see PE programmes moving towards a focus on the identification of 'gifted and talented' performers, the measurement of body mass index and/or the 'improvement' of teaching techniques to create more cost-effective curriculum (Evans & Davies, 2015).

Aligned with this neoliberal thinking, policy development has also led to new forms of funding and governance in which profit and non-profit making organisations have become more involved in the delivery of schooling, initial teacher education and continuing professional development (Harris, Cale & Musson, 2011). Consequently, the private sector has become more involved in public service activities normally associated with the state (Ball, 2012). As Penney and Mitchell discuss further (Chapter 11), the curriculum, and curriculum reform, have now become part of an open market in which teachers may no longer be the main providers of PE. In particular, as researchers have identified, primary teachers' lack of confidence to teach PE (Morgan & Bourke, 2008) has seen outsourcing provision become an attractive 'reform' solution to combat the persistent shortfalls of primary PE (Griggs, 2008). However, as outsourcing becomes more apparent, attention has been drawn to the possible long-term de-professionalisation of PE (Macdonald, 2011) and the re-framing of both political and professional visions of what the curriculum may become (Penney, Petrie & Fellows, 2014; see Chapter 11 by Penney & Mitchell).

As these neoliberal concepts around 'use-value' have begun to take hold, they have re-awoken the long-standing concerns about the status of PE (McCullick, 2014). Evans (2013) has suggested that these approaches to governance, organisation and delivery are already changing the nature of PE. With more 'interested parties' influencing the direction of school PE, the profession needs to find a clear voice within this crowded and contested space. Furthermore, our own experience shows it is critical that this voice spans political and professional arenas, and addresses curriculum reform with the understanding that there is a need for policy coherence across school and university sectors. In recent years, we have been fortunate in Scotland to go some way towards achieving such coherence in our primary PE work. With support from government agencies, we were able to work with key stakeholders in our efforts to reorient the primary PE curriculum (Jess et al., 2011) whilst simultaneously developing in-depth professional learning focused on the development of 'a profession' with the skills and knowledge to deliver this curriculum vision (Carse, 2015). While successful at a number of levels, this experience has also helped us recognise the dynamic nature of the policy arena and the precarious, fluid and often short-lived relationships within this context. Consequently, amidst these emerging internal and external dynamics, we acknowledge clear challenges for the stance the profession takes in relation to shifting patterns of provision and, perhaps more critically, the control of the PE discourses (Penney et al., 2014).

Implications for practice and future directions

As we consider the future, we recognise the progress the PE profession has made over the last 60–70 years. Both the historical and contemporary contexts contribute to experiences of, and prospects for, curriculum reform. While there may be ongoing concerns about the multi-activity approach and the marginalisation of primary PE, recent developments suggest new ways of thinking are beginning to align with contemporary curriculum models that articulate with a range of educational benefits (Bailey et al., 2009). Importantly, we see some progress towards overarching frameworks focusing on the integration of these new models (Kirk, 2013) and better connections of experiences across and beyond the school (Rovengo, 2006). We therefore suggest that the profession is starting to make notable progress in its quest to create curriculum frameworks that are educationally sound, robust and flexible enough to adapt to ever-changing political agendas and also act as the foundation to underpin these official texts.

We also acknowledge that the last 30 years has seen the profession interacting with a growing list of policy actors, mostly from outside the traditional education arena. While these interactions have helped elevate PE's position within many schools, they raise questions about the future ownership of PE curriculum reform, particularly when reports highlight limited involvement from the education sector in debates, developments and funding. Hence, while some progress has been made, if the profession is to engage productively with these external policy actors, a key challenge will be to effectively negotiate and influence events in the crowded policy arena. In saying this we acknowledge that finding a 'policy voice' may be a long-term project involving close collaboration between teachers, professional associations and universities, and requiring new ways of thinking about policy and curriculum (Penney, 2013). From a curriculum perspective, we agree with Kirk (2010) that universities will have a key role to play as catalysts in creating and developing the context for innovation as "it is only universities that provide the spaces for the critical intellectual work required to inform our judgements about public education, pedagogy and curriculum" (p. 141). As such, universities "will be the seedbeds for curriculum reform of physical education teachers' education" (p. 144) and "ideal hubs for the organisation of networks and partnerships" (p. 145). However, while universities may be key to curriculum reform and teacher education, we believe it is 'positive and powerful' professional associations that will be critical in raising professional standards, increasing credibility and transparency among the public and also becoming the 'policy voice' of the profession in its negotiations within the complex policy arena (Hargreaves & Shirley, 2009). Therefore, while we acknowledge that the synergy between the PE profession and policy stakeholders will continue to be a dynamic and messy process, we suggest that the emergence of educationally oriented initiatives within the profession has the potential to present PE as a more contemporary and adaptable subject with the capacity to make a valuable and sustained contribution to education across the globe.

Summary of key findings

- PE was introduced to the school curriculum in the late nineteenth century based on health concerns rather than its educational value.
- The dominant mind-body dualist view influencing education in western societies has resulted in PE consistently seeking to justify its presence in the curriculum.
- Throughout most of the twentieth century, governments had limited engagement in curriculum matters and the PE profession was able to create its own vision for the subject.
- In the latter part of the twentieth century, the multi-activity approach dominated PE and continues to do so in many countries. However, concerns are regularly voiced about the nature of this approach, particularly its educational value and positivist delivery method.
- Recently, holistic, participative, interactive and situated curriculum and pedagogy initiatives have been developed by the PE profession.
- With government involvement now more common, the policy landscape has become more crowded as the health, sport and education sectors vie to influence the nature of PE curriculum.
- Governments' focus on neoliberal 'use-value' has re-awoken concerns about the status of PE.
- As a relatively new subject area, given the political constraints and the issues of status and positioning, the PE profession's gradual and non-linear progress towards a robust educationally justifiable subject area is to be expected.
- The stance the PE profession takes in relation to shifting patterns of curriculum reform and provision will have a significant impact on the profession's ability to influence PE futures.

Reflective questions for discussion

1. How should PE address the concerns about the 'one-size-fits-all' multi-activity approach that continues to dominate practice in many countries?
2. How should the PE profession approach the task of articulating a rationale to connect with contemporary educational agendas?
3. How should PE position itself in relation to health and sport agendas?
4. What actions should the PE profession take to become a more influential 'player' in crowded policy arenas?

References

Ayers, P., Sawyer, W. & Dinham, S. (2004). Effective teaching in the context of a Grade 12 highstakes external examination in New South Wales, Australia. *British Educational Research Journal, 30*(1), 141–165.

Azzarito, L., & Ennis, C. (2003). A sense of connection: toward social constructivist physical education. *Sport, Education and Society, 8*(2), 179–197.

Bailey, R. P., Armour, K., Kirk, D., Jess, M., Pickup, I. & Sandford, R., (2009). The educational benefits claimed for physical education and school sport: An academic review. *Research Papers in Education, 24*(1), 1–27.

Ball, S. (2008). *The education debate.* Bristol: Policy Press.

Ball, S. (2012). *Global education inc. New policy networks and the neo-liberal imaginary.* London: Routledge.

Bunker, D., & Thorpe, R. (1982). A model for the teaching of games in secondary schools. *Bulletin of Physical Education, 18*(1), 5–8.

Burrows, L., & Ross, B. (2003). Introduction. In B. Ross & L. Burrows (Eds.), *It takes two feet: Teaching physical education and health in Aotearoa New Zealand* (pp. 13–18). Palmerston North, New Zealand: Dunmore Press.

Butler, J., & Griffin, L. (2010). *More teaching games for understanding, moving globally.* Champaign, IL: Human Kinetics.

Carney, C., & Armstrong, N. (1996). The provision of physical education in primary initial teacher training courses in England and Wales. *European Physical Education Review, 2*(1), 64–74.

Carse, N. (2015). Primary teachers as physical education curriculum change agents. *European Physical Education Review, 21*(3), 309–324.

Chow, J., Davids, K., Button, C., Shuttleworth, R., Renshaw, I. & Araujo, D. (2007). The role of nonlinear pedagogy in physical education. *Review of Educational Research, 77*(3), 251–278.

Cothran, D. (2001). Curricular change in physical education: Success stories from the front line. *Sport, Education and Society, 6*(1), 67–79.

Day, C., & Smethem, L. (2009). The effects of reform: Have teachers really lost their sense of professionalism? *Journal of Educational Change, 10,* 141–157.

English Department for Education. (2013). *National curriculum in England: PE programmes of study.* www.gov.uk/government/publications/national-curriculum-in-england-physical-education-programmes-of-study

Evans, J. (2004). Making a difference? Education and 'ability' in physical education. *European Physical Education Review, 10*(1), 95–109.

Evans, J. (2013). Equity and inclusion in physical education PLC. *European Physical Education Review, 20*(3), 319–334.

Evans, J., & Davies, B. (2015). Neoliberal freedoms, privatisation and the future of physical education. *Sport, Education and Society, 20*(1), 10–26.

Faucette, N., Nugent, P., Sallis, J. F. & McKenzie, T. L. (2002). 'I'd rather chew on aluminium foil': Overcoming classroom teachers' resistance to teaching physical education. *Journal of Teaching in Physical Education, 21*(3), 287–308.

Fernandez-Balboa, J. (1997). *Critical post-modernism in human movement, physical education and sport.* Albany, NY: State University of New York Press.

Fitzclarence, L., & Tinning, R. (1990). Challenging hegemonic physical education: Contextualising physical education as an examinable subject. In D. Kirk & R. Tinning (Eds.), *Physical education, curriculum and culture* (pp. 169–191). London: Falmer Press.

Fletcher, S. (1984). *Women first: The female tradition in English physical education, 1880–1980.* London: Athlone.

Gallahue, D., McLenaghan, B. & Luedke, G. (1975). *A conceptual approach to moving and learning.* New York: John Wiley & Sons.

Gard, M. (2008). Producing little decision makers and goal setters in the age of the obesity crisis. *Quest, 60*(4), 488–502.

Goodson, I. (1987). *School subjects and curriculum change.* London: Falmer Press.

Graber, K., Locke, L., Lambdin, D. & Solmon, M. (2008). The landscape of elementary school physical education. *Elementary School Journal, 108*(3), 151–159.

Green, K. (2004). Physical education, lifelong participation and 'the couch potato society'. *Physical Education and Sport Pedagogy, 9*(1), 73–86.

Griggs, G. (2008). Outsiders inside: The use of sports coaches in primary schools. *Physical Education Matters, 3*, 33–36.

Hardman, K., & Marshall, J. J. (2000). *World-wide survey of the state and status of school physical education: Final report.* Manchester, UK: University of Manchester.

Hardman, K., & Marshall, J. (2005). Physical education in schools in European context: Charter principles, promises and implementation realities. In K. Green & K. Hardman (Eds.), *Physical education: Essential issues* (pp. 39–65). London: Sage.

Hargreaves, A., & Shirley, D. (2009). *The fourth way: The inspiring future for educational change.* New York: Corwin Press.

Harris, J., Cale, L. & Musson, H. (2011). The effects of a professional development programme on primary school teachers' perceptions of physical education. *Professional Development in Education, 37*(2), 291–305.

Hastie, P. (2012). *Sport Education: International perspectives.* London: Routledge.

Hastie, P. A., & Siedentop, D. (2006). The classroom ecology paradigm. In D. Kirk, D. Macdonald & M. O'Sullivan (Eds.), *The Handbook of physical education* (pp. 214–225). London: Sage.

Hirst, P. (1968). Liberal education and the nature of knowledge. In R. Archambault (Ed.), *Philosophical analysis and education* (pp. 113–138). London: Routledge & Kegan Paul.

Hirst, P. H. (1993). Education, knowledge and practices. In R. Barrow & P. White (Eds.), *Beyond liberal education: Essays in honour of Paul Hirst.* London: Routledge.

Houlihan, B., & Green, M. (2006). The changing status of school sport and physical education: Explaining policy change. *Sport, Education and Society, 11*(1), 73–92.

James, P., Leach. R., Kalamara, E. & Shayeghi, M. (2001). The worldwide obesity epidemic. *Obesity Research, 9*(4), 228–233.

Jess, M. (2012). The future of primary PE: A 3–14 developmental and connected curriculum. In G. Griggs (Ed.), *An introduction to primary physical education* (pp. 37–54). London: Routledge.

Jess, M., Atencio, M. & Thorburn, M. (2011). Complexity Theory: Supporting curriculum and pedagogy developments in Scottish physical education. *Sport Education and Society, 16*(1), 179–199.

Jess, M., Keay, J. & Carse, N. (2014). Primary physical education: A complex learning journey for children and teachers. *Sport, Education and Society,* DOI:10.1080/13573322.2014.979142

Jewett, A. E., & Bain, L. L. (1985). *The curriculum process in physical education.* Dubuque, IA: Wm. C. Brown.

Kerr, J. H., & Rodgers, M. M. (1981). Primary school physical education: Non-specialist teacher preparation and attitudes. *The Bulletin of Physical Education, 17*(2), 13–20.

Kirk, D. (1992). *Defining physical education: The social construction of a school subject in post-war Britain.* London: Falmer Press.

Kirk, D. (2001). Schooling bodies through physical education: Insights from social epistemology and curriculum history. *Studies in Philosophy and Education, 20*(6), 475–487.

Kirk, D. (2010). *Physical education futures.* London: Routledge.

Kirk, D. (2013). Educational value and models-based practice in physical education. *Educational Philosophy and Theory, 45*(9), 973–986.

Kirk, D., & Kinchin, G. (2004). Situated learning as a theoretical framework for sport education. *European Physical Education Review, 9*(3), 221–236.

Kirk, D., & Macdonald, D. (1998). Situated learning in physical education. *Journal of Teaching in Physical Education, 17*, 376–387.

Kirk, D., Macdonald, D. & O'Sullivan, M. (2006). *The handbook of physical education.* London: Sage.

Kirk, D., Tinning, R. & Macdonald, D. (1997). The social construction of pedagogic discourse in physical education teacher education in Australia. *Curriculum Journal, 8*(2), 271–298.

Locke, F. L. (1992). Changing secondary school physical education. *Quest, 44*, 361–372.

Macdonald, D. (2011). Like a fish in water: Physical education policy and practice in the era of neoliberal globalization. *Quest, 63*(1), 36–45.

Macdonald, D., & Brooker, R. (1997). Assessment issues in a performance-based subject: A case study of physical education. *Studies in Educational Evaluation, 23*(1), 83–102.

Maton, K. (2011). Segmentalism: The problem of building knowledge and creating knowers. In D. Frandji & P. Vitale (Eds.), *Knowledge, pedagogy and society: International perspectives on Basil Bernstein's sociology of education* (pp. 126–140). Abingdon, UK: Routledge.

McCullick, B. (2014). From the cheap seats: One consideration of school-based PE's position in contemporary American schools. *Physical Education and Sport Pedagogy, 19*(5), 533–544.

Montague, A. (2012). *Using physical education and sport to raise school standards, better evidence-based education.* York: University of York.

Morgan, P., & Bourke, S. (2008). Non-specialist teachers' confidence to teach PE: The nature and influence of personal school experiences in PE. *Physical Education and Sport Pedagogy, 13*(1), 1–29.

Ovens, A., Hopper, T. & Butler, J. (Eds.). (2013). *Complexity thinking in physical education: Reframing curriculum, pedagogy and research.* London: Routledge.

Ozoliņš, J., & Stolz, S. (2013). The place of physical education and sport in education. *Educational Philosophy and Theory, 45*(9), 887–891.

Paffenbarger, R. S., Hyde, R. T., Wing, A. L. & Hsieh, C. (1986). Physical activity, all-cause mortality, and longevity of college alumni. *New England Journal of Medicine, 314*(10), 605–613.

Penney, D. (2008). Playing a political game and playing for position. Policy and curriculum development in health and physical education. *European Physical Education Review, 14*(1), 33–50.

Penney, D. (2013). From policy to pedagogy: Prudence and precariousness; actors and artefacts. *Asia-Pacific Journal of Health, Sport and Physical Education, 4*(2), 189–197.

Penney, D., & Chandler, T. (2000). Physical education: What futures? *Sport, Education & Society, 5*(1), 71–87.

Penney, D., & Evans, J. (1999). *Policy, politics and practice in physical education.* London: F&N Spon.

Penney, D., & Jess, M. (2004). Physical education and physically active lives: A lifelong approach to curriculum development. *Sport, Education and Society, 9*(2), 269–287.

Penney, D., Jess, M. & Thorburn, M. (2006). Improving the house of cards: Productive pressures for curriculum reform in secondary physical education. Paper presented at the *Australian Association for Research in Education Conference*, Adelaide, 27th–30th November.

Penney, D., Petrie, K. & Fellows, S. (2014). HPE in Aotearoa New Zealand: The re-configuration of policy and pedagogic relations and privatization of curriculum and pedagogy. *Sport, Education and Society, 20*(1), 42–56.

Peters, R. S. (1966). *Ethics and education.* London: Allen & Unwin.

Peters, R. S. (1983). Philosophy of education. In P. Hirst (Ed.), *Educational theory and its foundational disciplines.* London: Routledge & Kegan Paul.

Petrie, K., & lisahunter. (2011). Primary teachers, policy, and physical education. *European Physical Education Review, 17*(3), 325–339.

Physical Education Association (PEA). (1987). *Physical education in schools: Report of a commission of enquiry.* Ling House, UK: PEA.

Puhse, E., & Gerber, M. (Eds.). (2005). *International comparison of physical education: Concepts, problems, prospects.* Oxford: Meyer.

Quay, J., & Peters, J. (2008). Skills, strategies, sport, and social responsibility: Reconnecting physical education. *Journal of Curriculum Studies, 40*(5), 601–626.

Rizvi, F., & Lingard, B. (2010). *Globalizing education policy.* London: Routledge.

Rovengo, I. (2006). Situated perspectives on learning. In D. Kirk, D. Macdonald & M. O'Sullivan (Eds.), *The handbook of physical education* (pp. 262–275). London: Sage.

Sicilia-Camacho, A., & Brown, D. (2007). Revisiting the paradigm shift from the versus to the non-versus notion of Mosston's Spectrum of teaching styles in physical education pedagogy: A critical pedagogical perspective. *Physical Education & Sport Pedagogy, 13*(1), 85–108.

Siedentop, D. (1982). Movement and sport education: Current reflections and future images. Paper presented at the *Commonwealth and International Conference on Sport, Physical Education, Recreation and Dance*, Brisbane, Australia.

Siedentop, D. (1994). *Sport Education: Quality PE through positive sport experiences.* Champaign, IL: Human Kinetics.

Thorburn, M., & Horrell, A. (2011). Power, control and professional influence: The curious case of physical education in Scotland. *Scottish Educational Review, 43*(2), 71–83.

Thorburn, M., Jess, M. & Atencio, M. (2009). Connecting policy aspirations with principled progress? An analysis of current physical education challenges in Scotland. *Irish Educational Studies, 28*(2), 207–221.

Tinning, R., & Fitzclarence, L. (1994). Physical education for adolescents in the 1990s: The crisis of relevance. *Changing Education, 1*(2), 1–5.

Wallhead, T., & O'Sullivan, M. (2005). Sport Education: Physical education for the new millennium? *Physical Education and Sport Pedagogy, 10*(2), 181–210.

Webb, R., & Vulliamy, G. (1999). Changing times, changing demands: A comparative analysis of classroom practice in primary schools in England and Finland. *Research Papers in Education, 14*(3), 222–255.

Whitson, D., & MacIntosh, D. (1990). The scientization of physical education: Discourses of performance. *Quest, 42*(1), 40–51.

Williams, B., & Macdonald, D. (2015). Explaining outsourcing in health, sport and physical education, *Sport, Education and Society, 20*(1), 57–72.

Wright, J. (2004). Critical inquiry and problem-solving in physical education. In J. Wright, D. Macdonald & L. Burrows (Eds.), *Critical inquiry and problem-solving in physical education.* London: Routledge.

11

REFORMING CURRICULA FROM THE OUTSIDE-IN

Dawn Penney, MONASH UNIVERSITY, AUSTRALIA

& Stephen Mitchell, KENT STATE UNIVERSITY, USA

The starting points for this chapter are some of the characteristics of contemporary curriculum reform in physical education (PE) that other chapters in this part have touched on. In particular, the chapter engages with the growing complexity of 'the curriculum space' that is associated with PE in schools and the increasing influence and involvement of government and other organisations in shaping the direction and momentum of curriculum reform. Put simply, the chapter reflects that in many instances, very significant pressures, investment and impetus for changes to the experiences that are provided in PE curriculum time are coming from sources other than national, state or local education authorities. We direct attention to a body of research that has sought to better understand the influence of so-called 'external' organisations and initiatives that have emerged from various health, physical activity and sport interests and policy imperatives. The chapter recognises that curriculum reform may not be an explicit intention of many of the agencies and organisations that offer 'physical education' services and resources to schools. We contend, however, that reform is an important, albeit subtle effect of changing models of provision of PE, physical activity and sport in schools. Hence, the chapter explores ways in which contemporary political and policy dynamics are influencing developments in official policy and in the pedagogical practice of 'physical education curriculum' (see also Jess & Gray, Chapter 10). It also provides further insight into teachers' positioning and influence in curriculum reform (as discussed by Petrie, Chapter 12) and pursues the implications of the developments described in relation to concerns for equity and inclusion in PE (see Wilkinson, Chapter 13), and for enhanced 'quality'.

The notion of 'quality' in discussions about PE curriculum is something that we recognise as contested and that this chapter seeks to encourage reflection on amidst changing patterns of curriculum provision. We are also aware of the need to be clear in our use of various terminology. At the same time, however, we acknowledge that blurred boundaries in use of terminology has long been a feature of PE curriculum reform and remains something that is itself influential in the sorts of reforms that we address here. Discursive shifts including, for example, the move towards increasing adoption of the term 'PESS' (Physical Education and School Sport) in policy developments in the UK (see Jess & Gray, Chapter 10; Wilkinson, Chapter 13), illustrate that a change in language may reflect or reinforce particular directions in and for 'physical education'. Similarly, as many readers will recognise, conversations with students, teachers, principals, parents and/or other individuals involved in policy developments, invariably illustrate that the terms physical education, physical activity and sport are frequently interchanged. International and national policy statements continue to provide definitions that simultaneously articulate distinctions and relationships. In this chapter we refer particularly to statements made in the UNESCO (2015) *Quality Physical Education Guidelines for Policy-Makers*, while also illustrating distinctions being blurred amidst various policy initiatives and changing policy contexts. Notably in our view, the UNESCO (2015) guidelines make it very clear that any discussion about quality must engage with matters of equity and inclusion and, furthermore, must be a discussion that extends to the many stakeholders in PE curriculum and curriculum reform. Ultimately, we therefore challenge the labelling of some organisations and agencies as 'external' and advocate for a shift in thinking about who is involved, via various means in the curriculum reform 'space' of PE.

The notions of policy *spaces, contexts* and *networks*, are key constructs that we discuss further in the theoretical overview below. We explore 'curriculum' and hence 'curriculum reform' as a social and political construct, and locate the issues pursued in this chapter within the political frames of neoliberal and market discourses. We reaffirm, however, that in any exploration of curriculum reform, a historical perspective is important. The following section reflects that there is always a need to look at origins of events and consider, particularly, series of events that often indirectly create circumstances in which particular directions for curriculum reform become possible, are considered legitimate and/or desirable – or equally, are deemed impossible or inappropriate to pursue. Our theoretical discussion extends this thinking. The section that then follows, focusing on trends and issues associated with the changing space of PE curriculum reform, provides in-depth insights from a number of international contexts. We then consider the implications of the research studies and theoretical insights provided for evidence-based policy, curriculum and pedagogical practice in PE and present both possible and probable future directions for research and practice moving forward. The chapter concludes with a summary of key findings and reflective questions that are designed to prompt critical engagement with the issues we have raised.

Historical perspective

This chapter is grounded in notions of shifting curriculum landscapes and relations that are anchored in broader ideological and political changes *to*, and *in*, education and broader social policy. As Evans and Davies (2015a) recently acknowledged, changing public-private relations "has taken different forms in different countries, localities and contexts with widely differing pre-existing balances between private and public provision and degrees of autonomy afforded to established 'partners' in State provision" (p. 1), and furthermore is "always mediated and shaped by national and local politics, economic contingencies and levels of prosperity and austerity" (p. 1). This provides an important reminder, first, that the involvement of non-government agencies in education is, in many instances, not new. Second, it highlights that amidst global trends, it is critical to engage with the particularities of their articulation in any specific national and local context. Yet a parallel message from Evans and Davies (2015a, p. 2) is equally strong, namely that it is the "sheer scale, scope and penetration" of privatisation that is "what is new" in education and indeed, PE. Hence, in this section, we use a historical perspective to direct attention to a complex mix of continuities and changes over time. We take on board Penney, Petrie and Fellows' (2015) prompt to look beyond a surface impression of change and examine the structural and power-relations that have variously been reaffirmed, transformed and progressively normalised amidst changes that span the "governance, organisation, delivery and purposes" (Evans & Davies, 2015a, p. 2) of PE curriculum. We point to the need to consider curriculum continuities as well as changes that feature amidst the growing prominence of market discourses and practices in PE.

It is pertinent to note that the history of PE and specifically PE curriculum reform is a story of various interests, understandings and professional practices gaining legitimacy – and of educational discourses often having marginal status. Physical education having a low status in broader curriculum debates and being a low priority for funding and/or other resource allocations, are familiar features of curriculum reform internationally. In many instances PE curriculum reform amounts to a somewhat uncomfortable re-negotiation of relations between internal and external discourses to reach a new 'settlement' (Luke, Woods & Weir, 2013) in what has long been acknowledged as a complex and contested policy space (Houlihan, 2000). Insights from sport sciences, coaching and, similarly, developments in health knowledge and practices have all influenced PE curriculum over time and have provided the foundation for reform in official curriculum texts and pedagogical practices (see for example, Kirk, 1992). From a historical perspective then, what were once seen as 'new practices' become legitimised and normalised through uptake and enactment. Past curriculum reforms have also involved particular discourses of health, physical activity and sport being re-positioned, gaining status or being sidelined by politicians, individuals accorded authority in official curriculum development and/or, teachers. As Jess and Gray's chapter (10) also shows, a situation of PE welcoming and/or needing to look beyond education for support and investment, is not new.

Evans and Davies' (2015a) comments indicate, however, that the global influence of neoliberal and market discourses is such that developments in several countries now point to contexts of reform having been transformed as we have moved from *commercialisation* to *privatisation* of education. They explain that while the former has been seen in education systems internationally for several decades, the latter "is not just incidental or piecemeal involvement of private enterprise *in* education … but, rather, marketisation of education in and of itself" (Evans & Davies, 2015a, p. 2, original emphasis). In the next section we further explore concepts that are central to understanding this distinct shift in relations between public and private interests in education and PE, and the implications of the shift for curriculum reform.

Theoretical insights

As indicated above, the research in PE that this chapter focuses on relates to changing relations between the public and private sector in the provision of educational services. It reflects scholarship in education and PE that has responded to the growth (in extent and influence) of market economies, politics and ideology, associated particularly with neoliberalism and 'Third Way' thinking (see e.g. Ball, 2007; Evans & Davies, 2015a, 2015b; Macdonald, 2011) and that has sought to extend conceptualisations of the contemporary politics and processes of PE curriculum reform (see e.g. Penney et al., 2015) and the role and influence of teachers within that (see e.g. Macdonald, 2015; Powell, 2015). Insights from education policy sociology, sociology of education more broadly and curriculum theory specifically, are brought together here to inform discussion of concepts and conceptualisations relevant to our interest in the changing dynamics and landscape of curriculum reform in PE.

The concept of privatisation is central to the research and issues discussed here. Ball (2007, p. 13) provides a timely reminder that privatisation "has a long history" and suggests that to understand 'what is new' amidst recent developments in education, it is arguably "more appropriate to think about '*privatisations*'" (p. 13, our emphasis). As he points out, production of textbooks, testing programmes, equipment and building projects are all things that have long featured as 'privatisation' in education and that are easily recognisable features of the broad context of PE curriculum provision. The distinction that Ball (2007, p. 13) draws in relation to contemporary privatisation, relates to (i) the *scale* of involvement of various types of organisation in education (including private and not-for-profit companies, voluntary and community organisations, and national government organisations); (ii) the *nature* of involvement of these organisations, with historical patterns and boundaries of involvement "thoroughly breached" such that private sector participation now extends to *any* aspect of educational resources and services; and (iii) the parallel "fundamental re-design of the public sector", encompassing state involvement in and responsibility for, education. Ball (2007, p. 13) identifies the state as "increasingly re-positioned as the guarantor" rather than provider or financer of education. He also draws our attention to Hatcher's (2000) distinction between *exogenous privatisation*, involving "private companies entering education to take over directly responsibilities, services or programmes" (Ball, 2007, p. 14) and *endogenous privatisation*, which "refers to changes in the behaviour of public sector organisations themselves, where they act as though they were businesses, both in relation to clients and workers, and in dealings with other public sector organisations" (p. 14). Evans and Davies (2015a, 2015b) refer to the representation of exogenous and endogenous privatisation as respectively, privatisation *of* education (concerned with relations between State and private sectors) and the privatisation *in* education (concerned with relations *within* institutions). Taken together, the two notions convey the complexity of contemporary public/private relations in education and, we contend, PE curriculum. Directly and indirectly, we see *privatisations* impacting curriculum reform processes and directions in PE and below we draw on a growing body of international research to illustrate this. In doing so, we endeavour to take on board Ball's (2007) emphasis that analysis needs to avoid "lazy binaries" and "move beyond a simple juxtaposition of public/private to explore the blurrings and elisions between them" (p. 15). Considering these issues specifically in relation to curriculum reform in PE we also draw particular attention to Ball's (2007) observations that "privatisation can have paradoxical effect, good and bad together, and that the small particulars of privatisation might contribute to larger-scale social and political changes" (p. 15). We critically review what insights recent research in PE has provided and highlight the need for more research that can extend insights into the collective and longer-term impact of changing patterns of resourcing and provision of PE curriculum 'services' (design, teaching, testing) in relation to ongoing and prospective future reforms.

Discourse

Discourse has been a key tool in PE research focusing on curriculum reform and seeking to bring historical, political and sociological issues to the fore in analyses. Work in education policy sociology positions discourses as "influential particularly in providing possibilities of political thought and thus policy" (Ball, 2007, p. 1) and generating "subject positions, social relations and opportunities within policy" (p. 2). Ball and colleagues' work (e.g. Ball, 1994, 2007; Ball, Maguire & Braun with Hoskins & Perryman, 2012; Bowe, Ball & Gold, 1992) and research in PE drawing on the theoretical frameworks and conceptualisations articulated in this work, has sought to reveal the overt and more subtle ways in which particular discourses come to be included, excluded, legitimised, privileged and marginalised in and amidst curriculum reform processes (see also Penney, Chapter 9). Particularly relevant to this chapter is the dynamic interplay between discourses 'within and beyond' PE. Our contention is that shifts in the discourses that dominate the broader education and public sector space are impacting curriculum reform in PE and changing the 'possibilities for thought' about it moving forward.

Outsourcing

Outsourcing is another concept relating to the notion of privatisation/s in and of education and PE that is important to consider. Outsourcing can be seen as a form or element of privatisation. Drawing on Lair (2012), Williams and Macdonald (2015) explain outsourcing as "characterised by the movement of activities to a market-based organizational location from some other market or non-market location" (p. 57). They acknowledge that the practice is not new. The focus again is instead on the changing nature and extent of the practice, such that they describe it as "complex, controversial and pervasive" (p. 57); "an exogenous form of privatisation that coincides and coalesces with a number of endogenous forms of privatisation" (p. 69). As we discuss further below, theirs and others' research shows that the contemporary practice of outsourcing encompasses the systematic provision of PE learning experiences and 'delivery' of curriculum. This chapter reflects our view that opportunities and possibilities for curriculum reform need to be understood in the context of growing acceptance of outsourcing as an educationally sound and legitimate practice in PE.

Other concepts discussed by Ball (2007) help extend understanding of how outsourcing and privatisation more broadly relate to curriculum reform processes and relations in PE. Ball (2007) highlights that the changes in education policy that we associate with growth in privatisation in/of education need to be acknowledged as progressively transformative, such that "Each move makes the next thinkable, feasible and acceptable" (p. 19) even if the appearance is of disjointed or uncoordinated developments (Whitfield, 2001, cited in Ball, 2007). We argue that the directions pursued (and able to be pursued) in contexts of curriculum reform need to similarly be understood as reflecting the progressive culmination of a complex set of policy developments and the effects that they have over time on what is regarded as legitimate and desirable curriculum practice in PE. Ball (2007) further explains progressive transformation of education (and the public sector more broadly) as "both creative and destructive, a process of attrition and re-invention" (p. 19). We contend that this notion is highly pertinent in examining the trends and effects that we describe further below, centring on the increasing presence and influence of 'external providers' in PE curriculum. Whitfield (2001, cited in Ball, 2007, p. 20) has further identified three facets of transformation that potentially add depth to analyses of the privatisation and future of PE curriculum: "*destabilisation, disinvestment* and *commodification*" (our emphasis). The first facet involves a "discourse of derision" underpinning repeated criticism of public service. The second facet, Ball (2007) indicates could be termed "re-investment" rather than disinvestment, involving the redistribution of funding both within and away from the public sector. Third, commodification works to make "transformation possible by re-working forms of service, social relations and public processes into forms that are measurable and thus contractable and marketable" (p. 24). Ball (2007) explains that commodification "is both then cause and effect in relation to privatisation" (p. 24). Below we discuss research that evidences the commodification of PE and, more specifically, PE curriculum and the 'curriculum work' of teachers. We reaffirm Penney's (Chapter 9) emphasis of the need to understand curriculum reform as an increasingly complex process that involves an array of organisations and actors and the accompanying need to employ new theoretical tools to explore re-configured policy and curriculum relations.

Network Theory

'Network Theory', developed in education by Ball and Junemann (2012), enables the notion of governance in and of education to be re-framed. In research it enables us to reveal the changing landscape of PE as a policy (curriculum) 'space' that features changing policy and pedagogic relations (Penney et al., 2015). As Penney et al. (2015) have discussed, Ball and Junemann's (2012) theoretical work particularly prompts us to consider what curriculum reform scenarios are currently deemed (and will in the future be deemed) "possible, and eventually, obvious and necessary" (Ball & Junemann, 2012, p. 24), and what the curriculum effects of "the displacement and replacement of [curriculum] actors" (Penney et al., 2015, p. 53) within reconfigured policy and curriculum networks will be. This brings us back to significance of discourses and the need for research to explore the representation and positioning of various discourses within restructured curriculum networks. Penney et al. (2015) have drawn on Ball and Junemann's (2012) work to highlight that we should not assume that changing network relations (and, hence, knowledge relations) will precipitate distinct shifts in long-established patterns of dominance of particular discourses in curriculum reform in PE.

Macdonald (2015) adds the concept of *knowledge brokering* to the theorising of the action and, arguably, professional *responsibility* of individuals (and particularly teachers) within the increasingly complex local and global networks that we can associate with education and more specifically PE curriculum and curriculum reform conceptualised as a complex and ongoing political, policy and pedagogical process (see also Penney, Chapter 9; Petrie, Chapter 12). The concept of knowledge brokering importantly identifies brokers as intermediaries and mediators of knowledge services, systems and discourses that currently, or may in the future, feature as part of the education and, specifically, PE networks. We suggest that in contexts that are reframed by neoliberalism and privatisations in and of education, *brokering* is an integral and important aspect of developments associated with "official", "implicit" and "prudential" curriculum policy (Connelly & Connelly, 2013; Leahy, Burrows, McCuaig, Wright & Penney, 2016; see Penney, Chapter 9), and a valuable conceptual tool for analyses of reform of official curriculum texts and curriculum practices in PE.

To conclude this section it is pertinent to acknowledge that individually and collectively the concepts that we have discussed relate to changing, blurred and contested knowledge relations and boundaries in/of PE (Evans & Davies, 2015b; Macdonald, 2015; Penney, Chapter 9; Penney et al., 2015; Williams & Macdonald, 2015). They are tools that we employ in seeking to better understand contemporary contexts of curriculum reform and their consequences for curriculum reform. We try to reveal the shortcomings of binary language and conceptualisations, including who and what is now seen as 'internal' or 'external' to PE, or as 'outside' and 'within' the policy field and the profession.

Current trends and issues

The preceding discussion has highlighted that changes in political and economic contexts globally and locally are central concerns in considering 'trends and issues' associated with outsourcing and the involvement of various 'external providers' in PE curriculum. From the outset it is important to reiterate that while global developments are clearly impacting education policies and provision within national, state-based and local contexts, the particularities of each context are crucial to acknowledge. Hence, we fully expect variations in how pertinent or pressing the issues that we raise will seem, and urge readers to contextualise the points discussed in relation to their own specific political, policy and institutional settings.

'External providers' – key players in the physical education curriculum space?

The insights that research internationally provides about the involvement of various agencies, governmental and non-governmental, commercial and charitable, in the development and delivery of PE curriculum repeatedly points to notable shifts in the presence and influence of so-called 'external' agencies and organisations in curriculum matters. The theoretical discussion above highlighted that this is characteristic of education as a whole, such that it is far more appropriate to think of curriculum development and reform processes in terms of networks and network relations, than bounded and linear structures. In the case of PE, we emphasise that while there is an undeniable history of 'external agencies' having interest, involvement and influence in PE curriculum reform in policy arenas and in schools, recent research raises critical issues about (i) the number and range of organisations active and influential in shaping PE curriculum policy and provision and, in some contexts, the growing (dominant) influence of particular organisations; (ii) the ways in which 'external providers' are gaining curriculum influence; and (iii) prospective implications for how curriculum reforms will play out in practice. In relation to our first two points, it is useful to explore the involvement of agencies in arenas associated with official curriculum policy developments, and then beyond that, in terms of involvement and influence in what Connelly and Connelly (2013, see above) refer to as "implicit" and "prudential" curriculum policy.

Previous research in PE, particularly relating to National Curriculum developments in England and Wales, evidenced the direct involvement of key representatives from professional sport and from business in the official processes of curriculum reform in PE (Penney & Evans, 1999). Subsequent research in the UK has further conveyed shifting power-relations within and across the policy domains of education, sport and health, such that contexts of ongoing official curriculum reform have been characterised by the prominence of discourses with origins in fields other than education (see, for example, Houlihan & Green, 2006; Kirk, 2006; Thorburn & Horrell, 2011). Analysis of policy and curriculum developments in New Zealand has further illustrated the emergence of increasingly complex policy networks, with changing structural and funding relations amongst agencies and organisations in the education, sport and health policy sectors (Penney et al., 2015; Petrie & lisahunter, 2011). This research has also revealed that such developments can act as a catalyst for a host of organisations to play a direct and indirect role in the interpretation and enactment of PE curriculum (Petrie, Penney & Fellows, 2014). From their research findings Petrie et al. (2014) have argued that the proliferation of 'external providers' offering a variety of curriculum resources and services should not be equated with enhanced breadth in PE curriculum. Rather, they point to clear prospects of curriculum narrowing, with many organisations focusing attention on the same, selective elements of curriculum requirements associated with PE. In the USA these elements are in the form of the SHAPE America National Standards and Grade-Level Outcomes (Society of Health and Physical Educators, 2014) that, while being reasonably broad in domain scope, serve to focus the curriculum development efforts of state and local educational agencies. In a sense the standards also act to focus the involvement of other external agencies, in that commercial agencies usually develop their materials with a focus on the national standards and grade level outcomes. This said, from a network perspective, it is also important to acknowledge that these other external agencies are, essentially, SHAPE's competitors. For example teachers and school districts might purchase the (for profit) standards-based SPARK curriculum,[1] but those same teachers are probably not SHAPE America members.

Newly composed and configured policy communities, and a corresponding new set of influential policy actors who can be seen as critical in establishing and legitimising particular network relations, are amongst the features that Ball (2007) identifies with changing governance in and of education. In England, these features were arguably epitomised amidst the development of specialist schools, including specialist sports colleges that became the hub of and catalyst for numerous programmes and initiatives associated with PE and school sport, involving a mix of public and private funding sources. The Youth Sport Trust (YST), established in 1995 from philanthropic funding, vividly illustrated Ball's (2007) point that the incorporation of philanthropy into state policy can provide "a form of 'fast' and often very personal policy action" (p. 126). That action was overt and influential within government arenas and resulted in a period of unprecedented government and non-government investment in PE and school sport provision. A glance at the YST website and the list of its programmes and partners reflects that the charitable organisation was, and remains, instrumental in facilitating significant commercial investment and involvement in 'curriculum matters'. The policy developments and initiatives that it was instrumental in formulating and establishing fundamentally changed both contexts of curriculum provision in schools and the context for official curriculum reform. It is an example of an organisation with people skilled in forging 'partnerships' and influential network relations that directly and indirectly impact official curriculum policy; an organisation active in the production of "implicit curriculum policy" (Connelly & Connelly, 2013, see above), and in the provision of resources and services associated with curriculum enactment. Pertinent to this chapter, the YST was an 'external' organisation that rapidly moved to a central policy position within PE and that facilitated and sanctioned the involvement of many other external agencies in reform of policy and practice relating to PE curriculum provision and the provision of opportunities beyond the curriculum.

In the USA the most prominent parallel to the YST in terms of its role in forging multiple partnerships relevant to PE curriculum policy and provision, is SHAPE America, formerly known as the American Alliance for Health, PE, Recreation and Dance (AAHPERD). In contrast to the YST, SHAPE is a professional member-based organisation. It has a mission "to advance professional practice and promote research related to health and PE, physical activity, dance, and sport" (retrieved from www.shapeamerica.org/about/) and to provide resources for and advocacy on behalf of its 15,000 members. Through partnerships with other external corporate, not-for-profit and governmental agencies, including with the American Heart Association, the Centers for Disease Control and the President's Council on Fitness, Sports and Nutrition, SHAPE America seeks to impact PE curriculum and instruction in schools and to influence legislation at both the federal and state levels. While this influence has been pervasive, it is important to reiterate the significance of state legislation in driving the day-to-day operation of schools. Achievement standards are adopted and implemented at the state level, with varying degrees of accountability in terms of student learning for PE teachers and school districts. Most states have adopted or adapted the SHAPE America standards, though again there is little systematic assessment of student achievement (SHAPE America, 2006). It is also important to recognise the impact that the varied political landscape, and especially differing Republican and Democratic philosophies, has on local educational landscapes. In states with a Republican controlled legislature, such as Ohio in the Mid-West, the prevailing political orientation towards school operating standards is one of 'local control'. Essentially this means that politicians seek to devolve responsibility for decision making to the local level, under the assumption that school district boards and district superintendents are best informed as to how their schools should operate in terms of curriculum and procedures, provided that federal and state mandates are met. In these circumstances, different prospects arise for the development of new networks; there are greater 'freedoms' regarding allocation of resources and, therefore, the contracting of various educational services.

Outsourcing curriculum 'services' in physical education

As indicated above, Ball's (2007) discussion of privatisations in and of education brings to the fore the range of services that can be linked to processes of curriculum reform. This includes the contracting of advice on future developments and/or the production and revision of syllabus documents and associated materials (such as sample examination papers for examination PE syllabi), and the contracting of the provision of physical and/or technical infrastructure to support the implementation of reforms. It also encompasses production of supporting resources including textbooks, other teacher materials, assessment and reporting frameworks; the design and provision of professional development for teachers charged with implementing curriculum reforms; and the provision of staff who can be contracted to deliver aspects of new curricula. Readers in different countries and jurisdictions will recognise these as services that, in the case of PE, have been or are currently 'contracted out' at a system or individual school level.

Some services are embedded within reconfigured education systems as an integral dimension of curriculum reform. For example, schools in the UK and internationally that choose to offer an examination course in PE from one of the various examination boards (such as OCR, AQA, edexcel, or WJEC[2]) 'buy into' the associated applicable assessment system. The production of materials and resources that 'support' or 'accompany' examination PE syllabi internationally illustrates the way in which "implicit curriculum policy" (Connelly & Connelly, 2013) can be critical in shaping interpretations and enactment of formal curriculum policy, and the extent to which the direction of and possibilities for reform may well be in the hands of commercial companies. The production and distribution of textbooks for examination PE courses has long been acknowledged as 'big business' and the examination PE space can certainly see linkages and tensions emerge between commercial and curriculum reform interests. The dominance of particular texts within national or state-based markets may prove an important factor in consideration of (and 'consultation' about) reforms. Individuals who have been members of advisory groups or boards associated with the development of formal curriculum policy (and associated assessment policy, thus including examination writers or markers) may also be accorded high status as writers of textbooks and/or other resources and services (including provision of professional development courses for teachers and examination preparation courses for students). The texts, resources and supporting courses that are made available all shape, sometimes in profound ways, readings and enactment of new official curriculum (Brown & Penney, 2016).

Beyond examination PE, recent research in England, Australia and New Zealand has shown that outsourcing of various elements of 'core' PE curriculum provision (offered as part of the compulsory curriculum for all students) and the outsourcing of provision that is designed (and marketed) to 'value add' to curriculum experiences, are both now firmly established features of the contemporary PE landscape (Griggs, 2008, 2010; Lavin, Swindlehurst & Foster, 2008; Petrie et al., 2014; Williams, Hay & Macdonald, 2011). Williams et al.'s (2011) research involving primary and secondary schools in Queensland usefully identified outsourcing as cross-cutting the government and non-government school sectors in Queensland. Their survey findings also revealed that provision of particular activities constituted 'instructional services' that were being outsourced. From a curriculum reform perspective, the "ten most frequently outsourced" services give a clear appearance of alignment with a multi-activity curriculum model. Further, the most frequently cited reason for outsourcing was "to access external suppliers' expertise" (Williams et al., 2011, p. 407; see also Williams & Macdonald, 2015). Petrie et al.'s (2014) and Williams et al.'s (2011) research both point to the need to consider patterns of supply of services in looking at apparent demand preferences and in considering the implications of current outsourcing for curriculum reform. In both instances, the suggestion is that the services provided by the dominant players in the PE outsourcing market may well reaffirm the established dominance of sport-based discourses.

In the USA, both not-for-profit and commercial programmes are similarly familiar features of contemporary PE provision. Such programmes generally support, rather than replace, curriculum offerings and teachers. Varying degrees of outsourcing occur in those states that permit student 'waivers' for PE, most often by allowing participation in activities such as interscholastic sports, marching band and cheerleading to count as the required PE credit for high school graduation. This occurs in approximately 50% of states, with a further 25% of states permitting high school students to earn their PE credit through commercial online offerings that are often not taught by a licensed PE teacher (SHAPE America, 2006). Perhaps the best example of not-for-profit involvement in PE in the USA is *Fuel Up to Play 60*, an in-school nutrition and physical activity programme developed by the National Dairy Council and the National Football League, in collaboration with the US Department of Agriculture. As the title suggests, the focus of the programme is on healthy nutrition and the accumulation of sixty minutes of physical activity per day, during and outside of each school day. The most used commercial programme is the SPARK packaged curriculum, with lesson plans developed for elementary, middle and high school PE, along with before, during and after school physical activity ideas. These curriculums have been used extensively, with research to support programme efficacy in terms of impact on physical activity and fitness levels of elementary students (Sallis et al., 1997); academic achievement (Sallis et al., 1999); and sustainability (Dowda, Sallis, McKenzie, Rosengard & Kohl, 2005).

Focusing specifically on the 'supply' side of outsourcing, Petrie et al.'s (2014) research pointed to the significant role that cross-sector government funding mechanisms in New Zealand are playing in facilitating particular patterns of outsourcing, with many physical activity, sport and health-related programmes offered free of charge to schools as a result of the distribution of direct and indirect funding from both sport and health policy initiatives. Their findings also counter the notion that an increasing proliferation of providers of services can be assumed to equate to greater diversity in the range of PE related 'curriculum' services being offered to schools. Powell's (2015) analysis reaffirms the complex mix of government, not-for-profit and commercial funding and interests behind outsourced PE programmes stemming from the NZ$82 million government initiative *Kiwisport*, and specifically associates *Kiwisport* with helping "to reproduce the 'PE is the same as coaching sport skills' discourse" (Powell, 2015, p. 78). New Zealand is by no means the only context where this discourse remains dominant and has been openly legitimated by policies and funding initiatives. In England initiatives featuring joint funding from education and sport have similarly been designed to support growth in outsourcing of co- or extra-curricular programmes to specialist sport providers and coaches (see Flintoff, 2003, 2008; Wilkinson & Penney, 2015). These developments reaffirm the significance of policy contexts in shaping prospects and possibilities for ongoing and future curriculum reform.

Destabilisation and disinvestment in physical education curriculum

This section reflects that the sort of systemic change in "the fabric of education and physical education" (Evans & Davies, 2015b, p. 18) that we have discussed has been by design rather than accident. As Ball (2007) posits, the notions of destabilisation and disinvestment play a critical role in making the growth in presence and status of new players and services in curriculum provision both possible and necessary. From this perspective, the widespread and sustained curriculum marginality of PE in comparison to other curriculum areas, the extent to which discourses of standards and accountability direct curriculum reform attention to other areas, and (at least in some jurisdictions) a lack of confidence, expertise and training in PE for primary teachers (see for example, Petrie & lisahunter, 2011) are all conditions contributing to, and being used to legitimate both the supply and uptake of PE curriculum services and resources. They are also all factors underlying the growth of many and varied new partnerships, alliances and networks as the mechanisms to produce and deliver these services. A context of sustained disinvestment in PE curriculum can, for example, be seen as fundamental to the profile that the YST in England has attained and to the policy initiatives and networks that it has played a central role in leveraging. Similarly, Petrie and lisahunter (2011) point to other players effectively filling a void left by education in the PE curriculum space in New Zealand.

Powell's (2015, p. 75) contention that we need to simultaneously view the term assemblage as a noun ("the privatisation assemblage") and a verb ("to assemble"), and his analysis of the 'product' and 'process' in New Zealand, conveys the dynamic relationship and critical interplay between policy action and policy contexts. His ethnographic research also illustrates the link that Ball (2007) emphasises, between changing policy communities and changes in discourses, such that new networks need to be seen as legitimating new curriculum actors and new curriculum narratives. Powell (2015, p. 86) identifies views about "the purpose of PE, what quality PE looks like, who the PE expert should be" as all things that are "re-assembled" amidst and through the privatisation assemblage. Classroom teachers are de-skilled and their work de-professionalised within and by the assemblage; the 'expertise' of external providers and the quality of the services they are providing, is simultaneously accepted and legitimated as a natural and desired policy solution to a constructed policy problem (Powell, 2015; see also Ball, 2007; Evans & Davies, 2015b; Flintoff, 2003). In the next section we direct attention to other research that prompts us to consider curriculum discourses that are potentially marginalised amidst the trends we have discussed.

Quality and equity amidst privatisations in/of curriculum?

Evans and Davies (2015a) recently asked: "what legitimacy will innovative, radical and inclusive PE (in early years learning, schools and ITE) have in an education market where social justice is *not* a primary concern?" (p. 3, original emphasis). Here we therefore focus on matters of equity in PE and draw attention to research findings that reaffirm the need to continue to probe the implications of reforms that are stimulated and facilitated by new political, economic and policy agendas and relations. A point of reference for our discussion is the 2015 publication from UNESCO, *Quality PE Guidelines for Policy-makers*. In particular, the guidelines established that a commitment to inclusion, with difference positively embraced and the contribution that all participants bring to PE valued, is an essential and integral aspect of quality PE (UNESCO, 2015, pp. 8–9). The pronouncement prompts us to ask what impact the sorts of reconfiguration of the PE curriculum 'space' that we have described above, are having in relation to notions of 'quality' and concerns for equity and inclusion in PE.

Flintoff's (2008) research focusing on the School Sport Partnership Programme in England illustrated that initiatives that legitimate the established dominance of arguably narrow competitive sport discourses and serve to further conflate provision of sport and provision of quality PE, may do little to meaningfully advance gender equity in PE. Flintoff's (2008, p. 407) research highlighted that while the programme "was providing more opportunities for children, including girls and young women, to be physically active, within and beyond the curriculum", in parallel it revealed "how the scope and range of opportunities developed was limited by a competitive sport discourse". She concluded that the provision arising "has done little to include the vast majority of girls and young women (as well as some boys) and especially who have not already identified themselves as 'sporty' or interested in this particular kind of physical activity" (Flintoff, 2008, p. 407). More recently, Wilkinson and Penney (2015) pointed to the tension between discourses that are central to the increased involvement of external agencies (and, specifically, sport coaches and sport organisations) in extra-curricular provision and concerns for equity in relation to both ability and gender in PE. While the developments that their research explored did not directly relate to curriculum provision, we highlight the potential (often indirect) impact that the discourses that are legitimated amidst such developments can have on thinking about what constitutes quality PE curriculum provision and practice (see also Williams & Macdonald, 2015). Flintoff's (2008) caution of the inadequacies of "equality politics" (p. 407) and developments framed by discourses of access remain highly pertinent for any curriculum reform in PE. As we discuss below, there is a clear need for more research that pursues how patterns of long-standing inequity in PE are being impacted by the range of "privatisations" (Ball, 2007) of PE curriculum matters that research indicates are emerging if not yet fully established in curriculum discourse and practice (see also Evans & Davies, 2015a, 2015b).

'Quality' in this context is not merely a contestable concept. It is also now a highly marketable entity. 'Quality' provision of PE services and quality assurance, have, in some places, themselves become commercialised entities through formal accreditation or recognition schemes and endorsements. For example, tucked into the latest issue of *Physical Education Matters*, the professional journal from the Association for Physical Education (afPE) in the UK, is an A4 glossy flier, advertising resource packs called "PE CORE ACTIVITIES" produced by 1st4sport.com, "endorsed and supported" by afPE, and designed to support teachers in "effective delivery of the national curriculum PE programmes of study" (1st4sport.com, 2015). The AfPE has also been proactive as an association in promoting its "Quality Mark" award scheme "to celebrate and develop the quality of PE and Sport (PES) in schools" (Abrahams & Roberts, 2014, p. 1). In concluding their recent research review of the scheme, Abrahams and Roberts (2014) stated that "Tools that validate externally the quality of leadership, management, teaching and learning in PES should be encouraged and the afPE quality mark is a suitably robust protocol that is a sustainable driver for high quality PESS for young people" (p. 4). It is also an income generator for the association and a marketing tool for schools. Similarly in the USA, to 'set the standard' SHAPE America packages its National Standards and Grade-Level Outcomes for K-12 PE in a glossy publication, complete with a suggested curriculum framework, instructional strategies for implementation, assessment suggestions and ideas for using technology during instruction. Again this publication is a commercial product contributing to SHAPE America revenues. It further endorses the complex nature of privatisation activities and their impact on PE curriculum matters.

Implications for evidence-based practice and future directions

In considering implications of the trends and issues discussed, we reiterate that the "privatised education terrain" (Evans & Davies, 2015a) is far from uniform and nor is it stable. The localised form and effects will mean that what people recognise as key implications for PE curriculum reform now and into the future, will vary. Furthermore, we also recognise that what one recognises as implications and how one views them (as for example, either concerning or somewhat incidental) will reflect personal political and professional viewpoints. The majority of the research cited above is aligned with socio-critical scholarship and has been undertaken with the explicit agenda of asking questions of developments that are, arguably, in danger of never being voiced amidst the rolling process of more and more diverse privatisations becoming an established aspect of PE globally and locally. Amidst that process, we contend that researchers and PE professionals in schools, teacher education and curriculum authorities have an ongoing professional responsibility to critically and actively engage with new and emerging policy communities and the shifting discourses and relations that are a part of them. Albeit in varying ways (depending where are we are located geographically and what our role in relation to PE curriculum is), the terrain has changed, necessitating that we think differently about how to influence curriculum reform and that we seek to work with a potentially diverse collection of individuals and organisations in that endeavour. Ball (2007) made a telling point in stating: "There is no going back to a past in which the public sector as a whole worked well and worked fairly in the interests of all learners. There was no such past" (p. 187). PE curriculum can be viewed similarly. The terrain of and for reform is different, but in important respects the central challenge remains unchanged; can we do better in delivering on quality *and* equity than we have in the past? The research findings that we have presented indicate that the critical challenges are associated with how we work with and influence thinking in policy contexts and communities that privilege particular discourses in curriculum debates. The risks are that curriculum reform decisions and discussions at many levels are reframed in narrow economic terms and, within this process, what it is to be physically educated and what constitutes a quality PE curriculum is also redefined (see Evans & Davies, 2015a, 2015b; Penney et al., 2015; Williams & Macdonald, 2015). In these circumstances, we contend that it is essential that teachers and teacher educators engage seriously with the notion of physical educators becoming (and needing to be) skilled "knowledge brokers" (Macdonald, 2015) and informed, astute "policy actors" (Penney, 2013).

In our view, the issues that we have discussed are ones that need to be at the core of initial teacher education and professional learning in PE, and future research. "[P]rivatisation is an ongoing and contested process, not a complete, predictable nor necessarily foregone one" (Ball, 2007, p. 185). We arguably know all too little about the knowledge and skills required for teachers and teacher educators to act in the above ways amidst contexts that will continue to change. Research and researchers have a key role to play in extending current knowledge and we by no means wish to portray that as a simple task. As Evans and Davies (2015a) highlighted, outsourcing and the associated trends that we have described continue to proliferate and be taken up "without an 'evidence base' beyond that provided by its proponents" (p. 5), and, furthermore, often without a desire for alternative evidence bases to be established.

Summary of key findings

- Privatisations (Ball, 2007) in and of education have significantly changed the landscape of and context for curriculum reform in PE.
- Multiple agencies, spanning private and public sectors, are directly and indirectly influential in shaping reform of official curriculum texts (mandates). They are also active in producing resources that connect with reforms and in offering services to support the ongoing implementation of reforms. The composition of the networks associated with PE curriculum reform and the specific roles and influence of various agencies, reflects the interplay of global, national and state political, economic and professional contexts.
- Outsourcing of services that directly or indirectly relate to curriculum reform includes the production of texts, curriculum support resources, assessment frameworks and reporting systems, inspection and quality assurance services, and provision of professional learning for teachers.

- Long-standing patterns of limited government investment in PE curriculum, initial teacher education and professional learning for PE, have helped to create the opportunity for, perceived need for and justification of, growing privatisation in and of the PE curriculum 'space'.
- Teachers and teacher educators have a crucial role to play as "knowledge brokers" (Macdonald, 2015) in curriculum reform in PE.
- It is critical to consider continuities alongside changes in relation to PE curriculum. In particular, there is no guarantee that privatisations signal enhanced quality or greater equity in PE.

Reflective questions for discussion

1. What issues and developments discussed in this chapter appear familiar, or in contrast 'foreign'?
2. What key changes do you associate with (i) privatisation *in* PE, and (ii) privatisation *of* PE?
3. Who do you see as the 'major players' influencing curriculum reform in PE?; and what *discourses* are therefore being privileged or, in contrast, marginalised in PE curriculum development?
4. What do teachers need to know as "knowledge brokers" (Macdonald, 2015) working in increasingly complex PE curriculum networks?
5. What are the prospects for greater equity in contexts of increasing privatisations in and of PE curriculum?

Notes

1 Sport, Physical Activity and Recreation for Kids (SPARK) was developed at San Diego State University in the late 1980s and early 1990s, with the goals of combating rising levels of childhood obesity. See www.sparkpe.org/what-is-spark/.
2 OCR is the Oxford, Cambridge and RSA Examinations board; AQA is the Assessment and Qualifications Alliance; edexcel qualifications are now owned by Pearson; WJEC is the Welsh Joint Examination Council.

References

1st4sport.com. (2015). *New resources: Physical education core activities.* Retrieved from www.1st4sport.com/s-38-new-resources-physical-education-core-activities.aspx.

Abrahams, M., & Roberts, I. (2014). *Understanding the impact and value of engagement in the Association for Physical Education's Quality Mark Award.* Reading, UK: Association for Physical Education.

Ball, S. J. (1994). *Education reform: A critical and post-structuralist approach.* Buckingham; Philadelphia: Open University Press.

Ball, S. J. (2007). *Education plc. Understanding private sector participation in public sector education.* Abingdon, Oxon: Routledge.

Ball, S. J., & Junemann, C. (2012). *Networks, new governance and education.* Bristol: The Policy Press.

Ball, S. J., Maguire, M. & Braun, A., with Hoskins, K., & Perryman, J. (2012). *How schools do policy: Policy enactment in secondary schools.* Abingdon, Oxon: Routledge.

Bowe, R., Ball, S. J. & Gold, A. (Eds.). (1992). *Reforming education and changing schools: Case studies in policy sociology.* London: Routledge.

Brown, T. & Penney, D. (2016). Interpretation and enactment of Senior Secondary Physical Education: Pedagogic realities and the expression of Arnoldian dimensions of movement. *Physical Education and Sport Pedagogy,* DOI: 10.1080/17408989.2015.1123239.

Connelly, F. M., & Connelly, G. C. (2013). Curriculum policy guidelines. Context, structure and functions. In A. Luke, A. Woods & K. Weir (Eds.), *Curriculum syllabus design and equity: A primer and model* (pp. 54–73). New York: Routledge.

Dowda, M. C., Sallis, J. F., McKenzie, T. L., Rosengard, P. R. & Kohl, H. W. (2005). Evaluating the sustainability of SPARK physical education: A case study of translating research into practice. *Research Quarterly for Exercise and Sport, 76*, 11–19.

Evans, J., & Davies, B. (2015a). Physical education, privatisation and social justice. *Sport, Education and Society, 20*(1), 1–10.

Evans, J., & Davies, B. (2015b). Neoliberal freedoms, privatisation and the future of physical education. *Sport, Education and Society, 20*(1), 10–26.

Flintoff, A. (2003). The School Sport Co-ordinator Programme: Changing the role of the physical education teacher? *Sport Education and Society, 8*(2), 231–250.

Flintoff, A. (2008). Targeting Mr. Average: Participation, gender equity and school sport partnerships. *Sport, Education and Society, 13*(4), 393–411.

Griggs, G. (2008). Outsiders inside: The use of sports coaches in primary schools. *Physical Education Matters, 3*(1), 33–36.

Griggs, G. (2010). For sale – primary school physical education. £20 per hour or nearest offer. *Education 3-13: International Journal of Primary, Elementary and Early Years Education, 38*(1), 39–46.

Hatcher, R. (2000). Profit and power: Business and education action zones. *Education Review, 13*(1), 71–77.

Houlihan, B. (2000). Sporting excellence, schools and sports development: The politics of crowed policy spaces. *European Physical Education Review, 6*(2), 171–193.

Houlihan, B., & Green, M. (2006). The changing status of school sport and physical education: Explaining policy change. *Sport, Education and Society, 11*(1), 73–92.

Kirk, D. (1992). *Defining physical education: The social construction of a school subject in postwar Britain.* London: Falmer Press.

Kirk, D. (2006). The 'obesity crisis' and school physical education. *Sport, Education and Society, 11*(2), 121–133.

Lair, C. D. (2012). Outsourcing and the contracting of responsibility. *Sociological Inquiry, 82*(4), 557–577.

Lavin, J., Swindlehurst, G. & Foster, V. (2008). The use of coaches, adults supporting learning and teaching assistants in the teaching of physical education in the primary school. *Physical Education Matters,* Spring, ix–xi.

Leahy, D., Burrows, L., McCuaig, L., Wright, J. & Penney, D. (2016). *School health education in changing times: Curriculum, pedagogies and partnerships.* London: Routledge.

Luke, A., Woods, A. & Weir, K. (2013). Curriculum design, equity and the technical form of the curriculum. In A. Luke, A. Woods & K. Weir (Eds.), *Curriculum, syllabus design and equity: A primer and model* (pp. 6–39). New York: Routledge.

Macdonald, D. (2011). Like a fish in water: Physical Education policy and practice in the era of neoliberal globalization. *Quest, 63*(1), 36–45.

Macdonald, D. (2015). Teacher-as-knowledge-broker in a futures-oriented health and physical education. *Sport, Education and Society, 20*(1), 27–41.

Penney, D. (2013). From policy to pedagogy: Prudence and precariousness; actors and artefacts. *Asia-Pacific Journal of Health, Sport and Physical Education, 4*(2), 189–197.

Penney, D., & Evans, J. (1999). *Politics, policy and practice in physical education.* London: FN Spon, an Imprint of Routledge.

Penney, D., Petrie, K. & Fellows, S. (2015). HPE in Aotearoa New Zealand: The re-configuration of policy and pedagogic relations and privatization of curriculum and pedagogy. *Sport, Education and Society, 20*(1), 42–56.

Petrie, K., & lisahunter. (2011). Primary teachers, policy, and physical education. *European Physical Education Review, 17*(3), 325–339.

Petrie, K., Penney, D. & Fellows, S. (2014). Health and physical education in Aotearoa New Zealand: an open market and open doors? *Asia-Pacific Journal of Health, Sport and Physical Education, 5*(1), 19–38.

Powell, D. (2015). Assembling the privatisation of physical education and the 'inexpert' teacher. *Sport, Education and Society, 20*(1), 73–88.

Sallis, J. F., McKenzie, T. L., Alcaraz, J. E., Kolody, B., Faucette, N. & Hovell, M. F. (1997). The effects of a 2-year physical education program (SPARK) on physical activity and fitness in elementary school students. *American Journal of Public Health, 87*, 1328–1334.

Sallis, J. F., McKenzie, T. L., Kolody, B., Lewis, M., Marshall, S. & Rosengard, P. (1999). Effects of a health-related physical education on academic achievement: Project SPARK. *Research Quarterly for Exercise and Sport, 70*, 127–134.

Society of Health and Physical Educators [SHAPE America]. (2006). *Shape of the nation report: Status of physical education in the USA.* Reston, VA: SHAPE America.

Society of Health and Physical Educators [SHAPE America]. (2014). *National standards and grade-level outcomes for K-12 Physical Education.* Champaign, IL: Human Kinetics.

Thorburn, M., & Horrell, A. (2011). Power, control and professional influence: The curious case of Physical Education in Scotland. *Scottish Educational Review, 43*(2), 71–83.

Whitfield, D. (2001). *Public services or corporate welfare: Rethinking the nation state in the global economy.* London: Pluto Press.

Wilkinson, S. D., & Penney, D. (2015). The involvement of external agencies in extra-curricular physical education: Reinforcing or challenging gender and ability inequities? *Sport, Education and Society.* doi: 10.1080/13573322.2014.956714.

Williams, B., Hay, P. J., & Macdonald, D. (2011). The outsourcing of health, sport and physical education work: A state of play. *Physical Education and Sport Pedagogy, 16*(4), 399–416.

Williams, B. J., & Macdonald, D. (2015). Explaining outsourcing in health, sport and physical education. *Sport, Education and Society, 20*(1), 57–72.

UNESCO. (2015) *Quality physical education guidelines for policy-makers.* Paris: UNESCO.

12

CURRICULUM REFORM WHERE IT COUNTS

Kirsten Petrie, UNIVERSITY OF WAIKATO, NEW ZEALAND

As other chapters in this part of the handbook reaffirm, curriculum reform is a constant in educational settings, and can be viewed from a number of perspectives. Regardless of the sector of education we work in we have most likely all experienced curriculum reform associated with 'imposed change', or played a part in a complex process of negotiation between interested parties, be they government departments, school heads, boards of governors, classroom teachers, and parent communities (see Penney, Chapter 9). Curriculum reform can feel as if it has been imposed with haste and with what appears to be limited consultation or trialling, or it may seem to be advanced after an extensive and seemingly fraught period of negotiation between physical education (PE) experts, 'invested' outsiders, and government departments (as is often the case with national curriculum statements). In other instances, it may be a rich and fulfilling endeavour by a group of individuals trying to enact curriculum change at the local level. As Macdonald (2003) argued, and this chapter further reflects, whatever the origins or intentions of curriculum reform in PE it is teachers who are at the centre of curriculum reform, as they are responsible for the day-to-day implementation of any curriculum framework and requirements. From this perspective, curriculum reform happens daily in schools as teachers develop their own PE programmes, lessons, and assessment tasks in response to, and in the context of, various broader reform agendas and requirements (Ball, Maguire & Braun with Hoskins & Perryman, 2012; Priestley, 2011).

Given the centrality of the teachers amidst reform efforts, it would seem logical that teachers have a key role as drivers of any curriculum developments, regardless of the focus, object, rationale, scale of the reform. Kirk and Macdonald (2001, p. 565) posited:

> What might the consequences be for generating and then sustaining good practice if teachers were involved as partners, not only in the reform projects that produce new instructional discourse, but also in the maintenance of mandates during implementation?

In spite of this expressed desire to move beyond top-down approaches to curriculum reform, it would appear that teachers' roles in reform in PE have remained remarkably unchanged, and there has been little progress in effectively supporting teachers to be partners, let alone drivers of curriculum reform that has the potential to enhance equity and opportunities in PE. Why is this?

'Silencing' and/or 'sidelining' teachers

Over time and across continents the impetus, focus, object, rationale, and scale of curriculum reform can be seen to vary greatly, yet it would appear that teachers' roles in reform movements have remained remarkably unchanged (Calderhead, 2001). Current global and many national policy contexts appear to intensify conditions that preclude teachers from being heard in curriculum reform agendas and undermine their position and professionalism as 'curriculum reformists' (see below). Of course, the positioning and role of individual teachers of PE amidst reform varies significantly. Research into the life and career histories of PE teachers (Armour & Jones, 1998) illustrates how different cultural-discursive, material-economic, and social-political preconditions (Kemmis & Grootenboer, 2008) influence individual teachers. With that in mind it is important to caution against discussion of factors that impact on teachers' roles in curriculum reform as if teachers are a generic group. It is essential that as the reader, you remind yourself throughout the discussion that teachers operate across a spectrum of authority, involvement, and personal investment in curriculum reforms. In some instances teachers will be leading initiatives, in others they will be clearly recipients of reform. Furthermore, it is also important to acknowledge the inter-related nature of the many and ever changing factors in the complex landscape that is curriculum reform in PE. While I necessarily discuss factors independently, in reality they are intrinsically linked and operate collectively to mediate, shape, and form the praxis of teachers.

The policy context

Contemporary curriculum research in PE has increasingly directed attention to the significance of ideological and political contexts for reforms that have and may in the future be seen in PE. Neoliberal agendas, enacted differently in different educational contexts, are identified as permeating all aspects of education and PE (Macdonald, 2004, 2011; Pope, 2013). The Global Education Reform Movement (GERM) (Sahlberg, 2006), has directed attention to conditions that frame teachers' work, as practice in schools has become characterised by the marketisation of schools, performance pay, extensive accountability measures, charter schools, narrowing of curriculum, and productivity agendas. Many of these issues have been discussed in other chapters, however, it is important to briefly consider what they mean for teachers as curriculum reformists.

Teachers of PE face demanding reform agendas that are variously associated with curriculum, pedagogy, and assessment, whilst concurrently working in school settings that are persistently "being sucked into a vortex of endless demands, and reduced to a problem-solving institution to whose doors the social ills of society are laid" (Hopmann & Kunzli, 1997, pp. 259–260). This is evident internationally in PE curriculum reform with the extent of attention directed towards improved physical health outcomes associated particularly with nutrition and physical activity, and a parallel perpetual focus on enhancing sporting performance. In many parts of the western world, a focus on nutrition and physical activity in PE in response to claims and concerns associated with levels of childhood obesity has seen extensive investments made by governments into schools to help address this issue (Evans, Rich, Davies, & Allwood, 2008). The public health agenda places an impetus on teachers to get children 'more activity more often', and, furthermore, to ensure that children are monitored (by tools such as Fitnessgram) and that they self-monitor, as they 'learn' about nutrition, healthy eating, physical activity, and sport (Gard & Plium, 2014). Such reform agendas are arguably focused on finding superficial answers to complex questions, which shift attention away from local priorities and the specific needs of individual learners. Further, as highlighted in Chapter 11 (Penney & Mitchell) when frameworks for reform and for learning are increasingly determined by 'experts' outside of schools and/or outside of PE (for example: economists, epidemiologists, politicians), teachers become further sidelined from curriculum decision-making.

The neoliberal environment thus "increasingly encourages teachers [and arguably university-based researchers] to conceptualise their work in terms of what can be easily measured and quantified, and tend to value those things above the more complex, human dimensions of education practice" (Groundwater-Smith, Mitchell, Mockler, Ponte, & Ronnerman, 2012, p. 58). The dominant focus on accountability measures and the need for teachers and researchers to provide quantifiable evidence can profoundly affect educators' decisions about what matters most as they contemplate and/or respond to curriculum reform. Both the position of PE amidst wider reform and what is deemed important in PE, are prospectively impacted. The context that increasingly is reported as characterising education amidst neoliberalism is one that pressures teachers towards adopting the *policy* approach to reform that has become favoured by many governments; that is, teachers may resort to accepting standardised, decontextualised PE programmes and packages, at times offered by outside providers, in an endeavour to ensure that they and their students are 'measuring' up against the desired standards (see also Chapter 11, Penney & Mitchell). As highlighted by Petrie, Penney and Fellows (2014) in New Zealand, these developments have the potential to notably skew the direction of curriculum reform, narrow PE curriculum and precipitate disconnected programmes of learning that may do little to meet the unique needs of individual students.

Contexts of curriculum reform dominated by discourses of standards and performativity also carry very real possibilities of an escalation in performance anxieties amongst teachers as efforts to 'please' the head teacher (principal), board of governors or trustees, and/or education review offices contribute to a culture of compliance (Hargreaves & Goodson, 2006). Acting in agentic ways, thinking imaginatively about the needs of individual students and ensuring that there are more equitable opportunities for all learners in PE classes may be regarded as potentially a costly professional decision. Such approaches may jeopardise a teacher's ability to measure up against the outcomes privileged in 'quality teaching standards' and 'performance pay' principles. The political and policy context is thus fundamental in shaping the potential for teachers to opt to act as curriculum reformists in PE. Following Darling-Hammond (2011), Groundwater-Smith et al. (2012, p. 56) note that "punitive measures against teachers for perceived ineffectiveness and poor practice are unlikely to be as successful as generative professional learning in creating a strong and effective teaching profession" who feel empowered to lead, invest in, and engage with reform.

Whose 'knowledge' is valued in curriculum reform?

Countering the above emphasis is the recognition that teachers undoubtedly drive curriculum developments and decision-making in their own classroom, to construct curriculum that is localised and specific to their students' needs (Priestley, 2011). Many teachers actively seek out innovations to enhance their teaching and improve student learning in PE, they adopt or adapt new curriculum and pedagogical models, read material on the Internet, share ideas on social media, engage in teaching as inquiry or reflection, and introduce new activities to their curriculum. In doing so teachers generate their own theories about teaching and learning and, therefore, about what constitutes good practice in PE. Such 'bottom-up' approaches to curriculum reform are often reliant on individual teachers, whose agency in their own classrooms infrequently translates into changing the nature of PE beyond their own school gates.

Curriculum reform at this level is frequently viewed as practical knowledge, or "knowledge *in* practice" (Cochran-Smith & Lytle, 1999, p. 250). This notion appears to place teacher driven reform as inferior to more highly valued theoretical or formal knowledge, "knowledge *for* practice" (Cochran-Smith & Lytle, 1999, p. 250), generated by university-based researchers and government departments. Not only is the latter knowledge the predominant source of 'information' drawn on in the development of many curriculum reform agendas, it also positions teachers as recipients and consumers of information that will enable them to implement change and improve their understandings and practices. As such, teachers are then expected to deliver a curriculum constructed by agents and agencies external to the school context (Penney, 2006). As Ball et al. (2012) suggest: "Teachers, and an increasingly diverse cast of 'other adults' working in and around schools, not to mention students, are written out of the policy process or rendered simply as ciphers who '*implement*' " (p. 2, emphasis added).

Research within and beyond PE continues to point to teachers' role in curriculum reform as that of recipients and implementers of 'well meaning' and 'evidenced-based' curriculum initiatives, with an underlying suggestion that many teachers do not have the knowledge to engage in curriculum planning (Ward & Doutis, 1999) as their expertise does not extend beyond the knowledge of their local context students, school, and resources (Kirk & Macdonald, 2001). A 'divide' thus characterises the conception, process, and experience of much curriculum reform in PE – as opposed to an emphasis upon working in ways that draw on the collective knowledge of all members to the education community.

While teachers' voices may not be privileged in many official curriculum reforms in PE, in most instances teachers get opportunities to provide feedback on draft policy documents, and some may have opportunities to act as members of panels or advisory groups that inform developments. Teachers are thus typically 'consulted' on and about reform, but many questions remain, including – how many teachers are given or take up the opportunity to engage in the dialogue associated with reform and in what ways? And when they do engage, are they listened to?

Curriculum reform as a transaction

As other chapters in this handbook discuss, professional learning can be framed in many ways. It is something that, arguably, demands more critical attention in relation to curriculum reform in PE. Under the guise of professional learning work between university-based or government-based 'experts' and schools, PE curriculum reforms are, in many instances, essentially 'dumped' on teachers as 'experts' share new knowledge about curriculum models, and improved approaches to assessment and pedagogical approaches. These professional learning opportunities often take the form of abbreviated workshops or once/year professional development days framed around somewhat disjointed topics – often sponsored by school district administrators (Armour & Yelling, 2004; Macdonald, 2004). Teachers gravitate to these simplistic reform efforts in search of the next new idea, game, ready-made lesson, possibly as a pragmatic response to workload pressures (Petrie, 2012), and because such 'reform' efforts are less threatening as they do not challenge the status quo. Such approaches suggest that curriculum reform is linear and transactional, that is, 'new' knowledge is directly 'sold' to teachers ready for enactment.

The processes associated with the development and dissemination of many curriculum reform materials openly reaffirm transactional or linear thinking about knowledge relations and curriculum reform and, in so doing, marginalise teachers and teachers' knowledge. From this perspective, materials developed by university or government-based 'experts' are passed down to teachers 'with support' that it is envisaged will allow them to adapt them "for their local context" (Kirk & Macdonald, 2001, p. 565). As discussed further in Penney and Mitchell (Chapter 11) an array of other 'experts' are now active in the development of curriculum reform materials that 'support' delivery of PE in schools (Penney, Petrie, & Fellows, 2015; Powell, 2014; Powell & Gard, 2014; Williams, Hay, & Macdonald, 2011). This research highlights that the transactional nature of such reform activities carries the potential to exacerbate the narrowing and commodification of PE curriculum around a fixed body of knowledge and skills (that is more likely to fit within dominant physical health and sporting discourses) with limited reference to local contexts. It arguably signals a move towards curriculum reform that sees PE becoming increasingly standardised, formulaic, and quantifiable – especially when we consider that pre-packaged resources, designed to support teachers to reform PE curriculum, pedagogy, and assessment are employed and adopted by teachers "as a practical and sensible solution to the problem of curriculum time, resources, and 'skills' " (Apple & Jungerk, 1990, p. 248), and in some sectors a lack of confidence. The use of such materials, provided by 'experts' and designed in ways to support the curriculum reform and the 'reskilling' of teachers, can thus work to deskill the teachers (Apple, 1982; Smyth, Dow, Hattam, Reid, & Shacklock, 2000) as they divorce the conceptualisation of the resource from the delivery or execution. As the transactional approach and neoliberal context combine, teachers' abilities to adapt resources to their local contexts and the needs of their learners are marginalised or eroded, and large-scale national agendas take precedence. For PE curriculum reform, the danger is that teachers' contextual work will become less relevant, and their knowledge of individual learning needs will count for very little. Furthermore, the transactional approach does little to advance collaborative or significant reform in PE curriculum.

Space and time to think 'reformatively'

As discussed above, political and economic forces drive a reform movement that places schools in a constant state of flux and correspondingly teachers on a treadmill of change. It is important to reiterate that teachers are not only dealing with reform directly concerned with curriculum, pedagogy, and/or assessment. They are simultaneously working in school contexts that are being reshaped by a multitude of reform agendas, many of which at first glance may appear to sit outside of the 'core business' of PE curriculum, but can easily morph into daily responsibilities. As Ball et al. (2012) highlight, teachers are variously charged with contributing to and implementing policies and associated with national assessment programmes (National Standards, Senior Subject Qualifications), mental health, school uniforms, break times, and behaviour management. All schools are also grappling with broader curriculum reform initiatives, such as eLearning, student-centred pedagogies, culturally responsive pedagogies, and engaging student voice. The multitude of reform initiatives facing teachers is accentuated in many primary school settings, where classroom generalist teachers are expected to engage not only with PE developments, but also curriculum reform associated with all other learning areas. It is not surprising, then, that teachers of PE are at times overwhelmed by expectations to engage and contribute to 'reform'. What matters most, what initiatives should be priorities, and how does all of this get balanced against the imperative to raise performance? What are the incentives and possibilities for teachers to invest in generating curriculum reform in PE?

Agency, infidelity, and slippage

Even when "policies 'done' in schools are 'written' by governments, their agencies or other influential stakeholders" (Ball et al., 2012, p. 2) teachers demonstrate their agency as they act in resistance to the prescribed reform. Teachers' agency is expressed in all attempts to interpret, contest, and adapt curriculum policy in ways that have meaning for them and their learners. These responses further reflect recognition of the need to reshape and contextualise curriculum reform in response to multiple aspects of context – including the physical spaces and resources available, the diverse culture and social context of school communities, and the human capital to support reform efforts. At times such efforts have been seen as teachers being unfaithful or demonstrating infidelity to curriculum reform initiatives, reinforcing the low status accorded to teachers' knowledge and skills in relation to reform. Yet, as Ball et al.'s (2012, p. 3) recent work has highlighted, policy texts – and more specifically, curriculum texts, "have to be translated from text to action – put 'into' practice – in relation to history and to context, with the resources available", by teachers. Teacher agency is then, integral and essential to curriculum reform that will be contextually appropriate and effective. Hence, there are significant problems in framing the notion of "slippage" (Bowe & Ball with Gold, 1992; Penney & Evans, 1999) as inherently problematic or a shortcoming amidst curriculum reform endeavours. What works in one context, with one group of learners, may turn out to be a disaster in another. Therefore, in contrast to teachers being unfaithful to 'mandated' curriculum reforms in PE, agency in adaptation to meet the needs of learners in any specific context, can be seen as a central facet of teacher professionalism.

This is of course a very teacher centric view, so it is important to also note that teachers speak back to policy through their actions for a diverse range of reasons, some personal, others professional. As long as there are teachers willing to try new things and to learn with colleagues as part of their work as teachers, there will also be teachers who never engage with reform or innovation, and/or who actively find ways to accommodate reforms within unchanged curriculum and pedagogical practice as documented by Curtner-Smith (1999). Amidst any externally driven reform in PE, there will always be teachers who 'do what they have always done', some who will align with visions for quality and equity, and some who will not (see Chapter 13, Wilkinson). Alongside this, and in an education landscape in which performativity is rewarded, we are, however, more likely to see teachers 'playing the system' and adopting possibly questionable practices. This has become evident in the USA in relation to standardised test scores, with entire districts 'fudging' results to evidence 'enhanced' student achievement (Nichols & Berliner, 2007). While addressing issues of teacher performance is beyond the scope of this chapter, it is important to be conscious of how reform agendas, especially those fostered by neoliberal discourses, may influence professional cultures, teachers' actions, and the scope and expression of agency in relation to PE curriculum reform.

Centring teachers as leaders in curriculum reform

The nature of many reform efforts means that the relationship between practitioners and policy makers is destined to remain complex. Yet, as long as teachers are silenced or sidelined in and amidst talk of curriculum reform in PE, there will be limited opportunities for teachers of PE to be drivers of curriculum reforms that make a meaningful difference for learners beyond their own classrooms. As Macdonald (2003) and Penney (2006) have previously discussed, there is a need to move from conceptualisations of curriculum reform as top-down or bottom-up and, instead, look to partnership approaches, that "contribute to educator-driven, educator-directed and educator-led arrangements and which, in turn, we argue, nurture informed and strategic change" (Kemmis et al., 2014, p. 179). There is then, the opportunity to dissolve the theory practice dualism, and work in and for curriculum reform in PE in ways that allow "legitimate theory building [to] occur at the intersection of university and school sites of practices" (Groundwater-Smith et al., 2012, p. 16).

There is, however, a dearth of literature in the field of PE about how curriculum reform can be generated alongside collaborative non-hierarchical partnership approaches. The early work of Tinning, Macdonald, Tregenza, and Boustead (1996) went some way to attempting to utilise action research as a professional development approach and subsequently curriculum change. Since then there has been a growing body of evidence demonstrating collaborative approaches to professional learning in PE, where community of learners include both university-based lecturers and teachers in schools (see Chapter 10 by Jess and Gray). Yet there is still limited evidence of such approaches being adopted as part of system-level programmes of PE curriculum reform where teachers are positioned as curriculum developers and leaders, as opposed to implementers. Here it is also important to note that a collaborative practitioner research focused approach to curriculum reform that is underpinned by commitments to dissolve historic knowledge hierarchies, may constitute a valuable professional learning opportunity both for university partners and school-based practitioners. The sections that follow extend theoretical and empirical insights into such an approach.

Future directions: collaborative practitioner research

Collaborative (critical, transformative, action) practitioner research can be viewed as a way to support teachers to be drivers of and partners in curriculum reform. Building on the traditions of action research, Kemmis et al. (2014), Groundwater-Smith, et al. (2012), and Coburn and Stein (2010) amongst others, continue to progress the notion of collaborative research approaches, that involve the academy working to support teachers to take ownership and develop their capacity as curriculum drivers and researchers in their own right. The emergent and iterative nature of collaborative practitioner research (Paulus, Woodside, & Ziegler, 2008) is underpinned by "the assumption that inquiry is an integral, not separate, part of practice, and that learning from practice is an essential task of practitioners" (Cochran-Smith & Donnell, 2006, p. 509). The adoption of a collaborative practitioner research framework to curriculum reform thus provides a space to explore PE curriculum in ways that are organic, systematic, participatory, emancipatory, and driven by shared desires to problematise, whilst working toward collective decision-making. Curriculum reform that is undertaken within a culture of collaboration and where critical colleagueship (Lord, 1994) underpins practice has the potential to generate new dialogue and theorising about PE curriculum in schools. Groundwater-Smith et al. (2012, p. 79) explain that a "collaborative and critical perspective, means that through inquiry, meetings and discussions, teachers become aware of trends and policy shifts that are happening around them and can take up an activist perspective by broadening their decision-making and scope of action". The approach also aligns closely with the notion of a community of practice (Lave & Wenger, 1991) that has been adopted as a model to support the professional learning of teachers of PE. In addition, the philosophies that underpin Kaupapa Māori research (Bishop, 1998; Smith, 1999, 2005) as a model of respectful collaborative, culturally responsive, and respectful partnerships are useful to consider amidst efforts to advance curriculum reform from a collaborative standpoint. As the following section emphasises, a collaborative practitioner research approach rejects views of curriculum reform as neat, transactional, or linear. Instead the research and curriculum reform process is both fluid and messy.

Collaborative practitioner research and curriculum reform in practice

While within the PE community there is extensive evidence of research that has problematised practice (Evans, Davies, & Wright, 2004; Gard, 2011; Wright, Macdonald, & Burrows, 2004), it is significantly more challenging to find evidence of collaborative practitioner research being utilised to inform PE curriculum reform, development, and implementation. In the USA, and drawing from the collective work of Coburn and Stein (2010), there seems to be a push for collaborative curriculum reform models where university researchers design curriculum (programmes and/or resources) and then work with teachers to trial the 'reform' and make modifications to improve the product, before sharing it with others. In the USA and elsewhere, protocols have reflected a need for the process and impact of curriculum reforms to be scientifically measurable and replicable for the purposes of up-scaling. These agendas have similarly shaped reform efforts elsewhere, for example, in research directed towards the reform of assessment practices in senior secondary PE in Western Australia (Penney, Jones, Newhouse, & Campbell, 2012).

In other examples from the USA (Engle, 2010; Gosin, Dustman, Drapeau, & Harthun, 2003) teachers' work is posited as more central to the reform, as they partner with academic researchers to 'solve the problems' that have been predetermined by the 'academic' partners. Teachers are partners, and to some extent there is evidence of transformation of practice, however, it appears to be within bounds of achieving a predetermined purpose or as respondents to predesigned materials, and enacted in ways that the teachers are still to some extent 'subservient' to the expertise of others. As Kemmis (2006) cautions, we need to be wary of *inadequate action research*, where practitioner research is used as an implementation tool to get teachers and students to conform to particular notions of schooling, and to reinforce particular or narrow notions of PE curriculum, pedagogies, or assessments. Groundwater-Smith et al. (2012) stress that "the very act of engaging in critical or transformative practitioner research is thus to swim against the tide of current global discourses in education" (p. 58). This is of course not easy to accomplish, especially amidst research and/or professional learning aligned to implementation phases of curriculum reform. A further challenge internationally, is that in order to get research funding that allows for the sustained time needed to undertake collaborative practitioner research, projects have to align with state agendas and requirements, over and above localised classroom needs. Discussion in other chapters in this section illustrates that some efforts are nevertheless being made to build elements of resistance into such alignment and to pursue reform agendas that go beyond seeking 'quick fix' solutions to complex issues and dilemmas. The following section serves to highlight that the *ways* in which we seek to do this are as critical as the intent. It illustrates a collaborative practitioner research framework being used to develop 'new' understandings that are contextualised, localised, framed alongside social justice agendas, and with a desire to ensure educational opportunities cater to diverse needs.

Reimagining health and physical education in New Zealand primary schools

My own work (Petrie, Burrows, & Cosgriff, 2014; Petrie et al., 2013) with partners from academia and local schools goes some way to demonstrating how collaborative practitioner research can place teachers at the centre of curriculum reform. Notions of collaborative practitioner research and the *Teaching as Inquiry* process outlined in *The New Zealand Curriculum* (NZC) (Ministry of Education, 2007, p. 35), were tools used to help us make sense of current practice and refocus teaching and learning in health and physical education (HPE) to better reflect the needs and interests of all learners. This project provided an opportunity to reimagine what was taught in primary school HPE and engage in what could be regarded as 'radical' curriculum reform within the broad frame of HPE as conceptualised and presented in the NZC. Four primary school teachers joined with three university lecturers to build knowledge about current practices in HPE, expand repertoires, and reconstruct practice, before implementing and evaluating innovative HPE approaches in their classrooms. Teacher and student interviews and in class tasks prompted collective concerns about students' narrow conceptions about health, physical activity, and bodily appearance, raising questions about the role current HPE practices in schools play in contributing to these perspectives. This led us to question what we teach in the name of HPE, why we teach it, and how we teach it. In reforming the curriculum we collectively wanted to explore ways to better support the diverse needs of *all* learners and challenge students and ourselves to think and do differently in relation to HPE. To support this process it was necessary to establish conditions that gave all partners the space to engage in reflective dialogue. Our collective efforts to reform curriculum thus relied on:

- time to talk, think, discuss, debate and imagine;
- respectful partnerships where the shared expertise of all team members was acknowledged and drawn on;
- awareness of how our view of teaching and learning is influenced by our own assumptions, values, and beliefs, as well as the complexity of the landscapes in which we work;
- living with the discomfort of not knowing, and therefore being willing to grapple with, question, and dither about what teaching and learning in PE could become.

As this work has been disseminated some have queried the depth of change, or ask if the same would be possible with a different group of teachers or on a bigger scale. Others have suggested that it was a professional development activity as opposed to a collaborative research programme. Others may query it being foregrounded in relation to discussion of curriculum reform. Yet, we contend that a key to the shifts in thinking and practice evidenced in this research, demonstrate how collaborative practitioner research is professional learning and development for all partners and, furthermore, can undoubtedly facilitate curriculum reform. We learnt from each other, and in doing so were able to collectively come to new and richer understandings of PE curriculum and practice. Our curriculum reform agenda was a collective action, in response to the contextual needs of students and the local communities in which we work. Such work was not based on the premise that the 'experts' told teachers the answer(s). Rather, the research process involved a constant reshuffling of roles. The university partners became co-teachers, resource suppliers, and sounding boards for new ideas, and the teachers became both the generators and collectors of data, practitioner researchers, and activist professionals. In utilising this approach "we have taken the time to grapple with the discomfort of not knowing, engage in reflective dialogue, talking and dithering, and come to a place of reconfiguring and reimagining HPE together" (Petrie, Burrows, et al., 2014, p. 54). Our reimagining has made for significant shifts in how we all view what constitutes quality HPE for learners in primary school settings, and how this 'new curriculum' can be enacted in ways that ensure more equitable outcomes for all students. Sadly, while a range of attempts have been made to disseminate our learning to practitioner audiences (see Duggan, 2013; Keown & Petrie, 2013; Naera, 2013; Petrie with Devcich, 2013), the status of HPE in our communities remains limited by the demands of performative agendas associated with numeracy and literacy standards. In this context, the impact of this curriculum reformation has had limited extension beyond local schools.

Facilitating curriculum reform grounded in collaborative practitioner research

Collaborative practitioner research as a model of curriculum reform, requires education 'leaders' with the skills and willingness to do partnership in genuine and ethical ways that meaningfully supports teachers as drivers of curriculum reform, and that is effective in creating equitable learning opportunities for students of PE. Transformative, emancipatory partnerships between university researchers and teachers require a move beyond notions of privileging 'academic' theory and knowing over practice-informed theories generated by teachers. It also requires a move beyond simplistic, transactional, linear conceptualisations of curriculum reform. Arguably both shifts should be easy for a PE community that to a significant extent has prided itself on adopting a socio-critical perspective, and as seeking to ensure that practices in PE are equitable, contextually relevant, and meaningful for diverse learners and communities. What knowledge and therefore whose voices counts in relation to curriculum reform thus remains a critical issue for the field as it does for education more broadly (Ball, 1990; Ball et al., 2012). We cannot seek to suggest partnership is the way forward when we continue to create and legitimate hierarchies of knowledge in the way we speak of curriculum and reform. Future reform efforts must, therefore, position and seek to strengthen PE teaching as a research informed and a research informing profession, where teachers are both generators and utilisers of research (Lingard & Renshaw, 2010).

There are a growing number of texts and journal publications (for starters see Coburn & Stein, 2010; Cochran-Smith & Donnell, 2006; Groundwater-Smith et al., 2012; Kemmis et al., 2014; Locke, Alcorn, & O'Neill, 2013) available to assist teachers of PE and university partners to position themselves as curriculum reformists. Across these there are some guiding principles (listed below) that facilitators of research directed towards curriculum reform need to attend to in their efforts to undertake Collaborative Practitioner Research that 'makes a difference'. Furthermore, responsibility rests with the instigator/s of any reform agenda to consider what they can do to ensure that the process is one of collaborative co-construction that values the knowledge of all, and that keeps equity issues to the fore talk about of curriculum reform in PE (see Chapter 13, Wilkinson).

1. All partners value the *shared expertise* of the group, respecting each other's knowledge and experiences, and are willing to engage in learning with each other. In doing so there is scope for strengthening each other's position by building and enhancing relations.
2. Interventionist models with predetermined outcomes determined by academics are parked in favour of *listening to local concerns*. The challenge is "how best to address the difficult work of challenging accepted practices in order to develop the conditions that can genuinely enrich teachers' learners, rather than simply managing them to a predetermined solution" (Groundwater-Smith et al., 2012, p. 88).
3. Decisions are made *collegially*. This can only occur when partnerships are founded on genuine relationships, where there is an ongoing process of respectful negotiation and re-negotiation, and fortified by rapport and trust. This is key to fostering confidence and capacity in the use of teacher professional judgement, grounded in robust professional knowledge.
4. There is an atmosphere where practical as well as theoretical knowledge is acknowledged and valued. *Reciprocity* allows practitioners to challenge academic partners about theories and research, while academics can query practitioners' practice knowledge. Together there is the scope to develop knowledge of practice (Cochran-Smith & Lytle, 1999), when partners possess the ability to ask questions that are respectful, and yet challenging.

5. Members of the partnership are selected with care. It is necessary to ensure that each person has *a disposition and the capacity to be respectful of others*. This will require a concentrated effort to ensure that academic researchers, as partners, are not condescending of teachers and their work, but instead can demonstrate relational practice that enables others, and which supports a move beyond transactional models of working.

6. Explore opportunities to incorporate people who are not already perceived as experts in the field as they may provide fresh ideas in the process of challenging discourses that pervade the 'known' ways of thinking and doing in PE. This has the potential to create generative partnerships and allow for new ways of thinking that expand narrow perspectives.

7. Act as an *outstanding academic partner* (Ewing et al., 2010). This requires university partners to: give generously of their time and demonstrate a commitment to the school and projects; take the time to understand how schools operate; adopt a critical stance as opposed to pushing one agenda; demonstrate a willingness to provide learning opportunities (timely, contextualised) for team members and others; question their own sense of powerlessness and query our ethics around power relations (Locke et al., 2013); and, finally, have the quality and magnitude of professional knowledge relevant to project and translatable in local context. Such an approach will provide a platform for the academic partner to shift between the roles of expert, learner, mentor, and critical friend.

Summary of key findings

Teachers continue to be positioned as implementers, as opposed to developers, of curriculum reform by a range of contextual barriers including global reform movements, government and school policies and practice, teachers' status as knowledge generators, and curriculum reform process. The silencing of teachers in curriculum reform limits teacher agency and the potential for curriculum development that is contextually and culturally relevant. A Collaborative Practitioner Research approach, based on genuine non-hierarchical partnerships, presents an opportunity to reconceptualise how curriculum reform occurs in ways that are transformative and emancipatory for all. Education policy makers must reconsider ways of working with teachers to ensure teachers feel valued and motivated to engage and spend precious energy on this laborious task of curriculum reform. Reforming our own practices, as curriculum developers, would help counter teacher peripherality in PE curriculum reform agendas.

Reflective questions for discussion

1. What drives curriculum reform? The needs of the students, the local community, national, or global interests?
2. Who drives curriculum reform? Whose voices are really valued in curriculum reforms at school, local, or national level – where are teachers' and student voices?
3. Whose knowledge counts in this curriculum reform and therefore, how genuine is the 'partnership'?
4. What does contextually relevant curriculum reform entail?
5. What does it take to operate effectively as a partner in curriculum reform efforts?

References

Apple, M.W. (1982). *Education and power.* Boston: Routledge & Kegan Paul.

Apple, M., & Jungerk, S. (1990). 'You don't have to be a teacher to teach this unit': Teaching, technology, and gender in the classroom. *American Educational Research Journal, 27*(2), 227–251.

Armour, K. M., & Jones, R. L. (1998). *Physical education teachers' lives and careers: PE, sport and educational status.* London: Falmer Press.

Armour, K., & Yelling, M. (2004). Continuing professional development for experienced physical education teachers: Towards effective provision. *Sport, Education and Society, 9*(1), 95–114.

Ball, S. (1990). *Politics and policy making: Explorations in policy sociology.* London: Routledge.

Ball, S. J., Maguire, M., Braun, A., with Hoskins, K., & Perryman, J. (2012). *How schools do policy: Policy enactment in secondary schools.* Abingdon, Oxon: Routledge.

Bishop, R. (1998). Freeing ourselves from neo-colonial domination in research: A Maori approach to creating knowledge. *International Journal of Qualitative Studies in Education, 11*(2), 199–219.

Bowe, R., Ball, S., with Gold, A. (1992). *Reforming education and changing schools: Case studies in policy sociology.* London: Routledge.

Calderhead, J. (2001). International experiences of teaching reform. In V. Richardson (Ed.), *Handbook of research on teaching* (4th ed., pp. 777–802). Washington, D.C.: American Educational Research Association.

Coburn, C. E., & Stein, M. K. (Eds.). (2010). *Research and practice in education: Building alliances, bridging the divide.* New York: Rowman & Littlefield Publishers.

Cochran-Smith, M., & Donnell, K. (2006). Practitioner inquiry: Blurring the boundaries of research and practice. In J. L. Green, G. Camilli, & P. B. Elmore (Eds.), *Handbook of complementary methods in education research* (pp. 503–517). Washington, D.C.: Lawrence Erlbaum Associates; Published for the American Educational Research Association.

Cochran-Smith, M., & Lytle, S. L. (1999). Relationships of knowledge and practice: Teacher learning in communities. *Review of Research in Education, 24*(1), 249–305.

Curtner-Smith, M. (1999). The more things change the more they stay the same: Factors influencing teachers' interpretations and delivery of national curriculum physical education. *Sport, Education and Society, 4*(1), 75–97.

Darling-Hammond, L. (2011). *The flat world and education, 2011, John Dewey memorial lecture.* Paper presented at the annual conference of the Association for Supervision and Curriculum Development, San Francisco.

Duggan, D. (2013). Moving beyond the cringe: Planning with purpose. *Journal of Physical Education in New Zealand, 46*(2), 23–24.

Engle, R. (2010). The Middle-School Mathematics through Applications Project: Supporting productive collaborations during two different phases of curriculum design. In C. E. Coburn & M. K. Stein (Eds.), *Research and practice in education: Building alliances, bridging the divide* (pp. 19–35). New York: Rowman & Littlefield Publishers.

Evans, J., Davies, B., & Wright, J. (Eds.). (2004). *Body knowledge and control: Studies in the sociology of physical education and health.* London: Routledge.

Evans, J., Rich, E., Davies, B., & Allwood, R. (2008). *Education, disordered eating and obesity discourse: Fat fabrications.* New York: Routledge.

Ewing, R., Groundwater-Smith, S., Mockler, N., Loughland, T., Simpson, A., Smith, D., … Brooks, D. (2010). *Meta analysis of quality teaching action learning project.* Sydney: University of Sydney.

Gard, M. (2011). *The end of the obesity epidemic.* London: Routledge.

Gard, M., & Plium, C. (2014). *Schools and public health: Past, present, future.* Lanham, MD: Lexington Books.

Gosin, M. N., Dustman, P. A., Drapeau, A. E., & Harthun, M. L. (2003). Participatory action research: Creating an effective prevention curriculum for adolescents in the Southwestern US. *Health Education Research, 18*(3), 363–379.

Groundwater-Smith, S., Mitchell, J., Mockler, N., Ponte, P., & Ronnerman, K. (2012). *Facilitating practitioner research: Developing transformational partnerships.* Abingdon, Oxon: Routledge.

Hargreaves, A., & Goodson, I. (2006). Educational change over time? The sustainability and nonsustainability of three decades of secondary school change and continuity. *Educational Administration Quarterly, 42*(1), 3–41.

Hopmann, S., & Kunzli, R. (1997). OP-ED close our schools! Against current trends in policy making, educational theory and curriculum studies. *Journal of Curriculum Studies, 29*(3), 259–266.

Kemmis, S. (2006). Participatory action research and the public sphere. *Educational Action Research*, *14*(4), 459–476.

Kemmis, S., & Grootenboer, P. (2008). Situating praxis in practice. In S. Kemmis & T. Smith (Eds.), *Enabling praxis: Challenges for education* (Vol. 1, pp. 37–62). Rotterdam: Sense Publishers.

Kemmis, S., Wilkinson, J., Edwards-Groves, C., Hardy, I., Grootenboer, P., & Bristol, L. (2014). *Changing practices, changing education*. Singapore: Springer.

Keown, S., & Petrie, K. (2013). Making physical education a positive experience for all: A primary school teachers' perspective. *Physical Education Matters*, *8*(2), 50–52.

Kirk, D., & MacDonald, D. (2001). Teacher voice and ownership of curriculum change. *Journal of Curriculum Studies*, *33*(5), 551–567.

Lave, J., & Wenger, E. (1991). *Situated learning: Legitimate peripheral participation*. Cambridge, UK: Cambridge University Press.

Lingard, B., & Renshaw, P. (2010). Teaching as a research-informed and research-informing profession. In A. Campbell & S. Groundwater-Smith (Eds.), *Connecting inquiry and professional learning in education* (pp. 26–39). London: Routledge.

Locke, T., Alcorn, N., & O'Neill, J. (2013). Ethical issues in collaborative action research. *Educational Action Research*, *21*(1), 107–123.

Lord, B. (1994). Teachers' professional development: Critical colleagueship and the role of professional communities. In N. Cobb (Ed.), *The future of education: Perspectives on national standards in education* (pp. 175–204). Michigan: College Entrance Examination Board, The University of Michigan.

Macdonald, D. (2003). Curriculum change and the post modern world: Is the school curriculum-reform movement an anachronism? *Journal of Curriculum Studies*, *35*(2), 139–149.

Macdonald, D. (2004). Curriculum change in health and physical education: The devil's perspective. *Journal of Physical Education New Zealand*, *37*(1), 70–83.

Macdonald, D. (2011). Like a fish in water: Physical education policy and practice in the era of neoliberal globalization. *Quest*, *63*(1), 36–45.

Ministry of Education. (2007). *The New Zealand Curriculum*. Wellington, New Zealand: Learning Media.

Naera, J. (2013). Searching for the 'wiggle-room': Negotiating the non-negotiate in primary schools. *Principals Today*, *97*, 16–17.

Nichols, S. L., & Berliner, D. C. (2007). *Collateral damage: How high-stakes testing corrupts America's schools*. Cambridge, MA: Harvard Education Press.

Paulus, T., Woodside, M., & Ziegler, M. (2008). Extending the conversation: Qualitative research as dialogic collaborative process. *The Qualitative Report*, *13*(2), 226–243.

Penney, D. (2006). Curriculum construction and change. In D. Kirk, D. Macdonald, & M. O'Sullivan (Eds.), *The handbook of physical education* (pp. 565–579). London: Sage.

Penney, D., & Evans, J. (1999). *Politics, policy and practice in physical education*: London: E & FN Spon.

Penney, D., Jones, A., Newhouse, P., & Campbell, A. (2012). Developing a digital assessment in senior secondary physical education. *Physical Education and Sport Pedagogy*, *17*(4), 383–410.

Penney, D., Petrie, K., & Fellows, S. (2015). HPE in Aotearoa New Zealand: The reconfiguration of policy and pedagogic relations and privatisation of curriculum and pedagogy. *Sport, Education and Society*, *20*(1), 42–56.

Petrie, K. (2012). Enabling or limiting: The role of pre-packaged curriculum resources in shaping teacher learning. *Asia-Pacific Journal of Health, Sport and Physical Education*, *3*(1), 15–32.

Petrie, K., Burrows, L., & Cosgriff, M. (2014). Building a community of collaborative inquiry: A pathway to re-imagining practice in health and physical education. *Australian Journal of Teacher Education*, *39*(2), 45–57.

Petrie, K., Burrows, L., Cosgriff, M., Keown, S., Naera, J., Duggan, D., & Devcich, J. (2013). *Everybody counts? Reimagining health and physical education in primary schools*. Wellington, New Zealand: Teaching Learning Research Initiative.

Petrie, K., with Devcich, J. (2013). Re-visioning what it means to be active: An interview. *Journal of Physical Education New Zealand*, *46*(1), 16–17.

Petrie, K., Penney, D., & Fellows, S. (2014). Health and physical education in Aotearoa New Zealand: An open market and open doors? *Asia-Pacific Journal of Health, Sport and Physical Education*, *5*(1), 19–38.

Pope, C. (2013). The jagged edge and the changing shape of health and physical education in Aotearoa New Zealand. *Physical Education and Sport Pedagogy*, *19*(5), 500–511.

Powell, D. (2014). Assembling the privatisation of physical education and the 'inexpert' teacher. *Sport, Education and Society*, *20*(1), 73–88.

Powell, D., & Gard, M. (2014). The governmentality of childhood obesity: Coca-Cola, public health and primary schools. *Discourse: Studies in the Cultural Politics of Education, 36*(6), 854–867.

Priestley, M. (2011). Schools, teachers, and curriculum change: A balancing act? *Journal of Educational Change, 12*(1), 1–23.

Sahlberg, P. (2006). Education reform for raising economic competitiveness. *Journal of Educational Change, 7*(4), 259–287.

Smith, L. T. (1999). *Decolonizing methodologies: Research and indigenous peoples.* London/Dunedin, New Zealand: Zed books and University of Otago Press.

Smith, L. T. (2005). Building a research agenda for indigenous epistemologies and education. *Anthropology & Education Quarterly, 36*(1), 93–95.

Smyth, J., Dow, A., Hattam, R., Reid, A., & Shacklock, G. (2000). *Teachers' work in a globalizing economy.* London: Falmer Press.

Tinning, R., Macdonald, D., Tregenza, K., & Boustead, J. (1996). Action research and the professional development of teachers in the health and physical education field: The Australian NPDP experience. *Educational Action Research, 4*(3), 389–405.

Ward, P., & Doutis, P. (1999). Toward a consolidation of the knowledge base for reform in physical education. *Journal of Teaching in Physical Education, 18*(4), 382–402.

Williams, B., Hay, P., & Macdonald, D. (2011). The outsourcing of health, sport and physical educational work: A state of play. *Physical Education & Sport Pedagogy, 16*(4), 399–415.

Wright, J., Macdonald, D., & Burrows, L. (Eds.). (2004). *Critical inquiry and problem-solving in physical education.* London: Routledge.

13

EQUITY AND INEQUITY AMIDST CURRICULUM REFORM

Shaun D. Wilkinson, NORTHUMBRIA UNIVERSITY – NEWCASTLE, UK

Equity and inequity have long been a focus of attention in physical education (PE) and are matters often at the fore in discussions about curriculum reform (e.g. Australian Government, 2014; Daipi, 2004; Department for Education [DfE], 2014). Inequities in education, sport, health and/ or wider society may all underpin calls for curriculum reforms in education as a whole, or in PE specifically. In parallel, curriculum reforms continue to be critiqued in terms of their direct and indirect consequences for equity (e.g. Curtner-Smith, 1999; Penney & Evans, 1999). Talk of developing and enacting PE curriculum in ways that will advance and support greater equity is, therefore, not new. Such talk remains, however, characterised by the use of a variety of terms that have different meanings in international educational policy discourse, and that highlight that equity is not straightforward to address. This chapter therefore opens by examining key terms and constructs. Discussing equity, equality and inclusion reaffirms the need to interrogate the particular understandings of terms, and the social and political agendas that are reflected in curriculum reforms and curriculum research in PE.

As Penney discusses in Chapter 9, curriculum reform is always to some extent a product of history, but also something that is fundamental in shaping the future of PE. The second section of this chapter therefore connects historical insights with some of the contemporary issues and curriculum reform agendas that are being pursued internationally in PE. I examine a number of 'landmark reforms' in education and PE to illustrate particular trends, shifting foci and changing understandings of equity being expressed in different contexts. Discussion reflects a concern to move beyond rhetoric in considering equity in PE, and critically engage with the direct and subtle ways in which the interface between policy texts and contexts play out in practice to variously support or inhibit equity in PE. Attention then turns to theoretical resources and perspectives that have variously informed approaches to equity research in the field over time, their respective merits, apparent limitations and the advances in understanding that they have provided. I discuss the different contributions that social constructivist, socio-cultural, feminist, post-structural and socio-critical scholarship in PE have provided to understandings of equity. This provides a basis from which to critically review current trends and issues pertaining to equity and inequities amidst curriculum reforms in PE. I reaffirm that how equity is conceptualised in curriculum developments, and similarly, in research, is key to understanding what aspects of practice will be challenged or in contrast, left untouched – and, as a consequence, continue to be legitimated. I apply findings and conclusions from this review to consider implications for evidence-based policy development and professional practice in PE. The final sections of the chapter address potential directions for future research and practice that will support further advances in equity, and recall key findings.

Restrictions of space mean that I address selected issues, developments and perspectives. Throughout, I endeavour to illustrate the cross-cultural and international relevance of the various topics, equity-driven reforms and research insights that are explored. At the same time, I stress that particular cultural, social and policy contexts are always important to consider. Hence, I encourage readers to critically reflect on the specificities of their context from professional, social, cultural, political and historical perspectives, as they attempt to relate to the findings reported.

Equality, equity and inclusion: contested terms and social constructs

This section examines three key constructs that feature in policy and curriculum developments in PE internationally: equality, equity and inclusion. Distinguishing and defining the terms is a challenging undertaking, and one that, arguably, we cannot expect agreement upon. Indeed, while the concepts enjoy considerable currency in the PE literature and explicitly feature in a raft of educational policy reforms bearing on PE worldwide, they also have a long and contested history. This spans political, policy, professional and research arenas that pertain to PE and reflects differing interests in and perspectives on inclusion, equality and/or equity. Over 20 years ago, Evans and Davies (1993, p. 12) highlighted that, "their meanings are conveniently transient and depend upon the specifics of social, political or fiscal interests which dominate political or educational contexts of the day. Because they derive their agendas from and are used in such contexts they are inevitably contested." Accordingly, this chapter emphasises the need to appreciate the subtleties, nuances and distinctions between the terms as used over time and within any specific context of educational policy-making, professional practice, and research internationally.

In education and PE, *equality* has typically referred to all people being treated the same, with equality therefore tending to be defined as a technical concern with the distribution of opportunities amongst different social groups (Evans & Davies, 1986, 1993). This pretence of 'equal treatment' has been contested, with attention directed to the limits of claimed equality in relation to both 'access' and 'opportunity'. The emphasis is that a focus on uniformity fails to recognise that not all students are equally disposed or resourced to relate to, for example, the curriculum on offer. Nor are they equally able to take advantage of ostensibly egalitarian education or PE environments. In simple terms, talk of equality that is framed in terms of ensuring that all students have access to a particular set of PE curriculum and/or co-curricular experiences fails to engage with the differentiated nature of students' individual engagement with, and experiences of, curriculum. Contemporary educational rhetoric has begun to acknowledge the shortcomings of technical definitions of, and approaches to, 'equality' and 'equal opportunity'. For example, the recent Gonski Review of Funding for Schooling in Australia (Gonski et al., 2011) noted that promoting greater educational equality of opportunity does not imply that all students should be treated in the same way, but rather, that students need to be treated differently to equalise educational opportunities. Similarly, the Equality Act in England noted that some people may need extra help to get equal chances (DfE, 2014). From an equity perspective, the significant feature of both these recent developments is that positive engagement with difference is recognised as fundamental to creating situations in which all students have equal chances and/or opportunities in education. The discourse employed has a qualitative dimension and positions a notion of fairness aligned with social justice as at the heart of *equity* as a construct (Evans & Davies, 1986, 1993).

Once again, I stress that perspectives on equity vary and, accordingly, so too do definitions of it, and approaches to, it. The Organisation for Economic Co-operation and Development's [OECD] (2012) stance on equity is, however, a significant international reference point. Notably, the OECD also draws links between equity, fairness and inclusion, in stating that: "Equity in education means that personal or social circumstances such as gender, ethnic origin or family background, are not obstacles to achieving educational potential (fairness) and that all individuals reach at least a basic minimum level of skills (inclusion)" (p. 9). This stance challenges us to critically reflect on the obstacles that curriculum reforms associated with PE have focused attention on, with what effect, and to also consider what should be recognised as a basic minimum level of skill in PE.

In the PE field, Stidder and Hayes (2013, p. 9) have summarised equity in education in terms of "fairness and respect for all pupils where forms of oppression and discrimination are removed from the classroom setting". Sections below pursue the forms of oppression and discrimination that have been acknowledged in curriculum reforms in PE and that feature in contemporary debates, and critically examine the role of curriculum reform in seeking their 'removal' from PE lessons. The many issues associated with trying to 'deliver' both fairness and inclusion either through or amidst curriculum reform in PE are very evident. In relation to inclusion, a focus on "ensuring a minimum standard of education for all" (Gonski et al., 2011, p. 105) differs markedly to the use of inclusion (particularly in the US) centring on disabled children, and others identified as having 'special educational needs' [SEN] in mainstream educational contexts. Inclusion interpreted more broadly has extended this vision to "those regarded as being at educational risk due to marginalisation as a result of minority group status" (Forlin, 2004, p. 187), and increasingly to the aim of maximising educational opportunities for 'all' students. For example, the Ministry of Education in New Zealand [MoE-NZ] explicitly identified the revised curriculum as inclusive in the sense that it "is non-sexist, non-racist, and non-discriminatory" and "it ensures that students' identities, languages, abilities, and talents are recognised and affirmed and that their learning needs are addressed" (MoE-NZ, 2007, p. 9). Developments elsewhere, including, for example, Singapore (e.g. Daipi, 2004), England (e.g. DfE, 2013), Australia (e.g. Australian Government, 2014) and Canada (e.g. MoE-C, 2014), similarly foreground a desire to ensure that 'all' students, irrespective of their background, ability or circumstances, have the opportunity to learn and succeed in education. Subsequent sections therefore adopt this broad stance on inclusion. Amidst enduring political demands for inclusion, equity and equality of access and/or opportunity in education systems worldwide, discussion first provides a historical perspective, looking at selected developments in PE curriculum from an equity perspective.

The historical context: curriculum and equity-driven reforms in physical education

Over time, numerous reforms have aimed at ensuring equality and/or equitable experiences for students in PE internationally. I focus on specific policy developments that can be regarded as 'landmarks' for PE in curriculum terms, and that illustrate complexity and ongoing uncertainty in relation to the meanings being given to equity in PE. The examples that follow affirm that equality, equity and inclusion are fluid concepts and contested issues. They illustrate that curriculum reforms are at times clear responses to broader social and political shifts in thinking about equity and that, in other instances, the impact of reforms prompt fresh thinking and renewed debate about equity in PE.

Title IX

In 1972, amidst feminist activism, the United States [US] Congress passed Title IX of the Educational Amendments [herein Title IX] to the 1964 Civil Rights Act. Its passage brought about the first US federal law to mandate gender equality in all areas of public education, including PE. Title IX stated that "no person in the United States shall, on the basis of sex, be excluded from participation in, be denied the benefits of, or be subjected to discrimination under any education program or activity receiving federal financial assistance" (United States Department of Labor, 2007). Title IX can be understood as a liberal feminist initiative, underpinned by an assumption that equality for girls and women could be achieved through legal means and social reform, with a prime focus on changing existing structures and institutional policies so that opportunities and resources may be shared more equally between girls/women and boys/men. Hence, for PE in many US middle and high schools, a direct implication of Title IX was a legal requirement to restructure the provision of curriculum from gender-segregated classes to mixed-sex groups, except in relation to contact sports. As I discuss further below, this consequence of Title IX cannot be assumed as universally positive for girls or boys with various levels of ability in PE. Title IX also denied cultural differences, with it assumed that once girls experienced equal opportunity with respect to curriculum, instruction and expectations for performance in gender-integrated PE classes, an increase in opportunities to learn and develop their skills would follow (Nilges, 1998; Vertinsky, 1992). More recent theoretical and empirical work in PE (e.g. Azzarito, 2012; Evans & Bairner, 2013; Flintoff & Scraton, 2001; Paechter, 2003) highlights that this position failed to take into account the marginalisation and disadvantage that some students will experience amidst dominant ideologies of masculinity and femininity. It similarly overlooked that resources, abilities and previous experiences are all distributed differently among individuals within any social or cultural group, as well as between groups – and all of these factors can impact opportunities and experiences. Hence, although mixed-sex grouping was deemed fundamental to the provision of a gender-equitable PE program, as Scraton (1986, p. 89) trenchantly observed, "not only is equal access problematic for girls, while stereotypes of masculinity and femininity prevail, but there is a danger that these stereotypes will be reinforced by giving equal access to an unequal situation". Vertinsky (1992) reported that coeducational PE classes proved to be no panacea and were to a large extent an invitation to girls to participate in 'the PE of boys'. Indeed, amidst 'reform' a focus on performance in 'traditional' team sports as a basis of the PE curriculum was not challenged by Title IX. This characteristic in itself has been associated with disadvantage for girls amidst demands for fairness based on equality, and as the next example highlights, has been challenged internationally from an equity perspective (see below).

The National Curriculum for Physical Education in England and Wales

In England and Wales, the development of a National Curriculum, arising from the Education Reform Act [ERA] in 1988, was heralded as a significant step towards providing equality of opportunity for all children in government funded education (Penney, 2002). The ERA established access to a National Curriculum that would include PE as a constituent of the core curriculum, as a statutory entitlement for all students in government funded schools in England and Wales. In this sense, it was a landmark reform. The introduction of a National Curriculum for PE [NCPE] in 1992 (DfE/Welsh Office, 1992) officially and forcefully established the principle of an equal opportunity for students to access a 'broad and balanced' PE curriculum, encompassing varied areas of activity. Yet, research informed by education policy sociology (see below) revealed the NCPE and its definition of 'breadth and balance' in curriculum as reflecting central government's view of PE as synonymous with particular forms of sport and, more specifically, as continuing to legitimate the primacy of 'traditional' games in PE curriculum (Graham with Tytler, 1993; Penney & Evans, 1999; Williams & Woodhouse, 1996). This orientation towards a 'sport-based' PE curriculum remains prominent. A feature of the most recent NCPE, introduced by the coalition government in September 2014, is a continued emphasis, amongst other things, on developing physical competence and excellence in competitive team sports/games in schools (DfE, 2013).

Penney and Evans' (1999) research clearly evidenced that as a curriculum frame, the NCPE was openly designed to accommodate notable differences in PE curriculum provision both within and between schools. Seemingly sound arguments underpin such flexibility in curriculum requirements associated with reforms on this scale, not least that schools and teachers must be able to align curriculum with varied contexts and needs. Yet, research focusing on the NCPE (e.g. Curtner-Smith, 1999; Flintoff & Scraton, 2001; Kenway, Willis, Blackmore, & Rennie, 1998; Penney & Evans, 1999; Williams & Bedward, 2001) highlighted that flexibility amidst reform also meant that inequities in breadth and quality of experience and long-standing practices of sex-differentiated PE, could continue, as could the privileging of a school curriculum that had greater relevance to boys than to girls and which reflected a particular and Eurocentric version of physical activity.

In revisions to the NCPE (e.g. DfE, 1995; Department for Education and Employment/ Qualifications and Curriculum Authority [DfEE/QCA], 1999; QCA, 2007), successive texts have featured stronger and broader positioning of notions of equality of opportunity and inclusion, that acknowledge multiple categories of oppression such as gender and disability while recognising their overlap and inter-connectedness. The 1999 and 2007 orders, for example, included both general and subject specific inclusion statements reflecting a desire to meet the specific needs of students from an intersection of marginalised groups.

Amidst National Curriculum 'reforms' and broader United Kingdom [UK] government policy statements of a commitment to social inclusion, however, evidence of widespread change in the curriculum and pedagogies of PE has remained elusive. Stidder (2013, p. 26) asserts that the introduction of the NCPE "was an opportunity for PE teachers to move beyond conventional approaches and re-define the way in which boys and girls experienced their PE lessons in schools". Yet, in the overwhelming majority of schools in England and Wales, competitive sports and team games continue to dominate the PE curriculum (Quick, Simon & Thornton, 2010), and traditionally gender-demarcated patterns of provision remain largely unaltered in many contemporary secondary school contexts (Green, 2008). Curtner-Smith (1999) and Penney and Evans's (1999) research specifically highlighted that the flexibility inherent in official curriculum policy enabled 'new curriculum' to be adapted and accommodated within established practice and ideologies. In some instances, therefore, 'implementation' of the NCPE saw a continuation of boys and girls being given access to a separate and different PE curriculum, each reflecting traditional stereotypical perceptions of gender. According to Green, Smith, Thurston and Lamb (2007, p. 68), this outcome "is unsurprising given that contemporary PE is built on a history of sex segregation", with traditions becoming embedded as legitimate practice: "distinct male and female traditions expressed in quasi separate girls' and boys' departments, teaching differing activities to sex-specific teaching groups and holding, by degrees, differing perceptions regarding suitable content and teaching methods". The history that Green et al. (2007) refer to can similarly be viewed as limiting in relation to concerns for PE curriculum to reflect and respond to cultural and ethnic diversity. In this regard, the NCPE curriculum requirements largely reaffirmed a historical vision of PE curriculum that was culturally narrow – or certainly, left things open enough for monocultural interpretation to prevail (Figueroa, 1993). Like Title IX, the NCPE thus reaffirms history as critical to understanding the advances and limits to equity that are associated with any official curriculum reform. Figueroa's (1993, p. 100) observation that for those teachers "committed to multicultural, antiracist, and equal opportunities education", "ambiguities" in official curriculum texts "provide some openings", is an important reminder of the central role that teachers play in curriculum reform and in relation to equity in PE (see also Chapter 12 by Petrie).

Reforming physical education and school sport: PESSCL and PESSYP

The Physical Education and School Sport Club Links [PESSCL] and Physical Education and Sport Strategy for Young People [PESSYP] in England and Wales, strictly speaking, are not 'curriculum' reforms. However, they are notable examples of policy developments that have had clear implications for PE curriculum, and that have impacted on the context in which National Curriculum policy is understood and enacted. Discussion thus reaffirms that curriculum reform in PE needs to always be located in relation to broad policy contexts and political agendas that extend beyond education. It also supports the proposition developed in more depth in Chapter 11 (Penney & Mitchell), that curriculum reform in PE is being driven to an important extent from 'the outside in'.

The national PESSCL (Department for Education and Skills/Department for Culture, Media and Sport [DfES/DCMS], 2003) and PESSYP (Youth Sport Trust, 2009) strategies represented unprecedented UK government investment in provision of PE and sport for young people. Centring on investment in 'partnership-based' models of provision of PE and school sport [PESS], the initiatives openly spanned the education and sport policy boundaries, but also directly connected with the UK government's wider policy of social inclusion. The explicit intent was to encourage more young people to participate in structured sport and physical activity opportunities, particularly those from groups who have previously been under-represented (Flintoff, 2003). Research (e.g. Flintoff, 2008; Green, 2008; Wilkinson & Penney, 2014) has, however, called into question whether such provision serves to challenge or reaffirm discourses and practices that legitimate and contribute to the ongoing perpetuation of inequities in PE, physical activity and sport. Indeed, notwithstanding the underlying emphasis on social inclusion within PESSCL and PESSYP, Flintoff's (2008) research centring on school sport partnerships drew attention to the significance of pedagogy in relation to the prospect that coaching sessions for schoolchildren would express discourses of inclusion. Green (2008) and Wilkinson and Penney (2014) have also noted that discourses of sporting excellence and/or competitive sport tend to provide the dominant frame for commercial sports coaches' involvement in provision of physical activity opportunities in schools, and may act to deflect educational priorities and concerns to extend equity.

Green (2008), Flintoff (2008) and Wilkinson and Penney's (2014) research highlights that it cannot be assumed that new initiatives centring on 'partnership-based' development of PE and/ or sport in schools, will signal a move towards greater inclusivity and/or equity. More specifically, the reforms appear to have done little to challenge a long-established discourse of 'more of the same for the more able' associated with the organisation and delivery of extra-curricular PE and sport (e.g. Penney & Harris, 1997). As I discuss further below, narrow conceptualisations of 'ability' in PE remain an important source of inequity. In this regard, it is notable that the PESSCL strategy included a distinct 'Gifted and Talented' work strand, explicitly aimed at recognising, supporting and developing talented young "sports people" (DfES/DCMS, 2003, p. 1). As Penney and Evans (2013) have highlighted, critical issues to consider amidst such developments are who is identified as 'gifted and talented' in contexts of PE and/or school sport, and what, specifically, the initiatives advocate for in relation to provision for 'gifted and talented' students.

Theoretical perspectives and shifting views on equity and curriculum reform

Previous sections have reflected that over time, various theoretical perspectives have informed research addressing curriculum reform and equity in PE. This section points to some of the shifts in theoretical thinking over time and the issues that these have brought to the fore. The above discussion of research insights associated with Title IX and the NCPE to some extent reflected the prominence of feminist scholarship in the field, placing relations and differences between women/girls and men/boys at the centre of analysis, and positioning gender as a key dimension of overall identity and a determinant of behaviour. Messner and Sabo (1990, p. 1) remind us, however, that "there is no single feminist school of thought but rather a multifaceted mosaic of feminist visions and practices". The 'mosaic' is clearly evident in research in PE that has used various feminist perspectives and concepts to consider, for example, how PE and sport discourses shape and regulate how girls experience their bodies (e.g. Oliver & Lalik, 2001, 2004a), the hidden curriculum as a 'gender' issue (e.g. Bain, 1986; Varpalotai, 1987) and students' constructions of masculinity and femininity (e.g. Nilges, 1998; Paechter, 2003). As a central focus in wider feminist research in PE and critical analysis of curriculum reform, the hidden curriculum directs attention to implicit, unconscious ways in which students come to learn knowledge, attitudes, values, norms and assumptions (Nutt & Clarke, 2002). It is a theoretical construct that focuses on implicit messages conveyed in and through the daily routines and rituals of PE teachers' pedagogic practice, and grounded in the structure and content of curriculum. From an equity perspective, it gives visibility to 'taken-for-granted' assumptions, educational processes and practices that continue to generate and legitimate inequity in PE. Research by Varpalotai (1987) in Canada and Bain (1986) in the US, for example, highlighted how the hidden curriculum, embedded in curricula and practice, transmits powerful implicit gender-related messages to girls and boys about participation, behaviour, capabilities, masculinity and femininity. Other, more recent studies (e.g. Azzarito, 2012; Wilkinson & Penney, 2014) have similarly documented how the hidden curriculum expressed in and through the gender-differentiated patterns of provision in PE perpetuate inequities by maintaining girls'/boys' marginal engagement with stereotypically masculine/feminine team games in the curriculum. Accordingly, we see that gender-based distinctions in PE curriculum may discourage and ultimately suppress boys and girls from opportunities to explore and reconstruct alternative expressions of physical and gender identity – identities which step outside of and cross traditional stereotypical polarities and boundaries of masculinity and femininity. In essence, as Wilkinson and Penney (2014, p. 5) have noted, "participation in activities that continue to have an underlying association with culturally dominant versions of femininity or masculinity is far from value free".

Feminist perspectives continue to evolve. Influenced particularly by the critiques of black and disabled feminists (e.g. Lloyd, 1992; Mirza, 1997), the use of the category 'boy'/'girl' or other universalistic terms including 'black' or 'disability' are now recognised as highly problematic, and unitary notions or categories of oppression and, similarly, 'single issue' analyses, are increasingly challenged (e.g. Flintoff, Fitzgerald & Scraton, 2008). As Penney and Evans (2002) observed, historically, much of the feminist and critical research on equity and PE has tended to take such an approach, focusing, for example, on gender, race, class and sexuality as essentially discrete social categories. The contrasting position that they advocated for acknowledges the complexities inherent in multiple identities and subjectivities. From this intersectional perspective, students' gendered identities are understood as intertwined with, and simultaneously mediated by, other intersecting or cross-cutting social identities including class, age, race, ethnicity, ability, disability, sexuality, and other specificities, and gender is conceptualised as a dynamic, fluid and relational category related to other aspects of identity (Azzarito & Solmon, 2005; Flintoff et al., 2008).

Recent work has begun to respond to calls to expand theoretical understandings of 'difference' and provide more comprehensive and nuanced perspectives on the ways students' lived experiences of PE – and, furthermore, curriculum reform efforts, are differentially mediated by their multiple identities. For example, Hay and Macdonald (2010a, 2010b) explored how the interrelated influences of ability, gender and social class impacted on students' sense of self, potential achievement and learning opportunities within senior secondary PE. Fitzgerald's (2005) analyses of the embodied experiences of young disabled people within a PESS context revealed how orthodox conceptions of ability in PE run counter to the ways in which dominant notions of disability are recognised and understood. Research by Azzarito (2012) and Oliver and Lalik (2004b) in the US, and Hill (2013) and Kay (2006) in England, has revealed how racialised and cultural aspects of gender relations impact on how boys and girls experience their bodies and Western models of PE and physical activity. Elsewhere, O'Flynn's (2010) analysis of an elite school and a government school in Australia, points to the ways particular 'classed' subjectivities are discursively reproduced and reaffirmed in relation to participation in and provision of sport and physical activity in particular school settings. The challenges that findings such as this present for future research are considered below.

Equity, inclusion and reform in physical education: trends and issues

As already illustrated, research shows that notable historical traditions and established ways of thinking about and enacting curriculum invariably prevail in PE, despite, and to some extent because of, curriculum 'reforms'. From an equity perspective, curriculum stability remains an important ongoing trend in PE and an important issue to engage with.

> For all the talk of reform in PE in England and Wales and elsewhere, we can reflect that in important respects very little has changed in the curricula and pedagogies of PE. Notable inequities have been sustained not only in 'official' policy documents, but also in their implementation. (Penney & Evans, 1999, p. 138)

As indicated above, flexibility embedded in curriculum reform stands out as enabling the accommodation of new requirements within unchanged and potentially inequitable practice. Preceding discussion has also highlighted the potential for cultural narrowness and gender inequity to continue to be legitimated by curriculum that features and values a limited range of movement contexts, skills and knowledge. Chapter 11 (Penney & Mitchell) discusses a growing body of research that reveals that changing contexts and policy relations are shaping curriculum reform in PE and/or the conditions in which responses are formulated by schools and teachers (Penney, Petrie & Fellows, 2015). Both policy texts and policy contexts can thus be seen as contributing to an ongoing acceptance and dominance of sport and physical activity discourses as the prime point of reference for PE curriculum. Irrespective of whether they are stimulated by educational or other agencies (see Penney & Mitchell, Chapter 11) there is little evidence that curriculum reforms are embedding requirements that actively extend notions of ability in PE. Hunter's (2004, p. 181) comment that the "discursive space of the good student in PE is shaped by characteristics of competence, competition, comparison, display, skill, and fitness" within a context of PE as sport, highlights the implications for learning and learners. Alternative, culturally distinct and/or creative, aesthetic and non-performance aspects of movement educa-tion are marginalised and effectively disregarded as valuable – they do not contribute to one's recognition as 'able'. This exclusionary consequence of curriculum – that it is restrictive in the abilities that it acknowledges, is now well documented (e.g. Evans, 2004; Fitzgerald, 2005; Hay & Macdonald, 2010a, 2010b).

Taking a broader view, differences in the quality and scope of curriculum provision continue amidst reforms, and it remains the case that students are differently positioned to benefit from the 'opportunities' provided. In this regard, PE curriculum and reforms remain largely blind to (or in denial of) social inequities beyond schools. As Evans and Bairner (2013) have illustrated, the playing field beyond schools is far from 'level' and without acknowledgement of social dis-advantage, curriculum reform in PE is destined to perpetuate current inequities in society.

Implications and challenges for evidence-based policy and practice

Preceding sections have raised many issues for curriculum authorities, teachers, teacher educa-tors and researchers to consider. In focusing on the implications of theoretical and empirical insights, Evans and Davies' (1993, p. 18–19) comments on equity are a good starting point: "the issue must not be whether differences can be dissolved … but how they can be celebrated in ways which negate prejudice and stereotyping and at the same time respect individual cul-tural identity". Adopting this stance, and in the light of findings highlighted thus far, a number of challenges are evident. PE curriculum reform clearly needs to start from a more sophisti-cated understanding of difference/s in PE (informed by notions of intersectionality) and those developing official curriculum frameworks and interpreting them need to consider ways in which reform can enable and celebrate the expression of a greater range of identities and abil-ities in PE. Physical educationalists internationally need to work collectively to generate more practical examples of curriculum structures, requirements and practices that explicitly seek to do this. Future reform also needs to commit to equity being at the fore of aligned thinking and requirements relating to curriculum, pedagogy and assessment (see Penney, Chapter 9). Assessment, particularly, is a prospectively powerful avenue via which to push for greater equity in educational experiences and achievement (e.g. Hay & Penney, 2013). The OECD'S (2012, p. 9) emphasis that in education systems characterised by quality and equity "the vast majority of students have the opportunity to attain high level skills, regardless of their own personal and socio-economic circumstances", has further implications for curriculum reform in PE. Perhaps most contentious is the challenge to reach agreement upon the PE 'skill set' that should be an entitlement for all students. That agreement is a necessary prerequisite to future curriculum re-form directed towards the 'quality and equity' that the OECD advocates for.

Future directions for curriculum policy, practice and research

As mentioned in the theoretical perspectives section of this chapter, researchers in PE have begun to respond to calls for an intersectional approach to understanding the complexities of students' lived and differentiated experiences in and of PE. Despite a growing body of em-pirical work, however, gaps remain in our understanding of the ways curriculum reform and enactment in schools impact students' *multiple* identities, especially in contexts of PESS. For ex-ample, with exceptions (e.g. Azzarito, 2012; Oliver & Lalik, 2004b; Wilkinson & Penney, 2014), the hidden curriculum in PE has typically been reported as 'a gender issue'. Further research exploring the complexities of other aspects of students' identity and the ways in which they intersect with gender would be a welcome addition in extending analyses of the perspectives of young people to find out more about their experiences of reform associated with PESS. As Chapter 11 (Penney & Mitchell) reflects, another area worthy of further research is the 'outsourcing' of PESS. Indeed, in England and Wales, Central Europe, Australia, New Zealand as elsewhere, the services of 'external' providers, most notably peripatetic sports coaches, commercial and non-commercial sporting organisations, and sports clubs in the community, are integral to the provision of PE, physical activity and/or sport within and beyond the curriculum. Developments have signalled new policy and curriculum relations and the impact of these shifting relations in equity terms is undoubtedly important for future research to pursue.

Summary of key findings

- Curtner-Smith (1999) and Penney and Evans (1999) provided vivid insight into the frequently reported gap between policy rhetoric and the realities of curriculum reform in PE. Their research serves as a salutary reminder that educational policy legislation, in itself, does not automatically affect a shift in teachers' perspectives and ideologies. Accordingly, 'reforms' alone may yield few changes in either forms of curriculum organisation, content and pedagogic practice.
- Research has highlighted that the sex-differentiated structure of PE (e.g. Nutt & Clarke, 2002), PESS as a policy space (Penney & Evans, 1999) and the policy trend towards increased use of 'external' resources and coaches being central to provision of sport in schools (e.g. Flintoff, 2008), can all reaffirm discourses and practices that legitimate and contribute to the ongoing perpetuation of longstanding inequities that arise from narrow conceptualisations of ability, masculinity and femininity.
- Research in England (e.g. Evans, 2004; Fitzgerald, 2005) and Australia (e.g. Hay & Macdonald, 2010a, 2010b) has revealed that many students are designated as low ability in PE, not because they lack ability per se, but rather because their interests and abilities are marginalised by systems of judgement and curriculum that are not inclusive of diverse abilities – and that remain unchallenged by 'reforms'.

Reflective questions for discussion

The following questions prompt readers and/or practitioners to critically reflect on the material presented with a view to extending their capacity to maximise the opportunities that curriculum reform presents to advance equity in PE.

1. How can we create a curriculum that is more inclusive for students from all social groups? What are the strengths and limitations of using the notion of 'social group' as a starting point for thinking about equity and curriculum reform?
2. What changes to content would shape a 'more inclusive' PE curriculum? Why?
3. How has PE's association with sport and particularly 'traditional games' impacted on how ability is viewed? What evidence do you have for this?
4. What curriculum directions are emerging from, or reinforced by, 'partnership-based' delivery models in PE, or by the outsourcing of PE? Are these developments extending PE learning opportunities for all students?
5. What is being learnt through the hidden curriculum in PE and what are the effects of this learning?

References

Australian Government. (2014). *Review of the Australian curriculum*. Retrieved 13 October 2014 from https://docs.education.gov.au/system/files/doc/other/review_of_the_national_curriculum_final_report.pdf.

Azzarito, L. (2012). 'I've lost my football...': rethinking gender, the hidden curriculum, and sport in the global context. In S. Dagkas & K. M. Armour (Eds.), *Inclusion and exclusion through youth sport* (pp. 72–86). London: Routledge.

Azzarito, A., & Solomon, M. A. (2005). A reconceptualization of physical education: The intersection of gender/race/social class. *Sport, Education and Society*, 10(1), 25–47.

Bain, L. L. (1986). Description of the hidden curriculum in secondary physical education. *Research Quarterly*, 47(2), 154–160.

Curtner-Smith, M. D. (1999). The more things change the more they stay the same: Factors influencing teachers' interpretations and delivery of National Curriculum Physical Education. *Sport, Education and Society*, 4(1), 75–95.

Daipi, H. (2004). *Singapore's journey to 'inclusive education'*. A speech presented at Ministerial Forum on child-friendly learning environments. Retrieved 15 October 2014 from www.moe.gov.sg/speeches/2004/sp20040526.htm.

Department for Education. (1995). *Physical education in the National Curriculum*. London: HMSO.

Department for Education. (2013). *Reform of the National Curriculum in England*. Retrieved 15 October 2014 from www.ism.org/.../National_Curriculum_-_consultation_document.pdf.

Department for Education. (2014). *The Equality Act 2010 and schools*. Retrieved 15 October 2014 from www.gov.uk/government/uploads/system/uploads/attachment_data/file/315587/Equality_Act_Advice_Final.pdf.

Department for Education/Welsh Office. (1992). *Physical education for ages 5 to 16: Final report of the National Curriculum Physical Education working group*. London: HMSO.

Department for Education and Employment/Qualifications and Curriculum Authority. (1999). *Physical education: The National Curriculum for England*. London: HMSO.

Department for Education and Skills/Department for Culture, Media and Sport. (2003). *Learning through PE and school sport: A guide to the physical education, school sport and club links strategy*. Nottinghamshire: Author.

Evans, J. (2004). Making a difference? Education and 'ability' in physical education. *European Physical Education Review*, 10(1), 95–108.

Evans, J., & Bairner, A. (2013). Physical education and social class. In G. Stidder & S. Hayes (Eds.), *Equity and inclusion in physical education and sport* (pp. 141–159). London: Routledge.

Evans, J., & Davies, B. (1986). Sociology, schooling and physical education. In J. Evans (Ed.), *Physical education, sport and schooling: Studies in the sociology of physical education* (pp. 11–37). London: Falmer Press.

Evans, J., & Davies, B. (1993). Equality, equity and physical education. In J. Evans (Ed.), *Equality, education and physical education* (pp. 11–27). London: Falmer Press.

Figueroa, P. (1993). Equality, multiculturalism, antiracism and physical education in the National Curriculum. In J. Evans (Ed.), *Equality, education and physical education* (pp. 90–104). London: Falmer Press.

Fitzgerald, H. (2005). Still feeling like a spare piece of luggage? Embodied experiences of (dis)ability in physical education and school sport. *Physical Education and Sport Pedagogy*, 10(1), 41–59.

Flintoff, A. (2003). The school sport co-ordinator programme: Changing the role of the physical education teacher? *Sport, Education and Society*, 8(2), 231–250.

Flintoff, A. (2008). Targeting Mr. Average: Participation, gender equity and school sport partnerships. *Sport, Education and Society*, 13(4), 393–411.

Flintoff, A., Fitzgerald, H. & Scraton, S. (2008). The challenges of intersectionality: Researching difference in physical education. *International Studies in Sociology of Education*, 18(2), 73–85.

Flintoff, A., & Scraton, S. (2001). Stepping into active leisure? Young women's perceptions of active lifestyles and their experiences of school physical education. *Sport, Education and Society*, 6(1), 5–21.

Forlin, C. (2004). Promoting inclusivity in Western Australian schools. *International Journal of Inclusive Education*, 8(2), 185–202.

Gonski, D., Boston, K., Greiner, K., Lawrence, C., Scales, B. & Tannock, P. (2011). *Review of funding for schooling – final report*. Canberra, Australia: Department of Education, Employment and Workplace Relations.

Graham, D. with Tytler, D. (1993). *A lesson for us all: The making of the National Curriculum*. London: Routledge.

Green, K. (2008). *Understanding physical education*. London: Sage.

Green, K., Smith, A., Thurston, M. & Lamb, K. (2007). Gender and secondary school National Curriculum Physical Education: Change alongside continuity. In I. Wellard (Ed.), *Rethinking gender and youth sport* (pp. 68–83). London: Routledge.

Hay, P. J., & Macdonald, D. (2010a). The gendering of abilities in Senior PE. *Physical Education and Sport Pedagogy*, 15(3), 271–285.

Hay, P. J., & Macdonald, D. (2010b). Evidence for the social construction of ability in physical education. *Sport, Education and Society*, 15(1), 1–18.

Hay, P. J., & Penney, D. (2013). *Assessment in physical education: A sociocultural perspective*. London: Routledge.

Hill, J. (2013). 'If you miss the ball, you look like a total muppet!' Boys investing in their bodies in physical education and sport. *Sport, Education and Society*, 20(6), 762–779.

Hunter, L. (2004). Bourdieu and the social space of the PE class: Reproduction of Doxa through practice. *Sport, Education and Society*, 9(2), 175–192.

Kay, T. (2006). Daughters of Islam: Family influences on Muslim young women's participation in sport. *International Review for the Sociology of Sport*, 41(3), 357–373.

Kenway, J., Willis, S., Blackmore, J. & Rennie, L. (1998). *Answering back: Girls, boys and feminism in schools*. London: Routledge.

Lloyd, M. (1992). Does she boil eggs? Towards a feminist model of disability. *Disability and Society*, 7(3), 207–221.

Messner, M. A., & Sabo, D. F. (1990). Introduction: Toward a critical feminist reappraisal of sport, men, and the gender order. In M. A. Messner & D. F. Sabo (Eds.), *Sport, men and the gender order* (pp. 1–16). Champaign, IL: Human Kinetics.

Ministry of Education. (2007). *The New Zealand curriculum*. Wellington: Learning Media.

Ministry of Education. (2014). *Equity and inclusive education in Ontario schools*. Retrieved 15 October 2014 from www.edu.gov.on.ca/eng/policyfunding/inclusiveguide.pdf.

Mirza, H. (1997). *Black British feminism: A reader*. London: Routledge.

Nilges, L. M. (1998). I thought only fairy tales had supernatural power: A radical feminist analysis of Title IX in physical education. *Journal of Teaching in Physical Education*, 17(1), 172–194.

Nutt, G., & Clarke, G. (2002). The hidden curriculum and the changing nature of teachers' work. In A. Laker (Ed.), *The sociology of sport and physical education: An introductory reader* (pp. 148–166). London: RoutledgeFalmer.

O'Flynn, G. (2010). The business of 'bettering' students' lives: Physical and health education and the production of social class subjectivities. *Sport, Education and Society*, 15(4), 431–445.

Oliver, K. L., & Lalik, R. (2001). The body as curriculum: Learning with adolescent girls. *Journal of Curriculum Studies*, 33(3), 303–333.

Oliver, K. L., & Lalik, R. (2004a). Critical inquiry on the body in girls' physical education classes: A critical poststructural perspective. *Journal of Teaching in Physical Education*, 23(2), 162–195.

Oliver, K. L., & Lalik, R. (2004b). 'The beauty walk': Interrogating whiteness as the norm for beauty within one school's hidden curriculum. In J. Evans & B. Davies (Eds.), *Body knowledge and control: Studies in the sociology of physical education and health* (pp. 115–129). London: Routledge.

Organisation for Economic Co-operation and Development. (2012). *Equity and quality in education: Supporting disadvantaged students and schools*. OECD Publishing.

Paechter, C. (2003) Power, bodies and identity: How different forms of physical education construct varying degrees of masculinity and femininity in secondary schools. *Sex Education*, 3(1), 47–59.

Penney, D. (2002). Equality, equity and inclusion in physical education and sport. In A. Laker (Ed.), *The sociology of sport and physical education: An introductory reader* (pp. 110–128). London: RoutledgeFalmer.

Penney, D., & Evans, J. (1999). *Politics, policy and practice in physical education*. London: Taylor & Francis.

Penney, D. & Evans, J. (2002). Talking gender. In D. Penney (Ed.), *Gender and physical education: Contemporary issues and future directions* (pp. 13–23). London: Routledge.

Penney, D., & Evans, J. (2013). Who is physical education for? In S. Capel & M. Whitehead (Eds.), *Debates in physical education* (pp. 157–170). London: Routledge.

Penney, D., & Harris, J. (1997). Extra-curricular physical education: more of the same for the more able? *Sport, Education and Society*, 2(1), 41–54.

Penney, D., Petrie, K. & Fellows, S. (2015). HPE in Aotearoa New Zealand: The reconfiguration of policy and pedagogic relations and privatisation of curriculum and pedagogy. *Sport, Education and Society*, 20(1), 42–56.

Qualifications and Curriculum Authority. (2007). *Physical education programme of study key stage 3*. Retrieved 22 October 2014 from www.qca.org.uk/curriculum.

Quick, S., Simon, A. & Thornton, A. (2010). *PE and school sport survey 2009/10*. London: Department for Education.

Scraton, S. (1986). Images of femininity and the teaching of girls' physical education. In J. Evans (Ed.), *Physical education, sport and schooling: Studies in the sociology of physical education* (pp. 71–95). London: Falmer Press.

Stidder, G. (2013). The value of reflexivity for inclusive practice in physical education. In: S. Hayes and G. Stidder (Eds.), *Equity and inclusion in physical education and sport* (pp. 17–33). London: Routledge.

Stidder, G., & Hayes, S. (2013). Equity and inclusion in physical education: Themes and perspectives for practitioners. In S. Hayes & G. Stidder (Eds.), *Equity and inclusion in physical education and sport* (pp. 1–16). London: Routledge.

U.S. Department of Labor. (2007). *Title IX, education amendments of 1972*. Retrieved 22 October 2014 from www.dol.gov/oasam/regs/statutes/titleix.htm.

Varpalotai, A. (1987). The hidden curriculum in leisure: An analysis of girls' sport subculture. *Women's Studies International Forum, 10*(4), 11–22.

Vertinsky, P. A. (1992). Reclaiming space, revisioning the body: The quest for gender sensitive physical education. *Quest, 44*(3), 373–396.

Wilkinson, S. D., & Penney, D. (2014). The involvement of external agencies in extra-curricular physical education: Reinforcing or challenging gender and ability inequities? *Sport, Education and Society*, DOI: 10.1080/13573322.2014.956714.

Williams, A., & Bedward, J. (2001). Gender, culture and the generation gap: Student and teacher perceptions of aspects of National Curriculum Physical Education. *Sport, Education and Society, 6*(1), 53–66.

Williams, A., & Woodhouse, J. (1996). Delivering the discourse: Urban adolescents' perceptions of physical education. *Sport, Education and Society, 24*(1), 29–32.

Youth Sport Trust. (2009). *The PE and Sport Strategy for Young People: A guide to delivering the five hour offer*. Loughborough, UK: Author.

PART IV

Adapted physical activity

Introduction

Many physical educators realize that the educational process is intricately tied to health and developmental parameters (e.g., motor, physical, affective, cognitive, etc.) integrated into school curricula. Students with disability, for instance, show an increased risk for poor health due to sedentary lifestyles and are routinely deprived of opportunities to practice sports and engage in exercise programs. Segregation's insidious effects reach well beyond school environments, limiting access for individuals with disability and, due to society's discriminatory attitudes, impact every aspect of our complex communities.

Pedagogical practices are continuously influenced by politics, human rights movements, globalization of messages, cultural differences, and economic constraints. Societal and individual beliefs sometimes have contradictory influences in the context of schools and institutions and in different countries. On the one hand, on many occasions beliefs have become political movements that have positively impacted laws and school policies, methods, technology, and accessibility. Conversely, cultural beliefs often have reinforced stereotypes and prejudice against disability that can make entire societies resistant to change. Worldwide, these "mixed" contexts result in academic training that is disjointed, reflecting a reality of economic and cultural bias.

The issues of *diversity* and *inclusion* in the field of education require new theoretical viewpoints to meet the demands of the twenty-first century. In Chapter 14, I present a *dynamic systems* perspective and apply it to contexts of practices in adapted physical activity (APA) (e.g., developmental and recreational activities, sports activities, etc.). A goal of this chapter is to explain how to promote and facilitate full participation in various programs of physical activity for students with disability. In APA teaching contexts, it is vital that teachers follow principles of maximum participation and non-sedentary engagement. As the main guiding requirement for developing teacher and professional competencies, the principles of dynamic systems theory can help educators design meaningful pedagogical practices for PE activities. This chapter reconciles medical knowledge and advances and scientific evidence, with disability rights recommendations, to meet rehabilitative and educational needs, whether in clinical settings, in sports, or in APA programs. In this chapter, I provide a discussion of how the educational context reflects a self-organizing system (e.g., a PE class in action), with sub-systems (e.g., teachers, staff, students, all of which are immersed in an immediate, ever-changing learning environment), openly exchanging a flow of patterned energy (i.e., information) and dynamically cooperating and affecting each other. Using dynamic system concepts, I illustrate examples of cooperative solutions and attitude constraints, using the *disability rights* paradigm.

In Chapter 15, *Advances in disability and motor behavior research*, Rosa Angulo-Barroso and Teri Todd define the concept of disability from a biopsychosocial standpoint. From a motor behavior perspective, the authors discuss the complex phenomenon of an individual with disability, constrained by motor tasks, who is interacting with the environment. The authors introduce current theories that explain developmental changes in motor performance. They offer a task analysis model (e.g., Gentile's two-dimensional taxonomy of motor skills) to explain how motor skills can accommodate individual constraints and ensure success. Following Gentile's taxonomy, motor skills are divided into two broad categories: body orientation in quiet and dynamic tasks, and object manipulation. They discuss how to increase difficulty levels to sequence skill progressions appropriate to an individual's potential. To introduce critical components of designing a PE practice or task, Chapter 15 content is divided into six key elements of motor behavior: (a) attention and (b) motivation as part of the person's intrinsic characteristics, (c) demonstration, (d) feedback, (e) amount and distribution of practice, and (f) variability and specificity of practice. The authors summarize research findings in the areas of motor behavior (i.e., development, control, and learning) to demonstrate their potential applications in the field of APA.

When inclusion in schools became a major human rights issue, much of the world responded positively to international organizations that emphasized the adoption of the new *disability rights* paradigm, even changing their country's legislation to reflect this innovative approach. Although in some countries disability rights is a reflection of diversity in political, economic, and cultural issues and impacts the education of individuals with disability, many countries continue to use the traditional *medical model* of disability, practicing segregation policies in their school systems. In Chapter 16, I collaborate with a group of distinguished international scholars to report the major strides in higher education curricular development that recently have occurred throughout the world (North, Central, and South America; Europe, Asia, Africa, and the Middle East). We trace how many societies and their institutions (e.g., schools, legislative systems, and political and economic situations, among others) have shaped new demands for diversity in teaching and service delivery. Some countries, such as those in Europe and North America, historically have been leaders in developing assertive policies regarding APA professional competencies, as illustrated in their official standards in APA and in inclusion policies.

The *inclusion model*'s focus on welcoming students with disability into the regular classroom is a theoretically and pedagogically sound approach to the education of all students. Teachers' training, beginning at the preservice level, is critical to successful inclusion. Lauren Lieberman and Martin Block – Chapter 17, *Inclusive settings in adapted physical activity: a worldwide reality?* – introduce a debate about the inclusive curriculum. They discuss theoretical paradigms and pedagogical practices within the context of political and economic situations that span from local to worldwide perspectives. Coming from an inclusion perspective in modern schools, as well as from the broader sense of health promotion, critical issues for discussion include how to combine resources, knowledge, and experience – from both general and special education – to successfully provide a comprehensive, appropriate education to all children, with and without disabilities.

Indeed, worldwide, inclusive legislation is gradually becoming a reality. However, research shows that, almost universally, there is a common barrier to the practice of inclusion in school, regardless of a region's socioeconomic status. That is, teachers and students without disabilities simply do not feel prepared to include students with disability. Furthermore, the absence of assertive policies related to teacher training still is the teacher's main complaint in international surveys. To assist teachers in providing quality experiences, Lieberman and Block contextualize inclusion issues within the Theory of Planned Behavior, discussing possible solutions for inclusive practices, using examples from different cultures.

In synthesis, this Adapted Physical Activity section, in an attempt to contextualize APA pedagogy and practices from an international perspective, runs the risk of appearing to present more problems than solutions. My international experience in the field of APA and my long-time interest in dynamic systems concepts indicate that positive solutions for teaching PE in inclusive (or non-inclusive) contexts can emerge from critical, far-from-ideal situations (e.g., poverty). What future teachers and professionals in APA need to understand is that learners are unique, and their educational environments often are skewed by cultural and economic restrictions, and by their individual experiences with being disabled or not. They need to understand that, although we have theoretical foundations and recommendations for practice, there is no *single* solution for effectiveness. As educators, each of us is a critical part of a diverse, ever-changing system (the teaching-learning environment) and can act in very powerful ways to enhance the educational environment for *all* participants.

Eliane Mauerberg-deCastro
São Paulo State University, Brazil

14

THEORY AND PRACTICE IN ADAPTED PHYSICAL EDUCATION

The disability rights paradigm in synchrony with complex systems concepts

Eliane Mauerberg-deCastro, São Paulo State University, Brazil

In the physical education (PE) field, whether specifically in adapted (APE) or not, a developmental-behavioral model strongly influences the body of knowledge, and, consequently, the pedagogical practices of teachers and professionals. More recently, the body of knowledge in adapted physical activity (APA) has incorporated a complex systems conceptual approach to explain and improve pedagogical practices, particularly APE in inclusive settings. However, in the educational context of schools and institutions, the reality of pedagogical practices has "evolved" along with politics, human rights movements, globalization of messages, cultural differences, and economic constraints. Additionally, the deep influences of societal and individual beliefs have reinforced stereotypes and prejudices against disability. In this chapter, I will first introduce complex system concepts from a dynamic systems perspective to explain practices in APE (e.g., developmental and recreational activities, sports activities, etc.). Then, I will critically discuss issues that can adversely affect educational practices, in particular, physical education (i.e., medical model of disability, poverty, and stereotypes). I will conclude by describing how complex systems concepts are integrated into disability issues in the PE social context of inclusive schools, with particular emphases on human rights, cultural (e.g., violence), and economic situations (e.g., poverty).

Knowledge, attitudes, and APE practices

The foundations of core knowledge in the APA area constitute many varied knowledge components. For example, teachers may stress legislation, historical aspects of the area, human rights, situations and consequences of exclusion, biological and psycho-social foundations, and so forth, all aimed to promote and facilitate full participation in sports and many formats of physical activity for students with disability. In school settings, the reality of inclusion requires PE teachers and APA specialists to expand their perceptions about diversity and be accountable in their commitment to education for all students. Physical educators employ practices that are aligned with pedagogical principles, core knowledge about the learning phenomenon, developmental bases of children and youth, and philosophical and scientific foundations inherited from social sciences, psychology, health, and human biology.

Paradox: Although school PE is struggling with materializing inclusion and with high rates of sedentary lifestyle, a new generation of young Brazilian students with disability is being encouraged to engage in sports programs at school. Although no guarantee of year-round sport opportunities exists, they have been captivated by incentive programs by the Brazilian Paralympic Committee:

• Since 2006, the Brazilian Paralympic Committee has successfully organized the School Paralympics for elementary and high school students nationwide.

• In 2012, 1,200 athletes from 24 states gathered in the city of São Paulo to compete in one of the largest games for young students with disability (www.cpb.org.br/).

• The most recent national games for non-disabled students had nearly 3,000 participants. These competitions began in 1969 (Brazil, 2013).

Pedagogists are required to bridge the enormous gap between theory and practice. This is true when working with and educating students with disability, whether in general physical education or as specialists in APA.[1]

Besides achieving the goals of academic excellence, pedagogical methods continue to evolve in many different cultures to meet diversity, inclusion legislation, and demands for life-long integration in society (e.g., forming a family, raising children, having a professional career, community leadership, being fit and healthy, and so forth). Moreover, educating heterogeneous groups of students requires the management not only of school policies, curricular content, and teaching tools and methods, but also adjusting the beliefs of diverse groups (including those of the teacher). To fully understand why pedagogical practice has been inefficient in addressing diversity in the sense of full and efficient student participation, it is important to take into consideration the greatest barriers in human behavior and institutions themselves: *attitudes* and *exclusion*.

Is there a possibility for a new theoretical viewpoint in the name of diversity?

Slay (2002) claimed that a learning environment is a *socio-technical complex system*. As an open system, human physical activity can be conceptualized as a *dynamic system*, organized to reflect task-constrained learning, and is inseparable from environmental and socio-cultural factors. The disability condition is a multilayered organism constraint that continuously responds to task demands, whether successfully adapting or not. The same logic can be applied to age, gender, body proportions, past experiences, etc. These are all elements (i.e., organism/intrinsic constraints) of a diverse, unique learner.

A pedagogical theory relies on curriculum success that, in turn, is materialized through the learning process of pupils (Cunningham, 1992). According to Mennin (2010), learning results in continuously evolving adaptive responses. A school curriculum – considered a set of teachers' instructions, models, and pedagogical efforts working in cooperation with students – prompts contexts of endless problems and solutions and reflects self-organization of this complex system: the context of teaching-learning.

Whether from an inclusion perspective of modern schools or from a broader sense of health promotion, APA is a field in which individuals provide pedagogical opportunities to one another (i.e., from a teacher's perspective, student-to-student, or from the school's perspective). These members – while interacting during a learning experience – reflect *self-organizing systems* (e.g., a

PE class in action) and *subsystems* (e.g., members of the class immersed in a continuously changing environment) that are openly exchanging the flow of patterned energy (i.e., information), dynamically cooperating, and affecting one another. The dynamic systems perspective can be described from many points of view: the student, the teacher, the moment-to-moment interaction between a student with disability and a peer without disability within a task context or constraint, or the entire class dynamic. Such (deliberate) descriptions (by someone who is aware of the class context or its participants) take place in different time scales: an instant, the duration of a given task, a given developmental stage, or any other arbitrary timeframe.

According to Mauerberg-deCastro and Angulo-Kinzler (2001), the dynamic systems approach emphasizes the importance of *heterarchical* multiple subsystems and provides a unified analysis of the emergent behavior (i.e., learning something; mastering a skill; coping with rejection; showing concern for others, etc.). This means that individuals' priority, hierarchy, biological functions, and social interactions lose their validity as individual issues and give place to a holistic understanding of learning and adaptive behavior embedded in the actual task environment. For example, a young child with Down syndrome can exhibit difficulties in walking and, when going upstairs, she may decide to crawl instead of walk. However, if she is determined to carry a baby-sized doll along, going upstairs might force her to stand in order to hold the doll while completing the journey. The developmental pressure is not always based on the most effective practice of the behavior (e.g., walking), which can be mastered through practice; instead, a moment of decision can be of critical meaning to a behavior's emergence. The doll in this example becomes a critical context to the Down syndrome child's walking. Furthermore, the task becomes more complex when she steps up a staircase while managing the weight and size of this relatively large load (i.e., the baby-sized doll).

Pedagogical practices for meaningful PE activities for all

An adapted PE program put into practice is a subsystem (a sequence of instructions logically selected) embedded in a larger system (i.e., the context of the school as institution, its curriculum, and pedagogical methodology). Physical contexts are manipulated and relatively controlled by the teacher (for safety reasons and motivation enhancement), yet the rate of interactions among students is variable. Such teaching strategies are continuously changing as a class session progresses.

Exchanges between teacher and students are bounded by rules of cooperation. As a pedagogical practice materializes, these rules cannot be simplified based on typical individuals, even though typically developing students also are complex and unique. While a number of commonalities between individuals exist (e.g., order of milestones in common stages of motor development), the stochastic nature of students' interactions (i.e., not completely predictable moment-to-moment) provides a context for uncertainty in teaching. It is common for children with autism to express their perception of instructions differently than typically developing children, as well as to resist changing environments. Non-disabled children usually adapt to their autistic peers' ways of communicating and responding to others, and modify their own expectations and responses accordingly. Yet, adaptation continuously evolves in this ecosystem (i.e., the classroom, including the student with autism) and, hopefully, committed and skilled teachers are able to convey information that is useful to control and facilitate learning.

In order to best instruct students with disabilities, teachers must manage the teaching context by "juggling" relationships to achieve cooperation, utilize technology and physical resources and the environment to enhance students' skill acquisition, and continuously assess the results of their efforts while implementing curricula. Teachers often adapt inclusive

PE classes through the modification of instructions, variations of task requirements, and, sometimes, through the use of peer tutoring models (Klavina & Block, 2008; Lieberman & Houston-Wilson, 2009), etc. (Figure 14.1). It is important to remember that all students are more engaged when a task's goal is clear (e.g., going from point A to point B; hitting a target ten times, etc.). Many PE curricular activities have clear and obvious goals: for example, sports. The process of achieving goals occurs, essentially, through competition – against one-self, or against someone else.

Competition can be observed in PE class, especially when students reach the teen years and feel the need for affiliations and social affirmation. Sports inherently include these components. Teachers (and coaches) of students with disabilities must take the opportunity to teach moral values, and, through sports, promote respect for rules, acceptance of adversaries' successes, how to cope with failure, exploit opportunities for showing the determination to "try again," winning with responsibility, fair play, and the development of leadership.

The presence of students with disability in an inclusive school setting provides the ideal opportunity for everyone to experience and express positive attitudes, and ultimately to de-velop friendship. Teachers should appreciate the fact that diverse students – with and without disability – comprise a dynamic system, one that can be an amazing context in which educators can learn how to teach. They help to define the educator's purpose.

Physical educators, as well as any other educator, must realize that their practices instan-taneously affect not only class dynamics, but, in the long term, students' lifestyle choices and attitudes. Each and every student is part of a unique culture, and, as they interact, they exchange experiences that affect one another. Teachers should determine educational, developmental, health-related, and, often, therapeutic goals when teaching in inclusive contexts (or in adapted physical activity or individualized PE programs). Regardless of who the learners are, there are

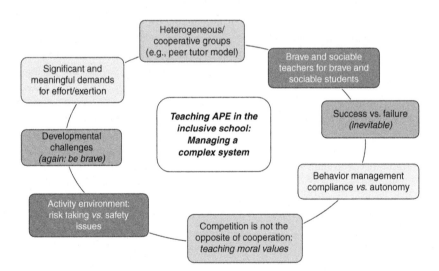

Figure 14.1 The management of a PE class requires finding solutions that are born within the system's dynamics. The system's collective elements are: students (their culture, values, history, expectations, courage with the unknown, compliance and autonomy, etc.), the teacher (his or her pedagogical choice for practice, experience, resilience to challenges, flexibility, cooperative relations with the institution, peers, and students, etc.) and the PE tasks or PE content (developmental value of activities, embedded rehabilitation potential, meaningful exercise requirements, predicted task success/failure rate, etc.)

principles that guide professional activities in any teaching context. Sherrill (2004) introduced several principles in APA. She claimed that, based on the developmental status of students and their adaptive potential, teachers must provide a safe activity environment; select activities that are functionally relevant for a variety of motor skills (ecological validity); and promote positive contexts for socialization, fun, and altruistic relationships.

The systematic physical activity program or PE class should manipulate rates of practice, task variability, levels of task difficulty, and other factors that facilitate or compete with behavioral outcomes. Teachers are able to exert influence on how students increase or lower their levels of motivation and arousal, and on how they focus attention. Teachers manipulate task requirements to increase physical efforts and improve tolerance to fatigue. Furthermore, teachers understand that, collectively, these factors make the class dynamics almost impossible to predict, and yet, they can establish appropriate goals and efficiently manage the group based on their teaching experiences, creativity, sensitivity, awareness, and goodwill. It is a wonder how this "ecosystem" of relations, stochastic, yet somewhat predictable, apparently flows into order (Figure 14.2).

Whatever the chosen activities in a PE program, it must provide a certain level of freedom, enjoyment, and be flexible to stimulate creativity. Sometimes pleasure and joy are lost during those activities that emphasize repetition or restricted participation (one based on the adult's perception of target learning). Gestures or performance requirements such as those that occur in sports can be quite individual, but, eventually, given meaningful and motivating practice opportunities, individuals self-organize actions. Movements or actions in sport or other PE activity are restricted by the (bio)mechanics of the target skill (e.g., presence of a physical

Figure 14.2 Diverse skills: students finding a single solution for a collective task (photo: D. F. Campbell, 2013)

disability), or restricted by the task goal (e.g., adapting target skill to the task, such as when playing sitting volleyball). Because teachers are part of dynamic settings (students, class material/equipment, task at hand), they need to be actively engaged with demonstrations, clearly and objectively communicate instructions that are accessible, be consistent with rules and participation requirements, and provide (when necessary) physical support for safety and touch contact for encouragement.[2]

There are many cultural, social, and legal issues surrounding how teachers actively engage a class of students in instruction. In APE, these issues are part of the educational process and cannot be ignored. Sometimes, family members, students, school administrators, and peer teachers can work cooperatively to identify the best strategies for implementing pedagogical methods with coherence and best practices, and in modifying methods for students with disabilities.

APA teachers often struggle to find appropriate teaching strategies that are politically correct and inclusive of students with disability. For example, because, in general, students with spinal cord injury have issues with body image, these can become more evident in a swimming class. In the health section of a PE class, a sensitive teacher must discuss with the entire class issues about the biased, unrealistic media standards about looks and "being cool" (Campbell, 2015; Seabrook, McChesney, & Miller, 2001). The same PE curricula require PE teachers to educate all students about medical needs, healthy habits, and being fit; the disability topic in such contexts cannot be ignored. Teachers can invite a student that has a disability to take an active role in educating peers about his and other disability conditions. This tutoring context helps to empower all students, as well as the teacher.

Such practical contexts and assumptions often are recognized as a local dynamic of those involved (students, teachers, and associated helpers such as *para-educators*). As a dynamic system, teaching and learning processes also reflect previous influences that go beyond the classroom to curricular planning. Traditionally, curricular planning has followed or has been influenced by theoretical approaches and models of practices in rehabilitation. In this case, even in inclusive settings, the traditional (and often criticized) medical model is a great influence on the educational system worldwide.

In the past, the medical model of disability was perhaps the greatest barrier to the development of a democratic, human rights-centered approach. However, in some countries today as well as some Brazilian regions, segregated education still prevails, whether due to economic reasons (e.g., many countries in Sub-Saharan Africa and South America) or by social choice (e.g., Hong Kong, Indonesia, Saudi Arabia). This model likely influences how educators, and, in particular, physical educators, deliver APA services and teach students with disabilities (Elsheikh & Alqurashi, 2013; Kurniawati, Minnaert, Mangunsong, & Ahmed, 2012; Mauerberg-deCastro, 2007; Sit, Lindner, & Sherrill, 2002; Peresuh & Barcham, 1998).

Therefore, educators need to be familiar with medical conditions and technological advances that are incorporated into the routine of living with a disability. Another issue that educators need to be knowledgeable about is the influence that media plays in multicultural settings, such as in inclusive schools, and, broadly, on inclusive environments (Campbell & Mauerberg-deCastro, 2011).

In the history of disability rights, a variety of events have reinforced the belief that individuals who do not meet certain societal patterns (e.g., behavioral or even aesthetic appearance) or expectations (e.g., independence, self-reliance, even economic success), should be "outcasts." This belief is seated in the medical model of disability (Figure 14.3), which insidiously influences attitudes that justify exclusion.

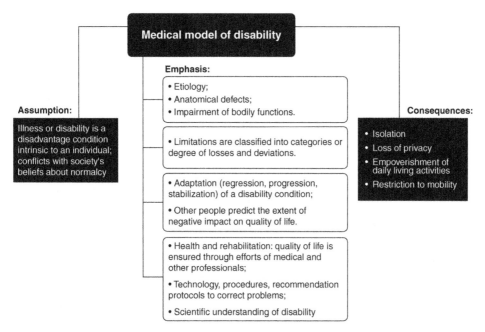

Figure 14.3 Assumption, emphasis, and consequences associated with the medical model of disability

Integrating medical advances and science to serve rehabilitation and APA

Educators and physical educators in many parts of the world have begun to embrace spontaneous, creative, and enriching teaching-learning environments for students with developmental problems (Block, 2015; Lieberman & Houston-Wilson, 2009; Mauerberg-deCastro, 2011; Winnick, 2000). Medical advances in science, the modernization of methods of treatment, and a complex multi-disciplinary relationship among various professionals dealing with health and rehabilitation have affected the traditional medical model's influence and are becoming increasingly more widespread across disciplines. For example, in Europe, the traditions of clinical psychology, neuropsychology, and psychiatry have merged into new disciplines. One such area is the French *psychomotricity*, which is a specialized professional field first established in the Hospital of Salpetriére in 1950 (Brunelle & Beauchesne, 1983). *Psychomotricity* became a popular method for teaching young children in pre-schools because of its emphasis on psychomotor development. The rapid developments within the *psychomotricity* field resulted in pedagogical applications, particularly for students with learning "inadaptations." In the 1970s, the National Centers of Psychomotor Formation, endorsed by the French National Ministry of Education, began the certification of educators and physical educators using *psychomotricity* as a means for providing psychopedagogical help (i.e., the Psychopedagogical Help Group, GAAP, according to Brunelle and Beauchesne, 1983).

Today, the medical field is benefiting from new scientific knowledge about disabilities, resulting in shifting influences and new conceptual frameworks about disability. Such knowledge has affected programs, treatment protocols, and policies, and has even influenced the way in which entire communities perceive disability. For example, when the media uses neutral or positive language to disseminate news about medical conditions of people with disability or health impairment, this exerts positive influences on attitudes and increases the general population's acceptance towards these individuals. Recently, such dissemination of information has occurred via TV programs (e.g., news story-telling, soap operas, miniseries, mainstreaming Paralympics and other sports practiced by disabled athletes, etc.), the Internet, school forums, integrated sports tournaments, all giving positive visibility to the issue of disability (Inimah, Mukulu, & Mathooko, 2012). This positive dissemination of information influenced the World Health Organization's decision to redefine the measurement and classification systems (i.e., IFC – International Classification of Functioning, Disability and Health) associated with disability. The IFC has contributed to an understanding of disability that goes beyond the notion of biological or clinical dysfunction and includes positive aspects of body functions, activities, roles in society, and environmental facilitation within the context of disability (WHO, 2011).

Institutions' support and facts

The practice of sports represents a positive tradition for institutions and entire cultures, and reflects not only the prestige of elite sports, but promotes the benefits of health and rehabilitation for almost everyone (DePauw & Gavron, 2005; Vanlandewijck et al., 2007). Sports participation for many students starts in school, yet students with disability may be largely ignored or dismissed from PE classes, even when an institution provides only a few options in a curriculum that must comply with legislation and inclusion policies. Worldwide, particularly in countries with emerging economies, many students with disability are provided with medical excuses or are denied access to physical education under the premise that they are "unfit" due to disability. However, an increasing range of physical education services is a growing reality, thanks to incentives, inclusive programs, and legislation by many local and international organizations. See, for example, existing international recommendations about inclusion by the United Nations' World Programme of Action Concerning Disabled Persons (United Nations [UN], 2010). Also, there is a growing body of national legislation in the U.S. (e.g., the Individuals with Disabilities Education Act, United States Government, 2002; Winnick, 2000) and organizational policies such as 60 minutes of daily physical activity for children and adolescents, recommended by the U.S. Department of Health and Human Services (United States Government, 2002). In APE/APA, the U.S. national certification program, Adapted Physical Education National Standards Project [APENS] (National Consortium for Physical Education and Recreation for Individuals with Disabilities, 2008), the 2008–2010 European Standards in APA (EUSAPA) project (Klavina & Kudláček, 2011), the Thematic European Network on Adapted Physical Activity (DePotter et al., 2003), and Special Olympics provide clear guidelines for APE practices and reform worldwide. Special Olympics, with 80,000 sport and physical activity events year-round, reaches 4.4 million people with intellectual disabilities in 170 countries (Special Olympics, 2015). Outstanding resources are available to support and promote APE programs of excellence via literature, conferences, and online support (e.g., Adapted Physical Education Assessment Scale II, Society of Health and Physical Educators [SHAPE], 2015).

According to Bouffard and Reid (2012), the movement toward *Evidence-Based Practice and Adapted Physical Activity (EBP)* in the field of APA has received ample support by scholars who have attempted to demonstrate the efficiency and effectiveness of various forms of interventions, or of other positive outcomes from APA practice. Although for Bouffard and Reid (2012), *best practice* is a debatable concept, it guides organizations and even governmental policies (*No Child Left Behind*, United States Government, 2002).

Indeed, the need for APE programs is on the rise, particularly in U.S. school systems. Zhang (2011), using a market-based perspective and U.S. national reports (i.e., 27th Annual Report; USDE, 2007; Kelly, 1995), analyzed employment rates of APE teachers and APE services for students with disabilities in public schools across the nation. The results showed that, in the U.S., employment of fully certified APE teachers fills only 24% of the need, leaving a 76% shortage nationally of APE teachers with full certifications.

Incorporating a democratic, complex system approach to pedagogical practices

In modern societies, services are now bridging hybrid and holistic paradigms in order to provide health, wellness, rehabilitation, and education to individuals with disabilities (Mauerberg-deCastro, 2001, 2006, 2007; Roush & Sharby, 2011). For example, international programs such as the UN (2001), UNICEF (2015), and WHO (2011) defend disability and civil rights. Emerging principles for the "normalization" and social role valorization of people with disabilities (Wolfensberger, 1972), and the disability movement (e.g., Special Olympics, International Paralympic Committee) have played a special role in inspiring new ways of intervention and education, promoting equal opportunities for all.

In APA, success in delivering physical activity and sport relies on professionals sensitive to human rights and with a critical view that nurtures the adaptive potential of individuals. These professionals facilitate and transform through experiences with their students and athletes, both with and without disabilities. In such a democratic context, individuals' transformative experiences reflect a model of positive social-political commitment to diversity.

The social model of disability

The *social model of disability* is widely advocated through civil rights movements, international unified concepts of inclusion, and disability movements. It is a model that focuses on the human rights of minorities, and, according to *Disabled World*:

> The social model of disability sees the issue of "disability" as a socially created problem and a matter of the full integration of individuals into society. In this model, disability is not an attribute of an individual, but rather a complex collection of conditions, many of which are created by the social environment. Hence, the management of the problem requires social action and is the collective responsibility of society at large to make the environmental modifications necessary for the full participation of people with disabilities in all areas of social life. The issue is both cultural and ideological, requiring individual, community, and large-scale social change. From this perspective, equal access for someone with an impairment/disability is a human rights issue of major concern. (*Disabled World*, 2015, n.p.)

The social model of disability does not dismiss the importance of biomedical practices used to reduce the effects of impairments and to adapt assistive technology (WHO, 2011). In this sense, adaptive processes are emergent from organism constraints (e.g., organism functions modified by intervention, or the use of devices for assistive mobility or to achieve sport excellence, and so forth) and range from the individual to social environment constraints (e.g., an entire community dismantling stereotypes to ensure rights and equality for all). Figure 14.4 illustrates a series of intrinsic constraint factors related to an individual with disability and a series of environmental constraints (extrinsic) within social, political, and even physical contexts that interplay as dynamic interactions in the social model of disability.

A society's propensity to form stereotypes is one of the consequences of a negative understanding of disability (Campbell & Mauerberg-deCastro, 2011). The medical model of disability historically reinforced a variety of such stereotypes, including concepts about health.[3]

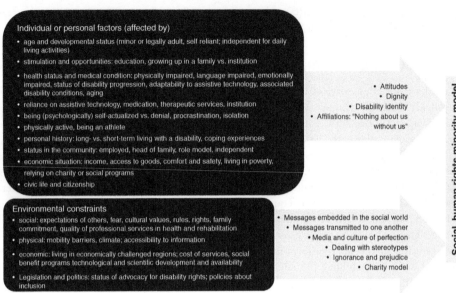

Figure 14.4   Concepts of the social model of disability "brought out" from environmental and personal constraints and directed to events and experiences by people with disability (adapted from the World Health Organization model, WHO, 2011)

Concepts related to stereotypes about disability affect all people, including individuals with disability themselves. For example, students with intellectual disability are at the highest risk for rejection by peers when compared with those with other types of disability (Varughese & Luty, 2010). Moreover, individuals with physical disability, for example, tend to be annoyed with the possibility that others would perceive them as having intellectual limitations (Mauerberg-deCastro, 2011).

Being physically active can prevent many complications related to disability. In fact, a sedentary lifestyle doubles the risk for disability for everyone. Consequences of a sedentary lifestyle often result in higher rates of obesity, mental health disorders, and poor cardiovascular fitness (Walsh, Kerr, & van Schrojenstein Lantman-de Valk, 2003). This is particularly true for students with intellectual disability, who, according to Silva, Santos, and Martins (2006), have significantly higher risk for developing obesity than their non-disabled peers. Weight gain adds another opportunity to be stereotyped, besides those associated with disability, and increases chances for bullying.

A majority of children with disability are further compromised educationally by many factors. They may experience constant health problems affecting attendance, segregation or being subjected to improper educational methods, participation in inclusive settings in which bullying is routine, and expectations for low academic performance and lowered standards and requirements, among other problems. Uneducated families with a member with disability will struggle harder than an educated family. In poverty, knowledge about opportunities and civil rights is not easily accessible.

Both oppressive and transformative situations are an integral part of students' individual experiences. Education is a process of shaping these situations towards a cooperative, coping, sharing, constructive, and transformative social experience. In teaching, some negative situations are impossible to eradicate. *Collective states* of a school class are filled with "ups" and

Figure 14.5 Dancing with the teacher. A collective state rising from interacting dynamic elements (e.g., partners, rope extension, music, a moving wheelchair) (photo: E. Mauerberg-deCastro, 2012)

"downs" during social learning interactions; students (disabled and not disabled), working with their teachers, forge their identities to a great extent by being a part of these "states" (Figure 14.5).

Although individuals can be thought of as part of many communities and with many roles, each *affects* her or his community in various ways. The disability condition is the result of many interactive factors or constraints (e.g., age, an individual's history, physical and psychological strengths and weaknesses, growing up in poverty versus abundance, cultural influences, etc.). *Collectively*, many constraints and opportunities exert an impact on identity formation and affiliations.

James Charlton and South African fellows Michael Masutha and William Rowland (Charlton, 1998) introduced the slogan, "Nothing about us without us," the 1990s, to voice their deep concern with the fact that individuals with disability were historically dismissed from participating in decision making policies and voicing their choices in a variety of contexts (e.g., education, sports, family affairs, work force), among other issues.

Educators' untold reality

An integral part of every educator's pedagogical perspective should be the critical understanding of the reality of disability[4] and the impact of the prevalent association of disability with poverty and inadequate educational environments – even when inclusive. Physical educators, for example, often rely on scarce sources of funding for developing their PE programs, whether in schools or other kinds of institutions.

In many cultures, PE is improvised and dismissed from school curricula, and obeying laws related to inclusion, developing resources, and teacher in-service training are not priorities (Bines & Lei, 2011; Mauerberg-deCastro, 2006). In developing countries' schools, PE teachers often are faced with classes that reflect not only the diversity of students' motor skills but situations that range from simple problems (e.g., placing a ramp for access of a wheelchair) to serious ones (e.g., programs to prevent and resolve violence towards disability; delivering safe PE classes to prevent harm to students with disability) (Kim, 2013; Orunaboka & Nwankwo, 2011). In such communities, PE teachers often teach outdoors or in non-fixed locations (Onyewadume, 2007; Orunaboka & Nwankwo, 2011). In Brazil, disabled students in PE classes approach their teachers with a variety of problems that reflect their daily struggles to attend school and to deal with violence (Albino, Zeiser, Bassani, & Vaz, 2008; Castro, Vaz, Oliveira, & Pinto, 2013). PE teachers teaching in schools in poor neighborhoods often must confront and assist students both with and without disabilities, deal with life-consuming issues such as hunger, domestic violence, and peer bullying. PE teachers also deal with the effects of poverty on families and their disabled students. These concerns include students being tired due to extensive demands of work or home chores, abuse by parents, or coming to PE wearing improper clothes, perhaps without shoes, or suffering from poor hygiene, and untreated illnesses (Devries et al., 2014; Mushoriwa, 2001; Onyewadume, 2007).

PE teachers often are restricted due their institution's economic problems. Teachers may teach without sport equipment appropriate for use by students with disabilities, inadequate PE facilities with limited or no accessibility for students with disability. Without trained assistants (or *para-educators*) to help with individuals with special needs, teachers must manage large classes while attempting to meet the needs of students with disabilities. In some locations, inadequate security permits outlaw gangs to operate inside schools, while the general population's ignorance about disabilities in general often results in oppression and violence toward disabled people (Mauerberg-deCastro, 2007).

Often, in school curricula, administrators and other educators place less importance on PE classes relative to their overall contribution to academic achievement (Petrie & lisahunter, 2011). Inconsistencies also occur in recognizing the value of core theoretical physical activity and sports knowledge as it relates to health. Brazilian school curricula[5] in many states require that PE teachers allocate one hour to teaching theoretical concepts out of their two weekly contact hours (Mauerberg-deCastro et al., 2013). Introducing theoretical content in PE does not help recognition of PE as an academic field if students do not have opportunities or the initiative to engage in actual and meaningful PE practice.

Inclusive and regular PE contexts: something is not working

Whether or not a methodological approach is theoretically sound for PE in school, reality of teaching is another matter. Unfortunately, for Brazilian students (and for others from different countries), engagement with physical activity is dangerously low. For example, Brazilian youth, including those who are disabled, are less and less engaged in physical activity, exposed to a fast-growing incidence of obesity, and increasing metabolic diseases. The incidence of overweight Brazilian males has tripled since the 1970s, from 18.5% to 60%. Obesity quadrupled, from 2.8% to 12.4%. Women's overweight and obesity values have doubled (IBGE, 2010). Children 5–9 years old are overweight

(34%) or obese (14%) (UNECLAC, 2010). Currently, inactive lifestyle shows that 60% of Brazilian children and youth are sedentary. There is a problem with PE in school in this country. Regardless of methods or philosophical approaches, worldwide, in industrialized countries children and youth are suffering the consequences of a sedentary lifestyle. School PE is failing to engage students in a meaningful exercise regime.

A study by Bejerot, Edgar, and Humble (2011) revealed that poor motor skills are strong risk factors for students to become targets of school bullying. Further, students with disabilities are likely targets of psychological (75%) and physical (2%) forms of violence, or both (23%). These victims, according to this study, can become bullies as well (28% of the cases). Individuals in inclusive settings are extremely vulnerable to violence.

In Brazil, teacher who are incapable of class management authority and discipline resort to ignoring students and withdrawing rather than intervening during situations of violence that occur among students. This allows them to be exposed to the tyranny of bullies and leaves them defenseless in situations that lead to injuries and pain inflicted by others (Arendt, 1992). The result of violence is a sense of victimization by students.

The PE class can be a paradoxical context. On the one hand, in well-taught and well-managed classes, students feel free to enjoy themselves, develop social awareness, and cultivate and enrich their learning communities. Indeed, positive PE experiences result in more socially adjusted students. While on the other hand, an unskilled teacher may not be able to prevent violence, causing student discomfort. Roman and Taylor (2013) found that a teacher's lack of PE experience was associated with student victimization from bullying. The question is, then, how can teachers transform PE from a negative context of victims and tyrants into a positive experience for all, particularly for students with disability, who frequently are the objects of deeply rooted stereotypical attitudes?

Physical educators are confronted with complex social contexts. Diverse students manifest a range of needs, desires, previous experiences, perceptions, and opinions of others along with varying skill levels (motor, social, cognitive, and emotional) (Bredahl, 2013). Teachers who are sensitive to complex interactions can build a positive environment that reflects school policies, protects students' vulnerabilities to conflict and violence, provides peer support, builds on family dynamics, and marshals economic resources. Together, these complex factors play into the reality of teaching practices and toward the goals of developing an inclusive and successful curriculum.

Final considerations

Although the political scenario and policy making in the field of PE have evolved to embrace diversity, the daily reality of teaching, in large part, has not. While inclusive programs are expanding globally, there is a universal trend toward complaints from PE teachers who feel they are unprepared to deal with students with disability. However, from moment to moment the teaching process includes both positive and negative components. A class can simultaneously have students who apply themselves and others who do not. From moment to moment, this, too, can change. Wise, committed teachers are aware of such challenges. *This* is the dynamic system principle of adaptation and occurs whether or not a student has a disability. Too, the wise, committed teacher knows that learning is not linear. A class of students – and the teacher – comprise a non-deterministic, quasi-random, self-organizing, collective *system*. PE teachers are more likely to figure out solutions to conflicting scenarios in inclusive settings if they take an active role within this system. For example, young students seem to enjoy lessons in which their teachers join with them in playing games just for the sake of teaming with someone so good. Teen students might prefer to have a class visitor who demonstrates excellence in a sport, for example. Athletes with disability are perfect candidates for this role. Creative teachers actively lead their students to discover solutions to problems. These teachers do not excuse themselves when students are lost in the beginning of the process of learning something.

It is impossible to ignore the importance of history when dealing with individuals with diversity. All individuals (e.g., students, teachers, staff) are affected by institutional traditions and policies, moral values and societal expectations, life goals, resources and technology, legacies of political oppression, and an ever-changing (globally influenced) society. Moving from the traditional "medical model" to rights- and diversity-based thinking about disability can cause a change in views. No longer is disability treated as a medical condition to be cured. People with disabilities are included rather than treated as outcasts. However, some educators have not yet caught up with these social and political changes. Teachers and educators will continue to be challenged to truly embrace these policies, enhancing the effectiveness of their teaching to include and care for individuals with disability.

Reflective questions for discussion

1. What are the major differences between the *medical model* of disability and the *social model* of disability?
2. Although the medical model of disability is considered the greatest barrier to the development of a democratic, human rights-centered approach, discuss other problematic issues regarding access and quality of education for all students, including those with disability, from an international perspective.
3. Briefly discuss organism/intrinsic constraints of a student with disability (e.g., cerebral palsy) in an APA context (e.g., playing soccer), and specify how a teacher might manipulate the teaching environment to promote success in learning.
4. Discuss how the teacher, students with and without disability, the school system (including planned curricula), and society (e.g., parents, messages via TV) comprise a dynamic system in the context of teaching-learning.

Notes

1 The term *adapted physical activity* (APA) is an umbrella concept to broadly define the professional and pedagogical activity of physical educators in general. APA encompasses the physical activity delivered in the school context and, herein, is adopted as *adapted physical education* (APE).
2 In many European countries and in the United States, schools have introduced a mandatory "non-touch" policy to discipline the routine of teachers and students of all ages in order to control harassment, bullying, and other perceived negative events associated with physical contact (Farlow, 1994). In general, this policy is quite controversial from the perspective of "touch withdrawal." Physical contact for certain age students, condition of disability, behavioral situations with students, safety issues, or simply social acquaintance are important, necessary, and sometimes, unavoidable. In PE settings in different parts of the world, there are

cultural and legal aspects that vary extensively. In some countries, not touching a student during instruction might be considered unsafe and, even, a sign of dislike, discrimination, or confrontation. And, quite often, physical activities require students to touch or physically contact each other.

3 According to Peterson, Puhl, and Luedicke (2012), physical educators (e.g., PE teachers, coaches, and in-training PE teachers or coaches), particularly male teachers and coaches, who display negative attitudes towards overweight students, tend to recommend weight control based solely on appearance instead of objective measures of health and physical performance.

4 According to the UN 2001 Statistical Database on Disability, an estimated 1.7% of the world's population has some kind of disability; 0.7% of this total consists of children under 14 years old (Filmer, 2008; UN, 2001). Today, determining the prevalence of disability within the population is much more complex because about one third of people with disability are older individuals. Rates of disability are much higher among those aged 80–89 years, increasing 3.9% each year after this. By 2050, experts predict that nearly 20% of the global population 60 years or older will be disabled (UN Enable, 2012). According to the UN Enable 2010 WPA report, in most countries, at least one person out of ten is disabled, and at least 25% of any population is adversely affected by the presence of disability. Furthermore, wars, refugee camps, and epidemics of disease make the scenario of incidence of disabilities much more prevalent. This world reality has an economic implication. Indeed, poverty is highly correlated with disability. Whether a country is economically developed or developmentally challenged, the combination of limited income and cost of living has a greater impact on the lives of families of people with a disability as compared to the rest of the community (WHO, 2011). As adults, half of individuals with disability are unemployed, need help from social programs and charity, and most live in poverty and isolation (Filmer, 2008). People with disability have increased risk for poor health due to sedentary lifestyle, resulting in lack of opportunities for practicing sports and exercise (Martinez-Leal et al., 2011; Mckeon, Slevin, & Taggart, 2013).

5 Paulo Freire's critical theory, endorsed by the nation's Ministry of Education, was largely integrated into the *socio-anthropological body culture* approach in Brazilian PE school curricula.

References

Albino, B. S., Zeiser, C. C., Bassani, J. J., & Vaz, A. F. (2008). Acerca da violência por meio do futebol no ensino de educação física: Retratos de uma prática e seus Dilemas [Awareness of violence by the means of teaching soccer in physical education: Picturing the practice and its dilemmas]. *Pensar a Prática, 11*, 139–147.

Arendt, H. (1992). *Entre o passado e o futuro [Between the past and the future]*. São Paulo, Brazil: Perspectiva.

Bejerot, S., Edgar, J., & Humble, M. B. (2011). Poor performance in physical education – a risk factor for bully victimization. A case–control study. *Acta Pediatrica, 100*, 413–419.

Bines, H., & Lei, P. (2011). Disability and education: The longest road to inclusion. *International Journal of Educational Development, 31*, 419–424.

Block, M. E. (2015). *An inclusive approach to adapted physical education*. Baltimore: Paul H. Brookes.

Bouffard, D., & Reid, G. (2012). The good, the bad, and the ugly of evidence-based practice. *Adapted Physical Activity Quarterly, 29*, 1–24.

Brazil. (2013). *Jogos Escolares da Juventude: Histórico [High School Youth Games: History]*. Ministério do Esporte. Retrieved August 21, 2014, from www.esporte.gov.br/index.php/institucional/alto-rendimento/jogos-escolares-brasileiros/historico.

Bredahl, A.-M. (2013). Sitting and watching the others being active: The experienced difficulties in PE when having a disability. *Adapted Physical Activity Quarterly, 30*, 40–58.

Brunelle, L. & Beauchesne, H. (1983). O campo terapêutico da psicomotricidade [The therapeutic field of psychomotricity]. In: J. J. Guillarme (Ed.), *Educação e reeducação psicomotoras [Psychomotor education and re-education]* (pp. 122–129). Porto Alegre, Brazil: Artes Médicas.

Campbell, D. F. (2015). *Television violence and young adults in Brazil: A content analysis of the popular telenovela, "Malhação"* [Doctoral dissertation]. São Paulo State University, Brazil.

Campbell, D. F., & Mauerberg-deCastro, E. (2011). Estereótipos e deficiência: a mídia e a cultura da perfeição [Stereotypes and disability: Media and the culture of perfection]. In E. Mauerberg-deCastro (Ed.), *Atividade física adaptada [Adapted physical activity]* (2nd edn) (pp. 83–112). Ribeirão Preto, Brazil: Novo Conceito.

Castro, J. T., Vaz, A. F., Oliveira, M. A. T., & Pinto, F. M. (2013). Violência em aulas de educação física: Corporalidade, docência e formação [Violence in physical education classes: Corporeality, teaching and training]. *Revista Iberoamericana De Educación, 62,* 19–37.

Charlton, J. I. (1998). *Nothing about us without us: Disability oppression and empowerment.* Berkeley and Los Angeles: University of California Press. Retrieved June 22, 2010, from http://books.google.com/books?id=ohqff8DBt9gC&lpg=PA3&pg=PA3#v=onepage&q&f=false.

Cunningham, D. J. (1992). Beyond educational psychology: Steps toward an educational semiotic. *Educational Psychology Review, 4,* 165–194.

DePauw, K., & Gavron, S. (2005). *Disability sport* (2nd edn). Urbana-Champaign, IL: Human Kinetics.

DePotter, J. C., Van Coppenolle, H., Djobova, S., Dobreva, I., Wijns, K., & Van Peteghem, A. (Eds.). (2003). *Vocational training in adapted physical activity.* Leuven, Belgium: THENAPA.

Devries, K. M., Child, J. C., Allen, E., Walakira, E., Parkes, J., & Naker, D. (2014). School, violence, mental health, and educational performance in Uganda. *Pediatrics, 133,* e129–e137.

Disabled World. (2015). Definitions of the models of disability. Retrieved January 22, 2015, from www.disabled-world.com/definitions/disability-models.php.

Elsheikh, A. S., & Alqurashi, A. M. (2013). Disabled future in the Kingdom of Saudi Arabia. *Journal of Humanities and Social Science, 16,* 68–71.

Farlow, B. J. (1994). *No-touch policies in the public school setting.* Paper presented at the Annual Meeting of the National Organization on Legal Problems of Education (San Diego, CA, November 1994). Retrieved December 10, 2014, from http://eric.ed.gov/?id=ED379750.

Filmer, D. (2008). Disability, poverty, and schooling in developing countries: Results from 14 household surveys. *The World Bank Economic Review, 22,* 141–163.

IBGE. (2010). *Pesquisa de Orçamentos Familiares 2008–2009 [Survey of Family Budgets 2008-2009].* Retrieved January 12, 2013, from www.ibge.gov.br/home/presidencia/noticias/imprensa/ppts/0000000108.pdf.

Inimah, G. M., Mukulu, E., & Mathooko, P. (2012). Literature review on media portrayal of people with disabilities in Kenya. *International Journal of Humanities and Social Science, 2,* 223–228. Retrieved March 20, 2015, from www.ijhssnet.com/journals/Vol_2_No_8_Special_Issue_April_2012/27.pdf.

Kelly, L. (1995). *Adapted physical education national standards / National Consortium for Physical Education and Recreation for Individuals with Disabilities.* Champaign, IL: Human Kinetics.

Kim, Y. W. (2013). Inclusive education in Korea: Policy, practice, and challenges. *Journal of Policy and Practice in Intellectual Disabilities, 10,* 79–81.

Klavina, A., & Block, M. E. (2008). The effect of peer tutoring on interaction behaviors in inclusive physical education. *Adapted Physical Activity Quarterly, 25,* 132–158.

Klavina, A., & Kudláček, M. (2011). Physical education for students with special education needs in Europe: Findings of the EUSAPA project. *European Journal of Adapted Physical Activity, 4,* 46–62.

Kurniawati, F., Minnaert, A., Mangunsong, F., & Ahmed, W. (2012). Empirical study on primary school teachers' attitudes towards inclusive education in Jakarta, Indonesia. *Procedia Social and Behavioral Sciences, 69,* 1430–1436.

Lieberman, L. J., & Houston-Wilson, C. (2009). *Strategies for inclusion* (2nd edn). Champaign, IL: Human Kinetics.

Martínez-Leal, R., Salvador-Carulla, L., Linehan, C., Walsh, P., Weber, G., Van Hove, G. … Kerr, M. (2011). The impact of living arrangements and deinstitutionalisation in the health status of persons with intellectual disability in Europe. *Journal of Intellectual Disability Research, 55,* 858–872.

Mauerberg-deCastro, E. (2001). Abordagens teóricas do comportamento motor. Conceitos dinâmicos aplicados aos processos adaptativos e à diversidade do movimento [Theoretical approaches of motor behavior. Dynamic concepts applied to adaptive processes and movement diversity]. In M. G. Guedes (Ed.), *Aprendizagem Motora [Motor Learning]* (pp. 105–125). Lisbon, Portugal: Edições FMH.

Mauerberg-deCastro, E. (2006). Atividade motora adaptada para crianças com atraso no desenvolvimento. A ação pedagógica segundo a abordagem dos sistemas dinâmicos [Adapted motor activity for children with developmental delay. The pedagogical action following the dynamic systems approach]. In D. Rodrigues (Ed.), *Atividade motora adaptada [Adapted motor activity]* (pp. 55–65). São Paulo, Brazil: Artes Medicas.

Mauerberg-deCastro, E. (2007). Adapted physical activity in Brazil: History, theoretical foundations, and professional action. *Journal of the Brazilian Society of Adapted Motor Activity, 12,* S64–S73. Retrieved March 18, 2016, from www.rc.unesp.br/ib/efisica/isapa/vol12no12007suplemento.pdf.

Mauerberg-deCastro, E. (2011). *Atividade física adaptada [Adapted physical activity]* (2nd edn). Ribeirão Preto, Brazil: Novo Conceito.

Mauerberg-deCastro, E., & Angulo-Kinzler, R. (2001). Vantagens e limitações das ferramentas usadas para investigar padrões de comportamento motor segundo a abordagem dos sistemas dinâmicos [Advantages and limitations of tools used to analyze motor behavior patterns according to dynamic systems approach]. In L. Teixeira (Ed.), *Avanços em comportamento motor [Advances in motor behavior]*. (Vol. 1) (pp. 35–57). São Paulo, Brazil: Movimento.

Mauerberg-deCastro, E., Paiva, A. C. S., Figueiredo, G. A., Costa, T. D. A., Castro, M. R., & Campbell, D. F. (2013). Attitudes about inclusion by educators and physical educators: Effects of participation in an inclusive adapted physical education program. *Motriz, 19*, 649–661.

Mennin, S. (2010). Self-organisation, integration and curriculum in the complex world of medical education. *Medical Education, 44*, 20–30.

Mckeon, M., Slevin, E., & Taggart, L. (2013). A pilot survey of physical activity in men with an intellectual disability. *Journal of Intellectual Disabilities, 17*, 157–167.

Mushoriwa, T. (2001). A study of attitudes of primary school teachers in Harare towards the inclusion of blind children in regular classes. *British Journal of Special Education, 28*, 142–147.

National Consortium for Physical Education and Recreation for Individuals with Disabilities. (2008). *Adapted physical education national standards* [APENS]. Retrieved January 6, 2015, from http://apens. org/.

Onyewadume, I. U. (2007). Adapted physical activity in Africa: Problems and the way forward. *Journal of the Brazilian Society of Adapted Motor Activity, 12*, S58–S63. Retrieved March 18, 2016, from www.rc.unesp. br/ib/efisica/isapa/vol12no12007suplemento.pdf.

Orunaboka, T. T., & Nwankwo, G. O. (2011). Safety precautions in the teaching of adapted physical education in primary and post primary schools in Rivers State of Nigeria. *International Journal of Academic Research in Business and Social Sciences, 1*, 129–136. Retrieved April 3, 2015, from www.hrmars.com/ admin/pics/93.pdf.

Peresuh, M., & Barcham, L. (1998). Special education provision in Zimbabwe. *British Journal of Special Education, 25*, 75–80.

Peterson, J. L., Puhl, R. M., & Luedicke, J. (2012). An experimental investigation of physical education teachers' and coaches' reactions to weight-based victimization in youth. *Psychology of Sport and Exercise, 13*, 177–185.

Petrie, K., & lisahunter (2011). Primary teachers, policy, and physical education. *European Physical Education Review, 17*, 325–339.

Roman, C. G., & Taylor, C. J. (2013). A multilevel assessment of school climate, bullying victimization, and physical activity. *Journal of School Health, 83*, 400–407.

Roush, S. E., & Sharby, N. (2011). Disability reconsidered: The paradox of physical therapy. *Physical Therapy, 91*, 1715–1727.

Seabrook, J., McChesney, R., & Miller, M. C. (2001). *The merchants of cool: The symbiotic relationship between the media and teens*. Retrieved March 18, 2016, from www.pbs.org/wgbh/pages/frontline/ shows/cool/.

Society for Health and Physical Education [SHAPE]. (2015). *Adapted physical education assessment scale II*. Retrieved April 6, 2015, from www.shapeamerica.org/prodev/workshops/adapted/apeasii.cfm.

Sherrill, C. (2004). *Adapted physical activity, recreation and sport* (6th edn). Dubuque, IA: McGraw-Hill.

Silva, D. L, Santos, J. A. R., & Martins, C. F. (2006). Avaliação da composição corporal em adultos com Síndrome de Down [Assessment of body composition in adults with Down syndrome]. *Arquivos de Medicina, 20*, 103–110.

Sit, C. H. P., Lindner, K. J., & Sherrill, C. (2002). Sport participation of Hong Kong Chinese children with disabilities in special schools. *Adapted Physical Activity Quarterly, 19*, 453–471.

Slay, J. (2002). Human activity systems: A theoretical framework for designing learning for multicultural settings. *Educational Technology & Society, 5*. Retrieved July 1, 2004, from http://ifets.ieee.org/periodical/vol_1_2002/v_1_2002.html.

Special Olympics. (2015). *What we do*. Retrieved March 10, 2015, from www.specialolympics.org/.

UN. (2001). Guidelines and principles for the development of disability statistics. *Statistics on special population groups*, Series Y, No. 10. New York: Statistics Division.

UN. (2010). *World programme of action concerning disabled persons*. Retrieved August 23, 2014, from www. un.org/disabilities/default.asp?id=23.

UNECLAC. (2010). *Social Panorama of Latin America 2010 of the United Nations Economic Commission for Latin America and the Caribbean*. Retrieved January 10, 2011, from www.eclac.cl/cgi-bin/getProd.asp?xml=/ publicaciones/xml/1/41801/P41801.xml&xsl=/dds/tpl-i/p9f.xsl&base=/tpl-i/top-bottom.xsl.

221

UN Enable. (2012). *Keeping the promise: Realizing the Millennium Development Goals for persons with disabilities towards 2015 and beyond.* Retrieved August 29, 2014, from www.un.org/esa/socdev/enable//disiydp. htm.

UNICEF. (2015). *The United Nations Children's Fund.* Retrieved March 10, 2015, from www.unicef.org/.

United States Government. (2002). Public law 107–110 – No child left behind act. Retrieved March 18, 2015, from www.cdc.gov/healthyyouth/npao/pdf/selecttools_resourceslist.pdf.

USDE. (2007). *Twenty-Seventh Annual Report to Congress on the Implementation of the Individuals with Disabilities Education Act, Parts B and C.* U.S. Department of Education. Retrieved December 1, 2014, from http://www2.ed.gov/about/reports/annual/osep/2005/parts-b-c/index.html.

Vanlandewijck, Y., Van Biesen, D., Verellen, J., Reynders, S., Meyer, C., & Van de Vliet, P. (2007). Socio-economic determinants of paralympic success. *Journal of the Brazilian Society of Adapted Motor Activity, 12,* S16–S22. Retrieved March 18, 2016, from www.rc.unesp.br/ib/efisica/isapa/vol12no-12007suplemento.pdf.

Varughese, S. J., & Luty, J. (2010). Stigmatised attitudes towards intellectual disability: A randomised cross-over trial. *Psychiatric Bulletin, 34,* 318–322.

Walsh, P. N., Kerr, M., & van Schrojenstein Lantman-de Valk, H. M. (2003). Health indicators for people with intellectual disabilities: A European perspective. *European Journal of Public Health, 13,* S47–S50.

Winnick, J. P. (2000). *Adapted physical education and sport* (3rd edn). Urbana-Champaign, IL: Human Kinetics.

World Health Organization [WHO]. (2011). *World report on disability.* Author. Retrieved December 30, 2015, from www.who.int/disabilities/world_report/2011/en/.

Wolfensberger, W. (1972). The principle of normalisation in human services. *The International Social Role Valorization Journal, 3,* 7–12.

Zhang, J. (2011). Quantitative analysis about market- and prevalence-based needs for adapted physical education teachers in the public schools in the United States. *The Physical Educator,* Fall, 140–149.

15

ADVANCES IN DISABILITY AND MOTOR BEHAVIOR RESEARCH

Rosa Angulo-Barroso & Teri Todd,

CALIFORNIA STATE UNIVERSITY AT NORTHRIDGE, USA

In this chapter we define the concept of disability from a biopsychosocial perspective. Disability is not limited to the person but is a complex phenomenon that encompasses constraints within the body and interactions with the environment. A person who cannot stand independently is limited in certain motor skills, for example, downhill skiing. With the use of a sit ski, however, she can successfully ski down a mountain. Adapting the task to accommodate individual constraints does not change the disability, but permits the person with the disability to move successfully. We will present current disability-specific research with the hope that educators will apply the concepts to those who will benefit. More information on specific disabilities can be found on the U.S. Department of Education website (http://idea.ed.gov).

We present Gentile's two-dimensional taxonomy of motor skills, where the environmental factors and function of the actions are essential to understanding the demands that a task places on a child (Gentile, 1987). For example, objects and people in the environment might be stable or move, and there may or may not be a change in condition between trials. The second part of the taxonomy is related to the function of the action and is divided into two broad categories; body orientation, still or moving, and object manipulation, which may or may not be present. Understanding the progression of difficulty within the taxonomy helps educators prepare skill progressions that are appropriate to the individual. For example, when teaching a child to play tee ball, he might start with hitting a ball off a tee with his hand, and, when successful at looking at the ball and aiming, advance to using a bat.

In this chapter we also define motor behavior and present a brief explanation of the most accepted theories to explain changes in motor performance. Finally, six key elements of motor behavior are discussed: (a) attention and (b) motivation as part of the person's intrinsic characteristics, (c) demonstration, (d) feedback, (e) amount and distribution of practice, and (f) variability and specificity of practice. These last three elements are critical components in the preparation of practice conditions. For example, if a child with cerebral palsy [CP] wants to improve her throwing pattern, the teacher can increase the child's attention and motivation levels by making the task relevant to the child using either a game or a functional goal. Similarly, teachers may offer demonstrations prior to the child initiating the practice as well as during the practice as needed. As practice progresses, the practitioner can offer instructions to improve performance together with demonstrations while encouraging peer observation of performance when possible. Further, practitioners can facilitate instruction by drawing the child's attention to the number of repetitions and total practice time to avoid fatigue, permitting sufficient practice to improve performance. Finally, teachers can sequence tasks, such as progressions of throwing difficulty, to emphasize variability of practice by introducing different target distances, target sizes, and weight and/or shape of the throwing object. If the purpose of instruction is to enhance a specific movement pattern or objective, then practitioners can emphasize more practice in the desired specific conditions.

Disability and categories

Teaching students with disabilities may appear a daunting task; however, understanding *how* disability affects movement and applying that knowledge to modify instruction and the environment will help ensure success. Individual constraints can be taken into consideration and provide the basis for modifications to the environment, task, and instruction to ensure student success. An example would be slowing the tempo of a game by changing equipment, for instance, a beach ball instead of volleyball, to accommodate children who require additional time for motor planning.

Disabilities can be broken down into several broad categories based on functionality. Over the past two decades there has been a move away from the medical model to biopsychosocial models (World Health Organization [WHO], 2013). The current biopsychosocial model proposed by WHO focuses on the individual's functional abilities and the role of contextual factors in facilitating or creating barriers to optimal function. This chapter does not go in depth into specific disabilities, as diagnostic labels do not provide in-depth information about a child's functional ability. For instance, two children with the same diagnostic label may require vastly different supports. Consider these two children, each with a physical disability; one student has a significant impairment in all four limbs and uses a power wheelchair; the other student had a below-the-knee amputation of the left leg, was fitted with a state-of-the-art prosthetic, and is able to walk, run, and hop unassisted. Each student has a physical disability but requires very different supports to function successfully. Diagnostic labels provide a starting point, and more information about the 13 categories of disability outlined by IDEA can be found in http://idea.ed.gov (see Table 15.1). Practitioners can obtain guidance on evidence-based practices for specific disabilities, but this information must be applied on an individual basis matching each person's abilities and constraints. For instance, a teaching or intervention strategy researched for individuals with a physical disability may also work well for a child with autism spectrum disorder who moves unsteadily.

Understanding the impact of structural and/or functional impairment is important when planning a PE lesson. Disability is a complex phenomenon that always includes a problem within a person's body and interaction with features of the person and their environmental context (WHO, 2013). Recognizing the differences in body function or structure and the malleability of contextual factors sets the scene for adapting activities for success (King, Rigby, & Batorowicz, 2013). Variability of motor abilities is very large in children with disabilities. Children may not follow typical trajectories of motor development. However, all children can learn motor skills and benefit from physical activity. Educators need to evaluate each child's abilities and limitations and adapt the task and environment accordingly (Block, 2000).

Task analysis and motor skill classification

One of the first things one might want to consider when preparing motor skill instruction to a diverse group of students is how to analyze the skill. Task analysis in APE is used primarily for

Table 15.1 Categories, definitions, and functional impairment of varied disability conditions (U.S. Department of Education, Individuals with Disabilities Education Act [IDEA])

Category	IDEA definition	Functional impairment
1. Autism	A developmental disability significantly affecting verbal and nonverbal communication and social interaction, generally evident before the age of 3. Other characteristics include engaging in repetitive activities and stereotyped movements, resistance to environmental change or change in daily routines, and unusual responses to sensory experience.	Difficulty in social communication and interaction Generally poor motor skills Atypical attention patterns Resistance to environmental change High prevalence of sensory seeking or avoiding behaviors
2. Deaf-blindness	Concomitant (simultaneous) hearing and visual impairments, the combination of which causes such severe communication and other developmental and educational needs that cannot be accommodated in special education programs for children with deafness or children with blindness.	Difficulty in receiving information from the environment Imitation is difficult Modification to instruction is necessary
3. Deafness	A hearing impairment so severe that a child is impaired in processing linguistic information through hearing that adversely affects a child's educational performance.	May not receive auditory cues Verbal instructions may be inadequate
4. Emotional disturbance	A condition exhibiting one or more of the following characteristics over a long period of time and to a marked degree that adversely affects a child's educational performance: a) inability to learn that cannot be explained by intellectual, sensory, or health factors; b) inability to build or maintain satisfactory interpersonal relationships with peers and teachers; c) inappropriate feelings under normal circumstances; d) a general pervasive mood of unhappiness or depression; e) tendency to develop physical symptoms or fears associated with personal or school problems.	Difficulty interacting with peers Difficulty following instructions May have strong reactions during team activities May be reluctant to participate in activities, alone or in groups
5. Hearing impairment	An impairment in hearing, whether permanent or fluctuating, that adversely affects a child's educational performance but is not included under the definition of "deafness."	Difficulty or inability to hear verbal instructions and cues May not hear cues, such as whistles or buzzers, during activities
6. Intellectual disability	Significantly subaverage general intellectual functioning, existing concurrently with deficits in adaptive behavior and manifested during the developmental period that adversely affects a child's educational performance.	Motor skill development lags behind same age peers without disabilities Difficulty comprehending instruction, especially multi-step May require more practice and instruction to learn a new skill or activity

Table 15.1 (*cont.*)

Category	IDEA definition	Functional impairment
7. Multiple disabilities	Concomitant impairments, the combination of which causes such severe educational needs that they cannot be accommodated in special education programs solely for one of the impairments.	Small group or 1:1 instruction for best results Great variability in individual characteristics
8. Orthopedic impairment	A severe orthopedic impairment that adversely affects a child's educational performance. Includes impairments caused by a congenital anomaly, disease, and other causes (cerebral palsy, amputations, fractures, or burns that cause contractures).	Difficulty with locomotor activities, possibly object control, also May use mobility devices such as wheelchairs, walkers, crutches Modifications to activities and the environment aid accessibility and success
9. Other health impairment	Having limited strength, vitality, or alertness, including a heightened alertness to environmental stimuli, which results in limited alertness with respect to the educational environment, that: a) is due to a chronic or acute health problem; b) adversely affects a child's educational performance.	May fatigue easily May be limited in the type of activities in which the child can participate Environmental stimuli (e.g., pollen) may need to be reduced by changing environments
10. Specific learning disability	A disorder in one or more of the basic psychological processes involved in understanding or in using language, spoken or written, that may manifest itself in the imperfect ability to listen, think, speak, read, write, spell, or do mathematical calculations.	Great variability in individual characteristics May have difficulty comprehending instructions, especially in group situations Use of multimedia presentation of information recommended
11. Speech or language impairment	A communication disorder such as stuttering, impaired articulation, language impairment, or voice impairment that adversely affects a child's educational performance.	May need extra time when communicating with instructor or teammates May use a communication device
12. Traumatic brain injury	An acquired injury to the brain caused by an external physical force, resulting in total or partial functional disability or psychosocial impairment, or both, that adversely affects a child's educational performance.	Great variability in individual characteristics depending on location and extent of damage to the brain May exhibit physical, cognitive, and/or behavioral deficits
13. Visual impairment, including blindness	An impairment in vision that, even with correction, adversely affects a child's educational performance. The term includes both partial sight and blindness.	May not receive visual cues and demonstration May have poorly developed spatial skills, including body awareness and laterality Intrinsic feedback may not be available

Definitions are taken from U.S. Department of Education Individuals with Disabilities Education Act (IDEA) http://idea.ed.gov/Sec.300.8.

three purposes: (a) to analyze complex skills to identify component parts; (b) to provide instructional content for skill acquisition (Goodwin, 2003); and (c) to assess motor skill performance (Seaman, DePauw, Morton, & Omoto, 2007). When analyzing a skill, it is helpful to remember that the skill performance does not occur in a vacuum. A complex person in a particular environment is performing the task. The characteristics and interplay between three elements: the person, the environment, and the task, are critical to better understand the motor learner's performance (Newell, 1991). When teaching children with differing abilities, Newell's model can provide a structure for adapting movement, activities (Pope, Breslin, Getchell, & Liu, 2012). Teachers should consider the learner's individual characteristics, including structural features like neuromuscular development and level of maturation; as well as functional aspects, such as attention capability and level of motivation, among others. Similarly, teachers should pay attention to environmental characteristics of the instructional setting, assessing whether the environment will facilitate the learning process. Finally, the demands that the task imposes on the learner also should be carefully evaluated. To do so, one can use Gentile's taxonomy to define the degree of complexity and organization of the task at hand. With time, all three components: person, environment, and task, may change, and, therefore, different expressions of movement performance may be observed (see Figure 15.1). Teachers can design and implement optimal practice conditions when they understand these person, environment, and task characteristics.

Gentile (1987) developed a two dimensional taxonomy of motor skills that provides a useful way to analyze motor skills taking into account environmental context and function of the action. The taxonomy is a helpful tool in identifying logical sequences when developing a progression of skill instruction. Gentile identified two environmental factors that often change in physical activity settings: regulatory conditions and inter-trial variability. *Regulatory condition* refers to objects or other people in the environment that can be stationary or in motion. This environmental condition regulates how the mover adapts to be successful. *Inter-trial variability*, defined as change from one trial to the next, is either present or absent. Combining these two factors results in four categories: closed tasks, consistent tasks, variable tasks, and open tasks. Batting a ball off a tee is

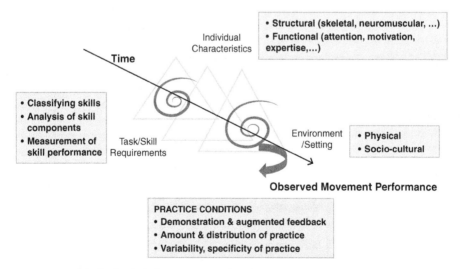

Figure 15.1 Model of individual characteristics, task, and environment across time. These three elements change over time, and, together shape the observed performance characteristics of an individual. The three elements, their interactions, and how they change across time need to be considered in the design of the practice conditions

an example of where the environment is stable and inter-trial variability is absent, representing a closed task. An example of an open task would be a football player catching the football while avoiding his opponents. Consistent and variable tasks have one stationary and one changing factor. Difficulty increases as the environmental factors become less stable.

The second part of Gentile's (1987) taxonomy is related to the function of the action. Gentile defined *action* as "the observable outcome resulting from the performer's purposeful interaction with the environment" (Gentile, 2000, p. 113). Gentile recognized two broad categories of action that vary within a task: body orientation and object manipulation. *Body orientation* can vary between being still (body stability) and moving (body transport). *Manipulation* refers to all actions "on objects to change or maintain their positions" and is present or absent. Hitting a golf ball off a golf tee requires body stability plus manipulation; swimming 50 yards requires body transport and no manipulation. When the two functions are combined, four categories are created: body stability no manipulation, body stability plus manipulation, body transport no manipulation, and body transport plus manipulation. Gentile's taxonomy has been used successfully in physical therapy and rehabilitation settings for individuals with a variety of disabilities (Niemeijer, Schoemaker, Bouwien, & Smits-Englesman, 2006; Wüest, van de Langerberg, & De Bruin, 2014). With practice this model can become a viable framework to create skill progressions in PE for any developmental level (Adam, 1999).

When both of these factors are placed into a table, 16 categories emerge (see Figure 15.2). Difficulty increases from upper left to the lower right-hand corner of the taxonomy. This table can aid instructors in preparing skill progressions and planning a variety of activities to meet multiple skill levels. Categories in the top left-hand side are suitable for beginners and students with low skill. The framework is also helpful in sequencing activities to move from a closed

Classification of Motor Tasks
(Gentile's Taxonomy)

		Environmental Context			
		Stationary		In Motion	
		No ITV	ITV	No ITV	ITV
Stability	No Manipulation	1A	1B	1C	1D
Stability	Manipulation	2A	2B	2C	2D
Transport	No Manipulation	3A	3B	3C	3D
Transport	Manipulation	4A	4B	4C	4D

(Left axis label: Function of Action)

Figure 15.2 Classification of motor tasks based on Gentile's taxonomy. This classification system has two dimensions (function of the action and environmental context), which in turn are subdivided into two levels each, originating a total set of 16 levels of motor skills (adapted from Gentile, 1987)

environment to more open game situations. In the first category (1A) the regulatory conditions are stationary, inter-trial variability absent, stable body, and no manipulation. The student has an opportunity to attend to body position and task execution. As the child becomes more confident, teachers can manipulate the environment or function of the task to incrementally increase difficulty. For instance, kicking a ball at a target while moving is an example of decreasing environment stability and increasing demands of the action.

PE teachers will find this taxonomy extremely helpful when designing multi-level instruction within a lesson. Stations may be set up which include a variety of categories. For instance when practicing throwing, one student may stand still and throw at a stationary target with the same size ball each trial (1B), while another student may be still and throw to another student who is wheeling across the gym (4B); at another station both the thrower and catcher may be moving, as in wheelchair basketball (4D). Each student is practicing throwing at a level that provides him or her optimal challenge and learning. Teachers using this framework can accommodate learners with different ability levels, permitting them to participate simultaneously in the lesson. A child with mobility impairment may be more comfortable throwing at a stationary target while another child in the class chooses the station with both thrower and catcher moving.

Key elements in motor behavior

Motor behavior, as a discipline, encompasses both theoretical and applied studies. Although theoretical perspectives are important to practitioners working with children with disabilities because they provide a foundation that guides and justifies some practice decisions, the studies that focus on applied aspects of motor behavior will be more directly related to their pedagogical applications. In the following section of this chapter we will focus on six key aspects that a practitioner should consider when designing the practice conditions for a child with disability: (a) attention, (b) motivation, (c) demonstration, (d) augmented feedback, (e) amount and distribution of practice, and (f) variability and specificity of practice.

Attention

Attention is defined as "(a) the act or state of applying the mind to something; (b) a condition of readiness for such attention involving, especially a selective narrowing or focusing of consciousness and receptivity" (Merriam–Webster's online dictionary, n.d.) and is an important part of learning and performing motor skills. The ability to selectively attend to pertinent cues and disregard irrelevant cues in the environment develops throughout early childhood and is often established by the time children begin formal education (Ruff & Capozzoli, 2003). However, some children struggle with establishing and maintaining attention. Motor performance of children with attention deficit hyperactivity disorder (ADHD), autism spectrum disorders (ASD), intellectual disabilities (ID), and other developmental delays may be affected by an inability to establish and maintain selective attention to environmental cues relevant to the task (Belmonte & Yurgelun-Todd, 2003; Gligorović & Durović, 2014; Tamm et al., 2010).

The importance of attention to motor performance is sometimes not completely recognized or taken into full consideration. It is important that practitioners evaluate a student's ability to attend while giving instruction and to maintain attention to relevant cues in the environment while completing the task (Cratty, 2004). Once this information is established, Gentile's model can be used as a guide to successfully design the task and environment for success. In a case study of a 5-year-old child with cerebral palsy, Kenyon and Blackington (2011) applied Gentile's model to the task of ascending a playground slide ladder. In their research the occupational therapist reported that the child was easily distracted and required multiple cues to stay on task. The treatment team systematically modified the task and the environment to provide increasing demands until the child was able to climb the ladder safely in a busy playground full of visual and auditory events that could be distracting. At the start the team had the child practice in a controlled environment with no distractions and no manipulation, simply stepping in place (1B). When the child was successful, they initiated the task of climbing a slide ladder. When the child was successful, the team moved the activity to an environment with more distractions until eventually the task was performed at the busy playground. This is one example of how Gentile's model can be applied to a specific task for a student with attention problems.

Certain problems with attention are prevalent for children with specific types of disabilities. ADHD is characterized by the core symptoms of inattention, impulsivity, and hyperactivity (American Psychiatric Association [APA], 2014). Inattentiveness is the limited ability to remain attentive for the time needed to perform or understand a certain task (APA, 2014). Children with ADHD have difficulty paying attention long enough to understand how to perform a task or activity and then experience challenges staying on-task long enough to complete the activity. Children with ADHD are typically behind their peers in motor performance and it has been hypothesized that skill acquisition is hampered by a deficit in sustaining attention (Burden & Mitchell, 2005). Short, direct bouts of instruction can be advantageous for children with ADHD. Additionally, individuals with ADHD may require less immediate repetition to learn a movement (Adi-Japha, Fox, & Karni, 2011) and benefit from repeating the movement at a different time.

The majority of children with ASD show atypical attention. A recent study of over 350 youth with ASD revealed significant impairments in both focused and sustained attention (Chien, Gau, Chiu, & Tsai, 2014). Additionally, individuals with ASD experience difficulty when shifting attention from one stimulus to another (Ozonoff, South, & Miller, 2000) and allotting attention in expected ways (Afshari, 2012). Problems with attention are thought to contribute to the core features of ASD and should be taken into consideration when choosing the task and environment. A variety of instructional strategies have been developed to enhance attention such as decreasing distractions in the environment, emphasizing relevant cues, using short instructional periods interspersed with frequent breaks, and teaching self-monitoring techniques to stay on task. Motor performance can be negatively affected by poor attention (Breslin & Rudisill, 2013).

When providing instruction and feedback to students with intellectual disability (ID) it is beneficial to emphasize an external focus of attention to enhance motor skill acquisition. A recent study by Chiviacowsky and colleagues compared the effect of instructions that directed attention to internal (movement of the body) *versus* external (movement of the object) elements of a throwing task for children with ID (Chiviacowsky, Wulf, & Avila, 2013). The children whose attention was directed towards the object, in this case where the beanbag landed, performed better than the group who were told to focus on their throwing limb.

Motivation

Motivation to engage in the physical activity presented to the learner is critical to success. Though it is widely known that children and adults with disabilities are less active than the non-disabled population, research on motivation and physical activity for individuals with disabilities is relatively scarce (Saebu, Sorensen, & Halvari, 2013). For the past two decades, Wehmeyer and colleagues have supported a self-determination framework to explore motivation for individuals with ID and other developmental disabilities (Wehmeyer & Abery, 2013). Self-determination theory is a metatheory which purports that three psychological needs are directly related to motivation: autonomy, competence, and relatedness (Deci & Ryan, 1985; also see Chapters 41 & 44, this volume). When individuals perceive that their needs are met, intrinsic motivation increases, leading to greater levels of participation. Wehmeyer and colleagues provide a framework of skills and attitudes that increase self-determined behavior. For instance realistic goal setting, self-monitoring, and self-reinforcement are all skills that can increase self-determined behavior and motivation (Wehmeyer & Abery, 2013). This framework offers promise when applied to the motor domain. Several theories of self-determination exist and all have a common basis: self-determination is a person-environment interaction. As people are able to act autonomously in a self-regulated and psychologically empowered manner their intrinsic motivation increases.

The self-determination framework was recently tested (Saebu et al., 2013) with young adults with physical disabilities and proved robust. Forty-four clients of a rehabilitation program answered a questionnaire based on self-determination theory in relation to the physical activity program provided by the rehabilitation clinic. The clients participated in the physical activity program three to five hours per day, six days per week. Clients indicated that autonomy support, optimal challenge, and social benefits increased intrinsic motivation, which, in turn, resulted in more physical activity.

Educators can provide opportunities for self-determined action by promoting choice, goal setting, problem solving, and self-regulation. Todd and Reid (2006) included individual goal setting and self-monitoring during a snowshoeing/jogging program for high school students with ASD. Participation in the program increased as students worked to meet their goals. Individual, task, and environmental constraints must be taken into consideration when setting attainable goals; this will increase the chance of student success.

Demonstration

Demonstration and imitation are important motor learning elements. Children learn motor skills by watching others, and teachers rely on demonstration to teach motor skills to their students. Children with ASD in particular have deficits in imitation and rarely imitate actions (Ingersoll, 2008; Williams, Whiten, & Singh, 2004) and thus do not benefit as much from demonstrations. However, demonstrations can be modified to be more effective. Cueing children to attend to specific movements, for instance, asking a child to look at your hands when demonstrating how to hold a bat will help children focus their attention on the task you want to demonstrate.

Imitation tasks can be divided into three categories: postural movements, actions on objects, and oro-facial movements; children with ASD show impaired imitation in all areas (Rogers, Hepburn, Stackhouse, & Weiner, 2003). However, children with ASD have greater success imitating tasks that involve actions on objects (Zachor, Ilanit, & Itzchak, 2010). This pattern also has been seen in children without disabilities and those with developmental delays (Stone, Ousley, & Littlefore, 1997). There is consensus in the literature that children with autism show fewer imitation deficits when tasks are goal-directed, meaningful, and have object-related actions. Custance, Mayer, Kumar, Hill, and Hearton (2014) recently conducted an experiment that added extrinsic, non-social rewards to object-related imitation tasks. Results suggested there was

231

no difference between children with and without ASD on imitation tasks. These findings can help educators choose appropriate tasks when preparing physical activity lessons.

Augmented feedback

In general, feedback refers to any type of information about a movement that has been performed. Feedback can enhance learning and performance of motor skills. Some feedback is inherent within a task, referred to as intrinsic feedback. This can include sensory-perceptual information that results from the performance of the movement through various sensory inputs, including vision, touch, proprioception, and hearing. Feedback can also be provided from external sources, such as from a teacher or peer. This feedback, known as extrinsic or augmented feedback, includes information in addition to intrinsic feedback from an outside source. The use of feedback is critical when learning and performing motor skills, however there may be challenges created by different impairments that teachers should take into consideration when planning lessons or activities.

Evidence-based practice research for children with intellectual disability recommends that instructors provide feedback in the form of movement outcome errors when learning a motor task. Teachers or peers can provide information on the accuracy of a throw (distance from target) or the length of a jump to augment the intrinsic information received by the mover. Tangible results provide meaningful information and aid in motor performance. A recent study compared this traditional technique to a reduced error protocol during a throwing task (Capio, Poolton, Sit, Eguia, & Masters, 2013). The researchers reasoned that the cognitive demands required to process complex information provided through feedback might impede acquisition of a skill. Researchers assigned one group of children to an error reduced (ER) group, while they placed a student comparison group in an error strewn group (ES). The ER group practiced throwing at a large target, while those in ES threw at a small target. The ER large target group made fewer errors, which is related to an instructional technique commonly known as errorless learning (Alberto & Troutman, 2006). The large target for the ER group was systematically made smaller, eventually matching the target of the ES group. The participants were asked to aim at the + in the square. Success was counted as hitting anywhere in the square target. The feedback provided immediately after the task was implicit to the task, and provided whether participants hit the target or not. At the conclusion of this task sequence, the children in the ER group performed better than the ES group. Although traditional extrinsic feedback relies heavily on cognitive processes to correct for movement errors and improve skill performance, this may be difficult for children with ID. Decreasing cognitive demands, by reducing the amount of information provided, and setting up the environment to promote success proved effective for this group of children. The researchers reasoned that reduced reliance on cognitive processes was beneficial during motor performance. When working with children with ID, it is important to understand how feedback is processed and the cognitive demands these processes may require to ensure that the information received is beneficial. Intrinsic feedback benefits motor learning when the environment is carefully constructed.

Students with ASD may benefit from visual information more than other forms. Sensory integration problems are common among people with ASD and may make it difficult to use intrinsic information received during motor skill performance. Visual feedback has proven important for children with ASD. A recent study by Yang and colleagues confirmed that children with ASD have motor coordination problems and rely on visual feedback to adjust movements and successfully complete motor tasks (Yang, Lee, & Lee, 2014). When visual feedback was eliminated during a reaching task, motor coordination and movement time were affected.

When teaching children with ASD it is important to choose tasks and environments that provide visual feedback. Additionally, it is helpful to cue the individual to important aspects of the feedback provided.

Providing feedback to children with visual impairments can pose a challenge for educators. Visual feedback implicit to a task is not readily accessible to learners with low or no vision. Furthermore, conventional information regarding body position and movement provided by the instructor may not be very meaningful to these students. A recent study evaluated spatial skills, including body awareness, laterality, directionality, and perspective taking (Koustriava & Papadopoulos, 2012). When giving feedback to students with visual impairments about a movement, researchers commonly give information that involves use of these skills. For instance they might tell a child that the ball landed two feet left of the target, or that they did not step with their right foot. The researchers found that spatial skills in children with low and no vision were not developed in many children. They concluded that this lack of knowledge was not due to the visual impairment but to incomplete development. Therefore, based on this research, educators should assess a child's spatial skills and adjust feedback accordingly. If a child is not sure where certain body parts are, how they move, or cannot differentiate between left and right, then this must be taken into consideration when providing feedback. For example, when teaching a child who cannot identify his left and right foot to step with the contralateral foot while throwing, a teacher can place visual cues on the floor for the student to step on with the correct foot. Three textured poly-spots, two placed side-by-side for the child to stand on and one in front of the foot that should step forward, will help the child know when he steps on the spot if he has used the correct foot.

Amount and distribution of practice

When considering the amount of practice to be scheduled for a learner, one can follow the general principle that more time for *motor practice is better* to improve performance and learning as long as fatigue is avoided. For example, young children better adapt their motor performance to a split belt treadmill where one leg moves faster than the other while walking, if they are provided with more previous experience or practice (Patrick et al., 2014). In addition to the amount of practice, educators might consider how to distribute this practice and whether the educator and learner should co-design the practice schedule.

It is widely accepted that for children without disability, practice should be *distributed as compared to a massed* schedule of practice that involves continuous practice with shorter and fewer breaks (Lee & Genovese, 1988; Shea, Lai, Black, & Park, 2000). A distributed schedule of practice allows more time for information processing and motor consolidation, minimizes fatigue, and may assist in motivation. Therefore, the preferred form of practice will include breaks for rest, observation of demonstration, self-evaluation, and error detection. However, an exception can be found in the literature, where children with ASD did not benefit from a distributed schedule of practice as compared to a massed schedule (Wek & Husak, 1989). Potentially, children with ASD's limited capacity to acquire and use task-intrinsic (information generated by the body) as well as task-related information (information generated by an external source like the practitioner or peers) may account for this result.

Another established account regarding practice schedule is that for children without disability *self-controlled practice* is better than a schedule imposed by the practitioner (Wulf, Raupach, & Pfeiffer, 2005). For instance, Post, Fairbrother, and Barros (2011) reported that a self-controlled amount of practice facilitated motor learning since those individuals who chose their practice schedules were more accurate during a transfer task. Interestingly, this same group of individuals also recalled the number of trials completed more effectively, suggesting that self-controlled practice has implications beyond task-specific factors. The added knowledge about the performance in itself via self-controlled practice, in addition to the cognitive processes (memory, for example) involved in motor learning, is a combination that recently has been acknowledged by motor learning scholars as important in the integration of motor learning concepts into PE (Rukavina & Jeansonne, 2009). Rukavina and Jeansonne (2009) propose that when students have an understanding of the learning process it can enhance motivation and their ability to select appropriate strategies for each unique learning situation. It is very plausible that similar effects might be detected in children with disabilities as long as self-controlled aspects of the practice are well matched with the individual's capacities.

Although self-controlled practice may be beneficial to skill learning, reducing the overall amount of practice has been observed to be advantageous under self-controlled conditions (Post et al., 2011). If this is the case, then teachers have a challenge when designing a PE lesson or intervention session. The task must both ensure sufficient practice and permit the learner to benefit from a self-controlled practice schedule. Therefore, educators need to consider the delicate balance between the learner's capacities and task demands to decide the self-controlled practice level optimal for each unique learner and situation.

Additionally, individual differences will influence the learner's use of self-controlled practice. For example, children who requested feedback during the execution of successful practice learned a throwing task better when compared to those children who received the same amount of feedback but not necessarily timed with the success of their practice (Chiviacowsky, Wulf, de Medeiros, Kaefer, & Tani, 2008). Wulf (2007) hypothesized that certain individual characteristics, such as levels of motivation and information processing capacity, may interact with self-controlled practice. In other words, Wulf suggests that self-controlled practice enhances the learner's motivation that, in turn, can generate deeper information processing, improving motor learning (Wulf, 2007).

Although the benefits of self-controlled practice also seem applicable to children with disabilities, further research is necessary and needs to examine the extent to which benefits of self-controlled practice can be generalized to children with disabilities. Thus far, such benefits have been found in patients with Parkinson disease (Chiviacowsky, Wulf, Lewthwaite, & Campos, 2012) and in a young adult with Down syndrome (Chiviacowsky, Wulf, Machado, & Rydberg, 2012). In these two studies, adults with different disabilities benefited from self-controlled feedback when learning a motor task (balancing for patients with Parkinson and a linear positioning task in the Down syndrome study) compared to a group of adults with the same disability that received the same amount and frequency of feedback but on a predetermined schedule. Again, being able to determine when feedback is needed may engage more cognitive processing and motivate the performer further compared to a pre-established schedule. It seems that self-controlled feedback enhances learning in individuals with disabilities.

Variability and specificity of practice

Whether the frequency of practice follows one or another schedule, practitioners will have to make decisions about the content to be included within the practice sessions and whether this content should be more or less variable (Porretta, 1990; Zipp & Gentile, 2010). In general, two forms of content practice have been defined: blocked, also called constant, and random, also called variable. There are advantages and disadvantages to each. Constant practice refers to repetitive practice of the same task. It has been shown to be more effective for improving specific task performance. When a motor skill is well learned, it typically demonstrates a high level of stability. On the contrary, random practice is defined by practice that involves varying the task demands over practice trials, purposefully destabilizing the skill performance. This type of variable practice has been hypothesized to improve adaptability and therefore transfer of learned skills to other skills of similar characteristics (Matsouka, Trigonis, Simakis, Chavenetidis, & Kioumourjoglou, 2010).

Different levels of practice conditions (from constant to random) may lead to different levels of stabilization, and the level of stabilization, in turn, will influence the child's adaptation capability. Previous research demonstrated that better adaptation is achieved with a schedule of constant followed by random practice (Barros & Corrêa, 2006; Corrêa, Benda, Meira Junior, & Tani, 2003). Constant practice facilitates the formation of a movement pattern, and the subsequent random practice prepares the child to more easily adapt to new contextual demands (Corrêa et al., 2003; Lai, Shea, Wulf, & Wright, 2000). Furthermore, additional constant practice prior to random practice may not facilitate adaptive motor responses in the face of a new demand because excess of constant practice tends to make the motor skill more rigid (Corrêa et al., 2010).

Whether the benefits of a constant followed by a random schedule of practice are applicable to children is not clear, but recent research replicating the findings of research with adults to children suggested that random practice facilitates motor learning (Granda Vera & Montilla, 2003; Ste-Marie, Clark, Findlay, & Latimer, 2004). Limited research would suggest that the nature and degree of benefits may depend on the task complexity and the child's age (Jarus & Gutman, 2001; Zipp & Gentile, 2010). Nevertheless, a small study conducted with children with Down syndrome demonstrated better performance on a transfer task of throwing to a more distant target under a random practice schedule (Baker, 2002). Also, children with dystonia, who have increased variability in their movements, are able to compensate their movement pattern appropriately in response to further increased variability (Chu, Sternad, & Sanger, 2013). Finally, in a study conducted with children with intellectual disabilities, variability of practice in a random schedule resulted in better performance in a throwing transfer task as compared to a constant schedule of practice (Matsouka et al., 2010). Together, these findings may suggest that children with disability may benefit from variable schedule of practice. Practicing skills within a constant context may involve repetition initially, but variability should be added to improve adaptability, enhancing transfer of the learned skills to different contexts.

Future research is necessary in the field of motor behavior in children with disabilities since many unanswered questions remain related to practice session design and content. However, the motor behavior principles presented in this chapter can be a great aid when practitioners are confronted with designing physical activity sessions for students with physical disabilities. Further, as the field of web-based technology and electronic devices continue to improve, these technologies could be incorporated as potential facilitators to enhance physical activity in individuals with disabilities, enhancing implementation of motivational routines and affording individualized progressive programs (Di Tore & Raiola, 2012; Wuang, Chiang, Su, & Wang, 2011).

Summary of key findings

- When viewed from a biopsychosocial perspective, disability is not limited to the person but encompasses constraints within the body and interactions with the environment (WHO, 2013). Dynamical systems theory provides a framework for understanding the interaction of the person, task, and environment.

- Individual constraints experienced by learners with disabilities can be accommodated through changing the demands of the task and environment.
- Gentile's taxonomy of motor skills is a helpful model to systematically modify the closed to open characteristics of the task and environment to increase the demands on learners with disabilities.
- Attention problems are common among children with disabilities and can impact learning and performance.
- Instructors can focus on movement outcomes using an external focus to obtain best results (Chiviacowsky et al., 2013).
- Goal setting, problem solving, and choice can increase self-determined behavior for individuals with disability and can have a positive impact on their motivation to engage in physical activity (Wehmeyer & Abery, 2013).
- Children with ASD are better able to imitate actions that they perceive as meaningful and actions that require the use of objects, for instance, throwing a ball. These findings have direct implications when demonstrating actions.
- When teaching children with disabilities, instructors should ensure that feedback matches the person's abilities.
- Children with visual impairments have been found to have poorly developed body awareness, laterality, and directionality.
- Because children with ID struggle with high cognitive demands of feedback, feedback should be limited.
- Because self-controlled practice has proven helpful for motor learning for individuals without disabilities, this concept should be examined for people with disabilities.
- Constant practice facilitates the formation of a movement pattern for individuals with disabilities, while subsequent random (variable) practice prepares the child with disabilities to more easily adapt to new contextual demands.

Reflective section with a study case

Six-year-old Suzie loves to listen to music, carry her favorite doll, and swim. Suzie has ASD and attends first grade in her neighborhood school. Suzie's teacher has prepared a lesson designed to teach skills needed to play soccer. The focus of the lesson is on kicking a receivable pass. The teacher begins the lesson by explaining why kicking and passing a ball is important and demonstrates how to kick with the instep of the foot to direct the pass to a player who moves to receive it. Following the demonstration the teacher directs the class to divide into two groups and practice passing the ball to one another from a short distance. After passing back and forth for some time the class is directed to a goal kicking activity. This lesson is well received by the majority of the students and they are engaged in the activities. Suzie, however, does not seem to pay attention to the instructions, and then does not understand the task at hand. She is frustrated, wanders away, and does not participate. The teacher wonders how he might modify the instruction and activity to assist Suzie so she may participate successfully.

1. Using Newell's model, identify individual constraints that Suzie may face. List the environmental and task characteristics of the lesson.
2. Gentile's taxonomy of motor skills is helpful when planning multilevel activities. Using the taxonomy, plan three activities for Suzie that progress in skill level and could be set up as stations during the passing activity so she is optimally challenged.

3. Children with ASD experience difficulties in attention and motivation. Explain how the task and environment can be set up for Suzie, including delivery of demonstration and feedback, to optimize participation, motor learning, and skill performance.
4. When teaching a motor skill to students with disability, program practice and variability need to be taken into consideration. Describe ways in which Suzie's teacher can provide the best conditions to practice this skill to facilitate transfer to a game situation.

References

Adam, D. L. (1999). Develop better motor skill progressions with Gentile's taxonomy of tasks. *Journal of Physical Education, Recreation, and Dance, 70*(8), 35–38.

Adi-Japha, E., Fox, O., & Karni, A. (2011). Atypical acquisition and atypical expression of memory consolidation gains in a motor skill in young female adults with ADHD. *Research in Developmental Disabilities, 32*, 1011–1020.

Afshari, J. (2012). The effect of perceptual-motor training on attention in the children with autism spectrum disorders. *Research in Autism Spectrum Disorders, 6*, 1331–1336.

Alberto, P. A., & Troutman, A. C. (2006). *Applied behavior analysis for teachers* (7th edn). Upper Saddle River, NJ: Merrill/Prentice Hall.

American Psychiatric Association (APA). (2014). *Diagnostic and statistical manual of mental disorders* (5th edn). Washington, D.C.: Author.

Baker, B. J. (2002). An investigation of the relative effects of blocked and random practice on the learning of ballistic motor skills in typically developing children and children with Down syndrome. University of Washington, ProQuest, UMI Dissertations Publishing: 3072055.

Barros, J. A. C., & Corrêa, U. C. (2006). Practice schedule and adaptive process in motor learning: Effects of task specificity. *Journal of Sport & Exercise Psychology, 28*, S30.

Belmonte, M. K., & Yurgelun-Todd, D. A. (2003). Functional anatomy of impaired selective attention and compensatory processing in autism. *Cognitive Brain Research, 17*, 651–664.

Block, M. E. (2000). *A teacher's guide to including students with disabilities in general physical education.* Baltimore: Paul H. Brookes Publishing.

Breslin, C. M., & Rudisill, M. E. (2013). Relationships among assessment time, time on task, and motor skill performance in children with autism spectrum disorder. *Adapted Physical Activity Quarterly, 30*, 338–350.

Burden, M. J., & Mitchell, D. B. (2005). Implicit memory development in school-aged children with attention deficit hyperactivity disorder (ADHD): Conceptual priming deficit? *Developmental Neuropsychology, 28*(3), 779–807.

Capio, C. M., Poolton, J. M., Sit, C. H., Eguia, K. F., & Masters, S. W. (2013). Reduction of errors during practice facilitates fundamental movement skill learning in children with intellectual disabilities. *Journal of Intellectual Disability Research, 57*, 250–305.

Chien, Y., Gau, S. S., Chiu, Y., & Tsai, W. (2014). Impaired sustained attention, focused attention, and vigilance in youths with autistic disorder and Asperger's disorder. *Research in Autism Spectrum Disorders, 8*, 881–889.

Chiviacowsky, S., Wulf, G., & Avila, L. T. G. (2013). An external focus of attention enhances motor learning in children with intellectual disabilities. *Journal of Intellectual Disability Research, 57*, 627–634.

Chiviacowsky, S., Wulf, G., de Medeiros, F. L., Kaefer, A., & Tani, G. (2008). Learning benefits of self-controlled knowledge of results in 10-year-old children. *Research Quarterly for Exercise and Sport, 79*, 405–410.

Chiviacowsky, S., Wulf, G., Lewthwaite, R., & Campos, T. (2012). Motor learning benefits of self-controlled practice in persons with Parkinson's disease. *Gait & Posture, 35*, 601–605.

Chiviacowsky, S., Wulf, G., Machado, C., & Rydberg, N. (2012). Self-controlled feedback enhances learning in adults with Down syndrome. *Revista Brazileira de Fisoterapia, 16*, 191–196.

Chu, V. W. T, Sternad, D., & Sanger, T. D. (2013). Healthy and dystonic children compensate for changes in motor variability. *Journal of Neurophysiology, 109*, 2169–2178.

Corrêa, U. C., Benda, R. N., Meira Júnior, C. M., & Tani, G. (2003). Practice schedule and adaptive process in the acquisition of a manual force control task. *Journal of Human Movement Studies, 44*, 121–138.

Corrêa, U. C., Massigli, M., de Camargo Barros, J. A., Gonçalves, L. A., de Oliviera, J. A., & Tani, G. (2010). Constant-random practice and the adaptive process in motor learning with varying amounts of constant practice. *Perceptual and Motor Skills, 110*, 442–452.

Cratty, B. (2004). Adapted physical education: Self-control and attention. *Focus on Exceptional Children, 37*, 66–72.

Custance, D. M., Mayer, J. L., Kumar, E., Hill, E., & Hearton, P. F. (2014). Do children with Autism re-enact object movements rather than imitate demonstrator actions? *Autism Research, 7*, 28–39.

Deci, E. L., & Ryan, R. M. (1985). *Intrinsic motivation and self-determination in human behavior.* New York: Plenum.

Di Tore, P. A., & Raiola, G. (2012). Exergames in motor learning. *Journal of Physical Education and Sport, 12*, 358–361.

Gentile, A. M. (1987). Skill acquisition: Action, movement, and neuromotor processes. In J. H. Carr, R. B. Shepherd, J. Gordon, A. M. Gentile, & J. M. Held (Eds.), *Movement science: Foundations for physical therapy in rehabilitation.* Gaithersburg, MD: Aspen Publishers.

Gentile, A. M. (2000). Skill acquisition: Action, movement, and neuromotor process. In J. H. Carr & R. B. Shepherd (Eds.), *Movement science: Foundations for physical therapy in rehabilitation* (2nd edn) (pp. 111–187). Gaithersburg, MD: Aspen Publishers.

Gligorović, M., & Durović, B. (2014). Inhibitory control and adaptive behavior in children with mild intellectual disability. *Journal of Intellectual Disability Research, 58*, 233–242.

Goodwin, D. L. (2003). Instructional approaches to the teaching of motor skills. In R. D. Steadward, G. D. Wheeler, & E. J. Watkinson (Eds.), *Adapted physical activity* (pp. 255–284). Edmonton, AB: University of Alberta Press.

Granda Vera, J., & Montilla, M. M. (2003). Practice schedule and acquisition, retention, and transfer of a throwing task in 6-yr.-old children. *Perceptual Motor Skills, 96*, 1015–1024.

Ingersoll, B. (2008). The effect of context on imitation skills in children with autism. *Research in Autism Spectrum Disorders, 2*, 332–340.

Jarus, T., & Gutman, Z. (2001). Effects of cognitive processes and task complexity on acquisition, retention and transfer of motor skills. *Canadian Journal of Occupational Therapy, 12*, 280–289.

Kenyon, L. K., & Blackinton, M. T. (2011). Applying motor-control theory to physical therapy practice: A case report. *Physiotherapy Canada, 63*, 345–354.

King, G., Rigby, P., & Batorowicz, B. (2013). Conceptualizing participation in context for children and youth with disabilities: An activity setting perspective. *Disability and Rehabilitation, 35*(18), 1578–1585.

Koustriava, E., & Papadopoulos, K. (2012). Are there relationships among different spatial skills of individuals with blindness? *Research in Developmental Disabilities, 33*, 2164–2176.

Lai, Q., Shea, C. H., Wulf, G., & Wright, D. L. (2000). Optimizing generalized motor program and parameter learning. *Research Quarterly for Exercise and Sport, 71*(1), 10–24.

Lee, T. D., & Genovese, E. D. (1988). Distribution of practice in motor skill acquisition: Learning and performance effects reconsidered. *Research Quarterly for Exercise and Sport, 59*, 277–287.

Matsouka, O., Trigonis, J., Simakis, S., Chavenetidis, K., & Kioumourjoglou, E. (2010). Variability of practice and enhancement of acquisition, retention and transfer of learning using an outdoor throwing motor skill by children with intellectual disabilities. *Studies in Physical Culture and Tourism, 17*, 157–164.

Merriam-Webster's online dictionary. (n.d.). Attention. Retrieved December, 15, 2014, from www.merriam-webster.com/dictionary/attention.

Newell, K. M. (1991). Motor skill acquisition. *Annual Reviews of Psychology, 42*, 213–237.

Niemeijer, A. S., Schoemaker, M. M., & Smits-Engelsman, B. (2006). Are teaching principles associated with improved motor performance in children with developmental coordination disorder? A pilot study. *Journal of American Physical Therapy Association, 86*, 1221–1230.

Ozonoff, S., South, M., & Miller, J. (2000). DSM-IV-defined Asperger disorder: Cognitive, behavioral, and early history differentiation from high-functioning autism. *Autism, 4*, 29–46.

Patrick, S. K., Musselman, K. E., Tajino, J., Ou, H-C., Bastian, A. J., & Yang, J. F. (2014). Prior experience but not size of error improves motor learning on the split-belt treadmill in young children. *PloS ONE, 9*(3), e93349.

Pope, M., Breslin, C. M., Getchell, N., & Liu, T. (2012). Using constraints to design developmentally appropriate movement activities for children with Autism Spectrum Disorder. *Journal of Physical Education, Recreation, and Dance, 83*, 35–42.

Porretta, D. L. (1990). Current theoretical aspects of motor learning research in mentally handicapped individuals. *Clinical Kinesiology, 44*, 33–37.

Post, P. G., Fairbrother, J. T., & Barros, J. A. C. (2011). Self-controlled amount of practice benefits learning of a motor skill. *Research Quarterly for Exercise and Sport, 82*, 474–481.

Rogers, S. J., Hepburn, S. L., Stackhouse, T., & Wehner, E. (2003). Imitation performance in toddlers with autism and those with other developmental disorders. *Journal of Child Psychology and Psychiatry and Allied Disciplines, 44*, 763–781.

Ruff, H. A., & Capozzoli, M. C. (2003). Development of attention and distractibility in the first 4 years of life. *Developmental Psychology, 39*, 877–890.

Rukavina, P. B., & Jeansonne, J. J. (2009). Integrating motor-learning concepts into physical education. *Journal of Physical Education, Recreation and Dance, 80*(9), 23–30.

Saebu, M., Sorensen, M., & Halvari, H. (2013). Motivation for physical activity in young adults with physical disabilities during a rehabilitation stay: A longitudinal test of self-determination theory. *Journal of Applied Social Psychology, 43*, 612–625.

Seaman, J. A., DePauw, K. P., Morton, K. B., & Omoto, K. (2007). *Making connections: From theory to practice in adapted physical education* (2nd edn). Scottsdale, AZ: Holcomb Hathaway, Publishers.

Shea, C. H., Lai, Q., Black, C., & Park, J. H. (2000). Spacing practice sessions across days benefits the learning of motor skills. *Human Movement Science, 19*, 737–760.

Ste-Marie, D. M., Clark, S. E., Findlay, L. G., & Latimer, A. E. (2004). High levels of contextual interference enhance handwriting skill acquisition. *Journal of Motor Behavior, 36*, 115–126.

Stone, W. L., Ousley, O. Y., & Littleore, C. D. (1997). Motor imitation in young children with autism: What's the object? *Journal of Abnormal Child Psychology, 25*, 475–485.

Tamm, L., Hughes, C., Ames, L., Pickering, J., Silver, C. H., Stavinoha, P., ... Emslie, G. (2010). Attention training for school-aged children with ADHD: Results of an open trial. *Journal of Attention Disorders, 14*(1), 86–94.

Todd, T., & Reid, G. (2006). Towards self-managing physical activity for individuals with autism spectrum disorder. *Focus on Autism and Other Developmental Disabilities, 21*, 167–177.

Wehmeyer, M. L., & Abery, B. H. (2013). Self-determination and choice. *Intellectual and Developmental Disabilities, 51*, 399–411.

Wek, S. R., & Husak, W. S. (1989). Distributed and massed practice effects on motor performance and learning of autistic children. *Perceptual and Motor Skills, 68*, 107–113.

Williams, J. H. G., Whiten, A., & Singh, T. (2004). A systematic review of action imitation in autism spectrum disorder. *Journal of Autism and Developmental Disorders, 34*, 285–299.

World Health Organization. (2013). *International classification of functioning, disability and health* (ICF). Exposure draft for comment. October, 2013. Geneva: WHO.

Wuang, Y.-P., Chiang, C.-S., Su, C.-Y., & Wang, C.-C. (2011). Effectiveness of virtual reality using Wii gaming technology in children with Down syndrome. *Research in Developmental Disabilities, 32*, 312–321.

Wüest, S., van de Langenberg, R., & de Bruin, E. D. (2014). Design considerations for a theory-driven exergame-based rehabilitation program to improve walking of persons with stroke. *European Review of Aging and Physical Activity, 11*, 119–129.

Wulf, G. (2007). Self-controlled practice enhances motor learning: Implications for physiotherapy. *Physiotherapy, 93*, 96–101.

Wulf, G., Raupach, M., & Pfeiffer, F. (2005). Self-controlled observational practice enhances learning. *Research Quarterly for Exercise and Sport, 76*, 107–111.

Yang, H., Lee, I-Chen, Lee, & I-Ching. (2014). Visual feedback and target size effects on reach-to-grasp tasks in children with autism. *Journal of Autism and Developmental Disabilities, 44*, 3129–3139.

Zachor, D. A., Ilanit, T., & Itzchak, E. B. (2010). Autism severity and motor abilities correlates of imitation situations in children with autism spectrum disorders. *Research in Autism Spectrum Disorders, 4*, 438–443.

Zipp, G. P., & Gentile, A. M. (2010). Practice schedule and the learning of motor skills in children and adults: Teaching implications. *Journal of College Teaching and Learning, 7*, 35–42.

16

AN INTERNATIONAL PERSPECTIVE IN PHYSICAL EDUCATION AND PROFESSIONAL PREPARATION IN ADAPTED PHYSICAL EDUCATION AND ADAPTED PHYSICAL ACTIVITY

Eliane Mauerberg-deCastro, SÃO PAULO STATE UNIVERSITY, BRAZIL

Aija Klavina, LATVIAN ACADEMY OF SPORT EDUCATION, LATVIA

Martin Kudláček, PALACKY UNIVERSITY OLOMOUC, CZECH REPUBLIC

Cindy Sit, CHINESE UNIVERSITY OF HONG KONG, HONG KONG

Serap Inal, YEDITEPE UNIVERSITY, TURKEY

Teacher preparation of physical educators (PE) in adapted physical activity (APA) or adapted physical education (APE) requires multi-, inter-, and cross-disciplinary foundations (Sherrill, 2004a). Similar to the education needed for all physical educators, APE specialists' education must cover diverse topics (e.g., human development, motor behavior, etc.). Additionally, they should understand a range of models intended to expand knowledge and skills of those who teach, coach, or deliver services to individuals with disabilities (Mauerberg-deCastro, 2011). APA curricula in higher education should require PE students to experience diversity during the performance of challenging tasks while they learn how to solve educational problems (Figure 16.1). Furthermore, PE teachers who expand their critical thinking and advocacy skills also develop professional confidence, people skills, and the ability to effectively contribute to policy making (Andre & Mandigo, 2013; Lund, Wayda, Woodard, & Buck, 2007).

The purpose of this chapter is to describe the status of teacher and professional preparation in APA around the world, whether for curriculum development, pre-service, in-service, or simply for expanding the notions on human relationships and civil rights. First, we present an overview of teacher preparation and service delivery demands in PE from an international perspective. Here, we demonstrate the major strides in higher education curriculum development

Figure 16.1 Undergraduate students in a problem-solving team task during an APA class
(photo: E. Mauerberg-deCastro)

that have taken place in the Americas – North, Central, and South; and in Europe, Asia, Africa, Oceania, and the Middle East. We also discuss how many societies and their institutions (e.g., schools, legislative systems, political and economic institutions, among others) have shaped demands for diverse teaching and service deliveries. Some countries, such as in Europe and in North America, historically have initiated more assertive policies regarding APA professional competences, as demonstrated in their official standards for APA.

Delivery of services to students with special needs

During the nineteenth century, delivery of rehabilitation services and special education had a common intervention strategy, often guided by medical or clinical needs (Mauerberg-deCastro, 2011; Roush & Sharby, 2011). These provisions reflected the reality of intervention for individuals with disability in specialized institutions – usually psychiatric hospitals. Today, advancements in special education have merged with the requirements of general education curricula in regular schools. Leading international organizations for human rights, such as the *World Programme of Action Concerning Disabled Persons* (UN, 2010) recommended this practice of inclusion. However, many countries and societies around the world have not completely abandoned the institutional model in education (Mushoriwa, 2001; Wong, 2008); others have no education plans at all.

The China National Basic Database of Disabled Population revealed that over 7 million of the 29.47 million individuals with disability nationwide received rehabilitation services in 2014. However, students with disability with special educational needs still received government-supported educations, as well as PE, in special schools or institutions (CDPF, 2008).

In Zimbabwe, provisions for special education started after 1980. This initiative reflected moral and religious beliefs rather than basic civil rights; however, there were no academic plans for students with disability (Peresuh & Barcham, 1998). According to these authors, the few special schools that attempted to provide inclusive settings lacked specialized teachers and support from psychologists, speech therapists, physiotherapists, and medical doctors.

Even in inclusive schools, exclusion and segregation of students with disability are insidious and negatively influence administrative decisions, equal opportunity policies, and educational attitudes (Bines & Lei, 2011; Monteiro & Manzini, 2008). Although, worldwide, enormous strides have been made in the protection of rights of individuals with disability and in lawfully ensuring their integration into society, the actual implementation of these accomplishments is quite paradoxical. For example, despite the Indonesian government's efforts – since 1978 – to promote inclusive schooling, there has been a *decline* in the number of integrated schools and students enrolled in inclusive schools (Heung & Grossman, 2007). In the Islamic Sheria countries, legal provisions to protect human rights include those that guarantee dignity for individuals with disabilities (Al-Jadid, 2013). However, these legal protections cannot ensure that the general community feels comfortable about the inclusion of such students (Al-Gain & Al-Abdulwahab, 2002; Al-Jadid, 2013). This is true, as well, in other parts of the Middle East: Egypt, Syria, Jordan, and Lebanon.

We find examples of inconsistencies between legislation, policy, and reality worldwide. Kurniawatia, Minnaert, Mangunsong, and Ahmed (2012) pointed out that, although the 1945 Constitution of the Republic of Indonesia ensured that all citizens – including those with disabilities – would have equal rights and full access to society, only recently have schools in Indonesia become inclusive. New Zealand schools also suffer with the imposition of legislation on school curricular policies that appear disconnected from school reality (Petrie & lisahunter, 2011). School reliance on "external providers" for exercise and other physical activities are in contradiction with the holistic, socio-cultural, and critical approach to PE, especially when considering educational needs of children, including those with disability.

Concerns regarding generalist teachers teaching students with special needs

In many countries, when educating students with disabilities, the requirement of generalist primary school classroom teachers in taking responsibility for the entire curriculum, including the teaching of PE, can also compromise quality of education (Petrie & lisahunter, 2011). It is important to address these problems and considerations relative to teacher preparation and pre-service programs in higher education in the APA area. This is true especially because, worldwide, legislation related to inclusive education is expanding (although there may not yet be many practical examples of success). Therefore, this chapter describes political, historical, geographical, and cultural scenarios that illustrate situations in different parts of the world that affect the education of individuals with disability, and challenge future educators – in particular, those in PE. We will begin with a discussion of the common influences on education of students with disabilities in almost all cultures of the world: *segregation* and the *medical model of disability*.

Education, segregation, and inclusion: history of the *medical model of disability*, diversity, and human rights

The heritage: eradication of defiance

Since the Middle Ages, entire cultures, especially in the Western world, have made efforts and committed resources to eradicate what they have perceived as "deviant," "bizarre," or simply "different" individuals. Eradication was seen as central to "preserving the purity" of races, behavior, creed, and family values. Political traditions as well as religious beliefs reflected the notion that individuals with disabilities were threats to what was considered "normal." Medical institutions and physicians were the "protectors" of societies, those who dealt with deadly plagues and epidemics. Historically, these medical professionals took an active part in eradicating the "abnormality of the deviant ones" (Mauerberg-deCastro, 2011).

The founding of the Salpetriere Hospital in Paris in 1656 marked the establishment of the medical model in psychiatric practice. Until the early nineteenth century, the hospital facilities harbored the mentally ill, prostitutes, orphans, the elderly, deported individuals from French colonies around the world, and other economic and social outcasts. Hospitals, hospices, and prisons all were places designated to house individuals considered "deviant" (Goode, 1999). This widespread incarceration of individuals with a variety of developmental and health problems can be considered the origin of the *medical model of disability*. In general, the medical model guided and determined methods for treatment, rehabilitation, education and medical-pedagogical methods such as those of Jean-Marc-Gaspard Itard in the early 1800s. These methods were precursors of special education services.

The development of segregated services

Special education (segregated) services replaced the psychiatric institutional approach. From 1920 to 1960, schools for children and youngsters with disability in the United States were rare, and the treatment of children with developmental disabilities in institutions and hospitals was still a common practice (Figure 16.2). Special education for children with disabilities began in 1930. With the exception of severe cases, in the United States, educational programs in regular schools with separate special classes were created in the 1950s for several disability conditions (Smith, Polloway, Patton, & Dowdy, 1998). Specific institutions for special education served

Figure 16.2 Institutionalized individuals with Down syndrome often displayed psychiatric behavior (film frame from 1970. Courtesy of M. Adrian)

specific types of disability and, today, this is still a common situation in many countries, especially those with poor and developing economies.

Efforts to educate children with disability began in France, where their eligibility was determined through intellectual quantification tests. In 1905, Alfred Binet and Theodore Simon developed an individual intelligence test that was administered to French students (Hardman, Drew, & Egan, 1999). In the United States and Europe, the first disabled individuals to receive education, although segregated, were those who were deaf, blind, and children diagnosed as slow learners. This trend also was observed in Brazil with the foundation of the Imperial Institute of Blind Boys (1854), and later the Imperial Institute of the Deaf and Dumb (1887), both in Rio de Janeiro (Mauerberg-deCastro, 2011). The first schools for students with intellectual disability were established in Salvador (a division of what currently is known as the Hospital Juliano Moreira), State of Bahia, and in Rio de Janeiro (School of Mexico), in 1874 (Januzzi, 1985). In 1954, the Association of Parents and Friends of the Exceptional (Associação de Pais e Amigos dos Excepcionais), known as "APAE," was founded. Today, APAE is the largest special education institution for intellectual disability in Brazil. Despite the fact that in 2006 the rate of inclusion of students with disability in regular schools was over 46% and has increased enrollment by 493% in the last ten years, according to the MEC-Multi-Year Plan Assessment Report of 2008–2011 (Brazil, 2011), this nationwide institution shows no signs of downsizing its segregated services (APAE Brasil, 2014).

Professional training

In the past, physicians controlled educational approaches, rehabilitation, and even entire school models, and the medical model of disability guided the training of professionals and educators in higher education programs (MacKenzie, 1909; Rathbone, 1934). For example, during the first half of the twentieth century in the history of Brazilian education, as well as in other countries, schools were subjected to the medical-psychological screening of students, which complied with a *hygienist* approach to school curricula, and which was government-enforced (Wanderbroock Junior & Boarini, 2007), particularly in the PE curricula (Góis Junior & Lovisolo, 2003). Over the course of history and continuing until today, in many nations the medical model influences policy making, methods and service delivery, attitudes of staff, and even conceptual foundations. This is true not only with regard to the institutions that house patients or students, but also to the development of higher education curricula for professional training and pre-service teaching.

In many societies and entire countries, the medical model influenced a hygienist conception, advocated during government dictatorships, such as in Brazil, Chile, Argentina, Mexico, Nazi Germany, and many Asian countries. Sports education during the Ottoman Empire in Turkey, for example, was limited to military schools (Celik & Bulgu, 2010). Military calisthenics exercises were the key style in teaching PE. The hygienist conception in PE, as well as in other classes, aimed to ensure that citizens would be physically and mentally healthy. Students with low IQ-tested intellectual levels were undesirable, and, once detected, were isolated from their peers. "Normal" students were equated with being strong, clean, obedient, agreeable, and ready to defend their nation against threats to the majority (Wanderbroock Junior & Boarini, 2007). Diversity of race, creed, culture, political views, working women, sexual orientation, conditions of health and disability, among other situations, were likely threats to the model. Therefore, the heads of institutions and State governments enforced disciplinary or corrective measures to "resolve deviating situations."

In the Brazilian education system, from the beginning of school installations during the 1800[1] Colonial State until the end of the last military dictatorship in the early 1980s, schools followed curricula established by the Catholic Church or the State, or both (Maciel & Shigunov Neto, 2006). Today, although a mandatory Federal law requires all courses in PE in public and private colleges and universities (over 500 PE undergraduate courses nationwide) to have a core course in special physical education or APE (Brazil, 1987), students with disability do not have meaningful access to PE in their schools. In part, this is due to confusion about the goals of physical activity as a means for education, rehabilitation, and health. Moreover, professionals and educators do not feel that they are well prepared to work with special education needs integrated with regular students, much less to work with the students with severe or multiple disabilities. Attitudes seem to be the biggest problem for both professionals and society.

The general concept of the *medical model* refers to an approach to physical and biological aspects of pathological conditions aimed at finding medical treatments based on diagnosed symptoms, syndromes, and afflictions of the human body (Mosby's Medical Dictionary, 2009). It is important to emphasize that, although controversial, early methods of diagnosis, treatment, and prevention in the medical field were intended to be neutral and scientific. The *medical model of disability*, however, is a negative conception about a person with a disability. Disability within the medical model is recognized as a *problem* caused by disease, impairment, lesion, trauma, or other health condition that requires medical treatment by professionals in order to provide the "best" medical solution or a "cure." Questioning the *medical model of disability* does not dismiss the role and importance of medical science in keeping people alive, in healing and providing therapeutic alternatives in medication, intervention, and assistive technology.

Professional preparation and teaching of APE for physical educators

Early development of special services (and eventually in the fields of APA and sports) on the American continents was geographically centered in North America (Cratty, 1975; Lowman, Colestock, & Cooper, 1928; Winnick, 1986). However, there is no question that European immigration during the eighteenth, nineteenth, and twentieth centuries strongly influenced the delivery of such services. Even today, the leadership and advancement of North America in science, rehabilitation methods, and technology, legislation, and philosophical aspects continue to be in contrast with the rest of the regions of the American continent.

Segregation and inclusion in school

In many societies, teaching and service delivery in APA require academic preparation at different levels of specialization (e.g., undergraduate, graduate, or post-graduate studies), but often we find situations in real life applications that reveal the need for further development in the area. One problematic situation, especially in societies with emerging economies, is that teachers and professionals in the field tend to improvise their practices when faced with diverse/heterogeneous classes. Some reported that they are not prepared to teach students with disability, even if they had pre-service training in an institution with a good academic reputation (Bines & Lei, 2011; Mauerberg-deCastro et al., 2013). In general, teachers experience negative feelings about teaching students with disabilities if they believe they received insufficient training on how to handle students with disability (Kudláček & Barret, 2010).

Standards of professional practice

In the United States, although increasing progress in APA has taken place since the 1950s, many APA leaders have admitted that professional preparation is complex and subject to widespread barriers (Auxter, Pyfer, Zittel, Roth, & Huettig, 2010). In the last decades of the last century, for example, school teachers' limitations in core APA knowledge prevented the full provision of appropriate PE services to individuals with disabilities (Kelly, 1995). In 1991, professionals came together to identify standards of professional practice for teaching students with disabilities. The National Consortium for Physical Education and Recreation for Individuals with Disabilities (NCPERID), in conjunction with the National Association of State Directors of Special Education (NASDSE), and Special Olympics International, organized an "Action Seminar" directed by Dr. Luke Kelly that resulted in the NCPERID publication, *Adapted Physical Education National Standards Project* (APENS, 1995; Kelly, 1995). The APENS became a national certification program in APE that established knowledge standards for physical educators in APA prior to their involvement in teaching children with disabilities (APENS, 1995).

Discrepancies between legislative recommendations and reality regarding students with disability's access to meaningful physical activity opportunities is common in both developed and developing countries with economic and political challenges. In Canada, for example, Nowicki, Brown, and Stepien (2013) observed that, although inclusive education is lawfully required, the exclusion of students with intellectual and learning disabilities suggests the need to establish strategies so that all children can be socially proactive in inclusive classrooms. Children with and without disability need to be involved in cooperative fellowships that will help them find solutions to achieve academic, social, health, and fitness goals.

Curriculum and instruction in APE/PA

Physical educators benefit from biological and clinical information about disabilities that can help them understand the health/medical issues and functional needs of their students with disability. However, teacher preparation curricula seldom explicitly address core and pedagogical content knowledge associated with *what* and *how* future PE teachers should deliver exercise or motor skill activity to diverse groups that include students with disabilities. Although program content often defines individuals according to their disability, instructors often fail to justify how and why activities and exercises meet educational needs of students with disability. Thus, the medical model of disability continues to influence APA instruction, evident in the pervasive organization of practices based on disability.

The early content of courses and curricula in APA was based on textbooks and literature that included topics of disability using: predominantly clinical terminology; classification systems based on anatomical defects; etiology of diseases and conditions leading to damage or impairment, functional abnormalities. *Exercise in Education and Medicine*, published in 1909, 1915, and 1923 by R. Tait MacKenzie (physician and professor at McGill University in Canada until 1904 and then at the University of Pennsylvania), and *Corrective Physical Education*, launched in 1934, with seven editions, by Josephine Rathbone (physical therapist, physical educator, and professor at Columbia University), were examples of textbooks on the subject of physical activity for medical conditions and used by college students in the area of PE and later in kinesiology.

Table 16.1 Sections and topics (chapters) in the textbook, *Adapted Physical Activity*, by
Mauerberg-deCastro (2005, 2011; adapted from Mauerberg-deCastro, 2005, 2011)

Sections	Topics related to APA and disabilities
Cross-disciplinary, historical, social, and political bases of APA	• Definition, concepts, and goals of PE, APE, and APA • Historical foundations in APA and sports; medical model of disability; institutionalization and methods of segregation • Stereotypes and disability; "culture of perfection"; media and violence; media role in attitudes and social stigma; advocacy for civil rights; prejudice and discrimination; stereotypes and minorities; role of PE teachers and responsibilities
Biological, psychological, and social foundations in APA	• Throughout lifespan; risk and prevention, classification systems, environmental vs. inherited; health problems and chronic conditions that cause disabilities • Motor development and delays; theories about the child and adaptive functions; human development; perceptual-motor development; motor control and motor learning • Clinical, behavioral, and educational characteristics of the blind, deaf, deaf-blind children, individuals with intellectual disability, and learning disability • Psychiatric disorders and behavioral problems in the adult and the child; pervasive developmental disorders, autism; problems of conduct; methods of behavior management; legal and ethical aspects • Language, perception, communication and expression; sensorial and perceptual impairments • Clinical, physiological, and biomechanical aspects of spinal cord injuries, amputation, and other physical disabilities; applications from the exercise sciences
Pedagogical trends in PE, exercise, curriculum development, and assessment	• Organization of APA: curriculum, objectives, and goals; principles in APA; ecological and dynamic systems approaches to rehabilitation and teaching APA • Toys, equipment, play, PA practices. Design and organization for pedagogical and therapeutic purposes; moral and cognitive development • Aquatics, dance, sports (Special Olympics; Paralympics); nature activities (radical sports; sustainability in sport and PE practices); alternative/holistic practices and healing (massage techniques, yoga, and meditation; humor and music in PE; animal assisted activity/therapy) • APA and the inclusive school; pedagogical methods, theories in education; trends and current facts in inclusion • Health, wellness, and exercise programs: active vs. inactive lifestyle • Evaluation, instruments, and assessment protocols

PE curricula and APA courses in higher education institutions often endorse the recommendations of international advocacy programs for education, and these also appear in international documents such as Education For All (EFA) (UNESCO, 2009) and the *World Report on Disability* (WHO, 2011). These recommendations reflect concerns with early intervention, facilitation of development, health, rehabilitation, inclusion and accessibility, among others.

In 2005, Mauerberg-deCastro proposed a new way to organize APA curricula in Brazilian higher education programs when she published the first Brazilian-only authored textbook,

Adapted Physical Activity (*Atividade Física Adaptada*). The curricula were divided into three sections of core knowledge, which included 1) history, society, and generalities about APA; 2) biological, psychological, and social foundations; and, 3) pedagogical trends in PE, exercise, curriculum development, and assessment. Although basic medical/clinical information appears in several chapters, she warns readers of the negative impact of the medical model of disability for guiding professionals and educators in their practices related to individuals with disabilities of all ages, cultural, and socioeconomic backgrounds (Table 16.1).

Advances in APA curricula and modern theoretical foundations in the USA, Canada, Australia, and most of Europe refer to interdisciplinary, cross-disciplinary, and multidisciplinary knowledge. APA programs for children in primary school, for example, integrate findings in infant development and, particularly, in motor development. This example provides professionals with an understanding about adaptations (e.g., postural control during mobility tasks) that children with disability exhibit over time (e.g., cerebral palsy), and how physical activity can be integrated into health, education, and rehabilitation initiatives.

Curriculum development in APA: the European experience

The European Union (EU) is an international organization that links 27 countries and operates with a broad influence to formulate, shape, and implement European policy. The European Commission (EC) is the central body of the EU that establishes and defines common policies for member countries. In 1972, the EC responded to the outcome of the first European summit, in which government leaders agreed that education would be the most important vehicle to lead Europe into a new era (European Commission, 2002). Among the Commission's strategic objectives was "Facilitating the access of all to education and training systems." A basic principle of the objective was that all citizens should have equal access to education and training.

Legislation, political, and economic situations of the region: goals and challenges in the APA area

The European Council's Declaration (European Commission, 2001) recognized physical education and sport as having an important role in European society. In order to give strategic orientation to the role of PE and sport in Europe and to enhance the visibility of PE and sport in EU policy making to raise public awareness, the EC published the document, "White Paper in Sport" (European Commission, 2007). This initiative aimed to improve social inclusion and integration through sport for all, using European programs and resources.

Guiding principles and models in pedagogical practices: service deliveries

Two large-scale European projects were implemented during the last decade that articulate the APA situation in Europe. The Thematic European Network on Adapted Physical Activity (THENAPA) involved more than 30 experts from 28 EU countries (DePotter et al., 2003), while the European Standards in APA (EUSAPA) project (2008–2010) involved more than 20 APA experts from 10 EU countries (Klavina & Kudláček, 2011).

The THENAPA project identified four professional tracks for APA specialization: physical education, sport performance, recreation, and rehabilitation. The EUSAPA project later explored the status of APA relative to academic standards (i.e., specific competencies and learning outcomes) in the three APA areas (sport, education, and rehabilitation). It provided a useful contribution to the development of an international academic framework to guarantee the quality of professional training in the fields of APA at the European level (European Standards in Adapted Physical Activity, 2010).

Two international study programs in Europe offer specializations in APA. The first was the Erasmus Mundus Master in Adapted Physical Activity (EMMAPA), a two-year Master's program (120 credits) offered jointly by the organizing universities and associate partners of the EMMAPA Consortium. As the EMMAPA program is terminating in 2016, a new international program is now in place, the International Master's in Adapted Physical Activity (IMAPA). The IMAPA combines the expertise of more than 20 universities and organizations throughout Europe. The IMAPA is housed at the University of Leuven (KU Leuven, Belgium) and at the University of Olomouc (Czech Republic).

The second international program, the European University Degree in Adapted Physical Activity (EUDAPA), is located at the Haaga-Helia University of Applied Sciences (Finland) (Vilhu, 2013). In countries (e.g., Ireland, Latvia, Poland, Portugal, and the United Kingdom [UK]) where APA does not exist as an official profession, other professionals (e.g., PE teachers, physiotherapists, and coaches) with backgrounds in APA provide APA services.

It seems clear that many school-aged students with disabilities do not have or have limited opportunity to participate on equal terms in education, including PE (Klavina & Kudláček, 2011). In most European countries, teachers are required by law to enroll a student with a disability in their class (Lienert, Sherrill, & Myers, 2001). Despite the EUSAPA project, there is great diversity in the educational systems, legislation, terminology, and teacher training programs in Europe regarding APE. For example, in Belgium, Portugal, Ireland, Latvia, and Poland, legislation does not explicitly mention APE (Klavina & Kudláček, 2011). In Finland APE can be delivered by teachers in daycare, in the classroom/special education class, in basic education, by PE teachers, and/or APE teachers, while in France, APA is explicitly considered a lawful profession. French professionals with APE bachelor's degrees can lead physical activity sessions in the areas of health and rehabilitation for persons with motor or psychological disabilities, but not in the area of coaching.

Throughout Europe, higher education institutions include studies in APE. Many have legislation that includes statements about specialized areas to support special education needs (SEN), with PE identified as one of these areas. For example, the University of Coimbra requires all students to enroll in the APE curriculum. In Latvia, however, APE is not explicitly mentioned in the laws. The requirements for pedagogical staff such as teachers working in educational settings include a diploma in higher education in a specific subject such as sport education. Several compulsory APE study courses are taught as part of sport science and health care programs at the Latvian Academy of Sport Education in Riga. In Poland, teachers in APE (called "special PE") are expected to participate in special life-long learning courses, continuing to develop APA-related competencies. Legislation in the UK prohibits discrimination in education and supports inclusive education.

Overall, PE is a compulsory part of education in most European countries. What differs is the amount of allocated teaching hours for PE across Europe, the approach to curricula, and the competencies of PE teachers. For example, during the last decade time allocated for PE has increased in 16% of the EU countries, remained the same in 68% of the countries, and has declined in 16% of these countries (Hardman, 2008). While students with disabilities are included in general education settings with growing frequency across Europe, there is a lack of guidelines related to functions, knowledge, and skills for APE professionals who work with school-aged students with SEN.

The Asian perspective in teacher preparation and service delivery in adapted physical activity and curriculum development

Special vs. inclusive education

The distinctive historical background in the Asian education system for children with disabilities or special education needs affects teacher preparation and service delivery in APA in unique ways. For example, even though Japan signed the Convention on the Rights of Persons with Disabilities in 2007 and ratified it in 2014 (Yasui, 2014), education for children with disabilities continues to be segregated on the basis of the severity and type of disability (Numano, 2013).

Governmental policies and disabilities: the Asian pioneers

The Republic of Korea, more commonly known as South Korea, is considered a pioneering Asian country in the field of special education legislation. In 1977, it lawfully mandated that free public education and related services should be provided to individuals with disabilities (Seo, Oakland, Han, & Hu, 1992). Inclusive education for students with disabilities or special education needs began in the mid-1990s, and, today, about 71% of students with disabilities receive inclusive education in community schools (Kim, 2013). It is likely that the 1988 Summer Olympic Games in Seoul inspired individuals with disabilities to advocate for their right to services and education.

Likewise, Taiwan's Constitution also protects the rights of children to receive education and special education (i.e., Taiwan Special Education Act and Taiwan People with Disabilities Rights Protection Act). Since 2012, approximately 87.2% of students with disabilities attended regular elementary schools, 84.4% junior high schools, and 73.1% senior high schools (Ministry of Education, Republic of China, 2014).

In Hong Kong, a special education policy provision first introduced in 1977 (called the "White Paper") advocated for the inclusion of children with disabilities in regular schools. Supported by the Disability Discrimination Ordinance (DDO, 1996) and by the Code of Practice in Education of 2001 (Poon-McBrayer & Lian, 2002), special schools are a tradition in Hong Kong (Sit, Lindner, & Sherrill, 2002). Conversely, in Indonesia, the cultural ideology of a community affects the school inclusion movement. It is common for community members to perceive persons with disabilities (*Cws'n*) as infectious and a disgrace to families.

Teacher preparation to work with students with disability

Most Asian countries have little tradition with professional or teacher preparation in APE or APA. For example, although Japan has a long history of APA and sports, no certification in APA or APE is required. Because no specific APA/APE departments exist in Japanese universities, pre-service and in-service training is problematic (Hong, 2014). Sports instructors or coaches primarily develop experiences in the area of disability in associations or national rehabilitation centers (Lin, 2003). It is encouraging that Japan won the bid for hosting the Summer Paralympic/Olympic Games 2020. Individuals with and without disabilities see this opportunity as an influential situation for promoting sports at elite and grass-root levels in their country (Yasui, 2014).

In the Republic of Korea, although the third 5-year Development Framework for Special Education (2008–2012) advocated the importance of professionalism in special education for regular education teachers, less than 25% of inclusive teachers have training in special education (Kim, 2013). The Yong-In University, led by Professor Kim Ki-Hong, established the first APE department in 1993. Ewha Women's University, led by Prof. Hong Yang-Ja, also was proactive in providing APA training (Sherrill, 2004b). The majority of Korean doctoral-level university professors received their doctoral degrees overseas, such as in the United States. Lin (2003) reported that 42 of 106 departments of PE offered courses in APE in 1997.

After the installation of the National Sports Promotion Act in 2005, the Korea Sports Association for the Disabled (KOSAD) and the Korean Paralympic Committee (KPC) were established in 2005 and 2006, respectively. Their purpose was to promote sports and leisure activities and offer training programs to elite athletes and coaches.

In Taiwan, very few universities offer formal teacher education programs. The National Taiwan Sport University established the Department of Adapted Physical Education in 2002 to offer bachelor and master degree courses in APE. Additionally, at the University of Taipei, the Graduate Institute of Transition and Leisure Education for Individuals with Disabilities offers training for special education teachers (Pan, 2014). The Taiwan Department of Education has also provided in-service and professional training in APE on a regular basis since 1992 (Sherrill, 2004b).

Hong Kong teachers receive formal teacher education training, but not necessarily in special education, even if they teach children with disabilities or SEN in special or regular schools. PE teachers with no special education training can teach in special schools. The Hong Kong Paralympic Committee & Sports Association for the Physically Disabled (HKPC&SAPD), and the Hong Kong Sports Association for Persons with Intellectual Disability (formerly HKSAM) offer regular training via workshops to local sports instructors, coaches, and PE teachers. Three universities in Hong Kong (i.e., Chinese University of Hong Kong, Hong Kong Baptist University, and University of Hong Kong) offer research in higher degree programs such as a PhD specialization in APA.

In Indonesia, despite limited knowledge and skills of teachers working with students with disabilities, inaccessibility of many school and community facilities, and negative attitudes of people towards inclusive education, the implementation of Curriculum 2013 included APE in 2014/2015 (Nasichin, 2014). It was an encouraging leap forward in the APA area in that country.

Sports and APA organizations behind professional qualification

In most of the Asian countries there are concerns about the shortage of qualified professionals, APE curricula, and APA programs. In light of such needs, the Asian Society for Adapted Physical Education and Exercise (ASAPE) was founded in Seoul, Korea in 1986. The ASAPE aims at advancing scientific research on APE and programs for individuals with disabilities in Asia (ASAPE, 2012) and holds a three-day International Symposium of ASAPE every two years. Key members of ASAPE include South Korea, Japan, Taiwan, Indonesia, and Hong Kong.

The Korean Society of Adapted Physical Activity and Exercise (KOSAPE) was founded in 1990. KOSAPE is an active member of ASAPE and regularly organizes national and international sports science congresses. For example, KOSAPE hosted the International Symposium for ASAPE twice (1996 and 2008), and the International Symposium of Adapted Physical Activity (ISAPA) in 2003. (This is not the same ISAPA as discussed below, the Indonesian Society for Adapted Physical Activity.) KOSAPE also organized the APA session in 2014 during the Asian Games International Sport Science Congress in Incheon.

The Japanese Society for Adapted Physical Education and Exercise (JASAPE) played a leading role in promoting research activities at national and international levels. To facilitate research and inquiry in APA, JASAPE welcomes researchers to publish their work in the *Japanese Journal of Adapted Sport Science*. Additionally, JASAPE hosted the International Symposium for ASAPE four times (1989, 1991, 1998, and 2006), as well as ISAPA in 1993. Professor Kyonosuke Yabe at Nagoya University and Professor Hong Yang-Ja at Ewha Women's University were the founding presidents of ASAPE and they are considered pioneers in the field of APA in Asia.

In Taiwan, there are two organizations in APA, namely, the Taiwan Association for Adapted Physical Activity and Health (TAPAS), led by Dr. Lin Man-Hua; and the Taiwan Society of Adapted Physical Activity (TSAPA), led by Dr. Huang Yueh-Guey. TAPAS organized the International Symposium for ASAPE in 1994 and 2000.

In Indonesia, Dr. Nasichin, together with Asian researchers and practitioners, established the Indonesian Society for Adapted Physical Activity (ISAPA) in 2002. ISAPA hosted the International Symposium for the Asian Society of Adapted Physical Education (ASAPE) in 2004 and 2010. ISAPA organized a series of joint workshops in APE with Professor Hideo Nakata from the University of Tsukuba in 2004–2008. Hong Kong, although with no APA professional organization, is an active member of the ASAPE and hosted the International Symposium for ASAPE in 2002 and 2012.

Curriculum development in APA: the Middle East experience

Many countries in the Middle East (ME) signed major international documents proclaiming the importance of integrating individuals with disabilities into civic, social, vocational, and educational contexts (Brown, 2005; UNESCO, 2000). However, in the field of PE, besides the limited knowledge of teachers, students with disabilities are still segregated, and many have restricted access to technology and rehabilitation (Emam & Mohamed, 2011; Hardman & Marshall, 2010). Turkey, Iran, and Israel have achieved some advances in inclusive education and APA that could be considered exemplary models of inclusive education for other Middle Eastern countries.

Overall, although PE is compulsory in school settings at any level, there are no common goals in the Middle Eastern region due to the cultural and educational politics of these countries. However, APA is a new concept for many countries, and, while we can observe examples of inclusive education, many barriers to children with disabilities continue to exist, not only due to inaccessibility of programs, but also to a lack of skilled teachers and APA specialists.

Access to APA education

Turkey

The Turkish Civil Law that was first issued in 1926, reorganized and modernized in 2000, states that men and women should have equal rights in all aspects of life. Additionally, the law ensures that "no one can be deprived of education," and, also, "the state is responsible to take the necessary measures to ensure education and employment of disadvantaged individuals in order to integrate them within society and to improve their status in society." PE provisions for students with disabilities started in the late 1990s. Children were usually given medical dismissal from PE classes, or they remained sitting and watching their friends during PE classes. In 2000, the Ministry of Education, universities, and non-governmental organizations began to support the inclusion of children with disabilities. Children with hearing and visual impairments, physical disabilities, and mild intellectual disabilities were encouraged to join regular schools in their districts according to their levels of education. Unfortunately, these children still face barriers to accessibility (especially regarding mobility) in regular schools, although transportation is available to a limited number of special schools.

The United Nations Convention on rights of Persons with Disabilities (2006) was signed by Turkey in 2009. Although the International Disability Rights Monitor of the Regional Report of Europe (2007) claims that Turkey lawfully ensures legal protection of disability rights, the application of such provisions in real life shows weaknesses. Especially problematic are issues of accessibility, health services, housing, and communication. Regarding the education and employment status of individuals with disabilities, Turkey was categorized as having "some basic protection" among the European countries, with no PE provisions for students with disabilities at this time.

Iran

In Iran, individuals with disabilities were recognized officially early in the twentieth century through charitable religious and cultural activities. The first school for children with visual disabilities opened in 1920 in Tabriz. Later, kindergarten schools were opened for children with hearing disabilities. Private education centers started in 1950 in Tehran for students with other disabilities. Special education laws and regulations approved initially in the early 1990s and revised in 2004 provided all Iranian students, including those with intellectual disabilities considered to be "educable," with the right to receive eight years of free mandatory education. This new vision was based on international trends supporting the development of inclusive special education. Today, Iran is considered the most inclusive among the Middle Eastern countries. Iranian children with disabilities participate in APA prior to attending elementary school and continue after graduation, participating in programs provided through welfare organizations (Adibsereshki, Tajrishi, & Mirzamani, 2010).

APE is a curricular component within the educational program of physical education in pre-school and primary school because of the curricular emphasis on basic movement skills through games and play. However, there is a shortage of PE teachers with interest in working with APA/PE at the secondary level. Additionally, APA/PE pedagogical approaches for students with disabilities are not yet implemented in the country (Adibsereshki et al. 2010).

Israel

In Israel, students with disabilities are increasingly included in regular schools. A survey performed in 1995–1997 reported that among the students with disabilities, only about 25% attended special schools, with the majority integrated in regular schools. In 2005, 75% of students with disabilities were recognized as eligible for supportive educational measures (Hutzler & Levi, 2008). Although Israel has specific programs to support inclusion of children with disabilities in PE (Hardman & Marshall, 2010), Hutzler and Levi (2008) claimed that, because generalist teachers were expected to manage entire classes of students including one or more with disability, teaching becomes an integrated, rather than inclusive, context (Hutzler, Fliess, Chacham, & Van den Auweele, 2002). In this case, students with disabilities are supposed to adapt on their own to the regular class environment.

Arab States in the Middle East

Most of the Arab States in the Middle East have representative signatures on major international documents about inclusion (Brown, 2005; UNESCO, 2000). Nevertheless, in reality, many countries struggle with economic, political, social, geographic, and professional obstacles to ensuring quality education for individuals with disabilities (Brown, 2005; EFA

Regional Report for Arab States, UNESCO, 2011; Weber, 2012). Despite civil wars and conflicts, Egypt, Syria, Jordan, and Lebanon have a long history and stable educational system rooted in the Arab culture. They all recognize the rights of students with disabilities, and particularly their rights to education, although the concept of inclusion is a novel one (Al Attiyah & Lazarus, 2007). In reality, access of students with disabilities to regular schools is still limited.

Egypt

Egypt has recently legalized inclusive education by issuing mandatory guidelines for school inclusion in 2009 and 2011. Since then, schools have admitted students with disabilities to pre-school and primary school settings. However, the quality of education for students with disabilities and teacher qualifications to teach students with disabilities remains controversial (Emam & Mohamed, 2011). Specialized teacher education is an important element in the structuring of classes based on the concept of inclusion (Adibsereshki et al., 2010). However, education to encourage parents to accept and support inclusive education is critical for effective and widespread implementation. A similar problem exists in other countries in the Middle East (Hardman & Marshall, 2010; Sadek & Sadek, 2000).

Saudi Arabia

Saudi Arabia has a well-organized educational program for citizens, from the elementary to university level. However, for students with disabilities, education is provided through segregated special education schools. Al-Gain and Al-Abdulwahab (2002) emphasized the negative consequences of this segregation to the Saudi perspective. Saudis continue to view individuals with disabilities as being homebound and helpless, having low quality of life, and presenting continuing dependence. The Ministry of Education began the special education program for children with visual disabilities in 1958 for boys, and in 1965 for girls. The first special education school was opened for children with auditory disabilities in 1964. However, the first institute for children with intellectual disabilities did not open until 1971 for both genders (Al-Jadid, 2013). Since then, the number of special education schools gradually increased to reach the majority of students with disabilities, although education that includes PE is offered in gender-segregated settings (Al-Gain & Al-Abdulwahab, 2002). In 2000, the disability code pledged that individuals with disabilities should have access to free and appropriate medical, psychological, social, educational, and rehabilitative services through public agencies (Al-Jadid, 2013). However, these laws have not been implemented extensively due to architectural and educational barriers (Al-Gain & Al-Abdulwahab, 2002; Elsheikh & Alqurashi, 2013).

Inclusive education in Saudi Arabia has been implemented primarily in international schools, and, only recently, inclusion has been extended to children with mild disabilities in government schools. As Alsalhe (2013) noted, although teachers express positive attitudes toward their students with disabilities, unfortunately, they lack knowledge of how to manage students' behaviors, especially those with learning disabilities. Therefore, teacher education for inclusive education, including APE curricular studies, should emphasize: methods of delivering activities and teaching skill to persons with disabilities; identification and management of pervasive behavior of children with developmental disorders; and the concept of *inclusion* towards students with disabilities.

Qatar

Special education in Qatar started for boys with hearing disabilities in 1975. In 1996, an international private school began educating children with learning disabilities in English. In 1998, blind children began receiving access to primary school. In 2002, this opportunity was extended to the secondary level schools. Schools for students with developmental disabilities and autism spectrum disorders were first provided in 1999, and later in 2006 included students with learning disabilities (Al Attiyah & Lazarus, 2007).

Adapted physical education/activity in higher education

APE and APA in higher education are, unfortunately, not common disciplines in the Middle Eastern countries. In Iran, APE is a curricular component within the educational program for PE teachers in the universities. In Turkey, APA is a required course in all departments of physical education and sports, and is an elective course for departments of trainer education and sports management (Inal & Subaşi, 2007).

In Turkey, there are more than 80 universities offering PE and sports programs for the bachelor of science degrees, with an obligatory course in APE since the year 2000. Although graduate studies programs in sports began in the late 1980s, the APA discipline did not start until the late 1990s. Physical education and sports programs at Marmara University, in 2002, and at Istanbul University, in 2007, opened modular programs on APE/APA as elective programs covering the last two years of the educational period (Inal & Subaşi, 2007). Marmara and Istanbul universities organized comprehensive and enhanced courses in APE/APA, and, for the first time, graduate students fulfilled the requirements in these areas (Inal & Subaşi, 2007).

APE/APA symposia and educational courses were included in scientific programs organized countrywide. Additionally, the 19th Symposium of Adapted Physical Activity (ISAPA), in 2013, was organized in Istanbul. Recently, two congresses were organized in APE and sports by two universities: the first in Middle Anatolia University of Selcuk in 2011, and the second in South East University of Batman. There is also a quarterly on-line bulletin that gathers information on APA/APE. In Israel, the Council of Higher Education requires APA in higher to begin at the bachelor's level. However, this four-year program also focuses on rehabilitation and preventive issues, in addition to APA. There is an increasing interest to include pre-service and in-service training in APA for PE teachers (Hutzler et al., 2002). The 20th International Symposium of Adapted Physical Activity (ISAPA), which met in June of 2015, may help Israel implement their training philosophy.

In Egypt, the Carnegie Faculty from the United Kingdom shared their pioneering training program on inclusive PE with the faculty at Helwan University. This program emphasized the development of teachers' management skills with inclusive classes (Emam & Mohamed, 2011), as well as preparation of teachers to work with various disability conditions and learning difficulties.

APA future considerations

Even in countries and regions around the world with high standards and resources in education, the provision of PE and sports for all students, including disabled ones, continues to present challenges. Common problems include unrealistic models of education and rehabilitation, particularly in inclusive settings (e.g., medical model; models of normalcy, standard health parameters, and academic achievement). Educators, peers, and society's negative attitudes toward individuals with disabilities, and the exclusion of individuals with disability from decision-making policy groups, are likely responsible for the enormous gap between high standards for inclusion and the reality of sedentary conditions, poor health, and limited quality of life. Professional leaders at once experience both "leaps of greatness" and "falls for lack of vision."

Teacher training programs and higher education curricula in the field of APE or APA often do not reflect modern school practices. Other than mandatory inclusive school legislation, university curricula and teacher educators continue to struggle to convey effective content and practice to adequately prepare pre-service teachers to be educators in APE/APA environments. Programs, no doubt, will improve, however, if theoretical foundations can be integrated with practical application to provide effective, realistic, and varied hands-on opportunities for pre-service and in-service APE educators.

There are a number of common issues and challenges faced by professionals and practitioners in the field of APA in many parts of the world. For example, a lack of or insufficient teacher education training can result in teachers without competence and knowledge of curricular planning, instructional skills, and behavioral management skills to work effectively with children with disabilities. Given the importance of physical activity in the promotion of health and well-being of individuals with disabilities, there is a pressing need to seek measures to overcome such challenges through the development and provision of formal APE/APA teacher education training. Additionally, the mobilization of APA/PE resources such as how to do effective curricular planning and facility use, high impact research that informs practice, and the exchange of knowledge of and expertise in APA among researchers and practitioners in different countries will enhance physical experiences for students with disabilities. These opportunities can assist children, youngsters, adults, and older adults with disabilities to stay active and healthy, minimizing their health risks and maximizing their opportunities for empowerment and living life with dignity.

Students with and without disability rely on educators who are committed to help them to find successful strategies for learning, whether in inclusive or segregated settings, or during individualized education programs. When APE/PA teaching excellence becomes a reality, empowerment is a natural consequence for all (Figure 16.3). Although support for APE/PA educators can be enhanced through laws, community awareness programs, effective, research-based training programs, and modern curricula, the public's attitudes become more positive through opportunities for frequent contact with individuals with disabilities. Thus, diversity of experiences is critical for both the public and students with disabilities, making the process a truly social, dignifying experience.

Reflective questions for discussion

1. Discuss the major challenges in poor countries with regard to education and APA opportunities.
2. What are the common educational challenges among regions such as the Middle East, Europe, Latin America, Asia, and Oceania?
3. Identify countries that have achieved legislative goals with regard to inclusion, yet still are unable to fully implement them. Explain the reasons.
4. Summarize the main historical issues regarding education and individuals with disability.
5. What are the main challenges to teachers in the field of APA to ensuring health and rehabilitation for people with disability?

Figure 16.3   Learning something fun: teaching and providing social support (photo: E. Mauerberg-deCastro & D. F. Campbell)

Note

1 Prior to 1808, the year that Portugal's Royal Family arrived in Brazil, schooling in the colony was very limited. From 1549 until 1759, the Jesuit education period, and then from 1760 until 1808, the Pambalini education period, education was erratic, improvised, and existed only to serve the economic interests of the Portuguese conquerors (Maciel & Shigunov Neto, 2006). Special education schools were installed first as a philanthropic endeavor, often connected to hospitals, e.g., schools for the intellectually disabled appeared in Salvador, State of Bahia, as part of a hospital, and in Rio de Janeiro (School of Mexico) in 1874 (Januzzi, 1985). Important institutions with special education curricula appeared in the first part of the twentieth century: Pestalozzi School (1932), the Association of Parents and Friends of the Exceptional (APAE) (1954), Paraná Institute of the Blind (1939). Some, like the APAE, expanded nationwide: Today there are more than 2,000 institutions. In 1963, the first governmental supported program of special education was installed in the State of Paraná. Most governmental efforts to insert special education classes in regular schools began in the 1960s, but they were duplicated in the existing segregated school system, providing little incentive to the regular school system.

References

Adibsereshki, N., Tajrishi, M. P., & Mirzamani, M. (2010). The effectiveness of a preparatory students programme on promoting peer acceptance of students with physical disabilities in inclusive schools of Tehran. *Educational Studies, 36*, 447–459.

Al Attiyah, A., & Lazarus, B. (2007). Hope in the life: The children of Qatar speak about inclusion. *Childhood Education, 83*, 366–369.

Al-Gain, S. I., & Al-Abdulwahab, S. S. (2002). Issues and obstacles in disability research in Saudi Arabia. *Asia Pacific Disability Rehabilitation Journal, 13*, 45–49.

Al-Jadid, M. S. (2013). Disability in Saudi Arabia. *Saudi Medicine Journal, 34*, 453–460.

Alsalhe, T. A. (2013). Adapted physical education in Middle East countries. *Hacettepe Journal of Sports Sciences, 24*, 105–110.

Andre, M. H., & Mandigo, J. L. (2013). Analyzing the learning of the taking personal and social responsibility model within a new physical education undergraduate degree program in El Salvador. *The Physical Educator, 70*, 107–134.

APAE Brasil. (2014). *Experiências da Rede Apae na inclusão escolar* [*Experiences of the APAE Network in inclusive school*]. Retrieved January 22, 2015, from www.apaebrasil.org.br/artigo.phtml?a=11398.

APENS. (1995). *Adapted Physical Education National Standards*. Retrieved January 22, 2015, from http://apens.org/15standards.html.

Asian Society for Adapted Physical Education and Exercise [ASAPE]. (2012). *History of ASAPE*. Retrieved September 22, 2014, from www.asape.net/about-asape/history.

Auxter, D., Pyfer, J., Zittel, L., Roth, K., & Huettig, C. (2010). *Principles and methods of adapted physical education and recreation* (11th edn). New York: McGraw-Hill.

Bines, H., & Lei, P. (2011). Disability and education: The longest road to inclusion. *International Journal of Educational Development, 31*, 419–424.

Brazil. (1987). Parecer n°215/87. Conselho Federal de Educação. Ministério da Educação e Cultura [Decision 215/87. Federal Board of Education. Ministry of Education and Culture].

Brazil. (2011). *Avaliação do Plano Plurianual 2008–2011 – MEC* [*School MEC-Multi-Year Plan Assessment Report of 2008–2011*]. Retrieved August 12, 2014, from http://portal.mec.gov.br/index.php?option=com_content&view=article&id=8966:lula-plano-plurianual-privilegia-educacao&catid=222&Itemid=164.

Brown, R. C. (2005). Inclusive education in Middle Eastern cultures. In D. Mitchell (Ed.), *Contextualizing inclusive education: Evaluating old and new international perspectives* (pp. 253–278). New York: Routledge Taylor & Francis Group.

CDPF. (2008). China Disabled Persons' Federation. Statistical Communiqué on the Development of the Work on Persons with Disabilities in 2014. Retrieved May 5, 2016, from www.cdpf.org.cn/englishold/statistics/201507/t20150717_522174.html.

Celik, V. O., & Bulgu, N. (2010). Physical education and sport on westernized movements in the last Ottoman period [Selcuk Universitesi Sosyal Bilimler Enstitusu Dergisi]. *Journal of Selcuk, 24*, 137–147.

Cratty, B. J. (1975). *Remedial motor activity for children*. Philadelphia: Lea & Febiger.

DePotter, J. C., Van Coppenolle, H., Djobova, S., Dobreva, I., Wijns, K., & Van Peteghem, A. (Eds.). (2003). *Vocational training in adapted physical activity*. Leuven, Belgium: THENAPA.

EFA Regional Report for Arab States, UNESCO Regional Bureau for Education in the Arab States, Beirut. (2011). Retrieved August 12, 2014, from www.uneso.org/beirut.

Elsheikh, A. S., & Alqurashi, A. M. (2013). Disabled future in the Kingdom of Saudi Arabia. *Journal of Humanities and Social Science, 16*, 68–71.

Emam, M. M., & Mohamed, A. H. H. (2011). Preschool and primary school teachers' attitudes towards inclusive education in Egypt: The role of experience and self-efficiency. *Procedia- Social & Behavioral Sciences, 29*, 976–985.

European Commission. (2001) *Treaty of Nice*. Retrieved September 19, 2014, from http://europa.eu/legislation_summaries/institutional_affairs/treaties/nice_treaty/index_en.htm.

European Commission, Directorate General for Education and Culture. (2002). *Education and training in Europe: Diverse systems, shared goals for 2010*. The work programme on the future objectives of education and training systems, Luxembourg: Office for Official Publications of the European Community.

European Commission: House of Commons Culture, Media and Sport Committee. (2007). *European Commission: White Paper on Sport*, 4–8.

European Standards in Adapted Physical Activity. (2010). *European Federation in Adapted Physical Activity*. Retrieved September 19, 2014, from http://eusapa.upol.cz/.

Góis Junior, E., & Lovisolo, H. R. (2003). Descontinuidades e continuidades do movimento higienista no Brasil do século XX [Discontinuities and continuities of the hygienic movement in Brazil of the twentieth century]. *Brazilian Journal of Sports Science, 25*, 41–54.

Goode, E. (1999). On behalf of labeling theory. In H. N. Pontell (Ed.). *Social Deviance* (3rd ed., pp. 86–96). New Jersey: Prentice-Hall.

Hardman, K. (2008). The situation of physical education in schools: A European perspective. *Human Movement, 9*(1), 5–18.

Hardman, K., & Marshall, J. (2010). The state and status of physical education in schools in international context. *European Physical Education Review, 6*, 203–229.

Hardman, M. L., Drew, C. J., & Egan, M. W. (1999). *Human exceptionality: Society, school, and family* (6th edn). Boston: Allyn and Bacon.

Heung, V., & Grossman, D. (2007). Inclusive education as a strategy for achieving education for all: Perspectives from three Asian countries. *International Perspectives on Education and Society, 8*, 155–180.

Hong, Y. J. (2014). *The study of adapted physical activity in Japan.* Invited speech, 2014 Incheon Asian Games, International Sport Science Congress, Incheon, Korea.

Hutzler, Y., Fliess, O., Chacham, A., & Van den Auweele, Y. (2002). Perspectives of children with physical disabilities on inclusion and empowerment: Supporting and limiting factors. *Adapted Physical Activity Quarterly, 19*, 300–317.

Hutzler, Y. & Levi, I. (2008). Including children with disability in physical education: General and specific attitudes of high-school students. *European Journal of Adapted Physical Activity, 1*(2), 21–30. Retrieved December 10, 2014, from http://eujapa.upol.cz/index.php/EUJAPA/article/download/8/7.

Inal, H. S., & Subaşı, F. (2007). Academic education in the field of disabled sports in Turkey. *Revista da Sobama, 12*, 182–186.

Januzzi, G. (1985). *A luta pela educação do deficiente mental no Brasil [The fight for the education of mentally handicapped in Brazil].* São Paulo, Brazil: Editora Autores Associados.

Kelly, L. (1995). *Adapted Physical Education National Standards.* Champaign, IL: Human Kinetics.

Kim, Y. W. (2013). Inclusive education in Korea: Policy, practice, and challenges. *Journal of Policy and Practice in Intellectual Disabilities, 10,* 79–81.

Klavina, A., & Kudláček, M. (2011). Physical education for students with special education needs in Europe: Findings of the EUSAPA Project. *European Journal in Adapted Physical Activity, 4*, 46–62.

Kudláček, M., & Barret, U. (2010). Adapted physical activity as a profession in Europe. *European Journal of Adapted Physical Activity, 4*, 7–16.

Kurniawati, F., Minnaert, A., Mangunsong, F., & Ahmed, W. (2012). Empirical study on primary school teachers' attitudes towards inclusive education in Jakarta, Indonesia. *Procedia Social and Behavioral Sciences, 69*, 1430–1436.

Lienert, C., Sherrill, C., & Myers, B. (2001). Physical educators' concerns about integrating children with disabilities: A cross-cultural comparison. *Adapted Physical Activity Quarterly, 18*, 1–17.

Lin, M. H. (2003). The qualification and training system for adapted physical activities in North East Asia. In B. C. Chow and C. H. P. Sit (Eds.), *Disability sport, adapted physical education and physical activity: Research to practice.* Hong Kong: Hong Kong Baptist University and the University of Hong Kong.

Lowman, C. L., Colestock, C., & Cooper, H. (1928). *Corrective physical education for groups.* New York: A.S. Barnes and Co.

Lund, J., Wayda, V., Woodard, R., & Buck, M. (2007). Professional dispositions: What are we teaching prospective physical education teachers? *Physical Educator, 64*, 38–47.

Maciel, L. S. B., & Shigunov Neto, A. (2006). A educação brasileira no período pombalino: Uma análise histórica das reformas pombalinas do ensino [The Brazilian education in the Pombaline period: A historical analysis of Pombal education reforms]. *Educação e Pesquisa, 32*, 465–476. Retrieved August 30, 2014, from www.scielo.br/pdf/ep/v32n3/a03v32n3.

MacKenzie, T. L. (1909). *Exercise in education and medicine.* Philadelphia: Saunders.

Mauerberg-deCastro, E. (2005). *Atividade física adaptada [Adapted physical activity].* Ribeirão Preto, Brazil: TecMed.

Mauerberg-deCastro, E. (2011). *Atividade física adaptada [Adapted physical activity]* (2nd edn). Ribeirão Preto, Brazil: Novo Conceito.

Mauerberg-deCastro, E., Paiva, A. C. S., Figueiredo, G. A., Costa, T. D. A., Castro, M. R., & Campbell, D. F. (2013). Attitudes about inclusion by educators and physical educators: Effects of participation in an inclusive adapted physical education program. *Motriz, 19*, 649–661.

Ministry of Education, Republic of China. (2014). *Education in Taiwan 2013–2014.* Retrieved September 20, 2014, from https://stats.moe.gov.tw/files/ebook/Education_in_Taiwan/2013-2014_Education_in_Taiwan.pdf.

Monteiro, A. P. H., & Manzini, E. J. (2008). Mudanças nas concepções do professor do ensino fundamental em relação à inclusão após a entrada de alunos com deficiência em sua classe [Changes in conceptions of elementary school teacher in relation to the inclusion of the entry of students with disabilities in its class]. *Revista Brasileira de Educação Especial [Brazilian Journal of Special Education], 14*, 35–52.

Mosby's Medical Dictionary. (2009). *Medical dictionary* (9th edn). St. Louis: Elsevier.

Mushoriwa, T. (2001). A study of attitudes of primary school teachers in Harare towards the inclusion of blind children in regular classes. *British Journal of Special Education, 28*, 142–147.

Nasichin, S. H. (2014). *Invited country report on adapted physical activity in Indonesia.* 13th International Symposium of Asian Society for Adapted Physical Education and Exercise, Fuzhou, China.

Nowicki, E. A., Brown, J., & Stepien, M. (2013). Children's thoughts on the social exclusion of peers with intellectual or learning disabilities. *Journal of Intellectual Disability Research, 58*, 346–357.

Numano, T. (2013). *Schools for special needs education in Japan.* Retrieved September 20, 2014, from www.nier.go.jp/English/educationjapan/pdf/201303SSN.pdf.

Pan, C.Y. (2014). *Invited country report on adapted physical activity in Taiwan.* 13th International Symposium of Asian Society for Adapted Physical Education and Exercise, Fuzhou, China.

Peresuh, M., & Barcham, L. (1998). Special education provision in Zimbabwe. *British Journal of Special Education, 25*, 75–80.

Petrie, K. & lisahunter. (2011). Primary teachers, policy, and physical education. *European Physical Education Review, 17*, 325–339.

Poon-McBrayer, K. F., & Lian, M. G. (2002). *Special needs education.* Hong Kong: Chinese University of Hong Kong.

Rathbone, J. L. (1934). *Corrective physical education.* Philadelphia: Saunders.

Regional Report of Europe. (2007). *International Disability Rights Monitor (IDRM).* Chicago: International Disability Network.

Roush, S. E. & Sharby, N. (2011). Disability reconsidered: The paradox of physical therapy. *Physical Therapy, 91*, 1715–1727.

Sadek, F. M., & Sadek, R. C. (2000). Attitudes towards inclusive education in Egypt & implications for teachers' preparation and training. *International Special Education Congress (ISEC).* University of Manchester. Retrieved September 20, 2014, from www.isec2000.org.uk/.

Seo, G., Oakland, T., Han, H. S., & Hu, S. (1992). Special education in South Korea. *Exceptional Children, 58*, 213–218.

Sit, C. H. P., Lindner, K. J., & Sherrill, C. (2002). Sport participation of Hong Kong Chinese children with disabilities in special schools. *Adapted Physical Activity Quarterly, 19*, 453–471.

Sherrill, C. (2004a). *Adapted physical activity, recreation and sport: Crossdisciplinary and lifespan* (6th edn). Dubuque, IA: McGraw-Hill.

Sherrill, C. (2004b). *Young people with disability in physical education/physical activity/sport in and out of schools: Technical report for the World Health Organization.* Retrieved September 20, 2014, from www.icsspe.org/sites/default/files/YOUNGPEOPLE.pdf.

Smith, T. E., Polloway, E. A., Patton, J. R., & Dowdy, C. A. (1998). *Teaching students with special needs in inclusive settings* (2nd edn). Boston: Allyn and Bacon.

UN. (2010). *World Programme of Action Concerning Disabled Persons.* Retrieved August 23, 2014. from www.un.org/disabilities/default.asp?id=23.

UNESCO. (2000). *Regional Report for Education in the Arab States.* Beirut: UNESCO Regional Office for Education in the Arab States.

UNESCO. (2009). *Overcoming Inequality: Why governance matters.* Contribution of higher education and research to education for all (EFA). Retrieved August 25, 2014, from http://unesdoc.unesco.org/images/0018/001800/180085e.pdf.

Vilhu, J. (2013). *EUDAPA European University Diploma in Adapted Physical Activity.* International Symposium in Adapted Physical Activities, Istanbul (Turkey), Abstract Book, p. 25.

Wanderbroock Junior, D., & Boarini, M. L. (2007). Educação higienista, contenção social: A estratégia da Liga Brasileira de Hygiene Mental na criação de uma educação sob medida (1914–45) [Hygienist education, social containment: The Brazilian League of Mental Hygiene strategy in creating a tailored education (1914–45)]. VII Jornada do HISTEDBR "O trabalho didático na história da educação." [7th HISTEDBR "Teaching workshop in educational history"]. Campo Grande, Brazil. Retrieved January 10, 2015, from www.histedbr.fe.unicamp.br/acer_histedbr/jornada/jornada7/_GT1%20PDF/EDUCA%c7%c3O%20HIGIENISTA%20GT1.pdf.

Weber, A. S. (2012). Inclusive education in the Gulf Cooperation Council. *Journal of Educational and Instructional Studies in the World, 2*, 85–97.

WHO. (2011). *World Report on Disability.* World Health Organization.

WHO. (2012). *World Health Statistics. A snapshot of Global Health.* World Health Organization. Retrieved June 5, 2014, from www.who.int/gho.

Winnick, J. P. (1986). History of adapted physical education: Priorities in professional preparation. *Adapted Physical Activity Quarterly, 3*, 112–117.

Wong, D. K. P. (2008). Do contacts make a difference? The effects of mainstreaming on student attitudes towards people with disabilities. *Research in Developmental Disabilities, 29*, 70–82.

Yasui, T. (2014). *Invited country report on adapted physical activity in Japan.* 13th International Symposium of Asian Society for Adapted Physical Education and Exercise, Fuzhou, China.

17

INCLUSIVE SETTINGS IN ADAPTED PHYSICAL ACTIVITY

A worldwide reality?

Lauren J. Lieberman, THE COLLEGE AT BROCKPORT, USA

& Martin Block, UNIVERSITY OF VIRGINIA, USA

In September 2014 Ecuadorian leaders met to discuss inclusion of children with disabilities in education. These officials recognized they had a long way to go as there were no laws in Ecuador for inclusion of children with disabilities. Yet, in some rural schools children with physical disabilities were being included seamlessly and without question because it was the right thing to do.

In this chapter we address inclusion from a global perspective. We begin by defining inclusion and describing international efforts to enhance legislation and teacher skills, while pointing out common barriers. We then use the Theory of Planned Behavior as a theoretical framework from which to discuss inclusion. Lastly, we explore major issues related to inclusive practice around the world outlining several possible solutions within a variety of different cultures. The chapter concludes with suggestions for future research.

What is inclusion?

Inclusion describes the philosophy of merging special and general education (Block, 2016; Lipsky & Gartner, 1987; Stainback & Stainback, 1990; see also Chapter 32 by Makopoulou & Thomas, this volume). The term reflects a philosophy in which all children, regardless of abilities or disabilities, are educated within the same environment; an environment where each child's individual needs are met (Downing, 2001; Stainback & Stainback, 1990; Stainback, Stainback, & Bunch, 1989). The philosophy of inclusion is perhaps best summed up by the following statement: "Although some children, especially those with severe and multiple disabilities, may have unique ways of learning, separating them from others who learn in a different way is unnecessary and could prevent them from achieving their full potential" (Downing, 2001, p. xii). It also is important to note that an inclusion philosophy goes beyond simply physically placing a child in a general education classroom. As noted by Stainback and Stainback (1990, p. 3), "An inclusive school is a place where everyone belongs, is accepted, supports, and is supported by his/her peers and other members of the school community in the course of having his/her educational needs met." Rapp and Arndt (2012, p. 30) point out that "Inclusion is an attitude not a place." For example, in physical education a child with cerebral palsy and an intellectual disability and uses a walker may participate in a soccer/football unit with a peer tutor for support using a ball larger than a typical soccer ball. Rule accommodations require that she receive the ball in a play before either team could attempt to score. The teacher also could have another student use a wheelchair or walker on the other team to even out the sides.

Children with disabilities enrolled in an inclusive physical education class should receive an individually determined, appropriate program with supplementary services and supports to meet their unique needs. In addition, these services also are provided to the child with a disability within the general education environment (Block, 2016; Downing, 2001; Lieberman & Houston-Wilson, 2009). In terms of physical education services, this means that an adapted physical education specialist, a trained general physical education specialist, a trained teacher assistant, or trained peer tutor provides individually determined goals, objectives, and accommodations within the general physical education setting. This concept of bringing services to the general education setting provides continual opportunities for children with disabilities to interact with, learn from, and form friendships with peers while ensuring that they receive an appropriate, individualized program (Hodge, Lieberman, & Murata, 2012). For example, a child learning to push his wheelchair or walk using crutches can be included in a general physical education primary school class. When children are playing a dodging and fleeing game with lots of running, the child with the physical disability can participate in the game and practice moving his wheelchair or walking on crutches. The advantage of having him in general physical education is that the stimulating environment motivates him to move around with his peers, and he receives added opportunities to interact with peers without disabilities.

Another critical tenet of the inclusion philosophy is that children with disabilities are the responsibility of both general and special education staff (Individuals with Disabilities Education Act – IDEA; United States Government, 2004). Unlike traditional self-contained programs in which the special education teacher (with the support of related services personnel) was solely responsible for a child's education, in inclusive programs all the school staff are responsible, making sure that each child's educational program is carried out appropriately (Hodge et al., 2012). The inclusion philosophy suggested that only through the merger of resources, knowledge, and talents of general and special education can both children with and without disabilities receive a comprehensive, appropriate education. General education teachers need continual support and training to make such a merged system work. In addition, the use of various co-teaching arrangements (the general and special education teacher dividing and sharing class instruction) can be an effective way to facilitate inclusive programs. Grenier (2011) showed how having an adapted physical educator support a child in a general physical education class allowed the child to be successfully included without disrupting other students or burdening the general physical educator. Many societies, although attempting to comply with international recommendations for inclusion, do not have policies or resources for teacher training or priorities in budgeting additional personnel for helping teaching inclusive classes.

United States federal intervention: Individuals with Disabilities Education Act and least restrictive environment

Because children with disabilities benefit from interactions with children without disabilities, the United States government enacted the Education for All Handicapped Children Act in 1975 (PL 94–142). Now known as the Individuals with Disabilities Education Act (IDEA), this landmark legislation guaranteed the rights of individuals with disabilities to a free, appropriate public education. Included in this legislation was a provision designed to ensure that children with disabilities are placed in general education programs with opportunities to interact with peers without disabilities as often as possible. Termed the *least restrictive environment (LRE)* in IDEA, the provision directs public agencies:

1. To the maximum extent appropriate, children with disabilities, including children in public or private institutions or other care facilities, are educated with children who are not disabled; and
2. That special classes, separate schooling, or other removal of children with disabilities from the regular educational environment occurs only when the nature or severity of the disability is such that education in regular classes with the use of supplementary aids and services cannot be achieved satisfactorily. (20 U.S.C. 1412 [5][B])

This law requires that the LRE for students with disabilities is, whenever possible, the same environment in which students without disabilities receive their education. Clearly, students with disabilities should be placed in general schools and general classrooms (including general physical education) whenever possible (Aufsesser, 1991; Turnbull, 1990).

Inclusion around the world

In 1994, the United Nations Educational, Scientific, and Cultural Organization (UNESCO, 1994) emphasized the right to inclusive education via the Salamanca Statement and Framework for Action on Special Needs Education. As a result, governments around the world began enacting legislation and policy to ensure children with disabilities were included in the public school system, not in separate schools (Pecora, Whittaker, Maluccio, & Barth, 2012). This international trend of including students with disabilities in general education can be seen in general physical education (GPE) classes across the globe in places such as the Czech Republic (Kudláček, Válková, Sherrill, Myers, & French, 2002), Ireland (Meegan & MacPhail, 2006), the Republic of (South) Korea (Jeong & Block, 2011), Greece (Panagiotou, Evaggelinou, Doulkeridou, Mouratidou, & Koidou, 2008), Israel (Hutzler & Levi, 2008), Portugal (Campos, Ferriera & Block, 2014), and Japan (Sato, Hodge, Murata, & Maeda, 2007). The following sections provide a review of the state of inclusion in select places around the world.

Legislation promoting inclusive education

Many countries have enacted legislation to support an inclusive philosophy and to move away from traditional models of sending children with disabilities to special schools. Italy and Brazil, for example, enacted legislation in 1988 requiring the inclusion of students in general education settings in regular schools, while other countries, such as Ecuador, have more recently followed this trend (Brazil, 1988). In the mid 1990s Brazil enacted the *Guidelines and Bases of National Education* (Law 9.394/96, Brazil, 1996) promoting a nationwide public awareness about inclusion. This law asserted that all children have the right to education (article 205), and that children who have special educational needs must have access to education "preferably in the public regular school system." More recently Brazil enacted the *National Policy on Special Education from the Perspective of Inclusive Education* (Brazil, 2007) to ensure the inclusion of children with special education needs in regular public schools. The policy applies to three distinct groups: children with physical, sensory, and intellectual disabilities; children with pervasive developmental disorders (Autism Spectrum Disorder, Attention Deficit and Hyperactivity Disorder, Learning Disabilities); and talented/gifted children.

Similarly, beginning in 1986, Portugal enacted public education laws to promote equality of opportunity in education and to provide improvements in the quality of teaching for students with disabilities. These laws have increased considerably the inclusion of students with disabilities in regular education (Campos et al., 2014). In the Republic of Korea, two powerful laws related to inclusion of children with disabilities in public school have increased opportunities for these children to participate with their peers in regular classes. The Anti-Discrimination Against and Remedies for Persons with Disabilities Act (ADARPD; Korea Ministry of Health and Welfare, 2010), and the Act on Special Education for Persons with Disabilities and Others (SEPD; Ministry of Education, Science and Technology, 2013) permitted school districts and Special Education Support Committees to manage inclusive education. Within SEPD, Article 21 (Integrated Education), heads of each school are required to make an effort to implement integrated education when carrying out various types of policies regarding education. In addition, Article 13 of ADARPD forbids daycare facilities, elementary and secondary education institutions from rejecting persons with disabilities. Further, an educational officer must provide career planning education and information suitable to the abilities and characteristics of persons with disabilities in regard to job training, career planning, and information (ADARPD; Korea Ministry of Health and Welfare, 2010). These laws are required so that students with disabilities can have proper education depending on their level and type of disability.

A greater number of students with disabilities included in general schools

As a result of legislation and changing public opinion, more children with special education needs around the world are now receiving their education in general education schools. In Brazil, results of the 2012 School Census indicate increased enrollment in public school special education. According to preliminary results from the Brazil School Census (Brazil, 2013), the enrollment of students with disabilities in public schools over the last 10 years has increased 493%. Recently, data from Portugal showed 98% of students with SEN attended general schools compared to 75% in 1997 (Rodrigues & Nogueira, 2010). These figures place Portugal in the group of European countries with the highest rate of inclusion education for students with disabilities. Other European countries, however, have been slower to enact more inclusive models of educating students with SEN. For example, Latvia, Hungary, and Belgium still rely on special schools more than most other European countries (World Health Organization, 2011).

As was the case in Europe, some countries in Asia are making more progress towards including students with disabilities in general schools while others still rely mostly on special schools. In South Korea 79,711 students with disabilities received special education in 2010. Of those, 55,935 (70%) received their education with peers in the general school environment, while 23,776 (30%) received their education in special schools (Ministry of Education, Science, and Technology, 2011). In contrast, conversations with researchers in China suggest that the majority of students with disabilities still attend special schools (personal correspondence, Wang Yongshun, Beijing Sport University, October 15, 2014). In some continents such as in Africa and South America information about this issue is not always easy to retrieve given the language barrier, and lack of accessibility/dissemination of information in international publications and scientific development.

Experiences of students with special education needs in physical education

While statistics from Brazil, Portugal, Korea, Israel, and other countries are encouraging, APA scholars and educators argue that the data do not accurately reflect the reality of the situation. For example, one researcher from Brazil noted that many children with disabilities, particularly those with more severe disabilities, still remain functionally excluded from general education settings (Mauerberg-deCastro et al., 2013). Similarly, a researcher in Portugal noted that, although current legislation in Portugal recognizes the importance of inclusion of students with disabilities, most schools, teachers, and students without disabilities are not prepared to include students successfully. In addition, the existence of policies promoting inclusive philosophies are not by themselves sufficient to guarantee the implementation of inclusive practice in Portuguese schools. In South Korea many principals still refuse to accept students with special education needs, and a recent research study found that half of the physical education teachers chose not to include students with disabilities in their general programs (Jeong & Block, 2011). In less developed countries including many on the African continent, the Caribbean, and the People's Republic of China many parents feel embarrassment and shame for having a child with a disability. The local culture pushes parents to either keep their child at home or send them to special schools. The result is outright exclusion and placement in special schools (Yang, Jia-Hong, Yu-Liu, & Kudláček, 2012).

There have been several studies from across the world exploring experiences of inclusion in GPE from the perspective of students with SEN (Asbjørnslett & Hemmingsson, 2005 [Norway]; Bredahl, 2013 [Norway]; Fitzgerald, 2005 [United Kingdom]; Fitzgerald & Stride, 2012 [United Kingdom]; Hutzler, Fliess, Chacham, & van den Auweele, 2002 [Israel]; Spencer-Cavaliere & Watkinson, 2010 [Canada]). While these studies reported many benefits of being included in GPE, they also reported negative experiences expressed by the students with disabilities. The two most common themes that accompany negative experiences were: feeling different and lack of competence. Feeling different was reported due to (a) type of activities in which the students were involved (e.g., playing different activities in PE instead of soccer, individual activities instead of class activities), (b) locations in which the activities were taking place (e.g., away from the class or in a separate room), (c) teacher assigned social roles or activity positions (e.g., spectator, goalie, scorekeeper), (d) teacher granted exemptions and preferential treatment (e.g., waiving the requirement of going outside in the cold weather), (e) interruptions of and dependency on a personal assistant, and (f) students' own sense of physicality.

The second most common theme noted was students' perceptions of lack of competence (Asbjørnslett & Hemmingsson, 2008 [Norway]; Bredahl, 2013 [Norway]; Fitzgerald, 2005 [United Kingdom]; Fitzgerald & Stride, 2012 [United Kingdom]; Spencer-Cavaliere & Watkinson, 2010 [Canada]). GPE provides many opportunities for making one's abilities, skills, and behaviors clearly visible (Tannehill, MacPhail, Halbert, & Murphy, 2013). Interviews revealed that if students with a disability had difficulties performing a skill or controlling their movements or behaviors due to their disability, they felt they were being looked at by peers, causing feelings of embarrassment, incompetence, and inadequacy. Such feelings were even more prevalent when peers without disabilities were frustrated with the challenges the students with disabilities faced (e.g., becoming angry when students did not catch a ball) (Bredahl, 2013).

Beliefs about students with disabilities

As reported in the previous section, for PE teachers to effectively include children with disabilities, it is important for them to know which behaviors help students feel included and excluded in PE class. In addition, it is important to understand teachers' attitudes and beliefs and what helps them facilitate the inclusion process. This section reviews research related to children without disabilities' attitudes and beliefs. This section is followed by an examination of teacher perspectives on the inclusion of children with disabilities.

Beliefs of students without disabilities

A number of research studies have suggested that beliefs of students without disabilities play a critical role in fostering feelings of acceptance, respect, and perceived competence in students with a disability (e.g., André, Louvet, & Deneuve, 2013 [France]; Asbjørnslett & Hemmingsson, 2008 [Sweden]; Kalymon, Gettinger, & Hanley-Maxwell, 2010; Obrusnikova, Block, & Dillon, 2010 [U.S.A.]; Obrusnikova, Dillon, & Block, 2011 [U.S.A.]; Seymour, Reid, & Bloom, 2009 [Canada]; Spencer-Cavaliere & Watkinson, 2010 [Canada]. More specifically, researchers have found a majority of middle school-aged students without disabilities have positive beliefs toward playing with a peer with a disability in their GPE classes. This perspective seems to lead to stronger intentions to play with this peer (Campos et al., 2014 [Portugal]; Obrusnikova et al., 2011, 2012 [U.S.A.]; Papaioannou, Evaggelinou, & Block, 2014 [Greece]; Verderber, Rizzo, & Sherrill, 2003 [U.S.A.]). The most frequently cited attributes of the student without a disability associated with favorable beliefs are being female (Obrusnikova et al., 2011; Obrusnikova & Dillon, 2012; Verderber et al., 2003), having stronger social responsibility goals (i.e., students with secure, positive relationships with their teachers and peers), and having stronger task-involved goals (i.e., students who focus on the skill development and demonstration of competence rather than focusing on trying to win) (Obrusnikova & Dillon, 2012).

In contrast, attributes of students with disabilities associated with less favorable beliefs or experiences by students without disabilities were (a) having different interests and lower competence levels (André et al., 2013; Kalymon et al., 2010; Obrusnikova et al., 2010; Seymour et al., 2009), (b) not spending time interacting with students without disabilities during and outside of school (Kalymon et al., 2010; Seymour et al., 2009), (c) affecting safety in GPE (Obrusnikova et al., 2010; Verderber et al., 2003), (d) having a lower social status among peers (Kalymon et al., 2010; Obrusnikova et al., 2010), (e) being given differential treatment by adults (Kalymon et al., 2010), and (f) being assisted by an adult (Kalymon et al., 2010).

General physical educators' beliefs about inclusion and teaching students with disabilities

Research suggests GPE teachers have mixed opinions regarding inclusion. While many GPE teachers are not opposed to including SEN in their classes, some do not feel adequately prepared or knowledgeable about strategies to accommodate these students (Crawford, O'Reilly, & Flanagan, 2012 [Ireland]; Fejgin, Talmor, & Erlich, 2005 [Israel]; Hodge et al., 2009 [USA]; Jeong & Block, 2011 [South Korea]; Jerlinder, Danermark, & Gill, 2010 [Sweden]; Lieberman, Houston-Wilson, & Kozub, 2002 [USA]; Lienert, Sherrill, & Myers, 2001 [Germany]; Mauerberg-deCastro et al., 2013 [Brazil]; Meegan & MacPhail, 2006 [Ireland]; Özer et al., 2013 [Turkey]; Sato et al., 2007 [Japan]; Vickerman & Coates, 2009 [United Kingdom]). For example, in Ireland, research by Meegan and MacPhail (2006) indicated that physical education teachers do not feel adequately prepared to accommodate students with SEN in physical education classes. This may be the result of limited preparation as noted by Barry-Power (2010) who found a low number of physical education teachers had received initial teacher training or the opportunity to gain further training once qualified in the area of special needs and inclusion.

Key barriers to inclusion consisted of unsuitable access to facilities, game-dominated physical education, and negative attitudes of students without disabilities towards classmates with SEN. Meegan and MacPhail (2006) also highlighted areas of PE teacher neglect including the development of individual education plans (IEP) and input into the IEP planning process. Additionally, the role and training of special needs assistants (SNAs) to aid in the inclusion of students with disabilities in physical education needs further investigation and development. Training and utilizing teacher assistants (or paraeducators) has been reported in other countries as well (e.g., Davis, Kotecki, Harvey, Oliver, 2007 [U.S.A.], Haycock & Smith, 2011 [United Kingdom]).

Favorable beliefs

Among the teacher-related variables associated with more favorable beliefs were being female (Fejgin et al., 2005 [Israel]; Meegan & MacPhail, 2006 [Ireland]), having adequate academic preparation (Obrusnikova, 2008 [U.S.A.]; Özer et al., 2013 [Turkey]; Tripp & Rizzo, 2006 [U.S.A]), having positive clinical experiences (Jerlinder et al., 2010 [Sweden]; Obrusnikova, 2008; Özer et al., 2013; Tripp & Rizzo, 2006), receiving information about the student's label or disability (Grenier, 2011; Tripp & Rizzo, 2006), and having a higher level of perceived competence to work with students with disabilities (Obrusnikova, 2008; Özer et al., 2013; Tripp & Rizzo, 2006).

The most common student-related variables associated with GPE teachers' favorable beliefs were the type and degree of a student's disability. GPE teachers held less favorable beliefs toward teaching students with severe disabilities or those who exhibited inattentiveness, hyperactivity, or had emotional-behavioral disorders (Ammah & Hodge, 2006; Hersman & Hodge, 2010; Hodge et al., 2009; Obrusnikova, 2008; Sato et al., 2007). Difficulties teachers experienced in accommodating a wide range of abilities and managing student behaviors during GPE instruction seem to adversely affect their self-confidence and perceived behavioral control (Hersman & Hodge, 2010; Hodge et al., 2009; Jeong & Block, 2011; Sato et al., 2007). Still, there are GPE teachers who accept the challenge of teaching students with severe disabilities because they become motivated to educate themselves on how to modify instruction and activities to meet their students' needs (Grenier, 2006; Hersman & Hodge, 2010; Hodge et al., 2009).

Assisting teachers to provide quality experiences

Hersman and Hodge (2010) and Özer et al. (2013) reported that better quality professional training, positive clinical experiences, and adequate support and teaching conditions are critical in facilitating a teacher's sense of behavioral control associated with teaching efficacy. However, consistent with prior research on inclusion (e.g., LaMaster, Gall, Kinchin, & Siedentop, 1998), many GPE teachers do not perceive their professional preparation, clinical experiences, support, and teaching conditions to be adequate (Fejgin et al., 2005; Hersman & Hodge, 2010; Jerlinder et al., 2010; Vickerman & Coates, 2009). For example, GPE teachers in Israel complained they do not receive support and professional help from the other instructional team members such as school counselors, special education teachers, and APE teachers (Fejgin et al., 2005).

Teaching conditions

In other studies (e.g., Ammah & Hodge, 2006; Hersman & Hodge, 2010; Hodge et al., 2009), teachers were concerned with various contextual issues such as lack of adequate equipment, limited instructional space, and large or overcrowded classes, particularly when working with students with emotional and behavioral disorders (Fejgin et al., 2005). Teachers perceived that contextual issues negatively affected teaching method selection, lesson pace, classroom safety, students' motivation to participate in activities, and the type of social interaction between students with and without disabilities (Fejgin et al., 2005; Hersman & Hodge, 2010; Suomi, Collier, & Brown, 2003). If GPE teachers are not provided the means to support students with SEN in general physical education, then inclusion will not be effective and teachers will not be in favor of having students with disabilities in their classes (Fejgin et al., 2005; Vickerman & Coates, 2009).

Analysis of international culture in the area of inclusive education related to the Theory of Planned Behavior

Teachers' attitudes are an important determinant of behavior in educational settings and one of the most important factors for successful implementation of inclusion in GPE. Teachers' beliefs toward inclusion are extremely important to understand especially related to their evolution. From a psychological perspective behavioral beliefs link the behavior of interest to expected outcomes (see also Kulinna & Cothran, Chapter 36, this volume). A behavioral belief is the subjective probability that the behavior will produce a given outcome. Ajzen (1991) also claims that, although a person may hold many behavioral beliefs with respect to any behavior, only a relatively small number are readily accessible at a given moment.

One of the most significant theories relating to this attitude-behavior relationship is Ajzen's (1991), Theory of Planned Behavior (TPB) which evolved from the Theory of Reasoned Action (TRA) (Fishbein, 1967). TPB assumes that an individual's intention to perform a given behavior is the best predictor of that behavior (Francis et al., 2004; Martin & Kudláček, 2010; Meegan & MacPhail, 2006; Verderber et al., 2003). As a general rule, the more favorable the individual's attitude and subjective norm and the greater their perceived control, the stronger the individual's intention to perform the behavior (Ajzen, 2002).

When applied to teaching students with disabilities in physical education, the TPB suggests that teaching is influenced by several psychological factors including teachers' beliefs regarding students' behavioral outcomes and evaluations, the expectations placed on them, their motivation to comply with such expectations, as well as the presence or absence of factors and resources that may help or hinder these students and their teaching. For example, a teacher who believes she can include a child who has a visual impairment in a floor hockey unit might ask the vision teacher questions, talk to the student herself, and e-mail the student's previous teacher to gain information. Once she learns about tasks that have and have not worked previously, the teacher trains several peer tutors, borrows and deflates a bell ball to slow down the game a bit so that all students can play more successfully. She could add a beeper to the back of the goal on the offensive side to orient the student who is blind. In this example, it took the students two weeks to get used to the variations, but then everyone was playing red faced, sweating, and having a ball! This teacher believed she could include this student and went out of her way to make it happen. Many teachers that do not have this belief might say this unit is too dangerous, the puck moves too fast, and the child should dance or play exergames during this unit (Perkins, Columna, Lieberman, & Bailey, 2013).

Summary of current trends and issues

Globally, physical education teachers' lack of training in inclusion is the biggest barrier to educating children with disabilities. International research examining preparation of preservice PE and SEN teachers indicates that initial teacher training providers are inconsistent in the amount of time spent addressing the issue and the nature of curricular content (Vickerman & Coates, 2009). The lack of training leads teachers to feel inadequate, and, as a result, children with disabilities are often unnecessarily excluded from physical education (Mauerberg-deCastro et al., 2013; Özer et al., 2013, Sato et al., 2007). Addressing lack of training that is so pervasive in the literature could assist PE teachers to deal more effectively with these situations as they arise.

Another major theme found in recent research examining inclusion involved contextual issues within the teaching environment, such as lack of adequate space, inadequate paraeducator training, lesson pace, and overcrowded classes, and lack of adequate or necessary equipment (Fejgin et al., 2005; Hersman & Hodge, 2010). These issues can be major barriers to skill acquisition for any child, and especially children with disabilities. The lack of equipment, even basic equipment, such as wheelchairs for children with mobility impairments, and other resources is often due to lack of funding but also may be caused by lack of availability of appropriate and necessary equipment. For example, developing countries may not have access to goalballs used for students with visual impairments. In addition, PE teachers often are unaware of the relevance of this game for students with visual impairments.

Implications for evidence-based practice

Social attitudes are frequently documented as a major hindrance to inclusion (Lieberman & Houston-Wilson, 2009). Role models can dispel myths about the ability levels of individuals with disabilities. High performing athletes with disabilities like Marla Runyan, Natalie du Toit, Dartanyan Crocket, Chris Ahrens, and Tatyana McFadden also can change the way people see individuals with disabilities. In addition, more disability awareness programming must be implemented in schools to help able-bodied children perceive the potential abilities of all individuals with disabilities (Lieberman & Houston-Wilson, 2009).

As described previously, major barriers to inclusion are lack of teacher training and attitudes among peers and teachers. It appears that these barriers can be explained, in part, using the Theory of Planned Behavior. For example, when teachers do not understand how inclusion will affect the outcome of the child's performance, they are unlikely to have a positive attitude toward inclusion. The universal lack of physical education teacher education training for inclusive settings often leads to a lack of understanding about the benefits of inclusion and the way to include students effectively. Professors in higher education also must be trained and encouraged to discuss the benefits of inclusion and teach effective strategies, such as universal design for learning, differentiating instruction (Gregory & Chapman, 2013), peer tutoring (Lieberman & Houston-Wilson, 2009), as well as methods to train and utilize paraeducators, to ensure the appropriate inclusion of children with disabilities (Block, 2016) (see Table 17.1).

In the future researchers across the world must address the issue of negative attitudes and stereotypes about individuals with disabilities. Researchers also must perform intervention studies to verify the effects of disability awareness, peer tutoring, paraeducators' training, modifying activities, and improving attitudes toward disabilities. Lastly, they must create curricula for college professors to adequately instruct professional preparation students on inclusive strategies for physical education.

Table 17.1 Strategy, definition, and resources related to Universal Design for Learning, Differentiating Instruction, peer tutoring, and training paraeducators in inclusive settings

Strategy	What it is	Resources
Universal Design for Learning	The provision of UDL in physical education helps to meet the needs of all learners in terms of: what they learn, how they learn, and why they learn. By purposefully, intentionally, and proactively designing the curriculum the teachers can foster the development of expert learners (Rapp, 2014).	Lieberman & Houston-Wilson, 2009 Rapp, 2014 Rapp & Arndt, 2012
Differentiating Instruction	Differentiated Instruction offers several options for learning, and it does not assume that each individual child would need a separate, unique adaption. For example, a student with cerebral palsy who has balance and coordination challenges is in a throwing and catching unit. Rather than creating a unique accommodation for this student, the teacher proactively created a number of ways to experience, practice, and measure success in throwing and catching for all students including the use of scarves and balloons for catching and different distances and size targets for throwing. These "differentiated" options for throwing and catching are available to all students and not specifically designed for the student with a disability. As a result, this student has the opportunity to be successfully included in the unit not by having unique, individual accommodations but by taking advantage of the planned differentiated options offered to all children in the class.	Ellis, Lieberman, & LeRoux, 2009
Peer tutoring	Peer tutoring is when children with disabilities are paired with a child with a mild disability or no disability. The peer tutor instructs and gives feedback to the child with the disability. Instruction can be unidirectional or bidirectional.	Cervantes, Lieberman, Magnesio, & Wood, 2013; Klavina & Block, 2013
Training paraeducators	Paraeducators, also known as teacher aides, teacher assistants, or special needs assistants are utilized to support the lead teacher. Paraeducators can be trained and used effectively in physical education to assist in teaching, feedback, safety, behavior, and motivation.	Hodge, Lieberman, & Murata, 2012 Lieberman, 2007 Lieberman & Houston-Wilson, 2009

Reflective questions for discussion

1. What is inclusion? To what extent can laws and policies enhance opportunities for inclusion? Use international examples to support your answer.
2. Historically, how has inclusion changed over the years? Did you attend schools and participate in GPE with students with disabilities? Did you view this experience positively or negatively? Provide examples to support your answer.
3. What are the major barriers to inclusion around the world? How are these different from barriers to effective teaching and learning in GPE?
4. What are some solutions to the barriers to inclusion found in this chapter? What other possible solutions might create more positive experiences for teachers and students with and without disabilities?
5. What steps can you take to improve the lives of children with disabilities in your classes, community, and country?

References

Ajzen, I. (1991). The theory of planned behavior. *Organizational Behavior and Human Decision Processes, 50*, 179–211.

Ajzen, I. (2002). Perceived behavioral control, self efficacy, locus of control, and the theory of planned behavior. *Journal of Applied Social Psychology, 32*, 665–683.

Ammah, J. O., & Hodge, S. R. (2006). Secondary physical education teachers' beliefs and practices in teaching students with severe disabilities: A descriptive analysis. *High School Journal, 89*, 40–54.

André, A., Louvet, B., & Deneuve, P. (2013). Cooperative group, risk-taking and inclusion of pupils with learning disabilities in physical education. *British Educational Research Journal, 39*, 677–693.

Asbjørnslett, M., & Hemmingsson, H. (2008). Participation at school as experienced by teenagers with physical disabilities. *Scandinavian Journal of Occupational Therapy. 15*, 153–161.

Aufsesser, P. M. (1991). Mainstreaming and the least restrictive environment: How do they differ? *Palaestra, 7*, 31–34.

Barry-Power, D. (2010). *The inclusion of students with disabilities in mainstream post-primary physical education from the perspective of the physical education teacher.* Thesis submitted in fulfillment of the requirement for the Degree of Masters of Arts at The Waterford Institute of Technology, Ireland.

Block, M. E. (2016). *An inclusive approach to adapted physical education.* Baltimore: Paul H. Brookes.

Brazil. (1988). *Constituição da República Federativa do Brasil [Constitution of the Federative Republic of Brazil].* Brasília, DF: Senado Federal/Secretaria Especial de Editoração e Publicações.

Brazil. (1996). *Congresso Nacional. Lei n. 9.394 estabelece as diretrizes e bases da educação nacional [National Congress. Law n. 9394 establishes guidelines and bases of national education].* Diário Oficial da União n. 248, de 23/12/96 – Seção I, p. 27833. Brasília.

Brazil. (2007). *Política Nacional de Educação Especial na perspectiva da Educação Inclusiva.* Brasília: Secretaria de Educação Especial/MEC.

Brazil. (2013). *Dados do Censo Escolar 2013 estão disponíveis para consulta [School Census 2013 are available].* Ministério Educação e Cultura, Secretaria Educação Especial. Retrieved October 10, 2015, from www.brasil.gov.br/educacao/2014/03/dados-do-censo-escolar-2013-estao-disponiveis-para-consulta.

Bredahl, A-M. (2013). Sitting and watching the others being active: The experienced difficulties in PE when having a disability. *Adapted Physical Activity Quarterly, 30*, 40–58.

Campos, M. J., Ferreira, J. P., & Block, M. E. (2014). Influence of an awareness program on Portuguese middle and high school students' perceptions toward peers with disabilities. *Psychological Reports, 115*, 1–16.

Cervantes, C. M., Lieberman, L. J., Magnesio, B., & Wood, J. (2013). Peer tutoring: Meeting the demands of inclusion in today's general physical education settings. *Journal of Physical Education, Recreation & Dance, 81*, 43–48.

Crawford, S., O'Reilly, R., & Flanagan, N. (2012). Examining current provisions, practice and experience of initial teacher training providers in Ireland preparing pre service teachers for the inclusion of students with special educational needs in physical education classes. *European Journal of Adapted Physical Activity*, *5*, 23–44.

Davis, R. W., Kotecki, J. E., Harvey, M. W., & Oliver, A. (2007). Responsibilities and training needs of paraeducators in physical education. *Adapted Physical Activity Quarterly*, *24*, 70–83.

Downing, J. (2001). *Including students with severe and multiple disabilities in typical classrooms* (3rd edn.). Baltimore: Paul H. Brookes.

Ellis, K., Lieberman, L. J., & Leroux, D. (2009). Using differentiated instruction in physical education. *Palaestra*, *24*, 19–23.

Fejgin, N., Talmor, R., & Erlich, I. (2005). Inclusion and burnout in physical education. *European Physical Education Review*, *11*, 29–50.

Fishbein, M. (1967). A consideration of beliefs, and their role in attitude measurement. In M. Fishbein (Ed.), *Readings in attitude theory and measurement* (pp. 257–266). New York: John Wiley & Sons.

Fitzgerald, H. (2005). Still feeling like a spare piece of luggage? Embodied experiences of (dis)ability in physical education and school sport. *Physical Education and Sport Pedagogy*, *10*, 41–59.

Fitzgerald, H., & Stride, A. (2012). Stories about physical education from young people with disabilities. *International Journal of Disability, Development and Education*, *59*, 283–293.

Francis, J. J., Eccles, M. P., Johnston, M., Walker, A., Grimshaw, J., Foy, R., ... Bonetti, D. (2004). *Constructing questionnaires based on the theory of planned behaviour: A manual for health services researchers.* Centre for Health Services Research, University of Newcastle upon Tyne, UK.

Gregory, G. H., & Chapman, C. M. (2013). *Differentiated instructional strategies.* Thousand Oaks, CA: Corwin.

Grenier, M. A. (2006). A social constructionist perspective of teaching and learning in inclusive physical education. *Adapted Physical Activity Quarterly*, *23*, 245–260.

Grenier, M. A. (2011). Co-teaching in physical education: A strategy for inclusive practice. *Adapted Physical Activity Quarterly*, *28*, 95–112.

Haycock, D., & Smith, A. (2011). To assist or not to assist? A study of teachers' views of the roles of learning support assistants in the provision of inclusive physical education in England. *International Journal of Inclusive Education*, *15*, 835–849.

Hersman, B. L., & Hodge, S. R. (2010). High school physical educators' beliefs about teaching differently abled students in an urban public school district. *Education and Urban Society*, *42*, 730–757.

Hodge, S., Lieberman, L. J., & Murata, N. (2012). *Essentials of teaching adapted physical education: Culture, diversity, and inclusion.* Scottsdale, AZ: Holcomb Hathaway.

Hodge, S. R., Ammah, J. O. A., Casebolt, K. M., LaMaster, K., Hersman, B., Samalot-Rivera, A., & Sato, T. (2009). A diversity of voices: Physical education teachers' beliefs about inclusion and teaching students with disabilities. *International Journal of Disability, Development and Education*, *56*, 401–419.

Hutzler, Y., Fliess, O., Chacham, A., & van den Auweele, Y. (2002). Perspectives of children with physical disabilities on inclusion and empowerment: Supporting and limiting factors. *Adapted Physical Activity Quarterly*, *19*, 300–317.

Hutzler, Y., & Levi, I. (2008). Including children with disability in physical education: General and specific attitudes of high-school students. *European Journal of Adapted Physical Activity*, *1*, 21–30.

Jeong, M., & Block, M. E. (2011). Physical education teachers' beliefs and intentions towards teaching students with disabilities. *Research Quarterly for Exercise and Sport*, *82*, 1–8.

Jerlinder, K., Danermark, B., & Gill, P. (2010). Swedish primary-school teachers' attitudes to inclusion: The case of PE and pupils with physical disabilities. *European Journal of Special Needs Education*, *25*, 45–57.

Kalymon, K., Gettinger, M., & Hanley-Maxwell, C. (2010). Middle school boys' perspectives on social relationships with peers with disabilities. *Remedial and Special Education*, *31*, 305–316.

Klavina, A., & Block, M. E. (2013). Training peer tutors to support children with severe, multiple disabilities in general physical education. *Palaestra*, *27*, 208–213.

Korea Ministry of Health and Welfare. (2010). *Anti-Discrimination against and remedies for persons with disabilities act.* Seoul, Korea: Author.

Kudláček, M., Válková, H., Sherrill, C., Myers, B., & French, R. (2002). An inclusion instrument based on planned behavior theory for prospective physical educators. *Adapted Physical Activity Quarterly*, *19*, 280–299.

LaMaster, K., Gall, K., Kinchin, G., & Siedentop, D. (1998). Inclusion practices of effective elementary specialists. *Adapted Physical Activity Quarterly*, *15*, 64–81.

Lieberman, L. J. (Ed.) (2007). *A paraprofessional training guide for physical education.* Champaign, IL: Human Kinetics.

Lieberman, L. J., & Houston-Wilson, C. (2009). *Strategies for inclusion* (2nd edn.). Champaign, IL: Human Kinetics.

Lieberman, L. J., Houston-Wilson, C., & Kozub, F. (2002) Perceived barriers to including students with visual impairments and blindness into physical education. *Adapted Physical Activity Quarterly, 19*, 364–377.

Lienert, C., Sherrill, C., & Myers, B. (2001). Physical educators' concerns about integrating children with disabilities: A cross-cultural comparison. *Adapted Physical Activity Quarterly, 18*, 1–17.

Lipsky, D. K., & Gartner, A. (1987). *Beyond separate education: Quality education for all*. Baltimore: Paul H. Brookes.

Martin, K., & Kudláček, M. (2010). Attitudes of pre-service teachers in an Australian university towards inclusion of students with physical disabilities in general physical education programs. *European Journal of Adapted Physical Activity, 3*, 30–48.

Mauerberg-deCastro, E., Paiva, A. C. S., Figueiredo, G. A., Costa, T. D. A., Castro, M. R., & Campbell, D. F. (2013). Attitudes about inclusion by educators and physical educators: Effects of participation in an inclusive adapted physical education program. *Motriz, Rio Claro, 9*, 649–661.

Meegan, S., & MacPhail, A. (2006). Irish physical educators' attitude toward teaching students with special educational needs. *European Physical Education Review, 12*, 75–97.

Ministry of Education, Science and Technology. (2011). *2011 annual report of special education*. Seoul, Korea: Author.

Ministry of Education, Science and Technology. (2013). *Special education laws for persons with disabilities and others*. Seoul, Korea: Author.

Obrusnikova, I. (2008). Physical educators' beliefs about teaching children with disabilities. *Perceptual and Motor Skills, 106*, 637–644.

Obrusnikova, I., Block, M., & Dillon, S. (2010). Children's beliefs toward cooperative playing with peers with disabilities in physical education. *Adapted Physical Activity Quarterly, 27*, 127–142.

Obrusnikova, I., & Dillon, S. R. (2012). Students' beliefs and intentions to play with peers with disabilities in physical education: Relationships with achievement and social goals. *Journal of Teaching in Physical Education, 31*, 311–328.

Obrusnikova, I., Dillon, S. R., & Block, M. E. (2011). Middle school student intentions to play with peers with disabilities in physical education: Using the theory of planned behavior. *Journal of Developmental and Physical Disabilities, 23*, 113–127.

Özer, D., Nalbant, S., Ağlamış, E., Baran, F., Samut, P. K., Aktop, A., & Hutzler, Y. (2013). Physical education teachers' attitudes towards children with intellectual disability: The impact of time in service, gender, and previous acquaintance. *Journal of Intellectual Disability Research, 57*, 1001–1013.

Panagiotou, A., Evaggelinou, C., Doulkeridou, A., Mouratidou, K., & Koidou, E. (2008). Attitudes of 5th and 6th grade Greek students toward the inclusion of children with disabilities in physical education classes after a Paralympic education program. *European Journal of Adapted Physical Activity, 1*(2), 31–43.

Papaioannou, C., Evaggelinou, C., & Block, M. E. (2014). The effect of a disability camp program on attitudes towards the inclusion of children with disabilities in a summer sport and leisure activity camp. *International Journal of Special Education, 29*, 1–9.

Pecora, J. K., Whittaker, J. K., Maluccio, A. N., & Barth, R. P. (2012). *The child welfare challenge: Policy, practice and research* (3rd edn.). New Brunswick, NJ: Aldine Transaction.

Perkins, K., Columna, L., Lieberman, L. J., & Bailey, J. (2013) Parental perceptions toward physical activity for their children with visual impairments and blindness. *Journal of Visual Impairments and Blindness, 107*, 131–142.

Rapp, W. (2014). *Universal design for learning in action*. Baltimore: Paul H. Brookes.

Rapp, W., & Arndt, K. (2012). *Teaching everyone: An introduction to inclusive education*. Baltimore: Brookes.

Rodrigues, D., & Nogueira, J. (2010). Educação especial e inclusiva em Portugal: Factos e opções [Special and inclusive education in Portugal: Facts and options]. *Revista Education Inclusiva, 3*, 97–109.

Sato, T., Hodge, S. R., Murata, N. M., & Maeda, J. K. (2007). Japanese physical education teachers' beliefs about teaching students with disabilities. *Journal of Sport Education and Society, 12*, 211–230.

Seymour, H., Reid, G., & Bloom, G. A. (2009). Friendship in inclusive physical education. *Adapted Physical Activity Quarterly, 26*, 201–219.

Spencer-Cavaliere, N., & Watkinson, J. E. (2010). Inclusion understood from the perspectives of children with disability. *Adapted Physical Activity Quarterly, 27*, 275–293.

Stainback, S., & Stainback, W. (1990). Inclusive schooling. In W. Stainback & S. Stainback (Eds.), *Support networks for inclusive schooling* (pp. 3–24). Baltimore: Paul H. Brookes.

Stainback, W., Stainback, S., & Bunch, G. (1989). A rationale for the merger of regular and special education. In W. Stainback, S. Stainback & M. Forest (Eds.), *Educating all students in the mainstream of regular education* (pp. 15–28). Baltimore: Paul H. Brookes.

Suomi, J., Collier, D., & Brown, L. (2003). Factors affecting the social experiences of students in elementary physical education classes. *Journal of Teaching in Physical Education, 22,* 186–202.

Tannehill, D., MacPhail. A., Halbert, G., & Murphy, F. (2013). *Research and practice in physical education.* London: Routledge.

Tripp, A., & Rizzo, T. (2006). Disability labels affect physical educators. *Adapted Physical Activity Quarterly, 23,* 310–326.

Turnbull, H. R. (1990). *Free appropriate public education: The law and children with disabilities* (3rd edn.). Denver, CO: Love.

UNESCO. (1994). *Salamanca statement and framework for action.* World Conference on Special Needs Education: Access and Quality. Retrieved March 22, 2016, from http://unesdoc.unesco.org/images/0009/000984/098427eo.pdf.

United States Government. (2004). *Public Law* 94–142. *Individuals with Disabilities Education Act (IDEA).* 108th Congress Public Law 446. Retrieved May 5, 2014, from www.gpo.gov/fdsys/pkg/PLAW-108publ446/html/PLAW-108publ446.htm.

Verderber, J. M. S., Rizzo, T. L., & Sherrill, C. (2003). Assessing student intention to participate in inclusive physical education. *Adapted Physical Activity Quarterly, 20,* 26–45.

Vickerman, P., & Coates, J. (2009). Trainee and recently qualified physical education teachers' perspectives on including children with special educational needs. *Physical Education and Sport Pedagogy, 14,* 137–153.

World Health Organization. (2011). *World report on disability.* Geneva, Switzerland: World Health Organization Library Cataloguing-in-Publication Data.

Yang, L., Jia-Hong, W., Yu-Liu, T., & Kudláček, M. (2012). Inclusion and tactics: Research on prospective physical education teachers' intentions and attitudes toward inclusive physical education. *Journal of Beijing University of Physical Education, 35,* 88–94.

PART V

Transformative pedagogies in physical education

Introduction

There is a growing and diverse literature on what is termed *transformative pedagogy*. It is seen in such diverse fields of practice as architecture, environmental sustainability and education. Much of this literature is inspired by the writings of scholars such as Aronowitz and Giroux (1985), Bowles and Gintis (1976), Freire (1972) and Giroux (1983).

Ukpokodu (2009) defines transformative pedagogy as an activist pedagogy combining the elements of constructivist and critical pedagogy that empowers students to examine critically their beliefs, values and knowledge with the goal of developing a reflective knowledge base, an appreciation for multiple perspectives and a sense of critical consciousness and agency (Ukpokodu, 2009, p. 43).

Taking Ukpokodu's lead, this part considers the constructivist, dialogic, critical and reflective nature of transformative pedagogy as a democratic educational spirit and an educational philosophy rather than a particular pedagogy.

Physical education has not been isolated from the discourses that inform transformative pedagogy. Moreover, physical education pedagogy has a considerable literature on critical pedagogy, constructivist informed pedagogy and reflective practice. There are numerous examples of advocacy for PE's role in social change and some analyses of the potential impact of social change on PE (see references in the chapter by Tinning in this collection). Indeed many social changes have provided, and will continue to provide, challenges to PE. However, notwithstanding all of this, to date, within the PE literature there is limited connection with transformative pedagogy as a specific concept.

In this part the authors consider the concept of transformative pedagogy in regard to physical education. Importantly, we all take the position that transformative pedagogy is a term for what is a broad church of transformative pedagog*ies*. The overall question that orients the chapters in this part is "what might genuinely be regarded as transformative pedagogies in PE and what have been their success?"

This section begins with Richard Tinning's chapter (18) which provides an overview of the discourse communities (both in PE and education more generally) that 'gives voice' to the critical agenda of transformative pedagogy and considers the possibilities and difficulties of engaging transformative pedagogies within physical education. In particular it explores the possibilities for transformative pedagogies to bring about both personal and social change.

In Chapter 19, Alan Ovens examines the practices that provide a means for enacting transformative pedagogies in physical education teacher education programmes (PETE). Acknowledging that *advocating for* transformative practice is not the same as *doing* transformative practice Ovens suggests that the very possibility of transformative practice appears contingent on a range of social, political and material factors that constitute the landscape of teacher education. For Ovens, the *doing* of a transformative practice in PETE is about enabling a setting where the practices of teaching can be reflexively interrogated.

Kimberley Oliver and David Kirk argue in Chapter 20 that early advocacy for critical pedagogy in physical education was not easily translated into practice. Tracing the main theoretical approaches to conceptualising the body, its social construction and the experience of embodiment in physical education, they then use an example from activist research with girls in PE to show how a focus on embodiment as integral to a transformative pedagogy requires a radical reconstruction of physical education.

Katie Fitzpatrick and Eimear Enwright explore 'transformative' pedagogies of physical education (PE) in Chapter 21 and consider what these approaches might mean for addressing issues of gender sexuality in the field. They suggest that transformative approaches to PE require attention to the social and political contexts within which they occur, and which articulate with practice in complex ways at the intersection of body, culture and practice.

According to Fiona Dowling and Robyne Garrett (Chapter 22), narrative inquiry has the potential to bring about enhanced understanding about the social world of PE and to transform its social inequalities. Positioning narrative inquiry in a historical context, they then present an overview of the most relevant research carried out during the past decade. The collective findings of the various studies foreground a discussion about how narrative inquiry can be developed in the future within the field of PE (theoretically and practically), and in particular, address what narrative pedagogical strategies might be useful, and why, for the purpose of transforming inequitable relations.

Drawing upon the relatively new area of study of critical obesity scholarship, Erin Cameron, Moss Norman and LeAnne Petherick employ the notion of *transformative pedagogy* in Chapter 23 to challenge scholars, students and professionals in the field of physical education to critically consider the construction and representation of the so-called 'obesity epidemic'. In an attempt to disrupt both the pervasiveness of dominant obesity discourse, the critical obesity pedagogy they describe uses what they call "obesity stories" to deconstruct commonly held assumptions about bodies, weight and health, and to expose the injustices of a culture that assigns moral value to body weight.

In the last chapter (24) in this part, in *Transformative pedagogy in physical education and the challenges of young people with migration backgrounds*, Dean Barker and Suzanne Lundvall provide an overview of scholarship dealing with ethnicity and cultural diversity in relation to PE. They identify two central themes that have occupied scholars over the last two decades: Muslim girls' experiences, and teachers' preparedness to respond to increasing cultural pluralism. In synthesising this literature, the chapter underscores recurring issues, central findings and implications for practitioners, as well as identifying themes that require further theoretical and practical attention.

Richard Tinning
University of Queensland, Australia

References

Aronowitz, S., & Giroux, H. (1985). *Education under siege*. South Hadley, MA: Bergin & Garvey.

Bowles, S., & Gintis, H. (1976). *Schooling in capitalist America*. New York: Basic Books.

Freire, P. (1972). *Pedagogy of the oppressed*. New York: Penguin.

Giroux, H. (1983). *Theory and resistance in education: A pedagogy of opposition*. South Handley, MA: Bergin & Garvey.

Ukpokodu, O. (2009). Pedagogies that foster transformative learning in a multicultural education course: A reflection. *Journal of Praxis in Multicultural Education, 4*(1), DOI: 10.9741/2161–2978.1003.

18

TRANSFORMATIVE PEDAGOGIES AND PHYSICAL EDUCATION

Exploring the possibilities for personal change and social change

Richard Tinning, UNIVERSITY OF QUEENSLAND, AUSTRALIA

In writing about a certain disposition with regard to education, Kenway, Bigum, and Fitzclarence (1995) used the term the *critical project* to describe a set of shared views around three key themes: the unity of educational theory and practice; the historical formation, social construction, and continual reconstruction of education and educational institutions; and the possibilities of education for emancipation and active and productive participation in a democratic society (Rizvi, 2011, p. 151). The critical project is inspired by a sense of *criticality* (Rizvi, 2011) that embraces the ethics of social justice and the principles of critical theory.

When we consider how Ukpokodu (2009) defines transformative pedagogy we can immediately see that she is talking about a pedagogy (this includes multiple pedagogies) that is underpinned by a *criticality* and which can be thought to be part of the *critical project*. To paraphrase her definition, we can say that by means of certain pedagogical practices, students have their beliefs, values, and knowledge transformed and, as a result, are not only empowered with a critical consciousness and a sense of greater agency over their own lives, but also to influence the lives of others via activism. There are two dimensions of change that are implicit in transformative pedagogy – personal change and social change. There is also an assumption that empowerment at the individual level will lead to a social transformation in the form of a more democratic, equitable, and liberal social world. As Storrs and Inderbitzin (2006) argue, "Transformative pedagogy and a learning-centered paradigm are at the heart of a liberal education" (p. 176).

In this chapter I will consider transformative pedagogies as a manifestation of the *critical project* and present a cautionary account of what might be claimed in regard to transformative pedagogy in physical education (PE) from a personal and social change perspective. For example, in addition to what needs to be transformed in PE, what do we really think can be transformed through PE? Can we really empower students to make changes in their lives in relation to their beliefs and values that are consistent with liberal democratic ideals? Moreover, if PE is to make a contribution to the making of critical citizens and liberal democratic ideals, should this be its foremost task? – its main objective? In my view we need to keep the potential for PE to make such contributions in perspective.

In regard to the field of health and physical education (HPE), Leahy, O'Flynn, and Wright (2013) argue that

> critical approaches in HPE have been the subject of much research and writing. Overwhelmingly the emphasis has tended to be to argue for, and seek to demonstrate how a socio-critical or critical pedagogical approach might be implemented in teaching movement and/or health education. (p. 176)

This observation is an important beginning for this chapter because it allows for the distinction between scholarship that argues *for* the critical project (advocacy) and scholarship that reports *on* actual attempts to implement the critical project. In order to progress this observation I will suggest that transformative pedagogy can be thought of as a discourse community that includes scholarship *for* and *on* the critical project.

Transformative pedagogy as a discourse community

Transformative pedagogy can be thought of as a discourse community. As a concept, discourse community links the power discourses have to create specific perspectives for interpreting the world, with the affiliations people make with particular groups or communities that circulate such discourses (Ovens & Tinning, 2009). Importantly, discourse communities can be constituted of smaller discourse communities and, in the case of transformative pedagogy these include, but are not limited to, the discourse communities of critical pedagogy (Wink, 2011), critical action research (Carr & Kemmis, 1986), critical teaching (Kincheloe & Steinberg, 1998), "liberatory pedagogy" (Freire, 1972), critical inquiry (Zeichner, 1983), critical approaches (Leahy et al., 2013), and critical reflection (Waring & Evans, 2015). Accordingly, in this chapter when I write of, for example critical pedagogy, I will do so with the understanding that it is part of the larger discourse community of transformative pedagogy.

To date, there is limited specific use of transformative pedagogy as a specific term within the PE literature. However, the discourses that describe transformative pedagogy are found within advocacy *for* and research *on* critical pedagogy (e.g. Bain, 1990; Culpan & Bruce, 2007; Fernandez-Balboa, 1995; Garrett & Wrench, 2011; Kirk, 1986; Penney & Waring, 2000; Wright, 1999); on gender and PE (e.g. Azzarito & Solmon, 2009; Dowling, 2006; Fisette & Walton, 2014; Fitzpatrick, 2013a; Larsson, Redelius, & Fagrell, 2010; Oliver, 2001; Wright & King, 1990); on sexuality and PE (e.g. Clarke, 1992; Griffin, 1981; Sykes, 1998; Wright, 1991); on race and ethnicity (e.g. Carroll & Hollinshead, 1993; Dagkas & Benn, 2006; Fitzpatrick, 2011b, 2013b; Flintoff, 2014; Knez, Macdonald, & Abbott, 2012); on obesity and PE (e.g. Burrows & Wright, 2004; Fitzpatrick, 2011a; Gard & Wright, 2001; Garrett, 2006); on disability and equity in PE (e.g. Dowling, Fitzgerald, & Flintoff, 2012; Evans & Davies, 1993); and on knowledge in PE/physical education teacher education (PETE) (e.g. Kårhus, 2010; Kirk, 1992; Nyberg & Larsson, 2014).

Numerous scholars in PE have specifically examined critical pedagogy 'in action' to see if it 'delivered' on its claims. In the PETE context the work of Curtner-Smith (2007), Gore (1990), Hickey (2001), Ovens (2004), and Philpot (2015) provide evidence that the best of intentions are often difficult to realize, to make real. It is also noteworthy that critical pedagogy has not been a focus across all countries that have scholarship and research in PE and PETE. By far the largest concentration of critical scholars in PE publishing in English journals tend to be working in the UK, Australia, New Zealand, Canada, USA, Sweden, and Norway, with almost nothing registered in Asian countries such as Japan and Korea. Maybe this all says something about receptivity to the liberal democratic ideal of the critical project. There are also obvious language barriers to this observation. Germany, for example, has a long history of work on critical theory, but it's mostly published in German.

A voice from within the 'big tent'

In progressing with this cautionary account of transformative pedagogies and PE, I need to explicitly confirm my long-time commitment to the ideals of transformative pedagogy. As I have argued elsewhere (Tinning, 2002), I have long been happy to place myself within what Lather (1998) called the critical pedagogy 'big tent'. This 'big tent' could also be described as housing those who, in the language of this Handbook section, advocate for transformative pedagogies.

Positive achievements and cautionary observations

There is no doubt that over the past 30 years, physical education as a field of study has shown a growing interest in the *critical project*. Not only have critical discourses influenced academic writing and research in PE, they also have been 'taken up' in some curriculum reform documents (for example within Australia and New Zealand). An Australian example is instructive here. In 1990 we saw the introduction of National Curriculum guidelines that were underpinned by the principles of social justice, diversity, and supportive environments. This prompted Macdonald and Kirk (1999) to argue that this official discourse meant that HPE teachers in Australia now have a "responsibility to teach the socially critical liberal curriculum as defined by the State" (p. 140). Subsequent curriculum manifestations in Australia have kept a similar ethic.

To see many of the issues critical pedagogy advocates raised in the 1980s now being addressed within the official discourse of our field is surely a small victory for those of us in the 'big tent' of critical pedagogy – those of us who champion transformative pedagogy. However, my enthusiasm for this apparent victory is tempered since, in my view, the social justice discourses that are central to transformative pedagogy have become mainstreamed and have often been appropriated by some teachers and administrators for reasons at considerable distance from their original intention. In this regard McLaren (1998) argues that because postmodern critical pedagogy has an emphasis on values such as diversity and inclusion, its language is easily co-opted by neo-liberalism and has become an ally of new capitalism and neo-liberal educational policy.

While Rovegno and Kirk (1995) claim "that socially critical work has shown that empowerment and emancipation are central goals of physical education" (p. 453), the terms emancipation and empowerment are rather ill-defined in PE and elsewhere. Giddens (1991) provides a useful conception of what he terms emancipatory politics: "a generic outlook concerned above all with liberating individuals and groups from constraints which adversely affect their life chances … Emancipatory politics is concerned to reduce or eliminate *exploitation, inequality* and *oppression*" (pp. 210–211, original emphasis). When we apply this observation to the history of the critical project in physical education we see that it has been more concerned with a rather restricted and individualized notion of emancipation. The concern has been more with the freedom of an individual to participate in the movement culture, become self-reliant or independent rather than with the broader sense of emancipation underpinning critical pedagogy. It seems that most physical education teachers are typically more concerned with what Giddens (1991) terms 'life politics'. As a "politics *of* choice" (Giddens, 1991, p. 214, original emphasis) life politics does not primarily concern itself with the conditions that liberate us in order to make choices. Since there is evidence that some PE teachers are insensitive to social issues, elitist, sexist, 'pragmatic sceptics', anti-intellectual, and conservative in their politics (Dewar, 1989; Macdonald, Hunter, Carlson, & Penney, 2002) we can surmise that they are probably more concerned with life politics than emancipatory politics, and it is likely that in their teaching they also embody this orientation.

Disquiet in the tent

Notwithstanding its ethical purpose, over the past two decades critical pedagogy has become the target of considerable critique, not just from the conservative Right, but also from many feminists and others on the educational Left who might be expected to share similar political agendas to the critical pedagogues. These criticisms have been concerned with both practical and conceptual issues (e.g. Biesta, 1998; Buckingham, 1998; Ellsworth, 1989; Gore, 1993; Lather, 1989; Luke & Gore, 1992). The fact that much of this criticism comes from many who were originally advocates for critical pedagogy (for example Gore, 1990) is a healthy sign for those still committed to the critical project and the whole idea of transformative pedagogy.

In reflecting on her own experiences of the limitations of critical pedagogy, Kohli (1998) argued that there were limits to the power of rational dialogue to change deeply held beliefs. In this regard, Gur-Ze'ev (1998) argues for a more sceptical, less utopian "counter education that does not promise collective emancipation" (p. 471). Not only have questions been raised about the actual influence of critical pedagogy on classroom practice, but also about the (very) possibility of critical pedagogy itself. Beista (1998) reminds us that since critical pedagogy is founded on the Enlightenment ideal of emancipation through critical reflexivity, fundamental questions about the possibility of a critical pedagogy are raised by poststructuralist critiques of the Enlightenment project. Lather (1998) is also persuaded by poststructural theory and its critique of Enlightenment ideals and she comes to the conclusion that "[i]mplementing a critical pedagogy in the field of schooling is impossible" (p. 495).

The physical education literature has also reported confusion and disquiet in regard to the scholarship on critical pedagogy. First, there is confusion because it seems that there is not a common understanding of what critical pedagogy actually is, or might be. In their study of the critical pedagogy practice of a number of physical education teacher educators (PETEs), Muros and Fernández-Balboa (2005) found that most of these teacher educators were quite confused regarding their own pedagogical theory, purposes, and methods, and displayed important contradictions in their own practice.

Disquiet is revealed in O'Sullivan, Siedentop, and Locke's (1992) article 'Towards collegiality: Competing viewpoints among teacher educators' in which they challenged what they considered to be the often 'overzealous' language used by some 'radicals' in the prosecution of their critical pedagogy 'mission', the perceived high moral ground taken by them, and the lack of evidence to support many of their claims. As I have argued elsewhere (Tinning, 2002), the early critical pedagogy literature does contain some rather forceful language (e. g. in describing the limitations of traditional pedagogies), it does take a high moral ground in its advocacy for 'freedom from oppression and unjust social practices', and it does contain claims for which there is little available empirical evidence. However, one can read this criticism as essentially a criticism of the rhetorical style of the critical scholars rather than of their underpinning mission. Importantly, O'Sullivan herself is clearly an advocate for the ideals of the critical project (see, for example, Enright & O'Sullivan, 2010) and her disquiet was related more to the style of writing than the social ethic underpinning it.

Fernández-Balboa (2015), a PETE and former resident in the 'big tent', offers an iconoclastic critique of transformative pedagogies in which he claims that there is a real "possibility that teachers and teacher educators, including those who call themselves 'transformative', may be in a sort of ideological cave [like Plato's allegory of the cave] wherein their notion of reality is limited and limiting". Fernández-Balboa (2015) asks how can we be sure that as advocates of transformative pedagogy we are not deluding ourselves as to its potential? Fernández-Balboa also takes issue with Ukpokodu's (2009) definition of transformative pedagogy and its capacity to inspire what he calls 'true transformation'. He argues it does not include any concrete purposes and, therefore, poses a considerable threat to its application. He also sees a problem with its epistemological perspective and suggests that if you try to assign a concrete meaning to each of the concepts presented within that definition (e.g. "empower students", "examine critically", "reflective knowledge base", "critical consciousness and action"), you will soon appreciate the multiple interpretations possible for each case. Thus, two people holding similar intentions (not to mention if they held opposite ones) may have serious difficulties to provide a reliable definition of "TP" (transformative pedagogy).

Notwithstanding these critiques of the definitional, theoretical, and epistemological foundations of transformative pedagogy, there are also some very practical issues that need to be considered.

What counts as transformative pedagogy?

If an individual makes transformative changes to their attitudes, beliefs, and or behaviour as a direct result of a particular pedagogy, can we call this a transformative pedagogy? For example, many of the young men who were engaged with Don Hellison's (2003) Responsibility Model actually changed the way they behaved in the gym in positive ways that are consistent with some aspirations of transformative pedagogy, but can we call Hellison's pedagogy a transformative pedagogy? A similar question can be asked of Cooperative Learning (Dyson & Casey, 2012), Sport Education (Siedentop, 1994), Teaching Games for Understanding [TGfU] (Rossi, 2000; Kirk & McPhail, 2002), and, most recently, Sport for Development (Rossi & Rynne, 2014).

Interestingly, Oliver and Kirk (Chapter 20, this volume) in concluding their chapter on 'transformative pedagogies for challenging body culture in physical education', suggest that

> researchers need to move beyond paradigmatic approaches to adopt a more pragmatic position. This position needs to focus, we suggest, on three questions: 'Can we make the situation for these youth and children better than it is currently?', 'What would be better?', and 'How might we go about this task?'

While sympathetic to the pragmatist perspective, I am left thinking that, if these are the orienting questions for transformative pedagogy then surely the work of Don Hellison (Responsibility), Daryl Siedentop (Sport Education), and Ben Dyson (Cooperative Learning) would also fit the criteria. However, if we think of these as instructional or pedagogical models (Metzler, 2011), then the Oliver and Kirk pragmatic position lacks some of the essential features of transformative pedagogy. As Ukpokodu (2009) defines it, it is an *educational perspective* concerned with questions of justice, democracy, and ethics, and cannot be thought of as an instructional model that can be learned and operationalized as a performance. Thought of in this way, transformative pedagogy is more of an educational philosophy than a particular pedagogy. It is not a set of practices that can be reproduced (on demand as it were) irrespective of context.

On the other hand, if we privilege the ontological and epistemological dimensions of the idea of transformative pedagogy while ignoring the transformative *possibilities* of certain pedagogical models, are we merely securing the boundaries of the discourse community and shutting out other possibilities? There are no right or wrong answers here – only certain shared agreements (e.g. about what stands for justice, democracy, and ethics) between members of the transformative pedagogy discourse community.

Transformative pedagogy and personal change

While Socrates was reported as asserting that "an unexamined life is not worth living", it is important to understand that the examined life is not without its problematic side – what we might call its 'collateral damage'. Underpinning a transformative pedagogy seems to be the development of a sort of sociological way of thinking (see Eimear's story in this collection). This is akin to what Mills (1970) calls the *sociological imagination* that necessitates, above all, "being able to 'think ourselves away' from the familiar routines of our daily lives in order to look at them anew" (Giddens, 1994, p. 18). The development of such a sociological imagination would necessitate some reflection on one's own personal epistemology. This personal epistemology is philosophy at the individual level and reflects how we think about knowledge and knowing (Hofer, 2010). It is a kind of reflexive project of the self.

However, this is not an easy project. How shall we understand the self is a question that has captured the attention of many fields of study over time. There are philosophical approaches (e.g. Descartes, 1641); psychological theories (Lasch, 1984); psychoanalytic theories (Elliott, 1995; Kristeva, 1991); postmodern theories (Gee, 1990), and social theories (Elliott, 1995) that might be brought to bear to better understand the self, and in particular the self in regard to teaching and learning.

Transformative pedagogies require students to critically challenge their beliefs, values, and knowledge with the intent of developing a sense of critical consciousness and agency. Critical reflection, a process that is central to transformative pedagogy, is highly oriented around the self and, as Brookfield (1994) noted, it is "not without risk. It should not be undertaken lightly given its potential impact to destabilize both individuals and organizational systems" (p. 213). We do know that the results of using transformative pedagogy can be unpredictable. Devís-Devís and Sparkes' (1999) account of the Spanish PETE student named Guillem who burnt his book provided a vivid account of the power of critiquing dominant values and ideas. Devís-Devís and Sparkes (1999) suggested that:

> The case of Guillem reveals how the simple act of being confronted with views that challenge one's taken-for-granted assumptions about the world, one's cherished beliefs, preferred identities and sense of self can be an excruciating experience for some students, who experience it in the form of a crisis. (p. 147)

The link between student identit(ies) and what they might learn from (and about) the socially critical curriculum is clearly demonstrated in this example. The potential 'slippage' between what is intended to be learnt and what is understood, is clearly evident. Oliver and Lalik (2004) "wonder whether learning critique alone might not leave adolescents with feelings of frustration and helplessness" (p. 122). Kenway and Bullen (2001) remind us that we need to be very careful of using pedagogical encounters that embarrass or degrade students' values, choices, and commitments. With similar sentiment on the limits of critique, Crowdes (2000) claims that in many classes in which critical pedagogies are used, students "are often left with their fairly extensive sociological vocabularies and socially aware minds detached from their bodies and agency in matters of conflict resolution and change" (p. 35). Accordingly, she argues for the use of pedagogic strategies that join somatic and sociological perspectives. In both school

PE and in the field of Kinesiology more generally, when we do engage in critical pedagogies it is usually rather strong in the sociological and rather weak in the somatic.

In regard to changing the self (personal change) Homer's *Odyssey* conveys something of the issue facing those of us who attempt to 'make reflective citizens of PE students'. As Zigmunt Bauman (2000) relates the story, apparently some of Odysseus's sailors were turned into hogs by Circe (Greek goddess of magic) and they relished their new condition so much so that they ran away from Odysseus when he attempted to rub a magic herb on them which would restore them to human form. However one pig was caught and, having been transformed back into a man, was far from grateful for his release and furiously attacked his liberator.

> So you [Odysseus] are back, you rascal, you busybody? Again you want to nag us and pester, again you wish to expose our bodies to dangers and force our hearts to take ever-new decisions? I was so happy, I could wallow in the mud and bask in the sunshine, I could gobble and guzzle, grunt and squeak, and be free from meditations and doubts: 'What am I to do, this or that?' Why did you come?! To fling me back into that hateful life I led before? (in Bauman, 2000, p. 18)

In the course of this storytelling Bauman asks: "Is liberation (read emancipation) a blessing or a curse"? (p. 18). In thinking of some of the negative reactions to the underpinning ideology of reflective practice that some PETE students display we must recognize that 'success' will always be, at best, only partial. Most people do not want to have their views and opinions challenged ... even if it might mean that they make a better contribution to a more equitable and just society. For example, many PETE students do not welcome being 'emancipated' from their 'false consciousness' regarding the obesity crisis (see Chapter 23 by Cameron et al., this volume).

Indeed, Eimear Enright (in Chapter 21 by Fitzpatrick & Enright, this volume), in providing an example of their 'transformative work with young people' provides evidence that her transformative pedagogy (a visual diary task) was a "transformation of sorts" for two of her students who speak about "seeing things they hadn't noticed before" and "looking at our own lives in different ways". However, she then qualifies this success by saying that

> for a minority of students in this course the visual diary task specifically was "a waste of time ... that took away from time we could be doing practical stuff" (Anonymous male student). This student voice reminds us that while we can work to create conditions which might support transformation, we can never be sure that our efforts will be well received or will actually lead to transformation.

Enright's observations are also confirmed by Ukpokodu (2009) who claims that pre-service and in-service teachers tend to exhibit resistance and defensiveness that negate their ability to experience transformative learning.

PE and social change (possibilities?)

There are numerous examples of advocacy for PE's role in social change (see Sage, 1993) and some analyses of the potential impact of social change on PE (see, for example Macdonald, 2014). A number of critical scholars have argued that the intent of critical pedagogy is to move beyond critique with the explicit objective of transforming social inequality and empowering those without power. In this regard, transformative pedagogy has the dual aim of educating about social inequity, identifying and highlighting oppressive structures, *and* educating for emancipation, actively dismantling oppressive structures and engaging in change. Waring and Evans (2015), in writing about critical reflection (which is part of the transformative discourse community), claim that

> [u]nderpinning the concept of critical reflection is an emphasis on transformation in-formed by social and political analysis of contexts. A key question is the extent to which engagement in critical reflection enables teachers and their students to become *successful change agents.* (p. 173, my emphasis)

This ethic has found voice in some contemporary (H)PE curricula which explicitly expect that students should not only become critical consumers of physical culture, but they should also *take action* in the community to address oppression where they see it. For example, one of the aims of the 1999 New Zealand HPE curriculum was that students should "participate in creative healthy communities and environments by taking responsible and critical action" (p. 7). Although such expectations are compatible with the *activist* dimension of the Ukpokodu (2009) definition, the question remains, are they realistic?

There is no doubt that broader social changes have provided, and will continue to provide, challenges to PE, but there is little evidence of PE offering significant challenges to broader social conditions. For example, we can think of the social change in regard to sexist language that has permeated all (or most) Western democracies. Addressing the changing expectations regarding language use has influenced PE (see Wright & King, 1990), not the other way around. In all discussions of PE for social change, we need to keep a sense of perspective regarding what can realistically be achieved. Hyperbole is seldom useful.

Keeping a sense of perspective

As I am writing about the possibilities for PE to be transformative, I am confronted with the news of the tragedy of the *Charlie Hebdo* killings in Paris. This act of terror was many things, not the least of which was a full-frontal attack on the ideals of the liberal democracy. I am left think-ing whether it is possible that by empowering students by means of transformative pedagogies "to examine critically their beliefs, values, and knowledge … [and] an appreciation for multiple perspectives" (Ukpokodu, 2009, p. 43) we could help avoid such horrors. But of course that is just a pipedream, for the fundamentalist thinking that underpins the Islamic jihad does not wel-come an examination of beliefs. Like all fundamentalist groups (religious or other), uncritical obedience to one interpretation of a text is what is expected. Fundamentalist thinking is clearly the antithesis of criticality (Rizvi, 2011) and is anathema to liberal democratic perspectives.

There is no doubt that certain experiences can be transformative. For example, I vividly re-member the impact that reading the *The Women's Room* (French, 1977) had on me back in the 1970s. However, just because something facilitates a transformation does not meant that there has been a transformative pedagogy involved. I'm sure that when Marilyn French wrote *The Women's Room* she wasn't intending to be pedagogical. There was no explicit pedagogical intent (see Tinning, 2010), but nevertheless it had a transformative effect.

Attributing an effect to transformative pedagogy is not a simple matter. 'Connecting the dots' (Klein, 2000), or making connections between actions, events, and ideas is a difficult process. Moreover, attributing a single cause to complex events is naïve, if not impossible. For example *the Arab Spring* revolutionary wave of demonstrations and protests, riots, and civil wars that began in Egypt around December, 2010 and spread throughout the countries of the

Arab League was not simply a protest at the corrupt and dictatorial government of President Mubarak. While recognizing the significant influence that social media played in mobilizing the protestors, other contextual matters also were important. For example it occurred at a time when there was a drought in Kansas and Russia that resulted in a substantially reduced wheat crop and an increased price of wheat. Both are major suppliers of grain to Egypt for the making of bread. As Rami Zurayk (2011) observed: "Although the Arab revolutions were united under the slogan 'the people want to bring down the regime' not 'the people want more bread', food was a catalyst".

Maybe we can claim that many of the participants in the Arab Spring uprisings had, as a result of a combination of circumstances, become empowered to change their circumstances – to overrun their oppressive governments. But can we say that this was the result of any transformative pedagogy? This raises the question of what, precisely, do we want to be the result of transformative pedagogies in PE? Is it the case that when students become 'armed' with a new consciousness, they will be empowered to overthrow the 'oppressive' regime of modern schooling? Other than a few remaining fans of Ivan Illich (1971) and his de-schooling movement, it is probably not what the advocates of transformative pedagogies have in mind. But how about 'overthrowing' the oppressive regime of body culture, the dominance of the male sports curriculum, and sexist practices that we have learned constitutes much of contemporary PE?

In thinking about this issue we need to remind ourselves of the things that we do know for certain. Such knowledge forms the context in which any attempt to 'do' transformative pedagogy must be understood. We know, for example, that some kids in PE classes are alienated and marginalized by their gender, ethnicity, sexuality, body type, or physicality. But we also know that in heterogeneous PE classes not all students are alienated or turned off by PE and we know that sport offers a great deal to many young people. Further, we know that over the past three decades the impact of schooling on the lives of young people is diminishing (Steinberg & Kincheloe, 1997), that the influence of social media on their lives is increasing (Sirna, 2014), and, despite the good intentions of some PE teaching, the cult of the body continues to be pervasive and powerful (Tinning, 2010). It is within this context that the possibilities for a transformative pedagogy in PE must be understood.

A closing word

Answers to the best way(s) of achieving the aims of transformative pedagogies for PE will not be found only within the restricted academic discourse community of transformative pedagogy. In thinking about the aspirations of transformative pedagogy as outlined by Ukpokodu (2009), it seems to me that a certain openness to knowledge and ways of knowing is required, rather than a rather tribal commitment to a particular academic discourse community.

In this regard Giroux (1992) discussed his own shift in both his politics and his theoretical work as *border crossing*. For Giroux, this border crossing took him to trans-disciplinary perspectives that crossed the theoretical divides of critical pedagogy, post-structuralism, cultural studies, social theory. Fitzpatrick's (2013a) recent book *Critical Pedagogy, Physical Education and Urban Schooling* provides a good example of such border crossing in PE critical research. Fitzpatrick used critical ethnography to provide an in-depth account of urban youth in the subjects of health education and PE. Her work crossed the discursive boundaries of youth studies, feminist theory, cultural studies, and educational theory. However, as Evans and Davies (2011) point out, there is no doubt that some borders seem particularly difficult to cross.

Developing an openness to border crossing is not an easy task. Evans and Davies (2011) argue that limited (restricted) theoretical perspectives develop early in one's academic training and that many research students "enter research environments with 'eyes wide shut' to the possibilities that other perspectives and forms of theory and understanding might offer" (p. 275). Indeed, new researchers are often asked "what are you? A Foucauldian? A critical theorist?" (Gard, 2011, p. 32). There are clearly identity making and stereotyping processes at work here that have the potential to seriously limit the potential for any border crossing.

Finally, the mission of the *critical project* remains as important in PE today as it did in the 1970s and 1980s and *criticality* is still a necessary disposition to prosecute the mission. However, as we prosecute the agenda of the critical project through transformative pedagogies we should keep in mind the target 'audience' of our work. While there is undoubtedly an increasing critical project inspired literature produced by the critical discourse community in PE, there is little evidence that the aims of transformative pedagogy are increasingly being realized. Rather, the audience of such literature is typically other academics in the discourse community and not the teachers and students who are meant to be empowered or emancipated. It is clear that prosecuting an academic career within the competitive university environment demands increasing high-level scholarship and critical scholars are advancing in this regard. However, the ideals of transformative pedagogy require more than sophisticated theorizing, they also require getting our hands 'dirty' in the messiness of practice and to learn what it actually takes to 'transform'. Balancing these tensions will not be easy.

Reflective questions for discussion

1. Why is it that we have not seen a 'take up' of the critical project in Asian countries like Japan, South Korea, and Hong Kong? It's popular in Europe and many Anglophone countries but why not in Asia?
2. What are the key tenets of transformative pedagogy?
3. What is the relationship between transformative pedagogy and critical pedagogy, and critical reflection?
4. What factors might limit the possibilities of transformative pedagogy?
5. What are some of the possible unplanned consequences of engaging transformative pedagogy in the classroom?

References

Azzarito, L., & Solmon, M. (2009). An investigation of students' embodied discourses in physical education: A gendered project. *Journal of Teaching in Physical Education, 28*(2), 173–191.
Bain, L. (1990). A critical analysis of the hidden curriculum in physical education. In D. Kirk & R. Tinning (Eds.), *Physical education, curriculum and culture: Critical issues in the contemporary crisis* (pp. 23–42). Basingstoke, UK: Falmer Press.
Bauman, Z. (2000). *Liquid modernity*. Cambridge, UK: Polity Press.
Biesta, G. (1998). Say you want a revolution … Suggestions for the impossible future of critical pedagogy. *Educational Theory, 48*(4), 499–510.
Brookfield, S. (1994). Tales from the dark side: A phenomography of adult critical reflection. *International Journal of Lifelong Education, 13*(3), 203–216.
Buckingham, D. (Ed.) (1998). *Teaching popular culture: Beyond radical pedagogy*. London: University College London Press.
Burrows, L., & Wright, J. (2004). The discursive production of childhood, identity and health. In J. Evans, B. Davies & J. Wright (Eds.), *Knowledge & control: Studies in the sociology of physical education and health* (pp. 83–96). London: Routledge.
Carr, W., & Kemmis, S. (1986). *Becoming critical: Education, knowledge and action research*. London: Falmer Press.

Carroll, B., & Hollinshead, G. (1993). Ethnicity and conflict in physical education. *British Educational Research Journal, 19*(1), 59–76.

Clarke, G. (1992). Learning the language: Discourse analysis in physical education. In A. Sparkes (Ed.), *Research in physical education and sport: Exploring alternative visions* (pp. 146–166). London: Falmer Press.

Crowdes, M. (2000). Embodying sociological imagination: Pedagogical support for linking bodies to minds. *Teaching Sociology, 28*, 28–40.

Culpan, I., & Bruce, J. (2007). New Zealand physical education and critical pedagogy: Refocusing the curriculum. *International Journal of Sport and Health Science, 5*, 1–11.

Curtner-Smith, M. (2007). The impact of a critically oriented physical education teacher education course on pre-service classroom teachers. *Journal of Teaching in Physical Education, 26*(1), 35–56.

Dagkas, S., & Benn, T. (2006). Young Muslim women's experiences of Islam and physical education in Greece and Britain: A comparative study. *Sport, Education & Society, 11*(1), 21–38.

Descartes, R. (1641). *Meditations on first philosophy*. Cambridge, UK: Cambridge University Press.

Devís-Devís, J., & Sparkes, A. (1999). Burning the book: A biographical study of a pedagogically inspired identity crisis in physical education. *European Physical Education Review, 5*(2), 135–152.

Dewar, A. (1989). Recruitment in physical education teaching: Toward a critical approach. In T. Templin & P. Schempp (Eds.), *Socialization into physical education: Learning to teach* (pp. 39–58). Indianapolis: Benchmark Press.

Dowling, F. (2006). Physical education teacher educators' professional identities, continuing professional development and the issue of gender equality. *Physical Education and Sport Pedagogy, 11*(3), 247–263.

Dowling, F., Fitzgerald, H., & Flintoff, A. (Eds.). (2012). *Equity and difference in physical education, youth sport and health: A narrative approach*. London: Routledge.

Dyson, B., & Casey, A. (2012). *Cooperative learning in physical education: A research based approach*. London: Routledge.

Elliott, A. (1995). *Subject to ourselves: Social theory, psychoanalysis and postmodernity*. Oxford: Blackwell.

Ellsworth, E. (1989). Why doesn't this feel empowering? Working through the repressive myths of critical pedagogy. *Harvard Educational Review, 59*(3), 297–324.

Enright, E., & O'Sullivan, M. (2010). 'Carving a new order of experience' with young people in physical education: Participatory action research as a pedagogy of possibility. In M. O'Sullivan & A. MacPhail (Eds.), *Young people's voices in physical education and sport* (pp. 163–185). London: Routledge.

Evans, J., & Davies, B. (1993). Equality, equity and physical education. In J. Evans & B. Davies (Eds.), *Equality, equity and physical education* (pp. 11–27). London: Falmer Press.

Evans, J., & Davies, B. (2011). New directions, new questions? Social theory, education and embodiment. *Sport, Education & Society, 16*(3), 263–279.

Fernández-Balboa, J.-M. (1995). Reclaiming physical education in higher education through critical pedagogy. *Quest, 47*, 91–114.

Fernández-Balboa, J.-M. (2015). *Transformative pedagogy in physical education? (Un)dreaming the (im)possible dream*. Unpublished paper, Universidad Autónoma of Madrid, Spain.

Fisette, J., & Walton, A. (2014). 'If you really knew me' … I am empowered through action. *Sport, Education and Society, 19*(2), 1–22.

Fitzpatrick, K. (2011a). Obesity, health and physical education: A Bourdieuean perspective. *Policy Futures in Education, 9*(3), 353–366.

Fitzpatrick, K. (2011b). Trapped in the physical: Maori and Pasifika achievement in HPE. *Asia Pacific Journal of Health, Sport and Physical Education, 2*(3–4), 35–51.

Fitzpatrick, K. (2013a). *Critical pedagogy, physical education and urban schooling*. New York: Peter Lang.

Fitzpatrick, K. (2013b). Brown bodies, racialisation and physical education. *Sport, Education and Society, 18*(2), 135–153.

Flintoff, A. (2014). Tales from the playing field: Black and minority ethnic students' experience of physical education teacher education. *Race, Ethnicity and Education, 17*(3), 346–366.

Freire, P. (1972). *Pedagogy of the oppressed*. New York: Penguin.

French, M. (1977). *The women's room*. New York: Summit Books.

Gard, M. (2011). *The end of the obesity epidemic*. London: Routledge.

Gard, M., & Wright, J. (2001). Managing uncertainty: Obesity discourses and physical education in a risk society. *Studies in Philosophy and Education, 20*(6), 535–549.

Garrett, R. (2006). Critical storytelling in physical education teacher education. *European Physical Education Review, 12*(3), 339–360.

Garrett, R., & Wrench, A. (2011). Negotiating a critical agenda in middle years physical education. *Australian Educational Researcher, 8*(3), 239–255.

Gee, J. (1990). *Social linguistics and literacies: Ideology in discourse.* London: Falmer Press.

Giddens, A. (1991). *Modernity and self-identity: Self and society in the late modern age.* Cambridge, UK: Polity Press.

Giddens, A. (1994). *Beyond left and right: The future of radical politics.* Cambridge, UK: Polity Press.

Giroux, H. (1992). *Border crossings: Cultural workers and the politics of education.* London: Routledge.

Gore, J. (1990). Pedagogy as text in physical education teacher education: Beyond the preferred reading. In D. Kirk & R. Tinning (Eds.), *Physical education, curriculum and culture: Critical issues in the contemporary crisis* (pp. 101–138). Basingstoke, UK: Falmer Press.

Gore, J. (1993). *The struggle for pedagogies: Critical and feminist discourses as regimes of truth.* New York: Routledge.

Griffin, P. (1981). One small step for personkind: Observations and suggestions for sex equity in coeducational physical education classes. *Journal of Teaching in Physical Education, (Introductory Issue) 1*(1), 12–18.

Gur-Ze'ev, I. (1998). Toward a non-repressive critical pedagogy. *Educational Theory, 48*(4), 463–486.

Hellison, D. (2003). *Teaching responsibility through physical activity.* Champaign, IL: Human Kinetics.

Hickey, C. (2001). "I feel enlightened now, but ...": The limits to the pedagogic translation of critical social discourses in physical education. *Journal of Teaching in Physical Education, 20*(3), 227–246.

Hofer, B. (2010). Personal epistemology in Asia: Burgeoning research and future directions. *The Asia-Pacific Educational Researcher, 19*(1), 179–184.

Illich, I. (1971). *Deschooling society.* Harmondsworth, UK: Penguin.

Kårhus, S. (2010). Physical education teacher education on the education market – who's defining what physical education teachers need to know? *Physical Education and Sport Pedagogy, 15*(3), 227–241.

Kenway, J., Bigum, C., & Fitzclarence, L. (1995). New education in new times. *Journal of Education Policy, 9*(4), 317–333.

Kenway, J., & Bullen, E. (2001). *Consuming children: Education-entertainment-advertising.* Buckingham, UK: Open University Press.

Kincheloe, J. & Steinberg, S. (Eds.). (1998). *Unauthorized methods: Strategies for critical teaching.* New York: Routledge.

Kirk, D. (1986). A critical pedagogy for teacher education: Toward an inquiry-oriented approach. *Journal of Teaching in Physical Education, 5*(4), 230–246.

Kirk, D. (1992). Physical education, discourse, and ideology: Bringing the hidden curriculum into view, *Quest, 44,* 35–56.

Kirk, D., & MacPhail, A. (2002). Teaching games for understanding and situated learning: Rethinking the Bunker-Thorpe model. *Journal of Teaching in Physical Education, 21*(2), 177–192.

Klein, N. (2000). *No logo.* London: Flamingo.

Knez, K., Macdonald, D., & Abbott, R. (2012). Challenging stereotypes: Muslim girls talk about physical activity, physical education and sport. *Asia-Pacific Journal of Health, Sport and Physical Education, 3*(2), 109–122.

Kohli, W. (1998). Critical education and embodied subjects: Making the poststructural turn. *Educational Theory, 48*(4), 511–519.

Kristeva, J. (1991). *Strangers to ourselves.* London: Harvester.

Larsson, H., Redelius, K., & Fagrell, B. (2010). Moving (in) the heterosexual matrix: On heteronormativity in secondary school physical education. *Physical Education and Sport Pedagogy, 14*(1), 1–17.

Lasch, C. (1984). *The minimal self: Psychic survival in troubled times.* New York: W.W. Norton.

Lather, P. (1989). Staying dumb? Student resistance to liberatory curriculum. In P. Lather (Ed.), *Getting smart! Empowering approaches to research and pedagogy* (pp. 163–190). London: Routledge.

Lather, P. (1998). Critical pedagogy and its complicities: A praxis of stuck places. *Educational Theory, 48*(4), 487–497.

Leahy, D., O'Flynn, G., & Wright, J. (2013). A critical 'critical inquiry' proposition in health and physical education. *Asia-Pacific Journal of Health, Sport & Physical Education, 4*(2), 175–187.

Luke, C., & Gore, J. (Eds.). (1992). *Feminisms and critical pedagogy.* New York: Routledge.

Macdonald, D. (2014). Is global neo-liberalism shaping the future of physical education? *Physical Education and Sport Pedagogy, 19*(5), 494–499.

Macdonald, D., & Kirk, D. (1999). Pedagogy, the body and Christian identity. *Sport, Education and Society, 4*(2), 131–142.

Macdonald, D., Hunter, L., Carlson, T., & Penney, D. (2002). Teacher knowledge and the disjunction between school curricula and teacher education. *Asia-Pacific Journal of Teacher Education, 30*(3), 259–275.

McLaren, P. (1998). Revolutionary pedagogy in post-revolutionary times: Rethinking the political economy of critical education. *Educational Theory, 48*(4), 431–462.

Metzler, M. (2011). *Instructional models for physical education.* Champaign, IL: Human Kinetics.

Mills, C. (1970). *The sociological imagination.* Harmondsworth, UK: Penguin.

Muros, B., & Fernández-Balboa, J. M. (2005). Physical education teacher educators' personal perspectives regarding their practice of critical pedagogy. *Journal of Teaching in Physical Education, 24*(3), 243–264.

Nyberg, G., & Larsson, H. (2014). Exploring 'what' to learn in physical education. *Physical Education and Sport Pedagogy, 19*(2), 123–135.

Oliver, K. (2001). Images of the body from popular culture: Engaging adolescent girls in critical inquiry. *Sport, Education and Society, 6*(2), 143–164.

Oliver, K., & Lalik, R. (2004). 'The beauty walk': Interrogating whiteness as the norm for beauty within one school's hidden curriculum. In J. Evans, B. Davies & J. Wright (Eds.), *Body knowledge and control: Studies in the sociology of physical education and health* (pp. 115–130). London: Routledge.

O'Sullivan, M., Siedentop, D., & Locke, L. (1992). Toward collegiality: competing viewpoints among teacher educators. *Quest, 22,* 266–280.

Ovens, A. (2004). *The (im)possibility of critical reflection: The lived experience of reflective practice in teacher education.* Unpublished PhD, The University of Queensland.

Ovens, A., & Tinning, R. (2009). Reflection as situated practice: A memory-work study of lived experience in teacher education. *Teaching and Teacher Education, 25,* 1125–1131.

Penney, D., & Waring, M. (2000). The absent agenda: Pedagogy and physical education. *Journal of Sport Pedagogy, 6*(1), 4–38.

Philpot, R. A. (2015). Critical pedagogies in PETE: An Antipodean perspective. *Journal of Teaching in Physical Education, 34*(2), 316–332.

Rizvi, F. (2011). Contesting criticality in a scholarship diaspora. In R. Tinning & K. Sirna (Eds.), *Education, social justice and the legacy of Deakin University* (pp. 145–157). Rotterdam/Boston: Sense Publishers.

Rossi, T. (2000). Socially critical pedagogy and the 'production of skilled performers': Further considerations of teaching and learning in physical education. *Journal of Physical Education New Zealand, 33*(3), 43–53.

Rossi, A., & Rynne, S. (2014). Sport development programmes for Indigenous Australians: Innovation, inclusion and development, or a product of 'white guilt'? *Sport in Society, 17*(8), 1030–1045.

Rovegno, I., & Kirk, D. (1995). Articulations and silences in socially-critical work on physical education: Toward a broader agenda. *Quest, 47*(4), 447–474.

Sage, G. (1993). Sport and physical education and the new world order: Dare we be agents of social change. *Quest, 45,* 151–164.

Siedentop, D. (1994). *Sport education: Quality PE through positive sport experiences.* Champaign, IL: Human Kinetics.

Sirna, K. (2014). Social media: Virtual environments for (re)constructing knowledge on health & bodies? In K. Fitzpatrick & R. Tinning (Eds.), *Health education: Critical perspectives* (pp. 118–128). London: Routledge.

Steinberg, S., & Kincheloe, J. (Eds.). (1997). *Kinderculture: The corporate construction of childhood.* Boulder, CO: Westview Press.

Storrs, D., & Inderbitzin, M. (2006). Imagining a liberal education: Critically examining the learning process through simulation. *Journal of Transformative Education, 4*(2), 175–189.

Sykes, H. (1998). Turning the closets inside/out: Towards a queer-feminist theory in women's physical education. *Sociology of Sport Journal, 15*(2), 154–173.

Tinning, R. (2002). Towards a 'modest' pedagogy: Reflections on the problematics of critical pedagogy. *Quest, 54*(3), 224–241.

Tinning, R. (2010). *Pedagogy and human movement: Theory, practice, research.* London: Routledge.

Ukpokodu, O. (2009). Pedagogies that foster transformative learning in a multicultural education course: A reflection. *Journal of Praxis in Multicultural Education, 4*(1), DOI: 10.9741/2161-2978.1003.

Waring, M., & Evans, C. (2015). Making sense of critical reflection. In M. Waring & C. Evans (Eds.), *Understanding pedagogy: Developing a critical approach to teaching and learning* (pp. 161–186). Abingdon, Oxon: Routledge.

Wink, J. (2011). *Critical pedagogy: Notes from the real world.* Boston: Pearson.

Wright, J. (1991). Gracefulness and strength: Sexuality in the Seoul Olympics. *Social Semiotics, 1*(1), 49–66.

Wright, J. (1999). Changing gendered practices in physical education: Working with teachers. *European Physical Education Review, 5*(3), 181–197.

Wright, J., & King, R. (1990). "I say what I mean," said Alice: An analysis of gendered discourse in physical education. *Journal of Teaching in Physical Education, 10,* 210–225.

Zeichner, K. (1983). Alternative paradigms for teacher education. *Journal of Teacher Education, 34*(3), 3–9.

Zurayk, R. (2011, 17 July). Use your loaf: Why food prices were crucial in the Arab spring. *The Observer.*

19

TRANSFORMATIVE ASPIRATIONS AND REALITIES IN PHYSICAL EDUCATION TEACHER EDUCATION (PETE)

Alan Ovens, UNIVERSITY OF AUCKLAND, NEW ZEALAND

This chapter examines the practices that provide a means for enacting transformative pedagogies in physical education teacher education programmes (PETE). By transformative pedagogy I mean an approach that aims to enable neophyte teachers to examine what educational, moral, and political commitments help guide their work as professional teachers and to encourage and engender critical citizenship, reflective thinking, social consciousness, and disposition for social justice (Ukpokodu, 2009, p. 47). The philosophical arguments for and against such a pedagogy, particularly as it is enacted as a form of critical pedagogy, have already been well discussed by a number of different authors (for example, see Fernández-Balboa, 1995, 1997; Gore, 1993; Kirk, 1986; O'Sullivan, Siedentop, & Locke, 1992; Sicilia-Camacho & Fernández-Balboa, 2009; Tinning, 2002, 2006) and will not be revisited here. In fact, there has been an enthusiastic advocacy for PETE to address social inequality and foster social justice stretching back for at least 30 years (Tinning, 2006). At the same time, there has been a corresponding number of concerns raised about the inability to render such an orientation in effective pedagogical practice (for example, Curtner-Smith, 2007; Gore, 1990; Devís-Devís & Sparkes, 1999; Hickey, 2001; Standal & Moe, 2013; Ruiz & Fernández-Balboa, 2005; Velija, Capel, Katene, & Hayes, 2008). This has led Tinning (2002) to declare that *advocating for* critical pedagogy is not the same as *doing* critical pedagogy. In other words, what has been an ideologically attractive idea has struggled to demonstrate that it is either feasible in pedagogical terms or effective in changing future teacher behaviour. In this chapter I discuss the problematic nature of doing transformative pedagogy in PETE and review some of the aspirations and realities of enacting such a pedagogy in practice.

In considering predominant models or theories used to research PETE, Tinning (2006) provided a very good analysis of the key theoretical orientations that have been used over the last 20–30 years. He identified these as the behaviouristic, personalistic, traditional/craft, and critical orientations. Initially, much of this work conceived professional learning as a form of socialisation (Lawson,1986;Templin & Schempp, 1989). According to Green (2010), socialisation "refers to the processes through which people are taught (directly or indirectly, explicitly or implicitly, intentionally or unintentionally) and internalise the values, beliefs, expectations, knowledge, skills, habits and practices prevalent in their groups and societies" (Green, 2010, p. 167). Research into socialisation has provided valuable insights into the role that early experiences in schools and sport have on shaping learning in PETE settings as well as the processes that professional and occupational socialisation have on the education and professional learning of PE teachers. However, in building on this, and celebrating a growing eclecticism of theories being used since Tinning's 2006 analysis, it is evident that those working in the field of transformative pedagogy are using a variety of theoretical positions to inform their work. It is now increasingly common to find transformative inspired PETE research drawing from areas such as gender studies, postmodernism, neo-materialism, postcolonialism, queer theory, figurational sociology, poststructuralism, self-study, and neo-Marxism. In the following discussion I draw on complexity thinking (Ovens, Hopper, & Butler, 2012) as one way of acknowledging how this growing transdisciplinarity provides increased awareness of the situated, contingent, contested, and interconnected nature of professional PETE settings and to better highlight those progressive practices that might be useful in enacting a form of transformative pedagogy with PETE students.

The complexity of transformative practice

When considering whether transformative practice is possible, the research evidence tends to provide a rather unsatisfactory answer of, "it depends". Its very possibility appears contingent on a range of social, political, and material factors that constitute the landscape of teacher education and that enable the forms of student subjectivity and sets of experiences that act collectively to enable a transformation taking place. Viewing teacher education as emerging from a constellation of factors in play at a particular moment problematises the notion that there is a universal concept called 'transformative pedagogy' that can be applied as some recipe for action in PETE programmes. Instead, it replaces it with a view that pedagogical practice is partial, decentred, and grounded in the particulars of history, place, and language. From this perspective, there is no subject or identity fashioned outside of its own history and contingency (Giroux, 2009). Instead, there is a sensitivity to the emergent nature of transformative pedagogy as the precondition of its agency and a recognition that, whatever practices are enacted in PETE settings, they are enabled by a system of social relations and differentiations constituted by multiple, interpenetrating, and layered systems (Alhadeff-Jones, 2012). Put more simply, it is rarely possible to succeed in enacting a transformative pedagogy in PETE when the teacher educator works alone. Likewise, the ability of programmes to be transformative is rarely mono-causal (Mordal-Moen & Green, 2012). Improving the possibility for transformative practice appears to involve attending to the creation and sustenance of social systems operating at different levels of the education system as much as it does on using particular methods and strategies in PETE lessons (Lorente & Kirk, 2013).

The enabling influence of a supporting policy environment

At the macro level, it can be argued that the ethos that underpins a particular national or state education system influences the possibility for transformative pedagogy in practice. Certainly, the current neoliberal climate framing much of the education sector discourse, with its emphasis on standards, measurement, and competitive individualism, seems to close down the opportunities for enacting forms of pedagogy oriented around issues of social justice, democracy, and critique (Apple, 2006). In the past, it has been argued that attempts to help PETE students become socially and pedagogically critical are undermined by the strong influence of their traditional training and the conservative micropolitics of schools (Fernández-Balboa, 2000). More recently, Kårhus (2010, 2012) observed how neoliberalism and its associated efforts to introduce market dynamics into Higher Education in Norway affected how the national providers in the field of sport and physical education configured their degree programmes, and this in turn affected the content knowledge of the PETE programmes involved.

In recent times some glimmer of hope has been provided by curriculum developers in different national contexts who have drawn on social-justice discourses to help frame new school curriculum developments. For example, as Tinning (2012) notes, the contemporary Australian curriculum documents state that teachers in the learning area of Health and Physical Education (HPE) have a responsibility to [teach] the socially critical liberal curriculum as defined by the State and that these clearly articulate the principles of diversity, social justice, and supportive environments. Similarly, the writers of the New Zealand HPE curriculum moved PE from a very technocratic conception to a position that favoured a more socio-critical pedagogy (Culpan & Bruce, 2007). As a result, New Zealand schools are expected to "reconceptualise their orientations in order to meet the new socio-critical thrust of which bi-culturalism is a unique, important and critical aspect" (Culpan & Galvan, 2012, p. 40). While the nature of 'social justice' may be highly contested in such policy texts (Rivzi & Lingard, 2011; Tinning, 2004), the use of such discourses can be seen as encouraging alternative pedagogies to emerge in school settings.

Such policy texts may influence two key factors that have traditionally constrained the transformative potential of teacher education. The first is that the prior knowledge and beliefs that student teachers bring to PETE programmes have been seen as a major influence on what and how students learn in teacher education. There is strong support for the idea that PETE students draw on their own experiences of PE and have already developed their own beliefs about PE and teaching from school, sport, friends, family, and the media (Curtner-Smith, 2007; Velija et al. 2008). This allows for the possibility that future students, who emerge from critically oriented school programmes, may be better able to problematise the subject area and engage with the emancipatory politics that structures their PETE programme. The second factor regards the schooling contexts and dispositions expected of them as teachers. Typically, there has been a tension between university and school contexts (Standal, Mordal-Moen, & Moe, 2014). However, when curriculum policy supports a critical orientation, the possibility for a more consistent professional language and set of discursive practices between schools and university settings increase and work to support the transformative aspirations of the PETE programme students are part of (Zeichner, 2010).

The enabling influence of the institutional environment

At the institutional level of teacher education (typically university settings), the collective constitution of programmes, the forms of pedagogical experiences they enable, the subjectivities of all the participants, and the structure of relationships between all the participants affect the possibility of transformative pedagogy. The collective entanglement of these factors shapes the political and cultural arena in which student experiences and subjectivity are produced and mediated. Support for this notion is provided by Mordal-Moen and Green (2012) in their study of PETE in one Norwegian university. They suggest that the particular configuration of factors, including student expectations, the nature of school mentoring, the orientations of the teacher educators, the research culture of the university, all collectively created a programmatic culture that is likely to sustain and reinforce the conservative philosophies of the teacher educators rather than support the development of transformative pedagogies. Likewise, in their study of 17 PETE educators, Ruiz and Fernández-Balboa (2005) found that more than half of their teacher educators did not fully understand the principles and purposes of critical pedagogy as presented in the literature and this had a strong influence on how they enacted critical pedagogy in practice. Another example is provided by Ovens and Tinning (2009) who concluded that the nature of the student teachers' reflectivity was contingent on the discursive community the student was part of, suggesting that the potential for a transformative pedagogy is dependent on the professional learning and work culture in which the student is situated.

The enabling influence of pedagogical practice

At the individual course or module level, the way theory becomes manifest in practice also influences the transformative potential of that practice. Theory is not only the content being taught, but can also shape the instructional practices and structures being used to teach the content. Giroux (1994) cautions that this can set up a tension between what he calls a *theory of pedagogy* and a *pedagogy of theorising*. The distinction is subtle but important. When the teaching in a course is oriented around a theory of pedagogy, the core ideas and concepts central to that pedagogy become knowledge to be learnt or absorbed by student teachers and applied in school contexts. The implication is that in the desire to enact a transformative pedagogy, it becomes reduced to theory taught through a transmission pedagogy where the teaching is either telling (the lecture), modelling (the demonstration lesson or microteaching), or apprenticeship (the practicum) (Ovens, 2013). In contrast, when the teaching in a course is oriented around a pedagogy of theorising, the focus shifts to examining how the core ideas and concepts central to transformative practice become enacted within and lived through the instructional practices and structures of the course.

As Segall (2002) points out, the issue here is that, while PETE students may be encouraged to ask critical questions *in* their teacher education courses, they are often not encouraged to ask the same question *of* their teacher education courses. For example, teacher educators encourage students to think about how teachers and schools meet the individual needs of their students, but rarely do they ask them how their teacher education lessons meet their own individual needs as student teachers. As Segall (2002) notes, if theory is not reflexively applied to understanding one's lived practice, the pedagogy involved becomes an exercise in separating theory from practice, while effectively disguising the process of doing so. By teaching a detached theory of social justice, power, oppression, and privilege, students are anesthetised from challenging their own education and the methods used to ensure that theory is disconnected from everyday practice because it becomes content to be learnt rather than lived (Segall, 2002)

To summarise the first half of this chapter, a sensitivity to the complexity of transformative pedagogy in PETE ensures that the mere use of methods, such as writing reflective journals, teaching critical theory, or using more democratic forms of assessment, does not lead with any certainty to making a pedagogy transformative. Rather, the potential for enacting a transformative pedagogy relates to how the use of such methods is embedded within specific relations of power that enable a transformative learning culture to emerge. This is not meant to suggest that teacher educators should avoid engaging with innovative, democratic, and alternative forms of practice. Instead, it acts as an important caveat on those who seek certainty and expect a utopian form of collective emancipation (Tinning, 2012).

With this in mind, the remainder of this chapter is focused on ways teacher educators working in PETE enact forms of pedagogy "that empowers students to examine critically their beliefs, values, and knowledge with the goal of developing a reflective knowledge base, an appreciation for multiple perspectives, and a sense of critical consciousness and agency" (Ukpokodu, 2009, p. 43). The aim in discussing these is not to suggest they are an effective way of teaching about social issues, nor that they are recipes that work in each situation. Transformative pedagogies are always tailored to individual contexts (Gur-Ze'ev, 1998; Hinchey, 2006). Rather, the aim is to demonstrate how each enacts a form of pedagogy in line with a set of values and beliefs that may, by becoming part of a broader assemblage, help highlight particular social issues and be transformative for PETE students.

Negotiated learning

The idea that the teacher educator may negotiate what content is taught in a course, how it is taught, and how the course work undertaken by students contributes to a final grade, has been one way of deliberately making transparent the power relations and hierarchical structures that are part of the fabric of academic fields and teacher education programmes and regulations for accreditation (Boud & Falchikov, 2006; Lorente & Kirk, 2013). Negotiated learning goes beyond providing students with options from which they may choose, such as selecting projects of interest or selecting from two or three provided by the teacher. The two most common approaches to negotiated learning are that of inviting students to be co-contributors to course design and the use of individual grading contracts (Boud & Falchikov, 2006). In the first approach, the students enrolled in a particular PETE course are provided with the opportunity to participate in contributing to the design of the individual course or module they are enrolled in. In the second, the coursework options, marking, and processes for aggregating assessment information into a final grade are mutually negotiated between the course lecturer and students on an individual basis.

The critical element in each approach is not that students merely participate in the design of course and assessment procedures, but that each approach promotes a democratic educational process that engages students in thinking about issues of power, equality, and social justice (Giroux, 2009). This does not mean that the teacher educator is out of the equation, nor does it mean a sharing of power. Rather, the teacher educator is using their authority to create opportunities for students to co-participate in the design process. The teacher educator is involved in a process of negotiation, not the handing over of all decision making to the student. In other words, the implementation challenge for the teacher educator is one of setting boundaries about which course/grading aspects are negotiable and being willing to engage in dialogue around the needs, interests, rights, and responsibilities of the student in relation to their own professional learning.

As a long-time proponent of transformative pedagogies, Ross (2010) describes how he used a self-assessment strategy with first and fourth year PETE students. The goals of integrating this technique into classwork were to foster individual and collective thoughtfulness, to encourage students to examine their own realities, to question 'truth' or 'fact', and to determine how 'fact' has influenced personal actions and beliefs. Coupled with his approach to teaching that constantly challenged students' entrenched beliefs, he required students to collate a dossier or record of their own work in response to how they were engaging with the ideas presented. At the end of the course they met with him to propose what mark they believed best represented their level of learning and the final decision was by consensus between the lecturer and student. Many of the students reported that they found the approach thought-provoking, challenging, and transformational.

We have never been questioned like this before. For most of us questions and answers were shallow places without much real thought, only spoon-feeding without much real thought. This was the beginning of the critical thinking impressed upon us ... How do I evaluate what I have learned when the process is not black or white? I cannot put this on paper. I do not know where it will lead or how much farther there is to go in this journey. (RB, 2000 as cited in Ross, 2010, p. 210)

In reporting on their ongoing work with negotiated grading contracts, Brubaker and Ovens (2012) systematically reflect on the issues involved with implementing alternative grading practices. Overall, the study affirms the idea that organising a more democratic classroom involves using the teacher educator's authority to create opportunities for students to be more actively involved in defining their learning. The study also highlights the difficulty of practising an alternative pedagogy in university settings organised around conventional assessment practices, particularly in respect to issues related to time, student anxiety, and necessity to report achievement in institutionally approved ways.

In Spain, Lorente and Kirk (2013) used an action research design to develop the use of democratic assessment strategies in Lorente's teaching of an optional assessment course for PETE students. By using forms of negotiated assessment with her students, Lorente aimed to create a learning culture that enabled students to engage in critical dialogue, experience democratic participation, and critically analyse the social messages that impact on assessment practices. The research reports a range of benefits from using negotiated assessment, including consistency with course learning outcomes, the ability to adjust assessment methods for particular groups, a high level of student engagement and motivation, increased student reflectivity, and awareness of their own learning processes. They conclude by stating that, "for student teachers in particular, we argue that the experience of participating in democratic forms of assessment is vital if they are to have the confidence and knowledge to apply these practices in their own work with students in schools" (p. 92).

Storytelling

Using storytelling in the form of fictional narratives or retold experiences has been one way to provoke critical thinking and foster critical and inclusive approaches to teaching in PETE settings. Storytelling is simultaneously a means to express identity, communicate, and connect with others; describe experience; and construct knowledge. Garrett (2006) reports on how she incorporated the practice of critical storytelling into an undergraduate PETE class. In this study, 60 undergraduate primary and secondary school PETE students were presented with stories written by five women about the lived experiences of their body, gender, and physical activity (see Garrett, 2004). The PETE students were asked to read the stories and consider how they, as student teachers, could create change, challenge, and/or support the storyteller in a PE setting. They were then asked to prepare written responses for three of the five stories prior to engaging in a group discussion. All of the written and verbal exchanges between the PETE students were compiled by the research team and analysed to identify dominant themes. The results from this qualitative coding exercise suggested that the students experienced significant transformation in their thinking. More specifically, they reported engaging in much deep, critical reflection about their practice, their role as educators, and the lived experience of their (female) students. Further, many reported a deepening of their capacity to empathise with the other. The researchers attributed the effectiveness of the pedagogy to the 'realness' of the stories and the ability for so many of the students to personally relate.

Peer teaching

As a pedagogy for teacher education, peer teaching aims to shift the organisation and structure of the lesson away from a lecturer-focused, transmission style of teaching to one where students participate in a learning community focused on the practice of teaching. Specifically, peer teaching involves the students taking turns to teach their peers and learning from being in the teaching role, receiving peer feedback, engaging in discussion, and reflecting on the experience (Garbett & Ovens, 2010). The aim is to create a learning context embedded in the practice of teaching in which students can experience and reflect on the relational complexities and dilemmas of teaching, the situational nature of professional knowledge, and the role of discernment and decision making in the act of teaching (Garbett & Ovens, 2010; Wilson & I'Anson, 2006). In this way, the knowledge for teaching is not represented as certain or generic, but enacted as a way of solving the specific pedagogical problems embedded in the teaching situation opening up possible teachable moments for the teacher educator to open this knowledge to challenge and reflection.

Ovens (2014) describes how he uses peer teaching with fourth-year PETE students to create a conceptual space where students can unpack and reflect on their prior knowledge. Using a self-study research methodology (Ovens & Fletcher, 2014) he has found there is support for the idea that working in smaller teaching groups can be particularly effective for enabling deeper thinking as students are able to discuss new ideas and share diverse viewpoints. However, the efficacy of such an approach is dependent on the pedagogical skill of the teacher educator to focus attention on students' pedagogical decision making and reframe their understandings through reflection. It is also dependent on the perception of authenticity of participants in the peer teaching activity and how the vulnerability created in such an intensive activity could be protected (Ovens, 2014). In respect to authenticity, he focuses on the importance of distinguishing between students *acting* in the role of teacher and *enacting* the role of teacher. Acting implies the task is framed by the participants as a theatrical performance in contrast to enacting, which implies the performance is enmeshed with, and emerges from, the immediate context. Focusing student attention on this distinction became important to structuring the experience.

When the students acted bored, the situation became a parody of a school classroom; the authenticity was low and the opportunity for meaningful learning from the activity was reduced. However, if the students were actually bored during a lesson taught by one of their peers, it became something that could be discussed meaningfully. What acts, ideas, and words promoted the disengagement that led to boredom? How does a teacher cope with a diverse range of students – whose interests were being served? In such discussions the participants were able to share their genuine feelings and thoughts (Ovens, 2014).

Case studies

Student-authored case studies, as a form of shared inquiry, have been presented as a transformative and effective teaching (pedagogical) tool in some PETE environments. In these examples, case studies were defined as "richly detailed, contextualized, narrative accounts of situations or experiences related to a given field that are intended to promote critical thinking about real-life events" (Levin, 1995, p. 63). In the United States, Richards, Hemphill, Templin, and Eubank (2012) introduced a culminating case study project in a junior PETE seminar course. Students were then required to draft a sample case study based on a topic or issue of great import to training PE teachers. Each case study was developed over the course of a 12-week term and went through a series of peer and instructor review processes. The purpose of the exercise was to promote critical thinking and reflection on the part of the student. According to the authors, the case-study writing process was successful. Students chose to address meaningful and salient issues that were likely to arise in real-world settings. They also demonstrated personal growth and evidence of critical self-reflection (Richards et al., 2012).

Lesson-study

Like case studies, lesson-studies are a form of shared inquiry that are aimed at structuring an inquiry-oriented approach to professional learning (Lieberman, 2009). In lesson-study, the students are organised into groups to collaboratively design and investigate a 'research lesson' they teach in an applied or authentic setting (Fernandez, 2010). The process includes cycles composed of collaborative planning, teaching, lesson observation, analytic reflection, and ongoing revision. As part of the process, lesson-study groups develop a written reflective report of their work (Fernandez, 2010).

Working with a group of elementary-school PETE students in the US, Cluphf and Vogler (2008) reported using a lesson-study-based approach with their students. In this study, students reported an increase in knowledge of the subject matter, methods of instruction, and increased motivation and self-efficacy (Cluphf & Vogler, 2008). In a follow-up study Cluphf, Lux, and Scott (2012) explored students' perceptions of using lesson-study in practicum. For this exercise, students were asked to work collaboratively with their associate or cooperating teacher (CT) to design and conduct a series of PE lessons. Over the course of their final practicum, these students were interviewed at regular intervals about the experience. Each participant (n=4) reported improvements in planning and personal confidence; however, they also reported struggles to overcome a visible power differential between themselves and their CT. In conclusion, they report that the students improved in their ability to understand, operationalise, and contextualise their learning in a real-world setting (school) (Cluphf et al., 2012).

Place-based pedagogies

There is a growing awareness of the important link between 'place' and pedagogy, particularly in respect to how and what learning is enabled. A strong example of using place to provoke and extend PETE students' cultural understanding and values is provided by Legge (2008). She describes how, in the mid-1990s, she approached an *iwi* (Māori tribe) in Northland, New Zealand and requested access to their Mārae as pedagogical experience for second-year Bachelor of Physical Education (BPE) students. A Mārae is a series of buildings constructed to form the cultural hub or home point for a Māori tribe. By requesting access to the Mārae, Legge was intentionally seeking more than an opportunity to teach about the cultural knowledge of the Māori. It was expected that participation in a first-hand, situated (or immersive) learning experience within the traditional Mārae setting would support cultural understandings that were necessary for later instruction in culturally responsive pedagogies. Immersion in the Mārae setting was also expected to provoke more meaningful and authentic experiences with the values and customs inherent to the indigenous Māori as well as extend the ethic of outdoor and experiential learning for students in the BPE programme (Legge, 2010). Over the course of their visit, which is generally four to five days, students were confronted with new experiences that enable them to question their dominant cultural values to "locate their personal identity, cultural differences and understanding of the world alongside the Māori world-view" (Legge, 2008, p. 89). According to Legge (2010), this experience has numerous transformative effects on the students' identities, personal belief systems, world-views, and personal practice as training PE teachers. Most notably, it has challenged the students to develop specific cultural skills that enable them to cross the divide between the familiar (their own culture) and the unfamiliar (Māori) (Legge, 2010). In the process, they have confronted assumptions, stereotypes, and misunderstandings about the 'other' and became more culturally competent pre-service teacher applicants (Legge, 2010).

Inquiry-oriented practicum learning

The practicum experience has been long valued as a core location for learning about teaching (Zeichner, 2010). It recognises that many of the lessons students will learn about teaching can only be done in the context of a school, working alongside, and with, experienced teachers and immersed in the culture and problems of everyday practice. The practicum provides an ideal location for students to investigate the nature of school environments and appreciate the diversity and complexity of modern schools, but only if it moves beyond an apprenticeship approach to structuring the experience (Tinning, 1987).

In their attempt to challenge the status quo and encourage critical reflection from PETE students about the purpose and design of PE in contemporary schools, Oliver et al. (2013) have developed an innovative field-based model for delivering a secondary PETE methods course. In their participatory action research study there were 11 pre-service teacher education student participants from a university in the Southwest USA. Each student, along with the course coordinator, met with youth from a local high school (aged 14–15) and, over the course of the semester, designed a PE curriculum that privileged the student voice and gave precedence to the needs of these youth. By the end of the term, the authors reported significant transformations in the pre-service teacher's attitudes, understandings, and beliefs about the purpose and design of school-based PE. They also reported the emergence of a new sense of identity or community amongst those involved in the study (Oliver et al., 2013). Within the new community of learners individuals reported a repositioning of the power dynamic between youth, pre-service teachers, and professors. According to one student, in her past experiences,

> it was an authoritarian figure commanding everybody down here whereas Dr. Oliver has created a way to help us be a part of the decision making and … take into consideration what we feel and how we feel about it and if we don't like something then she'll work with us and try to figure out how to fix it while it's still accomplishing what she wants to get accomplished … She has created a sense of community with our class modelling how to do it with [youth]. (Oliver et al., 2013, p. 8)

Reflecting on the 'doing' of transformative pedagogy in PETE

A core focus for many educators researching and rethinking their practice as PETE teacher educators has been on understanding how to enable a transformative pedagogy in their own unique context. As the preceding examples show, a variety of strategies and settings have been used with varied degrees of success in the PETE environment. In general, each enacts a transformative pedagogy as a form of professional learning that emerges from within a particular political and cultural arena where forms of student experience and subjectivity are produced and mediated in ways that enable students to engage in critical activities that may challenge the status quo, reconstruct social-political-historical knowledge, question dominant ideologies, and make public the histories of those marginalised, disenfranchised, and/or disaffected. Underlying these efforts is an acknowledgement that teacher education is a setting where the practices of teaching must be interrogated, particularly as they shape, produce, and challenge student subjectivities and experiences central to working in contemporary schooling contexts and that are themselves implicated in the social and the political of life in modern society. It is important to remember that the social and political are present in all pedagogies, since it is the discursive nature of any practice that makes it seem natural, neutral, apolitical, and asocial. The very idea of transformative pedagogy is to expose and problematise the already social and political in those practices.

In general, students appear to initially struggle to embrace unconventional approaches and push back against the unfamiliar, particularly if these experiences are confined to individual courses or activities. There is support for the idea that, over time, sustained involvement in transformative pedagogical experiences does lead to deeper and more critical thinking about the purpose of education, one's personal disposition, stereotypes, and previously held beliefs as well as the needs and interests of the students, but that such outcomes are difficult to predict and do not constitute some desire for a collective empowerment. Rather, the intention is more modest (Tinning, 2002), aiming instead to enact a common core of values in practice that themselves enable students to participate in informed and skilful ways in their role as educators in twenty-first century society. Unfortunately, at present, the efficacy, or long-term effects, of using these transformative pedagogies have yet to be examined in detail. It is certainly a gap in the literature and an area for future study.

Reflective questions for discussion

1. Why would it be rarely possible to succeed in enacting a transformative pedagogy in PETE when the teacher educator works alone?
2. How do the discourses circulating at the macro- and meso-levels of the education system influence how transformative pedagogy is enacted at the micro-level of the individual course?
3. What is the difference between a theory of pedagogy and a pedagogy of theorising?
4. How should the teacher educator use the pedagogical strategies discussed to ensure they are 'transformative' and not simply 'innovative'?

References

Alhadeff-Jones, M. (2012). Transformative learning and the challenges of complexity. In E. W. Taylor & P. Cranton (Eds.), *Handbook of transformative learning: Theory, research and practice* (pp. 178–194). San Francisco: Jossey-Bass.

Apple, M. (2006). *Educating the 'right' way: Markets, standards, God and inequality* (2nd edn). London: Routledge.

Boud, D., & Falchikov, N. (2006). Aligning assessment with long-term learning. *Assessment & evaluation in higher education, 31*(4), 399–413. doi: 10.1080/02602930600679050.

Brubaker, N., & Ovens, A. (2012) Implementing individualized grading contracts: Perspectives of two teacher educators. In J. R. Young, L. B. Erickson, & S. Pinnegar (Eds.) *Extending inquiry communities: Illuminating teacher education through self-study.* Proceedings of the 9th International Conference on Self-Study of Teacher Education Practices, Herstmonceux Castle, East Sussex, England. Provo, UT: Brigham Young University.

Cluphf, D., Lux, K., & Scott, V. (2012). Investigating PETE majors' perceptions of lesson study as a capstone experience. *The Physical Educator, 69,* 228–247.

Cluphf, D., & Vogler, E. W. (2008). Collaborative lesson planning in physical education: A case study. *The ICHPER-SD Journal of Research in Health, Physical Education, Recreation, Sport and Dance, 3,* 86–94.

Culpan, I., & Bruce, J. (2007). New Zealand physical education and critical pedagogy: Refocusing the curriculum. *International Journal of Sport and Health Science, 5,* 1–11.

Culpan, I., & Galvan, H. (2012). Physical education in New Zealand: A socio-critical and bi-cultural positioning. *Journal of Physical Education and Health, 1*(1), 31–42.

Curtner-Smith, M. (2007). The impact of a critically oriented physical education teacher education course on preservice classroom teachers. *Journal of Teaching in Physical Education, 26*(1), 35–56.

Devís-Devís, J., & Sparkes, A. (1999). Burning the book: A biographical study of a pedagogically inspired identity crisis in physical education. *European Physical Education Review, 5*(2), 135–152.

Fernandez, M. (2010). Investigating how and what prospective teachers learn through microteaching lesson study. *Teaching and Teacher Education, 26,* 351–362.

Fernández-Balboa, J.-M. (1995). Reclaiming physical education in higher education through critical pedagogy. *Quest, 47*, 91–114.

Fernández-Balboa, J.-M. (1997) Physical education teacher preparation in the postmodern era: Toward a critical pedagogy. In J.-M. Fernandez-Balboa (Ed.), *Critical postmodernism in human movement, physical education and sport* (pp. 121–138). New York: State University of New York Press.

Fernández-Balboa, J.-M. (2000). Micropolitical perspectives of prospective physical educators. *Journal of Sport Pedagogy, 6*(1), 1–33.

Garbett, D., & Ovens, A. (2010). Peer teaching: Learning twice. In J. Jesson, V. M. Carpenter, M. McLean, M. Stephenson, & Airini (Eds.). *University teaching reconsidered: Justice, practice, inquiry* (pp. 184–192). Wellington, NZ: Dunmore Publishing.

Garrett, R. (2004). Negotiating and physical identity: Girls, bodies and physical education. *Sport, Education and Society, 9*(2), 223–37. Doi:10.0180/1357332042000233958.

Garrett, R. (2006). Critical storytelling in physical education teacher education. *European Physical Education Review, 12*(3), 339–360. Doi: 10.1177/1356336X06069277.

Giroux, H. (1994). *Disturbing pleasures.* New York: Routledge.

Giroux, H. (2009). Teacher education and democratic schooling. In A. Darder, M. Baltodano, & R. Torres (Eds.), *The critical pedagogy reader* (2nd ed., pp. 438–459). New York: Routledge.

Gore, J. (1990). Pedagogy as 'text' in physical education teacher education. In D. Kirk & R. Tinning (Eds.), *Physical education, curriculum and culture: Critical studies in the contemporary crisis* (pp. 101–138). London: Falmer Press.

Gore, J. M. (1993). *The struggle for pedagogies. Critical and feminist discourses as regimes of truth.* New York: Routledge.

Green, K. (2010). *Key themes in youth sport.* London: Routledge.

Gur-Ze'ev, I. (1998). Towards a nonrepressive critical pedagogy. *Educational Theory, 48*(4), 463–486.

Hickey, C. (2001). "I feel enlightened now, but…": The limits to the pedagogical translation of critical social discourses in physical education. *Journal of Teaching in Physical Education, 20*(3), 227–246.

Hinchey, P. (2006). *Being a critical educator: Defining a classroom identity, designing a critical pedagogy.* New York: Peter Lang.

Kårhus, S. (2010). Physical education teacher education on the education market – who's defining what physical education teachers need to know? *Physical Education and Sport Pedagogy, 15*(3), 227–241.

Kårhus, S. (2012). Providers, consumers and the horizons of the possible: A case study of marketization and physical education teacher education pedagogical discourse. *Sport, Education and Society, 17*(2), 245–259. Doi: 10.1080/13573322.2011.607953.

Kirk, D. (1986). A critical pedagogy for teacher education: Toward an inquiry-oriented approach. *Journal of Teaching in Physical Education, 5*(4), 230–246.

Lawson, H. A. (1986). Occupational socialization and the design of teacher education programs. *Journal of Teaching in Physical Education, 5*, 107–116.

Legge, M. (2008). A snapshot of place based learning in a marae context: An autoethnographic account. *New Zealand Journal of Outdoor Education, 2*(4), 87–102.

Legge, M. (2010). Chapter 13: E noho marae: Transforming learning through direct Maori cultural experience. In J. Jesson, V. M. Carpenter, M. McLean, M. Stephenson, & Airini (Eds.), *University teaching reconsidered: Justice, practice, inquiry* (pp. 139–149). Wellington, NZ: Dunmore Publishing.

Levin, B. B. (1995). Using the case study method in teacher education: The role of discussion and experience in teachers' thinking about cases. *Teaching and Teacher Education, 11*(1), 63–79.

Lieberman, J. (2009). Reinventing teacher professional norms and identities: The role of lesson study and learning communities. *Professional Development in Education, 35*(1), 83–99.

Lorente, E., & Kirk, D. (2013). Alternative democratic assessment in PETE: An action-research study exploring risks, challenges and solutions. *Sport, Education and Society, 18*(1), 77–96.

Mordal-Moen, K., & Green, K. (2012). Neither shaking nor stirring: A case study of reflexivity in Norwegian physical education teacher education. *Sport, Education and Society, 19*(4), 415–434.

Oliver, K. L., Oesterrich, H. A., Aranda, R., Archeleta, J., Blazer, C., de la Cruz, K., Martinez, D., McConnell, J., Osta, M., Parks, L., & Robinson, R. (2013). 'The sweetness of struggle': Innovation in physical education teacher education through student-centered inquiry as curriculum in a physical education methods course. *Physical Education and Sport Pedagogy, 20*(1), 1–19. Doi: 10.1080/1740898 9.2013.803527.

O'Sullivan, M., Siedentop, D., & Locke, L. F. (1992). Toward collegiality: Competing viewpoints among teacher educators. *Quest, 44*, 266–280.

Ovens, A. (2013). Criticality in HPE: Think Piece 6: Disturbing practice in teacher education. *New Zealand Physical Educator, 46*(2), 20–21.

Ovens, A. (2014). Disturbing practice in teacher education through peer-teaching. In A. Ovens & T. Fletcher (Eds.), *Self-study in physical education: Exploring the interplay between scholarship and practice* (pp. 87–98). London: Springer.

Ovens, A., & Fletcher, T. (2014). *Self-study in physical education: Exploring the interplay between scholarship and practice.* London: Springer.

Ovens, A., Hopper, T., & Butler, J. (2012). *Complexity thinking in physical education: Reframing curriculum, pedagogy and research.* London: Routledge.

Ovens, A., & Tinning, R. (2009). Reflection as situated practice: A memory-work study of lived experience in teacher education. *Teaching and Teacher Education, 25*(8), 1125–1131. Doi:10.1016/j.tate.2009.03.013.

Richards, K. A., Hemphill, M. A., Templin, T. J., & Eubank, A. M. (2012). Student-authored case studies as a learning tool in physical education teacher education. *Journal of Physical Education, Recreation & Dance, 83*(3), 47–52.

Rizvi, F., & Lingard, B. (2011). Social equity and the assemblage of values in Australian higher education. *Cambridge Journal of Education, 41*(1), 5–22. Doi: 10.1080/0305764X.2010.549459.

Ross, B. (2010). Student self-assessment within a Frierean pedagogy. In J. Jesson, V. M. Carpenter, M. McLean, M. Stephenson, & Airini (Eds.), *University teaching reconsidered: Justice, practice, inquiry* (pp. 202–213). Wellington, NZ: Dunmore Publishing.

Ruiz, B., & Fernández-Balboa, J. (2005). Physical education teacher educators' personal perspectives regarding their practice of critical pedagogy. *Journal of Teaching in Physical Education, 24,* 243–264.

Segall, A. (2002). *Disturbing practice: Reading teacher education text.* New York: Peter Lang.

Sicilia-Camacho, A., & Fernández-Balboa, J-M. (2009). Reflecting on the moral bases of critical pedagogy in PETE: Toward a Foucaultian perspective on ethics and the care of the self. *Sport, Education and Society, 14*(4), 443–463. Doi: 10.1080/13573320903217166.

Standal, Ø. F., & Moe, V. F. (2013). Reflective practice in physical education and physical education teacher education: A review of the literature since 1995. *Quest, 65*(2), 220–240. Doi: 10.0180/00336297.2013.773530.

Standal, Ø. F., Mordal-Moen, K. M., & Moe, V. F. (2014). Theory and practice in the context of practicum: The perspectives of Norwegian physical education student teachers. *European Physical Education Review, 20*(2), 165–178. Doi: 10.1177/1356336x13508687.

Templin, T. J., & Schempp, P. G. (Eds.). (1989). *Socialization into physical education: Learning to teach.* Indianapolis: Benchmark Press.

Tinning, R. (1987). Beyond the development of utilitarian teaching perspectives: An Australian case study of action research in teacher preparation. In G. T. Barrette, R. S. Feingold, C. R. Rees, & M. Pieron (Eds.), *Myths, models and methods in sport pedagogy.* Champaign, IL: Human Kinetics.

Tinning, R. (2002). Toward a 'modest pedagogy': Reflections on the problematics of critical pedagogy. *Quest, 54,* 224–240.

Tinning, R. (2004). Rethinking the preparation of HPE teachers: Ruminations on knowledge, identity, and ways of thinking. *Asia-Pacific Journal of Teacher Education, 32*(3), 241–253. Doi:10.1080/1359866042000295406.

Tinning, R. (2006). Theoretical orientations in physical education teacher education. In D. Kirk, D. Macdonald, & M. O'Sullivan (Eds.), *The handbook of physical education* (pp. 369–385). London: Sage Publications.

Tinning, R. (2012). A socially critical HPE (aka physical education) and the challenge for teacher education. In B. Down & J. Smyth (Eds.), *Critical voices in teacher education: Explorations of educational purpose.* Dordrecht, The Netherlands: Springer.

Ukpokodu, O. (2009). The practice of transformative pedagogy. *Journal on Excellence in College Teaching, 20*(2), 32–67.

Velija, P., Capel, S., Katene, W., & Hayes, S. (2008). Does knowing stuff like PSHE and citizenship make me a better teacher?: Student teachers in the teacher training figuration. *European Physical Education Review, 4*(3), 389–406.

Wilson, G., & I'Anson, J. (2006). Reframing the practicum: Constructing performative space in initial teacher education. *Teaching and Teacher Education, 22,* 353–361.

Zeichner, K. (2010). Rethinking the connections between campus courses and field experiences in college- and university-based teacher education. *Journal of Teacher Education, 61*(2), 89–99.

20

TRANSFORMATIVE PEDAGOGIES FOR CHALLENGING BODY CULTURE IN PHYSICAL EDUCATION

Kimberly L. Oliver, NEW MEXICO STATE UNIVERSITY, USA

& David Kirk, UNIVERSITY OF STRATHCLYDE, UK

The boys say that we are dumb, stupid and wouldn't last five seconds [in sports] and that you're a woman and you need to stay in your place … We can bring all the fifth grade girls in and interview them and ask them how they feel when boys say different things to them. I believe it will help, because it's not fair for us girls – Maggee Mae, 10 years old. (Oliver & Hamzeh, 2010, pp. 43–44)

According to Ukpokodu (2009), transformative pedagogy is a form of activist pedagogy that places the learner at the centre of educational processes and is concerned to foster both critical consciousness and agency. Tinning (Chapter 18, this volume) has noted there is a range of socially critical discourses in the physical education (PE) research literature which relates to the concept of transformative pedagogy. Advocacies for forms of critical pedagogy in and through PE appeared in the 1970s and steadily gained momentum through the 1980s and 1990s (Devis, 2006). But the translation of this early advocacy into practice that could lead to social change was not easily attained. O'Sullivan, Siedentop, and Locke (1992) criticized advocates of critical pedagogy for failing to show what they labelled 'radical' PE would look like at the level of school programmes. This criticism echoed Dewey's (1938) observation that progressive educators face a more difficult task than traditional educators to develop programmes since they cannot fall back on existing practices, but must create genuinely new and alternative pedagogical forms.

We suggest that this challenge to realize advocacy in the practice of transformative PE pedagogies has continued to the present, with some exceptions that we will outline later in this chapter. The task is even more difficult when we consider pedagogies that challenge body culture in PE. This is because conceptualizations of the body and associated terminology vary both with advocates' purposes and with the theoretical perspectives they employ. There is no settled or dominant conceptualization, no well-developed theoretical position, and no widely accepted methodology for studying and practising transformative pedagogy that challenges body culture in PE. There have however been developments in train since the late 1990s, particularly associated with activist approaches to working with girls in PE, that may provide guidance on how further work in this area can proceed.

We begin the chapter with a brief account of the historical context for this topic, in which we note some of the main theoretical approaches to conceptualizing the body, its social construction, and the experience of embodiment in PE. Next, we consider issues in work on the body in PE since the 1980s with a particular emphasis on more recent trends, as we elaborate in further detail the theoretical discussions and advocacies for challenging body culture. In the final sections, we focus on the emerging line of research centred on activist approaches to working with girls in PE as an example of the successful translation of advocacy into practice that includes pedagogies of embodiment as integral to new forms of PE. We use this example to guide our thinking on some future directions for what might genuinely be regarded as transformative pedagogies in PE that have potential to make a difference for the better in the lives of young people.

Trends and issues in work on the body in physical education

Notions of the body in culture have been in the literature in PE since at least the late 1980s, though this use has been patchy in several respects. Where a concept of the body specifically is used, it is often not defined (e.g. Velija & Kumar, 2009). Additionally, while the body is some-times mentioned infrequently (Vertinsky, 1992) or not at all (Wright & King, 1990), it is clear that the authors concerned have much to say about the body and body culture. Physical edu-cation researchers have used a number of terms related to the body such as embodied identi-ties (Kirk & Tinning, 1994), embodied subjectivities (Wright, 1995), body narratives (Oliver, 1999), physicality (McDermott, 2000), habitus (Gorely, Halroyd, & Kirk, 2003), body-meanings (Azzarito, Solmon, & Harrison, 2006), the embodiment of gender (Velija & Kumar, 2009), and the physical self (Crocker et al., 2006).

Despite the lack of consistent terminology and an apparent reluctance to define the term, there is an implicit consensus in the literature on the importance of the body and body culture in PE, particularly in relation to girls. All of this work, without exception, takes an anti-dualist stance (Dewey, 1938). In an early contribution drawing on phenomenology and existentialism, Whitehead (1990) claimed that every human is an indivisible whole and that embodiment and personhood are inseparable. Satina and Hultgren (2001) similarly note (quoting Heidegger) that "We do not 'have' a body; rather, we 'are' bodily" (p. 521). They go on to charge that Cartesian dualism not only separates body and mind, but also then devalues the body compared with the intellect and in so doing objectifies the body as a thing that can only be understood as an object. In her critique of this dualist tendency in education, Whitehead argued that the body-as-lived is "the ongoing axis of thought and knowing" and is thus of primary importance in education (Whitehead, 2010, p. 26).

Building on a monist perspective, several authors have provided insights into what Young (1980, p. 140) called "the *situation* of being a woman in a particular society". Young had argued against the prevailing wisdom of the time in motor development research with young children that despite evidence of a "more or less typical style of running like a girl, climbing like a girl, swinging like a girl, hitting like a girl", this distinctively female way of moving is not due to some 'feminine essence' but is, instead, learned. In a patriarchal social order women learn to move in a confined field because they learn that "feminine bodily existence is self-referred to the extent that the feminine subject posits her motion as the motion that is *looked at*" (p. 148).

Other authors have developed Young's notion of the situation of being a woman in relation to school PE and other organized physical activity. Wright and King (1990, p. 222), for example, noted that there is considerable ambiguity surrounding girls' engagements with PE. On the one hand,

and consistent with Young's analysis, girls are "constructed by patriarchal discourses of femininity that work to constrain and restrain their behaviour"; but on the other hand, in PE lessons "they are expected to be active, competitive, and achievement-oriented". The net effect, according to Wright and King, is that conventional ways of being feminine consistently undermine expectations in PE regarding "activity, achievement and effort" and reproduce the gender relations of the wider society.

Vertinsky (1992, p. 382) supported this analysis of Wright and King and noted that part of the source of the contradictions girls experience is that they are in co-educational classes compared unfavourably with the male standard as the norm, where girls are portrayed "as 'deficient' males or passive victims of restrictive gender-stereotyped attitudes and practices". Writing in a different context, of adult women in aerobics classes, Markula (1995) noted these same ambiguities, but in this context draws our attention to women's contrasting behaviour in private and public spaces. She argued that women are privately critical (among friends) of priorities of the authoritative discourse of aerobics that laud the ideal body type, but publically conformist rather than transgressive. Returning to the topic of girls and PE, Wright (1995) argued that the male standard as norm is manifest in the dominance of team games traditionally associated with males, while activities traditionally associated with females such as dance are viewed as marginal. Echoing Young, Vertinsky (1992, p. 375) summed up the situation of girls in PE, where they learn "to experience their bodies as fragile encumbrances, as objects and burdens, rather than as living manifestations of action and intention. As a consequence, many readily learned to underestimate their bodily capacity for sport and games". Vertinsky (1992, p. 390) recognized the need for a different approach to PE in order to address these ambiguities and contradictions that characterize the situation of girls. She argued that there is a need for a form of "PE that emphasizes agency, action and the possibility of transformation and focuses on more than the single attainment target of physical activity". As such,

> teachers … would do well to encourage girls to talk about their bodies, how they feel about their sizes and shapes, and the different ways their bodies can move. These views of the body can then be discussed in terms of dominant messages that girls get about their bodies in this culture… (p. 389)

Several scholars have responded to this call to make spaces in the curriculum that allow girls to name and critique the patriarchal discourses surrounding their embodiment (e.g. Enright & O'Sullivan, 2010; Fisette, 2010; Oliver, 1999; Oliver & Lalik, 2004a).

Armour (1999) argued that since PE is 'body-focused', physical educators should make this focus explicit. This is because PE "can have a major role to play in the establishment of pupils' embodied identity" (p. 10). Satina and Hultgren (2001, p. 530) argued for the development of a 'pedagogy of embodiment' that offers girls opportunities to "develop and express self-affirming views of their body in an atmosphere that does not replicate culturally imposed limitations". In one of the earliest activist projects of working with girls in PE, Oliver and Lalik (2001) developed the notion of the 'body-as-curriculum', explaining that they "wanted to develop a curriculum of the body that would begin with girls' experiences, interests and concerns with their bodies, rather than featuring adults' perspectives exclusively" (p. 307). Further studies have added support to these calls to create what Vertinsky (1992) named as gender-sensitive forms of PE, with Gorely et al. (2003) and Azzarito and Solmon (2006, p. 94) arguing "a 'gender-relevant' critical pedagogy should be employed in PE classes to offer alternative constructions of embodied femininities and masculinities", while Crocker et al. (2006, p. 197) advocate that "interventions focused on the physical self and body image need to target young adolescents, if not children".

309

The possibilities for creating transformative pedagogies that are gender-sensitive must, however, address the issue of the male standard as the norm and the treatment of girls as "deficient" males (Vertinsky, 1992). This issue is part of the wider gender order of society. With respect to embodiment, Bourdieu (2001, p. 67) noted that when we come to consider masculine domination, we must account not only for the social and economic circumstances in societies that favour men over women, but the embedding of these social structures in the body itself.

Bourdieu noted that the power of masculine domination is such that women who play sport take many risks, including having their femininity and sexuality called into question. But these risks precisely make his point; the subversion of the gender order through an active and acting body provokes strong reactions in some men and women since it appears that the 'natural order of things' itself is being brought into question.

The ways in which girls as active and acting bodies might practise the physically active life are, as Markula (1995) noted, differentiated according to private and public spaces. Azzarito and Sterling (2010), in a study of minority ethnic girls in England, noted that public spaces were seen by the girls to be male spaces and therefore fraught with risk, and their preferences for physical activity were overwhelmingly in the private space of home. While we have noted the unfavourable comparison of girls to the male standard as norm, we might also consider along with Hills (2007) that these standards operate even in girl-only PE environments, and that girl-only spaces are not necessarily safer for less skilled girls if they lack social status or a friendship group. Moreover, Evans (2006, p. 557) claims that along with peer scrutiny and criticism, "the evaluative gaze of the teachers exerts power over the pupils, intensifying the gaze and other comments from peers (fear of ridicule), and also self-criticism (fear of inadequacy)".

This literature suggests unequivocally that pedagogies of embodiment in which the study of the social construction of the body becomes an essential part of the curriculum are key to the development of transformative forms of PE. Vertinsky (1992) argued that "it is unlikely that one single approach will serve the interests of all girls – in all sporting contexts … A gender sensitive perspective is thus one that lets patterns of discrimination themselves determine what action to take to eliminate bias" (p. 383). We consider this comment to be underpinned by a pragmatist perspective that asks how might we improve the situation for both girls and boys in PE? While there is no one-size-fits-all answer to this question, the literature would suggest that creating spaces for girls, in particular, to study embodiment is a critical element in any transformative approach to PE.

Activist approaches to challenging body culture in physical education

That's sick … Too muscular … I just think women should be feminine … not where you can see the muscle 'cause I think that's masculine – Alysa, age 13. (Oliver, 1999, p. 239)

Given the continuing challenge of girls' experiences of PE, and given the predominance of writing on embodiment in references to girls, gender, and PE, we focus this section on recent and ongoing activist research with girls and their teachers in PE as an example of transformative pedagogy.

Feminist authors (Bordo, 1989; Collins, 1990; hooks, 1995; Vertinsky, 1992; Wolf, 1991) claim that the "body plays a crucial role in the reciprocal relationship between women's private and public identities. The social meanings publicly attached to the body can become internalized and exert powerful influences on women's private feelings of self-worth" (Oliver & Lalik, 2001, p. 305). A key feature of activist work involved in engaging adolescent girls in PE involves teachers creating spaces in their curriculum for girls to critically explore their embodiment (e.g. Enright & O'Sullivan, 2013; Goodyear, Casey, & Kirk 2013; Hamzeh, 2012; Oliver & Lalik, 2001, 2004a). A pedagogy of embodiment helps girls "name the discourses that shape their lives and regulate their bodies ... [in order to support] girls' efforts to develop strategies for identifying, resisting, and disrupting forms of enculturation that threaten their health and limit their life chances" (Oliver & Lalik, 2004a, pp. 162–163). These studies, as well as others' work on girls' embodiment (e.g. Azzarito & Solmon, 2009; Garrett, 2004; Hills, 2006) provide strong evidence that while purposeful physical activity is necessary to girls' engagements in PE, it is *not* sufficient by itself. Offering girls the opportunities to explore their embodiment *is* central to creating relevant PE for girls.

In working toward understanding how to centralize embodiment pedagogically, activist scholars in PE have consistently approached their work with girls from an anti-dualist stance, have actively sought ways to help girls name experiences of their bodies that are often at a pre-conscious level in order for girls to be able to reflect on those experiences critically, and worked to support girls' sense of physicality in movement. First, activists' work with embodied pedagogies disrupts the debilitating mind/body dualism that privileges and values the mind while objectifying the body as something to be controlled, manipulated, and 'looked at' (Grumet, 1988; hooks, 1995). This mind/body dualism far too often plagues our systems of education (Garrison, 1997; Kirk, 1992), our pedagogical practices (Satina & Hultgren, 2001), and our traditional PE curricula (Oliver & Garrison, 1996; Wright, 1995). Starting from the perspective that *how* girls experience their bodies underpins their learning, activists have intentionally sought to make girls' bodies central in their curricula needs (Enright & O'Sullivan, 2010; Fisette, 2011; Oliver, 1999, 2001; Oliver & Lalik, 2000, 2001, 2004a). Placing the body at the centre disrupts the mind/body dualism of traditional practice thereby creating the cracks necessary for better understanding how girls read, internalize, resist, or reject forms and processes of oppression that threaten their health as well as their abilities, interests, and willingness to learn to value the physically active life. These cracks also create the spaces for better understanding girls' hopes – in other words – spaces for not just the language of critique but also the language of possibility (Fine, 1994; Giroux, 1997). In this context, Giroux (1997, p. 132) writes

> A critical pedagogy has to begin with a dialectical celebration of the languages of critique and possibility – an approach which finds its noblest expressions in a discourse integrating critical analysis with social transformation [around] problems rooted in the concrete experiences of everyday life.

As activists have made girls' everyday experiences of their bodies central to PE (Enright & O'Sullivan, 2010; Fisette, 2011; Oliver, Hazmeh, & McCaughtry, 2009; Oliver & Lalik, 2001), they have come to understand the circulating discourses that shape girls' subjectivities, have been able to search for places to explore girls' agency, and have worked collaboratively with girls to practise change (Oliver, 2010). The results have been a much clearer understanding of *how* girls experience their bodies through dominant cultural narratives that objectify and demean girls' bodies, as well as *how* and *where* they resist these same oppressive narratives, and *how* they identify what they want to change (Fisette, 2011; Oliver & Lalik, 2001, 2004a). Fisette (2012) and Oliver and Hamzeh's (2010) work illustrates this point:

> I don't like sexist things ... the whole female ball thing that really annoys me even though they are easier to throw. It's just the whole point that he's making us think that we can't

throw the bigger ones ... I think if he puts them out, he shouldn't call them female balls, just be like, 'Here's smaller ones, throw them if you want. Anyone can throw them.' (Fisette, 2013, p. 196)

Kim: Marie you said that sometimes the boys won't let the girls play because they have the wrong color of skin and they had taken a picture of you [Maggee Mae] ...

Maggee Mae: Yeah ... they told me I couldn't play because I was a girl and I was Black ... Sometimes I know that at the fifth-grade recess, some of the boys don't want the girls to play because they are girls, and I think that is a problem because we should all be able to do what we want to do; we should be able to play what we want to play. (Oliver & Hamzeh, 2010, p. 43)

A second way that activist scholars have worked with embodied pedagogies is by actively seeking ways to help girls name their experiences of their bodies that are often at a pre-conscious level. Greene (1995, p. 23) writes

Only when the taken-for-granted is subject to questioning, only when we take various, sometimes unfamiliar perspectives on it, does it show itself as what it is – contingent on many interpretations, many vantage points, unified (if at all) by conformity or by unexamined common sense. Once we can see our givens as contingencies, then we may have the opportunity to posit alternative ways of living and valuing and to make choices.

Part of what activist scholars have consistently done is to find ways to help girls name the meanings of their bodily experiences. An example from Oliver's work is this task: "Go through the magazines and cut out pictures and/or text that are of interest to you and categorize your pictures/text any way you want" (Oliver, 2001, p. 148). Many of the findings from activist work have come only after using creative methods such as this for assisting girls to find ways to put language to experiences that are difficult to explain in part because so many of these experiences operate on a pre-conscious level. Visual methodologies such as: magazine explorations and critiques (Enright & O'Sullivan, 2013; Oliver & Lalik, 2000, 2001, 2004a); photographic inquiry (Oliver & Hamzeh, 2010; Oliver et al., 2009; Oliver & Lalik, 2004a, 2004b); photographic essays (Oliver & Lalik, 2004a); scrap booking (Enright & O'Sullivan, 2010, 2012; Hamzeh, 2012); mapping (Enright & O'Sullivan, 2010; Hamzeh & Oliver, 2012; Oliver, 1999); and drawing (Oliver, 1999; Fisette, 2014) have all been methods that activists have used to assist girls in the process of naming issues that influence their embodiment.

In addition to using visual methods as a means for girls to put language to experience, activist scholars have also used a variety of techniques to help girls further elaborate experiences that are only partially explained. For example, asking girls to imagine a world where particular things no longer existed (i.e. people didn't care how they looked, there was no such thing as 'normal' female behaviour, there was no longer racism) was found useful in helping girls better describe the circumstances with which they currently experienced their bodies (Oliver, 1999). Asking girls to talk about what 'other girls' might think about their bodies was another technique useful in creating public settings where girls would talk about issues of embodiment that were important to them (e.g. anorexia and bulimia; teen pregnancy).

Through the process of trying to assist girls to find ways to name experiences that influence their embodiment so that they can start to look at these experiences from a variety of vantage points (Greene, 1995), what activists have learned is that this process takes time, patience, and creativity. Girls need multiple opportunities for exploring their embodiment because it is through these multiple and varied opportunities that they are able to better articulate what they know and feel. For example, in Oliver's (2001) work 13-year-old African American girls were writing about the magazine images they had selected as a way to represent messages that girls receive about their bodies. One of the girls, Alexandria, looked up and said

"I have a concept I want to talk about." She went on to explain that, "some girls at our school are pregnant". The group began discussing how they were curious to know what it "felt like to be pregnant" and how important it was to have their "mothers" to talk with because "they don't talk about it [teen pregnancy] at school". Brandi mentioned that when they were in 5th grade they saw a film but that "then most people didn't have questions and everyone was too embarrassed to ask questions". She continued by saying, "Now everybody got all these questions and there ain't nobody to ask".

(Oliver, 2001, p. 160)

This is just one of many types of conversations activists have had in their work with girls. What is important about assisting girls to name their experiences is that adults can begin to better understand just how important girls' embodiment is to their interest in learning to be healthy adults.

A third way activist scholars have worked toward understanding how to centralize girls' embodiment pedagogically is through their supporting and nurturing girls' sense of physicality in movement. What is pivotal to the success of such endeavours was these scholars' willingness to support girls' physicality on the girls' terms, rather than on some preconceived adult notion of 'what should be'. Here is where we see how girls' notions of embodiment lie beneath the surface. To illustrate our point we use an example from a study by Oliver and her colleagues (Oliver et al., 2009). In 2005–2006 Oliver worked with two groups of 10–11-year-old Mexican American, Hispanic, and White 5th grade girls in a poor, rural border community about 40 minutes from Juarez Mexico. The girls were selected by their PE teacher to work with Oliver one day per week for the entire school year. The teacher labelled these girls as either not liking PE or not liking physical activity in general. The study aimed to work with these girls to help them identify barriers to their physical activity enjoyment and participation and work with them to negotiate the barriers within their control so as to increase their opportunities for engaging in physical activity.

The girls were given cameras at the beginning of the study and asked to photograph things that helped them be physically active and things that either prevented them from being active or prevented them from enjoying physical activity. Through this process the girls explained that being a 'girly girl' often prevented them from being physically active because girly girls 'don't want to sweat', 'mess up their hair and nails', they didn't want to 'mess up their nice clothes', and sometimes they liked to wear 'flip flops'.

What Oliver began to learn as time went on was that these girls were using the idea of "being girly girl" as an excuse for not engaging in PE. Over time they started to talk about how when the teacher was having them play something they didn't like such as football, soccer, basketball, and Frisbee that they used excuses such as "we don't want to sweat" or "we don't want to mess up our clothes" as a way of getting out of the activity that wasn't meeting their particular needs. Below is a conversation Oliver had with the girls as they were explaining about why they didn't like these sports:

Maltilde says, 'because the boys kick your feet', 'trip you on purpose', 'push you down', 'they won't give you the ball', and 'grab your hair'. So I asked them whether it was the sport they didn't like or the way that sport was being played. I said, 'So if the boys are

313

kicking you or tripping you or pulling your hair or not giving you the ball those kinds of things …' Sunshine cut me off and says, 'You feel left out and hurt.' I continued, 'I'm trying to figure out, if there are a lot of girls that are girly girls or identify as girly girls, they should be able to be active in ways that are …' Sunshine cuts me off again and says, 'Suitable for them.' I continue, 'Yes, that are suitable, wouldn't you think?' … Sunshine goes on to explain that if girls 'felt comfortable with themselves they would be able to do physical activity'.

(Oliver et al., 2009, p. 102)

Oliver came to better understand from these girls that not only did they not like the content in PE – the traditional team sports – but they also did not like how the activities were played when boys were involved, did not like getting hurt or being left out, and wanted to be able to play and 'feel comfortable with themselves'. So, rather than play in situations they identified as unsuitable or dangerous, they chose not to participate. And what is so concerning here is that because their excuses 'not wanting to sweat or mess up their clothes' are SUCH normalized discourses around girls' disengagement in PE, no one questioned whether there might be some other reason they didn't want to play.

Rather than try to get the girls to critique how the notion of "girly girl" was contributing to their disengagement Oliver suggested that they work collaboratively to negotiate their barriers by making up games girls could play while simultaneously being "girly girl". So what they did was to create a book of games for days the girls "didn't want to sweat" or "didn't want to mess up their clothes", "break a nail", "didn't want to mess up their hair", and days that the girls wore flip flops. Through the process of Oliver working to support these girls' physicality of movement on their terms what started to happen was that the content of the games they created actually contradicted many of their self-identified girly girl barriers. That is, while they may have been making up games for days where they did not want to sweat or mess up their nice clothes, many of the actual games involved running, jumping, chasing, and fleeing – in other words, the possibility of sweating or getting their clothes dirty. Take for example, runaround kickball. The girls created this game for the days they didn't want to mess up their nice clothes. It involved kicking a ball and then the team that kicked all ran the bases while the outfielders collected the ball and then chased the girls running the bases trying to catch them. This study was conducted in a desert community, thus they played the game in the dust so the possibility of the girls messing up their clothes was pretty certain. Many of their games had these types of contradictions.

What Oliver learned was that IF we want girls to learn to value the physically active life we need to start from where girls ARE, and assist them in finding activities that THEY find valuable and relevant and enjoyable, regardless of what we think. This example highlights just how central girls' embodiment is to their physical activity participation and that we cannot trivialize or dismiss this centrality if we hope to assist girls in becoming physically active for life.

Future directions for transformative pedagogies that challenge body culture in physical education

What the example of activist work with girls in PE shows is how a focus on embodiment as integral to a transformative pedagogy requires a radical reconstruction of PE. In addition to pedagogies of embodiment, activist work typically employs student-centredness, inquiry-based education centred *in* action, and listening to respond over time (Oliver & Kirk, 2015). Future directions for transformative pedagogies, which challenge body culture in PE, similarly require the construction of new and creative alternatives to traditional practices and to imagine new possibilities for the substance and conduct of the subject in schools.

Moreover, given the lack of consistency of purposes, theoretical frameworks, and methods within the PE literature on the body in culture, we think researchers need to move beyond paradigmatic approaches to adopt a more pragmatic position that, through the influence of Dewey (1938) and others, lies at the root of transformative pedagogies (Ukpokodu, 2009). This position needs to focus, we suggest, on three questions: 'can we make the situation for these youth and children better than it is currently?', 'what would be better?', and 'how might we go about this task?'. Provided we answer the first question in the affirmative, we suggest there is no one future best way or right answer to how we go about making a difference for the better in the lives of young people.

Summary of key findings

- Concerns about body culture have been in the PE literature since at least the 1970s, with an acceleration of numbers of publications from the early 1990s to the present.
- Within this literature, advocacy for pedagogies that challenge body culture has dominated over the practice of alternative and potentially transformative pedagogies.
- The body in culture has been conceptualized in a variety of ways, depending on authors' purposes and theoretical perspectives, and includes historical, philosophical, sociological, and psychological theories.
- There is as a consequence no uniform methodology for studying or practising transformative pedagogies that challenge body culture.
- Despite this lack of uniformity, there has been a consensus on the importance of body culture in PE as a topic for transformative pedagogy.
- One example of transformative pedagogy in which embodiment is integral is provided in the work of activist researchers with girls in PE.
- In working toward understanding how to centralize embodiment pedagogically, activist scholars in PE have consistently approached their work with girls from an anti-dualist stance.
- Activist researchers have also actively sought ways to help girls name experiences of their bodies that are often at a pre-conscious level in order for girls to be able to reflect on those experiences critically.
- Activist scholars have worked to support girls' sense of physicality in movement.
- Future development of transformative pedagogies that challenge body culture in PE can benefit from asking three pragmatic questions to inform our work with young people.

Reflective questions for discussion

1. What might be the purposes of a transformative pedagogy that challenges body culture?
2. What theories and methods best seem to inform transformative pedagogies that challenge body culture?
3. What should be the future priorities for developing transformative pedagogies that challenge body culture in PE?
4. How do transformative pedagogies that challenge body culture require a shift in conceptualizing what counts for PE?
5. What might come of generations of young people who grow up with a critical lens toward body culture? How might this change what is possible for PE?

References

Armour, K. M. (1999). The case for a body-focus in education and physical education. *Sport, Education and Society, 4,* 5–15.

Azzarito, L. & Solmon, M. A. (2006). A poststructural analysis of high school students' gendered and racialized bodily meanings. *Journal of Teaching in Physical Education, 25,* 75–98.

Azzarito, L. M., & Solmon, M. A. (2009). An investigation of students' embodied discourses in physical education: A gendered project. *Journal of Teaching in Physical Education, 28*(2), 173–191.

Azzarito, L. M., Solmon, M. A., & Harrison, L. (2006). '…If I had a choice, I would…' A feminist post-structural perspective on girls in physical education. *Research Quarterly for Exercise and Sport, 77*(2), 222–239.

Azzarito, L., & Sterling, J. (2010). 'What it was in my eyes': Picturing youths' embodiment in 'real' spaces. *Qualitative Research in Sport and Exercise, 2*(2), 209–228. DOI: 10.1080/19398441.2010.488029.

Bordo, S. R. (1989). The body and the reproduction of femininity: A feminist appropriation of Foucault. In A. M. Jaggar & S. R. Bordo (Eds.), *Gender/body/knowledge: Feminist reconstructions of being and knowing* (pp. 13–33). New Brunswick, NJ: Rutgers University Press.

Bourdieu, P. (2001). *Masculine domination.* Cambridge, UK: Polity.

Broekhoff, J. (1972). Physical education and the reification of the human body. *Gymnasion, 9,* 4–11.

Collins, P. H. (1990). *Black feminist thought: Knowledge, consciousness, and the politics of empowerment, perspectives on gender,* Vol. 2, Boston, MA: Unwin Hyman.

Crocker, P. R., Sabiston, C. M., Kowalski, K. C., McDonough, M. H., & Kowalski, N. (2006). Longitudinal assessment of the relationship between physical self-concept and health-related behavior and emotion in adolescent girls. *Journal of Applied Sport Psychology, 18,* 185–200. DOI: 10.1080/10413200600830257.

Devis, J. (2006). Socially critical research perspectives in physical education. In D. Kirk, D. Macdonald, & M. O'Sullivan (Eds.), *Handbook of physical education* (pp. 37–58). London: Sage.

Dewey, J. (1938). *Education and experience.* New York: Macmillan.

Enright, E., & O'Sullivan, M. (2010). 'Can I do it in my pyjamas?' Negotiating a physical education curriculum with teenage girls. *European Physical Education Review, 16*(3), 203–222.

Enright, E., & O'Sullivan, M. (2012). Producing different knowledge and producing knowledge differently: Rethinking physical education research and practice through participatory visual methods. *Sport, Education and Society, 17*(1), 35–55.

Enright, E., & O'Sullivan, M. (2013). 'Now, I'm magazine detective the whole time': Listening and responding to young people's complex experiences of popular physical culture. *Journal of Teaching in Physical Education, 32,* 394–418.

Evans, B. (2006). 'I'd feel ashamed': Girls' bodies and sports participation. *Gender, Place & Culture: A Journal of Feminist Geography, 13*(5), 547–561.

Fine, M. (1994). Dis-stance and other stances: Negotiations of power inside feminist research. In A. Gitlin (Ed.), *Power and method: Political activism and educational research* (pp. 13–35). New York: Routledge.

Fisette, J. L. (2010). Getting to know your students. *Journal of Physical Education and Dance, 81*(7), 42–49. DOI: 10.1080/07303084.2010.10598508.

Fisette, J. L. (2011). Exploring how girls navigate their embodied identities in physical education. *Physical Education and Sport Pedagogy, 16*(2), 179–196.

Fisette, J. L. (2013). 'Are you listening?': Adolescent girls voice how they negotiate self-identified barriers to their success and survival in physical education. *Physical Education and Sport Pedagogy, 18*(2), 184–203.

Fisette, J. L. (2014). Activity #18: Giving voice to the moving body through pictures and drawings. In J. K. Dowdy & K. Cushner (Eds.), *Reading between the lines: Activities for developing social awareness literacy* (pp. 109–114). Lanham, MD: Rowman & Littlefield.

Garrett, R. (2004). Negotiating a physical identity: Girls, bodies and physical education. *Sport, Education and Society, 9*(2), 223–237.

Garrison, J. (1997). *Dewey and Eros: Wisdom and desire in the art of teaching.* New York: Teachers College Press.

Giroux, H. A. (1997). *Pedagogy and the politics of hope: Theory, culture, and schooling.* Boulder, CO: Westview Press.

Goodyear, V., Casey, A., & Kirk, D. (2013). Slights, cameras, inaction: Using flip cameras in cooperative learning to explore girls' (dis)engagement in physical education. In L. Azzarito & D. Kirk (Eds.), *Pedagogies, physical culture, and visual methods* (pp. 47–61). New York: Routledge.

Gorely, T., Holroyd, R., & Kirk, D. (2003). Muscularity, the habitus and the social construction of gender: Towards a gender relevant physical education. *British Journal of Sociology of Education, 24,* 429–448.

Greene, M. (1995). *Releasing the imagination: Essays on education, the arts, and social change.* San Francisco: Jossey-Bass.

Grumet, M. (1988). *Bitter milk: Women and teaching.* Amherst, MA: University of Massachusetts Press.

Hamzeh, M. (2012). *Pedagogies of deveiling: Muslim girls & the Hijab discourse.* North Carolina: Information Age.

Hamzeh, M., & Oliver, K. L. (2012). 'Because I am Muslim, I cannot wear a swimsuit': Muslim girls negotiate participation opportunities for physical activity. *Research Quarterly for Exercise and Sport, 83*(2), 330–339.

Hills, A. (2006). Playing the field(s): An exploration of change, conformity and conflict in girls' understandings of gendered physicality in physical education. *Gender and Education, 18*(5), 539–556.

Hills, L. (2007). Friendship, physicality, and physical education: An exploration of the social and embodied dynamics of girls' physical education experiences. *Sport, Education and Society, 12*(3), 317–336.

hooks, b. (1995). *Killing rage: Ending racism.* New York: Henry Holt.

Kirk, D. (1992). *Defining physical education: The social construction of a school subject in postwar Britain.* London: Falmer.

Kirk, D., & Tinning, R. (1994). Embodied self-identity, healthy lifestyles and school physical education. *Sociology of Health and Illness: A Journal of Medical Sociology, 16*(5), 600–625.

Markula, P. (1995). Firm but shapely, fit but sexy, strong but thin: The postmodern aerobicizing female bodies. *Sociology of Sport Journal, 12*, 424–453.

McDermott, L. (2000). A qualitative assessment of the significance of body perception to women's physical activity experiences: Revisiting discussions of physicalities. *Sociology of Sport Journal, 17*, 331–363.

Oliver, K. L. (1999). Adolescent girls' body-narratives: Learning to desire and create a 'fashionable' image. *Teachers College Record, 101*(2), 220–246.

Oliver, K. L. (2001). Images of the body from popular culture: Engaging adolescent girls in critical inquiry. *Sport, Education & Society, 6*, 143–164.

Oliver, K. L. (2010). The body, physical activity and inequity: Learning to listen *with* girls *through* action. In M. O'Sullivan & A. MacPhail (Eds.), *Young people's voices in physical education and youth sport* (pp. 31–48). London: Routledge.

Oliver, K. L., & Garrison, J. (1996). A narrative journey: Beyond the myth of the mind/body and self/society dualisms. *Proceedings of the Fortieth Annual Meeting of the South Atlantic Philosophy of Education Society*, 55–65.

Oliver, K. L., & Hamzeh, M. (2010). 'The boys won't let us play': 5th grade *mestizas* publicly challenge physical activity discourse at school. *Research Quarterly for Exercise and Sport, 81*(1), 39–51.

Oliver, K. L., Hamzeh, M., & McCaughtry, N. (2009). 'Girly girls *can* play games'/'*Las niñas pueden jugar tambien*': Co-creating a curriculum of possibilities with 5th grade girls. *Journal of Teaching in Physical Education, 28*(1), 90–110.

Oliver, K. L., & Kirk, D. (2014). Towards an activist approach to research and advocacy for girls and physical education. *Physical Education and Sport Pedagogy, 19*, 1–15.

Oliver, K. L., & Kirk, D. (2014). *Girls, gender and physical education: An activist approach.* London: Routledge.

Oliver, K. L., & Lalik, R. (2000). *Bodily knowledge: Learning about equity and justice with adolescent girls.* New York: Peter Lang.

Oliver, K. L., & Lalik, R. (2001). The body as curriculum: Learning with adolescent girls. *The Journal of Curriculum Studies, 33*(3), 303–333.

Oliver, K. L., &. Lalik, R. (2004a). Critical inquiry on the body in girls' physical education classes: A critical poststructural analysis. *Journal of Teaching in Physical Education, 23*(2), 162–195.

Oliver, K. L., & Lalik, R. (2004b). 'The beauty walk, this ain't my topic': Learning about critical inquiry with adolescent girls. *The Journal of Curriculum Studies, 36*(5), 555–586.

O'Sullivan, M., Siedentop, D., and Locke, L. (1992). Toward collegiality: Competing viewpoints among teacher educators. *Quest, 44*(2), 266–280.

Satina, B., & Hultgren, F. (2001). The absent body of girls made visible: Embodiment as the focus in education. *Studies in Philosophy and Education, 20*, 521–534.

Velija, P., & Kumar, G. (2009). GCSE physical education and the embodiment of gender. *Sport, Education and Society, 14*(4), 383–399.

Vertinsky, P. A. (1992). Reclaiming space, revisioning the body: The quest for gender-sensitive physical education. *Quest, 44*(3), 373–396.

Ukpokodu, O. N. (2009). Pedagogies that foster transformative learning in a multicultural education course: A reflection. *Journal of Praxis in Multicultural Education, 4*(1), Article 4. DOI: 10.9741/2161-2978.1003.

Whitehead, M. (1990). Meaningful existence, embodiment and physical education. *Journal of the Philosophy of Education, 24*, 3–14.

Whitehead, M. (2010). *Physical literacy: Throughout the lifecourse.* London: Routledge.

Wolf, N. (1991). *The beauty myth: How images of beauty are used against women.* London: Random House.

Wright, J. (1995). A feminist poststructuralist methodology for the study of gender construction in physical education: Description of a study. *Journal of Teaching in Physical Education, 15*, 1–24.

Wright, J., & King, R. C. (1990). 'I say what I mean,' said Alice: An analysis of gendered discourse in physical education. *Journal of Teaching in Physical Education, 10*(2), 210–225.

Young, I. M. (1980). Throwing like a girl: A phenomenology of feminine body comportment motility and spatiality. *Human Studies, 3*, 137–156.

21

GENDER SEXUALITY AND PHYSICAL EDUCATION

Katie Fitzpatrick, UNIVERSITY OF AUCKLAND, NEW ZEALAND

& Eimear Enright, UNIVERSITY OF QUEENSLAND, AUSTRALIA

In this chapter, we aim to explore 'transformative' pedagogies of physical education (PE) and consider what these approaches might mean for addressing issues of gender sexuality[1] in the field. We do not assume that there is a singular transformative approach but we do argue that some pedagogies have greater potential to be transformative than others. Specifically, we look at how transformative approaches might directly challenge narrow norms of gender sexuality in PE. It is important to note here that the word 'transformative' is used in a wide variety of ways in education (for example, Cummins & Sayers, 1995; Taylor & Cranton, 2012). In this chapter, we draw on critical approaches to transformative pedagogy that align with the field of critical pedagogy (Freire, 1970; Giroux, 2011; hooks, 2010; Kincheloe, 2008) and the sociology of the body (Evans, Davies, & Wright, 2004; Gard & Wright, 2005; Shilling, 2012). In so doing, we suggest that transformative approaches to PE require attention to the social and political contexts within which they occur, and which articulate with practice in complex ways. This is crucial in considering issues of gender sexuality because, as we explain below, these are expressed in PE settings at the intersection of body, culture, and practice (Butler, 1999; Shilling, 2012).

We begin by defining transformative pedagogy and then explaining our theoretical approach to gender sexuality. We use the two terms here together (as gender sexuality, rather than as gender *and* sexuality) because we argue that these are intertwined. We then consider work in the field of PE, and education more generally, directly addressing issues of gender sexuality. In the second half of the chapter we offer a few examples of transformative approaches to gender sexuality from our own practice. We discuss these as 'moments' or possibilities rather than suggesting they are fully articulated modes of practice.

Transformative pedagogy

Typologies come with the obvious risk of glossing over specificities and differences. While acknowledging the potential for reductionism, Wink (2005) suggests that thinking about pedagogy as one of transmissive, generative, or transformative provides a useful starting point for teacher reflection. Similar three point typologies abound in the literature, such as Miller and Seller's (1990) – transmissional, transactional, and transformational – and Cummins' (2005) – transmissive, constructivist, and transformative. This consistency in terminology reflects a broadly shared set of educational concerns: control and power sharing, what counts as legitimate knowledge, how meaning is constructed, and intended learning outcomes.

Transmissive pedagogy, sometimes referred to as traditional pedagogy (Rogers, 1969) or 'banking education' (Freire, 1970), is premised on the beliefs that the teacher's job is to impart knowledge to students, and that teachers' knowledge is more legitimate than students'. In the transmissive classroom, the teacher initiates and controls interactions, knowledge is most often viewed as fixed and inert, and learning equates to memorisation. Scholars have also claimed that transmissive pedagogies presuppose docile, passive students in classrooms characterised by a lot of teacher talk and a lot of student listening (Freire, 1970; Giroux, 2011).

The roots of generative pedagogy, sometimes called progressive, constructivist, social constructivist, or experiential pedagogy, can be traced at least as far back as to the work of Dewey and Montessori. In the generative classroom, knowledge is conceptualised as catalytic, meaning it is the catalyst or inspiration for further inquiry (Cummins & Sayers, 1995). Advocates of the generative classroom favour learning that is collective and collaborative. However, these approaches have been criticised for focusing too narrowly on the teaching and learning relationship and failing to articulate a coherent vision of the broader social implications of instruction. For example, Reyes (1992) has suggested that generative pedagogies may be just as blind as transmissive pedagogies to diverse social realities within and beyond the classroom.

Transformative pedagogy is sometimes used interchangeably with critical pedagogy (Wink, 2005). Cummins and Sayers (1995) describe it as an orientation that draws on collaborative critical inquiry to relate curricular content to students' lives, and focuses on the analysis and transformation of social realities. Ukpokodu (2009) defines it as "an activist pedagogy combining the elements of constructivist and critical pedagogy" and notes that it aims to empower "students to examine critically their beliefs, values, and knowledge with the goal of developing a reflective knowledge base, an appreciation for multiple perspectives, and a sense of critical consciousness and agency" (Ukpokodu, 2009, p. 43).

Irrespective of how it is defined, it is an orientation to pedagogy firmly rooted in Freirean, critical, and feminist theories that, for its advocates, seeks to be grounded in the lives of students and is participatory, activist, culturally sensitive, academically rigorous, hopeful, and critical. Student voice in this regard is central and "describes the many ways in which youth actively participate in school decisions that affect their lives and the lives of their peers" (Mitra, 2008, p. 20). The student voice movement supports a shift in the status of students in schools from passive objects to active participants, and student voice advocates often position their work as transformative (Hodgkin, 1998).

Transformative pedagogy in physical education

In the last 30 years, many scholars in the field of PE have observed the limitations of transmissive and generative approaches, and advocated instead for transformational pedagogies. While they have not necessarily used these terms, work in critical pedagogy, critical inquiry, and the politics of the field are clearly concerned with transformation. Perhaps because of its explicit focus on movement, bodies, and physicality, scholars have claimed that PE is potentially a key site for transformative practice (Fitzpatrick, 2010; Gard, 2006). Although the literature gives more attention to theoretical critique (Azzarito & Solmon, 2005; Fernández-Balboa, 1995, 1997; Kirk & Tinning, 1990; Wright, Macdonald, & Burrows, 2004), numerous examples of transformative practice do exist, some of which address gender, sexuality, and, specifically, the PE experiences of girls. Feminist, critical, and activist scholars have, for example, demonstrated how producing knowledge in collaboration with girls can support them in transforming oppressive practices within their local PE and physical activity contexts (Enright & O'Sullivan. 2010, 2012; Fisette 2011; Fisette & Walton 2014; Hamzeh & Oliver, 2012; Oliver, Hamzeh, & McCaughtry, 2009; Oliver & Kirk, 2014; Oliver & Lalik, 2001, 2004a, 2004b). Although less numerous, pedagogical studies concerned with reshaping constructions of masculinity have also been reported (Gard, 2003a, 2003b, 2004a; Hickey & Fitzclarence, 1999; Tischler & McCaughtry, 2011). Others illustrate what a critical multicultural pedagogy might look like and draw attention to the impact of narrow gendered and racialised discourses on notions of the physical (Azzarito, 2009; Fitzpatrick, 2010, 2013). With respect to sexuality and gender identities, other scholars have addressed the ways that PE marginalises particular gender expressions, and silences the experiences of lesbian, gay, bisexual, transgender, and queer youth (Clarke, 2000; Coll, O'Sullivan, & Enright, 2013; McGlashan, 2013; Sykes, 2011) and teachers (Clarke, 1997, 1998a, 1998b, 1998c, 2002, 2003; Squires & Sparkes, 1996; Sykes, 2001; Woods, 1992). There is, however, a dearth of work based on transforming practices in school PE around issues of sexuality (Fitzpatrick & McGlashan, in press; Sykes, 2011).

There are many commonalities across these pedagogical studies; they all espouse a commitment to student centred, critical, culturally aware, and democratic education. While interpretations of these terms may differ, above all this work emphasises the importance of understanding the subtleties of context. Transformative pedagogy is not a pedagogical 'model' that can be easily transplanted from one context to another. It is "the outcome of particular struggles and is always related to the specificity of particular contexts, students, communities, and available resources" (Giroux, 2011, p. 4). In relation to gender sexuality then it is important to attend to the specificities of both geographical contexts and how the body is gendered and sexualised in PE in different ways across sites. How scholars then approach gender sexuality theoretically is important. In order to transform inequitable practices, we need to understand the ontological bases for assumptions about gender sexuality and how these ultimately inform practice in the field.

Gender sexuality, the body, and theory

The field of PE, like other sites, is undoubtedly a site of gendered practice. Unlike other sites, however, and in its connection with sporting cultures, PE seems to produce particularly heightened expressions of gender sexuality. This is perhaps to do with the focus on physicality and the centrality of the body within the field (Dismore, 2007; Shilling, 2004), although Youdell (2005) argues that schools circumscribe gender in ways that are more delimiting than other spaces. Nevertheless, schools and PE are both framed by wider discourses of the body that form gender and sexuality in particular ways. Scholars have approached these issues from different theoretical perspectives, including naturalistic, socially constructed, in relation to social justice and disadvantage, and body capital (Shilling, 2012). In the field of PE, issues of inclusion and disadvantage have dominated (Clarke, 2006; Dagkas & Armour, 2012; Ennis, 1999; Flintoff & Scraton, 2006; Oliver & Hamzeh, 2010; Penney, 2002; Wright, 1996, 1997) although in sociologically oriented scholarship, a number of theoretical approaches have been used. While Connell's (1989, 1995) notion of hegemonic masculinity has been influential (e.g. Brown & Rich, 2002; Messner & Sabo, 1990; Parker & Curtner-Smith, 2012; Skelton, 1993), in the last 15 years, the theoretical perspectives of Judith Butler, Michel Foucault, and Pierre Bourdieu have been particularly significant.

Butler and Foucault

Butler (1999) argues that gender is constituted in relation to sexuality via, what she calls, the 'heterosexual matrix'. She argues that sex is "produced precisely through the regulatory practices that generate coherent identities through the matrix of coherent gender norms" (pp. 24–25). This requires "discrete and asymmetrical oppositions between 'feminine' and 'masculine' where these are understood as expressive attributes of 'male' and 'female'" (p. 24). Youdell (2005) explains this as a sex–gender–sexuality constellation. Such a constellation, she argues, constitutes sex, gender, and sexuality in particular ways "that open up possibilities and set limits for 'who' a student can be" (p. 250). She argues that within the constellation:

> the female body is already feminized, the feminine is already heterosexual, the hetero-feminine is already female. Sex–gender–sexuality, then, are not causally related; rather, they exist in abiding constellations in which to name one category of the constellation is to silently infer further categories. (p. 256)

The power of this constellation concerns the levels of intelligibility rendered. Youdell (2005) points out that for one to step outside of the constellation – or to embody an unexpected variation – is a move towards unintelligibility. So, the masculine-woman is questionable and is assumed to be lesbian. The masculine-heterosexual-woman is bordering on unintelligible. Such levels of unintelligibility potentially disrupt the gender-sexuality norms, although they may also reinforce them. Indeed, Youdell (2005) argues that, even when young people disrupt the constellation they also reinforce it because their 'difference' is quickly labelled as abhorrent or dismissed as the exception to the rule. Gender and sexuality then, according to this framework, are in constant articulation and are socially constructed, rather than naturalistic. Sykes (2011) argues that Butler's notion that heterosexuality is the original 'normal' from which other sexualities emanate "enables us to think about why there is continual, repetitive anxiety about learning, becoming and 'proving' normal heterosexuality in PE spaces" (p. 25). A number of scholars in the field have found Butler's thinking productive for challenging gender sexuality norms (see, for example, Clarke, 2004; Hills & Croston, 2012; Larsson, 2014; Larsson, Redelius, & Fagrell, 2011; Martino & Beckett, 2004).

Shilling (2012) argues that, along with Butler, Foucault's (1977, 1978) work has also been enormously influential in understanding gender, sexuality, and the body (and Butler, indeed, draws heavily on Foucault). The work of Foucault has proven productive in critiquing gendered representations and expressions of the body in PE (e.g. Garrett, 2004; Kirk, 2000; Larsson, 2013; McCuaig, 2007; Wright, 1997) and other physical contexts, such as sport and exercise (e.g. Markula & Pringle, 2006).

Along with Butler, Foucauldian thinking has also been critiqued for its dismissal of the material body (Larsson, 2014; Shilling, 2012) and, therefore, biological expressions of gender sexuality. As Shilling (2012) observes, "Butler's view of the performative constitution of bodies is suggestive, but it overlooks how embodiment and materiality themselves participate in performances and are not just effects of those enactments" (p. 214). Larssen (2014) points out that there is an undeniable tension in the field of PE pertaining to issues of the material body versus the body as social construction.

Bourdieu

The notion of physical capital mediates this position somewhat by acknowledging both the socially located nature of the body and, therefore, gender sexuality, but also the embodied and physical expressions of culture (Shilling, 2012). Scholars employing the notion of physical capital draw on the sociology of Pierre Bourdieu (1977, 1984, 1986, 1990) and theorise culture, and specifically social class, as resident and recognisable in the body via habitus (dispositions, expressions, and world view). Habitus is in constant dynamic articulation with the field (the social context in which it is formed) and is thus a bodily expression of cultural expectations, norms, and what Bourdieu understands as social capital. Capital takes many forms but is the recognition of prestige, power, and status within the field; essentially what stands for success.

McNay (1999) argues that Bourdieu's ideas apply particularly well to gender concerns because they highlight the materiality of the body and the expression of culture via bodily hexis. Shilling (2012) argues that bodily practices (including gendered forms of movement) are formed both by and within the contexts one engages in over time. Situated action then results from cultural context and individual strategic involvement in that context. Physical capital is both developed and employed strategically within a social field, according to the boundaries of that field and the possibilities for development. Skeggs (2004) argues "embodiment is the product of the composition and volumes of capital that can be accrued and carried by the body and the fit between the habitus (the disposition organising mechanism) and the field" (p. 22). In PE contexts, certain gendered habitus are a fit with the field while others are not; related norms of gender sexuality are then inscribed and reinscribed within the field in ongoing ways. This has a great deal to do with how the field of PE reproduces rather than disrupts norms, and how particular forms of femininity and masculinity are rewarded and reproduced. PE scholars have employed Bourdieu's notions of capital, field, and habitus to better understand gendered relations of power in the field (e.g. Brown, 2005; Fitzpatrick, 2013; Gorely, Holroyd, & Kirk, 2003; Hills, 2007; Hunter, 2004).

If we are to transform the field of PE and challenge the multiple ways the field reproduces narrow gender sexuality norms, we suggest that transformative approaches (rather than the transmissive or constructivist approaches we discussed earlier) hold the greatest potential. Transformative pedagogies both acknowledge the gendered nature of the field and aim to directly address relations of power, drawing on various theoretical perspectives to produce praxis. In the final section of this chapter, we offer examples of transformative pedagogies from our own practice. We do not offer these here as any kind of universal answer or suggest others should take up these specific approaches. We are, rather, responding to the critique that there are too few examples of applied critical practice in education and in PE (Wright, MacDonald, & Burrows, 2004). These small examples are offered here with the intention of sharing transformative practice, however messy, fraught, context-specific, and imperfect.

Doing transformative gender sexuality practice in physical education

Katie: teacher education and transformative practice

If we accept that gender sexuality is both socially constructed and material, then addressing these issues in the field requires an analysis of both social context and materiality, including bodily expression and experience. hooks (2010) argues that critical approaches to issues of power in education begin with personal experiences. One approach to transformative pedagogies in PE might be personal biographies (for example, Dowling, 2012). These can help to name and expose the norms of cultural practice we live. Bourdieu understands this via the metaphor of a fish in water. He explains that the fish cannot see the water, the cultural norms, it is swimming in: "when habitus encounters a social world of which it is the product, it finds itself 'as a fish in water', it does not feel the weight of the water and takes the world about itself for granted"

(Bourdieu in interview with Wacquant, 1989, cited in Grenfell & James, 1998 p. 16). I (Katie) use this metaphor in my own undergraduate teaching to facilitate students to begin to see the water we are all swimming in and to identify how norms of gender sexuality (and other issues) are reproduced in PE.

I teach a course called 'curriculum issues in health and PE'. The students in the course are all studying to be teachers of health and PE in secondary schools, and the course is completed in the final year of a four-year programme. As part of the course, students are required to read bell hooks' account of her experiences in her book, *Teaching Critical Thinking: Practical Wisdom* (2010). hooks begins the book with an account of growing up and attending university amid racially segregated communities in the USA in the middle of the twentieth century. She talks directly about the racism and sexism she experienced in education contexts, but she also highlights the importance of the teachers who humanised and who attended to the experiences and struggles of students. The students in my class are then required to write personal biographies of their PE experiences at the intersection of gender, sexuality, ethnicity, culture, and social class. They can represent these in creative ways via story, narrative, and poetry. Following this task, we explore a range of issues in the fields of health and PE (these two subjects are interwoven in curriculum in New Zealand) and we draw on a range of literature in the field which questions gender sexuality, ability, racialisation, body size, health, and so forth (for example: Burrows & Wright, 2004; Gard, 2004b; Hokowhitu, 2008; Rich, Holroyd, & Evans, 2004; Sykes & McPhail, 2008). For their next assignment, the students each have to form what I call a 'bold statement'. This statement is an argument for something they would like to change or advocate for or against. It must be related to health and PE and is a kind of 'moot' which they argue for and defend orally in front of the class. They must draw on research evidence to support their argument.

One of the students from my class in 2014, Will Elliot, presented his argument to the class and then submitted his bold statement as an opinion piece to the *New Zealand Physical Educator.* This publication is sent to all schools and is a mixture of practitioner-based articles and research articles. Therein, Will argued that girls and boys should not be separated for PE lessons, as is the case in some schools. He drew on the literature to argue that:

> The messages we send about the reasons why we would separate female students from males says something in itself. The arguments for single sex PE often include that females are intimidated by males which can often be construed as females are not as dominant at sport as males are. These serve to reinforce the power relationships which privilege males over females.
>
> What's more, by separating classes based on their observable physical attributes we are alienating those students who may appear male or female based on the way they look, but actually identify with other genders. In doing so, we would reinforce the idea of heteronormativity.
>
> I argue that many of the issues which single sex PE claim to remedy are not actually remedies at all, they are just pushing the issues to one side, rather than confronting them in classes. Additionally I believe that arguments for single sex PE often cite girls' non participation as an issue. I believe this issue is perhaps more of a reflection on a teacher's pedagogy in that they have created a class environment which is not inclusive. (Elliot, 2014, p. 15)

What is significant about Will's argument is that, while he was undoubtedly influenced by the readings and discussions in the class and the perspectives of other students, his bold statement, like those of other students, came from his own concerns about gender sexuality practice in schools. He was drawing on praxis to argue for change and transformation in the field of PE in a specific way that linked directly to the practice of schools.

Eimear: on seeing and being in a heteronormative world

The flâneur was a bourgeois man of nineteenth century French society, able to walk through the streets of the newly renovated Paris experiencing the sights, sounds, and smells of modern life, while still maintaining a distance from that which he observed. As a connoisseur of the streets, the flâneur was not only "just looking" (Bowlby, 1985), but rather seeing and being in the world in ways that intrinsically revealed meaningful, cultural critique and commentary (Ritzer, 2007). Introducing the concept of the 'flâneur' to my (Eimear's) PE teacher education (PETE) students was the starting point for a visual diary task I engaged students with on a third year sociology course. We began by acknowledging the historical background of the term, and considering the gendering of the flâneur as masculine and the excluded/invisible feminine flâneuse (Wolff, 1985). We then discussed what it might mean to be a flâneur/flâneuse in the twenty-first century. We drew on Kenway and Bullen's (2008) notion of 'the youthful cyber-flâneur' to help us think about the focus of inquiry, the landscape travelled, and the tools that might be used in contemporary flânerie:

> …today the object of the young cyberflâneur's inquiry is the global cultural economy and he or she is not limited by territoriality or time. The young cyberflâneur uses information and communications technologies (ICTs) as tools for inquiry and digital technologies for the production of visual and written commentary and critique. (Kenway & Bullen, 2008, p. 24)

I then introduced the visual diary task, which centred on gender. Students were asked to keep a four-week visual diary of their gendered PE, sport, and physical activity experiences. I prompted them to focus this diary on a variety of facets of their everyday lives, including watching televised sporting events, attending sport events, their own sport and leisure worlds, and sports media. I also suggested they consider exploring both the physical world and the virtual geographies that ICTs allow them to access. As cyberflâneurs the students drew on multiple genres (photographs, advertisements, social media, news stories, sports shows, sports club communications and websites, and so on) and chose to embed multi-media formats (image and text, audio and video, hyper text and hyper links) in their interactive visual diaries to reflect upon and articulate their critique. Students gathered advertisements, photographs of their own sporting clubs, pictures of toys and books, sports websites, flyers for sports attire, social media postings, blog sites, YouTube clips, and much more. They wrote short narratives about these photos in their diaries. These diaries then became the focus of classroom debate and also individual essays, where students were asked to make sense of their diary and the social construction of gender in relation to the literature we had been reading (e.g. Bernstein, 2002; Burrows & Wright, 2004; Coakley & Pike, 1998; Dewar, 1987; Gorely et al., 2003; Sykes & McPhail, 2008). Discussion of the visual diaries revolved around how gender norms are inscribed in how people move, gesture, eat, dress, talk, and act, assumptions of heterosexuality, cultural myths and stereotypes, media coverage of women in sport, and how omnipresent little symbols of gender sexuality differentiation are.

In anonymous course feedback two PETE students shared the following:

> I thought it was going to be an airy-fairy [course] to begin with but first impressions were wrong. The visual diary made me start to see things I hadn't noticed before. You

step outside of yourself. I'm a male and I'm going to be a PE teacher ... Embarrassed that I hadn't been more critical of media coverage of females before this. Normally, I wouldn't be one for the more theoretical [courses], but this worked. (Anonymous Male Student)

Loved the [course]. The visual diary was the best part of it. Taking the photos, collecting other images and texts, making a diary from them, looking at our own lives in a different way and having conversations about what this might mean for the students we teach. I think it's changed my perspectives on gender a lot. I didn't think about how gender inequality affects everyone before. I'm challenged now to do something about gender inequality in sport and in PE ... (Anonymous Female Student)

These two students evidence a transformation of sorts. They speak about 'seeing things they hadn't noticed before' and 'looking at our own lives in different ways'. Like Katie's example of transformative practice in teacher education, these students have been involved in a process of naming and exposing the norms of cultural practice that we live. The diary task and their positioning as flâneurs/flâneuses required them to 'step outside of [themselves]' and led to some of them articulating a transformative intent. Worth highlighting here, however, is that for a minority of students on this course this visual diary task specifically was "a waste of time ... another [course] that took away from time we could be doing practical stuff" (Anonymous male student). This student voice reminds us that while we can work to create conditions which might support transformation, we can never be sure that our efforts will be well received or will actually lead to transformation.

Transformative work with young people

We have both taught in transformative ways and researched transformative practice with young people in schools (see Enright & O'Sullivan, 2012, 2013; Fitzpatrick, 2010, 2013; Fitzpatrick & Russell, 2015). During this work we have learnt a lot about the importance of valuing student voice, employing collaborative and reciprocal methodologies, and the centrality of relationships with youth. Critically, research with youth is only truly transformative if it engages young people with the politics by which they live. In this sense, such research should focus on the issues that are important for young people in their own communities and seek to enhance their knowledge of these issues and their ability to act for social change. Of course, researchers are working within and among relations of power with young people. Being the 'adult researcher' among school students is simultaneously a position of power and one of alienation. The researcher in this setting has no real purpose: s/he is not a teacher or a student but some kind of intermediary, perhaps an observer, a pedagogue, a provocateur, an activist, a listener, and so forth. These depend on the kind of research being undertaken, the questions being asked, and the context. Young people are also dealing with wider power inequities at the intersection of gender sexuality, ethnicity, culture, and social class. The notion of youth voice cannot be naïve to these issues and researchers seeking student voice must consider who is given more/less voice and why (Rodríguez & Brown, 2009). Youth research scholars are in agreement that forming trusting relationships with young people is central to successful research of this kind (Cammarota & Fine, 2008; Madison, 2012; Tobin & Kincheloe, 2006), but it is also invariably messy and imperfect. We advocate for researchers in this sense to be especially sensitive to the voices of youth, for therein lies real potential for truly transformative pedagogies.

Final thoughts

In this chapter, we have attempted to explore the potential for transformative work in PE that attends to issues of gender sexuality. It is important to note that, while there is no singular approach to transformative practice, this work comes from and attends to concerns of social justice, exclusion, and inequities in the field. These are apparent in PE in complex ways, and theories of gender sexuality, as well as current research in the field, remind us how insidious gendered relations of power are. Nevertheless, scholars and educators working in critical ways to expose and challenge narrow norms of gender sexuality in PE have shown that transformational work with young people in schools and in teacher education is both possible and productive, especially when this work is done with the meaningful reciprocal engagement of young people themselves.

Reflective questions for discussion

1. Why do the authors use the terms 'gender sexuality' together (rather than 'gender *and* sexuality' or 'gender, sexuality')?
2. Why is it important to understand various theoretical approaches to gender sexuality?
3. What might transformative approaches to PE in your context look like?
4. How might these differ from transmissive or generative approaches?
5. The authors state that transformative teaching is not a model. What are the limitations of models-based practice, and why are these not typically transformative?

Note

1 We use the term gender sexuality here (rather than 'gender, sexuality' or 'gender and sexuality') to highlight the interconnectedness with which these two concepts are both read and performed (Butler, 1999). We explain this in more detail further below.

References

Azzarito, L. (2009). The panopticon of physical education: Pretty, active and ideally white. *Physical Education and Sport Pedagogy, 14*(1), 19–39.

Azzarito, L., & Solmon, M. A. (2005). A reconceptualization of physical education: The intersection of gender/race/social class. *Sport, Education and Society, 10*(1), 25–47.

Bernstein, A. (2002). Is it time for a victory lap? Changes in the media coverage of women in sport. *International Review for the Sociology of Sport, 37*(3–4), 415–428.

Bourdieu, P. (1977). *Outline of a theory of practice* (R. Nice, Trans.). Cambridge, UK: Cambridge University Press.

Bourdieu, P. (1984). *Distinction: A social critique of the judgment of taste* (R. Nice, Trans.). London: Routledge & Kegan Paul.

Bourdieu, P. (1986). The forms of capital. In J. Richardson (Ed.), *Handbook of theory and research for the sociology of education* (pp. 241–258). Westport, CT: Greenwood Press.

Bourdieu, P. (1990). *The logic of practice* (R. Nice, Trans.). Malden, MA: Polity Press.

Bowlby, R. (1985). *Just looking: Consumer culture in Dreiser, Gissing and Zola.* New York: Methuen.

Brown, D. (2005). An economy of gendered practices? Learning to teach physical education from the perspective of Pierre Bourdieu's embodied sociology. *Sport, Education and Society, 10*(1), 3–23.

Brown, D., & Rich, E. (2002). Gender positioning as pedagogical practice in teaching physical education. In D. Penney (Ed.), *Gender and physical education: Contemporary issues and future directions* (pp. 80–99). London: Routledge.

Burrows, L., & Wright, J. (2004). The good life: New Zealand children's perspectives on health and self. *Sport, Education and Society, 9*(2), 193–205.

Butler, J. (1999). *Gender trouble: Feminism and the subversion of identity.* London: Routledge.

Cammarota, J., & Fine, M. (2008). Youth participatory action research: A pedagogy for transformational resistance. In J. Cammarota & M. Fine (Eds.), *Revolutionizing education: Youth participatory action research in motion* (pp. 1–12). New York: Routledge.

Clarke, G. (1997). Playing a part: The lives of lesbian physical education teachers. In G. Clarke & B. Humberstone (Eds.), *Researching women and sport* (pp. 36–49). London: Macmillan.

Clarke, G. (1998a). 'Working out': Lesbian teachers and the politics of (dis)location. *Journal of Lesbian Studies, 2*(4), 85–99.

Clarke, G. (1998b). Voices from the margins: Lesbian teachers in physical education. PhD dissertation, Leeds Metropolitan University.

Clarke, G. (1998c). Queering the pitch and coming out to play: Lesbians in physical education and sport 1. *Sport, Education and Society, 3*(2), 145–160.

Clarke, G. (2000). Crossing borders: Lesbian physical education students and the struggles for sexual spaces. In S. Scraton & B. Watson (Eds.), *Sport, leisure identities and gendered spaces* (pp. 75–94). Eastbourne, UK: Leisure Studies Association.

Clarke, G. (2002). Difference matters: Sexuality and physical education. In D. Penney (Ed.), *Gender and physical education: Contemporary issues and future directions* (pp. 41–56). London: Routledge.

Clarke, G. (2003). There's nothing queer about difference: Challenging heterosexism and homophobia in physical education. In S. Hayes & G. Stidder (Eds.), *Equity and inclusion in physical education and sport: Contemporary issues for teachers, trainees and practitioners* (pp. 91–104). London: Routledge.

Clarke, G. (2004). Threatening space: (Physical) education and homophobic body work. In J. Evans, B. Davies, & J. Wright (Eds.), *Body knowledge and control: Studies in the sociology of physical education and health* (pp. 191–203). London: Routledge.

Clarke, G. (2006). Sexuality and physical education. In D. Kirk, D. Macdonald, & M. O'Sullivan (Eds.), *Handbook of physical education* (pp. 723–740). London: Sage.

Coakley, J. J., & Pike, E. (1998). *Sport in society: Issues and controversies.* Boston, MA: Irwin/McGraw-Hill.

Coll, L., O'Sullivan, M., & Enright, E. (2013, December). 'How come girls can wear earrings and guys can't?': Students regulating and resisting gender and sexuality norms in school. Paper presented at the Australian Association for Research in Education (AARE) Annual Conference, Adelaide, Australia.

Connell, R. W. (1989). Cool guys, swots and wimps: The interplay of masculinity and education. *Oxford Review of Education, 15*(3).

Connell, R. W. (1995). *Masculinities.* Los Angeles: University of California Press.

Cummins, J. (2005). A proposal for action: Strategies for recognizing HL competence as a learning resource within the mainstream classroom. *Modern Language Journal, 89*, 585–592.

Cummins, J., & Sayers, D. (1995). *Brave new schools: Challenging cultural illiteracy through global learning networks.* New York: St. Martin's Press.

Dagkas, S., & Armour, K. (Eds.). (2012). *Inclusion and exclusion through youth sport.* Abingdon, UK: Routledge.

Dewar, A. M. (1987, December). The social construction of gender in physical education. *Women's Studies International Forum, 10*(4), 453–465.

Dismore, H. (2007). The attitudes of children and young people towards physical education and school sport, with particular reference to the transition from Key Stage 2 to Key Stage 3. Unpublished PhD, Canterbury Christ Church University.

Dowling, F. (2012). A narrative approach to research in physical education, youth sport and health. In F. Dowling, H. Fitzgerald, & A Flintoff (Eds.), *Equity and difference in physical education, youth sport and health: A narrative approach* (pp. 37–59). London: Routledge.

Elliot, W. (2014). Co-educational schools should not implement single sex physical education: An opinion piece by Will Elliot (year 4 BPE student, University of Auckland). *New Zealand Physical Educator, 47*(2), 15.

Ennis, C. D. (1999). Creating a culturally relevant curriculum for disengaged girls. *Sport, Education and Society, 4*(1), 31–49.

Enright, E., & O'Sullivan, M. (2010). 'Can I do it in my pyjamas?' Negotiating a physical education curriculum with teenage girls. *European Physical Education Review, 16*(3), 203–222.

Enright, E., & O'Sullivan, M. (2012). Physical education 'in all sorts of corners': Student activists transgressing formal physical education curricular boundaries. *Research Quarterly for Exercise and Sport, 83*(2), 255–267.

Enright, E., & O'Sullivan, M. (2013). 'Now, I'm magazine detective the whole time': Listening and responding to young people's complex experiences of popular physical culture. *Journal of Teaching in Physical Education, 32*(4), 394–418.

Evans, J., Davies, B., & Wright, J. (Eds.). (2004). *Body knowledge and control: Studies in the sociology of physical education and health.* London: Routledge.

Fernández-Balboa, J.-M. (1995). Reclaiming physical education in higher education through critical pedagogy. *Quest, 47*(1), 91–114.

Fernandez-Balboa, J.-M. (Ed.). (1997). *Critical postmodernism in human movement, physical education and sport.* Albany, NY: State University of New York Press.

Fisette, J. L. (2011). Negotiating power within high school girls' exploratory projects in physical education. *Women in Sport and Physical Activity Journal, 20*(1), 73–90.

Fisette, J. L., & Walton, T. A. (2014). 'If you really knew me' … I am empowered through action. *Sport, Education and Society, 19*(2), 131–152. doi:10.1080/13573322.2011.643297

Fitzpatrick, K. (2010). A critical multicultural approach to physical education. *Critical Multiculturalism: Theory and Praxis, 177.*

Fitzpatrick, K. (2013). *Critical pedagogy, physical education and urban schooling.* New York: Peter Lang.

Fitzpatrick, K., & McGlashan, H. (2016). Rethinking straight pedagogy: Gender sexuality and PE. In D. Robinson, & L. Randall (Eds), *Social justice in physical education: Critical reflections and pedagogies for change* (pp. 102–121). Ontario: Canadian Scholars Press.

Fitzpatrick, K., & Russell, D. (2015). On being critical in health and physical education, *Physical Education and Sport Pedagogy, 20*(2), 159–173.

Flintoff, A., & Scraton, S. (2006). Girls and physical education. In D. Kirk, D. Macdonald, & M. O'Sullivan (Eds.), *Handbook of physical education* (pp. 767–783). London: Sage.

Foucault, M. (1977). *Discipline and punish: The birth of the prison.* New York: Vintage Books.

Foucault, M. (1978). *The history of sexuality, Vol. 1: An introduction.* New York: Pantheon Books.

Freire, P. (1970). *Pedagogy of the oppressed.* New York: Continuum.

Gard, M. (2003a). Being someone else: Using dance in anti-oppressive teaching. *Educational Review, 55*(2), 211–223.

Gard, M. (2003b). Moving and belonging: Dance, sport and sexuality. *Sex Education, 3*(2), 105–118.

Gard, M. (2004a). Movement, art and culture: Problem-solving and critical inquiry in dance. In J. Wright, D. Macdonald, & L. Burrows (Eds.), *Critical inquiry and problem-solving in physical education* (pp. 93–104). London: Routledge.

Gard, M. (2004b). An elephant in the room and a bridge too far, or physical education and the 'obesity epidemic'. In J. Evans, B. Davies, & J. Wright (Eds.), *Body knowledge and control: Studies in the sociology of physical education and health* (pp. 68–82). London: Routledge.

Gard, M. (2006). More art than science? Boys, masculinities and physical education. In D. Kirk, D. Macdonald, & M. O'Sullivan (Eds.), *Handbook of physical education* (pp. 784–795). London: Sage.

Gard, M., & Wright, J. (2005). *The obesity epidemic: Science, morality and ideology.* London: Routledge.

Garrett, R. (2004). Gendered bodies and physical identities. In J. Evans, B. Davies, & J. Wright (Eds.), *Body knowledge and control: Studies in the sociology of physical education and health* (pp. 140–156). London: Routledge.

Giroux, H. (2011). *On critical pedagogy.* New York: Continuum Books.

Gorely, T., Holroyd, R., & Kirk, D. (2003). Muscularity, the habitus and the social construction of gender: Toward a gender relevant physical education. *British Journal of Sociology Education, 24,* 429–448.

Grenfell, M., & James, D. (1998). *Bourdieu and education: Acts of practical theory.* London: Falmer Press.

Hamzeh, M., & Oliver, K. (2012). 'Because I am Muslim, I cannot wear a swimsuit': Muslim girls negotiate participation opportunities for physical activity. *Research Quarterly for Exercise and Sport, 83*(2), 330–339.

Hickey, C., & Fitzclarence, L. (1999). Educating boys in sport and physical education: Using narrative methods to develop pedagogies of responsibility. *Sport, Education and Society, 4*(1), 51–62.

Hills, L. (2007). Friendship, physicality, and physical education: An exploration of the social and embodied dynamics of girls' physical education experiences. *Sport, Education and Society, 12*(3), 317–336.

Hills, L., & Croston, A. (2012). 'It should be better all together': Exploring strategies for 'undoing' gender in coeducational physical education. *Sport, Education and Society, 17*(5), 591–605.

Hodgkin, R. (1998). Partnership with pupils. *Children UK, 17,* 11.

Hokowhitu, B. (2008). Understanding the Maori and Pacific body: Towards a critical physical education. *New Zealand Physical Educator, 41*(3), 81–91.

hooks, b. (2010). *Teaching critical thinking: Practical wisdom.* New York: Routledge.

Hunter, L. (2004). Bourdieu and the social space of the physical education class: Reproduction of Doxa through practice. *Sport, Education and Society, 9*(2), 175–192.

Kenway, J., & Bullen, E. (2008). The global corporate curriculum and the young cyberflaneur as global citizen. In N. Dolby & F. Rizvi (Eds.), *Youth moves: Identities and education in global perspective* (pp. 17–32). New York & London: Routledge.

Kincheloe, J. (2008). *Critical pedagogy primer.* New York: Peter Lang.

Kirk, D. (2000). Gender associations: Sport, state schools and Australian culture. *The International Journal of the History of Sport, 17*(2–3), 49–64.

Kirk, D., & Tinning, R. (Eds.). (1990). *Physical education, curriculum and culture: Critical issues in the contemporary crises.* Lewes, UK: Falmer.

Larsson, H. (2013). Sport physiology research and governing gender in sport – a power–knowledge relation? *Sport, Education and Society, 18*(3), 334–348,

Larsson, H. (2014). Materialising bodies: There is nothing more material than a socially constructed body. *Sport, Education and Society, 19*(5), 637–651.

Larsson, H. Redelius, K., & Fagrell, B. (2011). Moving (in) the heterosexual matrix: On heteronormativity in secondary school physical education. *Physical Education and Sport Pedagogy, 16*(1), 67–81.

Madison, D. S. (2012). *Critical ethnography: Method, ethics, and performance* (2nd edn). Thousand Oaks, CA: Sage.

Markula, P., & Pringle, R. (2006). *Foucault, sport and exercise: Power, knowledge and transforming the self.* London: Routledge.

Martino, W., & Beckett, L. (2004). Schooling the gendered body in health and physical education: Interrogating teachers' perspectives. *Sport, Education and Society, 9*(2), 239–251.

McCuaig, L. (2007). Sitting on the fishbowl rim with Foucault: A reflexive account of HPE teachers' caring. *Sport, Education and Society, 12*(3), 277–294.

McGlashan, H. (2013). Dare to be deviant: Reflective experiences of gay youth in physical education. Unpublished Masters of Professional Studies Dissertation. University of Auckland.

McNay, L. (1999). Gender, habitus and the field: Pierre Bourdieu and the limits of reflexivity. *Theory, Culture & Society, 16*(1), 95–117.

Messner, M. A., & Sabo, D. F. (Eds.). (1990). *Sport, men, and the gender order: Critical feminist perspectives.* Champaign, IL: Human Kinetics.

Miller, J. P., & Seller, W. (1990). *Curriculum perspectives and practices.* Toronto, ON: Copp Clark Pitman, Ltd.

Mitra, D. L. (2008). Amplifying student voice. *Educational Leadership, 66*(3), 20–25.

Oliver, K., & Hamzeh, M. (2010). 'The boys won't let us play': Fifth-grade Mestizas challenge physical activity discourse at school. *Research Quarterly for Exercise and Sport, 81*(1), 38–51.

Oliver, K. L., Hamzeh, H., & McCaughtry, N. (2009). 'Girly girls can play games'/'Las niñas pueden jugar tambien': Co-creating a curriculum of possibilities with 5th grade girls. *Journal of Teaching in Physical Education, 28*(1), 90–110.

Oliver, K. L., & Kirk, D. (2014). Towards an activist approach to research and advocacy for girls and physical education. *Physical Education and Sport Pedagogy, 21*(3), 313–327.

Oliver, K. L., & Lalik, R. (2001). The body as curriculum: Learning with adolescent girls. *The Journal of Curriculum Studies, 33*(3), 303–333.

Oliver, K. L., & Lalik, R. (2004a). Critical inquiry on the body in girls' physical education classes: A critical poststructural analysis. *Journal of Teaching in Physical Education, 23*(2), 162–195.

Oliver, K. L., & Lalik, R. (2004b). 'The beauty walk, this ain't my topic': Learning about critical inquiry with adolescent girls. *The Journal of Curriculum Studies, 36*(5), 555–586.

Parker, M. B., & Curtner-Smith, M. D. (2012). Sport Education: A panacea for hegemonic masculinity in physical education or more of the same? *Sport, Education and Society, 17*(4), 479–496.

Penney, D. (Ed.). (2002). *Gender and physical education: Contemporary issues and future directions.* London: Routledge.

Reyes, M. de la Luz. (1992). Challenging venerable assumptions: Literacy instruction for linguistically different students. *Harvard Educational Review, 62*, 427–446.

Rich, E., Holroyd, R., & Evans, J. (2004). 'Hungry to be noticed': Young women, anorexia and schooling. In J. Evans, B. Davis, & J. Wright (Eds.), *Body, knowledge and control: Studies in the sociology of physical education and health* (pp. 173–190). London: Routledge.

Ritzer, G. (Ed.). (2007). *The Blackwell encyclopedia of sociology* (Vol. 1479). Malden, MA: Blackwell Publishing.

Rodríguez, L. F., & Brown, T. M. (2009). From voice to agency: Guiding principles for participatory action research with youth. *New Directions for Youth Development, 2009*(123), 19–34.

Rogers, C. (1969). *Freedom to learn.* Columbus, OH: Merrill.

Shilling, C. (2004). Physical capital and situated action: A new direction for corporeal sociology. *British Journal of Sociology of Education, 25*(4), 473–487.

Shilling, C. (2012). *The body and social theory*. London: Sage.

Skeggs, B. (2004). Context and background: Pierre Bourdieu's analysis of class, gender and sexuality. In L. Atkins & B. Skeggs (Eds.), *Feminism after Bourdieu* (pp. 19–33). Oxford, UK: Blackwell Publishing.

Skelton, A. (1993). On becoming a male physical education teacher: The informal culture of students and the construction of hegemonic masculinity. *Gender and Education, 5*(3), 289–303.

Squires, S., & Sparkes, A. (1996). Circles of silence: Sexual identity in physical education and sport. *Sport, Education and Society, 1*(1), 77–101.

Sykes, H. (2001). Understanding and overstanding: Feminist-poststructural life histories of physical education teachers. *Qualitative Studies in Education, 14*(1), 13–31.

Sykes, H. (2011). *Queer bodies: Sexualities, genders and fatness in physical education*. New York: Peter Lang.

Sykes, H., & McPhail, D. (2008). Unbearable lessons: Contesting fat phobia in physical education. *Sociology of Sport Journal, 25*(1), 66–96.

Taylor, E. W., & Cranton, P. (Eds.). (2012). *The handbook of transformative learning: Theory, research and practice*. San Francisco: John Wiley & Sons Ltd.

Tischler, A., & McCaughtry, N. (2011). Physical education is not for me: When boys' masculinities are threatened. *Research Quarterly for Exercise and Sport, 82*(1), 37–48.

Tobin, K., & Kincheloe, J. (2006). *Doing educational research: A handbook*. Rotterdam, The Netherlands: Sense.

Ukpokodu, O. (2009). The practice of transformative pedagogy. *Journal on Excellence in College Teaching, 20*(2), 43–67.

Wink, J. (2005). *Critical pedagogy: Notes from the real world*. Boston: Pearson.

Wolff, J. (1985). The invisible flâneuse: Women and the literature of modernity. *Theory, Culture & Society, 2*(3), 37–46.

Woods, S. (1992). Describing the experiences of lesbian physical educators: A phenomenological study. In A. C. Sparkes (Ed.), *Research in physical education and sport: Exploring alternative visions* (pp. 90–117). London: Falmer Press.

Wright, J. (1996). The construction of complementarity in physical education. *Gender and Education, 8*(1), 61–80.

Wright, J. (1997). The construction of gendered contexts in single sex and co-educational physical education lessons. *Sport, Education and Society, 2*(1), 55–72.

Wright, J., MacDonald, D., & Burrows, L. (Eds.). (2004). *Critical inquiry and problem-solving in physical education*. London: Routledge.

Youdell, D. (2005). Sex-gender-sexuality: How sex, gender and sexuality constellations are constituted in secondary schools. *Gender and Education, 17*(3), 247–270.

22

THE TRANSFORMATIVE POSSIBILITIES OF NARRATIVE INQUIRY

Fiona Dowling, NORWEGIAN SCHOOL OF SPORT SCIENCES, NORWAY

& Robyne Garrett, UNIVERSITY OF SOUTH AUSTRALIA, AUSTRALIA

Narrative inquiry

Narrative inquiry is best described as an approach to research that is cross-disciplinary and extremely diverse theoretically and methodologically (Riessman, 2008). Narrative research in PE reflects this variety (Dowling, Garrett, lisahunter, & Wrench, 2015). Common across the disparate perspectives is, however, the notion that narration is fundamental to human meaning-making: we construct ourselves via the stories we tell. Individual and collective embodied experience is mediated, and indeed, made 'real' via the linguistic shaping and telling of stories, and the processes of their consumption. Narratives are thus inevitably relational. The teller and the 'listener' are active meaning-making agents, and 'small' or what we can call personal stories are inevitably linked to 'big' or societal stories that are socio-economically and culturally situated.

Stories are crafted at the intersections of identity axes and socio-cultural locations such that a young woman, for example, who narrates a tale of disaffection in PE classes inevitably draws upon biographical experiences as well as public discourses of gender, gender (in)equality in PE, and education more broadly. The narrative scholar's research agenda will similarly be a narrative reflecting personal circumstances, PE's research agenda, and educational research agendas in local, national, and global perspectives.

Narratives are thus imbued with power. Because of their different life experiences and resources, individuals in PE (students, parents, teacher educators, researchers) have different access to narrative repertoires and are differentially positioned with regard to 'hearing' and interpreting stories. Moreover, stories can be (ab)used to meet a range of political ends. Whilst recognising power at play it is, of course, important to recognise the agentic possibility of learning to retell or re-story one's experience by using new repertoires and by constructing counter-narratives of resistance to challenge repressive stories (Harris, Carney, & Fine, 2001). Collective narratives of resistance can lead to the re-structuring of the inequitable matrices of public stories. Feminists and critical race theorists have long since recognised the potential for narratives to disrupt taken-for-granted social practices and evoke social change (hooks, 1997), as have critical pedagogues (e.g. Freire, 1971). Clearly the latter is of pertinence to our discussion of transformative pedagogies.

In that light, this chapter will explore the potential of narrative inquiry to bring about enhanced understanding about the social worlds of PE contexts and to transform social inequalities within them. We will start by discussing how we perceive narrative inquiry, transformative pedagogies, and the social injustices that are prevalent in PE today. We will position narrative inquiry in a historical context and thereafter present an overview of the most relevant research carried out during the past decade. The collective findings of the various studies will foreground a discussion about how narrative inquiry can be developed in the future within the field of PE (theoretically and practically), and in particular, address what narrative pedagogical strategies might be useful, and why, for the purpose of transforming inequitable relations.

Transformative pedagogies

Turning to our understanding of transformative pedagogies, we share Giroux's (2011) belief that the fundamental challenge facing educators today within the current climate of neo-liberalism is

> the need to provide the conditions for students to address how knowledge is related to the power of both self-definition and social agency. Central to such a challenge is providing students with the skills, knowledge, and authority they need to inquire and act upon what it means to live in a substantive democracy, to recognise anti-democratic forms of power, and to fight deeply rooted injustices in a society and world founded on systemic economic, racial and gender inequalities. (p. 72)

Against a societal backcloth of broad social inequalities, physical educators might, for example, more specifically need to help students understand how power operates in constructing contemporary PE lessons as a space where greater numbers of young men feel at home compared to young women; how White, Eurocentric physical movement traditions dominate today's curriculum; how certain body shapes are valued more than others; how some young people engage in destructive self-monitoring body regimes whereas others resist them; or why some sports activities dominate PE lesson content whilst other movement forms are marginalised. PE teachers aiming to create transformative pedagogical classrooms would, in other words, aim to provide learning environments in which students can develop skills for critical analysis and self-reflection, become knowledgeable and willing to make moral judgements, and act in socially responsible ways as integral to the ongoing process of democratisation (Giroux, 2011). Cognisant of postmodern and postcolonial theories we acknowledge the need to perceive democracy as an on-going, unfinished project rather than being defined by a definitive formula (Giroux, 2011).

Drawing upon the wealth of philosophical perspectives that inform the broad field of critical pedagogy, such transformative pedagogical classrooms would be founded upon developing a culture of PE and schooling that supports the empowerment of the culturally marginalised and economically disenfranchised and unmasks claims like 'all' students have equal access to learning in PE. They would draw attention to the historicity of PE knowledge and practice and promote a dialectical view of knowledge that functions to unveil the connections between objective knowledge and the cultural norms, values, and standards of society. They would show how ideology operates at a deep, psychological personal level as well as in society at large and demystify the asymmetrical power relations and social arrangements that sustain the hegemonic interests of the ruling class. Transformative classrooms would also incorporate a theory of resistance and counter-hegemony and show how theory and practice are inextricably linked to our understanding of the social world and the actions we take. Finally they would illuminate the rights and freedom of students to become subjects of their world (Darder, Baltodano, & Torres, 2003). Central to this approach to education is the dialogical relationship between students and teacher and a problem-solving pedagogy. Rejecting traditional notions of the teacher as expert who transmits privileged knowledge, a critical pedagogy builds on the premise that students learn from teachers and teachers learn from students via engaging in dialogue and analysis that serve as a foundation for reflection and action (Darder et al., 2003). Students and teachers alike can become emancipated via the development of a critical social consciousness ('conscientisation'): they develop a deepening awareness of the social realities that shape their lives and discover capacities to re-create them.

Reflecting debates in education research more broadly, we acknowledge that there has been widespread criticism of a critical pedagogical approach to PE in schools and in teacher education from those who disagree with its premises (e.g. O'Sullivan, Siedentop, & Locke, 1992) and from advocates who have encountered the challenges of its implementation (e.g. Gore, 2003; Ruiz & Fernández-Balboa, 2005). We will not rehearse the arguments here but agree with Tinning's (2002) call for a 'modest' critical pedagogy and address them below as they relate to our discussion of narrative inquiry. On taking a closer look at how narrative inquiry and a modest critical pedagogy may complement each other and transform social relations, we believe they enable teacher educators and students to individually and collaboratively critically analyse the lived experiences of individuals in PE and sport, as well as the broader structures that shape them (Oliver, 1998). In particular they enable the voices of the marginalised to be 'heard' and through their recognition of the socio-historical construction of knowledge pave the way for past 'truths' to be relinquished and challenged by alternative claims. They are both interested in interrogating and disrupting notions of master narratives and the processes of co-construction of truths (whose voice is heard, whose is silenced, and with what consequences?). They reject simplistic, universal knowledge claims and resist closure, acknowledging the complexity, moral ambiguity, and fragmentary nature of ways of knowing. They are both founded upon the principle that practice and theory are inevitably interrelated. Moreover, a modest critical pedagogy and narrative inquiry recognise that knowledge is both cognitive and emotionally embodied, as well as political; transformation most often occurs in unstable moments at the intersections of the (un)conscious and in relation to imagined (more just) worlds.

Narrative inquiry in physical education research: its historical context and current issues

Narrative research focusing on social injustices in PE contexts has been carried out in the broad field of qualitative research and draws upon different ontological and epistemological positions, mirroring narrative inquiry in general. Whilst recognising the vital role that interpretive narrative research has played in paving the way for more critical narrative inquiry, we shall nevertheless concentrate upon studies that have explicitly been concerned with the concepts of critical pedagogy, emancipation, and social transformation. (For readers interested in tracing more general developments in narrative inquiry in PE see Armour, 2006 and Dowling et al., 2015.)

Our discussion is limited to research publications written in English and can be seen to promote neo-colonial values, which is not our intention. The review is not exhaustive and there are inevitably oversights for which we apologise. We aim, however, to provide the reader with a feel for the emerging field and exemplify the similarities as well as the diversity in theoretical and methodological concerns. Narrative inquiry as a strategy in critical pedagogy research and practice can best be characterised as a new and emerging field. The first studies appeared in the late 1990s and there has been a significant increase during the past five years. Some scholars have been concerned with sharing their experiences of using critical pedagogy in their classrooms whilst others have had a greater focus on composing resources for critical pedagogy. A number of studies spotlight pre-service teachers' experiences of potentially transformative learning situations whereas others illuminate the critical pedagogical worlds of teacher educators; a few inquiries straddle both. We will start by taking a closer look at the latter.

Tinning (1997) was a pioneer in using narrative in critical pedagogy. He developed a postgraduate course monograph that integrated personal, fictional tales from the classroom with multiple theoretical texts to illuminate the links between personal, political, and intellectual commitments, and values and beliefs in education. Another influential scholar in the field of PE/sport is Sparkes. Much of his early research was located within a broader discussion of the philosophy of science, challenging traditional positivist and postpositivist ways of knowing in PE culture and signposting the way for postmodern sensibilities. In 1997, he published an innovative paper in which he firmly rooted the discussion within a critical pedagogical framework. The paper addresses a number of issues ranging from his own awareness of oppressed gay voices in PE teacher education (PETE), his moral duty as a teacher educator to transform power relations that lead to oppression, and a growing recognition of the seeming dissonance between his espoused critical pedagogical philosophy and his actual teaching practices. Acutely aware that simply changing the course content of a module entitled 'Ideologies in PE' to include articles on sexual identity, "might smack of tokenism, particularly in an academic world that suffocates itself with the rhetoric of political correctness without any real hunger for tasting the dangers of political action" (Sparkes, 1997, p. 26), he embarked upon creating an evocative ethnographic fiction in order to engage students in critical reflection. He aimed to inform, awaken, and disturb pre-service teachers' involvement in social processes that can be oppressive. By appealing to their narrative mode of knowing he intended "to cut through the scientised comfort zone of many students and allow them to explore often ignored or repressed dimensions of their own subjectivity" (Sparkes, 1997, p. 34). The ethnographic fiction is a tale about a gay PE teacher, a successful rugby player, a one-time popular jock, who is forced to lead a double life for fear of being stigmatised on account of his sexual identity. The story shows glimpses of family relations, the need to constantly negotiate challenging PE student situations, and the workings of heterosexual norms in schools and society beyond. Citing Ellis (1995), Sparkes aimed to draw readers to question the authenticity of the text, to reflect upon its contingencies and not least, their complicity in its existence. By refraining from providing the reader with theoretical explanations for the tale, his intention, like that of Barone's (1995), was to enable the reader to tell self-stories and furthermore to engage in educational storytelling and sharing about possible interpretations of the 'fiction'. Herein lies the narrative and critical pedagogical strategy for bringing about possible transformation although Sparkes readily admits that for many students the story concerns 'Other' PETE environments and it is seldom easily interwoven into individual student narratives.

'Giving' Voice

Indeed, a central lesson to be drawn from the paper, of equal importance today as it was nearly two decades ago, is the issue of 'voice'. Sparkes (1997) addresses the dilemma of how to invite students to discuss inequalities and injustices in a non-threatening and supportive manner in a classroom which is inevitably wrought with power relations. He draws attention to the power dynamics in 'giving voice' to the marginalised – the narrative about the gay PE teacher is inextricably linked to Sparkes' own heterosexual, privileged majority narrative – and the inevitable co-construction of knowledge. The reader is integral to a story's construction and its consumption is unpredictable: is it taken on board, re-worked, and/or rejected? Whilst Sparkes witnessed students' engagement with the text he highlights the impossibility of knowing whether their 'critical' reflection acts as an "occasion for conspiracy", leading them to borrow the story as a means for improving reality. The latter is a theme Sykes and Goldstein (2004) develop in their anti-homophobia work in PETE. They contend that juxtaposing narratives is necessarily unpredictable in the critical pedagogical classroom drawing upon postmodern pedagogy and queer theory. Recognising that meaning is perpetually being deferred and grasped, teachers and students alike must accept uncertain outcomes not least when acknowledging that the unconscious also plays a part in how we come to know.

Sykes and Goldstein's (2004) Canadian study, whilst also addressing sexual identity, moves beyond Sparkes' (1997) paper to explore the potential of more participatory engagement with the creation of texts as well as their consumption. Using a video based on interview data with gay and lesbian PE teachers, as well as interview transcriptions, students in an elective course were invited to deconstruct and disrupt institutionalised and individual expressions of homophobia and heterosexism in schools by writing and enacting a performance ethnography. This embodied enactment of 'Others' and subjective experiences of discrimination could potentially lead to 'shifting positions' in the visual classroom when someone recognises "a stuck place, a point of resistance, a moment that cannot be understood … a practice of coping in a fecund and affirmative way without knowing what must be done" (Sykes & Goldstein, 2004, p. 58). In keeping with the notion of dialogical teaching and learning and the concept of praxis, the teacher educators and students alike were engaged in this process of problem-solving. One of the students reflected afterwards that she was more willing to take up the position of an activist in anti-homophobic work although this was not voiced by others. Once again we are therefore left with the impression that any transformation appears to be confined to a politics of recognition rather than a politics of redistribution (Apple, 2008).

Garrett's (2006) study using critical storytelling as a means of giving voice to girls' marginalised voices in Australian PE and to interrupt PETE students' overwhelming positive and uncritical experience of PE as a school subject provides yet another example of the varying degrees of success with regard to transforming students' positions. The project sought to combine multiple levels of critical analysis and practice. First, young women's stories from PE classes were co-constructed with the teacher educator/researcher to recreate feelings of marginalisation. Second, pre-service teachers were asked to read these narratives made available online and to respond to them as part of an on-going dialogue with fellow PETE students about processes of domination in PE. Third, as a result of this dialogue, the pre-service teachers were asked to develop and teach micro teaching sessions that reflected possible means of resisting discriminatory teaching and learning situations identified in the girls' stories. Conversations between the teacher educators and pre-service teachers revealed how some students developed greater empathy and emotional connections to the imagined PE worlds of marginalised students whereas others reported merely superficial engagement with their plights. In 2011, Garrett and Wrench built upon these findings and sought to use critical storytelling to address a range of inequity issues. They concluded that a major challenge in critical pedagogical classrooms using narrative inquiry is pre-service teachers' (in)ability to engage in high level abstraction required to translate stories, via theory, into their practice.

Resistance to narrative ways of knowing

Another finding across several studies (e.g. Dowling, Fitzgerald, & Flintoff, 2015; Garrett & Wrench, 2011; Sparkes, 1997) is the resistance shown to narrative ways of knowing from both students and teacher educator colleagues. Steeped in bio-behavioural ways of knowing, dominant PETE discourses marginalise narrative modes of knowing, as they also tend to marginalise teacher educators who promote narrative inquiry and critical pedagogy. By crafting a 'writerly rather than a readerly text', Dowling, Fitzgerald, and Flintoff (2015) invite readers to fill in the blanks of their collective narrative about trying to create more socially just classrooms in PETE by filling them with personal meaning from outside the text. Their study re-visits Sparkes' (1997) observation about the seeming disjuncture between espoused critical pedagogical intentions and teacher educators' practice. By sharing glimpses from some collective biographies in PETE they aim to provoke collective critical reflection amongst teacher educators concerning the extent to which taken-for-granted assumptions about knowledge claims are problematised. The study reveals how personal interests can dominate curricula initiatives and silence other equally relevant issues. The authors attempt to show the cracks in the rational dialogue of the Enlightenment and argue for the need to be more circumspect in our claims to know about how best to achieve emancipatory outcomes, echoing the earlier concerns of Gore (1990, 2003) and Tinning (2002). The postmodern study demonstrates the fragmentary and often contradictory nature of attempting to transform classrooms and pre-service teachers'/teacher educators' beliefs. It highlights the vulnerability of engaging in this type of work in academia, steeped as it is in traditional forms of knowing, but simultaneously reminds us of the rewards found in creating the conditions for the 'teachable moment' of possible transformation. Imbued with human emotions, the insecure pedagogical space of recognising that a familiar story can be told in a new way and reveal cracks in an authoritative tradition, can prove exhilarating and is a motivation for critical pedagogues to continue to swim against the technocratic tide.

Teacher educator self-reflexive narratives

In fact, a recent development in critical narrative inquiry is the increase in studies about PE teacher educators' narratives from the collaborative and dialogical classroom. Rather than merely inviting pre-service teachers to interrogate their storylines, scholars/teacher educators have turned a conscious gaze upon themselves and their relations to the production of knowledge and power in PE. Flintoff, Dowling, and Fitzgerald (2015) combine narrative inquiry, critical race theory, and a Whiteness lens to disrupt dominant ideas about 'race' and reveal the powerful silences in PETE research concerning antiracism. Sykes (2014) uses self-reflexive personal narratives to 'un-settle' assumptions about theories and methodologies used to research sexuality, gender, and sex in sport studies, in particular to illustrate how scientific racism and Western theoretical imperialism underpins much contemporary knowledge. By telling and sharing personal stories she becomes engaged in the process of relinquishing taken-for-granted truths in the belief that this can open up new imagined ways of being and her narratives invite the reader to (re)visit her/his own 'colonial closet'. Together these studies represent a clear shift in PE's critical pedagogy narrative from an early position that easily could be characterised as bordering on the dogmatic and founded upon restricted notions of emancipation (Tinning, 2002) to a position that grapples with the complexities of the on-going process of democratisation and social theory.

Counter-narratives

A relatively large number of studies fall into the category of providing PE culture with counter-narratives. Positioning their research within a critical pedagogical framework narrative scholars present evocative stories from a range of oppressive structures with which to 'talk back' and "expose the lies which hold together the ideological armour of privilege, domination and oppression" (Harris et al., 2001, p. 14). Acknowledging that teaching is a political act, Flintoff (2014) provides tales from the previously silenced voices of black and minority ethnic pre-service teachers in PETE to show how 'race', ethnicity, and gender are interwoven in individuals' embodied, everyday experiences of learning how to teach. Stride (2014) crafts analytic narratives to draw the reader into the agentic experiences of South Asian, Muslim girls in school PE/physical activity as a means to trouble stereotypes of them as passive, frail, and oppressed. Fitzgerald and Stride (2012) and Berg Svendby and Dowling (2012) challenge ableism in PE and deficit narratives of young people with disabilities. In 2012, an entire collection of counter-narratives celebrating difference in PE, youth sport, and health was published (Dowling, Fitzgerald, & Flintoff, 2012) that also included discussions of re-storying and deconstructing tales. It remains to be seen whether these studies can contribute to transformation but they symbolise the sustained interest in narrative inquiry as a possible tool for critical pedagogy.

Implications for evidence-based practice for current physical education challenges

Narrative inquiry does not provide the same kind of evidence as expected in some academic circles (Sparkes, 1997). It can appear removed from the techno-rational knowledge and truths of the bio-sciences and bio-behavioural research. While the form and content of narrative work are inseparable, texts are not intended to have one fixed meaning or social reality. Rather narrative researchers write authentic stories that mirror local realities and honour participants. They also recognise their constitutive role in crafting the texts when they attempt to capture the complexities, nature, and feeling of lived experience. In line with the principles of critical pedagogy in postmodern times, the way stories are written and whose voices are prioritised, have major implications for how they are understood and acted upon in transformative ways. Therefore in judging the quality of narrative work as an evidence base we are less inclined to draw from positivist thinking and ask whether a narrative is valid, reliable, or mirrors an objective reality. Rather it is more appropriate to ask: Is it useful? Is it connected and consistent? Does it 'cohere' with other research? In critical and transformative work narratives need to be authentic in the sense of being 'true to life' (Eisner, 1997; Smith, 2009). They need to persuade us to revisit taken-for-granted values and practices and provide a catalyst to develop empathetic understandings of 'the world of others'. Stories should affect us in sensory as well as emotional and cognitive ways and should avoid closure in order to allow for new stories to evolve (Dowling, 2012).

Current and on-going challenges within PE extend to interrogating and demystifying dominant notions of gender, sexuality, performance, whiteness, and 'healthy' bodies that continue to underpin PE curriculum and pedagogy. Transformation comes with respecting difference in terms of ethnicity, gender, and body size as well as challenging self-regulatory technologies, performance codes, and a techno-rational version of PE that continues to alienate. In negotiating these dominant power relations interrogation is needed of the structures and cultures that shape participants' stories within frameworks that celebrate, constrain, or oppress (Sparkes, 2006). This work is not without its challenges and must be positioned within a social and cultural landscape. The on-going and pervasive pedagogical work of the media continues to present narrow ideals around acceptable and healthy bodies which are becoming increasingly globalised. So too, in the absence of on-going professional development and narrow curriculum initiatives, the personal investment and subjective identities of many experienced teachers/educators in a techno-rational version of PE limits their openness to alternative versions. However, most powerful and limiting in the contemporary moment are neo-liberal schooling and university agendas that focus on accountability, self-regulation, and performance outcomes. These structural frameworks work to homogenise and globalise educational policy, curriculum, and pedagogy (Lingard, 2010). They can marginalise learning areas like PE and create risks for those who challenge hegemonic truths where, by standing out as radical, we become visible and thus vulnerable (Shor & Friere, 2003).

In taking a transformative role, critical and narrative research in PE promotes a dialectical view of knowledge and unveils the social arrangements that sustain inequity. It is not just about the generation of knowledge for research, but helping participants produce knowledge about themselves (Enright & O'Sullivan, 2011) as well as the skills and authority to act upon their lives. In supporting Foucault's (1979) assertion that 'power produces knowledge and knowledge produces power' the potential in narrative work is for young people to deconstruct dominant discourses, gendered ideals, and embodied identities. Teachers, too, can recognise their roles in the process of identity formation and enculturation as a means to produce alternative narratives. However, in working toward praxis where theory and practice are inextricably linked, noticing and understanding are not enough. Whilst narrative inquiry may open the door for multiple voices to be heard, transformation is enacted through awareness as well as action beyond practices that reproduce gendered, classed, raced, and narrow forms of physicality. This action is essential to provide the transformative spaces that allow a multiplicity of meanings about bodies, health, and physicality.

Future directions

This chapter has outlined how narrative scholars have developed their knowledge claims upon a range of ontological and epistemological theories. Whilst many claims have been made around the potential of narrative inquiry to bring about transformative change, changes in thinking, feeling, and understanding do not always lead to changes in practice, pedagogy, and outcomes for students. In altering power dynamics, giving voice and co-constructing knowledge we accept uncertain outcomes that are fragmented and sometimes contradictory. While it is difficult to say anything definitive about narrative genres, given their diversity and incompleteness, it is just as important not to collapse stories into categories where personal narratives are always more complex than any 'cultural analysis' can indicate (Squire, 2008, p. 57). Certainly circumspection is needed when making claims of emancipatory outcomes. While it is important to acknowledge what knowledge is gleaned from this research and in what ways these insights have informed practice, we must not overstate outcomes of change and transformation. So too, when researchers leave sites after data has been generated, participants can be left with more questions than answers. Dialogue might serve as the foundation for reflection but problem-solving and activism is then needed to take theory out of the abstract and into reality (Darder et al., 2003).

Nor do we wish to replace 'what is broken' by casting new norms and models upon others. In acknowledging insights from postmodernism, the challenge for transformation is to create a process that opens up possibilities for equality and inclusion in PE without substituting a new 'replacement' position or practice that is 'better' for an old one (Bain, 1997, p. 188). Rather, we aspire to develop self-conscious and self-critical practices that allow multiple representations in an on-going process of democracy (Giroux, 2011). In following Denzin (2010), we believe in a future characterised by mutual respect for different waves of qualitative inquiry and the types of knowledge insights they provide, as well as nurturing collaborative dialogue between narrative inquiry and activist research that is based on a body of narrative work (Oliver & Kirk, 2016). In striving toward linking theory and practice, praxis can be found in collaborative projects that work to identify the transformative, dialogical, counter-hegemonic strategies, practices, and pedagogy that provide multiple mainstreams and stories of success. Narrative research with its attention to temporality reminds us that our research agendas, methodologies, and theoretical lenses are neither decontextualised nor ahistorical. We must not discount persistent findings as 'old news' but rather hear 'new stories' framed within ever evolving and emerging theories that unveil new and novel insights (Dowling, Garrett, lisahunter, & Wrench, 2015).

In challenging neo-liberal agendas and moving toward praxis, a principal question for narrative inquirers is not the study of authorised curriculum revisions but rather how teachers and students make sense of curriculum in light of the social spaces and histories of their schools, the stories of their lives, and interactions with increasingly complex groups. This focus embraces a constructivist position that is different from traditional methods where students are assumed to be passive knowledge receivers and teachers are experts in executing the transmission of approved subject matter (Craig, You, & Oh, 2012, p. 272). Rather, the teacher is repositioned to negotiate curriculum 'alongside the lives of learners' (Murphy & Pushor, 2010). As self-acting agents rather than self-regulatory, teachers and students can tell stories, relive and retell, provoke changes in practices, and socially change the educational landscape. Stories of collaborative curriculum-making are meaningful not only to those who have lived and experienced them but to others for whom collaborative curriculum-making might inspire PE stories to live by (Craig, You, & Oh, 2013).

As a form of pedagogy, narrative has a potential to do critical work. It encourages critical thinking and creates spaces where those most affected in PE can speak on their own behalf and define who they are and who they want to be. It provides a framework for interaction and the challenge of hegemony by drawing attention to the centrality of lived experience and appreciating the intricate relationships between learning, teaching, and life (Chan, 2012). In creating pedagogies of possibility participants can be authors of change and generate stories of success that others might build on. Narrative inquiry can also contribute politically. It can contribute to equality, particularly in ways that perceive difference as a resource rather than a problem. Narrative can help us to work towards a re-negotiation of PE that broadens the legitimate learning spaces and directs us to new forms of physical expression. It offers a democratic and inclusive approach to knowledge construction that can meet the research challenges of a global postmodern world (Dowling, Garrett, lisahunter, & Wrench, 2015).

We must continue to listen. We must keep asking whose voices are not being heard. If we do not continue to take small steps and produce spaces where those most affected can articulate their experiences and their embodiment then nothing will slow the forces of dominant discourses and socially constructed ideals that continue to disempower.

Reflective questions for discussion

1. In the light of research findings that reveal persistent inequalities in PE contexts, such as girls' disengagement (e.g. Garrett, 2006) or the marginalisation of students with a disability (e.g. Berg Svendby & Dowling, 2012; Fitzgerald & Stride, 2012), how can critical narrative inquiry contribute to a greater understanding of the complex ways in which these inequalities occur?
2. If dialogue and problem-solving are central features of a critical pedagogical PE class, how can narrative ways of knowing contribute to these learning strategies?
3. In an education system that currently valorises certainty of learning outcomes, what barriers might an educator espousing narrative inquiry encounter and how can they be resisted?
4. How can narrative inquiry help deconstruct the ways in which certain truths in PE become more valued than other truths? e.g. why bio-behavioural narratives dominate practice.

References

Apple, M. (2008). Is deliberated democracy enough in teacher education? In M. Cochran-Smith, S. Feiman-Nemser, D. J. McIntyre, & K. Demers (Eds.), *Handbook of research on teacher education: Enduring questions in changing contexts* (3rd ed., (pp. 105–110). New York: Routledge & the Association of Teacher Educators.

Armour, K. (2006). The way to a teacher's heart: Narrative research in physical education. In D. Kirk, D. MacDonald, & M. O'Sullivan (Eds.), *The handbook of physical education* (pp. 467–485). London: Sage.

Bain, L. (1997). Transformation in the postmodern era: A new game plan. In J. Fernandez-Balboa (Ed.), *Critical postmodernism in human movement, physical education and sport* (pp. 183–196). Albany, NY: State University of New York Press.

Barone, T. (1995). Persuasive writings, vigilant readings, and reconstructed characters: The paradox of trust in educational storysharing. In J. Amos Hatch & R. Wisniewski (Eds.), *Life history and narrative* (pp. 63–74). London: Falmer Press.

Berg Svendby, E., & Dowling, F. (2012). Negotiating the discursive spaces of inclusive education: Narratives of experience from contemporary PE. *Scandinavian Journal of Disability Research, 15*(4), 361–378. http://dx.doi.org/10.1080/15017419.2012.735200

Chan, E. (2012). The transforming power of narrative in teacher education. *Australian Journal of Teacher Education, 37*(3), 111–127.

Craig, C., You, J., & Oh, S. (2012). Why school-based narrative inquiry in physical education? An international perspective. *Asia-Pacific Journal of Education, 32*(3), 271–284.

Craig, C., You, J., & Oh, S. (2013). Collaborative curriculum making in the physical education vein: A narrative inquiry of space, activity and relationship. *Journal of Curriculum Studies, 45*(2), 169–197.

Darder, A., Baltodano, M., & Torres, R. (2003). Critical pedagogy: An introduction. In A. Darder, M. Baltodano, & R. Torres (Eds.), *The critical pedagogy reader* (pp. 1–21). London: RoutledgeFalmer.

Denzin, N. (2010). *The qualitative manifesto: A call to arms.* Walnut St, CA: Left Coast Press.

Dowling, F. (2012). A narrative approach to research in PE, youth sport and health. In F. Dowling, A. Flintoff, & H. Fitzgerald (Eds.), *Equity and difference in physical education, youth sport and health: A narrative approach* (pp. 37–59). London: Routledge.

Dowling, F., Fitzgerald, H., & Flintoff, A. (Eds.). (2012). *Equity and difference in physical education, youth sport and health: A narrative approach.* London: Routledge.

Dowling, F., Fitzgerald, H., & Flintoff, A. (2015). Narratives from the road to social justice in PETE: Teacher educator perspectives. *Sport, Education & Society, 20*(8), 1029–1047. http://dx.doi.org/10.1080/13573322.2013.871249

Dowling, F., Garrett, R., lisahunter, & Wrench, A. (2015). Narrative inquiry in physical education research: The story so far and its future promise. *Sport, Education & Society, 20*(7), 924–940. http://dx.doi.org/10.1080/13573322.2013.857301

Eisner, E. (1997). The new frontier in qualitative research methodology. *Qualitative Inquiry, 3*, 259–273.

Enright, E., & O'Sullivan, M. (2011). 'Producing different knowledge and producing knowledge differently': Rethinking physical education research and practice through participatory visual methods. *Sport Education and Society, 17*(1), 35–55.

Fitzgerald, H., & Stride, A. (2012). Stories about physical education from young people with disabilities. *International Journal of Disability, Development and Education, 59*(3), 283–293.

Flintoff, A. (2014). Tales from the playing field: Black and minority ethnic students' experience of physical education teacher education. *Race, Ethnicity and Education, 17*(3), 346–366. http://dx.doi.org/10.1080/13613324.2013.832922

Flintoff, A., Dowling, F., & Fitzgerald, H. (2015). Working through whiteness, race and (anti)racism in physical education teacher education. *Physical Education and Sport Pedagogy, 20*(5), 559–570. http://dx.doi.org/10.1080/17408989.2014.962017

Foucault, M. (1979). *Discipline and punish: The birth of the prison.* Harmondsworth, UK: Penguin.

Freire, P. (1971). *Pedagogy of the oppressed.* New York: Seabury.

Garrett, R. (2006). Critical storytelling as a teaching strategy in physical education teacher education. *European Physical Education Review, 12*(3), 339–360.

Garrett, R., & Wrench, A. (2011). Negotiating a critical agenda in middle years physical education. *Australian Educational Researcher, 8*(3), 239–255.

Giroux, H. (2011). *On critical pedagogy.* New York & London: Continuum.

Gore, J. (1990). Pedagogy as text in physical education. In D. Kirk & R. Tinning (Eds.), *Physical education, curriculum and culture: Critical issues in the contemporary crisis* (pp. 101–138). London: Falmer Press.

Gore, J. (2003). What can we do for you! What can 'we' do for 'you'? Struggling over empowerment in critical and feminist pedagogy. In A. Darder, M. Baltodano, & R. D. Torres (Eds.), *The critical pedagogy reader* (pp. 331–348). London: Routledge.

Harris, A., Carney, S., & Fine, M. (2001). Counter work: Introduction to 'Under the covers: theorising the politics of counter stories'. *International Journal of Critical Psychology, 4,* 6–18.

hooks, b. (1997). Representing whiteness in the black imagination. In R. Frankenberg (Ed.), *Displacing whiteness. Essays in social and cultural criticism* (pp. 165–179). Durham, NC & London: Duke University Press.

Lingard, B. (2010). Policy borrowing, policy learning: Testing times in Australian schools. *Critical Studies in Education, 51*(2), 129–147.

Murphy, M., & Pushor, D. (2010). Teachers as curriculum planners. In C. Kridel (Ed.), *Encyclopedia of curriculum studies* (pp. 657–658). Thousand Oaks, CA: Sage.

Oliver, K. (1998). A journey into narrative analysis: A methodology for discovering meanings. *Journal of Teaching in Physical Education, 17,* 244–259.

Oliver, K., & Kirk, D. (2016). Towards an activist approach to research and advocacy for girls and physical education. *Physical Education and Sport Pedagogy, 21*(3), 313–327. http://dx.doi.org/10.1080/1740898 9.2014.895803.

O'Sullivan, M., Siedentop, D., & Locke, L. (1992). Toward collegiality: Competing viewpoints among teacher educators. *Quest, 44,* 266–280.

Riessman, C. Kohler. (2008). *Narrative methods for the human sciences.* London: Sage.

Ruiz, B. Muros, & Fernández-Balboa, J.-M. (2005). Physical education teacher educators' personal perspectives regarding their practice of critical pedagogy. *Journal of Teaching in Physical Education, 14,* 243–264.

Shor, I., & Freire, P. (2003). What are the fears and risks of transformation? In A. Darder, M. Baltodano, & R. Torres (Eds.), *The critical pedagogy reader* (pp. 479–510). New York: RoutledgeFalmer.

Smith, J. (2009). Judging research quality: From certainty to contingency. *Qualitative Research in Sport and Exercise, 1*(1), 91–100.

Sparkes, A. C. (1997). Ethnographic fiction and representing the absent other. *Sport, Education and Society, 2*(1), 25–40.

Sparkes, A. (2006). Exploring body narratives. *Sport Education and Society, 4*(1), 17–30.

Squire, C. (2008). Experience-centred and culturally-orientated approaches to narrative. In M. Andrews, C. Squire, & M. Tamboukou (Eds.), *Doing narrative research* (pp. 41–63). London: Sage.

Stride, A. (2014). Let US tell YOU! South Asian, Muslim girls tell tales about physical education. *Physical Education and Sport Pedagogy, 19*(4), 398–417.

Sykes, H. (2014). Un-settling sex: Researcher self-reflexivity, queer theory and settler colonial studies. *Qualitative Research in Sport, Exercise and Health, 6*(4), 583–595.

Sykes, H., & Goldstein, T. (2004). From performed to performing ethnography: Translating life history research into anti-homophobia curriculum for a teacher education program. *Teaching Education, 15*(1), 41–61.

Tinning, R. (1997). *Pedagogies for physical education. Pauline's story.* Deakin, Geelong, Australia: Deakin University.

Tinning, R. (2002). Toward a 'modest pedagogy': Reflections on the problematics of critical pedagogy. *Quest, 54,* 224–240.

23

SHIFTING STORIES OF SIZE

Critical obesity scholarship as transformative pedagogy for disrupting weight-based oppression in physical education

Erin Cameron, MEMORIAL UNIVERSITY OF NEWFOUNDLAND, CANADA

Moss Norman & LeAnne Petherick, UNIVERSITY OF MANITOBA, CANADA

Media headlines blare "Obesity Epidemic Becomes Worldwide Phenomenon" (Millner, 2014), reflecting and fueling societal concerns about a supposed global "obesity" epidemic (World Health Organization [WHO], 1998). Pop culture has profited enormously from this obesity panic by emphasizing appearance-standards and weight loss in lifestyle magazines, television shows, reality television programs, and television documentaries. Even respected health professionals have joined the obesity panic discourse, likening it to terrorism – "Unless we do something about it, the magnitude of the dilemma will dwarf 9/11 or any other terrorist attempt" (Associated Press, 2010, para. 2).

Such "obesity" rhetoric has effectively fueled a culture that relies on making people feel badly about their bodies and themselves. Consider for a moment the pictures that are most often used with obesity-related news articles. Cooper (2007) calls it the "headless fatties" phenomenon, that is, dehumanizing depictions of headless people that serve to reinforce notions of "obesity" as non-human. She writes, "the body becomes symbolic: we are there but we have no voice, not even a mouth in a head, no brain, no thoughts or opinions. Instead we are reduced and dehumanized as symbols of cultural fear" (para. 3). Such depictions, alongside the digitally modified photos that trim people in magazines, on television, and in the movies, serve to inform society about normative bodies. Bordo (1993) suggests that such visual texts serve as pedagogical tools that are "training our perception in what's a defect and what is normal" (p. xviii). Crucially, this war is not just being waged on printed pages, television screens, or computers of the popular media. As early as 1985, Tinning (p. 10) argued that the professional discipline of physical education was complicit in perpetuating a "cult of slenderness," and now, he and others argue, it remains complicit in perpetuating the dominant obesity discourse (Tinning, Philpot, & Cameron, in press).

The dominant obesity discourse refers to the hyperbolic claims about "obesity," that falsely link fatness with personal irresponsibility, laziness, and lack of willpower; all of which primarily profits the weight loss industry (Campos, 2004). In fact, a significant body of critical obesity scholarship now provides evidence that many overweight people do not suffer from poor health or incur more health care costs; rather, it is only at extreme ends of the Body Mass Index (BMI) spectrum that serious health problems predominantly occur (see Durazo-Arvizu, McGee, Cooper, Liao, & Luke, 1998; Flegal, Graubord, Williamson, & Gail, 2005). In *The Obesity Epidemic*, Gard and Wright (2005) argue that obesity science has remained stagnant since the 1880s and that the media continue to rely on old studies that misconstrue and misrepresent facts. Within this critical obesity scholarship, an increasing number of physical education and kinesiology scholars are now adding their voices and offering critical perspectives on health, bodies, and weight.[1]

Despite the growth of critical obesity scholarship in many different fields, including physical education, to date there remains a dearth of research on the pedagogical approaches used to effectively challenge the dominant obesity discourse (Cameron, 2015a). Of the little research that does exist, it is clear that critical obesity pedagogy not only challenges students to critically examine their beliefs, values, and knowledge (Boling, 2011; Guthman, 2009), but it can also challenge social institutions, such as physical education and kinesiology faculties, to become aware of the embodied injustices being enacted through dominant discourses. In this sense, critical obesity pedagogy satisfies the criteria that Ukpokodu (2010) articulates as a form of transformative pedagogy. At a time when educational institutions are needing to promote themselves as diversity-focused (Mitchell, 2003) and equity-conscious (Ahmed, 2007), it is time for the field of physical education to pay attention to the negative impacts of weight-based oppression and to address this important social justice issue so that everybody, regardless of size, may feel supported in pursuing their healthy-(active)-at-any-size lives.

In this chapter, we begin by exploring the stories we, in the kinesiological sciences,[2] tell about "obesity" and its relationship to health. We examine how these stories have implications for both the people that they are about – that is, individuals labeled as having an unhealthy weight – as well as for the professionals who define themselves by, through, and within this discourse – that is, kinesiologists and physical educators. In focusing on stories, we aim to pry open what appears to be the one, singular, and seemingly unassailable "Truth" about body shape and size and its relationship to health (that is, dominant obesity discourse), and reveal the multiple, contradictory, and inconclusive small 't'-truths or stories that complicate the one Truth. To re-focus our attention on stories is by no means to suggest that obesity stories are trivial and that they can be easily dismissed. The essayist, Thomas King (2003), writes that, the "truth about stories is that that is all we are" (p. 2). Stories, in other words, mediate how we see ourselves and others. They shape how we relate to the world. Therefore, our intent in disrupting the notion of one singular truth is a decidedly political endeavor as we aim to instigate questions in those who read this chapter, such as: How do the dominant stories we tell about "obesity" function? Who do such stories privilege? Who do they oppress? In telling this particular story, what other stories are foreclosed? And, perhaps most importantly, we engage our readers to ask themselves, if stories are all that we are, as King suggests, then what kind of story do we, as physical educators, want to be? Do we want to tell stories that teach people to hate their bodies as, we argue, dominant obesity stories do?

We begin our chapter by situating physical education within a historical context and discuss the dominant trends towards more techno-scientific approaches to human movement and health and the adoption of the dominant obesity discourse. We then explore the implications of the dominant obesity discourse within physical education and how scholars are beginning to challenge this discourse through critical obesity pedagogy that endeavors to deconstruct commonly held assumptions about bodies, weight, and health, and to expose the injustices of a culture that assigns moral value to body weight. Lastly, like the other chapters in this section, we frame our chapter through transformative pedagogy, the idea that it's not *just* about justice and fairness, but it is also about dialogic learning (Britzman, 2003) with the aim to educate for social justice. As such, critical obesity pedagogy can be seen as being part of a bigger effort to "make sure that the future points the way to a more socially just world" (Giroux, 2007, p. 2).

A historical context: disciplining bodies in physical education

Physical education has a long history of responding to national initiatives that aspire to change the body size, shape, and fitness levels of Canadian children, not just for health, but also for social, national, economic, and market-driven interests (Francis & Lathrop, 2014; Lathrop & Francis, 2011; Singleton & Varapolatai, 2006). In this way, physical education curricula were (and are) always designed and implemented within particular social and cultural contexts that have vested interests in how bodies are produced – literally educated, trained, and shaped. By examining key moments in the history of physical education in Canada we can see how inter-sections of political and economic investment shape corporeal training of bodies. For example, in 1844 Egerton Ryerson, the head of Upper Canada education, lobbied for physical education programs to emphasize drill and gymnastic training. This was reflective of systems of European fitness training as a means to encourage a national investment in state protection while at the same time emphasizing a need for the broader population to acquire and maintain a healthy body (Singleton & Varapolatai, 2006). While ostensibly utilitarian in focus, the moral underpin-ning of this model of training was apparent in Ryerson's proclamation that "physical weakness produces moral evil" (Ryerson, 1848, cited in Lathrop & Francis, 2011, p. 64).

In addition to being morally laden, the training of bodies has been (and continues to be) a highly gendered and classed endeavor. Early physical training practices in Canada focused on drills and skills for boys that mirrored the requirements of military training regimes (Singleton, 2009). Training for girls in physical education, on the other hand, focused on acquiring grace-ful movements and light calisthenics, the skills that were thought necessary to being a "proper" young woman at the time (Lathrop & Francis, 2011). Similarly, with the Strathcona Trust, the emphasis remained on rigorous physical fitness regimes similar to those endorsed by Eggerton Ryerson, but the State investment was intensified, as only those schools adopting the Trust's *Syllabus for Physical Training for Schools* were eligible for funding. As with Ryerson's focus, the Syllabus also had a decidedly imperial and military flavor as it was directly adapted from prac-tices deployed in British navy and army training protocols (Lathrop & Francis, 2011). As na-tional concerns shifted, so too did priorities within physical education curricula.

While the focus in physical education curricula of the late nineteenth and early twentieth century was aimed at preparing boys and young men for military service, and girls and young women for middle-class ideals of feminine domesticity, the focus in the late twentieth cen-tury turned to health and fitness for the "national good." Here, citizens were incited to work on their bodies as a means of supporting the home front by becoming healthy, responsible, and non-burdensome workers, mothers, and consumers. In this way, the front line, as it were, switched from that of an external threat in the form of war with other nations, to the home front where the war was on loose living, such as over-eating, physical inactivity, and flabby bod-ies. In other words, as the purpose of physical education changed in accordance with emerging national "crises," the military metaphor nevertheless stayed consistent, such that in the early twenty-first century the United States Surgeon General, Richard Carmona, exclaimed that "obesity is the terror within" (Associated Press, 2010, para. 2).

With the emergence of obesity as a national concern, and the widespread moral assump-tion that obesity was attributable to laziness and physical inactivity (Gard & Wright, 2005), physical education has claimed a position of professional prominence in the "war on obesity" and physical education teachers have been positioned as "frontline" combatants in this "war" (Burrows & Wright, 2004). Here, physical educators are expected to be able to shape bodies into taut, muscular, lean forms poised to tackle the challenges of everyday responsible citizenship. This brief (and admittedly superficial) historical overview has demonstrated that stories of physical inactivity and fitness are as much, if not more so, about prevailing moral and ideological concerns of the time as they are about objective scientific rationalizations of health and wellbeing. Indeed, physical education curricula are responsive to these stories, adapting in accordance with the "crises" of the time. Whether this is the need for "in shape and fit for duty," healthy and productive factory workers, responsible housewives and mothers, or conscientious body consumers feverishly struggling to attain an impossible and highly commodified bodily ideal (Macdonald, 2011; Wright, 2014), school-based physical and health education has occupied an important position in shaping bodies in accordance with these various national "crises" and prevailing market forces.

Although political, social, and economic factors influenced physical education curricula, these influences were often difficult to discern because they were buried within the seemingly neutral language of positivist science. Teaching about how to be a physically educated body (Petherick, 2013) has historical connections to various forms of science. As one example of how ideological influences are obscured through scientific classification, Vertinsky (2002) conducts a historical examination of the physiognomy used in physical and health education contexts. Here, "height, girth, and body shape classifications [were] tied to specific character traits," thus merging seemingly benign bodily quantifications with prevailing social assumptions about what bodies *should* look like (p. 95). When embedded in scientific language, these social constructions of embodiment take on an aura of "truth." In her thorough examination of William Sheldon's pseudo-scientific work on physiognomy, Vertinsky finds that his patterns of body somatotyping and character trait connection, were largely debunked by medical and psychology experts at the time, yet Sheldon's classifications continued to be taught in physical education curricula long after the science underlying them was discredited. In fact, the authors of this chapter learned about Sheldon's somatotyping in our undergraduate kinesiology degrees some 40 years after the credibility of these classifications had been undermined. Some scholars, faculty, and students reading this chapter may be familiar with ecto-, endo-, and meso-morphic body classifications in physical education contexts as the size and shape of the body is used to encourage or direct students towards specific sports. Vertinsky (2002) argues that when we measure bodies, we are not measuring human nature, but rather "enforcing normalcy" (Davis, 1995). We are giving form to the bodies we measure by insisting that the bodies that do not conform to socially constructed norms – such as those found in the body classifications of Sheldon – require remedial attention in the form of physical training and discipline. Obesity science, with its practices of measuring and categorizing bodies, has similar implications within today's physical and health education, as we explore in more detail in the following sections.

A skinny utopia? Trends in physical education related to dominant obesity discourse

In recent times, physical education departments and faculties in the North American context have adopted a more techno-scientific approach to human movement within their curricula; some have even re-branded to the more scientific sounding name, "kinesiology" (Andrews, 2008; Pronger, 2002; Vertinsky, 2009). These shifts reflect broader economic and cultural trends that have prompted educational institutions and curricula to increasingly become subjected to a market imperative, where knowledge must demonstrate measurable use-value to the educational institution, its students, and the broader economy. Within this context, kinesiological knowledge is increasingly treated as a commodity that is simultaneously consumed by potential students who aim to secure white collar, professional careers while it is traded within the broader knowledge economy, competing with other knowledges for supremacy (Newman, Albright, & King-White, 2011). For the discipline of kinesiology, increasing the use-value of its knowledge commodities has largely been achieved through building stronger connections to what Murray and his colleagues (Murray, Holmes, Perron, & Rail, 2008) have referred to as the "medical-industrial-academic complex," a term used to describe the ever deepening – and highly problematic – connections between health, market forces, and universities. Within this context, kinesiology's brand revolves around selling the promise of transforming bodies into supposedly healthier, fitter, more beautiful forms. As preventative approaches to health have come to prominence, and physical activity is increasingly recognized as an important part of "obesity" prevention, kinesiological sciences moved from its position on the disciplinary margins into the center with its new-found position in the allied health sciences.

The application and expansion of medical authority and technologies in the name of life and health is a process that Conrad (1992) has referred to as medicalization. Such a process not only ignores the resounding evidence behind the social determinants of health (Raphael, 2009), but it ignores one of the greatest flaws of the dominant obesity discourse – how it is measured. The most commonly used method of measuring "obesity" is BMI, a ratio of weight-to-height, that classifies people into distinct weight categories (Health Canada, 2003). Despite the fact that BMI is widely used in obesity science research and is promoted by the World Health Organization (WHO), it has come under intense criticism for being a very misleading measure of fat. This is because it does not take into consideration a multitude of factors such as muscle mass, bone density, water content, sex, age, and race, all of which have been shown to influence the results (Anderson, 2012; Burkhauser & Cawley, 2008). Furthermore, a shift in BMI categories in the late twentieth century by the National Institutes of Health (NIH) has led to confusing interpretations about the pervasiveness of the "obesity epidemic," where millions of Americans become overweight and obese overnight (Saguy, 2013).

Given the BMI's controversial history, why does the scientific community – including those working under the disciplinary umbrella of kinesiological sciences – remain silent about, if not enthusiastically supportive of inconclusive and contradictory evidence that forms the foundation for obesity truth claims? In other words, most of us in the field of kinesiology – undergraduates and faculty alike – know the limitations of BMI and its relationship to health. We can recite the so-called "obesity paradox," or the perplexing relationship where excess weight can simultaneously increase life-threatening diseases, while lowering mortality rates, particularly for older adults (Flegal, Kit, Orpana, & Graubard, 2013). We can also tell you about the contested knowledge around whether overall BMI scores or fat distribution on the body, especially in the abdominal area, are best predictors of health status. Given the exercise focus, we also know well the "fat or fit" debate that pits overall cardiovascular fitness against body fat as the primary risk predictor, with many of our students enthusiastically recounting the evidence suggesting it is possible to be both "fat *and* fit" (Gaesser, 2002). Yet, despite knowing all of these paradoxical and contradictory knowledges, seldom do these crystallize into a concerted critique of "obesity science" or "obesity epidemic" rhetoric. Instead, the use of BMI is ubiquitous and gaining popularity with an explosion of online "BMI calculators." Hence, complex and controversial details that do not align with dominant "obesity" truths are often excluded on the grounds that they are unquantifiable, and thus irrational, aspects that cannot be included under the umbrella of scientific fact.

In this way, "obesity science" is as much about disregarding and foreclosing those stories that complicate and disrupt the coherence of the one, over-arching truth as it is about the objective presentation of scientific facts. Dominant obesity discourse, therefore, works to silence and disregard some stories and storytellers, while privileging and triumphantly celebrating other stories as well as those who tell them (i.e., obesity experts) (Norman, Rail & Jette, 2016). But why is this the case? Why does "obesity" seem to elude scientific scrutiny, when it very clearly is not simply an excess percentage of adipose tissue but rather a story about how changing ideas and contexts are influencing the way individuals think, feel, and act towards body size (Cameron, 2014)? As Klein (2001) reflects on the historical contexts and perceptions of fatness, he writes "until this century no one has ever dreamed of living in a skinny land. Fat has always been the shape of Utopia. Now, of course, the prejudice against fat seems universal and eternal; and thin belongs to what is truly good and beautiful" (p. 35). The answer to these questions, we suggest below, has as much to do with deeply embedded, visceral even, assumptions about obesity and embodiment as it does with a rational consideration of the facts.

The student body and the kinesiology curriculum

It is important to remember that what we know and how we feel about others says as much about *us* as it does about those *others* that we know and feel a particular way about. In other words, when we tell stories about obesity in our courses (e.g., that obesity = ill-health, and that exercise = cure), in important ways, we are speaking about our discipline and the role it plays in the "war on obesity." But we are also speaking about our own bodies – faculty and student bodies alike – as we work to discipline ourselves, purportedly making the "right choices" about healthy eating and active living. In this regard, we agree with Guthman (2009), who writes that anxiety and resistance to learning about critical obesity scholarship has to do with the deep emotional and personal investment individuals have in their own body projects – the policing and disciplining of bodies to achieve the taut lean, bodily lines that have come to be read as "healthy" within our current context. Despite the critiques of critical obesity scholars, stories about individual lifestyle modification, self-discipline, and controlling health by managing the contours of the flesh are central to kinesiological pedagogies and praxis.

In the kinesiological sciences, obesity truths and a techno-scientific approach to obesity are not peripheral to the curriculum, but actually *form* the curriculum. Once in the field, we are taught techniques for dividing the irreducible diversity of human morphology into relatively simple normative categories of embodiment (such as those provided by somatotyping or BMI charts). Then we are taught how to manipulate or alter the body into the normal-ideal categories (i.e., normal weight) through techniques that approach the body in machine-like ways (such as, the mechanical metaphor of the energy balance model of body weight). These lessons are incredibly seductive for those of us in the discipline. This is because we do not simply learn these new techniques for bodily control as abstract concepts, but many of us apply those techniques to our own lives, taking even greater control of the flesh and, in the process, learning the pleasures – dangerous, as they may be – associated with accumulating power over the body (Foucault, 1980; Pronger, 1998). In important ways, therefore, students in the kinesiological sciences quite literally come to embody the curriculum in a manner that students in most other faculties will not. In this sense, the techno-scientific approach to the body not only *forms* the curriculum of the kinesiological sciences, but also *forms* the contours of the "student body."

Our students and faculty alike are genuinely excited to share these experiences of bodily manipulation and control with others. We want to "help" others and we feel that we can "help" people by giving them the power to take control over their bodies. This point is an important one because we don't want to undermine what is, in most cases, a genuine and well-intentioned desire on the part of faculty and students to "help" others. Rather, our critique is directed at the profession more broadly, which we have argued is largely defined and gains its professional legitimacy over and against those fat and "obese" others who, we learn, are in need of "help" to re-gain control over their lives. Tellingly, this relationship and how kinesiological sciences defines itself against the out-of-control fat body (i.e., the body that eats too much, does not exercise enough, and cannot control its desires) is an example of thin *professional* privilege, a concept that builds upon the notion of "thin privilege" (Bacon, 2009). Underlying the kinesiological sciences is an imperative to change the difference of the other (that is, fatness) into the sameness of the self (that is, thinness), while only passingly accounting for the complex array of factors that influence body shape, size, and their relationship to health. In drawing attention to how "thin privilege" – whether professional or personal – is less a physical manifestation of individual willpower than a cherished cultural story, forged at a particular historical moment at the nexus of class, race, sexual, and gender privilege, we hope to disrupt a sense of certainty that too often accompanies the imperative to change the lives of others.

A "shadow epidemic": the rise of weight bias and discrimination

Dominant obesity discourse has triggered what Daghofer (2013) calls a "shadow epidemic" (p. 6), whereby as "obesity" concerns have escalated so have anti-fat attitudes leading to increasing weight bias and discrimination. This trend is evident within educational research where scholars draw attention to increasing rates of weight-based oppression, often expressed as fat phobia and fat bullying (Puhl & Heuer, 2009). For example, school policies and curriculum focus on very limited notions of health and as a result are having potentially damaging consequences for young people's developing sense of self (Evans, Rich, Davies, & Allwood, 2008; Rice, 2007).

Much of the educational research has focused on the prevalence and impact of weight bias in K-12 school contexts. For example, research has shown that teachers tend to have significant weight bias (Greenleaf & Weiller, 2005; Peters & Jones, 2010), curriculum serves to reinforce dominant obesity discourse (Azzarito, 2007; Gard, 2008), and schools often are "totally pedagogised micro-societies … driven by a culture of individualism, one of whose manipulating mantras is 'obesity discourse' " (Evans et al., 2008, p. 6).

In post-secondary contexts, weight bias has been found to be significant among university students in the fields of medicine (Puhl & Heuer, 2009), nursing, psychology (Waller, Lampman, & Lupfer-Johnson, 2012), nutrition (Puhl, Wharton, & Heuer, 2009), physical education and kinesiology (Greenleaf, Martin, & Rhea, 2008; O'Brien, Hunter, & Banks, 2007), and outdoor and environmental education (Russell, Cameron, Socha, & McNinch, 2013). Faculty members are also not immune to weight bias.[3]

While research documenting the prevalence of weight bias continues to grow, there is a need for more research that explores teaching and learning strategies that help shift the story of size. To date, a handful of critical obesity scholars have explored specific strategies aimed at reducing anti-fat attitudes (for literature reviews see Daníelsdóttir, O'Brien, & Ciao, 2010; Puhl & Heuer, 2009). Others have reflected upon teaching experiences related to critical obesity pedagogy (see Boling, 2011; Cameron, 2015a; Fisanick, 2007; Guthman, 2009; Tirosh, 2006; Watkins, Farrell, & Doyle-Hugmeyer, 2012) and created teaching resources to support educators (Cameron, 2015b; Clifford, 2013; Hopkins, 2011). But, there clearly is a need for more research in this area and for sharing of resources to aid educators in having "critical discussions and lessons with students about bodies in an attempt to avoid or at least mitigate the detrimental impacts of living in a fat-hating society that pathologizes fatness and vilifies fat bodies" (Fullbrook, 2012, p. 68).

Implications – a developing critical obesity pedagogy

To date, some writing has explored ideas that could help inform a developing critical obesity pedagogy more generally (e.g., Cameron et al., 2014; Cameron & O'Reilly, 2015; Fullbrook, 2012; Kirk, 2006; Russell et al., 2013; Sykes, 2011; Tinning et al., in press). While such writing has brought to light how educational institutions serve as pedagogical sites for reproducing normative ideas about the healthy "thin" body, such writing has also highlighted the important role transformative pedagogies, such as critical obesity pedagogy, could play in helping to shift from technocratic and unjust-orientated physical education towards a socially just and inclusive-orientated physical education. Seemingly central to a developing critical obesity pedagogy are the following key constructs:

(a) Language: Overall, language focused around monitoring weight, dieting, or exercising has the potential to create harm. Providing messages around the importance of active living and healthy, balanced eating for *all* bodies, regardless of size and shape, avoids potential harm while still communicating essential health messages.

(b) Consciousness: Some suggest that by simply talking about the dominant obesity discourse and the resulting negative consequences of weight stigma is to alter one's consciousness. Areas where awareness raising is particularly important are regarding the harms of focusing on weight and, conversely, of the benefits of a health-centered approach.

(c) Intersectionality: Many believe that body size serves as yet another axis of signification used to categorize, differentiate, and dehumanize. To date, obesity discourse has shown to be sexist, heterosexist, classist, racist, and ableist.

(d) Embodiment: The body's existence as a pulsating, thinking, and feeling entity shall not be forgotten. The dominant obesity discourse separates body and personhood, but critical obesity pedagogy embraces the interconnected ways the body exists in the world.

(e) Context: While the dominant obesity discourse decontexualizes, critical obesity pedagogy emphasizes contextuality. An understanding of the social, political, cultural, and historical contexts of obesity is helpful for deconstructing and disrupting "obesity" rhetoric.

(f) Deconstruction: Finally, in foregrounding the multiple, complex, and contextually situated stories that often remain unaccounted for in dominant obesity discourse, critical obesity pedagogy aims to disrupt and deconstruct obesity discourse by pluralizing the stories about body shape, size, and health (Pringle & Pringle, 2012). Here, the goal is not to replace one truth with another, equally dubious truth, but to foster a critical and reflective consciousness that incites people to engage with the stories they tell, and consider the effects these stories have, both for the self and others.

If the "war on obesity" is the overarching battle strategy and if the positivist approach to body size and shape forms the foundational conditions upon which our physical education-kinesiological discussions about the body, physical activity, and health must proceed, then what we offer in our teaching is a tactic for speaking back to, and feeling differently about, dominant constructions of obesity and fatness. For us, the tactic emerges not from the hallowed laboratories of the university, but in the fluid and interstitial spaces that are opened up through the "practices of everyday life" itself (de Certeau, 1984). It refers to those difficult to pin down, but impossible to ignore, embodied *feelings* about movement as well as those irreducibly complex ways of *doing* movement that do not easily align with dominant constructions of health. The tactic also operates in those inevitable and impossible to close gaps in the knowledge in obesity science, such as those obesity paradoxes we discussed earlier that, when brought into the classroom, have the potential to erode, distract, disrupt, pluralize, and re-imagine the "obesity truths" that we have come to accept almost out of habit.

Future directions

Shifting the oppressive practices that shame "obese" bodies in our field is imperative if we are committed to transforming our spaces into places where bodies can be emancipated rather than derogated. Transformative approaches to PE, applying Pinar's (2004) identification of the need to "complicate conversations" in curriculum theory, can be applied to the pedagogical and curriculum work transpiring in physical education and kinesiology. Identifying the ways the "hard" sciences masquerade in front and on top of the visceral embodied, and softer and more palatable aspects of the moving body require an engagement with complicating conversations. There is a need to engage in dialogues about the living, breathing, moving body as a series of stories, mediating how we see ourselves and each other. By disrupting and challenging the historic, and dominant ways of seeing, measuring, assessing, training, and educating our students the possibilities for dismantling the oppressive weight-biases circulating amongst our discipline may flourish. Transformative pedagogy, using critical theoretical perspectives, offers an opportunity to focus on equity, inclusion, and social justice to tell different stories about bodies, health, and human movement.

To conclude this chapter, we would like to offer a few key directions that we feel would help to shift the story of size in the field of physical education and begin to disrupt the harmful consequences of weight-based oppression.

1. Weight bias reduction should be a priority, particularly in physical education and physical activity settings.
2. Critical obesity scholarship offers critical and transformative potential to the field of physical education and should be given more prominence.
3. Critical obesity scholarship should be taught within physical education teacher education.
4. More research is needed around effective pedagogical strategies for teaching critical obesity scholarship.
5. More resources should be developed around effective critical obesity pedagogy.

Reflective questions for discussion

1. What stories have you heard about "obesity"?
2. How do these stories speak to your own body and to the bodies of others?
3. Do these stories present diverse body shapes and sizes in a positive or negative way? How can negative stories be altered to form a more positive and welcoming context?
4. Do these stories create safe and empowering spaces for bodies of all shapes and sizes to engage physical activity?
5. How could we tell different stories to create safe and empowering activity spaces?
6. How could shifting the story help to transform the field of physical education?

Notes

1 For example, scholars from Canada (Moss Norman, LeAnne Petherick, Erin Cameron, Elaine Power, Lisa McDermott, Genevieve Rail), the USA (Shannon Jette, Carolyn Vander Schee), England (Emma Rich, David Kirk, John Evans), New Zealand (Richard Pringle, Lisette Burrows, Katie Fitzpatrick), Australia (Richard Tinning, Michael Gard, Jan Wright, Deana Leahy, Louise McCuaig), the United Arab Emirates (Lily O'Hara), and Sweden (Mikael Quennerstedt), are playing an integral role in disputing the scientific rationalizations of obesity, drawing attention to the historical, cultural, social, and political contexts of obesity discourse, and highlighting the negative stereotypes perpetuated by the dominant obesity discourse within physical education and kinesiology contexts.
2 We use the term "kinesiological sciences" to reflect the fluid and related landscapes of physical education and kinesiology in the North American context where schools and faculties of physical education have increasingly adopted the name Kinesiology. Moreover, many physical education teachers certified within the last decade or so will have undergraduate degrees in kinesiology.
3 An especially egregious example is when Geoffrey Miller, an evolutionary psychologist, tweeted, "Dear obese PhD applicants: If you don't have the willpower to stop eating carbs, you won't have the willpower to do a dissertation. #truth" (Kingkade, 2013). Miller's tweet caused far-reaching outrage, motivating his university to conduct size acceptance and diversity training throughout the university (Wentworth, 2013). Miller's is a recent example of how weight can have a direct impact on post-secondary educational experiences, acceptances, and achievement.

References

Ahmed, S. (2007). You end up doing the document rather than doing the doing: Diversity, race equity and the politics of documentation. *Ethnic and Racial Studies*, *30*(4), 590–609.

Anderson, J. (2012). Whose voice counts? A critical examination of discourses surrounding the body mass index. *Fat Studies*, *1*(2), 195–207.

Andrews, A. (2008). Kinesiology's inconvenient truth and the physical culture studies imperative. *Quest*, *60*(1), 45–62.

Associated Press. (2010, July 7). Obesity bigger threat than terrorism? *CBSNews Website*. Retrieved from www.cbsnews.com.

Azzarito, L. (2007). 'Shape up America!': Understanding fatness as a curriculum project. *Journal of the American Association for the Advancement of Curriculum Studies*, *3*, 1–25.

Bacon, L. (2009). Reflections on fat acceptance: Lessons learned from privilege. Retrieved from www.LindaBacon.org.

Boling, P. (2011). On learning to teach fat feminism. *Feminist Teacher*, *21*(2), 110–123.

Bordo, S. (1993). *Unbearable weight: Feminism, western culture and the body*. Los Angeles: University of California Press.

Britzman, D. (2003). *Practice makes practice: A critical study of learning to teach* (2nd edn). Albany, NY: State University of New York Press.

Burkhauser, R.V., & Cawley, J. (2008). Beyond BMI: The value of more accurate measures of fatness and obesity in social science research. *Journal of Health Economics*, *27*(2), 519–529.

Burrows, L., & Wright, J. (2004). The discursive production of childhood, identity and health. In J. Evans, B. Davies, & J. Wright (Eds.), *Body knowledge and control: Studies in the sociology of physical education and health* (pp. 83–95). New York, NY: Routledge.

Cameron, E. (2014). *Throwing their weight around: A critical examination of faculty experiences with challenging dominant obesity discourse in post-secondary education* (Doctoral dissertation). Lakehead University, Thunder Bay, ON.

Cameron, E. (2015a). Toward a fat pedagogy: A study of pedagogical approaches aimed at challenging obesity discourse in post-secondary education. *Fat Studies: An Interdisciplinary Journal of Body Weight and Society*, *4*(1), 28–45.

Cameron, E. (2015b). Teaching resources for post-secondary educators who challenge dominant "obesity" discourse. *Fat Studies: An Interdisciplinary Journal of Body Weight and Society*, *4*(2), 212–226.

Cameron, E., Oakley, J., Walton, G., Russell, C., Chambers, L., & Socha, T. (2014). Moving beyond the injustices of the schooled healthy body. In I. Bogotch & C. Shields (Eds.), *International handbook of educational leadership and social (in)justice* (pp. 687–704). New York, NY: Springer.

Cameron, E., & O'Reilly, C. (2015). Sizing up stigma: Weighing in on the issues and solutions to diabetes and obesity stigma. *Biochemistry & Cell Biology*, *93*(5), 430–437.

Campos, P. (2004). *The obesity myth: Why America's obsession with weight is hazardous to your health*. New York, NY: Penguin.

Clifford, D. (2013). Health at every size curriculum. *HAES Curriculum Website*. Retrieved from http://haescurriculum.com/about/.

Conrad, P. (1992). Medicalization and social control. *Annual Review of Sociology*, *18*(1), 209–232.

Cooper, C. (2007). Headless fatties. Charlotte Cooper Website. Retrieved from http://charlottecooper.net/publishing/digital/headless-fatties-01-07.

Daghofer, D. (Ed.). (2013). From weight to well-being: Time for shift in paradigms? A discussion paper on the inter-relationships among obesity, overweight, weight bias, and mental well-being. *Provincial Health Services Authority Website*. Retrieved from www.phsa.ca/populationhealth.

Daníelsdóttir, S., O'Brien, K., & Ciao, A. (2010). Anti-fat prejudice reduction: A review of published studies. *Obesity Facts*, *3*(1), 47–58.

Davis, L. (1995). Constructing normalcy: The bell curve, the novel, and the invention of the disabled body in the nineteenth century. In *Enforcing Normalcy: Disability, deafness and the body*. New York, NY: Verso.

de Certeau, M. (1984). *The practices of everyday life*. Berkeley, CA: University of California Press.

Durazo-Arvizu, R., McGee, D., Cooper, R., Liao, Y., & Luke, A. (1998). Mortality and optimal body mass index in a sample of the U.S. population. *American Journal of Epidemiology*, *147*(8), 739–749.

Evans, J., Rich, E., Davies, B., & Allwood, R. (2008). *Education, disordered eating and obesity discourse: Fat fabrications*. New York, NY: Routledge.

Fisanick, C. (2007). "They are weighted with authority": Fat female professors in academic and popular cultures. *Feminist Teacher*, *17*(3), 237–255.

Flegal, K., Graubord, B., Williamson, D., & Gail, M. (2005). Excess deaths associated with underweight, overweight, and obesity. *Journal of the American Medical Association*, *29*(15), 1861–1867.

Flegal, K. M., Kit, B. T., Orpana, H., & Graubard, B. I. (2013). Association of all-cause morality with overweight and obesity using standard Body Mass Index categories: A systematic review and meta-analysis. *Journal of American Medical Association*, *309*. 71–82.

Foucault, M. (1980). *Power/knowledge: Selected interviews and other writings, 1972–1977*. New York, NY: Pantheon Books.

Francis, N., & Lathrop, A. (2014). Here we go all around the mulberry bush. Problematizing "progress" in Ontario's elementary school curriculum: 1900 to 2000. *The Journal of Educational Dance*, *14*, 27–34.

Fullbrook, A. (2012). You have nothing to lose! Using culturally relevant pedagogy in secondary education to make space for body acceptance (Masters thesis). Retrieved from ProQuest Dissertations and Theses. (ISBN 9780494919880)

Gaesser, G. (2002). *Big fat lies: The truth about your weight and health*. Carlsbad, CA: Gurze Books.

Gard, M. (2008). Producing little decision makers and goal setters in the age of the obesity crisis. *Quest*, *60*(4), 488–502.

Gard, M., & Wright, J. (2005). *The obesity epidemic*. London: Routledge.

Giroux, H. (2007). Introduction: Democracy, education and the politics of critical pedagogy. In P. McLaren & J. Kincheloe (Eds.), *Critical pedagogy: Where are we now?* (pp. 1–5). New York, NY: Peter Lang.

Greenleaf, C., Martin, S., & Rhea, D. (2008). Fighting fat: How do fat stereotypes influence beliefs about physical education? *Obesity*, *16*(2), S53–S59.

Greenleaf, C., & Weiller, K. (2005). Perceptions of youth obesity among physical educators. *Social Psychology of Education*, *8*(4), 407–423.

Guthman, J. (2009). Teaching the politics of obesity: Insight into the neoliberal embodiment and contemporary biopolitics. *Antiopode*, *41*(5), 110–1133.

Health Canada. (2003). Canadian guidelines for body weight classification in adults. *Health Canada Website*. Retrieved from www.hc-sc.gc.ca/fn-an/alt_formats/hpfb-dgpsa/pdf/nutrition/weight_book-livres_des_poids-eng.pdf.

Hopkins, P. (2011). Teaching and learning guide for: Critical geographies of body size. *Geography Compass*, *5*(2), 106–111.

King, T. (2003). 'You'll never believe what happened' is always a great way to start. In T. King (Ed.), *The truth about stories* (pp. 1–29). Toronto, ON: House of Anasi Press.

Kingkade, T. (2013, July 2). Geoffrey Miller claims mocking obese people on twitter was research: University disagrees. *Huffington Post Website*. Retrieved from www.huffingtonpost.ca/.

Kirk, D. (2006). The 'obesity crisis' and school physical education. *Sport, Education, and Society, 11*(2), 121–133.

Klein, R. (2001). Fat beauty. In J. E. Braziel & K. LeBesco (Eds.), *Bodies out of bounds: Fatness and transgression* (pp. 19–38). Los Angeles: University of California Press.

Lathrop, A., & Francis, N. (2011). Children who drill are seldom ill! The rise and fall of a "female tradition" in Ontario elementary school education 1850s to 2000. *Historical Studies in Education, 23*(1), 61–90.

Macdonald, D. (2011). Like a fish in water: Physical education policy and practice in the era of neoliberal globalization. *Quest, 63*(1), 36–45.

Millner, J. (2014, January 8). Obesity epidemic becomes worldwide phenomenon. *NewScientist Website*. Retrieved from www.newscientist.com.

Mitchell, K. (2003). Educating the national citizen in neoliberal times: From the multicultural self to the strategic cosmopolitan. *Transactions of the Institute of British Geographers, 48*(4), 387–403.

Murray, S., Holmes, D., Perron, A., & Rail, G. (2008). Towards an ethics of authentic practice. *Journal of Evaluation in Critical Practice, 14*, 682–689.

Newman, J., Albright, C., & King-White, R. (2011). Staying fat: Moving past the exercise-industrial-complex. In L. Scherff & K. Spector (Eds.), *Culture, relevance and schooling: Exploring the unknown* (pp. 103–124). Lanham, MD: Rowman & Littlefield.

Norman, M. E., Rail, G., & Jette, S. (2016). Screening the un-scene: De-constructing the (bio)politics of story telling in a Reality Makeover weight loss series. In D. McPhail, J. Ellison, & W. Mitchinson (Eds.), *Obesity in Canada: Historical and critical perspectives.* (pp. 342–372). Toronto, ON: University of Toronto Press.

O'Brien, K. S., Hunter, J. A., & Banks, M. (2007). Implicit anti-fat bias in physical educators: Physical attributes, ideology and socialization. *International Journal of Obesity, 31*(2), 308–314.

Peters, D., & Jones, R. (2010). Future sport, exercise, and physical education professionals' perceptions of the physical self of obese children. *Kinesiology, 42*(1), 36–43.

Petherick, L. (2013). Producing the young biocitizen: Secondary school students' negotiation of learning in physical education. *Sport, Education and Society, 18*(6), 711–730.

Pinar, W. F. (2004). *What is curriculum theory?* Mahwah, NJ: Lawrence Erlbaum.

Pringle, R., & Pringle, D. (2012). Competing obesity discourses and the critical challenges for health and physical educators. *Sport, Education and Society, 17*(2), 143–161.

Pronger, B. (1998). Post-sport: Transgressing boundaries in physical culture. In G. Rail (Ed.), *Sport and postmodern times: Culture, gender, sexuality, the body and sport* (pp. 277–298). Albany, NY: State University of New York Press.

Pronger, B. (2002). *Body fascism: The salvation in the technology of fitness.* Toronto, ON: University of Toronto Press.

Puhl, R., & Heuer, C. (2009). The stigma of obesity: A review and update. *Obesity, 17*(5), 941–964.

Puhl, R., Wharton, C., & Heuer, C. (2009). Weight bias among dietetics students: Implications for treatment practices. *Journal of the American Dietetic Association, 109*(3), 438–444.

Raphael, D. (2009). *Social determinants of health: Canadian perspectives* (2nd edn). Toronto, ON: Canadian Scholars' Press.

Rice, C. (2007). Becoming "the fat girl": Acquisition of an unfit identity. *Women's Studies International Forum, 30*(2), 158–174.

Russell, C., Cameron, E., Socha, T., & McNinch, H. (2013). "Fatties cause global warming": Fat pedagogy and environmental education. *Canadian Journal of Environmental Education, 18*, 27–45.

Ryerson, E. (1848). The importance of physical education. *The Journal of Education for Upper Canada, 1*, 336.

Saguy, A. (2013). *What's wrong with fat?* New York, NY: Oxford University Press.

Singleton, E. (2009). From Command to constructivism: Canadian secondary school physical education curriculum. *Curriculum Inquiry, 39*(2), 321–342.

Singleton, E., & Varapolatai, A. (2006). *Stones in the sneaker: Active theory for secondary school physical education and health education.* London, ON: The Althouse Press.

Sykes, H. (2011). *Queer bodies: Sexualities, genders & fatness in physical education.* New York, NY: Peter Lang.

Tinning, R. (1985). Physical education and the cult of slenderness: A critique. *ACHPER National Journal, 107*(Autumn), 10–14.

Tinning, R., Philpot, R., & Cameron, E. (in press). Critical pedagogy, physical education, and obesity discourse: More advocacy than pedagogy. In D. Robinson, L. Randall, & W. Harvey (Eds.), *Critical pedagogy within physical education: Problematizing sociocultural, political, and institutional practices and assumptions.* Canadian Scholars Press.

Tirosch, Y. (2006). Weighty speech: Addressing body size in the classroom. *The Review of Education, Pedagogy, and Cultural Studies, 28*(3–4), 267–279.

Ukpokodu, O. (2010). Pedagogies that foster transformative learning in a multicultural education course: A reflection. *Journal of Praxis in Multicultural Education, 4*(1), 1–9. DOI: 10.9741/ 2161–2978.1003.

Vertinsky, P. (2002). Embodying normalcy: Anthropometry and the long arm of William Sheldon's somatotyping project. *Journal of Sport History, 29*(2), 95–133.

Vertinsky, P. (2009). Mind the map or mending it: Qualitative research and interdisciplinary in Kinesiology. *Quest, 61*(1), 39–51.

Waller, T., Lampman, C., & Lupfer-Johnson, G. (2012). Assessing bias against overweight individuals among nursing and psychology students: An implicit association test. *Journal of Clinical Nursing, 21*(23–24), 3504–3512.

Watkins, P. L., Farrell, A., & Doyle-Hugmeyer, A. (2012). Teaching fat studies: From conception to reception. *Fat Studies: An Interdisciplinary Journal of Body Weight and Society, 1*(2), 180–194.

Wentworth, K. (2013). Professor Geoffrey Miller Censured by UNM. *The University of New Mexico Newsroom Website.* Retrieved from http://news.unm.edu/newsmedia/advisories.

World Health Organization [WHO]. (1998). Obesity: Preventing and managing the global epidemic. *Report of a WHO Consultation on Obesity.* Geneva, CH: World Health Organization.

Wright, J. (2014). Beyond body fascism: The place for health education. In K. Fitzpatrick & R. Tinning (Eds.), *Health education: Critical perspectives* (pp. 233–248). New York, NY: Routledge.

24

TRANSFORMATIVE PEDAGOGY IN PHYSICAL EDUCATION AND THE CHALLENGES OF YOUNG PEOPLE WITH MIGRATION BACKGROUNDS

Dean Barker, UNIVERSITY OF GOTHENBURG, SWEDEN

& Suzanne Lundvall, THE SWEDISH SCHOOL OF SPORT AND HEALTH SCIENCES, SWEDEN

Global migration continues to impact societies and their education systems in the 2010s. Schools in many countries are becoming more culturally diverse, a process that is having implications for school managers, teachers, students, and their families. Physical educators have been greatly affected by this trend. In the last ten years, scholarship dealing with the implications of burgeoning cultural diversity has increased substantially. In this chapter, we chart the main developments in this research. We have identified two main threads. The first relates to Muslim girls and PE, the second to teachers' cultural competence in contexts of growing diversity. In addition, we will also consider a smaller set of disconnected studies that, while not constituting threads in terms of on-going discussions, make useful contributions to our understanding of cultural difference in PE.

Before beginning in earnest we would like to make several preliminary comments. First, we want to draw attention to the 'local' nature of the research reviewed in this chapter. Globally, many physical educators are experiencing pluralism. However, because nations have different socio-political histories when it comes to ethnicity and migration, specific emphases of discussions can vary significantly. Second and related, while we aim to be comprehensive in a chapter such as this, we cannot claim to be exhaustive. With an almost exclusive reliance on research published in English, the chapter could be charged with extending the ethnocentrism that some of our colleagues below condemn (Benn, Dagkas, & Jawad, 2011). In this respect, the chapter should be read as a synthesizing contribution but not as an all-embracing summary. Finally, this discussion can be read against a backdrop of transformative pedagogies and the idea that education should help students to "examine critically their beliefs, values and knowledge with the goal of developing ... an appreciation of multiple perspectives, and a sense of critical consciousness" (Ukpokodu, 2009, p. 43). While this might sound like an appropriate framework to employ given the topic, only some of the scholarship below makes explicit claim to being transformative in Ukpokodu's sense. Our intention is not to evaluate the research against a standard by which some of its authors never agreed to be judged. Instead, we are concerned to discuss how transformative thinking might open up future research enterprises in the area.

Historical overview

Ethnicity has been a topic of interest for general education theorists and sport scholars for many years. Carrington and Williams' (1988) chapter, 'Patriarchy and ethnicity: The link between school physical education and community leisure activities' identified a range of contributing factors associated with ethnicity. From survey work in Northern England, Carrington and Williams surmised that ethnicity accentuated high participation rates of males and low participation rates of females in extra-curricular sports. The authors proposed that ethnic minority girls' lack of confidence in their physical capabilities was particularly pertinent to physical educators: "This [lack of confidence] suggested that questions could be raised about the quality and effectiveness of Physical Education and in particular about the adequacy of institutional responses to cultural diversity in this area of the curriculum" (Carrington & Williams, 1988, p. 84). In attempting to assess PE quality, the authors interviewed teachers in PE and other school subjects. The main themes emerging from their empirical work – parental concern, institutional constraints on staff, the low status of PE in some cultures, and problems encountered in mixed-sex swimming lessons – have become recurring themes in later investigations.

The idea that the PE field was not responding effectively to increased pluralism was taken up by Carroll and Hollinshead (1993) in their widely cited investigation published in the *British Educational Research Journal*. These researchers set about exploring minority students' experiences in PE lessons, providing detailed insights into how students of mainly Bangladeshi and Pakistani descent perceived PE in the early 1990s. Empirical work led the authors to suggest that despite schools abandoning assimilationist and integrationist policies in favour of multicultural ones, assimilationist ideas continued to inform practice. Significantly, the paper was sharply critiqued by Siraj-Blatchford (1993) in the same journal issue, largely in relation to the notion of 'culture clash'. Siraj-Blatchford claimed that Carroll and Hollinshead had not managed to escape their Eurocentric worldview and had failed to perceive 'participation in PE' from the Muslim community's position.

Not long after the appearance of Carroll and Hollinshead's paper, a text that has become widely cited in the North American context appeared in *Quest*. DeSensi (1995) introduced the ideas of intercultural sensitivity and multiculturalism, which for educational purposes involved helping students learn about individuals with different backgrounds but centrally, helping students come to know themselves. DeSensi (1995) asserted that multicultural education involves helping students move from a state of ethnocentrism, where they may deny cultural difference and/or make negative evaluations of other cultures, to a state of ethnorelativism, which involves recognizing and appreciating cultural difference. The paper inspired interest in culturally relevant, culturally sensitive, and ethno-relative pedagogies in the United States. Scholars have developed and empirically investigated these approaches in later research (see, for example, Burden, Columna, Hodge, & Martínez de la Vega Mansilla, 2013; Hastie, Martin, & Buchanan, 2006, discussed in more detail below).

In the same year that DeSensi's piece appeared, several practically oriented papers were published in physical education journals. *Strategies* included a text titled, 'How to stop stereotyping students' (Lyter-Mickelberg, 1995). The *Journal of Physical Education, Recreation and Dance* ran a feature called, 'Women of color: Perspectives within the profession'. The line of discussion followed in the feature was grounded in the question of professional preparedness: "Given the cultural diversity that exists in the United States, just how well-prepared are today's teachers to meet the needs of minority students? Will HPERD professionals be able to meet the needs of a more linguistically and culturally diverse student population?" (Corbett, 1995, p. 26). Butt and Pahnos (1995) also called for a multicultural focus in the same journal. And it is perhaps not coincidental that Don Hellison's (1995) hugely influential book, *Teaching Responsibility Through Physical Activity* with a focus on inner-city youth was published in the same year.[1]

In short, the mid-1990s saw a modest groundswell in interest in ethnic diversity from physical educators. American scholars drew on tenets of multicultural education, a trend that continues today. British theorists tended to be more eclectic in their theoretical positioning but in general, tended to shy away from multiculturalist perspectives.[2] This historical note is important when considering the following sections as it goes some way in explaining the 'national bias' to the research threads in the review. In saying this, the notion that PE was (or is) unprepared for changing societies has continued to be a common theme for research across national borders.

Current trends and issues

The following section is divided into three subsections. The first deals with Muslim girls and PE, while the second is concerned with the PE field's capacity to handle increasing cultural heterogeneity in classrooms. The third comprises a small collection of loosely related investigations that focus on students and their experiences and perceptions within PE contexts.

Muslim girls and physical education

By far the most researched topic concerning cultural diversity and PE in recent times is the participation of Muslim girls. Reasons for this focus are manifold and include but are certainly not limited to the growing victimization of Muslims, Islamophobia, and an enduring assumption that religious beliefs prevent Muslim girls from participating in PE and sport (Stride, 2014; Walseth, 2015). Many scholars have adopted case study or qualitative research methods working within an interpretive perspective. As a result, it has provided substantial insights into how different parties, including teachers, parents, and of course, the girls themselves, make sense of 'Muslim females' participation in PE lessons'. Many of these researchers have conducted studies in the United Kingdom where many Muslims identify as British Asians and have Pakistani, Indian, or Bangladeshi ancestry (Benn, Jawad, & Al-Sinani, 2013; Dagkas, Benn, & Jawad, 2011). Although international scholars also have contributed comparative work on this topic (Benn & Pfister, 2013; Dagkas & Benn, 2006), due to the preponderance of British literature, we know more about this context than others.

It seems clear from this work that there are four situations that limit many Muslim girls' PE participation. Existing research suggests that: (i) dress codes that require girls to expose parts of their bodies; (ii) dance lessons that contain movements which could be seen as sexually provocative; (iii) swimming lessons where males are present; and (iv) religious festivals that require girls to participate in vigorous physical activity while they are fasting, *can* all prevent Muslim girls from taking part in PE lessons or be met with disapproval from girls' families (Benn & Pfister, 2013; Dagkas et al., 2011). Most commentators point out, though, that many Muslim girls have positive attitudes towards PE, enjoy participating, and can articulate health and educational benefits of the school subject (Dagkas & Benn, 2006). Indeed, variability and heterogeneity are consistent themes in the literature and Muslim girls' inclusion in PE lessons is contingent on an abundance of factors. Both Stride (2014) and Knez, Macdonald and Abbott (2012) stress for example, that Muslim families expect girls to embody Islamic discourses associated with honour and modesty but that these expectations nonetheless vary substantially with interpretations of the Qu'ran. For some parents, PE practices are largely supported by Islam and participation is seen as consistent with notions of care of the body. For others these same practices are seen as highly problematic (Knez et al., 2012). Muslims' value conflict can be intensified with parental fears of Westernization, loss of ethnic identities, and the abandonment of tradition and culture (Benn & Pfister, 2013). In these situations, forms of compromise between families and schools become necessary but more difficult to achieve.

Unsurprisingly, variation exists regarding the way schools and teachers respond to Muslim girls. Scholars have found evidence of inclusive school practices such as allowing girls to wear tracksuits, change and shower privately, and be excused from intense physical activities during Ramadan (Dagkas & Benn, 2006). Many schools have clear policies on school expectations and provide teachers with senior management support (Dagkas et al., 2011). Researchers also have found that such practices are implemented inconsistently. Schools that serve predominantly one minority group appear to be more successful in meeting the needs of their students. Conversely, schools that serve diverse local communities with high levels of religiosity, are under-resourced, and/or have teachers who are unsure of boundaries between Islamic and cultural practices typically have greater difficulties meeting the needs of their students. Teachers across – and even within – schools diverge greatly in terms of both their preparedness to meet students' needs and their knowledge of cultural and religious requirements (Dagkas & Benn, 2006). In cross-cultural comparative work in this area, Dagkas and colleagues (2011) suggest that it is not just teachers' attitudes and the school environment that affect teachers' work but also broader socio-historical factors found within a national culture. They point out that differing views on cultural relations within societies such as Greece and Britain, for example, result in Greek teachers reporting fewer problems and feeling less anxious about working with Muslim students than do their British peers (Dagkas & Benn, 2006).

As well as intra-religious variation, several scholars have pointed to inter-cultural similarity, notably that Muslim girls often experience exclusive practices in PE in similar ways to non-Muslim girls (Knez et al., 2012). Similarities have led scholars to consider multiple layers of identity (Dagkas et al., 2011) and while there has long been an acknowledgement that class and gender combine with ethnicity to affect people's subjectivities, intersectional theories have only slowly entered discussions related to cultural diversity in PE (Azzarito & Solomon, 2005; Flintoff, Fitzgerald, & Scraton, 2008). Noting that 'single issue' research sometimes fails to capture the complexity of experiences, Flintoff and colleagues (2008) provide a discussion of what they see as imperatives when working with intersectional theory. Flintoff reiterated this perspective in her work with Webb, emphasizing the methodological challenges of researching minority students' experiences of PETE (Flintoff & Webb, 2012).

Scholars explore the broad problem of girls' non-participation in this research thread. While many caution against simple, one-size-fits-all solutions, commentators have collectively made recommendations for change. Dagkas et al. (2011) propose that to increase participation, decisions around dress codes and gender organization need to be based on understanding difference, reiterating "flexibility is key to success in developing inclusive policy and practice" (p. 237). Working in a Norwegian context, Walseth (2015) suggests that a focus on testing physical skills is particularly demotivating for Muslim girls and that teachers should do this sparingly. Walseth further proposes that teachers need to be more sensitive to Muslim girls' embodied faith and ensure that boys do not dominate lessons. Azzarito (2009) provides a more general recommendation, claiming that physical educators should provide girls with a space to create alternative narratives. Hamzeh and Oliver (2012), like Knez and colleagues (2012), contend that teachers should avoid narrow stereotypes, develop deep understanding of girls' experiences, and build collaborative relationships with girls and their families. Interestingly, scholars have suggested that PE activities, themselves, are rarely problematic; instead problems result from "situational contexts" (Benn et al., 2011). This idea is somewhat at odds with holistic perspectives that frame pedagogy as interaction between subject matter, teacher, and student (see, for example, Amade-Escot, 2006).

Teachers' cultural competence

The second major research thread dealing with cultural diversity and PE has centred on the consequences for teachers of changing student demographics in their classes. A foundation argument that emerged in early publications and has continued to orient researchers' attention has been that, if physical educators are to provide equitable experiences, they need to meet challenges resulting from increasing pluralism (Benn et al., 2011). Scholars considering teachers' cultural competence have posited that: (1) 'traditional' (often read as 'current') PE practices are unlikely to meet the needs of children living in 'new' cultural milieus; and (2) since teachers continue to be recruited from a white middle class, considerable 'cultural distance' is likely to exist between teachers and their pupils (Burden, Hodge, Bryant, & Harrison, 2004; Flory & McCaughtry, 2011). Much of the work examining teachers' cultural competence has been conducted in the United States utilizing multiculturalist frameworks (see DeSensi, 1995). This research has examined how teachers and their programmes might become more culturally responsive, relevant, and sensitive (Mowling, Brock, & Hastie, 2011).

Although relatively few studies have illustrated empirically physical educators' underpreparedness to work with cultural diversity, there is some evidence to support this claim. Investigations have shown for instance that teachers in the US are frequently monolingual, experience communication difficulties with English language learners, have varying knowledge of cultural and religious requirements of minority groups, and at least some feel ill-prepared to work with heterogeneous groups (Columna, Foley, & Lytle, 2010). Many of the teachers in Columna and colleagues' (2010) descriptive survey acknowledged that cultural diversity is valuable, but indicated that they experience difficulties implementing culturally responsive pedagogies. Dagkas and Benn's (2006) examination of PE in Greece and Britain showed that a number of practitioners believed their training had not prepared them for multicultural classes. Instead, these teachers suggested they had learned to deal with diversity on the job.

Accounts of transformative interventions in PE also are relatively rare. Hastie et al. (2006) drew on Ladson-Billing's (1995) work with culturally relevant pedagogies to develop a stepping[3] unit with African-American children. Reporting reasonable levels of success, Hastie and colleagues experienced apprehension related to teaching unfamiliar content which was closely connected to their pupils' cultural heritage. Apprehension was also foregrounded in Rovegno and Gregg's (2007) insightful account of teaching a Native American folk dance unit to a third grade at a predominantly African-American elementary school. The account raises a raft of dilemmas that relate to issues such as structural inequality, authenticity, and teacher knowledge. At the same time, the authors encourage pedagogues to experiment with ways of helping children to appreciate pluralism. In slightly different ways, both accounts suggest that anxiety may be a necessary part of changing traditional power relationships (see also Flory & McCaughtry, 2011). Importantly, Hastie et al.'s research raises the question of why there are few people from minority groups working in academia, a topic given thorough consideration by Hodge and Wiggens (2010) in a North American context and Lundvall and Meckbach (2012) in a Swedish context.

Teachers' reports of lack of preparedness have put Physical Education Teacher Education (PETE) under the spotlight. In an early paper, Burden and colleagues (2004) suggested that teacher education programmes tend to be ethnocentric and do not recognize ways in which they privilege white perspectives. Shortcomings in PETE programmes are, according to Burden et al. (2004), in line with the teachers' concerns in the Dagkas and Benn (2006) investigation. This may point to a prime reason why beginning teachers encounter problems when working in culturally diverse schools. In a similar vein, Benn and Dagkas (2006) argue that although schooling has changed with society, higher education lags behind. In considering diversity training in PETE programmes, two themes have emerged: the need for reflection and the need for cross-ethnic contact.

Burden and colleagues (2004) emphasize the need to increase PETE students' capacities for reflection around cultural difference as a central strategy of helping beginning teachers deal with diversity. They recommend that teacher educators ensure that novice teachers reflect on the assumptions they have about learners. Rather than providing one-off courses in multiculturalism, Burden et al. suggest that teacher educators introduce multiculturalist content across courses. Continuing work in this area, Burden (2011) maintains that PETE educators are responsible for learning about PETE students' constructions of minority cultures. Burden et al. (2013) expand on these ideas in a more recent paper, proposing that teacher educators should help beginning teachers to "willingly and critically examin[e] their own attitudes and beliefs about, and attitudes toward student diversity" (Burden et al., 2013, p. 177), gain knowledge about students' values, cultural norms, and languages; and develop language objectives in order to improve communication.

Providing possibilities for cross-racial contact has also been touted as an important strategy for enhancing the cultural responsiveness of PETE programmes. Calls for increased cross-cultural contact have been made largely in recognition of the fact that PETE cohorts have tended to be homogenous in a number of respects including socio-economic status, religion, and ethnicity. Benn and Dagkas (2006) allude to the persistence and scope of this pattern, noting that recruitment and retention of ethnic minority teachers has been a national concern in Britain since at least the 1980s.

To offset this tendency, Burden et al. (2013) propose more "aggressive" recruitment of minority group individuals into higher education. As an alternative strategy, Columna and colleagues (2010) suggest that PETE programmes provide "real life experiences whereby [PETE students] are exposed to diverse cultures" (p. 308). Benn and Dagkas (2006) provide an interesting counter to these contentions, suggesting that teachers are more likely to develop attitudes and knowledge of other cultures as a result of their personal experiences *outside* of their pre-service teacher training. These assertions raise questions about the limits of PETE and what might realistically be achieved within teacher education, a point to which we will return.

Benn and Dagkas (2006) make an additional comment regarding teacher education, noting that single-sex PETE training in Britain was halted in the mid-1980s. They suggest that while this may have led to increased gender equity, mixed-sex training for PE now works against the inclusion of Muslim women in PETE programmes. In an attempt to be more inclusive, the researchers grouped Muslim primary school trainees together so that they could receive training in a gender-segregated context. The women reported feeling more comfortable but at the same time, the investigators noted that the strategy meant denying other students opportunities to learn about Islam.

A final topic contributing to discussions on the implications of changing demographics for teachers is the issue of language proficiency. Recently, Burden et al. (2013) suggested that limited English proficiency can restrict communication and lead to poor educational performance in PE. They proposed using ethnolinguistically relevant pedagogies and the ability to communicate with students from diverse backgrounds is an essential skill. This analytic paper follows a series of more practically oriented pieces aimed at providing teachers with strategies to work with English Language Learners (ELLs). Columna, Senne, and Lytle (2009) for example, provide recommendations for how Euro-American teachers can communicate effectively with Hispanic parents. Clancy and Hruska (2005) work from the assumption that PE provides an excellent setting for supporting language acquisition and give suggestions for how PE teachers can help ELLs improve their English, a theme that has also been addressed by Bell and Lorenzi (2004).

Ethnicity and experiences of physical education

As noted at the outset of the chapter, researchers are conducting studies that do not directly run into the threads dealing with either Muslim girls' participation or teachers' cultural competence. Nonetheless, these studies shed light on the issue of cultural diversity and PE. This research complements the work above and hence has the potential to extend our understanding of PE practice in times of increasing plurality.

Experiences of pupils with migration backgrounds in PE have garnered a modest amount of researcher attention. Unlike their female counterparts, Muslim boys' participation in Western forms of PE has remained out of frame for many scholars. Farooq and Parker (2009) provide an exception. These researchers conducted an ethnographic investigation of Muslim adolescent males' constructions of masculinities in a Muslim independent school. They show how the students and schools place high value on PE and sport. A significant part of this value lies in PE's perceived cathartic dimension and many of the participants describe PE and sport as means to expulse negative feelings and become more disciplined. Indeed, echoing earlier work on muscular Christianity (Mangan, 2000), PE and sport are viewed as practices through which boys could come closer to "what God wanted them to be" (Farooq & Parker, 2009, p. 289).

Fitzpatrick (2011) provides an examination of PE in the lives of Maori and Pasifika youth in New Zealand, suggesting that for these groups too, PE holds an important place albeit for different reasons. Through ethnographic work, she highlights the contradictory meanings that PE assumes for these young people. PE is, according to Fitzpatrick (2011), linked to friendship, playfulness, and critical engagement but is also a space where large brown bodies are marginalized and framed as athletic but intellectually lacking. In a second paper, Fitzpatrick (2013) notes that PE manages to maintain its non-academic status despite considerable academic engagement required at senior high school. This, she argues, has specific relevance for Maori and Pacific Island young people in terms of educational engagement. An important contribution of this paper relates to 'Renee', a student teacher of Maori descent. Using Bourdieu's concepts of habit and field, Fitzpatrick provides a vivid illustration of how ethnic minority students can succeed and progress in the field of PE and at the same time are forced to move between indigenous private spheres and Eurocentric academic and professional spheres (see also Hodge & Wiggens, 2010; Lundvall & Meckbach, 2012).

Barker and colleagues' (2014) work from Switzerland stresses the highly individualized nature of young people's PE experiences. In contrast to Farooq and Parker (2009) and Fitzpatrick (2011, 2013), Barker et al. (2014) pick up on the ambivalence some young people with migration backgrounds feel towards the school subject. Focusing on three cases, Barker and colleagues show how PE can be enjoyable and rewarding, restrictive and frustrating, or boring and embarrassing depending on how it intersects with young people's discursive histories. Central arguments are that generalizations common within popular discourses work to homogenize people with migration backgrounds and that one's ethnicity can have subtle and unexpected effects on the ways that pupils make sense of PE.

Finally, the body is a theme that has attracted race and ethnicity scholars' attention in the field of PE (e.g. Fitzpatrick, 2011, 2013). Azzarito (2009) noted, for example, that PE students' constructions of ideal bodies were gendered and racialized. She pointed out that while many students resisted talking explicitly about race in relation to bodies, the ideal body was typically white. Working with British Asian girls, Hill and Azzarito (2012) conducted a participatory visual ethnography to investigate the gendered and racialized nature of body discourses. They noted that young people's body narratives provide them with multiple readings of bodies and that the ways that girls make sense of themselves as active bodies have consequences for whether they engage with sport or physical activity.

Future directions and questions of change

A significant question at this point is: where will physical education scholars direct their attention in the future? There seem to be several areas that deserve further exploration. First, and foremost, despite a number of investigations describing contexts and attitudes, few are explicitly pedagogical in nature. Taking pedagogy as an activity that simultaneously involves curriculum, teacher, and learner, there is a need to account for how pedagogies are currently enacted and how they might be reconsidered, revised, or re-enacted in contexts of cultural heterogeneity. Indeed, if our intention is to facilitate transformative learning, there is a need to trial new content and new forms of teaching and share these experiences with others.

Inclusive and socially just practices are undoubtedly taking place and, in line with a more general thrust in current research, researchers might pay greater attention to 'transformative' sites where things are 'working'. More could be learned from cases where cultural diversity is seen as an advantage and where diverse forms of cultural knowledge are practised and valued. More concretely, scholars might examine schools and PETE programmes that have culturally heterogeneous cohorts and situations in which students from minority groups are thriving. Alternatively, scholars might collaborate with teachers and teacher educators who are doing exceptional work with their students. These kinds of cases have been reported but often only peripherally. A concerted focus on the circumstances that contribute to these situations could provide valuable insights that could revitalize current practices.

Theorists and practitioners might also consider the aims of school curricula and how these affect physical educators' work with minority groups. There has been much discussion about the objectives of PE as well as the rationale and 'ideal form' of the subject (Bailey et al., 2009; Kirk, 2010). These discussions have specific relevance to ethnicity and vice versa. Programmes based on the notion of 'maximum physical activity for health' are likely to elicit very different reactions from Muslim families (or Sikh, Hindu, or Catholic families) compared to programmes based on socio-critical principles that can involve quite radical challenges to traditional norms and values. Simply put, there is a need to go beyond framing PE as a neutral, positive activity where increasing participation is automatically desirable, to question how the nuanced politics of PE interacts with pupils' own political and identity projects.

In a similar vein, some thought should be given to claims that PE is able to remedy broader social ills and that physical educators should extend their focus to include areas such as pupils' language proficiency. Some scholars have argued convincingly that PE's educational claims are already too diffuse (McKenzie & Lounsbery, 2009) and – in line with the name of the school subject – that it would be prudent to focus our attention on learning in the physical domain (Evans, 2004). An awareness of the discussion would appear to have significant bearing on future research endeavours in the area of ethnicity and PE.

Intersectionality provides a key concept for further research. Gender and ethnicity as theoretical constructs have been combined in a handful of investigations and more work is surely needed. Yet socio-economic class remains conspicuous by its almost total absence. It seems if not preposterous then at least very strange that in discussions of ethnicity and PE, few scholars have questioned how markers of ethnic difference that lead to marginalization and stigmatization combine with limited access to social and economic capital to affect individuals' PE experiences. Sociological studies of schooling have long demonstrated that class plays an important role in educational achievement (Bernstein, 1971). An important challenge for physical educators is to explain how class processes play out in culturally diverse PE settings.

We would like to finish with a rather philosophical point regarding future directions. Stuart Hall (2000) proposed that the meeting of cultures is agonistic and never completed. It is a moment that is ambiguous, and "without the promise of celebratory closure or transcendence of the complex" (p. 235). Scholarship on PE and ethnicity might too be framed as part of an on-going process, a site where we write and re-write ethnic (and gender, ability, class, and age) discourses to create new ways of thinking about what we are doing in the name of PE. Rather than see scholars' task as changing the nature of PE *for good* (in both senses of the word), we might see scholarship as part of an on-going discussion that is reflexive in the sense that it will influence our own and others' practices. Research is and will remain essentially incomplete in the sense that it will not provide the final word on ethnicity and PE. This point may be disheartening, liberating, or both but it is a point that we believe deserves consideration when embarking on new projects.

Summary of key findings

- For the most part, existing research can be grouped into two main threads: that dealing with Muslim girls and PE and that which considers physical educators' responses to cultural diversity. Additionally, there are a small number of investigations focusing on the experiences and perceptions of young people from minority groups.
- Muslim girls have garnered increasing attention in the last two decades due to migration and the increasing presence of cultural discourses (including Islamophobic discourse and the idea that Islam is incompatible with women's sport and physical activity).
- Scholars have suggested that: (i) dress codes that require girls to expose parts of their bodies; (ii) dance lessons that contain movements which could be seen as sexually provocative; (iii) swimming lessons where males are present; and (iv) religious festivals that require girls to participate in vigorous physical activity while they are fasting, can but do not necessarily prevent Muslim girls from taking part in PE lessons.
- Whether girls fully engage with PE will depend on: familial interpretations of Islam; flexibility of teachers and schools with factors such as dress codes and changing arrangements; and the interest of girls themselves. Programme content does not appear to be a decisive factor when it comes to participation.
- A number of schools are changing to meet the needs of Muslim girls, however progress has been inconsistent and patchy. Schools that serve diverse local communities, are under-resourced, meet high levels of religiosity, and/or have teachers that know little about Islam have been generally less successful.
- The notion that traditional forms of PE do not meet the needs of increasingly diverse populations and that change is indispensable has constituted a persistent argument in literature on ethnicity and PE.
- Some studies have shown that PE teachers tend to be monolingual, have limited knowledge of minority groups, and experience communication difficulties when dealing with these groups.
- A number of scholars have suggested that PETE programmes tend to be ethnocentric and privilege White, European ways of seeing the world. These scholars contend that PETE

programmes need to counter this theme to better prepare teachers for current and future teaching contexts.

- Two key ways of improving PETE programmes have been identified: facilitating student reflection in the area of race and ethnicity, and providing opportunities for cross-cultural contact.
- Some research exploring students' experiences of PE suggests that PE holds an important place in the lives of young people from minority groups. Other research, however, highlights ambivalence towards PE.
- Emerging research suggests that bodies are both gendered and racialized and that this has significant consequences for physical educators and their work with bodies.

Reflective questions for discussion

1. While trends undoubtedly exist, variability and heterogeneity are consistent themes in the literature on cultural diversity and PE. How should physical educators deal with the fact that even within one minority group (such as 'Muslim girls'), significant differences may exist between individuals in the ways that PE is perceived and experienced?
2. Some scholars have suggested that PETE programmes should provide "real life experiences whereby [students] are exposed to diverse cultures" (Columna et al., 2010, p. 308). Do you agree? Justify your answer.
3. There is relatively little research on a number of minority groups and their experiences and perceptions of PE. Why do you think this is? Can you think of groups that have not caught the attention of scholars but might warrant exploration?

Notes

1 In 1997, Kincheloe and Steinberg suggested that 'inner city issues' is often used as a kind of shorthand to signify that race is being discussed. In Hellison's work, race certainly played an important role, even if Hellison did not theorize it explicitly.

2 Hesse (2000) suggests that multiculturalist theory gained less traction in Britain as it came under increasing attack in the 1980s. Hesse suggests that its focus on the celebration of cultural identities was "demonized by the Left as a dangerous distraction to the anti-racist struggle and by the Right as a virulent undermining of the British way of life" (p. 9). Further, multicultural discussions had emerged largely in primary and secondary school contexts and as a political discourse, it was "profoundly under-theorized" (p. 19). According to Hesse, multiculturalism had an entirely different development in the United States. Debates concerning multiculturalism had taken place at universities and, in the 1990s, these debates had extended into the fields of gender and the politics of knowledge. Considerations of multiculturalism involved exploring democratic ideals of citizenship as well as the epistemology of many academic disciplines.

3 Stepping, according to Hastie and colleagues, is often seen as a type of African-American dance. Technically though it is not a dance but "a series of synchronized, rhythmical body movements that are combined with chants and, often, verbal play" (p. 296). Musical instruments are not used and, instead, body movements such as clapping and stamping are used to produce rhythms.

References

Amade-Escot, C. (2006). Student learning within the didactique tradition. In D. Kirk, M. O'Sullivan, & D. Macdonald (Eds.), *Handbook of research in physical education* (pp. 347–365). Thousand Oaks, CA: Sage.

Azzarito, L. (2009). The Panopticon of physical education: Pretty, active and ideally white. *Physical Education and Sport Pedagogy, 14*(1), 19–39.

Azzarito, L., & Solomon, M. A. (2005). A reconceptualization of physical education: The intersection of gender/race/social class. *Sport, Education and Society, 10*(1), 25–47.

Bailey, R., Armour, K. M., Kirk, D., Jess, M., Pickup, I., & Sandford, R. (2009). The educational benefits claimed for physical education and school sport: An academic review. *Research Papers in Education, 24*(1), 1–27.

Barker, D. M., Barker-Ruchti, N., Gerber, M., Gerlach, E., Sattler, S., & Pühse, U. (2014). Youths with migration backgrounds and their experiences of physical education: An examination of three cases. *Sport, Education and Society, 19*(2), 186–203.

Bell, N. D., & Lorenzi, D. (2004). Facilitating second language acquisition in elementary and secondary physical education classes. *Journal of Physical Education, Recreation & Dance, 75*(6), 46–51.

Benn, T., & Dagkas, S. (2006). Incompatible? Compulsory mixed-sex Physical Education Initial Teacher Training (PEITT) and the inclusion of Muslim women: A case-study on seeking solutions. *European Physical Education Review, 12*(2), 181–200.

Benn, T., Dagkas, S., & Jawad, H. (2011). Embodied faith: Islam, religious freedom and educational practices in physical education. *Sport, Education and Society, 16*(1), 17–34.

Benn, T., Jawad, H., & Al-Sinani, Y. (2013). The role of Islam in the lives of girls and women in physical education and sport. In Z. Gross, L. Davies, & A. Diab (Eds.), *Gender, religion and education in a chaotic postmodern world* (pp. 255–270). New York: Springer.

Benn, T., & Pfister, G. (2013). Meeting needs of Muslim girls in school sport: Case studies exploring cultural and religious diversity. *European Journal of Sport Science, 13*(5), 567–574.

Bernstein, B. (1971). *Class, codes and control* (Vol. 1). London: Routledge.

Burden Jr, J. W. (2011). Exploring cross-racial contact: Implications for PETE pre-service teachers' color-blind racial attitudes. *Journal of Studies in Education, 1*(1), 1–16.

Burden Jr, J. W., Columna, L., Hodge, S. R., & Martínez de la Vega Mansilla, P. (2013). Ethnolinguistically relevant pedagogy: Empowering English language learners in physical education. *Quest, 65*(2), 169–185.

Burden Jr, J. W., Hodge, S. R., Bryant, C. P., & Harrison, L. (2004). From colorblindness to intercultural sensitivity: Infusing diversity training in PETE programs. *Quest, 56*, 173–189.

Butt, K. L., & Pahnos, M. L. (1995). Why we need a multicultural focus in our schools. *Journal of Physical Education, Recreation & Dance, 66*(1), 48–53.

Carrington, B., & Williams, T. (1988). Patriarchy and ethnicity: The link between school physical education and community leisure activities. In J. Evans (Ed.), *Teachers, teaching and control in physical education* (pp. 83–96). London: Falmer Press.

Carroll, B., & Hollinshead, G. (1993). Ethnicity and conflict in physical education. *British Educational Research Journal, 19*(1), 59–76.

Clancy, M. E., & Hruska, B. L. (2005). Developing language objectives for English language learners in physical education lessons. *Journal of Physical Education, Recreation & Dance, 76*(4), 30–35.

Columna, L., Foley, J. T., & Lytle, R. K. (2010). Physical education teachers' and teacher candidates' attitudes toward cultural pluralism. *Journal of Teaching in Physical Education, 29*(3), 295–311.

Columna, L., Senne, T. A., & Lytle, R. (2009). Communicating with Hispanic parents of children with and without disabilities. *Journal of Physical Education, Recreation & Dance, 80*(4), 48–54.

Corbett, D. (1995). Women of color: Perspectives within the profession. *Journal of Physical Education, Recreation and Dance, 66*(7), 25–27.

Dagkas, S., & Benn, T. (2006). Young Muslim women's experiences of Islam and physical education in Greece and Britain: A comparative study. *Sport, Education and Society, 11*(1), 21–38.

Dagkas, S., Benn, T., & Jawad, H. (2011). Multiple voices: Improving participation of Muslim girls in physical education and school sport. *Sport, Education and Society, 16*(2), 223–239.

DeSensi, J. T. (1995). Understanding multiculturalism and valuing diversity: A theoretical perspective. *Quest, 47*, 34–43.

Evans, J. (2004). Making a difference? Education and ability in PE. *European Physical Education Review, 10*(1), 95–108.

Farooq, S., & Parker, A. (2009). Sport, physical education, and Islam: Muslim independent schooling and the social construction of masculinities. *Sociology of Sport Journal, 26*(2), 277–295.

Fitzpatrick, K. (2011). Stop playing up!: Physical education, racialization and resistance. *Ethnography, 12*(2), 174–197.

Fitzpatrick, K. (2013). Brown bodies, racialisation and physical education. *Sport, Education and Society, 18*(2), 135–153.

Flintoff, A., Fitzgerald, H., & Scraton, S. (2008). The challenges of intersectionality: Researching difference in physical education. *International Studies in Sociology of Education, 18*(2), 73–85.

Flintoff, A., & Webb, L. (2012). 'Just open your eyes a bit more': The methodological challenges of researching black and minority ethnic students' experiences of physical education teacher education. *Sport, Education and Society, 17*(5), 571–589.

Flory, S. B., & McCaughtry, N. (2011). Culturally relevant physical education in urban schools: Reflecting cultural knowledge. *Research Quarterly for Exercise and Sport, 82*(1), 49–60.

Hall, S. (2000). Conclusion: The multi-cultural question. In B. Hesse (Ed.), *Un/Settled multiculturalisms: Diasporas, entanglements, 'transruptions'* (pp. 209–241). London: Zed Books.

Hamzeh, M., & Oliver, K. L. (2012). 'Because I am Muslim, I cannot wear a swimsuit': Muslim girls negotiate participation opportunities for physical activity. *Research Quarterly for Exercise and Sport, 83*(2), 330–339.

Hastie, P., Martin, E., & Buchanan, A. M. (2006). Stepping out of the norm: An examination of praxis for a culturally-relevant pedagogy for African-American children. *Journal of Curriculum Studies, 38*(3), 293–306.

Hellison, D. R. (1995). *Teaching responsibility through physical activity.* Champaign, IL: Human Kinetics.

Hesse, B. (2000). Un/settled multiculturalisms. In B. Hesse (Ed.), *Un/Settled multiculturalisms: Diasporas, entanglements, 'transruptions'* (pp. 1–30). London: Zed Books.

Hill, J., & Azzarito, L. (2012). Representing valued bodies in PE: A visual inquiry with British Asian girls. *Physical Education & Sport Pedagogy, 17*(3), 263–276.

Hodge, S. R., & Wiggens, D. K. (2010). The African American experience in physical education and kinesiology: Plight, pitfalls, and possibilities. *Quest, 62,* 35–60.

Kincheloe, J. L., & Steinberg, S. R. (1997). *Changing multiculturalism.* Buckingham, UK: Open University Press

Kirk, D. (2010). *Physical education futures.* London: Routledge.

Knez, K., Macdonald, D., & Abbott, R. (2012). Challenging stereotypes: Muslim girls talk about physical activity, physical education and sport. *Asia-Pacific Journal of Health, Sport and Physical Education, 3*(2), 109–122.

Ladson-Billing, G. (1995). Toward a theory of culturally relevant pedagogy. *American Educational Research Journal, 32*(3), 465–491.

Lundvall, S., & Meckbach, S. (2012). Widening participation in sport-related studies in higher education: An exploratory study of symbolic struggles. *Sport, Education and Society, 17*(5), 671–686.

Lyter-Mickelberg, P. (1995). How to stop stereotyping students. *Strategies, 8*(6), 16–21.

Mangan, J. A. (2000). *Athleticism in the Victorian and Edwardian public school: The emergence and consolidation of an educational ideology* (3rd edn.). London: Frank Cass.

McKenzie, T. L., & Lounsbery, M. A. (2009). School physical education: The pill not taken. *American Journal of Lifestyle Medicine, 3,* 219–225.

Mowling, C. M., Brock, S. J., & Hastie, P. (2011). African-American children's representation of personal and social responsibility. *Sport, Education and Society, 16*(1), 89–109.

Rovegno, I., & Gregg, M. (2007). Using folk dance and geography to teach interdisciplinary, multicultural subject matter: A school-based study. *Physical Education and Sport Pedagogy, 12*(3), 205–223.

Siraj-Blatchford, I. (1993). Ethnicity and conflict in physical education: A critique of Carroll and Hollinshead's case study. *British Educational Research Journal, 19,* 77–82.

Stride, A. (2014). Let US tell YOU! South Asian, Muslim girls tell tales about physical education. *Physical Education and Sport Pedagogy, 19*(4), 398–417.

Ukpokodu, O. N. (2009). Pedagogies that foster transformative learning in a multicultural education course: A reflection. *Journal of Praxis in Multicultural Education, 4*(1), 4.

Walseth, K. (2015). Muslim girls' experiences in physical education in Norway: What role does religiosity play? *Sport, Education and Society, 20*(3), 304–322.

PART VI

Analyzing teaching

Introduction

There are many reasons why we want to know more about how teachers teach their subject matter. Researchers are interested in studying excellent teachers to better understand the elements of effective teaching and to use this information to better prepare preservice teachers. Likewise, novice or struggling teachers can benefit from feedback from teacher assessments to improve their skills and better manage their classrooms. Principals and supervisors use formative assessments of teaching as primary tools to assist teachers to learn new strategies or improve current practice, while teachers receive summative assessments associated with annual or periodic reviews to provide information for school or grade level placement or other personnel decisions.

Recently, in the United States, the analysis of teaching has taken on heightened intensity as teacher job security and salaries have become tied directly to classroom performance, particularly student learning. Neoliberal perspectives on high stakes testing have led to finger-pointing when students do not score well on these tests or do not improve from year to year based on external metrics of success. The natural next step is to assess the teaching learning environment and particularly teaching behavior as the source of the problem.

For the last decade, however, physical educators have been buffered from the more punitive forms of teacher evaluations due to the peripheral position and perceived low status of physical education within the school environment. With most of the high stakes testing and teacher evaluations targeted at literacy and mathematics, physical educators, though forced to teach increasingly larger classes, for shorter time periods, and with fewer resources, have not received the same level of scrutiny as have their classroom colleagues. Increasingly, though, the federal government has offered large state level multimillion dollar grants, such as "No Child Left Behind" and the most recent "Race to the Top," as carrots to entice states and school districts to evaluate teachers in all subject areas as one condition to receive this funding (United States Department of Education [USDE], 2001, 2009). Many state Departments of Public Instruction have taken on the task of designing evaluation systems to assess teacher effectiveness in all subject areas, including physical education.

The chapters in this part look at a range of trends and issues associated with teaching analysis and teacher effectiveness. In the first chapter (25), McCullick, Gaudreault, and Ramos open this part with a comprehensive review of research associated with teacher accountability in the United States. They begin by describing many of the concerns associated with the teacher accountability movement and highlight the contradictory research results that provide the foundation on which teacher effectiveness decisions are currently being made. They then distinguish between performance-based and student growth/value-added accountability models currently competing for acceptance in states and school districts across the United States. Performance-based models evaluate the teaching process, while student growth models evaluate teachers using student outcomes (typically based on student scores on high stakes achievement tests). The authors explain the theory and policies associated with these two approaches and detail a number of issues associated with use of these teacher evaluation models in the classroom and gymnasium.

It appears clear that physical education teachers are experiencing teacher accountability initiatives and are assuming a precarious place in the high stakes environment. These efforts to hold teachers directly responsible for student learning in their classes shows a blatant ignorance of or disregard for the plethora of factors that are known to impact students' opportunities to learn. Physical education professionals at every school level will need to understand the consequences of value-added, student growth accountability models to have even a reasonable chance of steering clear of the pitfalls.

Performance-based models have been used for many years in education and physical education to provide formative feedback and assessments to teachers in physical education. Subramaniam and Wuest's chapter (26) examines several methods for measuring teaching in physical education. After a brief history of research on the measurement of teaching in physical education, they describe several quantitative methods with particular emphasis on systematic observation systems. While systematic observation has a rich history in physical education beginning with the work of Cheffers (1977) and Metzler (1983), these systems are finding new and varied purposes when coupled with wireless technologies and mobile device applications. The authors conclude by glimpsing the future of ecologically valid instruments that allow researchers to measure student learning in authentic game play settings.

This section concludes with Cale's (27) analysis and critique of the issues surrounding teaching about active lifestyles. She summarizes and critiques the research evidence on the role of physical education as a positive influence on young people's physical activity. She then considers issues teachers face when teaching about active lifestyles. This includes critiquing current lifestyles pedagogy and some common practices, notably fitness testing. Although highly touted when first developed, fitness tests have not proven to be as motivating to students as once predicted. Unfortunately, they hold potential to become the "high stakes" tests in physical education similar to the standardized tests in reading and mathematics used to evaluate classroom teacher effectiveness. Cale explains that fitness tests/student test scores can become the "student growth" measure used to compare physical education teachers and evaluate their "effectiveness." She provides a powerful critique of these tests and concludes with a futuristic assessment of issues and concerns for the future.

Catherine D. Ennis
University of North Carolina at Greensboro, USA

Stephen J. Silverman
Teachers College, Columbia University, USA

References

Cheffers, J. (1977). Observing teaching systematically. *Quest, 28*(1), 17–28.

Metzler, M. (1983). Using academic learning time in process-product studies with experimental teaching units. In T. Templin & J. Olson (Eds.), *Teaching in physical education* (pp. 185–196). Champaign, IL: Human Kinetics.

United States Department of Education [USDE]. (2001). *The 'No Child Left Behind' Act (public law PL 107–11).* Washington, DC: Author. Retrieved from www2.ed.gov/nclb/landing.jhtml.

United States Department of Education [USDE]. (2009). *American Recovery and Reinvestment Act of 2009 (ARRA),* Section 14005–6, Title XIV, (Public Law 111–5). Washington, DC: Retrieved from www2. ed.gov/programs/racetothetop/legislation.html.

25

TEACHER ACCOUNTABILITY AND EFFECTIVE TEACHING IN PHYSICAL EDUCATION

Bryan A. McCullick, UNIVERSITY OF GEORGIA, USA

Karen Lux Gaudreault, UNIVERSITY OF WYOMING, USA

& Nilo C. Ramos, OKLAHOMA STATE UNIVERSITY, USA

In many professions, relatively simple calculations and logically linked outcome measures determine one's effectiveness. Two such examples are sales and law. The evaluation of sales professionals is based on the dollar amount brought in on a yearly basis while prosecuting attorneys' effectiveness is usually dependent on the number of cases won and lawbreakers brought to justice. To our knowledge, few debate whether these measures are fair let alone valid and reliable. Many would accept the premise that if a real estate agent sold $1 million worth of real estate in a calendar year then he was an 'effective' sales professional. Similarly, a prosecuting attorney who won 50 % or more of her cases would be regarded almost universally as an effective lawyer. Although there is room for debate, it is safe to say that, in both cases, a direct line can reasonably be drawn between the individual's work and the outcome.

When it comes to evaluating teacher effectiveness, however, the process and confounding factors make the practice considerably less straightforward. If it were easy to measure good teaching by readily determined metrics such as profit margins or winning records in the courtroom, there would be little need for this text to address the topic. As it is, the identification of teaching that results in student learning is an exercise that is marred with a multitude of variables and an inability to control for them. Teacher effectiveness literature indicates the importance of understanding that directly connecting teacher behavior and student achievement and "equat[ing] effectiveness with success in producing achievement gain" (Brophy & Good, 1986, p. 328) is a slippery slope at best.

Perhaps the culprit preventing effective teaching from easy measurement of student achievement is that "the difficulty in identifying the concept of effectiveness in teaching lies in the complexity of teaching" (Rink, 2014, p. 408). That is, a teacher's 'product' – student learning, is heavily influenced by a host of dynamics beyond the control of schools and teachers. Even the research base identifying what teacher behaviors are most indicative of teacher effectiveness has cautioned that a relationship between effective teaching behaviors and student learning is not as easily conceptualized because "in reality, instruction always occurs within particular contexts" (Brophy & Good, 1986, p. 369) and those contexts heavily influence student achievement.

This 'context' makes equating teacher behaviors with student achievement such a dubious task. The nature of schools and other overwhelming variables such as students' previous school experiences, resources outside of school necessary to practice and learn, and opportunities within home life mediate the effects of teacher behaviors on student learning (Darling-Hammond, Amrein-Beardsley, Haertel, & Rothstein, 2012). Any individual who has spent one day in a school could attest to this assertion. Incredulously, it is those writing and enacting policy who seemingly fail to recognize the complexity of this issue. In turn, it allows for a much 'cleaner' determination of teacher performance. Conversely, there are many concerns resulting in myriad issues associated with labeling teachers effective or ineffective since the bulk of research indicates that most popular modes of teacher evaluation are "fraught with inaccuracies and inconsistencies" (p. 8). As a result, these individuals stand as advocates for using student achievement gains to measure teacher effectiveness and, eventually, make personnel decisions.

For physical education (PE) teachers the evaluation of teacher effectiveness provides additional concerns. A majority of research and debate about teacher effectiveness guiding state and national policy centers on the classroom with little attention being paid to content areas that are taught in different contexts. PE scholars have given much attention to teacher effectiveness research but only recently has the debate on evaluating PE teachers' effectiveness based on student performance been brought to the forefront (Roberts, 2014). As with the debate regarding teachers in 'regular' classrooms, the debate regarding PE teacher effectiveness has similar problems. Specifically, the amount of instructional time, class sizes, and available resources are areas in which teaching in the gymnasium is different from the classroom. At the same time, PE brings with it additional complexities of marginalization, lack of resources, isolation, and its historical connection to coaching sport, all of which make for a strong argument that in PE drawing a connection between teacher effectiveness and student outcomes becomes an even flimsier proposition than in any other subject area.

While hardly anyone would take a stance that teachers should not be held *reasonably* accountable for effective teaching, the debate seems to center on *how* teachers are held accountable, what measures determine it, and the impact on teachers' professional lives when employment, advancement, and rewards are tied to these measures. Therefore, the purpose of this chapter is three-fold and will highlight: (a) confounding dynamics in the evaluation of teacher effectiveness, (b) widely used models of assessment, and (c) the impact of this movement on the teaching of PE and PE teachers. The chapter concludes with reflections on where teachers, physical education teacher education (PETE) researchers, and faculty should focus their efforts in the near future.

Confounding dynamics in the evaluation of teacher effectiveness

For a concise and well-presented history on the genesis and proliferation of the teacher accountability movement in the United States, we direct readers to Metzler (2014). In short, over the last 30-plus years despite evidence to the contrary, the position that teachers should be held accountable and that there are valid and reliable measures that can assuredly indicate which teachers contribute most to student learning (Milanowski, 2004) has continued to gain support. Shockingly, the movement has pressed on and even advanced in the face of evidence suggesting that making teacher effectiveness determinations based on student outcomes is precarious, at best. Given less attention, however, are the complications that make this issue an area of fervent debate. While far from a comprehensive list, those complications are: (a) uncontrollable factors, (b) contradictory research results, (c) ineffective staffing practices, and (d) resources.

Uncontrollable factors

Regardless of the subject matter, perhaps, the most influential hindrance to the validity of teacher effectiveness measures is that of the factors influencing student learning outside the teacher's and school's sphere of influence. Unlike the example of the real-estate sales professionals whose products and performance are easily linked, student learning and being prepared to learn is heavily dependent on factors beyond even the student's control. Perhaps the most influential of these factors is the student's socio-economic status (SES) and associated "sub-components" that have far-reaching impact on resources which contribute most to student achievement (Hattie, 2013). Additionally, data suggest that influencing student achievement are factors such as teacher turnover (Ronfeldt, Loeb, & Wyckoff, 2013) and parental aspirations and expectations (Hong & Ho, 2005).

At the same time, students bring with them a number of factors that affect their own achievement. Among others, children's prior school achievement, dispositions and attitudes, and pre-school experiences appear to have the most powerful effect on student achievement (Hattie, 2013). Arguably, while schools and teachers can possibly foster these, the evidence suggests that they are best done so in pre-schools. Whether children are able to get those experiences, however, is not within the control of the school or teacher.

Contradictory research results

We give more attention to this subject in a subsequent section of this chapter, but the body of knowledge on teacher evaluation measures is inconsistent. There are scholars positing that "rigorous teacher evaluation system can be substantially related to student achievement" (Milanowski, 2004, p. 34), while others claim that, even those systems which are statistically strong, produce ratings that "differ substantially from class to class and from year to year, as well as from one statistical model to the next" (Darling-Hammond et al., 2012, p. 9). Further complicating the issue is that both sides put forth strong arguments that would leave even the most independent arbitrator unconvinced that either had the stronger case. In the end, not only have scholars put forth much effort to create and test evaluation models, but they have also worked just as hard at convincing others of their position. Without consensus, this leaves policy makers to their own devices when taking a side. When those policy makers are individuals with little knowledge of teaching, learning, and how schools operate, expediency takes precedent over appropriateness.

Ineffective staffing practices

Perhaps the single-most controversial outcome of the teacher evaluation debate concerns how evaluation results should influence personnel decisions. Teacher evaluations are usually linked to retention, promotion, or salary increases. Economists have recognized that one purpose of employee evaluation is to motivate employees to improve their work (Taylor & Tyler, 2011). However, they also recognize that one problem with this is that "evaluation induced improvements may … be transient if the incentives only operate on behavior that contributes to an evaluation score. By contrast, the effects may be more likely to persist if the evaluation spurs employees' investment in human capital" (p. 1).

Teacher evaluation, at best, can be a vital component of teacher development. However, as Murphy, Hallinger, and Heck (2013) noted, the definition of the term evaluation connotes a superior-subordinate relationship fraught with the tensions that accompany it – especially when the results of the evaluation "are used to make decisions about the terms of employment" (p. 349).

The idea that measuring teacher value based on student outcomes is seemingly too complex to allow the same approaches used in business and other professions to be applied to teaching.

Resources

Arguing against the high cost of evaluating teaching is low-hanging fruit for anyone opposed to teacher evaluation and is hardly adequate to dissuade those interested in using evaluation to improve schools. However, one cannot ignore the time and money required to conduct meaningful teacher evaluations. Without a well-funded and well-designed evaluation, a partial or compromised teacher evaluation can result, causing personnel and political repercussions.

Ideally, the basic tenet driving teacher evaluation and accountability is the intent of improving students' experiences in schools. The evidence, it appears, indicates that if this is the end-point, then spending "time and energy in areas other than teacher evaluation" (Murphy et al., 2013, p. 352) is perhaps a more efficient way of reaching it. There is little doubt that expending significant funds is required for the assessment of teacher effectiveness. In the United States, spending on education is often a topic that follows political party lines and possibilities for consensus are low. Inevitably, policy makers find compromise by agreeing to use the easiest and most cost-effective manner of conducting evaluations, often leading to the use of invalid and unreliable instruments and hiring untrained evaluators to conduct the evaluations. Both lead to poor data and have far-reaching implications for teachers, schools, and, most importantly, children.

Models of teacher evaluation

Educational reforms in the last 50 years focusing on teacher quality have been concurrent with an increase in federal policies related to teacher effectiveness (Cohen-Vogel, 2005). Consequently, the improvement of teacher evaluation systems has received amplified attention as a way to increase teacher effectiveness and student achievement.

There has been a recent push at the national level in the United States for school reform with an emphasis on teacher accountability and quality. The federal government's introduction of 'No Child Left Behind' in 2002 and the 'Race to the Top' (RTTT) competition in 2009 intensified the focus on improving accuracy of teacher evaluation systems to measure teacher effectiveness. Outcomes of these systems are used for high-stakes teacher decisions such as tenure, salary increases, and dismissal. As a result, holistic teacher evaluation systems have emerged employing standards-based, multi-dimensional, and formative approaches using student outcome data. Since individual states and school districts have freedom to define and quantify teacher effectiveness, many have developed their own teacher evaluation systems based on established, modified, or locally developed models.

Primarily, teacher evaluation systems are composed of two types of models: (a) *performance-based* and (b) *student growth*. *Performance-based* models evaluate teacher quality with a focus on teacher-controlled variables such as teaching skills, dispositions, professional development, and assessment of student learning. *Student growth* models are statistical models that use norm-referenced statistics and may use non-teacher controllable factors associated with student achievement (e.g., student's background and school characteristics) to calculate student growth. In essence, *performance-based* models evaluate *process* while *student growth* models evaluate *outcomes* to measure teacher effectiveness. The following discussion on teacher evaluation models in the United States and internationally will provide a description and examples of these models.

The *performance-based* models emerging in recent decades include *teacher performance assessments* and *standards-based evaluations*. *Teacher Performance Assessments* began in 1987 with the National Board for Professional Teaching Standards' (NBPTS) evaluations for accomplished teachers (Darling-Hammond, 2010). Teachers voluntarily chose to participate in these evaluations and collected and organized evidence of their performance in a portfolio with lesson plans, student learning evidence, and video-recorded teaching lessons with commentaries. Trained experts scored these artifacts with rubrics that evaluated dimensions of teaching. California adopted this method to assign additional pay for teachers who had attained NBPTS certification. The Council of Chief State School Officers (CCSSO) following the NBPTS criteria created the Interstate New Teacher Assessment and Support Consortium (InTASC) standards. The InTASC standards have been incorporated in an evaluation approach used by the Council for the Accreditation of Educator Preparation (CAEP) for teacher education programs accreditation.

Standards-based evaluations are based on teaching standards grounded in teaching and learning research literature (Darling-Hammond, 2010). One example is the *Danielson Framework* which is a set of research-based instructional components aligned with CCSSO's InTASC standards. It can be used to evaluate teachers' planning and preparation, classroom environment, instruction, and professional responsibilities. Another example is the *Marzano Teacher Evaluation Model* which can be used to evaluate teachers' classroom strategies and behaviors, planning and preparing, reflection, collegiality, and professionalism. Both are designed to increase conversations among practitioners for enhancing teaching skills while also being used for evaluation, professional development, mentoring, and coaching. These instruments utilize indicators such as analysis of lesson and unit plans, classroom observations, teacher participation in the community, student feedback, and teacher conversations to provide research-based evidence of teacher practices associated with student outcomes.

In addition to using models that evaluate teacher performance, teacher evaluation systems incorporate *student growth* models in their assessment of teacher effectiveness. The most commonly used models include Value-Added Models (VAMs) and Student Growth Percentiles (SGPs). Federally funded Race to the Top initiatives require states to adopt data on student growth as a measure of teacher effectiveness. Thus, government policy and funding have been instrumental in driving recent use of *student growth* models in teacher evaluation systems (Sledge & Pazey, 2013).

VAMs' objective is to measure teachers' yearly contributions to student learning and achievement based on standardized tests while accounting for student background and other factors related to student achievement beyond the teacher's control (e.g., attendance and economic status). These models use hierarchical linear modeling to predict individual student scores using the students' previous scores while accounting for specific variables and then compare the prediction to the student's actual score and other students' scores with similar performances. The difference between the scores is attributed to the impact, or value that the teacher 'added' to the students' actual scores. States have assigned various values to VAMs in teacher evaluation. Arizona requires that VAMs must be weighted between 35 and 50% of the teacher evaluation while Colorado, Florida, and Idaho require a minimum of 50% (Baker, Oluwole, & Green, 2013).

SGPs differ from VAMs in that they do not account for student differences and student background. SGPs use a statistical method that calculates the relationship between a student's current and previous scores in comparison to the student's peers. Thus, if a student has a SGP of 90, it means that the student had more growth than 90% of similar students.

Internationally, countries have opted to use *performance-based* models alone or have complemented these models with *student growth* models. It appears that while the United States uses standardized assessments to measure educational quality, other countries are focusing on instructional practices and curriculum quality, using multiple measures (mainly formative evaluations) to improve teaching instead of punishing educators or schools for low performance (Conley, 2015). Stewart (2011) noted that, in countries that employing high-performance measures such as Canada and Finland, teachers and principals are encouraged to discuss student progress, while annual teacher evaluations in Singapore and China use multiple measures such as classroom observations, community involvement, and contributions to their school. These countries rely on school-level accountability systems based on a variety of "school improvement goals, professional contributions, and indicators of student well-being" (p. 19) instead of relying solely on student achievement data. In other high-achieving countries such as South Korea, little attention is given to teacher evaluations (Darling-Hammond, 2010). Instead, these countries focus on effectiveness in the teacher preparation, support, and development to increase student achievement.

Other countries have developed student growth model-based teacher evaluation systems similar to those in the United States. In Chile, the discussion about teacher quality is centered on teacher characteristics related to students' achievement in standardized tests and evaluation of teacher competencies (Santelices, Galleguillos, Gonzáles, & Taut, 2015). Lingard (2010) indicated that a "global trend – represented by the Anglo-American [student outcomes] model – [which] has been towards standardization" (p. 139) has driven policy changes in Australia and England, but not in other countries such as Finland, Scotland, and Wales.

Issues associated with teacher evaluation models

Researchers continue to explore the use of *performance-based* and *student growth* models in teacher evaluation systems (e.g., Goldhaber & Hansen, 2010; Kane & Staiger, 2012). In addition to questions surrounding their effectiveness and accuracy, findings suggest the majority of evaluations do not identify areas for teacher improvement. School districts do not consistently use results to provide beginning teachers with additional help and poor teacher performance, in general, is unaddressed (Weisberg, Sexton, Mulhern, & Keeling, 2009). Issues such as these have contributed to doubt undermining practitioners' belief in these systems. Consensus among policy makers, practitioners, and researchers is that the majority of teacher evaluation systems do not provide school district administrators with assistance in personnel decision-making or in teacher improvement (Darling-Hammond et al., 2012; Strunk, Weinstein, & Makkonen, 2014).

Performance-based models are grounded in research connecting teacher performance to student achievement. Used in teacher evaluation systems for many years, these models confirm that if teachers demonstrate/possess (or not) characteristics linked to student learning, they may be deemed (in)effective. Although there is little doubt these methods can be effective (e.g., Cantrell & Kane, 2013; see www.metproject.org), other issues related to accuracy (due to human error) and teacher impact (attribution of student learning to the teacher) indicate teachers are only one factor impacting student achievement. Models do not consider multiple variables impacting student learning such as home and community challenges and support, peer culture and achievement, prior schooling and teachers, and other school factors such as instructional time, class size, and curriculum materials (e.g., Darling-Hammond et al., 2012).

Student growth models have received increased attention in recent years due to policy changes based on beliefs that these models can be used effectively to evaluate teacher quality. In fact, *student growth* models may be the hottest issue in education and are being used in teacher evaluations resulting in high-stakes decisions such as dismissal, tenure, and financial reward. VAMs have been the most commonly used *student growth* model in teacher evaluation systems. Researchers and statisticians have recognized the benefits of VAMs (e.g., Ballou, Sanders, & Wright, 2004; Goldhaber & Hansen, 2010). Theoretically, VAMs can indicate the impact an individual teacher had on an individual student, and consequently, the teacher's effectiveness. Conversely, researchers and scholars are raising issues around the use of VAMs in the evaluation of teachers (e.g., Darling-Hammond et al., 2012; Mathis, 2013; Sahlberg, 2011). According to Gabriel and Lester (2013), four methodological issues dominate the literature: (a) error rates, (b) test effects, (c) model biases, and (d) inherent problems of achievement tests.

Studies have indicated VAMs' error rates make them inconsistent (e.g., Schochet & Chiang, 2010). Sass (2008) explored the changes of VAM scores of teachers in Florida and California who were in the bottom 20%. In the following year, between 20% to less than 35% of those teachers stayed in the same category, 35% to around 45% moved up to average level while 20% to over 40% scored above average (highest category).

Research on test effects has pointed out that the type of test used, time of the year taken, and stakes (or perceived importance) of the test can significantly change teachers' VAM scores (Bill & Melinda Gates Foundation, 2010). Papay's (2011) study indicated that almost 50% of teachers would have received a different category in their evaluation if the test itself, or time taken, were different. In a review of research examining potential bias in VAMs, Gabriel and Lester (2013) cited finding that minority teachers have more unstable general VAMs scores. These findings may be due to inclusion of variables in the model such as demographics, previous tests scores, and even the nonrandomized selection of students to teachers. The authors also pointed out that the use of students' achievement test scores in VAMs assumes that these tests are an accurate measure of student learning and achievement, ignoring the inherent issues associated with standardized tests.

The issues surrounding VAMs result in a cautious approach to their use. Considering that at least one in four teachers may be misevaluated, critics argue that restraint is essential, especially in high-stakes decisions. Relying solely on VAM models could lead to ethical, legal, and practical issues, as VAMs are highly unreliable from test to test, classroom to classroom, and from year to year (Mathis, 2013). Sahlberg (2011) summarized this position stating that using only student test scores to evaluate individual teachers was inappropriate. Although VAM models have raised issues about their use in high-stakes decisions, supporters continue to call for more research to validate VAMs for teacher evaluation (Ballou et al., 2004).

Another *growth* model that is receiving attention is Student Growth Percentiles (SGPs). According to Baker et al. (2013), the popularity of SGPs is due to a lack of investigations on their validity and their design does not estimate teacher effectiveness. In fact, the authors warned, "student growth percentiles are not intended for attribution of responsibility for student progress to either the teacher or the school" (p. 8). Proponents of SGPs indicate that this model provides a simple and easy indication to stakeholders (parents, teachers, and administrators) of how much improvement a student had from year to year when compared to the students' peers, which not only displays how much a student improved, but also what is the range of improvement expected for students with the same level of performance (e.g., Betebenner, 2011). The few available studies on SGPs have indicated that they should not be used in teacher evaluations because SGPs do not consider factors that are beyond a teacher's control, and consequently, unfair for rewarding teacher performance or making high-stakes decisions (Ehlert, Koedel, Parsons, & Podgursky, 2012; Goldhaber & Walch, 2012).

As the number of states adopting *student growth* models into their teacher evaluation systems is increasing, there is a growing number of research studies investigating the relationship and consistency between *performance-based* and *student growth* models. The literature can be classified into studies exploring this relationship in (a) research contexts and (b) practice (Strunk et al., 2014). This differentiation highlights the methodologies and assumptions used in the studies and the implications for stakeholders involved in the use of these measures. Strunk et al. (2014) noted the studies using research contexts have used sample sizes from 24 (Grossman, Loeb, Cohen, & Wickoff, 2013) to 3000 teachers (MET project) measuring multiple evaluation tools and have found moderate to low correlations between observation-based measures and VAMs. These studies have found a positive and moderate correlation between standardized tests and observational measures, due to issues associated with these tools that include observers' consistency, types of measures used, and student bias toward teachers (Strunk et al., 2014). Recently, Morgan Hodge, Trepinski, and Anderson (2014) investigated the stability of teacher performance (observation evaluations) and effectiveness (standardized test scores) over a five-year period. The results indicated that neither evaluation method was highly stable over multiple years while the relationship, though small, between the methods was relatively stable over time.

In an attempt to solve issues associated with teacher evaluation systems, scholars and researchers have proposed different approaches. Taken together, these initiatives suggest a comprehensive system using multiple measures to create a fair and accurate evaluation of teacher effectiveness. Formative approaches focused on improving teachers' weaknesses and teaching strategies are best balanced with summative approaches; although measures that de-emphasize test scores require more work, they may potentially have greater impact on instruction and improvement of education (Mathis, 2013). According to Weisberg et al. (2009), evaluation systems should: (a) be comprehensive with clear performance standards, multiple rating options, and regular feedback to teachers; (b) have trained administrators and evaluators who are regularly monitored and held accountable for using evaluations effectively; (c) use evaluations in high-stakes decisions such as reward, promotion, and dismissal; and (d) adopt low-stakes options in dismissal policies. Darling-Hammond et al. (2012) suggested most effective teacher evaluation systems are based on professional standards – with multiple observations, multiple data sources, implemented by expert evaluators, and used to provide timely and meaningful feedback to teachers. All key stakeholders (e.g., principal and teachers) must be involved in the development process. The most effective systems are specific for each teacher grade level, subject area, and experience levels (Clayton, 2014).

Overall, the literature has specified that more research is essential to improve our understanding of present evaluation systems and models. Additionally, scholars indicate that, due to the varied contexts of individual schools, there is no consensus on one evaluation system that may work across all grade levels and subjects. Despite this, the literature points to the need for meaningful changes to teacher evaluation systems to make them successful in accurately and fairly evaluating teacher effectiveness.

Physical education teacher evaluation and implications

Teacher evaluation in PE has been available for many years. Evaluators have relied on *performance-based* models using general evaluation tools (e.g., Danielson Framework for Teaching and Marzano Teacher Evaluation Model) and specific tools such as the PE Teacher Evaluation Tool (National Association for Sport and Physical Education [NASPE], 2007) to assess teacher practice and evaluate teacher effectiveness. Similar to other teacher evaluations, issues include the accuracy of the measure and knowledge of the evaluator about the subject. The fact remains that PE is the only school subject that requires and teaches performance of movement physical skills. This exacerbates the issue and suggests that most principals do not have the expertise or time to learn PE-specific evaluation tools. Combined with a lack of priority, it is no surprise that there has been little emphasis given to the accurate evaluation of PE teachers.

Recent incentives and renewed support for the use of student achievement data in the evaluation of teachers may soon extend to PE. The problem is that currently, due in part to the fact PE is not considered a core subject, with some exceptions (e.g., *PE Metrics*, NASPE, 2010, 2011) standardized testing in PE is rare. Fitness testing is the most commonly used among physical educators, even as criticism of its accuracy and negative effects on teaching practices remain (Mercier & Doolittle, 2013). In the same way classroom teachers may teach students to the test, physical educators could train students to do well on fitness testing (see Cale, Chapter 27, this volume). Furthermore, the use of fitness tests can negatively affect students' perceptions toward physical activity. Most importantly, fitness testing does not necessarily represent students' knowledge, skills, and dispositions. Welk (2008) noted a limitation of fitness testing is that it measures the product or outcome rather than the underlying behaviors that promote physical activity and fitness. While it can help students develop physical activity and fitness goals, it should be only one tool to help assess students' dispositions and knowledge towards physical activity and, consequently, teacher effectiveness.

Another alternative that could assist administrators with PE teacher evaluation and PE's pursuit of legitimacy is the creation of achievement data by the PE teachers themselves. This practice is hardly novel; as Mercier and Doolittle (2013) suggested, assessments have been the "third leg" (p. 38) of PE pedagogy (curriculum, instruction, and assessment) and support for their use by organizations including NASPE, NBPTS, and CAEP have addressed the use of assessments for instructional improvement and standard alignment. Mercier and Doolittle's work provides guidelines for specific summative assessments (e.g., observations, written tests, and physical activity log with parental signature) that can be used to measure student achievement and provide evidence of teaching and program quality. Chief among them, student-learning objectives (SLOs) should guide selection of summative assessments that would demonstrate student achievement on goals for the unit, semester, or year. Sources of this type of assessments include *PE Metrics* (NASPE, 2010, 2011) and state level assessments designed by scholars. To make these assessments effective, several steps are needed: (a) a supportive environment between teachers and administrators; (b) teacher training and digital data tracking and recording; (c) effective communication with parents and students, especially if results are used for grade and school records; and (d) stakeholder understanding and value for the assessment process.

Lack of knowledge and concern from administration

Regardless of instructional level, building level principals have a significant impact on the culture and function of their respective school(s). Further, scholars have found that principal leadership has the ability to impact teacher efficacy (Soehner & Ryan, 2011). For physical educators, this can negatively impact their feelings and perceptions of their workplace as studies have shown many principals do not value physical education (Stringer, 2004). Stevens-Smith (2007) found that nearly 25% of the principals in her study described physical education as a low-priority course.

Further, most principals lack the knowledge about what constitutes a quality physical education program. They are unaware of state and national standards for physical education programming and teaching and, as a result, are ill-equipped to effectively evaluate physical educators' teaching behaviors in the gym or curriculum. This is compounded by administrators' personal, often negative, experiences as students in physical education.

Referred to as the 'apprenticeship of observation' (Lortie, 1975), administrators spent countless hours developing their conceptions of physical education and physical education teachers likely immersed in programs that could be described as 'roll the ball out' or 'busy, happy, good.' As a result, their notions of physical education subject matter and those who teach it are grounded in these images and impressions leading to inaccurate ideas about the physical educator working in their building under their supervision. With respect to evaluation and assessment, this might mean that principals enter the gym only looking to determine if children are well managed and physically active. As a result, many PE teachers' evaluations and assessments of teaching behavior by these principals may lack value, fail to contribute to teacher development, and might be characterized as inaccurate.

Impact on physical education and its teachers

Principal leadership has a significant impact on the well-being and motivation of teachers (Eyal & Roth, 2011). As any teacher will tell you, a principal can make a significant difference in the climate of a building, the morale of teachers and staff, and the overall culture of a school. Further, principal leadership has the potential to influence the status of PE in schools and may impact how others in school view the value of physical education (Blankenship & Coleman, 2009). Michigan teachers in a study by Sun, Youngs, Yang, Chu, and Zhao (2012) reported receiving very few evaluations and assessments by their principals. Of the 88 principals included, only 26% evaluated their teachers each year, 40% of the teachers reported being evaluated every three years, and 6% reported that their principal had never evaluated them. If physical educators are not observed by administration, it is unlikely they will receive meaningful feedback to enhance their teaching. As a result, a physical educator's development, growth, and improvement is dependent upon their abilities to reflect, self-assess, and seek out opportunities to connect with other teachers in their building or other physical educators in their school district.

Future directions

A chapter on this topic would be incomplete without addressing the increased need for advocacy associated with teacher evaluation. We will present recommendations relative to the respective constituents who would implement them. These constituents are (a) P-12 physical education teachers, and (b) PETE faculty and researchers.

P-12 physical education teachers

Physical educators should actively engage in their own advocacy efforts at the grass roots level. Physical educators should collect and share formative and summative assessments to document student performance and achievement. Assessments inform teacher decisions regarding curriculum, lesson planning, and lesson progression. Sharing this information within the school with other teachers, parents, administration, and students is one additional powerful advocacy tool. Professional organizations and scholars repeatedly urge practitioners to use and share data on student achievement to demonstrate the benefits of quality physical education. Given the current context of schools and educational policy, it is imperative that physical educators demonstrate the valuable place of PE and effective teaching in their schools.

PETE faculty and researchers

PETE faculty and researchers are essential to addressing the issue of teacher effectiveness and accountability. While not their sole province, teacher educators are usually in the best position to provide principals with specific evaluation materials geared toward measuring PE teacher effectiveness.

PETE faculty can assist school administrators to select and use effective evaluation tools and blend information from evaluation methods to produce reliable and valid teacher evaluations. Professional organizations such as SHAPE America and the Special Interest Group (SIG) of the American Educational Research Association (AERA) can develop relationships with principals, state legislators, and state school boards to address problems with teacher evaluation.

On a more local level, PETE faculty can make valuable contributions by nurturing relationships with school district administrators (not just PE teachers) to educate them and enhance awareness of quality physical education and reliable and valid assessments of teacher effectiveness in PE. Further, PE teachers who are more aware and have a deeper understanding of the impact of assessment and evaluation on their careers are better prepared to advocate for themselves and their programs. Programmatically, PETE programs should:

- ensure graduates can self-analyze and discuss additional evaluation resources to gain effective and valuable feedback about their teaching;
- increase instruction on multiple ways to assess students in PE school programs;
- ensure that pre-service teachers develop and apply assessments during their student teaching experience;
- train corps of mentor teachers to assist pre-service teachers in developing and using assessments during their student teaching experience and early field experiences.

PETE scholars who are engaged in research also have a large part to play. Currently, the body of work on issues surrounding teacher evaluation, effectiveness, and accountability in PE is limited. Future studies can enhance our knowledge of principals' perceptions of PE and encourage them to increase their knowledge of PE. In terms of PE-specific advocacy strategies, the field is nearly barren and the following areas of scholarship would be worthy of attention:

- identification of strategies necessary for improved evaluation of PE teachers by administration and significant others in the workplace;
- analyses of different evaluation systems implemented for PE teachers;
- the effects of this emphasis on PETE programs and PETE students' assessment;
- exemplar studies of PETE programs' efforts to increase emphasis on assessment;
- the relationship between teacher use of assessment and principal evaluation.

While the current state of teacher evaluation and accountability presents unique challenges for physical education and those who teach it, strategies presented here may provide a beginning to improving this process. Effective teacher evaluation has the potential to improve teaching practices, student learning, and demonstrate PE teachers' pedagogical skill.

Reflective questions for discussion

1. Discuss the major concerns surrounding teacher assessment.
2. Of the approaches to assessment discussed in this chapter, which would be the most appropriate for PE?
3. What types of assessment information can PE teachers provide to principals to assist in this process?

4. If you taught a workshop for principals to teach them about 'best practices' in teacher evaluation in PE, what topics and experiences would you include in the workshop?

5. Once teachers have been assessed how can this information be used to assist teachers to improve their performance and enhance student learning?

References

Baker, B. D., Oluwole, J., & Green, P. C. III (2013). The legal consequences of mandating high stakes decisions based on low quality information: Teacher evaluation in the race-to-the-top era. *Education Policy Analysis Archives, 21*(5), 1–67.

Ballou, D., Sanders, W., & Wright, G. (2004). Controlling for student background in value-added assessment of teachers. *Journal of Educational and Behavioral Statistics, 29*(1), 37–65.

Betebenner, D. W. (2011). A technical overview of the student growth percentile methodology: Student growth percentiles and percentile growth projections/trajectories. The National Center for the Improvement of Educational Assessment, Dover, NH. Retrieved from www.nj.gov/education/njsmart/ performance/SGP_Technical_Overview.pdf.

Bill & Melinda Gates Foundation. (2010). *Learning about teaching: Initial findings from the Measures of Effective Teaching Project.* Seattle, WA: Author.

Blankenship, B. T., & Coleman, M. M. (2009). An examination of 'wash-out' and workplace conditions of beginning physical education teachers. *Physical Educator, 66*(2), 97–111.

Brophy, J., & Good, T. (1986). Teacher behavior and student achievement. In M. C. Wittrock (Ed.), *Handbook of research on teaching* (3rd edn) (pp. 328–375). New York, NY: Macmillan.

Cantrell, S., & Kane, T. J. (2013). Ensuring fair and reliable measures of effective teaching: Culminating findings from the MET project three-year study (policy and practice brief). Measures of Effective Teaching (MET) project, Bill & Melinda Gates Foundation.

Clayton, C. D. (2014). Understanding current reforms to evaluate teachers: A literature review on teacher evaluation across the career span. *Excelsior: Leadership in Teaching and Learning, 8*(2), 52–71.

Cohen-Vogel, L. (2005). Federal role in teacher quality: 'Redefinition' or policy alignment? *Educational Policy, 19*(1), 18–43.

Conley, D. T. (2015). A new era for educational assessment. *Education Policy Analysis Archives, 23*(8). http:// dx.doi.org/10.14507/epaa.v23.1983. This article is part of EPAA/AAPE's Special Series on *A New Paradigm for Educational Accountability.* Guest Series Edited by Dr. Linda Darling-Hammond.

Darling-Hammond, L. (2010). *The flat world and education. How America's commitment to equity will determine our future.* New York, NY: Teachers College Press.

Darling-Hammond, L., Amrein-Beardsley, A., Haertel, E., & Rothstein, J. (2012). Evaluating teacher evaluation. *The Phi Delta Kappan, 93*(6), 8–15.

Ehlert, M., Koedel, C., Parsons, E., & Podgursky, M. (2012). *Selecting growth measures for school and teacher evaluations.* National Center for Analysis of Longitudinal Data in Education Research (CALDAR). Working Paper #80.

Eyal, O., & Roth, G. (2011). Principals' leadership and teachers' motivation: Self-determination theory analysis. *Journal of Educational Administration, 49*(3), 256–275.

Gabriel, R. & Lester, J. N. (2013). Sentinels guarding the grail: Value-added measurement and the quest for education reform. *Education Policy Analysis Archives, 21*(9). This article is part of EPAA/AAPE's Special Issue on *Value-Added: What America's Policymakers Need to Know and Understand,* Guest Edited by Dr. Audrey Amrein-Beardsley and Assistant Editors Dr. Clarin Collins, Dr. Sarah Polasky, and Ed Sloat. Retrieved from http://epaa.asu.edu/ojs/article/view/1165.

Goldhaber, D., & Hansen, M. (2010). Implicit measurement of teacher quality. *American Economic Review: Papers & Proceedings, 100* (May 2010), 250–255. Retrieved from www.aeaweb.org/articles. php?doi=10.1257/aer.100.2.250.

Goldhaber, D., & Walch, J. (2012). Strategic pay reform: A student outcomes-based evaluation of Denver's ProComp Teacher Pay Initiative. *Economics of Education Review, 31*, 1067–1083.

Grossman, P., Loeb, S., Cohen, J., & Wyckoff, J. (2013). Measure for measure: The relationship between measures of instructional practice in middle school English language arts and teachers' value-added scores. *American Journal of Education, 119*(3), 445–470.

Hattie, J. (2013). *Visible learning: A synthesis of over 800 meta-analyses relating to achievement.* London: Routledge.

Hong, S., & Ho, H. Z. (2005). Direct and indirect longitudinal effects of parental involvement on student achievement: Second-order latent growth modeling across ethnic groups. *Journal of Educational Psychology, 97,* 32–42.

Kane, T. J., & Staiger, D. O. (2012). *Gathering feedback from teaching: Combining high-quality observation with student surveys and achievement gains* (research paper). Measures of Effective Teaching (MET) project, Bill & Melinda Gates Foundation.

Lingard, B. (2010). Policy borrowing, policy learning: Testing times in Australian schooling. *Critical Studies in Education, 51*(2), 129–147.

Lortie, D. C. (1975). *School teacher: A sociological inquiry.* Chicago: University of Chicago Press.

Mathis, W. (2013). *Research-based options for education policymaking.* Retrieved from http://greatlakes-center.org/docs/Policy_Briefs/Research-Based-Options/PB-OPTIONS.pdf.

Mercier, K., & Doolittle, S. (2013). Assessing student achievement in physical education for teacher evaluation. *Journal of Physical Education, Recreation & Dance, 84*(3), 38–42.

Metzler, M. W. (2014). Teacher effectiveness research in physical education: The future isn't what it is supposed to be. *Research Quarterly in Exercise and Sport, 85,* 14–19.

Milanowski, A. (2004). The relationship between teacher performance evaluation scores and student achievement: Evidence from Cincinnati. *Peabody Journal of Education, 79*(4), 33–53.

Morgan, G. B., Hodge, K. J., Trepinski, T. M., & Anderson, L. W. (2014). The stability of teacher performance and effectiveness: Implications for policies concerning teacher evaluation. *Education Policy Analysis Archives, 22*(95), 1–18.

Murphy, J., Hallinger, P., & Heck, R. H. (2013). Leading via teacher evaluation: The case of the missing clothes? *Educational Researcher, 42*(6), 349–354.

National Association for Sport and Physical Education. (2007). *Physical education teacher evaluation tool.* Reston, VA: Author.

National Association for Sport and Physical Education. (2010). *PE metrics: Assessing national standards 1–6 in elementary school.* Reston, VA: Author.

National Association for Sport and Physical Education. (2011). *PE metrics: Assessing national standards 1–6 in secondary school.* Reston, VA: Author.

Papay, J. P. (2011). Different tests, different answers: the stability of teacher value-added estimates across outcome measures. *American Educational Research Journal, 48*(1), 163–193.

Rink, J. E. (2014). Measuring teacher effectiveness in physical education. *Research Quarterly in Exercise and Sport, 84,* 407–418.

Roberts, G. (2014). Time to demonstrate how we impact student learning. *Research Quarterly in Exercise and Sport, 85,* 27–30.

Ronfeldt, M., Loeb, S., & Wyckoff, J. (2013). How teacher turnover harms student achievement. *American Educational Research Association Journal, 50,* 4–36.

Sahlberg, P. (2011). The fourth way of Finland. *Journal of Educational Change, 12,* 173–185.

Santelices, M. V., Galleguillos, P., González, J., & Taut, S. (2015). Un estudio sobre la calidad docente en Chile: El rol del contexto en donde enseña el profesor y medidas de valor agregado. *Psyhke, 24*(1), 1–14.

Sass, T. (2008). *The stability of value-added measures of teacher quality and implications for teacher compensation policy.* Washington, DC: Calder.

Schochet, P. Z., & Chiang, H. S. (2010). *Error rates in measuring teacher and school performance based on students' test score gains* (NCEE 2010–4004). Washington, DC: National Center for Education Evaluation and Regional Assistance, Institute of Education Sciences, U.S. Department of Education.

Sledge, A., & Pazey, B. L. (2013). Measuring teacher effectiveness through meaningful evaluation: Can reform models apply to general education and special education teachers? *Teacher Education and Special Education, 36*(3), 231–246.

Soehner, D., & Ryan, T. (2011). The interdependence of principal school leadership and student achievement. *Scholar-Practitioner Quarterly, 5*(3), 274–288.

Stevens-Smith, D. (2007). High-stakes testing and the status of physical education. *Journal of Physical Education, Recreation and Dance, 78*(8), 10.

Stewart, V. (2011). Raising teacher quality around the world. *Educational Leadership, 68*(4), 16–20.

Stringer, A. J. (2004). *Middle school principals' perceptions of physical education and their influence on physical education programs* (Doctoral dissertation, University of North Carolina at Greensboro).

Strunk, K., Weinstein, T., & Makkonen, R. (2014). Sorting out the signal: Do multiple measures of teachers' effectiveness provide consistent information to teachers and principals? *Education Policy Analysis Archives, 22*(100). http://dx.doi.org/10.14507/epaav22.1590.

Sun, M., Youngs, P., Yang, H., Chu, H., & Zhao, Q. (2012). Association of district principal evaluation with learning-centered leadership practice: Evidence from Michigan and Beijing. *Educational Assessment, Evaluation and Accountability, 24*(3), 189–213.

Taylor, E. S., & Tyler, J. H. (2011). The effect of evaluation on performance: Evidence from longitudinal student achievement data of mid-career teachers. Washington, DC: National Bureau of Economic Research Working Paper No. 16877.

Weisberg, D., Sexton, S., Mulhern, J., & Keeling, D. (2009). *The widget effect: Our national failure to acknowledge and act on differences in teacher effectiveness.* Brooklyn, NY: New Teacher Project. Retrieved from http://tntp.org/assets/documents/TheWidgetEffect_2nd_ed.pdf.

Welk, G. J. (2008). The role of physical activity assessments for school-based physical activity promotion. *Measurement in Physical Education and Exercise Science, 12,* 184–206.

26

MEASUREMENT OF TEACHING IN PHYSICAL EDUCATION

Prithwi Raj Subramaniam & Deborah A. Wuest, ITHACA COLLEGE, USA

Teaching is a complex multidimensional act involving teachers and students working in partnership to teach and learn from each other (Campbell, Kyriakides, Muijs, & Robinson, 2003; Danielson, 2001; Muijs, Campbell, Kyriakides, & Robinson, 2005; Rink, 2013; Shulman, 1986; Siedentop, 2002; Silverman, 1994). To gain some degree of insight into the complexities involved in the teaching act requires a systematic approach in conducting research and collecting data that are reliable and valid. Quantitative measures that produce valid and reliable scores on student outcome measures are "essential first steps" (Locke, 1977, p. 11) for measuring teaching and enabling researchers to establish causal links between the multiple variables influencing teaching and student learning (Floden, 1986; Rink, 2013). Causal connections between teaching and learning and the interaction of multiple variables in the teaching context can also be established through carefully designed interventions with a clear focus on the desired outcome measure.

How researchers collect data and the type of data collected vis-à-vis outcome measures have a direct impact on the measurement of teaching. Siedentop (2002, p. 427) states that "good data are the key to successful research." Such data permit researchers to provide valid and reliable interpretations and generalizations on effective teaching and learning. Using quantitative measures to gather data allows researchers to gain a deeper understanding of the teaching-learning relationship in making informed decisions to improve teaching practice and student achievement. In an era of standards-based systems of accountability, such data on measurement of teaching become invaluable to teachers and other stakeholders in education. This chapter will acquaint the reader with a brief history of research on measurement of teaching in physical education (PE), quantitative methods of measuring teaching in PE, and suggested directions for future research on teacher effectiveness.

A brief history of measurement of teaching in physical education

Efforts to measure teaching effectiveness originated in classroom research and have been greatly influenced by the seminal work of Dunkin and Biddle (1974). Dunkin and Biddle advanced a model for the study of teaching that emphasized the interaction between four constructs – presage variables, process variables, product variables, and contextual variables. Early efforts to study teacher effectiveness were based on the process-product paradigm (Shulman, 1986) utilizing direct systematic observation of teacher behaviors, student behaviors, and the interaction between teachers and students in an effort to understand the relationship between teacher and student variables (Graber, 2001; Lee, 2003; Lee & Solmon, 2005; Rink, 2003). The lack of consistent results, however, coupled with recognition of the complex nature of teaching, the interdependence of student and teacher behaviors, and impact of teacher behaviors on student learning led to a shift to the mediating process paradigm.

In the mediating process paradigm, scholars examined the role of student behaviors as mediators of instruction. Researchers viewed students as active and controlling agents in the learning process (Lee, 2003; Lee & Solmon, 2005; Rink, 2003; Siedentop, 2002). Pedagogy researchers began to use time-based and response-based variables as proxy measures of student achievement using systematic observation (Siedentop, 2002; van der Mars, 2006). The mediating process-product paradigm also extends to classroom ecology (Doyle, 1977) in the study of teaching effectiveness. Using task analysis Doyle emphasized the complex nature of classroom ecology and the influential nature of teacher-student interactions (Hastie & Siedentop, 1999, 2006; Placek & Locke, 1986; Siedentop, 2002; Tousignant & Siedentop, 1983). With the changing conception of teaching and learning, the quest to understand how cognitive processes influence thinking and decision making became an important area of inquiry. Studying student and teacher cognition provided a lens to understand how cognition mediates learning (Lee, 1997, 2003; Lee & Solmon, 2005; Solmon, 2006; see Solmon's Chapter 33 in this volume).

Quantitative methods of measuring teaching in physical education

Nixon and Locke (1973) created the impetus for systematic observation of teaching by urging PE pedagogy researchers to engage in more descriptive-analytic research. As a corollary to this stimulus, the Teachers College Data Bank Project produced the first descriptive time data on how teachers spent their time in the gymnasium (Anderson & Barrette, 1978). Systematic observation quickly became the *sine qua non* in the measurement of teaching in the field. There was a surge in the development of observation instruments to observe teacher and student behavior through direct observation or via videotape (Placek & Locke, 1986; Silverman, 1991; van der Mars, 2006). The proliferation of direct systematic observation instruments ultimately resulted in the compilation of a compendium containing specialized instruments for use in PE and sport settings (Darst, Zakrajsek, & Mancini, 1989).

Systematic observation approach

Systematic observation is an explicit observation methodology that involves precise specification of what is to be observed, ignored, and recorded (McKenzie & van der Mars, 2015; Michaels, 1983; van der Mars, 1989a). Direct systematic observation involves trained observers to observe, encode, and recode the behavior of participants (Carlson & McKenzie, 1984; McKenzie & van der Mars, 2015; Michaels, 1983). This methodology can provide specific quantitative (i.e., activity type, frequency, and duration) and qualitative (i.e., context) data (Carlson & McKenzie, 1984; McKenzie & van der Mars, 2015; van der Mars, 1989a). A large majority of research on teaching in PE (RT-PE) involving instructional time, sometimes described as opportunity to learn, has depended on direct systematic observation to collect data (Darst et al., 1989; van der Mars, 2006). Typically, researchers using systematic observation use one or more of the four basic observation tactics: event recording, duration recording, interval recording, and momentary time sampling (Carlson & McKenzie, 1984; McKenzie & van der Mars, 2015; van der Mars, 1989b). These tactics are used to measure/estimate the frequency and/or duration of teacher and student behavior (van der Mars, 1989b, 2006).

Event recording

Event recording is the appropriate tactic for collecting data when the event and/or behavior are repeatable. The repeated occurrence of an event or behavior results in a frequency of that event or behavior. Event recording provides data on the frequency of occurrence of a *discrete event* by tallying the number of times that event occurred. In essence, it provides a frequency count of behavior and the raw data are converted to rate per minute and percent total, and sometimes are reported as ratios (McKenzie & van der Mars, 2015; van der Mars, 1989b). It is important that the behaviors to be observed are clearly defined prior to using this observation tactic to collect data. Van der Mars (1989b) cautions against the use of event recording when a behavior occurs at extremely high rates because keeping count of the extremely high rate of behavior and maintaining reliability could become problematic. Another instance when this tactic is inappropriate is when a behavior or event lasts for an extended period of time. In this case, the frequency data do not convey the duration of the behavior and the validity of the data could be jeopardized (van der Mars, 1989b).

Several studies have used event recording independently or in combination with other systematic observation tactics (e.g., Ashy, Lee, & Landin, 1988; Byra & Coulon, 1994; Lee & Ward, 2009; Rhoades & Woods, 2012; Silverman, 1985, 1988; Silverman, Subramaniam, & Woods, 1998; Solmon & Lee, 1996). An event recording tool currently gaining popularity among RT-PE researchers is the Game Performance Assessment Instrument (GPAI) (Oslin, Mitchell, & Griffin, 1998; van der Mars, 2006) that permits data collection in authentic game play settings.

Duration recording

Duration recording is the appropriate technique to use when systematic observation involves time-dependent variables. This is the preferred technique when the focus is on a temporal dimension of a discrete behavior or event that has a clear beginning and ending (Carlson & McKenzie, 1984; van der Mars, 1989b, 2006). Duration recording is used in measuring continuous behaviors that last for extended periods of time, and the data are typically expressed in minutes or percent of observed time (Carlson & McKenzie, 1984; McKenzie & van der Mars, 2015; van der Mars, 1989b, 2006).

This direct systematic observation is used to collect data on how time is used by students and teachers. The collection of data on time-based variables allows researchers to assess the duration of time a class/student or teacher engages in a particular behavior (Carlson & McKenzie, 1984). Early studies on time-based variables used duration recording (e.g., Anderson & Barrette, 1978; McKenzie, Clark, & McKenzie, 1984). These studies provided the initial conceptualization and systematic understanding of time-dependent variables in the gymnasium (Metzler, 1989). As researchers' conceptualization and understanding of time became more refined, they began to use duration recording in combination with other direct observation tactics (e.g., Cusimano, 1987; Silverman, 1985).

Interval recording

If the intent is to measure the (non)occurrence of a behavior during specified time intervals, then interval recording is the appropriate direct observation method. Typically, interval length ranges from 3 to 10 seconds (McKenzie & van der Mars, 2015; van der Mars, 2006). Interval recording is a form of discontinuous time-based measurement (Carlson & McKenzie, 1984). Data obtained in interval recording are converted to percentage of intervals (McKenzie & van der Mars, 2015; van der Mars, 1989b, 2006). Observers have the choice of selecting either the *partial-interval recording* or the *whole-interval recording*. In the former procedure, even a fleeting occurrence of the behavior would be coded whereas in the latter procedure the behavior must be present for the whole length of the interval (McKenzie & van der Mars, 2015; van der Mars, 1989b).

The recognition that instructional time could be used as a proxy for student achievement (Siedentop, Tousignant, & Parker, 1982) paved the way for the systematic observation instrument, Academic Learning Time-Physical Education (ALT-PE), to become a widely used means for collecting time-dependent data in PE using the interval recording tactic (Dodds, 1983; Mancini, Wuest, Clark, & Ridosh, 1983; Metzler, 1983; Placek & Randall, 1986; Shute, Dodds, Placek, Rife, & Silverman, 1982; Silverman, Dodds, Placek, Shute, & Rife, 1984; Silverman, Tyson, & Marrs-Morford, 1988). Interval recording can provide estimates of both frequency and duration of behaviors which makes it the most widely used observation tactic (McKenzie & van der Mars, 2015; van der Mars, 1989b, 2006).

Momentary time sampling

The occurrence of individual or group behavior can be measured using momentary time sampling. In this tactic, the coding decision about a behavior occurs at the end of each observational interval (McKenzie & van der Mars, 2015; McNamee & van der Mars, 2005; van der Mars, 1989b). Interval lengths in this direct systematic observation method generally range from 1 to 10 minutes (van der Mars, 1989b). Data are typically expressed as percent of total intervals (individuals) or percent of total number of people observed across all samples (group) (McKenzie & van der Mars, 2015). This tactic has the advantage of permitting observers to use the time in between observations to collect other relevant data (McKenzie & van der Mars, 2015; van der Mars, 1989b). On the other hand, there is the potential for over- or underestimating observed behavior since momentary time sampling only provides an estimate of the occurrence of the behavior (McKenzie & van der Mars, 2015; van der Mars, 1989b, 2006).

System for Observing Fitness Instruction (SOFIT) is the most widely used momentary time sampling instrument in RT-PE. This systematic observation tool has been used successfully in large intervention studies to simultaneously assess physical activity, lesson context, and teacher behavior (McKenzie & van der Mars, 2015). Several studies have used momentary time sampling to study teacher behavior and physical activity in PE (e.g., Chow, McKenzie, & Louie, 2009; Faucette & Patterson, 1990; Kulinna, Silverman, & Keating, 2000; Logan, Robinson, Webster, & Rudisill, 2015; van der Mars, Rowe, Schuldheisz, & Fox, 2004).

Advantages and limitations of systematic observation

There are several advantages of using systematic observation as a methodology in measuring teaching. First, it is a direct method with strong internal (or content) validity that can provide objective data. Second, it permits observers to record behaviors that occur naturally in the teaching context. Third, specific behaviors or events can be targeted to better understand how the teaching environment impacts learning. Fourth, systematic observation provides the lens for researchers to scrutinize the teaching act in a systematic way for analysis, critique, and refinement (Cheffers, 1977). Fifth, the results of descriptive-analytic studies provide the basis for conducting experimental and evaluative studies (Anderson, 1971). Finally, the data obtained using systematic observation (e.g., frequency, minutes, percent) are easily understood by teachers and administrators (McKenzie & van der Mars, 2015).

Systematic observational methods also have several limitations including observer effects or reactivity. Teachers' awareness of the observer's presence is likely to affect their behavior consciously or unconsciously (Muijs, 2006). For some teachers, awareness of being observed increases the frequency of targeted behaviors and in the process has the potential to influence data fidelity (McKenzie & van der Mars, 2015; Michaels, 1983). Another limitation of systematic observation is the potential for observer bias. Systematic error or bias occurs when human observers are involved no matter how careful the observer is (Michaels, 1983).

Observers' judgmental decisions and inferences during encoding could pose a reliability issue as well. This issue can be minimized through proper training prior to data collection. There also is the potential for observer drift (misinterpretation of defined categories and coding conventions through the passage of time) which warrants recalibration to re-establish reliability (McKenzie & van der Mars, 2015; Michaels, 1983). The variability of a teacher's behavior within and between lessons may be overlooked when data are expressed in percentage or frequency counts (Kyriacou & Newson, 1982).

In addition, using distinct categories of behavior fragments the teaching process by imposing the observer's predetermined selection of important elements of behavior which may not be congruent with the teacher's intentions (Casey & Taylor, 2004; Grant, Ballard, & Glynn, 1986). Moreover, the categories adopted are not sensitive to the quality of the teacher's behavior. For example, observers are not able to discern the quality of questioning when the focus of the coding category is questioning frequency (Kyriacou & Newson, 1982; Michaels, 1983; Muijs, 2006). Additionally, a teacher's behavior may convey meaning to students that cannot be captured through direct observation using systematic observation instruments. Also, the focus on targeted behavior fails to capture the dynamic quality of teacher-student interaction in the learning context (Kyriacou & Newson, 1982; Muijs, 2006). Systematic observation instruments were developed to measure teaching based on direct instruction and may not be a good fit for some model-based instruction. Finally, direct observations of teacher behavior are mere snapshots and do not provide a full picture of teacher behavior in the overall scheme of teaching and learning. They are not intended to measure teacher cognition such as teacher beliefs or subject matter knowledge (Muijs, 2006). Based on the aforementioned limitations of direct systematic observation to analyze teaching effectiveness, caution should be exercised in interpreting such data on teaching effectiveness.

Systematic observation paved the way to studying teaching effectiveness in a more systematic manner in PE and produced the foundational knowledge to our understanding of the teaching-learning process in the gymnasium. There is an extensive body of literature using systematic observation as a data collection method in teacher effectiveness research investigating the relationship between time (and opportunity) and student learning that has generated a descriptive database on time variables in PE (van der Mars, 2006). There also is a growing body of literature on systematic observation tools and physical activity in the school setting. Systematic observation has its advantages and limitations like any other data collection methodology. It will continue to be used appropriately to capture certain types of data in teaching effectiveness research. The traditional paper-and-pencil approach to systematic observation, however, is being supplemented by new technology to facilitate the collection of quality data on teaching effectiveness. The following section will address the use of technology in collecting observational data.

Technology and observational data

Technology has become a powerful tool for collecting observational data in PE. When studying teaching effectiveness, researchers can incorporate appropriate technology to collect and analyze data effectively and efficiently both in terms of teaching behaviors and student outcomes. Researchers' ability to interface computing devices and software has contributed to greater ease in the use of systematic observation tools and an influx of new tools and methodologies for use in research efforts to measure outcome variables (McKenzie & van der Mars, 2015).

Systematic observation users, once tied to paper-and-pencil approaches to data collection, now benefit from portable, compact computer devices – laptops, tablets, and smartphones – that expedite data collection (Castellano, Perea, Alday, & Mendo, 2008). The growing presence of smartphones and tablets and the development of systematic applications ("apps") for the popular iOS (Apple) and Android platforms contribute to greater ease in observation of variables of interest.

Technological advancements in software have facilitated observers' use of various systematic observation tools. Advances cited by McKenzie and van der Mars (2015) include the ability to store videotaped data for later coding, facilitating initial as well as ongoing reliability checks. Stored records make it possible to code videos with other systematic observation instruments, gaining a different perspective on what has transpired. Other advances that hold promise for use in the study of teacher effectiveness are better synchronization of data from multiple sources, including those from systematic observations of teachers and/or students, videos, sensors such as those capturing heart rate or movement, and data from assessments of student outcomes (Zimmerman, Bolhuis, Willemsen, Meyer, & Noldus, 2009). The ability to accurately and reliably synchronize data provides a more complete picture of the teaching-learning process.

Videotaping has long been a staple of movement observation and continues to be an important technique in the assessment of student learning. Advances in video recording and analysis have revolutionized videography. Additionally, the development of mobile devices (tablets and smartphones) and a host of "apps" for analysis and visual representation of performance have facilitated this process. The shift from analog to digital formats has made video easier to use and analyze. The ability to wirelessly transmit video to cloud storage, a computer, or to a mobile device makes the video readily available for analysis. New software and apps (e.g., Coach's Eye, Ubersense, Dartfish Express) create easily understood, visual representations of the data, thus enhancing the ability of teachers and/or their students to analyze their performance, while providing a permanent record for later analysis or sharing.

The miniaturization of sensors with increased storage capacity and rapid data processing along with wireless data transmission and increased affordability offer new possibilities for assessment (Kelly, 2014; McKenzie & van der Mars, 2015; Zimmerman et al., 2009). Wearable sensors, such as pedometers, heart rate monitors, accelerometers, and combined accelerometer and heart rate monitors provide a means of objectively measuring physical activity and its various components. Butte, Ekelund, and Westerterp (2012) discuss various devices, best practices, and future development.

The development of "smart" sports equipment with embedded or attached sensors offers another means to assess sports skill performance, while creating a permanent record and quantifiable data on parameters of interest. Companion apps store information and turn raw data into easily understood displays representing specific performance aspects. Tennis racquets, basketballs, and soccer balls with embedded sensors and sensors to attach to golf clubs and bats now exist, and more "smart" equipment and sensors, along with companion apps, are in development and will likely be available for many popular sports (Kelly, 2014).

Game play is the preferred venue for the authentic assessment of skills and tactical knowledge in many sports. It is challenging to provide a valid and reliable assessment of both players' skills and tactics exhibited during game play. However, current videographic technology coupled with more sophisticated software makes it possible to address this need. Chow, Tan, Lee, and Button (2014) describe how an automated motion-tracking system can be used in PE to authentically assess the tactical dimensions and skill execution during game play. Installation of a video camera directly above the court captures the movements of players. The A-Eye software refines the data, allowing players to be tracked automatically and continuously. Analysis yields information on players' behavior during play, offering insights relative to differences in court coverage and skills execution, such as passing and receiving, or tennis stroke execution. It can also be used effectively to examine players' movements in net and territorial games. The A-Eye provides quantifiable records for teachers to use for student assessment. Capturing information over a number of lessons allows teachers to document students' progress. Chow et al. (2014) note the "relevance and validity of using the A-Eye to examine performance efficiency is strong" (p. 456), "allowing for the more effective, objective and reliable measures of game performance and movement behaviors" (p. 460). Further, it has "good potential in addressing difficulty in the measurement of game performance" (p. 460) in PE.

There is, however, one caution to keep in mind when using technology as a tool for collecting observational data. Technology is like any other systematic observational instrument that requires rigorous procedures (e.g., calibration, training, etc.) for researchers to produce reliable and valid data. The quality of data should not be compromised when using technology to assist in collecting observational data. Technology is subject to measurement error just as are human observers.

Technological advances have provided and will continue to provide greater ease in the use of systematic observation tools in teacher effectiveness research. Advances in software, video recording and analysis, wearable sensors, and automated motion tracking system allow researchers to collect data expeditiously and measure outcome variables objectively. Researchers should practice caution when using technology because technology in itself does not guarantee or improve data accuracy. Using technology in concert with systematic observation instruments has the potential to yield quality data.

Conclusion and future directions

Researchers use systematic observation to procure reliable and accurate data on teachers' instructional behavior and student outcomes. Systematic observation has provided a rich body of literature on teaching effectiveness. Early studies relied on duration recording to collect data on how teachers and students used instructional time in PE. The acceptance of instructional time as a proxy for student achievement led PE pedagogy researchers to use interval recording for collecting time-dependent data. Event recording is used to collect data when the event and/or behavior are repeatable. A renewed approach to using event recording emerged as a result of a shift from technique-based to game-based approaches to teaching (e.g., GPAI) coupled with authentic assessment practices (Mitchell, Oslin, & Griffin, 2003; Oslin et al., 1998). Momentary time sampling tools (e.g., SOFIT) have been used successfully in large-scale physical activity intervention studies to code behavior at the end of each observational interval. It should be pointed out that these methods have been used independently or in combination with other systematic observation tactics in teacher effectiveness research.

Future teacher effectiveness research needs to focus on developing more ecologically valid instruments that allow researchers to measure student learning in authentic game play settings. Data obtained using these instruments can provide credible evidence of student learning. For example, students not in possession of the ball in territorial games would be coded as not accruing ALT-PE using the interval recoding tactic. However, from a tactical awareness perspective, they are still actively engaged in off-the-ball tactics such as positioning, guarding, and supporting (van der Mars, 2006). While measuring these behaviors in isolation does not fully capture the essence of student learning, using more sophisticated instruments, aided by technology, can assist in enhancing performance assessment.

The broadening conception of teacher accountability and teaching effectiveness (Good, 2014; Kyriakides, Campbell, & Christofidou, 2002) is dependent on accurate ways to measure teacher behavior and student learning. In the future systematic observation instruments will need to be more sensitive to context and instructional models to provide valid and reliable measures. Systematic observation instruments that yield authentic student performance data during game play settings, such as the GPAI (Oslin et al., 1998), can serve this function well. Although using standalone direct observation tactics may not be appropriate to encapsulate the complexity of teaching, combining several direct observation tactics in a single study has the potential to provide rich data on teaching effectiveness. More advanced observation systems can facilitate the design of developmentally appropriate assessment tasks that permit students to demonstrate their learning in authentic game play (van der Mars, 2006).

The changing landscape in games instruction requires measurement tools that are more sensitive in assessing student learning. In this regard, hybrid systematic observation tools that link time/opportunity with newer variables such as decision making and execution will enable researchers to assess student learning in holistic and authentic ways (Rink, 1996; van der Mars, 2006).

Systematic observation tactics use varying coding formats (e.g., interval length, length of observe/record intervals), but there is a paucity of research investigating the variability of coding formats. This is particularly important in ascertaining how far the interval length can be stretched in a particular activity without losing data accuracy (McKenzie & van der Mars, 2015). For example, McNamee and van der Mars (2005) found that interval lengths up to 90 seconds can provide acceptable levels of accuracy for physical activity data in physical education.

There also is a dire need to engage in longitudinal studies to track teaching effectiveness over time in PE. Our counterparts in health have been successful in tracking student behavior changes using longitudinal studies (Summerfield, 2001). The dearth of longitudinal studies in teacher effectiveness research in PE can be attributed to a lack of consensus on outcome measures and the lack of available practical, reliable, and valid measures of student achievement, other than fitness.

Researchers will rely more on technology in the future to collect observational data using smartphones and apps and incorporating automated motion-tracking systems (Chow et al., 2014) to complement and supplement systematic observational data in authentic game play settings. The advent of affordable drones with enhanced capabilities such as wireless transfer of video offers the possibility of more sophisticated data related to game play performance for the entire game, including off-the-ball actions. Possibilities for research expand with the potential to incorporate such technology in conjunction with systematic observation instruments like the GPAI (Oslin et al., 1998).

Future research on teacher effectiveness also will rely on technology-based data collection tools in large-scale multi-site research projects (McKenzie & van der Mars, 2015). A team of researchers will have the capability to access data collected from different sites simultaneously.

Data also can be shared and transferred readily among researchers with expertise in diverse areas allowing for multifaceted analyses. Additionally, systematic observation data collected using technology in both quantitative and qualitative studies can complement and supplement teacher effectiveness research resulting in powerful findings that will help us better understand the complex multidimensional act of teaching.

Progress has been made in measuring teaching effectiveness in PE by shifting our focus from studying individual variables to multiple variables and their influence on teaching and learning using systematic observation tools and technology. Regardless of the systematic observation tactic or technology used to collect data, it is critical that the data produced – whether from observations of teaching or measures of student learning – are valid and reliable.

Summary of key findings

- Teaching is a complex act. RT-PE has evolved from traditional studies examining individual variables associated with teacher behavior and student outcomes to more contemporary research investigating multiple variables. Systematic observation has been used successfully in the measurement of teaching in efforts to better understand the teaching-learning process.
- Descriptive-analytic research in PE using systematic observation pioneered the creation of a descriptive database on instructional time variables.
- Event recording, duration recording, interval recording, and momentary time sampling are the four basic observation tactics used in systematic observation. Researchers have used them independently or in combination to study the multidimensional act of teaching. A rich body of literature on PE teacher effectiveness research has evolved from systematic observational data.
- Systematic observation is suited to collecting many types of data in teacher effectiveness research. Collecting valid, reliable, and accurate data is the pulse of systematic observation.
- Technological advancements have made major contributions in collecting and analyzing data effectively and efficiently using systematic observational tools.

Reflective questions for discussion

1. In what ways can systematic observation be used to measure multidimensional elements of teaching? Are there some aspects of teaching that are simply too complex to measure using systematic observation?
2. How can researchers measure the changing roles of teachers and their influence on student learning in teacher effectiveness research?
3. What constraining factors limit researchers' ability to use systematic observation to measure all relevant dimensions in teaching?
4. How and to what extent can Danielson's framework be adapted to systematically observe teachers in PE?
5. In what ways are researchers using technology to study teaching and teacher effectiveness?
6. To what extent does the use of technology-based data collection tools affect data accuracy in teacher effectiveness research?
7. What trade-offs do researchers have to confront in teacher effectiveness research using systematic observation and technology?

References

Anderson, W. G. (1971). Descriptive-analytic research on teaching. *Quest, 15*(1), 1–8.

Anderson, W. G., & Barrette, G. T. (Eds.). (1978). What's going on in gym: Descriptive studies of physical education classes. *Motor skills: Theory into practice* [Monograph 1].

Ashy, M. H., Lee, A. M., & Landin, D. K. (1988). Relationship of practice using correct technique to achievement in a motor skill. *Journal of Teaching in Physical Education, 7*, 115–120.

Butte, N. F., Ekelund, U., & Westerterp, K. R. (2012). Assessing physical activity using wearable monitors: Measures of physical activity. *Medicine and Science in Sports & Exercise, 44*, S5–S12.

Byra, M., & Coulon, S. C. (1994). The effect of planning on the instructional behaviors of preservice teachers. *Journal of Teaching in Physical Education, 13*, 123–139.

Campbell, R. J., Kyriakides, L., Muijs, R. D., & Robinson, W. (2003). Differential teacher effectiveness: Towards a model for research and teacher appraisal. *Oxford Review of Education, 29*, 347–362.

Carlson, B. R., & McKenzie, T. L. (1984). Computer technology for recording, storing, and analyzing temporal data in physical activity settings. *Journal of Teaching in Physical Education, 4*, 24–29.

Casey, C. E., & Taylor, A. W. (2004). Teacher education research in physical education. *Avante, 10*(2), 24–31.

Castellano, J., Perea, A., Alday, L., & Mendo, A. H. (2008). The measuring and observation tool in sports. *Behavior Research Methods, 40*, 898–905.

Cheffers, J. (1977). Observing teaching systematically. *Quest, 28*(1), 17–28.

Chow, B. C., McKenzie, T. L., & Louie, L. (2009). Physical activity environmental influences during secondary school physical education. *Journal of Teaching in Physical Education, 28*, 21–37.

Chow, J. Y., Tan, C. W. K., Lee, M. C. Y., & Button, C. (2014). Possibilities and implications of using a motion-tracking system in physical education. *European Physical Education Review, 20*, 444–446.

Cusimano, B. E. (1987). Effects of self-assessment and goal setting on verbal behaviors of elementary physical education teachers. *Journal of Teaching in Physical Education, 6*, 166–173.

Danielson, C. (2001). New trends in teacher evaluation. *Educational Leadership, 58*(5), 12–15.

Darst, P. W., Zakrajsek, D. B., & Mancini, V. H. (1989). *Analyzing physical education and sport instruction* (2nd edn). Champaign, IL: Human Kinetics.

Dodds, P. (1983). Relationships between academic learning time and teacher behaviors in a physical education majors skills class. In T. Templin & J. Olson (Eds.), *Teaching in physical education* (pp. 173–184). Champaign, IL: Human Kinetics.

Doyle, W. (1977). Paradigms for research on teacher effectiveness. In L. S. Shulman (Ed.), *Review of research in education* (Vol. 5, pp. 163–198). Itasca, IL: Peacock.

Dunkin, M., & Biddle, B. (1974). *The study of teaching.* New York, NY: Holt, Rhinehart & Winston.

Faucette, N., & Patterson, P. (1990). Comparing teaching behaviors and student activity levels in classes taught by PE specialists versus nonspecialists. *Journal of Teaching in Physical Education, 9*, 106–114.

Floden, R. E. (1986). Research on effects of teaching: A continuing model for research on teaching. In M. C. Wittrock (Ed.), *Handbook of research on teaching* (3rd ed., pp. 3–16). New York, NY: Macmillan.

Good, T. L. (2014). What do we know about how teachers influence student performance on standardized tests: And why do we know so little about other student outcomes? *Teachers College Record, 116*(1), 1–41.

Graber, K. (2001). Research on teaching in physical education. In V. Richardson (Ed.), *Handbook of research on teaching* (4th ed., pp. 491–519). Washington, DC: American Educational Research Association.

Grant, B., Ballard, K. D., & Glynn, T. (1986). Directions in research on teaching physical education. *Educational Psychology, 6*(1), 19–35.

Hastie, P., & Siedentop, D. (1999). An ecological perspective on physical education. *European Physical Education Review, 5*(1), 9–29.

Hastie, P. A., & Siedentop, D. (2006). The classroom ecology paradigm. In D. Kirk, D. Macdonald, & M. O'Sullivan (Eds.), *The handbook of physical education* (pp. 214–225). Thousand Oaks, CA: Sage.

Kelly, H. (2014, December 31). Smart sports equipment turns phones into coaches. Retrieved from http://edition.cnn.com/2014/11/28/tech/innovation/smart-sports-equipment/.

Kulinna, P. H., Silverman, S., & Keating, S. D. (2000). Relationship between teachers' belief systems and actions toward teaching physical activity and fitness. *Journal of Teaching in Physical Education, 19*, 206–221.

Kyriacou, C., & Newson, G. (1982). Teacher effectiveness: A consideration of research problems. *Educational Review, 34*(1), 3–12.

Kyriakides, L., Campbell, R. J., & Christofidou, E. (2002). Generating criteria for measuring teacher effectiveness through a self-evaluation approach: A complementary way of measuring teacher effectiveness. *School Effectiveness and School Improvement: An International Journal of Research, Policy and Practice, 13*, 291–325.

Lee, A. M. (1997). Contributions of research on student thinking in physical education. *Journal of Teaching in Physical Education, 16,* 262–277.

Lee, A. M. (2003). How the field evolved. In S. Silverman & C. Ennis (Eds.), *Student learning in physical education: Applying research to enhance instruction* (2nd ed., pp. 9–25). Champaign, IL: Human Kinetics.

Lee, A. M., & Solmon, M. A. (2005). Pedagogy research through the years in RQES. *Research Quarterly for Exercise and Sport, 76,* S108–S121.

Lee, M., & Ward, P. (2009). Generalization of tactics in tag rugby from practice to games in middle school physical education. *Physical Education and Sport Pedagogy, 14,* 189–207.

Locke, L. F. (1977). Research on teaching physical education: New hope for a dismal science. *Quest, 28,* 2–16.

Logan, S. W., Robinson, L. E., Webster, E. K., & Rudisill, M. E. (2015). The influence of instructional climate on time spent in management tasks and physical activity of 2nd grade students during physical education. *European Physical Education Review, 2,* 195–205.

Mancini, V., Wuest, D., Clark, E., & Ridosh, N. (1983). In T. Templin & J. Olson (Eds.), *Teaching in physical education* (pp. 197–208). Champaign, IL: Human Kinetics.

McKenzie, T. L., Clark, E. K., & McKenzie, R. E. (1984). Instructional strategies: Influence on teacher and student behavior. *Journal of Teaching in Physical Education, 3*(2), 20–28.

McKenzie, T. L., & van der Mars, H. (2015). Top 10 research questions related to assessing physical activity and its context using systematic observation. *Research Quarterly for Exercise and Sport, 86,* 13–29.

McNamee, J., & van der Mars, H. (2005). Accuracy of momentary time sampling: A comparison of varying interval lengths using SOFIT. *Journal of Teaching in Physical Education, 24,* 282–292.

Metzler, M. (1983). Using academic learning time in process-product studies with experimental teaching units. In T. Templin & J. Olson (Eds.), *Teaching in physical education* (pp. 185–196). Champaign, IL: Human Kinetics.

Metzler, M. (1989). A review of research on time in sport pedagogy. *Journal of Teaching in Physical Education, 8,* 87–103.

Michaels, J. W. (1983). Systematic observation as a measurement strategy. *Sociological Focus, 16,* 217–226.

Mitchell, S. A., Oslin, J. L., & Griffin, L. L. (2003). *Sport foundations for elementary physical education.* Champaign, IL: Human Kinetics.

Muijs, D. (2006). Measuring teacher effectiveness: Some methodological reflections. *Educational Research and Evaluation: An International Journal of Theory and Practice, 12,* 53–74.

Muijs, D., Campbell, J., Kyriakides, L., & Robinson, W. (2005). Making the case for differentiated teacher effectiveness: An overview of research in four key areas. *School Effectiveness and School Improvement, 16,* 51–70.

Nixon, J. E., & Locke, L. (1973). Research on teaching in physical education. In M. W. Travers (Ed.), *Second handbook of research on teaching* (pp. 1210–1242). Chicago: Rand McNally.

Oslin, J. L., Mitchell, S. A., & Griffin, L. L. (1998). The Game Performance Assessment Instrument (GPAI): Development and preliminary validation. *Journal of Teaching in Physical Education, 17,* 231–243.

Placek, J. H., & Locke, L. F. (1986). Research on teaching physical education: New knowledge and cautious optimism. *Journal of Teacher Education, 37*(4), 24–28.

Placek, J. H., & Randall, L. (1986). Comparison of academic learning time in physical education: Students of specialists and nonspecialists. *Journal of Teaching in Physical Education, 5,* 157–165.

Rhoades, J. L., & Woods, A. M. (2012). National board certified physical education teachers task presentations and learning environments. *Journal of Teaching in Physical Education, 31,* 4–20.

Rink, J. E. (1996). Tactical and skill approaches to teaching sport and games [Monograph]. *Journal of Teaching in Physical Education, 15,* 397–516.

Rink, J. E. (2003). Effective instruction in physical education. In S. Silverman & C. Ennis (Eds.), *Student learning in physical education: Applying research to enhance instruction* (2nd ed., pp. 165–186). Champaign, IL: Human Kinetics.

Rink, J. E. (2013). Measuring teacher effectiveness in physical education. *Research Quarterly for Exercise and Sport, 84,* 407–418.

Shulman, L. S. (1986). Paradigms and research programs in the study of teaching: A contemporary perspective. In M. C. Wittrock (Ed.), *Handbook of research on teaching* (3rd ed., pp. 3–36). New York, NY: Macmillan.

Shute, S., Dodds, P., Placek, J., Rife, F., & Silverman, S. (1982). Academic learning time in elementary school movement education: A descriptive analytic study. *Journal of Teaching in Physical Education, 1*(2), 3–14.

Siedentop, D. (2002). Ecological perspectives in teaching research. *Journal of Teaching in Physical Education*, *21*, 427–440.

Siedentop, D., Tousignant, M., & Parker, M. (1982). *Academic Learning Time-Physical Education Coding Manual: 1982 Revision*. Unpublished manual, The Ohio State University.

Silverman, S. J. (1985). Relationship of engagement and practice trials to student achievement. *Journal of Teaching in Physical Education*, *5*, 13–21.

Silverman, S. J. (1988). Relationship of presage and context variables to achievement. *Research Quarterly for Exercise and Sport*, *59*, 35–41.

Silverman, S. (1991). Research on teaching in physical education. *Research Quarterly for Exercise and Sport*, *62*, 352–364.

Silverman, S. (1994). Research on teaching and student achievement. *Sport Science Review*, *3*(1), 83–90.

Silverman, S., Dodds, P., Placek, J., Shute, S., & Rife, F. (1984). Academic learning time in elementary school physical education (ALT- PE) for student subgroups and instructional activity units. *Research Quarterly for Exercise and Sport*, *55*, 365–370.

Silverman, S. J., Subramaniam, P. R., & Woods, A. M. (1998). Task structures, student practice, and skill in physical education. *Journal of Educational Research*, *91*, 298–306.

Silverman, S., Tyson, L., & Marrs-Morford, L. M. (1988). Relationships of organization, time, and student achievement in physical education. *Teaching and Teacher Education*, *4*, 247–257.

Solmon, M. A. (2006). Learner cognition. In D. Kirk, D. Macdonald, & M. O'Sullivan (Eds.), *The handbook of physical education* (pp. 226–241). Thousand Oaks, CA: Sage.

Solmon, M., & Lee, A. M. (1996). Entry characteristics, practice variables, and cognition: Student mediation of instruction. *Journal of Teaching in Physical Education*, *15*, 136–150.

Summerfield, L. M. (2001). School health education. In V. Richardson (Ed.), *Handbook of research on teaching* (4th ed., pp. 472–490). Washington, DC: American Educational Research Association.

Tousignant, M., & Siedentop, D. (1983). A qualitative analysis of task structures in required secondary physical education classes. *Journal of Teaching in Physical Education*, *3*, 47–57.

van der Mars, H. (1989a). Systematic observation: An introduction. In P. W. Darst & D. B. Zakrajsek (Eds.), *Analyzing physical education and sport instruction* (2nd ed., pp. 3–17). Champaign, IL: Human Kinetics.

van der Mars, H. (1989b). Basic recording tactics. In P. W. Darst & D. B. Zakrajsek (Eds.), *Analyzing physical education and sport instruction* (2nd ed., pp. 19–51). Champaign, IL: Human Kinetics.

van der Mars, H. (2006). Time and learning in physical education. In D. Kirk, D. Macdonald, & M. O'Sullivan (Eds.), *The handbook of physical education* (pp. 191–213). Thousand Oaks, CA: Sage.

van der Mars, H., Rowe, P. J., Schuldheisz, J. M., & Fox, S. (2004). Measuring students' physical activity levels: Validating SOFIT for use with high-school students. *Journal of Teaching in Physical Education*, *23*, 235–251.

Zimmerman, P. H., Bolhuis, J. E., Willemsen, A., Meyer, E. S., & Noldus, L. P. J. J. (2009). The Observer XT: A tool for the integration and synchronization of multimodal signals. *Behavior Research Methods*, *41*, 731–735.

27

TEACHING ABOUT ACTIVE LIFESTYLES

Lorraine Cale, LOUGHBOROUGH UNIVERSITY, UK

The importance of a physically active lifestyle is now well recognised with comprehensive reviews revealing physical activity (PA) in children and young people to have both physical and psychological benefits (e.g. Janssen & LeBlanc, 2010; National Institute for Clinical Excellence [NICE], 2007; Stensel, Gorely & Biddle, 2008; United States Department of Health and Human Services [USDHHS], 2008). Despite this, there are ongoing concerns globally over the PA levels of many youngsters. For example, the most recent World Health Organization's Health-Behaviour in School-aged Children (HBSC) Survey reported less than half of young people in almost every country meet current PA recommendations (Currie et al., 2008).

If young people are to enjoy and benefit from a physically active lifestyle, they need to be equipped with the knowledge, skills, competence and confidence to do so. Few would argue that an appropriate avenue for this is through physical education (PE) and that teaching about active lifestyles should therefore be a key component of PE curricula. Indeed, the adoption and maintenance of a physically active lifestyle is an established goal of the subject in many countries (e.g. Australian Curriculum, Assessment and Reporting Authority [ACARA], 2012; Department for Education, 2013; National Association for Sport and Physical Education [NASPE], 2004), with governments increasingly looking to schools as a convenient form of public health investment (Armour & Harris, 2013).

This chapter focuses on teaching about active lifestyles as an explicit objective of PE. First, it considers the PE context and the opportunities the subject affords in this regard. It then summarises and critiques the evidence on the effectiveness of PE in positively influencing young people's PA, before considering some of the issues faced in teaching about active lifestyles. This includes critiquing current pedagogy and some common practices, notably the practice of fitness testing. The chapter concludes with a summary of the key findings and some key questions with respect to teaching about active lifestyles.

PE as a context for teaching about active lifestyles

PE provides a very suitable context for teaching about active lifestyles for a number of reasons. Via its dual focus on 'learning to move' and 'moving to learn', it provides opportunities to be active and educates students about and through physical activity (Harris, 2010). PE is also compulsory or at least a well established component of the school curriculum in many countries, thus providing a captive audience and access to all or most young people at a time of high receptiveness (Cale & Harris, 2005; Fox & Harris, 2003). At the same time, caution is needed concerning what the subject can realistically achieve (Cale, Harris & Chen, 2014; Harris, 2010). PE has a range of objectives and providing and teaching about health and health-related PA is only one of its many goals (Lounsbery, McKenzie, Trost & Smith, 2011). Furthermore, PE accounts for less than 2% of young people's time (Cale & Harris, 2013; Fox & Harris, 2003), at least half of which can justifiably involve only light or physically passive activity (Stratton, Faircloth & Ridgers, 2008). Given such constraints, it is suggested that whilst PE clearly makes a contribution to young people's PA, it cannot by itself address their PA needs (Fox, Cooper & McKenna, 2004; McKenzie & Lounsbery, 2009) nor ensure they meet PA recommendations.

Indeed, the role of PE in promoting active lifestyles and public health more broadly, has and continues to be debated (Armour & Harris, 2013; O'Sullivan, 2004; Quennerstedt, 2008). O'Sullivan (2004) notes that, although there seems to be agreement that PE should promote health-enhancing PA, there are disagreements over the degree to which it should focus on public health goals. Armour and Harris (2013, p. 209) argue that "much of the international PE community is uncertain about the precise nature of appropriate health knowledge to be covered in PE, the proper role for PE in health and the level of responsibility the profession should accept for children's (let alone adults') health outcomes". Others, meanwhile, are critical of PE's unquestioned 'allegiance to health', how it legitimates itself on this basis, and the uncritical, simplistic and narrow way in which schools and teachers engage in health issues in the curriculum and in their pedagogical practices (Burrows & Wright, 2004; Evans, 2007; Evans & Rich, 2011; Gard & Wright, 2001; Wellard, 2012). This latter issue and some pedagogical practices are explored later in the chapter.

The effectiveness of PE in promoting active lifestyles

A review of the evidence base concerning the effectiveness of PE in promoting active lifestyles provides some indication of what the subject can realistically achieve. A number of studies have evaluated the effectiveness of PE or other school-based PA interventions over the years and reviews of these have been published (e.g. Almond & Harris, 1998; Cale & Harris, 2005; 2006; De Meester, van Lenthe, Spittaels, Lien & De Bourdeauhuij, 2009; Demetriou & Honer, 2012; Dobbins et al., 2009; Dobbins, Husson, DeCorby & La Rocca, 2013; Harris & Cale, 1997; Kahn et al., 2002; Kriemler et al., 2011; Stone, McKenzie, Welk & Booth, 1998; van Sluijs, McMinn & Griffin, 2007). Whilst most focused on school-based or PA interventions broadly, all include studies in which PE has been the key intervention. The interventions themselves generally included providing information about the benefits of physical activity, increasing the amount of time pupils spent on PA during the school day, as well as increasing the amount of PA during existing PE lessons or PA sessions. Some of the specific teaching strategies and means by which they did this are outlined later.

The early reviews conducted by Harris and Cale (1997) and Almond and Harris (1998) included studies of formally evaluated health-related PE programmes. The authors reported that such programmes can achieve positive outcomes in physiological, clinical, behavioural, cognitive and affective measures (Almond & Harris, 1998; Harris & Cale, 1997), concluding the evidence to be "encouraging and sufficiently convincing" (Harris & Cale, 1997, p. 99). Stone et al. (1998) conducted a review of PA interventions in youth that included a total of 14 school-based studies. Improvements in knowledge and attitudes related to PA were generally found and some studies reported significant increases in moderate to vigorous (MV) PA during PE classes (see

Li, Chapter 38, this volume). Few positive findings, however, were reported for out-of-school PA. Kahn et al. (2002) undertook a systematic review of the effectiveness of various approaches to increasing PA in which 13 of the 26 studies evaluated the effectiveness of modified PE. They concluded that there is strong evidence that school-based PE can be effective in increasing PA levels and improving physical fitness.

Based on previous reviews and the evidence, Cale and Harris (2005; 2006) highlighted the trends, characteristics and issues concerning school-based interventions designed to increase young people's PA. The authors reaffirmed earlier reviews that school-based PE programmes can achieve a range of positive outcomes and be effective, highlighting meaningful improvements in young people's PA, fitness, knowledge and attitudes (Cale & Harris, 2005; 2006).

In 2007, van Sluijs et al. (2007) conducted a systematic review on the effectiveness of interventions to promote PA in children and adolescents. They identified 57 studies, 47 of which were school-based. Effective interventions documented increases ranging from an additional 3 minutes of PE-related PA to 283 minutes per week of overall PA, and a 59% increase in the number of participants being regularly active (van Sluijs et al., 2007).

De Meester et al.'s (2009) review summarised the effectiveness of PA interventions among European teenagers, identifying a total of 20 studies and including 15 school-based. The review revealed school-based interventions to be effective in improving PA levels in the short term. However, these improvements were limited to school-related PA with no conclusive transfer to leisure time PA (De Meester et al., 2009).

The review by Kriemler et al. (2011) both summarised recent reviews of school-based PA or fitness interventions and systematically reviewed newly published intervention studies. The authors identified 20 new studies with the interventions being implemented by PE experts, classroom teachers or a combination. The results revealed 47–65% of the interventions to be effective, with the effect mostly seen in school-related PA. All 20 studies revealed a positive intervention PA effect in-school, out-of-school or overall, and 6 of 11 studies showed a fitness increase. Kriemler et al. (2011) concluded that the results provide strong evidence for the positive effect of school-based interventions on children and adolescents' PA.

Demetriou and Honer (2012) reviewed the effectiveness of school-based interventions with a PA component on three target levels: health and fitness; psychological determinants; and PA. The review identified 129 intervention studies implemented during PE or regular school hours, the majority of which were found to achieve significant effects on motor performance (69.7%), PA (56.8%) and knowledge of PA (87.5%).

Dobbins et al. (2009; 2013) conducted two systematic reviews examining the effectiveness of school-based interventions in promoting PA and fitness in children and adolescents. The 2013 review included 44 school-based studies. The authors concluded there is some evidence to suggest that school-based PA interventions are effective in increasing the proportion of children who engage in MVPA during school hours. Intervention group participants were also found to spend more time in MVPA, less time watching television, and to have improved aerobic capacity or fitness.

Collectively the above reveal that school-based PA interventions, many of which include PE as a key component, can provide positive outcomes for young people. It is noteworthy though that most reviews report interventions to be successful in increasing PA during school hours and in PE, but less so in influencing PA out of school. The exception is the recent updated review by Kriemler et al. (2011) which shows intervention effects beyond school-based PA. From a public health perspective this is an important finding which suggests schools and PE may have a greater influence on PA than previously thought. Scholars, however, acknowledge the need for further research and for more high quality interventions (De Meester et al., 2009; Demetriou

& Honer, 2012; Fox & Harris, 2003; Kriemler et al., 2011; van Sluijs et al., 2007) as limitations and risk of bias in the studies are recognised (Dobbins et al., 2013).

Despite the short-term effects, researchers have also failed to provide evidence of the long-term impact of school-based interventions (De Meester et al., 2009; Dobbins et al., 2013; Kriemler et al., 2011). This has led some authors to be more sceptical about the impact of PE on PA (e.g. Armour & Harris, 2013; Trost, 2006). For example, Armour and Harris (2013) note there is little "evidence to suggest that PE in most countries has achieved anything significant in terms of encouraging lifelong engagement in PA" (p. 202). That said, one notable Canadian study conducted in the 1970s, the Trois-Rivieres Pont-Rouge study, examined the long-term health consequences of a PE intervention and provides at least some evidence of sustained impact (Trudeau et al., 1998; 1999). At follow-up over 20 years later, the intervention students demonstrated better motor fitness and reported better health and more positive attitudes towards PA (Trudeau & Shephard, 2008).

Noteworthy is that the reviews consistently highlight the potential of multicomponent interventions in promoting PA in particular, rather than isolated education or curricular changes (De Meester et al., 2009; Kriemler et al., 2011; van Sluijs et al., 2007). Whilst varying greatly, the interventions often focused on one or more changes, for example, to the school curriculum, PE lessons, routines, the environment, or involved teacher training and/or educational materials. PE interventions or components typically involved more lessons or lesson time, changing lesson content or pedagogy, enhancing curriculum materials or incorporating classroom-based instruction. From the reviews and studies, however, it is not possible to identify which specific components are effective or more effective. Scholars have acknowledged the limited information often provided about the interventions themselves, notably in terms of their content and mode of implementation, as problematic (Cale & Harris, 2005; De Meester et al., 2009; Stone et al., 1998; van Sluijs et al., 2007). On one level, this hampers stratification and analyses of potential effective components and on a practical level, it makes study replication and guidance for future research, interventions and practice difficult (Cale & Harris, 2005). With limited guidance, schools are reluctant to implement new programmes. Indeed, Lounsbery et al. (2011) identified the difficulties in encouraging the widespread adoption of evidence-based PE programmes by schools.

In their review, Cale and Harris (1998) observed that where programme content was outlined, it was often not especially innovative or the type which would appeal to many young people. From the more recent reviews (e.g. Dobbins et al., 2013; van Sluijs et al., 2007) this also still seems to be the case. For example, vigorous activity, endurance training/exercise or didactic instruction and repetitive activity featured in some programmes (e.g. see studies by Bayne-Smith et al., 2004; Dorgo et al., 2009; Ewart, Young & Hagberg, 1998; Stephens & Wentz, 1998; Walther et al., 2009; Wang et al., 2008; Weeks, Young & Beck, 2008, summarised and cited in Dobbins et al., 2013). Whilst such activities may positively influence short-term fitness gains, they are narrow in focus, may be inappropriate and unappealing to many young people, and are therefore unlikely to be successful in promoting lifetime PA. Other studies meanwhile relied heavily on classroom or computer-based theoretical instruction (e.g. see studies by Frenn et al., 2005; Palmer, Graham & Elliott, 2005; Perry, Kelder & Klepp, 1994 summarised and cited in van Sluijs et al., 2007), the drawback of which is that such instruction is sedentary and focuses on information transmission rather than experiential learning.

More encouragingly, a number of studies cited within the reviews did incorporate more positive approaches. For example, some programmes provided tailored interventions and feedback and lower intensity and non-competitive PA with emphasis on fun, well-being, variety or choice (see Haerens et al., 2006; Sallis at al., 2003; Simon et al., 2004; Story et al., 2003, summarised and cited in van Sluijs et al., 2007), or peer-led or self-directed sessions (see Pangrazi, 2003; Perry et al., 1987 in van Sluijs et al., 2007). Similarly, other studies included the development of self-management and behavioural skills for PA such as self-monitoring, goal setting and/or the enhancement of self-esteem and confidence (e.g. Angelopoulos, Milionis, Grammatikaki, Moschonis & Manios, 2009; McManus et al., 2008; Peralta, Jones & Okely, 2009; Wilson et al., 2011; Young, Phillips, Yu & Haythornthwaite, 2006 in Dobbins et al., 2013).

Pedagogy underpinning teaching about active lifestyles

A number of factors are clearly important in determining the effectiveness of PA interventions and programmes and their subsequent successful, wider adoption into schools and PE curricula. Not least, this includes the underpinning pedagogy and quality of their delivery. However, limitations in the pedagogy traditionally applied to teaching about active lifestyles have been acknowledged and knowledge about effective PE-for-health pedagogies or models has been identified as a significant gap in the field (Armour & Harris, 2013; Haerens, Kirk, Cardon & De Bourdeaudhuij, 2011). Armour and Harris (2013) note how, although there has been much interest in health-focused curriculum activities and interventions, less attention has been paid to the development of pedagogies to be used in the health dimension of PE. Additionally, they claim that the curriculum, programmes and activities have traditionally been the driver to the educational process, rather than the needs of the learners, yet they argue implicit in effective PE-for-health pedagogies should be a reversal of this, with pedagogy and learners' needs being at the core (Armour & Harris, 2013).

In the absence of knowledge about appropriate pedagogies, it is perhaps not surprising that concerns have been expressed over the teaching of the area in practice. Further, a few notable factors seem to be heightening these concerns and hampering progress. First, Alfrey and Gard (2014) and Kirk (2010) argue that the PE profession is resistant to change and it is widely acknowledged how sport techniques, competitive sport and team games which focus on performance and fitness have dominated, and continue to dominate PE and teachers' philosophies and practices (Green, 2009; Kirk, 2010; McKenzie & Kahan, 2004; Trost, 2006). When teaching about active lifestyles, scholars suggest many apply the same sport, performance and fitness oriented approach (Alfrey, Cale & Webb, 2012; Harris & Leggett, 2015 Puhse et al., 2011), centring on narrow, limited, instrumental and sometimes questionable outcomes and activities. Alfrey and Gard (2014, p. 4) note how literature has portrayed a picture of the profession as "steadfastly resistant to change away from the dualistic and instrumental understandings of health and the body", towards more "progressive and student-centred practices and pedagogies". Rather, Haerens et al. (2011) and Quennerstedt (2008) highlight the need for a broader approach which focuses on development in the cognitive, psychomotor, behavioural and affective domains and the adoption of a socially critical perspective to teaching and learning about active lifestyles.

Scholars have furthermore raised concerns over many PE teachers' inadequate health knowledge and narrow, limited and even flawed understandings, arising from their often limited training and/or engagement in relevant professional development (Alfrey et al., 2012; Armour & Harris, 2013; Castelli & Williams, 2007; McKenzie, 2007; see also Chapter 31 by Haerens et al.). If PE teachers lack the knowledge, training and pedagogies to deliver the area well, as evidence suggests many do, then it seems unlikely that health aspirations, in this case enhanced student learning and engagement in PA, will be realized (Armour & Harris, 2013). In recognition of this issue, Haerens et al. (2011) are developing a learner-centred pedagogical model for health-based PE, the central theme of which is 'valuing a physically active life' (see also, Sun, Chen, Zhu &

Ennis, 2012; see also Thorburn, Chapter 6; Ennis, Chapter 8). However, more work on establishing effective pedagogies for health is required (Armour & Harris, 2013).

As a result of the above, many PE teachers' delivery of active lifestyles is likely to be traditional, narrow and simplistic, and may involve some questionable or undesirable practices which may also mitigate against young people's learning and engagement in PA. Examples of such practices include adopting a hardline approach to exercise, forcing young people into strenuous exercise, fitness regimes involving dull, boring and repetitive drill type activities, weighing and measuring, and fitness testing (Cale & Harris, 2009b; Rich, 2010). One of these alleged questionable practices, namely fitness testing, remains a standard feature of PE practice (Gard & Wright, 2001) and is therefore given particular consideration.

The role of fitness testing in teaching about active lifestyles

Fitness testing is commonplace within PE and is mandatory in some countries and states (Alfrey & Gard, 2014; Cale et al., 2014; Cooper et al., 2010; Corbin, 2010). Indeed, a recent study in Australia found fitness testing to be the most popular context for teaching about health (Alfrey & Gard, 2014). Yet, controversy has surrounded fitness testing in young people for many years and it has and continues to be a popular topic of debate (e.g. Cale et al., 2014; Cale & Harris, 2009a; Cohen, Voss & Sandercock, 2014; Liu, 2008; Lloyd, Colley & Tremblay, 2010; Naughton, Carlson & Greene, 2006; Silverman, Keating & Phillips, 2008; Wrench & Garrett, 2008). Cale and Harris (2009a) note the issues raised most commonly with fitness testing focus on the type, validity, reliability, ethics and value or purpose of testing young people. The latter is primarily the focus here in so far as the value or purpose of testing serves to contribute to teaching about (and promoting) active lifestyles.

Advocates of fitness testing in schools claim that it promotes healthy lifestyles, physical fitness and PA, learning and educational goals, positive attitudes, motivates young people to maintain or enhance their physical fitness or PA, and facilitates goal setting and self-management skills (Australian Council for Health, PE and Recreation [ACHPER], 2004; Corbin, 2010; Keating, Silverman & Kulinna, 2002; Silverman et al., 2008). A further rationale for testing and for which there is now growing support is the link between health-related fitness and health outcomes in children (Lloyd et al., 2010; Ortega, Ruiz, Castillo & Sjostrom, 2008; USDHHS, 2008). Whether fitness tests do actually serve many of these purposes is, however, debatable and their value has been questioned (e.g. Cale & Harris, 2009a; Keating, 2003; Naughton et al., 2006; Rice, 2007; Stewart Stanec, 2009). Keating (2003) cites three facts that cast doubt on the role of fitness testing in improving fitness and PA levels: a) children have failed to show improvements in fitness and have become less physically active; b) the percentage of overweight youth has increased substantially in recent years; and c) the proportion of inactive adults has also increased dramatically. Similarly, based on a review of the literature and a study of the views and experiences of stakeholders and experts in the field, Cale and Harris (2009a) noted there was little evidence to support the notion that fitness testing promotes healthy lifestyles and PA. To the contrary, they and others have cautioned that testing can be counterproductive to this goal in that it can be unpleasant, uncomfortable, embarrassing and meaningless for many young people, and that scores can be inaccurate, misleading, unfair and de-motivating (Cale & Harris, 2009a; Naughton et al., 2006; Rice, 2007). Cale and Harris (2009a) concluded that fitness testing may therefore represent a misdirected effort and that PE time could be better spent.

Equally, Cale and Harris (2009a) and Silverman et al. (2008) recognise the potential educational role of fitness testing, viewing this as an essential outcome if testing is to be justified and afforded precious PE time. The educational worth of fitness testing can be considered in terms of what young people learn through testing, their experiences of testing, and the impact of these. Surprisingly, researchers have paid relatively little attention to these aspects and when they have, the findings appear to be mixed. Hopple and Graham (1995) investigated children's perspectives and understanding of the mile run test. They found that children generally showed little or no understanding of why they were being asked to complete the test and that many disliked taking it. Likewise, Luke and Sinclair (1991) reported unfavourable attitudes towards fitness tests, whilst Keating (2003) reported some youngsters did not value or take testing seriously. More recently though, Mercier and Silverman (2014) found students overall to hold a slightly positive attitude towards testing, although acknowledged that amongst these were students with highly negative attitudes. Prospective and qualified PE teachers have furthermore reported many young people to dislike or not enjoy fitness testing (Alfrey & Gard, 2014; Cale & Harris, 2009a; Corbin, 2010; Wrench & Garrett, 2008). Reflecting on the potential dangers of institutional testing, Corbin (2010) expressed concern over the percentage of elementary teachers reporting children crying during testing whilst, based on their findings, Wrench and Garrett (2008) concluded how the "continuing unproblematic use of fitness testing in schools and universities might actually cause more pain than pleasure" (p. 342). These concerns are significant given that young people's enjoyment and experiences of fitness testing are likely to impact upon their future participation and motivation to participate in PA (Keating et al., 2002; Silverman et al., 2008; Wiersma & Sherman, 2008). Students' perspectives and attitudes within PE and how these influence their engagement are explored in Part VIII.

Additional issues regarding fitness testing include the individualistic nature and performative culture reflected in and reinforced through fitness testing, as well as the use of some questionable testing practices (Alfrey & Gard, 2014; Cale & Harris, 2009a; Cale et al., 2014; Wrench & Garrett, 2008). Targeting the individual and individual behaviour change fails to acknowledge factors in the physical and social environment that influence PA. Because young people have little control over, or decision-making opportunities with respect to their lifestyles and behaviours (Cale & Harris, 2009a), this also raises questions over the efficacy and ethics of curricula that assume this level of personal control (Gard & Wright, 2001; Wrench & Garrett, 2008). Key concerns with the performative culture (which celebrates comparison, measurement, assessment and accountability) in testing are that it reduces health to variables which can be measured, and puts individuals under pressure to work on, evaluate and judge their bodies against unattainable social ideals and to meet standards over which they have little or no control (Evans, 2007; Evans & Rich, 2011).

Cale et al. (2014) identified a number of questionable and potentially problematic 'performative' fitness testing practices, for example, the use of maximal fitness tests (most notably the multistage fitness test which is a progressive shuttle run test which requires individuals to exercise to exhaustion), the public posting of fitness test scores, and the public monitoring of students' weight or body composition. Questions have been asked over the appropriateness of the multistage fitness test for young people in that it was developed for use with elite, adult populations (Winsley, 2003), carries an element of risk (Association for Physical Education, 2008; Eve & Williams, 2000) and can be overly public and misused (Cale & Harris, 2009b; Pangrazi, 2006; Wrench & Garrett, 2008) and thereby undermine the confidence of, and embarrass some young people (Cale et al., 2014). On the issue of monitoring weight, Cale and Harris (2009b, p. 143) argue that it is not necessary to "measure children … to tell them something that they already know, and more importantly, no child needs to be measured to be helped to enjoy being physically active". The continued uncritical focus on testing is thus questionable on pedagogical grounds and suggests that the needs of many learners are being overlooked. Interestingly, some teachers themselves are now questioning the role of fitness testing and certain fitness testing practices (Alfrey & Gard, 2014; Cale et al., 2014). In their study, Alfrey and Gard (2014) found that some health and PE teachers had reservations about fitness testing, were unsure why they used tests, and had begun to reflect on the dangers and shortcomings of testing as a context for learning.

So far a rather bleak picture has been painted with regard to the value of fitness testing in PE, raising questions as to why the practice continues. Arguably a sound reason for fitness testing is the belief that it can potentially enhance learning about, as well as engagement in, active lifestyles. Silverman et al. (2008) are of the view that fitness testing can be used in positive ways to enhance the educational experience as well as promote good attitudes in children, whilst Lloyd et al. (2010) advise that the fear of assessment should not out-weigh the potential pedagogical benefits to students. Rather than simply being critical of school-based testing, we therefore need to take a look at the pedagogical approach to the testing and testing practice. In recognition of inappropriate and poor fitness testing practice, Corbin (2010) argues that quality PE that allows students to practise, understand and prepare for testing is essential if they are to see the value and personal benefits. In addition, it is imperative that any testing is learner- rather than activity-centred, which should consequently help to eradicate some of the possible pitfalls and negative experiences. In sum, scholars argue that if testing is appropriately employed, subjected to informed critique, and incorporated as just one component of a broad and holistic educational programme, it can be a valuable component of the PE curriculum and play a role in promoting active lifestyles (Cale & Harris, 2009a; Cale et al., 2014; Lloyd et al., 2010; Rowland, 2007; Silverman et al., 2008).

Finally to ensure best practice, teachers need access to training, guidance, support and opportunities for open professional dialogue about fitness testing (Alfrey & Gard, 2014; Cale & Harris, 2009b; Cale et al., 2014; Silverman et al., 2008). Various fitness testing guidelines for young people have been published over the years, including some recent recommendations by Cale et al. (2014) which focus on 'monitoring' within the PE curriculum more broadly, and which cover health and PA monitoring as well as fitness testing. The recommendations include key principles, messages and values teachers should strive to adopt in their practice plus guidance on content, organisation and delivery (Cale et al., 2014). Crucially, they encourage a holistic, critical and learner-centred approach, and for teachers to encourage their students likewise to be critically reflective of practice.

Summary of key findings

To summarise, below are the main findings, points and some key questions stemming from this chapter with respect to teaching about active lifestyles.

- It is generally accepted that PE provides a suitable context for teaching about active lifestyles. However, there is ongoing debate over the specific role and responsibility it should have for public health and health outcomes.
- Evidence reveals that school-based PA interventions, many of which include PE as a key component, can be effective and provide a number of positive outcomes for young people.
- Gaps in the evidence and limitations in the studies to date make it difficult to replicate studies and identify which types or aspects of school-based programmes are effective or most effective.
- Scholars consider the underpinning pedagogy and quality of delivery also to be key in PA and PE interventions and programmes. Unfortunately, researchers acknowledge limitations

in the pedagogy traditionally applied to teaching about active lifestyles and a lack of knowledge about effective PE-for-health pedagogies or models.

- In the absence of knowledge about appropriate pedagogies, concerns have been expressed about the way active lifestyles are taught and teachers' ability and effectiveness to deliver this area effectively. Additional factors which heighten these concerns include the PE profession's resistance to change, some PE teachers' sport, performance and fitness philosophies, and their limited health knowledge, training and/or engagement in relevant professional development.
- As a consequence, many PE teachers' delivery of active lifestyles is likely to be traditional, narrow and simplistic, and involve some misinformed, questionable or undesirable practices.
- Some scholars see fitness testing within PE as a questionable practice and yet it is commonplace and continues to be an ongoing topic of debate.
- Advocates of fitness testing in schools have justified its use on various grounds. Notably they argue that it promotes healthy lifestyles and PA, although there is little evidence to support this claim.
- The main issues discussed here with fitness testing relate to the value or purpose of testing young people in so far as it contributes to teaching about (and promoting) active lifestyles, the individualistic nature and performative culture reflected in and reinforced through testing, and to some questionable testing practices.
- Some scholars argue that if fitness testing is appropriately and critically employed, and incorporated as just one component of a broad and holistic educational programme, it can be a valuable component of the PE curriculum and play a role in promoting healthy lifestyles and PA.
- To ensure best practice, teachers need access to and opportunities for training, guidance, support and open professional dialogue about fitness testing in young people.

Reflective questions for discussion

1. When teaching about active lifestyles, what student learning outcomes are realistic for PE?
2. How can teachers maximise PE's potential to engage young people in active lifestyles?
3. How can scholars and researchers support PE teachers to adopt evidence-based PA and PE programmes and draw on research to inform their practice?
4. How can scholars, curriculum developers and specialists encourage and support PE teachers to develop effective PE-for-health pedagogies?
5. What learner-centred pedagogical practices are most likely to engage children and youth in in-class physical activity?
6. How can instructional practices be modified and adapted to encourage less fit and lower ability students to engage meaningfully in physical activity?

References

Alfrey, L., Cale, L., & Webb, L. A. (2012). Physical education teachers' continuing professional development in health-related exercise. *Physical Education and Sport Pedagogy, 17*(5), 477–491. DOI: 10.1080/17408 989.2011.594429.

Alfrey, L., & Gard, M. (2014). A crack where the light gets in: A study of health and physical education teachers' perspectives on fitness testing as a context for learning about health. *Asia-Pacific Journal of Health, Sport and Physical Education, 5*(1), 3–18.

Almond, L., & Harris, J. (1998). Interventions to promote health-related physical education. In S. Biddle, J. Sallis & N. Cavill (Eds.), *Young and active? Young people and health-enhancing physical activity – evidence and implications* (pp. 133–149). London: Health Education Authority.

Angelopoulos, P. D., Milionis, H. J., Grammatikaki, E., Moschonis, G., & Manios, Y. (2009). Changes in BMI and blood pressure after a school based intervention: The CHILDREN study. *European Journal of Public Health, 19*(3), 319–325.

Armour, K., & Harris, J. (2013). Making the case for developing new PE-for-health pedagogies. *Quest, 65*(2), 201–219.

Association for Physical Education. (2008). *Safe practice in physical education.* Leeds, UK: Coachwise.

Australian Council for Health, Physical Education and Recreation [ACHPER]. (2004). *Australian fitness education award: Teacher Manual* (rev. edn). Adelaide: Author.

Australian Curriculum, Assessment and Reporting Authority [ACARA]. (2012). *The health and physical education curriculum f-10.* Sydney: Author.

Bayne-Smith, M., Fardy, P. S., Azzollini, A., Magel, J., Schmitz, K. H., & Agin, D. (2004). Improvements in heart health behaviors and reduction in coronary artery disease risk factors in urban teenaged girls through a school-based intervention: The PATH program. *American Journal of Public Health, 94*(9), 1538–1543.

Burrows, L., & Wright, J. (2004). The discursive production of childhood, identity and health. In J. Evans, B. Davies & J. Wright (Eds.), *Body knowledge and control* (pp. 83–96). London: Routledge.

Cale, L., & Harris, J. (1998). The benefits of health-related physical education and recommendations for implementation. *The Bulletin of Physical Education, 34*(1), 27–41.

Cale, L., & Harris, J. (Eds.). (2005). *Exercise and young people. Issues, implications and initiatives.* Basingstoke, UK: Palgrave Macmillan.

Cale, L., & Harris, J. (2006). School based physical activity interventions: Effectiveness, trends, issues, implications and recommendations for practice. *Sport, Education and Society, 11*(4), 401–420.

Cale, L., & Harris, J. (2009a). Fitness testing in physical education: A misdirected effort in promoting healthy lifestyles and physical activity? *Physical Education and Sport Pedagogy, 14*(1), 89–108.

Cale, L., & Harris, J. (2009b). *Getting the buggers fit* (2nd edn). London: Continuum.

Cale, L., & Harris, J. (2013). Physical education and health: Considerations and issues. In S. Capel & M. Whitehead (Eds.), *Debates in physical education* (pp. 74–88). Abingdon, Oxon: Routledge.

Cale, L., Harris, J., & Chen, M. H. (2014). Monitoring health, activity and fitness in physical education: Its current and future state of health. *Sport Education and Society, 19*(4), 376–397.

Castelli, D., & Williams, L. (2007). Health-related fitness and physical education teachers' content knowledge. *Journal of Teaching in Physical Education, 26*(1), 3–19.

Cohen, D., Voss, C. & Sandercock, R. H. (2014). Fitness testing for children: Let's mount the Zebra! *Journal of Physical Activity and Health, 12*(5), 597–603. DOI: http://dx.doi.org/10.1123/jpah.2013-0345.

Cooper, K. H., Everett, D., Meredith, M. D., Kloster, J., Rathbone, M. & Read, K. (2010). Preface: Texas statewide assessment of youth fitness. *Research Quarterly for Exercise and Sport, 81*(3), ii–iv.

Corbin, C. B. (2010) Texas Youth Fitness Study: A commentary. *Research Quarterly for Exercise and Sport, 81*(3), S75–S78.

Currie, C., Gabhainn, S., Godeau, E., Roberts, C., Smith, R., Currie, D., Picket, W., Richter, M., Morgan, A., & Barnekow, V. (Eds.). (2008). Inequalities in young people's health: International report from the HBSC 2005/06 Survey. *WHO policy series: Health policy for children and adolescents*, Issue 5, Copenhagen: WHO Regional Office for Europe.

De Meester, F., van Lenthe, J. J. Spittaels, H., Lien, N., & De Bourdeauhuij, I. (2009). Interventions for promoting physical activity among European teenagers: A systematic review. *International Journal of Behavioural Nutrition and Physical Activity, 6*(82), 1–11.

Demetriou, Y., & Honer, O. (2012). Physical activity interventions in the school setting: A systematic review. *Psychology of Sport and Exercise, 13*, 186–196.

Department for Education. (2013). Programmes of study for physical education. Key stages 3 & 4. https://www.gov.uk/government/uploads/system/uploads/attachment_data/file/239086/SECONDARY_national_curriculum_-_Physical_education.pdf.

Dobbins, M., DeCorby, K., Robeson, P. et al., (2009). *School-based physical activity programs for promoting physical activity and fitness in children and adolescents aged 6 to 18.* Cochrane Database of Systematic Reviews, Issue 1.

Dobbins, M., Husson, H., DeCorby, K., & La Rocca, R. L. (2013). *School-based physical activity programs for promoting physical activity and fitness in children and adolescents aged 6 to 18.* Cochrane Database of Systematic Reviews, Issue 2.

Dorgo, S., King, G. A., Candelaria, N. G., Bader, J. O., Brickey, G. D., & Adams, C. E. (2009). Effects of manual resistance training on fitness in adolescents. *Journal of Strength & Conditioning Research, 23*(8), 2287–2294.

Evans, J. (2007). Health education or weight management in schools? *Cardiometabolic Risk and Weight Management, 2*(2), 12–16.

Evans, J., & Rich, E. (2011). Body policies and body pedagogies: Every child matters in totally pedagogised schools? *Journal of Education Policy, 26*(2), 311–329.

Eve, N., & Williams, D. (2000). Multistage fitness test in secondary schools: Advice on safety. *Bulletin of Physical Education, 36*(2), 110–114.

Ewart, C. K., Young, D. R., & Hagberg, J. M. (1998). Effects of school-based aerobic exercise on blood pressure in adolescent girls at risk for hypertension. *American Journal of Public Health, 88*(6), 949–951.

Fox, K., Cooper, A., & McKenna, J. (2004). The school and promotion of children's health-enhancing physical activity: Perspectives from the United Kingdom. *Journal of Teaching Physical Education, 23*, 338–358.

Fox, K., & Harris, J. (2003). Promoting physical activity through schools. In J. McKenna & C. Riddoch (Eds.), *Perspectives on health and exercise* (pp. 181–201). Basingstoke, UK: Palgrave Macmillan.

Frenn, M., Malin, S., Brown, R. L., Greer, Y., Fox, J., Greer, J., et al. (2005). Changing the tide: An internet/video exercise and low-fat diet intervention with middle-school students. *Applied Nursing Research, 18*, 13–21.

Gard, M., & Wright, J. (2001). Managing uncertainty: Obesity discourses and physical education in a risk society. *Studies in Philosophy and Education, 20*, 535–549.

Green, K. (2009). Exploring the everyday 'philosophies' of physical education teachers from a sociological perspective. In R. Bailey & D. Kirk (Eds.), *The Routledge physical education reader* (pp. 183–206). London: Routledge.

Haerens, L., Deforche, B., Maes, L., Cardon, G., Stevens, V., & De Bourdeaudhuij, I. (2006). Evaluation of a 2-year physical activity and healthy eating intervention in middle school children. *Health Education Research, 2*(6), 911–921.

Haerens, L., Kirk, D., Cardon, G., & De Bourdeaudhuij, I. (2011). Toward the development of a pedagogical model for health-based physical education. *Quest, 63*, 321–338.

Harris, J. (2010). Health-related physical education. In R. Bailey (Ed.), *Physical education for learning: A guide for secondary schools* (pp. 26–36). London: Continuum.

Harris, J., & Cale, L. (1997). How healthy is school PE? A review of the effectiveness of health-related physical education programmes in schools. *Health Education Journal, 56*, 84–104.

Harris, J., & Leggett, G. (2015). Influences on the expression of health within physical education curricula in secondary schools in England and Wales. *Sport, Education and Society, 20*(7), 908–923.

Hopple, C., & Graham, G. (1995). What children think, feel and know about physical fitness testing. *Journal of Teaching in Physical Education, 14*(4), 408–417.

Janssen, L., & LeBlanc, A. G. (2010). Systematic review of the health benefits of physical activity and fitness in school-aged children and youth. *International Journal of Behavioural Nutrition and Physical Activity, 7*, 7–40.

Kahn, E. B., Ramsey, L. T., Brownson, R. C., Health, G. W., Howze, E. H., & Powell, K. E. (2002). The effectiveness of interventions to increase physical activity. *American Journal of Preventive Medicine, 22*(4S), 73–107.

Keating, X. D. (2003). The current often implemented fitness tests in physical education programs: Problems and future directions. *Quest, 55*, 141–160.

Keating, X. D., Silverman, S., & Kulinna, P. H. (2002). Preservice physical education teacher attitudes toward fitness tests and the factors influencing their attitudes. *Journal of Teaching in Physical Education, 21*, 193–207.

Kirk, D. (2010). Four relational issues and the bigger picture. In D. Kirk (Ed.), *Physical education futures* (pp. 97–120). Abingdon, Oxon: Routledge.

Kriemler, S., Meyer, U., Marin, E., van Sluijs, E. M. F., Andersen, L. B., & Marin, B. W. (2011). Effect of school-based interventions on physical activity and fitness in children and adolescents: A review of reviews and systematic update. *British Journal of Sports Medicine, 45*, 923–930.

Liu, Y. (2008). Youth fitness testing: If the 'horse' is not dead, what should we do? *Measurement in Physical Education and Exercise Science, 12*, 123–125.

Lloyd, M., Colley, R., & Tremblay, M. S. (2010). Advancing the debate on fitness testing for children: Perhaps we're riding the wrong animal. *Pediatric Exercise Science, 22*, 176–182.

Lounsbery, M. A. F., McKenzie, T. L., Trost, S., & Smith, N. J. (2011). Facilitators and barriers to adopting evidence-based physical education in elementary schools. *Journal of Physical Activity and Health, 8*(1), S17–S25.

Luke, M. D., & Sinclair, G. D. (1991). Gender differences in adolescents' attitudes toward school physical education. *Journal of Teaching in Physical Education, 11*, 31–46.

McKenzie, T. L. (2007). The preparation of physical educators: A public health perspective. *Quest, 59*, 346–357.

McKenzie, T., & Kahan, D. (2004). Impact of the Surgeon General's report: Through the eyes of physical education teacher education. *Journal of Teaching in Physical Education, 23*, 300–317.

McKenzie, T. L., & Lounsbery, M. A. F. (2009) School physical education: the pill not taken. *American Journal of Lifestyle Medicine, 3*(3), 219–225.

McManus, A. M., Masters, R. S. W., Laukkanen, R. M. T., Yu, C. C. W., Sit, C. H. P., & Ling, F. C. M. (2008). Using heart-rate feedback to increase physical activity in children. *Preventive Medicine, 47*(4), 402–408.

Mercier, K., & Silverman, S. (2014). High school students' attitudes toward fitness testing. *Journal of Teaching in Physical Education, 33*, 269–281.

National Association for Sport and Physical Education [NASPE]. (2004). *Moving into the future: National standards for physical education* (2nd edn), Reston, VA: Author.

National Institute for Health and Clinical Excellence [NICE]. (2007). Physical activity and children: Review 1: Descriptive epidemiology. NICE Public Health Collaborating Centre: www.nice.org.uk.

Naughton, G. A., Carlson, J. S., & Greene, D. A. (2006). A challenge to fitness testing in primary schools. *Journal of Science and Medicine in Sport, 9*, 40–45.

Ortega, F. B., Ruiz, J. R., Castillo, M. J., & Sjostrom, M. (2008). Physical fitness in childhood and adolescence: A powerful marker of health. *International Journal of Obesity, 32*, 1–11.

O'Sullivan, M. (2004). Possibilities and pitfalls of a public health agenda for physical education. *Journal of Teaching in Physical Education, 23*, 392–404.

Palmer, S., Graham, G., & Elliott, E. (2005). Effects of a web-based health program on fifth grade children's physical activity knowledge, attitudes and behaviour. *American Journal of Health Education, 36*(2), 86–93.

Pangrazi, R. P. (2006). *Dynamic physical education for elementary school children* (15th edn). Boston, MA: Allyn & Bacon.

Pangrazi, R. P., Beighle, A., & Vehige, T. (2003). Impact of Promoting Lifestyle Activity for Youth (PLAY) on children's physical activity. *Journal of School Health, 73*, 317–321.

Peralta, L. R., Jones, R. A., & Okely, A. D. (2009). Promoting healthy lifestyles among adolescent boys: The Fitness Improvement and Lifestyle Awareness Program RCT. *Preventive Medicine, 48*(6), 537–542.

Perry, C. L., Kelder, S. H., & Klepp, K. (1994). Community-wide cardiovascular disease prevention in young people. Long-term outcomes of the Class of 1989 Study. *European Journal of Public Health, 4*, 188–194.

Perry, C. L., Klepp, K. I., Halper, A., Dudovitz, B. S., Golden, D., Griffin, G., et al. (1987). Promoting healthy eating and physical activity patterns among adolescents: A pilot study of 'Slice of Life'. *Health Education Research, 2*(2), 93–103.

Puhse, U., Barker, D., Brettschneider, W. D. Feldmeth, A. K., et al. (2011). International approaches to health-oriented physical education: Local health debates and differing conceptions of health. *International Journal of Physical Education, 3*, 2–15.

Quennerstedt, M. (2008). Exploring the relation between physical activity and health: A salutogenic approach to physical education. *Sport, Education and Society, 13*(3), 276–283.

Rice, C. (2007). Becoming 'the fat girl': Acquisition of an unfit identity. *Women's Studies International Forum, 30*, 158–174.

Rich, E. (2010). Obesity assemblages and surveillance in schools. *International Journal of Qualitative Studies in Education, 23*(7), 803–821.

Rowland, T. W. (2007). Fitness testing in schools: Once more around the track. *Pediatric Exercise Science, 19*, 113–114.

Sallis, J. F., McKenzie, T. L., Conway, T. L., Elder, J. P., Prochaska, J. J., Brown, M., Zive, M. M., Marshall, S. J. & Alcaraz, J. E. (2003). Environmental interventions for eating and physical activity: A randomized controlled trial in middle schools. *American Journal of Preventive Medicine, 24*(3), 209–217.

Silverman, S., Keating, X. D., & Phillips, S. R. (2008). A lasting impression: A pedagogical perspective on youth fitness testing. *Measurement in Physical Education, 12*, 146–166.

Simon, C., Wagner, A., DiVita, C., Rauscher, E., Klein-Platat, C., Arveiler, D., Schweitzer, B., & Triby, E. (2004). Intervention centred on adolescents' physical activity and sedentary behaviour (ICAPS): Concept and 6-month results. *International Journal of Obesity, 28*, S96–S103.

Stensel, D. J., Gorely, T., & Biddle, S. J. H. (2008). Youth health outcomes. In A. L. Smith & S. J. H. Biddle (Eds.), *Youth physical activity and sedentary behaviour: Challenges and solutions* (pp. 31–57). Champaign, IL: Human Kinetics.

Stephens, M., & Wentz, S. (1998). Supplemental fitness activities and fitness in urban elementary school classrooms. *Family Medicine, 30*(3), 220–223.

Stewart Stanec, A. D. (2009). The theory of planned behavior: predicting teachers' intentions and behavior during fitness testing. *Journal of Teaching in Physical Education, 28*, 255–271.

Stone, E. J., McKenzie, T. L., Welk, G. J., & Booth, M. L. (1998). Effects of physical activity interventions in youth: Review and synthesis. *American Journal of Preventive Medicine, 15*(4), 298–315.

Story, M., Sherwood, N. E., Himes, J. H., Davis, M., Jacobs, D. R., Cartwright, Y., et al. (2003). An after-school obesity prevention program for African-American girls: The Minnesota GEMS pilot study. *Ethnicity & Disease, 13*(1 Suppl 1), S54–S64.

Stratton, G., Fairclough, S. J., & Ridgers, N. (2008). Physical activity levels during the school day. In A. L. Smith & S. J. H. Biddle (Eds.), *Youth physical activity and sedentary behaviour: Challenges and solutions* (pp. 321–350). Champaign, IL: Human Kinetics.

Sun, H., Chen, A., Zhu, X., & Ennis, C. D. (2012). Learning science-based fitness knowledge in constructivist physical education. *Elementary School Journal, 113*(2), 215–229.

Trost, S. (2006). Public health and physical education. In D. Kirk, M. O'Sullivan & D. Macdonald (Eds.), *Handbook of physical education* (pp. 163–187). London: Sage.

Trudeau, F., Laurencelle, L., Tremblay, J., et al. (1998). Follow-up of the Trois-Rivieres growth and development longitudinal study. *Pediatric Exercise Science, 10*, 3768–3777.

Trudeau, F., Laurencelle, L., Tremblay, J., et al. (1999). Daily primary school physical education: Effects on physical activity during adult life. *Medicine in Science and Sports and Exercise, 31*, 111–117.

Trudeau, F., & Shepard, R. J. (2008). Is there a long-term health legacy of required physical education? *Sports Medicine, 38*(4), 265–270.

United States Department of Health and Human Services [USDHHS]. (2008). *Physical activity guidelines advisory committee report.* Washington, DC: Author.

van Sluijs, E. M. F., McMinn, A. M., & Griffin, S. J. (2007). Effectiveness of interventions to promote physical activity in children and adolescents: Systematic review of controlled trials. *British Medical Journal, 335*, 703.

Walther, C., Gaede, L., Adams, V., Gelbrich, G., Leichtle, A., Erbs, S., et al. (2009). Effect of increased exercise in school children on physical fitness and endothelial progenitor cells: A prospective randomized trial. *Circulation, 120*(22), 2251–2259.

Wang, L. Y., Gutin, B., Barbeau, P., Moore, J. B., Hanes, J. Jr, Johnson, M. H., et al. (2008). Cost-effectiveness of a school-based obesity prevention program. *Journal of School Health, 78*(12), 619–624.

Wellard, I. (2012). Body-reflexive pleasures: Exploring bodily experiences within the context of sport and physical activity. *Sport, Education and Society, 17*(1), 21–33.

Wiersma, L. D., & Sherman, C. P. (2008). The responsible use of youth fitness testing to enhance student motivation, enjoyment, and performance. *Measurement in Physical Education and Exercise Science, 12*, 167–183.

Winsley, R. J. (2003). The suitability of the multistage fitness test to assess children's aerobic fitness. *European Journal of Physical Education, 8*(1), 19–28.

Wrench, A., & Garrett, R. (2008). Pleasure and pain: Experiences of fitness testing. *European Physical Education Review, 14*(3), 325–346.

PART VII

Educating teachers 'effectively' from PETE to CPD

Introduction

This part is about learning to teach. Each chapter addresses a different aspect of this fascinating topic ranging from understanding how learning theory informs research and practice, to analysing issues in physical education teacher education (PETE) and continuing professional development (CPD), and considering teacher learning in two highly topical areas: health and inclusion. Yet, even though each chapter has a distinct focus, they are also linked by two shared understandings. The first is that in order to be effective in meeting pupils' diverse and dynamic learning needs, physical education (PE) teachers must learn continuously throughout their careers. The second understanding is that whereas the term 'effective' is used widely to characterise – and scrutinise – contemporary teaching and learning, it is a highly contested concept that warrants critical analysis. None of the chapters, therefore, offers easy certainties or comforting recipes for success to inform learning/teaching in PE, PETE or CPD. Instead the authors invite readers to engage with the issues, review with circumspect enthusiasm the material presented, enter the debates with informed enthusiasm and, perhaps, reflect afresh on practice and/or research.

Handbooks serve a number of functions, one of which is to act as an authoritative point of reference in a field. To that end, the chapter authors have provided historical overviews of their topics and summarised key international literature. This, however, does not go far enough. In any considerations of learning and teaching there are a wide range of implicit and explicit views on the 'correct' purposes of teaching; what 'should' be learnt; the 'best' ways to learn, the 'proper' role of teachers and, by implication, the 'best' ways to educate – or train – them (terms which, in themselves, generate debate). Competing views on these topics are in a constant struggle for supremacy. This also explains why 'effectiveness' is such a slippery concept in teaching, learning to teach and education more widely. Ko, Sammons and Bakkum (2013) conducted a review of the research and evidence on effective teaching and highlighted a need to unpack the concept of effectiveness by addressing questions such as:

- Effective in promoting which outcomes? This relates to the goals of education for students.
- Effective over what time period? This relates to the idea of change and improvement over time.

- Effective for whom? This relates to effectiveness in promoting outcomes for different groups of students (e.g. by gender or ethnic/language group). (p. 5)

These authors conclude that defining effectiveness is never straightforward and they question "whether it is appropriate to think in simple categories such as more effective or less effective teachers or teaching" (p. 40). This is an interesting question that also applies to the ways in which we decide to educate teachers and it is a theme that runs through all of the chapters in this part of the handbook.

In the first chapter, Quennerstedt and Maivorsdotter add a further layer to questions about effectiveness by focussing on the complexity of learning. Drawing on Sfard's (1998) metaphors of learning as *acquisition* and *participation*, they review some of the most commonly used learning theories and consider the ways in which they impact upon our understanding of learning, teaching and research: "What is certain is that the different assumptions underpinning learning theories lead to different assumptions about how teachers could and should teach, and such understandings – rarely made explicit – lead researchers to ask different questions in educational research" (p. 420). They also highlight matters of some concern. A review of research published over the last ten years in key journals in our field reveals that the learning theories underpinning and informing research are rarely made explicit in publications, and that there is a pressing need to develop new learning theories in and for PE. Addressing both of these concerns is essential to enhancing teacher learning.

The chapter by McCuaig and Enright pursues the notion of effectiveness in the context of PETE by grounding their review in Hunter's (1994) notion of 'principled positions'. They point out that discussions about effectiveness usually rest on notions of an 'ideal' teacher and they discuss three examples of principled positions in PE (physically competent, healthy citizen and socially critical actor) and explore the implications for PETE. These authors draw on the work of McCuaig and Hay (2013) to argue for the value of focussing on understanding the principled positions of others. Moreover, in setting reflective questions, they ask readers to spend some time interrogating their personal principled positions including origins and implications. In conclusion, the chapter suggests that much work remains to be done: "Some five decades on, an expansive body of research, advocacy and critique has done little to resolve the challenges we face in establishing agreed criteria for PETE effectiveness" (p. 440).

Shifting from PETE to CPD, the chapter by Parker and Patton focusses on teacher professional learning from the point of initial certification through to retirement. These authors begin by arguing that "although there is a growing recognition of the importance of CPD for the professional growth of teachers, numerous questions remain about the nature of *optimally effective* CPD" (p. 447). A review of the international literature on CPD in both education and PE suggests that we have made little progress from Guskey's (2002) claim that what is required is an 'optimal mix' of CPD types and formats for each teacher at each career stage. The evidence suggests, however, that we are a long way from achieving anything close to an effective, personalised CPD offering. The authors also highlight concerns about CPD that is designed to introduce new teaching ideas without due consideration of impact on student learning, and there is certainly a lack of research that captures such impact. They also point to a largely neglected concern: that of the educational needs of CPD facilitators and providers. In concluding, these authors make a plea for more robust studies – including quantitative research – to try to better understand the impact of different CPD approaches on teachers' and pupils' learning. This, they argue, may lead to the development of more 'effective' forms of CPD.

While previous chapters have focussed on learning and teaching at a generic level, the next two focus on more specific aspects of professional practice in contemporary PE. Haerens, Aelterman, De Meester and Tallir address the challenges of developing PE teachers' pedagogies in the field of health. There can be little question that this is a key contemporary concern. 'Health' has become entwined with PE's aims and aspirations and, in some countries, this has resulted in a change of name for the subject (HPE, for example). The authors note, however, that this growth has not led to consensus on the most important goals and learning outcomes of health-based PE. There are disagreements about the definition of health in and beyond PE contexts, and on whether PE should be involved in developing fitness or merely increasing physical activity levels – or neither.

Haerens et al. review the literature on goals such as physical fitness development, increasing physical activity, motor development and stimulating autonomous motivation. They conclude that to better support teachers, more research is needed "regarding possible mechanisms that determine the effectiveness of training in health-based PE at the teacher level" (p. 467). Moreover, we need more transparency in studies on different teacher education approaches in order to support teachers in this field. Similar to Parker and Patton in the previous chapter, and Quennerstedt and Maivorsdotter in the earlier chapter on learning theory, Haerens et al. make a plea for research to be reported in more consistent ways to facilitate the development of a cumulative body of knowledge. They also suggest that teachers need to be more centrally involved in the design and content of CPD in the area of health.

In the final chapter in this section, Makopoulou and Thomas consider ways in which we might support teachers to develop 'effective inclusive pedagogies'. The authors note that, over time, the agenda in this field has shifted from 'special educational needs' and 'mainstreaming' to inclusion, which is about equal access and opportunities for all. The authors draw on the work of Reiser to argue:

> Inclusion is about the child's right to participate and the school's duty to make learning more meaningful and relevant for all, particularly those learners most vulnerable to exclusionary pressures. Inclusion is based on "a paradigm shift from a deficit model of disability to one of social/human rights" (Rieser, 2013, p. 1). (p. 473)

What this means is that the development of inclusive pedagogies can be regarded as one of the tenets of any claims to be an 'effective' teacher. Yet, the review undertaken in this chapter highlights numerous unresolved questions about how best to support teachers to learn in this field. The authors argue that more research of all kinds is needed – descriptive, evaluation and experimental – to inform policy and practice. Here again, a need for greater conceptual clarity is signalled and, similar to Haerens et al., it is suggested that CPD programmes should be better grounded in teachers' experiences.

As was noted earlier, these chapters fulfil the functions of a handbook in that they have surveyed and summarised their topics. The bibliographies alone will serve as rich material for new researchers. In addition, the explicit attempt to tackle thorny questions of 'effectiveness' has raised a number of questions for further critical reflection. A common theme to emerge is an urgent need for the PE-related research base to be more helpful for practice. Pleas are made in these chapters, for example, for research that is more transparent at all levels – including making explicit the learning theories underpinning studies – and that is more consistent and detailed in the reporting of findings. These are serious concerns and it could be argued that they stem from the persistent theory/research-practice gap that characterises the field (see Armour, 2014, for a fuller discussion). The evidence presented in this part confirms my view that finding new mechanisms to bridge this gap is one of the most pressing challenges to be tackled in our field.

Kathleen M. Armour
University of Birmingham, UK

References

Armour, K. M (Ed.). (2014). *Pedagogical cases in physical education & youth sport*. London: Routledge.

Guskey, T. R. (2002). Professional development and teacher change. *Teachers and Teaching, 8*(3), 381–391.

Hunter, I. (1994). *Rethinking the school: Subjectivity, bureaucracy, criticism*. St Leonards, NSW: Allen & Unwin.

Ko, J., Sammons, P. & Bakkum, L. (2013). *Effective teaching: A review of the research and evidence*. Reading: CfBT Education Trust. Retrieved 3 October 2015, from http://cdn.cfbt.com/~/media/cfbtcorporate/files/research/2013/r-effective-teaching-2013.pdf.

McCuaig, L., & Hay, P. J. (2013). Principled pursuits of 'the good citizen' in health and physical education. *Physical Education and Sport Pedagogy, 18*(3), 282–297.

Rieser, R. (2013). *Educating teachers for children with disabilities: Mapping, scoping and best practices exercise in the context of developing inclusive education*. Bhutan: UNESCO.

Sfard, A. (1998). On two metaphors for learning and the dangers of choosing just one. *Educational Researcher, 27*(2), 4–13.

28

THE ROLE OF LEARNING THEORY IN LEARNING TO TEACH

Mikael Quennerstedt & Ninitha Maivorsdotter, ÖREBRO UNIVERSITY, SWEDEN

Learning is a complex matter, and it is difficult to find generally accepted definitions of or clear boundaries for what learning is or can be understood as. However, given the centrality of learning in education, it is imperative to consider how researchers, teachers, coaches and other stakeholders within the field of physical education (PE) approach and address it. The purpose of this chapter is to introduce central learning theories in relation to PE and to present an overview of current research regarding the role of learning theory in learning to teach. In this context, current trends and implications for research and practice are discussed.

What can be considered as learning and, in consequence, a learning theory? A wide definition of learning is that proposed by Knud Illeris (2007, p. 3) as "any process that in living organisms leads to permanent capacity change and which is not solely due to biological maturation or ageing". This will almost certainly include theories ranging from Howard Gardner's theory of multiple intelligences to Michel Foucault's writings about power and knowledge. A different and more delineated option is the classical division between learning theories based on different philosophical frameworks, such as behaviourist, cognitivist and constructivist theories of learning (Macdonald, 2004), the latter of which is often divided into individual/cognitive and social constructivism (Cobb & Bowers, 1999).

In this chapter we use Anna Sfard's (1998) two metaphors of learning to structure the chapter: *the acquisition metaphor* and *the participation metaphor*. This division of different learning theories helps to map basic assumptions the theories entail both in general and in research in PE. In the chapter the metaphors are used to facilitate an understanding of learning and its consequences for learners, teachers and researchers. We do not have the space to give a comprehensive overview of, for example, theories of reproduction, teaching, motivation, power relations, system theory or modern brain research all of which have consequences for learning. Instead we focus on theories explicitly focusing on *what* and *how* people learn.

Historical overview

As problematised in *The Handbook of Physical Education* edited by Kirk, Macdonald and O'Sullivan (2006), research in PE has generated relatively few studies explicitly using learning theories to explore how individuals learn. According to Rink (1999) this also applies to the use of learning theory in relation to research on teaching in PE. In the body of research presented in the 2006 handbook, it is noted that interest in learning in PE research primarily starts in the 1970s with so-called time-based research, even if earlier studies focusing on the acquisition of motor skills also were closely related to issues of learning (van der Mars, 2006). These studies implicitly start with a behaviourist orientation to learning, where teachers' actions are considered as directly linked to student behaviour in terms of learning as a product of the teaching process (Hastie & Siedentop, 2006). Other chapters in the handbook reveal the introduction of the classroom ecology paradigm in the 1980s as a response to the earlier process-product paradigm (Hastie & Siedentop, 2006). This research took an interest in students' responses to tasks in the classroom, and how teachers and students act together in PE practice. Another perspective critical of the process-product paradigm emerged from cognitivist research. Solmon (2006) argued that PE research on learner cognition has its roots in the motor learning literature but that a movement towards issues of cognitive mediation, student and teacher perceptions and motivational research had significant impact.

Much of the constructivist research in PE can, with inspiration from Cobb and Bowers (1999), be labelled social constructivism. Some research does exist within an individual constructivist orientation with a basis in, for example, Piaget, but this is not the majority (Rovegno & Dolly, 2006). Instead it was social constructivist research including situated perspectives of learning that from the 1990s influenced PE research. This strand of research has, according to Rovegno and Dolly (2006) and Rovegno (2006), introduced the situated nature of knowledge into the field. Several studies focusing on how individuals act in socio-cultural settings have been published. These include studies focusing on different dimensions of learning, for example Teaching Games for Understanding, or teacher knowledge and teacher learning (Rovegno, 2006).

Overview of learning theories

In this chapter Sfard's (1998) metaphors of acquisition and participation help us to structure current conceptualisations of learning and can be used to scrutinise some of the basic assumptions of learning found in different theories. Sfard details the ways in which educational research oscillates between these two metaphors and, what she calls, competing ontologies. This leads to different answers regarding the question of what learning *is* and how we *really* learn (cf. Quennerstedt, Öhman & Armour, 2014).

Learning as acquisition

The acquisition metaphor, which has dominated research on learning for a long time, includes a wide range of learning theories. According to Sfard (1998), these assumptions about learning are discernible in behaviourism, cognitivism, individual constructivism following the works of Vygotsky, research using Piaget and in some interactionist theories of learning. Even where there are significant differences between some of the theories (see Table 28.1), a common assumption is that knowledge is something external that individual learners can acquire, internalise or assimilate in existing schemas or patterns of behaviour. In other words, learning is about acquisition and gaining possession of something through changed behaviour (as in Skinner's behaviourism) or active reconstruction (as in Piaget's individual constructivism). Here, knowledge is a commodity; something that people have or possess.

Learning is usually understood as a change in behaviour in behaviourist theories, or in terms of concept development in most cognitive learning theories. In Piaget's theories, for example, concepts are modified and, as a consequence, existing schemas of knowledge are reconstructed. Knowledge can accordingly be applied, transferred and shared. According to these theories, people learn through reception, construction of meaning, internalisation, discovery, appropriation or accumulation; teachers teach by delivering, conveying, facilitating or fostering the development of knowledge. Thus, learning as acquisition means that knowledge is something that individual learners have and own, and that can be transferred between different contexts as individuals build experience. Studies within this metaphor often focus mainly on the individual with less emphasis on context.

Learning as participation

On the other hand, understanding learning as participation involves viewing knowledge as an aspect of a practice or activity (cf. Illeris, 2007). According to Sfard (1998), this view of learning can be found in sociocultural learning theories building on, for example, Vygotsky's use of concepts such as communities of practice, legitimate peripheral participation and apprenticeship (cf. Lave & Wenger, 1991; Wertsch, 1998). It also is expressed in research using the classic works of John Dewey, Donald Schön's notions of the reflective practitioner, Michael Polanyi's theory of tacit and embodied knowledge and in more recent attempts to further theorise learning in terms of 'learning as becoming' (Hodkinson, Biesta & James, 2007).

A basic assumption that links these theories is an understanding that knowledge is situated, mediated and centred on the ability to act in a certain practice. Knowing something is about becoming a 'member' of a particular practice, activity or discourse, as in situated learning theories (e.g. Lave & Wenger, 1991), or as a relation between action and its cultural, institutional and historical contexts, as in many sociocultural learning theories (e.g. Wertsch, 1998). This involves a shift from understanding knowledge as *having*, to knowledge as *doing*.

Issues of learning in the participation metaphor are always considered in light of the interplay between an individual and the environment, and are often connected to the ability to communicate. Learning is, accordingly, something social that occurs in communication and participation in different contexts. In the participation metaphor, it is assumed that people learn through interaction, communication, taking part and thus gaining access to different contexts. As a consequence, teachers teach by creating cooperative learning environments, communication, negotiation and guiding learners in and through inquiry in social contexts.

In short, learning as participation involves people becoming members of and participants in different practices. Knowledge is thus seen as an aspect of a practice, discourse or activity. Studies based on this metaphor often begin with the location in which the learning takes place

Table 28.1 Metaphorical mapping (adapted from Sfard, 1998, p. 7)

	Acquisition metaphor Behaviourist orientation	Acquisition metaphor Cognitivist orientation	Participation metaphor
Goal of learning	Individual enrichment	Individual enrichment	Community building
Learning	Acquisition of behaviours, behavioural change	Knowledge acquisition, information processing	Becoming a participant
Student	Recipient	Recipient, reconstructor	Participant, apprentice
Teacher	Provider	Mediator	Expert participant, guide
Knowledge	Different behaviours	Individual or collective structures	Aspect of practice, discourse, activity
Knowing	Having, possessing	Having, possessing	Participating, communicating

and sometimes downplay individual experiences and, as a result, tend to be criticised for being unable to explain transfer of learning (Sfard, 1998).

Of course, few contemporary learning theories in education or PE can be categorised wholly within either the acquisition or the participation metaphor. Most theories acknowledge, to some extent, individual aspects of the learner as well as sociocultural influences. The conceptualisation of learning within both metaphors, however, has been influenced by debates centring on individual-environment dualism (Hodkinson et al., 2007). What is certain is that the different assumptions underpinning learning theories lead to different assumptions about how teachers could and should teach, and such understandings – rarely made explicit – lead researchers to ask different questions in educational research.

Current trends and issues

The trends and issues presented in this section are based on a review of studies published in the following journals between 2004 and 2014: *Sport, Education and Society, Physical Education and Sport Pedagogy, Journal of Teaching in Physical Education, European Physical Education Review, Quest* and *Research Quarterly for Exercise and Sport*. The key inclusion criteria for the search were: (i) that the word 'learning' was present in the abstract or key word list; (ii) there was a focus on the role of learning theory in learning to teach; and (iii) the studies were published in English (which also is a limitation). As a result, this section is based on a synthesis of the abstracts of about 300 articles. Sfard's (1998) metaphors will again be used as the organising framework.

Learning as acquisition

Within understandings of learning as acquisition, individual-environment dualism underpins two predominant trends in PE research, namely studies based on *motor learning theories* and those drawing from *cognitive learning theories*. Historically, these trends have been based on similar assumptions; i.e. that learning is something external that the learner can acquire, and researchers within these fields explore learning with focus primarily on the individual rather than the environment. There are, however, also differences in understandings of where learning actually takes place; for example learning as embodied or in the mind through reflection.

Studies exploring *motor learning* have focused on the body in terms of observable, gross bodily behaviour to identify cause and effect. Studies often take a 'functional' approach to teaching and emphasise the use of feedback and reward systems to change and modify behaviour (cf. Wallian & Wei Chang, 2006). Numerous studies have explored motor learning in PE from these premises and show, for example, the positive effects of using self-controlled feedback (e.g. Chiviacowsky & Wulf, 2005) and the benefits of allowing individuals to control their own practice schedule to improve their motor skills (e.g. Keetch & Lee, 2007). In the last decade, more traditional views of motor learning have been influenced by new concepts, such as those featured in sociocultural perspectives of learning (Chow, 2013; Wallian & Wei Chang, 2006). Studies like these have led to diversity, new research questions and methodological developments where the relation between the individual and the environment is taken into account to some extent (e.g. Renshaw, Chow, Davids & Hammond, 2010; Robinson & Goodway, 2009).

Other PE research has focused on the body as being 'governed' by the mind. Studies like this often take their point of departure in *learning cognition* and are sometimes based on *constructivist* perspectives of learning (e.g. Chen, Rovegno, Cone & Cone, 2012). In this field of research, learner perceptions and learning strategies tend to be at the centre of inquiry, and the ensuing studies have shed light on areas such as how peers can influence learning outcomes in PE (e.g. Ward & Lee, 2005) or the misunderstandings, pedagogical difficulties and resistance that can arise when teachers learn to teach (e.g. McCaughtry, Sofo, Rovegno & Curtner-Smith, 2004). Related to this are studies using pedagogical content knowledge (PCK) as developed by Shulman (e.g. Ayvazo, Ward & Stuhr, 2010). Although this research often focuses on issues of teaching and teacher knowledge rather than learning, PCK has been used in relation to how teaching influences pedagogy and, as consequence, learning (e.g. McCaughtry, 2004; Stran & Curtner-Smith, 2010).

The review demonstrates that studies taking learning as acquisition as their starting point have been helpful in identifying significant qualitative shifts in movement skills, student and teacher thinking, problematic instances of knowledge acquisition, and factors that facilitate and inhibit learning. The use of an acquisition approach to learning thus positions teachers' learning as a process of learning how to become a provider of knowledge or a mediator of student learning (see Table 28.1).

Learning as participation

Research within the learning as participation metaphor is also underpinned by assumptions emanating from the individual-environment dualism. Researchers within this field tend to focus on the environment, with less emphasis on the importance of the individual and individual learning (cf. Hodkinson et al., 2007).

In PE research, learning as participation is clearly expressed in Kirk and Macdonald's influential article 'Situated learning in physical education' (1998). Drawing on the work of Lave and Wenger (1991), the article underpinned a large number of later studies that used a *situated perspective on learning* (e.g. Curtner-Smith & Sofo, 2004; Sinelnikov, 2009). The situated approach highlights the context-embedded character of learning, its social dimensions and the importance of authentic participation based on membership of a social group (Kirk, 2012; MacPhail, Kirk & Kinchin, 2004; Metzler, Lund & Gurvitch, 2008). When reviewing the literature it became clear that there were numerous studies using, or more implicitly basing their studies in, a situated perspective. For example, such studies include: an understanding and exploration of learning using pedagogical models including Teaching Games for Understanding (TGfU) (e.g. Griffin, Brooker & Patton, 2005; Tan, Chow & Davids, 2012), cooperative learning (e.g. Dyson, Griffin & Hastie, 2004; Goodyear, Casey & Kirk, 2014) and Sport Education (e.g. Kirk, 2012; Wallhead & O'Sullivan, 2005).

Parallel with the development in English-speaking journals of viewing learning as participation, in France the *didactique tradition* began to attract the attention of a wider audience in PE research. It is important to note, however, that the didactic tradition of educational research in Europe had been prominent for at least 35 years (Amade-Escot, 2006). Studies within this tradition shed light on qualitative accounts and analyses of critical moments in the teaching process when content is brought into play, such as the dynamics of implicit negotiations between teachers and students over content issues, and the co-construction of meaning underpinning classroom interactions (Amade-Escot, 2005). In these studies, knowing content is about becoming a 'member' of the classroom practice (e.g. Wallhead & O'Sullivan, 2007).

Emphasis on the social environment also appears in research using what we term a *sociocultural perspective*, where learning is explored as a sociocultural process. Studies drawing on a sociocultural perspective of learning, for example using the work of Bourdieu, Bernstein or Vygotsky, have been important in research on PE (cf. Cliff, 2012; Evans, Davies & Rich, 2009; Light, 2011;

Quennerstedt et al., 2014), and continue to contribute new research insights (e.g. Bäckström, 2014; Dowling & Kårhus, 2011; Strandbu & Steen-Johnsen, 2014). For example, drawing on post-Vygotskian theory, Barker, Quennerstedt and Annerstedt (2015) show the flexible and fluid nature of 'expertness' in group work in PE, both in the unpredictable nature of member interactions and in the challenging role that teachers adopt when they include group work in their classes. Furthermore, Bernstein's recontextualising principle in pedagogic discourse has not only been used to explore curriculum and assessment (cf. Penney, 2013), but also to understand learning (e.g. Evans, De Pian, Rich & Davies, 2011; Ivinson, 2012). For example, in Evans et al.'s (2009) well-cited article 'The body made flesh: Embodied learning and the corporeal device', the authors address a number of problems concerning how researchers have understood and explored the bodily aspect of learning in PE.

More recently, research based on a *pragmatist framework* that includes the works of Dewey or Schön has been used to explore learning in PE (e.g. Nyberg & Larsson, 2014; Quennerstedt, 2013). Here the focus is on how individuals and environment transform and are transformed by each other in an ongoing process (Quennerstedt, Öhman & Öhman, 2011). In these studies researchers open what they call 'the black box of learning' by empirically exploring how learning occurs when individuals interact in different contexts (e.g. Andersson, Östman & Öhman, 2015; Maivorsdotter & Wickman, 2011). For example, Maivorsdotter and Lundvall (2009) explore ways in which student teachers learn basketball and gymnastics. They demonstrate that the student teachers' former experiences of sport play a crucial role in the ways in which they are able to learn. Moreover, tension between norms and values in competitive sport and those promoted in teacher education created contradictory feelings of pleasure/displeasure in the learning process.

The need to explore learning as a complex phenomenon in different contexts has also recently been raised and addressed by studies making use of a perspective on learning known as *complex learning theory*. This theory rests upon epistemology and assumptions drawing from social constructivist theories of learning (Light, 2008), and researchers argue that this theory has certain purchase in postmodern times that, it is argued, are characterised by uncertainty, multiplicity and contradiction (e.g. Atencio, Jess & Dewar, 2012; Jess, Atencio & Thorburn, 2011).

Conclusions

Although learning is clearly central to PE, a review of research published in key journals in the field and that have the term 'learning' in their keywords or abstracts suggests that such studies tend to focus on *content* and issues of *teaching* or *coaching* (cf. Quennerstedt et al. 2014). Quennerstedt and colleagues observed that studies that do focus on learning tend to *discuss* learning rather than analyse what and how people learn drawing from explicit theories of learning (cf. also Ward & Lee, 2005). The review does illustrate, however, that learning is, in essence, a complex concept. Moreover, as Akkerman and Van Eijck (2013, p. 60) remind us, the learner at the centre of PE practices is multi-faceted and has to be recognised as a "whole person who participates in school as well as in many other practices". The number of variables operating in any pedagogical encounter is vast and, in order to cope with this complexity, teachers need to be supported by research using a clear learning theory framework simply to make sense of what is happening in any particular class (Quennerstedt et al., 2014). A conclusion that can be drawn from the issues raised in this chapter is that while the range of theories used in research has extended, no single theory will do the 'whole job' of identifying and analysing all the learning processes occurring during one single lesson in PE.

Implications for teaching

Many of the studies in the review start from an assumption that PE is quite problematic in its current state. There also is evidence of pressure to clarify the role of PE in increasing physical activity levels in contrast, perhaps, to its more traditional focus on educational values. Regardless of the different positions on this debate, however, pedagogy and learning remain central aspects of PE.

For teachers learning to teach, as well as for others interested in learning in PE, the fact that researchers tend not to be explicit about the assumptions they have made about learning and knowledge is problematic. If researchers are not clear about the learning theories that drive what they do in research, it is difficult to see how they can claim to be analysing learning in any depth. In view of this, it also is pertinent to consider the role of learning theory in learning to teach. In order to successfully develop their teaching, teachers need to be familiar with a wide range of learning theories. All learning theories have their strengths and limitations, and it seems obvious to suggest that teachers learning to teach have to be able to reflect on learning from different theoretical perspectives.

The research review further indicates that both within the acquisition and the participation metaphors there are two lines of research explicitly dealing with learning to teach. The first is research that focuses on developing practice, and the second is research that aims to produce results and theoretical ideas that could be used as tools for reflection. What both of these lines of thought have in common is that they are interested in helping teachers to act in different ways with different consequences. There are, however, also differences. One line of inquiry is about developing strategies, lessons and models in order to test or work with teachers in various pedagogical interventions, such as models-based instruction, pedagogical models or teaching interventions aiming at increasing levels of physical activity. In these studies, the focus often is on 'quality outcomes' and testing what works and does not work in PE practice. Here, the emphasis tends to be upon changing teaching practice and developing 'best practice' and this has clear consequences for teacher education.

The other line of inquiry uses theoretical tools to map a problem, ask questions and support empirical study. Here, the studies focus on what students learn and how teachers teach in order to understand the learning that is happening. This research tends to suggests that findings can lead to reflective and nuanced decision-making among practitioners, thereby potentially leading to new discussions and new ways of thinking about teaching. The consequences for teacher education and teacher professional development lie in promoting career-long growth of teachers' professional knowledge and critical judgement.

The two lines of research make different assumptions about how to address what has been called the gap between practice and research. However, both lines of inquiry indicate that PE teachers need to know more about *what* students learn, *how* students learn and also *why* this learning is important. For this, it is essential that teachers develop additional tools with which to explore the practices in which they are involved. This is yet another example of the indisputable fact that in addition to being in a constant process of learning to teach, teachers also are themselves engaged in a constant process of learning to learn.

Future directions

Research exploring learning in PE has been undertaken from different theoretical perspectives in recent decades, and each perspective has its benefits and limitations. In the more recent research we reviewed there also are signs of a more varied use of learning theories. In comparison to other curriculum areas such as mathematics education or science education, there has been limited debate in PE about the value and use of different learning theories (Quennerstedt et al., 2014). Sfard (1998) argues that in many fields, proponents of the two metaphors of learning are involved in academic discussions about central issues that separate their perspectives. Yet, the fact that there is debate in these areas is not necessarily problematic; rather, the problem is that the debate is not vigorous enough in the field of PE.

This chapter shows that learning is a complex concept. In order to grasp the complexity inherent in learning, theories such as 'body pedagogies' and 'complex learning theory' might be useful. In addition, rhizomatic ideas building on the work of Gilles Deleuze and Félix Guattari (cf. Enright & Gard, 2016), or 'new materialist' theories from, for example, Karen Barad (Larsson & Quennerstedt, 2012) are stressed by some researchers as ways of qualifying the investigation of learning in PE. Together with a need for methodological development, this theoretical diversification is important for the field because it supports more varied studies of teaching and learning in different contexts. Together with the theories being made explicit, this means that results could more easily be cumulative and that research findings across studies would have greater coherence.

The field also needs what can be called theory-generating research. Even though we now see an emergence of the use of learning theories in studies of different contexts, the field also needs to use insights from empirical and theoretical explorations in order to develop theories about teaching and learning in PE in relation to issues such as citizenship, embodiment, class, gender, sexuality and ethnicity. In this way, different aspects of embodied learning can be theorised and critical aspects of learning in relation to society at large taken into account.

With the strong focus on research using learning theory in schools, especially in the older age groups, there also is great value in researching other fields, both within and outside school. For example, there are gaps in the literature concerning studies using learning theories in movement practices in primary schools and preschools. This means that the practices in which young children engage are seldom represented in research. The tendency is for research to cover PE in general, and neglect knowledge about the growth, experiences, practices and standpoints of young children. Also, in contexts outside school there is a gap when it comes to youth sports and studies of *learning* in high performance sports and adult participation are also scarce. In terms of future directions, it is pertinent to mention the emergence of new studies of critical inquiry into learning in relation to digital media and 'pedagogies of technology'. These consider how technology is used in PE in school, and also how digital technologies of health (for example apps in mobile phones) shape learning processes, affecting how and what is learnt about health. This is a clear area of development for the future.

Summary of key findings

- In the field of PE, an acquisition metaphor has dominated in terms of both behaviouristic and cognitive theories of learning.
- In the last 20 years the acquisition metaphor has been challenged by theories in the participation metaphor, most notably by research based on situated learning theory.
- There is strong evidence of studies on school interventions regarding learning, and studies based on situated learning theory and pedagogical models.
- Two main lines of scholarly debate related to learning theories in teaching were found in the literature: the first is research that develops and tests 'quality outcomes' and 'best practice', and the second is research that promotes 'tools for reflection' through empirical results and theoretical ideas.

- The review of research reveals a persistent lack of explicit identification of learning theory underpinning and informing the research.
- There is a need for more theory-generating research that is grounded in explicit theories of learning in order to develop new theories in PE settings.

Reflective questions for discussion

In order to further scrutinise the role of learning theory in learning to teach we suggest the reading, discussion and analysis of significant learning theories within both the acquisition and participation metaphors. Questions that can be discussed in relation to the field of PE include:

1. What does a certain learning theory explain or fail to explain in terms of teaching and learning?
2. How do we as teachers or researchers know whether a student or learner has learned anything, and if they have, how do we know what this is?
3. If we teach a student about the relation between physical activity and health, what kind of citizen does that student then become? Also, if a student is a certain kind of citizen, what does s/he learn about the relation between physical activity and health?
4. What must a teacher know in order to become a better teacher? What would make them a better teacher, and in relation to what? Why is the suggested knowledge important?
5. What should teachers know about learning in order to make reflective and nuanced decisions in the gym?

References

Akkerman, S. F., & Van Eijck, M. (2013). Re-theorising the student dialogically across and between boundaries of multiple communities. *British Educational Research Journal, 39*(1), 60–72.

Amade-Escot, C. (2005). Using the critical didactic incidents method to analyze the content taught. *Journal of Teaching in Physical Education, 24*(2), 127–148.

Amade-Escot, C. (2006). Student learning within the didactique tradition. In D. Kirk, D. Macdonald & M. O'Sullivan (Eds.), *The handbook of physical education* (pp. 347–365). London: Sage.

Andersson, J., Östman, L. & Öhman, M. (2015). I am sailing – towards a transactional analysis of 'body techniques'. *Sport, Education and Society, 20*(6), 722–740.

Atencio, M., Jess, M. & Dewar, K. (2012). 'It is a case of changing your thought processes, the way you actually teach': Implementing a complex professional learning agenda in Scottish physical education. *Physical Education and Sport Pedagogy, 17*(2), 127–144.

Ayvazo, S., Ward, P. & Stuhr, P. T. (2010). Teaching and assessing content knowledge in preservice physical education. *Journal of Physical Education, Recreation & Dance, 81*(4), 40–44.

Bäckström, Å. (2014). Knowing and teaching kinaesthetic experience in skateboarding: An example of sensory emplacement. *Sport, Education and Society, 19*(6), 752–772.

Barker, D., Quennerstedt, M. & Annerstedt, C. (2015). Inter-student interactions and student learning in health and physical education: A post-Vygotskian analysis. *Physical Education and Sport Pedagogy, 20*(4), 409–426.

Chen, W., Rovegno, I., Cone, S. L. & Cone, T. P. (2012). An accomplished teacher's use of scaffolding during a second-grade unit on designing games. *Research Quarterly for Exercise and Sport, 83*(2), 221–234.

Chiviacowsky, S., & Wulf, G. (2005). Self-controlled feedback is effective if it is based on the learner's performance. *Research Quarterly for Exercise and Sport, 76*(1), 42–48.

Chow, J. Y. (2013). Nonlinear learning underpinning pedagogy: Evidence, challenges, and implications. *Quest, 65*(4), 469–484.

Cliff, K. (2012). A sociocultural perspective as a curriculum change in health and physical education. *Sport, Education and Society, 17*(3), 293–311.

Cobb, P., & Bowers, J. (1999). Cognitive and situated learning perspectives in theory and practice. *Educational Researcher, 28*(2), 4–15.

Curtner-Smith, M., & Sofo, S. (2004). Preservice teachers' conceptions of teaching within sport education and multi-activity units. *Sport, Education and Society, 9*(3), 347–377.

Dowling, F., & Kårhus, S. (2011). An analysis of the ideological work of the discourses of 'fair play' and moral education in perpetuating inequitable gender practices in PETE. *Physical Education and Sport Pedagogy, 16*(2), 197–211.

Dyson, B., Griffin, L. L. & Hastie, P. (2004). Sport education, tactical games, and cooperative learning: Theoretical and pedagogical considerations. *Quest, 56*(2), 226–240.

Enright, E., & Gard, M. (2016) Media, digital technology and learning in elite sport: A critical response to Hodkinson, Biesta and James. *Physical Education and Sport Pedagogy 21*(1), 40–54.

Evans, J., Davies, B. & Rich, E. (2009). The body made flesh: Embodied learning and the corporeal device. *British Journal of Sociology of Education, 30*(4), 391–406.

Evans, J., De Pian, L., Rich, E. & Davies, B. (2011). Health imperatives, policy and the corporeal device: Schools, subjectivity and children's health. *Policy Futures in Education, 9*(3), 328–340.

Goodyear, V. A., Casey, A. & Kirk, D. (2014). Hiding behind the camera: Social learning within the cooperative learning model to engage girls in physical education. *Sport, Education and Society, 19*(6), 712–734.

Griffin, L. L., Brooker, R. & Patton, K. (2005). Working towards legitimacy: Two decades of Teaching Games for Understanding. *Physical Education and Sport Pedagogy, 10*(3), 213–223.

Hastie, P., & Siedentop, D. (2006). The classroom ecology paradigm. In D. Kirk, D. Macdonald & M. O'Sullivan (Eds.), *The handbook of physical education* (pp. 214–225). London: Sage.

Hodkinson, P., Biesta, G. & James, D. (2007). Understanding learning cultures. *Educational Review, 59*(4), 415–427.

Illeris, K. (2007). *How we learn: Learning and non-learning in school and beyond.* London: Routledge.

Ivinson, G. (2012). The body and pedagogy: Beyond absent, moving bodies in pedagogic practice. *British Journal of Sociology of Education, 33*(4), 489–506.

Jess, M., Atencio, M. & Thorburn, M. (2011). Complexity theory: Supporting curriculum and pedagogy developments in Scottish physical education. *Sport, Education and Society, 16*(2), 179–199.

Keetch, K. M., & Lee, T. D. (2007). The effect of self-regulated and experimenter-imposed practice schedules on motor learning for tasks of varying difficulty. *Research Quarterly for Exercise and Sport, 78*(5), 476–486.

Kirk, D. (2012). Sport education, critical pedagogy and learning theory: Toward an intrinsic justification for physical education and youth sport. *Quest, 58*(2), 255–264.

Kirk, D., & Macdonald, D. (1998). Situated learning in physical education. *Journal of Teaching in Physical Education, 17*(2), 376–387.

Kirk, D., Macdonald, D. & O'Sullivan, M. (Eds.). (2006). *The handbook of physical education.* London: Sage.

Larsson, H., & Quennerstedt, M. (2012). Understanding movement: A sociocultural approach to exploring moving humans. *Quest, 64*(4), 283–298.

Lave, J., & Wenger, E. (1991). *Situated learning: Legitimate peripheral participation.* Cambridge, UK: Cambridge University Press.

Light, R. (2008). Complex learning theory – its epistemology and its assumptions about learning: Implications for physical education. *Journal of Teaching in Physical Education, 27*(1), 21–37.

Light, R. L. (2011). Opening up learning theory to social theory in research on sport and physical education through a focus on practice. *Physical Education and Sport Pedagogy, 16*(4), 369–382.

Macdonald, D. (2004). Understanding learning in physical education. In J. Wright, L. Burrows & D. MacDonald (Eds.), *Critical inquiry and problem-solving in physical education* (pp. 16–29). London: Routledge.

MacPhail, A., Kirk, D. & Kinchin, G. (2004). Sport education: Promoting team affiliation through physical education. *Journal of Teaching in Physical Education, 23*(2), 106–122.

Maivorsdotter, N., & Lundvall, S. (2009). Aesthetic experience as an aspect of embodied learning: Stories from physical education student teachers. *Sport, Education and Society, 14*(3), 265–279.

Maivorsdotter, N., & Wickman, P.-.O. (2011). Skating in a life context: Examining the significance of aesthetic experience in sport using practical epistemology analysis. *Sport, Education and Society, 16*(5), 613–628.

McCaughtry, N. (2004). The emotional dimensions of a teacher's pedagogical content knowledge: Influences on content, curriculum, and pedagogy *Journal of Teaching in Physical Education, 23*(1), 30–47.

McCaughtry, N., Sofo, S., Rovegno, I. & Curtner-Smith, M. (2004). Learning to teach sport education: Misunderstandings, pedagogical difficulties, and resistance. *European Physical Education Review, 10*(2), 135–155.

Metzler, M. W., Lund, J. & Gurvitch, R. (2008). The diffusion of model-based instruction by establishing communities of practice. *Journal of Teaching in Physical Education, 27*(4), 449–456.

Nyberg, G., & Larsson, H. (2014). Exploring 'what' to learn in physical education. *Physical Education and Sport Pedagogy, 19*(2), 123–135.

Penney, D. (2013). Points of tension and possibility: Boundaries in and of physical education. *Sport, Education and Society, 18*(1), 6–20.

Quennerstedt, M. (2013). Practical epistemologies in physical education practice. *Sport, Education and Society, 18*(3), 311–333.

Quennerstedt, M., Öhman, M. & Armour, K. (2014). Sport and exercise pedagogy and questions about learning. *Sport, Education and Society, 19*(7), 885–898.

Quennerstedt, M., Öhman, J. & Öhman, M. (2011). Investigating learning in physical education – a transactional approach. *Sport, Education and Society, 16*(2), 159–177.

Renshaw, I., Chow, J.Y., Davids, K. & Hammond, J. (2010). A constraints-led perspective to understanding skill acquisition and game play: A basis for integration of motor learning theory and physical education praxis? *Physical Education and Sport Pedagogy, 15*(2), 117–137.

Rink, J. E. (1999). Instruction from a learning perspective. In C. Hardy & M. Mawer (Eds.), *Learning and teaching in physical education* (pp. 149–168). London: Falmer.

Robinson, L. E., & Goodway, J. D. (2009). Instructional climates in preschool: Children who are at-risk. Part I: Object-control skill development. *Research Quarterly for Exercise and Sport, 80*(3), 533–542.

Rovegno, I. (2006). Situated perspectives on learning. In D. Kirk, D. Macdonald & M. O'Sullivan (Eds.), *The handbook of physical education* (pp. 262–274). London: Sage.

Rovengo, I., & Dolly, J. P. (2006). Constructivist perspectives on learning. In D. Kirk, D. Macdonald & M. O'Sullivan (Eds.), *The handbook of physical education* (pp. 242–261). London: Sage.

Sfard, A. (1998). On two metaphors for learning and the dangers of choosing just one. *Educational Researcher, 27*(2), 4–13.

Sinelnikov, O. A. (2009). Sport education for teachers: Professional development when introducing a novel curriculum model. *European Physical Education Review, 15*(1), 91–114.

Solmon, M. (2006). Learner cognition. In D. Kirk, D. Macdonald & M. O'Sullivan (Eds.), *The handbook of physical education* (pp. 226–241). London: Sage.

Stran, M., & Curtner-Smith, M. (2010). Impact of different types of knowledge on two preservice teachers' ability to learn and deliver the Sport Education model. *Physical Education and Sport Pedagogy, 15*(3), 243–256.

Strandbu, Å., & Steen-Johnsen, K. (2014). Bourdieu knew more than how to play tennis!: An empirically based discussion of habituation and reflexivity. *Sport, Education and Society, 19*(8), 1055–1071.

Tan, C. W. K., Chow, J. Y. & Davids, K. (2012). 'How does TGfU work?': Examining the relationship between learning design in TGfU and a nonlinear pedagogy. *Physical Education and Sport Pedagogy, 17*(4), 331–348.

van der Mars, H. (2006). Time and learning in physical education. In D. Kirk, D. Macdonald & M. O'Sullivan (Eds.), *The handbook of physical education* (pp. 292–311). London: Sage.

Wallhead, T., & O'Sullivan, M. (2005). Sport education: Physical education for the new millennium?. *Physical Education and Sport Pedagogy, 10*(2), 181–210.

Wallhead, T., & O'Sullivan, M. (2007). A didactic analysis of content development during the peer teaching tasks of a sport education season. *Physical Education and Sport Pedagogy, 12*(3), 225–243.

Wallian, N., & Wei Chang, C. (2006). Development and learning of motor skill competencies. In D. Kirk, D. Macdonald & M. O'Sullivan (Eds.), *The handbook of physical education* (pp. 191–213). London: Sage.

Ward, P., & Lee, M. (2005). Peer-assisted learning in physical education: A review of theory and research. *Journal of Teaching in Physical Education, 24*(3), 205.

Wertsch, J.V. (1998). *Mind as action*. Oxford: Oxford University Press.

29

EFFECTIVE PHYSICAL EDUCATION TEACHER EDUCATION

A principled position perspective

Louise McCuaig & Eimear Enright, UNIVERSITY OF QUEENSLAND, AUSTRALIA

In the Sage *Handbook of Physical Education* (Kirk, Macdonald, & O'Sullivan, 2006), Richard Tinning (2006) demonstrates the ready access that scholars have to rich and extensive reviews of teacher education. His commentary draws attention to literature provided by, for example, Feiman-Nemser (1996), Peck and Tucker (1971) and Zeichner (1983), as well as physical education teacher education (PETE) specific reviews offered by Fernández-Balboa (1997), Macdonald (1997), O'Sullivan (1996), Rink (1993), and Vendien and Nixon (1985). Such work has been enriched by comprehensive reviews of specific PETE approaches, including reviews of reflective teaching (Tsangaridou & Siedentop, 1995), PETE models and curricular (Collier, 2006), and sport education approaches (Hastie, de Ojeda, & Luquin, 2011). Noting the dominance of English language and American scholarship, Tinning also highlights the usefulness of studies by Crum (1996) and Hanke (2001), to which we would add the work of colleagues from Canada (Melnychuk, Robinson, Lu, Chorney, & Randall, 2011) and Hong Kong (Wang & Ha, 2009a).

In our efforts to provide a modest contribution to this body of work, we do not wish to replicate previous reviews and critiques. Instead, we build this review on the exploration of an implicit criterion upon which the effectiveness of PETE has been judged – namely the capacity to produce teachers who can deliver 'effectively,' the skillful, fitness, and socio-critical objectives of school PE programs. We begin with a brief historical appraisal of the emergence, advocacy, and critique of 'effectiveness' as a construct within the context of PE and PETE scholarship. Following this, we offer an alternative philosophical review of past and current perspectives on PETE effectiveness according to Hunter's (1994) notion of principled positions. We nominate three principled position cases (physically competent, healthy citizen, and socially critical actor), and identify their role in shaping the advocated approaches to, and evaluation of, PETE effectiveness. In concluding this section, we identify three enduring questions of who (PETE recruits and educators), what (curriculum content), and how (pedagogical approaches), that all three cases share in their visions of an effective PETE. Next we explore the powerful influence of an emerging accountable child and performative teacher principled position, and the impact of a global accountability movement on the measurement of effective teaching in PE and PETE

(Metzler, 2014; Ward, 2013). In light of our commentary we offer some directions for future research and a summary overview of the research informing an effective PETE.

A range of caveats necessarily accompanies these efforts. While our review provides a sense of how PETE has been constructed in particular contexts, points in time, and with ends in mind, it nevertheless privileges certain voices and histories, most notably from sources that are readily available in the English language. As with Collier (2006), we also call upon readers to be mindful of the marginalization of voices within scholarly literature that has resulted in fewer opportunities to engage with the perspectives of women, practitioners, and minority populations. We also take inspiration from the classicist Nussbaum (1994), who acknowledges the presentation of a "somewhat idiosyncratic account of certain themes" (p. 6), which in our case reflects the lenses of our own biographies (female, socio-critical PETE educators and researchers) that we have employed on PETE research. With these cautionary notes in mind, we turn now to the historical emergence of effective teaching as an influential criterion of PETE programs.

Historical review: the case for and against PETE effectiveness

In this historical review we first pursue a clarification of concepts and theoretical orientations that will provide the foundations upon which we conduct a broader review of PETE effectiveness (see also Rink, 2013; Ward, 2013). As Cochran-Smith and Zeichner (2005) warn, establishing what stands for teacher effectiveness is characterized by complexity and an array of disagreement. Notwithstanding this state of affairs, early research and advocacy reveal considerably less ambiguity. Nuanced general and PE specific treatments of the emergence and popularity of teaching effectiveness reveal some common themes. Effective teaching arose within the burgeoning influence of educational psychology and behaviorist traditions, predominantly gained purchase within American settings, focused initially on teacher characteristics and behaviors, with a later shift towards student learning and performance (Kyriacou, 1997; Muijs & Reynolds, 2011; Rink, 2013; Solmon & Garn, 2014; Tinning, 2006; Ward, 2013).

Prior to the 1960s, studies of teacher effectiveness were characterized as 'black-box' research (Ward, 2013) that involved inputs such as teacher attributes, student performance outputs, and analytic efforts to establish causal relationships in the absence of an interrogation of classroom activities. As Muijs and Reynolds (2011) explain, attempts to open the classroom 'black box' typically employed a process-product paradigm involving a pre-test measurement, a post-test, and comprehensive observations of classroom behaviors to determine the impact of teacher characteristics on student achievement. According to American PETE scholars, the Dunkin and Biddle (1974) model comprising of presage, context, process, and product variables, in addition to the later research of Brophy and Good (1986), underpinned the development of direct instruction strategies for teacher effectiveness in PE, focusing on dimensions such as student activity time, active monitoring, structured learning experiences, and feedback (Metzler, 2014; Rink, 2013; Ward, 2013). Scholars, including Metzler (2014), Tinning (2006), and Ward and Barrett (2002) maintain that PETE specific endeavors employing behaviorist approaches owe much to Daryl Siedentop. In the influential *Developing Teaching Skills in Physical Education* (Siedentop, 1976, 1983; Siedentop & Tannehill, 2000), Siedentop (1983) defines effective teaching as that which keeps "students appropriately engaged in the subject matter a high percentage of the available time, within a warm, nurturant climate" (p. 43). Conversely, ineffective teaching occurs when PE students are simply "overinstructed and underpracticed" (Siedentop & Tannehill, 2000, p. 28). According to Siedentop, improving teaching skills is reliant on opportunities to practice instructional skills, and the provision of reliable feedback by teacher educators who conduct systematic observation and measurement of performance (Siedentop, 1983, Siedentop & Tannehill, 2000).

Importantly for our purposes, Kyriacou (1997) observes that shared definitions of the relationship of effective teaching to intended learning outcomes, has been accompanied by "very little consensus about the relative importance of different educational outcomes which are taken to be the goals of effective teaching" (p. 8). As Ward (2013) succinctly summarizes, "what counts is influenced by ideological and paradigmatic positions" (p. 431). Yet, although defining teacher effectiveness might be fraught with challenges, PE and PETE research reflect an enduring quest for 'effectiveness.' Recently, for example, the PE and PETE profession's sustained interest in establishing a definitive understanding of effective teaching is evident in a special topics series in the *Research Quarterly in Exercise Science* (RQES) journal. This series included a range of perspectives and responses to the contemporary determinants of teacher effectiveness (Dyson, 2014; Ennis, 2014; Lindsay, 2014; McKenzie & Lounsbery, 2013, 2014; Metzler, 2014; Pišot, Plevnik, & Štemberger, 2014; Rink, 2013, 2014; Solmon & Garn, 2014; Ward, 2013, 2014).

Nonetheless, the relative dominance of a behaviorist oriented quest for effective teaching in PETE has been troubled, most notably by those critiquing the construct's connotations of a technocratic rationality and performative pedagogy, underpinned by a logic that reduces teaching to "a discrete series of skills that could be isolated, practiced, and applied in a systematic manner" (Tinning, 1991, p. 7). Critics have also questioned the reliance on teacher-centeredness that produces "transmission-oriented and cognitively less demanding tasks" (Macdonald, 2004, p. 19). Dyson (2014) notes the problematics of these issues and references to "curriculum fidelity instead of student learning outcomes" (p. 145). In response, commentators typically refer to 'quality' teaching which, Dyson (2014) argues, moves "attention beyond a focus merely on issues of effectiveness in relation to the achievement of pre-specified objectives" (p. 145). No doubt reflecting this sustained critique, conceptions of effective teaching have gradually been cast adrift from their explicit behaviorist moorings and have instead co-opted diversity of definitions concerning the usefulness or impact of preferred approaches to teaching and learning.

Theoretical overview: principled positions on PETE effectiveness

Mindful of these issues, in the following section we focus attention on the observations of Kyriacou (1997), Solmon and Garn (2014), and Ward (2013) that evaluating teacher effectiveness necessarily depends on *what* educational outcomes are considered important and are intended. For O'Sullivan (1996), educational outcomes pursued by PETE educators involve a "vision of what it means to be a good teacher" and what it "means to have a program that produces such educators" (p. 132). From their earliest inception, Lee and Solmon (2005) suggest that PETE programs have endeavored to respond to "concerns about the type of individual needed to direct and organise health and physical education" (p. 109) and the knowledge, skills, and dispositions required to "make them effective" (p. 109).

Developing further this idea that an effective PETE is intimately related to the construction of the 'ideal' teacher of PE, we suggest that Hunter's (1994) principled position notion provides a useful tool for this review. As Hunter (1994) argued, critics of schooling tend to evaluate programs of education according to the partial or failed "realisation of certain underlying principles" (Hunter, 1994, p. xv), which reflect different positions that all "cohere around the notion of an ideal formation of the person" (p. xv). Definitions of the ideal person or citizen are critical to education as they articulate the 'problems' to be solved through the 'solution' of schooling. In proposing PE as a solution to the problem of an active, healthy citizenry, stakeholders have offered diverse claims and rationales for PE programs (Bailey et al., 2009), which

McCuaig and Hay (2013) argue, reflect contextually specific principled conceptions of the ideal 'product' of PE.

Inevitably, principled positions informing the construction of the ideal 'product' of school PE also influence the research, design, delivery, and advocacy of PETE. Our canvassing of the literature published in the English language reveals the dominance of three principled positions informing notions of an effective PE and PETE. These positions find expression in Ward's (2014) nomination of the public health, academic, and sociological instrumental ends shaping PE, to which he adds his own 'holy grail' of enjoying movement. Similarly, PETE literature and research tends to cohere around three principled positions, or cases, that shape arguments for and against teacher effectiveness: the physically competent participant, healthy citizen, and socially critical actor. In the following section we briefly outline these principled position 'cases,' to illustrate how notions of the ideal PE *and* ideal teacher of PE, have resulted in the advocacy of particular theoretical frameworks, curriculum content, pedagogical practices, and recruits to service these positions. This work does not attempt to provide an exhaustive analysis of, or even address, all seminal literature. Rather we draw on an eclectic range of literature and research to illustrate some of the conflicting principled positions on what individuals will need to know and be able to do as graduates of an effective PETE program.

Case 1: PETE effectiveness for physically competent participants

According to the physically competent participant position, school PE programs and their teachers provide the training ground for a life-long capacity for, and participation in, sports and physical activities (McCuaig & Hay, 2013). PETE researchers and educators operating from this position consider an effective PETE graduate to be one who can teach, analyze, and enhance children's fundamental and game oriented movement capacities (Siedentop, 2002). For advocates of this position, what stands for competence, that is what PE students know and can do in terms of human movement, is of critical importance.

From its earliest origins, PE and PETE have allocated attention to what students and their teachers could *do*, as opposed to what they *knew about*, human movement (McCuaig & Tinning, 2010). For over a century, the primary objective of this principled position has been students' acquisition of fundamental neuro-muscular skills, such as running, jumping, catching, and throwing. In early British and Australian PE curricula, such skills were likened to the core academic skills of reading, writing, and arithmetic (Great Britain Board of Education [GBBOE], 1933), while American commentators argued that "physical illiteracy should be as abhorrent to the broad-minded educator as so-called mental illiteracy" (Laporte, 1933, p. 10). In these early decades, the physical performance, stance, and shape of teachers' bodies was expected to provide students with a living illustration of the standard to which pupils must aspire (McCuaig & Tinning, 2010). Dramatic increases in the quantity and sophistication of motor learning research during the 1960s and 1970s further clarified these rationales, resulting in a "dominant perspective that considered teachers of PE to be primarily responsible for facilitating the acquisition of motor skills" (Lee & Solmon, 2005, p. S110). As outlined in the previous section, direct instruction approaches in PE and PETE from this time onwards emphasized the delivery of a progression of learning from skills to mini-games/strategies to whole game play, with provision of specific corrective feedback and systematic practice (Macdonald, 2004). More recently, the advocacy of fundamental skills has (re) emerged as physical literacy, the precise conceptualization of which attracts considerable debate (Lloyd, 2011; Whitehead, 2010). Given an enthusiasm for literacy across global educational institutions (McCuaig, Coore, & Hay, 2012), physical educators and policy makers have sought to harness the potential of the concept of *physical* literacy. For example, current standards for PE in the

United States state that the "goal of physical education is to develop physically literate individuals who have the knowledge, skills, and confidence to enjoy a lifetime of healthful physical activity" (Society for Health and Physical Educators [SHAPE], 2014).

Yet, an enduring emphasis on what PE and PETE students can do with respect to human movement was challenged in the 1960s by critics who turned their attention to the knowledge dimensions underpinning movement and teaching competence. This turn of events reveals a subtle and sustained tension operating across two 'registers' within this principled position, notably the intelligent performer and the physically able participant. Advocates aligning with the intelligent performer register have sought to elevate the cognitive importance and educational credentials of PE and PETE (Armour & Jones, 1998; Bailey et al., 2009). Despite earlier requirements for PETE students to master understanding of anatomy, physiology, hygiene, and body mechanics, Franklin Henry's seminal paper ushered in a renewed 'academicization' of PE in school and tertiary settings (Bain, 1990). In a later elaboration, Henry (1978) argued that a theoretical and scholarly body of knowledge unique to PE exists, the acquisition of which "is assumed to be an adequate and worthy objective … without any demonstration or requirement of practical application" (p. 13). Henry (1978) was to predict that "an increasing proportion of graduates in the academic discipline will not wish to become teachers" (p. 27). These shifts privileging the 'know' over the 'do' of physical performance generated an increasing emphasis on the acquisition of sub-disciplinary knowledge that underpinned efforts to produce intelligent performers (Kirk, 1983).

This heightened interest in cognitive matters in PE was strengthened within PETE research and practice with the release of Shulman's knowledge framework. As Tsangaridou (2006b) explains, Shulman (1986, 1987) argued that too much attention had been allocated to teachers' managerial and organizational capacities with little research addressing the "complexities of teacher understanding and transmission of content knowledge" (Tsangaridou, 2006b, p. 505). In response, Shulman devised a seven category framework of teachers' knowledge that included the core subject-matter or content knowledge, pedagogical content knowledge, and curricular knowledge. To this day, much advocacy and critique of PETE effectiveness draws on Shulman's classification to propose strategies that best enhance prospective PE teachers' knowledge for practice. More on this later.

These decades also marked an emerging critique of the dominance of didactic and paternalistic teaching in school and tertiary settings (Leahy, Burrows, McCuaig, Wright, & Penney, 2015; Macdonald, 2004). In contrast, learning was newly conceptualized as a dynamic, constructive process between learners, teachers, and the learning environment. Consequently, teaching strategies that engaged learners in the processes of inquiry, problem-solving, and rational decision-making were increasingly devised and promoted (Macdonald, 2004). These developments contributed to the *Teaching Games for Understanding* [TGFU] model (Bunker & Thorpe, 1982), and later tactical knowledge (Gréhaigne & Godbout, 1995) and *Play Practice* (Launder, 2001) approaches. Building on these developments, PE and PETE educators operating from the physically competent position have more recently sought to maximize the potentialities of both physical and cognitive registers through a curricular and pedagogical strategy commonly referred to as models-based instruction (MBI). Much of the theoretical articulation and practical guidance of MBI has been provided by Mike Metzler (Iserbyt, Ward, & Martens, 2015; Metzler, 2011), whose handbook identifies eight instructional models for PE. Advocates claim that each model represents a "plan of action that, when faithfully implemented, leads to achievement of the desired learning outcomes" (Fletcher & Casey, 2014, p. 406). A models-based approach to PE and PETE has been identified "as a foundational pedagogical content knowledge and as a definition of 'best practice' in physical education" (Gurvitch, Blankenship, Metzler, & Lund, 2008, p. 480).

Although contemporary PETE educators have noted the paucity of MBI research in PETE (Fletcher & Casey, 2014) and a limited global reach (Curtner-Smith, 2012), Metzler (2014) argues that a substantial resource of knowledge is currently under construction which will guide those who "train teachers to use those models to the fullest potential of their respective designs" (p. 16). This body of work includes Metzler's ongoing research with colleagues (Gurvitch et al., 2008; Metzler, 2014), Curtner-Smith's (1997, 1999, 2001, 2007, 2012; Curtner-Smith, Hastie, & Kinchin, 2008; Curtner-Smith & Sofo, 2004b; Hastie & Curtner-Smith, 2006) rich and sustained interrogation of MBI in PETE, in addition to contributions from Asian scholars (Wang & Ha, 2009b) and European physical educators (Casey, 2014; Casey & Fletcher, 2012; Deenihan & MacPhail, 2013; Fletcher & Casey, 2014). Research findings from this literature demonstrate the need for PETE students to first participate as learners across all models, experiencing and observing the teaching of each model by expert PETE educators. Implementation of the newly acquired practices should then be accompanied by considerable guidance and support (Gurvitch et al., 2008). For some, effective preparation involves a "broad base of MBI related pedagogical content knowledge" (Gurvitch et al., 2008, p. 481), while others recommend a gradual introduction of content to reflect teacher confidence, student readiness, and the school contexts of professional experience (Deenihan & MacPhail, 2013). Australian physical educators (Pill, Penney, & Swabey, 2012) have, however, raised concerns about an impoverished MBI in PETE, preferring to advocate for a sport literacy approach underpinned by more integration across the models. While these recommendations may reflect Metzler's (2011) claim that there is "no one best way to teach physical education" (p. 9), there does nevertheless appear to be an enthusiasm across recent literature for a fidelity approach to model implementation within and beyond PETE (Hastie & Casey, 2014).

In conclusion, the literature presented within this case reveals the nuanced perspectives and approaches adopted by those who envision PE and PETE programs according to the physically competent principled position. It also has revealed the sustained influence of a behaviorist tradition, an influence that is no less evident in the second of our principled position case studies, that of the healthy citizen.

Case 2: PETE effectiveness for healthy citizenship

As McCuaig and Hay (2013) demonstrate, PE professionals have embraced the healthy citizenship principled position, advocating an "explicit link between school PE and the healthy growth and development of children's bodies" (p. 285). Postural matters dominated early conceptions of healthy living (McCuaig, 2008), so it is not surprising to discover claims that "if the class or the individual stands badly there has certainly been some failure in the teaching" (GBBOE, 1933, p. 12). Later in the twentieth century, Hellison (1973) confirmed that the "primary objective of early physical education programs was, without a doubt, physical health" (p. 1) and to this day, many physical educators continue to adopt, and critique, the position that a good citizen is an active, healthy citizen (Leahy et al., 2015). Moral fortitude and a good character also have been considered vital components of the healthy citizen, with games and sports facilitating emotional control, respect for others, obedience to rules, and a willingness to try wholeheartedly within challenging circumstances (McCuaig, 2008). Advocates of PE as a positive source of social and moral education have proposed a broader remit of responsible and healthy lifestyles, with the respected work of Hellison (1985, 1995), offering "genuinely alternative forms of social organization in physical education classes in an attempt to redress the social conditions placing some young people's wellbeing at risk" (Rovegno & Kirk, 1995, p. 451).

As the twentieth century unfolded, conceptions of the healthy self were to undergo considerable renovation, resulting in an expanded repertoire of characteristics that did not focus exclusively upon the physicality of young bodies, an absence of disease, or a hygienic consciousness. However, the past two decades have witnessed a revival of public health as a pre-eminent remit of PE, particularly in response to a rising incidence of childhood obesity (Cale, Harris, & Chen, 2007; Lindsay, 2014; McKenzie & Lounsbury, 2013; Sallis & McKenzie, 1991; Telford, Cunningham, Telford, & Abhayaratna, 2012; Trost, 2006; Welk, Eisenmann, & Dollman, 2006). As with the case of physical competency, advocates across the globe have claimed that "the primary teaching goal should be to prepare [students] for a lifetime of physical activity" (Lee & Solmon, 2005, p. S115). From the healthy citizen perspective, therefore, contemporary PETE programs can be considered effective when they are grounded in public health goals and health promotion theory (McKenzie & Lounsbery, 2013, 2014) and evaluated according to graduates' achievement of public health outcomes (McKenzie & Lounsbery, 2013). Assessment of these goals can be best established through, for example, the System for Observing Fitness Instruction Time (SOFIT) tool, a measure of students' engagement in moderate to vigorous physical activity within school settings (McKenzie & Lounsbery, 2013).

In his advocacy of the healthy citizen principled position, McKenzie (2007) argues that PETE programs can effectively prepare PE teachers when they

- specifically focus on children's behavioral and psychological responses to exercise and physical activity and consider topics such as correlates of childhood physical activity, ecologic models explaining physical activity behavior, and environmental engineering, that promote activity-friendly environments;
- teach potential instructors how to develop student behavior-change skills, such as planning, goal setting, self-monitoring, self-reinforcement, soliciting social support, overcoming barriers to physical activity, and resisting negative influences on physical activity and health;
- establish a working knowledge of behaviors associated with food, nutrition, and eating. (p. 353)

These recommendations capture the explicit articulation between public health initiatives and the purposes of school PE that has been an enduring characteristic of the healthy citizen principled position. As noted earlier, health oriented PE programs continue to ground desired outcomes according to an explicit use of behavioral principles within the context of school PE and PETE endeavors (Ward & Barrett, 2002; Welk et al., 2006).

Notwithstanding this support, advocacy for a public health oriented PE has attracted considerable critique, with scholars such as Gard and Wright (2001, 2005) challenging the hegemony of obesity discourses, rampant individualism, and modes of bodily surveillance that characterize these approaches. Additionally, health educators have questioned the narrow definition of health adopted by PETE educators; one that privileges diet and exercise over topics such as drug and alcohol use, relationships and sexual education, body image, mental health, and food studies, to name but a few (Fetro, 2000; Leahy & McCuaig, 2014). In the Australian context, Tinning (2004) suggests that practicing and preservice teachers alike, resist contemporary topics on the social view of health, sexuality, and social justice principles as this curriculum content is inconsistent with their preconceived notions of what a PE teacher should be teaching. Much of this latter commentary and research has been underpinned by a socio-critical analysis of health oriented PE programs, a perspective that we will now explore.

Case 3: PETE effectiveness and socially critical actors

Our final case study finds substantial expression in commentary provided by Juan-Miguel Fernández-Balboa (1997) and his call to reclaim PE in higher education through a critical pedagogy. In stating his hopes for PETE, Fernández-Balboa (1997) aspires to the creation of transformative intellectuals, who are

> able to construct and question knowledge, critically connect education with the broader sociocultural contexts and influences, and act politically and ethically to transform and improve schools and the profession. From this perspective, I argue that teacher education must include not only (a) the body of knowledge to be taught in schools, but also (b) knowledges and skills to be able to teach in, and transform, schools; (c) knowledges and skills to advance the profession; and (d) knowledges and skills to create a better society. (p. 162)

This advocacy more broadly represents the turn towards a socially critical perspective for PE and PETE (Devís-Devís, 2006; Kirk & Tinning, 1990; Philpot, 2015; Rovegno & Kirk, 1995). The socially critical principled position underpinning subsequent programs of PE and PETE privileges the capacity of learners to recognize and challenge the impact of social forces on their own and others' efforts to lead active, healthy lives. For many socio-critically oriented faculty the focus on biophysical sciences at the expense of humanities and social sciences leaves PETE graduates ill-prepared for the complexity of work with post-modern youth (Melnychuk et al., 2011). As Cliff (2012) explains, educators who adopt a socially critical perspective consider the social component of 'socio-cultural' perspectives to involve interrogation of "power and social relations, political and economic factors," whilst the cultural invites an exploration of "shared ways of thinking and acting" (p. 296). Physical educators adopting this position devise PETE courses that explore and question the status quo, hope that their students "will be aware of injustices, feel a sense of agency to address those injustices and, ultimately, choose to act by participating in social movements and organizing around these issues" (Swalwell, 2013, p. 2). Educators who advocate the socially critical tradition emphasize the teaching and modelling (by teachers) of social justice principles (Cliff, 2012; Penney & Chandler, 2000), including those who have focused their attention on assessment in PE (Hay & Penney, 2012). In the late 1980s Linda Bain (1988) argued that one of the fundamental contributions of PE was the promotion of social justice. Similarly, inherent in Penney and Chandler's (2000) vision for PE was "a professional commitment to addressing social justice" (p. 76).

Interestingly, the socio-critical principled position has gained less advocacy within American PETE programs (Curtner-Smith & Sofo, 2004a) than that of countries such as Australia and New Zealand (Philpot, 2015), Britain (Brown & Evans, 2004), Scandinavia (Dowling, 2006; Larsson & Redelius, 2008), and Canada (Melnychuk et al., 2011). This situation within the context of PE and PETE has possibly evolved in response to suggestions that "more has been written about advocacy for critical pedagogy than on how it might be operationalized" (Philpot, 2015, p. 319). Such concerns also have been raised by Tinning (2002), an ardent advocate of socio-critical perspectives, who has nonetheless ruminated over the ambitious goals of this perspective. In his deliberations, Tinning (2002) has called upon socio-critical colleagues to adopt a modest PETE pedagogy given the 'pedagogical soup' of values, identities, and beliefs within which PETE educators conduct their courses (Tinning, 1995). In seeking to address the advocacy-practice gap in PETE, Philpot (2015) offers a categorization and explanation of six pedagogical approaches that might promote a more "enlightened interpretation" (p. 320). Learning experiences in PETE seeking to promote a socio-critically oriented graduate include: problematization of knowledge, reflection, power sharing through democratic classrooms; dialogue; and border crossing (Philpot, 2015). In one of the few interrogations of an American PETE program employing a socio-critical strategy, Curtner-Smith and Sofo (2004a) found that their ambitious attempts to inspire a social justice orientation amongst their students had "virtually no impact on them at all" (p. 134). Upon reflection, these PETE scholars recommended more scaffolding of students' engagement with these issues across their degree to enhance an effective traction within later courses of the program.

For many advocates, however, the 'status quo' to be challenged in a socio-critical PETE is that dissonance between contemporary PE programs grounded in social justice principles and the discourses of sexism, racism, individualism, or homophobia that have been found to influence practicing and pre-service teachers of PE (Clarke, 2006; Curtner-Smith & Sofo, 2004a; Flintoff & Scraton, 2006; Harrison Jr. & Belcher, 2006; Tinning, 2002). It is within this context that the practice of critical reflection has achieved a privileged status. Although Fendler (2003) and Tinning (2006) note the dominance of teacher reflection within general teacher education, for socio-critically oriented PETE educators, teacher effectiveness requires more than the technical or practical reflection skills identified by Van Manen (Mallett, 2004). Indeed Tsangaridou and Siedentop (1995) recognize the need for reflection beyond simple pedagogical decision-making, given the "increasing concern about the moral and political dimensions of teaching" (p. 212). Thus reflection does not simply imply a consideration of "what works in a lesson to maintain peace and order" (Tinning, Macdonald, Wright, & Hickey, 2001, p. 269), but also engages "issues relating to schooling and education as inherently political and ideological social structures" (Tinning et al., 2001, p. 280). Critical reflection has been identified as a necessary precursor to action, where PETE students are encouraged to pose questions of their practice, challenge taken-for-granted assumptions, and constantly question "why physical education is approached in this way and who it is that benefits" (Tinning et al., 2001, p. 283). This deeper level interrogation of personal values, moral perspectives, socio-political factors and their influence on teachers and schools is tightly wedded to the advocacy of a critical pedagogy (Attard & Armour, 2005; Ovens & Tinning, 2009). It also highlights one of the most consistent approaches operating across all principled perspectives on PETE effectiveness, a situation which we will now explore in our summary of this historical review.

Historical and theoretical summary

Tracking the historical trajectory of PETE effectiveness has offered us insight into how various principled positions have shaped the emergence of methodologies and theoretical frameworks which have sometimes been "abandoned, sometimes thrived, and sometimes, with gradual changes, continued to contribute to our understanding of the teaching-learning process" (Lee & Solmon, 2005, p. S108). Such shifts across time reflect the "repetitive irresolvable debates" (Hunter, 1994, p. 154) about PETE effectiveness, and how PETE has been forced to reinvent itself, or at least be seen to do so, in response to ongoing educational, cultural, and institutional change (Kirk, Macdonald, & Tinning, 1997). As with other PETE reviews (e.g., Lee & Solomon, 2005; O'Sullivan & Doutis, 1994; Tinning, 2006) we note that such debates often cohere around three broad questions of: who should be recruited into PETE programs, what content they should receive (Siedentop, 2002; Ward, 2013) and how they should learn this content (Tinning, 1991, 2002, 2010). Others in this text address these in more depth, but in this section we briefly explore the debates and challenges pertaining to recruits and teachers in PETE that operate across the principled position case studies.

In their ruminations on the increasing interest of reflection practices within PETE, Tsangaridou and Siedentop (1995) consider arguments that PETE candidates were becoming "more conservative, likely to be authoritarian, restricted in their cognitive development, less analytical, more other directed, less flexible and conformist in their values" (p. 232). Such concerns reflect the enduring and ubiquitous questioning of the 'baggage' that recruits bring to their PETE programs (Armour & Jones, 1998; Macdonald & Kirk, 1996, 1999; Templin & Schempp, 1989; Tinning, 2002, 2004). Whether it be for postural excellence, skillful performance, or as exemplary models of physical activity or fitness, questions regarding the physical capacities of recruits reflect Wilmore's perspective that "What we are communicates more than what we say" (quoted in Tinning, 1990, p. 25). Following the seminal work of Lortie (1975) and Schempp (1989) however, a more dominant theme has been that of changing the beliefs and values of prospective teachers, which has posed both a barrier to, and criterion of, effective PETE (Ennis, 1994; Matanin & Collier, 2003; Pajares, 1992; Tsangaridou, 2006a). For example, from the physically competent perspective, a lasting commitment to MBI requires a deliberate strategy for changing PETE students' beliefs (Gurvitch et al., 2008), while socio-critical scholars argue that critical pedagogies require students to "question and (re)consider their own beliefs" (Philpot, 2015, p. 326). Hong Kong colleagues argue (Wang & Ha, 2009b) that challenging PETE students' prior experience and knowledge requires complex human resourcing and balancing of theoretical knowledge and professional application. The values and physical attributes of PETE recruits also have figured in debates on the acquisition of specific knowledges through PETE, with Rovegno's (1993) early research indicating that the development of PETE students' PCK is a complex process requiring careful consideration of "prospective teachers' prior knowledge, values, and beliefs" (Lee & Solmon, 2005, p. S112). In contrast, Siedentop (2002) claims that the reduction in PETE students' skillful movement and dominance of PCK has resulted in PETE graduates who are "so unprepared in the content area that they would be described as 'ignorant' if the content area were a purely cognitive knowledge" (p. 369).

Regardless of principled position, searching questions concerning who enters and who teaches in PETE programs reveal the complexity of capturing a decisive model of PETE effectiveness. Even so, as our next section demonstrates, a new suite of principled positions may be in the process of addressing these matters.

Current trends and issues: accountability, performativity, and digital technologies

Our efforts to date have acknowledged the diversity of locations in space and time of PETE programs, and their articulation with distinct principled positions on school PE and PETE. Notwithstanding this relative eclecticism, recent scholarship indicates that instead of new cases for or against PETE effectiveness, we are approaching a situation that might be described as 'case closed.' For example, drawing on the research of Ball (2003), we argue that the principled position diversity of the PE profession has been effaced by an all-encompassing neoliberalism that is expressed through the bureaucratic principled positions of the accountable student and performative teacher.

Over a decade ago, Ball (2003) identified managerialism and performativity within global education reform efforts that offered "a politically attractive alternative to the state-centred, public welfare tradition of education provision" (p. 215). Describing performativity as a "mode of regulation that employs judgements, comparisons and displays as a means of incentive, control, attrition and change" (p. 216), Ball argued that teachers experience considerable tension between metric performances and authentic pedagogical relationships. The very objectives and language of teacher education accreditation bears witness to a neoliberal emphasis on account-ability. According to advocates (Ingvarson, Elliot, Kleinhenz, & McKenzie, 2006), "accreditation can help to raise professional status and drive quality improvements within the pre-service sec-tor" (Ingvarson et al., 2006, p. 2). For Macdonald (2011) however, contemporary PE is imbued with neoliberalism, and the profession appears eager to "accept and accrue more of the vestiges of this ideology as a way of buying into the dominant policy agendas" (p. 36).

Reflecting this sentiment, the profession's quest to secure an 'effective' PETE can be found in Lawson's (1986) call for more stringent and faithfully implemented accreditation and certifica-tion standards. At that time, an unparalleled critique of education and schooling resulted in a raft of policies designed to improve the quality of teacher education programs, including changing the ways in which teachers were recruited and rewarded (Tannehill & O'Sullivan, 1990). By the turn of the century, an increasingly rigorous program of PETE accreditation was to become a global phenomenon (Ingvarsen et al., 2006). While some countries have been required to meet PETE-specific standards and measures, others have been linked to general standards of teacher professionalism (Tinning, 2006; Ward, 2013). In what we suggest was a remarkably prescient observation, Tannehill and O'Sullivan (1990) predicted that, "unless the physical education pro-fession becomes more informed of what is happening in teacher testing at state and national levels, physical educators will be left to react to others' decisions on how teachers of physical education should be judged" (p. 238).

Such issues dominated the recent commentary on effective teaching in RQES (Ennis, 2014; Metzler, 2014; Rink, 2013, 2014; Solmon & Garn, 2014; Ward, 2013). For Ward (2013), "teacher effectiveness should be situated within the contemporary teacher evaluation policies that exist at both state and federal levels" (p. 294). More broadly, Rink (2014) argues that the standards and assessment movement provides opportunities for shared visions. Other scholars debate the merits of 'who' will evaluate PE and PETE programs, and 'how' (Ennis, 2014; McKenzie & Lounsbery, 2013; Metzler, 2014), leading Ennis (2014) and Ward (2014) to reiterate the im-portance of measuring student *learning* as opposed to using proxy variables such as physical activity. As with Ennis (2014), Karp and Woods (2008), Rink (2014), Solmon and Garn (2014), Australian scholars Hay and Penney (2012) argue that a growing assessment and accountability culture demands that PETE students and faculty alike must "better understand assessment from a theoretical, conceptual and practical basis" (p. 129).

Yet, there also are some teacher educators who argue that the quest for rigorous account-ability and an enthusiasm for assessment has come at considerable cost. For example, Tinning (2006) argues that as PETE is increasingly shaped by stakeholders external to the profession, our "program orientations will probably become less eclectic, more conservative and less adventur-ous" (p. 381). No-one better captures the angst associated with these external influences than Metzler (2014) and his colleagues who suggest that instead of encouraging PETE students to display innovative MBI practices, perhaps it is more appropriate to "default to simplistic, tradi-tional, direct instruction" (p. 18) for their teaching performance assessment. Succinctly summa-rizing the challenge to PETE, Metzler (2014) states that "subtly at first, but now fully apparent, any evidence-based agenda we might offer to define and guide best practice has been co-opted by policymakers and other external forces in the name of teacher evaluation, accountability and quality" (p. 18). To date, there is little sign that the incessant audit culture (Ball, 2003) currently dominating the education landscape will abate, reinforcing Ayers and Housner's (2008) concern that we may regret the fact that our research has paid little attention to this critical domain.

Other researchers have identified the need for more research on the intersections between emergent digital technologies and PETE effectiveness. Interestingly, assessment often pro-vides the rationale for the inclusion of technology as a means of enhancing PE and PETE effectiveness. According to McKenzie and Lounsbery (2013), effective teaching involves the use of technologies, such as pedometers and accelerometers, that are designed to "help students set daily physical activity goals and to monitor their progress" (p. 425). Although there is currently a great deal of interest in the use of digital technology in PE, there is also an – as yet – unaddressed risk that the transformative potential of digital technology may not be realized in PE. In contrast to McKenzie's position, Gard (2014) has described the punitive overtones associated with digital technology as a mechanism for making schools and students more accountable for public health outcomes. On the other hand, there is the less dramatic but equally unfortunate possibility that digital technology will be used in PE and PETE to deliver more of the same, an outcome that has regularly been reported by educational researchers in other curriculum areas (for example Smeets, 2005). An educational world characterized by increasing technological innovation and sustained desire for accountability informs our final section on future research agendas.

Implications for future research and practice

In the remaining commentary we identify some notable silences in the literature and raise some possibilities to be considered for future research. First, our review has revealed that the principled positions of university-based researchers dominate the literature on PETE effectiveness. This is, perhaps, unsurprising, considering some of the observations made in the wider education literature. Cochran-Smith and Zeichner (2005), for example, have suggested there is "little research that includes the perspectives, questions and voices of cooperating teachers and prospective teachers" (p. 16). While some British scholars have been addressing this gap (e.g., Chambers, 2014), we suggest that future research partnerships could be more attentive to the voices of all key stakeholders, including the pre-service teachers with whom we work, cooperating teachers, principals, and students in schools.

Second, we identified the increasing imperatives of a global accountability culture and the incorporation of digital technologies within PETE, and this speaks to a much needed, and internationally diverse, extended body of knowledge. In the area of assessment and accountability, some two decades on from Tannehill and O'Sullivan's call for more information, there are signs that the profession has begun to undertake new research and consider its implications for teacher preparation (Hay, 2006; MacPhail & Halbert, 2010; Redelius & Hay, 2012). There is, however, still much to learn, particularly with respect to the response of PETE, and its educators, to burgeoning regimes of teacher accreditation. In the area of digital technologies, there are clear research gaps. While the incorporation of digital technology has been a point of sustained discussion in the PE literature since the late 1990s (e.g., Gard, 2014), the focus has primarily been on school PE and the implications for pupils. Although recently, Casey and Goodyear investigated teacher learning and digital technologies (Goodyear, Casey, & Kirk, 2014), we still have little empirical work providing insight into the potential and challenges of the digital in supporting effective PETE. What, for example, are the kinds of PETE experiences necessary to prepare pre-service teachers to think critically about the role of the digital in physical education, while also preparing them to use technology to achieve student learning objectives?

Finally, in a chapter on learning to teach in PE, it is worth recalling that O'Sullivan (2003) advocated the need for long-term programs of scholarship in PETE that question, amongst other things, what we know about the connections between what pre-service physical educators do and what students learn. While a range of scholars have undertaken sustained, cohesive interrogations of PETE over a number of decades, including Daryl Siedentop, Richard Tinning, Mary O'Sullivan, and Matthew Curtner-Smith, few have pursued longitudinal studies of effect/impact which follow the graduates of teacher education programs into their early years of teaching (Cochran-Smith & Zeichner, 2005). While research has sought to elicit students' perspectives (e.g., Enright & O'Sullivan, 2010), pre-service teachers' perspectives (e.g., McMahon & MacPhail, 2007), teachers' perspectives (e.g., Curtner-Smith, 2001), and teacher educators' perspectives (e.g., McEvoy, Heikinaro-Johansson, & MacPhail, 2015) on what constitutes effective PE and PETE, there is a clear need for more substantial, systematic, and connected, longitudinal research with all stakeholders. Indeed, McEvoy and her co-authors (2015) identify a need for more research beyond the US context, larger quantitative studies, and a maximization of the possibilities offered by practitioner inquiry approaches.

Summary

To conclude, from the principled position perspective we are bound to acknowledge Hunter's (1994) warning against "secular holiness" and to support his arguments that scholars should "develop a far more pluralistic and supple bearing towards the ethical and organisational reality of the school system" (p. 164). Curriculum historians have shown that curricula in higher education institutions, like subjects in schools, are dynamic amalgams that are in a constant process of contestation and reconstruction as they fight for status, resources, and esteem (Goodson, 1983). In seeking to understand others' principled positions we may facilitate a deeper respect for the "restraints imposed by the plurality of persons, disciplines, conducts and objectives" (McCuaig & Hay, 2013, p. 295) that together, shape, restrict, or strengthen the profession's desire to produce effective teachers of PE. We also note Skinner's (1963) counsel that "behavior – human or otherwise – remains an extremely difficult subject matter" (p. 509). Some five decades on, an expansive body of research, advocacy, and critique has done little to resolve the challenges we face in establishing agreed criteria for PETE effectiveness. Nonetheless, the following questions offer some interesting routes into considering these issues locally.

Reflective questions for discussion

1. How is effectiveness 'measured' on the PETE program with which you are/have been associated?
2. What principled positions do you hold and how have you become aware of them?
3. In your local and national contexts, what external agencies are influencing what PETE looks like, and how are they shaping PETE programs?
4. What are your views about the embodied dimension of PETE pedagogies?
5. How is technology influencing what effective physical education teacher education is and how could it impact upon what it might become?
6. What role could/should critical analysis play in PETE?
7. What could models-based practice contribute to the development of an 'effective' PETE?

References

Armour, K. M., & Jones, R. L. (1998). *Physical education teachers' lives and careers: PE, sport, and educational status.* London: Psychology Press.

Attard, K., & Armour, K. M. (2005). Learning to become a learning professional: Reflections on one year of teaching. *European Journal of Teacher Education, 28*(2), 195–207.

Ayers, S. F., & Housner, L. D. (2008). A descriptive analysis of undergraduate PETE programs. *Journal of Teaching in Physical Education, 27*(1), 51–67.

Bailey, R., Armour, K., Kirk, D., Jess, M., Pickup, I., & Sandford, R. (2009). The educational benefits claimed for physical education and school sport: An academic review. *Research Papers in Education, 24*(1), 1–27.

Bain, L. L. (1988). Beginning the journey: Agenda for 2001. *Quest, 40*(2), 96–106.

Bain, L. L. (1990). Physical education teacher education. In W. R. Houston, M. Haberman, & J. P. Sikula (Eds.), *Handbook of research on teacher education* (pp. 758–781). New York: Macmillan.

Ball, S. (2003). The teacher's soul and the terrors of performativity. *Journal of Education Policy, 18*(2), 215–228.

Brophy, J., & Good, T. L. (1986). Teacher behavior and student achievement. In M. C. Wittrock (Ed.), *Handbook of research on teaching* (3rd edn) (pp. 328–375). New York: Macmillan.

Brown, D., & Evans, J. (2004). Reproducing gender? Intergenerational links and the male PE teacher as a cultural conduit in teaching physical education. *Journal of Teaching in Physical Education, 23*, 48–70.

Bunker, D., & Thorpe, R. (1982). A model for the teaching of games in secondary schools. *Bulletin of Physical Education, 18*(1), 5–8.

Cale, L., Harris, J., & Chen, M. (2007). More than 10 years after "the horse is dead…": Surely it must be time to dismount? *Pediatric Exercise Science, 19*, 115–131.

Casey, A. (2014). Models-based practice: Great white hope or white elephant? *Physical Education and Sport Pedagogy, 19*(1), 18–34.

Casey, A., & Fletcher, T. (2012). Trading places: From physical education teachers to teacher educators. *Journal of Teaching in Physical Education, 31*(4), 362–380.

Chambers, F. C. (Ed.). (2014). *Mentoring in physical education and sports coaching.* London: Routledge.

Clarke, G. (2006). Sexuality and physical education. In D. Kirk, D. Macdonald, & M. O'Sullivan (Eds.), *The handbook of physical education* (pp. 723–739). London: Sage.

Cliff, K. (2012). A sociocultural perspective as a curriculum change in health and physical education. *Sport, Education and Society, 17*(3), 293–311.

Cochran-Smith, M., & Zeichner, K. M. (2005). *Studying teacher education: The report of the AERA panel on research and teacher education.* Mahwah, NJ: American Educational Research Association.

Collier, C. (2006). Models and curricula of physical education teacher education. In D. Kirk, D. Macdonald, & M. O'Sullivan (Eds.), *The handbook of physical education* (pp. 386–407). London: Sage.

Crum, B. (1996). *Conceptual divergences in European PE teacher & sport coach education programmes: A pilot study.* Paper presented to the Danish Sport Confederation, Copenhagen.

Curtner-Smith, M. (1997). The impact of biography, teacher education, and organizational socialization on the perspectives and practices of first-year physical education teachers: Case studies of recruits with coaching orientations. *Sport, Education and Society, 2*(1), 73–94.

Curtner-Smith, M. (1999). The more things change, the more they stay the same: Factors influencing teachers' interpretations and delivery of National Curriculum Physical Education. *Sport, Education and Society, 4*(1), 75–97.

Curtner-Smith, M. D. (2001). The occupational socialization of a first-year physical education teacher with a teaching orientation. *Sport, Education and Society, 6*(1), 81–105.

Curtner-Smith, M. (2007). The impact of critically oriented physical education teacher education on pre-service classroom teachers. *Journal of Teaching in Physical Education, 26*(1), 35–56.

Curtner-Smith, M. (2012). Preparing preservice physical education teachers to teach sport education. In P. Hastie (Ed.), *Sport Education: International perspectives* (pp. 151–165). London: Routledge.

Curtner-Smith, M. D., Hastie, P. A., & Kinchin, G. D. (2008). Influence of occupational socialization on beginning teachers' interpretation and delivery of Sport Education. *Sport, Education and Society, 13*(1), 97–117.

Curtner-Smith, M., & Sofo, S. (2004a). Influence of a critically oriented methods course and early field experience on pre-service teachers' conceptions of teaching. *Sport, Education and Society, 9*(1), 115–142.

Curtner-Smith, M., & Sofo, S. (2004b). Preservice teachers' conceptions of teaching within Sport Education and multi-activity units. *Sport, Education and Society, 9*(3), 347–377.

Deenihan, J. T., & MacPhail, A. (2013). A preservice teacher's delivery of Sport Education: Influences, difficulties and continued use. *Journal of Teaching in Physical Education, 32*(1), 166–185.

Devís-Devís, J. (2006). Socially critical research perspectives in physical education. In D. Kirk, D. Macdonald & M. O'Sullivan (Eds.), *The handbook of physical education*, (pp. 37–58). London: Sage.

Dowling, F. (2006). Physical education teacher educators' professional identities, continuing professional development and the issue of gender equality. *Physical Education and Sport Pedagogy, 11*(3), 247–263.

Dunkin, M. J., & Biddle, B. J. (1974). *The study of teaching.* New York: Holt, Rinehart & Winston.

Dyson, B. (2014). Quality physical education: A commentary on effective physical education teaching. *Research Quarterly for Exercise and Sport, 85*(2), 144–152.

Ennis, C. D. (1994). Knowledge and beliefs underlying curricular expertise. *Quest, 46*(2), 64–175.

Ennis, C. D. (2014). The role of students and content in teacher effectiveness. *Research Quarterly for Exercise and Sport, 85*(1), 6–13.

Enright, E., & O'Sullivan, M. (2010). 'Can I do it in my pyjamas?' Negotiating a physical education curriculum with teenage girls. *European Physical Education Review, 16*(3), 203–222.

Feiman-Nemser, S. (1996). *Teacher mentoring: A critical review.* ERIC Clearing House on Teaching and Teacher Education. Retrieved from www.ericdigests.org/1997-1/mentoring.html.

Fendler, L. (2003). Teacher reflection in a hall of mirrors: Historical influences and political reverberations. *Educational Researcher, 32*(3), 16–25.

Fernández-Balboa, J. M. (1997). Knowledge base in physical education teacher education: A proposal for a new era. *Quest, 49*(2), 161–181.

Fetro, J.V. (2000). Commentary on 1988–1998 national practices in K-12 health education and physical education teacher certification. *Journal of Health Education, 31*(3), 150–155.

Fletcher, T., & Casey, A. (2014). The challenges of models-based practice in physical education teacher education: A collaborative self-study. *Journal of Teaching in Physical Education, 33*(3), 403–421.

Flintoff, A., & Scraton, S. (2006). Girls and physical education. In D. Kirk, D. Macdonald, & M. O'Sullivan (Eds.), *The handbook of physical education* (pp. 767–783). London: Sage.

Gard, M. (2014). eHPE: A history of the future. *Sport, Education and Society, 19*(6), 827–845.

Gard, M., & Wright, J. (2001). Managing uncertainty: Obesity discourses and physical education in a risk society. *Studies in Philosophy and Education, 20*(6), 535–549.

Gard, M., & Wright, J. (2005). *The obesity epidemic: Science, morality, and ideology.* New York: Routledge.

Goodson, I. (1983). Subjects for study: Aspects of a social history of curriculum. *Journal of Curriculum Studies, 15*(4), 391–408.

Goodyear, V. A., Casey, A., & Kirk, D. (2014). Tweet me, message me, like me: Using social media to facilitate pedagogical change within an emerging community of practice. *Sport, Education and Society, 19*(7), 927–943.

Great Britain Board of Education [GBBOE]. (1933). *Syllabus of physical training for schools.* London: HMSO.

Gréhaigne, J. F., & Godbout, P. (1995). Tactical knowledge in team sports from a constructivist and cognitivist perspective. *Quest, 47*(4), 490–505.

Gurvitch, R., Blankenship, B. T., Metzler, M. W., & Lund, J. L. (2008). Student teachers' implementation of model-based instruction: Facilitators and inhibitors. *Journal of Teaching in Physical Education, 27*(4), 466–486.

Hanke, U. (2001). Research on physical education teacher and coach education (published in German) 1999–2000. *International Journal of Physical Education, 38*(1), 17–23.

Harrison, Jr. L., & Belcher, D. (2006). Race and ethnicity in physical education. In D. Kirk, D. Macdonald, & M. O'Sullivan (Eds.), *The handbook of physical education* (pp. 740–751). London: Sage.

Hastie, P. A., & Casey, A. (2014). Fidelity in models-based practice research in sport pedagogy: A guide for future investigations. *Journal of Teaching in Physical Education, 33*(3), 422–431.

Hastie, P. A., & Curtner-Smith, M. D. (2006). Influence of a hybrid Sport Education – Teaching Games for Understanding unit on one teacher and his students. *Physical Education & Sport Pedagogy, 11*(1), 1–27.

Hastie, P. A., de Ojeda, D. M., & Luquin, A. C. (2011). A review of research on sport education: 2004 to the present. *Physical Education and Sport Pedagogy, 16*(2), 103–132.

Hay, P. (2006). Assessment for learning in physical education. In D. Kirk, D. Macdonald, & M. O'Sullivan (Eds.), *The handbook of physical education* (pp. 312–325). London: Sage.

Hay, P., & Penney, D. (2012). *Assessment in physical education: A sociocultural perspective.* London: Routledge.

Hellison, D. (1973). *Humanistic physical education.* Englewood Cliffs, NJ: Prentice-Hall.

Hellison, D. (1985). *Goals and strategies for teaching physical education.* Champaign, IL: Human Kinetics.

Hellison, D. (1995). *Teaching responsibility through physical activity.* Champaign, IL: Human Kinetics.

Henry, F. M. (1978). The academic discipline of physical education. *Quest, 29*(1), 13–29.

Hunter, I. (1994). *Rethinking the school: Subjectivity, bureaucracy, criticism.* St Leonards, NSW: Allen & Unwin.

Ingvarson, L., Elliott, A., Kleinhenz, E., & McKenzie, P. (2006). Teacher education accreditation: A review of national and international trends and practices [Monograph]. *Teacher Education, 1*, 1–93.

Iserbyt, P., Ward, P., & Martens, J. (2015). The influence of content knowledge on teaching and learning in traditional and Sport Education contexts: An exploratory study. *Physical Education and Sport Pedagogy, 20*(2), 174–185.

Karp, G. G., & Woods, M. L. (2008). Preservice teachers' perceptions about assessment and its implementation. *Journal of Teaching in Physical Education, 27*(3), 327–346.

Kirk, D. (1983). Theoretical guidelines for 'Teaching for Understanding'. *Bulletin of Physical Education, 9*, 41–45.

Kirk, D., MacDonald, D., & O'Sullivan, M. (Eds.). (2006). *Handbook of physical education.* London: Sage.

Kirk, D., Macdonald, D., & Tinning, R. (1997). The social construction of pedagogic discourse in physical education teacher education in Australia. *The Curriculum Journal, 8*(2), 271–298.

Kirk, D., & Tinning, R. (Eds.). (1990). *Physical education, curriculum and culture: Critical issues in the contemporary crisis.* Hampshire, UK: Falmer Press.

Kyriacou, C. (1997). *Effective teaching in schools: Theory and practice.* London: Nelson Thornes.

Laporte, W. R. (1933). Physical education contributes to the Seven Cardinal Principles. *The Journal of Health and Physical Education, 4*(3), 10–71.

Larsson, H., & Redelius, K. (2008). Swedish physical education research questioned – current situation and future directions. *Physical Education and Sport Pedagogy, 13*(4), 381–398.

Launder, A. G. (2001). *Play practice: The games approach to teaching and coaching sports.* Champaign, IL: Human Kinetics.

Lawson, H. A. (1986). Occupational socialization and the design of teacher education programs. *Journal of Teaching in Physical Education, 5*, 107–116.

Leahy, D., Burrows, L., McCuaig, L., Wright, J., & Penney, D. (2015). *School health education in changing times: Curriculum, pedagogies and partnerships.* London: Routledge.

Leahy, D., & McCuaig, L. (2014). Disrupting the field: Teacher education in health education. In K. Fitzpatrick & R. Tinning (Eds.), *Health education: Critical perspectives* (pp. 220–232). London: Routledge.

Lee, A. M., & Solmon, M. A. (2005). Pedagogy research through the years in RQES. *Research Quarterly for Exercise and Sport, 76* (sup2), S108–S121.

Lindsay, E. L. (2014). Effective teaching in physical education: The view from a variety of trenches. *Research Quarterly for Exercise and Sport, 85*(1), 31–37.

Lloyd, R. J. (2011). Awakening movement consciousness in the physical landscapes of literacy: Leaving, reading and being moved by one's trace. *Phenomenology & Practice, 5*(2), 73–92.

Lortie, D. (1975). *The limits of socialization.* Chicago: University of Chicago Press.

Macdonald, D. (1997). Researching PETE: An account of explicit representations and covert knowledges. In J. Wright (Ed.), *Researching in physical and health education* (pp. 23–39). Wollongong, Australia: Faculty of Education, University of Wollongong.

Macdonald, D. (2004). Understanding learning in physical education. In J. Wright, D. Macdonald, & L. Burrows (Eds.), *Critical inquiry and problem-solving in physical education* (pp. 16–31). London: Routledge.

Macdonald, D. (2011). Like a fish in water: PE policy and practice in the era of neoliberal globalization. *Quest, 63*, 36–45.

Macdonald, D., & Kirk, D. (1996). Private lives, public lives: Surveillance, identity and self in the work of beginning physical education teachers. *Sport, Education and Society, 1*(1), 59–75.

Macdonald, D., & Kirk, D. (1999). Pedagogy, the body and Christian identity. *Sport, Education and Society, 4*(2), 131–142.

MacPhail, A., & Halbert, J. (2010). 'We had to do intelligent thinking during recent PE': Students' and teachers' experiences of assessment for learning in post-primary physical education. *Assessment in Education: Principles, Policy & Practice, 17*(1), 23–39.

Mallett, C. J. (2004). Reflective practices in teaching and coaching: Using reflective journals to enhance performance. In J. Wright, D. Macdonald, & L. Burrows, L. (Eds.), *Critical inquiry and problem-solving in physical education* (pp. 147–158). London: Routledge.

Matanin, M., & Collier, C. (2003). Longitudinal analysis of preservice teachers' beliefs about teaching physical education. *Journal of Teaching in Physical Education, 22*(2), 153–168.

McCuaig, L. (2008). *Teaching the art of healthy living: A genealogical study of H-PE and the moral governance of apprentice citizens.* Doctor of Philosophy, University of Queensland.

McCuaig, L., Coore, S., & Hay, P. J. (2012). Reducing dissonance along health–education fault lines: Health-literacy advocacy and the case for efficacious assessment. *Asia-Pacific Journal of Health, Sport and Physical Education, 3*(1), 3–15.

McCuaig, L., & Hay, P. J. (2013). Principled pursuits of 'the good citizen' in health and physical education. *Physical Education and Sport Pedagogy, 18*(3), 282–297.

McCuaig, L., & Tinning, R. (2010). HPE and the moral governance of p/leisurable bodies. *Sport, Education and Society, 15*(1), 39–61.

McEvoy, E., Heikinaro-Johansson, P., & MacPhail, A. (2015). Physical education teacher educators' views regarding the purpose(s) of school physical education. *Sport, Education and Society*, (ahead-of-print), 1–13.

McKenzie, T. L. (2007). The preparation of physical educators: A public health perspective. *Quest, 59*(4), 345–357.

McKenzie, T. L., & Lounsbery, M. A. (2013). Physical education teacher effectiveness in a public health context. *Research Quarterly for Exercise and Sport, 84*(4), 419–430.

McKenzie, T. L., & Lounsbery, M. A. (2014). The pill not taken: Revisiting physical education teacher effectiveness in a public health context. *Research Quarterly for Exercise and Sport, 85*(3), 287–292.

McMahon, E., & MacPhail, A. (2007). Learning to teach sport education: The experiences of a pre-service teacher. *European Physical Education Review, 13*(2), 229–246.

Melnychuk, N., Robinson, D. B., Lu, C., Chorney, D., & Randall, L. (2011). Physical education teacher education (PETE) in Canada. *Canadian Journal of Education/Revue Canadienne de L'éducation, 34*(2), 148–168.

Metzler, M. W. (2011). *Instructional models for physical education*. Scottsdale, AZ: Holcomb Hathaway, Publishers.

Metzler, M. W. (2014). Teacher effectiveness research in physical education: The future isn't what it used to be. *Research Quarterly for Exercise and Sport, 85*(1), 14–19.

Muijs, D., & Reynolds, R. (2011). *Effective teaching: Evidence and practice*. London: Sage.

Nussbaum, M. (1994). *The therapy of desire: Theory and practice in Hellenistic ethics*. Princeton, NJ: Princeton University Press.

O'Sullivan, M. (1996). What do we know about the professional preparation of teachers? In S. Silverman & C. Ennis (Eds.), *Student learning in physical education: Applying research to enhance instruction* (pp. 315–337). Champaign, IL: Human Kinetics.

O'Sullivan, M. (2003). Learning to teach physical education. In Silverman & C. Ennis (Eds.), *Student learning in physical education: Applying research to enhance instruction* (2nd edn) (pp. 275–294). Champaign, IL: Human Kinetics.

O'Sullivan, M., & Doutis, P. (1994). Research on expertise: Guideposts for expertise and teacher education in physical education. *Quest, 46*(2), 176–185.

Ovens, A., & Tinning, R. (2009). Reflection as situated practice: A memory-work study of lived experience in teacher education. *Teaching and Teacher Education, 25*(8), 1125–1131.

Pajares, F. (1992). Teachers' beliefs and educational research: Cleaning up a messy construct. *Review of Educational Research, 62*(3), 307–332.

Peck, R. F., & Tucker, J. A. (1971). *Research on teacher education*. Research and Development Center for Teacher Education, University of Texas at Austin.

Penney, D., & Chandler, T. (2000). Physical education: What future (s)? *Sport, Education and Society, 5*(1), 71–87.

Philpot, R. (2015). Critical perspectives in PETE: An Antipodean perspective. *Journal of Teaching in Physical Education, 34*, 316–332.

Pill, S., Penney, D., & Swabey, K. (2012). Rethinking sport teaching in physical education: A case study of research based innovation in teacher education. *Australian Journal of Teacher Education, 37*(8), 118–138.

Pišot, R., Plevnik, M., & Štemberger, V. (2014). Effective teaching in physical education: Slovenian perspective. *Research Quarterly for Exercise and Sport, 85*(2), 153–156.

Redelius, K., & Hay, P. J. (2012). Student views on criterion-referenced assessment and grading in Swedish physical education. *Physical Education & Sport Pedagogy, 17*(2), 211–225.

Rink, J. E. (1993). Teacher education: A focus on action. *Quest, 45*, 308–320.

Rink, J. E. (2013). Measuring teacher effectiveness in physical education. *Research Quarterly for Exercise and Sport, 84*(4), 407–418.

Rink, J. E. (2014). Teacher effectiveness in physical education – Consensus? *Research Quarterly for Exercise and Sport, 85*(3), 282–286.

Rovegno, I. (1993). Content-knowledge acquisition during undergraduate teacher education: Overcoming cultural templates and learning through practice. *American Educational Research Journal, 30*(3), 611–642.

Rovegno, I., & Kirk, D. (1995) Articulations and silences in socially critical work on Physical Education: Toward a broader agenda. *Quest, 47*, 447–474.

Sallis, J. F., & McKenzie, T. L. (1991). Physical education's role in public health. *Research Quarterly for Exercise and Sport, 62*(2), 124–137.

Schempp, P. (1989). Apprenticeship-of-observation and the development of physical education teachers. In T. Templin & P. Schempp (Eds.), *Socialization into physical education: Learning to teach* (pp. 13–38). Indianapolis, IN: Benchmark Press.

Shulman, L. (1986). Those who understand: Knowledge growth in teaching. *Educational Researcher, 15*(2), 4–14.

Shulman, L. (1987). Knowledge and teaching: Foundation of the new reform. *Harvard Educational Review, 57*(1), 1–22.

Siedentop, D. (1976). *Developing teaching skills in physical education*. Mountain View, CA: Mayfield.

Siedentop, D. (1983). *Developing teaching skills in physical education* (2nd edn). Mountain View, CA: Mayfield.

Siedentop, D. (2002). Content knowledge for Physical Education. *Journal of Teaching in Physical Education, 21*(4), 368–377.

Siedentop, D., & Tannehill, D. (2000). *Developing teaching skills in physical education* (4th edn). Mountain View, CA: Mayfield.

Skinner, B. F. (1963). Operant behavior. *American Psychologist, 18*(8), 503–515.

Smeets, E. (2005). Does ICT contribute to powerful learning environments in primary education? *Computers and Education, 44*(3), 343–355.

Society of Health and Physical Educators [SHAPE]. (2014). *National standards and grade level outcomes for K-12 physical education*. Champaign, IL: Human Kinetics.

Solmon, M. A., & Garn, A. C. (2014). Effective teaching in physical education: Using transportation metaphors to assess our status and drive our future. *Research Quarterly for Exercise and Sport, 85*(1), 20–26.

Swalwell, K. (2013). 'With great power comes great responsibility': Privileged students' conceptions of justice-oriented citizenship. *Democracy and Education, 21*(1), Article 5. Retrieved from http://democracyeducationjournal.org/home/vol21/iss1/5.

Tannehill, D., & O'Sullivan, M. (1990). Teacher testing and implications for physical education. *Journal of Teaching in Physical Education, 9*, 227–239.

Telford, R. D., Cunningham, R. B., Telford, R. M., & Abhayaratna, W. P. (2012). Schools with fitter children achieve better literacy and numeracy results: Evidence of a school cultural effect. *Pediatric Exercise Science, 24*(1), 45–57.

Templin, T., & Schempp, P. (1989). An introduction to socialization into physical education. In T. Templin & P. Schempp (Eds.), *Socialization into physical education: Learning to teach* (pp. 1–11). Indianapolis, IN: Benchmark Press.

Tinning, R. (1990). *Ideology and physical education: Opening Pandora's box*. Geelong, Australia: Deakin University Press.

Tinning, R. (1991). Teacher education pedagogy: Dominant discourses and the process of problem setting. *Journal of Teaching Physical Education, 11*, 1–20.

Tinning, R. (1995). We have ways of making you think, or do we? Reflection on 'training' in reflective teaching. In C. Paré (Ed.), Better Teaching in P. E.?: Think About It! *Proceedings of the international seminar on training of teachers in reflective practice in physical education*. Quebec: Department des Science de L'activite' Physique, Universite' du Quebec a Trois-Rivieres.

Tinning, R. (2002). Towards a 'modest pedagogy': Reflections on the problematics of critical pedagogy. *Quest, 54*(3), 224–240.

Tinning, R. (2004). Rethinking the preparation of Health and Physical Education teachers: Ruminations on knowledge, identity and ways of thinking. *Asia-Pacific Journal of Teacher Education, 32*(3), 241–253.

Tinning, R. (2006). Theoretical orientations in physical education teacher education. In D. Kirk, D. Macdonald, & M. O'Sullivan (Eds.), *The handbook of physical education* (pp. 369–385). London: Sage.

Tinning, R. (2010). *Pedagogy and human movement: Theory, practice, research*. London: Routledge.

Tinning, R., Macdonald, D., Wright, J., & Hickey, C. (2001). *Becoming a physical education teacher, contemporary and enduring issues*. Sydney: Prentice Hall.

Trost, S. G. (2006). Public health and physical education. In D. Kirk, D. Macdonald, & M. O'Sullivan (Eds.), *The handbook of physical education* (pp. 163–187). London: Sage.

Tsangaridou, N. (2006a). Teacher beliefs. In D. Kirk, D. Macdonald, & M. O'Sullivan (Eds.), *The handbook of physical education* (pp. 486–501). London: Sage.

Tsangaridou, N. (2006b). Teachers' knowledge. In D. Kirk, D. Macdonald, & M. O'Sullivan (Eds.), *The handbook of physical education* (pp. 502–515). London: Sage.

Tsangaridou, N., & Siedentop, D. (1995). Reflective teaching: A literature review. *Quest, 47*, 212–237.

Vendien, C., & Nixon, J. (1985). *Physical education teacher education: Guidelines for sport pedagogy*. New York: John Wiley & Sons.

Wang, C. L. J., & Ha, A. (2009a). The teacher development in physical education: A review of the literature. *Asian Social Science, 4*(12), 3.

Wang, C. L. J., & Ha, A. (2009b). Pre-service teachers' perception of Teaching Games for Understanding: A Hong Kong perspective. *European Physical Education Review, 15*(3), 407–429.

Ward, P. (2013). The role of content knowledge in conceptions of teaching effectiveness in physical education. *Research Quarterly for Exercise and Sport, 84*(4), 431–440.

Ward, P. (2014). A response to the conversations on effective teaching in physical education. *Research Quarterly for Exercise and Sport, 85*(3), 293–296.

Ward, P., & Barrett, T. (2002). A review of behavior analysis research in physical education. *Journal of Teaching in Physical Education, 21*(3), 242–266.

Welk, G., Eisenmann, J., & Dollman, J. (2006). Health-related physical activity in children and adolescents: A bio-behavioral perspective. In D. Kirk, D. Macdonald, & M. O'Sullivan (Eds.), *The handbook of physical education* (pp. 665–684). London: Sage.

Whitehead, M. (Ed.). (2010). *Physical literacy: Throughout the lifecourse.* London: Routledge.

Zeichner, K. M. (1983). Alternative paradigms of teacher education. *Journal of Teacher Education, 34*(3), 3–9.

30

WHAT RESEARCH TELLS US ABOUT EFFECTIVE CONTINUING PROFESSIONAL DEVELOPMENT FOR PHYSICAL EDUCATION TEACHERS

Melissa Parker, UNIVERSITY OF LIMERICK, IRELAND

& Kevin Patton, CALIFORNIA STATE UNIVERSITY – CHICO, USA

Nearly a century ago, John Dewey (1916) remarked that if we teach today as we taught yesterday, children are robbed of today and tomorrow. We contend the same could be said about the continuing professional development (CPD) of teachers. Yet, although there is a growing recognition of the importance of CPD for teacher growth, numerous questions remain about the nature of *optimally effective* CPD.

In teaching, CPD refers to a variety of educational experiences designed to improve teachers' practice and pupils' learning outcomes (Darling-Hammond & McLaughlin, 2011). Throughout their careers, teachers experience a vast array of CPD activities with the potential to enhance their knowledge, skills, and dispositions, thus improving practice and contributing to their growth as professionals. Historically, much CPD was rather passive in nature. The most commonly reported formats were school based in-service days, structured workshops, conference attendance, and university-linked courses. Over the past decade, however, CPD approaches that view teacher learning as, "interactive and social, based in discourse and community practice" (Desimone, 2011, pp. 68–69) have emerged. These CPD formats highlight formal and informal learning within communities.

Defining continuing professional development

CPD refers to a variety of educational experiences related to an individual's work and is designed to improve practice and outcomes (Darling-Hammond & McLaughlin, 2011). These opportunities may be voluntary or mandatory, individual or collaborative, and formal or informal (Desimone, 2011). Nabhania, O'Day Nicolas, and Bahous (2014) identify several embedded models of CPD shown to enhance teaching practices: action research/inquiry, networking, coaching strategies, and self-monitoring/self-reflection. Examining these strategies and their possible impact on CPD is a worthwhile endeavor as these more contemporary iterations of CPD are considered a powerful mechanism for teacher growth and development.

While many points can be taken from the professional development literature there is surprisingly little agreement about what constitutes 'effective' CPD. Guskey (1995), among others, has argued that each individual teacher needs an 'optimal mix' of formats and approaches. This argument raises further questions about the purposes of CPD and the relative effectiveness of different approaches at different career stages.

Depending on the CPD's purpose, the context, and school culture within which it resides, there are numerous viewpoints on characteristics defining effective CPD. In one instance, effectiveness may relate to teacher engagement or the extent to which the environment and actions of the CPD process increase teacher commitment. In other cases, CPD might be linked to teacher development and improved practice. Effectiveness also may relate to CPD's impact on improving students' cognitive, psychomotor, and affective learning outcomes. With such varying purposes it is easy to see how the concept of 'effective' CPD is somewhat contested and diffuse in meaning. In line with DiPaola and Hoy's (2014) goal for CPD as "building the capacity of teachers to help students learn" (p. 101), we argue, however, that effective CPD can be linked to teacher engagement, teaching practice, *and* student learning. The intent of this chapter is to provide a comprehensive overview of the current international knowledge base on CPD for physical education teachers (PE-CPD), to consider questions about effectiveness and their implications for future PE-CPD design, and to identify areas for further investigation.

Historical overview

Inquiry into PE-CPD is relatively new. Early beginnings in the United States included descriptions of two programs. In the first, Anderson (1982) and his students at Teachers College developed and studied CPD for local school districts, while the second, 'Second Wind,' was a CPD resource for PE teachers in the Massachusetts area (Griffin & Hutchinson, 1988). Two doctoral dissertations were among the first empirical PE-CPD studies in the USA. In 1983, O'Sullivan's dissertation documented changes in selected teaching behaviors as a result of systematic data collection and discussion. Faucette's (1984) dissertation investigated enhancers and inhibitors of in-service education. She continued her line of research addressing principals' roles in CPD (Faucette & Graham, 1986) linking elementary PE teachers' concerns to their implementation of changes proposed within the CPD program (Faucette, 1987). By the early 2000s, four major CPD projects added to the emerging literature: the Franklin Academy of Physical Education (a PDS school in Columbus, Ohio) (Stroot, O'Sullivan, & Tannehill, 2000), the Saber Tooth Project in Nebraska (Ward, 1999), the South Carolina assessment project (Rink & Williams, 2003), and Armour and Yelling's (2004) investigation into the provision of PE-CPD in the UK.

These early projects yielded two foundational CPD variables shaping contemporary CPD research. First, CPD process investigations provided clear pictures of barriers to and facilitators of successful CPDs (e.g., Armour & Yelling, 2004; Doutis & Ward, 1999; Ha, Lee, Chan, & Sum, 2004; Kirk & MacDonald, 1998; Pissanos & Allison, 1996; Pope & O'Sullivan, 1998; Rovegno & Bandhauer, 1997; Schwager & Doolittle, 1988; Stroot et al., 2000). Second, the majority reported teachers' perceptions of the impact of CPD (Faucette & Graham, 1986; Ha et al., 2004; Kirk & MacDonald, 1998; Schwager & Doolittle, 1988), although these researchers did not indicate the actual CPD's impact on teaching practices or student learning.

Theoretical frameworks for examining teachers' professional development

Macdonald et al. (2002) offered five perspectives within which to situate PE-focused peda-gogical research: positivist, interpretive, socially critical, poststructuralist, and feminist. A small number of experimental CPD studies used a positivist perspective with systematic observations of behavior followed by planned interventions (e.g., McKenzie, Alcaraz, Sallis, & Faucette, 1998; O'Sullivan, 1983). Similarly, a few poststructuralist researchers sought to understand technolo-gies of power in relation to CPD (e.g., Macdonald, Mitchell, & Mayer, 2006). To date, very few scholars have used socially critical or feminist perspectives to study PE-CPD.

Instead, most PE-CPD researchers have used interpretive perspectives. These perspectives are rooted in "the premise that social organizations are constructed based on purposeful actions of individuals as they negotiate their social roles and define status within the collective social group" (Macdonald et al., 2002, p. 138). Falling within the interpretive perspective, social con-structivist theories are frequently utilized for examining teachers' CPD both historically (e.g., Pissanos & Allison, 1996; Rovegno & Bandhauer, 1997) and recently (e.g., Armour & Yelling, 2007; Makopoulou & Armour, 2011a; Patton, Parker, & Pratt, 2013). While multiple definitions of constructivism exist, Fosnot (2005, p. 34) summarizes constructivist learning as "an interpre-tive, recursive, non-linear building process by active learners interacting with their surround – the physical and social world."

Situated learning theory, a social constructivist approach to learning that underpins the con-cept of communities of practice (CoP), provides a meaningful framework for examining teach-ers' ongoing CPD (e.g., Deglau & O'Sullivan, 2006; Kirk & Macdonald, 1998; Parker, Patton, Madden, & Sinclair, 2010). Lave and Wenger's (1991) model of situated learning proposes that learning involves a process of CoP engagement, emphasizing the relationship between knowl-edge and situations in which it is acquired and used. As CoP develop their own understandings of their practices and profession, this framework allows researchers to examine places and spaces where teachers engage in actions about their work with students.

Current trends and issues

Effective CPD is on-going and sustained

Most CPD encourages teachers to change some aspect of their practice, ultimately requiring them to acquire new knowledge to foster increased student learning (Vetter, 2012). Traditional one-shot CPD formats may provide teachers with information, yet it is clear that these "forms of CPD provision ... are often ineffective in supporting teachers to learn in ways that can en-hance practice" (Armour & Yelling, 2007, p. 178). Professional development of this type is un-likely to help teachers to become continuous learners and innovative thinkers.

Scholars argue that to support teachers CPD must be on-going, sustained, and reflective (Betchel & O'Sullivan, 2007; Parker et al., 2010; Parker, Patton, & Tannehill, 2012). Moreover, as many teachers work largely in isolation, they find it difficult to identify opportunities to en-gage in critical reflection (O'Sullivan & Deglau, 2006). Thus, long-term CPD is best punctuated by opportunities to work collaboratively with others on-site to practice changes to teaching. Developing teachers' interest and capacity in such dialogue requires time if teacher learning is to be supported and nurtured (O'Sullivan & Deglau, 2006).

On-going and sustained CPD in-and-of-itself appears to be a necessary but insufficient condition for teacher growth. Instead, it is important to allocate sessions to time intensive CPD pedagogies. These pedagogies provide teachers with opportunities to learn new pedagogical skills (Ince, Goodway, Ward, & Lee, 2006) and transfer skills between contexts (Petrie, 2010). As a result teachers more fully understand the change process, better engage with the CPD program, gain a sense of ownership, and value the changes undertaken (Murphy & O'Leary, 2012; Parker et al., 2010; Patton & Griffin, 2008a, 2008b).

Furthermore, sustained CPD facilitates the development of community, another essential component for effective CPD (Atencio, Jess, & Dewar, 2012; Keay & Lloyd, 2009; Parker et al., 2010). When studying a Scottish CoP designed for primary specialist PE teachers, Atencio et al. (2012) found problems when this CPD was subsequently expanded to a large scale, centrally driven project. The expansion resulted in a series of one-off, short duration workshops that did not replicate the former sense of community, ownership, and empowerment in the original program. Teachers, instead, reported feeling isolated and marginalized in their practice.

Effective CPD is based on teachers' needs and interests

When CPD provides teachers with opportunities to participate in decision-making about what and how they will learn, and how they will use these knowledge and skills, teachers report increased ownership of and commitment to CPD (Armour & Yelling, 2007; Deglau & O'Sullivan, 2006; Parker et al., 2010; Tannehill & Murphy, 2012). This teacher-centered CPD approach does not limit the agenda to local teacher-generated content; instead, effective CPD addresses the wider political and structural schools requirements while simultaneously acknowledging teachers' needs and interests. Easton (2008) argues that the most powerful active learning opportunities are embedded in teachers' work, beginning with teachers' assessments of their students' needs and identifying their own areas for learning. PE research indicates that effective CPD encourages teachers to take an active role in shaping their practice by initiating, sustaining, and directing CPD content and focus (Makopoulou & Armour, 2011b).

Evidence suggests that CPD is most relevant when it focuses on teachers' real work in schools with young people, addressing their unique school contexts, and acknowledging teachers' prior knowledge and experience. Contextually based CPD responds to local conditions and can be delivered in a variety of formats and modes to meet the wide range of teachers' learning needs. Importantly, high quality CPD successfully balances teachers' needs with a broader vision for the CPD initiative within the wider educational context (O'Sullivan & Deglau, 2006; Parker et al., 2010). Hunuk, Ince, and Tannehill (2012) found that participation in teacher-centered CPD focusing on specific students' needs resulted in changed teaching practices and culture. As a result, pupils increased their engagement in PE, triggering continued teacher professional and personal learning. O'Sullivan and Deglau (2006) reported that when teachers are empowered and treated as professionals and leaders, with meaningful control over the substance of CPD experiences, they are more willing to share their ideas and learn from each other (Armour & Yelling, 2007; Casey, 2012; Patton et al., 2013).

Effective CPD includes opportunities within learning communities

There is growing acceptance of the benefits of communities of practice (CoP) that extend opportunities for teacher learning beyond the workplace (Atencio et al., 2012; Deglau & O'Sullivan, 2006; Hunuk et al., 2012; Parker et al., 2010). Within these structures, teachers learn from and with one another, growing a culture of collaboration (Duncombe & Armour, 2004). Known by a variety of names (e.g., teacher inquiry communities, professional learning communities, CoP) these communities all focus on teacher learning. Among the most studied teacher collectives is the concept of the CoP, characterized by a common purpose, shared social practices and engagement, and a collective repertoire of experiences, practices, and stories (Wenger, 1998). Through CoP, teachers developed curriculum (Parker et al., 2010), designed CPD to meet their unique needs (Tannehill & Murphy, 2012), overcome contextual factors that impeded their use of pedagogical models (Goodyear & Casey, 2015), and changed their pedagogical practices (Hunuk et al., 2012; Parker, Patton, & Sinclair, 2016; Patton et al., 2005). Within a CoP, learning can be deep, focused on growth, and grounded in an understanding of teacher practice (Parker et al., 2012). In some cases the result is sustained pedagogical and curricular innovation over time (Deglau & O'Sullivan, 2006; Parker et al., 2016).

Communities of practice also have the capacity to engender camaraderie and respect between participants (Parker et al., 2012), providing safe environments for risk taking, reflecting on failures as well as sharing successful programs and practices (Wenger, 1998). This environment facilitates the creation of a shared vision through debate about key issues, theory, and practice (Parker et al., 2010), provoking "critical and even uncomfortable discussions in order to challenge teachers' pre-existing views of physical education" (Atencio et al., 2012, p. 127). When examining CPD provision in the UK, Keay and Lloyd (2009) reported that CoPs were "seen by most providers as a valuable networking opportunity that might alleviate feelings of isolation and have a positive impact on their work" (p. 669) and that, when developed appropriately, led to increased professionalism.

Because communities of practice evolve in unpredictable and non-linear ways, often in relation to contradiction and change (Atencio et al., 2012), their development and maintenance is rarely easy. Effective creation and continuance of CoP appear to be related to many factors including: levels of support, catalysts for change, visions for student learning, understanding personal and professional relationships, and desires to engender a sense of empowerment (Parker et al., 2010; Parker et al., 2012). Conversely, if all or most of these aspects are not present, CoP may fail to achieve agreed-upon goals (Atencio et al., 2012).

Effective CPD are supported

CPD should enhance teachers' engagement in lifelong learning. To achieve this goal, administrators need to provide continuous support to facilitate teachers' efforts to alter their teaching (Armour, 2010). Unfortunately, adequate support is not always a component of CPD. In many cases, traditional CPD have been fragmented, creating a gap between teachers' aspirations for pupils and the CPD availability and support (Armour & Makopoulou, 2012; Armour & Yelling, 2004).

Despite many barriers to effective CPD, considerable evidence exists that effective CPD is possible with adequate support. Supporting factors identified in CPD literature include time, support from other teachers and key stakeholders, and resources. Time during teachers' regular working hours to engage in professional learning is an important (and often neglected) support for effective CPD (Parker et al., 2012). Time can come in several forms including time away from teaching to observe others teach, share, and learn new skills and strategies, and experiment with new curricular ideas (Betchel & O'Sullivan, 2006; Deglau & O'Sullivan, 2006). When CPD policies or projects build in time for collaborative work during regular school hours, teachers can engage in intensive and sustained professional learning activities (Parker et al., 2010; O'Sullivan & Deglau, 2006).

Scholars also point out that effective CPD is characterized by support from other teachers and key stakeholders (e.g., Armour & Makopoulou, 2012; Betchel & O'Sullivan, 2007; Parker et al., 2010; Pratt, 2015). Further, in effective CoP, they identify the importance of teachers helping teachers (Armour & Yelling, 2004), collective participation (Armour & Makopoulou, 2012), and mentoring (McCaughtry, Cothran, Hodges-Kulinna, Martin, & Faust, 2005; Patton et al., 2005). This type of collective participation encourages sharing knowledge, providing the basis for peer support while stimulating teacher reflection (Pratt, 2015; Sinelnikov, 2009). In addition, principals or head teachers (Betchel & O'Sullivan, 2007), university partners (Parker et al., 2010; Ward, 1999; Ward & O'Sullivan, 2006), other school administrators (Parker et al., 2010; Prusak, Pennington, Graser, Beighle, & Morgan, 2010), and students (Betchel & O'Sullivan, 2007) are highly influential when encouraging teachers to make and sustain CPD-related changes to their practice. Lastly, research confirms that support in the form of equipment resources enables teachers to improve their instruction (McCaughtry, Martin, Hodges-Kulinna, & Cothran, 2006; Ward & O'Sullivan, 2006).

Effective CPD acknowledges teachers as learners in an active and social environment

A key factor inhibiting teachers' ability to learn and change their practices is being treated as 'passive learners' (Makopoulou & Armour, 2011a). Teachers should be treated as active learners, instead of being 'trained' to be compliant (Easton, 2008). In PE, an essential goal of CPD is to help teachers view themselves as active (Armour, 2010; Makopoulou & Armour, 2011b). This requires teachers to conceptualize their learning as an intentional, dynamic, social, and active process. For this type of learning to occur, effective CPD focuses on inquiry and reflection, with teachers constructing their own meaning and understanding through social engagement in relevant CPD tasks and activities (O'Sullivan & Deglau, 2006; Patton, Parker, & Neutzling, 2012).

The crux of active learning environments is providing opportunities for teachers to engage in CPD activities, such as action research (Casey, 2012), observing and receiving feedback on teaching (Sinelnikov, 2009), and making presentations and/or writing for publication (Deglau & O'Sullivan, 2006; Patton et al., 2013). The format for these activities includes group discussion (Deglau, Ward, O'Sullivan, & Bush, 2006), chat rooms and use of social media (Goodyear, Casey, & Kirk, 2014; Martin, McCaughtry, Hodges-Kulinna, & Cothran, 2009), as well as observing expert teachers and/or being observed while teaching (Martin et al., 2009; Sinelnikov, 2009), and developing curriculum (Parker et al., 2010). Arranging for teachers to play a central role in designing and implementing initiatives for their own learning supports active participation (O'Sullivan & Deglau, 2006) and encourages continued involvement in the design of their own learning.

A critical factor in the social nature of teacher learning is the development of positive, trusting, personal, and professional relationships among stakeholders (Armour, 2006; Patton et al., 2013). Armour and Yelling (2007) reported that teachers placed a high value on learning collaboratively in informal networks or communities. Similarly, Keay (2006) argued that CPD providers need to recognize the importance of collaborative learning for teachers and actively incorporate opportunities for its development. Participating in informal social events as an element of CPD allows teachers and facilitators to begin to know each other on a more personal basis, helping to enhance trust and build strong collegial relationships (Parker et al., 2010; Ward & O'Sullivan, 2006).

Effective CPD enhances teachers' pedagogical skills and content knowledge

Armour and Yelling (2004) point out that effective PE-CPD is discipline-specific, allowing teachers to engage with a set of teaching, assessment, observation, and reflection experiences focused on "curriculum and pedagogy for learning in physical education" (p. 109). Such activities provide learning experiences related to teachers' daily work, affording opportunities for teachers to consider why and how the content they offer their students is organized and delivered (O'Sullivan & Deglau, 2006). These content and pedagogy-specific CPD opportunities stimulate the teachers' interest, encouraging their greater participation and facilitating change toward inclusion of content knowledge and effective teaching practices (e.g., Hunuk et al., 2012; Patton & Griffin, 2008a).

Hunuk et al. (2012) found that through participation in a CoP, teachers increased their health related fitness (HRF) and assessment knowledge. Similarly, in a study of middle school PE teachers, Patton and Griffin (2008a) reported increased alignment between instructional and assessment practices. In work with urban teachers, CPD has resulted in increased self-efficacy for teaching various curriculum aspects, including motor skills, fitness, personal and social responsibility (Martin et al., 2009; Martin, McCaughtry, Kulinna, Cothran, & Faust, 2008), and an increased willingness to use technology (Ince et al., 2006). Looking at the issue from another perspective, Alfrey, Cale, and Webb (2012) attribute teachers' deficiency in HRF content knowledge to a general lack of teacher engagement with CPD specifically related to health and lifelong physical activity.

From a pedagogical perspective, Petrie (2010) found that primary generalist teachers benefited from opportunities to transfer classroom pedagogical strategies and skills to the PE context. These learning opportunities, however, need to be balanced and connected with opportunities to develop PE content knowledge. Likewise, when studying CPD associated with sport education, Sinelnikov (2009) found that teachers adopted pedagogical behaviors associated with content (e.g., choosing captains), considered benchmark elements of the model. Similarly Patton and Griffin (2008a) reported increased use of indirect pedagogies to facilitate student-oriented small-sided games and peer assessment.

Effective CPD is facilitated with care

Armour and Yelling (2007) noted CPD providers "need to tread a careful line, simultaneously being leaders (providing expert input, helping teachers to work together) and followers" (p. 195). This type of facilitation acknowledges teachers' individual contexts, hears their voices, and identifies their assets; thus considering deficiencies in a non-judgmental manner (Deglau & O'Sullivan, 2006; Parker et al., 2010; Patton et al., 2013). Effective facilitators encourage teacher capacity-building through engagement in self-improvement and a focus on student learning (Patton & Parker, 2014). For example, Goodyear and Casey (2015) reported that a facilitator, termed a 'boundary spanner,' was a catalyst for the adoption and sustained use of a pedagogical innovation, thereby facilitating teachers' use of action research, driving social energy, and supporting the subsequent emergence of a CoP.

Successful facilitation acknowledges that teachers actively construct new meaning based on prior knowledge and experiences, recognizes the influences of others in a social environment, and emphasizes the relevance of formal knowledge in teacher growth and development (Patton et al., 2012). Traditionally, CPD providers are hired solely based on their expertise to engage in one-directional content delivery. In contrast, effective facilitators are teacher-centered, providing structured experiences proposed by the teachers themselves and without dictating responses (Patton & Parker, 2014; Patton et al., 2012; Patton et al., 2013).

This "pedagogy of facilitation" (Poekert, 2011) engages teachers in meaningful ways to learn new skills and content. Patton et al. (2013) identify pedagogies that actively engage teachers such as trying out content, reporting back to the group, and sharing lessons learned with others via public dissemination. By 'teaching without telling,' facilitators used various participant-centered pedagogical strategies to make CPD meaningful. This strategy contributed to the development of an environment that encouraged teachers to become active participants in the creation of knowledge.

Effective CPD focus on improving student learning outcomes

Research also suggests that teachers perceive CPD to be impactful and sustainable when related to student-achievement gains (Darling-Hammond, Wei, Andree, Richardson, & Orphanos, 2009; Hattie, 2009). Although assessing the causal link between professional development and student achievement may be the most important outcome of CPD, it is also the most difficult, if not impossible, aspect (Kerka, 2003). CPD that is intensive and includes application of knowledge to teachers' planning and instruction is most likely to influence teachers' practices, in turn, positively affecting student achievement (Desimone, Porter, Garet, Yoon, & Birman, 2002; Knapp, 2003). Unfortunately, developers too often plan and conduct CPD with the aim of introducing a new teaching practice or policy rather than assisting teachers to develop a robust understanding of the impact on student learning.

Researchers typically use either proxy measures (e.g., MVPA, HR) (Johns, Ha, & MacFarlane, 2001; McKenzie, Sallis, Kolody, & Faucette, 1997; Woods & Lynn, 2001), or process variables (Ward, 1999) to assess student learning outcomes that result from PE-CPD. Few studies have specifically measured the impact of substantial CPD as improvements in student learning outcomes. McKenzie et al. (1998) reported improvements in children's manipulative skills. They concluded that PE programs delivered by physical education specialists and classroom teachers with substantial CPD training could improve the quality of children's manipulative skills (catching and throwing). Likewise, Hunuk et al. (2012) concluded that a CoP based on teachers' specific needs increased their students' learning and positively changed teachers' teaching culture. Results of their experimental study demonstrated that treatment-group students' health-related fitness knowledge significantly improved from pre- to post-test on a health-related fitness knowledge test. Finally, while CPD was not the focus of the study, Iserbyt, Ward, and Martens (2015) reported that an intensive one-on-one CPD format enhanced teachers' content knowledge resulting in student learning gains in swimming.

Implications for evidence-based CPD practice

The literature reviewed in this chapter indicates that effective CPD requires considerable time, and that time must be carefully structured, purposefully directed, and focused on content, pedagogy, or both. In 1982, Anderson reflected on PE-CPD's future indicating that:

> If teacher educators are to have a meaningful role in this [PD] effort, not only will they have to assist in the creation and maintenance of new formats for inservice education, they will need to devise new ways of working with inservice teachers that acknowledge the voluntary, collaborative and collegial nature of their relationships. (p. 16)

While much more is known about the high-intensity, situated, and collaborative learning required for effective CPD, in some ways Anderson's challenge has yet to be realized. In our own experience, although some innovative practices are reported, there have been few major changes over the last three decades in the way that much PE-CPD is conducted. There is still a need, therefore, to work towards new formulations and structures (Armour & Yelling, 2007).

Several pragmatic questions also arise when considering how to best design and implement effective CPD for teachers. For example, research results suggest that CPD is most effective when driven by teacher-generated topics (directly related to the wider political and structural requirements of schools) in close-knit communities with common goals. If this is true, large school districts are challenged to run multiple, small CPD learning communities with both a common conceptual focus and varied goals consistent with diverse teacher populations/contexts. Thus far, in physical education, this has proven to be a tall order that school districts have been largely unable to fulfil. Hence, in spite of these challenges, schools must create opportunities for teachers to grow and develop in their practice so that they, in turn, can help students grow and develop knowledge and ability to think critically. This is especially relevant "when the growing acknowledgement of its [CPD] effect upon pupil learning is recognised" (Alfrey et al., 2012; p. 488). It is surely time to use what is known to influence and impact policy and to change CPD formats for the majority of teachers.

Evaluation of CPD

Quality CPD evaluation provides meaningful information that can be used to make thoughtful, responsible decisions about CPD processes and effects. The purpose of evaluation is to determine the value of specific CPD activities; asking questions such as "Are CPD activities achieving their intended results (i.e., teacher engagement, teaching practice, and/or student learning)?" To guide evaluation, Guskey (2002) argues there is a need to go beyond simplistic evaluation to collect and analyze five critical levels of information: (a) participants' reactions, (b) participants' learning, (c) organizational support and change, (d) participants' use of new knowledge and skills, and (e) student learning outcomes. With each succeeding level, the process of gathering evaluation information becomes more complex. Further, because each level builds on the previous, success at one level is usually necessary for success at higher levels (Guskey, 2002). In PE-CPD literature reviewed in this chapter, evaluation efforts are most often limited to the first three levels. For example, studies most often report teachers' initial satisfaction with the experience (level 1) and, less frequently, reflect new knowledge and skills (level 2), and the school or district's advocacy, support, accommodation, facilitation, and recognition (level 3). CPD stakeholders find evaluation, especially in the higher levels advocated by Guskey, to be problematic as researchers often study CPD after the fact instead of being involved in planning and conduct from its inception. Evident from this review is that purposeful PE-CPD evaluation in the areas of degree and quality of implementation and student learning outcomes (levels 4 and 5) has not figured prominently in the PE-CPD literature, warranting further investigation. This call for systematic information gathering and analysis as central components of the planning for and study of CPD increases its potential for success (Guskey, 2002).

Future directions

Despite a growing body of research examining CPD in a PE context, more research is needed to explore the direct and indirect outcomes of CPD. Such studies should aim at describing what, how, and under what conditions teachers positively engage in CPD, resulting in sustained professional learning. Specifically, those responsible for planning and implementing CPD need better tools to critically assess and evaluate the effectiveness of what they do (Guskey & Yoon, 2009) as well as investigate the critical role that principals and key stakeholders play in supporting the unique needs of specialist teachers.

Relatively few studies systematically document established changes to teachers' actual teaching practices. Vescio, Ross, and Adams (2008) acknowledge empirical validation of changes as an important step in documenting CPD outcomes. These authors note that "understanding the outcomes of these endeavors on teaching practice and student learning is crucial, particularly in today's era of scarce resources and accountability" (p. 81). Much CPD research leaves readers to question the relationship between CPD and improvements in student learning. Only a handful of PE studies examined student learning as a direct outcome of CPD (see Hanuk et al., 2012; McKenzie et al., 1998). Indeed, Guskey and Yoon (2009, p. 498) argue that robust, trustworthy evidence examining the specific CPD aspects that contribute to learning/improvements is "in dreadfully short supply and that dedicated efforts to enhance the body of evidence are sorely needed." Therefore, CPD planning should begin with discussions of specific CPD goals, identification of evidence that best reflects goal achievement, and evaluation methods to collect evidence that is meaningful and defensible.

Additionally, more frequent use of quantitative studies and alternative theoretical frameworks may provide a much needed macro perspective and illuminate issues that may have been overlooked through an overreliance on interpretive theory. These steps can document systematic changes to teachers' pedagogies and practices focusing CPD goals on student learning outcomes. These more robust research platforms can increase education leaders' and policymakers' understanding and support for the most effective forms of CPD (Darling-Hammond et al., 2009).

Summary of key findings

The existing literature suggests that 'effective' CPD is a contested term having diverse meanings and linked to multiple outcomes. Nonetheless, there is evidence to suggest that CPD is more likely to be effective when it:

- is on-going and sustained;
- addresses wider political and structural requirements of schools while recognizing teachers' needs and interests;
- acknowledges teachers as learners in an active and social environment;
- includes collaborative learning opportunities within communities of physical educators;
- enhances teachers' pedagogical skills and content knowledge;
- is facilitated with care;
- is supported;
- focuses on changes in the quality of students' learning; and
- includes an integrated plan to evaluate Guskey's (2002) five levels leading to increases in student learning outcomes.

Reflective questions for discussion

1. Researchers have employed interpretive theories to guide much of the existing PE-CPD research. What has the field learnt from the evidence produced using this lens, what has been masked, and what might be learnt by using other theoretical lenses?
2. Why is 'effective' CPD a contested concept?
3. Given the current 'effective' CPD knowledge base, why has CPD provision been so slow to change and what can be done to alter that?
4. What is currently known about the relationship between CPD and improvements in student learning and why is the evidence base so limited?
5. How might CPD be evaluated in the context of different purposes?
6. How could education leaders and policymakers make better use of evidence from the evaluation of CPD activities and programmes?

References

Alfrey, L., Cale, L., & Webb, L. (2012). Physical education teachers' continuing professional development in health related exercise. *Physical Education and Sport Pedagogy, 17,* 477–491, DOI: 10.1080/1740898 9.2011.594429

Anderson, W. G. (1982). Working with inservice teachers: Suggestions for teacher educators. *Journal of Teaching in Physical Education, 1*(3), 15–21.

Armour, K. (2006). Physical education teachers as career-long learners: A compelling agenda. *Physical Education and Sport Pedagogy, 11*(3), 203–207.

Armour, K. (2010). The physical education profession and its professional responsibility … or … why '12 weeks paid holiday' will never be enough. *Physical Education and Sport Pedagogy, 15,* 1–13.

Armour, K., & Makopoulou, K. (2012). Great expectations: Teacher learning in a national professional development programme. *Teaching and Teacher Education, 28,* 336–346.

Armour, K., & Yelling, M. (2004). Continuing professional development for experienced physical education teachers: Towards effective provision. *Sport, Education and Society, 9,* 95–114.

Armour, K., & Yelling, M. (2007). Effective professional development for physical education teachers: The role of informal, collaborative learning. *Journal of Teaching in Physical Education, 26,* 177–200.

Atencio, M., Jess, M., & Dewar, K. (2012). "It is a case of changing your thought processes, the way you actually teach": Implementing a complex professional learning agenda in Scottish physical education. *Physical Education and Sport Pedagogy, 17,* 127–144, DOI:10.1080/17408989.2011.565469

Bechtel, P., & O'Sullivan, M. (2006). Effective professional development – What we now know. *Journal of Teaching in Physical Education, 25,* 363–378.

Bechtel, P., & O'Sullivan, M. (2007). Enhancers and inhibitors of teacher change among secondary physical educators. *Journal of Teaching in Physical Education, 26,* 221–235.

Casey, A. (2012). Practitioner research: A means of coping with the systemic demands for continual professional development. *European Physical Education Review, 19*(1), 76–90.

Darling-Hammond, L., & McLaughlin, M. (2011). Policies that support professional development in an era of reform. *Phi Delta Kappan, 92*(6), 81–92.

Darling-Hammond, L., Wei, R., Andree, A., Richardson, N., & Orphanos, S. (2009). *Professional learning in the learning profession: A status report on teacher development in the United States and abroad.* Dallas, TX: National Staff Development Council.

Deglau, D., & O'Sullivan, M. (2006). The effects of a long-term professional development program on the beliefs and practices of experienced teachers. *Journal of Teaching in Physical Education, 25,* 379–396.

Deglau, D., Ward, P., O'Sullivan, M., & Bush, K. (2006). Professional dialogue as professional development. *Journal of Teaching in Physical Education, 25,* 413–427.

Desimone, L. M. (2011). A primer on effective professional development. *Phi Delta Kappan, 92*(6), 68–71.

Desimone, L., Porter, A., Garet, M., Yoon, K., & Birman, B. (2002). Effects of professional development on teachers' instruction: Results from a three year longitudinal study. *Education Evaluation and Policy Analysis, 24,* 81–112.

Dewey, J. (1916). *Democracy and education.* New York: Macmillan.

DiPaola, M., & Hoy, W. K. (2014). *Improving instruction through supervision, evaluation, and professional development.* Charlotte, NC: Information Age.

Doutis, P., & Ward, P. (1999). Teachers' and administrators' perceptions of the Saber-tooth project reform and of their changing workplace conditions. *Journal of Teaching in Physical Education, 18,* 417–427.

Duncombe, R., & Armour, K. (2004). Collaborative professional learning: From theory to practice. *Journal of In-service Education, 30*(1), 141–166.

Easton, L. B. (2008). From professional development to professional learning. *Phi Delta Kappan, 89*(10), 755–759.

Faucette, N. (1984). *Implementing innovations: A qualitative analysis of the impact of an in-service program on the curricula and teaching behaviors of two elementary physical education teachers* (Unpublished doctoral dissertation). University of Georgia, Athens, GA.

Faucette, N. (1987). Teachers' concerns and participation styles during in-service education. *Journal of Teaching in Physical Education, 6,* 425–440.

Faucette, N., & Graham, G. (1986). The impact of principals on teachers during inservice education: A qualitative analysis. *Journal of Teaching in Physical Education, 5,* 79–90.

Fosnot, C. T. (2005). *Constructivism: Theory, perspectives, and practice.* New York: Teachers College Press.

Goodyear, V., & Casey, A. (2015). Innovation with change: Developing a community of practice to help teachers move beyond the 'honeymoon' of pedagogical renovation. *Physical Education and Sport Pedagogy, 20*(2), 186–203.

Goodyear, V., Casey, A., & Kirk, D. (2014). Tweet me, message me, like me: Using social media to facilitate pedagogical change within an emerging community of practice. *Sport, Education and Society, 19*(7), 927–943.

Griffin, P., & Hutchinson, G. (1988). Second Wind: A physical education program development network. *Journal of Teaching in Physical Education, 7*, 184–189.

Guskey, T. (1995). Professional development in education: In search of the optimal mix. In T. Guskey & M. Huberman (Eds.), *Professional development in education: New paradigms and practices* (pp. 114–131). New York: Teachers College Press.

Guskey, T. (2002). Does it make a difference? Evaluating professional development. *Educational Leadership, 59*(6), 45–51.

Guskey, T. R., & Yoon, K. S. (2009). What works in professional development? *Phi Delta Kappan, 90*(7), 495–500.

Ha, A., Lee, J. C. K., Chan, D. W. K., & Sum, R. K. W. (2004). Teachers' perceptions of in-service teacher training to support curriculum change in physical education: The Hong Kong experience. *Sport, Education and Society, 9*, 421–438.

Hattie, J. A. C. (2009). *Visible learning: A synthesis of over 800 meta-analyses relating to achievement.* London: Routledge.

Hunuk, D., Ince, M. L., & Tannehill, D. (2012). Developing teachers' health-related fitness knowledge through a community of practice: Impact on student learning. *European Physical Education Review, 19*(1), 3–20.

Ince, M. L., Goodway, J. D., Ward, P., & Lee, M. (2006). Effects of professional development on the technological competency and attitudes toward the use of technology of urban physical education teachers. *Journal of Teaching Physical Education, 25*, 397–412.

Iserbyt, P., Ward, P., & Martens, J. (2015). The influence of content knowledge on teaching and learning in traditional and Sport Education contexts: An exploratory study. *Physical Education and Sport Pedagogy,* DOI: 10.1080/17408989.2015.1050662

Johns, D., Ha, A., & Macfarlane, D. (2001). Raising activity levels: A multidimensional analysis of curriculum change. *Sport, Education and Society, 6*, 199–210, DOI: 10.1080/13573320120084272

Keay, J. (2006). Collaborative learning in physical education teachers' early-career professional development. *Physical Education & Sport Pedagogy, 11*, 285–305.

Keay, J., & Lloyd, C. (2009). High-quality professional development in physical education: The role of a subject association. *Professional Development in Education, 35*, 655–676, DOI: 10.1080/19415250902879584

Kerka, S. (2003). *Does adult educator professional development make a difference: Myths and realities.* Washington, DC: ERIC Publications.

Knapp, M. (2003). Professional development as a policy pathway. *Review of Research in Education, 27*, 109–157.

Kirk, D., & MacDonald, D. (1998). Situated learning in physical education. *Journal of Teaching in Physical Education, 17*, 376–387.

Lave, J., & Wenger, E. (1991). *Situated learning: Legitimate peripheral participation.* Cambridge, UK: Cambridge University Press.

Macdonald, D., Kirk, D., Metzler, M., Nilges, L., Schempp, P., & Wright, J. (2002). It's all very well, in theory: Theoretical perspectives and their applications in contemporary pedagogical research. *Quest, 54*, 133–156.

Macdonald, D., Mitchell, J., & Mayer, D. (2006). Professional standards for physical education teachers' professional development: Technologies for performance? *Physical Education and Sport Pedagogy, 11*(3), 231–246.

Makopoulou, K., & Armour, K. (2011a). Physical education teachers' career-long professional learning: Getting personal. *Sport, Education and Society, 16*, 571–592.

Makopoulou, K., & Armour, K. (2011b). Teachers' professional learning in a European learning society: The case of physical education. *Physical Education and Sport Pedagogy, 16*, 417–433.

Martin, J., McCaughtry, N., Hodges-Kulinna, P., & Cothran, D. (2009). The impact of a social cognitive theory-based intervention on physical education teacher self-efficacy. *Professional Development in Education, 35*, 511–529.

Martin, J., McCaughtry, N., Hodges-Kulinna, P., Cothran, D., & Faust, R., (2008). The effectiveness of mentoring-based professional development on physical education teachers' pedometer and computer efficacy and anxiety. *Journal of Teaching in Physical Education, 27*, 68–82.

McCaughtry, N., Cothran, D., Hodges-Kulinna, P., Martin, J., & Faust, R. (2005). Teachers mentoring teachers: A view over time. *Journal of Teaching in Physical Education, 24*, 326–343.

McCaughtry, N., Martin, J., Hodges-Kulinna, P., & Cothran, D. (2006). What makes teacher professional development work? The influence of instructional resources on change in physical education. *Journal of In-service Education, 32*, 221–235.

McKenzie, T., Alcaraz, J., Sallis, J., & Faucette, N. (1998). Effects of a physical education program on children's manipulative skills. *Journal of Teaching in Physical Education, 17*, 327–341.

McKenzie, T., Sallis, J., Kolody, B., & Faucette, N. (1997). Long-term effects of a physical education curriculum and staff development program: SPARK. *Research Quarterly for Exercise and Sport, 68*, 280–291.

Murphy, F., & O'Leary, M. (2012). Supporting primary teachers to teach physical education: Continuing the journey. *Irish Educational Studies, 31*, 297–310.

Nabhania, M., O'Day Nicolas, M., & Bahous, R. (2014). Principals' views on teachers' professional development. *Professional Development in Education, 40*, 228–242.

O'Sullivan, M. (1983). The effects of inservice education on the teaching effectiveness of inservice physical education teachers. *Dissertation Abstracts International, 44*(6), 1724A. (University Microfilms No. AA18318413).

O'Sullivan, M., & Deglau, D. (2006). Principles of professional development. *Journal of Teaching in Physical Education, 25*, 441–449.

Parker, M., Patton, K., Madden, M., & Sinclair, C. (2010). From committee to community: The development and maintenance of a community of practice. *Journal of Teaching in Physical Education, 29*, 337–357.

Parker, M., Patton, K., & Sinclair, C. (2016). "I took this picture because …": Accessing teachers' depictions of change. *Physical Education and Sport Pedagogy, 21*(3), 328–346.

Parker, M., Patton, K., & Tannehill, D. (2012). Mapping the landscape of Irish physical education professional development. *Irish Educational Studies, 31*, 311–327.

Patton, K., & Griffin, L. L. (2008a). Three physical education programs' adaptive approaches to change: "How can I spin that so it works for me?" *Sport, Education, and Society, 13*, 433–450.

Patton, K., & Griffin, L. L. (2008b). Examining teacher change: Two teachers' experiences and patterns of change in a physical education teacher development project. *Journal of Teaching in Physical Education, 27*(3), 272–291.

Patton, K., Griffin, L. L., Sheehy, D., Arnold, R., Gallo, A. M., Dodds, P., Pagnano, K., Henninger, M., & James, A. (2005). Navigating the mentoring process in a teacher development project: A situated learning perspective. *Journal of Teaching in Physical Education, 24*, 302–325.

Patton, K., & Parker, M. (2014). Facilitators' views of successful professional development. *Physical Education & Sport Pedagogy, 19*(1), 60–75.

Patton, K., Parker, M., & Neutzling, M. (2012). Tennis shoes required: The role of the facilitator in professional development. *Research Quarterly for Exercise and Sport, 83*(4), 522–532.

Patton, K., Parker, M., & Pratt, E. (2013). Meaningful learning in professional development: Teaching without telling. *Journal of Teaching in Physical Education, 32*, 441–459.

Petrie, K. (2010). Creating confident, motivated teachers of physical education in primary schools. *European Physical Education Review, 16*, 47–64.

Pissanos, B., & Allison, P. (1996). Continued professional learning: A topical life history. *Journal of Teaching in Physical Education, 16*, 2–19.

Poekert, P. (2011). The pedagogy of facilitation: Teacher inquiry as professional development in a Florida elementary school. *Professional Development in Education, 37*(1), 19–38.

Pope, C., & O'Sullivan, M. (1998). Culture, pedagogy and teacher change in an urban high school: How would you like your eggs done? *Sport, Education and Society, 3*, 201–226.

Pratt, E. (2015). *Physical education teachers' perceptions of the role of support mechanisms within contemporary professional development.* Unpublished doctoral dissertation. University of Northern Colorado, Greeley, CO.

Prusak, K., Pennington, T., Graser, S., Beighle, A., & Morgan, C. (2010). Systemic success in physical education: The East Valley phenomenon. *Journal of Teaching in Physical Education, 29*, 85–106.

Rink, J., & Williams, L. (2003). Developing and implementing a state level assessment program. *Journal of Teaching in Physical Education, 22*, 473–511.

Rovegno, I., & Bandhauer, D. (1997). Norms of the school culture that facilitated teacher adoption and learning of a constructivist approach to physical education. *Journal of Teaching in Physical Education, 16,* 401–425.

Schwager, S., & Doolittle, S. (1988). Teachers' reactions to activities in ongoing program development. *Journal of Teaching in Physical Education, 7,* 240–247.

Sinelnikov, O. A. (2009). Sport Education for teachers: Professional development when introducing a novel curriculum model. *European Physical Education Review, 15*(1), 91–114.

Stroot, S., O'Sullivan, M., & Tannehill, D. (2000). Weaving a web of relationships. In M. Johnson, P. Brossan, D. Cramer, & T. Dove (Eds.), *Collaborative reform and other improbable dreams: The challenges of professional development schools* (pp. 233–245). Albany, NY: State University of New York Press.

Tannehill, D., & Murphy, G. (2012). *Teacher empowerment through a community of practice: The urban school initiative.* Paper presented at the American Alliance for Physical Education, Recreation and Dance, Boston, MA.

Vescio, V., Ross, D., & Adams, A. (2008). A review of research on the impact of professional learning communities on teaching practice and student learning. *Teaching and Teacher Education, 24*(1), 80–91.

Vetter, A. (2012). Teachers as architects of transformation: The change process of an elementary school teacher in a practitioner research group. *Teacher Education Quarterly, 39*(1), 27–49.

Ward, P. (1999). Design of the Saber-tooth Project [Monograph]. *Journal of Teaching in Physical Education, 18,* 403–416.

Ward, P., & O'Sullivan, M. (2006). Professional development in urban settings. *Journal of Teaching in Physical Education, 25,* 348–362.

Wenger, E. (1998). *Communities of practice: Learning, meaning and identity.* Cambridge, UK: Cambridge University Press.

Woods, A., & Lynn, S. (2001). Through the years: A longitudinal study of physical education teachers from a research based professional preparation program. *Research Quarterly for Exercise and Sport, 72,* 219–231.

31

EDUCATING TEACHERS IN HEALTH PEDAGOGIES

Leen Haerens, Nathalie Aelterman, An De Meester &
Isabel Tallir, GHENT UNIVERSITY, BELGIUM

There have been considerable debates about physical education (PE)'s role in public health. Researchers, PE teacher educators and PE teachers have not only critically interrogated whether it is valuable, attainable and feasible to try to promote young people's health through PE (e.g. Bailey et al., 2009), but proponents of health-based PE also hold distinctive visions about how teachers can realize it in practice. In other words, even among those in favour of health-based PE, there is currently no consensus on the most relevant goals and learning outcomes. These differences are contingent not only on the definition of health as including physical, social, intellectual and psychological aspects, but also on the specific perspectives and emphases taken within each of these definitions (e.g. is enhancing physical health about improving fitness or increasing activity levels?). In this chapter we will discuss the role of physical activity (PA) in PE from several different goal perspectives.

The PA consequences of different PE goal priorities

Physical fitness development as a goal of health-based PE

Numerous research and policy studies support the role of physical fitness in PE. With large-scale, cross-sectional, longitudinal and even prospective population studies among adults providing evidence for a relationship between physical fitness, cardiorespiratory health and risks for mortality (Boreham & Riddoch, 2001), PE teachers have long been expected to improve and monitor students' physical fitness. Indeed, a common memory many adults hold of their PE experiences during childhood and adolescence is likely to be participation in physical fitness testing (Hopple & Graham, 1995).

In the 1990s in the US, The National Standards for PE (National Association for Sport and Physical Education, 1995) stated that students should achieve and maintain a health-enhancing level of physical fitness. At the same time, books (e.g. Pate & Hohn, 1994) were published on how the PE curriculum could be redesigned and restructured to teach lifetime fitness skills and attitudes. In Scotland and Australia, a number of innovative (yet ultimately unsustainable) daily health-related PE programmes emerged during this period (Kirk, 1991). In Europe, The Committee for Development of Sport developed the European Tests of Physical Fitness (Eurofit; Adam, Klissouras, Ravazolla, Renson & Tuzworth, 1988) recommended that Eurofit tests should

461

be adopted for the purpose of measuring and assessing the physical fitness of school-aged children through PE. As a consequence, many PE teachers around the world started to incorporate and measure balance, coordination, flexibility, speed and reaction time, muscular strength as well as cardiorespiratory fitness and endurance testing in their lessons. Moreover, practices involving weighing children and taking skinfold measures were increasingly implemented (e.g. Wright & Dean, 2007) because overweight and increased body fat were found to be inversely related to physical fitness and were suggested as major risk factors for cardiovascular ill-health and mortality among adults (Boreham & Riddoch, 2001).

During the past two decades, however, the effectiveness of such fitness-oriented testing practices has been the subject of some debate given that there is no evidence to suggest they are effective in stimulating young people to become more active (Cale & Harris, 2002; Trost, 2004). Moreover, fitness testing often is perceived as unpleasant, uncomfortable and embarrassing. The information children generate from scores is largely redundant and even negative in that it can stimulate social comparison of test scores (Cale & Harris, 2009; Hopple & Graham, 1995).

Acknowledging that fitness testing may be problematic on a number of grounds, authors have published guidelines on how fitness testing and monitoring can be implemented in more positive ways (Cale & Harris, 2002; Keating & Silverman, 2004). Hopple and Graham (1995) suggest a need for students to better understand the purpose of the fitness testing. Others point out that students can be stimulated to self-assess their fitness levels (e.g. Castelli & Williams, 2007; Keating, 2003; Welk, 2008). These strategies can act as a basis upon which to design health pedagogies if the aim was simply to monitor and improve students' fitness, however, there are important critiques of fitness-based approaches to health-based PE. Specifically, Trost (2004) suggests that physical fitness is strongly affected by heredity and sports participation outside PE, emphasizing the limited role PE can play in improving physical fitness. A second critique relates to the broad educational remit of PE beyond merely promoting physical fitness. Although the purely fitness-oriented view of health-based PE currently receives rather little support in the research literature, studies in the USA (e.g. Ferguson, Keating, Bridges, Guan & Chen, 2007) and the UK (Alfrey, Cale & Webb, 2012) show that many PE teachers continue to include fitness testing and monitoring in their practice and many US school districts and states collect and monitor fitness test scores.

Increasing PA as the major goal of health-based PE

The first national physical activity guidelines were based on the amount of physical activity required for the development of cardiovascular physical fitness (Boreham & Riddoch, 2001; Fulton, Garg, Galuska, Rattay & Caspersen, 2004). From the 1990s onwards, however, researchers argued that simply transposing adult fitness guidelines onto school-aged children had a negative impact on young people's experiences in physical activity and sport (e.g. Trost, 2004). Several organizations then developed recommendations for appropriate amounts of physical *activity* (PA) rather than focusing on physical *fitness* (Fulton et al., 2004).

In line with these shifts in focus from physical fitness to PA, a well-established and widely recognized group of researchers in the USA began advocating for increased PA levels in PE classes (McKenzie & Lounsbery, 2014; Sallis et al., 2012; Trost & van der Mars, 2009). This was based on growing evidence that health benefits can be accrued very quickly (e.g. decreases in overweight and obesity). In recent publications, Sallis et al. (2012) use the term 'health optimising PE' (HOPE) to refer to PE lessons that keep students active at moderate to vigorous (MVPA) intensity levels for more than 50% of the lesson time, engage all students regardless of physical ability and significantly contribute to students' overall PA levels. Another important HOPE goal is to teach students self-management skills, such as self-monitoring, self-evaluation and self-reinforcements, to further increase overall activity levels (McKenzie et al., 1996).

In accordance with the PA during PE focus, researchers have developed numerous interventions to train teachers to promote the highest possible activity levels in PE lessons. The Sports, Play and Active Recreation for Kids (SPARK) programme is one of the most thoroughly investigated and widely used PE programmes in existence (McKenzie, Sallis & Rosengard, 2009). The SPARK programme consists of lessons with a health-fitness and a motor-sport skill focus. SPARK trainers coach teachers to implement sample units and lessons plans, simultaneously mentoring them to improve class management and instructional skills, increasing children's activity levels. Following SPARK, the Middle School Physical Activity and Nutrition (M-SPAN) intervention similarly focuses on increasing teachers' awareness of the need for active PE, assisting teachers in designing and implementing active PE curricula, and developing teachers' class management and instructional skills (McKenzie et al., 1996; McKenzie et al., 2009). Elementary PE teachers adopting the Child and Adolescent Trial for Cardiovascular Health (CATCH, McKenzie et al., 1996), receive a written PE curriculum (guidebook) and supporting materials (Activity Box), participate in a 6–9 hour training, and on-site consultation at school in alternate weeks at the completion of the training.

When the instructional focus is on increasing activity levels during PE, much can be learned from the way teachers were trained in intervention studies such as SPARK, M-Span and CATCH. Specifically, the results revealed sustainable impacts of the training with many teachers still using the materials provided after the studies ended (e.g. Dowda, Sallis, McKenzie, Rosengard, & Kohl, 2005). One key factor in intervention success was the sustained, on-site support. This addressed the tendency for children's PA levels to return to baseline levels if teachers were not provided with long-term guidance (Dowda et al., 2005; McKenzie et al., 2003). This finding mirrors the wider literature on effective and ineffective teachers' professional development (Clarke & Hollingsworth, 2002).

Despite reported beneficial effects on students' PA levels, scholars also have critiqued these programmes. One source of criticism states that increasing PA during PE will never suffice to improve health. During the past 20 years, numerous studies have assessed PE lessons for their potential to increase PA. For example, PA has been measured using heart rate monitors, pedometers, accelerometers, and through numerous observational systems (e.g. System for Observing Fitness Instruction Time, (SOFIT); McKenzie, Sallis & Nader, 1992). Findings indicated tremendous variability in the number of minutes of PA students accrue as well as in the intensity of in-class PA, depending on a range of factors, including goals and lesson content (Pate, O'Neill & McIver, 2011). Most studies record rather low levels of MVPA in traditional elementary (Cardon, Verstraete, De Clereq & De Bourdeaudhuij, 2004) and secondary lessons with an average MVPA engagement of approximately 10–25 minutes per 30 minute lesson (Aelterman et al., 2012; Fairclough & Stratton, 2005; Slingerland, Ooman & Borghouts, 2011). Although Bassett et al. (2013) suggested that mandatory PE can contribute 23 minutes of MVPA per day, few lessons reach these averages unless the lesson is planned specifically to increase PA. Current evidence suggests that without additional PE instructional time (Haerens, De Bourdeaudhuij, Maes, Cardon & Deforche, 2007; Van Acker et al., 2011), promoting MVPA only during PE will remain an inadequate strategy for enhancing children's health. Thus, PA promotion should be combined with many other strategies throughout the school day to promote adequate PA during school hours.

Other critics express concern about limiting the PE focus to merely promoting active lifestyles. Advocates of highly active PE lessons come mainly from the public health field, suggesting that maximizing PA during PE is needed to combat obesity and chronic diseases. These researchers argue that PE teachers need to prioritize public health goals over all other PE goals (e.g. McKenzie & Lounsbery, 2014; Trost, 2004). They argue the current focus on a wide range of diverse learning outcomes is a reason PE has not made positive impact on public health. In this ongoing debate, advocates for a balanced PE approach (e.g. Ennis, 2011) argue that school-based PE is more than PA and should have a comprehensive educational focus on motor skill, sport, personal and social development as well as PA. Advocates of this perspective point out that some lessons that rank low in PA intensity, may have been of poor quality or simply focused on cognitive and affective goals, long considered central to educational approaches to PE.

Aelterman et al. (2012) and Chow, McKenzie and Louie (2009) showed that different activities and sports produce different activity intensity levels, suggesting that lessons with a predominant focus on increasing intensity levels should prioritize higher MVPA intensity sport activities over those with lower intensities. Thus, one critical question to be addressed when emphasizing MVPA is activity type – should teachers choose a series of Zumba lessons, for example, because students will probably be very active; or lessons in which students work together on dance choreography, provoking thoughtful conversation and reflective decision making, but at a much lower physical activity intensity. Lindsay (2014) points out that other lessons in which students work in stations, read instructions from task cards and keep track of their scores while learning a sport shooting technique might result in submaximal activity levels, but valuable linkages with maths (adding the scores) and reading (instructions for each station) can be made.

Enhancing motor skill development as the major goal for health-based PE

The dominant curriculum model used in PE worldwide is the multi-activity model (Siedentop, Mand & Taggert, 1986). In this model, teachers typically develop direct styles of instruction to teach the techniques of a wide range of sports such as soccer, basketball, gymnastics or athletics in blocks of 4–6 weeks (Curtner-Smith & Sofo, 2004). This sports-based approach to PE, which emphasizes mastery in a certain sport (Jewett, Bain & Ennis, 1995), is not considered optimal in facilitating the realization of health-related goals. Trost (2004), for example, argues that a sports-based approach tends to serve athletically gifted children's needs and interests at the expense of less gifted children who have greater need for regular PA.

Despite the critiques of the multi-activity model, however, researchers are increasingly arguing that the development of motor skills in and through PE should not be overlooked in a health promoting perspective. Children between the ages of 3 and 5 years quickly expand their array of motor skills, and studies have indicated that motor competence is critically sensitive to change until about the age of 12 (Fransen et al., 2014; Gallahue & Donnelly, 2003). In particular, Gallahue, Ozmum and Goodway (2012) point out the development and mastery of fundamental motor skills, including locomotor (e.g. skipping, running, galloping) and object control skills (e.g. throwing, catching, kicking), are essential building blocks for more complex movement and sport skills (e.g. Seefeldt, 1980). Several studies have demonstrated that motor skill development is reciprocally associated with PA (e.g. Stodden et al., 2008). Moreover, although the evidence from experimental, longitudinal or prospective studies is still limited, more authors are suggesting that well-developed fundamental motor skills are a prerequisite to engagement in – and enjoyment of – regular PA for health (Logan, Robinson, Wilson & Lucas, 2012).

Since studies have revealed that fundamental motor skills do not develop naturally through maturational processes or when children engage in free play (Gallahue et al., 2012; Van Beurden et al., 2003), researchers continue to investigate how motor competence is developed through PE programmes, especially for younger aged children (Lubans, Morgan, Cliff, Barnett & Okely,

2010). If the focus is on stimulating motor development, much can be learned from prior structured motor skill intervention studies (e.g. Ericsson & Karlsson, 2014; Goodway, Crowe & Ward, 2003), which have shown that motor delayed children can significantly improve their fundamental motor skills through relatively short structured and organized interventions. Specifically, interventions consisted of relatively short (9 weeks with two 35 minute sessions per week) periods during which children participated in planned movement activities that were developmentally and instructionally appropriate (Gagen & Getchell, 2006). In these studies, fundamental motor skills were learned, practised and reinforced (Goodway & Branta, 2003; Robinson & Goodway, 2009; Valentini & Rudisill, 2004).

In terms of developing health pedagogies, however, there are some important lessons in the current motor development literature. First, the majority of interventions were implemented by researchers themselves (Apache, 2005; Goodway & Branta, 2003; Goodway et al., 2003; Robinson & Goodway, 2009; Valentini & Rudisill, 2004). There is less information supporting motor skill development where limited instructional time and/or novice teachers are included purposefully in the research design. More information also is needed examining the effects of teacher training and teachers' fidelity to the target programme during implementation (Apache, 2005; Logan et al., 2012). In addition, there is some evidence to suggest that PE teachers have limited ability to improve students' motor performance due to limited instructional time (Ennis, 2011; Lounsbery & Coker, 2008). Future researchers should focus on understanding more about the feasibility of asking teachers and educators to influence motor skill development in PE.

Another lesson relates to the dominant focus in existing research in the area of motor development of younger children with delayed motor development patterns. More studies are needed to assess the effectiveness of such approaches for all children, including older and normally motor developed children, who are all participating in PE. Finally, it is currently unclear whether and how existing test batteries (Cools, De Martelaer, Vandaele, Samaey & Andries, 2010) devised to accurately measure motor competence might serve the realization of PE goals. Many issues and concerns that were discussed in regard to fitness testing would also apply to motor skill development (e.g. risks for increased social comparison).

Stimulating autonomous motivation as the major goal of health-based PE

During the past few years, researchers have increasingly argued that PE can promote active and healthy lifestyles when the curriculum consists of personally relevant, interesting and enjoyable activities encouraging young people to develop strong personal interests in sport and PA (Haerens, Kirk, Cardon, De Bourdeaudhuij & Vansteenkiste, 2010; Lindsay, 2014). This perspective is supported by motivation theories such as Self-Determination Theory (Deci & Ryan, 2000; see Chapters 39–44, this volume), suggesting that when students find activities inherently interesting, meaningful and enjoyable, or when these activities hold personal relevance or value, students are more likely to engage in these activities outside PE (Haerens et al., 2010; Haerens, Kirk, Cardon & De Bourdeaudhuiji, 2011; Van de Berghe, Vansteenkiste, Cardon, Kirk & Haerens, 2012). This health-based PE approach prompts physical educators to acquire knowledge and understanding of behavioural (e.g. social cognitive theory) and motivational theories (e.g. Self-Determination Theory), to become the "motivating coach" who promotes young people's lifelong PA engagement (Trost, 2004). In addition to motivational insights and skills, this view also requires teachers to have a sound technical understanding of PA teaching methods and strategies to support different aged students' safe and effective health-related PA participation.

There is an extensive body of research showing that secondary school students learn more and are more active when they enjoy and value the activities offered (e.g. Aelterman et al., 2012; Jaakkola, Liukkonen, Laakso & Ommundsen, 2008; Lonsdale, Sabiston, Raedeke, Ha & Sum, 2009; Xiang's Chapter 40, this volume). The focus on valuing and enjoying PA requires a pedagogical shift, however, from physical, behavioural and motor learning outcomes towards affective and motivational learning outcomes. Thus, fostering students' enjoyment and value of PE requires an alternative approach to be adopted by the teacher when interacting with students. Specifically, whereas an exclusively directive teaching style might be effective for increasing PA or stimulating motor development, it might not be appropriate for achieving affective and cognitive learning outcomes. This is because the latter may require students to accept, endorse and internalize information in the process of coming to know and value the benefits of a physically active life, and to become relatively independent decision-makers (Haerens et al., 2011). Within this philosophy on health-based PE, teachers provide opportunities for students to act and think for themselves in terms of how to choose and organize physical activities that are easily transferable into leisure time (Harris, 2000; Whitehead & Fox, 1983). In addition, teachers clarify expectations and facilitate student learning by prompting students with information on activity-related guidelines and the benefits of an active lifestyle, and providing them with strategies for becoming more active. This approach is not explicitly aimed at eliciting high MVPA levels or maximizing opportunities to develop physical fitness or motor skills. Yet, recent intervention studies in which teachers are trained to incorporate such a motivating approach have documented beneficial effects on students' engagement and skill development during the lesson, and their future PA intentions (e.g. Kirk & Tinning, 1994). Haerens et al. (2011) developed a pedagogical model for health-based PE (HBPE) with the theme of 'valuing and enjoying a physically active lifestyle' as its conceptual foundation, although the model's effectiveness has not yet been tested in traditional multi-activity sports-based settings (Armour & Makopoulou, 2012).

Training teachers in health pedagogies

In the USA, where alarm over increases in the incidence of obesity and diabetes have led to the formulation of new standards by the Society of Health and Physical Education (SHAPE), pre-service and in-service continuing professional development (CPD) programmes for teachers are shifting quickly towards a more health-based approach (Cothran, McCaughtry, Kulinna & Martin, 2006). Yet, in many other countries there is evidence that professional development tends to focus on sport-specific update courses such as games, dance and gymnastics (Armour & Makopoulou, 2012; Armour & Yelling, 2004), with rather less content available on health-based PE. So, as Armour and Harris (2013) and Cothran et al. (2006) suggest, as long as PE teachers lack the content knowledge and pedagogies to deliver health-based PE effectively, it seems unlikely that health aspirations will be realized. This issue becomes even more problematic when PE teachers themselves are not aware of the existing knowledge gaps (e.g. Castelli & Williams, 2007) and therefore see little need to modify their current practices (e.g. Clarke & Hollingsworth, 2002).

To add a further complication, there is evidence that given the diverse ideologies on HBPE and related learning outcomes, many researchers, PE teacher educators and PE teachers are uncertain about the precise nature of HBPE, making it difficult to develop training in health pedagogies (Armour & Makopoulou, 2012; Puhse et al., 2011). There is a wealth of studies proposing designs of effective CPD programmes (for overviews see Kahn et al., 2002; Kriemler et al., 2011; Lonsdale et al., 2013; Parker & Patton's Chapter 30, this volume). Although these studies offer valuable information describing curricula content leading to significant change (e.g. effectively increasing PA during PE, improving fundamental motor skills), there are fewer studies addressing the underlying mechanisms that determine whether teachers adopt effective health pedagogies after engaging in a CPD programme. Studies conducted in the USA have demonstrated that 'top down' implementation of predefined health-related curricula tends to fail when long-term guidance is lacking. This may be due to the fact that teachers are overwhelmed by the amount of information and the imposed changes conflict with the teachers' school context and their current beliefs about effective PE (Cothran et al., 2006). These findings correspond to findings in the wider CPD literature shifting a focus on change as something that is done to teachers who are relatively passive participants to change as a complex process that involves teachers' active learning through reflective participation in training and practice (e.g. Clarke & Hollingsworth, 2002).

For CPD training to be effective, teachers must be offered time and support to analyse different forms of health-related PE, taking into account their beliefs and context needs (Deglau & O'Sullivan, 2006). They also need practice-relevant ideas with clear benefits for their personal practice (Armour & Yelling, 2004, 2007; Guskey, 2002; O'Sullivan & Deglau, 2006). Specifically, when CPD guides in-service teachers in developing and health-based PE, teachers can experience what works in their specific context, and develop confidence to implement different forms of health-based PE (see Deglau & O'Sullivan, 2006 for an example). Teachers then also need continuous follow-up support and guidance on strategies to integrate new information with their existing knowledge and current curriculum (Cothran et al., 2006; Dowda et al., 2005; McKenzie et al., 2003). By stimulating (self-)reflection (e.g. Reason & Bradbury, 2008) throughout this process, teachers can gradually discover which perspectives and approaches align with their personal convictions and current practice, and can iteratively refine their approaches through a process of enacting and reflecting (Clarke & Hollingsworth, 2002). For example, Deglau and O'Sullivan (2006) showed how an approach involving a 15 month programme including eight workshops, several debriefing sessions and more than 126 contact hours resulted in effective changes to practice. Teachers in this study demonstrated a willingness to implement new curricula, share new innovations and ideas with others, and contribute to the implementation of innovations in their broader professional community.

Future directions

Current validations of different approaches to health-based PE through research are predominantly situated at the pupil level (e.g. improved motor competencies, increased activity levels). More research is needed regarding possible mechanisms that determine the effectiveness of health-based PE training at the teacher level (e.g. teaching practices, beliefs). This corresponds to the suggestions made by Kriemler et al. (2011) and Lonsdale and colleagues (2013), who argue that in future research there is a need for more transparent reporting of intervention strategies and CPD organization. To illustrate with just one of many examples, Van Beurden et al. (2003) conducted an intervention that aimed at enhancing motor skill development while at the same time obtaining high activity levels during PE. In their study, they mention that their intervention incorporated professional development for teachers by means of four workshops, but apart from a general description of what these workshops were about, it remains unclear how the intervention was delivered to the teachers, and which strategies could explain the changes teachers made to their way of teaching. To address this omission, it would be preferable for future studies to be embedded in the wider professional development literature (e.g. Clarke & Hollingsworth, 2002), so that teacher change and an understanding of the likely mechanisms that brought about the change are studied more systematically.

There also is a strong need to involve teachers themselves in the development and optimization of teacher training, not only in terms of content (e.g. developing realistic and sound practical examples), but also delivery methods (Aelterman et al., 2013). Through involving teachers in health-based PE CPD development, teachers themselves can become the social agents who help train other professionals in the field (Clarke & Hollingsworth, 2002; Deglau & O'Sullivan, 2006).

Summary of key findings: overarching and shared views

Debates are ongoing about which types of programmes are effective in promoting health, and which should be disseminated on a larger scale (e.g. Canadas, Veiga & Martinez-Gomez, 2014). Interestingly, many public health advocates share a view of what HBPE is *not* about. One message that comes across very clearly is that the mixing of health goals with the dominant goals of sport-based, multi-activity PE programmes risks undermining sustained implementation of any health-based initiative. There is little evidence to suggest that PE students can learn health-related goals in a sport-specific skills and mastery-oriented activity-based approach (Jewett et al., 1995).

There are also several shared ideas across each of the presented views on HBPE.

- The ultimate goals of and rationale for HBPE in each of the described approaches all relate to increasing young people's engagement in sport and physical activity for enhanced health outside PE.
- Health pedagogies require an interdisciplinary and developmental approach, which, in turn, requires the provision of new training for both pre-service and in-service teachers. Such training would need to develop broader perspectives on the relationships between physical fitness, PA, motor development and health, along with insights into social, psychological and behavioural theories that are prominent in health promotion.
- Moreover, a change in teachers' philosophies about teaching and learning in PE would be required, from a disciplinary mastery orientation towards an integration of self-actualization and social reconstruction orientations (Harris, 2000; Jewett et al., 1995).
- Indeed, shared pedagogical approaches across the four health-based PE perspectives involves students' self-assessing and monitoring their progress in situations where positive experiences are reinforced and the use of social comparisons is avoided.
- Literature revealed that effective change requires considerable additional PE teacher training that is sustained. Further, in-service training needs to encourage teachers' participation, input, testing and implementation of different forms of health-based PE.

Reflective questions for discussion

(Imagine) You are a physical education teacher in secondary school …

- In what sense do you think you have a role to play in stimulating and motivating your pupils to remain or become active *beyond the context of the PE lesson*?
- Think about a typical lesson you delivered during the past month.
  - Think about the goals and the concrete learning activities. Do they align with one or more of the four perspectives on health-based PE? Can you think of two strengths and two criticisms of the approach you have taken?
  - Could you redesign the activity in light of a different health-based approach?

- In what sense would you change your goals?
- How would you then change your activities? Can you think of two concrete adaptations you would make (e.g. how could you include self-assessment, facilitate positive experiences, avoid social comparison)?
- How would you change your instructions and feedback? On what would you focus?
- What do you think the community of PE teachers needs to implement health-related PE effectively? As a professional, what role could you play to support the profession in meeting these needs?
- What are the barriers to implementing health-based PE in schools in your area?
- What opportunities do PE teachers have to expand their role to provide health-based leadership to all members of their school community?
- What learning theories have been prevalent in health-based PE programmes? As you anticipate the future, in what ways can new approaches to HBPE expand students' understanding of PA and assist them to be more physically active outside of schools?

References

Adam, C., Klissouras, V., Ravazollo, M., Renson, R. & Tuxworth, W. (1988). *European test of physical fitness*. Rome, Council of Europe, Committee for the Development of Sport.

Aelterman, N., Vansteenkiste, M., Van Keer, H., De Meyer, J., Van De Berghe, L. & Haerens, L. (2013). Development and evaluation of a training on need-supportive teaching in physical education: Qualitative and quantitative findings. *Teaching and Teacher Education, 29*, 64–75.

Aelterman, N., Vansteenkiste, M., Van Keer, H., Van De Berghe, L., De Meyer, J. & Haerens, L. (2012). Students' objectively measured physical activity levels and engagement as a function of between-class and between-student differences in motivation towards physical education. *Journal of Sport and Exercise Psychology, 34*(4), 457–480.

Alfrey, L., Cale, L. & Webb, L. A. (2012). Physical education teachers' continuing professional development in health-related exercise. *Physical Education and Sport Pedagogy, 17*(5), 477–491.

Apache, R. R. G. (2005). Activity-based intervention in motor skill development. *Perceptual and Motor Skills, 100*(3), 1011–1020.

Armour, K., & Harris, J. (2013). Making the case for developing new PE-for-health pedagogies. *Quest, 65*(2), 201–219.

Armour, K. M., & Makopoulou, K. (2012). Great expectations: Teacher learning in a national professional development programme. *Teaching and Teacher Education, 28*(3), 336–346.

Armour, K. M., & Yelling, M. (2004). Professional 'development' and professional 'learning': Bridging the gap for experienced PE teachers. *European Physical Education Review, 10*, 71–93.

Armour, K. M., & Yelling, M. (2007). Effective professional development for physical education teachers: The role of informal, collaborative learning. *Journal of Teaching in Physical Education, 26*(2), 177–200.

Bailey, R., Armour, K., Kirk, D., Jess, M., Pickup, I. & Sandford, R. (2009). The educational benefits claimed for physical education and school sport: An academic review. *Research Papers in Education, 24*(1), 1–27.

Bassett, D. R., Fitzhugh, E. C., Heath, G. W., Erwin, P. C., Frederick, G. M., Wolff, D. L., Welch, W. A. & Stout, A. B. (2013). Estimated energy expenditures for school-based policies and active living. *American Journal of Preventive Medicine, 44*(2), 108–113.

Boreham, C., & Riddoch, C. (2001). The physical activity, fitness and health of children. *Journal of Sports Sciences, 19*(12), 915–929.

Cale, L., & Harris, J. (2002). National fitness testing for children – issues, concerns and alternatives. *The British Journal of Teaching Physical Education, 33*(1), 32–34.

Cale, L., & Harris, J. (2009). Fitness testing in physical education: A misdirected effort in promoting healthy lifestyles and physical activity? *Physical Education and Sport Pedagogy, 14*(1), 89–108.

Canadas, L., Veiga, O. L. & Martinez-Gomez, D. (2014). Enhancing public health through physical education in Spain: A call to action. *Gaceta Sanitaria, 28*(5), 432–433.

Cardon, G., Verstraete, S., De Clereq, D. & De Bourdeaudhuij, I. (2004). Physical activity levels in elementary-school physical education: A comparison of swimming and nonswimming classes. *Journal of Teaching in Physical Education, 23*(3), 252–263.

Castelli, D., & Williams, L. (2007). Health-related fitness and PE teachers' content knowledge. *Journal of Teaching in PE, 26*(1), 3–19.

Chow, B. C., McKenzie, T. L. & Louie, L. (2009). Physical activity and environmental influences during secondary school physical education. *Journal of Teaching in Physical Education, 28*(1), 21–37.

Clarke, D., & Hollingsworth, H. (2002). Elaborating a model of teacher professional growth. *Teaching and Teacher Education, 18*, 947–967.

Cools, W., De Martelaer, K., Vandaele, B., Samaey, C. & Andries, C. (2010). Assessment of movement skill performance in preschool children: Convergent validity between MOT 4–6 and M-ABC. *Journal of Sports Science and Medicine, 9*(4), 597–604.

Cothran, D. J., McCaughtry, N., Kulinna, P. H. & Martin, J. (2006). Top-down public health curricular change: The experience of physical education teachers in the United States. *Journal of Teaching in Physical Education, 32*(4), 533–547.

Curtner-Smith, M. D., & Sofo, S. (2004). Preservice teachers' conceptions of teaching within sport education and multi-activity units. *Sport Education and Society, 9*(3), 347–377.

Deci, E. L., & Ryan, R. M. (2000). The 'what' and 'why' of goal pursuits: Human needs and the self-determination of behavior. *Psychological Inquiry, 11*(4), 227–268.

Deglau, D., & O'Sullivan, M. (2006). The effects of a long-term professional development program on the beliefs and practices of experienced teachers. *Journal of Teaching in Physical Education, 25*, 379–396.

Dowda, M., Sallis, J. F., McKenzie, T. L., Rosengard, P. & Kohl, H. W. (2005). Evaluating the sustainability of SPARK physical education: A case study of translating research into practice. *Research Quarterly for Exercise and Sport, 76*(1), 11–19.

Ennis, C. D. (2011). Physical education curriculum priorities: Evidence for education and skillfulness. *Quest, 63*(1), 5–18.

Ericsson, I., & Karlsson, M. (2014). Motor skills and school performance in children with daily physical education in school: A 9-year intervention study. *Scandinavian Journal of Medicine & Science in Sports, 24*(2), 273–278.

Fairclough, S., & Stratton, G. (2005). 'PE makes you fit and healthy'. Physical Education's contribution to young people's physical activity levels. *Health Education Research, 20*(1), 14–23.

Ferguson, R. H., Keating, X. F. D., Bridges, D. M., Guan, J. M. & Chen, L. (2007). California secondary school physical education teachers' attitudes toward the mandated use of the Fitnessgram. *Journal of Teaching in Physical Education, 26*(2), 161–176.

Fransen, J., Deprez, D., Pion, J., Tallir, I. B., D'hondt, E., Vaeyens, R., Lenoir, M. & Philippaerts, R. M. (2014). Changes in physical fitness and sports participation among children with different levels of motor competence: A 2-year longitudinal study. *Pediatric Exercise Science, 26*(1), 11–21.

Fulton, J. E., Garg, M., Galuska, D. A., Rattay, K. T. & Caspersen, C. J. (2004). Public health and clinical recommendations for physical activity and physical fitness: Special focus on overweight youth. *Sports Medicine, 34*(9), 581–599.

Gagen, L. M., & Getchell, N. (2006). Using 'constraints' to design developmentally appropriate movement activity for early childhood education. *Research Quarterly for Exercise and Sport, 74*, 36–47.

Gallahue, D. L., & Donnelly, F. C. (2003). *Developmental physical education for all children* (4th edn). Champaign, IL: Human Kinetics.

Gallahue, D. L., Ozmum, J. C. & Goodway, J. D. (2012). *Understanding motor development: Infants, children, adolescents, adults* (7th edn). New York: McGraw-Hill Companies, Inc.

Goodway, J. D., & Branta, C. F. (2003). Influence of a motor skill intervention on fundamental motor skill development of disadvantaged preschool children. *Research Quarterly for Exercise and Sport, 74*(1), 36–46.

Goodway, J. D., Crowe, H. & Ward, P. (2003). Effects of motor skill instruction on fundamental motor skill development. *Adapted Physical Activity Quarterly, 20*(3), 298–314.

Guskey, T. R. (2002). Professional development and teacher change. *Teachers and Teaching: Theory and Practice, 8*, 381–391.

Haerens, L., De Bourdeaudhuij, I., Maes, L., Cardon, G. & Deforche, B. (2007). School-based randomized controlled trial of a physical activity intervention among adolescents. *Journal of Adolescent Health, 40*(3), 258–265.

Haerens, L., Kirk, D., Cardon, G. & De Bourdeaudhuij, I. (2011). Toward the development of a pedagogical model for health-based physical education. *Quest, 63*(3), 321–338.

Haerens, L., Kirk, D., Cardon, G., De Bourdeaudhuij, I. & Vansteenkiste, M. (2010). Motivational profiles for secondary school physical education and its relationship to the adoption of a physically active lifestyle among university students. *European Physical Education Review, 16*(2), 117–139.

Harris, J. (2000). *Health-related exercise in the national curriculum: Key Stage 1 to 4.* Champaign, IL: Human Kinetics.

Hopple, C., & Graham, G. (1995). What children think, feel, and know about physical-fitness testing. *Journal of Teaching in Physical Education, 14*(4), 408–417.

Jaakkola, T., Liukkonen, J., Laakso, T. & Ommundsen, Y. (2008). The relationship between situational and contextual self-determined motivation and physical activity intensity as measured by heart rates during ninth grade students' physical education classes. *European Physical Education Review, 14*(1), 13–31.

Jewett, A., Bain, L. & Ennis, C. D. (1995). *The curriculum process in physical education.* Dubuque, IA: Brown & Benchmark.

Kahn, E. B., Ramsey, L. T., Brownson, R. C., Heath, G. W., Howze, E. H., Powell, K. E., Stone, E. J., Rajab, M. W., Corso, P. & Briss, P. A. (2002). The effectiveness of interventions to increase physical activity: A systematic review. *American Journal of Preventive Medicine, 22*(4), 73–108.

Keating, X. F. D. (2003). The current often implemented fitness tests in physical education programs: Problems and future directions. *Quest, 55*(2), 141–160.

Keating, X. F. D., & Silverman, S. (2004). Teachers' use of fitness tests in school-based physical education programs. *Measurement in Physical Education and Exercise Science, 8,* 145–165.

Kirk, D. (1991). Daily physical education research: A review and critique. *Daily physical education: Collected papers on health based physical education in Australia.* Geelong. Australia: Deakin University Press.

Kirk, D., & Tinning, R. (1994). Embodied self-identity, healthy life-styles and school physical-education. *Sociology of Health & Illness, 16*(5), 600–625.

Kriemler, S., Meyer, U., Martin, E., Van Sluijs, E. M. F., Andersen, L. B. & Martin, B. W. (2011). Effect of school-based interventions on physical activity and fitness in children and adolescents: A review of reviews and systematic update. *British Journal of Sports Medicine, 45*(11), 923–930.

Lindsay, E. L. (2014). Effective teaching in physical education: The view from a variety of trenches. *Research Quarterly for Exercise and Sport, 85*(1), 31–37.

Logan, S., Robinson, L., Wilson, A. & Lucas, W. (2012). Getting the fundamentals of movement: A meta-analysis of the effectiveness of motor skill interventions in children. *Child Care Health and Development, 38*(3), 305–315.

Lonsdale, C., Rosenkranz, R. R., Peralta, L. R., Bennie, A., Fahey, P. & Lubans, D. R. (2013). A systematic review and meta-analysis of interventions designed to increase moderate-to-vigorous physical activity in school physical education lessons. *Preventive Medicine, 56*(2), 152–161.

Lonsdale, C., Sabiston, C. M., Raedeke, T. D., Ha, A. S. C. & Sum, R. K. W. (2009). Self-determined motivation and students' physical activity during structured physical education lessons and free choice periods. *Preventive Medicine, 48*(1), 69–73.

Lounsbery, M., & Coker, C. (2008). Developing skill-analysis competency in physical education teachers. *Quest, 60*(2), 255–267.

Lubans, D. R., Morgan, P. J., Cliff, D. P., Barnett, L. M. & Okely, A. D. (2010). Fundamental movement skills in children and adolescents: A review of associated health benefits. *Sports Medicine, 40*(12), 1019–1035.

McKenzie, T. L., Li, D. L., Derby, C. A., Webber, L. S., Luepker, R. V. & Cribb, P. (2003). Maintenance of effects of the CATCH physical education program: Results from the CATCH-ON Study. *Health Education & Behavior, 30*(4), 447–462.

McKenzie, T. L., & Lounsbery, M. A. (2014). The pill not taken: Revisiting physical education teacher effectiveness in a public health context. *Research Quarterly for Exercise and Sport, 85*(3), 287–292.

McKenzie, T. L., Nader, P. R., Strikemiller, P. K., Yang, M. H., Stone, E. J., Perry, C. L., Taylor, W. C., Epping, J. N., Feldman, H. A., Luepker, R. V. & Kelder, S. H. (1996). School physical education: Effect of the child and adolescent trial for cardiovascular health. *Preventive Medicine, 25*(4), 423–431.

McKenzie, T. L., Sallis, J. F. & Nader, P. R. (1992). SOFIT – System for Observing Fitness Instruction Time. *Journal of Teaching in Physical Education, 11*(2), 195–205.

McKenzie, T. L., Sallis, J. F. & Rosengard, P. (2009). Beyond the stucco tower: Design, development, and dissemination of the SPARK physical education programs. *Quest, 61*(1), 114–127.

National Association for Sport and Physical Education [NASPE]. (1995). *Moving into the future: National Standards for Physical Education.* Reston, VA: NASPE.

O'Sullivan, M., & Deglau, D. (2006). Chapter 7: Principles of professional development. *Journal of Teaching in Physical Education, 25*(4), 441–449.

Pate, R. R., & Hohn, R. C. (1994). A contemporary mission for physical education. In R. R. Pate & R. C. Hohn (Eds.), *Health and fitness through physical education.* Champaign, IL: Human Kinetics.

Pate, R. R., O'Neill, J. R. & McIver, K. L. (2011). Physical activity and health: Does physical education matter? *Quest, 63*(1), 19–35.

Puhse, U., Barker, D., Brettschneider, W. D., Feldmeth, A. K., Gerlach, E., McCuaig, L., McKenzie, T. L. & Gerber, M. (2011). International approaches to health-oriented physical education: Local health debates and differing conceptions of health. *International Journal of Physical Education, 3*, 2–15.

Reason, P., & Bradbury, H. (2008). *The Sage handbook of action research: Participative inquiry and practice.* Thousand Oaks, CA: Sage.

Robinson, L. E., & Goodway, J. D. (2009). Instructional climates in preschool children who are at-risk. Part I: Object-control skill development. *Research Quarterly for Exercise and Sport, 80*(3), 533–542.

Sallis, J. F., McKenzie, T. L., Beets, M. W., Beighle, A., Erwin, H. & Lee, S. (2012). Physical education's role in public health: Steps forward and backward over 20 years and hope for the future. *Research Quarterly for Exercise and Sport, 83*(2), 125–135.

Seefeldt, V. (1980). Developmental motor patterns: Implications for elementary physical education. In G. Roberts & D. Landers (Eds.), *Psychology of motor behavior and sport* (pp. 314–323). Champaign, IL: Human Kinetics.

Siedentop, D., Mand, C. & Taggart, A. (1986). *Physical education teaching and curriculum strategies for grades 5–12.* Palo Alto, CA: Mayfield.

Slingerland, M., Ooman, J. & Borghouts, L. (2011). Physical activity levels during Dutch primary and secondary school physical education. *Journal of Physical Activity & Health, 6*, 866–878.

Stodden, D. F., Goodway, J. D., Langendorfer, S. J., Roberton, M. A., Rudisill, M. E., Garcia, C. & Garcia, L. E. (2008). A developmental perspective on the role of motor skill competence in physical activity: An emergent relationship. *Quest, 60*(2), 290–306.

Tinning, R., & Kirk, D. (1991). *Daily physical education: Collected papers on health based PE in Australia.* Geelong, Australia: Deakin University Press.

Trost, S. G. (2004). School physical education in the post-report era: An analysis from public health. *Journal of Teaching in Physical Education, 23*(4), 318–337.

Trost, S. G., & van der Mars, H. (2009). Why we should not cut physical education. *Educational Leadership, 67*(4), 60–65.

Valentini, N. C., & Rudisill, M. E. (2004). An inclusive mastery climate intervention and the motor skill development of children with and without disabilities. *Adapted Physical Activity Quarterly, 21*(330), 347.

Van Acker, R., De Bourdeaudhuij, I., De Martelaer, K., Seghers, J., Kirk, D., Haerens, L., De Cocker, K. & Cardon, G. (2011). A framework for physical activity programs within school-community partnerships. *Quest, 63*(3), 300–320.

Van Beurden, E., Barnett, L. M., Zask, A., Dietrich, U. C., Brooks, L. O. & Beard, J. (2003). Can we skill and activate children through primary school physical education lessons? 'Move it Groove it': A collaborative health promotion intervention. *Preventive Medicine, 36*(4), 493–501.

Van Den Berghe, L., Vansteenkiste, M., Cardon, G., Kirk, D. & Haerens, L. (2012). Research on self-determination in physical education: Key findings and proposals for future research. *Physical Education and Sport Pedagogy, 19*(1), 97–121.

Welk, G. J. (2008). The role of physical activity assessments for school-based physical activity promotion. *Measurement in Physical Education and Exercise Science, 12*, 184–206.

Whitehead, J., & Fox, K. (1983). Student centred physical education. *Bulletin of Physical Education, 19*(2), 21–30.

Wright, J., & Dean, R. (2007). A balancing act. Problematising prescriptions about food and weight in school health texts. *Journal of Didactics and Educational Policy, 16*(2), 75–94.

32

EDUCATING TEACHERS FOR EFFECTIVE INCLUSIVE PEDAGOGIES

Kyriaki Makopoulou & Gary Thomas,

UNIVERSITY OF BIRMINGHAM, UK

Several authors in this volume (see the Adapted Physical Activity part in this volume) have discussed some of the possibilities and challenges in adapted physical education. In this chapter, the focus shifts towards the notion of inclusion which in recent years has become an important aspect of educational policies internationally (United Nations Educational, Scientific and Cultural Organization [UNESCO], 2013; see also Chapter 17 by Lieberman & Block, this volume). Inclusive education differs from previously held notions of 'integration' and 'mainstreaming', which tended to be concerned principally with 'special educational needs' and implied learners changing or becoming 'ready for' accommodation by the mainstream. By contrast, the term 'inclusive education' now acknowledges the importance of equal access and equal opportunities for all (not just those with Special Educational Needs and Disabilities – SEND). It is about rejecting segregation or exclusion of learners for whatever reason – ability, gender, language, care status, family income, disability, sexuality, colour, religion, or ethnic origin. It also encourages the modification of the environment (i.e. the structure, organisation, learning, curriculum, and assessment practices of schools) so that diverse learning needs can be met, whatever the origin or nature of those needs.

Inclusion is about the child's right to participate and the school's duty to accept by making learning more meaningful and relevant for all, particularly those learners most vulnerable to exclusionary pressures. Inclusion is based on "a paradigm shift from a deficit model of disability to one of social/human rights" (Rieser, 2013, p. 1). It is considered a pathway to mitigate the negative effects of poverty, social, racial, ethnic inequalities, and cultural disintegration (UNESCO, 2008). It is thus underpinned by a strong social agenda. Educating young people about the value of learning (and living) with others and understanding that diversity is a resource and asset to their educational and life experiences is paramount (European Agency for Development in Special Needs Education [EADSNE], 2012). The notion of inclusion has therefore clear implications for how teachers teach (and how and what teachers learn), with inclusive pedagogies being the foundation of effective teaching and learning.

The purpose of this chapter is to examine how teachers can be educated to adopt effective inclusive pedagogies that meet the diverse needs of the student population. Some of the challenges and barriers encountered will be discussed and possibilities for future teacher education programmes will be considered. The chapter begins with an historical overview of how our understanding of inclusion has changed over time. We then present the principles of effective inclusive teaching followed by an analysis of the literature on the nature and quality of existing initial teacher education (ITE) and Continuing Professional Development (CPD) programmes. We will then consider the implications for evidence-based practice by drawing upon a national CPD programme on inclusive Physical Education (PE) in England and conclude with points for future research and practice on inclusive education.

Historical overview

Inclusive education emerged out of 'special' education. The establishment of special schools in the nineteenth century and before was based on an instinct to expect and to identify difference and disability and occurred simultaneously with the growth of the eugenic and psychometric movements which focused on the systematic medicalisation of the body and mind (Hodkinson, 2012; see also chapters 14 & 16 by Eliane Mauerberg-deCosta et al., this volume). These 'sciences' gave the logical foundations and practical tools for educators to establish the quality of every student and to make decisions about who would be part of, and who would be separated from, the mainstream education provision. However, after the Second World War, such mechanisms began to lose credibility as educators began to think more deeply about the effects of separation, including the devaluing of the separated minority.

The 1960s saw the rise of the Civil Rights movement, initially concerned mainly with 'race' and subsequently expanded to other groups that experienced discrimination, segregation, and oppression. In the 1970s and 1980s, as a result of the heightened importance of social justice internationally, action was being demanded to eliminate exclusion and segregation (Thomas, 2013). Within this anti-discriminatory climate, parents/carers of students educated in special schools began to challenge the decisions of authorities and professionals; and there was subsequently a clear move towards their placement into mainstream schools (Nepi, Fioravanti, Nannini, & Peru, 2015). In England, this was legitimatised by the 1978 Warnock Report and the subsequent 1981 Education Act. In the US, major changes in inclusive education took place during the 1960s during which period the foundations for developing a positive learning environment and access to effective education for disabled students were laid (United States Department of Education [USDE], 2008).

Significant developments in educational theory, such as the resurgence of interest in progressive education, also contributed to the realisation that the notion of (dis)ability and its relationship to achievement should be challenged. More specifically, arguments that success or failure at school were *constructed* rather than *within-child* led educators to question beliefs about the crystal-hard relationship that had been assumed to exist between ability and achievement. Academics over several decades (e.g. Coles, 1997, Rouse, 2007) have argued that children fall behind at school for a host of reasons, most of them having little or nothing to do with 'dysfunctions' in the workings of their brains. Based on socio-cultural understanding of learning, the notion of inclusion therefore "promotes a view of human difference as an aspect of every person, rather than something that characterises or differentiates some learners from others" (Rouse & Florian, 2012, p. i). Consequently, it is not 'diagnosis' and separate treatment that are important for success in schools, but rather the existence of the *right conditions for learning*.

There have been several reports that emphasise this point. Articulations of these new developments in ways of thinking, in policy and in law include: The UN *Convention on the Rights of the Child* which in 1989 set out children's rights in respect of freedom from discrimination and in respect of the representation of their wishes and views; and the UNESCO Salamanca Statement (1994) which called on all governments to give the highest priority to inclusive education. The Human Rights Act passed in 1998 contained an anti-discrimination article and brought the European Convention on Human Rights into UK legislation. British courts must now adhere to the convention. The Disability Discrimination Act (1995) also contained provisions to ensure that disabled pupils are not treated less favourably than other pupils. In the US, the Individuals with Disabilities Education Improvement (*IDEA*) Federal Law stated that children with disabilities have the right to be educated in the Least Restrictive Environment (LRE) (i.e. a child's school placement must be as close as possible to the child's home and the child is educated in the school he or she would attend if not disabled). Under IDEA and other related laws, the need for quality teachers was recognised to ensure the appropriate education of children with disabilities.

However, in spite of a number of progressive changes in legislation, achieving inclusion and reducing underachievement continues to be one of the biggest problems faced by schools across Europe (EADSNE, 2010). Whilst there is very little robust evidence on the effects of inclusion on the achievement of pupils with diverse needs (Nepi et al., 2015), concerns have been raised that SEND children (in England) are still vulnerable to exclusion from the culture, curriculum, and community of mainstream schools (Runswick-Cole, 2011). In this context, there are strong voices questioning the extent to which inclusion is a 'sound educational practice' for everyone (Hodkinson, 2012). Their arguments have rested principally on the "impracticability of inclusion, its ideological or values-based provenance, and the pedagogic and social benefits of special education" (Hick & Thomas, 2008, p. xxii).

The maintenance of exclusionary practices, if and when applicable can be partly explained by examining the impact of other political, educational, and socio-economic influences on school systems (Bourke, 2009). Naraian, Ferguson, and Thomas (2012) argued that the policy of inclusion is fundamentally incompatible with the marketisation of education and the standards-driven, outcomes-based philosophy that underpins much of educational endeavours in recent years. In the context of competitive, selective, and socially divisive policies (Hick & Thomas, 2008), the future of schools is determined to a large extent by how well their students perform in standardised tests. In the US, for example, the 2001 federal No Child Left Behind Act demanded that *all* students demonstrate proficiency in reading and mathematics by 2014 (Naraian et al., 2012). This example provides a clear illustration of the 'framework of exceptionality' (Hick & Thomas, 2008) in which teachers and schools find themselves. Similar targets dominate the UK educational system and it has been argued that in this environment, it is often the case that SEND children are viewed as "inefficient consumers of scarce resources" (Goodley & McLaughlin, 2011, p. 5). But there also are concerns about the prevailing stereotypes about the presence, participation, and achievement of other groups of learners that appear to reflect and perpetuate deficit-orientated explanations of failure.

Research suggests that the relationship between school performance and deprivation is so close that the two variables appear to be simply alternative measures of the same thing (Blane, White, & Morris, 1996). It also seems that learners from minority ethnic communities have long been disproportionately targeted by special education (Hick & Thomas, 2008). In this context, institutional racism has become a widely recognised concept in the UK, and in a government commissioned report, it was acknowledged that persisting inequalities take new forms:

> Whilst overt racism (at least on the part of staff) is now unusual in schools, discrimination against the grandchildren and great grandchildren of the early Black migrants persists in the form of culturally unrepresentative curricula and low expectations of attainment and behaviour on the part of staff. (Department for Education and Skills [DfES], 2006, p. 3)

Riehl (2000) presented compelling evidence demonstrating that "the challenges and opportunities posed by diversity are growing" (p. 57). So, this issue is complex and questions remain about the means by which effective inclusive education can be achieved in practice (Runswick-Cole, 2011). There are many and varied ways of helping to develop more inclusive practices in education and physical education and the following section looks at some of these in an attempt to answer questions about what schools and teachers can do to offer a truly inclusive education experience to all young people.

Theoretical framework

As pupils arrive in schools from different backgrounds, and with different prior experiences, needs, (dis)abilities, and aspirations, the key challenge for schools and teachers is to provide a coordinated, informed, and tailored support to students who differ in important ways (Dyson, Howes, & Roberts, 2002). The issue of inclusion necessitates school-level action. Research suggests that schools which have an inclusive, participatory culture display a number of consistent characteristics (Winter & O'Raw, 2010). However, no matter how inclusive schools might think they are, they all need to engage in ongoing critical reflection about their ethos, forms of organisation, curriculum, and teaching/learning/assessment practices to ensure that, within an ever-evolving student population, barriers are removed. To this end, the Index of Inclusion (Booth & Ainscow, 2002) was developed with the aim to support the inclusive development of schools. Although there is a large body of literature on school organisation around inclusion (e.g. EADSNE, 2004), because of limited space, this section focuses on the central principles of teaching and learning with the intention of offering practitioners a framework of thinking about effective inclusive pedagogy.

Research designed to explore questions about teaching and learning for inclusion is relatively scarce. However, the available evidence seems to point towards some key principles that reflect a powerful and reflective pedagogy that has been developing over the last 100 years (Hartley, 2009). John Dewey, an influential American educational philosopher in the first half of the twentieth century, argued that pupils should participate actively in decisions that affect their learning. For Dewey, "the child is the starting point, the centre, and the end" (cited in Flanagan, 1994, p. 4). Likewise, the fundamental argument underpinning the 'child-centred' educational philosophy of the 1960s was that education should "start with the needs of the child" (Hartley, 2009, p. 427). Since these early elaborations, the development of pedagogical approaches grounded in constructivist and socio-cultural perspectives of learning (e.g. cooperative, reciprocal learning, learning communities) enable young people to 'learn together rather than separately' (Dyson et al., 2002) and to be involved in their own education in a meaningful way.

A persistent theme in making inclusive learning a reality in schools is pupil choice (and pupil voice). Offering pupils opportunities to *choose* what, how, and where they learn represents a fundamental step towards a truly inclusive pedagogical approach. In this case, reflecting existing rhetoric about the importance of personalising learning, students are not consumers but co-creators of their educational experiences (Makopoulou, 2011). This requires that teachers engage in dialogue with learners and their families in order to understand and respect their diversities and to "jointly create suitable and attainable conditions for achieving relevant and pertinent learning opportunities" (UNESCO, 2008, p. 11).

Separate programmes should also be viewed with scepticism. Offering separate instruction and promoting individual work (with a learning support assistant) locates those students who are perceived to be lagging behind at the margins of the classroom (Florian & Black-Hawkins, 2011). In sharp contrast, a key element of an inclusive learning environment is "not the individualisation but the diversification of the educational provision" (Blanco, 2009, p. 11). Learner diversity needs to be thoroughly understood and considered in the planning phase, instead of taking a 'one size fits all' approach 'on the basis of an average student' only to then subsequently "carry out individualised actions to respond to the needs of specific students" (Blanco, 2009, p. 14). Inclusive pedagogy therefore means that teachers "extend what is ordinarily available" and "reduce the need to mark some learners as different" (Florian & Black-Hawkins, 2011, p. 826).

In the US, IDEA (federal law) supported the provision of 'culturally relevant instruction' for diverse learners in regular classroom environments, which revolved around the following principles (USDE, 2008, p. 41):

- linking assessments of student progress directly to the instructional curricula rather than abstract norms to standardised tests;
- creating classroom environments that reflect different cultural heritages and accommodate different styles of communication and learning;
- developing and implementing family-friendly practices to establish collaborative partnerships with parents/carers.

Similar questions about the effective inclusion of all learners seem to have troubled PE academics and teachers over a number of years. The debate began in the 1960s when it was recognised that students vary in *physical ability* for a host of reasons and that teaching the 'correct' technique based on a 'model in teacher's mind' is neither achievable nor appropriate: "A technique suitable for one may be limiting for another with different physical or mental attributes" (Knapp, 1964, p. 14). Knapp (1964) suggested that effective instruction should rather build upon the interests and abilities of each individual. Given the time of its publication, this radical and progressive proposition problematised taken-for-granted normative practices that continue to enforce a 'constitutional divide' between 'perfected naturalised humanity' and the 'imperfect bodies' (Campbell, 2009) who fail to perform according to pre-determined standards.

Since then, the 'struggle' to meet and support learners' diverse needs in PE settings has been embedded – albeit not always explicitly – in a range of topical publications. The most striking example of an expanded view of PE pedagogy is the US-based 'Spectrum of teaching styles'. Introduced by Mosston over 40 years ago and further developed by Mosston and Ashworth (2010) over the decades, the spectrum is testimony to the substantial consensus of PE experts that teachers must draw upon a range of teaching styles (demonstrating 'mobility ability') to respond in a personalised way to learners' diversities. Within the spectrum, the inclusion teaching style (where teachers present learners with different entry points) highlights the importance of giving students choice over what and how they learn. In this way, learners are self-regulated and learning is viewed as "something they do for themselves rather than as something that is done to or for them" (Mosston & Ashworth, 2010).

The 'inclusion spectrum', developed by Ken Black and Pam Stevenson in the UK, offers another theoretical and practical framework for enhancing learning experiences and outcomes for all. More specifically, it is predicated that all pupils will be included and challenged to progress in their learning if and when their teachers differentiate activities by Space, Task, Equipment, or People (STEP) and by adopting different approaches to teaching and learning. These include 'open' (i.e. all play together), 'modified' (i.e. adapt activities using the STEP tool), 'parallel' (i.e. ability groups), or 'separate' (i.e. temporary interventions aligned with the lesson learning objectives) activities – or through a process called 'reverse integration' as all pupils participate in disability sport (Stevenson, 2009). Underpinned by the social model of disability, the inclusion spectrum has not been without its critiques. Fitzgerald (2012, p. 445) argued that encouraging teachers to "modify or tinker with sport based skills and the composition of the groups receiving instruction" does little to question and unsettle prevailing 'normative practices'. The inclusion model has not been subjected to intense empirical investigation about its effects and effectiveness; it is thus difficult to consider it to be a universally agreed and 'proven' model for effective inclusive practice.

Understanding students' diverse learning needs lies at the heart of effective inclusive practices. In recent years, it is widely accepted that assessment must be used in ways that enhance student learning by engaging learners in understanding where they are in their learning, where they need to go next (but the destination could be different for different learners), and how best to get there (Frapwell, 2010). There also is consensus that high quality assessment must be 'valid' and 'reliable'. However, inside the assessing systems of schools there are in fact few objective standards (that are not normative). In their absence, there remains little more than the comparison of one student with another. It is on such comparisons that beliefs about ability rest and are perpetuated (Evans & Penney, 2008). Therefore, assessment can be seen and practised as a process for enabling and legitimising the hierarchisation and judgement of students (Thomas, 2013).

Thomas (2013) has recently claimed that "a strong case needs to be made for a new kind of thinking and policy about inclusion" (p. 474), if the ambitious rights-based and outcomes-based arguments that underpin inclusion are to be realised. This needs policy makers, researchers and practitioners to draw upon present-day ideas about thinking, learning and teaching and to reject twentieth century thinking on exceptionality. In this context, Initial Teacher Education (ITE) and Continuing Professional Development (CPD) programmes can play an important role.

Current trends and issues

Research evidence suggests that the quality of teachers is an important factor determining student learning and achievement. In the US, the No Child Left Behind Act (NCLB, 2002) required the presence of well-qualified teachers in every classroom and the use of evidence-based practice to optimise student learning (USDE, 2008). Internationally, it is acknowledged that in order to offer a truly inclusive experience, teachers need to engage in high quality ITE and CPD programmes. When effective, it is in these settings that teachers' understandings about the importance of inclusive teaching and learning are developed and expanded, attitudes and perceptions about student diversity are examined, and the ways they understand, approach, and respond to learners' differences are scrutinised (Florian & Rouse, 2009; Forlin, 2010; UNESCO, 2008, 2013). However, although the vision and goals of inclusive education are clearly outlined in European and international policies, over the last decade there are claims that preparing and supporting teachers for inclusive classrooms is "one of the most important challenges facing teacher education today" (Voltz, 2003, p. 5).

Findings from the Teaching and Learning International Survey showed that ITE is not having enough impact on teacher preparedness for inclusive education (Organisation for Economic Co-operation and Development [OECD], 2009). Other studies also suggest that teachers do not feel adequately prepared to respond to the challenges of diverse learners, raising fundamental questions about the quality and effectiveness of available provision (Rieser, 2013). Teachers often express fear, anxiety, and reluctance to include learners with special needs in mainstream schools (Forlin, 2010). These findings can be partly explained by evidence indicating that despite major policy reforms, ITE programmes have yet to undergo the anticipated and necessary large-scale curriculum changes to align with these requirements (Hodkinson, 2010; Rieser, 2013). An urgent reconsideration of the curriculum in the whole continuum of teacher education from ITE to CPD is thus needed (EADSNE, 2010).

In a recent publication by UNESCO (2013), a range of curriculum-related challenges in ITE were identified; one of the most pertinent being the apparent lack of a broad understanding of inclusion (Rieser, 2013). The ITE curriculum often is based on concepts of segregation and special education with little if any consideration given to other groups of learners who face exclusionary pressures. Linked to this, it is often the case that inclusion is treated as a 'stand-alone topic' (with specifically designed one-off modules on SEND students) or a 'specialist issue' (additional placements in special schools) rather than embedded as a key principle of effective teaching (UNESCO, 2013). However, such professional learning experiences reinforce narrow interpretations of the notion of inclusion and perpetuate prevailing beliefs that children who experience learning or other difficulties or disabilities are the responsibility of specialist trained teachers (EADSNE, 2010).

Large discrepancies between the content of ITE curriculum and the practical knowledge and skills teachers need to implement inclusive education in schools have also been identified (European Training Foundation, 2010). Researchers question programmes that are heavily lecture-based and which are delivered by teacher educators who lack expertise and 'practical wisdom' (UNESCO, 2013). The issue here is not the enhancement of trainee teachers' theoretical knowledge per se – as teacher knowledge is a significant factor affecting student achievement (Timperley & Alton-Lee, 2008). The problem exists and escalates when (trainee) teachers have limited opportunities to understand the key principles of effective inclusive pedagogies and to reflect upon their own beliefs, attitudes, and values; factors which appear to shape the ways teachers organise the learning environment (Forlin, Loreman, Sharma, & Earle, 2009). Critical theorists also suggest that trainee teachers need more and better opportunities to engage critically with the causes (e.g. historical, socio-cultural, ideological) of discriminatory and oppressive practices in education (Ballard, 2003). Instead of focusing on the development of instructional competences in a narrow and technicist way, it is therefore considered paramount that ITE (and CPD) programmes focus on the formation and modification of attitudes and cultures that influence the way teacher knowledge is put into practice.

In ITE settings, this necessitates extensive and high quality school placements. Research suggests that it is only through opportunities to engage with diverse learners in authentic contexts that trainee teachers can develop an in-depth understanding of child development and diversity in context (UNESCO, 2013). To ensure quality in provision, strong collaborative partnerships between ITE programmes and schools need to be developed and sustained, offering school staff and teacher educators opportunities to draw and build upon their different forms of expertise (McIntyre, 2009). The purpose of school placements should not only revolve around the application of taught competencies but also pursue a mutual transformative agenda so that all partners involved: develop, review and evolve ways of teaching with the primary aim of responding to individual differences.

Although the research evidence on the challenges and opportunities within current ITE programmes is accumulating, very little research on the nature and quality of existing CPD programmes on inclusion is available. Contrary to other national strategies (e.g. numeracy, literacy), CPD for inclusion is considered a neglected area with only limited and largely fragmented CPD opportunities offered to teachers (Hodkinson, 2012). Existing research (e.g. Stubbs, 2008) has examined the nature and quality of different CPD forms (e.g. school-based provision with access to a mentor, short courses) and findings largely reflect the wider CPD literature on how best to support teachers to learn (see Chapter 16 by Mauerberg-deCastro et al., this volume). However, there is very little understanding on what teachers learn about inclusion in CPD settings, the extent to which this knowledge reflects current and broad conceptualisations of inclusive pedagogy, whether the opportunities teachers have to 'ponder the rhetoric and reality' of effective inclusion of diverse learners in their schools (Riehl, 2000, p. 56), and how (or whether) this learning impacts upon their practices. It is therefore clear that the evidence base of CPD on inclusion needs to be expanded. The project reported in the following section sought to address this gap.

Implications for evidence-based practice

In 2013, a national CPD programme on 'Inclusive Physical Education' (IPE-CPD) was launched in England. Funded by a UK business and managed by the Youth Sport Trust (an independent charity supporting school PE in England) this programme was offered (and is still being offered) to all primary and secondary teachers and other adults (e.g. teaching assistants, sport coaches) involved in the education of children. Its aim was to increase the confidence and competence of school staff to deliver high quality IPE experiences to all students, including pupils with Special Educational Needs and Disabilities (SEND; see also Chapter 16, Mauerberg-de Castro et al., this volume, for discussion of teacher confidence to teach students with disability). The 'inclusion spectrum' provided the theoretical framework (or 'theory of instruction'; Wayne, Yoon, Cronen, & Garet, 2008) for the programme.

Delivered in a 'traditional' format, through a one-off, day-long (6 hours) workshop, the content and structure of the programme were designed (and reviewed) by 'experts' on inclusion but the delivery was the responsibility of approximately 40 trained tutors. The authors were commissioned by the YST to carry out an independent evaluation with the goal to provide evidence of programme impact on participants' confidence to deliver high quality IPE (objective 1) and to capture the quality of CPD implementation (objective 2). A range of both qualitative and quantitative methods were employed, including interviews with tutors (n=15), systematic observations of workshops (n=20), participant questionnaires (n=750), and follow-up interviews with school staff and students with the aim to capture CPD impact in a more detailed way (Makopoulou, 2015). Drawing upon evidence from workshop observations, this section provides evidence on some aspects of its content and ways participants were supported to learn.

Evidence suggests that, at a theoretical level, this programme reflected the non-categorical definition of inclusion (offering tailored opportunities to every child) supported in the literature. However, despite this seemingly clear and shared conceptual understanding underpinning workshop design, some confusion and disparity was apparent in most of the workshops observed. Evidence showed that although most tutors made clear references to the need to understand inclusion broadly, the practical aspect of the workshop – dominated by examples about the inclusion of SEND students – was perhaps the space when/where tutors' conflicting and somewhat confused interpretations were most vividly evident. Although a few tutors offered advice on how to support the 'whole spectrum' (including the more able students), there was little (if any) elaboration on how to effectively educate a student population that is diverse in terms of race and ethnicity, social class, gender, or cultural/linguistic factors.

Given the purpose of this programme, the most striking finding was the limited (if any) meaningful connections made between the CPD experience and participants' existing practices. Observations showed that, in most cases, tutors allowed insufficient opportunity for participants to articulate how they addressed effective inclusion of all learners; to provide examples of good practice or to discuss potential challenges/barriers encountered. This lack of understanding of participants' existing practices and attitudes led to some tutors making a series of assumptions about the knowledge/skills participants needed (thus failing to ground the experience in participants' questions). Evidence also showed that only three tutors facilitated 'conceptual dissonance' (Timperley & Alton-Lee, 2008), by supporting participants to evaluate the adequacy of current practices, to analyse how these deviate from what is proposed in CPD, and to discuss or evaluate the effect of different approaches on their students.

Although most tutors did not tailor provision effectively, a key strength of this programme was the importance placed on fostering participants in rethinking student ability and achievement (Naraian et al., 2012). This was illustrated by discussions about the importance of planning based on teachers' understanding of what students 'can do' rather than delivering PE lessons grounded in misdirected and ill-informed assumptions about the difficulties students experience. In this sense, inclusion was promoted as a pedagogical approach that should be "firmly located within the sphere of individual students and their needs" (Hodkinson, 2010, p. 63). While discussing issues around monitoring progress, most tutors also questioned the idea that all students' achievement can and should be 'measured' in a single, narrow way and against 'normative' standards. Participants were rather advised that the emphasis should be on individual learning targets so that all students have opportunities to succeed.

This perspective resonates with existing progressive rhetoric on inclusion that fosters teachers to discover, acknowledge, and stimulate 'the open learning potential of each student' (UNESCO, 2008). There is evidence to suggest that such an approach diminishes inequalities in educational outcomes, especially for Black and Minority Ethnic students (Hick & Thomas, 2008). But, unquestionably, this approach somehow goes against the standards- and performance-based educational system in England. Questions yet to be explored through school case studies are the extent to which participants have opportunities (or are permitted) to explore the potential utility of this way of assessing and how evidence of progress can be captured in a way that the experiences and outcomes for diverse groups of students are not compromised.

Future directions

Research on curricular aspects of inclusive education is still at an emergent stage. Fundamental questions remain about the ways in which teachers support diverse learners to participate and achieve (descriptive research) as well as the effectiveness of their practices (evaluation research). Innovative approaches to inclusive teaching need to be tested (experimental research) so that rhetoric is grounded in robust evidence of processes and impact. Similar lines of inquiry need to be pursued in answering important questions about effective/ineffective ITE and CPD programmes. Research on the nature and impact of CPD opportunities on inclusion is particularly weak, lacking sufficient depth and specificity to guide policy and practice.

ITE and CPD provision programmes also need to be grounded in the best available research evidence in order to strengthen the ways in which teachers understand and respond to students' differences. Evidence from the evaluation of the IPE programme in England suggests that ensuring conceptual clarity, in both theoretical and practical situations, is an important step. However, more attention needs to be placed on the ways ITE and CPD providers interpret and apply existing theory and research. There also is a need to ensure that CPD programmes are grounded in teachers' experiences and questions, offering opportunities for meaningful critical engagement with instructional strategies and curriculum approaches (as well as teachers' practical wisdom) to ensure that attitudes and practices are challenged.

Summary of key findings

- Inclusion is about providing effective and tailored learning opportunities for every child (UNESCO, 2008).
- Teachers have a professional responsibility to shift away from 'one size fits all' approaches and to recognise instead that learners are diverse in numerous ways: life experiences, family history, social, economic, cultural, and ethnic background, prior experiences, personal interests, and (dis)abilities.
- The pedagogical foundation of inclusive teaching is grounded in progressive, constructivism, and social learning theories.
- Today, inclusive education, as a political, social, and educational concept, has been embraced while segregation and discrimination have been rejected and outlawed.
- Despite significant changes in legislation, evidence suggests that ITE programmes remain largely unchanged, grounded in principles of segregation and special education ('special', one-off modules or additional placements in special schools).
- There is evidence to suggest that preparing and supporting teachers for inclusive classrooms is a key challenge facing teacher education today.
- Very little research on the nature and quality of existing CPD programmes on inclusion is available.
- Evidence from the CPD programme in England suggests that tutors need further support to ensure that teachers develop new insights on how to identify and cater for student diversity, beyond the needs of SEND students.
- Teachers involved in the process must be permitted to inform the CPD provision based on their understandings, perspectives, questions, and practices (tailoring CPD provision).
- It is important that researchers work together to build a strong knowledge base that is not only grounded in robust research but that also has *sufficient depth and specificity* to guide CPD policy and practice.

Reflective questions for discussion

1. What is inclusive education?
2. Which students are we thinking about when we talk of 'inclusive education'?
3. What are the key elements of effective inclusive teaching?
4. What are the key challenges that need to be addressed to ensure that teachers are prepared to address student diversity effectively?

References

Ballard, K. (2003). The analysis of context: Some thoughts on teacher education, culture, colonization and inequality. In T. Booth, K. Nes, & M. Stromstad (Eds.), *Developing inclusive teacher education*. London: RoutledgeFalmer.

Blanco, R. (2009). Conceptual framework of inclusive education. In C. Acedo, M. Amadio, & R. Opertti (Eds.), *Defining an inclusive education agenda: Reflections around the 48th session of the International conference on Education*. Geneva: UNESCO.

Blane, D., White, I., & Morris, J. (1996). Education, social circumstances and mortality. In D. Blane, E. Brunner, & R. Wikinson (Eds.), *Health and social organisation: Towards a policy for the 21st century* (pp. 171–187). London: Routledge.

Booth, T., & Ainscow, M. (2002). *Index for inclusion: Developing learning and participation in schools*. Bristol: Centre for Studies in Inclusive Education.

Bourke, P. E. (2009). Professional development and teacher aides in inclusive education contexts: Where to from here? *International Journal of Inclusive Education, 13*(8), 817–827.

Campbell, F.K. (2009). *Contours of ableism: The production of disability and abledness.* Basingstoke: Palgrave Macmillan.

Coles, R. (1997). *The moral intelligence of children.* London: Bloomsbury.

Department for Education and Skills [DfES]. (2006). *Exclusion of black pupils: Priority review. "Getting it. Getting it right."* London: Author. Retrieved 31 August 2015, from www.standards.dfes.gov.uk/ethnic-minorities/resources/PriorityReviewSept06.pdf.

Dyson, A., Howes, A., & Roberts, B. (2002). *A systematic review of the effectiveness of school-level actions for promoting participation by all students.* London: Evidence for Policy and Practice Centre.

European Agency for Development in Special Needs Education [EADSNE]. (2004). *Inclusive education and classroom practice in secondary education: Literature review.* Odense, Denmark: Author.

European Agency for Development in Special Needs Education [EADSN]. (2010). *Teacher education for inclusion: International literature review.* Odense, Denmark: Author.

European Agency for Development in Special Needs Education [EADSNE]. (2012). *Teacher education for inclusion: Profile of inclusive teacher.* Odense, Denmark: Author.

European Training Foundation. (2010). *Mapping policies and practices for the preparation of teachers for inclusive education in contexts of social and cultural diversity: Former Yugoslav Republic of Macedonia.* [Country report – working document] (European Training Foundation).

Evans, J., & Penney, D. (2008). Levels of the playing field: The social construction of physical 'ability' in the physical education curriculum. *Physical Education and Sport Pedagogy, 13*(1), 31–47.

Fitzgerald, H. (2012). 'Drawing' on disabled students' experiences of physical education and stakeholder responses. *Sport, Education and Society, 17*(4), 443–462.

Flanagan, F. M. (1994). 'John Dewey', paper presented in *Programme 7 of 'The Great Educators', First Series*, broadcasted on 9 May 1994. Also available at: www.admin.mtu.edu/ctlfd/Ed%20Psych%20Readings/dewey.pdf (accessed 1 December 2009).

Florian, L., & Black-Hawkins, K. (2011). Exploring inclusive pedagogy. *British Educational Research Journal, 37*(5), 813–828.

Florian, L., & Rouse, M. (2009). The inclusive practice project in Scotland: Teacher education for inclusive education. *Teaching and Teacher Education, 25*(4), 594–601.

Forlin, C. (Ed.). (2010). *Teacher education for inclusion: Changing paradigms and innovative approaches.* London: Routledge.

Forlin, C., Loreman, T., Sharma, U., & Earle, C. (2009). Demographic differences in changing pre-service teachers' attitudes, sentiments and concerns about inclusive education. *International Journal of Inclusive Education, 13*(2), 195–209.

Frapwell, A. (2010). Assessment for learning. In R. Bailey (Ed.), *Physical education for learning: A guide for secondary schools.* London: Continuum.

Goodley, D. A., & McLaughlin, J. (2011). Does every child matter, post-Blair? The interconnections of disabled childhoods. ESRC End of Award Report, RES-062-23-1138. Swindon: ESRC.

Hartley, D. (2009). Personalisation: The nostalgic revival of child-centred education? *Journal of Education Policy, 24*(4), 423–434.

Hick, P., & Thomas, G. (2008). *Inclusion and diversity in education.* London: Sage.

Hodkinson, A. (2010). Inclusive and special education in the English educational system: Historical perspectives, recent developments and future challenges. *British Journal of Special Education, 37*(2), 61–67.

Hodkinson, A. (2012). Illusionary inclusion – what went wrong with New Labour's landmark educational policy? *British Journal of Special Education, 39*(1), 4–11.

Knapp, B. (1964). *Skill in sport: The attainment of proficiency.* London: Routledge & Kegan Paul.

Makopoulou, K. (2011). Personalising learning: A perfect pedagogy for teachers and coaches? In K. M. Armour (Ed.), *Introduction to sport pedagogy for teachers and coaches: Effective learners in physical education and youth sport* (pp. 244–257). London: Routledge.

Makopoulou, K. (2015). *Independent evaluation of the Sainsbury's Inclusive PE training programme.* Interim Report 5.

McIntyre, D. (2009). The difficulties of inclusive pedagogy for initial teacher education and some thoughts on the way forward. *Teaching and Teacher Education, 25*(4), 602–608.

Mosston, M., & Ashworth, S. (2010). *Teaching physical education* (2nd online edn). Retrieved 27 August 2010, from www.spectrumofteachingstyles.org/ebook.

Naraian, S., Ferguson, D. L., & Thomas, N. (2012). Transforming for inclusive practice: professional development to support the inclusion of students labelled as emotionally disturbed. *International Journal of Inclusive Education, 16*(7), 721–740.

Nepi, L. D., Fioravanti, J., Nannini, P., & Peru, A. (2015). Social acceptance and the choosing of favourite classmates: A comparison between students with special educational needs and typically developing students in a context of full inclusion. *British Journal of Special Education* (DOI: 10.1111/1467–8578.12096)

Organisation for Economic Co-operation and Development [OECD]. (2009). *Creating effective teaching and learning environments – first results from TALIS.* Retrieved April 4, 2016, from www.oecd.org/datao-ecd/17/51/43023606.pdf.

Riehl, C. J. (2000). The principal's role in creating inclusive schools for diverse students: A review of normative, empirical, and critical literature on the practice of educational administration. *Review of Educational Research, 70*(1), 55–81.

Rieser, R. (2013). *Educating teachers for children with disabilities: Mapping, scoping and best practices exercise in the context of developing inclusive education.* Bhutan: UNESCO.

Rouse, M. (2007). *Enhancing effective inclusive practice: Knowing, doing and believing.* Kairaranga, Wellington: New Zealand Ministry of Education.

Rouse, M., & Florian, L. (2012). *Teacher education for inclusive education: Final report of the inclusive practice project.* Retrieved 31 August 2015, from www.efds.co.uk/assets/0000/6672/OO195.pdf.

Runswick-Cole, K. (2011). Time to end the bias towards inclusive education? *British Journal of Special Education, 38*(3), 112–119.

Stevenson, P. (2009). The pedagogy of inclusive youth sport: Working towards real solutions. In H. Fitzgerald (Ed.), *Disability and youth sport* (pp. 119–131). London: Routledge.

Stubbs, S. (2008). *Inclusive education: Where there are few resources.* Oslo: The Atlas Alliance.

Thomas, G. (2013). A review of thinking and research about inclusive education policy, with suggestions for a new kind of inclusive thinking. *British Educational Research Journal, 39*(3), 473–490.

Timperley, H., & Alton-Lee, A. (2008). Reframing teacher professional learning: An alternative policy approach to strengthening valued outcomes for diverse learners. *Review of Research in Education, 32,* 328–369.

United Nations Educational, Scientific and Cultural Organization [UNESCO]. (2008). *Inclusive education: The way of the future.* International Conference Centre, Geneva, 25–28 November 2008.

United Nations Educational, Scientific and Cultural Organization [UNESCO]. (2013). *Promoting inclusive teacher education curriculum.* Bangkok: UNESCO.

United States Department of Education [USDE]. (2008). *Education and inclusion in the United States: An overview.* Washington, DC: Author.

Voltz, D. L. (2003). Collaborative infusion: An emerging approach to teacher preparation for inclusive education. *Action in Teacher Education, 25*(1), 5–13.

Wayne, A. J., Yoon, K., Cronen, P. S., & Garet, M. S. (2008). Experimenting with teacher professional development: Motives and methods. *Educational Researcher, 37*(8), 469–479.

Winter, E., & O'Raw, P. (2010). *Literature review on the principles and practices relating to inclusive education for children with special educational needs.* Trim, Ireland: National Council for Special Education.

PART VIII

The role of student and teacher cognition in student learning

Introduction

The study of student and teacher cognition is a key aspect in efforts to increase our understanding of the teaching and learning process. Thinking and decision making play an important role in physical education classes, ultimately determining how students interact and what they learn. Throughout this part, both students and teachers are characterized as active mediators in the teaching and learning process. The focus of the first three chapters is student cognition, including the perspectives and attitudes that students bring to physical education classes, how their competence beliefs affect their willingness to engage and their learning, and ways to structure the learning environment to facilitate thought processes that enable them to learn. Students are viewed as active and controlling agents in their learning rather than passive recipients of information.

Using cognitive mediation, metacognition, and self-regulation as theoretical bases, Solmon provides an historical overview of student cognitions in Chapter 33, *Student cognition: Understanding how students learn in physical education*. Researchers have provided evidence that an awareness of cognitive processes is important in gaining a clearer understanding of how students learn from teaching, and that the ways that teachers structure learning tasks can act to enhance or constrain cognitions that facilitate learning. Despite the promise evident in this line of research, however, over the past decade there have been relatively few studies investigating students' thoughts as they learn. Solmon argues that a focus on student learning is a critical element in demonstrating the worth of PE programs and calls for multi-level analyses that can explore social and individual factors related to self-regulated learning.

Both Garn and Webster highlight the complexities of student cognition in the PE context using multidimensional theoretical frameworks to structure and connect knowledge about PE from the student perspective. In Chapter 34, *Student physical self-concept beliefs*, Alex Garn focuses on students' physical self-concept beliefs, reflecting cognition aimed inwardly toward physical abilities commonly used and physical attributes on display in PE settings. Collin Webster concentrates on students' attitudes and perspectives in Chapter 35, *Student attitudes and perspectives*, reflecting cognition aimed outwardly toward experiences with teachers, pedagogy, curriculum, and peers in PE settings. Both Garn and Webster articulate the motivational, affective, and behavioral implications associated with students who make positive evaluations about themselves (i.e., physical self-concept) and their learning environment (i.e., attitudes). It is unclear, however, how students' physical self-concept beliefs and attitudes directly impact learning PE content. These chapters situate facets of student cognition as critical components of quality PE and engagement in health-enhancing behaviors.

The focus of the next two chapters shifts to cognitive aspects of teaching. Teachers are characterized as thoughtful and reflective practitioners, and it is acknowledged that their understanding of students' cognitive processes is a critical element in effective teaching. In Chapter 36, *Teacher beliefs and efficacy*, Pamela Kulinna and Donetta J. Cothran explore the complicated relationship between two key elements of teacher cognition: beliefs and efficacy. Teacher beliefs serve as a lens through which they interpret the environment, structure their knowledge, and make decisions. Prospective teachers enter teacher preparation programs with strongly established belief systems. Likewise, practicing teachers in professional development sessions also have strongly held beliefs refined through their teaching experiences. In order for professional development programs to be effective, it is imperative that these prior belief systems be considered. To understand how teachers' beliefs serve to facilitate, or alternatively impede, student learning, it is important for teachers to be aware of their belief systems and, as they develop their knowledge about teaching, that they reflect on those beliefs. Kulinna and Cothran describe how teachers' belief systems and values about the purposes of PE and about how students learn influence the decisions they make. Additionally, they point out that teachers must consider students' beliefs and values if they are to teach effectively.

Nate McCaughtry and Matthew Ferry outline the emotional dimensions of being a physical educator in Chapter 37, *The emotional dimensions of physical education teacher knowledge*. Teacher emotions and emotional understanding of students are identified as crucial elements for sustaining positive learning environments in PE and promoting the wellbeing of teachers and students. They make persuasive arguments about the role of teachers' emotions in decision-making processes that affect day-to-day practices. The emotional toil of coping with marginalization and low status within the broader school curriculum is also described. Despite these professional barriers, many physical educators are able to develop emotional knowledge of their students that helps create caring environments and strong teacher-student bonds. McCaughtry and Ferry argue that emotional knowledge of students or a lack of it helps explain a variety of common PE phenomena ranging from curricular planning and implementation to blaming students when lessons go awry.

In light of the recent concerns about the role of physical education in addressing public health concerns, this part concludes with a chapter that explores the interaction of teacher and student cognitions as they relate to beliefs about physical activity, health-related fitness, and obesity. In Chapter 38, *The nature and consequences of obesity bias in physical education: Implications for teaching*, Weidong Li examines how obesity bias, defined as anti-fat attitudes and stereotypical beliefs toward overweight individuals, affects teaching practices and student learning. He provides evidence that both implicit and explicit bias exist in PE classes on the part of teachers and students, and that those cognitions have a negative effect on student learning and engagement in physical activity. Specifically, obesity bias can lead to the marginalization of overweight students, negatively affecting their emotional wellbeing and social functioning. When this happens, the very students who are most in need of lessons that will enable them to develop skills and dispositions to be physically active are alienated from PE and physical activity, further increasing their health risk. In this concluding chapter, the social ecological model is offered as a conceptual framework to address issues related to the inclusion of overweight students by developing school-wide programs to reduce obesity bias and promote physically active lifestyles. That framework encompasses multiple levels that interact to influence a wide array of cognitions that affect student learning, including individual factors, the social and instructional context, school, family and community issues as well as society and public policy. This model can be used not only to guide efforts to promote cognitions that promote inclusion for overweight students, but also to structure the PE learning environment effectively for all students.

Melinda A. Solmon and Alex Garn
Louisiana State University, USA

33

STUDENT COGNITION

Understanding how students learn in physical education

Melinda A. Solmon, LOUISIANA STATE UNIVERSITY, USA

A survey of definitions using a web-based search engine reveals that the term cognition encompasses a wide array of processes and constructs that intersect as individuals comprehend their surroundings, give meaning to their experiences, acquire knowledge, make decisions, and develop plans of action. As Gage and Berliner (1992) observed more than two decades ago, cognition can be simply defined as "all the ways in which people think" (p. G-3). So, from a broad frame of reference, all thought processes, inclusive of beliefs, perceptions, attention, concentration, emotions, motivations, mental abilities, learning strategies, reasoning, and decision making are elements of cognition, given that they are related to how individuals acquire knowledge and make sense of their environments (Solmon, 2006). As McCaughtry and Ferry (Chapter 37, this volume) point out in their discussion of teachers' emotional understandings, the human experience is incredibly complex and holistic in nature. To isolate individual aspects of the holistic human experience is, by nature, contrary to that conceptualization and doing so poses a risk of dissecting the experience to the point that the comprehensive meaning is lost. Seemingly, however, it is necessary to isolate aspects of that complex human experience to better understand them before we can fully examine how they interact.

The focus of this part of the handbook is on the broad range of cognitions that form the basis of the human learning experience, including beliefs, knowledge, emotions, and perceptions that are examined in detail in other chapters. The emphasis of this chapter is on what we know about students' thought processes as they learn, and based on that, how teachers and practitioners in physical activity settings can structure the learning environment to engage students in cognitions that enable them to learn. Across domains of educational research, social cognitive theories have played an increasingly important role, and the value of studying the thoughts of learners in the context of social factors that affect cognitive processes has been acknowledged (Solmon, 2006). It is recognized that individual and social perspectives are both critically important in the teaching and learning process, and the myriad social and situational factors that profoundly influence cognition are addressed throughout this handbook. Although important findings relative to social factors as they affect individual learner cognition are addressed, the emphasis here will be on individual cognition.

The term cognition has generally been used interchangeably with thought processes (Peterson, 1988; Wittrock, 1986b). The study of thought processes as students learn is rooted in the work of John Dewey (1966, 1990), who characterized students as educational theorists who are active and controlling agents in their own learning. Dewey argued that students' views should inform the educational process, and his philosophy provides a rationale for the study of students' thought processes as an important research paradigm. A wide array of cognitive processes are critical elements in the teaching and learning process, including interpreting stimuli in the environment, selecting and paying attention to instructional cues, and deciding how to interact in classes. Examples of decisions that students make related to their cognitions that have a powerful impact on what they learn are associated with: how much effort to exert, whether or not to use strategies and/or seek help when they encounter difficulties, and whether they will persist in a learning activity or task.

A basic assumption of frameworks that incorporate a cognitive approach is that our actions are governed by thought (Roberts, 1992). That may not always be a tenable assumption, however, since our actions are not always preceded by thoughtful decision making. Sometimes we may act, or react, with little or no consciousness or awareness of our thought processes, or we may act without really thinking. Even though students may not be aware of their cognitions as they learn, a better understanding of the cognitive processes that foster learning will enable teachers and researchers to apply these findings to develop instructional strategies that will encourage students to think and act in ways that empower them to learn.

The purpose of this chapter is to review and synthesize recent literature that is related to student cognition in physical education (PE). Given space limitations, I rely on summaries of earlier work presented in previous volumes (Solmon, 2003, 2006) and focus on recent additions to the literature. To situate this body of work in the existing literature, I begin with a brief historical overview. Next, cognitive mediation, metacognition, and self-regulation are posed as theoretical bases that serve as frameworks for the investigation of student cognition, and motivation is situated as a cognitive process in this literature. The major findings of research on student cognition in PE settings are organized around four themes: (a) student characteristics that influence their ability to successfully engage in cognitive processes that will enable them to learn, (b) recent research that has focused on student learning, (c) studies that have used approaches grounded in metacognition and self-regulated learning, and (d) the relationship between cognitive function and PE, physical activity, and physical fitness. Based on those major findings, I present implications for practice that are supported by the research. I conclude by pointing out directions for future research, summarizing the key points, and posing reflective questions for discussion.

Brief historical perspective

In the broader field of research on teaching in PE, the motor learning literature is the context for the earliest research on the role of cognition. Cognitive concerns dominate the initial phase of learning a motor skill, as learners focus on information presented through instructions and demonstrations to understand the elements required in the task and to develop cognitive representations of the skill to be learned (Magill, 2001). As learners acquire a basic level of proficiency, motor performance becomes more automated and cognitive demands related to processing information about the skill are reduced, enabling learners to direct their attention to more technical aspects of the skill, specific points of technique, or strategies in using the skill. In their review in the early 1970s, Nixon and Locke (1973) surmised that the focus of research in teaching in PE up to that point had focused primarily on motor skill acquisition. They insightfully observed, however, that knowing how individuals learn skills does not necessarily translate to knowing how to help them learn skills. They called for researchers to begin asking substantive questions in research studies designed to learn how teachers can best help PE students learn, and understanding students' cognitions is an important element in doing that.

The process-product paradigm dominated educational research in the early 1970s. Process-product studies examined relationships between teacher behavior as the instructional process and measures of student achievement as the product variable. A strength of this approach was that studies were conducted in field based settings, and this line of research made a contribution to the knowledge base about effective teaching during this time frame. As the field of research on teaching evolved, however, limitations and inherent weaknesses in the application of the process-product paradigm became apparent. The lack of a theoretical basis was viewed as a serious deficiency, and basic assumptions of this approach were called into question. The shortcomings of this paradigm are documented in several reviews (e.g., Doyle, 1977; Lee & Solmon, 1992; Shulman, 1986; Wittrock, 1986b) and will not be reiterated in detail here. There is general agreement that the process-product research provided a structure to drive more sophisticated inquiry in the 1970s, but also that this approach represents a simplistic view of teaching that lacks the complexity to fully explore how students learn from teaching. Shulman (1986) points out that the reliance on overt, observable behaviors inherent in the paradigm disregards the cognitive activities of both students and teachers and argues that a clear understanding of how students learn from teaching must include the investigation of student cognition.

The shift in educational research from the process-product paradigm to approaches that incorporate the study of cognition parallels the cognitive revolution in psychology, characterized by MacKeachie (2000) as a shift from the behaviorist approaches dominant in the 1950s and 1960s to an emphasis on human cognition. A survey of the editions of the *Handbook of Research on Teaching* (Gage, 1963; Travers, 1973; Wittrock, 1986a) provides evidence of this. Peterson (1988) points out there is virtually no mention of students or learning in the chapter titles in the first two editions, which were dominated by a focus on teachers and teaching. An emphasis on students and cognition emerged in the third edition, as several chapters addressed issues related to student learning. Wittrock (1986b) provided a review of the research on students' thought processes and several other chapters address issues related to student learning and cognition. The fourth edition of that handbook (Richardson, 2001) continued to reflect an emphasis on learners and how their cognitions affect their learning. The publication of handbooks focused on self-regulation (Boekaerts, Pintrich, & Zeidner, 2000; Vohs & Baumeister, 2011; Zimmerman & Schunk, 2011) also support the contention that a focus on cognitive processes in learning continues to be an important line of inquiry.

Although there has been a continued focus on cognition and self-regulated learning across academic disciplines, the research on student cognition specific to PE has lagged behind other academic content areas. In 1999 Luke and Hardy characterized interest in students' thought processes in PE as "limited." Several scholars in PE, however, have examined aspects of student cognition in PE classes. That body of work has made a significant contribution to the knowledge base about effective teaching in that context as summarized in earlier reviews (Lee, 1997; Solmon, 2003, 2006). Despite the promise evident in this line of inquiry, and the acknowledgement that understanding how students learn is a critical element in research on effective teaching, my literature search for this chapter suggests that a focus on student thoughts as they learn has not been a point of emphasis in journals that publish research in PE over the past five years.

Theoretical bases and core elements in the study of student cognition

One of the criticisms of the early research using the process-product paradigm was the lack of a theoretical basis to guide the research. Examining direct relationships between instructional processes and learning products may have the capacity to determine "what works" but that simplistic approach cannot tell us why "it" works, how "it" works, or in what contexts "it" might be effective. Approaches that include a focus on cognition necessitated a paradigm shift to theoretical views with the capacity to provide an understanding of why different instructional approaches are effective and how students learn from teaching.

Theoretical perspectives used to investigate student cognitions are grounded in the view of learners as active and controlling agents in the learning process, as characterized in Dewey's (1966, 1990) work. Three broad categories of theories have been used to frame the study of cognition: cognitive mediation, constructivism, and critical theories such as post-structuralism. In this chapter I focus on research that is grounded in a mediational perspective, as constructivist and post-structuralist views are presented in other chapters in this volume. It is important to note, however, the assertions that meaningful learning is grounded in personal experience and that the understanding of formal instruction is mediated by myriad influences is central to these theoretical approaches. A cognitive constructivist perspective recognizes that learners develop (i.e., construct) their individual ways of knowing through active restructuring of existing knowledge from the framework of their personal experiences and understandings (Powell & Kalina, 2009). Through a feminist post-structural lens, learners are viewed as active agents who make choices and participate in defining their identities rather than passive participants in institutionalized processes (Azzarito, Solmon, & Harrison, 2006). These theoretical views are complementary in that they both emphasize that learning requires active, effortful involvement on the part of the learner. As research on student cognitions has evolved, the mediational framework has been operationalized to some degree in constructs of self-regulated learning and metacognition. Consistent with the cognitive mediational paradigm, the conceptualization of learners as active agents in their learning is central to those constructs. An additional consideration that is a core element in the study of cognition is motivation as an underlying cognitive process.

Cognitive mediation

Doyle (1977) describes the evolution of the mediating processes paradigm. In the two-factor process-product approach the link between teacher behavior and student achievement is conceptualized as a direct relationship. The cognitive mediational approach advances that model by expanding to a three-factor model that recognizes that mediating factors intervene in the relationship between what the teacher does and what students learn. From this perspective, it is recognized that learning does not automatically occur from teaching. Instead, learning occurs when students are actively engaged in the process, activating cognitions that enable them to learn from teaching. Teachers produce learning and achievement only to the degree that they activate students' cognitions.

Early work using the mediating processes paradigm relied on overt, observable variables such as time on task, observer estimates of attention, and task completion rates. Doyle (1977) criticized this limited conceptualization of student mediation and argued that researchers needed to move beyond that approach to investigate cognitive processes rather than the reliance on observations of behavior. Considering cognitive elements as mediators between teacher behavior and learning outcomes recognizes that students have different perceptions of teacher behaviors and other classroom events, and that based on those unique perceptions they think, act, and learn in individual ways. The critical link between teacher behavior and what is learned is students' active and controlling role in mediating the effects of teaching. From this perspective, the teacher's goal is to create a learning environment that encourages and enables students to think and act in ways that enable them to learn.

Using Doyle's work as a guide, Lee and Solmon (1992) urged scholars in PE to incorporate the study of student cognitions in research studies to gain a clearer understanding of how students learn from teaching. Dodds, Griffin, and Placek (2001) acknowledge that the cognitive mediational model provides a basis to investigate students' cognitions, but point out that the learners' domain specific knowledge is an important element that has often not been examined in the investigation of understanding how students learn from teaching. They argue that to fully understand learner cognition the development of student knowledge must be considered.

Metacognition and self-regulation

The rationale for investigating student cognitions is based on the assumption that, if we gain an understanding of how thought processes promote learning, we will be able to structure the learning environment and design tasks that enable students to use those cognitive processes effectively. Inherent in that assumption is that learners can exert a level of control over their cognitions if encouraged to do so. Wittrock (1986b) defined metacognition as an individual's knowledge about and control over their cognitive processes. It encompasses monitoring, planning, and evaluating efforts to master a task. Simply stated, metacognition is an individual's awareness of his or her thinking. Luke and Hardy (1999) advocated for the use of metacognition as a framework to study students' thoughts in PE, criticizing the existing research in PE for a tendency to "reduce the complexity of learning to a number of isolated variables, such as motivation, that remain adrift from any wider conceptual framework" (p. 175). Metacognition provides a structure to consider multiple variables rather than studying aspects of cognition in isolation, enabling researchers to examine cognition as a more authentic holistic process. As the investigation of student thought processes has evolved, recent research in PE (Chatzipanteli & Digelidis, 2011) and sport settings (Brick, MacIntyre, & Campbell, 2015) has used a metacognitive framework to study teaching and learning.

Self-regulation is a parallel concept to metacognition. According to Zimmerman and Schunk (2011), it is a process "whereby learners personally activate and sustain cognitions, affects, and behaviors that are systematically oriented toward the attainment of personal goals" (p. 1). Grounded in social cognitive theory, the construct of self-regulated learning encompasses cognitive, motivational, affective, and social contextual factors (McBride & Xiang, 2013). As active participants in their learning, students construct individual meanings, identify goals to guide their efforts, and develop strategies to work toward those goals (Pintrich, 2003). Consistent with characterizations of metacognition, planning, monitoring, and evaluating progress toward goals are central to self-regulated learning. The continuum of self-determination (Ryan & Deci, 2000) has been used by researchers to characterize levels of self-regulation (i.e., McBride & Xiang, 2013). Four levels of regulation have been used to operationalize based on the level of internalization of an individual's reason for engaging in an activity: (a) external (because I *have* to), (b) introjected (because I *ought* to), (c) identified (I see value in the activity and I *want* to), and (d) intrinsic (because I *enjoy* the activity). More internalized regulations are more autonomous and should lead to a higher quality of engagement (Ryan & Deci, 2000).

Motivation as a cognitive process

Achievement motivation is seen as a critical determinant of success and the educational literature is replete with studies investigating motivation. Scholars in PE and promotion of physical activity have followed suit, and a preponderance of recent research in PE pedagogy has been framed from a motivational perspective. Defined by Roberts (2001) as the "dispositions, social variables, and/or cognitions that come into play when a person undertakes a task at which he or she is evaluated, or enters into competition with others, or attempts to attain some standard of excellence" (p. 6), motivation is recognized as a cognitive process. Solmon (2003) character-ized motivation as a central construct that underlies more global cognitive processes. Motivation involves being willing to exert effort, to work at a challenging level, and to persist when difficulty is encountered, which ultimately leads to achieving goals. A plethora of theories have been used to investigate motivation, and the focus of many chapters in this volume is to closely examine recent research from various theoretical perspectives. It is beyond the scope of this chapter to provide an in depth account of motivation in PE, but it is not possible to examine student cogni-tion in isolation from motivation. From a practical standpoint, if an individual lacks motivation for a particular activity or task, cognitions will likely be geared toward avoiding engagement, so being motivated is a prerequisite for fostering cognitions that will lead to learning.

Current trends and issues

During the past two decades concern about the consequences of physical inactivity and rise in obesity levels has received increased attention from the media, from government agencies and commissions, and from the research community. Reviewing the list of published articles in the *Journal of Teaching in Physical Education, Research Quarterly for Exercise and Sport, Physical Education and Sport Pedagogy*, and *Sport, Education and Society* reveals a focus on pedagogies of the body, sport and culture, promotion of physical activity, the role of PE in the prevention of obesity, and understanding motivation in physical activity settings, but research studies focused on cogni-tions that influence student learning are comparatively sparse. Only a small proportion of studies focus on what, how, or if, students learn in PE classes and the cognitions that are involved in that process. Recently, scholars have advocated for the use of physical literacy (PL) as a framework for defining the focus of PE (Castelli, Centeio, Beighle, Carson, & Nicksic, 2014; Giblin, Collins, & Button, 2014; Kirk, 2013). PL is a philosophical view articulated by Whitehead (2010) that embraces a holistic perspective of the lived experience and rejects mind-body dualism. She conceptualized PL as the embodiment of the motivation, confidence, physical competence, knowledge and understanding that enable an individual to realize his/her innate potential through embodied experiences. Cognition is a fundamental element in conceptualization of PL. Although much has been written from this philosophical perspective, the measurement of PL as a learning outcome has not been clarified (Giblin et al., 2014) and to date, there is little, if any, data-based research using this framework.

The focus of this section on current issues and trends is on recent work. Earlier reviews (Solmon, 2003, 2006) have synthesized research by examining constructs involved in cognition by organizing research findings into categories outlining cognition as a scheme of processes as they might occur along a timeline. That is, I have emphasized that students enter instructional settings with an array of prior knowledge, experiences, and beliefs that serve as a lens or filter through which students perceive instruction and teacher behaviors. Based on their individual characteristics, students give unique meanings to classroom interactions. They do not all inter-pret instruction in the same way, and may or may not interpret what the teacher says in the way that is intended. Based on these perceptions, they make decisions about their engagement in learning activities. They choose whether to exert effort, to use strategies, to seek help when they encounter difficulties, as well as other decisions that determine whether or not they learn. Readers are referred to the review by Solmon (2006) for a detailed overview of earlier work. Consistent with the recent trend toward a more global view of cognition, four themes are used to organize the current trends and issues for this chapter. First, conditions and characteristics that have been identified as prerequisites for effective cognition are delineated. This is followed by a synthesis of recent work investigating student learning in specific domains. Next, the work using metacognition and self-regulation as a framework is presented. This section concludes with a brief summary of an area that has received an increasing amount of attention in recent years: the relationship between PE/physical activity/physical fitness with cognition and academic achievement.

Requisites for effective cognitive engagement

In order for students to actively engage in learning activities they must have a reason to do so. Earlier I described motivation as a central construct that underlies global cognitions. Motivation is associated with higher levels of cognitive engagement such as elaboration and critical thinking (Stolk & Harari, 2014). Regardless of the theoretical approach undertaken to explain motivation, it is clear that an individual must attach some level of value to an endeavor before she or he will be motivated to engage in and learn an activity. According to the expectancy value model (Eccles, 2005), subjective task values enable individuals to answer the question "Why should I do this activity?" Four dimensions or elements of value are outlined in the expectancy value framework: (a) intrinsic value (interest/enjoyment/satisfaction), (b) attainment value (importance of doing well), (c) utility value (usefulness), and (d) perceived cost (benefits vs. investment required). If students do not value an activity at some level, they are unlikely to invest their effort in learning. Students' past experiences, cultural backgrounds, socializing agents, and existing knowledge may predispose them to value certain activities, or alternatively to be alienated from class activities.

Some students come to PE settings with an intrinsic interest in physical activity and sport based on positive prior experiences that may include family involvement in physical activity and a history of success. Others, however, do not see inherent value in the content of PE. Several scholars have explored the social construction of bodily meanings and examined how media images and culture influence choices that students make regarding their involvement in PE (Azzarito & Kirk, 2013). That work has a strong focus on gender and privilege, as well as skill level, and is represented in other chapters in this volume. This research on body pedagogies is relevant to addressing the issue of value for students who, because of their backgrounds and prior experiences, are not attracted to PE. Spencer-Cavaliere and Rintoul (2012) provide evidence that PE continues to be an uncomfortable experience for some children. They examined students' perspectives about alienation in PE. The sixth graders in their study articulated feelings of powerlessness, meaningless, and isolation, leading to negative feelings and a lack of value. A study by Frisette (2013) demonstrates that listening to students' voices can inform teachers and researchers about ways to address concerns about value. The adolescent girls in her study were able to identify barriers they perceived to their involvement in PE and the ways that they were able to negotiate barriers to be successful.

In addition to finding value in a task, it also is critical that individuals believe they can experience some level of success in an activity. Even when individuals see value in an activity, if they do not believe that some level of success is possible, or that they can demonstrate some level of competence, it is unlikely that they will choose to exert effort on a task. Elliot and Dweck (2005) assert that competence is the conceptual core of motivation. The manner in which competence is evaluated is a key consideration. When competence is judged according to self-referenced (personal improvement) or task-referenced (mastering a task/achieving a goal) criteria then success is always a possibility. When the criteria for success or demonstrating competence are externally referenced relative to the performance of others, students with less experience and lower ability often believe that, no matter how much effort they exert, success (beating others in the class) is not a realistic possibility. When students are concerned about whether or not they can be successful, the focus of their cognitions is likely to shift from a focus on the task at hand to anxiety related concerns about maintaining self-esteem. Garn's chapter (Chapter 34, this volume) on students' self-concept beliefs provides insight into the influence ability beliefs have on student learning.

In addition to valuing the task and believing they can be successful, students must also be positioned to understand and interpret instruction. Webster (Chapter 35, this volume) provides a review of recent studies focused on students' perceptions of instruction. What is important with regard to cognition is to reiterate that individual students, based on their prior knowledge, experiences, and beliefs, do not always perceive instruction the same ways, and often do not perceive instruction in the manner in which the teacher intends (Solmon, 2006). In order to fully understand students' cognitions as they learn, it is important for teachers and researchers to determine the meanings that students construct based on their perceptions of instruction.

Learning domain specific knowledge

A discussion of student cognition is incomplete without the consideration of the development of students' domain specific knowledge (Dodds et al., 2001). Investigating how student knowledge develops is a labor intensive effort, and those efforts are complicated by the difficulty inherent in measuring what students actually learn. Another confounding issue relevant to student knowledge in PE is the lack of clarity about what is to be learned (Nyberg & Larsson, 2014). There has been an ongoing debate for decades concerning what the basis for content taught in school PE should be. That debate continues, driven to some degree by efforts to increase the status of PE to be recognized as a meaningful element in a core academic curriculum (Reid, 2013).

Studies that measure learning in PE classes are not commonplace, as time on task, appropriate practice trails, and more recently levels of in-class physical activity often are accepted as proxies for learning. Some researchers who have measured learning do so in the context of comparing one methodology or teaching approach to another. In many cases there is little if any consideration of why or how one method facilitates learning as compared to another, but some researchers have addressed that issue. There has been extensive investigation of the instructional effects of the Sport Education model (for a review see Araújo, Mesquita, & Hastie, 2014), as well as Teaching Games for Understanding (for a review see Stolz & Pill, 2014). Although both reviews point out methodological shortcomings and make suggestions for future research that focuses on how students learn, there is general support for the conclusion that teaching approaches that situate learning experiences in authentic contexts, as these models do, are effective in helping students to learn techniques and strategies by promoting cognitions that foster understanding of game play. Researchers also have investigated how the Spectrum of Teaching Styles affects student learning and engagement (Byra, Sanchez, & Wallhead, 2014). Although learning was not measured, Sanchez, Byra, and Wallhead (2012) concluded that students reported higher levels of cognitive involvement in the inclusion style, as compared to command and practice style lessons. Taken together, findings from these lines of research support the notion that the teaching approach used affects how and what students learn through the activation of their cognitions. In her commentary on curriculum priorities for PE, Ennis (2011) cautions that instructional models that merely engage students in moderate to vigorous physical activities undermine the educational focus on knowledge and skill development needed to foster students' dispositions to embrace physically active lifestyles. It is important for researchers to continue investigations relevant to student cognitions that promote the acquisition of domain specific knowledge to do that.

Metacognition and self-regulation

Consistent with the trend evident across educational research (Pintrich, 2003), over the past decade research in PE related to student cognition has been framed using the metacognition and self-regulation literature. Luke and Hardy (1999) advocated for the use of metacognition as a conceptual framework to guide research on student cognition, but to date there still has been relatively little research published that focuses on metacognition and self-regulated learning in PE. These approaches encompass a broad range of cognitions, including attentional focus, use of learning strategies, self-efficacy and confidence, self-evaluation, monitoring, and planning. From earlier work summarized by Solmon (2006), we know that structuring tasks sequentially at an appropriate level of difficulty and designing appropriate practice so that learners can experience success can decrease anxiety and stress and help students focus their attention on learning. Instructional cues can help individuals concentrate on key aspects of a learning task and when learners encounter difficulties, learning strategies can help them master tasks. The studies cited in the earlier review generally considered these variables in isolation, and the more recent work grounded in metacognition and self-regulation provides a more comprehensive picture of student cognitions.

Several researchers (e.g., McBride & Xiang, 2013) have used self-regulated learning to frame their investigations of motivation, but have not included a measure of learning in the research design, and that work is addressed in the section on motivation. A few studies have, however, included a pre-post design as an indicant of learning. Chatzipanteli and Digelidis (2011) used question prompts designed to activate students' metacognitive process while they performed a volleyball serve test. Participants completed five trials, and after a short break completed five additional trials where, after each attempt, they completed a survey designed to prompt metacognitive processes, including analyzing each trial, planning to improve performance, monitoring, evaluation, and reflection. Performance on the second set of trials was significantly better. Although the results support the notion that this technique can be used to promote metacognition and improve learning, the lack of a comparison-control group and the short duration of the instructional episode are methodological weaknesses in this study.

Kolovelonis and colleagues (Kolovelonis, Goudas, & Dermitzaki, 2010, 2011; Kolovelonis, Goudas, Dermitzaki, & Kitsantas, 2013; Kolovelonis, Goudas, Hassandra, & Dermitzaki, 2012) conducted a series of studies on self-regulated learning of skills in a PE setting. A strength of these studies is the use of an experimental design with different levels of treatments and control conditions, and the use of motor tasks (i.e., dart throwing and basketball dribbling) but the short time allocated for students to practice the task (16 minutes) is a limitation. They found that emulative practice with social feedback followed by self-control practice where students set goals and monitored their progress was effective in skill acquisition and promoting motivational beliefs (Kolovelonis et al., 2010, 2012, 2013). Self-recording also had a positive effect on skill performance (Kolovelonis, Goudas, & Dermitzaki, 2011). This line of studies provides evidence that when tasks are structured to promote students' involvement in their learning they not only perform better but also demonstrate more positive affect as compared to control conditions. Tasks that increase student autonomy and promote more internalized regulations foster both learning and higher levels of motivation.

Physical activity, physical fitness, physical education, and cognition

In the context of high stakes testing, school administrators have in many cases sought to decrease time for PE and other opportunities for children to be physically active to allocate increased time to prepare for standardized testing (Monnat, Lounsbery, & Smith, 2014). This trend has sparked efforts to support the argument that sacrificing time for children to be active in order to increase time spent in math and reading is not associated with increased test scores, and there is clear evidence that is true (Trudeau & Shepard, 2008). Correlational studies provide evidence that children who are physically active (Donnelly & Lambourne, 2011) and physically fit (Chomitz et al., 2009) perform better academically than those who are not, and that short bouts of physical activity during the school day improve attention-to-task for elementary school students (Mahar, 2011). The line of reasoning that PE and physical activity can improve cognition and may improve academic achievement scores in addition to improving children's health may be useful in efforts to ensure that PE requirements are not eroded. Care must be taken, however, to ensure that content of PE is valued in its own right as an important element in school curricula and that programs are not reduced to simply promoting high levels of physical activity at a target heart rate.

Implications for evidence-based practice

The knowledge base generated from research on student cognition supports several implications for teaching. First, practitioners must be aware of ways that prior knowledge, cultural experiences, and other characteristics affect whether or not students are motivated to learn in PE. In the current educational context, it is important that teachers ensure that students in their classes see value in the content being taught and that the instruction is meaningful to them. Additionally, care must be taken to structure activities so that students believe that they can be successful in the learning activity if they are willing to exert effort. A focus on personal improvement and task mastery, as opposed to normative comparisons, and sequencing tasks at an appropriate level of difficulty are important elements in structuring classes so that students can experience success. When those issues have been addressed, then teachers can focus on ways to provide instruction that will facilitate cognitions that enable students to learn.

Selection of curricular models and teaching approaches affects student cognitions, in that models that create more authentic situated learning experiences generally elicit a higher level of cognition than teaching approaches that rely solely on direct instruction. Inclusion of tasks that require students to analyze their performance, set goals, and monitor their progress can facilitate cognitive involvement and promote learning, facilitating higher levels of internalization and self-regulation. Lastly, because students do not always perceive instructional behaviors and class events as the teacher intends, it is an important endeavor for teachers to include checks for understanding in their lessons. Asking students what they are thinking, what they understand, and what suggestions they have for instruction can provide valuable insight into the ways that students learn (Koekoek, Knoppers, & Stegeman, 2009) and whether they are learning.

Future directions

The study of student cognition in PE is an important area of research that has not received much consideration in recent years. I have tried to make the argument that a research focus on student learning in PE is a critical element in demonstrating the importance of PE programs in schools and that this area deserves more attention. Much of the recent work has been conducted using experimental designs in contrived settings with very short instructional phases.

Although the pressure to publish a high quantity of research produces a system that encourages this, and these studies do make a contribution, research conducted in real world settings is needed. To gain a better understanding of student cognition, studies conducted in authentic field settings with practicing teachers using metacognitive/self-regulation frameworks are essential to promote a more comprehensive understanding of student learning. It also is critical that valid and reliable assessments of learning be included in studies that focus on student cognition. Given the complexity of the human learning experience, research designs that apply multi-level analyses that enable researchers to examine social and individual factors to explore metacognition and self-regulated learning hold promise.

Summary of key findings

- Cognition encompasses a wide range of thought processes related to knowledge acquisition including beliefs, perceptions, attention, concentration, emotions, motivations, learning strategies, reasoning, and decision making.
- In order for students to be motivated to learn by engaging in cognitive processes, they must see value in the content and believe that they have the ability to experience success if they exert effort.
- To understand how to foster student cognition that promotes learning, teachers and researchers must have an understanding of the individual meanings that students assign to instructional behaviors.
- Curriculum and teaching approaches that situate learning in authentic contexts are effective in increasing techniques and strategies that promote cognition and foster understanding of game play.
- Learning styles with higher levels of student autonomy and cognitive involvement (inclusion) are more effective at increasing student learning than those with direct teacher control (command & practices styles).
- The instructional approach used by the teacher can serve to enhance or constrain students' cognitive engagement.
- Metacognition and self-regulated learning provide frameworks that enable researchers to examine cognition from an integrated holistic perspective rather than isolating individual variables.
- Sequential task structuring and instructional cueing at an appropriate difficulty level can foster student success, decrease anxiety and stress, and enhance students' focus on learning.
- Learning activities can be structured to engage students in metacognitive processes that will translate to higher levels of internalization, self-regulation, and motivation.
- Tasks structured to promote student involvement in the learning process increase student performance and contribute to positive affect. Tasks that promote student autonomy and promote internalized regulation foster both learning and higher motivation levels.
- Activities that involve students in analyzing their performance, setting goals, developing strategies, and monitoring progress are associated with higher levels of learning.

Reflective questions for discussion

1. What should students be learning in PE, and how can we engender a culture shift within students and teachers to increase the focus on learning in school PE?
2. How can learning in PE be assessed?

3. How does the emphasis on physical activity promotion in schools enhance or constrain research on teaching and learning in PE?
4. How can teachers challenged with large class sizes, inadequate facilities and equipment, and students who are seemingly not motivated or interested in PE successfully incorporate learning activities in their curricula that will promote student cognition that promotes learning?

References

Araújo, R., Mesquita, I., & Hastie, P. (2014). Review of the status of learning in research on sport education: Future research and practice. *Journal of Sports Science and Medicine, 13*, 846–858.

Azzarito, L., & Kirk, D. (Eds.). (2013). *Pedagogies, physical culture, and visual methods.* New York: Routledge.

Azzarito, L., Solmon, M.A., & Harrison, L. (2006). "… If I had a choice, I would." A feminist post-structuralist perspective on girls in physical education classes. *Research Quarterly for Exercise and Sport, 77*, 222–239.

Boekaerts, M., Pintrich, P. R., & Zeidner, M. (Eds.). (2000) *Handbook of self-regulation.* San Diego: Academic Press.

Brick, N., MacIntyre, T., & Campbell, M. (2015). Metacognitive processes in the self-regulation of performance in elite distance runners. *Psychology of Sport and Exercise, 19*, 1–9.

Byra, M., Sanchez, B., & Wallhead, T. (2014). Behaviors of students and teachers in the command, practice, and inclusion styles of teaching: Instruction, feedback, and activity level. *European Physical Education Review, 20*, 3–19.

Castelli, D., Centeio, E., Beighle, A., Carson, R., & Nicksic, H. (2014). Physical literacy and comprehensive school physical activity programs. *Preventive Medicine, 66*, 95–100.

Chatzipanteli, A., & Digelidis, N. (2011). The influence of metacognitive prompting on students' performance in a motor skills test in physical education. *International Journal of Sports Science and Engineering, 5*, 93–98.

Chomitz, V. R., Slining, M. M., McGowan, R. J., Mitchell, S. E., Dawson, G. F., & Hacker, K. (2009). 416 A: Is there a relationship between physical fitness and academic achievement? 417: Positive results from public school children in the northeastern United States. *Journal of School Health, 79*, 30–37.

Dewey, J. (1990). *School and society and the child and the curriculum.* Chicago: University of Chicago Press. (Original work published in 1899).

Dewey, J. (1966). *Democracy and education.* New York: Free Press. (Original work published in 1916).

Dodds, P., Griffin, L. L., & Placek, J. H. (2001). A selected review of literature on the development of learners' domain-specific knowledge. *Journal of Teaching in Physical Education, 20*, 301–313.

Donnelly, J. E., & Lambourne, K. (2011). Classroom-based physical activity, cognition, and academic achievement. *Preventive Medicine, 52*, S36–S42.

Doyle, W. (1977). Paradigms of research for teacher effectiveness. *Review of Research in Education, 5*, 163–198.

Eccles, J. S. (2005). Subjective task value and the Eccles et al. model of achievement-related choices. In A. J. Elliot & C. S. Dweck (Eds.), *Handbook of competence and motivation* (pp. 105–121). New York: Guilford Press.

Elliot, A. J., & Dweck, C. S. (2005). Competence and motivation: Competence as the core of achievement. In A. J. Elliot and C. S. Dweck (Eds.), *Handbook of competence and motivation* (pp. 3–12). New York: Guilford Press.

Ennis, C. D. (2011). Physical education curriculum priorities: Evidence for education and skillfulness. *Quest, 63*, 5–18.

Frisette, J. L. (2013). Are you listening? Adolescent girls voice how they negotiate self-identified barriers to their success and survival in physical education. *Physical Education & Sport Pedagogy, 18*, 184–203.

Gage, N. L. (Ed.). (1963). *Handbook of research on teaching.* Chicago: Rand McNally.

Gage, N. L., & Berliner, D C. (1992). *Educational psychology* (5th edn). Boston: Houghton.

Giblin, S., Collins, D., & Button, C. (2014). Physical literacy: Importance, assessment, and future directions. *Sports Medicine, 44*, 1177–1184.

Kirk, D. (2013). Educational value and models-based practice in physical education. *Educational Philosophy and Theory, 45*, 973–986.

Koekoek, J., Knoppers, A., & Stegeman, H. (2009). How do children think they learn in physical education? *Journal of Teaching in Physical Education, 28*, 310–332.

Kolovelonis, A., Goudas, M., & Dermitzaki, I. (2010). Self-regulated learning of a motor skill through emulation and self-control levels in a physical education setting. *Journal of Applied Sport Psychology, 22*, 198–212.

Kolovelonis, A., Goudas, M., & Dermitzaki, I. (2011). The effect of different goals and self-recording on self-regulation of learning a motor skill in a physical education setting. *Learning and Instruction, 21*, 355–364.

Kolovelonis, A., Goudas, M., Dermitzaki, I., & Kitsantas, A. (2013). Self-regulated learning and performance calibration among elementary physical education students. *European Journal of Psychology of Education, 28*, 685–701.

Kolovelonis, A., Goudas, M., Hassandra, M., & Dermitzaki, I. (2012). Self-regulated learning in physical education: Examining the effects of emulative and self-control practice. *Psychology of Sport and Exercise, 13*, 383–389.

Lee, A. M. (1997). Contributions of research on student thinking in physical education. *Journal of Teaching in Physical Education, 16*, 262–277.

Lee, A., & Solmon, M. (1992). Cognitive conceptions of teaching and learning motor skills. *Quest, 44*, 57–71.

Luke, I., & Hardy, C. (1999). Appreciating the complexity of learning in physical education: The utilization of a metacognitive ability conceptual framework. *Sport, Education and Society, 4*, 175–191.

MacKeachie, W. (2000). Foreword. In M. Boekaerts, P. R. Pintrich, & M. Zeidner (Eds.), *Handbook of self-regulation* (pp. xxi–xxiii). New York: Academic Press.

Magill, R. (2001) *Motor learning: Concepts and applications* (6th edn). Boston: McGraw Hill.

Mahar, M. (2011). Impact of short bouts of physical activity on attention-to-task in elementary school children. *Preventive Medicine, 52*, S60–S64.

McBride, R., & Xiang, P. (2013). Self-regulated learning and perceived health among students participating in university physical activity classes. *Journal of Teaching in Physical Education, 32*, 220–236.

Monnat, S., Lounsbery, M., & Smith, N. (2014). Correlates of state enactment of elementary school physical education laws. *Preventive Medicine, 69*, S5–S11.

Nixon, J., & Locke. L. (1973). Research in teaching in physical education. In R. M. W. Travers (Ed.), *Second handbook of research on teaching* (pp. 1210–1242). Chicago: Rand McNally.

Nyberg, G., & Larsson, H. (2014). Exploring 'what' to learn in physical education. *Physical Education & Sport Pedagogy, 19*, 123–135.

Peterson, P. L. (1988). Teachers' and students' cognitional knowledge for classroom teaching and learning. *Educational Researcher, 17*(5), 5–14.

Pintrich, P. R. (2003). A motivational science perspective on the role of student motivation in learning and teaching contexts. *Journal of Educational Psychology, 95*, 667–686.

Powell, K., & Kalina, C. (2009). Cognitive and social constructivism: Developing tools for an effective classroom. *Journal of Education, 130*, 241–250.

Reid, A. (2013). Physical education, cognition, and agency. *Educational Philosophy and Theory, 45*, 921–933.

Richardson, V. (Ed.). (2001) *Handbook of research on teaching* (4th edn). Washington, D.C.: American Educational Research Association.

Roberts, G. C. (1992). Motivation in sport and exercise: Conceptual constraints and convergence. In G. C. Roberts (Ed.), *Motivation in sport and exercise* (pp. 3–29). Champaign, IL: Human Kinetics.

Roberts, G. C. (2001). Understanding the dynamics of motivation in physical activity: The influence of achievement goals on motivational processes. In G. C. Roberts (Ed.), *Advances in motivation in sport and exercise* (pp. 1–50). Champaign, IL: Human Kinetics.

Ryan, R., & Deci, E. (2000). Self-determination theory and the facilitation of intrinsic motivation, social development, and well-being. *The American Psychologist, 55*, 68–78.

Sanchez, B., Byra, M., & Wallhead, T. L. (2012). Students' perceptions of the command, practice, and inclusion styles of teaching. *Physical Education & Sport Pedagogy, 17*, 317–330.

Shulman, L. S. (1986). Paradigms and research programs in the study of teaching: A contemporary perspective. In M. C. Wittrock (Ed.), *Handbook of research on teaching* (3rd edn) (pp. 3–36). New York: Macmillan.

Solmon, M. (2003). Student issues in physical education classes: Attitude, cognition, and motivation. In S. J. Silverman & C. D. Ennis (Eds.), *Student learning in physical education: Applying research to enhance instruction* (2nd edn) (pp. 147–163). Champaign, IL: Human Kinetics.

Solmon, M. A. (2006). Learner cognition. In D. Kirk, D. Macdonald, & M. O'Sullivan (Eds.), *Handbook of research in physical education* (pp. 226–241). Thousand Oaks, CA: Sage.

Spencer-Cavaliere, N., & Rintoul, M. A. (2012). Alienation in physical education from the perspectives of children. *Journal of Teaching in Physical Education, 31*, 344–361.

Stolk, J., & Harari, J. (2014). Student motivations as predictors of high-level cognitions in project-based classrooms. *Active Learning in Higher Education, 15*, 231–247.

Stolz, S., & Pill, S. (2014). Teaching games and sport for understanding: Exploring and reconsidering its relevance in physical education. *European Physical Education Review, 20*, 36–71.

Travers, R. M. W. (Ed.). (1973). *Second handbook of research on teaching.* Chicago: Rand McNally.

Trudeau, F., & Shephard, R. (2008). Physical education, school physical activity, school sports, and academic performance. *International Journal of Behavioral Nutrition and Physical Activity, 5*, 10. doi 10.1186/1479-5868-5-10

Vohs, K. D., & Baumeister, R. F. (Eds.). (2011). *Handbook of self-regulation: Research, theory, and practice* (2nd edn). New York: Guilford Press.

Whitehead, M. (2010). *Physical literacy: Throughout the life course.* New York: Routledge.

Wittrock, M. C. (Ed.). (1986a). *Handbook of research on reaching* (3rd edn). New York: Macmillan.

Wittrock, M. C. (1986b). Students' thought processes. In M. C. Wittrock (Ed.), *Handbook of research on teaching* (3rd edn) (pp. 297–314). New York: Macmillan.

Zimmerman, B., & Schunk, D. (2011). Self-regulated learning and performance: An introduction and an overview. In B. Zimmerman & D. Schunk (Eds.). *Handbook of self-regulation of learning and performance* (pp. 1–12). New York: Routledge.

34

STUDENT PHYSICAL SELF-CONCEPT BELIEFS

Alex C. Garn, LOUISIANA STATE UNIVERSITY, USA

Effective learning tasks in physical education (PE) commonly call for students to simultaneously engage physically, cognitively, and psychosocially. Therefore, student-learning outcomes of quality PE programs generally focus on a variety of advancements physically (e.g., motor skill execution; physical activity participation), cognitively (e.g., application of health-related fitness knowledge; sport tactics), psychologically (e.g., self-efficacy; self-concept), and socially (e.g., interpersonal skills; social responsibility). Physical self-concept beliefs represent an individual's subjective sense of self physically (Fox & Wilson, 2008; Harter, 2012; Marsh, Martin, & Jackson, 2010). Physical self-concept is a key indicator of mental health (Fox, 1997) and promotes students' motivation (Garn & Wallhead, 2015) and physical activity behavior (Marsh, Papaioannou, & Theodorakis, 2006). Standage, Gillison, Ntoumanis, and Treasure (2012) argue that physical self-concept is an important outcome of quality PE and the physically challenging and interactive nature of PE makes it an optimal setting to investigate this construct (Barnes & Spray, 2013).

Self-concept plays a central role in physical perceptions of self. Although it is beyond the scope of this review to compare and contrast self-concept to other cognitive constructs (see Bong & Skaalvik, 2003 for an excellent review), it is important to note that self-concept is the more encompassing construct, while both self-efficacy and perceived competence are key components of the self-concept belief construct. In other words, self-efficacy focuses on individuals' beliefs about what they can accomplish in a specific situation based on their abilities, whereas self-concept focuses on how one defines and evaluates personal abilities (Bong & Skaalvik, 2003). Bong and Skaalvik also point out notable differences such as time orientation (i.e., self-efficacy = future-oriented; self-concept = past-oriented), specificity (self-efficacy = situational-specific; self-concept = domain-specific), and frame of reference (i.e., self-efficacy = performance-based; self-concept = personal, performance, and normative-based). Perceived competence is viewed as the core component of self-concept (Harter, 2012) and as such it reflects the cognitive component of self-concept beliefs. The inclusion of emotional reactions to competencies, considered an important aspect of the evaluative process, is one substantive difference between the two constructs. For example, students in PE with similar competence beliefs may have varying emotional reactions to those beliefs, which can cause differences in self-concept. In summary, self-efficacy and perceived competence are important components of a broader set of self-concept beliefs.

In this chapter I review PE research on student physical self-concept beliefs. I will explore the historical roots of self-concept research and the evolution of physical self-concept in the initial part of the chapter followed by detailed accounts of prominent physical self-concept theories commonly used to investigate PE students and settings. Themes focus on physical self-concept measurement, personal characteristics, and contextual factors that enhance and undermine physical self-concept development, and consequences associated with individual differences in physical self-concept. I also underscore substantive issues in need of greater exploration and conclude the chapter with recommendations on how physical self-concept research translates to PE best practices in teaching and learning. I emphasize the role of cognition in physical self-concept beliefs throughout the chapter.

The theoretical scope of this chapter is limited to multidimensional models of self-concept because they provide an authentic and useful perspective for understanding the construct (Fox & Wilson, 2008; Marsh, 1997; Shavelson, Hubner, & Stanton, 1976). Grounded in social cognitive principles of personality and individual difference, multidimensional models of self-concept assume that self-concept is organized in a complex hierarchical and domain-specific structure (Marsh et al., 2010). The superordinate level of multidimensional models of self-concept is global self-esteem, which represents an individual's overall sense of self (Fox & Wilson, 2008; Harter, 2012). Global self-esteem is the most stable and trait-like aspect of self-concept and is influenced by domain-specific self-concept beliefs (Shavelson et al., 1976).

Much of the current multidimensional self-concept research is based on the seminal work of Shavelson and colleagues (1976) who theorized that global self-esteem is derived from four main domain specific self-concepts: (a) academic/intellectual, (b) social, (c) emotional, and (d) physical. Within each self-concept domain resides more specific subdomains of self-concept. Shavelson et al. (1976) considered the subdomains of physical self-concept to be grounded in perceptions of physical ability and appearance. The common premise across frameworks is that individuals use self-concept subdomains to define and evaluate their respective domain-level self-concept. For example, a student may have favorable views of strength and sport self-concepts and unfavorable views of flexibility and endurance self-concepts (subdomain level), which impacts how she views her physical self (domain level). Self-concept also can be broken down further into facets (e.g., tennis ability) and subfacets (e.g., serving ability in tennis). The lowest and most specific levels of multidimensional self-concept models are characterized by interpretations of situational and contextual interactions with the environment. Students often use social comparison strategies in PE contexts to make judgments about their strength, endurance, sport competence, etc. (Barnes & Spray, 2013).

The role of cognition in self-concept

Fox and Wilson (2008) highlight the important role of cognition in self-concept development with their "self-director" metaphor. The self-director represents an individual's cognitive processes that organize, monitor, integrate, and protect her/his self-concept. Interactions with the environment are filtered through the self-director whereby experiences that generate enhancements to the self are emphasized while experiences that erode the self are minimized. The impact that appraisals of environmental interactions have on self-concept beliefs is embedded in culturally relevant norms and value systems. The self-director guides individuals toward culturally relevant contexts that facilitate a positive sense of self and away from contexts that detract from a positive sense of self. Similarly, appraisals of success are typically attributed to internal characteristics (e.g., ability; effort) to bolster one's sense of self while appraisals of failure often are attributed to external factors (e.g., luck; weather) to preserve one's sense of self (Weiner,

2000). In culturally relevant contexts where negative feedback is imminent, the self-director is likely to implement protective strategies such as self-handicapping (Rhodewalt & Vohs, 2005) or devaluing the context (Harter, 2012) to limit self-concept damage.

Initially physical self-concept research conducted in K-12 PE (Beasley & Garn, 2013) is emphasized. Studies focused on after-school physical activity programs (Martin, Garn, Shen, McCaughtry, & Nash, 2014) and school-based interventions (Annesi et al., 2007) also are reviewed.

Historical overview

Most current multidimensional theories of self-concept trace origins back to William James's (1890) *Principles of Psychology* (see Harter, 2003 for a concise historical overview). James differentiated between two interrelated aspects of the self, the "stream of thought" (James, 1890, p. 224) also known as the I-self and the "the consciousness of self" (James, 1890, p. 291) also known as the Me-self. The I-self consists of multiple psychological constructs including self-awareness, self-agency, self-continuity, and self-coherence. The Me-self is also multidimensional and constitutes the material-Self, social-Self, spiritual-Self, and pure-Ego. James denotes that the body is at the core of one's material-Self with specific body parts being more intimately involved in shaping the material-Self. The Me-self and its components set the stage for investigating multidimensional self-concept.

Contributions from social psychologists such as Cooley's (1922) theory of the looking glass self build on James' work, advancing understanding about self-concept development. However, the strong influence of behaviorism on psychology during the first part of the twentieth century in the United States diminished the study of self-concept (Harter, 2003). The role of cognition in personality development was more progressive during this time period in Europe (e.g., Freud's notions of ego development in psychoanalysis – see Freud, 2005; Binet's measures of intelligence – see Binet & Simon, 1916), contributing to greater acceptance of self-concept research worldwide. For example, Martin (1926) advocated for the study of multidimensional self-concept in Australia based on philosophy and critique of James, Binet, and Freud among others.

The emergence of humanistic psychology based on the work of Carl Rogers in the mid-twentieth century is another important historical juncture in the study of self-concept (Wylie, 1974). Rogers' (1951) work emphasized the active role of the individual in personality development, purporting a natural human inclination to pursue personal growth, self-actualization, and self-awareness. Rogers theorized that self-concept is an organized configuration of beliefs pertaining to personal characteristics, abilities, and interactions with the environment. Self-concept is strongest when individuals fully accept who they are and feel others do the same in what Rogers terms unconditional positive regard.

In the later part of the twentieth century, cognitive, social, and social-cognitive paradigms advanced to the forefront of psychological and educational research (Dweck & Leggett, 1988) as well as systematic investigation of multidimensional self-concept in exercise science (e.g., Sonstroem, 1978). In fact, Sonstroem's research often is credited as facilitating in–depth investigations of multidimensional self-concept in the physical domain (Fox, 1997). Sonstroem (1978) initially developed the psychological model for physical activity participation (PMPAP). The PMPAP followed the *skill development hypothesis* that presumed external behaviors and experiences of success lead to increases in internal development of self-esteem. However, Sonstroem proposed in the PMPAP that perceptions of physical ability and physical estimation of physical and sport skills mediated the relationship between physical activity behavior and self-esteem. For example, students' physical activity engagement in PE increases their ability beliefs and expectations for success, leading to self-esteem enhancements. The *self-enhancement hypothesis* also is included in the PMPAP whereby individuals actively seek to enhance self-esteem by engaging in external behaviors and environments that facilitate success. In the PMPAP, the relationship between self-esteem and physical estimation is considered reciprocal. Furthermore, physical estimation also is hypothesized to directly impact attraction to physical activity (i.e., personal interest), which directly influences physical activity. In other words, in the self-enhancement hypothesis aspect of the PMPAP, the relationship between self-esteem and physical activity behavior is mediated sequentially by physical estimation and attraction to physical activity. In simple terms, students actively engage in behaviors or seek out opportunities in PE they believe can increase self-esteem and avoid behaviors or situations that potentially decrease self-esteem. Taken together, the PMPAP represents a foundational multidimensional model of self-concept in the physical domain.

Systematic investigation of multidimensional physical self-concept in PE and school-based physical activity received increased attention in the late 1980s (e.g., Fox & Corbin, 1989; Marsh & Peart, 1988). For example, Marsh and Peart (1988) examined the impact of a 6-week, 14-session school-based physical fitness intervention on physical fitness and multidimensional self-concept in a sample of grade eight Australian girls. The three conditions of the intervention included: (a) emphasis on cooperative fitness activities and feedback; (b) emphasis on competitive fitness activities and feedback; and (c) control. Results indicated there was a large intervention effect on fitness for both the cooperative and competitive groups compared to the control. Students in the cooperative group, however, reported more positive physical ability and physical appearance self-concepts at the end of the intervention compared to other groups. Students in the competitive group reported the lowest levels of physical ability self-concept. Marsh and Peart noted that physical activity environments that stress competition and social comparison create few winners and many losers, which likely erodes physical ability self-concept.

While Sonstroem's work set the stage for preliminary investigations of multidimensional self-concept in the physical domain, it is the separate but notable accomplishments of Kenneth Fox and Herbert Marsh that have produced systematic investigation of multidimensional physical self-concepts with children and adolescents in PE settings. For both Fox and Marsh, a key factor in their physical self-concept theory development is the production and continued popularity of rigorous self-report measures. Specifically, the Physical Self-Perception Profile (PSPP; Fox & Corbin, 1989) and the Physical Self-Description Questionnaire (PSDQ; Marsh, Richards, Johnson, Roche, & Tremayne, 1994) are instruments with tightly interwoven theoretical and measurement alignment. These two theoretical frameworks are discussed in the next section.

Theoretical frameworks

Multidimensional physical self-concept theories share numerous theoretical assumptions. As noted earlier (see Table 34.1), theorists posit a hierarchical and domain-specific structure (Fox & Wilson, 2008; Marsh et al., 2010). The top of the hierarchy consists of the most general and stable form of self-concept, self-esteem. Facets become more domain-specific and contextually formed moving down the hierarchy. Interpretations of experiences and interactions in one's environment reside at the bottom of the hierarchy. Therefore, self-concept interventions are typically focused using a bottom–up approach. In other words, self-concept interventions are considered most effective when they target logical domain-specific, contextually driven facets of self-concept. For example, physical fitness-based interventions in PE would be most

Table 34.1 Comparison of proposed hierarchical structures of Marsh's Physical Self-Description Questionnaire and Fox's Physical Self-Perception Profile

Physical self-concept beliefs

Hierarchical level	Marsh's PSDQ	Fox's PSPP
Superordinate	Global self-esteem	Global self-esteem
Domain	Physical self-concept	Physical self-worth
Subdomain	Activity self-concept	Body attractiveness beliefs
	Appearance self-concept	Physical condition beliefs
	Body fat self-concept	Physical strength beliefs
	Coordination self-concept	Sport competence beliefs
	Endurance self-concept	
	Flexibility self-concept	
	Health self-concept	
	Sport self-concept	
	Strength self-concept	

successful targeting self-concepts related to physical endurance, muscular strength, flexibility, and body composition (e.g., Marsh, 1993; Marsh & Peart, 1988).

Physical self-concept is theorized as a core element in facilitating motivation, psychological well-being, and health-related behavior (Fox, 1997; Harter, 2012; Marsh Papaionannou, & Theodorakis, 2006). Craven and Marsh (2008) note that people who feel good about their appearance and physical capabilities are more likely to maximize physical potential, fitness, and mental health compared to those who do not. Physical self-concept is theorized as an important health outcome in and of itself as well as an antecedent, mediator, and moderator of health-related outcomes.

The skill development and self-enhancement hypotheses also are key theoretical assumptions in multidimensional self-concept theory. Applied to PE settings, students who experience success and receive positive behavioral feedback should increase multidimensional physical self-concepts while students exposed to failure and negative feedback will likely decrease self-concepts. Furthermore, students who view PE as an environment to enhance facets of physical self-concepts will likely be attracted to the context while students with the opposing perspective of PE will likely be indifferent. From a measurement standpoint, minor differences are present between Fox's and Marsh's notions of the specific facets of physical self-concept.

Fox's PSPP

Fox's theoretical framework (see Table 34.1) of physical self-concept is easily recognized by the use of the PSPP (Fox & Corbin, 1989) or the Children and Youth Physical Self-Perception Profile (CY-PSPP; Welk & Eklund, 2005), the measure typically used in K-12 PE settings. Global self-esteem resides at the top of Fox's framework but unidimensional measures are added to the PSPP to measure the apex of the model. Physical self-worth represents the global measure of physical self-concept on the PSPP, with four main dimensions of beliefs nested beneath physical self-worth: (a) physical conditioning, (b) sport competence, (c) body attractiveness, and (d) strength. The PSPP constructs are based on content analysis of qualitative interviews of undergraduate students involved in PE courses (Fox, 1997). The PSPP consists of 30 items presented in a structured alternative format (Harter, 2012) and answered using a four-point Likert scale. An example item for sport competence on the CY-PSPP is: "Some kids do very well at all kinds of sports BUT other kids don't feel that they are very good when it comes to sports" (Welk & Eklund, 2005). Students choose one of the two statements and decide if it is "really true for me" or "sort of true for me."

The CY-PSPP consistently demonstrates valid and reliable measurement characteristics with PE students in 3rd–6th grade (Welk, Corbin, Dowell, & Harris, 1997; Welk & Eklund, 2005). In validation studies by Welk and colleagues, the four dimensions of the CY-PSPP produce stable correlations with the strongest relationship occurring between physical conditioning and sport competence beliefs (range of r's = .64–.72) and the weakest relationship between strength beliefs and body attractiveness (range of r's = .44–.53). Body attractiveness was most closely associated with physical self-worth (range of r's = .76–.78) and the relationship between physical self-worth and global self-esteem (range of r's = .74–.75) was robust. In fact, the strength of relationships can be critiqued as a possible method effect based on the use of the structured alternative format (Marsh et al., 1994).

Marsh's PSDQ

Marsh's development of the PSDQ and a subsequent short version of the PSDQ (PSDQ-S; Marsh et al., 2010) is grounded in classic measurement theory and factor analysis. The PSDQ is a product of rigorous within-network and between-network empirical testing (see Marsh, 1997). Within-network testing involved validity (e.g., construct, discriminant; convergent via factor analysis) and reliability (e.g., internal consistency; test-retest) analysis of the hierarchical and multidimensional structure of the PSDQ. Once within-network support was achieved, between-network evidence was gathered, consisting of establishing a stable pattern of theoretically grounded relationships of PSDQ variables to other constructs (e.g., dimensions of fitness; physical activity; motivation).

A visual representation of the hierarchy and domains of Marsh's PSDQ (70 items) is provided in Table 34.1. Global self-esteem is located at the top of the hierarchy of the PSDQ with global physical self-concept located below. There are nine subdomains of physical self-concept beliefs including: (a) appearance, (b) body fat, (c) coordination, (d) endurance, (e) flexibility, (f) health, (g) physical activity, (h) sport competence, and (i) strength. The PSDQ uses short declarative statements (e.g., Physically, I am happy with myself) that are measured on a six-point false-to-true scale. These subdomains reflect appearance, health, and physical fitness components (Marsh, 1997).

The PSDQ-S

More recently, Marsh and colleagues developed a shorter form, PSDQ-S (40 items), to reduce participant burden (Marsh et al., 2010). In an exemplary validation investigation, Marsh et al. (2010) used six different samples across the lifespan including adolescent students (ages 12–18) with a total of 4,803 participants to establish within-network and between-network support for the PSDQ-S. Furthermore, multi-group confirmatory factor analysis of factorial invariance provided support for invariance across age, gender, and time for the PSDQ-S.

The correlation between global self-esteem and global physical constructs as measured by the PSDQ-S is robust (range of r's = .77–.84; Marsh et al., 2010). Global physical self-concept has the strongest relationships with appearance (r = .69) and coordination (r = .61) and lowest with health self-concept (r = .13). Flexibility self-concept and coordination share the strongest association among dimensions (r = .80) while sport competence and health self-concept share the weakest association ($r = .10$). In general, most of the nine dimensions of the PSDQ-S share a moderate, positive association. Marsh et al. (2010) recommend the use of the PSDQ-S with youth around the age of 12 years old (~ middle school students): however; testing the suitability of the PSDQ-S with younger children such as elementary PE students is needed. As individuals get older, it is theorized that the hierarchical nature of self-concept becomes more differentiated, which is demonstrated by smaller correlations among domain-related self-concepts.

The jingle-jangle fallacy

The jingle-jangle fallacy occurs when researchers assume that measures with the same labels measure the same constructs while the jangle fallacy occurs when researchers assume that measures with different labels measure different constructs (Marsh, 1994). Marsh and colleagues tested the jingle-jangle and the jangle fallacies using a multi-trait, multi-method design and analysis (Marsh, Asci, & Tomás, 2002). Marsh et al. (2002) tested the jingle-jangle and jangle fallacies with the PSDQ and PPSP in a large sample of Turkish university students enrolled in elective PE classes. Results yielded clear convergent validity for three factors across the PSDQ and PSPP: (a) global physical self-concept – global physical self-worth; (b) strength on both scales; and (c) sport competence on both scales. In other words, these subscales of the PSDQ and PSPP measure the same construct. Evidence also supported commonality on the appearance subscale of the PSDQ and the body attractiveness subscale of the PSPP; and the endurance subscale of the PSDQ and physical condition subscale of the PSPP. Therefore, of the 16 subscales of the PSDQ and PSPP (global self-esteem of PSPP was not included), there is both theoretical and empirical evidence for the overlap of five subscales. These results provided important information for making interpretations and generalizations across studies that use the PSDQ and PSPP in PE and other physical activity settings.

Current trends and issues

This section is a synthesis of physical self-concept research in PE settings focused on: (a) PE-related antecedents of student physical self-concept; and (b) physical self-concept as an antecedent of student engagement.

PE-related antecedents of physical self-concept

A crucial line of inquiry examines antecedents that maximize or inhibit the growth of physical self-concept in PE. Antecedents of multidimensional physical self-concept are covered within two models of multidimensional self-concept theory. First, the *internal/external frames of references model* (Barnes & Spray, 2013; Chanal & Sarrazin, 2007), which highlights the role of personal and social comparisons in physical self-concept development, is outlined. Next, findings pertaining to the *skill development hypothesis model* (Annesi et al., 2007; Fox, 1997), which explores the impact of physical activity behavior and engagement in PE on physical self-concept, are presented.

Internal/external frames of reference

Interpretations of environmental interactions present the foundation of hierarchical models of multidimensional self-concept. Internal/external frames of reference represent the personal and social comparison standards that individuals use in the environment to make appraisals of their self-concept (Barnes & Spray, 2013). An internal frame of reference occurs when individuals compare their achievements to previous achievements within the same environment (i.e., PE) as well as to their achievements in other environments (e.g., mathematics achievement; science achievement; etc.). If current achievement is determined to be lower than previous achievement and/or an individual believes she/he achieves at a higher level in other environments, self-concept is posited to diminish (Möller, Pohlmann, Köller, & Marsh, 2009). On the other hand, if current achievement is viewed as higher than previous achievement and/or the individual believes she/he achieves at a lower level in other environments, self-concept is posited to increase. With an internal frame of reference, self-concept can change regardless of normative standing. In other words, self-concept can decrease despite good normative standing.

An external frame of reference occurs when students use social comparisons from others as a frame of reference for their own achievements (Barnes & Spray, 2013; Chanal & Sarrazin, 2007; Möller et al., 2009). In general, positive social comparisons generate higher levels of self-concept while negative social comparisons produce lower levels of self-concept. There are, however, theoretical nuances associated with an external frame of reference. First, social comparison targets play a key role in the process of evaluation (Barnes & Spray, 2013). When the social comparison target(s) is/are believed to possess greater ability, it is considered an *upward comparison*. When the social comparison target(s) is/are believed to possess similar ability, it is considered a *lateral comparison* while social comparison target(s) considered to have lower ability is/are termed a *downward comparison*. Upward, lateral, and downward comparisons are defined as the *direction of comparison* for an external frame of reference (Chanal & Sarrazin, 2007).

External frames of reference can also be explicit and implicit. An *explicit external frame of reference* occurs when external comparisons of ability and achievement are consciously made toward specific individuals or small groups. For example, in PE a student may identify a friend or group of friends with whom to make social comparisons of ability. An *implicit external frame of reference* occurs when social comparisons are made unconsciously toward naturally occurring groups. In school settings such as PE, implicit frames of reference are typically measured as class-levels and/or school-levels of ability/achievement. A general theoretical prediction of implicit external frames of reference is termed the *big-fish-little-pond effect* (BFLPE; Marsh & Hau, 2003). The BFLPE denotes the hypothesis that students with similar ability will have lower self-concepts when they are in classes or schools with higher ability students (Möller et al., 2009). Higher self-concepts are possessed when students are in classes or schools with lower ability students. In statistical terms, the BFLPE represents a negative relationship between class-average/school-average of ability/achievement and self-concept.

Chanal and Sarrazin (2007) provide interesting evidence of the contrasting results about direction of comparisons and explicit/implicit frames of reference and physical self-concept development in French high school PE students. Results indicated that students were more likely to make upward comparisons in their explicit external frames of reference and these upward comparisons to small groups of targets were positively related to physical self-concept development. However, the BFLPE also was evident and more pronounced with implicit frames of reference. Chanal and Sarrazin postulate that when students in PE actively make upward comparisons, assimilating effects occur whereby motivation and modeling facilitate increases in physical self-concept. On the other hand, when students make upward comparisons unconsciously or with a limited locus of control, deleterious effects to self-concept result. A specific PE example may be helpful to clarify this complex issue. Students in class X complete a skills test that measures performance on a scale from 0 (poor performance) to 10 (excellent performance). Jennifer scores a 7 on the skills test and identifies Lisa (8) and Rhonda (9) as explicit external frames of references. Jennifer's physical self-concept may still increase because of assimilation effects and her control over the upward comparison targets. On the other hand, if the overall class average on the skills test was 9 (i.e., implicit upward comparison), Jennifer's physical self-concept would likely suffer (i.e., BFLPE). Taken together, social comparisons in PE led to an overall decline in physical self-concept despite the positive contributions of explicit upward comparisons toward small groups of peers.

Skill development hypothesis

Exploration of the skill development hypothesis of self-concept embodies another theoretical model that contributes to understanding about PE-related factors that act as antecedents to physical self-concept. To review, the skill development hypothesis states that external behaviors and appraisals of successful engagement lead to heightened self-concepts (Sonstroem, 1978). There is correlational (Beasley & Garn, 2013), longitudinal (Marsh, Papaionannou, & Theodorakis, 2006), and intervention (Morgan, Saunders, & Lubans, 2012) evidence supporting the skill development hypothesis in K–12 PE and/or school-based physical activity programs. Physical activity is the behavior most often (and almost exclusively) examined in tests of the skill development hypothesis while different models of motivation are most commonly used to denote successful engagement (Marsh, Papaionannou, & Theodorakis, 2006; Standage et al., 2012). In many cases, researchers frame these studies in a health perspective rather than a test of the skill development hypothesis because physical self-concept is considered a key indicator of mental health and psychological well-being (Craven & Marsh, 2008; Fox & Wilson, 2008; Standage et al., 2012). Nevertheless, the tenets of the skill development hypothesis of self-concept are supported.

A brief synopsis of intervention-based research testing different aspects of the skill development hypothesis is provided because of the broader generalizations that can be made from randomized controlled and quasi-experimental research designs (Annesi et al., 2007). Specifically, three school-based intervention studies that lasted approximately three months (Annesi et al., 2007), six months (Morgan et al., 2012), and nine months (Schneider, Dunton, & Cooper, 2008) are compared and contrasted. Two of the studies (i.e., Annesi et al., 2007; Schneider et al., 2008) explicitly used PE classes as the main delivery arm of the intervention while Morgan et al. (2012) used a multicomponent school-based approach. PE teachers were involved in all three studies. Intervention sessions ranged from two-to-three 45-minute sessions per week (Annesi et al.) to five 50-minute sessions per week (Schneider et al.) with children (Annesi et al.) and adolescents (Morgan et al.; Schneider et al.). Annesi et al. and Schneider et al. used the PSDQ while Morgan et al. used the CY-PSPP.

These studies revealed that school-based exercise interventions tend to have the greatest impact (i.e., moderate-to-large effect sizes) on physical self-concept in the first three to six months. Schneider et al. reported no main effects between the intervention and control groups: however; cardiovascular fitness moderated the relationship between group assignment and physical self-concept. Specifically, only students in the intervention group who demonstrated cardiovascular fitness enhancements reported increased levels of physical self-concept. Intervention-based increases also were detected in physical condition (Morgan et al.) and appearance (Annesi et al.) self-concepts in the shorter interventions. It also should be noted that PE appeared to have a stronger effect on physical self-concept than after-school programs (Annesi et al.); however; some research suggests that student involvement in both PE and after-school physical activity programs is optimal (Martin et al., 2014). Thus, it appears that multidimensional physical self-concept stabilizes and regresses to the mean after approximately six to nine months of participation in school-based exercise interventions.

Physical self-concept as an antecedent

Physical self-concept also can act as an antecedent to PE-related engagement and behaviors. Specifically, Craven and Marsh (2008) suggest that individuals who feel good about their domain-specific self-concept are more likely to engage, achieve, and enjoy interactions and activities within that domain. This section is focused on physical self-concept as an antecedent in the physical domain. Research pertaining to the self-enhancement hypothesis in PE and PE-related contexts will initially be examined followed by a review of studies focused on the *reciprocal effects model* (REM; Marsh, Papaionannou, & Theodorakis, 2006). The REM is tested by investigating bidirectional effects of the self-enhancement hypothesis and skill-development hypothesis.

Self-enhancement hypothesis

The self-enhancement hypothesis states that individuals actively seek out environments that provide opportunities to increase self-concept. An important premise of this hypothesis is the role that previous domain-specific self-concept plays as a determinant of future motivation, achievement, and behavior in that domain (Garn & Shen, 2015; Marsh, Chanal, & Sarrazin, 2006). Students with higher levels of domain-specific self-concept are more likely to engage and achieve in that setting while students with lower levels of domain-specific self-concept are less likely to engage and achieve (Ferla, Valcke, & Cai, 2009; Marsh, Trautwein, Ludtke, Köller, & Baumert, 2005). For example, in a large-scale German study, students with higher levels of mathematics self-concept were more likely to demonstrate higher levels of future interest and achievement compared to students with lower levels of mathematics self-concept (Marsh et al., 2005). There is much less investigation of the self-enhancement hypothesis in PE contexts compared to the skill development hypothesis. The few studies that have explored the self-enhancement hypothesis have done so within the REM.

Reciprocal effects model

Fox (1997), Marsh (1997), and Sonstroem (1978) all advocate for researchers to take a comprehensive approach to studying multidimensional physical self-concept by simultaneously investigating the skill development hypothesis and self-enhancement hypothesis. Marsh and colleagues termed this line of inquiry the REM (Marsh, Chanal, & Sarrazin, 2006; Marsh, Papaioannou, & Theodorakis, 2006). Marsh, Chanal, and Sarrazin (2006) investigated the REM in the context of junior high school PE (Grades 7, 8, 9; mean age = 13.50). Specifically, relationships between gymnastics self-concept and performance were examined over a ten-week PE unit. A total of three expert judges achieved excellent inter-rater reliability ($\alpha = .93$) when analyzing a videotape analysis of a set performance of exercises for over 400 boys and girls. Using multi-level analysis to account for variation at class and individual levels, findings supported the REM. Specifically, gymnastics self-concept at the beginning of the unit was a positive predictor of performance at the end of the program while controlling for performance at the beginning of the unit. Likewise, gymnastics performance was a positive predictor of self-concept at the end of the program while controlling for self-concept at the beginning of the unit.

Marsh, Papaioannou, and Theodorakis (2006) also found support for the REM in primary, middle, and high school PE contexts. In a large-scale study of over 2,500 Greek students from 200 PE classes, physical self-concept, motivational variables within the theory of planned behavior, and self-reported physical activity were examined at the beginning and end of a school year (approximately nine months). Findings revealed strong support for reciprocal effects between physical self-concept and self-reported physical activity after controlling for age and gender effects. The strongest support for reciprocal effects between physical self-concept and motivational variables occurred between physical self-concept and intentions for physical activity as well as perceived behavioral control. The REM was not supported between physical self-concept and attitudes toward physical activity. More recently, Garn and Shen (2015) examined a REM between physical self-concept and exercise basic psychological needs (i.e., exercise-related feelings of autonomy, competence, and relatedness) in university-level PE classes over the course of a semester. Findings supported the self-enhancement hypothesis, but not the REM. Specifically, only physical self-concept at the beginning of the semester was a positive predictor of feelings of autonomy, competence, and relatedness at the end of the semester while controlling for these basic psychological needs at the beginning of the semester. Clearly, more research testing different variations of the REM in PE contexts is needed to make broad generalizations of physical self-concept as both an antecedent and outcome to PE relevant variables.

Implications for evidence-based practice

There are a number of implications from multidimensional physical self-concept research that can translate into more effective practice by physical educators. Teacher strategies are proposed based on findings related to frames of reference, the skill development hypothesis, the self-enhancement hypothesis, and REM. First, students often use internal and external frames of reference simultaneously in PE (Barnes & Spray, 2013). The major complication for teachers is that multiple frames of reference create both positive and negative effects on students' physical self-concept (Chanal & Sarrazin, 2007). For example, ability grouping that forces implicit external comparisons of ability hinders physical self-concept. Likewise, creating "athletic PE" classes consisting of the most physically gifted students can produce a BFLPE and reduce physical self-concept whereas explicit external comparisons to individuals or small groups appears to enhance physical self-concept (Seaton, Marsh, & Craven, 2009). Therefore, physical educators must be highly aware of their students' social comparison strategies and find ways to structure the learning environment in ways that reduce forced comparisons and diminishes BFLPE. Marsh and colleagues consistently warn of the harmful nature of using highly selective grouping strategies in classrooms (Marsh & Hau, 2003; Seaton et al., 2009). Specifically, teachers that regularly group high ability students together are likely to intensify BFLPE, lowering self-concept compared to students of similar ability grouped in mixed ability structures. Highly competitive activities that stress normative feedback and external pressure also appear to strengthen BFLPE whereas the use of cooperative activities that builds a sense of belongingness can potentially reduce BFLPE (Marsh & Peart, 1988; Seaton et al., 2009).

Empirical findings of the skill development hypothesis, self-enhancement hypothesis, and REM are intrinsically linked and can be strategically translated into practice. Quality learning environments in PE should facilitate actualization of the skill development hypothesis. Physical educators who consistently implement effective skill progressions, small-sided games with maximum and equitable participation, and promote health-enhancing physical activity in meaningful ways are likely to enhance students' multidimensional physical self-concept (e.g., sport self-concept; physical condition sport-concept; strength self-concept; etc.). Likewise, PE practice can be enhanced when teachers are aware of their students' physical self-concept because students often make engagement-related choices based on their level of domain-specific self-concept (Marsh et al., 2005). In other words, teachers in tune with their students' varying degrees of self-concept can make modifications that create a better student–activity fit.

Future directions

There are a number of important directions that researchers investigating multidimensional physical self-concept can take to advance the current literature in PE. Despite the sophisticated instruments related to multidimensional physical self-concept, there is a continuing need to explore strengths and weaknesses of these measures. Currently, some scholars dispute the effects (i.e., increased method bias; reduced social desirability) of the structured alternative format of the PSPP (Marsh et al., 2002; Welk & Eklund, 2005), which needs to be clarified. Likewise, more within-network testing of the PSDQ and PSDQ-S in elementary PE classes is needed to determine the psychometric properties of these instruments in younger populations. Researchers also need to build on the noteworthy work of Chanal and colleagues by continuing to investigate internal/external frames of reference and the BFLPE in PE (Chanal & Sarrazin, 2007; Marsh, Chanal, & Sarrazin, 2006). Implementing field-based quasi-experimental research designs that manipulate frames of reference and ability grouping in PE could advance understanding of the relationship between social comparisons on physical self-concept. Further testing of PE-related factors that moderate BFLPE also is warranted. In terms of future testing of the skill development hypothesis and REM in PE settings, more researchers need to actually test skill development. To date, there is much more evidence associated with the role of physical activity behavior and physical self-concept within these two models than skill development.

Summary of key findings

- Judgments of positive self-concepts are vital for students to fulfill their potential and lead happy lives in and out of school (Craven & Marsh, 2008).
- Self-concept is a hierarchical and domain-specific psychological construct with global self-esteem at the apex and environmental interactions at the base.
- Multidimensional physical self-concept is the domain-specific construct closely linked to PE environments within self-concept theories (Fox, 1997; Marsh, Papaioannou, & Theodorakis, 2006).
- The *self-director metaphor* (Fox & Wilson, 2008) highlights the central role of cognition in physical self-concept appraisals and reflects the underlying assumptions of the self-enhancement hypothesis. Specifically, individuals actively seek out environments that promote self-concept and avoid or devalue environments that stunt self-concept growth. Therefore, physical educators must find ways to make PE an appealing context for physical self-concept development.
- Creating lessons that stress an internal frame of reference, cooperation, a sense of belonging and avoiding high levels of external pressure and homogenous ability grouping are strategies that support self-concept (Barnes & Spray, 2013; Chanal & Sarrazin, 2007; Marsh & Peart, 1988; Seaton et al., 2009).
- Skill development, motivated engagement, and physical activity participation also are avenues to enhancing students' multidimensional physical self-concept in PE contexts (Marsh, Chanal, & Sarrazin, 2006; Marsh, Papaioannou, & Theodorakis, 2006).

Reflective questions for discussion

1. What strategies can physical educators use to capitalize on the positive effects of individual and small group upward comparisons (i.e., explicit external frame of reference) while

minimizing the negative effects of implicit group comparisons (i.e., BFLPE) on students' physical self-concept in PE contexts?

2. Compare and contrast the theoretical tenets of Fox's and Marsh's theories of multidimensional physical self-concept. In what ways could these two frameworks be combined to advance understanding of multidimensional physical self-concept development in PE?

3. In what ways can physical educators' understanding of the self-director metaphor be used to enhance their practice in PE?

References

Annesi, J. J., Faigenbaum, A. D., Westcott, W. L., Smith, A. E., Unruh, J. L., & Hamilton, F. G. (2007). Effects of the Fit for Life protocol on physiological mood, self-appraisal, and voluntary physical activity changes in African-American preadolescents: Contrasting after-school care and physical education formats. *International Journal of Clinical and Health Psychology, 7*, 641–659.

Barnes, J. S., & Spray, C. M. (2013). Social comparison in physical education: An examination of the relationship between two frames of reference and engagement, disaffection, and physical self-concept. *Psychology in the Schools, 50*, 1060–1072.

Beasley, E., & Garn, A. C. (2013). An investigation of adolescent girls' global self-concept, physical self-concept, and identified regulation in physical education. *Journal of Teaching in Physical Education, 32*, 237–252.

Binet, A., & Simon, T. (1916). *The development of intelligence in children* (E. Kit, Trans.). Baltimore, MD: Williams & Wilkins.

Bong, M., & Skaalvik, E. M. (2003). Academic self-concept and self-efficacy: How different are they really? *Educational Psychology Review, 15*, 1–40.

Chanal, J. P., & Sarrazin, P. G. (2007). Big-fish-little-pond effect versus positive effect of upward comparisons in the classroom: How does one reconciliate contradictory results? *International Review of Social Psychology, 20*, 69–86.

Cooley, C. H. (1922). *Human nature and the social order.* New York: Charles Scribner's Sons.

Craven, R. G., & Marsh, H. W. (2008). The centrality of the self-concept construct for psychological well-being and unlocking human potential: Implications for child and educational psychologists. *Educational and Child Psychology, 25*, 104–118.

Dweck, C. S., & Leggett, E. L. (1988). A social-cognitive approach to motivation and personality. *Psychological Review, 95*, 256–273.

Ferla, J., Valcke, M., & Cai, Y. (2009). Academic self-efficacy and academic self-concept: Reconsidering structural relationships. *Learning and Individual Difference, 19*, 499–505.

Fox, K. R. (1997). The physical self and processes in self-esteem development. In K.R. Fox (Ed.), *The physical self: From motivation to well-being* (pp. 111–140). Champaign, IL: Human Kinetics.

Fox, K. R., & Corbin, C. B. (1989). The Physical Self-Perception Profile: Development and preliminary validation. *Journal of Sport and Exercise Psychology, 11*, 408–430.

Fox, K. R., & Wilson, P. M. (2008). Self-perceptual systems and physical activity. In T.S. Horn (Ed.), *Advances in sport psychology* (3rd ed., pp. 49–64). Champaign, IL: Human Kinetics.

Freud, S. (2005). *Group psychology and the analysis of the ego: The future of an illusion.* Frankfurt-on-Main: Fischer Verlag. (Original work published in 1921).

Garn, A. C., & Shen, B. (2015). Physical self-concept and basic psychological needs in exercise: Are there reciprocal effects? *International Journal of Sport and Exercise Psychology, 13*, 169–181.

Garn, A. C., & Wallhead, T. (2015). Social goals and basic psychological needs in high school physical education. *Sport, Exercise, and Performance Psychology, 4*, 88–99.

Harter, S. (2003). The development of self-representations during childhood and adolescence. In M. R. Leary & J. P. Tangney (Eds.), *Handbook of self and identity* (pp. 610–642). New York: The Guilford Press.

Harter, S. (2012). *The construction of self: Developmental and sociocultural foundations.* New York: The Guilford Press.

James, W. (1890). *Principles in psychology* (Vol. 1). New York: Henry Holt and Company.

Marsh, H. W. (1993). Physical fitness self-concept: Relations of physical fitness to field and technical indicators for boys and girls aged 9–15. *Journal of Sport & Exercise Psychology, 15*, 184–206.

Marsh, H. W. (1994). Sport motivation orientations: Beware of jingle–jangle fallacies. *Journal of Sport & Exercise Psychology, 16*, 365–380.

Marsh, H. W. (1997). The measurement of physical self-concept: A construct validation approach. In K. R. Fox (Ed.), *The physical self: From motivation to well-being* (pp. 27–58). Champaign, IL: Human Kinetics.

Marsh, H. W., Asci, F. H., & Tomás, I. M. (2002). Multitrait-multimethod analyses of two physical self-concept instruments: A cross-cultural perspective. *Journal of Sport and Exercise Psychology, 24*, 99–119.

Marsh, H. W., Chanal, J. P., & Sarrazin, P. G. (2006). Self-belief does make a difference: A reciprocal effects model of the causal ordering of physical self-concept and gymnastics performance. *Journal of Sports Sciences, 21*, 101–111.

Marsh, H. W., & Hau, K. T. (2003). Big-fish-little-pond effect on academic self-concept: A crosscultural (26 country) test of the negative effects of academically selective schools. *American Psychologist, 58*, 364–376.

Marsh, H. W., Martin, A. J., & Jackson, S. (2010). Introducing a short version of the Physical Self-Description Questionnaire: New strategies, short-form evaluative criteria, and applications of factor analysis. *Journal of Sport and Exercise Psychology, 32*, 438–482.

Marsh, H. W., Papaioannou, A., & Theodorakis, Y. (2006). Causal ordering of physical self-concept and exercise behavior: Reciprocal effects model and the influence of physical education teachers. *Health Psychology, 25*, 316–328.

Marsh, H. W., & Peart, N. (1988). Competitive and cooperative physical fitness training programs for girls: Effects of physical fitness on multidimensional self-concepts. *Journal of Sport and Exercise Psychology, 10*, 390–407.

Marsh, H. W., Richards, G., Johnson, S., Roche, L., & Tremayne, R. S. (1994). Physical Self-Description Questionnaire: Psychometric properties and multitrait-multimethod analysis to existing instruments. *Journal of Sport and Exercise Psychology, 16*, 270–305.

Marsh, H. W., Trautwein, U., Ludtke, O., Köller, O., & Baumert, J. (2005). Academic self-concept, interest, grades, and standardized test scores: Reciprocal effects models of causal ordering. *Child Development, 76*, 397–416.

Martin, A. H. (1926). The concepts of self and personality. *Australian Journal of Philosophy, 4*, 168–190.

Martin, J., Garn, A. C., Shen, B., McCaughtry, N., & Nash, B. (2014). Variations in multi-dimensional physical self-concept linked to physical education and physical activity clubs in underserved urban high school students. In J. H. Borders (Ed.), *The psychology of self-esteem: New research* (pp. 11–18). New York: Nova Science.

Möller, J., Pohlmann, B., Köller, O., & Marsh, H. W. (2009). A meta-analytic path analysis of the internal/external frame of reference model of academic achievement and academic self-concept. *Review of Educational Research, 79*, 1129–1167.

Morgan, P. J., Saunders, K. L., & Lubans, D. R. (2012). Improving physical self-perception in adolescent boys from disadvantaged schools: Psychological outcomes from the Physical Activity Leaders randomized controlled trial. *Pediatric Obesity, 7*, 27–32.

Rhodewalt, F., & Vohs, K. D. (2005). Defensive strategies, motivation, and the self: A self-regulatory process view. In A. J. Elliot & C. S. Dweck (Eds.), *Handbook of competence and motivation* (pp. 548–565). New York: The Guilford Press.

Rogers, C. (1951). *Client-centered therapy: Its current practice, implications and theory.* London: Constable.

Schneider, M., Dunton, G. F., & Cooper, D. M. (2008). Physical activity and physical self-concept among sedentary adolescent females: An intervention study. *Psychology of Sport and Exercise, 9*, 1–14.

Seaton, M., Marsh, H. W., & Craven, R. G. (2009). Earning its place as a pan-human theory: Universality of the big-fish-little-pond effect across 41 culturally and economically diverse countries. *Journal of Educational Psychology, 101*, 403–419.

Shavelson, R. J., Hubner, J. J., & Stanton, G. C. (1976). Self-concept: Validation of construct interpretations. *Review of Educational Research, 46*, 407–441.

Sonstroem, R. J. (1978). Physical estimation and attraction scales: Rationale and research. *Medicine and Science in Sports, 10*, 97–102.

Standage, M., Gillison, F. B., Ntoumanis, N., & Treasure, D. C. (2012). Predicting students' physical activity and health-related well-being: A perspective cross-domain investigation of motivation across physical education and exercise settings. *Journal of Sport and Exercise Psychology, 34*, 37–60.

Weiner, B. (2000). Intrapersonal and interpersonal theories of motivation from an attributional perspective. *Educational Psychology Review, 12*, 1–14.

Welk, G. J., Corbin, C. B., Dowell, M. N., & Harris, H. (1997). The validity and reliability of two different versions of the Children and Youth Physical Self-Perception Profile. *Measurement in Physical Education and Exercise Science, 1,* 163–177.

Welk, G. J., & Eklund, B. (2005). Validation of Children and Youth Physical Self-Perception Profile in younger children. *Psychology of Sport and Exercise, 6,* 51–65.

Wylie, R. C. (1974). *The self-concept: A review of methodological considerations and measuring instruments* (revised ed., Vol. 1). Lincoln, NE: University of Nebraska Press.

35

STUDENT ATTITUDES AND PERSPECTIVES

Collin A. Webster, UNIVERSITY OF SOUTH CAROLINA, USA

In its simplest characterization, the evolution of research on teaching can be described as a gradual shift in pursuit, away from "rigid prescriptions of effectiveness" (Rink, 2003, p. 166), and toward an understanding of how context, with its innumerable variations, influences the direction and outcome of instructional events. One result of this shift is the emergence of a new research paradigm in physical education (PE) that highlights the mediating role of the learner in the teaching-learning process (Solmon, 2003). An increased focus on cognitive mediation variables in student learning brought student attitudes and perspectives into sharper relief as a viable and necessary topic of inquiry within the field.

Despite gaining legitimacy, PE research on student attitudes and perspectives has made relatively slow progress compared to research on other mediating process variables. For instance, in the *Handbook of Physical Education* (Kirk, Macdonald, & O'Sullivan, 2006), limited attention is given to the topic. Solmon (2006) only briefly mentions student attitudes in a single paragraph of her chapter on learner cognition. In Dyson's (2006) chapter on student perspectives, he discusses the relative dearth of investigative attention given to such perspectives, citing various reasons such as time consuming qualitative methodologies needed to obtain in depth and accurate data that give authenticity to students' voices. Since 2006 the rate of published studies on student attitudes and perspectives has risen somewhat; however, it is fair to say that the field is still faced with many more questions than answers concerning how students feel about, and view, PE.

This chapter is organized to provide an overview of theoretical frameworks, methodologies, and empirical strands in published research on student attitudes and perspectives about PE since 2006. I will discuss issues and limitations involved with research in the domain, application of the current knowledge base to theory development and professional practice, and directions for future inquiry. Student perspectives and attitudes are broadly defined for this chapter as students' viewpoints, opinions, and/or judgments (Dyson, 2006). While this definition is understood to reflect multiple dimensions of student affect, certain variables of relevance are excluded from this chapter since they are given more attention in other chapters of this volume. In particular, psychometric research on student motivation, values, interests, and preferences is not a focus of this chapter.

Major conceptual/theoretical perspectives

Affective learning theory

The study of student attitudes and perspectives rests within a multidimensional framework that can be broadly defined in terms of student affect. Affect includes attitudes, interests, biases, emotions, motivations, and other variables that together inform a student's feelings and views related to a particular object or subject of concern (e.g., learning task, school subject, teacher). In the area of general education, Krathwohl, Bloom, and Masia (1964) introduced a five-level taxonomy of affective learning that focuses on students' developing relationships with class content. The two lower levels in the taxonomy, receiving and responding to class content, are defined by affective responses that require minimal engagement with the knowledge and skills taught in class. In PE, students at these levels might demonstrate receptivity to class content by dressing out for class, attending to the teacher, following the teacher's directions, and staying on task. The three higher levels in the taxonomy, valuing, organizing, and characterization, are defined by affective responses that reflect an increasing willingness to accept and take ownership of the knowledge and skills being taught in class. In PE, students at these levels might show that they value class content by applying skills they learn in class to other physical activity contexts and electing to take other courses focusing on similar content. They organize their values in a way that internalizes and prioritizes the class content, such that their value of the knowledge and skills "successively and pervasively becomes part of the individual" (Krathwohl et al., 1964, p. 28). Krathwohl et al.'s model is based on the assumption that progression from lower levels to higher levels of affect is relatively linear, such that modifications in a student's value for class content establish new relationships between the individual and the content that are relatively stable at each given level.

Webster, Mîndrilă, and Weaver (2011, 2013) applied Krathwohl et al.'s (1964) work to examine high school students' affective learning from an instructional communication perspective in a compulsory PE course. The researchers found support for a theoretical model that highlights the importance of the teacher's communication of content relevance to students. Relevance was an influential factor for students electing to take similar courses in the future (considered to reflect higher order affective responses in Krathwohl et al.'s taxonomy) and, ultimately, having stronger intentions to use the knowledge and skills learned in class once the course was finished. In addition, distinct affective learning profiles were identified across the sample of students. For example, one group consisted of students with above average scores on all measures (e.g., perceived teacher communication, lower and higher order affective responses, behavioral intentions). This group was comprised mostly of boys, students who participated in organized sports, and students who reported engaging in free-time physical activity at least 2–3 times per week. Another group, which consisted of students with below average scores on all measures, was comprised mostly of girls, relatively fewer sports participants, and fewer students who engaged in free-time physical activity. Overall, a variable-centered approach to understanding affective learning in PE supported a general pattern of causal assumptions (e.g., perceived content relevance influences higher order affective responses, which in turn influence behavioral intentions), while a person-centered approach highlighted subgroups of learners who may require specially tailored pedagogical intervention to increase affective learning and maximize the impact of PE.

Attitude theory

Krathwohl et al.'s (1964) work can be thought of as an overarching theory of affective learning. Other theoretical perspectives in the domain focus more narrowly on specific components of student affect. In PE research, perhaps the most prominent example can be found in psychometric research on student attitude. The particular importance of attitudes in students' affective learning can be placed within the theory of planned behavior (Ajzen, 1991), which focuses on the role of beliefs in goal-directed action. Specifically, three types of beliefs – behavioral, normative, and control – are proposed to underpin behavioral intentions. Behavioral beliefs inform an individual's attitudes and are based on expected and evaluated outcomes of engaging in a particular behavior, such as trying a new learning task in class or being physically active in one's free time. The more positive students' expectations and evaluations for outcome behaviors, the more favorable their attitudes toward the behavior will be. Attitude is viewed as a key predictor of intentions to engage in the targeted behavior. A more favorable attitude is expected to lead to stronger behavioral intentions, which are theorized to directly influence actual behavior. This perspective is meaningful in PE because as students get older, their attitudes toward PE decline (Subramaniam & Silverman, 2007). Moreover, student attitudes may influence future participation in physical activity (Silverman & Subramaniam, 1999).

Investigators have drawn from various conceptions to quantitatively assess student attitudes in K-12 PE. Silverman and Subramaniam (1999) reviewed the literature on student attitudes in PE and concluded that numerous measurement issues, especially the use of measures that reflected a unidimensional and potentially narrow conception of attitude, confound the results of earlier studies. Subsequently, Silverman and his colleagues employed rigorous psychometric procedures to develop improved, validated attitude measures that assess multiple dimensions of the construct (Mercier & Silverman, 2014a; Phillips & Silverman, 2012; Subramaniam & Silverman, 2000). This work and studies that have used the measures support a dual-component conceptualization of attitude, which includes both an affective and a cognitive aspect (Mercier & Silverman, 2014b; Subramaniam & Silverman, 2007). For example, Mercier and Silverman (2014b) found that attitude scores were higher on cognitive versus affective factors in relation to fitness testing for high school students. Although students understood and valued the importance of fitness tests, they did not enjoy taking the tests. The development of valid and reliable attitude measures has distilled distinct elements of the construct that can be examined to refine theoretical application in research. Additionally, these measures have allowed for more robust quantitative investigations of student attitudes in PE, which have in turn strengthened the translatability of attitude research for practice.

Constructivist and critical perspectives

The study of student affect also has been approached using constructivist and critical perspectives on learning. Constructivism frames learning as an active, as opposed to a passive, process. Learners actively engage in relating new information to existing knowledge structures constructing meaningful subject matter understandings (Crotty, 2003). Interpretive research couched in constructivist principles attempts to unearth these subjective understandings. Critical inquiry situates students' attitudes and perspectives amid historical, social, and political contexts, and foregrounds issues of equitability and justice in education (Crotty, 2003). Critically framed research seeks to reconcile educational disparities, usually as they relate to gender and race. While constructivist and critical epistemologies align with different agendas, both perspectives promote increased awareness of each student as unique and central in the teaching-learning process.

Azzarito's research examines PE student attitudes and perspectives drawing on constructivist and critical traditions grounded in feminist poststructuralism (e.g., Azzarito & Katzew, 2010; Azzarito & Solmon, 2006a, 2006b; Azzarito, Solmon, & Harrison, 2006; Hill & Azzarito, 2012). In one study, for instance, interviews with high school girls and their teacher were analyzed to examine ways in which students participated in or resisted PE (Azzarito et al., 2006). The results indicated that, although girls enjoyed and valued physical activity, they negotiated their participation within PE when they perceived activities that limited their choices and favored boys. Another example of a critical lens in the domain is research within a student voice framework. Enright and O'Sullivan (2013) adopted this framework and used qualitative data sources to examine adolescent girls' perspectives on popular physical culture. Findings showed that girls primarily derived their understanding about physicality from cultural artifacts that endorsed fad diets and cosmetics and reinforced negative self-perceptions and attitudes toward physical activity. Consistent with the student voice movement, this research challenges dominant discourses that surround and imbue educational policy and practice by seeking to authenticate and harness students' voices as a means to reframe school reform (Cook-Sather, 2002).

Key research findings

In this section I will summarize prominent focus areas and key findings from recent research on student attitudes and perspectives in PE. Study purpose and findings are organized into three general themes, (a) affective concepts and dimensions, (b) student characteristics, and (c) program context and characteristics. These themes illustrate evolving facets of the knowledge base and coalesce organizing frameworks used in previous reviews of research on student attitudes and perspectives (Dyson, 2006; Silverman & Subramaniam, 1999; Solmon, 2003). Themes are not always mutually exclusive, as some emphases/findings are relevant to more than one theme. In addition, due to space limitations and the overall intent of this handbook, what follows is not designed to serve as a systematic review of the research literature, but rather as an overview of the developing knowledge base. The studies reviewed are intended to provide illustrative examples of each theme. I include brief descriptions of theoretical frameworks and methods used in the studies to punctuate commonly used scientific approaches within and across themes and to give transparency to the findings.

Affective concepts and dimensions

As discussed in the previous section, a number of theoretically driven quantitative studies were conducted using psychometric approaches to define and examine aspects of student affect. These studies demonstrate that affective learning is driven by both cognitive and affective factors. The studies by Silverman and colleagues (Mercier & Silverman, 2014a, 2014b; Phillips & Silverman, 2012; Subramaniam & Silverman, 2000, 2007) consistently supported a dual-component attitude construct, which included a cognitive component (i.e., perceived usefulness of the attitude object) and an affective component (i.e., perceived enjoyment related to the attitude object). These attitude components are conceptually similar to variables measured by Webster et al. (2011, 2013), including perceived content relevance (the extent to which the student feels the class content can satisfy personal interests and goals) and willingness to take additional PE courses (a higher order affective response in Krathwohl et al.'s (1964) taxonomy). Webster et al.'s (2011, 2013) studies found these variables were related, though distinct, and each variable uniquely contributed to the construction of an affective learning typology among high school PE students.

The congruency between the affective attitude component (i.e., enjoyment) and higher order affective learning in Krathwohl et al.'s (1964) taxonomy (e.g., willingness to pursue additional learning within a subject area) reinforces other theoretical perspectives commonly applied in psychometric research on student cognition. For example, within self-determination theory, intrinsic self-regulation (being motivated purely through the enjoyment of doing an activity) is viewed as optimal for learning (Deci & Ryan, 1985). Similar to the ascent from lower to higher levels of affective response in Krathwohl et al.'s (1964) framework, the shift from extrinsic to intrinsic motivation in self-determination theory is understood to reflect the gradual internalization of a particular value (such as for PE content) leading to increased enjoyment.

The psychometric studies discussed above highlight key components of affective learning. In tandem with these studies, research examining PE students' perspectives of learning has helped further to operationalize affective dimensions and processes. Prusak, Davis, Pennington and Wilkinson (2013) conducted a mixed-methods study of fifth and sixth grade students' attitudes toward a district-wide mandated PE program. Qualitative data revealed that perceptions of usefulness and enjoyment underpinning the students' attitudes were strengthened when the learning environment and class activities provided opportunities to socialize, were believed to have an impact on health knowledge and behaviors, and were well managed with an engaging teacher.

Several studies provide deeper insight into the nature of enjoyment as an affective response. Dismore and Bailey (2011) explored children's perceptions of enjoyment at Key Stage 2 (ages 7–11) and Key Stage 3 (ages 11–14) in one borough in England. Students' attitudes toward PE were based in conceptions of fun and enjoyment, and these conceptions changed as students transitioned from Stage 2 to Stage 3. Older students viewed fun as linked to challenge, whereas younger students viewed it in terms of pleasurable responses to playing games. In another study, Garn and Cothran (2006) investigated university students' conceptions of fun. Participants were asked to describe the most fun they ever had in K-12 PE. Results underscored the importance of task/skill challenge in conceptions of fun and also pointed to other important factors, including students' relationships with their teacher and classmates and competition (some participants liked competition and others did not). Research with secondary school students in the U.S. and England found similar results (Smith & St. Pierre, 2009). Researchers purposefully selected student participants on the basis of survey responses indicating positive attitudes toward PE. They interviewed them to learn their perceptions of subject enjoyment. Factors that emerged as related to enjoyment included the themes associated with the teacher (e.g., teacher-student interactions, instructional strategies), social interactions with peers, students' own conceptions of ability, class activities (e.g., challenging activities, competitive activities), and the PE environment (a different physical setting from other school subjects).

Student characteristics

In recent literature, the second general theme associated with student attitudes and perspectives focuses on student characteristics. Most studies in this theme focus on gender. A number of studies on student attitude and perspectives identified differences between boys and girls or focused on girls' learning experiences. In psychometric studies discussed above, Mercier and Silverman (2014b) found that girls scored significantly lower than boys on the affective-feelings factor of their measure, which assessed attitude toward fitness tests. Webster et al. (2013) found that students who scored below average on all measures used to classify affective learning profiles were mostly girls.

Other psychometric studies also have reported results concerning gender. Nicaise, Cogerino, Bois, and Amorose (2006) examined high school students' perceptions of teacher feedback and perceptions of physical competence. The association between perceived teacher feedback and perceived physical competence was stronger for girls than boys. A study by Shen, McCaughtry, Martin, Fahlman, and Garn (2012) focused solely on girls' learning experiences. High school girls from inner-city schools completed measures of relatedness toward teachers and peers in PE. The students and their PE teachers also completed measures of the students' behavioral and emotional engagement. Results showed that relatedness played a direct role in both behavioral and emotional engagement in PE. Girls reporting higher relatedness were more likely to enthusiastically participate in class and exert effort in activities. In contrast, girls reporting lower relatedness were more likely to be bored and alienated in class. Students' relationship with their PE teachers was especially prominent in predicting engagement. This research builds on studies by Garn and Cothran (2006) and Smith and St. Pierre (2009), which highlight the importance of positive relationships to student affect in PE.

Qualitative studies investigating gender issues have also tended to focus on girls' experiences in PE. Gibbons and Humbert (2008) examined the coeducational PE experiences of middle school girls in Canada. Results indicated the girls felt their activity choices in PE were limited and did not usually enjoy the current offerings. The girls also perceived they were not given a sufficient chance to develop physical competence. Although they understood the importance of physical activity, they did not always value it, and felt the PE teacher favored boys more than girls.

Other studies conducted from a critical perspective resonate with these findings. Oliver, Hamzeh and McCaughtry (2009) conducted a feminist poststructuralist study of fifth grade girls' self-identified barriers to participation in physical activity and helped the girls to negotiate those barriers to increase their physical activity opportunities. Findings revealed that the girls employed a "girly girl" façade to avoid participating in activities they did not like within male-dominated spaces. With the researchers' help, girls co-constructed a curriculum of activities they found appealing. Stride (2014) reported similar results in a study examining South Asian Muslim girls' PE-based experiences in England. Key themes reinforced Oliver et al.'s (2009) concept that girls' physicality is fluid; they choose to resist or embody dominant discourses and practices. Some girls took active agency in negotiating their PE/activity experiences. Social relations were important to their PE enjoyment and participation. Overall, critical perspectives of gender and affect in PE demonstrate that girls experience barriers, reflecting the embodiment of oppressive, male-dominant social structures. They, however, also at times devise shrewd strategies to survive and even thrive in class (Azzarito et al., 2006; Fisette, 2011, 2013).

Another focus of research in this theme is the attitudes and perspectives of students of different skills levels. For example, Bernstein, Phillips, and Silverman (2011) examined middle school PE students' attitudes and perceptions of competitive activities. The researchers found that high skilled students enjoyed competing with their friends in PE because they felt it was fun and not high stakes like sport. Moderate skilled students enjoyed competitive activities when they perceived the activities as challenging and felt they were improving. Low skilled students enjoyed collaborating with their peers. However, findings also showed that low and moderate skilled students felt they had limited opportunities to learn because high skilled students dominated the activities. This research indicates that perceptions of enjoyment change with skill level.

Whereas earlier PE research emphasized low skilled students' attitudes and perspectives (e.g., Carlson, 1995; Portman, 1995), recent studies have shifted attention to high skilled or gifted and talented students. Crance, Trohel, and Saury (2013) examined a highly skilled French male high school student's experiences during two Sport Education-based PE handball lessons. Findings indicated that he worked to negotiate the application of skillfulness (developed though participation in an elite sport context) to the particular constraints of school PE (e.g., his less skilled peers, school rules). His learning experience was ultimately positive, defined by confronting challenges to his sport-based identity within the class and reshaping his role from athlete to tutor.

While some high skilled students may learn to function successfully within and contribute to the goal structure of school PE, research on students identified as gifted and talented raises concerns that PE may not always provide the necessary support structure to accommodate these students' learning needs. Operating within a student voice framework, Lamb and Lane (2013) investigated secondary students' perspectives on being in the gifted and talented PE program in England. Focus groups and a questionnaire were used to collect data. While students expressed appreciation for being recognized for their athletic skills, they also felt a disconnect between program and school goals. Issues, such the academic teachers' perceptions (e.g., being unaware the students were in the gifted and talented program, having misgivings about the time commitment involved as a participant in the program) and the toll that being a program participant had on students' social lives, led to a perceived tension between school and sport. When offered, mentoring helped to ease this tension; however, findings suggested that mentoring was limited and generally unstructured. Extending this work, Lamb and Aldous (2014) found that a university-based mentoring program, facilitated mostly through email exchanges, fostered an open dialogue between gifted and talented students and PE undergraduate student mentors and helped students balance academic work with PE participation. Although research on high skilled and gifted and talented students is still in its early stages, findings seem to suggest these students may perceive challenges to participating in school PE or balancing the demands of high level programming with other school responsibilities; however, these perceptions may be quelled with adequate external support.

Program context and characteristics

This theme consists of studies focused on students' attitudes and perspectives related to PE program context and characteristics. Most research in this theme is qualitative and centers on urban settings. Dyson, DiCesare, Coviello, and Dyson (2009) examined students' perspectives of middle school PE programs. Themes indicated students had both positive and negative perceptions of their programs. Positive perceptions were tied to socializing with peers, playing games, and feeling better from exercising. Negative perceptions were tied to overcrowded gyms, repetitive and boring lessons, gender inequity, and insufficiently challenging content. Urban students' perceptions of uninteresting or meaningless curriculum content also were evident in a study by James and Collier (2011). These researchers used a classroom ecology framework to examine an elementary PE class. Results showed that the teacher's management and instructional systems were weak and students perceived the content to have little relevance.

Some research has identified ways to improve the quality of urban PE programs. In a study with inner city teachers and children, Holt, Sehn, Spence, Newton, and Ball (2012) found that having a specialist teacher, establishing clear expectations during the lesson, and promoting children's perceptions of choice were important components of positive youth development. Flory and McCaughtry (2011) also addressed issues of meaningful learning experiences in urban PE. The researchers conducted a four-year study of PE programs in urban secondary schools from the perspective of cultural relevance. Enhancing students' perceptions of cultural relevance was linked to teachers' expressions of care and respect, use of caring and respectful language and communication, and selection of culturally meaningful curricular content. Care was central to teachers' concerns about both the over: of students and their mastery of the subject matter. Respect involved strateg. enacted to "flatten" social hierarchies, including those among students and betwe and teachers. Language and communication included strategies for minimizing l teaching based on issues related to English as a second language and urban con tion. Culturally relevant curricular content reflected students' interests and diverse perspectives.

Researchers have examined other program characteristics from students' perspectives including assessment practices and teacher appearance. In a study by Mercier and Silverman (2014b), high school students' attitudes toward fitness testing differed by type of fitness test; students preferred the Fitnessgram as opposed to the President's Challenge. Redelius and Hay (2012) examined secondary students' views on criterion-referenced assessment in Sweden. Despite clearly understanding the PE grading criteria, students did not believe teachers followed the stated criteria. Rather, they perceived that teachers graded based on student attitudes, dispositions, and behaviors. Gold, Petrella, Angel, Ennis, and Woolley (2012) conducted a study investigating middle school students' perceptions of their PE teacher, attitudes, and behavioral intentions. Students perceived teachers who appeared to be either normal weight or underweight as more knowledgeable about PE and more capable of motivating them to lead a healthy and active lifestyle. Girls preferred teachers who appeared underweight and had more favorable perceptions of these teachers than boys.

Overall, research over the last decade highlights several themes, pointing to the importance of perceived relevance, usefulness, enjoyment, and interpersonal relationships in fostering positive attitudes and perspectives in PE. While the major strands of this research focus on affective concepts and dimensions, student characteristics, program context and characteristics, promising new directions also are evident in the recent literature. For instance, studies have focused on students' perspectives of misbehavior (Cothran, Kulinna, & Garrahy, 2009), students' help seeking behaviors (Nye, 2008), and students' perceptions of alienation in PE (Spencer-Cavaliere & Rintoul, 2012). Findings from these emerging areas strengthen and reinforce many traditional themes reviewed in this chapter.

Implications for evidence-based practice

The research evidence presented in this chapter carries tentative implications for professional practice. It is clear, for example, that student attitudes and perspectives are malleable and linked to a range of variables within the PE classroom, including the teacher, the teacher's classroom behaviors (instructional, managerial, and social), other students, and class activities. It also is clear that a potentially wide range of affective learning profiles exists within PE classes; some students perceive little value in the subject, while other students may struggle to identify with PE.

Teachers may find that taking time to learn about students' backgrounds, interests, and ambitions creates opportunities to enhance instruction by selecting relevant content, tailoring expectations for student participation and learning, and strengthening teacher-student relationships. These changes may, in turn, promote positive attitudes and perspectives, especially for students with maladaptive affective profiles. It also may be possible for teachers to nurture these students' positive attitudes and perspectives by designing learning experiences that encourage student-student interaction. Selecting class activities based on students' interests may be particularly important to fostering favorable affective profiles among girls.

Future directions for research

The majority of studies on student attitudes and perspectives have focused on older children and adolescents, mostly in secondary school settings. While this trend is logical, based on the tendency for student attitudes in PE to sour as children age (Subramaniam & Silverman, 2007), the focus should expand to younger children in elementary PE to ensure that programs meet the needs of all students. Moreover, most research to date has been descriptive in nature. Such research is important and must continue, as it helps to identify groups in need of additional support. Concomitantly, researchers should endeavor to identify meaningful tasks that foster positive affect in PE. Research stemming from multiple strands and traditions can inform the selection of independent variables for such experiments. For example, psychometric studies indicate that affective outcomes may hinge on perceptions of class relevance. Girls tend to perceive less relevance in PE than boys (Shen, McCaughtry, Martin, Fahlman, & Garn, 2012; Webster et al., 2011, 2013). Qualitative studies based on constructivist and critical perspectives underscore the importance of teacher-student relationships in girls' attitudes and perspectives toward PE (Gibbons & Humbert, 2008; Nicaise et al., 2006; Stride, 2014). Based on these results, field-based trials that manipulate the nature, extent, and quality of teachers' communication of content relevance or the amount of interaction and personalization teachers employ with girls can provide answers to important questions related to students' attitudes and affect.

It also will be necessary to work toward a more comprehensive understanding of how student attitudes and perspectives fit broadly into a general theory of affective learning. Limited research exists to operationally define affective variables. Given that Krathwohl et al.'s (1964) work delineates a range of affective learning responses and illustrates the hierarchical relationships between such responses, this work can be applied in future research to frame conceptual, theoretical, and measurement approaches. Research along these lines also should identify antecedent variables that impinge on students' affective responses. Manipulating independent variables in practice (e.g., the teacher's instruction) is especially important in theoretical investigations so that results inform future research. The ultimate research goal should be to provide PE teachers, teacher educators, and policy makers with a strong evidence base that (a) demonstrates the importance of student affect to the major aims of PE, (b) identifies effective curricular and instructional strategies for enhancing students' affective learning, and (c) provides clear direction for implementing these strategies in schools.

Summary of key findings

- The major findings from the research reviewed in this chapter confirm that based on psychometric research, a student's attitude consists of two components – perceived usefulness and perceived enjoyment (Mercier & Silverman, 2014a, 2014b; Subramaniam & Silverman, 2000, 2007).
- These components, grounded in attitude theory, reflect key aspects of affective learning (i.e., perceived class relevance, interest in electing to take additional courses in the subject, and intentions to use the knowledge and skills learned in class after finishing the course).
- These two components were originally conceptualized in Krathwohl et al. (1964) and extended using an instructional communication perspective (Webster et al., 2011, 2013).
- Qualitative studies, many conducted in urban schools, support the concept that perceived usefulness and enjoyment underpin students' approach/avoidance tendencies within PE

(e.g., Cothran et al., 2009; Dyson et al., 2009; Flory & McCaughtry, 2011; James & Collier, 2011; Spencer-Cavaliere & Rintoul, 2012).

- This work examining students' perceptions of usefulness and enjoyment extend the conceptual and theoretical dimensions related to student affect.
- These components are tied to (a) social opportunities/relationships with peers (Dismore & Bailey, 2011; Dyson et al., 2009; Prusak et al., 2013; Smith & St. Pierre, 2009; Stride, 2014), (b) a belief that class activities have an impact on health knowledge and behaviors (Prusak et al., 2013), and (c) an organized, skillful, and engaging teacher (Holt et al., 2012; Prusak et al., 2013).
- Further, conceptions of enjoyment change with age (Dismore & Bailey, 2011) and skill level (Bernstein et al., 2011). Girls enjoy PE less than boys (Mercier & Silverman, 2014b; Webster et al., 2013) and tend to not view it as useful (Gibbons & Humbert, 2008; Webster et al., 2013).
- Teachers appear to influence students' attitudes and perspectives in PE (Flory & McCaughtry, 2011; Garn & Cothran, 2006; Gold et al., 2012; Holt et al., 2012; Shen et al., 2012).
- Teacher–student and student–student interactions may be particularly important in shaping girls' attitudes and perspectives toward PE (Nicaise et al., 2006; Shen et al., 2012; Stride, 2014).
- Girls are capable of navigating and negotiating their PE experiences to actively resist male-dominated discourses and events and, when given the opportunity, may create more personally meaningful opportunities to participate and learn (Azzarito et al., 2006; Fisette, 2011, 2013; Oliver et al., 2009; Stride, 2014).
- Highly skilled students may learn to scale their skillfulness within lesson constraints to accommodate program objectives (Crance et al., 2013).
- Mentoring or other forms of external support might be needed for such students when they are enrolled in specialized programs with demanding schedules and performance expectations as these programs may present or exacerbate competing priorities between PE, academics, and students' social lives (Lamb & Aldous, 2014; Lamb & Lane, 2013).

Reflective questions for discussion

1. Why might students' attitudes toward PE decline from childhood to adolescence? What could teachers do to nurture and sustain positive student affect?
2. Several psychometrically derived constructs, based on attitude theory and affective learning theory, were discussed in this chapter. How might these constructs fit into a theoretical framework explaining the affective learning process? What implications would the theory have for teachers?
3. What kinds of strategies could teachers use to foster students' enjoyment in elementary PE? How might these strategies change when teaching high school students?
4. Why do girls feel the need to carve paths of resistance in PE? What role could teachers play in reducing this need?
5. What are the key components of a mentoring program in PE for gifted and talented students? How would the program be designed to help students (a) adjust to working with less skilled peers and (b) learn to value and identify with the goals of the PE program?

References

Ajzen, I. (1991). The theory of planned behavior. *Organizational Behavior and Human Decision Processes, 50,* 179–211.

Azzarito, L., & Katzew, A. (2010). Performing identities in physical education: (En)gendering fluid selves. *Research Quarterly for Exercise and Sport, 81,* 25–37.

Azzarito, L., & Solmon, M. A. (2006a). A post-structural analysis of high school students' gender and racialized bodily meanings. *Journal of Teaching in Physical Education, 25,* 75–98.

Azzarito, L., & Solmon, M. A. (2006b). A feminist postructuralist view of student bodies in physical education: Sites of compliance, resistance and transformation. *Journal of Teaching in Physical Education, 25,* 200–225.

Azzarito, L., Solmon, M. A., & Harrison, L. (2006). "…If I had a choice I would…": A feminist post-structuralist perspective on girls in physical education. *Research Quarterly for Exercise and Sport, 77,* 222–239.

Bernstein, E., Phillips, S., & Silverman, S. (2011). Attitudes and perceptions of middle school students toward competitive activities in physical education. *Journal of Teaching in Physical Education, 30,* 69–83.

Carlson, T. B. (1995). We hate gym: Alienation from physical education. *Journal of Teaching in Physical Education, 14,* 467–477.

Cook-Sather, A. (2002). Authorizing students' perspectives: Toward trust, dialogue and change in education. *Educational Researcher, 31,* 3–14.

Cothran, D. J., Kulinna, P. H, & Garrahy, D. A. (2009). Attributions for and consequences of student misbehavior. *Physical Education and Sport Pedagogy, 14,* 155–167.

Crance, M., Trohel, J., & Saury, J. (2013). The experience of a highly skilled student during handball lessons in physical education: A relevant pointer to the gap between school and sports contexts of practice. *Physical Education and Sport Pedagogy, 18,* 103–115.

Crotty, M. (2003). *The foundations of social research: Meaning and perspective in the research process.* London: Sage.

Deci, E. L., & Ryan, R. M. (1985). *Intrinsic motivation and self-determination in human behavior.* New York: Plenum.

Dismore, H., & Bailey, R. (2011). Fun and enjoyment in physical education: Young people's attitudes. *Research Papers in Education, 26,* 499–516.

Dyson, B. (2006). Students' perspectives of physical education. In D. Kirk, D. Macdonald, & M. O'Sullivan (Eds.), *The handbook of physical education* (pp. 326–346). London: Sage.

Dyson, B., DiCesare, E., Coviello, N., & Dyson, L. (2009). Students' perspectives of urban middle school physical education programs. *Middle Grades Research Journal, 4,* 31–52.

Enright, E., & O'Sullivan, M. (2013). "Now, I'm magazine detective the whole time": Listening and responding to young people's complex experiences of popular physical culture. *Journal of Teaching in Physical Education, 32,* 394–418.

Fisette, J. L. (2011). Exploring how girls navigate their embodied identities in physical education. *Physical Education and Sport Pedagogy, 16,* 179–196.

Fisette, J. L. (2013). "Are you listening?": Adolescent girls voice how they negotiate self-identified barriers to their success and survival in physical education. *Physical Education and Sport Pedagogy, 18,* 184–203.

Flory, S. B., & McCaughtry, N. (2011). Culturally relevant physical education in urban schools: Reflecting cultural knowledge. *Research Quarterly for Exercise and Sport, 82,* 49–60.

Garn, A. C., & Cothran, D. J. (2006). The fun factor in physical education. *Journal of Teaching in Physical Education, 25,* 281–297.

Gibbons, S. L., & Humbert, L. (2008). What are middle-school girls looking for in physical education? *Canadian Journal of Education, 31,* 167–86.

Gold, R. R., Petrella, J. K., Angel, J. B., Ennis, L. S., & Woolley, T. W. (2012). The qualities of physical education teachers based upon students' perceptions of physical appearance. *Journal of Instructional Psychology, 39,* 92–104.

Hill, J., & Azzarito, L. (2012). Representing valued bodies in PE: A visual inquiry with British Asian girls. *Physical Education and Sport Pedagogy, 17,* 263–276.

Holt, N. L., Sehn, Z. L., Spence, J. C., Newton, A., & Ball, G. D. C. (2012). Possibilities for positive youth development through physical education and sport programs at an inner city school. *Physical Education and Sport Pedagogy, 17,* 97–113.

James, A. R., & Collier, D. (2011). An ecological examination of an urban sixth grade physical education class. *Physical Education and Sport Pedagogy, 16,* 279–293.

Kirk, D., Macdonald, D., & O'Sullivan, M. (Eds.). (2006). *The handbook of physical education.* London: Sage.

Krathwohl, D. R., Bloom, B. S., & Masia, B. B. (Eds.). (1964). *Taxonomy of educational objectives: Handbook II: The affective domain.* New York: McKay.

Lamb, P., & Aldous, D. (2014). The role of e-mentoring in distinguishing pedagogic experiences of gifted and talented pupils in physical education. *Physical Education and Sport Pedagogy, 19,* 301–319.

Lamb, P., & Lane, K. (2013). Pupil voice on being gifted and talented in physical education: "They think it's just, like, a weekend sort of thing." *Physical Education and Sport Pedagogy, 18,* 150–168.

Mercier, K., & Silverman, S. (2014a). Validation of an instrument to measure high school students' attitudes toward fitness testing. *Research Quarterly for Exercise and Sport, 85,* 81–89.

Mercier, K., & Silverman, S. (2014b). High school students' attitudes toward fitness testing. *Journal of Teaching in Physical Education, 33,* 269–281.

Nicaise, V., Cogerino, G., Bois, J. E., & Amorose, A. J. (2006). Students' perceptions of teacher feedback and physical competence in physical education classes: Gender effects. *Journal of Teaching in Physical Education, 25,* 36–57.

Nye, S. B. (2008). Students' help seeking during physical education. *Journal of Teaching in Physical Education, 27,* 368–384.

Oliver, K. L., Hamzeh, M., & McCaughtry, N. (2009). "Girly girls can play games"/"*Las niñas pueden jugar tambien*": 5th grade girls negotiate self-identified barriers to physical activity. *Journal of Teaching in Physical Education, 28,* 90–110.

Phillips, S. R., & Silverman, S. (2012). Development and validation of scores of an instrument to measure fourth and fifth grade student attitude toward physical education. *Measurement of Physical Education and Exercise Science, 16,* 316–327.

Portman, P. A. (1995). Who is having fun in physical education classes? Experiences of sixth grade students in elementary and middle schools. *Journal of Teaching in Physical Education, 14,* 445–453.

Prusak, K. A., Davis, T., Pennington, T., & Wilkinson, C. (2013). Children's perceptions of a district-wide physical education program. *Journal of Teaching in Physical Education, 33,* 4–27.

Redelius, K., & Hay, P. J. (2012). Student views on criterion-referenced assessment and grading in Swedish physical education. *Physical Education and Sport Pedagogy, 17,* 211–225.

Rink, J. E. (2003). Effective instruction in physical education. In S. J. Silverman & C. D. Ennis (Eds.), *Student learning in physical education: Applying research to enhance instruction* (2nd edn) (pp. 165–186). Champaign, IL: Human Kinetics.

Shen, B., McCaughtry, N., Martin, J. J., Fahlman, M., & Garn, A. C. (2012). Urban high-school girls' sense of relatedness and their engagement in physical education. *Journal of Teaching in Physical Education, 31,* 231–245.

Silverman, S., & Subramaniam, P. R. (1999). Validation of scores from an instrument assessing student attitude toward physical education. *Journal of Teaching in Physical Education, 19,* 97–125.

Smith, M. A., & St. Pierre, P. (2009). American and English secondary students' perceptions of enjoyment in physical education. *The Physical Educator, 66,* 209–221.

Solmon, M. A. (2003). Student issues in physical education classes: Attitudes, cognition, and motivation. In S. J. Silverman & C. D. Ennis (Eds.), *Student learning in physical education: Applying research to enhance instruction* (2nd edn) (pp. 147–163). Champaign, IL: Human Kinetics.

Solmon, M. A. (2006). Learner cognition. In D. Kirk, D. Macdonald, & M. O'Sullivan (Eds.), *The handbook of physical education* (pp. 226–241). London: Sage.

Spencer-Cavaliere, N., & Rintoul, M. (2012). Alienation in physical education from the perspectives of children. *Journal of Teaching in Physical Education, 31,* 344–361.

Stride, A. (2014). Centralizing space: The physical education and physical activity experiences of South Asian, Muslim girls. *Sport, Education and Society,* DOI: 10.1080/13573322.2014.938622

Subramaniam, P. R., & Silverman, S. (2000). The development and validation of an instrument to assess student attitude toward physical education. *Measurement in Physical Education and Exercise Science, 4,* 29–43.

Subramaniam, P. R., & Silverman, S. (2007). Middle school students' attitudes toward physical education. *Teaching and Teacher Education, 22,* 602–611.

Webster, C. A., Mîndrilă, D., & Weaver, G. (2011). The influence of state motivation, content relevance and affective learning on high school students' intentions to utilize class content following completion of compulsory physical education. *Journal of Teaching in Physical Education, 30,* 231–247.

Webster, C. A., Mîndrilă, D., & Weaver, G. (2013). Affective learning profiles in compulsory high school physical education: An instructional communication perspective. *Journal of Teaching in Physical Education, 32,* 78–99.

36

TEACHER BELIEFS AND EFFICACY

Pamela Hodges Kulinna, ARIZONA STATE UNIVERSITY, USA

& Donetta J. Cothran, INDIANA UNIVERSITY, USA

This chapter examines Physical Education (PE) teacher beliefs and efficacy and their relationship with teacher practice. We begin with a brief historical overview of topics followed by a discussion of the central theories supporting the literature on teachers' belief systems and efficacy. Next we summarize the literature related to PE teachers' beliefs and efficacy with particular attention to their relationship with teacher practice. The final section includes implications for evidence-based practice, future directions, and a summary of key findings.

Historical overview of teacher beliefs and efficacy

In the early 1980s the observational nature of teacher effectiveness research began to broaden to include teacher cognition. Moving beyond describing what teachers did or did not do in their classes, researchers began to focus on teachers' cognition and the decisions they make. Teacher cognition consists of beliefs and knowledge that interact to create a personal cognitive framework from which teachers perceive and act upon their environment. The concepts of beliefs and knowledge are complicated and interdependent and it is therefore hard to distinguish between them. Traditionally, knowledge has been defined as objective, definable, and measurable facts that can be agreed upon by scholars, while beliefs represent the experiential and evaluative aspects of cognition (Nespor, 1987). For example, a teacher may "know" the basic skills and rules of a sport, but how they choose to implement a particular sport unit will be based in large part on a personal decision-making process that includes what the teacher believes about the purposes of PE, the skills of most importance, how students learn best (and how individuals/specific groups of students might learn differently if at all), and teachers' role in the learning process, to name but a few belief considerations. Both knowledge and beliefs are continuously interacting to inform teachers' practices, although the personal and deeply held nature of beliefs makes them arguably more influential on practice (Pajares, 1992).

Self-efficacy is a specific and critical sub-set of a teacher's belief system. Specifically it refers to an individual's collective beliefs about her or his ability to initiate, engage, and complete a behavior at a certain level of competence. The concept of self-efficacy was introduced by Bandura (1977) as a theory to explain behavior and motivation. There is a large body of research and meta-analyses supporting the critical role that self-efficacy cognitions play in human behavior (e.g., Multon, Brown, & Lent, 1991). Teacher efficacy is related to teaching behaviors that foster student achievement (e.g., Ashton & Webb, 1986). Bandura stresses that efficacious teachers are more competent, develop a larger skill repertoire, manage their emotions more effectively, use more problem solving strategies, and persist longer in the face of failure than do less efficacious teachers (1997). More recently, the umbrella term, Social Cognitive Theory (e.g., Bandura, 1997, 2006), has been used as an overall cognitive framework that includes several core concepts including: (a) self-efficacy, (b) outcome expectations, (c) goal setting, (d) self-regulation, and (e) observational learning and modeling.

Teacher beliefs in PE

Teacher beliefs are key considerations in understanding teachers' decision making and actions. They play a key role for teachers due to the uncertain, isolated, and complex environments in which teaching occurs. This section provides an overview of some of the areas of research about teacher beliefs.

How do belief systems develop and change?

Lortie's (1975) seminal work noted that students enter teacher education programs with already well-developed educational belief systems due to their apprenticeship of observation in K-12 schooling. Specific to students' belief systems in physical education teacher education (PETE), O'Sullivan (2005) suggested that PETE students enter programs as conservative individuals who often prefer coaching over teaching and prioritize skill development. During the first five to ten years of teaching, teachers' beliefs change gradually to reflect combinations of beliefs and context constraints. In general experienced teachers' belief systems are relatively stable and resistant to change. There is, however, some indication that belief systems are malleable during the college years (e.g., Solmon & Ashy, 1995) and for experienced teachers when faced with changing contexts (Ennis, 1994).

Many curriculum reform initiatives depend on teachers' willingness and ability to change their beliefs. Davis and Andrzejewski (2009) suggest four specific steps for promoting belief change. First, the current beliefs must be made conscious so that teachers are actually aware of what they believe. For example, the Value Orientation Inventory (VOI; Ennis & Chen, 1993; Ennis & Hooper, 1988) could be used to help teachers examine their curricular values. Second, a situation must be created in which pre-existing beliefs are specifically questioned or tested. Working with pre-service teachers, Timken and van der Mars (2009) report success with case studies; while Sofo and Curtner-Smith (2010) suggest field experiences can provide a beliefs questioning and development environment. Next, teachers need to be helped to view the beliefs questioning and testing process as a professional challenge and not a threat to their personal identity. Finally they suggest that teachers must be provided with time to reflect and reconcile their pre-existing beliefs with the new information or context.

Teacher beliefs about the purposes of PE

Perhaps the largest body of literature specific to beliefs in PE is related to teachers' value orientations. Values are a cluster of beliefs around a specific issue used in an evaluation or prioritization process. Jewett, Bain, and Ennis (1995) suggested that teachers have unique value systems that prioritize the importance of the subject matter, the learner, and society in the education process and those priorities guide their decision making. They described five value orientations: (a) disciplinary mastery (DM), (b) self-actualization (SA), (c) learning process (LP), (d) social reconstruction

(SR), and (e) ecological integration (EI). Subsequent work in the area (Ennis & Chen, 1993, 1995; Ennis & Hooper, 1988) led to the development of an instrument (VOI) to assess value orientations as well as a re-conceptualization of the social reconstruction value orientation. That orientation is now described as social responsibility to better reflect the belief systems of teachers in the field. Both DM and LP value orientations focus on the traditional body of knowledge in PE (e.g., motor ability, fitness) and how students learn (e.g., learning how to learn). The other three domains focus more on the PE student's self and social development. In SA, the focus is on the student's needs/interests, while in SR it is on developing positive interpersonal relationships. Finally, EI has an integrated emphasis across all areas, that is, the foundational knowledge base, the student as self and learner, and the student's social development. Most teachers' value systems reflect a blend of value orientations, described as their value profile with each teacher's profile consisting of both high and low priority value orientations (Ennis & Zhu, 1991).

Research in numerous countries demonstrates the presence of each of the value orientations in a variety of teaching settings, although the context does seem to have a significant influence on the most common values. For example, Banville, Desrosiers, and Genet-Volet (2002) found that Canadian teachers gave a higher priority to the subject matter orientations and held a lower value for social skills, reflecting an opposite pattern to that found in a sample from the United States. Work by Chen, Lui, and Ennis (1997) demonstrated that Chinese PE teachers' values of DM and SA matched their US counterparts, although the groups differed on other value orientation priorities. Chinese teachers ranked LP and EI more highly while American teachers reported more value for SR.

Differences in belief systems are not limited to national contexts alone. In one study of US urban and rural teachers, teachers in the urban settings reported that SA and SR were higher priorities, while rural teachers rated DM and LP higher as outcome goals (Ennis & Chen, 1995). Working with teachers in Flanders Belgium, Behets and Vergauwen (2004) found differences by grade level with elementary teachers placing higher priority on DM and SA while secondary teachers reported more value for DM and SR. The authors suggest those differences may be influenced by national curricular innovations. Liu and Silverman (2006) also reported differences by grade level in their sample of teachers from Taiwan, reporting that gender, experience, level, and school location (urban or rural) were associated with teachers' values. Specifically, these authors reported that females tended to prioritize SR while more males valued DM and LP. More experienced teachers valued the LP orientation and elementary teachers were most likely to value SR. Finally more rural teachers valued DM and LP. Liu and Silverman (2006) concluded that Taiwanese physical educators prioritized self-concept, self-control, and social responsibility to allow for the coming together of body and spirit in their teaching.

Teachers, however, may also hold values that are not strictly educational in nature. Cothran and Ennis (1998) reported that PE teachers' top ranked class outcome was to provide a fun environment and their students reported similar beliefs about the importance of fun as a class outcome. Other research suggests teachers' first priority may be class management (e.g., Siedentop, Doutis, Tsangaridou, Ward, & Rauschenbach, 1994). Those two priority beliefs may be precursors to or concurrent steps with teachers' actualized educational value orientations.

Student learning

Teacher beliefs about student learning also are important to understand within the context of teacher expectancy, described by Martinek as the Pygmalion effect (Martinek, 1981). Trouilloud, Sarrazin, Martinek, and Guillet (2002) reported that teacher expectations do have self-fulfilling effects and strongly predict student achievement. Teacher expectations also affect students' perceived competence (Trouilloud, Sarrazin, Bressoux, & Bois, 2006). Teachers' beliefs about the amount of control they have over student learning is an area that needs more investigation. Further, researchers in this area found student teachers' beliefs about their ability to affect student learning decreased over their student teaching experience (Schempp, 1986). It is a fairly consistent finding that teachers interact differently with males and females in class (e.g., Nicaise, Cogerino, Fairclough, Bois, & Davis, 2007), although the identification and nature of beliefs underlying those differing interactions has not been explored.

Teacher beliefs about working with students with disabilities is also an important area of work (see Mauerberg-deCastro's chapter in this volume). Hodge and his colleagues reported that high school PE teachers had mostly favorable beliefs about inclusion; however, some teachers also indicated that they felt underprepared/unsupported to teach individuals with more severe disabilities (Hodge, Ammah, Casebolt, LaMaster, & O'Sullivan, 2004). Similarly, Obrusnikova (2008) suggested that PE teachers' beliefs systems toward teaching children with disabilities is generally positive, although there may be different levels of support associated with the type of disability. Steven (2008) found that teachers' attitudes towards inclusion were related to their practice. A more positive teacher attitude toward inclusion was positively linked to providing all students with significantly more practice attempts, at a higher level of success.

Do beliefs influence actions?

The beliefs-action link is a complicated one. For example, Ennis (1992) found that three elementary teachers engaged in a series of compromises when attempting to implement their espoused ideal program as measured by the VOI within the operational constraints of their school setting. One of those constraints is the teachers' belief in the value of maintaining order. Siedentop et al.'s (1994) examination of secondary teachers' value orientations and practice found that although teachers held clearly articulated curricular goals, those goals were secondary to class compliance and order. Ennis (1992) suggested that beliefs acted as one of several forces in the teachers' settings. Bill, for example, had a clear preference for a skill-based movement curriculum; however, the time students spent in skill practice was limited in his classes due to disruptive students and his lack of focus on student social development. Kulinna, Silverman, and Keating (2000) reported a similar mismatch between stated goals and actions when studying teachers with high and low belief systems about physical activity as an outcome priority for PE. When these teachers' instructional behaviors were measured with the System for Observing Fitness Instructional Time (SOFIT; McKenzie, Sallis, & Nader, 1991) instrument, there were no differences between groups in percent of class time spent in moderate to vigorous physical activity, fitness activities, or teacher-related fitness-related behaviors despite their reported belief differences. It seems possible in this case that the teachers' knowledge base about how to teach physically active lessons was a key constraint on their ability to achieve their stated priority.

Arguably the most influential aspect of beliefs on teacher actions is the role they play in knowledge utilization. Given that teachers are convinced of the truth of their beliefs, the beliefs act as a standard by which new information is judged. Information that supports existing beliefs is more readily accepted and integrated into the existing knowledge structure while incongruent information is rejected. For example, Ennis, Cothran, and Loftus (1997) found that teachers with different curricular belief systems organized their curricular knowledge structures differently. Those beliefs and knowledge interact to influence practice. Ennis, Mueller, and Hooper (1990) explored the role of teacher beliefs in their acceptance of a professional development program to promote curricular change. They found that some of the program concepts (e.g., shared decision making, cognitive focus) were accepted by many teachers across most value orientations. Interestingly, those same ideas were less likely to be adopted by teachers with a Disciplinary Mastery approach. Other types of teacher beliefs are related to self-efficacy, a person's beliefs about his or her ability to achieve in a particular situation.

Self-efficacy and PE teachers

Although not the only influence, self-efficacy is a key factor on an individual's willingness to engage in and maintain effort when involved in a task. This section provides a brief overview of some areas of self-efficacy research as well as an examination of factors that may influence efficacy, including the self-efficacy of classroom teachers required to teach PE.

Measuring PE teacher efficacy

Because self-efficacy is context specific, the development of measurement tools is quite challenging. Thus, an individual's efficacy may be different for different tasks or content. For example, a teacher may believe he or she will be more successful teaching dance than an invasion game. Yet even within the dance domain, that same teacher may feel more efficacious teaching younger children compared with adolescents or with a certain form of dance, such as folk dance, when compared to creative dance. As such the development of psychometrically sound instruments that can be used in a variety of settings is challenging. This leads many researchers to modify efficacy instruments from the general education field. However, a few instruments specific to PE have been developed. Martin and Kulinna (2003) developed a psychometrically sound instrument (Physical Education Teachers' Physical Activity Self-Efficacy Scale, PETPAS) to assess PE teachers' efficacy for teaching lessons with high levels of physical activity despite potential barriers.

Humphries, Hebert, Daigle, and Martin (2012) developed a valid and reliable tool (Physical Education Teaching Efficacy Scale; PETES) based on national teacher standards. The seven instrument efficacy-related factors in PETES include: (a) teaching content knowledge, (b) applying scientific knowledge, (c) accommodating skill differences, (d) teaching students with special needs, (e) implementing instruction, (f) providing assessment, and (g) using technology. The resulting PETES is a 35-item survey composed of seven efficacy factors and may serve as an overall measure of PE teaching efficacy.

Teacher efficacy and practice

Do teachers feel efficacious about teaching PE? That answer is very individualized and context specific; but in general, teachers do report a moderate level of efficacy in many studies. For example, descriptive results from Humphries et al.'s (2012) validation study showed that teachers were highly efficacious in accommodating student skill-level differences during instruction. A study of teachers using the PETPAS scale (Martin & Kulinna, 2003) also demonstrated that teachers were somewhat efficacious (e.g., approximately 60% on a scale of 0–100%) in their ability to overcome barriers (time, space, institution, students) they faced in teaching physically active classes. There was, however, a large range in teachers' efficacy scores relative to teaching physically active lessons. When a Turkish version of this scale was used with a sample of PE teachers, results indicated that teachers were overall less efficacious (ranged 31–55%) than their US counterparts (Gencay, 2009). Woods and Rhoades (2013) specifically examined teacher efficacy in a group of U.S. National Board Certified physical educators. Building on earlier work by Gibson and Demby (1984), the authors specifically differentiated between General Teaching Efficacy (GTE), when teachers believe that students can learn regardless of their capabilities or particular environment and Personal Teaching Efficacy (PTE), when teachers believe they can personally affect students' learning by their teaching behaviors (Woods & Rhoades, 2013). As might be expected given the targeted population, they found generally high reports of self-efficacy in this board certified group. Teacher Efficacy Scale scores for these teachers showed strong PTE scores and their PTE was higher than a measure of their GTE. Follow-up interviews with some participants suggested keys to their professional success. Factors differentiating them from non-board certified teachers were related to reflection, a deep commitment to teaching effectiveness, and a strong motivation to excel.

Does efficacy influence practice?

Similar to the complicated beliefs-teacher practice relationship, the relationship between teacher self-efficacy and practice is generally not a directly linear relationship. Working with PE teachers in Taiwan, Pan, Chou, and Hsu (2013) found that teachers' self-efficacy had a positive impact on measures of their teaching practices. Specifically, teachers' self-efficacy was positively related to their preparation for teaching, content taught, teaching strategies selected, and assessments used. Gorozidis and Papaioannou (2011) examined relationships among self-efficacy, achievement goals, attitudes, and intentions and teachers' adoption of a new curriculum. Teachers with a "mastery" achievement goal orientation and high self-efficacy had more positive attitudes, higher fidelity toward the curriculum, and higher intentions to continue teaching the curriculum in the future than teachers with a "performance approach" goal orientation. Conversely, scores of teachers with a performance-approach goal orientation had a small positive relationship with the implementation of teaching plans that were unrelated to intentions for future curriculum use. All teachers reported significantly higher levels of self-efficacy toward teaching daily lesson plans for the new national curriculum in Greece, compared to their self-efficacy in using student-centered teaching styles or their self-efficacy in promoting students' exercise self-regulation.

Hsiang (2013) also explored the influence of teacher efficacy. In this large-scale study involving over 400 teachers in Taiwan, teacher self-efficacy affected students' learning motivation, learning atmosphere, and learning satisfaction. In contrast, Martin, Kulinna, Eklund, and Reed (2001) did not find self-efficacy to be an influential component in understanding teachers' intentions to teach physically active PE classes. The difference in these findings may be due to the teachers in Martin et al.'s (2001) study indicating that they were quite efficacious about teaching physically active classes; although this may not appear to influence their intentions to make physically active physical education a priority.

Developing efficacy

There is clear evidence that self-efficacy can be enhanced via professional development for both pre-service and in-service teachers. For example, Zach, Harari, and Harari (2012) found that a four year PETE program positively affected students' efficacy with increases across the four years in both general teaching efficacy as well as PE teaching efficacy. Similarly, Gurvitch and Metzler (2009) explored the influence of either laboratory or field-based practicum experiences on pre-service teachers' efficacy. Although throughout the program the two groups' efficacy varied slightly, by the end of student teaching, they were similar. The authors suggest the high level of authenticity in student teaching was a powerful and similar experience across groups.

Professional development for in-service teachers is a primary avenue for teacher change. There is some evidence to suggest that professional development can enhance teacher self-efficacy.

Martin and colleagues studied the direct effects of a curriculum change project at the elementary level on teacher efficacy (Martin, McCaughtry, Kulinna, & Cothran, 2009). This unique research design examined the effects of two professional development options. One group of teachers received a traditional one day workshop on the new curriculum while a second group received similar training plus additional support after the initial workshop. Both groups showed a general positive trend in efficacy toward teaching the curriculum, while the latter group demonstrated significantly larger increases in efficacy toward overcoming barriers. Working with a mentor also may increase both professional development effectiveness and teachers' efficacy (Martin, McCaughtry, Kulinna, Cothran, & Faust, 2008). The same project also trained mentors and protégés in the use of technology with both groups increasing their reported pedometer and computer self-efficacy. An intriguing investigation by Mouton, Hansenne, Delcour, and Cloes (2013) suggests higher emotional intelligence is related to higher self-efficacy. Given that student-teacher relationships are a primary context factor for teacher success and enjoyment, the need for emotional intelligence is not unexpected. What is unknown is if programs to increase teacher emotional intelligence would have corresponding effects on teacher efficacy.

Classroom teachers' efficacy for teaching PE

Classroom teachers often are required to teach PE in elementary grades and a few studies have investigated their efficacy toward teaching PE. In one of the first studies to investigate classroom teachers' belief systems and PE teaching performance, Faucette and Patterson (2001) found that classroom teachers had "overwhelmingly negative attitudes toward the responsibility of teaching the subject" (p. 108). One study performed in Australia with classroom teachers from 37 schools reported that teachers had moderate levels of confidence in their ability to teach PE. Importantly, teachers who recalled more negative experiences during their pre-K-12 PE programs reported lower levels of PE teaching confidences and were less committed to sport and physical activities themselves (Morgan & Bourke, 2008). A single teacher education course was shown to help elementary classroom pre-service teachers begin developing their identities as PE teachers; however, there was insufficient exposure to change self-efficacy (Fletcher, Mandigo, & Kosnik, 2013).

Current trends and issues

Researchers will continue to examine the relationships among teacher cognition, beliefs, and self-efficacy. It is critical to know not only what teachers do in their classes but also why they choose to employ certain teaching behaviors. Only with that knowledge can professional developers effectively structure pre-service and in-service professional development programs to support and develop current beliefs and to help teachers change their belief systems to better meet student needs.

The advent of innovative approaches to education and physical education is contributing to changes in teachers' beliefs and efficacy. One such recent development in the field is that of US physical educators working within a Comprehensive School Physical Activity Program (CSPAP; Carson, Castelli, Beighle, & Erwin, 2014). Centeio, Erwin, and Castelli (2014) studied PE teachers' beliefs related to adopting CSPAP programming at their schools. The authors reported that PE teachers who participated in the training process were redefining their roles as PE teachers, expanding beyond teaching their PE classes to become organizers and promoters of physical activity across the school day. Within this transformation, teacher beliefs about physical education and their efficacy to take on new roles continue to grow.

Implications for evidence-based practice

Beliefs strongly impact practice at both the pre-service and in-service levels. At the pre-service level, it is imperative that educators realize the influence of candidates' strongly held entry beliefs. Teacher educators, working with pre-service teachers, can bring those beliefs to consciousness by planning and guiding specific experiences to create belief dissonance that can be resolved through reflection and positive new experiences. In-service teachers also need opportunities to recognize and explore new beliefs and options in a safe and guided way. Patton and Parker (2015) provide an excellent guide for planning effective professional development. Their suggestions include focusing on teachers' actual needs, approaching those needs from an active and social learning perspective. Both pre-service and in-service teachers need to realize that students, themselves, come to PE with their own beliefs about the class and effective teaching. Their ability to address those beliefs will be a key to teacher success (Cothran & Kulinna, 2006).

Future directions

Given the importance of teacher beliefs and efficacy, it is clear that more research is needed in the area. More complete understandings of pre-service teachers' entry beliefs will help in the design of stronger intervention programs. From a design perspective, additional intervention studies like Martin and colleagues' (Martin et al., 2009) and Gurvitch and Metzler's (2009) quasi-experimental designs are needed as scholars strive to identify high impact best practices.

Summary of key findings

- Although knowledge and beliefs both influence teacher cognition, knowledge often is defined as "facts" that can be agreed upon by scholars while beliefs are more experiential, evaluative, personal, and resistant to change (Nespor, 1987).
- Self-efficacy is a subset of an individual's beliefs specific to one's ability to initiate, engage, and complete a behavior at a certain level of competence (Bandura, 1977). Social Cognitive Theory is the umbrella term that includes self-efficacy and acknowledges the complexity and multi-dimensional nature of cognition and decision making.
- Values are a cluster of beliefs used in an evaluative manner. The Value Orientation Inventory (Ennis & Chen, 1993; Ennis & Hooper, 1988) is a widely used instrument to assess teachers' program values. Teacher curricular values are stable, but influenced by context.
- Teacher beliefs (e.g., student learning, students with disabilities) influence their practice and their students' experiences and subsequent learning opportunities. The beliefs-practice relationship, however, is not a directly linear one, with many factors affecting teacher practice.
- Measurement of teacher efficacy is challenging because it is very context specific. Most studies find teachers generally are efficacious in their teaching skills but those results vary widely for specific individuals.
- Self-efficacy does seem to impact teacher practice, although much like the beliefs-practice findings, the relationship is not a direct, linear one. The teaching environment is too complex for a single variable to explain fully teacher practice. Self-efficacy for specific tasks or content can be increased with effective professional development for pre-service or in-service teachers.
- Classroom teachers required to teach PE generally report negative beliefs about PE and low self-efficacy in their ability to teach it.

Reflective questions for discussion

1. Given the limited time and resources in most PE programs, difficult decisions must be made with regard to priority. Consider your current or future program and rank order the following program goals from highest to lowest importance: motor skill, physical activity, fitness knowledge, teamwork, fitness performance, self-control, academic integration, and fun. Focus on what you truly believe – do not worry about the "right answer" because there isn't one! What would a program based on your value ranking look like in practice? What barriers might there be to implementing your values and how could you overcome them?

2. If we randomly sampled a large number of PE classes across the country, we would no doubt find a vast majority of teachers using direct instruction to teach sport. What specific beliefs about PE, teachers, students, knowledge, and learning underlie those content and instructional decisions? Think of other instructional methods (e.g., cooperative learning, guided discovery) and content (e.g., outdoor education, personal fitness); what similar and alternate beliefs might underlie those educational options?

3. Based on your personal experiences as a student in K–12 PE, what content or activities do you believe your teachers felt most efficacious about teaching? How could you tell? Rate yourself on a 5 point scale with 5 being "highly confident" about your ability to teach in the following content areas: lifetime/recreational sports, net games, invasion games, outdoor recreation, aquatics, dance, fitness, and martial arts. What do those ratings mean for you as a teacher with regard to curricular decision making (What are you most likely to teach?) and professional development (What options could you pursue to increase your efficacy in an area?).

4. The local school district has hired you to design a professional development program. The district hopes to switch to a fitness focused program including formal fitness assessment at the secondary level but it has met significant teacher resistance to the plan. What current beliefs might the teachers have that you would need to understand and address? What types of experiences could you provide to address those beliefs and give teachers confidence in their ability to teach the new curriculum?

References

Ashton, P.T., & Webb, R. B. (1986). *Making a difference: Teachers' sense of efficacy and student achievement*. White Plains, NY: Longman.

Bandura, A. (1977). Self-efficacy: Toward a unifying theory of behavioral change. *Psychological Review*, *84*(2), 191–215. http://dx.doi.org/10.1037/0033-295X.84.2.191

Bandura, A. (1997). *Self-efficacy: The exercise of control*. New York: Freeman and Co.

Bandura, A. (2006). Guide for constructing efficacy scales. In F. Pajares & T. Urban (Eds.), *Adolescence and education, Volume 4: Self-efficacy beliefs of adolescents*. Greenwich, CT: Information Age Publishing.

Banville, D., Desrosiers, P., & Genet-Volet, Y. (2002). Comparison of value orientations of Quebec and American teachers: A cultural difference? *Teaching and Teacher Education*, *18*, 469–482.

Behets, D., & Vergauwen, L. (2004). Value orientations of elementary and secondary physical education teachers in Flanders. *Research Quarterly for Exercise and Sport*, *75*, 156–164.

Carson, R. L, Castelli, D. M., Beighle, A., & Erwin, H. (2014). School-based physical activity promotion: A conceptual framework for research and practice. *Childhood Obesity*, *10*(2), 100–106.

Centeio, E., Erwin, H., & Castelli, D. (2014). Comprehensive school physical activity programs: Characteristics of trained teachers. *Journal of Teaching in Physical Education*, *33*, 492–510.

Chen, A., Lui, Z., & Ennis, C. D. (1997). Universality and uniqueness of teacher educational value orientation. *Journal of Research and Development in Education*, *30*, 135–143.

Cothran, D. J., & Ennis, C. D. (1998). Curricula of mutual worth: Comparisons of students' and teachers' curricular goals. *Journal of Teaching in Physical Education*, *17*, 307–326.

Cothran, D. J., & Kulinna, P. H. (2006). Students' perspectives on direct, peer, and inquiry teaching strategies. *Journal of Teaching in Physical Education, 25*, 166–181.

Davis, H., & Andrzejewski, C. (2009). *Teacher beliefs*. Retrieved January 5, 2015, from www.education.com/reference/article/teacher-beliefs/.

Ennis, C. D. (1992). Curriculum theory as practiced: Case studies of operationalized value orientations. *Journal of Teaching in Physical Education, 6*, 287–300.

Ennis, C. D. (1994). Urban secondary teachers' value orientations: Social goals for teaching. *Teaching & Teacher Education, 10*, 109–120.

Ennis, C. D., & Chen, A. (1993). Domain specifications and content representativeness of the revised value orientation inventory (VOI-2). *Research Quarterly for Exercise and Sport, 64*, 436–446.

Ennis, C. D., & Chen, A. (1995). Teachers' value orientations in urban and rural school settings. *Research Quarterly for Exercise and Sport, 66*, 41–50.

Ennis, C. D., Cothran, D. J., & Loftus, S. J. (1997). The influence of urban teachers' beliefs on their knowledge organization. *Journal of Research and Development in Education, 30*, 73–86.

Ennis, C. D., & Hooper, L. M. (1988). Development of an instrument for assessing educational value orientations. *Journal of Curriculum Studies, 20*, 277–280.

Ennis, C. D., Mueller, L. K., & Hooper, L. M. (1990). The influence of teacher value orientations on curriculum planning within the parameters of a theoretical framework. *Research Quarterly for Exercise and Sport, 61*, 360–368.

Ennis, C. D., & Zhu, W. (1991). Value orientations: A description of teachers' goals for student learning. *Research Quarterly for Exercise and Sport, 62*, 33–40.

Faucette, N., & Patterson, P. L. (2001). Classroom teachers and physical education. *Education, 110*, 108–114.

Fletcher, T., Mandigo, J., & Kosnik, C. (2013). Elementary classroom teachers and physical education: Change in teacher-related factors during pre-service teacher education. *Physical Education and Sport Pedagogy, 18*, 169–183.

Gencay, O. A. (2009). Validation of the physical education teachers' physical activity self-efficacy scale with a Turkish sample. *Social Behavior and Personality, 37*, 223–230.

Gibson, S., & Dembo, M. (1984). Teacher efficacy: A construct validation. *Journal of Educational Psychology, 4*, 569–582.

Gorozidis, G., & Papaioannou, A. (2011). Teachers' self-efficacy, achievement goals, attitudes and intentions to implement the new Greek physical education curriculum. *European Physical Education Review, 17*, 231–253.

Gurvitch, R., & Metzler, M. W. (2009). The effects of laboratory-based and field-based practicum experiences on pre-service teachers' self-efficacy. *Teaching and Teacher Education, 25*, 437–443.

Hodge, A. J., Ammah, J., Casebolt, K., LaMaster, K., & O'Sullivan, M. (2004). High school general physical education teachers' behaviors and beliefs associated with inclusion. *Sport, Education and Society, 9*, 395–419. http://dx.doi.org/10.1080/13573320412331302458

Hsiang, Y. (2013). Relationships among teachers' self-efficacy and students' motivation, atmosphere, and satisfaction in physical education. *Journal of Teaching in Physical Education, 33*, 68–92.

Humphries, C. A., Hebert, E., Daigle, K., & Martin, J. (2012). Development of a physical education teaching efficacy scale. *Measurement in Physical Education and Exercise Science, 16*, 284–299.

Jewett, A. E., Bain, L. L., & Ennis, C. D. (1995). *The curriculum process in physical education*. Madison, WI: Brown and Benchmark.

Kulinna, P. H., Silverman, S., & Keating, X. D. (2000). Relationship between teachers' belief systems and actions toward teaching physical activity and fitness. *Journal of Teaching in Physical Education, 19*, 206–221.

Liu, H. Y., & Silverman, S. (2006). The value profile of physical education teachers in Taiwan, ROC. *Sport, Education and Society, 11*, 173–191.

Lortie, D. (1975). *Schoolteacher: A sociological study*. Chicago: University of Chicago Press.

Martin, J. J., & Kulinna, P. H. (2003). The development of a physical education teachers' physical activity self-efficacy instrument. *Journal of Teaching in Physical Education, 22*, 219–232.

Martin, J. J., Kulinna, P. H., Eklund, R. C., & Reed, B. (2001). Determinants of teachers' intentions to teach physically active physical education classes. *Journal of Teaching in Physical Education, 20*, 129–143.

Martin, J. J., McCaughtry, N., Kulinna, P. H., & Cothran, D. J. (2009). The impact of a social cognitive theory based intervention on teacher self-efficacy. *Professional Development in Education, 35*, 511–529. doi: 10.1080/19415250902781814

Martin, J. J., McCaughtry, N., Kulinna, P. H., Cothran, D., & Faust, R. (2008). The effectiveness of mentoring-based professional development on physical education teachers' pedometer and computer efficacy and anxiety. *Journal of Teaching in Physical Education, 27*, 68–82.

Martinek, T. (1981). Pygmalion in the gym: A model for the communication of teacher expectations in physical education. *Research Quarterly for Exercise and Sport, 52*, 58–67.

McKenzie, T. L., Sallis, J. F., & Nader, P. R. (1991). SOFIT: System for observing fitness instruction time. *Journal of Teaching in Physical Education, 11*, 195–205.

Morgan, P., & Bourke, S. (2008). Non-specialist teachers' confidence to teach PE: The nature and influence of personal experiences in PE. *Physical Education and Sport Pedagogy, 13*, 1–29.

Mouton, A., Hansenne, M., Delcour, R., & Cloes, M. (2013). Emotional intelligence and self-efficacy among physical education teachers. *Journal of Teaching in Physical Education, 32*, 342–354.

Multon, K. D., Brown, S. D., & Lent, R. W. (1991). Relation of self-efficacy beliefs to academic outcomes: A meta-analytic investigation. *Journal of Counselling Psychology, 18*, 30–38.

Nespor, J. (1987). The role of beliefs in the practice of teaching. *Journal of Curriculum Studies, 19*, 317–328.

Nicaise, V., Cogerino, G., Fairclough, S., Bois, J., & Davis, K. (2007). Teacher feedback and interactions in physical education: Effects of student gender and physical activities. *European Physical Education Review, 13*, 319–337.

Obrusnikova, I. (2008). Physical educators' beliefs about teaching children with disabilities. *Perceptual and Motor Skills, 106*, 637–44.

O'Sullivan, M. (2005). Beliefs of teachers and teacher candidates: Implications for teacher education. In F. Carreiro da Costa, M. Cloes, & M. Gonzalex (Eds.), *The art and science of teaching in physical education and sport*. Lisbon: Universidade De Tecnica.

Pajares, M. F. (1992). Teachers' beliefs and educational research: Cleaning up a messy construct. *Review of Educational Research, 62*, 307–332.

Pan, Y.-H., Chou, H-S., & Hsu, W-T. (2013). Teacher self-efficacy and teaching practices in the health and physical education curriculum in Taiwan. *Social Behavior and Personality, 42*, 241–250. doi.org/10.2224/sbp. 2013.41.2.241

Patton, K., & Parker, M. (2015). "I learned more at lunchtime": Guideposts for reimagining professional development. *Journal of Physical Education, Recreation & Dance, 86*(1), 23–29. doi: 10.1080/07303084.2014.978421

Schempp, P. (1986). Physical education student teachers' beliefs in their control over student learning. *Journal of Teaching in Physical Education, 5*, 198–204.

Siedentop, D., Doutis, P., Tsangaridou, N., Ward, P., & Rauschenbach, J. (1994). Don't sweat gym! An analysis of curriculum and instruction. *Journal of Teaching in Physical Education, 13*, 375–394.

Sofo, S., & Curtner-Smith, M. (2010). Development of pre-service teachers' value orientations during a secondary methods course and early field experience. *Sport, Education and Society, 15*, 347–365. doi: http://dx.doi.org/10.1080/13573322.2010.493314

Solmon, M. A., & Ashy, M. H. (1995). Value orientations of pre-service teachers. *Research Quarterly for Exercise and Sport, 66*, 219–230.

Steven, E. (2008). The effect of teachers' attitude toward inclusion on the practice and success levels of children with and without disabilities in physical education. *International Journal of Special Education, 23*, 48–55.

Timken, G., & van der Mars, H. (2009). The effect of case methods on preservice physical education teachers' value orientations. *Physical Education and Sport Pedagogy, 14*(2), 169–187.

Trouilloud, D. O., Sarrazin, P. G., Martinek, T., & Guillet, E. (2002). The influence of teacher expectations on student achievement in physical education classes: Pygmalion revisited. *European Journal of Social Psychology, 32*, 591–607.

Trouilloud, D. O., Sarrazin, P. G., Bressoux, P., & Bois, J. (2006). Relation between teachers' early expectations and students' later perceived competence in physical education classes: Autonomy-supportive climate as a moderator. *Journal of Educational Psychology, 98*, 75–86.

Woods, A. M., & Rhoades, J. (2013). Teaching efficacy beliefs of National Board Certified physical educators. *Teachers and Teaching, 19*, 507–526.

Zach, S., Harari, I., & Harari, N. (2012). Changes in teaching efficacy of pre-service teachers in physical education. *Physical Education and Sport Pedagogy, 17*, 447–462.

37

THE EMOTIONAL DIMENSIONS OF PHYSICAL EDUCATION TEACHER KNOWLEDGE

Nate McCaughtry, WAYNE STATE UNIVERSITY, USA

& Matthew Ferry, GEORGE MASON UNIVERSITY, USA

Much has been written over the years attempting to explain what it is like to be a physical educator. One consistent line of inquiry has sought to understand how physical educators experience the day-to-day life of the profession. Starting with Locke's (1974) description of "what the tourists never see," many scholars have described both the joys and satisfactions of teaching physical education (PE), along with its bumps and bruises (e.g., marginality, role conflict, lack of funding). This line of inquiry can be aptly labeled the emotional dimensions of the PE teaching occupation.

Slightly more recently and in a bit different direction, another line of inquiry has emerged seeking to address the question: What do effective teachers know that enables them to competently teach diverse groups of students? Most work in this area evolved from Shulman's (1987) classic categorizations of teachers' knowledge and has sought to classify and elaborate the wide-ranging areas of knowledge that effective teachers possess and ineffective teachers lack. The newest elaborations in this area have concentrated on describing the emotional knowledge that teachers possess or fail to possess about their students and its intersection with more disciplinary based forms of content, curriculum, and pedagogical knowledge (e.g., Hargreaves, 1998, 2001; McCaughtry, 2004, 2005; Rosiek, 2003). We label this second line of inquiry the emotional dimensions of knowledge about students.

In this chapter, we seek to connect these two areas of inquiry by suggesting that teacher emotion and emotional understanding lie at the heart of both. Although the linkages may not be readily apparent, our assertion that teaching PE is emotional practice (Denzin, 1984), or as some might say emotional labor (Hochschild, 1983), positions emotion both at the heart of physical educators' career satisfaction and progression and as foundational to their ability to connect with young people, facilitating their passion and desire to learn. Therefore, to adequately conceptualize the emotional dimensions of PE teacher knowledge it seems only logical to focus dually on the emotions embedded in the career experience, and then more succinctly on the intersection between emotions, students, and teachers.

We begin this chapter by providing a theoretical framework for conceptualizing teacher emotion in PE. This section is followed by a review of multiple lines of research literature falling into two broad categories: teachers' personal emotions as they relate to PE, and how teachers' emotional understanding of students informs their pedagogy. Next, we provide our thoughts on how this collective work can inform evidence-based practice and future areas of research, concluding with a summary of key findings and reflective questions for discussion.

Theoretical framework

As background for this review of the emotional dimensions of PE teacher knowledge, this section makes three theoretical points. First, teaching PE is emotional practice and best viewed through a pragmatic perspective on emotion and human experience (Denzin, 1984). Second, emotion is a central feature in how teachers experience their careers, including how they make decisions about teaching and their career development (Hargreaves, 2001). Third, the ways that teachers emotionally understand and connect with students intersect with all other forms of disciplinary knowledge (e.g., content, curriculum, pedagogical) to influence their thinking and decisions about teaching (Hargreaves, 1998; McCaughtry, 2004, 2005).

Emotion is one of the most nebulous and controversial terms in all of scholarly discourse. In some disciplines like cognitive psychology or cognitive neuroscience it has a very precise meaning and is differentiated from other similar physiological or psychological 'constructs.' In other fields like sociology its use is more general, encompassing a range of dispositions like affect and feelings. In this chapter, we adopt a more Deweyan pragmatic conception of emotion that not only fails to draw sharp boundaries between related emotion-like constructs (e.g., affect, feelings, efficacy, motivations, attitudes, values, etc.), but also makes the case that it is difficult, and even at times absurd, to attempt to differentiate the human experience into discrete qualities like cognition, emotion, physical, and so on. Long ago, Dewey (1958) argued that human experiences are at one and the same time cognitive, emotional, and physical:

> It is impossible to divide in a vital experience the practical, emotional and intellectual from one another and to set the properties of one over against the characteristics of the others. The emotional phase binds parts together into a single whole; "intellectual" simply names the fact that the experience has meaning; "practical" indicates that the organism is interacting with events and objects which surround it. (p. 55)

In essence, to more fully understand any human experience in its complexity, whether it be riding a bike, performing mathematical calculations, or teaching first graders to skip, we must remain open to the cognitive, emotional, and physical qualities of the experience and the ways they intersect within individuals and among groups. For Dewey (1958), not recognizing the holistic nature of human experience risks simply providing selective emphasis on certain qualities over others:

> The only way to avoid a sharp separation between mind which is the center of the processes of experiencing and the natural world which is experienced is to acknowledge that all modes of experiencing are ways in which some genuine traits of nature come to manifest realization. The favoring of cognitive objects and their characteristics at the expense of traits that excite desire, command action and produce passion, is a special instance of a principle of selective emphasis. (pp. 24–25)

Dewey's (1958) work reminds us to look at the human experience holistically and avoid the impulse to micro-parcel it into discrete psychological constructs or section out and privilege cognition over other forms of understanding. Hence, in this chapter we adopt a broad perspective on the concept of emotion and use it to attempt to make sense of a range of phenomena in PE teachers' lives and the research that portends to capture it. We do so while also recognizing the contradictions involved in both arguing for a holistic view of human experience while at the same time examining only one side of it, namely the emotional side.

While Dewey's writing often connected his pragmatic view of human experience with education by emphasizing how education can best be molded to 'the child,' others focus more attention on understanding the experience of teachers. Most importantly, scholars from diverse perspectives have identified teaching as emotional practice or emotional labor (Denzin, 1984; Hochschild, 1983; van Manen, 1995). As a helping profession, teachers are called on to understand their own emotions, interpret those of students, transform subject matter into meaningful experiences, and excite students to learn. As Hargreaves (1998) pointed out, schools are fast paced, communication-intensive, and emotionally draining places to work, much less thrive and survive. He argued that it is by understanding the emotional dimensions, or rather 'geographies,' that we can understand what it feels like to be an everyday teacher, and begin creating more emotionally viable systems of education that support teachers better and lead to less burnout and attrition (Hargreaves, 2001). It is also by examining the emotional dimensions of the teacher-student educative process that we can assist newer teachers in understanding their students as more than passive recipients in need of physical or cognitive growth and development. After all, we now fully realize based on the recent generation of research on youth perceptions of PE that students are far from passive recipients of instruction, and instead actively read the emotional landscapes of classrooms, adjusting their in-class effort and performance accordingly (e.g., Tischler & McCaughtry, 2011).

PE as a profession has benefitted immeasurably from the many diverse ways in which scholars have examined the *emotional dimensions of the physical education teaching occupation*. While research on teachers' working conditions and career development rarely uses an explicit emotion based theoretical lens, much of it has an emotional grounding or underpinning and as such contributes to our global understanding of what it feels like to be a teacher. For example, work in the areas of PE teacher marginalization (O'Sullivan, 1989), burnout (Carson, 2006), and induction (Stroot, 1993) shows us the feelings involved in teaching subject matter with lower status, few reward structures, high repetition, and intense reality shock when transitioning from comfortable teacher education programs into the hectic world of schools. Still other work in areas like teacher self-efficacy (Bandura, 1997), curricular value orientations (Ennis, Ross, & Chen, 1992), content decision making (Ferry & McCaughtry, 2013), and professional development (Patton, Parker, & Neutzling, 2012) illustrates how teachers' feelings about educational purposes and their role in the educational process affect their willingness to learn new strategies, offer a diverse range of movement content in their classes, and develop professionally. Collectively, work in these areas often says nothing explicit about teacher emotion, but when read more deeply, emotion seems to infiltrate the entire scope of how teachers experience their work. They choose to teach some content over others at least partly because of how they 'feel' about content. They participate in professional learning because of how they 'feel' about the content being presented, about the presenter, about their confidence in enacting new strategies, and about their role in the change process. And, they succeed, persevere, burn out, or leave the profession based on their ability to emotionally manage teaching a marginalized subject, find a fulfilling way to deal with stress, and navigate their first few uncertain years. As a result, a review about the emotional dimensions of PE teachers' knowledge must begin by capturing the diverse range of work that chronicles the life of teachers, because it is an irreducible part of knowing about teaching.

By contrast, a second line of inquiry into the *emotional dimensions of PE teachers' knowledge of students* has focused on the role that teachers' emotional understanding and connections with students plays in their thinking and decisions about content, curriculum, and pedagogy. In 1987, Lee Shulman proposed a categorization system to identify the types of knowledge that separate effective and less effective teachers (e.g., curricular, pedagogical, content, pedagogical content, and so on). Based on his and related typologies (e.g., Grossman, 1990), many scholars set about studying knowledge differences between novice and experienced teachers, especially in physical education (e.g., Rovegno, 1992, 1993, 1998; Schempp, Manross, Tan, & Fincher, 1998). McCaughtry (2004, 2005), however, soon argued that typologies of teacher knowledge often included a category of 'knowledge about students,' but more often than not this category focused exclusively on student cognitive or motor development issues such as developmental patterns, stages of development, common learning errors, learning cues and the like. According to McCaughtry (2004, 2005), a missing piece in the teacher knowledge puzzle was teachers' emotional knowledge of students. He found that, in reality, many of the thought processes and decisions that physical educators make regarding disciplinary issues like content, curriculum, and pedagogy are in fact 'filtered' through their emotional knowledge of and connections with students (McCaughtry, Barnard, Martin, Shen, & Kulinna, 2006). Said differently, expert and experienced PE teachers do things like structure curriculum, scaffold content, give feedback, manage classes, and evaluate students based in large part on how they emotionally understand and connect with learners.

This second line of inquiry into the *emotional dimensions of physical education teachers' knowledge of students* has unfolded in a number of directions. Some work has specifically sought to connect teachers' emotional knowledge of students with their pedagogical decision making (McCaughtry, 2004). Other studies have examined how PE teachers' pre-professional and professional socialization impacts their abilities to understand the emotional side of teaching students (Flory & McCaughtry, 2014). Still more studies have examined how teachers establish emotional connections with and among students in relation to socio-cultural issues like gender, race, and urbanization (Flory & McCaughtry, 2011).

Collectively, these various strands of inquiry illustrate the intersection between teachers' emotional knowledge of students and their more disciplinary forms of understanding. Expert and experienced teachers do not view students as developmental automatons receptive to mechanical content instruction and practice. Rather, the teacher emotion literature shows that a majority of teachers' instructional practices are interwoven with how they understand and interact with students emotionally, and we now realize that emotional understanding encompasses a great many things such as care, respect, flattening masculinity hierarchies, shared decisions making, and many others (Tischler & McCaughtry, 2014).

Emotional dimensions of the physical education teaching occupation

Locke's (1974) thorough examination of PE teachers' work lives revealed a continuum of (sometimes paradoxical) emotions inherent in their everyday realities. In the decades that followed some scholars have explicitly used emotion as a foundational construct when examining how teachers know different aspects of their work, while others have researched a particular topic from which teacher emotion was found to be a current that cut across the strand. Below we survey research concerning how teachers know their work and focus on the emotional dimensions inherent in the findings.

Marginalization

Teachers' feelings of marginalization are well-documented phenomena in the PE literature (O'Sullivan, 1989). Whipp, Tan, and Yeo's (2007) work with experienced teachers revealed a range of factors that informed their decision to leave the profession. Negative feelings associated with a lack of respect, a lack of genuine ability to make decisions and participate in meaningful professional development, and 'untenable' workloads all left the teachers with a sense that there were no real opportunities to advance beyond feelings of monotonous routine. In contrast, Lux and McCullick (2011) identified four strategies that one teacher used to navigate her work and avoid feelings of marginalization. These included building close relationships with parents, students, and the wider community; developing relationships with like-minded and respected faculty; acquiring a range of resources; and developing a close friendship with a colleague. While on the surface these may not appear to be 'emotional aspects' per se, it was clear in the findings, and in general, that positive emotional relationships and the process of building programs can be very rewarding and emotionally sustaining experiences.

Burnout

Relatedly, additional research has documented that teachers' work in marginalized environments over periods of time can give rise to feelings of teacher burnout (Carson, 2009). Teacher burnout is characterized by feelings of exhaustion, anxiety, being overwhelmed, and feeling isolated. Factors that can lead PE teachers to experience feelings of being burned out include "insufficient remuneration, unreasonable time pressures, role conflicts, lack of resources, feelings of isolation, a generally negative view of [PE] held by the wider school and community, and a lack of [PE] specific professional development" (Carson, 2009, p. 242). Carson (2006) found that feelings of burnout accumulated as the workday progressed. This was especially so for high burnout teachers. Further, daily feelings of burnout were associated with perceptions of performance, while efforts to control emotional expression increased levels of burnout. Compared to teachers with low to moderate feelings of being burned out, high burnout teachers were more likely to work in the most challenging contexts.

Teacher induction

Teachers who are in the induction phase of their socialization are in a critical transitionary stage, thus, it should not be surprising to learn that these experiences elicit a range of emotions (Curtner-Smith, 1997; Lawson, 1986; Schempp, Sparkes, & Templin, 1993; Stroot, 1993). Research on teacher induction is littered with salient emotion based descriptors such as, shock, surprise, grueling, challenge, boredom, worn out, isolated, fear, and doubt. For example, Flory and McCaughtry (2014) found a number of emotional currents among three new Caucasian educators as they related to teaching culturally relevant PE in racially and culturally diverse school environments, including fear and empathy, among others. For one teacher, working in an unfamiliar community and school setting fomented feelings of culture shock and fed negative affect surrounding the actions and behaviors of racially diverse minority students and families.

Self-efficacy

While not explicitly portrayed as an emotional dynamic, we see teacher self-efficacy as informative to teachers' emotions. Martin, McCaughtry, Hodges-Kulinna, and Cothran (2008) reported that teachers who had higher levels of self-efficacy toward teaching active PE classes were found to have more favorable attitudes, greater efficacy to overcome barriers, and stronger feelings of control when compared to teachers who were less efficacious. Teachers low in instructional self-efficacy were more likely to experience anger at undesirable student behavior, whereas teachers high in instructional self-efficacy were more apt to encourage and persist in helping their students learn (Bandura, 1997).

Teachers' curricular value orientations

Research on teachers' curricular value orientations (CVOs) is another way to view ways that emotion mediates how teachers know and enact their work. Ennis et al. (1992) found that teachers with a disciplinary mastery/learning process orientation were more readily able to maintain consistency between stated values and actual teaching behaviors. In contrast, teachers with an ecological integration/social reconstruction orientation found it more difficult to maintain this consistency, and the authors suggested a range of learner, instructional, and contextual features limited this group's ability to enact these values in their curricula. Indeed, research suggests that community and education contexts can influence how teachers' CVOs impact their pedagogy (Ennis & Chen, 1995). For a more extensive discussion of both teacher efficacy and CVOs see Kulinna and Cothran (Chapter 36, this volume).

Teachers' emotional connections to curricular content

Early studies from this strand have revealed secondary teachers' emotional connections to specific physical activities (e.g., love, comfort) to be a critically informing feature in how they perceive and ultimately choose curricular content. An initial study by Ferry and McCaughtry (2013) found that one group of secondary PE teachers' exclusive selection of sport was grounded in their biographically based love affairs with sport. Ferry and McCaughtry (2015) then examined teachers' curricular decision making with an eye toward understanding how content knowledge informed this practice. Far from being solely a neutral/cognitive kind of knowledge, knowing and performing different physical activities (PAs) pedagogically was a particularly gendered proposition for the teachers. They experienced 'comfort' teaching certain PAs, anxiety and fear at teaching PAs that clashed with their gendered knowledge and identities, and at times felt guilt for not stretching their comforts in order to diversify their curricula.

Teacher change

Considering the social and psychological difficulties traditionally associated with teacher change, this research is well positioned for review from a teacher emotion perspective. Patton et al. (2012) examined facilitators' knowledge and experience with ongoing PE professional development. They found that facilitators' considerations of the teachers' emotions were critically linked to making sure they understood what they were 'bringing to the table,' so they could create learning communities in which teachers felt safe and comfortable with the process. Cothran (2001) in her examination of six teachers' individual attempts at curricular change found that different stages of change elicited different emotions. Emotions ranged from dissatisfaction with the status quo to disappointment with what students were learning. They experienced feelings of frustration and tension as they implemented content and utilized instructional strategies that were foreign. On the positive side they demonstrated eagerness to share with others what they had developed, as well as satisfaction with the positive student engagement that resulted.

Emotional dimensions of teachers' knowledge of students

Research examining the emotional dimensions of teachers' knowledge of students and the ways in which it intersects with teaching practice started emerging in both the general education field (Day & Leitch, 2001; Hargreaves, 1998, 2001; Rosiek, 2003; Zembylas, 2002) and in PE (McCaughtry, 2004, 2005) during the late 1990s and early 2000s. In PE, McCaughtry (2004, 2005), for example, published a series of case studies specifically examining ways that emotional understanding of students influenced teachers' curricular decisions, in-lesson pedagogies, class management, and theories of learning/development. These papers emphasized a theoretical point about the importance of conceptualizing categories of teacher knowledge, like pedagogical content knowledge, as a unity between disciplinary forms of knowing about teaching and the inter-relational forms of knowing that teachers develop with students through practice.

Emotional knowledge of students and the induction process

Going beyond explicit attempts to describe teachers' emotional knowledge of students and its correlates with practice can yield valuable insight, and a number of research threads have done just that, though sometimes outside the bounds of emotion-specific terminology. For instance, researchers have used various socialization models to investigate how emotional knowledge of students is facilitated or hindered from developing during the pre-professional (before teacher training), professional (during teacher training), and induction (first three years as a teacher) stages. For example, Flory and McCaughtry (2014) traced three induction teachers' emotional biographies to illustrate how early experiences with families, community cultures, and youth sport eventually shaped their abilities to relate emotionally to urban students in their first teaching positions. Similarly, Wilkinson, Harvey, Bloom, Joober, and Grizenko (2013) demonstrated how early informal teaching and community work affected physical education teacher education (PETE) students' views about being caring teachers and understanding the educational experiences of students with disabilities.

Developing emotional knowledge of students during PETE training

Other PE scholars have examined the specific impact that professional teacher preparation in PETE programs has had on pre-service teachers' emotional understanding of students. Oliver and Oesterreich (2013), for instance, explained how using a 'student-centered curriculum as inquiry' approach to teacher education led to important emotional understanding and new ways of thinking about PE content selection among undergraduate PE majors. Similarly, McCaughtry and Rovegno (2003) showed that when pressed to avoid blaming students for classroom difficulties, pre-service teachers developed emotional understanding which helped them read the classroom landscape more effectively and connect better with students around learning. Klemola, Heikinaro-Johansson, and O'Sullivan (2013) likewise explained how 'social and emotional learning' modules enabled PETE students to listen to students' emotions better and respond more effectively to facilitate learning, and also how to use their own emotions to reduce students' off-task and inappropriate behaviors.

Intersection of emotional knowledge of students and socio-cultural issues

Researchers also have explored the intersection between teachers' emotional understanding of students and their pedagogical practice in relation to a number of socio-cultural factors, including gender, race, and urban contexts. McCaughtry (2004, 2006), for example, produced a series of studies that spotlighted one new physical educator's journey from naïve entry into teaching, to identification of gender injustices over time, and finally her political maneuvering and implementation of strategies working with girls to eliminate physical activity barriers and develop a more equitable educational environment. Her journey chronicled the development of emotional understanding and the pursuit of pedagogical and political reform.

Another strand of gender based teacher emotional work is evidenced by the participatory action research of scholars such as Azzarito and Katzew (2010), Enright and O'Sullivan (2012), Oliver and Hamzeh (2010), and Oliver, Hamzeh, and McCaughtry (2009). Collectively, this work examines strategies teachers and researchers working with young people use to build emotional understanding, critique physical culture and PA constraints, and envision/construct heightened critical consciousness and more equitable conceptions of self and PA opportunities.

Tischler and McCaughtry's (2014) work chronicling the interplay of multiple male masculinities in the PE context represents another lens through which to view teacher emotional understanding of students. Their study spotlighted how one male physical educator read the landscape and interplay of boys' masculinities in PE and the process through which he developed an adventure based system that both flattened and narrowed masculinity hierarchies, and in so doing produced a more equitable platform for all students to learn.

Beyond gender related issues, however, PE scholars also have examined teachers' emotional knowledge of students in relation to racial awareness/understanding and multicultural pedagogies. For example, Harrison, Carson, and Burden (2010) found that teachers of color possess greater multicultural teaching knowledge and skills than White teachers. White teachers educated in cities, however, possessed significantly greater multicultural teaching knowledge than those in rural areas. Somewhat similarly, Columna, Foley, and Lytle (2010) reported that female PE teachers value and implement cultural pluralism to a greater degree than their male counterparts and that both groups valued cultural pluralism more than they implemented it. Examining a service-learning program during post-hurricane Katrina disaster relief, Domangue and Carson (2008) described how participating in the experience built teachers' emotional understanding in the form of cultural competence through consistent engagement, cultural exposure, and engaged instruction.

Finally, several urban PE scholars have explained ways that knowledge of students serves as an 'emotional filter' through which teachers understand and operate in urban schools. McCaughtry et al. (2006) were the first to describe this filter effect by showing how the ways in which urban PE teachers emotionally understood their students influenced their approaches to dealing with educational challenges. These challenges included dealing with insufficient instructional resources, providing culturally relevant instruction, coping with school and community violence, selecting relevant content, and negotiating the 'culture of basketball.' Later, Flory and McCaughtry (2011) explained four key principles of culturally relevant physical education in urban schools that were grounded in emotional understanding between teachers and students. These were demonstrating global and discipline specific care, increasing respect by reducing hierarchies among students and between teachers and students, valuing multilingual and urban styles of communication, and teaching locally relevant and accessible physical activities.

Implications for evidence-based practice

Pre-service teachers can increase their emotional understanding of ways students engage in and learn PA. There are a number of different approaches and methods available to help PETE students develop, depending on the 'kind' of emotional understanding desired. For example, post-lesson processing with a specific focus on the influences of teacher and student emotion during lessons can help pre-service teachers learn to use emotion as a lens through which to more thoroughly interpret lesson events from the viewpoints of both teachers and students. Further, research on professional development has pointed to the importance of understanding and addressing teachers' emotions when designing and facilitating ongoing opportunities for growth when learning new content, curricular models, and instructional strategies, etc.

Developing an emotional understanding of one's students is not something that is a one-time or periodic pedagogical action. Rather, it should be viewed as an integral and continuous part of every area of a teacher's daily work. This is part of an ongoing cycle of learning about one's students, planning, and delivering instruction with this knowledge, assessing results, and seeking further understanding of one's students in relation to program goals. Effective teachers have an emotional understanding of their students that impacts every aspect of their teaching, including the selection and implementation of curricular models, content, and instructional strategies. Teachers expend great effort in hopes of decreasing the cultural gap between themselves and their students. They seek to increase pro-social rapport and understanding among and between students and create meaningful and educational engagement with a variety of PAs.

Some beginning teachers, especially Caucasian middle class teachers, may struggle to get past their own cultural templates and often view urban minority students from a 'deficit' perspective. Considering that Caucasians continue to dominate the teaching field, and that racially and culturally diverse urban schools are those in most need of effective teachers, PETE programs should strive to work more closely with districts and schools to create induction programs that explicitly help beginning (Caucasian) teachers enact more culturally relevant forms of pedagogy.

Future directions

In the wake of the great recession and the increasing presence of charter schools in the U.S. set in the wider education 'reform' narrative, researchers might ask how charter schools have addressed issues of preparing teachers to emotionally understand their students and the communities in which they live and attend school. If such schools are truly laboratories for what might 'work' and not work, then perhaps some important insights could be gained from teachers who work in these settings.

Induction programs also provide opportunities to explore how teachers negotiate emotional feelings during the first teaching years. While we continue to learn much about teacher socialization, induction, and burnout, research examining the nature and effectiveness of induction programs pairing university PETE programs with school districts has the potential to make a valuable contribution to the literature.

With the exception of some student centered research, much of the research on teachers' emotional understanding of their work and their students has been conducted in traditional schools in which the 'regular' school day has largely remained unaltered. Perhaps larger scale intervention studies that dramatically alter the form and flow of the school day, and thus students' and teachers' experience, could shed new light on how to better design and schedule educational environments to avoid some of the more common negative affect experienced by teachers and students in school PE.

Following the work of Carson (2006), and Lux and McCullick (2011), researchers should examine more thoroughly the emotional characteristics of low burnout/exceptional teachers. These unique individuals seem to sidestep many of the pitfalls that result in burnout and marginalization. Findings from this research could further the development of PETE, induction, and professional development programs that increase teacher retention, effectiveness, and happiness.

Finally, in recent years an increasing number of PETE courses, program efforts, textbooks, and research studies have included topics dealing explicitly with issues of teacher emotions. These can help pre-service teachers gain an authentic emotional understanding of their future students. Perhaps a review or comparative study of different approaches to emotional engagement might enhance our understanding of the strengths and areas of improvement within this emerging area of study.

Summary of key findings

- Teaching PE in a variety of settings often is accompanied by feelings of marginalization that can lead to feelings of burnout.
- Teachers' connections with the curricular content that they teach is a social, personal, and emotional process; perhaps more so than in any other way in which their knowledge of content could be viewed.
- Efforts to invoke teacher change must consider the teachers' emotional readiness and experiences.
- If professional development programs of all kinds are not viewed as emotionally safe environments, they will likely be less effective than they could be.
- Building close relationships with parents, students, and the wider community; developing relationships with like-minded and respected faculty; acquiring a range of resources; and developing a close friendship with a colleague are strategies teachers can use to work back against marginalizing environments (Lux & McCullick, 2011).
- Particular community and educational contexts will reward certain teacher value orientations more so than others. While secondary PE has historically been a space dominated by hyper masculinity and competitive team sport, research has shown that adventure based physical education can flatten and narrow masculinity hierarchies, and in doing so produce a more equitable platform for all students to learn.
- PETE programs that have components explicitly focused on pre-service teachers developing the ability to emotionally understand students can have a positive impact.
- Teachers' emotional knowledge and understanding of students is dynamic, ongoing, and cyclical. More disciplinary and cognitive forms of teachers' knowledge (such as PCK) does not exist separate from their emotional understanding of the socio-cultural and personal aspects of students' lives.
- All teachers, but especially Caucasian teachers, need to be particularly aware of, and diligently work toward developing accurate emotional understandings of minority students and the communities in which they live and attend school.

Reflective questions for discussion

1. Some research surveyed above was not grounded in teacher emotion theory, yet contained findings that document the role emotion plays in teachers' work. What other theoretical

frameworks and research strands might benefit from being approached or reviewed from a teacher emotion and/or student emotion perspective?

2. How might you respond to someone who suggests that knowing students from emotional, personal, and social and cultural perspectives too closely enters the realm of the personal, and is too dangerous to one's professional career in an age where being accused of sexual harassment and abuse is too readily a possibility?

3. Considering the literature cited on teacher burnout, marginalization, and induction, create an action plan to design a collaborative induction program linking a university PETE program and a school or school district. Use research on teacher education, socialization/induction, and professional development to help design the program.

4. The literature cited above discusses teacher and student emotion as a general phenomenon while also discussing specific emotions being tied to particular experiences in physical education. Create a schematic that outlines desirable and undesirable emotions experienced by both students and teachers in PE and the contexts in which they often take place.

5. Where negative/undesirable emotions exist (e.g., teachers and students are displeased; teacher is comfortable; students are bored) suggest concrete ways to alleviate or address undesirable emotions so that all parties have a more enjoyable and educational experience.

References

Azzarito, L., & Katzew, A. (2010). Performing identities in physical education: (En)gendering fluid selves. *Research Quarterly for Exercise and Sport, 81*, 25–37.

Bandura, A. (1997). *Self-efficacy: The exercise of control.* New York: Freeman.

Carson, R. L. (2006). *Exploring the episodic nature of teachers' emotions as it relates to teacher burnout.* UMI 3232157. Ann Arbor, MI: ProQuest Information and Learning Co.

Carson, R. (2009). "I have very little left to give": Understanding the emotional experiences of teachers and teacher burnout. In L. D. Housner, M. W. Metzler, P. G. Schempp, & T. J. Templin (Eds.), *Historic traditions and future directions of research on teaching and teacher education in physical education* (pp. 237–248). Morgantown, WV: Fitness Information Technology.

Columna, L., Foley, J. T., & Lytle, R. K. (2010). Physical education teachers' and teacher candidates' attitudes toward cultural pluralism. *Journal of Teaching in Physical Education, 29*, 295–311.

Cothran, D. J. (2001). Curricular change in physical education: Success stories from the front line. *Sport, Education and Society, 6*, 67–79.

Curtner-Smith, M. D. (1997). The impact of biography, teacher education, and organizational socialization on the perspectives and practices of first-year physical education teachers: Case studies of recruits with coaching orientations. *Sport, Education and Society, 2*, 73–94.

Day, C., & Leitch, R. (2001). Teachers' and teacher educators' lives: The role of emotion. *Teaching and Teacher Education, 17*, 403–415.

Denzin, N. (1984). *On understanding emotion.* San Francisco: Josey-Bass.

Dewey, J. (1958). *Experience and nature.* Mineola, NY: Dover Publications.

Domangue, E., & Carson, R. (2008). Preparing culturally competent teachers: Service-learning and physical education teacher preparation. *Journal of Teaching in Physical Education, 27*, 347–367.

Ennis, C. D., & Chen, A. (1995). Teachers' value orientations in urban and rural school settings. *Research Quarterly for Exercise and Sport, 66*, 41–50.

Ennis, C. D., Ross, J., & Chen, A. (1992). The role of value orientations in curricular decision making: A rationale for teachers' goals and expectations. *Research Quarterly for Exercise and Sport, 63*, 38–47.

Enright, E., & O'Sullivan, M. (2012). Physical education in all sorts of corners: Student activists transgressing formal physical education curricular boundaries. *Research Quarterly for Exercise and Sport Science, 83*, 255–267.

Ferry, M., & McCaughtry, N. (2013). Secondary physical educators and sport content: A love affair. *Journal of Teaching in Physical Education, 32*, 375–393.

Ferry, M., & McCaughtry, N. (2015). "Whatever is comfortable": Secondary physical educators' curricular decision making: Issues of knowledge and gendered performativity. *Journal of Teaching in Physical Education, 34,* 297–315.

Flory, S. B., & McCaughtry, N. (2011). Culturally relevant physical education in urban schools: Reflecting cultural knowledge. *Research Quarterly for Exercise and Sport, 82,* 49–60.

Flory, S. B., & McCaughtry, N. (2014). The influences of pre-professional socialization on early career physical educators. *Journal of Teaching in Physical Education, 33,* 93–111.

Grossman, P. (1990). *The making of a teacher.* New York: Teachers College Record.

Hargreaves, A. (1998). The emotional practice of teaching. *Teaching and Teacher Education, 14,* 835–854.

Hargreaves, A. (2001). The emotional geographies of teachers' relations with colleagues. *International Journal of Educational Research, 35,* 503–527.

Harrison, L., Carson, R., & Burden, J. (2010). Physical education teachers' cultural competency. *Journal of Teaching in Physical Education, 29,* 184–198.

Hochschild, A. R. (1983). *The managed heart: The commercialization of human feeling.* Berkeley, CA: University of California Press.

Klemola, U., Heikinaro-Johansson, P., & O'Sullivan, M. (2013). Physical education student teachers' perceptions of applying knowledge and skills about emotional understanding studied in PETE in a one-year teaching practicum. *Physical Education & Sport Pedagogy, 18,* 28–41.

Lawson, H. A. (1986). Occupational socialization and the design of teacher education programs. *Journal of Teaching in Physical Education, 5,* 107–116.

Locke, L. F. (1974). The ecology of the gymnasium: What the tourists never see. SAPECW Workshop, Gatlinburg, TN. (Eric Document No. ED 104 823).

Lux, K., & McCullick, B. A. (2011). How one exceptional teacher navigated her working environment as the teacher of a marginal subject. *Journal of Teaching in Physical Education, 30,* 358–374.

Martin, J. J., McCaughtry, N., Hodges-Kulinna, P., & Cothran, D. (2008). The influences of professional development on teachers' self-efficacy toward educational change. *Physical Education and Sport Pedagogy, 13,* 171–190.

McCaughtry, N. (2004). The emotional dimensions of a teacher's pedagogical content knowledge: Influences on content, curriculum and pedagogy. *Journal of Teaching in Physical Education, 23,* 30–47.

McCaughtry, N. (2005). Elaborating pedagogical content knowledge: What it means to know students and think about teaching. *Teachers and Teaching: Theory and Practice, 11,* 377–393.

McCaughtry, N. (2006). Working politically amongst professional knowledge landscapes to implement gender-sensitive physical education reform. *Physical Education and Sport Pedagogy, 11,* 159–179.

McCaughtry, N., Barnard, S., Martin, J., Shen, B., & Kulinna, P. (2006). Teachers' perspectives on the challenges of teaching physical education in urban schools: The student emotional filter. *Research Quarterly for Exercise and Sport, 77,* 486–498.

McCaughtry, N., & Rovegno, I. (2003). Development of pedagogical content knowledge: Moving from blaming students to predicting skillfulness, recognizing motor development, and understanding emotion. *Journal of Teaching in Physical Education, 22,* 355–368.

Oliver, K. L., & Hamzeh, M. (2010). "The boys won't let us play": Fifth grade Mestizas challenge physical activity discourse at school. *Research Quarterly for Exercise and Sport Science, 81,* 38–51.

Oliver, K. L., Hamzeh, M., & McCaughtry, N. (2009). 'Girly girls can play games' /'Las niñas pueden jugar tambien': Co-creating a curriculum of possibilities with fifth-grade girls. *Journal of Teaching in Physical Education, 28,* 1–22.

Oliver, K. L., & Oesterreich, H. A. (2013). Student centered inquiry as curriculum as a model for field-based teacher education. *Journal of Curriculum Studies, 45,* 394–417.

O'Sullivan, M. (1989). Failing gym is like failing lunch or recess: Two beginning teachers' struggle for legitimacy. *Journal of Teaching in Physical Education, 8,* 227–242.

Patton, K., Parker, M., & Neutzling, M. M. (2012). Tennis shoes required: The role of the facilitator in professional development. *Research Quarterly for Exercise and Sport, 83,* 522–532.

Rosiek, J. (2003). Emotional scaffolding: An exploration of the teacher knowledge at the intersection of student emotion and the subject matter. *Journal of Teacher Education, 54,* 399–412.

Rovegno, I. (1992). Learning to teach in a field-based methods course: The development of pedagogical content knowledge. *Teaching and Teacher Education, 8,* 69–82.

Rovegno, I. (1993). Content-knowledge acquisition during undergraduate cultural templates and learning through practice. *American Educational Research Journal, 30,* 611–642.

Rovegno, I. (1998). The development of in-service teachers' knowledge of a constructivist approach to physical education: Teaching beyond activities. *Research Quarterly for Exercise and Sport, 69*, 147–162.

Schempp, P. G., Manross, D., Tan, S. K., & Fincher, M. D. (1998). Subject expertise and teachers' knowledge. *Journal of Teaching in Physical Education, 17*, 342–356.

Schempp, P. G., Sparkes, A. C., & Templin, T. J. (1993). The micropolitics of teacher induction. *American Educational Research Journal, 30*, 447–472.

Shulman, L. S. (1987). Knowledge and teaching: Foundations of the new reform. *Harvard Educational Review, 57*, 1–22.

Stroot, S. A. (1993). Socialization into physical education. [Monograph]. *Journal of Teaching in Physical Education, 12*, 337–469.

Tischler, A., & McCaughtry, N. (2011). PE is not for me: When boys' masculinities are threatened. *Research Quarterly for Exercise and Sport, 82*, 37–48.

Tischler, A., & McCaughtry, N. (2014). Shifting and narrowing masculinity hierarchies in physical education: Status matters. *Journal of Teaching in Physical Education, 33*, 342–362.

Van Manen, M. (1995). *The tact of teaching: The meaning of pedagogical thoughtfulness.* London, ON: Althouse Press.

Whipp, P. R., Tan, G., & Yeo, P. T. (2007). Experienced physical education teachers reaching their "use-by date": Powerless and disrespected. *Research Quarterly for Exercise and Sport, 78*, 487–499.

Wilkinson, S., Harvey, W. J., Bloom, G. A., Joober, R., & Grizenko, N. (2013). Student teacher experiences in a service-learning project for children with attention-deficit hyperactivity disorder. *Physical Education and Sport Pedagogy, 18*, 475–491.

Zembylas, M. (2002). "Structures of feeling" in curriculum and teaching: Theorizing the emotional rules. *Educational Theory, 52*, 187–208.

38

THE NATURE AND CONSEQUENCES OF OBESITY BIAS IN PHYSICAL EDUCATION

Implications for teaching

Weidong Li, THE OHIO STATE UNIVERSITY, USA

The obesity epidemic in the United States is at the forefront of public health issues and concerns. Not only is obesity associated with many health risk factors and chronic diseases (U.S. Department of Health and Human Services [USDHHS], 1996) but it is also related to many psychosocial, emotional, and behavioral concerns. One significant contributing factor to the psychosocial, emotional, and behavioral issues experienced by overweight students is the negative bias that society holds against them. Overweight individuals are often stigmatized as being bad, ugly, stupid, lazy/unmotivated, incompetent, or unattractive due to their body weight (Puhl & Brownell, 2001).

Obesity bias refers to the tendency to judge overweight or obese individuals in a negative way based on assumed attributes or behaviors (Rukavina & Li, 2008). Obesity bias reflects an individual's anti-fat attitudes and stereotyped beliefs toward overweight students. These anti-fat attitudes and stereotyped beliefs can negatively impact teaching practices and overweight students' learning in PE (Greenleaf & Weiller, 2005; Li & Rukavina, 2012b; Peterson, Puhl, & Luedicke, 2012a; Puhl & Latner, 2007; Shore et al., 2008). Specifically, when compared to their normal weight peers, overweight students have lower academic achievement, have more tardiness and absences, receive more detentions, suffer more social isolation and marginalization with fewer friendship ties, encounter an increased risk of being bullied and harmed by their peers, have higher rates of depression, display lower self-esteem, and engage in less physical activity (e.g., Geier et al., 2007; Janssen, Craig, Boyce, & Pickett, 2004; Puhl & Latner, 2007; Shore et al., 2008).

The purpose of this chapter is to examine recent literature related to obesity bias in PE. In the first section, I describe different types of obesity bias and settings where it occurs, and explore how obesity bias varies according to race and gender. Next, obesity bias in PE classes is examined and the impact of obesity bias on overweight students' emotional well-being and behaviors is considered. This is followed by an overview of the strategies that overweight students use to cope against obesity bias or weight-related teasing and interventions that reduce obesity bias. I conclude with implications for evidence-based practice, future research directions, a summary of key findings from this line of research, and reflective questions for discussion. Many terms have been used to describe overweight individuals' experiences related to stereotypical views, including weight stigma, weight stigmatization, obesity stigmatization, obesity stigma, anti-fat attitudes, obesity bias, peer victimization, and weight bias. To be consistent, obesity bias is used throughout this chapter as a term that encompasses all of these constructs.

Foundations of obesity bias

There are two different types of obesity biases: implicit and explicit bias (Puhl & Brownell, 2001). Implicit bias refers to negative attitudes or behaviors that an individual expresses toward overweight people beyond their consciousness. It operates automatically when an environmental cue is present, for example, when a person laughs at a fat joke. Individuals often are unaware of their implicit bias. On the other hand, explicit bias refers to negative attitudes or behaviors that an individual consciously expresses toward overweight people. Explicit bias can take many different forms but is generally classified as being either covert/relational or overt/physical. Covert/relational explicit bias involves attitudes or behaviors intended to damage peer relationships, friendships, and social acceptance. Examples include social marginalization and isolation, teasing, mocking, joking, gossiping, rumor spreading, and name-calling (Neumark- Sztainer, Story, & Faibisch, 1998; Puhl & Latner, 2007; see also Cameron, Norman, & Petherick, Chapter 23). Overt/physical explicit bias involves physical attacks or threats such as pushing, punching, hitting, and kicking (Crick & Bigbee, 1998).

Obesity bias occurs in many different settings (Puhl & Latner, 2007). Employers in work places (Roehling, 1999), exercise scientists and practitioners (Chambliss, Finely, & Blair, 2004), and physicians and medical school students in health and medical settings (Schwartz, Chambliss, Brownell, Blair, & Billington, 2003; Weise, Wilson, Jones, & Neises, 1992) have all been reported to exhibit bias toward overweight or obese individuals. Classroom teachers, in-service and pre-service PE teachers, and peers also express bias towards overweight or obese individuals in educational settings (Bauer, Yang, & Austin, 2004; Li & Rukavina, 2012b; Neumark-Sztainer, Story, & Harris, 1999; Puhl & Brownell, 2006). Even family members such as parents can hold bias toward their children who are overweight or obese (Crandall, 1995).

Gender differences are evident with regard to explicit bias. In their review, Tang-Peronard and Heitmann (2008) found that overweight girls experience more stigmatization than overweight boys and are more socially marginalized with regard to friendships and romantic relationships. Overweight or obese boys are more likely to be the victims of overt/physical explicit bias (Griffiths, Wolke, Page, & Horwood, 2006; Pearce, Boergers, & Prinstein, 2002), while overweight or obese girls experience more relational forms of bias (Janssen et al., 2004; Neumark-Sztainer et al., 1998; Pearce et al., 2002).

Obesity bias begins at an early age (Margulies, Floyd, & Hojnoski, 2008; Su & Santo, 2011). Margulies et al. (2008) suggest that preschool children hold negative attitudes and judgments toward their obese peers. As children age, their negative attitudes and judgments toward overweight or obese peers get stronger (Klaczynski, Daniel, & Keller, 2009), and they tend to remain stable during transition from early adolescence to young adulthood (Haines, Hannan, van den Berg, Eisenberg, & Neumark-Sztainer, 2013). Given that the majority of previous studies are cross-sectional, there is a need for longitudinal studies that investigate developmental changes in obesity bias among children and adolescents. Information gathered from this line of research can provide insights on the development and refinement of effective intervention components to reduce obesity bias.

Obesity bias in PE

Given the public display of body sizes, ability, and skill levels in physical activity/sports set-tings, overweight students are particularly vulnerable for suffering obesity bias. Bias toward overweight students has been well documented in physical activity (Faith, Leone, Ayers, Heo, & Pietrobelli, 2002; Pierce & Wardle, 1997; Storch et al., 2007) and PE (Bauer et al., 2004; Fox & Edmunds, 2000; Li & Rukavina, 2012b; Trout & Graber, 2009) settings. The findings from this line of research have shown that many overweight students experience negative bias and weight-related teasing by their peers. Li and Rukavina (2012b) report that some overweight or obese students are not teased in PE due to a variety of reasons. There appear to be combin-ations of factors that permit some overweight children to avoid teasing and harassment. These factors may include school policy and environments, individual personality and traits (e.g., high levels of self-efficacy), athletic ability, social skills, cultural backgrounds, and academic ability. These findings provide insights to guide the development of strategies for PE teachers to use to minimize teasing and design interventions to protect overweight students from teasing (see also Cale, Chapter 27).

Research suggests that overweight students are stigmatized not only by their peers, but also by their PE teachers (Bauer et al., 2004; Greenleaf & Weiller, 2005; Li & Rukavina, 2012b; Peterson et al., 2012a). In-service PE teachers reported more negative attitudes toward overweight stu-dents than non-overweight students, assigned more positive adjectives to non-overweight students than overweight students, and had higher ability expectations for non-overweight stu-dents than overweight students. When physical educators hold obesity bias against overweight students it can hinder their effectiveness. There also is evidence showing that pre-service PE teachers possess obesity bias (Chambliss et al., 2004; O'Brien, Hunter, & Banks, 2007; Peters & Jones, 2010). Given that in-service and pre-service PE teachers exhibit obesity bias, the next step for researchers is to focus on how obesity bias affects teaching behaviors. There is a need to develop and test interventions to reduce obesity bias and to identify preventive and reactive strategies for teachers to minimize or eliminate obesity-related teasing in PE. Reduction of obesity bias can facilitate the creation of inclusive, positive learning climates where overweight or obese students can be motivated to be engaged in learning and physical activities in PE.

With the growing concern about obesity and sedentary behaviors among children and ado-lescents, numerous national reports and initiatives call for school PE to play a more prominent role in developing and maintaining a healthy, physically active lifestyle among children and ado-lescents (USDHHS, 1996, 2008). PE teachers are in a unique position to reinforce school-based programs on bias, and work with a variety of shareholders to combat the epidemic of obesity and physical inactivity by maximizing physical activity opportunities during school. Teachers can be agents of change, as their attitudes and behaviors shape students' attitudes and behaviors. They must be aware of and act upon the negative impact of obesity bias on overweight stu-dents' psychosocial and emotional development and health behaviors (Gray, Kahhan, & Janicke, 2009). Doing so can help teachers form appropriate attitudes and behaviors toward overweight students, thus providing fair, safe, and motivating environments to maximize engagement and learning for all students in PE.

Cardinal, Whitney, Narimatsu, Hubert, and Souza (2014) and Jalongo (1999) have empha-sized that obesity is a social justice issue. Findings from previous studies suggest some physical educators demonstrate a lack of awareness of student teasing in PE and rarely implement strat-egies to deal with weight-related teasing. Peterson, Puhl, and Luedicke (2012b) explored the role victimization plays in obesity bias in PE. They reported that PE teachers are more likely to intervene when overweight females are victims of weight-based harassment as compared to males. Male teachers, however, are less likely to take action to address this problem than are female teachers. It is critical for researchers and educators to examine current teacher preparation programs to address this diversity issue for pre-service teachers. An instructional module on obesity bias and strategies for dealing with obesity bias in PE should be integrated into both pedagogical and methods classes. Professional development workshops for in-service PE teachers would also benefit from the inclusion of an obesity module focused on content and teaching skills needed to create an inclusive environment for overweight students.

Little research has examined methods teachers can use to include overweight students in PE. Li and Rukavina (2012a) proposed a conceptual model to address inclusive issues with regard to overweight students. The Social Ecological Constraints Model outlines constraints at five different ecological levels (individual, PE instructional settings, school/family, community, and society) that can affect overweight or obese students' engagement and learning in PE, as reflected in Figure 38.1. These constraints can be associated with body weight, height, cognition, attitudes, peers, weight stigma, and educational policies. Findings from Rukavina, Doolittle, Li, Manson, and Beale (in press) support the use of the Social Ecological Constraints Model as a viable framework for research on inclusion of overweight students in PE. Research framed using this model can guide efforts to identify inclusive practices in PE settings and test their effectiveness in promoting overweight students' motivation and inclusion in PE.

Obesity bias negatively affects overweight students' emotional well-being and social functioning (e.g., Eisenberg, Neumark-Sztainer, Haines, & Wall, 2006; Gray, Janicke, Ingerski, & Silverstein, 2008; Storch et al., 2007). Negative effects are evident across all races and ethnic groups (Eisenberg, Neumark-Sztainer, & Perry, 2003). The effects of obesity bias on overweight students can be far-reaching. Overweight students who suffer obesity bias feel more lonely, have lower levels of self-esteem, are less satisfied with their body image, show higher levels of depression, and experience higher rates of suicidal ideation and attempts than their normal weight peers (Eisenberg et al., 2006; Gray et al., 2008; Storch et al., 2007).

Obesity bias not only affects emotional well-being and social functioning among overweight students but also negatively impacts their health behaviors (Gray et al., 2009). Compared to other

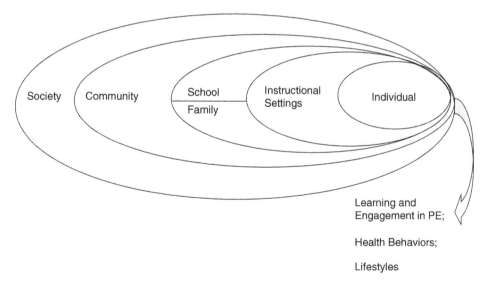

Figure 38.1 Social ecological constraint model for inclusion of overweight students into PE

students, overweight students suffering obesity bias are more likely to report increased weight concerns, hold negative attitudes toward sports, and report more barriers to be engaged in physical activity. They also are more likely to avoid physical activity, experience behaviors indicative of eating disorders, and engage in excessive amounts of screen time (Faith et al., 2002; Gray et al., 2008; Haines, Neumark-Sztainer, Eisenberg, & Hannon, 2006; Mellin, Neumark-Sztainer, Story, Ireland, & Resnick, 2002; Puhl & Luedicke, 2012). Overweight students who experience weight-related teasing may feel bad about themselves, self-conscious of their body weight, sad, excluded, and even depressed (Li & Rukavina, 2012b). They at times exhibit learned helplessness (Trout & Graber, 2009) and may avoid participation in activities (Bauer et al., 2004). Overweight students who are teased during sports or physical activities often express a preference for isolated, sedentary activities (Hayden-Wade et al., 2005), report less enjoyment in sports, and engage in less physical activity as compared to their normal weight peers (Faith et al., 2002; Storch et al., 2007).

The negative effects of obesity bias can be more detrimental if overweight students internalize obesity bias (Hilbert, Braehler, Haeuser, & Zenger, 2014). There is evidence that overweight individuals express obesity bias against their in-group (Schwartz, Vartanian, Nosek, & Brownell, 2006). Overweight individuals who internalize bias have more frequent binge eating, refuse to diet, and report lower core self-evaluation in response to obesity bias (Hilbert et al., 2014; Puhl & Latner, 2007). The internalization of obesity bias is a serious concern that can have a negative influence on overweight students' psychosocial and emotional well-being and their health behaviors, but more researchers need to explore this notion. A closer examination of the internalization of obesity bias by overweight and obese students is especially important in PE and physical activity since overweight students may internalize the idea that their body size limits how well they can perform in sports and games (Pierce & Wardle, 1997). The current literature on internalization of obesity bias has several limitations including focusing on adults, relying solely on correlational and descriptive designs, and using self-report surveys or open-ended questions to assess internalization of obesity bias. There is a need to focus more on children and adolescents and to employ other measures such as interviews, pictures, photography, and drawings to gain a deeper understanding of why and how the internalization occurs.

There is a vicious cycle of obesity, bias, and behaviors (Hayden-Wade et al., 2005). Overweight students who are stigmatized are more likely to experience negative affect and less likely to be physically active and exhibit healthy eating behaviors than their normal weight peers. Consequently, many overweight students are at risk to gain additional weight. Obesity bias during PE or physical activities can serve as a barrier for overweight students to engage in physical activity, and to adopt a physically active lifestyle (Bauer et al., 2004; Faith et al., 2002). In response to these biases, overweight students can choose to withdraw from their peers socially, engage in more sedentary activities, such as watching TV and playing video games, and overeating. Subsequently, they often are more socially isolated and can gain more weight, making them even more likely to avoid physical activity (Hayden-Wade et al., 2005). As a result, overweight children and adolescents may resist lifestyle interventions that target physical activity and healthy eating (Bosch, Stradmeijer, & Seidell, 2004).

Coping strategies against obesity bias or weight-related teasing

Not all overweight or obese students suffer adverse effects of obesity bias (Eisenberg et al., 2006). Moderating and mediating factors such as family ties and social activities can serve as a social buffer and alleviate the adverse effects of obesity biases (Faith et al., 2002; Mellin et al., 2002). Some overweight or obese students use various strategies to cope with stress and negative emotions produced by biased behaviors from their peers (Neumark-Sztainer et al., 1998).These include ignoring, self-talk, teasing back or physically fighting, and losing weight by dieting and exercise (Li, Rukavina, & Wright, 2012; Neumark-Sztainer et al., 1998; Puhl & Brownell, 2006).

Puhl and Brownell (2003) reviewed the literature to conceptualize coping strategies based on data from adult populations. Building on their review, Li and Rukavina (2009) conducted a conceptual review of coping mechanisms and factors affecting coping behaviors that overweight students can use in response to obesity bias in PE. A qualitative study using interviews on coping mechanisms in PE showed that overweight adolescents employed multiple strategies to cope with weight-related teasing (Li et al., 2012). Strategies were characterized as representative of seven mechanisms: self-protection, compensation, confrontation, seeking social support, avoidance/psychological disengagement, losing weight, and stress reduction. Adolescents' selection of these strategies was dependent on the situation. Most adolescents used trial and error to determine coping strategy effectiveness.

When adolescents employ coping mechanisms effectively, they may be shielded from the negative effects of obesity bias and may reduce future teasing incidents. One study has examined the effects of a therapeutic intervention program on reducing episodes of teasing and emotional distress among obese children (Panzer & Dhuper, 2014). Five 10–12-year-old children (3 boys, 2 girls) and their parents participated in a 6-session intervention program. Those children were purposely sampled because they frequently experienced obesity bias. At the end of the intervention, both children and parents demonstrated proficiency in explaining coping strategies and appropriate responses during simulated teasing situations. Two years after the intervention, findings showed a reduction in obese children's emotional distress and fewer episodes of teasing (Panzer & Dhuper, 2014). These results should be viewed with caution, however, due to small sample size, a potential growth effect, and the lack of a control group. Nevertheless, this study took the first step to develop, implement, and evaluate a program to equip obese children with coping strategies.

Research on coping mechanisms in PE is still in its infancy (Li & Rukavina, 2009).The information related to how overweight students cope with obesity bias in PE is limited and many questions remain unanswered. The findings generated by extending this line of research have potential to help overweight students better cope with obesity bias in PE.

Interventions for reducing obesity bias

Researchers have used intervention methods derived from several theoretical frameworks to develop intervention programs and test the effectiveness of these programs on bias reduction, including attribution theory, perspective taking, social conditions, consciousness-raising, experiential learning, and deconstructing negative stereotypes (Rukavina & Li, 2008). A discussion of these frameworks is beyond the scope of this chapter and readers are referred to Rukavina and Li (2008) for an overview. Only a few intervention studies have been conducted to reduce obesity bias and their effectiveness has been limited (e.g., Anesbury & Tiggemann, 2000; Bell & Morgan, 2000; Crandall, 1994; Puhl, Schwartz, & Brownell, 2005; Rukavina, Li, Shen, & Sun, 2010). Interventions were influential in changing students' beliefs about the controllability of obesity; however, they failed to reduce obesity bias toward overweight or obese peers (Anesbury & Tiggemann, 2000; Bell & Morgan, 2000). In other research, interventions proved effective in reducing explicit bias among adults by providing information on body shape and size controllability (Crandall, 1994; Puhl et al., 2005; Rukavina et al., 2010), evoking empathy (Rukavina et al., 2010; Teachman, Gapinski, Brownell, & Rawlins, 2003), through a service-learning project (Rukavina, Li, & Rowell, 2008), and in children through promoting size acceptance (Irving, 2000) and implementing a school-wide intervention program (Haines et al., 2006).

The majority of intervention studies designed to reduce implicit bias have been unsuccessful (e.g., Gapinski & Schwartz, 2006; Rukavina et al., 2010). Daniels (2008) suggests the limited success of interventions may be because studies have only targeted individuals rather than their social networks. Obesity bias exists in different forms and settings, and occurs in every corner of society. It also is reinforced by different sources at multiple levels (i.e., family, school, community, and society) (Neumark-Sztainer et al., 1999). Therefore, a social ecological framework is well positioned to guide future interventions on bias reduction (Daniels, 2008).

Puhl and Latner (2007) point out that limited research has been conducted to explore ways to reduce obesity bias among teachers. Hague and White (2005) developed and implemented a web-based educational module focusing on size acceptance to change student teachers' and school teachers' obesity bias. Despite methodological weaknesses including failure to establish treatment fidelity and short intervention duration, the findings showed a reduction of negative attitudes toward overweight individuals in the intervention groups when compared to the control group. Given that some classroom and PE teachers hold obesity bias, it is critical to identify effective strategies to reduce teachers' obesity bias and conduct interventions to test their efficacy with the goal of providing a fair, motivating, and inclusive learning climate for overweight students to be engaged in learning in classrooms and PE. These intervention studies can focus on increasing teachers' awareness of their own obesity bias and its negative effects on overweight students' psychosocial functions, emotions, and health behaviors, understanding of the causes of obesity, and equipping them with effective strategies to handle obesity bias (Neumark-Sztainer & Eisenberg, 2005).

Implications for evidence-based practice

PE teachers have great potential to create positive, inclusive learning environments where overweight students can be actively engaged in learning and physical activities. Evidence-based practices can empower teachers to achieve that goal. First, it is critical to encourage pre-service and in-service PE teachers to examine and challenge their own bias. In this way they can increase their awareness of the negative effects obesity bias can have on overweight students' psychosocial function, emotional well-being, and health behaviors. Second, advocates can work with administrators and all teachers to develop a no-teasing policy for a school-wide systematic implementation. Third, individuals within the school community can strive together to create a positive, inclusive learning climate to increase overweight students' self-efficacy and activity engagement. Fourth, interventions can be used to educate students to accept all body types and sizes and promote the belief that everyone has their own gifted areas. Fifth, teachers can work with overweight students to equip them with coping strategies and provide support for students being teased. Finally, using the social ecological constraint model (Li & Rukavina, 2012a) as a guide, PE teachers can work with shareholders to develop a school-wide program to reduce obesity bias and promote healthy, physically active lifestyles.

Future directions

The detrimental effects of obesity bias on overweight students in PE is well documented. As we move forward with investigations in this area, there is an urgent need for researchers to address research questions that inform teaching practices. The social ecological constraint model can be used to identify and evaluate strategies to reduce obesity bias among teachers, children, and adolescents. By alleviating the negative effects of bias internalization on overweight students' emotional well-being, social functions, and health behaviors, students can lead more productive, physically active lives. It also is important to identify preventive and reactive strategies teachers can use to minimize teasing in PE. Investigating how obesity bias affects PE teachers' teaching behaviors and how teachers can effectively include overweight students in PE can lead to significant gains in this area. From the student perspective, researchers need to examine the effects of inclusive practices and coping mechanisms on overweight students' motivation and behaviors in PE.

Summary of key findings

- Many overweight students are stigmatized not only by their peers in PE, but also by their PE teachers.
- Many overweight students experience negative bias and weight-related teasing in PE. Weight-related teasing occurs in multiple forms and different physical activity contexts.
- Overweight students who are stigmatized are more likely to experience negative affect and less likely to be physically active and to engage in healthy eating behaviors.
- Not all overweight or obese students suffer from the adverse effects of obesity bias. The adverse effects of obesity bias can be moderated and mediated by family ties, social activities, and coping mechanisms.
- Overweight adolescents can employ multiple strategies using different mechanisms to cope with weight-related teasing. Adolescents' selection of these strategies is dependent on their situation, and they use trial and error to determine the coping strategy effectiveness.
- Unfortunately, researchers to date have had only limited success in designing interventions to reduce explicit bias and have been even less successful in reducing implicit bias.
- Interventions that target all community members and that enhance both awareness and coping strategies are hypothesized to lead to the greatest success.

Reflective questions for discussion

1. How can we raise awareness of obesity bias and its consequences among all shareholders in our society? Design a specific action plan to raise the awareness of obesity bias and its consequences in your school or professional community.
2. Is there a need for obesity bias policies and legislation to prevent discrimination against overweight people? If so, what policies and legislation would be effective in reducing obesity bias? How can these policies and legislation be effectively implemented in schools and in PE?
3. What strategies are effective in reducing obesity bias? How can they be implemented?
4. What are effective teaching pedagogies and strategies for PE teachers to include overweight or obese students? How can PE teachers be encouraged to employ these in their teaching?
5. Compare and contrast different types of coping mechanisms and then develop a plan to teach these adaptive coping mechanisms to overweight students to protect themselves from suffering detrimental effects of obesity bias.

References

Anesbury, T., & Tiggerman, M. (2000). An attempt to reduce negative stereotyping of obesity in children by changing controllability beliefs. *Health Education Research, 15*, 145–152.

Bauer, K.W., Yang, Y.W., & Austin, S. B. (2004). "How can we stay healthy when you're throwing all of this in front of us?" Findings from focus groups and interviews in middle schools on environmental influences on nutrition and physical activity. *Health Education and Behavior, 31*, 34–46.

Bell, S. K., & Morgan, S. B. (2000). Children's attitudes and behavioral intentions toward a peer presented as obese: Does a medical explanation for the obesity make a difference? *Journal of Pediatric Psychology, 25*, 137–145.

Bosch, J., Stradmeijer, M., & Seidell, J. (2004). Psychosocial characteristics of obese children/youngsters and their families: Implications for preventive and curative interventions. *Patient Education and Counseling, 55*, 353–362.

Cardinal, B. J., Whitney, A. R., Narimatsu, M., Hubert, N., & Souza, B. J. (2014). Obesity bias in the gym: An under-recognized social justice, diversity, and inclusivity issue. *Journal of Physical Education, Recreation & Dance, 85*, 3–6.

Chambliss, H. O., Finley, C. E., & Blair, S. N. (2004). Attitudes toward obese individuals among exercise science students. *Medicine Science for Sports and Exercise, 36*, 468–474.

Crandall, C. S. (1994). Prejudice against fat people: Ideology and self-interest. *Journal of Personality and Social Psychology, 66*, 882–894.

Crandall, C. S. (1995). Do parents discriminate against their heavyweight daughter? *Personality and Social Psychology Bulletin, 21*, 724–735.

Crick, N. R., & Bigbee, M. A. (1998). Relational and overt forms of peer victimization: A multi informant approach. *Journal of Consulting and Clinical Psychology, 66*, 337–347.

Daniels, D. Y. (2008). Examining attendance, academic performance, and behavior in obese adolescents. *Journal of School Nursing, 24*, 379–387.

Eisenberg, M. E., Neumark-Sztainer, D., Haines, J., & Wall, M. (2006). Weight-teasing and emotional well-being in adolescents: Longitudinal findings from project EAT. *Journal of Adolescent Health, 28*, 675–683.

Eisenberg, M. E., Neumark-Sztainer, D., & Perry, C. L. (2003). Peer harassment, school connectedness, and academic achievement. *Journal of School Health, 73*, 311–316.

Faith, M. S., Leone, M. A., Ayers, T. S., Heo, M., & Pietrobelli, A. (2002). Weight criticism during physical activity, coping skills, and reported physical activity in children. *Pediatrics, 110*, e23.

Fox, K. R., & Edmunds, L. D. (2000). Understanding the world of the "fat kid": Schools help provide a better experience? *Reclaiming Child Youth: Journal of Emotion Behavior Problems, 9*, 177–181.

Gapinski, K. D., & Schwartz, M. B. (2006). Can television change anti-fat attitudes and behavior? *Journal of Applied Biobehavioral Research, 11*, 1–28.

Geier, A., Foster, G., Womble, L., McLaughlin, J., Borradaile, K., Nachmani, J., et al. (2007). The relationship between relative weight and school attendance among elementary school children. *Obesity, 15*, 2157–2161.

Gray, W. N., Janicke, D. M., Ingerski, L. M., & Silverstein, J. H. (2008). The impact of peer victimization, parent distress and child depression on barrier formation and physical activity in overweight youth. *Journal of Developmental and Behavioral Pediatrics, 29*, 26–33.

Gray, W. N., Kahhan, N. A., & Janicke, D. M. (2009). Peer victimization and pediatric obesity: A review of the literature. *Psychology in the Schools, 46*, 720–727.

Greenleaf, C., & Weiller, K. (2005). Perceptions of youth obesity among physical educators. *Social Psychology of Education, 8*, 407–423.

Griffiths, L. J., Wolke, D., Page, A. S., & Horwood, J. P. (2006). Obesity and bullying: Different effects for boys and girls. *Archives of Disease in Childhood, 91*, 121–125.

Hague, A., & White, A. (2005). Web-based intervention for changing attitudes of obesity among current and future teachers. *Journal of Nutrition Education and Behavior, 37*, 58–66.

Haines, J., Hannan, P. J., van den Berg, P., Eisenberg, M. E., & Neumark-Sztainer, D. (2013). Weight-related teasing from adolescence to young adulthood: longitudinal and secular trends between 1999 and 2010. *Obesity, 21*, 428–434.

Haines, J., Neumark-Sztainer, D., Eisenberg, M. E., & Hannon, P. J. (2006). Weight teasing and disordered eating behaviors in adolescents: Longitudinal findings from project EAT (eating among teens). *Pediatrics, 117*, 209–215.

Hayden-Wade, H. A., Stein, R. I., Ghaaderi, A. T. A., Saelens, B. E., Zabinski, M. F., & Wilfley, D. E. (2005). Prevalence, characteristics, and correlates of teasing experiences among overweight children vs. non overweight peers. *Obesity Research, 13*, 1381–1392.

Hilbert, A., Braehler, E., Haeuser, W., & Zenger, M. (2014). Weight bias internalization, core self-evaluation, and health in overweight and obese persons. *Obesity, 22*, 79–85.

Irving, L. (2000). Promoting size acceptance in elementary school children: The EDAP puppet program. *International Journal of Eating Disorder, 8*, 221–232.

Jalongo, M. (1999). Matters of size: Obesity as a diversity issue in the field of early childhood. *Early Childhood Education Journal, 27*, 95–103.

Janssen, I., Craig, W., Boyce, W., & Pickett, W. (2004). Associations between overweight and obesity with bullying behaviors in school-aged children. *Pediatrics, 13*, 1187–1194.

Klaczynski, P., Daniel, D. B., & Keller, P. S. (2009). Appearance idealization, body esteem, causal attributions, and ethnic variations in the development of obesity stereotypes. *Journal of Applied Developmental Psychology, 30*, 537–551.

Li, W., & Rukavina, P. (2009). A review on coping mechanisms against obesity bias in physical activity/education settings. *Obesity Reviews, 10*(9), 87–95.

Li, W., & Rukavina, P. (2012a). Including overweight or obese students in physical education: A social ecological constraint model. *Research Quarterly for Exercise and Sport, 83*(9), 570–578.

Li, W., & Rukavina, P. (2012b). The nature, occurring contexts, and psychological implications of weight-related teasing in urban physical education programs. *Research Quarterly for Exercise and Sport, 83*, 308–317.

Li, W., Rukavina, P., & Wright, P. M. (2012). Coping against weight-related teasing among overweight or obese adolescents in urban physical education. *Journal of Teaching in Physical Education, 31*, 182–199.

Margulies, A. S., Floyd, R. G., & Hojnoski, R. L. (2008). Body size stigmatization: An examination of attitudes of African American preschool-age children attending Head Start. *Journal of Pediatric Psychology, 33*, 487–496.

Mellin, A. E., Neumark-Sztainer, D., Story, M., Ireland, M., & Resnick, M. D. (2002). Unhealthy behaviors and psychosocial difficulties among overweight adolescents: The potential impact of familial factors. *Journal of Adolescent Health, 31*, 145–153.

Neumark-Sztainer, D., & Eisenberg, M. (2005). Weight bias in a teen's world. In K. D. Brownell, R. Puhl, M. B. Schwartz, & L. Rudd (Eds.), *Weight bias: Nature, consequences, and remedies* (pp. 68–79). New York: Guilford Press.

Neumark-Sztainer, D., Story, M., & Faibisch, L. (1998). Perceived stigmatization among overweight African American and Caucasian adolescent girls. *Journal of Adolescent Health, 23*, 264–270.

Neumark-Sztainer, D., Story, M., & Harris, T. (1999). Beliefs and attitudes about obesity among teachers and school health care providers working with adolescents. *Journal of Nutrition Education, 31*, 3–9.

O'Brien, K. S., Hunter, J. A., & Banks, M. (2007). Implicit anti-fat bias in physical educators: Physical attributes, ideology, and socialization. *International Journal of Obesity, 31*, 308–314.

Panzer, B. M., & Dhuper, S. (2014). Designing a group therapy program for coping with childhood weight bias. *Social Work, 59*, 141–147.

Pearce, M. J., Boergers, J., & Prinstein, M. J. (2002). Adolescent obesity, overt and relational peer victimization, and romantic relationships. *Obesity Research, 10*, 386–393.

Peters, D. M., & Jones, R. J. A. (2010). Future sport, exercise and physical education professionals' perceptions of the physical self of obese children. *Kinesiology, 42*, 36–43.

Peterson, J. L., Puhl, R. M., & Luedicke, J. (2012a). An experimental assessment of physical educators' expectations and attitudes: The importance of student weight and gender. *Journal of School Health, 82*, 432–440.

Peterson, J. L., Puhl, R. M., & Luedicke, J. (2012b). An experimental investigation of physical education teachers' and coaches' reactions to weight-based victimization in youth. *Psychology of Sport and Exercise, 13*, 177–185.

Pierce, J. W., & Wardle, J. (1997). Cause and effect beliefs and self-esteem of overweight children. *Journal of Child Psychology and Psychiatry and Allied Disciplines, 38*, 645–650.

Puhl, R. M., & Brownell, K. (2001). Bias, discrimination, and obesity. *Obesity Research, 9*, 788–805.

Puhl, R. M., & Brownell, K. D. (2003). Ways of coping with obesity stigma: Review and conceptual analysis. *Eating Behaviors, 4*, 53–78.

Puhl, R. M., & Brownell, K. D. (2006). Confronting and coping with weight stigma: An investigation of overweight and obese adults. *Obesity, 14*, 1802–1815.

Puhl, R. M., & Latner, J. (2007). Stigma, obesity, and the health of the nation's children. *Psychological Bulletin, 133*(4), 557–580.

Puhl, R. M., & Luedicke, J. (2012). Weight-based victimization among adolescents in the school setting: Emotional reactions and coping behaviors. *Journal of Youth and Adolescence, 41*, 27–40.

Puhl, R. M., Schwartz, M. B., & Brownell, K. D. (2005). Impact of perceived consensus on stereotypes about obese people: A new approach for reducing bias. *Health Psychology, 24*, 517–525.

Roehling, M. V. (1999). Weight-based discrimination in employment: Psychological and legal aspects. *Personnel Psychology, 52*, 969–1017.

Rukavina, P. B., Doolittle, S., Li, W., Manson, M., & Beale, A. (2015). Middle school teachers' strategies for including overweight students in skill and fitness instruction. *Journal of Teaching in Physical Education, 34*, 93–118. doi: 10.1123/jtpe.2013-0152.

Rukavina, P., & Li, W. (2008). School physical activity interventions: Do not forget about obesity bias. *Obesity Reviews, 9*, 67–75.

Rukavina, P. B., Li, W., Shen, B., & Sun, H. (2010). A service learning based project to change implicit and explicit bias toward obese individuals among Kinesiology pre-professionals. *Obesity Facts, 3*, 117–126.

Rukavina, P. B., Li, W., & Rowell, M. B. (2008). A service learning based intervention to change attitudes toward obese individuals in kinesiology pre-professionals. *Social Psychology of Education, 11*, 95–112.

Schwartz, M. B., Chambliss, O. H., Brownell, K. D., Blair, S., & Billington, C. (2003). Weight bias among health professionals specializing in obesity. *Obesity Research, 11*, 1033–1039.

Schwartz, M. B., Vartanian, L., Nosek, B., & Brownell, K. D. (2006). The influence of one's own body weight on implicit and explicit anti-fat bias. *Obesity Research, 14*, 440–447.

Shore, S., Sachs, M., Lidicker, J., Brett, S., Wright, A., & Libonati, J. (2008). Decreased scholastic achievement in overweight middle school students. *Obesity, 16*, 1535–1538.

Storch, E. A., Milsom, V. A., DeBraganza, N., Lewin, A. B., Geffken, G. R., & Silverstein, J. H. (2007). Peer victimization, psychosocial adjustment, and physical activity in overweight and at risk-for-overweight youth. *Journal of Pediatric Psychology, 32*, 80–89.

Su, W., & Santo, A. D. (2011). Preschool children's perceptions of overweight peers. *Journal of Early Childhood Research, 10*, 19–31.

Tang-Peronard, J. L., & Heitmann, B. L. (2008). Stigmatization of obese children and adolescents: The importance of gender. *Obesity Reviews, 9*, 522–534.

Teachman, B. A., Gapinski, K. D., Brownell, K. D., & Rawlins, M. (2003). Demonstrations of implicit anti-fat bias: The impact of providing causal information and evoking empathy. *Health Psychology, 22*, 68–78.

Trout, J., & Graber, K. C. (2009). Perceptions of overweight students concerning their experience in physical education. *Journal of Teaching in Physical Education, 28*, 272–292.

U.S. Department of Health and Human Services [USDHHS]. (1996). *Physical activity and health: A report of the Surgeon General.* Washington, DC: U.S. Government Printing Office.

U.S. Department of Health and Human Services [USDHHS]. (2008). *Physical activity guidelines for Americans.* Washington, DC: U.S. Government Printing Office.

Wiese, H. J. C., Wilson, J. F., Jones, R. A., & Neises, M. (1992). Obesity stigma reduction in medical students. *International Journal of Obesity and Related Metabolic Disorders, 16*, 859–868.

PART IX

Achievement motivation

Introduction

Motivation is a mental process that brings about and sustains goal-oriented actions (Pintrich & Schunk, 2002). Pioneer scholars, such as John Dewey, viewed motivation as an integral part of knowledge to be learned. He (1902) considered content that is not motivating to be an "evil" in education, stating, "What we mean by the mechanical and dead in instruction is this lack of motivation" (p. 354).

The learning environment has a direct and powerful influence on students' motivation to learn and achieve. In this paradigm, researchers study how environmental events, such as rewards or punishment, motivate or demotivate individuals. Researchers also study motivation from a developmental perspective, examining if individuals can learn to regulate their own motivation in an externally controlled environment and, if so, how they learn to use self-regulated motivation strategies to achieve success. Quite a few theories have evolved from these research paradigms. Examples from the early behaviorist theory family include conditioning theory (e.g., Skinner, 1953), drive theory (Woodworth, 1918), and purposive behaviorism (Tolman, 1932). Examples from the cognitive theory family include arousal theory (James, 1922), cognitive consistency theory (Heider, 1946), and humanistic theories (Maslow, 1954).

In the past three decades, research on physical education students' motivation has evolved into mainstream inquiry. This research is driven by a set of theoretical frameworks evolved from those mentioned above. They include expectancy-value theory, self-determination theory, achievement goal theory, and interest theory. Substantial evidence from this research has begun to transform ways researchers and practitioners understand learner motivation in PE (Chen, 2015). This rich body of evidence forms the knowledge base for this part.

The six chapters included in this part focus on issues critical to motivating children to learn in physical education and to apply what they learn to real life. The first chapter, Chapter 39, *Motivation research in physical education: Learning to become motivated*, serves as the introduction for the part. In it, Chen focuses on the important proposition that motivation, as a cognitive process, can be deliberately learned. In Chapter 40, *Expectancy-value based motivation for learning*, Ping Xiang summarizes research findings from expectancy-value theory. This theory attempts to explain which students' beliefs for success and realization of task values motivate them. In Chapter 41, *Maximizing student motivation in physical education: A self-determination theory perspective,* John Wang examines the research base supporting self-determination theory. By addressing issues associated with rewards and external regulations, Wang explores the role of self-determination theory in nurturing students' intrinsic motivation to achieve externally determined goals by satisfying their innate needs for autonomy, competence, and relatedness. In Chapter 42, *Individual and situational interest,* Bo Shen provides a comprehensive review of research findings on student interests. Many PE practitioners intuitively emphasize strategies to integrate "fun" into PE to motivate students. As part of a detailed review of theoretical and empirical perspectives, Shen addresses pros and cons of relying on personal and situational interests to motivate students in physical education.

In Chapter 43, *Adaptation or maladaptation of achievement goals in physical education,* Sami Yli-Piipari presents research evidence that students adapt or mal-adapt their personal goals (e.g., performance vs. mastery goals) to position themselves to fulfill teacher-imposed external goals. He illustrates how adaptive and maladaptive goals can lead students to different motivation paths. In the last chapter in this section, Chapter 44, *Motivation as a learning strategy,* Haichun Sun integrates findings from several theoretical perspectives to answer the important question: Can motivation provide viable learning strategies to enhance learning in physical education? She carefully examines the role of self-initiated motivation through strategies students plan and employ to control their thoughts, feelings, and actions to attain learning goals. Sun concludes that motivation may provide effective strategies to help learners align personal goals with learning goals, regulate their learning behaviors, and develop interest in PE.

A goal of this part is to provide relevant empirical evidence for PE researchers and practitioners interested in theoretical and practical applications of student motivation. Each chapter author draws on a common body of literature from the achievement motivation scholarly research base while developing a unique perspective on a particular motivation theory. Because of the common origins of motivation constructs, for example, perceived competence, readers will find that authors have developed the primary constructs in different ways emphasizing unique findings and providing insights into practical applications. Continuing with the standard Handbook format, each chapter provides a chapter-specific historic overview, theoretical framework or frameworks, review and critique of empirical research findings, and a discussion for future directions. These should help distinguish each chapter and theory and facilitate understanding the practical implications of achievement motivation and strategies PE teachers can use to motivate student learning.

Ang Chen
University of North Carolina at Greensboro, USA

References

Chen, A. (2015). Operationalizing physical literacy for learners: Embodying the motivation to move. *Journal of Sport and Health Science, 4,* 125–131.

Dewey, J. (1902). The child and the curriculum. In R. D. Archambault (Ed.) (1964) *John Dewey on education: Selected writings.* Chicago: The University of Chicago Press.

Heider, F. (1946). Attitudes and cognitive organization. *Journal of Psychology, 21,* 107–112.

James, W. (1922). What is an emotion? In K. Dunlap (Ed.), *The emotions* (pp. 11–30). Baltimore, MD: Williams & Wilkins.

Maslow, A. (1954). *Motivation and personality.* New York: Harper.

Pintrich, P. R., & Schunk, D. H. (2002). *Motivation in education: Theory, research and applications* (2nd edn). Upper Saddle River, NJ: Pearson Education, Inc.

Skinner, B. F. (1953). *Science and human behavior.* New York: Free Press.

Tolman, E. C. (1932). *Purposive behavior in animals and man.* New York: Appleton-Century-Crofts.

Woodworth, R. S. (1918). *Dynamic psychology.* New York: Columbia University Press.

39

MOTIVATION RESEARCH IN PHYSICAL EDUCATION

Learning to become motivated

Ang Chen, UNIVERSITY OF NORTH CAROLINA AT GREENSBORO, USA

Motivation research has occupied an important space in the PE literature. The findings have furnished extensive evidence for a deeper understanding of K-12 students' motivation to learn knowledge about physical activity and health, improve motor skills for sports and other physical activities, and develop personal fitness for health and performance. Consequences from childhood physical inactivity continue to challenge PE researchers to search for effective ways to motivate children to be physically active in and out of the school environment (Institute of Medicine, 2013).

These challenges are manifested on two fronts associated with changes in education and society in the twenty-first century. First, the most recent revision of the U.S. National Standards for PE (Society of Health and Physical Educators [SHAPE], 2014) establishes physical literacy as the ultimate goal for K-12 students. As an abstract idea (Whitehead, 2010), physical literacy seems to encompass a spectrum of components, including motivation, necessary for leading a physically active life. Although scholars are still debating whether it is feasible or realistic under the current school environment for the idea to take hold (Chen & Sun, 2015), a consensus is that children need to learn how to become motivated for physical activity in and out of school. Second, physical play is no longer the only leisure activity for children. The concept that a child must move physically to play is challenged by the reality of "cyber-space." Children now can literally plan and play a virtual but real game on screen with someone from across the world.

Under these academic and leisure contexts, motivating children in PE and beyond requires more effort than ever from educators. A critical issue is what to do to maximize the motivation effect. Emerging research evidence on content specificity (Ding, Sun, & Chen, 2013) suggests that motivation is content specific and can be learned along with PE content. It is the goal of this chapter to review research evidence related to motivation development and acquisition and elaborate the possibility of teaching motivation to K-12 PE students. In the following sections I will (a) give a very brief historical overview, (b) discuss frequently used theoretical frameworks, (c) review current trends and issues, and (d) provide conclusions based on the review. I will close the chapter with a set of questions for reflection and further discussions.

Historical overview

In a landmark survey of doctoral research from 1930 to 1946 (Cureton, 1949), motivation did not appear on any of the 420 dissertations in the 20 institutions granting doctoral degrees in PE. The first research on motivation as a construct seems to be a study of achievement motivation on risk taking by Glyn Roberts (1975). Before that, student motivation was understood through studies on students' degree of likings or interest (that is, individual interest as conceptualized today). For example, Driftmier (1933) studied high school girls' individual differences in interest as related to PE. She reported that the first two choices were rhythmic work (38% of the 245 girls) and stunts, tumbling, and pyramids (25%). In third place was marching tactics (9%). Basketball and tennis were among the least interesting activities with 2% and 1%, respectively. Although no motivation constructs were used in the study, Driftmier's intention seems to be obvious: to explore what could motivate girls to better participate in PE. Other data from the same study support this observation. For example, Driftmier also reported that on the first day of class, 100% of the girls preferred the new self-directed squad teaching method to the traditional teacher-class method. An overwhelming number of girls (61%) still preferred the self-direct method on the last day of class. In fact, this type of motivation-equals-liking understanding has persisted for many years overlapping with the research on theoretical constructs of motivation. For example, Browne (1992) conducted a study similar to that of Driftmier's (1933) on reasons girls selected PE. She reported that the top two reasons for high school girls to select PE were "I like physical activity" (99% of participants) and "Classes are fun" (95%).

It was not until the 1980s that motivation in PE was studied with established, mature theoretical frameworks and constructs. Most noticeably, all motivation theories originate from a cognitive perspective. They treat motivation, especially achievement motivation, as complex processes rather than a simple stimuli-responses loop. These theories include achievement goal theory (Nicholls, 1984), expectancy-value theory (Eccles, 1983), self-efficacy theory (Bandura, 1977), interest theory (Hidi, 1990), and self-determination theory (Deci, 1980).

Guided by these theories, motivation research in PE is almost completely focused on students. In their literature search, Chen, Chen, and Zhu (2012) identified over 200 published research reports focused on student motivation. Compared to this number, research on PE teacher motivation is rather scarce. This lack of empirical work has created a void in the literature and provided little generalizable evidence to address teacher motivation.

Theoretical frameworks

The achievement goal theory, expectancy-value theory, self-efficacy theory, interest theory, and self-determination theory are mature theories that have influenced motivation research in PE. Detailed descriptions of the theories are provided in other chapters in this handbook (see Solmon, Chapter 33). Here I present (a) a brief description of each theory and (b) a conceptual summary of their implications that inform current research.

Dominant theories in PE research

Achievement goal theory functions with an assumption that individuals not only are striving to achieve goals or outcomes that others determine for them but also are achieving the goals they choose by themselves. Researchers in psychology (e.g., Nicholls, 1984) have identified two goal orientations: an ego/performance goal orientation and a task/mastery goal orientation. Individuals with the ego/performance goal tend to become motivated when they perceive an opportunity to outperform others; whereas those with the task/mastery goal orientation become motivated to focus on the completion of the task at hand. Elliott and Harackiewicz (1996) further identified an approach-avoidance structure within each goal orientation. A mastery-avoidance goal, for example, motivates one to act to avoid difficult tasks, whereas a performance-avoidance goal motivates the individual to act to avoid showing incompetence. The theory also postulates that an environment can be performance- or task-prone. PE teachers can create either a performance-involving climate or a mastery-involving climate (Treasure, 1997). A particular goal orientation environment can strengthen learners' corresponding goal orientation (Todorovich & Curtner-Smith, 2002).

Expectancy-value theory suggests that competence-based expectancy beliefs for success and perceived value in the task are motivators for action (Eccles, 1983). Expectancy beliefs refer to one's judgment on the possibility of success in an activity. *Task values* are associated with the perceived worth or the benefits an activity may provide. Eccles and Wigfield (1995) proposed and validated a five-component theoretical model that contains expectancy beliefs and four task values. *Attainment value* is the importance the person acknowledges to him/herself when doing well in the activity. *Intrinsic or interest value* is the extent of enjoyment a task provides to the individual when completing the activity. *Utility value* refers to the usefulness of the activity to the person in current and future life. *Cost* is the negative consequence resulting from pursuing the activity. In PE, research evidence has shown that the theory is viable in predicting learner persistence and effort (Xiang, McBride, & Bruene, 2004), engagement and learning (Ding et al., 2013).

Interest theory conceptualizes motivation as a result of positive emotions from the interactions between the person and an object or activity. Interest is characterized by a high level of attention, intensive effort, and prolonged engagement with pleasant and successful feelings (Hidi, 2000). *Individual interest* refers to one's psychological preferences for an activity, while *situational interest* refers to an activity's appealing effect that triggers high level attention and engagement at the moment of person–activity interaction. In PE, situational interest has been validated as a multi-dimensional construct (Chen, Darst, & Pangrazi, 1999). Research evidence has shown that individual interest is associated with knowledge and skill gains, whereas situational interest is correlated with in-class physical activity levels (Chen & Darst, 2002; Chen, Martin, Ennis, & Sun, 2008).

Self-determination theory is an overarching theory for general motivation in life (Deci, 1980). Researchers assume that ultimately motivation derives from basic human psychological needs for competence, autonomy, and relatedness (Deci & Ryan, 1985). The theory further postulates that motivation comes from two basic sources, one is through regulations external to the individual and to the activity (*extrinsic motivation*); the other comes from the attraction and enjoyment the activity exerts on the individual (*intrinsic motivation*) (Deci & Ryan, 1985). Ultimate motivation derives from basic human psychological needs for competence, autonomy, and relatedness (Deci & Ryan, 1985). Research in PE has yielded limited evidence suggesting complex relations among the needs, regulation mechanisms, and extrinsic/intrinsic (Standage, Duda, & Ntoumanis, 2003, 2005).

Self-efficacy theorists believe that motivation depends on individuals'"judgments of the likelihood that one can organize and execute given courses of action required to deal with a prospective situation" (Bandura, 1980, p. 263). The judgments, in turn, are functions of efficacious information individuals gather from multiple sources including their own competence perceptions and others' input about their ability. In PE, research using the theory has been scarce, which makes it difficult to summarize the research findings and implication (Chen et al., 2012).

Implications

One overarching underpinning for these theories is the way individuals perceive competence. In a mastery environment such as schools, individuals rely on self-perceptions of competence to determine the degree of effort (a proxy measure of motivation) they are willing to put forth. In children, the underlying power of perceived competence can be the most important source of motivation (Harter, 1982, 1985). In the physical activity domain, Marsh and his colleagues (Marsh, Hey, Roche, & Perry, 1997) examined physical self-concept and self-efficacy illustrating the generalizability of the perceived competence construct.

This line of empirical work has revealed two fundamental conceptions or beliefs children rely on to judge their own competence: an incremental belief or an entity belief (Dweck, 1999). The entity belief is the conception that competence is a fixed capacity one is born with. The incremental belief is the conception that competence is incrementally developed with effort and experience. Interacting with the effort concept, the two beliefs lead children to attribute success or failure differently. Low effort (or display of less effort) in completing a task suggests high competence. In contrast, high effort in completing the same task indicates low competence (Eccles, Wigfield, & Schiefele, 1998). These conceptions result in very different motivational behaviors. In PE, Li, Lee, and Solmon (2008) found that college students who were led to the entity belief were more likely than those who were led to the incremental belief to attribute success or failure to "fixed" competence. They were less likely to display intrinsic motivation, and did not put forth as much effort in pursuing the tasks.

Interest is another underlying thread found across several theories, especially the interest theory and expectancy-value theory. Research has revealed convincing evidence that interest, especially situational interest, is a primary motivator in PE (Chen, Darst, & Pangrazi, 2001). In the expectancy-value theory, interest is one of the values children are likely to recognize and rely on for motivation (Wigfield & Eccles, 2002). Even for interest development, the role of perceived competence cannot be overlooked. Research evidence has shown a close connection between individual interest and competence. Children often are most interested in doing those activities they are capable of doing well (Renninger & Wozniak, 1985).

The research based on these theories has made it clear that motivation and motivated behavior derive from a set of beliefs, values, goals, and emotions. One or more of the entities interact with environmental factors to lead the individual to adopt either a motivational or amotivational mental process when approaching the task at hand. Because beliefs, values, goals, and some emotions are learned during individuals' development, it can be reasoned that motivation is an acquired mental state. An overall implication of the theories and their empirical research appears to be whether and how motivation can be taught to children and adolescents along with the content they are learning.

Current trends and issues

This section includes two parts. In the first part, the focus is on the current literature about motivation acquisition. It draws research evidence from studies using the dominant theoretical frameworks to illustrate how motivation is developed and whether motivation is a learnable entity. In the second part, I will focus on the issues in the current motivation research in PE by identifying the areas of research that most need to be strengthened.

Current research on "becoming motivated"

In education, motivation has been studied as a mental process that is developed and sustained along with knowledge growth. Motivation strategies are for teachers to use rather than for students to learn. Seldom has motivation been considered a "content" that can be taught to students. Emerging evidence seems to suggest, however, it is possible that motivation can be a learned/acquired asset for the learner (see Sun, Chapter 44).

Achievement goal theory

Children's goal orientations are nurtured and shaped by the immediate learning environment (Ames, 1992). Ames concluded that the classroom environment, as established by the teacher, presents numerous achievement-related cues to the learner. The goal-related cues are conveyed in six common instructional elements: task design (T), distribution of authority (A), success recognition (R), grouping structures (G), achievement evaluation (E), and time allocation (T) (Epstein, 1989). By absorbing the meaning of the cues, children learn what goals, mastery or performance, the teacher expects and will reward. As a result of using this TARGET strategy teachers can assist students to acquire a goal orientation.

In PE, Parish and Treasure (2003) conducted a correlational study with 442 middle school students and found a positive correlation (r = .555) between perception of a mastery climate and intrinsic motivation and a positive correlation (r = .505) between perception of a performance climate and amotivation. Wang, Liu, Chatzisarantis, and Lim (2010) examined the corresponding relationship between middle school students' (n = 781) perception of goal climates and their goal orientations with enjoyment in PE. They concluded that "when the teachers create an environment whereby personal improvement and mastery are valued, the students are more likely to adopt mastery-approach goal" (p. 335). The findings clearly indicate the association between goal climate and learner goal orientation.

Studies using quasi-experimental designs have shown promising evidence supporting the goal acquisition notion. Solmon (1996) manipulated the motivational climate by creating a mastery or a performance instruction setting for middle school students (n = 109) to learn juggling to determine if a particular climate could lead to a corresponding motivational belief and attribution. The results showed that students in the performance climate were more likely to attribute success to natural ability than students in the mastery climate. Todorovich and Curtner-Smith conducted two studies with third grade (n = 54, 2003) and sixth grade (n = 72, 2002) students. They manipulated the goal climate in the gymnasium. Results from both studies showed that the students taught with a particular goal climate developed that goal orientation.

Expectancy-value theory

Eccles and her colleagues' empirical and theoretical work has demonstrated that the expectancy beliefs for success and task values work together in developing motivational behaviors (e.g., Eccles et al., 1998; Wigfield & Eccles, 2002; see also Xiang, Chapter 40). One important finding from Eccles and her colleagues' work is that children are able to differentiate expectancy beliefs from task values at a young age. This ability to differentiate leads them to adopt different motivational paths. It is this differentiation that provides a basis for educators to consider ways to teach beliefs and values to encourage learners to acquire and sustain motivation.

Based on the motivation specificity hypothesis (Bong, 2001), Chen et al. (2008) examined elementary school students' (n = 298 from 48 intact classes) expectancy-value beliefs. They used different PE content (tasks) to examine the extent to which students could differentiate between expectancy beliefs and attainment, utility, interest, and cost values in the fitness development content they were studying. The results from correlation analyses on class means clearly showed that the students attached different task values to different fitness knowledge and exercise domains. The only exception was interest value which was invariantly high across all content domains in PE. Ding et al. (2013) further confirmed the expectancy-value specificity with a random student sample (n = 346) from eight Chinese middle schools. The results from both regression and structural equation modeling suggested that task values, especially the utility value, determined student achievement in learning fitness knowledge while expectancy beliefs determined achievement in learning motor skills.

These findings are especially meaningful for teaching PE. Because learning in PE encompasses and demands both physical as well as cognitive effort, results clearly indicate that learners may adopt differentiated motivational pathways to learn in the two distinct but related domains. The findings caution us to pay close attention to students' motivational processes when using these pathways.

Interest theory

Interest research has long established the link between individual interest (personal preferences for an entity/activity) and learning achievement (see also Shen, Chapter 42). Its close relationship with knowledge and values suggests the potential for individual interest to be "learnable." In other words, when a person begins to acquire knowledge or value, he/she simultaneously is acquiring an interest (or disinterest) associated with the knowledge or value. Hidi and Anderson (1992) hypothesized that situational interest can evolve into individual interest. When a child is exposed to an attractive activity/task over time, his/her situational interest will change from a "catching" type of interest to a "holding" type (Mitchell, 1993). Reinforced by knowledge and acquired values, situational interest can become stable and enduring individual interest.

In PE, Chen (1996) found that in secondary schools students are able to differentiate activities/tasks that catch their interest from those that do not. In follow-up research, Chen (1998) found that students are likely to become resistant when they perceive that the content is boring. In subsequent studies on situational interest, Chen and Darst (2001) manipulated the situational interest elements in tasks to determine the extent to which the content, by itself, contributed to situational interest. The results showed that the level of cognition in physical activity tasks is the determinant for situational interest. The findings reinforce the notion that through careful task design, PE teachers can help students acquire a sense of situational interest. There is little evidence, however, of students internalizing situational interest so that they acquire individual interest. Interest theorists (e.g., Hidi, 1990; Krapp, 1999) hypothesize that depending on what knowledge and skill the situational interest entails, the situational interest can evolve into individual interest. In other words, students can learn to become interested in the content they are learning if the knowledge and skills are taught with strong situational interest. The hypothesis is partially supported by a study in PE (Shen, Chen, Tolley, & Scrabis, 2003) in which boys who had low individual interest in learning dance became highly engaged in a dance unit when the teachers designed the content with strong situationally interesting tasks.

Self-determination theory

At the heart of self-determination theory is the notion that self-regulation coupled with rewards and punishment (e.g., grades by teachers) can motivate learners extrinsically (see also

Wang, Chapter 41). However, when the rewards are no longer available, the motivated behavior is likely to stop unless the learner has begun the valuing process to appreciate the regulation strategies being learned. In fact, teaching students to self-regulate their own behavior has been a central goal of schooling. Because children often do not possess formal content knowledge when starting school, they are less likely to demonstrate intrinsic motivation in the classroom. Learner motivation, therefore, depends on how well the teacher is able to help children adopt one or more self-regulation mechanisms: external regulation, introjected regulation, identified regulation, and integrated regulation (Deci & Ryan, 1985). The premise of moving a child from extrinsic motivation to intrinsic motivation lies in the expectation that children are able to understand and learn the self-regulation processes and eventually align with the values embedded in the process (reflected in adopting the identified and/or integrated regulations).

In PE, Ntoumanis (2001) found a positive association between perceived competence and introjected and identified regulations in PE. The findings indicate a possibility that learners who adopt introjected (performing to satisfy others) or identified (performing because they value the activity) regulations may become competent through learning in PE. This and other findings (e.g., Standage et al., 2003, 2005) imply that self-regulation mechanisms can be included as part of the formal content for students to learn and acquire. Once students have acquired self-regulation strategies, they should be able to develop and maintain motivation to learn and achieve what is expected of them.

Self-efficacy theory

Classroom research has clearly demonstrated that self-efficacy is learned through interactions between the student and the classroom environment. There is evidence showing when children move through a well-sequenced curriculum their self-efficacy increases because of increased knowledge and competence (Shell, Colvin, & Bruning, 1995). Ironically many reports have documented a decline in self-efficacy as children become older and progress through the upper school grades. Researchers and theorists attribute this decline to classroom factors such as a norm-referenced grading system and a competitive atmosphere (e.g., Eccles, Wigfield, & Schiefele, 1998), because these factors negatively affect students' self-appraisal processes.

In PE, studies on students' self-efficacy development are lacking. An early study (Chase, 1998) attempted to identify sources of self-efficacy information in PE. With a small sample of children (n = 24), Chase was able to differentiate sources of information for young children in elementary schools: success in performance for younger children and effort and success by social norm comparison for older ones. One study (Pan, 2014) using structure equation models attempted to determine the extent to which PE teachers' (n = 462) self-efficacy influenced students' (n = 2,681) motivation. The results revealed a large impact of teacher efficacy on student motivation (factor loading = .70). The results suggest the influential role of teacher self-efficacy in PE students' motivation (see Kulinna and Cothran, Chapter 36). More research is needed to determine whether the impact can lead to an increase in students' self-efficacy.

Current issues

A targeted review examining motivation acquisition suggests a possibility that motivation strategies may be taught to children and adolescents in PE and the strategies can be an integral part of PE content. To establish these relationships, we need additional research in the following areas to enrich our knowledge of motivation development: perceived competence and actual competence; gender differentiations in motivation; motivation and ethnicity identity; and knowledge and motivation. Researchers should develop new hypotheses to further study learner motivation not only as an individual mental process but also as a curricular and pedagogical process.

Perceived competence and actual competence

The theories and supporting evidence seem to point to a single factor that is the foundation for most motivation constructs: perceived competence (see also Garn, Chapter 34). Although psychological research has long identified several critical sources influencing competence conception development, pedagogical research has generated little evidence to show the relationship between perceived competence and actual competence. More importantly we need to know how to teach children to correctly use relevant competence information, such as effort, success, expectancy, standards, to motivate themselves. Children come to PE with misconceptions about many aspects of physical activity (Pasco & Ennis, 2015; Placek et al., 2001). Correcting these misconceptions can be the first step to developing a positive conception about competence beliefs.

Gender differentiations in motivation

It is acknowledged that children's conceptions about themselves and events around them are socially constructed as is the motivation process (Wentzel, 2004). Research has shown that boys and girls perceive their competence in different ways (Lee, Fredenburg, Belcher, & Cleveland, 1999), define success differently (Lee, Nelson, & Nelson, 1988), and believe gender-appropriateness in sports (Lirgg, George, Chase, & Ferguson, 1996). Solmon, Lee, Belcher, Harrison, and Wells (2003) conducted an interesting study with important implication for PE. They examined perceived gender appropriateness of hockey and a hockey skill (wrist shot) for male and female college students. Although students perceived hockey as a male sport and playing hockey was more male-appropriate than female-appropriate, their view about the specific skill was gender neutral. The female students who perceived hockey as gender neutral displayed stronger confidence in learning to play hockey than those females who believed it gender-inappropriate.

The finding from this study and others (e.g., Shen et al., 2003) have suggested gender appropriateness is a critical issue in motivating girls in PE. They also point out, however, that both female and male students can be motivated to learn if the content and tasks are structured carefully to enhance their perceived competence (Solmon et al., 2003) and interest (Shen et al., 2003). However, studies are urgently needed in this area to determine curricular and pedagogical characteristics that can motivate all students.

Motivation and ethnic identity

Although ethnic identity has been an important area of inquiry in education, specific research on ethnic minority student motivation is rarely found in the literature. Basch's (2011) literature review convincingly documented health consequences in minority adolescents due to the disparity in participation in physical activity. Given that motivation processes are socially constructed (acquired), it can be hypothesized that children growing up in different ethnic cultures may be adapted to the motivation process endorsed by the culture. Cultural studies in sport have clearly shown that when minority youths assume ethnically unique identities (Harrison, Harrison, & Moore, 2002), they are likely to follow ethnically unique ways to learn in the sport domain (Harrison, Moore, & Evans, 2006). Further, they are likely to engage in an assimilation process to fit into the mainstream culture while maintaining their own identity (Zieff, 2000). These studies have laid a foundation for additional, motivation-specific inquiries into the motivation processes the ethnic minority students adopt in PE.

Harrison (1995) articulated the link between cultural upbringing and possible subjective physical activity choices arguing that the link is a function of cultural assimilation in a community. An individual's upbringing can have a profound impact on the motivation process a child adopts in learning in PE. In an experimental study, Harrison (2001) found when students received an ethnicity-relevant cue for a physical activity, the information significantly amplified their prediction of their own performance, although it did not impact their actual performance. Vierling, Standage, and Treasure (2007) found that Hispanic students' satisfaction of autonomy need predicted their motivation toward physical activity, leading to enhanced physical activity participation and positive attitudes. Additional studies examining ethnic minority learner motivation are needed to better understand unique culturally influenced processes in motivation development.

Implications for evidence-based practice

One of the most salient implications of the research is that PE students may learn motivation strategies as a content. Based on motivation specificity, teachers can match content/ tasks with motivation strategies that are sensitive to content. For example, when teaching health-enhancing fitness activities, teachers can emphasize the value (importance and utility values) of the content. When promoting physical intensity, teachers can emphasize cognitive load along with physical load to show students how situational interest can motivate them to participate enthusiastically. Teachers also can teach students the appropriate ways to estimate or perceive their own competence using differentiated learning strategies that provide challenges appropriate to students' abilities. In these ways teachers can help students learn motivational processes.

Instructional climate

A well-structured motivating environment is the basis for teaching motivation to students. A mastery-oriented climate is necessary for learners to develop motivational processes focusing on completion of learning tasks rather than on ability comparison. PE teachers can create a mastery climate that focuses on mastering the knowledge and skills being taught. In the meantime, teachers should minimize the effect of competition among individual students, such as ranking student performance on a fitness test.

Self-regulation

One determinant for motivation development is the adoption of appropriate external regulation mechanisms. It is necessary to implement external regulations to enhance student extrinsic motivation. Physical educators should realize that, although we hope students will have intrinsic motivation, not all students will develop high intrinsic motivation for all physical activities. Extrinsic motivation through positive self-regulation is necessary so that students can start the process of internalizing extrinsic motivation under teachers' supervision and eventually become intrinsically motivated to participate in physical activities in which they have built competence.

Culturally relevant motivation

Cultural influence is a factor that can act as a powerful motivator. Limited evidence suggests that students with an ethnic minority background may demonstrate different types or degrees of motivation because of their upbringings. At present, there is little evidence to allow researchers to reach a conclusive determination about the extent ethnicity cultures influence motivation in PE. Physical educators should be sensitive about particular needs of ethnic minority students, especially the basic needs for autonomy, competence, and relatedness.

Gender equality

Research has provided extensive information examining gender and motivation. Research confirms that boys and girls can be mastery and performance oriented and can view their competence in different ways. Interestingly, they similarly value the benefits from regular physical activity and can be motivated by situational interest despite their different individual interests. Most importantly, most students like PE at least until they reach middle school age. In addition, students display gender-based preferences for sports (appropriateness) which can diminish when students direct their focus to specific skills and learning. The research findings are clear that the motivation strategies supported by the research evidence work effectively for both girls and boys.

It appears that although motivation has been studied as a psychological topic and motivation processes are indeed an individual mental process, motivation is also a curricular issue. Motivation, however, has rarely been studied as part of the curriculum. PE curriculum guide and textbooks usually do not include motivation strategies as part of instructional content to be taught. For children to develop and sustain strong motivation for physical activity, motivation needs to become part of the content in each PE lesson.

Future directions

We study motivation in PE with a hope that children will be able to motivate themselves for physical activity participation outside of PE. This expectation has become clear and increasingly important as is delineated in the current PE goals and standards (SHAPE, 2014). Adopting physical literacy as the goal of K-12 PE has designated learner motivation as one pillar in the curriculum (Whitehead, 2010).

Chen (2013) encouraged motivation researchers to move beyond current research paradigms to focus on: (a) the connection between individual dispositional variables (self-concept, values, expectancies) and environmental variables (motivation climates, policies, curriculum); (b) motivation specificity issues (what types of motivation can be learned for what activities, especially how to design motivating fitness activities for children); (c) the behavioral regulation processes that help internalize situational interest/motivation into self-initiated motivation; and (d) the transition processes that we can teach children to apply motivation learned in PE in after-school environments.

Summary of key findings

- Motivation research in PE has yet to change its focus due to the current change in PE goals and standards (SHAPE, 2014) and other policy changes in education.

- Motivation research has been based on five dominant achievement motivation theories: achievement goals, expectancy-value, interest, self-efficacy, and self-determination. Most studies are descriptive and use correlational designs.
- Learner motivation, although an individual mental process, can be learned and acquired during the process of learning PE.
- Perceived competence is an underlying factor responsible for several motivation sources: goal orientations, expectancy beliefs, and self-efficacy. It is also found associated with individual interest and intrinsic motivation.
- Studies on motivation with ethnic minority cultures are lacking. Studies with gender as a variable have generated informative findings. Male and females may view sports through "gendered" lenses, but may likely view physical activity knowledge and skills as "gender neutral." In addition, gender-appropriateness can be overcome by strong situational interest.
- Helping students learn motivation relies on creating a mastery-goal centered learning environment that deemphasizes social comparison of physical performance. Extrinsic motivation and its associated self-regulation may be helpful for developing positive motivation toward learning PE. Self-regulations can be acquired and should be part of the PE content. Future motivation research needs to further explore the way motivation is learned and internalized for children/adolescents to apply to non-school settings for an active lifestyle.

Reflective questions for discussion

1. In what ways will the PE Standards change affect motivation research in the twenty-first century?
2. Learner perceived competence is the underlying construct in several achievement motivation theories. Discuss the ways perceived competence and its function are viewed in these theories.
3. Motivation researchers believe motivation is based on the acceptance of certain beliefs, goals, values, and emotions. Why is this position important for studying motivation in PE?
4. Do you agree with the position that motivation can be learned and should be part of PE content? Explain your reasons and use research evidence to support them.
5. What implication can one draw from comparing Driftmier (1933) and Solmon et al. (2003) in terms of gender appropriateness?
6. In the limited studies with culturally diverse students (e.g., Vierling et al., 2007), theoretical frameworks developed with western, European student populations were used. Do you think this is a culturally relevant research practice? Why do you think so? Use evidence to support your arguments.

References

Ames, C. (1992). Classrooms: Goals, structures, and student motivation. *Journal of Educational Psychology, 84*, 261–271.

Bandura, A. (1977). Self-efficacy: Toward a unifying theory of behavioral change. *Psychological Review, 84*, 191–215.

Bandura, A. (1980). Causing the relationship between self-efficacy judgment and action. *Cognitive Therapy and Research, 4*, 263–268.

Basch, C. E. (2011). Physical activity and the achievement gap among urban minority youth. *Journal of School Health, 81*, 626–634.

Bong, M. (2001). Between- and within-domain relations of academic motivation among middle and high school students: Self-efficacy, task-value, and achievement goals. *Journal of Educational Psychology, 93*, 23–34.

Browne, J. (1992). Reasons for the selection or nonselection of physical education studies by year 12 girls. *Journal of Teaching in Physical Education, 11*, 402–410.

Chase, M. A. (1998). Sources of self-efficacy in physical education and sport. *Journal of Teaching in Physical Education, 18*, 76–89.

Chen, A. (1996). Student interest in activities in a secondary physical education curriculum: An analysis of student subjectivity. *Research Quarterly for Exercise and Sport, 67*, 424–432.

Chen, A. (1998). Perception of boredom: Students' resistance to a secondary physical education curriculum. *Research in Middle Level Education Quarterly, 21*, 1–20.

Chen, A. (2013). Special Topic: Top 10 research questions related to children physical activity motivation. *Research Quarterly for Exercise and Sport, 84*, 441–447.

Chen, A., & Darst, P. W. (2001). Situational interest in physical education: A function of learning task design. *Research Quarterly for Exercise and Sport, 72*, 150–164.

Chen, A., & Darst, P. W. (2002). Individual and situational interest: The role of gender and skill. *Contemporary Educational Psychology, 27*, 250–269.

Chen, A., Darst, P. W., & Pangrazi, R. P. (1999). What constitutes situational interest? Validating a construct in physical education. *Measurement in Physical Education and Exercise Science, 3*, 157–180.

Chen, A., Darst, P. W., & Pangrazi, R. P. (2001). An examination of situational interest and its sources in physical education. *British Journal of Educational Psychology, 71*, 383–400.

Chen, A., Martin, R., Ennis, C. D., & Sun, H. (2008). Content specificity of expectancy beliefs and task values in elementary physical education. *Research Quarterly for Exercise and Sport, 79*, 195–208.

Chen, A., & Sun, H. (2015). A great leap of faith: Editorial for *Journal of Sport and Health Sciences* special issue on physical literacy. *Journal of Sport and Health Science, 4*, 1–3.

Chen, S., Chen, A., & Zhu, X. (2012). Are K-12 students motivated in physical education? A meta-analysis. *Research Quarterly for Exercise and Sport, 83*, 36–48.

Cureton, T. K. (1949). Doctorate theses reported by graduate departments of health, physical education and recreation 1930–1946, inclusive. *Research Quarterly, 20*, 21–59.

Deci, E. L. (1980). *The psychology of self-determination.* Lexington, MA: D. C. Heath.

Deci, E. L., & Ryan, R. M. (1985). *Intrinsic motivation and self-determination in human behavior.* New York: Plenum.

Ding, H., Sun, H., & Chen, A. (2013). Expectancy-value and situational interest motivation specificity on engagement and achievement outcomes in physical education. *Journal of Teaching in Physical Education, 32*, 253–269.

Driftmier, E. (1933). Individual differences in interests and physical traits as related to high school girls in physical education. *Research Quarterly, 4*, 198–220.

Dweck, C. S. (1999). *Self-theories: Their role in motivation, personality, and development.* Philadelphia: Taylor & Francis.

Eccles, J. (1983). Expectancies, values, and academic behaviors. In J. T. Spence (Ed.), *Achievement and achievement motives* (pp. 75–146). San Francisco: Freeman.

Eccles, J. S., & Wigfield, A. (1995). In the mind of the achiever: The structure of adolescents' academic achievement related-beliefs and self-perceptions. *Personality and Social Psychology Bulletin, 21*, 215–225. doi:10.1177/0146167295213003

Eccles, J. S., Wigfield, A., & Schiefele, U. (1998). Motivation to succeed. In W. Damon (Series Ed.) & N. Eisenberg (Vol. Ed.), *Handbook of child psychology* (5th ed., Vol. 3, pp. 1017–1095). New York: J. Wiley.

Elliott, A. J., & Harackiewicz, J. M. (1996). Approach and avoidance achievement goals and intrinsic motivation: A meditational analysis. *Journal of Personality and Social Psychology, 70*, 461–475.

Epstein, J. (1989). Family structures and student motivation: A developmental perspective. In C. Ames & R. Ames (Eds.), *Research on motivation in education* (Vol. 3, pp. 259–295). San Francisco: Academic Press.

Harrison, Jr., L. (1995). African Americans: Race as a self-schema affecting physical activity choices. *Quest, 47*, 7–18.

Harrison, Jr., L. (2001). Perceived physical ability as a function of race and racial comparison. *Research Quarterly for Exercise and Sport, 72*, 196–200.

Harrison, Jr., L., Harrison, C. K., & Moore, L. N. (2002). African American racial identity and sport. *Sport, Education and Society, 7*, 121–133.

Harrison, Jr., L., Moore, L. N., & Evans, L. (2006). Ear to the Streets: The race, hip-hop, and sports learning community at Louisiana State University. *Journal of Black Studies, 36*, 622–634. DOI: 10.1177/0021934705276797

Harter, S. (1982). The perceived competence scale for children. *Child Development, 53*, 87–97.

Harter, S. (1985). Competence as a dimension of self-evaluation: Toward a comprehensive model of self-worth. In R. Leahy (Ed.), *The development of the self* (pp. 55–121). New York: Academic Press.

Hidi, S. (1990). Interest and its contribution as a mental resource for learning. *Review of Educational Research, 60*, 549–571.

Hidi, S. (2000). An interest researcher's perspective: The effects of extrinsic and intrinsic factors on motivation. In C. Sansone & J. M. Harackiewicz (Eds.), *Intrinsic and extrinsic motivation: The search for optimal motivation and performance* (pp. 309–339). New York: Academic.

Hidi, S., & Anderson, V. (1992). Situational interest and its impact on reading and expository writing. In K. A. Renninger, S. Hidi, & A. Krapp (Eds.), *The role of interest in learning and development* (pp. 215–238). Hillsdale, NJ: LEA.

Institute of Medicine. (2013). *Educating the student body: Taking physical activity and physical education to school.* Washington, DC: The National Academies Press.

Krapp, A. (1999). Interest, motivation, and learning: An educational–psychological perspective. *Learning and Instruction, 14*(1), 23–40.

Lee, A. M., Fredenburg, K., Belcher, D., & Cleveland, N. (1999). Gender differences in children's conceptions of competence and motivation in physical education. *Sport, Education and Society, 4*, 161–174.

Lee, A. M., Nelson, K., & Nelson, J. K. (1988). Success estimations and performance in children as influenced by age, gender, and task. *Sex Roles, 48*, 719–726.

Li, W., Lee, A. M., & Solmon, M. (2008). Effects of dispositional ability conceptions, manipulated learning environments, and intrinsic motivation on persistence and performance. *Research Quarterly for Exercise and Sport, 79*, 51–61. DOI: 10.1080/02701367.2008.10599460

Lirgg, C. D., George, T. R., Chase, M. A., & Ferguson, R. H. (1996). Impact of conception of ability and sex-type of task on male and female self-efficacy. *Journal of Sport & Exercise Psychology, 18*, 426–434.

Marsh, H. W., Hey, J., Roche, L. A., & Perry, C. (1997). Structure of physical self-concept: Elite athletes and physical education students. *Journal of Educational Psychology, 89*, 369–380.

Mitchell, M. (1993). Situational interest. *Journal of Educational Psychology, 85*, 424–436.

Nicholls, J. (1984). Achievement motivation: Conceptions of ability, subjective experience, task choice, and performance. *Psychological Review, 91*, 328–346.

Ntoumanis, N. (2001). A self-determination approach to the understanding of motivation in physical education. *British Journal of Educational Psychology, 71*, 225–242.

Pan, Y. H. (2014). Relationships among teachers' self-efficacy and students' motivation, atmosphere, and satisfaction in physical education. *Journal of Teaching in Physical Education, 33*, 68–92.

Parish, L. E., & Treasure, D. C. (2003). Physical activity and situational motivation in physical education: Influence of the motivational climate and perceived ability. *Research Quarterly for Exercise and Sport, 74*, 173–182. DOI: 10.1080/02701367.2003.10609079

Pasco, D., & Ennis, C. D. (2015). Third grade students' mental models of blood circulation related to exercise. *Journal of Teaching in Physical Education, 34*, 76–92.

Placek, J., Griffin, L., Dodds, P., Raymond, C., Tremino, F., & James, A. (2001). Middle school students' conceptions of fitness: The long road to a healthy lifestyle. *Journal of Teaching in Physical Education, 20*, 314–323.

Renninger, K. A., & Wozniak, R. H. (1985). Effect of interest on attentional shift, recognition, and recall in young children. *Developmental Psychology, 21*, 624–632.

Roberts, G. C. (1975). Sex and achievement motivation effects on risk taking. *Research Quarterly, 46*, 58–70.

Shell, D. F., Colvin, C., & Bruning, R. H. (1995). Self-efficacy, attributions, and outcome expectancy mechanisms in reading and writing achievement: Grade-level and achievement-level differences. *Journal of Educational Psychology, 87*, 386–398.

Shen, B., Chen, A., Tolley, H., & Scrabis, K. A. (2003). Gender and interest-based motivation in learning dance. *Journal of Teaching in Physical Education, 22*, 396–409.

Society of Health and Physical Educators [SHAPE]. (2014). *National standards & grade-level outcomes for K-12 physical education.* Champaign, IL: Human Kinetics.

Solmon, M. A. (1996). Impact of motivational climate on students' behaviors and perceptions in a physical setting. *Journal of Educational Psychology, 88*, 731–738.

Solmon, M. A., Lee, A. M., Belcher, D., Harrison, Jr., L., & Wells, L. (2003). Beliefs about gender appropriateness, ability, and competence in physical activity. *Journal of Teaching in Physical Education, 22,* 261–279.

Standage, M., Duda, J. L., & Ntoumanis, N. (2003). A model of contextual motivation in physical education: Using constructs from self-determination and achievement goal theories to predict physical activity intentions. *Journal of Education Psychology, 95,* 97–110.

Standage, M., Duda, J. L., & Ntoumanis, N. (2005). A test of self-determination theory in school physical education. *British Journal of Educational Psychology, 75,* 411–433.

Todorovich, J. R., & Curtner-Smith, M. D. (2002). Influence of the motivational climate in physical education on sixth grade pupils' goal orientations. *European Physical Education Review, 8,* 119–138.

Todorovich, J. R., & Curtner-Smith, M. D. (2003). Influence of the motivational climate in physical education on third grade students' task and ego orientations. *Journal of Classroom Interaction, 38,* 36–46.

Treasure, D. C. (1997). Perceptions of the motivational climate and elementary school children's cognitive and affective response. *Journal of Sport and Exercise Psychology, 19,* 278–290.

Vierling, K. K., Standage, M., & Treasure, D. C. (2007). Predicting attitudes and physical activity in an "at-risk" minority youth sample: A test of self-determination theory. *Psychology of Sport and Exercise, 8,* 795–817.

Wang, J. C. K., Liu, W. C., Chatzisarantis, N. L. D., & Lim, C. B. S. (2010). Influence of perceived motivational climate on achievement goals in physical education: A structural equation mixture modeling analysis. *Journal of Sport & Exercise Psychology, 32,* 324–338.

Wentzel, K. R. (2004). Understanding classroom competence: The role of social-motivational and self-processes. In R. Kail (Ed.), *Advances in child development and behavior* (Vol. 32, pp. 213–241). New York: Elsevier.

Whitehead, M. (Ed.). (2010). *Physical literacy throughout the life course.* New York: Routledge.

Wigfield, A., & Eccles, J. S. (2002). The development of competence beliefs, expectancies for success, and achievement values from childhood through adolescence. In A. Wigfield & J. S. Eccles (Eds.), *Development of achievement motivation* (pp. 1–10). San Diego, CA: Academic Press.

Xiang, P., McBride, R. E., & Bruene, A. (2004). Fourth graders' motivation in an elementary physical education running program. *The Elementary School Journal, 104,* 253–266.

Zieff, S. G. (2000). From badminton to the bolero: Sport and recreation in San Francisco's Chinatown, 1895–1950. *Journal of Sport History, 27,* 1–29.

40

EXPECTANCY-VALUE BASED MOTIVATION FOR LEARNING

Ping Xiang, TEXAS A&M UNIVERSITY, USA

Obesity is epidemic in the United States. It is reported that 16.9% of American children and adolescents from 2 through 19 years of age are considered obese (Ogden, Carroll, Kit, & Flegal, 2012). Physical inactivity is a major contributing factor for obesity during childhood and adolescence. Consequently, school physical education (PE) has been called upon to increase PA levels to help children and adolescents maintain healthy weight, in addition to accomplishing goals of helping students develop movement knowledge and competencies, acquire motor skills, and understand the values and enjoyment of physical activity (PA) (Society of Health and Physical Educators [SHAPE], 2014). How well school PE can address those goals is determined partially by students' motivation. One aspect of students' motivation, expectancy-value based motivation, developed by Eccles and her colleagues (e.g., Eccles et al., 1983; Eccles, Wigfield, & Schiefele, 1998; Wigfield & Eccles, 1992, 2000), refers to individuals' innate desire for success and their belief in their ability to achieve success in these endeavors.

In the last 15 years, expectancy-value theory has emerged as an influential theory in research on student motivation in PE/PA settings (e.g., Chen, Martin, Ennis, & Sun, 2008; Chen & Chen, 2012; Xiang, McBride, & Bruene, 2006; Yli-Piipari & Kokkonen, 2014). In this chapter I will describe three aspects of this theory and emphasize its applications to PE/PA. In the first section I will present the expectancy-value theory from both historical and contemporary perspectives with an emphasis on its four value components. The second section summarizes the empirical studies that have examined expectancy-value theory and its relations to student achievement outcomes (e.g., effort, performance, knowledge, intention for future participation in PE/PA, and learning) primarily in the context of PE. I will highlight current research trends and issues and summarize key findings from this research. In the third section I offer recommendations for future research and implications for evidence-based practice and propose reflective questions to further our understanding of issues around student expectancy-value based motivation for learning in PE.

Expectancy value theory

Understanding student motivation has long been of interest to researchers and practitioners in education and PE. This is because motivation influences student learning and achievement in schools. Although there are many definitions of motivation, Eccles and her colleagues (e.g., Eccles et al., 1998) argue that student motivation is best captured by the two most fundamental questions "Can I succeed?" and "Do I want to succeed?" The "Can I succeed?" question deals with students' expectancy beliefs in performing achievement tasks, whereas the "Do I want to succeed?" question concerns the values that students attach to those achievement tasks. With this belief, Eccles and her colleagues (e.g., Eccles et al., 1983; Eccles et al., 1998; Wigfield & Eccles, 1992, 2000) proposed the expectancy-value theory of achievement choice to explain effort, choice, and achievement-related behavior in achievement settings, including schools. When students' motivation is examined from the expectancy-value theory lens, it becomes known as *expectancy-value based motivation for learning*.

Historic overview of the expectancy-value theory

Eccles' expectancy-value theory of achievement choice (e.g., Eccles et al., 1983) is based on Atkinson's (1957) expectancy-value theory of achievement motivation. Atkinson postulated that achievement behaviors are influenced by achievement motives, expectancies for success, and incentive values. Eccles and her colleagues proposed that students' performance, persistence, and task choice are directly determined by their expectancy beliefs and task values. Expectancy beliefs include both expectancies for success and beliefs about ability to achieve success. Expectancies for success deal with students' sense of how well they will perform on an upcoming task or activity, while beliefs about ability are defined as students' perceptions of their ability to successfully complete different tasks or activities. Theoretically, the distinction between expectancies for success and beliefs about ability primarily hinge on the individual's time frame. For example, expectancies for success focus on the future, while beliefs about ability concern one's ability in the present. However, considerable empirical work has revealed these two constructs are significantly, positively, and highly correlated when assessed with children and adolescents in many school subject areas, including PE (see Eccles & Wigfield, 2002; Xiang, McBride, Guan, & Solmon, 2003). Factor analyses often identify these two constructs loading on a single factor, suggesting they are not distinguishable, at least not by children and adolescents. As a result, researchers now tend to integrate these two into one construct, often labeled expectancy-related beliefs, expectancy beliefs, or competence beliefs. The term expectancy beliefs will be used throughout this chapter.

Task values are defined as how much students value an activity. This construct directly addresses the issue, "Why should I choose this activity over others?" The task value construct consists of four values: attainment value (importance), intrinsic value (interest/enjoyment), utility value (usefulness), and cost (Eccles et al., 1983, also see Chapter 39 by Chen, this volume). Attainment value represents students' beliefs about the importance of doing well on a given activity and is associated with their identity, self-image, and core personal goals (e.g., achievement needs and competence needs). For example, some students consider aerobic exercise important when they view it as central to their effort to stay in shape. Intrinsic value refers to how much students enjoy or like an activity. Many elementary students consider parachute activities interesting because they gain much enjoyment or have fun from the activity. Utility value concerns students' perceptions of an activity's worthiness in relation to their current and future life. For instance, some students would consider running useful when they believe it is a lifelong, health-related PA. Cost is defined as negative aspects of engaging in an activity, such as loss of time and energy for other activities, and fear of failure. This construct has received much less research attention and, consequently, is not as well elaborated as the other positive values in the expectancy-value theory. It is important to note that these four task values are associated with different achievement outcomes. (See also Chapter 33 by Solmon in the volume for a summary of expectancy value theory in cognition.)

Although expectancy beliefs and task values (i.e., importance, interest, and usefulness) represent two distinct constructs, scholars assume they are positively related to each other (e.g., Eccles et al., 1983; Eccles et al., 1998). The positive correlation between these two constructs implies that students are likely to consider activities important, interesting, and useful when they feel competent in those activities. Researchers theorize that these two constructs are influenced, either directly or indirectly, by a host of social, cognitive, and cultural variables (e.g., Eccles et al., 1983; Eccles et al., 1998). For example, students' task-specific beliefs, achievement goals, and self-schemata directly influence their expectancy beliefs and task values, whereas their perceptions of socializers' attitudes and expectations for them, gender roles, and activity stereotypes have indirect influences on their expectancy beliefs. Additionally, the expectancy-value theory assumes that students' cultural milieu (e.g., cultural stereotypes of gender role) and their perceived competence characteristics such as their aptitude and their previous performance serve as distal determinants of expectancy beliefs and task values. In short, the influences on students' expectancy beliefs and task values are complex and require concerted efforts to understand them (e.g., Eccles et al., 1983; Eccles et al., 1998).

Current trends and issues

The expectancy-value theory has become an influential theoretical perspective to understand and explain student motivation and achievement outcomes in PE during the last 15 years (e.g., Ding, Sun, & Chen, 2013; Gao, 2009; Xiang et al., 2003, 2005, 2006; Zhu & Chen, 2013a). The research in this line of inquiry has provided empirical evidence that expectancy-value theory can be utilized to understand issues associated with PE students' motivation for learning. Findings are primarily consistent with those of classroom research and summarized below. Though this section focuses on the context of PE, findings from other settings necessary to facilitate our understanding of students' expectancy-value motivation are included as well.

Expectancy beliefs and task values: distinct but related constructs

The expectancy-value theory (e.g., Eccles et al., 1983) originated in the academic domain. Scholars hypothesized that expectancies for success, beliefs about ability, and task values (importance, interest, and usefulness) represented distinct constructs.

To apply this theory to the field of PE, researchers first examined whether PE students were able to distinguish these constructs. To this end, Xiang and her colleagues (2003) conducted a study with 414 second and fourth grade elementary school PE students. Students were asked to rate their beliefs about ability, expectancies for success, and task values for PE (as a school subject) and throwing (as a specific movement skill) on questionnaires with five-point scales. Results of exploratory factor analyses revealed a two-factor structure of beliefs about ability, expectancies for success, and separate task values for both PE and throwing. Specifically, items measuring beliefs about ability and expectancies for success loaded on one factor, while items measuring task values (importance, interest, and usefulness) loaded on the other factor. This finding supported previous classroom research indicating that beliefs about ability and expectancies for success were not empirically distinguishable (see Eccles & Wigfield, 2002). It also provided the first empirical evidence that expectancy beliefs and task values are distinct constructs for elementary PE students. Zhu, Sun, Chen, & Ennis (2012) confirmed this finding in a confirmatory factor analysis of expectancy value data for 811 students in grades 3–5.

Xiang et al.'s (2003) results also corroborated Eccles, Wigfield, Harold, and Blumenfeld's (1993) finding that students do not differentiate importance, interest, and usefulness during the elementary school years. However, Xiang, McBride, and Bruene (2004) did not report a similar finding from a factorial structure study of expectancy beliefs and task values among fourth graders in a PE running program. Confirmatory factor analysis yielded a four-factor model, expectancy beliefs, importance, interest, and usefulness, indicating fourth graders in this study were able to differentiate the three task values in running. Zhu and colleagues (2012) conceptualized importance, interest, and usefulness as three differential components underlying the construct of task values in elementary PE and reported that this structure was supported by a confirmatory factor analysis on data provided by 811 third–fifth graders (ages 8–11). The discrepancy in these findings may be a reflection of the difference in the data analysis methods utilized in these studies, exploratory factor analysis versus confirmatory factor analysis. This discrepancy also may be related to the theorization that motivation constructs are specific to domain/content/activity (e.g., Chen et al., 2008). This study is described in the section, "Content specificity of expectancy beliefs and task values" below.

Unlike the mixed findings for elementary school students, research findings regarding the differentiation among the three task values are more consistent for middle school students. In the domain of mathematics, Eccles and Wigfield (1995) reported that confirmatory factor analyses revealed importance, interest, and usefulness were recognized as three distinct constructs among students in grades 5 through 12 (ages 11–18). In PE, Gao (2009) examined differentiation among importance, interest, and usefulness components revealed in a confirmatory factor analysis with a sample of middle school PE students. Zhu and colleagues (2012) also reported this differentiation. Additionally, based on results of a confirmatory factor analysis, Ding and colleagues (2013) reported that Chinese middle school PE students were able to construe importance, interest, and usefulness as three distinct task values.

There are fewer studies documenting high school PE and college PA students' ability to differentiate among expectancy beliefs, importance, interest, and usefulness. Chen and Chen (2012) reported that high school students (i.e., ninth graders, ages 14–15) differentiated expectancy beliefs, importance, interest, and usefulness based on confirmatory factor analysis. Similarly, Gao and Xiang (2008) reported that college students differentiated these four expectancy-value constructs in weight training as revealed by a confirmatory factor analysis. This differentiation also extended to Chinese college students in PE (Chen & Liu, 2009). Obviously, the differentiation should be more extensively studied among PE high school and college students. Based on cognitive evaluation theories, Deci and Ryan (2000) theorize that older adolescents and adults identify with and integrate desirable values as primary motivation sources.

Though expectancy beliefs and task values are distinct constructs, Eccles and her colleagues assumed they were positively related to each other (e.g., Eccles et al., 1998). Correlations reported in studies with students from elementary to college PE/PA settings provide empirical data to support this assumption (Ding et al., 2013; Gao, 2009; Gao & Xiang, 2008; Gu, Solmon, & Zhang, 2012; Xiang, McBride, & Bruene, 2004). Xiang and colleagues (Xiang et al., 2003) found that the positive relationship between expectancy beliefs and task values (a composite variable) existed not only in PE but also in throwing for both second and fourth graders (ages 7–8 & 9–10, respectively). Positive relationships among expectancy beliefs, importance, interest, and usefulness also were observed in an elementary PE running program (Xiang et al., 2006).

Gao (2009) reported that expectancy beliefs, importance, interest, usefulness were positively related to one another for a sample of middle school PE students in his study. Such a positive link extended to a sample of Chinese middle school PE students (Ding et al., 2013). Chen and Chen (2012) targeted ninth graders in high school PE and made a similar observation that these expectancy-value constructs were positively correlated with one another. The positive relationships between expectancy beliefs and task values were retained among college students in PA classes (Gao, Kosma, & Harrison, 2009; Gao & Xiang, 2008; Gu, Solmon, Zhang, & Xiang, 2011).

In sum, consistent with the expectancy-value theory, PE students in elementary, secondary, and college were able to differentiate expectancy beliefs, importance, interest, and usefulness as expectancy-value constructs. These constructs were positively related to one another, supporting the hypothesis (e.g., Wigfield & Eccles, 2002; Xiang et al., 2003) that students are more likely to consider achievement activities important, interesting, and useful when they believe they have competence to complete them. Additionally, correlations might further indicate the opposite relationship. That is, once PE students acknowledge the value of tasks, they attempt to motivate themselves through increased positive perception of competence and beliefs of future success in completing the tasks.

Content specificity of expectancy beliefs and task values

Content specificity of motivation constructs refers to the fact that motivation constructs are specific (or sensitive) to the domain, content, or activity in which the individual is participating (e.g., Chen at al., 2008). This is because any given domain, content, or activity requires a unique set of knowledge and skills, that can influence students' motivation toward learning and their performances. Therefore, students' motivational variables (e.g., conceptions of ability) should be assessed at the specific domain level of the content or activity (Li & Xiang, 2007; Shen, McCaughtry, & Martin, 2008).

Eccles and colleagues (1993) reported the content specificity of expectancy beliefs and task values in math, reading, music, and sports. Specifically, they assessed 865 first-, second-, and fourth-grade (ages 6–10) students' expectancy beliefs and task values in these domains and found they had distinct expectancy beliefs and task values for each domain or activity. Other studies also have supported the content specificity of expectancy beliefs and task values in academic settings (e.g., Bong, 2001; Jacobs, Lanza, Osgood, Eccles, & Wigfield, 2002).

In PE, content specificity of expectancy beliefs and task values also has become a research focus. In a study with a random sample of elementary school students, Chen et al. (2008) investigated whether students' expectancy beliefs and task values (i.e., importance, interest, and usefulness) varied as a function of the three content areas: cardiorespiratory fitness, muscular fitness, and traditional skills/games. Multivariate analysis of variance and correlation analyses yielded results that generally support the hypothesis that expectancy beliefs and task values are specific to domain, content, or activity. For example, mean levels of students' expectancy beliefs, importance, and usefulness were found to be significantly higher for the cardiovascular fitness content than two other content areas. Ding et al. (2013) took this question a step further examining whether expectancy beliefs, task values (along with situational interest), emerged as differential predictors of exercise knowledge, badminton striking skill, basketball dribbling skill, and in-class PA. Though participants in their study were Chinese middle school PE students, results generally support the specificity construct. For example, regression analyses revealed expectancy beliefs predicted badminton striking skill; interest predicted basketball dribbling skill; usefulness predicted exercise knowledge, and situational interest predicted in-class PA.

In sum, expectancy beliefs and task values are specific not only to the content but also to achievement outcomes in PE. Researchers need to keep this in mind when attempting to expand the knowledge base on students' expectancy-value based motivation. Additionally, they need to consider the nature of motivation specificity when designing motivation strategies for

K-12 students. Additionally, research on content specificity of expectancy beliefs and task values needs to be extended to high school and college students.

Age and gender differences

As important demographic variables, students' age and gender have received considerable attention from PE pedagogy researchers (e.g., Gao & Xiang, 2008; Gu et al., 2012; Xiang et al., 2003; Yli-Piipari & Kokkonen, 2014). This work revealed some inconsistent findings concerning age and gender differences in students' expectancy beliefs and task values in PE settings. Xiang and colleagues (2003) reported that second (ages 6–7) graders held significantly higher expectancy beliefs and task values in both PE and throwing than did fourth (ages 9–10) graders. In a year-long follow-up study (Xiang, McBride, & Guan, 2004), second grade students now in third grade reported lower expectancy beliefs in PE, whereas the original fourth graders' expectancy beliefs in PE remained the same as they progressed to the fifth grade. Contrary to expectancy beliefs which increased, task values associated with PE declined as students progressed through grades 2–5. These findings partially support the classroom research that students' expectancy beliefs and task values generally decreased over the elementary school years (e.g., Eccles et al., 1998; Jacobs et al., 2002). More significantly, this research documented a decline in task values in PE when students transition from primary to intermediate grades.

Focusing on middle school PE students (grades 6–8), Gao (2009) found no age/grade-associated differences in expectancy beliefs. However, sixth and seventh (ages 11–13) graders were found to consider PE more important than eighth graders. Additionally, sixth graders viewed PE as more useful than eighth graders. Similarly, Zhu and Chen (2010) reported that middle school students in their study did not differ significantly in expectancy beliefs; but sixth graders scored significantly higher on the three task values (importance, interest, and usefulness) than their eighth grade counterparts. Contrary to these cross-sectional findings, Yli-Piipari, Jaakkola, Liukkonen, and Nurmi (2013) found that expectancy beliefs declined but task values (as a composite variable) increased for Finnish students who proceeded from the sixth grade (i.e., last grade level in elementary schools) to the ninth grade. It is likely that these discrepant findings may be due to differences in curriculum focus in the U.S. and Finland.

While the longitudinal data reported by Jacobs and colleagues (2002) revealed a rapid decline in expectancy beliefs in sports during high school years, particularly near the end of high school, no data are available concerning whether expectancy beliefs declined among high school PE students. The same observation can be made for the population of college students in PE/PA programs. There is a need to strengthen research with late-adolescent and young-adult populations to further understanding their expectancy-value-driven motivation for life-long PA.

Xiang and colleagues (2003) also examined gender differences in PE students' expectancy beliefs and task values. They investigated second and fourth graders' expectancy beliefs and task values in PE and throwing. They found that fourth-grade girls had lower expectancy beliefs in PE than boys. However, no gender differences were observed in fourth graders' expectancy beliefs and task values in running (Xiang, McBride, and Bruene, 2004; Xiang et al., 2006).

A similar picture was observed in students in secondary school PE. In a study of PE students in grades 6, 7, and 8, Gao (2009) reported that compared to girls, boys held higher expectancy beliefs and higher intrinsic value. In contrast, Gu and colleagues (2012) indicated that middle school boys and girls in their study did not score differently on expectancy beliefs and task values (as a composite variable). Based on longitudinal data with a sample of Finnish students who progressed from the sixth to ninth grade, Yli-Piipari and Kokkonen (2014) reported that grade 9 boys viewed PE as more useful than did girls.

There have been few studies examining gender differences among college students from the expectancy-value theory perspective. The limited research evidence shows gender differences emerged on expectancy beliefs only. Compared to female students, male students were found to feel more competent in activities such as dart-throwing (Gao et al., 2009) and weight lifting (Gao & Xiang, 2008).

Gender differences observed in expectancy beliefs and task values may reflect gender stereotypes that students hold for different activities. *Gender stereotypes* are defined as beliefs about the behaviors and characteristics of each sex (Del Boca & Ashmore, 1980). In the expectancy-value model, Eccles and her colleagues (1983) theorized that students' gender stereotypes are a personal factor that influences their expectancy beliefs, task values (attainment value, intrinsic value, and utility value), and activity choices. Students are more likely to develop positive expectancy beliefs and values for activities they believe are appropriate for their gender. As Lee (2002) pointed out, in PE/PA settings male students tend to have higher expectancy beliefs and values for masculine sports and physical activities (e.g., basketball and football), whereas female students feel more competent and place higher values in feminine sports and physical activities (e.g., dance and gymnastics). These gender differences have a potential to influence students' PA choices, effort, and willingness to participate. Further, adults' gender stereotypes also may influence how competently boys and girls perform in non-gender appropriate activities in PE classes.

Relations among expectancy beliefs, task values, and achievement outcomes

Much research guided by the expectancy-value theory thus far has focused on how students' expectancy beliefs and task values are related to their achievement outcomes. PE outcomes can include movement skill learning, performance, persistence, and intention for future participation (e.g., Chen & Chen, 2012; Ding et al., 2013; Gao, 2009; Gao & Xiang, 2008; Gu et al., 2012; Xiang et al., 2003, 2006; Xiang, McBride, & Bruene, 2004; Zhu & Chen, 2013a). This work provides strong evidence that although expectancy beliefs and task values are essential to achievement outcomes in PE settings, they have differential predictive powers.

Xiang and colleagues (2003, 2004, 2006) conducted several studies to examine expectancy beliefs and task values in relation to elementary school students' intentions for future participation in PE, intention for future participation in running, persistence/effort in running, and performance in a timed one mile run. Some findings converged: expectancy beliefs emerged as a stronger predictor of students' persistence/effort in running and timed one mile performance, whereas task values served as a stronger predictor of students' intention for future participation in PE and intention for future participation in running. Particularly, in the context of running programs in elementary school PE, the intrinsic value (interest) in running consistently emerged as a stronger predictor for students' intention for future participation in running than the expectancy beliefs and other task values.

Gao (2009) targeting students in grades 6, 7, and 8 reported that expectancy beliefs predicted cardiovascular fitness (measured by PACER), whereas expectancy beliefs, importance, and interest predicted PE engagement and satisfaction. In their study, Gu and colleagues (2012) also assessed sixth, seventh, and eighth grade students' cardiovascular fitness (measured by the PACER), PA engagement as a percentage of time engaged in MVPA (measured by accelerometers), and expectancy beliefs and task values. They found that expectancy beliefs emerged as predictors of students' cardiovascular fitness and PA engagement but not of task values (importance, interest, and usefulness).

587

Zhu and Chen (2010) examined middle school students' expectancy beliefs and task values in relation to their achievement of health-related fitness knowledge and badminton striking skills. Knowledge and skills were conceptualized and calculated as the change in student performance from pretest to posttest. They found that students' health-related fitness knowledge and badminton striking skills significantly improved over the course of one school year, but neither expectancy beliefs nor task values emerged as predictors of such improvements.

Although other researchers have focused on students' knowledge and movement skill, they did not assess achievement. For example, in their study of Chinese middle school students, Ding and colleagues (2013) reported that expectancy beliefs were predictive of students' badminton striking skill and basketball dribbling skill, whereas task values were predictive of their knowledge about exercise principles and benefits. In contrast, Chen and Chen (2012) found that neither expectancy beliefs nor task values predicted PE students' energy balance knowledge among a sample of 195 ninth graders.

Similar to findings observed in elementary and secondary school PE settings, expectancy beliefs and task values were found to predict a number of achievement outcomes in college PE/PA programs. Gao and Xiang (2008) reported that importance and interest were predictive of students' intention for future participation in weight training and in-class engagement (as measured by the workout logs recorded by students over the course of the semester). Conversely, expectancy beliefs were the only predictor of students' skill test performance. Focusing on college female students, Gu and colleagues (2011) found that expectancy beliefs predicted female students' class attendance, whereas importance, interest, and usefulness all predicted students' exercise choice (i.e., intention for future participation in PA classes). Chen and Liu (2008) extended the expectancy-value theory research to a sample of 368 Chinese college students and reported that interest and usefulness predicted students' decisions to continue PE, while importance predicted students' daily self-initiated PA. Surprisingly, expectancy beliefs were found not predictive of either outcome.

Implications for evidence-based practice

Research reviewed in this chapter has at least two important implications for evidence-based practice in PE. First, students' expectancy beliefs and task values are influential for their motivation and achievement outcomes. Students are more likely to value physical activities when they have positive ability beliefs and have high expectancies for success in those activities. Therefore, PE teachers might consider using motivation strategies to nurture students' expectancy beliefs and developing their task values to help children accomplish a range of achievement outcomes. One strategy for teachers to enhance PE students' expectancy beliefs is to adopt a differentiated learning perspective in task design. This strategy can provide opportunities for students to choose tasks at a difficulty and complexity level most appropriate to their competence optimizing success. Doing so will increase students' chances to succeed which in turn will facilitate the formation and maintenance of positive ability beliefs. Maximizing students' practice time in class is another strategy to enhance competence and positive ability beliefs. Although instructional time is a proxy variable for learning, using effective instruction to optimize student instructional time increases their opportunities to learn and master skill, sport, and fitness tasks. Mastery is a powerful tool to enhance PE students' ability beliefs and their expectations for performance success.

PE teachers should help students develop beliefs that PE is important, interesting, and useful by explicitly explaining the benefits of PE/PA activities. Understanding PE/PA benefits may help connect students' innate desire to move (intrinsic value) with their development of a value base centered on attainment value and utility value. With these connections in mind, students may realize the value of PE, especially those intrinsic values beyond immediate enjoyment. Providing students with a variety of interesting, enjoyable, relevant, meaningful, and challenging learning activities can be an effective approach to developing such a value system. These learning activities may create an experiential environment to strengthen students' beliefs that PE is not only interesting and enjoyable but also personally meaningful, important, and useful. According to the expectancy-value theory, this belief-value system will eventually begin to form the basis for learners' motivational decisions.

Second, it is important to realize that expectancy beliefs and task values play different roles in students' achievement outcomes. It is imperative for teachers to be aware of content specificity associated with learners' expectancy beliefs and task values and to use this knowledge to guide teaching practices. For example, if the goal is to help students perform well on a one mile run test at the end of the school year, teachers can provide students with a variety of running activities throughout the school year. These activities can develop and enhance students' positive beliefs about their ability to perform the final running test successfully. On the other hand, if the goal is to strengthen students' intention to participate in future running activities, teachers can structure running activities in a way that students find them useful, important, and interesting. Suggested activities might include: Allowing students to talk with their friends and/or listen to music as they run, having them run through obstacle courses, and using pedometers to record distances covered in other activities such as in soccer scrimmages or orienteering.

Future directions

Student motivation is a multifaceted construct that holds potential for enhancing students' experiences in PE and physical activities. Because motivation can derive from multiple sources. researchers should investigate multiple theoretical perspectives to gain a more complete picture of student motivation in PE. Although this chapter focuses primarily on the expectancy-value theory, several scholars (e.g., Ding et al., 2013; Gao, 2009; Gao et al., 2008; Xiang, Liu, McBride, & Bruene, 2011; Xiang, McBride, & Bruene, 2004; Zhang, Solmon, & Gu, 2012) have examined expectancy beliefs and task values along with constructs drawn from achievement goal theory, interest theory, self-efficacy theory, and self-determination theory in PE. Their work reveals that students are likely driven by different sources of motivation for different achievement outcomes. For example, in the study of Ding et al. (2013), task values predicted students' knowledge of exercise principles and benefits; expectancy beliefs predicted their movement skills performance; and situational interest predicted their engagement (as measured by accelerometers). Similarly, Zhang et al. (2012) conducted a study examining PE students' motivation using both self-determination and expectancy-value theories to look more broadly at a range of factors impacting performance.

Except for these efforts, research using multiple theoretical perspectives is scarce. For both theoretical clarification and practical effectiveness, more multidimensional studies are needed to provide a basis for enhancing student motivation in PE. As Chen (Chapter 39, this volume) has pointed out, both achievement goal theory and expectancy belief components in expectancy-value theory share an important underlying tenet, perceived competence, as the driving force for learner motivation. A better understanding of achievement goal-related issues and an ability to plan lessons and curriculum using these related strategies can help motivate students. For example, in studies (e.g., Xiang & Lee, 2002) investigating achievement goal theory, perceived motivation climate, defined as student perceptions of the achievement goals addressed by the teacher, was found to influence student motivation, performance, engagement, and learning. Unfortunately, little information is available concerning the relationships among expectancy beliefs, task values, and perceived motivational climate as they interact to influence PE students' expectancy beliefs.

Self-determination theory (Deci & Ryan, 2000; Ryan & Deci, 2002) is another example of an overarching motivation theory to address the multidimensional complexity of student motivation. SDT proposes that a critical source of students' motivation lies in their basic needs for autonomy, competence, and relatedness. How well school environments address these needs can determine, in part, students' motivation for learning and achievement. Therefore, the constructs of autonomy and competence may well be conceptually and functionally associated with the constructs of expectancy beliefs, and relatedness may be theoretically linked with task values. Multidimensional research programs in these areas can expand our knowledge about students' expectancy-value based motivation for learning.

A number of factors, such as gender roles, activity stereotypes, short- and long-term goals, and significant socializers' beliefs and behaviors influence expectancy beliefs and task values. Nevertheless, researchers have not examined these variables extensively in PE. This information can provide valuable insights into designing and implementing effective interventions to enhance students' expectancy beliefs and task values associated with physical activities.

With the exception of the work by Xiang and colleagues (Xiang et al., 2006), and Yli-Piipari et al. (2013), no research has addressed developmental changes in PE students' expectancy beliefs and task values over the school years. Additional longitudinal PE research is needed to understand how students' expectancy-value based motivation evolves as they progress from elementary through high school into college.

Because the expectancy-value model has not been extensively examined in high school and college PE/PA settings, there is a need for future research to target these two student populations. Additional research is needed to better understand critical ways that gender differences and cultural influences act on students' expectancy beliefs and task values. This line of inquiry can have important implications for PE instruction. This is particularly true as student populations grow ever more diverse and PE teachers work to respond to the increasing need for globalized education and PE.

As a task value, cost is assumed to have a compromising impact on student motivation. Although PE researchers (e.g., Chen & Chen, 2012; Chen & Liu, 2008, 2009; Zhu & Chen, 2013b) have conducted research to examine cost, this task value has not received the same level of research scrutiny in comparison to three other task values, importance, interest, and usefulness. As a result, there is little externally valid research evidence available concerning the types of costs that can compromise student motivation to participate in PE. More importantly, little is known about counter-measures teachers may use to address students' negative perceptions and barriers. Methodologically, cost has been assessed exclusively through open-ended questions (e.g., Chen & Chen, 2012; Chen & Liu, 2008, 2009; Zhu & Chen, 2013b). Consequently, the generalizability of these findings is limited. Future research is needed to develop measures with improved generalizability, permitting PE researchers to compare the four task values in relation to their predictive power for achievement outcomes.

Summary of key findings

- Despite some inconsistencies, the literature reviewed above generally points to several key findings.
- Consistent with the expectancy-value theory, expectancy beliefs, attainment value, intrinsic value, and utility value are distinct but related motivation sources, particularly for middle school PE students.

- Expectancy beliefs, attainment value, intrinsic value, and utility value are specific not only to the content/activity but also to educational outcomes in PE, supporting the concept of the content specificity of motivation constructs (e.g., Chen et al., 2008).
- Expectancy beliefs when measured objectively were predictive of students' performances and engagement, while task values were predictive of students' self-reported intention for future participation in PE, exercise choice, and engagement.
- Research that integrates expectancy-value theory with other theoretical frameworks is rare but necessary to further our understanding of student motivation in PE.
- To date, there are no consistent age or gender differences in students' expectancy beliefs or task values. Gender differences in students' expectancy beliefs and task values are most prevalent in perceptions of gender stereotyped physical activities.
- Multicultural, multiethnic frameworks are essential to expand our repertoire of strategies to motivate *every* child in this country and the world for life-long PA.

Reflective questions for discussion

1. How might PE teachers use expectancy-value theory to increase student PA intensity in PE?
2. How can teachers and curriculum developers use the relationship between expectancy beliefs and task values to enhance student motivation and achievement outcomes?
3. Discuss possibilities for using expectancy-value theory to motivate difficult to engage students in PE. Propose three general strategies appropriate for students with diverse perceptions of competence and task value.
4. Can motivation be taught? Some argue that motivation is a mental process that may not be teachable. What do you think? Take a position and provide your reasoning.
5. What strategies can teachers use to assist students to form and maintain positive ability beliefs in PE?
6. How might teachers use content specific motivation strategies to teach the (a) overload principle, (b) overhand throwing, and (c) line-dancing. Construct your answer based on expectancy-value theory and research findings about its content specificity.
7. Based on the author's discussion of future research directions related to expectancy-value theory, propose two research questions to move the field forward. Explain your rationale for studying your questions.

References

Atkinson, J. W. (1957). Motivational determinants of risk-taking behavior. *Psychological Review, 64*, 359–372. doi:10.1037/h0043445

Bong, M. (2001). Between- and within-domain relations of academic motivation among middle and high school students: Self-efficacy, task value, and achievement goals. *Journal of Educational Psychology, 93*, 23–34. doi:10.1037//0022-0663.93.1.23

Chen, A., & Liu, X. (2008). Expectancy beliefs and perceived values of Chinese college students in physical education and physical activity. *Journal of Physical Activity & Health, 5*, 262–274.

Chen, A., & Liu, X. (2009). Task values, cost, and choice decisions in college physical education. *Journal of Teaching in Physical Education, 28*, 192–213.

Chen, A., Martin, R., Ennis, C. D., & Sun, H. (2008). Content specificity of expectancy beliefs and task values in elementary physical education. *Research Quarterly for Exercise and Sport, 79*, 195–208.

Chen, S., & Chen, A. (2012). Ninth graders' energy balance knowledge and physical activity behavior: An expectancy-value perspective. *Journal of Teaching in Physical Education, 31*, 293–310.

Deci, E. L., & Ryan, R. M. (2000). The "what" and "why" of goal pursuits: Human needs and the self determination theory of behavior. *Psychology Inquiry, 11*, 227–268.

Del Boca, F. K., & Ashmore, R. D. (1980). Sex role stereotypes through the life cycle. In L. Wheeler (Ed.), *Review of personality and social psychology* (Vol. 1, pp. 163–192). Beverly Hills, CA: Sage.

Ding, H., Sun, H., & Chen, A. (2013). Impact of expectancy-value and situational interest motivation specificity on physical education outcomes. *Journal of Teaching in Physical Education, 32*, 253–269.

Eccles, J. S., Adler, T. F., Futterman, R., Goff, S. B., Kaczala, C. M., Meece, J., & Midgley, C. (1983). Expectancies, values and academic behaviors. In J. T. Spence (Ed.), *Achievement and achievement motives* (pp. 75–146). San Francisco: W. H. Freeman.

Eccles, J. S., & Wigfield, A. (1995). In the mind of the actor: The structure of adolescents' achievement task values and expectancy-related beliefs. *Personality and Social Psychology Bulletin, 21*, 215–225.

Eccles, J. S., & Wigfield, A. (2002). Motivational beliefs, values, and goals. *Annual Review of Psychology, 53*, 109–132. doi:10.1146/annurev.psych.53.100901.135153

Eccles, J. S., Wigfield, A., Harold, R. D., & Blumenfeld, P. (1993). Age and gender differences in children's self- and task perceptions during elementary school. *Child Development, 64*, 830–847.

Eccles, J. S., Wigfield, A., & Schiefele, U. (1998). Motivation to succeed. In W. Damon (Series Ed.) & N. Eisenberg (Vol. Ed.), *Handbook of child psychology* (5th ed., Vol. 3, pp. 1017–1095). New York: Wiley.

Gao, Z. (2009). Students' motivation, engagement, satisfaction, and cardiorespiratory fitness in physical education. *Journal of Applied Sport Psychology, 21*(Suppl1), S102–S115. doi: http://dx.doi.org/10.1080/10413200802582789

Gao, Z., Kosma, M., & Harrison, L., Jr. (2009). Ability beliefs, task value, and performance as a function of race in a dart-throwing task. *Research Quarterly for Exercise and Sport, 80*, 122–130.

Gao, Z., Lee, A. M., & Harrison, L., Jr. (2008). Understanding students' motivation in sport and physical education: From the expectancy-value model and self-efficacy theory perspectives. *Quest, 60*, 236–254.

Gao, Z., & Xiang, P. (2008). College students' motivation toward weight training: An application of expectancy-value model. *Journal of Teaching in Physical Education, 27*, 399–415.

Gu, X., Solmon, M. A., & Zhang, T. (2012). Using the expectancy-value model to examine students' physical activity engagement and cardiovascular fitness in physical education. *International Journal of Sport Psychology, 43*, 385–402.

Gu, X., Solmon, M. A., Zhang, T., & Xiang, P. (2011). Group cohesion, achievement motivation, and motivational outcomes among female college students. *Journal of Applied Sport Psychology, 23*(2), 175–188. doi: http://dx.doi.org/10.1080/10413200.2010.548847

Jacobs, J. E., Lanza, S., Osgood, E. W., Eccles, J. S., & Wigfield, A. (2002). Changes in children's self-competence and values: Gender and domain differences across grades one through twelve. *Child Development, 73*, 509–527.

Lee, A. M. (2002). Promoting quality school physical education: Exploring the root of the problem. *Research Quarterly for Exercise and Sport, 73*, 118–124. doi: 10.1080/02701367.2002.10609000

Li, W., & Xiang, P. (2007). Ability conceptions in physical education: Some measurement considerations. *Quest, 59*, 358–372.

Ogden, C. L., Carroll, M. D., Kit, B. K., & Flegal, K. M. (2012). Prevalence of obesity and trends in body mass index among US children and adolescents, 1999–2010. *JAMA, 307*(5), 483–490.

Ryan, R. M., & Deci, E. L. (2002). Self-determination theory and the facilitation of intrinsic motivation, social development, and well-being. *American Psychologist, 55*, 68–78.

Shen, B., McCaughtry, N., & Martin, J. (2008). The influence of domain specificity on motivation in physical education. *Research Quarterly for Exercise and Sport, 79*, 333–343.

Society of Health and Physical Educators [SHAPE]. (2014). *National standards & grade-level outcomes for K-12 physical education*. Champaign, IL: Human Kinetics.

Wigfield, A., & Eccles, J. S. (1992). The development of achievement task values: A theoretical analysis. *Developmental Review, 12*, 265–310.

Wigfield, A., & Eccles, J. S. (2000). Expectancy–value theory of motivation. *Contemporary Educational Psychology, 25*, 68–81. doi: 10.1006/ceps.1999.1015

Wigfield, A., & Eccles, J. S. (2002). The development of competence beliefs, expectancies for success, and achievement values from childhood through adolescence. In A. Wigfield & J.S. Eccles (Eds.), *Development of achievement motivation* (pp. 1–10). San Diego, CA: Academic Press.

Xiang, P., Chen, A., & Bruene, A. (2005). Interactive impact of intrinsic motivators and rewards on behavior and motivation outcomes. *Journal of Teaching in Physical Education, 24*, 179–197.

Xiang, P., & Lee, A. (2002). Achievement goals, perceived motivational climate and students' self-reported mastery behaviors. *Research Quarterly for Exercise and Sport, 73*, 58–65.

Xiang, P., Liu, Y., McBride, R. E., & Bruene, A. (2011). Longitudinal goal patterns and their effects on students' motivation in running programs. *Journal of Experimental Education, 79*(3), 295–317.

Xiang, P., McBride, R. E., & Bruene, A. (2004). Fourth graders' motivation in an elementary physical education running program. *Elementary School Journal, 104*, 253.

Xiang, P., McBride, R. E., & Bruene, A. (2006). Fourth-grade students' motivational changes in an elementary physical education running program. *Research Quarterly for Exercise and Sport, 77*, 195–207.

Xiang, P., McBride, R. E., & Guan, J. (2004). Children's motivation in elementary physical education: A longitudinal study. *Research Quarterly for Exercise and Sport, 75*, 71–80.

Xiang, P., McBride, R. E., Guan, J., & Solmon, M. (2003). Children's motivation in elementary physical education: An expectancy-value model of achievement choice. *Research Quarterly for Exercise and Sport, 74*, 25–35.

Yli-Piipari, S., Jaakkola, T., Liukkonen, J., & Nurmi, J. (2013). The effect of physical education students' beliefs and values on their physical activity: A growth mixture modelling approach. *International Journal of Sport and Exercise Psychology, 11*, 70–86. doi: http://dx.doi.org/10.1080/1612197X.2012.731191

Yli-Piipari, S., & Kokkonen, J. (2014). An application of the expectancy-value model to understand adolescents' performance and engagement in physical education. *Journal of Teaching in Physical Education, 33*, 250–268.

Zhang, T., Solmon, M. A., & Gu, X. (2012). The role of teachers' support in predicting students' motivation and achievement outcomes in physical education. *Journal of Teaching in Physical Education, 31*, 329–343.

Zhu, X., & Chen, A. (2010). Adolescent expectancy-value motivation and learning: A disconnected case in physical education. *Learning and Individual Differences, 20*, 512–516. doi: 10.1016/j.lindif.2010.04.013

Zhu, X., & Chen, A. (2013a). Adolescent expectancy-value motivation, achievement in physical education, and physical activity participation. *Journal of Teaching in Physical Education, 32*, 287–304.

Zhu, X., & Chen, A. (2013b). Motivational cost aspects of physical education in middle school students. *Educational Psychology, 33*, 465–481. doi: http://dx.doi.org/10.1080/01443410.2013.785043

Zhu, X., Sun, H., Chen, A., & Ennis, C. (2012). Measurement invariance of expectancy-value questionnaire in physical education. *Measurement in Physical Education and Exercise Science, 16*, 41–54.

41

MAXIMIZING STUDENT MOTIVATION IN PHYSICAL EDUCATION

A self-determination theory perspective

C. K. John Wang, NANYANG TECHNOLOGICAL UNIVERSITY, SINGAPORE

As we advance into the twenty-first century, we are entering a new world driven by use of technology, including driving, television, computers, and mobile devices. Alongside, there is a worldwide trend of reduced physical activity. A recent systematic review of 1769 studies by Ng and her colleagues (Ng et al., 2014) found that in 2013 the prevalence of obesity and over-weight in children and adolescents in developed countries was 23.8% for boys and 22.6% for girls. In developing countries, the prevalence of overweight and obesity has increased from 8.1% in 1980 to 12.9% in 2013 for boys and from 8.4% to 13.4% for girls in the same period. This is a worrying trend as childhood obesity and overweight has increased by 47% in the past 33 years, and there is an urgent need for actions to address this global epidemic. Physical education (PE) may be a vehicle to counter this trend. PE provides an existing organizational structure and op-portunities to reach all school-aged children and adolescents (5–16 years). Within such a 'captive audience' (grouped by class to attend compulsory lessons), children can benefit from a physical education program that provides the skills, knowledge, and confidence to participate in physical activity (PA) within or outside of PE. To achieve this aim, insight into the mechanism of moti-vation in PE among children and adolescents is an important area of research.

With this in mind, the purpose of this chapter is to provide an understanding of the motiva-tional processes in PE from a self-determination theory perspective (SDT; Deci & Ryan, 1985). Understanding student motivation from this perspective is the key to inform PE teachers and other practitioners of the fundamental mechanisms to effectively promote motivation in children and adolescents. The first part of this chapter will provide a brief historical overview of motiva-tion research. The second part will focus on the theoretical tenets of SDT including its five sub-theories or constructs. Next, the current research trends and findings in SDT will be highlighted within the subtheory framework. Thereafter, practical implications will be outlined in the con-text of PE teaching and learning and key findings will be summarized at the end of the chapter.

Historical overview

Weiner (1992) divides the development of motivational theories into three metaphors. Initially, the 'machine-like' or mechanistic metaphor included approaches such as Hull's (1943) drive theory. The mechanistic metaphor views humans as passive and motivated by a small set of drives (such as sex and avoidance of pain). Motivated behavior is equated with striving for equilibrium or homeostasis. As this approach is not adequate for addressing the complexities of human behavior, the 'god-like' metaphor, represented by cognitive theories, took over. Cognitive theories view motivation as a cognitive phenomenon and from this perspective humans have complete rationality in making fully informed choices (Weiner, 1992). Achievement theory (Atkinson, 1958; McClelland, 1961) and attribution theory (Weiner, 1972) are examples of this approach. The pioneering work of the cognitive theorists led to the development of a social cognitive approach that currently dominates the study of motivation. This is a 'judge-like' metaphor as described by Weiner (1992). In the social cognitive approach, human beings are seen as actively processing events (internal and external) with expectations regarding future consequences, rather than merely processing the information needed to guide the immediate action (Bandura, 1986).

The study of motivation has evolved toward a focus on the social environment. Under the conceptual umbrella of the social cognitive approach, two major theories commonly utilized in achievement motivation research are achievement goal theory (AGT; Ames, 1992; Dweck, 1986; Nicholls, 1989) and SDT (Deci & Ryan, 1985). In AGT, two major achievement goals operate in achievement settings. The first goal perspective focuses on self-referenced mastery or learning how to do a task and is commonly labeled as 'mastery' or 'task' goals. The second perspective emphasizes normative comparison of ability or performance relative to others and is normally labeled as 'performance' or 'ego' goals (Pintrich, 2000). Furthermore, variations in these goal perspectives are linked to different cognition, affect, and behavior. Specifically, a more motivationally adaptive pattern is predicted by mastery goals and a less motivationally adaptive pattern is associated with performance goals, depending on various factors (Ames, 1992; Dweck, 1986; Nicholls, 1989). See Elliot (2005) for detailed discussion about the AGT.

Building on White's (1959) effectance motivation and deCharms' (1968) personal causation, Deci and Ryan's (1985) SDT proposed that three psychological innate needs provide a basis for making predictions about the effects of the social environment on behaviors. SDT has differentiated the content of goals and the regulatory processes in predicting outcomes. In addition, SDT postulates (Deci & Ryan, 2000) that goal pursuit and behavioral regulation are influenced by the extent to which the three basic psychological needs are satisfied. In the last five years, SDT has dominated the literature in physical activity motivation due to its comprehensive ability to explain engagement and disengagement behaviors.

Theoretical framework

Empirical research examining SDT has generated five subtheories to explain motivated behavior. These subtheories, basic psychological needs theory, cognitive evaluation theory, organismic integration theory, causality orientations theory, and goal contents theory, will be briefly outlined in the following sections.

Basic psychological needs theory (BPNT)

From the SDT perspective, goals are driven by three basic psychological needs (Deci & Ryan, 1985; Ryan & Deci, 2000); the need for autonomy, competence, and relatedness (Deci & Ryan, 1985; Ryan, 1995). The need for autonomy is defined as the need to feel ownership of one's behavior (deCharms, 1968). The need for competence refers to individuals' need to produce desired outcomes and to experience mastery and effectiveness when dealing with their environment (Harter, 1978; White, 1959). The need for relatedness is the need to feel that one can relate to others and with the social world in general (Ryan, 1995). People are motivated to satisfy these needs because they are considered essential to the development of the self in terms of growth, social development, and personal well-being (Deci & Ryan, 1985, 1991; Ryan & Deci, 2000).

BPNT forms the core of SDT because without the needs concepts, explanations for intrinsically motivated behavior may not be complete (Deci & Ryan, 2000). Satisfaction of the three needs enhances intrinsic motivation. When intrinsically motivated, people engage in activities that interest them. They do so with a full sense of volition; without the presence of external rewards or constraints. On the other hand, if the three needs are thwarted, intrinsic motivation will be undermined. In this sense, psychologists predict mastery goals promote intrinsic motivation as the focus is on the activities as an end in itself, rather than a means to an end. Performance goals, on the other hand, are predicted to have a negative relationship with intrinsic motivation because the experience of engagement in the tasks is taken as a means to an end (Nicholls, 1989). Social contexts that support students' autonomy, competence, and relatedness promote intrinsic motivation. In particular, those that support autonomy will promote self-determined behavior. It is thus important to understand the influence of social context on intrinsic motivation.

Cognitive evaluation theory

Deci and Ryan (1985) proposed cognitive evaluation theory (CET) as a subtheory within SDT to specify social environment conditions within achievement-oriented situations that influence intrinsic motivation. There are four formal propositions proposed in CET. In the first proposition, CET states that intrinsically motivated activities are autonomous or self-determined. For intrinsic motivation to be enhanced, individuals must be led to perceive they are the 'origin' or agent (internal perceived locus of causality) of their behavior rather than 'pawns' (external perceived locus of causality). The second proposition further specifies that feelings of competence and optimal challenge enhance intrinsic motivation. Social-contextual events (e.g., rewards, communication, feedback) that promote one's feeling of competence will enhance intrinsic motivation for that activity, whereas those events that diminish one's sense of effectance will undermine intrinsic motivation. In addition, for perceived competence to enhance intrinsic motivation, people must experience their behavior to be self-determined. In other words, feelings of competence will enhance intrinsic motivation only if they derive from the context of autonomy (Ryan & Deci, 2000).

The third CET proposition describes the importance of functional significance (i.e., psychological meaning) of the external events perceived by the actors. These events can be perceived as either informational, controlling, or amotivating. Informational events are those perceived to convey feedback about the individual's competence and should, when positive, enhance intrinsic motivation. Controlling events are those perceived to apply pressure to act or think in a way the controlling party designates. Amotivating events are those that do not carry any feedback about competence or autonomy. When actors perceive external events as controlling or amotivating, their intrinsic motivation diminishes.

The final CET proposition focuses on events inside the person. Similar to external events, certain internal events such as thoughts and feelings can make the actor feel pressured to act in a less self-determined way. Ryan (1982) argues that ego involvement is a good example of these internal controlling events because individuals may feel their self-esteem hinges on the outcomes of their performance. This feeling leads to a decrease in intrinsic motivation.

In summary, CET highlights how social-contextual events can facilitate intrinsic motivation by supporting or satisfying people's need for autonomy and competence. Conversely, if these needs are not supported, intrinsic motivation will be undermined. However, Deci and Ryan (Deci & Ryan, 1985, 1991; Ryan & Deci, 2000) stressed that CET applies only to activities that hold intrinsic personal interest. For activities that are not interesting to an individual, the CET principles are not applicable. Deci and Ryan (1985) addressed issues associated with the nature of extrinsic motivation creating another SDT subtheory entitled organismic integration theory (OIT).

Organismic integration theory

Deci and Ryan (1985) suggested that extrinsic motivation varied according to the degree of self-determination. For example, certain PE activities such as distance running may not be interesting to students in the first instance but they have to participate. OIT explains the process through which externally regulated behaviors can be acquired or 'taken in' by the individual and transformed into more self-determined regulation. This process is described as 'internalization' and involves a shift from an external to internal locus of causality (Deci & Ryan, 1991) as individuals are led to rationalize the behavioral outcomes relevant to their need satisfaction. That is, the more internalized a behavioral regulation, the more it will be experienced as autonomous (Ryan & Connell, 1989).

Deci and Ryan (1985) have linked the concept of internalization to that of extrinsic and intrinsic motivation. They suggest that there are five main types of behavioral regulations located on the intrinsic-extrinsic continuum, each reflecting a qualitatively different 'reason' for acting out the behavior in question (see Figure 41.1). These are external, introjected, identified, integrated, and intrinsic forms of regulation. External regulation is the least self-determined form of extrinsic motivation and refers to behavior that is controlled by external means, such as rewards or external authority. An example of external regulation occurs when children participate in PE lessons because they want to avoid punishment from their teacher.

Introjected regulation refers to behavior that is internally controlled or self-imposed, such as acting out of feelings of guilt avoidance, or to attain ego-enhancements such as pride. It is characterized by feelings of 'ought,' 'should,' or 'must.' A child saying "I must exercise in order to feel good about myself" might illustrate this form of regulation.

In identified regulation, the behavior is a more self-determined form of extrinsic motivation, acting according to one's choice or values. It is characterized by feelings of 'want' rather than 'ought.' For example, a child saying, "I want to exercise to improve my fitness" exemplifies identified regulation. Although the activity is performed for an extrinsic reason (i.e., to improve fitness), it is internally regulated and self-determined.

Integrated regulation represents the most autonomous form of extrinsic motivation. This refers to behaviors that are in harmony with other structures within the self, that is, congruent

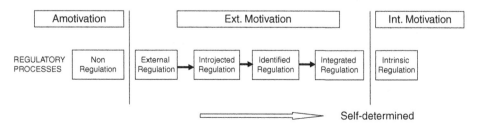

Figure 41.1   Schematic illustration of the self-determination continuum

to one's beliefs and values. For example, a runner may choose to complete repetitive resistance training to improve his performance.

Finally, intrinsically motivated behavior is behavior that is undertaken solely for its own sake or enjoyment. Saying, "I play soccer because I enjoy it" is an example of intrinsic motivation. This is the highest level of self-determination whereby the behavior is emanating fully from the self.

These five behavioral regulations can be viewed as a continuum ranging from highly internal to highly external in the following order: intrinsic, integrated, identified, introjected, and external. In addition to these behavioral regulations, a state of amotivation exists where the person's behavior has no personal causation and no intention to act. Amotivated people perceive a lack of contingency between their own actions and outcomes, or a lack of competence. Consequently, amotivation also occupies a separate category at the external end of the continuum.

Causality orientations theory

Focusing on individual differences in motivational orientations, causality orientations theory (COT) was formalized as the fourth subtheory (Ryan & Deci, 2008). COT explains motivational orientations, namely autonomy, control, and impersonal, as predictors of behavior and other aspects of personality. The autonomy orientation is defined as the experience of choice whereby individuals select available information to make choices and self-regulate in pursuit of self-selected goals. Such orientation emanates from an integrated sense of self. The control orientation involves controls in the environment or internally controlling imperatives such as should, have to, and must, whereby individuals experience pressure to act accordingly. Such orientation emanates an absence of choice with no integrated sense of self. The impersonal orientation is based on beliefs that behavior and outcomes are independent, resulting in the experience of incompetence. Such orientation leads to impersonal functioning that is erratic and non-intentional. One lacks competence or does not have the essential psychological structures to deal with life's challenges successfully (Deci & Ryan, 1985). Hence, COT is another subtheory that connects the self-determination continuum from OIT to the three classes of initiating and regulatory events: informational, controlling, and amotivating. These respective events relate to individuals' motivational orientations that subsequently relate to their self-determined, control-determined, and amotivated behaviors.

Goal contents theory

Goal contents theory (GCT) is the latest addition to the subtheories of SDT (Ryan & Deci, 2008). As mentioned in the previous section, goal pursuit is driven by the three psychological needs and well-being. Within the SDT framework, the contents of people's life goals tend to fall into extrinsic or intrinsic focus (Kasser & Ryan, 1996). Extrinsic goals or aspirations are goals such as gaining financial success, appearance, and fame and image. This type of goal reflects people's intention to impress others by gaining external or outwardly focused signs of worth. Extrinsic goals emphasize outcomes that are not linked to needs satisfaction. On the other hand, intrinsic goals or aspirations are goals such as health, affiliation, personal growth, and community contribution. Ryan and Deci (2008) argued that intrinsic goals focus on needs satisfaction for autonomy, competence, and relatedness.

SDT assumes that goal contents are linked to outcomes related to well-being above and beyond the effects of motivation (Ryan, Williams, Patrick, & Deci, 2009). People who strongly emphasize extrinsic goals and aspirations demonstrate low levels of psychological well-being

(Kasser & Ryan, 1996). In contrast, those who placed relatively strong importance on intrinsic goals and aspirations display high levels of well-being. These five inter-related subtheories represent a coherent SDT framework. For example, the BPNT is linked to OIT in that the three basic needs are the origins of the most autonomous forms of motivational regulations. The CET highlights the social and interpersonal contexts that may facilitate or undermine intrinsically motivated behaviors. The COT represents the personal orientation at a trait level and the GCT examines the goal content that individuals strive for. In the next section, research related to these five subtheories will be presented.

Current trends and issues

There has been extensive research examining the five SDT subtheories in various settings. In non-physical education settings, a meta-analysis conducted by Deci and his colleagues (Deci, Koestner, & Ryan, 1999) examined the effects of extrinsic rewards on intrinsic motivation. They reviewed 128 experimental studies published between 1971 and 1997. The results showed that all tangible rewards and expected rewards undermined free-choice intrinsic motivation. In the sub-levels of expected rewards, engagement-contingent, completion-contingent, and performance-contingent rewards all had undermining effects on free-choice intrinsic motivation. Although verbal rewards had a significant positive effect on free-choice intrinsic motivation, this effect was found for college students but not children. This study confirms that tangible rewards made contingent on task performance undermine intrinsic motivation for interesting tasks.

In addition to tangible rewards, a variety of experimental studies using varied tasks and age groups demonstrated that other factors, such as threat of punishment, externally set deadlines, evaluations, and competitive pressure, undermine intrinsic motivation. Researchers demonstrated that these events undermine people's feeling of self-determination because often they are perceived as controlling people's behavior (Deci et al., 1999).

In PE settings, Van de Berghe and his colleagues (Van de Berghe, Vansteenkiste, Cardon, Kirk, & Haerens, 2014) recently conducted a systematic review of SDT research. This review included a total of 74 publications that followed the motivational sequence based on the tenets of SDT (Teacher antecedents → Teacher need satisfaction and motivation → Need support in PE → Student need satisfaction → Motivation → Outcomes).

Nine studies examined the antecedents of teacher need satisfaction and motivation (e.g., Taylor & Ntoumanis, 2007) and found that teachers' beliefs, work pressures, and perception of student self-determination are related to teacher needs satisfaction and self-determination motivation to teach in PE classes. In addition, teacher high needs satisfaction positively related to more adaptive motivational strategies (needs support strategies). In general, the various aspects of the teaching context may thwart teachers' needs for autonomy, competence, and relatedness. This leads to teacher use of motivational strategies that prevent satisfaction of students' psychological needs (Taylor, Ntoumanis, & Smith, 2009). On the other hand, teacher satisfaction of the three psychological needs positively predicted teacher self-determined motivation, thereby leading to use of motivational strategies, such as gaining an understanding of students, provision of instrumental support, and provision of meaningful rationale (Taylor, Ntoumanis, & Standage, 2008).

According to CET, significant others' behaviors can impact individuals' intrinsic motivation (Deci & Ryan, 1985, 1991; Ryan & Deci, 2000; Vallerand & Losier, 1999). In the school context, teachers are probably the most influential people in the environment. The ways teachers interact with students can either facilitate or undermine their intrinsic motivation. Specifically, teachers can either communicate with a controlling style, such as giving directives, exerting pressure, or controlling the students' behavior, or interact in an autonomy-supportive way that enhances decision making and student choice. Several studies have shown that autonomy-supportive teachers enhance their students' intrinsic motivation, intentions to exercise during leisure time, and exercise behaviors (e.g. Chatzisarantis & Hagger, 2009; Standage, Duda, & Ntoumanis, 2003).

Further, research has shown the motivational benefits of more self-determined behavioral regulations in the PE contexts. For example, in Standage et al.'s (2003) study, intrinsic motivation was positively related to concentration, positive affect, and a preference for trying challenging tasks. Wang and Liu (2007) found that external and introjected regulations in PE were negatively related to enjoyment. On the other hand, identified regulation and intrinsic motivation were positively related to enjoyment and competence.

Researchers have begun to examine contextual events that support or inhibit the internalization process. Deci, Eghrari, Patrick, and Leone (1994) suggested that three contextual factors, providing a meaningful rationale, acknowledging the actor's perspective, and communicating choice rather than control, promote internalization. Providing a rationale that is meaningful to the actor can help the individual understand the value of performing the activity. Acknowledgment of conflict helps reduce internal pressure and also conveys respect from the actor's perspective to strengthen relatedness. Finally, rationale and acknowledgment need to be presented in an autonomy-supportive way rather than in a controlling manner.

Surprisingly, there were not many studies conducted in PE and sport settings examining the causal orientation theory. In the classroom domain, Deci, Schwartz, Sheinman and Ryan (1981) have shown the direct effects of teachers' autonomy orientation towards supporting children's intrinsic motivation. Children of more controlling teachers scored lower on measures of mastery orientation and perceived competence than children in classrooms of more autonomy-supportive teachers. In addition to showing less interest in learning and challenge, these children reported lower self-esteem than children exposed to autonomy-supportive teachers. Taylor et al. (2008) found that teachers' autonomous causality orientation positively predicted teacher self-determined motivation to teach.

Another area that has been greatly ignored is the goal content theory in PE settings. In one study, Vansteenkiste, Simons, Lens, Sheldon, and Deci (2004) found that framing an exercise activity in terms of an intrinsic goal attainment produced better performance compared to extrinsic goal framing. A handful of other studies examined the goal content of participants in recreational and competitive sport contexts (e.g., Chatzisarantis & Hagger, 2007; Vansteenkiste, Mato, Lens, & Soenens, 2007). In general, competitive athletes tended to focus on extrinsic goal aspiration compared with recreational athletes. Athletes who placed more importance on intrinsic goals reported higher well-being (Chatzisarantis & Hagger, 2007). Extrinsic goals were found to be associated with ego involvement and less task-involvement compared with intrinsic goals (Vansteenkiste et al., 2007). Although these findings may not be generalized to the physical education setting, the findings may serve as starting points for PE researchers to launch studies on goal framing issues in relation to student motivational processes in learning.

SDT can be applied in many domains, ranging from sport and exercise to health (e.g., Cheon, Reeve, & Moon, 2012; Ryan & Deci, 2008; Williams, Freedman, Ryan, & Deci, 1996), parenting (e.g., Grolnick, Ryan, & Deci, 1991), and education (e.g., Klassen, Perry, & Frenzel, 2012). Despite the extensive research on this topic, SDT is an empirically based open theory with much room for continued improvement in the specification and expansion of its propositions (Ryan & Deci, 2008). It seems true that SDT is a relevant guiding theory in the study of PE student motivation as well. It provides a comprehensive platform to connect motivation with the social contexts and events and cognitive processes. It also provides theoretical guidance in terms of leading PE students to internalize external values and regulations.

Implications for evidence-based practice

A recent study by Church and his colleagues (Church et al., 2012) extended support for the universal importance of SDT needs satisfaction in eight cultures. The study demonstrated that perceived need satisfaction predicted overall well-being to a similar degree in all eight cultures studied. Therefore, interventions that facilitate need satisfaction may enhance well-being across different cultures.

SDT provides unique contributions to our understanding of motivation. For example, it acknowledges that every individual has inherent growth tendencies and innate psychological needs that act as inner motivational resources to produce high quality engagement and optimal functioning (Reeve, 2012). The theory also acknowledges that not everyone is intrinsically motivated in a particular setting. Content can be structured to promote internalization of extrinsic motivation with practical implications for PE teachers derived from the SDT literature.

Use of adaptive motivational strategies

Connell and Wellborn (1991) proposed three broad types of motivational teaching strategies, autonomy-support, structure, and involvement. Autonomy-support teaching strategies focus on promoting students' internal locus of causality and increasing their feelings of volition. Autonomy-supportive teachers facilitate students' personal autonomy by taking students' perspective; identifying and nurturing students' needs, interests, and preferences; providing optimal challenges; highlighting meaningful learning goals; and presenting interesting, relevant, and enriched activities (Jang, Reeve, & Deci, 2010). For example, when teaching soccer, teachers can provide a meaningful rationale for students undertaking the activity, such as fun, teamwork, and/or fitness development. By providing a meaningful rationale in an autonomy-support manner, the teacher may facilitate the students in internalizing the values acknowledged externally, thereby increasing students' motivation to engage in the learning activities.

Structure refers to the amount and clarity of information that teachers provide to students about expectations and ways of effectively achieving desired educational outcomes (Skinner & Belmont, 1993). Students in a well-structured environment have a clear understanding of what is required of them to achieve the desired outcomes. Therefore, they can direct their effort to complete the activities. It is important for PE teachers to plan their lessons to include clear declarative and procedural objectives. For the provision of structure, teachers might want to initiate learning activities by offering clear and detailed expectations and instructions, offering helpful guidance and scaffolding to guide students to attain positive tangible outcomes from each task throughout the lesson. During the process, it is crucial for PE teachers to provide clear feedback to enhance students' perceptions of competence and perceived personal control throughout the lesson.

Finally, to encourage interpersonal involvement with student growth, Connell and Wellborn (1991) encouraged PE teachers to show personal interest and provide emotional support to students (demonstrating warmth, sympathy, humor, willingness to listen, and investing time and energy). Acknowledging students' inner conflicts may help in reducing apprehensions related to practicing new motor skills. Tessier, Sarrazin, and Ntoumanis (2010) argue that in-service and pre-service teachers acquire adaptive motivational strategies through physical education teacher education and in-service teacher training or intervention programs.

Satisfying the need for competence

The importance of perceived competence is emphasized in many motivation theories including SDT. PE teachers need to nurture and enhance students' sense of competence to assist them to develop intrinsic motivation in physical activity tasks. There are a few practical suggestions based on the research literature for enhancing students' need for competence. First, PE teachers need to provide successful lesson experiences for their students. Teachers need to differentiate activities for different abilities so that everyone can be optimally challenged at their own level and achieve success. Second, PE teachers need to praise students for the effort they put into the learning processes rather than just for the outcomes. In other words, PE teachers should create a mastery climate (Ames, 1992) such that the focus is on mastery of skills, self-improvement, and effort. Third, when students are practicing skills, PE teachers need to provide informative and positive feedback to inform students how to be successful, thereby improving their competence.

Minimizing use of external rewards

PE teachers need to be aware that external rewards can undermine intrinsic motivation. Any rewards, threats, and evaluation given within PE lessons may have undermining effects on students' intrinsic motivation. SDT suggests that when considering students' intrinsic motivation, it is more important to consider students' perceptions of the environment where an event takes place than to focus on the event itself (e.g., rewards, goals) (Deci & Ryan, 1985). External rewards need to convey informational feedback to the students rather than controlling feedback. The focus, instead, should be on enhancing students' autonomy and competence. For example, PE teachers should not reward/praise the highest goal scorer because students may perceive this as controlling feedback. Instead, if the high scorer has made significant improvement and given much effort in the game, the teacher should highlight that, thus using informational feedback to enhance the students' perceptions of competence.

Using contextual factors to promote internalization

PE teachers need to understand that not all students enjoy physical activities, and some may see PE as a source of stress. PE teachers can use three contextual factors (Deci et al., 1994) to promote internalization: providing a meaningful rationale, acknowledging the actor's perspective, and communicating choice rather than control. To effectively provide a meaningful rationale to students PE teachers need to acknowledge the reasons some students may not wish to participate. For example, they may have internal conflicts (external conditions and internal factors, e.g., poor weather conditions, fear, and avoidance of tasks) that make them reluctant to participate in the activity willingly. Acknowledging these conflicts helps teachers reduce internal pressure and also conveys respect for students. Thus, students may perceive the internalization process to be persuasive rather than coercive, further enhancing the relatedness between the teacher and students and fostering empathy and respect for the students as individuals. In addition, teachers need to present the rationale and acknowledgment in an autonomy-supportive way rather than in a controlling manner. The final contextual factor is maximizing students' perception of activity choice. Providing choice allows students to feel a sense of autonomy, control, and empowerment over their own behaviors. For example, students can be given the choice in sequencing activities or have a choice of activity in PE lessons.

Additionally, satisfying the need for relatedness can facilitate the internalization process. In fact, PE is an optimal context to assist learners to fulfill this need when teachers show genuine concern and respect for their students. Additionally, teachers can use different group-ing methods to foster relatedness among students, such as grouping students into teams for long periods of time so they can have a common identity in working towards a common task.

Promoting intrinsic goals

The inherent long-term goals of PE should be for health, positive interpersonal relationships, personal growth, and sense of community (Education Scotland, 2014). To optimize SDT strat-egies, PE teachers should stress the importance of intrinsic goals instead of highlighting sport stars. Instead, intrinsic goal aspirations contribute to needs satisfaction and well-being. One example of intrinsic goal framing in PE might be: "Increasing your cardio-vascular endurance enhances physical fitness and prevents many diseases, such as high blood pressure, diabetes, and obesity." An example of extrinsic goal framing is: "Performing fitness exercises will make you more physically attractive and prevent you from being fat."

Future directions

In general, SDT has generated many insights into the motivational forces underlying students' behavior in PE. There remain, however, a few key issues for future research. First, although in the academic domain, intrinsic motivation has been shown to demonstrate higher engagement, lower dropout, and better academic performance than extrinsic motivation (Deci et al., 1999), additional research is needed to examine this construct in PE. For example, Sun and Chen (2010) found no relationship between students' self-determined motivation and learning out-comes in PE. In this study, although PE students were intrinsically motivated, they learned little. There is a need for future research to revisit the link between motivation and effective learning outcomes in the PE domain.

Second, Van de Berghe et al.'s (2014) review of 74 SDT studies in PE found several limita-tions in design and methods. In fact 55.4% (41 out of 74 studies) of the study authors men-tioned study design as one of the main limitations of their studies. Additionally, sample sizes in these studies were small and the duration of the interventions was usually short (< 5 weeks). In addition, 39.3% of authors mentioned measurement issues as one of their concerns, including single item measurement and instrument reliability. Certainly, greater access to school envir-onments would permit studies with larger and multi-leveled samples, control groups, study replication, and increased duration (including longitudinal designs) greatly enhancing research validity and study design.

Finally, most of the SDT research in PE has focused on students, rather than on teachers. In any classroom setting, teachers are the agents of change and are responsible for setting up a conducive classroom structure for learning. It is thus important for future research to look into teacher-related contextual factors, possible antecedents of teacher behavior, and links to the SDT constructs. Again, effectively communicating the value of SDT findings and strategies to teachers is critical to facilitating their assistance and participation in research and then attending workshops to implement SDT into their daily practices.

Summary of key findings

- This brief overview of SDT and its research suggests a few key principles that have broad implications for practice in PE classrooms. SDT assumes that all humans possess inherent growth tendencies.

- Three innate psychological needs, autonomy, competence, and relatedness, are the nutrients for self-motivation and personality integration.
- The motivational sequence based on the tenets of SDT (Teacher antecedents → Teacher need satisfaction and motivation → Need support in PE → Student need satisfaction → Motivation → Outcomes) provides a systematic understanding of the causal inference of the key variables.
- Social-contextual factors have profound influence on the needs satisfaction of students in PE.
- It is important for PE teachers to understand their own needs satisfaction to facilitate student learning in the gymnasium. This will assist them to incorporate needs satisfaction in their instructions with the goal to involve, nurture, and vitalize these inner motivational resources, facilitating high quality engagement and learning in the classroom.
- Teachers also can teach adaptive motivational strategies. Effective motivational strategies can be acquired from an educational environment emphasizing autonomy-support, structure, and involvement.
- From the SDT's perspective, motivation is a multidimensional construct. Students can be motivated intrinsically, extrinsically, or both in physical activities.
- Facilitating the internalization process will help students develop more autonomous motivation.
- Students can be very successful when they internalize extrinsic motivation into intrinsic motivation. This finding can be a key to developing sustainable students. PE teachers can improve student motivation by creating environments that satisfied students' needs for autonomy, competence, and relatedness.
- Teachers can make intrinsic goals the main focus of PE. These goals can be associated with positive outcomes and well-being enhancing student enjoyment.
- Learning goals within the physical education curriculum should be linked to SDT's intrinsic goal framework for optimal student motivation.
- Administrators' and teachers' use of tangible and expected extrinsic rewards can undermine intrinsic motivation in PE and thus should be employed with caution.

Reflective questions for discussion

1. SDT focuses on three innate psychological needs (competence, autonomy, and relatedness) that are essential for self-growth and optimal functioning. How does the satisfaction of these needs lead to different types of motivation?
2. How do social contexts, such as those characterized by competition and rewards, influence PE students' intrinsic motivation? What strategies can teachers use to reverse the influences of these contextual factors?
3. What needs do some students satisfy through participation in sports and games? Classify these needs within the categories of extrinsic or intrinsic motivation. Are there any long-term benefits of extrinsic motivation? To what extent should teachers work to encourage intrinsic motivation while discouraging extrinsic?
4. What teaching strategies can PE teachers use to promote students' self-determined motivation? Describe factors that stop PE teachers from using such strategies.

References

Ames, C. (1992). Classrooms: Goals, structures, and student motivation. *Journal of Educational Psychology*, *84*, 261–271.

Atkinson, J. W. (1958). *Motives in fantasy, action and society*. Princeton, NJ: Van Nostrand.

Bandura, A. (1986). *Social foundations of thought and action: A social cognitive theory.* Englewood Cliffs, NJ: Prentice-Hall.

Chatzisarantis, N. L., & Hagger, M. S. (2007). The moral worth of sport reconsidered: Contributions of recreational sport and competitive sport to life aspirations and psychological well-being. *Journal of Sports Sciences, 25,* 1047–1056.

Chatzisarantis, N. L., & Hagger, M. S. (2009). Effects of an intervention based on self-determination theory on self-reported leisure-time physical activity participation. *Psychology and Health, 24,* 29–48.

Cheon, S. H., Reeve, J., & Moon, I. S. (2012). Experimentally-based, longitudinally-designed, teacher-designed, teacher-focused intervention to help physical education teachers be more autonomy supportive. *Journal of Sport and Exercise Psychology, 34,* 365–396.

Church, A. T., Ketigbak, M. S., Locke, K. D., Zhang, H., Shen, J., Vargas-Flores, J., ... Ching, C. M. (2012). Need satisfaction and well-being: Testing self-determination theory in eight cultures. *Journal of Cross Cultural Psychology, 44*(4), 507–534.

Connell, J. P., & Wellborn, J. G. (1991). Competence, autonomy and relatedness: A motivational analysis of self-esteem processes. In M. Gunnar & A. Sroufe (Eds.), *Minnesota symposium on child psychology* (pp. 43–77). Chicago: University of Chicago Press.

deCharms, R. (1968). *Personal causation: The internal affective determinants of behavior.* New York: Academic Press.

Deci, E. L., Eghrari, H., Patrick, B. C., & Leone, D. R. (1994). Facilitating internalization: The self-determination theory perspective. *Journal of Personality, 62,* 119–142.

Deci, E. L., Koestner, R., & Ryan, R. M. (1999). A meta-analytic review of experiments examining the effects of extrinsic rewards on intrinsic motivation. *Psychological Bulletin, 125*(6), 627–668.

Deci, E. L., & Ryan, R. M. (1985). *Intrinsic motivation and self-determination in human behavior.* New York: Plenum Press.

Deci, E. L., & Ryan, R. M. (1991). A motivational approach to self: Integration in personality. In R. Dienstbier (Ed.), *Nebraska symposium on motivation* (pp. 237–288). Lincoln, NE: University of Nebraska Press.

Deci, E. L., & Ryan, R. M. (2000). The "what" and "why" of goal pursuits: Human needs and the self-determination of behavior. *Psychological Inquiry, 11*(4), 227–268.

Deci, E. L., Schwartz, A. J., Sheinman, L., & Ryan, R. M. (1981). An instrument to assess adults' orientations towards control versus autonomy with children: Reflections on intrinsic motivation and perceived competence. *Journal of Educational Psychology, 73,* 642–650.

Dweck, C. S. (1986). Motivational processes affecting learning. *American Psychologist, 41,* 1040–1048.

Education Scotland. (2014). Health and wellbeing: Experiences and outcomes. Retrieved from www.educationscotland.gov.uk/learningandteaching/curriculumareas/healthandwellbeing/eandos/index.asp.

Elliot, A. J. (2005). A conceptual history of the achievement goal construct. In A. Elliot & C. Dweck (Eds.), *Handbook of competence and motivation* (pp. 52–72). New York: Guilford Press.

Grolnick, W. S., Ryan, R. M., & Deci, E. L. (1991). Inner resources for school-achievement: Motivational mediators of children's perceptions of their parents. *Journal of Educational Psychology, 83*(4), 508–517.

Harter, S. (1978). Effectance motivation reconsidered: Toward a developmental model. *Human Development, 1,* 34–64.

Hull, C. L. (1943). *Principles of behavior.* New York: Appleton-Century-Crofts.

Jang, H., Reeve, J., & Deci, E. L. (2010). Engaging students in learning activities: It is not autonomy support or structure, but autonomy support and structure. *Journal of Educational Psychology, 102,* 588–600.

Kasser, T., & Ryan, R. M. (1996). Further examining the American dream: Differential correlates of intrinsic and extrinsic goals. *Personality and Social Psychology Bulletin, 22*(3), 280–287.

Klassen, R. M., Perry, N. E., & Frenzel, A. (2012). Teachers' relatedness with students: An underemphasized aspect of teachers' basic psychological needs. *Journal of Educational Psychology, 104,* 150–165. doi: 10.1037/a0026253

McClelland, D. C. (1961). *The achieving society.* Princeton, NJ: Van Nostrand.

Ng, M., Fleming, T., Robinson, M., Thomson, B., Graetz, N., Margono, C., ... Barquera, S. (2014). Global, regional, and national prevalence of overweight and obesity in children and adults during 1980–2013: A systematic analysis for the Global Burden of Disease Study 2013. *The Lancet.* doi: 10.1016/S0140-6736(14)60460-8

Nicholls, J. G. (1989). *The competitive ethos and democratic education.* Cambridge, MA: Harvard University Press.

Pintrich, P. R. (2000). An achievement goal theory perspective on issues in motivation terminology, theory, and research. *Contemporary Educational Psychology, 25,* 92–104.

Reeve, J. (2012). A self-determination theory perspective on student engagement. In S. L. Christenson, A. L. Reschly, & C. Wylie (Eds.), *Handbook on research on student engagement* (pp. 149–172). New York: Springer.

Ryan, R. M. (1982). Control and information in the intrapersonal sphere: An extension of Cognitive Evaluation Theory. *Journal of Personality and Social Psychology, 43*(3), 450–461.

Ryan, R. M. (1995). Psychological needs and the facilitation of integrative processes. *Journal of Personality, 63*, 397–427.

Ryan, R. M., & Connell, J. P. (1989). Perceived locus of causality and internalization: Examining reasons for acting in two domains. *Journal of Personality and Social Psychology, 57*, 749–761.

Ryan, R. M., & Deci, E. L. (2000). Self-determination theory and the facilitation of intrinsic motivation, social development, and well-being. *American Psychologist, 55*(1), 68–78.

Ryan, R. M., & Deci, E. L. (2008). A self-determination theory approach to psychotherapy: The motivational basis for effective change. *Canadian Psychology and Health, 49*, 186–193.

Ryan, R. M., Williams, G. C., Patrick, H., & Deci, E. L. (2009). Self-determination theory and physical activity: The dynamics of motivation in development and wellness. *Hellenic Journal of Psychology, 6*, 107–124.

Skinner, E. A., & Belmont, M. J. (1993). Motivation in the classroom: Reciprocal effects of teacher behavior and student engagement across the school year. *Journal of Educational Psychology, 85*(4), 571–581.

Standage, M., Duda, J. L., & Ntoumanis, N. (2003). A model of contextual motivation in physical education: Using constructs from self-determination and achievement goal theories to predict physical activity intentions. *Journal of Educational Psychology, 95*, 97–110.

Sun, H., & Chen, A. (2010). An examination of sixth graders' self-determined motivation and learning in physical education. *Journal of Teaching in Physical Education, 29*, 262–277.

Taylor, I., & Ntoumanis, N. (2007). Teacher motivational strategies and student self-determination in physical education. *Journal of Educational Psychology, 99*, 747–760.

Taylor, I., Ntoumanis, N., & Smith, B. (2009). The social context as a determinant of teacher motivational strategies in physical education. *Psychology of Sport & Exercise, 19*, 235–243.

Taylor, I., Ntoumanis, N., & Standage, M. (2008). A self-determination theory approach to understanding antecedents of teachers' motivational strategies in physical education. *Journal of Sport & Exercise Psychology, 30*, 75–94.

Tessier, D., Sarrazin, P., & Ntoumanis, N. (2010). The effect of an intervention to improve newly qualified teachers' interpersonal style, students' motivation and psychological need satisfaction in sport-based physical education. *Contemporary Educational Psychology, 35*, 242–253.

Vallerand, R. J., & Losier, G. F. (1999). An integrative analysis of intrinsic and extrinsic motivation in sport. *Journal of Applied Sport Psychology, 11*, 142–169.

Van de Berghe, L., Vansteenkiste, M., Cardon, G., Kirk, D., & Haerens, L. (2014). Research on self-determination in physical education: Key findings and proposals for future research. *Physical Education and Sport Pedagogy, 1*, 97–121. doi: 10.1080/17408989.2012.732563

Vansteenkiste, M., Matos, L., Lens, W., & Soenens, B. (2007). Understanding the impact of intrinsic versus extrinsic goal framing on exercise performance: The conflicting role of task and ego involvement. *Psychology of Sport and Exercise, 8*(5), 771–794.

Vansteenkiste, M., Simons, J., Lens, W., Sheldon, K. M., & Deci, E. L. (2004). Motivating learning, performance, and persistence: The synergistic effects of intrinsic goal contents and autonomy-supportive contexts. *Journal of Personality and Social Psychology, 87*(2), 246–260.

Wang, C. K. J., & Liu, W. C. (2007). Promoting enjoyment in girls' physical education: The impact of goals, beliefs, and self-determination. *European Physical Education Review, 13*(2), 145–164.

Weiner, B. (1972). *Theories of motivation: From mechanism to cognition.* Chicago: Rand McNally.

Weiner, B. (1992). *Human motivation: Metaphors, theories, and research.* Newbury Park, CA: Sage.

White, R. W. (1959). Motivation reconsidered: The concept of competence. *Psychological Review, 66*, 297–333.

Williams, G., Freedman, Z., Ryan, R., & Deci, E. (1996). Motivational predictors of weight loss and maintenance. *Journal of Personality and Social Psychology, 70*(1), 115–126.

42

INDIVIDUAL AND SITUATIONAL INTEREST

Bo Shen, WAYNE STATE UNIVERSITY, USA

Interest is a powerful motivation source for children. Anyone who has watched children's enthusiasm when playing video games knows the truth to this claim. In educational psychology, interest has been a subject of children's motivation and development research (Renninger, Hidi, & Krapp, 1992). In the past 25 years, research examining the motivational function of interest in schools has generated much needed evidence to support interest as a critical variable in student motivation. These findings also suggest that educational interest is a strong motivator to children's learning. In physical education (PE), research on interest and interest-based motivation has produced meaningful results that may assist in developing motivation strategies appropriate to K-12 learners.

In this chapter, I first will give a brief historic overview of interest and introduce the basic dual-interest framework that scholars have used as the basis for most empirical work. Then I will provide an in-depth review of interest research findings in PE. In subsequent sections, I will discuss a hypothetical model for understanding the role of interest in motivation research, research implications in teaching PE, and future research directions. Finally, I will summarize the main points in this chapter and conclude with reflective questions to facilitate readers' discussions of central issues in interest-based research in PE.

Historical overview

Since Dewey's groundbreaking work, *Interest and Effort in Education* (1913), interest has long been recognized as an integral component in teaching and learning. Educational researchers (Alexander, 2005; Hidi, 2000; Krapp & Lewalter, 2001) have shown that interest can attract learners to participate actively in learning. Interest and achievement are significantly correlated in most school disciplines (Renninger, Sansone, & Smith, 2004). High interest levels can increase learners' engagement time, improve information storage, and enhance understanding. In PE, scholars have found that interest is one of the most important motivation constructs in predicting learners' engagement and intention for future PE participation (Chen & Ennis, 2004). To some extent, learners' interest can override the effects of extrinsic rewards and other motivational variables to direct and energize their involvement in learning and physical activity (PA) (Xiang, Chen, & Bruene, 2005).

In initial PE studies, researchers conceptualized interest as preferences or liking for specific physical activities. For example, Lumpkin and Avery (1986) surveyed university learners' preference for physical activities offered in colleges. They found that learners' interest in individual sports led many to enroll in individual sport courses. Van Wersch, Trew, and Turner (1992) investigated age and gender differences in preferences for physical activities as PE content. They found that both boys' and girls' interest in PE declined with increases in age. Although those findings demonstrate learners' strong interest in physical activities, they reveal little about the motivation effects of students' interest in PE.

It was not until the 1990s that researchers used the established theoretical construct of situational and individual interest to study students' PE interest. Recent researchers have used this theoretical approach to explore the motivation function of interest. Specifically, researchers focus on fundamental questions of under what circumstance do students seek and pursue some activities over others and how they develop new activity interest when they have not demonstrated prior interest. In addition, researchers have examined the association between interest and learning in PE. For example, many investigators have focused on connections between situational interest and learning variables, such as task designs, learning outcomes, PA involvement, effort, and intention (Chen & Darst, 2002; Chen & Shen, 2004; Shen & Chen, 2006, 2007).

Theoretical framework

As a motivation construct, *interest* refers to an individual's psychological state of engaging or reengaging with particular classes of objects, events, or ideas over time (Hidi & Renninger, 2006). Three major characteristics distinguish interest from other motivation structures. First, interest includes both affective and cognitive components. The affective component registers positive emotions accompanying engagement, while the cognitive component activates perceptual and representational conceptions related to engagement. While these two components are distinct, they often interact as one force that influences an individual's behavior. The second characteristic is that both the affective and cognitive interest components have biological foundations (Hidi, 2000). Neuroscientists (e.g., Panksepp, 2003) confirm that an individual's emotional system ingrained in the mammalian brain seeks interested activity. The brain's interest-search system is directly associated with individuals' engrained physical, cognitive, or symbolical engagement experiences with objects of interest (Hidi, 2000). The third characteristic is that interest is the outcome of an interaction between a person and a particular entity. Although interest originates within a person, the entity and the environment outline the *direction* of interest and contribute to its development and its emotional and cognitive outcomes. In other words, interest is content specific and arises as individuals interact with the phenomena in specific environments (Hidi & Renninger, 2006).

Types of interest

Two types of interest, individual interest and situational interest, have been the primary focus of educational research. *Individual interest* is described as an individual's relatively enduring predisposition to prefer engaging with certain objects, stimuli, and events (Hidi & Renninger, 2006). Interest researchers point out that individual interest is developed over time during a person's constant and consistent interaction with certain activities in a particular environment. It is based on increased knowledge, positive emotions, and increased value in these activities. *Situational interest*, on the other hand, is defined as an activity's momentary appealing effect on an individual in a particular context and at a particular moment (Hidi, 2000). Situational interest is generated by certain stimulating or rousing characteristics in an activity (e. g., novelty) and tends to be shared among individuals. Situational interest is based on a short, tentative relationship between a person and an activity at a given moment. Its motivation effect is short-lived but with high intensity (Hidi, 2000). In learning, situational interest results from learners' recognition of appealing features associated with a specific learning task that can catch and hold learners' attention and other cognitive functions for a period of time (Mitchell, 1993).

Although there is a fundamental distinction between individual interest and situational interest, they are not dichotomous phenomena that occur in mutual isolation. On the contrary, individual interest and situational interest often interact and influence each other's development (Hidi & Renninger, 2006). Situational interest may evoke or contribute to the development of a long-lasting individual interest, while high situational interest may enhance learners' engagement in learning activities that influence the formation of individual interest in a subject matter (Alexander, 2005).

In education, individual interest plays significant roles in knowledge acquisition, even after controlling for previous knowledge, intelligence, and text readability (Hidi & Renninger, 2006). Individual interest does not simply enhance the quantity of knowledge acquired (e.g., recalled text information) but has its most remarkable effect on the quality of learning (e.g., problem solving). Situational interest, sometimes known as "interestingness," also plays an important role in learning and academic achievement. Learners' high interestingness will lead to focused attention and mental readiness (Krapp & Lewalter, 2001). Hoffmann (2002) found that situational interest was more powerful than other factors (e.g., readability) in explaining differences in text comprehension and concluded that situational interest is a powerful determinant of learning. Hidi and Renninger (2006) further elaborate the dynamic relationship between situational interest and individual interest in terms of both affective and cognitive processes. Mitchell (1993) stated that situational interest involves processes to catch the appealing characteristics (i.e., those that trigger/stimulate students' emotions) and hold it (i.e., those that inspire students to search for personal meaning).

There are four phases of individual interest development. In the first phase, situational interest is *triggered*, sparked by environmental features such as information incongruence (curiosity), surprise, personal relevance, or character identification. The second phase, situational interest, is *maintained*, held or sustained through internalizing task meaningfulness and developing personal task involvement. Maintained situational interest involves focused attention and persistence over an extended time. Mitchell (1993) argued that triggered situational interest could be a precursor to individual interest development. During the third stage individual interest is *emerging* and is reinforced by positive feelings, stored knowledge, and developing values. This stage represents the beginning phases of a relatively enduring predisposition to actively seek repeated reengagement with particular content over time. The last stage, *well-developed* individual interest, is sustained when the emerging individual interest continues to be reinforced and validated with additional stored knowledge and values. A well-developed individual interest leads an individual to consider both task context and content in the problem solution process.

Interest and learning theory

Alexander (2004) introduced a *model of domain learning* (MDL) to describe interest development in relation to knowledge development in content domains. In MDL, interest, learning strategies, and prior knowledge are critical factors contributing to learning. In fact, interest act as a *coupling* component to strategy development and knowledge acquisition. Within the learning process, effects of interest change in association with the learner's progression through the acclimation, competency, and proficiency knowledge acquisition stages. Specifically, learners at different stages need to be motivated with situational interest or individual interest or a combination of both, and are likely to use different learning strategies to facilitate learning.

During the *acclimation* learning stage, learners have limited domain knowledge or skill. Their cognitive efforts are directed toward constructing a domain knowledge framework. During this stage, individuals' deep-seated interest in the domain is quite low and learners often are mostly concerned with task completion. Situational interest is learners' primary motivator, attracting them to the learning task and encouraging them to put forth continuous cognitive effort and energy. At the *competency* stage, learners are beginning to master key domain knowledge and skills. Although learners may continue to be attracted to situationally interesting task information, the situational interest is likely internalized into individual interest. The developing individual interest in the domain begins gradually to replace situational interest as a major motivator. Learning strategies supported by developing individual interest help learners reconstruct the domain knowledge structure by tuning and personalizing pieces of new information. At the *proficiency* stage, individual interest becomes learners' sole motivator. Learners have developed genuine individual interest in learning domain knowledge, motivating them to become more expert in applying effective learning strategies to master new knowledge. With increased quantity and quality of domain knowledge, proficient learners experience deep comprehension with ease. The theoretical framework of interest and the MDL have formed a theoretical platform that guides the conceptualization of most research studies on interest in PE. In the following section, I will summarize major findings from this line of research.

Current trends and issues

Currently, interest research in PE is characterized by a focus on studying situational interest and its motivation functions. In general, there are three intertwined research focuses. Researchers in the first research focus examine and verify the psychometric properties of the interest construct in physical activity settings. In the second focus, researchers identify associations between situational interest and other learning determinants, such as personal characteristics, while researchers in the third focus clarify the relations between interest-based motivation and PE learning achievement.

Focus 1: verification of the interest construct

In the first study examining situational and individual interest theory, Chen (1996) examined the relationship between meaningfulness of physical activities and situational interest in PE. The research purpose was to establish the characteristics of individual and situational interest. In this research, learners sorted 60 physical activities in the PE curriculum on a Q-scale based on the activities' situational interest, providing rationales for their sorting decisions. Chen revealed that learners' perceptions of situational interest in physical activities depended on their diverse personal interpretations of meaning in the activities and learning tasks, such as perceptions of novelty and enjoyment. Consistency between situational interest in an activity and personal interpretation of meaning motivated the learners to pursue continued participation in the activity. The findings provided evidence suggesting situational interest in PE could be a multi-source motivation construct.

Based on the assumption that situational interest is a content-specific, multi-source construct, Chen, Darst, and Pangrazi (1999) tested the tenability of a multi-source construct model of situational interest in middle school PE. Chen and colleagues found that students perceive physical activities as situationally interesting when they provided new information, demanded high-level attention, encouraged exploration, and generated instant enjoyment. The researchers concluded that situational interest in PE could be derived from five dimensional sources: novelty, optimal challenge, attention demand, exploration intent, and instant enjoyment. Sun, Chen, Ennis, Martin, and Shen (2008) further examined the multidimensional sources of situational interest in elementary school PE. Their results confirmed that the five dimensions were the primary sources of situational interest for elementary school students. Based on these consistent findings the researchers hypothesized that manipulating curriculum content and instructional tasks could influence situational interest.

Focus 2: situational interest and other determinants

Learning task design and situational interest

Cognitive and physical demands are two fundamental components that can be manipulative in PE learning task design. The interplay between the two components determines the acquisition of cognitive knowledge and physical skills. Chen et al. (1999) examined the effects of different cognitive and physical demands of learning tasks on situational interest. In their research, middle school students evaluated situational interest within four learning tasks representing various combinations of cognitive and physical involvement. The results showed that cognitive demand in a physical activity determines the level of situational interest. The students considered the tasks with high cognitive demand highly interesting, regardless of physical demands, while they evaluated tasks with low cognitive and physical demand particularly low in situational interest.

Gender and skill level and situational interest

Although Chen and his colleagues demonstrated that task design influences situational interest, gender and skill level also may play a moderating role in the learning process. In some instances PE continues to facilitate a gender stereotypical social environment where learners with higher prior skill levels, most of whom are boys, show higher interest in learning specific physical activities. Chen and Darst (2002) reported that boys and girls had different individual and situational interests in different learning tasks and that the difference might contribute to the knowledge and skills boys and girls have developed prior to taking part in PE. However, situationally interesting learning tasks were less sensitive to skill level and gender. In a subsequent study, Shen, Chen, Scrabis, and Tolley (2003) found that with effective instructional designing, situational interest was more likely to elicit high physical engagement than learners' gender and skill levels when learning an activity.

Goal orientation and situational interest

Situational interest in PE also has been investigated using achievement goals to predict learning. Shen, Chen, and Guan (2006) found that interest and achievement goals played inter-dependent roles in motivating middle school PE students. In this research, mastery goals had a strong influence on students' recognition of situational interest. Students with high mastery goals were more likely than students with low mastery goals to recognize situational interest in a learning task. The finding indicates that creating a mastery-oriented learning climate has strong potential to foster students' situational interest. Teachers, therefore, can increase students' motivation by structuring their learning climate to increase situational interest.

Focus 3: interest and learning

Learning outcomes and situational interest

Chen and Ennis (2004) stressed that there are two basic forms of learning outcomes in PE. One outcome is the acquisition of knowledge and skill usually measured with motor skills and knowledge tests. The other is physiological intensity, which produces health benefits from physical movement. Shen et al.'s study (2003) examined the effects of situational and individual interests on the learning outcomes in a dance unit. They found that situational interest was directly associated with PA intensity measured in steps taken during the lessons while individual interest was associated with measures of knowledge and skill performance. The findings clearly distinguished the functions for both interest types. Situational interest has a strong motivation effect on learners' engagement in the learning process. Students' level of individual interest in PE content may influence content mastery. For example, students who develop strong individual content interest may be willing to cognitively focus and physically practice until they achieve mastery.

Guided by MDL, Shen and Chen (2006) explored the interrelations among middle school PE students' prior knowledge, learning strategies, interest, physical engagement, and learning outcomes. The results highlighted interrelationship among learners' prior knowledge, learning strategies, and interest. Situational interest also influenced changes in learners' individual interest and was associated with learners' cognitive effort during the learning process. In a second study, Shen and Chen (2007) examined interactions between learners' PE profiles and their prior knowledge, learning strategies, and interest. Results from a cluster analysis emphasized relationships between learner characteristics as described in the MDL and situational interest. The findings provided initial evidence that optimizing situational interest within learning tasks could enhance PE learners' motivation. Although some learners enter the learning environment with low individual interest, teachers can manipulate curricular tasks to trigger high situational interest, nurturing the initial development of individual interest.

In other research investigating situational interest, Zhu et al. (2009) examined the extent to which situational interest motivation and cognitive engagement contributed to student achievement. In their research, Zhu and colleagues explored how completing lesson-related workbook assignments contributed to student achievement in learning health-related fitness knowledge in elementary PE. The researchers found that although situational interest contributed little to performance on workbook assignments and knowledge gain, the performance of correctly solving PE-oriented workbook problems contributed significantly to students' fitness knowledge gains. This emphasized the importance of engaging students in the learning process by encouraging them to attempt the workbook tasks. The findings supported the hypothesis that situational interest may have direct impact on participation and engagement, although it may not directly impact learning achievement. Teachers can manipulate task-oriented situational interest variables to enhance student motivation to engage in learning outcomes.

Seductive details

In lay-person's terms, situational interest can be understood as having fun, although having fun may not necessarily contribute to learning (Garner, Brown, Sanders, & Menke, 1992; Harp & Mayer, 1998). Although situational interest seems to have little direct impact on skill and knowledge acquisition, Garner et al (1992) proposed that the "fun" students experience in learning may represent *seductive details*. Seductive details attract students' attention and result in feelings of pleasure or fun but have little direct effect on student learning. Rather than content-based curriculum, seductive details are a characteristic of recreational PE in which students are entertained, and learning is not an outcome. In recreational PE, some students enjoy tasks or activities that do not lead to knowledge or skill acquisition. They become actively involved in participating in physical activities and report that "it is fun." But these experiences do not facilitate learning outcomes defined in the curriculum (Harp & Mayer, 1998).

Seductive details refer to enjoyable but unimportant information, materials, and activities that have little relevance to the content or learning process. Teachers intentionally insert seductive details into the learning process to make class fun and interesting. Seductive details, when serving as the motivational source, may lead to strong, positive emotion, rather than cognitive involvement with meaningful content (Harp & Mayer, 1998). Although seductive details can enhance learners' engagement with the learning process, they have little impact on learning and may even interfere with new knowledge and skills construction (Wade & Moje, 2000).

Shen, McCaughtry, Martin, and Dillon (2006) explored the effect of seductive details on learning net games in middle school PE. In particular, Shen et al. (2006) focused on the impact on learners' ability to identify and recall important knowledge- and skill-related content and their ability to transfer information to solve movement problems. Results showed that seductive details directly interrupted learners' recall of important movement information and interfered with their ability to transfer relevant information to solve movement problems in learning net games. The findings call attention to the importance of designing relevant situationally interesting tasks purposefully promoting situational interest while controlling seductive details. When teachers design effective motivational strategies in PE, it is imperative to avoid seductive details.

Implications for evidence-based practice

Students come to PE with diverse individual interests in a variety of different physical activities. It is difficult for physical educators to change or redirect students' individual interests to learning tasks that may not interest them (Chen, 2001). Conversely, situational interest can offer an alternative platform to enhance learner motivation. Teachers can manipulate situational interest to generate temporary but maximal motivation effects (Chen & Darst, 2001). Specifically, teachers can trigger and maintain situational interest through modifying certain aspects in the learning environment and contextual factors, such as learning climate, the task structure, and task presentation (Subramaniam, 2009, 2010). Teachers can manipulate task-based situational interest to deliberately couple knowledge and value to inspire and form strong individual interest (Hidi & Renninger, 2006). The interest-related research evidence discussed in this chapter can greatly impact teacher planning and practice.

Structuring a mastery learning climate

Learning environments can influence students' situational interest development (Darst, Chen, van der Mars, & Cusimano, 2001). By designing mastery learning climates in PE, teachers foster students' recognition of situational interest (Shen, Chen, & Guan, 2006). Mastery learning climates also are more effective than other factors (e.g., personal goals, prior knowledge) in enhancing student interest (Cury et al., 1996). In a mastery-learning climate, teachers personalize tasks and expectations to encourage students to enhance their effort, leading to improvement. By facilitating meaningful success in tasks, physical educators can create positive learning climates to trigger and maintain high situational interest among all students.

Designing instruction to enhance student choice

Providing students with choices in a learning context enhances situational interest (Iyengar & Lepper, 1999). Teachers show respect to PE students by recognizing their individual differences, inclinations, and behavioral feelings. Providing task choices that align students' individual interest with the content may help them understand the learning purpose and assist them to internalize their interest in learning tasks. When teachers offer students activity, partner, and equipment choices within differentiated tasks, they strengthen situational interest and facilitate interest internalization found in learning tasks.

Emphasizing cognitive demand

Chen and Darst (2001) emphasized that situational interest is a function of learning task design. Well-designed learning tasks trigger and maintain situational interest. Their research confirmed that cognitively engaging learning tasks are more likely to lead to situational interest than do rote practices and tasks with minimal cognitive demands. To optimize situational interest in learning tasks, teachers should consider increasing cognitive task demands rather than reducing physical task demands. A sound, situationally interesting learning task increases students' cognitive engagement and provides them with optimal cognitive challenge to enhance their attention and effort.

Providing exploration opportunities

Exploratory learning tasks generate instant enjoyment and lead to greater situational interest than command-oriented, teacher-directed tasks (Chen, Darst, & Pangrazi, 2001). When designed to provide differentiated success (e.g., choices of high, medium, and low difficulty levels within the same task), exploratory tasks arouse learners' perceptions of situational interest, increasing their intrinsic motivation to engage in the activity (Deci, 1992). Embedding exploration opportunities in learning differentiated tasks increases learners' curiosity, generating instant enjoyment, and evoking situational interest. It is particularly important for students to succeed in exploratory tasks reinforcing the connection between achievement and enjoyment.

Enriching novelty and challenge

When tasks are designed to challenge learners in novel activities, they are particularly effective in generating situational interest. Learners are more likely to experience situational interest when the activity is optimally challenging or novel to them. Conversely, students often demonstrate lack of interest when tasks are repetitive in nature and/or perceived as too easy or difficult (Shen, Winger, Li, Sun, & Rukavina, 2010). Situational interest will be subdued when students perceive there is "nothing new" in the activity. It is important for teachers to enrich tasks by enhancing novelty and optimal challenge in learning task design. As Subramaniam (2010) suggests,

> novelty can be as simple as finding a new way to organize students for practice or as complex as designing a new game using the skills that have been taught. Alternatively, novelty can also mean bringing in new ideas, games, or activities that students have not been exposed to previously. (p. 40)

Developing personally meaningful content

Learning tasks presented in a personally meaningful context empower students and enhance the development of situational and individual interest (Chen et al., 1999, 2001). Students are likely to view personally related or relevant tasks as more valuable and meaningful than isolated or disconnected tasks. Physical educators can enhance student engagement by presenting meaningful rationales and strong connections between tasks and students' personal lives. A personally meaningful rationale may trigger situational interest as well as aid students in understanding the value attached to the task in a personally meaningful way. Consequently, adding content value can inspire students to transition from situational to individual interest, increasing their motivation and enjoyment (Alexander, 2005).

Future directions

Experienced teachers know that different learning tasks can have unique appeal and hold different situational interest for different students. Just how a curriculum or a task evokes student interest has not yet been examined through empirical research. There are many opportunities for researchers to manipulate interest within curricular design. Currently, PE researchers tend to conceptualize motivation as a student psychological disposition, overlooking the role that curriculum content plays in students' interest-based motivation. In some cases, curriculum design and interest-based motivation have been studied separately. At times, physical educators may plan or design lessons and units with little consideration for the motivational effects of learning tasks (Chen & Ennis, 2004). When designing a motivation strategy, they may assume that interest is an entity independent from learning tasks or curriculum. In these situations, they may inadvertently emphasize seductive details (e.g., fun activities to attract student interest) as viable motivational strategies. Future researchers should compare the motivational impact of seductive details with integrated task designs that strengthen situational interest within the curriculum. A stronger link between interest-based motivation research and schooling will enhance the theoretical significance and practical impact of motivation research to the education community.

Motivation theories can provide evidence to support the optimal design of learning environments (Chen & Ennis, 2004; Lee, Whitehead, Ntoumanis, & Hatzigeorgiadis, 2008). Motivation models provides a foundation to study multiple motivation variables to explore, complement, extend, and synthesize existing knowledge (Duda & Hall, 2001). Interest and other motivation constructs (e.g., goal orientation, value, self-efficacy, etc.) can be integrated into a comprehensive framework to explain learning and motivation behavior in PE. Future research needs to explore the extent to which different motivational constructs can coexist within the same student.

Additionally, situational interest has been identified as a powerful motivator, especially for novice learners (Alexander, 2005). The construct in PE has been articulated to consist of multidimensional sources. Chen and Ennis (2004) propose that the structure of situational interest may vary because of its high sensitivity to the learning environment defined by the content, instructional strategies, and learners. Nevertheless, to date, the study of multidimensionality of situational interest and its function with learning is still in a very early stage. The function of situational interest dimensions on learning and in-class involvement largely remains unknown. There is an urgent need to examine how situational interest dimensions function in the PE content domain. This knowledge is critical to designing effective motivation strategies to enhance students' learning and involvement in PE.

Summary of key findings

- Interest can lead to instant engagement, enhance the quality of task engagement, and facilitate learning effectiveness.
- Individual interest is developed over time based on accumulated knowledge and skill. Individual interest is maintained by individuals' value systems and is difficult to change.
- Situational interest evolves through person–activity interactions. It is occasion-specific and maintained by situational factors.
- Situational interest is a multidimensional construct that includes novelty, cognitive challenge, high attention demand, exploration opportunities, and instant enjoyment.
- Situationally interesting tasks demand high cognitive attention. Tasks that are attractive to students are less sensitive to ability, gender, and age.
- Situationally interesting tasks can increase physical activity levels in PE lessons. In low situational interest tasks, learners are less likely to be motivated regardless of individual interest. Conversely, in high situational interest tasks, learners with high individual interest may show higher motivation to learn.
- Teachers can motivate learners by providing exploration opportunities in learning tasks, reinforcing achievement with enjoyment, and inspiring strong individual interest.
- Although seductive details can enhance learners' engagement with the learning process, they may have little impact on learning and can even interfere with the construction of new knowledge and skills.

Reflective questions for discussion

1. Describe ways that the three major interest characteristics distinguish the interest construct from other motivation constructs.
2. According to the model of domain learning, what are the significant learner characteristics at different learning stages? How can one develop motivating strategies effective for the students at each learning stages?
3. In small groups, design a number of situationally interesting activities for a fitness workshop incorporating the five sources of situational interest.
4. Think about a situational-individual interest story in your life – a story about how you became attracted to an activity and then how the activity has become your personal hobby. Describe how you may use it to remind yourself of your own motivational resiliency.
5. Although seductive details are situationally interesting and motivating, they have little impact on learning. Should PE teachers add "fun stuff" or sensations unrelated to the content to enhance students' engagement in PE classes? Take a pro or con position and explain your perspective using research evidence to support your arguments.

References

Alexander, P. A. (2004). A model of domain learning: Reinterpreting expertise as a multidimensional and multistage process. In D. Y. Dai & R. J. Sternberg (Eds.), *Motivation, emotion, and cognition: Integrative perspectives on intellectual functioning and development* (pp. 273–298). Mahwah, NJ: Lawrence Erlbaum.

Alexander, P. A. (2005). *Psychology in learning and instruction.* Upper Saddle River, NJ: Prentice Hall.

Chen, A. (1996). Student interest in activities in a secondary physical education curriculum: An analysis of student subjectivity. *Research Quarterly for Exercise and Sport, 67,* 424–432.

Chen, A. (2001). A theoretical conceptualization for motivation research in physical education: An integrated perspective. *Quest, 53,* 35–58.

Chen, A., & Darst, P. W. (2001). Situational interest in physical education: A function of learning task design. *Research Quarterly for Exercise and Sport, 72,* 150–164.

Chen, A., & Darst, P. W. (2002). Individual and situational interest: The role of gender and skill. *Contemporary Educational Psychology, 27,* 250–269.

Chen, A., Darst, P. W., & Pangrazi, R. P. (1999). What constitutes situational interest? Validating a construct in physical education. *Measurement in Physical Education and Exercise Science, 3,* 157–180.

Chen, A., Darst, P. W., & Pangrazi, R. P. (2001). An examination of situational interest and its sources. *British Journal of Educational Psychology, 71,* 383–400.

Chen, A., & Ennis, C. D. (2004). Goals, interest, and learning in physical education. *The Journal of Educational Research, 97,* 329–338.

Chen, A., & Shen, B. (2004). A web of achieving in physical education: Goals, interest, outside-school activity and learning. *Learning and Individual Differences, 14,* 169–182.

Cury, F., Biddle, S., Famose, J., Goudas, M., Sarrazin, P., & Durand, M. (1996). Personal and situational factors influencing intrinsic interest of adolescent girls in school physical education: A structure equation modeling analysis. *Educational Psychology, 16,* 305–315.

Darst, P. W., Chen, A., van der Mars, H., & Cusimano, B. E. (2001). Teacher, class size, and situational interest: Student responses to fitness routines. *Journal of Sport Pedagogy, 7,* 43–66.

Deci, E. L. (1992). The relation of interest to the motivation of behavior: A self-determination theory perspective. In K. A. Renninger, S. Hidi, & A. Krapp (Eds.), *The role of interest in learning and development* (pp. 43–69). Hillsdale, NJ: Lawrence Erlbaum.

Dewey, J. (1913). *Interest and effort in education.* New York: Houghton Mifflin.

Duda, J. L., & Hall, H. K. (2001). Achievement goal theory in sport: Recent extensions and future directions. In R. N. Singer, H. A. Hausenblas, & C. M. Janelle (Eds.), *Handbook of research in sport psychology* (2nd ed., pp. 417–434). New York: Wiley.

Garner, R., Brown, R., Sanders, S., & Menke, D. J. (1992). Seductive details and learning from text. In K. A. Renninger, S. Hidi, & A. Krapp (Eds.), *The role of interest in learning and development* (pp. 239–254). Hillsdale, NJ: Lawrence Erlbaum.

Harp, S. F., & Mayer, R. E. (1998). How seductive details do their damage: A theory of cognitive interest in science learning. *Journal of Educational Psychology, 90,* 414–434. http://dx.doi.org/10.1037/0022-0663.90.3.414

Hidi, S. (2000). An interest researcher's perspective: The effects of intrinsic and extrinsic factors on motivation. In C. Sansone & J. M. Harackiewicz (Eds.), *Intrinsic and extrinsic motivation: The search for optimal motivation and performance* (pp. 309–339). San Diego, CA: Academic Press.

Hidi, S., & Renninger, K. A. (2006). The four-phase model of interest development. *Educational Psychologist, 4,* 111–127.

Hoffmann, I. (2002). Promoting girls' learning and achievement in physics classes for beginners. *Learning and Instruction, 12,* 447–465.

Iyengar, S. S., & Lepper, M. R. (1999). Rethinking the role of choice: A cultural perspective on intrinsic motivation. *Journal of Personality and Social Psychology, 76,* 349–366.

Krapp, A., & Lewalter, D. (2001). Development of interest and interest-based motivational orientations: A longitudinal study in vocational school and work settings. In S. Volet & S. Jarvela (Eds.), *Motivation in learning context: Theoretical advances and methodological implications* (pp. 201–232). London: Elsevier.

Lee, M. J., Whitehead, J., Ntoumanis, N., & Hatzigeorgiadis, A. (2008). Relationships among values, achievement orientations, and attitudes in youth sport. *Journal of Sport & Exercise Psychology, 30,* 581–610.

Lumpkin, A., & Avery, M. (1986). Physical education activity program survey. *Journal of Teaching in Physical Education, 5,* 185–197.

Mitchell, M. (1993). Situational interest: Its multifaceted structure in the secondary school mathematics classroom. *Journal of Educational Psychology, 85,* 424–436.

Panksepp, J. (2003). At the interface of the affective, behavioral and cognitive neurosciences: Decoding the emotional feelings of the brain. *Brain and Cognition, 52,* 4–14.

Renninger, K. A., Hidi, S., & Krapp, K. (Eds.). (1992). *The role of interest in learning and development.* Hillsdale, NJ: LEA.

Renninger, K. A., Sansone, C., & Smith, J. L. (2004). Love of learning. In C. Peterson & M. E. P. Seligman (Eds.), *Character strengths and virtues: A classification and handbook* (pp. 161–179). New York: Oxford University Press.

Shen, B., & Chen, A. (2006). Examining the interrelations among knowledge, interests, and learning strategies. *Journal of Teaching in Physical Education, 25,* 182–199.

Shen, B., & Chen, A. (2007). An examination of learning profiles in physical education. *Journal of Teaching in Physical Education, 26,* 145–160.

Shen, B., Chen, A., & Guan, J. (2006). Using achievement goals and interest to predict learning in physical education. *The Journal of Experimental Education, 75,* 89–108.

Shen, B., Chen, A., Scrabis, K. A., & Tolley, H. (2003). Gender and interest-based motivation in learning dance. *Journal of Teaching in Physical Education, 22,* 396–410.

Shen, B., McCaughtry, N., Martin, J., & Dillon, S. (2006). Does "sneaky fox" facilitate learning? Examining the effects of seductive details in physical education. *Research Quarterly for Exercise and Sport, 77,* 498–506.

Shen, B., Winger, R., Li, W., Sun, H., & Rukavina, P. (2010). An amotivation model in physical education. *Journal of Teaching in Physical Education, 29,* 72–84.

Subramaniam, P. R. (2009). Motivational effects of interest on student engagement and learning in physical education: A review. *International Journal of Physical Education, 46,* 11–19.

Subramaniam, P. R. (2010). Unlocking the power of situational interest in physical education. *Journal of Physical Education, Recreation & Dance, 81,* 38–41.

Sun, H., Chen, A., Ennis, C., Martin, R., & Shen, B. (2008). An examination of the multidimensionality of situational interest in elementary school physical education. *Research Quarterly for Exercise and Sport, 79,* 62–70.

Van Wersch, A., Trew, K., & Turner, I. (1992). Post-primary school pupils' interest in physical education: Age and gender differences. *British Journal of Educational Psychology, 62,* 56–72.

Wade, S. E., & Moje, E. B. (2000). The role of text in classroom learning. In M. L. Kamil, P. B. Mosenthal, P. D. Pearson, & R. Barr (Eds.), *Handbook of reading research* (Vol. III, pp. 609–627). Mahwah, NJ: Erlbaum.

Xiang, P., Chen, A., & Bruene, A. (2005). Interactive impact of intrinsic motivators and extrinsic rewards on behavior and motivation outcomes. *Journal of Teaching in Physical Education, 24,* 179–197.

Zhu, X., Chen, A., Ennis, C. D., Sun, H., Hopple, C., Bonello, M., Bae, M., & Kim, S. (2009). Student situational interest, cognitive engagement, and learning achievement in physical education. *Contemporary Educational Psychology, 34,* 221–229.

43

ADAPTATION OR MALADAPTATION OF ACHIEVEMENT GOALS IN PHYSICAL EDUCATION

Sami Yli-Piipari, UNIVERSITY OF GEORGIA, USA

Most human behaviors are guided by specific goals. In educational settings, goals may derive from sources either external to the learner or within the learner. Currently, learner-generated goals are driving the research enterprise in goal research and, specifically, the study of achievement goal orientation constructs. In this chapter, I will provide a historic overview of this research, elaborate the dominant theoretical frameworks, and review the research evidence. I will then discuss the research implications for pedagogical practice and suggest future research directions. I will close with a summary of key findings in achievement goal research and pose reflective questions for further discussion.

Historical overview

Achievement motivation research can be traced to William James' inquiry (1890) on achievement and self-evaluation. Decades later, Henry Murray (1938) published *Explorations in Personality* in which he identified 27 motivation-related needs including the need for achievement. David McClelland (1961) conceptually developed the need for achievement in his book, *The Achieving Society*, in which he described three motivational needs: achievement motivation, authority/power motivation, and affiliation motivation. Parallel with McClelland's conceptualization, psychologist John Atkinson (1964) studied human motivation focusing on the joint influences of motivation to succeed and avoid failure in achievement situations.

Achievement motivation research began with John Nicholls' (1984) work surrounding Achievement Goal Theory (AGT). Roberts (2012) documented the development of research on achievement motivation by describing the exciting atmosphere in the Institute for Child Behavior and Development at the University of Illinois in Fall 1977, where Nicholls, Maehr, Dweck, A. Ames, C. Ames, Hill, Farmer, and Roberts met regularly with their students in seminars discussing and designing research examining motivation. These discussions led to several prominent achievement motivation models and theories. For instance, Dweck's inquiry into children's apparent helplessness in achievement contexts demonstrated that children with equal aptitude can respond very differently to failure due to their different goal conceptions toward tasks. Some children displayed a mastery response, whereas others displayed helplessness response patterns (Diener & Dweck, 1980) (also see implicit theories by Dweck, Chui, & Hong, 1995). These studies led to the conclusion that achievement goals represent an individual's purpose for engagement and to the identification of performance and learning goals often displayed by individuals in achievement contexts.

Nicholls (1984, 1989) published two influential AGT texts that evolved from his conceptual theorizing and worldview focused on equal educational opportunity. One of the tenets of AGT centers on whether individuals define success as self- or other-referenced. Individuals who adopt the self-referenced success orientation (mastery orientation) are interested in improving their skills or learning and demonstrate mastery of tasks. Conversely, individuals who assume the other-referenced success orientation (ego orientation) tend to demonstrate an ego-centered performance-based comparison to others (Nicholls, 1984). AGT has had a tremendous impact on PE and has generated an impressive plethora of PE studies that has advanced our knowledge about learner motivation.

Carole Ames (Ames, 1992a, 1992b, 1992c) first introduced the motivational climate concept to educational achievement motivation research. Her studies illustrated that task-involvement leads learners to the mastery goal orientation, while ego-involvement leads to the performance goal orientation (Ames, 1992a). The environmental determinants of motivational climate, according to Ames, include six teacher-controlled factors, Task, Authority, Rewards/Recognition, Grouping, Evaluation, and Time to complete tasks, described as the TARGET system. Students are likely to learn successfully in classrooms in which teachers assign Tasks suitable to students' development levels, share Authority with students, Reward effort, use heterogeneous Grouping strategies and criterion-referenced Evaluation, and maximize academic learning Time (Epstein, 1989).

In the 1990s, Andrew Elliot and his colleagues (Elliot, 1999; Elliot & Harackiewicz, 1996) incorporated the achievement and avoidance approaches into the mastery vs. performance goal structure, therefore, developing the two-goal theoretical model into a 2×2 structure: a) mastery-approach and b) mastery-avoidance goals and c) performance-approach and d) performance-avoidance goals (Elliot, 1999). The 2×2 Model postulates that individuals have needs or valence toward either achievement or avoidance (Roberts, 2012). It has generated a lot of interest in PE and sport since its inception.

The core of social-cognitive theories, such as achievement goal theories, is found in the complex interplay between environment and individual. The majority of contemporary PE research has examined these relationships. Researchers have focused on understanding the mediating role of achievement goals and orientations between the psychological environment created by the teacher, coach, parent, or learner and numerous outcomes. In these studies, researchers have conceptualized and examined psychological environments using Ames' (1992a) motivational climate concept or the three psychological needs structure from the Self-Determination Theory (Deci & Ryan, 1985, see Chapter 41 in this volume). Although Nicholls' (1984) dichotomous model has been widely used for scientific inquiry in PE, there has been a subtle shift toward Elliot's (1999) 2×2 framework. It may be that the 2×2 Model provides more plausible solutions to understand student motivation or the novelty of Elliot's ideas that have drawn scholars toward the 2×2 framework.

Theoretical frameworks and empirical evidence

Typically, PE teachers set psychomotor, cognitive, and affective learning goals for their students. Although these goals may relate to students' skill and health development, some students may not share their teachers' goals. Instead, students' goals may be adaptive or maladaptive in regard to the teachers' intended educational outcomes. Adaptive goals refer to motivational goals that enhance positive learning outcomes consistent with learning goals, whereas maladaptive student goals may lead to motivation goals that are inconsistent with learning goals. In PE, a key motivation question is how can teachers better enhance and direct student motivation to facilitate student participation in teacher-directed curricula and learning tasks.

AGT derives from an understanding of the interactions between achievement, competence/ability perception, and the social environment in which achievement is expected. The strength of AGTs is that the theories are taking account of this interplay and employing a social-cognitive approach, examining motivation and learning-related behaviors. An underlying assumption in social-cognitive theories is that individuals are active, intentional, and rational decision makers who, governed by their beliefs and values, will behave in certain ways in achievement contexts. In PE, for instance, students with adaptive achievement motivation voluntarily choose to participate with high intensity in tasks designed by the PE teacher. Conversely, students with maladaptive achievement motivation do not want to participate in teacher-designed tasks and, if teachers attempt to force their participation, the students' participation may be marginal with little effort and commitment. Therefore, researchers' theoretical goal when studying achievement motivation is to understand students' adaptive and maladaptive achievement goals and their impact on learning and participation.

Nicholls' AGT

AGT is a prominent framework used to understand PE and sport achievement behaviors (Nicholls, 1984, 1989). AGT provides a useful framework to understand *why* students either decide to engage in teacher-directed learning tasks and drills or refuse and sit on the bleachers. To understand the why, one must explore and understand students' purposes or goals for their actions. To understand motivation that directs and energizes behavior, researchers must consider the *purpose* of the achievement behavior and understand the *goals of actions* (Roberts & Treasure, 2012). Nicholls (1984) argued that the goal of action is a driving force that can be directed toward demonstrating competence or avoiding displaying incompetence. AGT states that individuals in achievement contexts can have multiple goals due to different reasons and purposes. These goal-related phenomenological meanings (or cognitive perceptions) are important because they govern intensity and effort of actions. Nicholls pointed out that individuals perceive their abilities (or competence) differently (Nicholls & Miller, 1983) and can have either undifferentiated or differentiated ability conceptions (Nicholls, 1984). With an *undifferentiated ability conception*, one perceives ability holistically and therefore is not able to differentiate ability from other factors such as effort, coincidence, or outside influences that may impact performance (Nicholls & Miller, 1983). An individual with a *differentiated ability conception* defines ability independently from these factors.

Whether individuals see ability as undifferentiated or differentiated, these conceptions have an important role in the ways they view success. One of the central AGT tenets is the *definition of success*, which can be viewed as self- or other-referenced. Individuals with the undifferentiated ability conception see success to be self-referenced, with interest in improving their skills or learning and demonstrating task mastery (Nicholls, 1984). Individuals with a differentiated ability conception see success as other-referenced and tend to focus on demonstrating performance in comparison to others (Nicholls, 1989). Self-referenced individuals participate in activities due to task-centered reasons and, thus, are likely to direct and maintain energy and effort more consistently compared to other-referenced individuals who participate due to ego-centered reasons. For instance in PE, students who see success as self-referenced demonstrate persistence in the face of adversity, while other-referenced students are hesitant to continue or give up easily if they see little chance to outperform others.

Achievement goal orientations

PE students who have the undifferentiated ability conception have a predisposition for task orientation. These predispositions are individuals' inherited tendencies to act in certain ways. Task-oriented students are inclined to focus on task completion and understanding, learning and developing skills, showing mastery, solving problems, seeking challenges, and persisting in the face of failure (Nicholls, 1984). Conversely, ego-oriented students approach tasks as a contest and aim to show superiority over peers. Roberts (2012) emphasized these predispositions should not be viewed as traits or needs but are dynamic "cognitive schemas" that may be altered in light of new information received when performing tasks. Additionally, Nicholls (1989) postulated that task and ego orientations are not mutually exclusive but vary independently and are, thus, orthogonal, meaning that students can be strong in either or both goal orientations simultaneously. In other words, they can perceive success as both gaining mastery and being better than others. Pensgaard and Roberts (2000) found evidence supporting the orthogonal relationship between the two goal orientations.

Adaptive and maladaptive goal profiles

Nicholls theorized that task-oriented individuals were more adaptive than ego-oriented learners, pointing out various positive task-oriented indicators of motivation, such as enhanced performance, intrinsic motivation, and positive affect (Nicholls, 1984). Conversely, he predicted that ego-oriented learners would be less motivationally adaptive. He postulated that these two goal orientations would interact with perceived ability/competence in achievement-related processes. Nicholls (1984) further argued that goal orientations work together with one's competence perception in determining the meaning of success and desired outcome. Task orientation appears to have minimal influence on perceived competence. Task-oriented individuals may display adaptive outcomes regardless of his/her competence perception levels because they often define success in association with effort. Individuals with both high ego orientation and high competence perception may select moderately difficult tasks to ensure success that they define as outperforming others. Individuals with a high ego orientation and a low competence perception, however, may select very easy or sometimes very difficult tasks so that they can attribute success or failure to competence rather than effort.

Goal orientations and learning outcomes

In PE, task orientation has been positively correlated with numerous positive outcomes, whereas empirical evidence on ego orientation has been mixed. Most studies have focused on motivational or mediating variables, such as motivational regulations, affective variables, and achievement-related strategies, assumed to facilitate learning achievement (see review by Biddle, Wang, Kavussanu, & Spray, 2003). In addition, researchers have examined the relationship between achievement orientations and more direct learning outcomes, such as effort, intensity, physical activity (PA), and fitness (Roberts, 2012).

Although studies have shown a positive relationship between task orientation and adaptive outcomes, a literature review by Biddle et al. (2003) found positive relationships between task orientation and perceived competence (14 out of 30 studies), task orientation and enjoyment

(36 out 48), and task orientation and behavioral variables (16 out of 25). Task orientation was found to have an inverse relationship with negative affect (13 out of 34). On the other hand, ego orientation had a positive relationship to competence perceptions in 14 studies (no relationship in 16 studies out of 30), no relationship to positive affect (31 studies out of 44), and a positive relationship to negative affect in 13 studies (no relationship in 20 studies out of 38). Ego orientation had no relationship to behavioral variables in 19 studies (out of 25).

Biddle et al. (2003) reviewed the literature from 2005 to 2014 noting that a positive relationship was found between task orientation and eight variables. These were (a) PA behavior (Yli-Piipari, Barkoukis, Jaakkola, & Liukkonen, 2013), (b) self-determined motivation (Murcia, Gimeno, & Gonzále-Cutre, 2010), (c) intrinsic motivation (Balaguer, Castillo, Duda, & Garcia-Merita, 2011; Bortoli, Bertollo, Filho, & Robazza, 2014; Chin, Khoo, & Low, 2012; Stuntz & Weiss, 2009), (d) identified regulation (Bortoli et al., 2014), (e) flow (Murcia et al., 2010), (f) satisfaction/enjoyment (Cunningham & Xiang, 2008; Newton, Watson, Kim, & Beacham, 2006; Stuntz & Weiss, 2009), (g) pleasant psycho-bio-social states (Bortoli, Bertollo, Comani, & Robazza, 2011), and (h) unpleasant psychological states (Bortoli, Bertollo, & Robazza, 2009). Not surprisingly, task orientation was negatively correlated with amotivation (Balaguer et al., 2011). In other studies, for example, two youth sport-related studies (Bortoli et al., 2009; Chin et al., 2012), the findings were mixed. In turn, the findings between ego orientation and outcomes were mainly non-significant. Biddle et al.'s (2003) review showed that ego orientation was positively related to introjected regulation (Balaguer et al., 2011), extrinsic regulation (Balaguer et al., 2011; Bortoli et al., 2014; Chin et al., 2012), amotivation (Chin et al., 2012), and anxiety (Abrahamsen, Roberts, & Pensgaard, 2008), and negatively correlated with self-determined motivation (Murcia et al., 2010).

The Trichotomous Model

Elliot and Harackiewicz (1996), revisiting McClelland's (1951) original theoretical work, argued that achievement motivation may have two goals, to obtain success or to avoid failure. They pointed out the need to expand the dichotomous achievement goal model to incorporate the independent approach and avoidance components within the performance (ego) goal orientation. This resulted in the Trichotomous Model that includes mastery goals, performance-approach goals (PAp), and performance-avoidance goals (PAv). In this model, Elliot and Harackiewicz (1996) assumed that mastery goals were very similar to task-oriented goals, in which participation is purported to improve one's skills and mastery. Conversely, performance goals have both definition and valence that lead to two independent ego-oriented goals, PAp and PAv goals. PAp goals imply that individuals seek to prove superior competence and gain positive evaluations for their abilities, whereas PAv goals suggest that individuals seek to prove that they are not incompetent and avoid negative evaluations of their competence from others (Elliot & Harackiewicz, 1996).

The Trichotomous Model has provided two important conclusions in terms of goal adaption and maladaption (Elliot & Church, 1997; Elliot & Harackiewicz, 1996). First, the model assumes that both PAp and mastery goals are characterized by an approach focus on potential positive outcomes (Elliot, 2005). Elliot and Harackiewicz (1996) reported that mastery goals and PAp goals were linked with positive outcomes, such as enjoyment and intrinsic motivation, whereas PAv was linked with low levels of enjoyment and intrinsic motivation (Elliot & Harackiewicz, 1996). Elliot (2005) further identified possible outcomes differences in terms of mastery and PAp goals showing that PAp goals can be more beneficial than the mastery goals in situations where task attainment depends on externally imposed criteria rather than intrinsic task interest. Second, the

Trichotomous Model appears to counter the goal-competence interaction assumption by providing evidence showing that motivational orientations are independent of perceived competence (Elliot & Harackiewicz, 1996). Elliot and colleagues view perceived competence as an antecedent of achievement goal adaption (Elliot, 2005; Elliot & Church, 1997). Because individuals' high competence perception may provide cues about success or failure possibilities, a competence perception may predict the adoption of both approach goals (mastery and PAp). On the contrary, low competence perceptions facilitate adapting PAv goals (Elliot, 2005; Elliot & Church, 1997).

The 2×2 Model

More recently, Elliot (Elliot, 1999; Elliot & McGregor, 2001) proposed an advanced 2×2 achievement goal framework. They reconceptualized mastery goals based on approach-avoidance distinctions introducing mastery-performance (MAp) and mastery avoidance (MAv) goals (Elliot, 1999; Elliot & McGregor, 2001). Although Elliot and colleagues agreed with previous literature indicating that mastery (task) goals led to positive learning and behavioral outcomes, they argued that these positive findings were due to research manipulations and measures primarily focused on positive mastery possibilities, while ignoring mastery avoidance aspects. In the 2×2 Model, MAv goals are conceptualized as avoiding self- or task-referenced incompetence. In other words, PE students may avoid situations they perceive will be difficult for them to show improvement or growth. Conversely, other PE students may view MAp goals as positively valenced goals enabling them to strive for skills and abilities advancing learning (Elliot, 1999). For instance PE students' goals for action may be to improve their skill or fitness levels. Thus, Elliot presented four achievement goals: MAp (focused on task-based or intrapersonal competence), MAv (focused on task-based or intrapersonal incompetence), PAp (focused on normative competence), and PAv (focused on normative incompetence). The 2×2 Model provides an alternative explanation for adaptive and maladaptive achievement goals. Elliot originally (1999) and retrospectively (2005) pointed out the difficulty of determining "a priori" which specific approach and avoidance goals relate to outcomes. He theorized, however, that approach goals (MAp and PAp) should lead to adaptive outcomes, while avoidance goals should lead to maladaptive outcomes (Elliot, 1999). Although Nicholls conceptualized that task goals would be adaptive and ego goals maladaptive for students with low competence perceptions, Elliot (1999, 2005) theorized that approach goals can be adaptive for all students as long as they hold the approach goal orientations rather than the avoidance orientation.

Physical education research

Papaioannou, Zourbanos, Krommidas, and Amatzouglou (2012) identified 33 studies (25 correlational, 5 experimental, 3 longitudinal) that used either the Trichotomous or the 2×2 model. They found that in 21 studies MAp goals and in 11 studies PAp goals were positively related to adaptive outcomes, such as PA participation, race performance, shuttle run performance (MAp only), academic performance (MAp only), pacer test performance, fitness, intrinsic motivation, relatedness, autonomy (MAp only), identified regulation (MAp only), metacognition, incremental theory (MAp only), utility value, intrinsic value, situational interest, satisfaction, effort, enjoyment, and positive affect. MAv (in 10 studies) and PAv (in 14 studies) goals typically were unrelated to adaptive outcomes. In 6 studies, PAv goals were positively related to maladaptive goals, such as external regulation, self-handicapping, test anxiety, and negative affect, whereas MAv goals were positively related to negative affect in 2 studies. Although Papaioannou et al.

(2012) did not find a positive relationship between MAp goals and maladaptive outcomes, they confirmed that PAp had a positive relationship with negative affect, test anxiety, and external regulation.

Since 2010, researchers have conducted 16 studies along this line of inquiry with 11 studies being correlational, 1 experimental, and 4 longitudinal. In general, MAp goals were positively related to intrinsic motivation and identified regulation (Gao, Podlog, & Harrison, 2012), effort/persistence (Gao et al., 2012), life satisfaction (Castillo, Duda, Álvarez, Mercé, & Balaguer, 2011), social affiliation/social recognition (Garn, Ware, & Solmon, 2011). In addition, the MAp goals had an indirect effect on pacer test results via self-efficacy (Gao, Xiang, Lochbaum, & Guan, 2013). Gao et al. (2013) found that PAp goals were positively related to pacer test results, intrinsic motivation and amotivation, and effort/persistence, while Garn et al. (2011) reported a positive relationship between PAp goals and social affiliation/recognition/status. Conversely, MAv goals were positively related only to pacer test results and effort/persistence (Gao et al. 2012). It should be noted, though, that this evidence was derived from only one study. PAv goals were positively related to amotivation (Gao et al. 2012), social affiliation/recognition (Garn et al., 2011), social physique anxiety (Balli, Erturan-İlker, & Arslan, 2014), and negatively to lower self-esteem (Castillo et al., 2011).

In summary, the research evidence confirms that task orientation and MAp goals are the most adaptive. Research findings also indicate that, although the ego orientation can be adaptive, it is dependent on individuals' competence perception and adoption of the approach-centered goals. Although there is empirical evidence of the adaptive impact of the ego orientation and PAp goals, the impact can be trivial in comparison with that of task orientation and MAp goals. In addition, task orientation and MAp goals are more positively correlated with a range of outcome measures than are the ego-orientation and PAp goals. Further, ego-orientation and PAp goals tend to be related to maladaptive outcomes, such as fear of failure, negative affect, and amotivation in general. Research findings using the 2×2 Model have repeatedly demonstrated that avoidance goals are the most maladaptive in terms of achievement.

Implications for evidence-based practice

Research evidence has provided a solid foundation to understand motivational goal processes and learning environments that nurture adaptive goal orientations. PE teachers should understand that students may operate according to their own goals rather than the goals that educators impose on them. Although externally imposed goals are consistent and similar, students' goals can be different and very diverse. PE teachers making daily decisions using TARGET can have an impact on student learning and engagement. Additionally, because students interpret instructional cues in different ways, they can perceive learning process and learning environments differently. Teachers can facilitate students' development of adaptive learning goals by adopting an individual teaching approach whenever possible.

In general, research findings clearly indicate that the mastery orientation is the most adaptive goal orientation. This cognitive schema defines characteristics required to be successful in most learning environments. It is highly desirable for PE teachers to nurture students' mastery orientation rather than an ego goal orientation. In so doing, it seems, PE students with both low and high competence perceptions can achieve success. Although the ego orientation can have adaptive learning effects (especially combined with individuals' high perception of competence), a high ego orientation may lead to undesirable outcomes, such as low sportsmanship, low value for rules, low moral functioning, and high self-reported cheating (Boixados, Cruz, Torregrossa, & Valiente, 2004; Lee, Whitehead, Ntoumanis, & Hatzigeorgiadis, 2008; Sage &

Kavussanu, 2007). It may be prudent for PE teachers to refrain from ego-supportive practices when teaching.

There is evidence showing that adapting approach achievement goals may counter undesirable influence from competence perceptions. Elliot and Harackiewicz (1996) hypothesized that individuals with both low and high competence perceptions can obtain adaptive outcomes if their goals are related to approach rather than avoidance tendencies. In other words, PE teachers should be aware that both MAp and PAp goals can lead to adaptive outcomes. During a fitness class, for example, not only may students with a high MAp be motivated to participate fully with the goal of fitness improvement but also students either with high PAp and high competence perception or high MAp and low competence perception may be motivated as well. Although the reasons may be different, these students can display positive, desirable adaptive motivation for learning.

Empirical evidence confirms that approach goals are positively related to PA and fitness-related performance (Garn & Sun, 2009; Wang, Biddle, & Elliot, 2007), competence (Castillo et al., 2011; Cetinkalp, 2012; Cuevas, Garcia-Calvo, & Contreras, 2013), intrinsic motivation (Barkoukis, Ntoumanis, & Nikitaras, 2007; Gao et al., 2012; Nien & Duda, 2008; Smith, Duda, Allen, & Hall, 2002; Wang, Koh, & Chatzisarantis, 2009), and effort and persistence (Garn & Sun, 2009; Gao et al., 2012). In addition, correlational evidence has shown stronger relationship between adaptive outcomes and MAp goals than between adaptive outcomes and PAp goals. Teachers, therefore, should emphasize MAp goals over PAp goals enhancing strategies.

Additional research findings have provided support to Elliot's (2005) assumptions that PAp goals may be more beneficial for individuals' performance than MAp goals in situations where task attainment depends on externally imposed criteria rather than intrinsic interest. Specifically, two studies examining competitive race performance and pacer test scores showed larger correlation coefficients between PAp goals and outcomes than between MAp goals and outcomes (Garn & Sun, 2009; Stoeber, Uphill, & Hotham, 2009). Although this evidence is descriptive, its implications for teaching should not be overlooked. Although the PAp goals may facilitate achievement in tasks with externally imposed criteria such as races and competitive events, they are likely to lead to maladaptive outcomes, such as external regulation (Barkoukis et al., 2007; Smith et al., 2002), and test anxiety (Smith et al., 2002). The evidence cautions PE teachers to become aware of long-term (negative) side effects when adopting and using strategies centered on the PAp tenets.

It appears that avoidance tendencies are detrimental for human achievement (Elliot, 1999). Both MAv and PAv goals are unrelated to adaptive outcomes, and PAv goals in particular may lead to maladaptive outcomes, such as high self-handicapping (Ommundsen, 2004), test anxiety (Smith et al., 2002), and low sport satisfaction (Papaioannnou, Ampatzoglou, Kalogiannis, & Sagovits, 2008). Nevertheless, limited evidence has shown that MAv (example: "*I don't want to do worse than last time*") may be beneficial to students who are studying to develop fitness (Wang, Lim, Aplin, Chia, McNeil, & Tan, 2008) or engaging in strenuous exercise (Lochbaum, Stevenson, & Hilario, 2009). PE teachers should be aware of the role that competence perception plays in determining the approach or avoidance paths. Elliot (1999) hypothesized that individuals with high competence perceptions may adopt approach goals, while those with low competence perceptions may adopt avoidance goals. When making instructional decisions, PE teachers should be aware of students' diverse skill and fitness levels, their likely competence perceptions and actual competence, and their likely achievement goal structures (MAp, MAv, PAp, and PAv). It seems imperative for teachers to create learning environments that nurture mastery rather than an avoidance approach.

Future directions

Although achievement goal research has been a popular topic for decades, lately, researchers have raised concerns regarding the conceptual disagreement over the most adaptive goal profiles. Even though the adaptive role of mastery goals on learning outcomes is well established, researchers' conceptual disagreements and inability to agree on the most suitable achievement goal profile may have weakened the AGT research. An important direction for future research is to further clarify the role of mastery in PE and in sport. Because the physical nature of PE differentiates it from other school content areas, PE researchers in the future should not rely solely on educational theories and conclusions but design innovative studies based on their unique understanding and standpoint. PE motivational climate interventions should focus on identifying and examining motivational pathways in all three outcome domains (psychomotor, cognitive, and affective) to more broadly understand the effects of different goal orientations on learning achievement in these domains.

Scholars agree that mastery goal orientation is the most adaptive orientation for learning-related outcomes. Given that much of sport-related PE content conveys a competitive element, future PE researchers should examine whether there are instances in which PAp goals are more beneficial than MAp goals in these competitive environments. It should be beneficial to learn whether PAp goals are motivating when a task is based on externally imposed criteria, a universal characteristic of activities/tasks in schools.

In the general education, achievement motivation scholars are examining the competence–achievement goal relationship. Lately, researchers have introduced the standards-based 3×2 Achievement Goal Model, arguing that individuals may define competence through task, self, or other evaluation and valence competence as a desirable possibility (i.e., success) or an undesirable possibility (i.e., failure) (Elliot, Murayama, & Pekrun, 2011). This model introduces the following goals: a *task-approach goal* focusing on the attainment of task-based competence (e.g., "doing the task correctly"), a *task-avoidance goal* focusing on the avoidance of task-based incompetence (e.g., "avoiding doing the task incorrectly"), a *self-approach goal* focusing on the attainment of self-based competence (e.g., "doing better than before"), a *self-avoidance goal* focusing on the avoidance of self-based incompetence (e.g., "avoiding doing worse than before"), an *other-approach goal* focusing on the attainment of other-based competence (e.g., "doing better than others"), and an *other-avoidance goal* focusing on the avoidance of other-based incompetence (e.g., "avoiding doing worse than others"). PE researchers should examine the theoretical conceptualization and utility of the multi-goal model in a range of PE content and learning environments.

Summary of key findings

- The mastery/task orientation in which students perceive PE success as self-referenced is the most adaptive achievement goal orientation in PE. Conversely, the performance/ego orientation, that is, perceiving PE success as other-referenced, can be either adaptive or maladaptive, depending on the participants' own competence perceptions.
- Researchers have shown that task and ego orientations are orthogonal. Individuals can simultaneously perceive PE success as gaining mastery or being better than others.
- Students may hold both approach and avoidance tendencies related to their goal orientations in achievement contexts.
- Performance approach goals have been theorized to be adaptive and avoidance goals maladaptive.

- Researchers have shown that MAp (focus on improvement) and PAp (focus on outperforming others) goals can be adaptive. Research evidence from MAv (avoiding tasks so as not to do worse than before) and PAv (avoiding tasks so as not to lose) goals have shown that avoidance goals are either non-related to outcomes or to maladaptive outcomes in PE contexts.
- Motivational climate is a concept closely related to achievement goal orientations.
- Motivational climate assumes that students perceive the learning environment to be either task- or ego-involving. Their perceptions can have a nurturing impact on their task and ego orientation.
- If students perceive learning climates to be task-involving, they are likely to develop a task orientation. On the contrary, researchers assume that students in ego-involving climates will develop ego orientations.

Reflective questions for discussion

1. If a PE student does not want to participate in the teacher-assigned tasks, how should the teacher address the problem? Please use research evidence when answering/discussing the question.
2. Do mastery-supportive PE teaching practices undermine highly competitive students' achievement motivation? Explain the rationale for your answer using research.
3. Do PE rules and regulations undermine students' achievement motivation? Explain the rationale for your answer using research.
4. From the perspective of AGT, what interventions/strategies should researchers/teachers implement to enhance students' achievement motivation? Explain why these interventions/strategies can be effective.

References

Abrahamsen, F. E., Roberts, G. C., & Pensgaard, A. M. (2008). Achievement goals and gender effects on multidimensional anxiety in national elite sport. *Psychology of Sport and Exercise, 9*, 449–464.

Ames, C. (1992a). Achievement goals and the classroom motivational climate. In D. H. Schunk & J. L. Meece (Eds.), *Student perceptions in the classroom* (pp. 327–348). Hillsdale, NJ: Lawrence Erlbaum Associates.

Ames, C. (1992b). Achievement goals, motivational climate, and motivational processes. In G. C. Roberts (Ed.), *Motivation in sport and exercise* (pp. 161–176). Champaign, IL: Human Kinetic.

Ames, C. (1992c). Classrooms: Goals, structures, and student motivation. *Journal of Educational Psychology, 84*(3), 261–271.

Atkinson, J. W. (1964). *An introduction to motivation.* Princeton, NJ: Van Nostrand.

Balaguer, I., Castillo, I., Duda, J. L., & Garcia-Merita, M. (2011). Associations between the perception of motivational climate created by coaches, dispositional goal orientations, forms of self-regulation and subjective vitality in young tennis players. *Revista de Psicologia del Deporte, 20*(1), 133–148.

Balli, Ö. M., Erturan-İlker, G., & Arslan, Y. (2014). Achievement goals in a Turkish high school PE setting: The predicting role of social physique anxiety. *International Journal of Educational Research, 67*, 30–39.

Barkoukis, V., Ntoumanis, N., & Nikitaras, N. (2007). Comparing dichotomous and trichotomous approaches to Achievement Goal Theory: An example using motivational regulations as outcome variables. *British Journal of Educational Psychology, 77*, 683–702.

Biddle. S. J. H., Wang, C. K. J., Kavussanu, M., & Spray, C. M. (2003). Correlates of achievement goal orientations in physical activity. *European Journal of Sport Science, 3*, 1–20.

Boixados, M., Cruz, J., Torregrossa, M., & Valiente, L. (2004). Relationships among motivational climate, satisfaction, perceived ability, and fair play attitudes in young soccer players. *Journal of Applied Sport Psychology, 16*(4), 301–317. doi:10.1080/10413200490517977

Bortoli, L., Bertollo, M., Comani, S., & Robazza, C. (2011). Competence, achievement goals, motivational climate, and pleasant psychobiosocial states in youth sport. *Journal of Sports Sciences, 29*(2), 171–180.

Bortoli, L., Bertollo, M., Filho, E., & Robazza, C. (2014). Do psychobiosocial states mediate the relationship between perceived motivational climate and individual motivation in youngsters? *Journal of Sports Sciences*, *32*(6), 572–582.

Bortoli, L., Bertollo, M., & Robazza, C. (2009). Dispositional goal orientations, motivational climate, and psychobiosocial states in youth sport. *Personality and Individual Differences*, *47*(1), 18–24.

Castillo, I., Duda, J. L., Álvarez, M. S., Mercé, J., & Balaguer, I. (2011). Motivational climate, approach-avoidance achievement goals and well-being in young soccer players. *Revista De Psicologia Del Deporte*, *20*(1), 149–164.

Cetinkalp, Z. K. (2012). Achievement goals and physical self-perceptions of adolescent athletes. *Social Behavior and Personality*, *40*(3), 473–480.

Chin, N. S., Khoo, S., & Low, W.Y. (2012). Self-determination and goal orientation in track and field. *Journal of Human Kinetics*, *33*, 151–161.

Cuevas, R., Garcia-Calvo, T., & Contreras, O. (2013). Motivational profiles in physical education: An approach from the 2×2 achievement goals theory. *Anales De Psicología*, *29*(3), 685–692.

Cunningham, G. B., & Xiang, P. (2008). Testing the mediating role of motivational climate in the relationship between achievement goals and satisfaction: Are the relationships invariant across sex? *Journal of Teaching in Physical Education*, *27*, 192–204.

Deci, E. L., & Ryan, R. M. (1985). *Intrinsic motivation and self-determination in human behavior*. New York: Plenum.

Diener, C. I., & Dweck, C. S. (1980). An analysis of learned helplessness: (II) The processing of success. *Journal of Personality and Social Psychology*, *39*, 940–952.

Dweck, C. S., Chui, C., & Hong, Y. (1995). Implicit theories: Elaboration and extension of the model. *Psychological Inquiry*, *6*(4), 322–333.

Elliot, A. J. (1999). Approach and avoidance motivation and achievement goals. *Educational Psychologist*, *34*, 169–189.

Elliot, A. J. (2005). A conceptual history of the achievement goal construct. In A. Elliot & C. Dweck (Eds.), *Handbook of competence and motivation*. New York: Guilford Press.

Elliot, A. J., & Church, M. A. (1997). A hierarchical model of approach and avoidance achievement motivation. *Journal of Personality and Social Psychology*, *72*, 218–232.

Elliot, A. J., & Harackiewicz, J. M. (1996). Approach and avoidance achievement goals and intrinsic motivation: A mediational analysis. *Journal of Personality and Social Psychology*, *70*, 461–475.

Elliot, A. J., & McGregor, H. A. (2001). A 2×2 achievement goal framework. *Journal of Personality and Social Psychology*, *80*, 501–519.

Elliot, A. J., Murayama, K., & Pekrun, R. (2011). 3×2 achievement goal model. *Journal of Educational Psychology*, *103*(3), 632–648.

Epstein, J. L. (1989). Family structures and students' motivation: A developmental perspective. In C. Ames & R. Ames (Eds.), *Research on motivation in education* (pp. 250–300). San Diego, CA: Academic Press.

Gao, Z., Podlog, L. W., & Harrison, L. (2012). College students' goal orientations, situational motivation and effort/persistence in physical activity classes. *Journal of Teaching in Physical Education*, *31*(3), 246–260.

Gao, Z., Xiang, P., Lochbaum, M., & Guan, J. (2013). The impact of achievement goals on cardiorespiratory fitness: Does self-efficacy make a difference? *Research Quarterly for Exercise and Sport*, *84*(3), 313–322.

Garn, A. C., & Sun, H. (2009). Approach-avoidance motivational profiles in early adolescence to a PACER fitness test. *Journal of Teaching in Physical Education*, *28*, 400–442.

Garn, A. C., Ware, D. R., & Solmon, M. A. (2011). Student engagement in high school physical education: Do social motivation orientations matter? *Journal of Teaching in Physical Education*, *30*(1), 84–98.

James, W. (1890). *The principles of psychology* (Vol. 1). New York: Holt.

Lee, M. J., Whitehead, J., Ntoumanis, N., & Hatzigeorgiadis, A. (2008). Relationships among values, achievement orientations, and attitudes in youth sports. *Journal of Sport & Exercise Psychology*, *30*(5), 588–610.

Lochbaum, M. R., Stevenson, S., & Hilario, D. (2009). Achievement goals, thoughts about intense physical activity, and exerted effort: A meditational analysis. *Journal of Sport Behavior*, *32*, 53–68.

McClelland, D. C. (1961). *The achieving society*. New York: Macmillan.

Murcia, J. A. M., Gimeno, E. C., & Gonzále-Cutre, D. (2010). The achievement goal and self-determination theories as predictors of dispositional flow in young athletes. *Anales de psicología*, *26*(2), 390–399.

Murray, H. A. (1938). *Explorations in personality*. New York: Oxford University Press.

Newton, M., Watson, D. L., Kim, M. S., & Beacham, A. O. (2006). Understanding motivation of underserved youth in physical activity settings. *Youth & Society*, *37*(3), 348–371.

Nicholls, J. G. (1984). Achievement motivation: Conceptions of ability, subjective experience, task choice, and performance. *Psychological Review*, *91*, 328–346.

Nicholls, J. G. (1989). *The competitive ethos and democratic education*. Cambridge, MA: Harvard University Press.

Nicholls, J. G., & Miller, A. T. (1983). The differentiation of the concepts of difficulty and ability. *Child Development*, *54*, 951–959.

Nien, C. L., & Duda, J. L. (2008). Antecedents and consequences of approach and avoidance achievement goals: A test of gender invariance. *Psychology of Sport and Exercise*, *9*, 352–372.

Ommundsen, Y. (2004). Self-handicapping related to task and performance approach and avoidance goals in physical education. *Journal of Applied Sport Psychology*, *16*(2), 183–197.

Papaioannou, A. G., Ampatzoglou, G., Kalogiannis, P., & Sagovits, A. (2008). Social agents, achievement goals, satisfaction and academic achievement in youth sport. *Psychology of Sport and Exercise*, *9*, 122–141.

Papaioannou, A. G., Zourbanos, N., Krommidas, C., & Amatzouglou, G. (2012). The place of achievement goals in the social context of sport: A comparison of Nicholls' and Elliot's models. In G. C. Roberts and D. C. Treasure (Eds.), *Advances in motivation in sport* (3rd edn) (pp. 59–90). Champaign, IL: Human Kinetic.

Pensgaard, A. M., & Roberts, G. C. (2000). The relationship between motivational climate, perceived ability and sources of distress among elite athletes. *Journal of Sport Sciences*, *18*, 191–200.

Roberts, G. C. (2012). Motivation in sport and exercise from an achievement goal theory perspective: After 30 years, where are we? In G. C. Roberts and D. C. Treasure (Eds.), *Advances in motivation in sport* (3rd edn) (pp. 5–58). Champaign, IL: Human Kinetics.

Roberts, G. C., & Treasure, D. C. (Eds.). (2012). *Advances in motivation in sport* (3rd edn). Champaign, IL: Human Kinetics.

Sage, L., & Kavussanu, M. (2007). The effects of goal involvement on moral behavior in an experimentally manipulated competitive setting. *Journal of Sport and Exercise Psychology*, *2*, 190–207.

Smith, M., Duda, J. L., Allen, J., & Hall, H. (2002). Contemporary measures of approach and avoidance goal orientations: Similarities and differences. *British Journal of Educational Psychology*, *2*, 154–189.

Stoeber, J., Uphill, M. A., & Hotham, S. (2009). Predicting race performance in triathlon: The role of perfectionism, achievement goals, and personal goal setting. *Journal of Sport & Exercise Psychology*, *31*(2), 211–245.

Stuntz, C. P., & Weiss, M. R. (2009). Achievement goal orientations and motivational outcomes in youth sport: The role of social orientations. *Psychology of Sport and Exercise*, *10*(2), 255–262.

Wang, C. K. J., Biddle, S. J. H., & Elliot, A. J. (2007). The 2×2 achievement goal framework in a physical education context. *Psychology of Sport and Exercise*, *8*, 147–168.

Wang, C. K. J., Koh, K. T., & Chatzisarantis, N. (2009). An intra-individual analysis of players' perceived coaching behaviours, psychological needs, and achievement goals. *International Journal of Sports Science & Coaching*, *4*, 177–192.

Wang, C. K. J., Lim, B. S., Aplin, N. G., Chia, Y. H. M., McNeil, M., & Tan, W. K. (2008). Students' attitudes and perceived purposes of physical education in Singapore: Perspectives from a 2×2 achievement goal framework. *European Physical Education Review*, *14*(1), 51–70.

Yli-Piipari, S., Barkoukis, V., Jaakkola, T., & Liukkonen, J. (2013). The effect of physical education goal orientations and enjoyment in adolescent physical activity: A parallel process latent growth analysis. *Sport, Exercise, and Performance Psychology*, *2*(1), 15–31.

44

MOTIVATION AS A LEARNING STRATEGY

Haichun Sun, UNIVERSITY OF SOUTH FLORIDA, USA

Motivation is a central construct that has been proved to enhance K-12 students' learning. During the learning process, some students encounter difficulties and obstacles that may discourage them from putting forth maximum effort. It is only natural that students who understand how to motivate themselves may learn more effectively. From this perspective, the motivation process, itself, can be understood as a unique learning strategy (Chen, 2013; Wang, Chapter 41, this volume). I will begin this chapter with an overview of selected contemporary motivation constructs or theories that are widely studied and applied in education, such as goal theory, interest-based theory, and self-determination theory. In the second section, I will review and critique selected PE research examining motivational strategies related to student learning. Finally, I will discuss the future of PE motivation research with respect to student learning.

Historical overview

Learning

Historically, conceptualizations of learning have evolved from a behaviorist to a cognitive perspective. Originally derived from British empiricist notions of knowledge acquisition (Reynolds, Sinatra, & Jetton, 1996), behaviorists conceptualize learning as a process of behavioral conditioning and reconditioning (Alexander, 2005). Although modern behaviorist learning theory acknowledges learning as a process involving more than reinforced behavioral experiences, the theory leaves little room to explain mind functioning (Reynolds et al., 1996) or the role and function of active thinking and reasoning in behavior (Alexander, 2005). During the 1950s~1960s, psychologists worked to clarify and explain the nature of learning (Shuell, 1986), generating new theories, such as constructivism.

One of the most noticeable and influential constructivist learning theories is social constructivism (Vygotsky, 1978). Social constructivism claims "learning is a necessary and universal aspect of the process of developing culturally organized, specifically human psychological function" (Vygotsky, 1978, p. 90). In other words, learning occurs when the learner internalizes the social experience by interacting with others. Vygotsky's concept of "Zone of Proximal Development (ZPD)" further emphasizes the role that knowledgeable and/or experienced others play in optimizing social interaction with novice learners to enhance learning.

Learning in physical education

Physical education is a unique discipline in education in that it concerns development of the psychomotor as well as the cognitive and affective domains (Rink, 2003). Learning theories in PE also have made the transition from behaviorism to cognitivism. Although curricula focus, in part, on motor learning, researchers agree that psychomotor learning is inseparable from the cognitive process (Jewett, Bain, & Ennis, 1995). In general, PE learning is defined as a relatively permanent behavioral change resulting from physical movement experiences associated with cognitive understandings of that movement (Rink, 2001). The concept of learning in physical education includes engagement in many physical tasks, cognitive understanding of the movements involved, and recognition of the importance of social interaction.

To further articulate PE learning, Ennis (2003) proposed a value-context model to describe relevant factors "directly affecting what, how, and how much students learn in physical education" (p. 114). In this model, student learning is central to schooling and directly influenced by the curriculum planning and teaching process. The planned curriculum and instruction inform the nature of the school context, which, in turn, influences student responses to the curriculum and instruction. This cycle emphasizes the *process* of curriculum decision-making and how curriculum determines and facilitates student learning in particular school and class environments. A curriculum and the context it creates, however, are influenced by the values and beliefs that are held by students, families, teachers, peer groups, and school administrators. These values and beliefs impact student learning directly. Lastly, the global and pervasive social environment in PE, defined as the societal climate of expectations and performance, ultimately determines specific learning outcomes. Evolution and changes to the U.S. National Standards in the past 20 years (National Association for Sport and Physical Education, 1995, 2004; Society of Health and Physical Education [SHAPE], 2014) have exemplified the tenets elaborated in the model. During the last two decades, societal expectation for health promotion and control of childhood obesity gradually has played a larger role in the standards shaping PE learning outcomes. This change, to a degree, has begun to redefine learning and the role of motivation in PE.

Motivation

Motivation is a mental process that energizes human beings to engage in activities and accomplish their goals (Pintrich & Schunk, 2002). Historically, motivation has played a different role in behaviorism and cognitivism. Behavioral theorists view motivation as a change in the frequency of a behavioral occurrence or response driven by stimuli external to the person. From the behavioristic viewpoint, motivation reflects a high possibility that an expected behavior will appear as people respond to external demands. In behaviorism individuals' feelings and thoughts are considered of little relevance in this stimulus-response loop. Conversely, cognitive theorists view motivation as an internal process that directs behaviors based on active, conscientious interaction among beliefs, values, affects, attributions, goals, perceptions of competence, and social comparison (Pintrich & Schunk, 2002).

Through the years, motivation has been conceptualized as having three psychological functions: (a) energizing or activating behavior (e.g., what engages learners or turns them away from learning); (b) directing behavior (e.g., why one activity is chosen over another); and (c) regulating behavior sustainability (e.g., why one persists toward a goal) (Alderman, 2008).

In education, students' motivation is characterized by their task choice, practice persistence, effort level when completing assignments, and demonstrated achievement (Wigfield & Eccles,

2002). From the cognitive perspective, educational motivation research supports the assumption that these characteristics are based on students' (a) achievement goal orientations (Nicholls, 1984), (b) interest in the content and environment (Renninger, Hidi, & Krapp, 1992), and (c) determination of behaviors (Deci & Ryan, 1985). In the past three decades, scholars have studied motivation theories involving these constructs or motivators in education and PE. In the following sections, I will briefly review theories integrally linked to learning knowledge and skills needed for active and healthful living.

Theoretical frameworks

Optimal learning occurs when students' needs for knowledge acquisition, motivation, and other desired educational outcomes are satisfied (Alexander, 2005). Learning is optimized when learners possess motivation to learn. Therefore, motivation is one of the most critical and important necessities for learners. Researchers have developed a number of theoretical models in the past 30 years in an attempt to better understand and explain motivated learning behavior and process (e.g., Sansone & Harackiewicz, 2000; Wigfield & Eccles, 2002).

Achievement Goal Theory (AGT)

Since 1980, researchers have articulated contemporary conceptions of achievement goals as students' goal orientations and goal structures within social environments that impact learning (Urdan, 1997). Research focuses on the nature of achievement goals including both a personal component (the goal that the student pursues) and a situational component (the goals students perceive as important in the environment such as learning objectives) that may orient students toward different achievement goals (Kaplan, Middleton, Urdan, & Midgley, 2002).

Goal orientation

Achievement goals emphasize the students' meaning or purpose for engaging in an achievement behavior (Molden & Dweck, 2000; Nicholls, 1984). Ames (1992) defines achievement goals as integrated patterns that combine beliefs, affect, and attribution to influence individual behavior intentions. In general, the achievement goals can determine individuals' ways to approach, participate in, and/or react to achievement related activities.

Achievement goals have been operationalized within a dual-goal structure featuring task/mastery and ego/performance-involved goals (Nicholls, 1984). More recently achievement goal researchers have extended the dual-goal theory to encompass a multiple goals construct. Elliot (1999) proposed that within mastery or performance goals, students take either an approaching or avoiding strategy to define and choose personally meaningful goals. Within the performance-approach goals strategy, students define achievement as demonstrating high ability in reference to peers' achievement, while the performance-avoidance goals lead students to avoid demonstrating low ability or appearing stupid or dumb. When the approach-avoidance distinction is applied to mastery goals (Elliot, 1997; Pintrich, 2000), students with mastery-avoidance goals attempt to avoid misunderstanding or demonstrating inability to master the material (Pintrich, 2003). Although motivation function within multiple goal constructs is complex, researchers have shown that the 2×2 achievement goals matrix effectively predicts and explains most motivational processes and outcomes (e.g., effort, persistence, performance; see Elliot, 2005).

Goal structure

In addition to students' personal goals, the achievement goal orientation also explores characteristics of learning environments that may influence students' goal orientation. Ames (1992) emphasized that care be taken in learning task design, use of rewards, evaluation, or recognition, and distribution of authority or responsibility. She argues that tasks characterized by variety, diversity, and challenge are more likely to encourage learner interest in learning, promoting mastery goal orientation. Goal structures holistically define the motivational climate in a learning context (Treasure, 2001). Basically, a mastery-oriented learning environment is related to adaptive or positive cognition, motivation, and affect patterns.

Interest Theory

Interest has been conceptualized as both individual/personal and situational (Krapp, Hidi, & Renninger, 1992). Individual interest refers to a person's psychological disposition in preference for an activity or action. Individual interest is a relatively stable and enduring disposition. Conversely, situational interest is defined as a psychological state elicited by aspects of the immediate environment, such as ways in which learning tasks are organized and presented.

Individual interest is specific to each individual. Renninger (2000) asserted that individual interest derives from stored knowledge and value. For individual interest to emerge, sufficient knowledge about the object is a necessary and sufficient condition. Students will be highly motivated and engaged in a learning task if they have high individual interest. From a practical educational perspective, however, Hidi and Anderson (1992) argue that using student individual interest as a primary motivational tool can be difficult because of the diverse nature of individual interest.

Situational interest, on the other hand, is characterized by spontaneity. A situationally interesting activity can immediately attract learners' attention, involve them in the process, and provide instant, positive feelings toward the activity (Hidi & Harackiewicz, 2000). Given its spontaneity, situational interest is considered a motivator that the teacher can control to some extent (Schraw, Flowerday, & Lehman, 2001). In PE, Chen, Darst, and Pangrazi (1999) validated a situational interest model characterized by novelty, challenge, attention demand, exploration, and instant enjoyment.

Self-Determination Theory (SDT)

In SDT, needs for competence, autonomy, and relatedness serve as the cornerstones of human motivation (Deci & Ryan, 1985). These needs provide a fundamental source of mental energy for human behaviors manifested in person-activity interactions in an environment, such as a classroom, gymnasium, or playground. Specifically, the first need, *competence*, refers to satisfaction in one's ability and feelings of effectiveness in ongoing activities. Perceptions of competence are positively related to intrinsic motivation. Deci and Ryan (1985) define *autonomy*, the second need, as the degree to which individuals perceive themselves as the origin or behavior source responsible for the initiation of the behavior. When experiencing autonomy, individuals regulate their behaviors by initiating and directing actions (Ryan & Powelson, 1991). Ryan and Deci (2000) define the third need, *relatedness*, as the extent to which individuals feel connected to others through activities and their sense of belonging both to their community and other individuals.

Deci and Ryan (e.g., 1985, 2000) conceptualized self-determination as a motivation process with three basic states, intrinsic motivation, extrinsic motivation, and amotivation. *Intrinsically* motivated individuals engage in activities both for the sake of the activity, itself, and the satisfaction inherent in performing the activity (Deci & Ryan, 1985). Intrinsic motivation is the fuel for action (Grolnick, Gurland, Jacob, & DeCourcey, 2002). It derives from person–activity interaction that people find interesting, optimally challenging, or aesthetically pleasing (Ryan & Deci, 2002) and resides in people's needs for autonomy, competence, and relatedness.

In reality, however, people often need to be motivated through means other than interest, challenge, or pleasant experiences. Motivation leading to enhanced performance in activities with inherently low interest, low challenge, and few pleasant experiences is referred to as *extrinsic motivation* (Deci & Ryan, 1985). Additionally, the absence of motivation or situations where an individual lacks the intention to act is described as *amotivation* (Ryan & Deci, 2000). An individual with amotivation feels incompetent, does not value what he/she does, does not expect a desired outcome, or feels lack of control in an environment (Deci & Ryan, 1985; Ryan & Deci, 2000).

Basic needs and the learning environment

Although self-determination is an individual-centered process, its development depends on a supportive environment, especially for school-age children. A hierarchical motivation model (Ryan & Deci, 2000; Vallerand & Losier, 1999; Vallerand & Rousseau, 2001) incorporating the fundamental SDT tenets delineates the sequential pattern of motivational processes. From this perspective, social environments lead to innate need satisfaction, which in turn leads to different types of motivational consequences. In general, a social environment can be autonomy-supportive or externally controlling, either facilitating or undermining intrinsic motivation. Therefore, school/classroom environments that satisfy students' needs for autonomy will enhance or facilitate their intrinsic motivation, resulting in adaptive behavior or outcomes.

In summary, contemporary researchers in achievement motivation have focused on a few powerful theories to explain students' learning-related motivation. It is clear that students can adopt different goals, interest, and regulations and adapt them to teacher-designed classroom climates or structures. The research forms a basis from which children's and adolescents' motivation to learn in PE can be studied and understood. In the next section, I will discuss current theoretically based research findings and their implications for learning.

Current trends, issues, and implications

Learning environments and climate research

Prominent motivation theories (e.g., STD, goal theory) are based on the assumption that teachers can create a motivating learning environment leading to positive/adaptive student behaviors and outcomes. For example, SDT researchers are studying social contexts that fulfill students' innate psychological needs enhancing self-determined motivation. When studying AGT, Ames and Ames (1984) suggested that teachers share authority or responsibility with students to support their autonomy in the learning process. Ames (1992) recommended teachers create a learning-conducive mastery goal environment by placing high value on meaningful mastery tasks rather than on competition, instead emphasizing self-reference standards in evaluation and offering opportunities for self-directed learning.

Self-determination research

To study SDT in PE learning contexts, researchers incorporated AGT to investigate students' self-determined motivation and perceived learning climates (mastery, performance, and origin) (Ntoumanis, 2001, 2005; Standage, Duda, & Ntoumanis, 2005). More specifically, researchers hypothesized that a mastery environment characterized by cooperation, self-referenced improvement, and opportunities to make choice/decisions will help students satisfy needs for relatedness, competence, and autonomy, respectively. Consequently the mastery environment will lead to greater motivation and achievement. Research evidence has revealed strong relationships between mastery contexts and satisfaction of the three innate needs. The performance climate, on the other hand, was not related to student perceived autonomy or relatedness. Overall, research findings confirm that the autonomy-supportive environment contributed to student need satisfaction of autonomy, competence, and relatedness (Standage, Duda, & Ntoumanis, 2003). From a curricular perspective, findings support constructivist curricular approaches in which PE learners are actively constructing content meanings and understandings as they interact socially. In this environment students are likely to master knowledge and skills, learn to empower themselves to construct shared meanings, and identify the most meaningful learning processes to maximize learning (Pollard, Thiessen, & Filer, 1997).

Satisfying the three needs, however, may yield complex PE outcomes. In recent years the childhood obesity crisis has encouraged public health advocates to champion the role of PE in public health. Promoting and increasing moderate-to-vigorous physical activity (MVPA) in PE has become a curricular strategy to achieve this mission (Sallis et al., 2012). Pedagogy scholars, in turn, have examined a range of teaching strategies to determine the most effective SDT-based interventions strategies to meet this goal. For example, Lonsdale et al. (2013) randomly assigned teachers and students to one of four conditions: 1) explaining relevance – explaining activity rationale and importance as related to students' lives; 2) providing choice – providing students with from two to four PA choices within the lesson; 3) complete free choice – providing students with needed equipment and limited teacher instructions; and 4) usual practice. Results revealed that, although students' perception of autonomy increased during both choice-based interventions (# 2 & 3 above), their self-determined motivation did not increase in any of the teaching strategy conditions. Free choice (#3) led to the greatest MVPA when compared with other conditions; but it did not foster motor skill development and health knowledge acquisition/mastery. Thus, preliminary evidence suggests that the role of SDT as a learning strategy needs additional empirical examination to understand its effect on learning.

Recently, researchers have cautioned that not all SDT tenets may be supported in empirical PE research. Gillison, Standage, and Skevington (2013) tested five different PE social contexts to examine the effect of intrinsic vs. extrinsic goals on outcomes, motivation, effort, enjoyment, and future intention to exercise on learner motivation and behavior outcomes. They compared the outcomes in the following different experimentally manipulated PE conditions: 1) autonomy supportive, intrinsic goal content; 2) controlling, intrinsic goal content; 3) autonomy supportive, extrinsic goal content; 4) controlling, extrinsic goal content; and 5) neutral climate, no goal content provided (control group). The intrinsic goal condition emphasized the goal of being physically fit and healthy, while the extrinsic goal emphasized looking good or outperforming others. Results showed that autonomy support and an intrinsic goal focus positively predicted measured outcomes, including motivation, effort, enjoyment, and future intention to exercise. The extrinsic goal focus, however, led students to the positive outcome of a greater appreciation for lesson values and stronger future exercise intention. Findings from these fitness and exercise-oriented lessons were contrary to theoretical SDT assumptions that typically apply in learning-oriented lessons. Scholars assume a negative relation (in learning-oriented lessons) between the controlling extrinsic goal and outcome. Although these findings were contrary to SDT tenets, they did not completely contradict previous findings (Gillison et al., 2013). Gillison et al. (2013) pointed out that these findings suggest that promoting extrinsic goals for an existing activity might have short-term positive effects on individuals' behavior and perceptions. These findings also suggest that PE researchers consider evaluating the longer-term effects of ongoing extrinsic goals/pursuits in future SDT classroom research.

AGT research

Another important strand of research on environment is from the AGT perspective. PE researchers examining achievement goal climate have provided strong evidence that PE teachers can manipulate goal climate. Todorovich and Curtner-Smith (2003), for example, manipulated achievement goal climate when investigating the influence of mastery and performance goal climates on third grade students' goal orientations (n = 80). Students were assigned to task or ego climate groups or a control group. The findings indicated that students in the task climate condition strengthened their task orientations, while those taught within an ego-involving climate strengthened their ego orientation. Interestingly, neither treatment impacted the other orientation.

Similar findings have been reported in a PE curriculum intervention study in which researchers created a task/mastery involved climate in 88 lessons (Digelidis, Papaioannou, Laparidis, & Christodoulidis, 2003). PE teachers taught junior high school students (n = 262) using a task-involving curriculum, while the control group (n = 521) was taught an unrelated curriculum. The students' goal orientations and perception of motivational climate were measured before and after the intervention. Results showed that students in the task-involved curriculum reported a stronger task-involvement climate and weaker ego-involvement climate than did those in the control curriculum. The students in the task goal-oriented climate had higher post task goal orientation scores and lower post ego orientation scores. This research evidence suggests that PE teachers can create and control the achievement goal climates and that students adapt to the desired goal orientation.

Researchers have demonstrated a direct connection between motivational climate and student motivated learning behavior (Standage et al., 2003; Theodosiou & Papaioannou, 2006). It appears that a mastery/task-involvement climate leads to positive motivation and behavior in learning. Specifically, Standage et al. (2003) found that students in a mastery goal-oriented environment tend to achieve high satisfaction levels with the mastery learning process using relevant metacognitive strategies for learning. In another example, Theodosiou and Papaioannou (2006) conducted a study involving 182 elementary, 365 junior high, and 235 senior high school students. In this study, although the researchers observed moderate positive relationships between mastery/task goal orientation and metacognitive learning strategies, they found no meaningful relationships between the strategies and the performance/ego-goal orientation. They did find that PE students with high task goal orientation were intrinsically motivated, valued the process of learning, and were likely to adopt self-regulatory cognitions and behaviors.

Research has not provided conclusive evidence on the relationship between the goal orientations, student motivation, and learning behavior outcomes. Although Shen, Chen, Scrabis, and Tolley (2003) found that students' goal orientations were not directly related to student in-class physical activity, other studies have indicated that mastery/task goal orientation strongly predicted students' in-class participation in MVPA (Chen & Shen, 2004; Dempsey, Kimiecik, &

Horn, 1993). Mastery/task goal orientation was also found to predict positive motivational or behavioral outcomes in some studies. Sarrazin, Roberts, Cury, Biddle, and Famose (2002) found that mastery goal-oriented students in a climbing task exerted more effort and performed better than did performance goal-oriented students.

The goal orientation-learning relationship, however, has not been observed in other studies. For example, Solmon and Boone (1993) found there was no difference in skill improvement between students with different goal orientations. Their findings suggested that in PE achievement goal orientations were not predictive of skill achievement. Berlant and Weiss (1997) further confirmed that students' motor skill acquisition was not associated with students' achievement goal orientations. In addition, Shen and colleagues (Chen & Shen, 2004; Shen et al., 2003) indicated that students' goal orientations were not directly related to skill and knowledge test outcomes. These results indicate it may be premature to conclude that the mastery/task goal orientation is superior to ego goal orientation with respect to inducing PE students' learning. Moreover, PE research suggests that performance goals may not be as maladaptive as Pintrich (2003) asserted in the dual-goal theory. For example, Wang, Chatzisarantis, Spray, and Biddle (2002) found that PE students' high performance/ego goal orientation predicted high levels of motivation toward leisure time physical activity (PA) participation when associated with high-perceived competence.

Researchers have examined motivational function within multiple goal constructs (approach and avoidance) on four goal profiles held by PE students: mastery, mastery avoidance, performance, and performance avoidance. Wang, Biddle, and Elliot (2007), for example, identified goal profiles through cluster analysis with a sample of Singapore adolescents (n = 995). Results revealed four distinct goal profiles: moderate, low, high, and mastery achievement goals. Each goal profile had a unique impact on PE students' motivational outcomes. As Wang et al. (2007) illustrated, the high category, consisting of high scores on all four achievement goals, were linked to the highest perceived competence and relatedness, lowest amotivation, highest reported effort, highest participation, least boredom, and greatest enjoyment in PE activities. Similarly, Garn and Sun (2009) examined the integration of achievement and social goal profiles with a group of U.S. middle school students (n = 214). A cluster analysis resulted in three goal profiles: high goals, low achievement goals and moderate social goals, and low social goals. Students with high goals reported significantly higher effort than students in other goal profile groups. Learning/performance outcome results, however, did not indicate any differences in PE students' goal profiles. Specifically, there were not statistically significant differences on students' PACER test performance across the three goal-profile groups.

It is worth pointing out that in both the Wang et al. (2007) and Garn and Sun (2009) studies, high avoidance goals did not necessarily lead to negative consequences when co-existing with other goals. Although Elliot (1997) hypothesized that in PE avoidance goals were associated with maladaptive outcomes, these findings seem to suggest a more complex and multidimensional goal structure. More studies are needed to enhance our understandings of goal constructs' motivational functions as related to PE learning.

Interest Theory

Researchers hypothesize that PE students' individual interest could be a significant and positive predictor of student performance (Chen & Darst, 2001; Shen et al., 2003; Zhu, Chen, & Parrott, 2014). Likewise, they acknowledge that, although situational interest appears to explain only a small amount of variance in student performance (Zhu et al., 2009; Zhu et al., 2014) it may positively influence students' learning strategy application. Shen and Chen (2006) found that situational interest was associated with PE students' cognitive efforts during the learning process. Guided by the Model of Domain Learning (MDL; Alexander, 2005), Shen and Chen (2006) explored the interrelations among middle school PE students' knowledge, interests, and use of learning strategies. They found a direct, significant relationship between situational interest and students' use of learning strategies. The researchers further reported that the association was independent of students' individual interest, suggesting that situational interest may have a significant impact on students' application of learning strategies regardless of their individual interest in the content.

There is very limited evidence, however, to support the relationship between situational interest and students' learning outcomes. In an earlier study, Shen et al. (2003) found no association between middle school students' (n = 57) knowledge and skill acquisition and situational interest. Similarly, in a more recent study, Zhu et al. (2009) measured third-grade students' (n = 670) situational interest, workbook problem solving performance, and knowledge gain and found that situational interest contributed little to students' knowledge gain in cardio-respiratory fitness content and workbook performance.

Although situational interest might not directly impact PE learning outcomes, researchers have hypothesized that it may have practical meaning to PE students. In general, different activities elicit different levels of situational interest. For example, Sun (2012) compared elementary school students' situational interest in an exergaming/active video game unit and a traditional fitness unit. The results showed that students' situational interest in exergaming was significantly higher than in the fitness unit at the beginning and end of instruction. Consistent with interest theory, Sun's studies (2012, 2013) revealed that students' situational interest declines over time regardless of their initial interest. Therefore, it is important for PE teachers to carefully design learning tasks to sustain students' situational interest.

Most PE learning tasks consist of both a physical movement component and an often neglected cognitive component (Schmidt & Lee, 2009). How a task is designed may offer different levels of situational interest to students. In a study examining the effects of different cognitive and physical learning task demands on situational interest, Chen and Darst (2001) found that cognitive demand in a physical activity greatly contributed to the level of situational interest. Middle school students in their sample (n = 242) considered tasks with high cognitive demand to be highly situationally interesting, regardless of the physical demands. Students judged tasks with both low cognitive and low physical demands particularly low in situational interest.

Recent studies examining cardiovascular tests also have provided evidence to help PE teachers choose appropriate activities. For instance, Zhu (2013) compared students' perceived situational interest in the PACER and the One-mile Run. In this study, many students reported higher situational interest in PACER than in the One-mile Run. Recently, Zhu et al. (2014) examined relationships between students' personal and situational interest and performance in the same two aerobic fitness tests. The results showed that, if adolescents perceive increased challenge, their performance in PACER and One-mile Run decreases. PE teachers can use these findings in task design and test administration to enhance students' situational interest in these tasks.

Self-determined motivation and learning

Deci, Koestner, and Ryan (1999) revealed that intangible rewards (e.g., positive verbal feedback) enhanced intrinsic motivation, whereas tangible rewards undermined it. The exception to this finding occurred when tangible rewards were given unexpectedly (without students' prior knowledge). Silverman, Tyson, and Krampitz (1992) investigated the relationship between PE teacher feedback and student achievement when learning the volleyball serve and forearm pass. Their findings suggest that both positive feedback (intangible rewards, praise, or reinforcement) and affective feedback (intended as motivation or to improve attitude) was significantly related to students' achievement. Silverman et al. (1992) proposed that positive or affective feedback might motivate students to continue practicing skills.

Koka and Hein's (2003) study conducted with 783 schoolchildren aged 12–15 in Estonia also examined the impact of teachers' feedback on students' intrinsic motivation. Results suggested that positive general feedback was a significant predictor for all observed dimensions of intrinsic motivation (i.e., enjoyment-interest, effort-importance, and competence), especially for perceived competence. In addition, they found a positive relationship between teachers' feedback directed toward knowledge and performance gains and students' perceived enjoyment-interest. Interestingly, the relationship between perceived positive specific feedback and intrinsic motivation as well as perceived competence was not evident in this study. Therefore, Koka and Hein (2003) suggested that PE teachers might need to provide positive general feedback or feedback concerning how to perform the skill to enhance both perceived competence and interest in activities as well as to facilitate intrinsic motivation. Moreover, they pointed out that when students are in the early learning stage, teachers might need to avoid using feedback that is too specific and precise, which might overload learners and interfere with the learning process.

In PE, intrinsic motivation is a predictor for many positive outcomes. These outcomes include concentration level (Ntoumanis, 2005; Standage et al., 2005), preference for attempting challenging tasks, positive affect (i.e., happy, satisfied, excited, and relaxed) (Standage et al., 2005), intention to be physically active after school (Ntoumanis, 2001, 2005; Standage et al., 2003), and effort (Ntoumanis, 2001). Not surprisingly, intrinsic motivation has a negative association with unpleasant feelings or emotions (e.g., feelings of disappointment, embarrassment) (Ntoumanis, 2005).

Despite theoretical hypotheses that external regulation would lead to maladaptive affective or undesirable cognitive consequences, no relationships have been established between external regulation and outcome measures, such as effort in class, intention for after-school physical activity (Ntoumanis, 2001), concentration level, and preferences for challenging tasks in PE (Standage et al., 2005). These PE findings suggest that, although external regulation may not yield adaptive or maladaptive outcomes, it does predict students' feeling of boredom (Ntoumanis, 2001), suggesting an association between strong teacher control and increased boredom in students.

When tangible learning outcomes were measured in SDT studies, the motivational function of self-determined motivation has remained unclear. Sun and Chen (2010) examined the relationship between sixth grade PE students' (n = 242) self-determined motivation and learning. Learning outcomes were students' health-related fitness knowledge and two motor skills (basketball control dribbling and badminton striking). Structural equation modeling results indicated that amotivation was negatively related to health-related fitness knowledge gain. Neither intrinsic nor extrinsic motivations impacted knowledge and skill achievement. Although students in this study reported high levels of self-determined motivation and low levels of amotivation, high motivation did not positively contribute to their learning achievement. The discrepancies in these studies may be due to different designs (i.e., correlational vs. experimental) or to the research setting where achievement in knowledge and skills may or may not have been the instructional focus. These inconsistent findings challenge researchers to continue their SDT studies to advance our understanding of the relationship between self-determined motivation and learning.

Future directions

Extensive research examining motivation has provided evidence that teachers can manipulate achievement goal orientation climates to facilitate learning. Further, they can adjust the autonomy-supportive environment and enhance situational interest. In so doing, they can help learners align personal goals with learning goals, regulate their learning behaviors, and develop interest in PE. There is a need, however, for more and stronger evidence relating the teachers' strategies and effort to student learning.

Rink (2001) defines learning as a relatively permanent behavioral change resulting from the experience of physical movement associated with cognitive understanding of the movement. Cognitive knowledge and motor skill acquisition are the central indicators defining student learning represented by student performance on knowledge and skill achievement tests (Chen & Ennis, 2004).

Student learning in PE has not been a central focus in research (Rovegno, 2006). In many studies reviewed in this chapter, researchers seldom included knowledge and skill acquisition as outcome measures. Instead, motivational correlates, such as students' affection, effort, concentration, and intention toward after-school PA, have been the main outcome measures. Although understanding these outcomes is helpful, research that emphasizes content-centered competence outcomes, such as knowledge and skill attainment, will be useful and meaningful for PE curricula that serve the academic mission of schooling.

Motivation researchers in PE share the core elements of social-cognitive tradition emphasizing that perceptions developed through social interactions are the central motivation source (Bandura, 1986). These interactions either motivate or demotivate learners by creating a sense of competence, defining successes, and generating interests. Emerging research evidence appears to suggest the motivation sources can be content specific (Chen, Martin, Ennis, & Sun, 2008). Future research is needed to identify content-relevant motivation sources that facilitate student development of a range of learning strategies consistent with the specific knowledge and skills to be mastered.

Theories discussed in this chapter generally propose that motivation is a process that learners adapt to external environments. Motivation is an innate mental process residing within a person that can be called upon as a resource for learning strategy development (Hidi & Harackiewicz, 2000). Relying on these resources, students may develop learning strategies associated with either adaptive or maladaptive AGT learning goals. These may be advantageous when enhancing personally meaningful outcomes (task values or interests) or leveraging challenges from the learning environment (SDT self-regulations). Understanding student motivation as learning strategies enables researchers and teachers to comprehend how students engage in learning to address environmental influences. This integrated, multidimensional theoretical perspective may help clarify the relationship between PE students' motivation and learning (Chen, Chen, & Zhu, 2012; Chen & Ennis, 2004; Pintrich, 2003). Well-designed descriptive studies using systematic or naturalistic observation tools will be needed in the near future to understand the internalization process as well as the interaction between motivation and learning (Shen, Chen, & Guan, 2007).

As a school subject, PE has emphasized the development of a healthy, physically active lifestyle. Accordingly, students must master a body of disciplinary knowledge that integrates biological-medical sciences, social-psychological sciences, and cultural humanities to achieve the goal of becoming physically literate (SHAPE, 2014). Because motivation plays important roles in students' learning, from a learning-centered perspective, motivation should be "linked explicitly to ways of knowing, understanding, and constructing meaning" (Oldfather & Dahl,

1994, p. 139). To facilitate the internalization process for optimal motivation, the PE teachers should provide students with social support to enhance learning (Deci & Ryan, 1985; Ryan & Deci, 2000). Future studies are needed to identify strategies that will assist students to learn more effectively in externally (teacher) controlled social environments, permitting them to internalize healthy, active lifestyle-related values and behaviors. Intervention studies can be a viable approach to investigate complex interactions among learning environments, curriculum/ task, motivation, and learning.

Summary of key findings

- The concept of learning is changing to reflect a deeper understanding of the relationship between cognition and behavior.
- Although PE learning often is behavioral, in-depth and relevant cognitive knowledge about the science of physical activity serves as a guide to students' decision-making and physically active behavior.
- Research on achievement goal orientations indicates that a mastery-goal adaptive motivation process can be an effective learning strategy to enhance students' focus on the learning processes.
- Research on the achievement goal climate demonstrates that teachers can successfully nurture a student's mastery goal orientation by creating a mastery goal-oriented learning environment.
- Researchers have confirmed that teachers can manipulate situational interest in curriculum planning and task design. Clearly, situational interest is an effective teaching strategy to attract students immediately to situationally interesting tasks regardless of their personal interest. Research findings, however, have not confirmed its effectiveness as a learning strategy to enhance student achievement.
- SDT research has strong potential to help students develop autonomous learning strategies. Findings have shown that teacher support for the three basic needs for autonomy, competence, and relatedness is effective in enhancing students' motivation to learn.
- Additionally, SDT research has demonstrated a possibility to develop self-regulated learning strategies to internalize the values of a desired behavior.
- Taken together, PE motivation researchers have built a substantial body of research supporting the hypothesis that PE students are motivated. However, the magnitude of each construct's motivational function may vary based on the role and description of context in this research.
- Of most concern in research examining PE motivation is researchers' outcome measure choices.
- Researchers have rarely studied learning variables, such as process measures (e.g., time on task, physical activity intensity) or achievement measures (e.g., knowledge or skill test, performance records). Thus researchers have assumed connections between students and achievement and have not adequately tested this relationship.
- Further, researchers have not explicitly and sufficiently studied students' learning strategies in parallel with motivation strategies.
- Future researchers should focus not only on the motivational correlates (e.g., affection, effort, etc.) but also learning behavior correlates (e.g., time on task, physical intensity, completion of written assignments) and learning achievement to further understand learning strategies students may adopt as their motivation outcomes.

Reflective questions for discussion

1. What is the common theoretical basis for all achievement motivation theories? Discuss why this common basis is so important when studying achievement motivation in education, in general, and in PE in particular.
2. SDT is a comprehensive theory that encompasses the functions of other achievement motivation theories. One of the most important SDT tenets is to provide individuals the opportunity to be autonomous (to own the decision, action, etc.) in their settings. Given that schools reflect tightly controlled environments, what strategies would be most effective in promoting autonomy while still providing an orderly learning environment?
3. Researchers have observed the link between motivation levels and learning achievement in classroom-based research, but rarely in PE. What limits PE researchers from establishing this critical link to fully understand the power of student motivation? What suggestions can you make for future research?
4. Students' PE motivation and their motivation in after-school settings may require different mental processes. For example, the PE motivation process can derive and be dominated by perceived competence, whereas the motivation in an after-school setting can be driven completely by individual interest. To what extent do motivation mechanisms/strategies learned in PE transfer to outside school settings making physically active behavior sustainable? Use research evidence to support your conclusion.

References

Alderman, M. K. (2008). *Motivation for achievement: Possibilities for teaching and learning* (3rd edn). New York: Routledge.

Alexander, P. A. (2005). *Psychology in learning and instruction*. Columbus, OH: Prentice-Hall.

Ames, C. (1992). Classrooms: Goals, structures, and student motivation. *Journal of Educational Psychology, 84*, 261–271.

Ames, C., & Ames, R. (1984). Goal structures and motivation. *The Elementary School Journal, 85*, 39–52.

Bandura, A. (1986). *Social foundations of thought and action: A social cognitive theory*. Englewood Cliffs, NJ: Prentice-Hall.

Berlant, A. R., & Weiss, M. R. (1997). Goal orientation and the modeling process: An individual's focus on form and outcome. *Research Quarterly for Exercise and Sport, 68*, 317–330.

Chen, A. (2013). Special Topic: Top 10 research questions related to children physical activity motivation. *Research Quarterly for Exercise and Sport, 84*, 441–447.

Chen, A., & Darst, P. W. (2001). Situational interest in physical education: A function of learning task design. *Research Quarterly for Exercise and Sport, 72*, 150–164.

Chen, A., Darst, P. W., & Pangrazi, R. P. (1999). What constitutes situational interest? Validating a construct in physical education. *Measurement in Physical Education and Exercise Science, 3*, 157–180.

Chen, A., & Ennis, C. D. (2004). Goal, interest, and learning in physical education. *The Journal of Educational Research, 97*, 329–338.

Chen, A., Martin, R., Ennis, C. D., & Sun, H. (2008). Content specificity of expectancy beliefs and task values in elementary physical education. *Research Quarterly for Exercise and Sport, 79*, 195–208.

Chen, A., & Shen, B. (2004). A web of achieving in physical education: Goals, interest, outside-school activity and learning. *Learning and Individual Differences, 14*, 169–182.

Chen, S., Chen, A., & Zhu, X. (2012). Are K–12 learners motivated in physical education? A meta-analysis. *Research Quarterly for Exercise and Sport, 83*, 36–48.

Deci, E. L., Koestner, R., & Ryan, R. M. (1999). A meta-analytic review of experiments examining the effects of extrinsic rewards on intrinsic motivation. *Psychology Bulletin, 125*, 627–668.

Deci, E. L., & Ryan, R. M. (1985). *Intrinsic motivation and self-determination in human behavior*. New York: Plenum.

Deci, E. L., & Ryan, R. M. (2000). The "what" and "why" of goal pursuits: Human needs and the self-determination of behavior. *Psychological Inquiry, 11*, 227–268.

Dempsey, J. M., Kimiecik, J. C., & Horn, T. S. (1993). Parental influence on children's moderate to vigorous physical activity participation: An expectancy-value approach. *Pediatric Exercise Science, 5*, 151–167.

Digelidis, N., Papaioannou, A., Laparidis, K., & Christodoulidis, T. (2003). A one-year intervention in 7th grade physical education classes aiming to change motivational climate and attitudes toward exercise. *Psychology of Sport and Exercise, 4*, 195–210.

Elliot, A. J. (1997). Integrating the "classic" and "contemporary" approaches to achievement motivation: A hierarchical model of approach and avoidance achievement motivation. In M. Maehr & P. Pintrich (Eds.), *Advances in motivation and achievement* (Vol. 10, pp. 243–279). Greenwich, CT: JAI Press.

Elliot, A. J. (1999). Approach and avoidance motivation and achievement goals. *Educational Psychologist, 34*, 169–189.

Elliot, A. J. (2005). A conceptual history of the achievement goal construct. In A. Elliot & C. Dweck (Eds.), *Handbook of competence and motivation* (pp. 52–72). New York: Guilford Press.

Ennis, C. D. (2003). Using curriculum to enhance student learning. In S. J. Silverman & C. D. Ennis (Eds.), *Student learning in physical education: Applying research to enhance instruction* (2nd ed., pp. 109–127). Champaign, IL: Human Kinetics.

Garn, A. C., & Sun, H. (2009). Approach-avoidance motivation in early adolescents: Exploring goal profiles and fitness testing. *Journal of Teaching in Physical Education, 28*, 400–421.

Gillison, F. B., Standage, M., & Skevington, S. M. (2013). The effects of manipulating goal content and autonomy support climate on outcomes of a PE fitness class. *Psychology of Sport and Exercise, 14*, 342–352.

Grolnick, W. S., Gurland, S. T., Jacob, K. F., & DeCourcey, W. (2002). The development of self-determination in middle childhood and adolescence. In A. Wigfield & J. Eccles (Eds.), *Development of achievement motivation* (pp. 148–171). San Diego, CA: Academic Press.

Hidi, S., & Anderson, V. (1992). Situational interest and its impact on reading and expository writing. In K. A. Renninger, S. Hidi, & A. Krapp (Eds.), *The role of interest in learning and development* (pp. 43–69). Hillsdale, NJ: Erlbaum.

Hidi, S., & Harackiewicz, J. M. (2000). Motivating the academically unmotivated: A critical issue for the 21st century. *Review of Educational Research, 70*, 151–179.

Jewett, A. E., Bain, L. L., & Ennis, C. D. (1995). *The curriculum process in physical education.* Madison, WI: Brown & Benchmark.

Kaplan, A., Middleton, M. J., Urdan, T., & Midgley, C. (2002). Achievement goals and goal structures. In C. Midgley (Ed.), *Goals, goal structures, and patterns of adaptive learning* (pp. 21–54). New York: Routledge.

Koka, A., & Hein, V. (2003). Perceptions of teachers' feedback and learning environment as predictors of intrinsic motivation in physical education. *Psychology of Sport and Exercise, 4*, 333–346.

Krapp, A., Hidi, S., & Renninger, K. A. (1992). Interest, learning, and development. In K. A. Renninger, S. Hidi, & A. Krapp (Eds.), *The role of interest in learning and development* (pp. 43–69). Hillsdale, NJ: Erlbaum.

Lonsdale, C., Rosenkranz, R. R., Sanders, T., Peralta, L. R., Bennie, A., Jackson, B., Taylor, I. M., & Lubans, D. R. (2013). A cluster randomized controlled trial of strategies to increase adolescents' physical activity and motivation in physical education: Results of motivating active learning in physical education (MALP) trial. *Preventive Medicine, 57*, 696–702.

Molden, D. C., & Dweck, C. S. (2000). Meaning and motivation. In C. Sansone & J. M. Harackiewicz (Eds.), *Intrinsic and extrinsic motivation: The search for optimal motivation and performance* (pp. 131–159). San Diego, CA: Academic Press.

National Association for Sport and Physical Education. (1995). *Moving into the future: National standards for physical education.* Reston, VA: Author.

National Association for Sport and Physical Education. (2004). *Moving into the future: National standards for physical education* (2nd edn). Reston, VA: Author.

Nicholls, J. G. (1984). Achievement motivation: Conceptions of ability, subjective experience, task choice, and performance. *Psychological Review, 91*, 328–346.

Ntoumanis, N. (2001). A self-determination approach to the understanding of motivation in physical education. *British Journal of Educational Psychology, 71*, 225–242.

Ntoumanis, N. (2005). A prospective study of participation in optional school physical education using a self-determination theory framework. *Journal of Educational Psychology, 97*, 444–453.

Oldfather, P., & Dahl, K. (1994). Toward a social constructivist reconceptualization of intrinsic motivation for literacy learning. *Journal of Reading Behavior, 26*, 139–158.

Pintrich, P. R. (2000). Multiple goals, multiple pathway: The role of goal orientation in learning and achievement. *Journal of Educational Psychology, 92*, 544–555.

Pintrich, P. R. (2003). A motivational science perspective on the role of student motivation in learning and teaching contexts. *Journal of Educational Psychology, 95,* 667–686.

Pintrich, P. R., & Schunk, D. H. (2002). *Motivation in education: Theory, research and applications* (2nd edn). Upper Saddle River, NJ: Pearson Education, Inc.

Pollard, A., Thiessen, D., & Filer, A. (1997). *Children and their curriculum: The perspectives of primary and elementary school children.* London: Falmer Press.

Renninger, K. A. (2000). Individual interest and its implications for understanding intrinsic motivation. In C. Sansone & J. M. Harackiewicz (Eds.), *Intrinsic and extrinsic motivation: The search for optimal motivation and performance* (pp. 373–404). San Diego, CA: Academic Press.

Renninger, K. A., Hidi, S., & Krapp, A. (1992). *The role of interest in learning and development.* Hillsdale, NJ: Erlbaum.

Reynold, R. E., Sinatra, G. M., & Jetton, T. L. (1996). Views of knowledge acquisition and representation: A continuum from experience centered to mind centered. *Educational Psychology, 31*(2), 93–104.

Rink, J. E. (2001). Investigating the assumptions of pedagogy. *Journal of Teaching in Physical Education, 20,* 112–128.

Rink, J. E. (2003). Effective instruction in physical education. In S. J. Silverman & C. D. Ennis (Eds.), *Student learning in physical education: Applying research to enhance instruction* (2nd ed., pp. 147–163). Champaign, IL: Human Kinetics.

Rovegno, I. (2006). Situated perspectives on learning. In D. Kirk, D. Macdonald, & M. O'Sullivan (Eds.), *Handbook of physical education* (pp. 262–274). Los Angeles: Sage.

Ryan, R. M., & Deci, E. L. (2000). Self-determination theory and the facilitation of intrinsic, social development, and well-being. *American Psychologist, 55*(1), 68–78.

Ryan, R. M., & Deci, E. L. (2002). An overview of self-determination theory. In E. L. Deci & R. M. Ryan (Eds.), *Handbook of self-determination research* (pp. 3–33). Rochester, NY: University of Rochester Press.

Ryan, R. M., & Powelson, C. L. (1991). Autonomy and relatedness as fundamental to motivation and education. *Journal of Experimental Education, 60*(1), 49–66.

Sallis, J. F., McKenzie, T. L., Beets, M. W., Beighle, A., Erwin, H., & Lee, S. (2012). Physical education's role in public health: Steps forward and backward over 20 years and HOPE for the future. *Research Quarterly for Exercise and Sport, 83,* 125–135.

Sansone, C., & Harackiewicz, J. (2000). *Intrinsic and extrinsic motivation: The search for optimal motivation and performance.* San Diego, CA: Academic Press.

Sarrazin, P., Roberts, G., Cury, F., Biddle, S., & Famose, J. P. (2002). Exerted effort and performance in climbing among boys: The influence of achievement goals, perceived ability, and task difficulty. *Research Quarterly for Exercise and Sport, 73,* 425–436.

Schmidt, R. A., & Lee, T. D. (2009). *Motor control and learning: A behavioral emphasis* (4th edn). Champaign, IL: Human Kinetics.

Schraw, G., Flowerday, T., & Lehman, S. (2001). Increasing situational interest in the classroom. *Educational Psychology Review, 13,* 211–224.

Shen, B., & Chen, A. (2006). Examining the interrelations among knowledge, interests, and learning strategies. *Journal of Teaching in Physical Education, 25,* 182–199.

Shen, B., Chen, A., & Guan, J. (2007). Using achievement goals and interest to predict learning in physical education. *The Journal of Experimental Education, 75*(2), 89–108.

Shen, B., Chen, A., Scrabis, K. A., & Tolley, H. (2003). Gender and interest-based motivation in learning dance. *Journal of Teaching in Physical Education, 22,* 396–409.

Shuell, T. J. (1986). Cognitive conceptions of learning. *Review of Educational Research, 56,* 411–436.

Silverman, S., Tyson, L., & Krampitz, J. (1992). Teacher feedback and achievement in physical education: Interaction with student practice. *Teaching & Teacher Education, 8,* 333–344.

Society of Health and Physical Educators [SHAPE]. (2014). *National standards & grade-level outcomes for K-12 physical education.* Champaign, IL: Human Kinetics.

Solmon, M. A., & Boone, J. (1993). The impact of student goal orientation in physical education classes. *Research Quarterly for Exercise and Sport, 64,* 418–424.

Standage, M., Duda, J. L., & Ntoumanis, N. (2003). Predicting motivational regulations in physical education: The interplay between dispositional goal orientations, motivational climate and perceived competence. *Journal of Sport Sciences, 21,* 631–647.

Standage, M., Duda, J. L., & Ntoumanis, N. (2005). A test of self-determination theory in school physical education. *British Journal of Educational Psychology, 75,* 411–433.

Sun, H. (2012). Exergaming impact on physical activity and interest in elementary physical education. *Research Quarterly for Exercise and Sport, 83,* 212–220.

Sun, H. (2013). Impact of exergames on physical activity and interest in elementary school students: A follow up study. *Journal of Sport and Health Science, 2,* 138–145.

Sun, H., & Chen, A. (2010). An examination of sixth graders' self-determined motivation and learning in physical education. *Journal of Teaching in Physical Education, 29,* 262–277.

Theodosiou, A., & Papaioannou, A. (2006). Motivational climate, achievement goals and metacognitive activity in physical education and exercise involvement in out-of-school settings. *Psychology of Sport and Exercise, 7,* 361–379.

Todorovich, J. R., & Curtner-Smith, M. D. (2003). Influence of the motivational climate in physical education on third-grade students' task and ego orientations. *Journal of Classroom Interaction, 38,* 36–46.

Treasure, D. (2001). Enhancing young people's motivation in youth sport: An achievement goal approach. In G. C. Roberts (Ed.), *Advances in motivation in sport and exercise* (2nd ed., pp. 79–100). Champaign, IL: Human Kinetics.

Urdan, T. C. (1997). Achievement goal theory: Past results, future directions. In M. L. Maehr & P. R. Pintrich (Eds.), *Advances in motivation and achievement, Vol. 10* (pp. 99–141). Greenwich, CT: JAI Press.

Vallerand, R. J., & Losier, G. F. (1999). An integrative analysis of intrinsic and extrinsic motivation in sport. *Journal of Applied Sport Psychology, 11,* 142–169.

Vallerand, R. J., & Rousseau, F. L. (2001). Intrinsic and extrinsic motivation in sport and exercise: A review using the hierarchical model of intrinsic and extrinsic motivation. In R. N. Singer, H. A. Hausenblas, & C. M. Janelle (Eds.), *Handbook of sport psychology* (2nd ed., pp. 389–416). New York: Wiley.

Vygotsky, L. S. (1978). *Mind in society: The development of higher psychological processes.* Cambridge, MA: Harvard University Press.

Wang, C. J., Biddle, S. J., & Elliot, A. J. (2007). The 2×2 achievement goal framework in a physical education context. *Psychology of Sport and Exercise, 8,* 147–168.

Wang, C. J., Chatzisarantis, N. L. D., Spray, C. M., & Biddle, S. J. H. (2002). Achievement goal profiles in school physical education: Differences in self-determination, sport ability beliefs, and physical activity. *British Journal of Educational Psychology, 72,* 433–445.

Wigfield, A. & Eccles, J. S. (2002). The development of competence beliefs, expectancies for success, and achievement values from childhood through adolescence. In A. Wigfield & J. S. Eccles (Eds.), *Development of achievement motivation* (pp. 91–120). San Diego, CA: Academic Press.

Zhu, X. (2013). Situational interest and physical activity in fitness testing: A need for pedagogical engineering. *International Journal of Sport and Exercise Psychology, 12,* 76–89.

Zhu, X., Chen, A., Ennis, C., Sun, H., Hopple, C., Bonello, M., Bae, M., & Kim, S. (2009). Situational interest, cognitive engagement, and achievement in physical education. *Contemporary Educational Psychology, 34,* 221–229.

Zhu, X., Chen, S., & Parrott, J. (2014). Adolescents' interest and performances in aerobic fitness testing. *Journal of Teaching in Physical Education, 33,* 53–67.

INDEX

Bold page number indicate figures, *italic* numbers indicate tables.